A Practitioner's Guide to
TAKEOVERS AND MERGERS
IN THE EUROPEAN UNION

A Practitioner's Guide to
TAKEOVERS AND MERGERS IN
THE EUROPEAN UNION

Fifth Edition

SWEET & MAXWELL

Published by City & Financial Publishing in 2008

Reprinted in 2010 by Thomson Reuters (Legal) Limited
(Registered in England & Wales, Company No 1679046. Registered Office
and address for service: 100 Avenue Road, London, NW3 3PF)
trading as City & Financial Publishing

Reprinted by Great Britain by
CPI Antony Rowe, Chippenham

British Library Cataloguing-in-Publication Data. A catalogue record for this book is
available from the British Library.

ISBN: 978 1905 121 304
This book has been compiled from the contributions of the named authors. The views expressed
herein do not necessarily reflect the views of their respective firms. Further, since this book is
intended as a general guide only, its application to specific situations will depend upon the
particular circumstances involved and it should not be relied upon as a substitute for obtaining
appropriate professional advice.

The law is stated as at 1 February 2008. Whilst all reasonable care has been taken in the preparation of this book, City & Financial Publishing and the authors do not accept responsibility for any
errors it may contain or for any loss sustained by any person placing reliance on its contents.

Biographies

Neil Harvey has been a corporate partner at Clifford Chance since 1986 specialising in domestic and international takeovers and mergers, both public and private. He is co-head of Clifford Chance's Global Consumer Goods and Retail Industry Group and a member of the CBI's Companies Committee.

Alex Nourry is a partner at Clifford Chance and head of the European Competition and Regulation group in London. He specialises in EC/UK competition law, including merger control/joint ventures, cartels/abuse of market power, sector inquiries/market investigations, licensing/distribution systems, State aid/public procurement, and regulation of utilities. Alex advises businesses across a wide range of industry sectors, energy, financial services, information technology and media/telecommunications and transport. Experience includes phase II investigations under the EC Merger Regulation, investigations and cases before the EC Commission, the Courts of the European Communities, the UK Competition Appeals Tribunal, and before the OFT and the Competition Commission.

Stefan Köck has been a partner of Freshfields Bruckhaus Deringer since 1995 and works in the Vienna office. His principal areas of practice are employment and corporate law. In corporate law matters, he specialises in mergers and acquisitions, corporate restructurings, and public takeovers.

Stefan Köck graduated from the University of Vienna School of Law in 1985 and was admitted to the Austrian Bar in 1993. He worked as assistant professor at the Department of Labour Law and Special Security at the University of Vienna. He graduated with a Master of Laws degree from the Northwestern University School of Law (Chicago, USA) and received his doctorate from the University of Vienna School of Law.

Chris Sunt is a partner at Freshfields Bruckhaus Deringer's Belgian corporate practice. He is a leading corporate and financial law practitioner in Belgium. His practice focuses mainly on corporate M&A and capital markets transactions and he also has renowned expertise in banking and finance work.

Chris studied law at the universities of Antwerp and Ghent. He received his LL.M. from Harvard Law School in 1980 and was a senior research assistant at Ghent University. He has been a member of the Brussels Bar since 1980. Chris is also a deputy judge at the Court of Appeal in Brussels.

Peter Petrov is a partner at Borislav Boyanov & Co. His principal practice areas are corporate and competition, financial markets, defence and communications. He attended Sofia University "St. Klement of Ochrida" School of Law (LL.M.) and the Academy of American and International Law. He has been admitted to the Sofia Bar Association.

Damian Simeonov is a partner at Borislav Boyanov & Co and head of the Finance Practice Group. He specialises in finance, TMT and M&A and has advised on some of the largest finance transactions in Bulgaria.

Damian was educated at the Legal Faculty of Sofia University (ML) and has attended a training course at the Academy of American and International Law, Dallas, Texas (1998). He is a member of the Sofia Bar Association, the International Bar Association, the Centre for International Legal Studies and is secretary of the Legal Development Foundation. He is actively engaged in SEE Legal (*www.seelegal.org*).

Elias Neocleous graduated in law from Oxford University in 1991 and is a barrister of the Inner Temple. He was admitted to the Cyprus Bar in 1993 and has been a partner in Andreas Neocleous & Co, Cyprus's leading law firm, since 1995. He currently heads the firm's corporate and commercial department as well as the specialist banking and finance, tax and company management groups.

Elias's main areas of practice are banking and finance, company matters, international trade, intellectual property, trusts and estate planning and taxation. He is Honorary Secretary of the Limassol Chamber of Commerce and Industry and a founder member of the Cyprus Society of Trust and Estate Practitioners, and serves on its committee.

He has many publications to his credit and is a co-author of *Introduction to Cyprus Law,* a comprehensive guide to the laws of Cyprus.

Kyriakos Georgiades graduated in law from Queen Mary, University of London in 1978 and was admitted as a solicitor of the Supreme Court of England and Wales in 1980. After several years as a partner in a successful regional practice in the South East of England he joined Andreas Neocleous & Co as a partner in 2004 and now heads the specialist corporate group within the firm's company and commercial department.

His main areas of practice are corporate law, shipping law, EU law and general commercial litigation. He has many publications to his credit and is a co-author of *Introduction to Cyprus Law,* a comprehensive guide to the laws of Cyprus.

Achilleas Malliotis graduated in government and law from the London School of Economics in 1999. He obtained an MA in European Integration at the University of Bradford in 2000 and a postgraduate Diploma in Law at the BPP Law School in 2001. He became a barrister of Lincoln's Inn in 2002 and was admitted to the Cyprus Bar in 2003. He is based in the Nicosia office of Andreas Neocleous & Co, specialising in company law and EU law.

Ivo Bárta is a partner at White & Case and one of its leading lawyers in the fields of mergers and acquisitions and financing in the Czech Republic and Slovakia. He also focuses on private equity, foreign direct investment, and general corporate transactions. He is admitted to practice in the Czech Republic and Slovakia. Mr Bárta was educated at the Comenius University, Slovakia (J.D. and Ph.D.); the University of Michigan, U.S.A. (LL.M.); and University of Leuven, Belgium (LL.M.). The latest independent publications (*Chambers Global, European Legal 500, IFLR1000, PLC Which Lawyer?*) evaluated him as a leading Czech and Slovak M&A and financing practitioner.

Mikkel Baaring Lerche is a partner in Bech-Bruun's Corporate/M&A practice group. With more than 20 years' experience in M&A work, he focuses primarily on cross-border transactions and private equity deals for both international and domestic clients, and his experience includes a number of public to private transactions. Mikkel Baaring Lerche is ranked as one of Denmark's leading M&A practitioners by, among others, *Chambers Global*, *Legal 500* and *IFLR*.

Philip Risbjørn co-heads Bech-Bruun's M&A Corporate department. He mainly advises foreign corporations and private equity funds on negotiated acquisitions and takeovers. He is particularly experienced in large multi-jurisdictional M&A transactions and controlled auctions and has considerable expertise in designing corporate structures and in advising on national and cross-border mergers, demergers and similar transactions. He holds a Master of Laws from the University of Copenhagen (1991), Denmark and an LL.M. from Cambridge University, England (1995). Philip Risbjørn is ranked as one of Denmark's leading M&A practitioners by, among others, *Chambers Global*.

Raino Paron is a cum laude graduate of the University of Tartu Faculty of Law. He holds a Masters of Law degree with distinction from Georgetown University Law Center. Raino has worked in the legal departments of the International Monetary Fund and International Bank for Reconstruction and Development. He has also served as the deputy manager of the economic department of the Pärnu City Government. Raino is the chairman of the Council of the Tallinn Stock Exchange's Arbitration Court. He is also the American Bar Association's Central and East European Business Law Group's country coordinator for Estonia. Raino has been a member of the Estonian Bar Association since 1996.

Marina Tolmatšova is a graduate of the University of Tartu Faculty of Law and a member of the Estonian Bar Association since 2003. Ms Tolmatšova specialises in M&A, corporate governance, banking and finance, capital markets and private equity.

Heili Haabu is a graduate of the University of Tartu Faculty of Law and a member of the Estonian Bar Association since 2004. Ms Haabu specialises in M&A, general corporate, corporate governance and labour law.

Tarja Wist is a founding partner of Waselius & Wist and an experienced expert in finance and capital markets law. She received her LL.M. degree from the Law Faculty of the University of Helsinki in 1989 and was admitted to the Finnish Bar in 1994, served as secretary to the Legislative Commission for Securities Market Law 1990–1993 and as a member of the working group of the Ministry of Finance for implementation of the Takeover Directive in 2004–2005.

Ms Wist chairs the Securities and Finance Law Expert Group of the Finnish Bar Association and the Financial and Banking Law Conferences sub-committee of the Banking Law Committee of the International Bar Association.

Tom Fagernäs joined Waselius & Wist in 2007. He received his LL.M. degree from the Law Faculty of the University of Helsinki in 2007.

Tom Fagernäs practises in the areas of M&A, capital markets and banking and finance. He is a co-writer of various articles on Finnish takeover laws.

Bertrand Cardi is based in the Paris office of Linklaters. He joined the firm in 1999, spent one year in the New York office and became a partner in 2004. His practice is focused on all areas of mergers and acquisitions with a specialisation on public offers and private equity-related transactions. He graduated from HEC Business School and the Assas University and has participated in the writing of a number of law review articles on French corporate and stock exchange law.

Thierry Vassogne has been the co-head of Linklaters Paris since 1998 after having been a partner at Gide Loyrette Nouel since 1981. His practice is focused on mergers and acquisitions, especially public M&A, as well as corporate litigation.

Marc Loy is based in the Paris office of Linklaters. He has been a partner at Linklaters since 1999 and was previously a partner in a French law firm. His practice is focused on public mergers and acquisitions and related litigation.

Georg Frowein has been a partner of Hengeler Mueller since 2002 and works in the Frankfurt office. He is a member of the Hengeler Mueller M&A practice group and specialises in corporate and real estate transactions. Georg Frowein studied law in Freiburg and Bonn and holds a doctorate degree (Dr. jur.) from the University of Heidelberg. In 1994, he obtained a Master of Laws (LL.M.) degree from the University of Michigan, Ann Arbor, USA. He is admitted to the Frankfurt and New York bars.

Frank Burmeister has been a partner of Hengeler Mueller since 2003 and works in the Frankfurt office. He is a member of the Hengeler Mueller M&A practice group and specialises in corporate and real estate transactions. Frank Burmeister studied law in Hamburg and holds a doctorate degree (Dr. jur.) from the University of Hamburg. He is admitted to the Frankfurt bar.

Katia Protopapa has been a partner of T.J. Koutalidis Law Firm since 1994. Her practice is focused on European community law; mergers, acquisitions and divestitures; company law; business law; commercial law: corporate law; transport law; agency and distributorships; and antitrust and trade regulation. She graduated from University of Athens School of Law and holds an LL.B; and from London University in 1989 with an LL.M. She is a member of the Athens Bar Association and the Hellenic Commercial Law Association.

Konrád Siegler is a partner of the Budapest office of Weil, Gotshal & Manges, where he leads the banking and finance and capital markets practice. Konrád obtained his law degree from Eötvös Loránd University, Faculty of Law in 1991 and currently lectures there on securities law. He is an arbitrator at the Money and Capital Markets Arbitration Court of Hungary and has been a member of the Budapest Bar since 1994.

Gábor Zoltán Szabó is a senior associate of the Budapest office of Weil, Gotshal & Manges, specialising in capital markets, corporate and finance transactions. Gábor has written several law review articles regarding different areas of Hungarian business law. He graduated from Eötvös Loránd University, Faculty of Law in 1995 and holds an LL.M. in international business law from the Central European University. He has been a member of the Budapest Bar since 1999.

Eithne FitzGerald is partner and head of Corporate Finance in A&L Goodbody, Dublin. She is a leading corporate finance and M&A lawyer in Ireland, handling both domestic and international cross-border transactions, including private equity. She also has a specialist interest in non-contentious insurance law and advises a number of international and Irish insurers. Eithne holds a legal degree from Trinity College, Dublin and a Diploma in European Law from University College, Dublin.

Eithne managed the London office of A&L Goodbody for three years in the 1990's and is highly recommended as an expert in a number of leading legal publications.

Nicolò Juvara is a partner of Norton Rose Group, based in Milan. He specialises in M&A and he also has extensive experience of advising on joint venture transactions. He has expertise in the areas of outsourcing and has specialist knowledge of the financial services and insurance industries. Nicolò is a member of the Tax and Legal Committee of AIFI (Italian Private Equity and Venture Capital Association) and of AIDA (Insurance Law International Association). He is a regular speaker at Italian and international conferences and author of numerous articles on matters dealing with financial services, insurance, corporate governance, MiFID and outsourcing. In the European Legal Experts 2008 Directory, he is recognised as a "leading lawyer" in the areas of corporate and M&A.

Rocco Santarelli is an associate of Norton Rose Group, based in Milan. He specialises in capital markets and M&A. He also has experience of advising on general corporate law and corporate governance matters relating to listed companies. Rocco is a graduate of LUISS University in Rome and earned a masters degree in Private International and Competition Law from the University of Milano-Bicocca.

Liga Hartmane is a partner and Head of the Trade and Technology Practice Group at Klavins & Slaidins LAWIN, specialising in competition law, commercial agency, franchising and distribution, mergers and acquisitions, and general corporate law. Ms Hartmane holds a Diploma in EC Competition Law (2005), University of London King's College, and has graduated from the University of Latvia Faculty of Law (dipl. iur. 2000, mag. iur. 2002). She has written numerous law review articles regarding Latvian antitrust and competition law and practice. Ms Hartmane has also held lecturing positions in Legal Theory, University of Latvia and at the Latvian Training Center for Judges.

Martins Gailis is an associate lawyer and a member of the Trade and Technology Practice Group at Klavins & Slaidins LAWIN, specialising in competition law, intellectual property law, and commercial agency, franchising and distribution. Mr Gailis has an LL.M. degree with distinction from the Riga Graduate School of Law (2005) and LL.B. degree in English and European Law from the University of Essex (2004). Mr Gailis has contributed to several law review articles regarding Latvian antitrust and competition law and practice, as well as in the field of intellectual property law in Latvia.

Dovilė Burgienė is a partner and head of Quality Management at Lideika, Petrauskas, Valiūnas ir partneriai LAWIN. He joined the firm in 1997 and was admitted in 2002. He holds a Master's Degree in Law from Vilnius University and a Master of Laws (LL.M.) degree in EU Law from Stockholm University. His practice areas are: corporate law, corporate governance, mergers and acquisitions; public private partnership; finance and securities. He is a member of the Lithuanian-British Association British Chamber of Commerce in Lithuania; Lithuanian Young Lawyers Association; European Forum, International Bar Association and the European Corporate Governance Institute.

Guy Harles is a founding partner at Arendt & Medernach and head of the Corporate, Tax and Intellectual Property Practice. He specialises in corporate work, where he advises on the structuring of international transactions, private equity investments, corporate reorganisations, mergers and acquisitions and corporate finance. He also has extensive knowledge in the fields of intellectual property. He frequently serves as an arbitrator.

He has been a member of the Luxembourg Bar since 1980 and Paris Bar since 1993. He presently serves as a president of the Luxembourg Association for Arbitration and Euroarbitrage. He was a reader on business law at the Centre Universitaire de Luxembourg, the Faculty of Law (University of Luxembourg) and Université Louis Pasteur (Strasbourg) from 1981 to 2007. Guy Harles holds a Master's degree in law from the Université Robert Schuman de Strasbourg (France), as well as an advanced degree (DESS in banking and finance) from the same university.

Katia Gauzès is a senior associate at Arendt & Medernach and works with the Corporate, Tax and Intellectual Property Practice, where she specialises in corporate law, advising major international companies, private equity firms and other investors in structuring and financing mergers and acquisitions, leveraged buy-outs and other private equity deals, corporate reorganisations and refinancings.

She has been a member of the Paris Bar since 2002 and has been admitted by the Luxembourg Bar to practice in Luxembourg under her French professional title. She holds a Master's degree in business law (Maîtrise droit des affaires) as well as a DESS degree in business law and tax (DESS droit des affaires et fiscalité) from the Université Paris II Panthéon-Assas (France). She also holds an MBA from the business school ESSEC in Paris (France).

Nicolai Vella Falzon, graduated at the University of Malta as Notary Public in 1995 and as Doctor of Laws in 1997; was admitted to the Bar of the Superior Courts of Malta in 1998 and currently practises in both the inferior and superior Courts of Malta; read for a Master of Laws degree LL.M. at the London School of Economics and Political Science (LSE) graduating in 1998; membership of professional bodies includes the Malta Chamber of Advocates and the Institute of Financial Services Practitioners; he is currently a partner at Fenech & Fenech Advocates and practices mainly in the international transactions/corporate practice department of the firm focusing in particular on civil, commercial and corporate law and litigation, particularly international transactions, mergers and acquisitions, asset finance, intellectual property law, competition law, aviation, and general commercial law matters.

Weero Koster is a partner at Norton Rose, Amsterdam and specialises in M&A transactions in the energy, infrastructure and other fields. Acknowledged as one of the leading energy lawyers in the Netherlands by both Chambers Global Guide and the European Legal 500, Weero's practice includes advising domestic and international energy companies on privatisations, mergers, acquisitions, divestitures and alliances. In addition to his corporate energy practice, Weero Koster has been involved in a number of project financing deals in the Netherlands. Weero has published numerous articles on energy law, merger control, product liability and international mergers and acquisitions. He is a regular conference speaker and teaches at the Law Institute for In-house Corporate Counsel. Weero is a member of the International Bar Association, the Netherlands Commercial Law Association and the Netherlands Securities Law Association.

Konrad Konarski is a partner at the international law firm Baker & McKenzie where he heads the capital market practice of the Warsaw office. He is a graduate of the Adam Mickiewicz University in Poland and licensed as an attorney in Poland. He specialises in legal advice to issuers, shareholders and underwriters in initial public offerings and mergers and acquisitions of listed companies. For the past 12 years he has participated in several dozen transactions on the Polish capital market, including international offerings of equity and debt instruments, and initial public offerings of foreign companies in Poland. He is an author or co-author of several articles and books on securities regulations and frequent speaker at conferences on capital market regulations and corporate governance. In 2003–2007 he was consistently nominated by *International Financial Law Review* as one of "The Leading Capital Market Lawyers" in Poland. He is also mentioned as recommended lawyer for capital markets and investment funds by *PLC Which lawyer?*, *Legal 500*, *IFLR 1000* and *Chambers*.

Nuno de Brito Lopes is a corporate law partner at PLMJ and was admitted to the Portuguese Bar Association in 1993. His resume includes: Member of IBA and CILS; Postgraduate degree in Securities Law, University of Lisbon Law School, 1998; Assistant Professor of *EU Law I*, Lusíada University, Lisbon (1993–1995); Sessions on *Corporate Law and the Corporate Fiscal Body*, Chartered Public Accountants' Training Period (2001); Conferences and Invited Professor of *Due Diligence, Mergers and Acquisitions* and *International Commercial Law*, INDEG/ISCTE's Management post-graduate courses (2002–2007); Iberian Lawyer Magazine Group of Experts (2007 to date). He has written several articles in international legal magazines on matters of Corporate Law and M&A.

Neil McGregor is the managing partner of McGregor & Partners S.C.A. and has overall responsibility for matters governed by English law. An honours graduate in law of the University of Aberdeen, he took up a posting in Bucharest as the first resident expatriate lawyer of Sinclair Roche & Temperley in 1996 and became partner in 2000. He was admitted to the Bucharest Bar and became the managing partner of the firm on its establishment in 2002. *(Neil may be contacted at : neil.mcgregor@mcgregorlegal.eu)*

Peter Šuba received his law degree from Comenius University in Bratislava, Slovakia, in 1998 and his LL.M. from Harvard Law School in 2003. He is a European partner with Squire Sanders. Mr Šuba has counselled and represented numerous Slovak and non-Slovak clients in corporate acquisitions, privatisations, venture capital investments, insurance claim settlements, real estate acquisitions and finance, telecommunications law, syndicated loans and capital markets transactions. Mr Šuba has represented and advised the Slovak Government in consortium with CA IB in the privatisation of the state Rail Cargo Company, a global real estate fund in a €60 million acquisition by share purchase of a deluxe hotel in Eastern Europe and a major British retail company in all stages of development of its largest hypermarket to date in Slovakia located in Bratislava Zlaté piesky.

Andrew Sandor graduated from Georgetown University Law Center and is a licensed American attorney. Mr Sandor's mergers and acquisitions experience includes advising a group of US private equity funds on the acquisition of a regional telecommunications company, a US multinational in the acquisition and later disposal of a Slovak manufacturer, a US floral products company in the acquisition of a Central European distributor, and a regional discount airline in raising early and later round financing.

Michal Luknár graduated from the Law Faculty, Comenius University and is a fully licensed Slovak advocate, member of the Slovak Bar Association. Mr Luknár advises clients on a large variety of matters relating to business and civil law matters. He focuses his practice on corporate law, drafting and reviewing contracts, performing legal due diligence and representing clients in litigation. Mr Luknár is experienced in representing foreign investors in the privatisation of Slovak steel works, petrochemical and energy distribution companies. Mr Luknár also assisted in the financial debt restructuring of a client playing an important role in the energy sector and currently he is also active in the field of PPP projects.

Srečo Jadek was born in 1957 and graduated from the Law Faculty of Ljubljana University, Slovenia in 1981. After traineeship at the Ljubljana Court, he became a sole practitioner in 1984 and took over his father's law office established in 1958. In 1993 he merged his office with the law office of Mr Pavle Pensa. Since then he has been senior partner in the law office Jadek & Pensa, which is repeatedly recommended as the leading Slovenian law firm by the foreign law firm rankings publications *Legal 500* and *Chambers*. Srečo Jadek is a member of the Slovenian bar, as well as the International Bar Association, Insolvency and Creditors' Rights Committee J. His main fields of activity are finance law, mergers and acquisitions, corporate law and investment funds law. He has been appointed bankruptcy/liquidation administrator by bankruptcy courts in several bankruptcy/liquidation proceedings since 1990. He also litigates commercial and civil cases.

Carlos de Cárdenas Smith is a partner based in the Madrid office of Uría Menéndez. He joined Uría Menéndez in 1989 and was made a partner in 1998. He headed the New York office from 1997 to 2000. Carlos focuses his practice on M&A, banking and finance. He has been a Commercial Law lecturer at the Universidad Pontificia de Comillas (ICADE) in Madrid, an author of a book on tender offers in Spain and co-author of several books on business law. He has worked on the most significant project and leveraged finance transactions in Spain and is head of the banking and finance practice of Uría Menéndez.

Alex Bircham is a junior lawyer based in the London office of Slaughter and May. He joined Slaughter and May in 2006 and qualified in 2008, spending six months on secondment at Uría Menéndez during this period Alex undertakes a wide range of work, including M&A and general corporate as well as banking and finance.

Anders Lundin holds law degrees from Stockholm University School of Law and New York University School of Law. He was an associate of Haight, Gardner, Poor & Havens, New York, 1978–79 and became an associate of the Swedish firm Lagerlöf & Leman in 1980 and was a partner from 1987–92, when he left the firm and participated in the foundation of Gernandt & Danielsson in which today he is a partner. Anders Lundin´s practice is focused on M&A, banking and finance and capital markets.

Krister Skoog holds law degrees from Stockholm University School of Law and QMW University of London School of Law. He became an associate of Gernandt & Danielsson in 2000. In 2001–02 he was a law clerk at the District Court of Stockholm. Krister Skoog´s practice is focused on M&A and capital markets.

Linnéa Ecorcheville holds law degrees from Lund University School of Law. She became an associate of Gernandt & Danielsson in 2006. From 2004–05, she was an associate of Linklaters Advokatbyrå in Stockholm. Linnéa Ecorcheville's practice is focused on M&A and capital markets.

Hergüner Bilgen Özeke
Founded in 1989, Hergüner Bilgen Özeke is a full service law firm in Turkey with major international clientele. The firm draws upon the individual domestic and international experience of its more than 100 fee earners.

Hergüner's clients include local companies doing business in and outside of Turkey, multinational companies and financial institutions doing business in Turkey or Turkish affiliates of multinational companies, as well as multilateral financial institutions.

The firm's practice areas cover all areas of law that are of interest to local and foreign businesses in Turkey, including in particular, mergers and acquisitions; energy and infrastructure; real estate; banking and finance; capital markets; privatisation; litigation; arbitration; competition law; intellectual property and environmental law.

Karen Davies is a senior associate at Clifford Chance. She specialises in public bids, mergers and demergers, private acquisitions and disposals, joint ventures, restructurings and equity issues of all types, both in the UK and across borders.

Contents

Chapter 1

Takeovers and Mergers in the European Union – an Overview

Neil Harvey and Alex Nourry
Partners
Clifford Chance LLP

1.1 Introduction

1.1.1 Background

Over the years 2004 to 2007, there was a significant increase in mergers and acquisitions ("M&A") activity both globally and in Europe. This encompassed both takeovers of public companies – the primary focus of this Guide – and acquisitions of private companies. Over 40 per cent of global M&A activity by volume in 2007 took place in Europe compared to approximately 30 per cent in 2000. This period was characterised by some very large public takeovers, including the battle for Dutch bank, ABN Amro, between Barclays and a consortium of European banks led by the Royal Bank of Scotland ("RBS") in the summer of 2007. The battle was won by the RBS consortium in October 2007 with a mainly cash bid worth €70 billion, allowing the consortium to secure the biggest bank takeover in history. Although the number of takeover deals with European targets grew by just under a third between 2005 and 2006, the value of such deals grew by almost 75 per cent in the same time period, with the trend continuing during the first half of 2007, signalling a significant rise in the size of these deals. Some of the factors and trends which fuelled such growth are examined below.

The majority of this activity took place in western Europe, but the markets of eastern Europe also experienced significant growth. The value of M&A activity in eastern Europe more than doubled between 2003 and 2006, rising to €77.25 billion.[1] However, the vast majority of such activity in eastern Europe comprised of private, not public, transactions.

Moving into 2008 with volatile stock markets and more pessimistic assumptions of economic growth, predictions of future levels of European takeover activity have become exceedingly difficult. Although there is still significant strategic takeover activity, e.g., in the mining/resources sector (BHP Billiton's bid for Rio Tinto Zinc and the potential bid by Vale for Xstrata) and brewing sector (the Carlsberg and Heineken consortium's bid for Scottish & Newcastle), there can be

---

[1] All exchange rates in this Chapter are based on the European Central Bank's average bilateral exchange rates for the particular year cited. Current figures are based on the average 2007 rate.

no doubt that the credit crunch that was triggered in August 2007 by the problems in the US sub-prime mortgage market has had a serious impact on market confidence generally and, in particular, on bidders' ability to finance larger acquisitions. Balanced against this, there will be the possibility for companies to make opportunistic acquisitions while stock market prices are depressed.

1.1.2 Recent trends and developments

1.1.2.1 Activity of private equity firms in the market

Private equity has played an increasingly important role in takeover activity during recent years.

Between 2003 and 2006, the aggregate capitalisation of the major global private equity funds,[2] grew from €20.77 billion to €84.42 billion. This growth was fuelled by low interest rates and the availability of funding.

In Europe, the number and size of private equity-driven M&A transactions have both shown strong growth. The number of private equity M&A transactions with European targets has more than doubled when comparing the first quarter of 2003 to the second quarter of 2007. The value of these deals grew during the same period from €15.03 billion to €131.34 billion.

This growth in private equity's influence culminated in headlining deals during 2006 and 2007, including some of the largest leveraged buy-outs in Europe. For example, in June 2007, Alliance Boots, one of the most famous names in British retail, became the first FTSE 100 company to be bought by a private equity firm after Kohlberg Kravis Roberts (the private equity house) and Stephano Pessina (the Boots deputy chairman) won an intense bidding competition with an increased bid of €16.22 billion.

Also, in March 2006, an acquisition vehicle controlled by private equity firms AlpInvest Partners, The Blackstone Group, The Carlyle Group, Hellman & Friedman, Kohlberg Kravis Roberts and Thomas H. Lee Partners, acquired the entire issued share capital of Nielsen Company, a public Dutch market research company. The deal was valued at just under €8.5 billion.

Central and eastern Europe has also seen the appearance of private equity in recent years. This has included takeovers of companies based in this region, such as Permira's public takeover of Hungarian chemicals company Borsodchem, and many pan-European deals with a significant central European component.

Although private equity deals, particularly the larger transactions, have been impacted severely by the credit crunch, it is expected that over time, as unsyndicated debt becomes absorbed and the debt markets settle down, private equity players will continue to be a dominant force in the takeover market.

1.1.2.2 Hedge funds and activist investors

Whilst private equity has become a mainstream player in the public takeover market over the last few years, hedge funds have also increased their profile on

---

[2] Funds valued at over €3.65 billion.

the takeover scene. Hedge funds have been increasingly using their financial muscle to buy up substantial shareholdings in public companies, thus accruing significant influence over how those companies are run, bought and sold.

In recent years, hedge funds have looked to achieve ever-higher returns, and have seen the possibilities provided by private equity's presence in the takeover market.

These funds, believed to be worth over €1.46 trillion globally, have been buying significant equity stakes or derivatives based on equity in public companies that were seen as likely targets for takeover, in particular by private equity funds. An example is to be found in the takeover battle for BAA, the British airports operator, in the summer of 2006. It was believed that hedge funds held around 20 per cent of BAA shares, and thus played a significant part in the bidding process, which was eventually won by Spanish infrastructure company, Grupo Ferrovial. Once successful, Ferrovial refinanced the deal, raising €13.20 billion worth of debt finance, including €2.93 billion worth of subordinated debt from the hedge funds.

A further example of the influence of hedge funds over major corporate trans-actions was in the bidding war for ABN Amro. The bid by the RBS consortium depended heavily on the Belgian bank Fortis, part of the RBS consortium, being able to pass a shareholders' resolution allowing Fortis to make a €13 billion rights issue in order to help fund the bid. Up until the resolution was passed, it was feared that hedge funds holding 30 per cent of Fortis's stock would try to influence the vote and derail the rights issue. However, in the end the resolution was successful and the rights issue was made.

1.1.2.3   The Middle East and Asia
Recent years have seen a significant and high-profile participation by Asian and Middle Eastern countries on the European takeover scene.

Gulf states have sought to employ the immense wealth garnered from their vast deposits of oil and natural gas in various forms of investments, including the global equity markets, as a means of reducing their economic dependence on their natural resources. Some countries and emirates in this region, in particular Dubai and Qatar, have developed their own financial markets and have succeeded in attracting many of the world's leading financial institutions. As discussed below, the relatively recent proliferation of Islamic financing has also had an impact in increasing the Gulf States' appetite for takeovers. This increase in available funds has meant that these countries have been able to partake in significant deals in the European takeover market.

In 2007, Delta Two, a Qatari-backed investment vehicle, held talks with the UK's third-largest supermarket chain, J Sainsbury, over a potential public-to-private buy-out valued at €15.49 billion (although this did not eventually proceed). Furthermore, with the Dubai Borse (a 28 per cent shareholder) and the Qatar Investment Authority (a 20 per cent shareholder) competing to take control of the London Stock Exchange, almost half of its shares were held by Middle Eastern investors.

1.1.2.4 *India and China*
India and China, with their rapidly expanding economies, have also been making incursions into the European takeover arena.

Since 2000, Indian companies – buoyed by a domestic boom, good availability of credit and a growing confidence to expand – have made great strides in the global markets. This growing investment by Indian companies in large foreign firms is exemplified by Tata Steel's success in winning an intense bidding war for the Anglo-Dutch steel maker Corus in January 2007 with an offer worth €9.06 billion. This followed Mittal Steel's takeover of Arcelor of Luxembourg in June 2006, which created the world's largest steel company. Tata has also emerged as a principal contender to buy Land Rover and Jaguar from Ford, although this would be a private M&A transaction if it proceeds.

China's substantial economic growth and influence has now spread into Europe as well, and, in particular, into the banking sector. For example, China Development Bank ("CDB"), one of the Chinese government's leading institutions, became a significant shareholder in Barclays when it took up an initial stake worth €3.6 billion, with an option to purchase up to a further €9.5 billion worth of shares if Barclay's bid for ABN Amro had proved successful. In the mining sector, Aluminium Corporation of China (Chinalco), together with US-based Alcoa Inc., acquired an indirect 12 per cent stake in Rio Tinto plc, in a surprise high profile dawn raid in February 2008.

1.1.2.5 *Islamic finance*
The continuing ability of Gulf-based entities (sovereign and corporate) to raise funds has been greatly influenced by the increasing sophistication and viability of Shari'a-compliant financial instruments, such as the *sukuk*, a Shari'a-compliant product that most closely resembles a "conventional" bond issue. It is predicted that the depth and volume of the Islamic finance market, and the *sukuk* market in particular, will continue to grow as investors become more comfortable with the parameters of Shari'a and the differences between the Shari'a principles applicable to financing and conventional financing.

Although the *sukuk* market is still developing, there have been some extremely large issues in recent years. For example, in 2006, Dubai Ports World ("DP World") made a €2.79 billion issue to fund its takeover of P&O. This trend seems set to continue with a number of *sukuk* currently in the pipeline for the financing or refinancing of leveraged buy-outs and other acquisitions as many investors see Islamic finance as a very fertile source of funding. One of the most interesting facets of current *sukuk* issues is that many investors purchasing *sukuk* are not Islamic and their decision to invest is purely driven by satisfaction of credit-risk related issues.

1.1.2.6 *Sovereign wealth funds*
Sovereign wealth funds have been growing rapidly in size and influence over the last few years. The US Treasury estimates their combined reserves to be between €1,094.49 billion and €1,824.15 billion. Notwithstanding their current scale, it is expected that these funds will continue to grow in size. Many of these funds are from the Middle East and Asia. Over the years, the governments of

these countries, which have benefited from significant deposits of oil and other natural resources, have built up large reserves of foreign currency.

Those countries that have prospered from their oil deposits have sought to use sovereign wealth funds as a way of buffering the effects of volatile oil prices and as long-term savings vehicles. The vast reserves that these countries possess have had a significant impact on more developed markets and regions. For example, Dubai International Capital owns a 3 per cent stake in Europe's EADS, maker of Airbuses and the Eurofighter. As mentioned above, the Dubai Borse and the Qatar Investment Authority hold large stakes in the London Stock Exchange, and the China Development Bank is now a major shareholder in Barclays, one of Europe's largest banking institutions. Further, in May 2007, the Chinese Government, through the Chinese Investment Corporation, invested €2.19 billion in the large US private equity firm, Blackstone.

A high-profile sovereign wealth fund is Temasek Holdings, which is backed by the Singapore Government, and is thought to manage a portfolio valued at an estimated €72.97 billion . Although its primary focus is on Asian markets and sectors, it holds some significant stakes in European companies. For example, it holds an 11 per cent shareholding in Standard Chartered Bank, which it purchased for €3.19 billion in 2006, and also invested €3.65 billion in a stake in Barclays during the British bank's unsuccessful bid for ABN Amro.

Concerns surrounding the influence of these large sovereign wealth funds have led to protectionist reactions. For example, the US Government passed a new law in July 2007 requiring its Committee on Foreign Investment to conduct a full 90-day investigation of takeovers of US companies by foreign government-owned funds, unless a member of the Cabinet determines it would not impair US national security.

France and Germany, led by Nicolas Sarkozy and Angela Merkel, have been the most vociferous campaigners for the EU to take a stricter stance on sovereign wealth funds. Despite Brussels' traditional attitude that the free movement of capital within the EU is a fundamental tenet of European law, EU ministers have proposed certain schemes that could be implemented to help reduce concerns surrounding large investment by foreign states. The EU has proposed a system of "golden shares" for Member State governments that could allow governments to stop foreign governments taking control of key industries. The trade commissioner argued that such a system could be legitimately used where foreign state-controlled funds sought to buy into European companies in sensitive industries, such as the defence industry. In contrast to these proposals from the EU, Germany is considering adopting a US-style model.

1.1.2.7 Credit crunch
August 2007 saw a dramatic fall in global share prices as investors suffered from the financial turmoil caused by the collapse in the US sub-prime mortgage market. Global stock markets were badly hit in the initial panic and equity prices plummeted. They then staged a gradual recovery but subsequently plummeted again early in 2008. This crisis has seen many large investment banks and also mortgage lenders both in the US and Europe suffer losses, acted as a catalyst for the Northern Rock crisis in the UK and has led generally to a drop in confidence

in the asset-backed securities market. More significantly for the takeovers market, the crisis has also led to a shortfall in the availability of funding for takeovers and acquisitions. M&A activity already started slowing down during the second half of 2007 and this has continued into 2008. Private equity activity (particularly with regard to larger transactions) has waned as the availability of loan finance has lessened. The true long-term impact of the credit crunch remains to be seen but it will almost certainly continue to influence the level of takeover activity adversely until confidence returns to the markets.

1.1.2.8   Pensions – transparency and funding issues

Company pension schemes, and more particularly their funding position, currently play a significant role in the European takeovers market. Since 1 January 2005, all companies listed on a European Stock Exchange have had to account for the cost of making pension provision for their employees under International Accounting Standard 19 ("IAS 19"). The requirement for some recognition of actuarial gains and losses in the accounts (i.e., the difference between the actuarial assumptions used in assessing the company's pension scheme funding and the actual outcome) has led to some EU companies with previously unfunded pension schemes (for example in Germany, Spain and France) having to pre-fund their schemes in order to reduce their deficits.

In the UK, legislation introduced in April 2005 has substantially increased the risks of acquiring a company with a UK defined benefit pension scheme. The Pensions Regulator (a creature of that legislation) has power (albeit to date very rarely used) to pursue a wide net of people, including associates of and persons connected with the employer, for contributions to, or financial support for, an underfunded scheme. Underfunding for this purpose is assessed on the full cost of buying out the liabilities with annuity and deferred annuity contracts (a very expensive option).

This legislation now affects many transactions with a UK element, particularly where the proposed deal is highly leveraged. Potential bidders are finding that it is often crucial to involve, and strike a deal with, the trustees of the pension scheme as part of any proposed takeover or merger. In addition, it is often desirable to seek clearance from the Pensions Regulator in respect of a transaction in order to obtain comfort that the Pensions Regulator will not use its legislative powers to impose significant financial obligations in relation to the target group's defined benefit pension schemes. Whilst clearance can be sought after the event, clearance obtained before the transaction offers greater certainty for business planning purposes during the transaction.

The Pensions Regulator's stance on whether or not parties to a corporate transaction should consider seeking clearance is set out in published guidance. However, this guidance is subject to change and evolving market practice. The Pensions Regulator recently "reminded" parties that the underlying principle for considering clearance is whether the transaction is financially detrimental to the ability of the pension scheme to meet its pension liabilities. If the transaction involves a significant weakening of the employer covenant (e.g., where it is highly leveraged), then it is (and is likely to remain) the Pensions Regulator's view that clearance is an appropriate consideration, irrespective of the funding position of the scheme involved. Furthermore, the Pensions Regulator encourages the trustees of the pension scheme to consider whether to seek additional funding/mitigation which is significantly higher than the amount required to achieve full funding under IAS 19.

The issue as to whether or not to seek clearance (and its consequential timing implications) is particularly important in the takeovers and mergers market given the Takeover Panel's stance that it will not allow bidders to make a formal bid which is conditional on clearance from the Pensions Regulator.

1.2 Merger control

1.2.1 The Regime

Possibly the most significant factor impacting levels of takeover and merger activity in Member States is EU competition law. Although, in principle, the Commission takes a positive view of major corporate reorganisations within the EU as a means to increase European industry's competitiveness, the Commission may oppose a transaction when it substantially undermines competition in the EU.

All transactions falling within the scope of the EC Merger Regulation ("ECMR") must be notified to the Commission. Where the ECMR applies to a transaction, the Commission has exclusive jurisdiction and the parties are only required to make one filing in the European Economic Area ("EEA") with the Commission (as opposed to multiple filings with national authorities). As at 31 January 2008, 3,696 transactions had been notified to the Commission under the ECMR. Of these transactions, at the time of writing, 20 had been prohibited by the Commission, the latest being *Ryanair/Aer Lingus* (Case M.4439), and 21 had been approved subject to conditions following either a first-phase or a second-phase investigation.

1.2.2 Applicability of the ECMR

As set out in the ECMR, all "concentrations" with a "Community dimension" must be notified to the Commission for approval before being implemented. The Commission Consolidated Jurisdictional Notice (the "Jurisdictional Notice") provides detailed guidance on filing thresholds, with the aim of enabling firms to establish more quickly (and in advance of any contact with the Commission), whether and to what extent their operations may be covered by the ECMR.

1.2.2.1 Concentrations
Concentrations are widely defined in the ECMR and include mergers, acquisitions and certain types of joint ventures. The determining factor is whether the transaction will lead to a lasting change in (direct or indirect) control over one or more undertakings.

The concept of a concentration under the ECMR includes the creation of all joint ventures which perform, on a lasting basis, all of the functions of an independent economic entity. It is not sufficient for the joint venture only to take over specific functions within the parent companies' business activities without having access to the market itself.

1.2.2.2 Control and decisive influence

The definition of control is very broad. It is sufficient for one party to acquire "the possibility of exercising decisive influence" over another company. Control can be exercised on a de facto or legal basis, regardless of the parties' shareholdings, and this can have important implications for minority shareholders. Therefore, the acquisition of any stake in a company must be carefully considered, in order to ascertain whether it confers either sole or joint control. The Jurisdictional Notice provides guidance in this regard.

Decisive influence may arise through the ownership of all or part of the company's assets or rights which confer decisive influence on the decision-making process of the company. It is therefore not necessary to show that the decisive influence is or will be actually exercised, although the possibility of exercising that influence must be effective (*see Cementbouw* v *Commission* Case T-282/01). Article 3(2) of the ECMR provides that the possibility of exercising decisive influence over an undertaking can exist on the basis of rights, contracts or any other means, either separately or in combination, and having regard to the considerations of fact and law involved. For example, in *Anglo American Corporation/Lonrho* (Case M.754), the Commission considered that Anglo American's 27.5 per cent stake in Lonrho enabled it to cast a majority of votes at shareholders meetings, allowing it to exercise decisive influence over – and thereby control – Lonrho. Anglo American was also the only major mining company holding shares in Lonrho, and the next-largest shareholder held only 3 per cent of Lonrho's shares. Decisive influence can also be constituted by veto rights going beyond normal minority protection rights of shareholders, for example where two or more companies can jointly exert decisive influence over the target's affairs, namely its budget, investment and appointment of management.

Even in the absence of specific veto rights, two or more minority shareholders may jointly control the joint venture where, together, they have the majority of the voting rights and they act together in exercising those voting rights. Such collective action can result from a legally binding agreement to this effect or it can occur on a de facto basis, for example, where strong common interests exist between the minority shareholders. In this respect, the Commission may look at voting behaviour in the pre-existing company's decision-making bodies (in particular, the shareholders meetings) over a period of time.

An important Commission decision regarding joint control is *Conagra/Idea* (Case M.010). Conagra was to acquire 20 per cent of a new joint venture's share capital entitling it to 26 per cent of the voting rights on the board of directors. Conagra also had rights to subscribe for additional shares of up to 50 per cent in total. A 75 per cent majority was required on the joint venture's board for such things as the approval of the annual budget, strategic plans, selection of management, investment and launching new products. The Commission considered that Conagra's ability to block decisions of the board requiring a 75 per cent majority went beyond the usual protection of a minority shareholder and therefore decided that Conagra had the right to exercise a decisive influence on the joint venture with the result that the acquisition was treated as a concentration.

Where investors subscribing for shares in the target company finance a transaction, there is a possibility they could exert decisive influence. For this reason, management buy-outs and other venture-capital type transactions may also fall within the scope of the ECMR (*see*, for example, *Industri Kapital/Dyno* (Case M.1813)). Whether such a conclusion can be reached will depend on the precise nature of the voting or contractual rights that the investors/subscribers have in the target company. Where such rights go beyond the usual protection afforded to minority shareholders, investors are likely to have joint control with the purchaser over the target.

1.2.2.3 Exceptions
The ECMR does not apply to certain acquisitions by credit institutions holding securities on a temporary basis, certain acquisitions in the context of insolvency proceedings, certain acquisitions by financial holding companies, or to intra-group restructurings.

1.2.2.4 Community dimension
If it is established that the transaction in question is a "concentration" (as described above), it is then necessary to consider whether the concentration meets certain turnover thresholds and therefore has a "Community dimension".

The relevant turnover is the amount derived during the last financial year from the sale of products or the provision of services after the deduction of sales rebates and taxes directly related to turnover. Special rules apply for the calculation of the turnover of financial and credit institutions and insurance companies.

Under the ECMR, a concentration has a Community dimension where:

(a)   the combined aggregate worldwide turnover of all of the companies concerned is more than €5 billion (this threshold is intended to exclude mergers between small and medium-sized companies);

(b)   the aggregate Community-wide turnover of each of at least two of the companies concerned is more than €250 million (this threshold is intended to exclude relatively minor acquisitions by large companies or acquisitions with only a minor European dimension); and

(c)   *unless* each of the companies concerned achieves more than two-thirds of its aggregate Community-wide turnover within one and the same Member State (this threshold is intended to exclude cases where the effects of the merger are felt primarily in a single Member State, where it is more appropriate for the national competition authorities to deal with it).

The ECMR also includes concentrations of a smaller size where it is likely that the transaction concerned would have been caught by multiple national merger-control regimes. Thus the ECMR also applies where:

(a)   the combined aggregate worldwide turnover of all of the companies concerned is more than €2.5 billion; and

(b)   the aggregate Community-wide turnover of each of at least two of the companies concerned is more than €100 million; and

(c)   the combined aggregate turnover of all of the companies concerned is more than €100 million in each of at least three Member States; and

(d)   in each of at least three of these Member States, the aggregate turnover of each of at least two of the companies concerned is more than €25 million;

(e)   *unless* each of the companies concerned achieves more than two-thirds of its aggregate Community-wide turnover within one and the same Member State.

The turnover thresholds under the ECMR have the effect of bringing within the Commission's jurisdiction transactions which take place outside the EU and where neither the parties nor the business concerned are principally European in nature. As long as a concentration has a Community dimension, it is irrelevant that none of the parties have a registered office, subsidiary or branch within the EU. For example, mergers between US companies (such as *Oracle/PeopleSoft* (Case M.3216)) may be caught where each of the merging companies have Community turnover in excess of €250 million, and satisfied the combined aggregate worldwide turnover threshold of €5 billion.

1.2.3   *Notification of a concentration*

All concentrations with a Community dimension must be notified to the Commission prior to their implementation and following: conclusion of the agreement, announcement of a public bid, or the acquisition of a controlling interest. Notification may also be made where the parties can demonstrate to the Commission a good-faith intention to conclude an agreement, for example following the signing of a letter of intent or, in the case of a public bid, where they have publicly announced an intention to make such a bid. The notification must be made on Form CO, as published by the Commission. Copies of the notification are sent to the competition authorities of the Member States.

A simplified procedure may be used for routine cases which do not involve significant competition issues. Such notifications are made on short Form CO, which requires less information than Form CO. However, a Form CO will be required where the Commission determines that it is necessary for an adequate investigation of possible competition concerns.

The Commission actively encourages the parties to initiate contact at the earliest opportunity and at least two weeks (or longer in more difficult cases) before the expected date of notification. It has in the past been cooperative in providing confidential guidance to parties in informal pre-notification contacts. Such contacts may be instrumental in avoiding a second-phase investigation, particularly if difficult issues are involved, as it effectively gives the Commission more time to examine the case.

1.2.3.1   *Suspension of the concentration*
The merger cannot be completed until it has been declared compatible with the common market. However, a duly notified public bid can proceed as long as the bidder does not exercise the voting rights attached to the securities in question

or does so only to "maintain the full value of those investments". The Commission may also on request grant a derogation from the obligation to suspend the concentration and will be guided by the effect of the suspension on the parties to the merger (for example, major financial risks) and on third parties, as well as the threat to competition posed by the concentration. However, in practice, the Commission has remained reluctant to grant derogations. As at 31 January 2008, only 95 derogations have been granted.

Parties can be fined if they implement a merger in contravention of the suspension requirements, although failure to comply with them does not affect the validity of the merger itself, as this will depend on the outcome of the Commission's investigation. Similar fines may be imposed for breach of any conditions attached to a clearance or for implementing a concentration in breach of a prohibition decision, as well as periodic fines to compel undertakings to comply with an obligation imposed by the Commission when it grants a derogation from the suspension period, any clearance conditions or prohibition decisions. Lesser fines may be imposed for failure to notify, late notification, or the submission of false or misleading information.

The Commission is using its fining powers with increasing frequency. For example, the Commission fined Tetra Laval €90,000 for providing incorrect or misleading information relating to the acquisition of Sidel (Case M.3255). Further, on 13 December 2007 the Commission announced that it had carried out dawn raids at the premises of two unidentified suspension PVC manufacturers in the UK (under Article 13 of the ECMR) for allegedly implementing a notifiable merger without first obtaining clearance from the Commission.

1.2.3.2 *Timing of the Commission's review*
Where a transaction falls within the ECMR, the Commission must make decisions "without delay". It has 25 working days in which to make its initial first-phase assessment. This is extended to 35 working days where the parties give undertakings to have the transaction cleared to give the Commission time to seek third-party comments on the proposed undertakings, or where a Member State makes a request that the merger be referred to it. The Commission must then either clear the transaction or open an in-depth second-phase investigation where it finds that the merger raises "serious doubts as to its compatibility with the common market".

In this second phase, the Commission has an additional 90 working days in which to approve (with or without conditions) or prohibit the transaction. This period is extended to 105 working days where the parties offer undertakings, unless they are offered within 55 working days after the opening of the in-depth investigation. These periods may also be extended once, for a maximum of 20 working days, at the request of the parties within 15 working days after the opening of the in-depth investigation, or any time by the Commission with the agreement of the parties.

Under the simplified procedure, concentrations that fulfil the requirements for clearance are declared compatible with the common market at the end of the first phase.

1.2.3.3 Undertakings

Parties may give undertakings to meet specific competition objections and thereby obtain clearance of the transaction. Undertakings can be given either in the first phase so as to avoid a second-phase investigation, or during the second phase. The Commission will consult with third parties concerning the undertakings offered. As set out in its Remedies Notice, the Commission prefers structural remedies (usually involving divestiture of assets) as opposed to behavioural commitments (such as licensing products or brands to third parties), and requires that any activities to be divested must consist of a viable business that can compete effectively with the merged entity. Parties may even be required to offer an "up-front buyer" for the business to be divested as a condition of final approval of the merger (*see*, for example, *Fortis/ABN Amro* (Case M.4844)).

If it becomes apparent that the Commission has serious concerns as to the compatibility of the transaction, the parties can withdraw their initial filing. This gives the parties the opportunity to restructure and renotify the deal to overcome the competition objections. This may help to avoid the opening of a second-phase investigation, the imposition of conditions or a prohibition decision. This approach was adopted by the parties in *Microsoft/Time Warner/ContentGuard* (Case M.3445), where the transaction was restructured and the notification withdrawn as the transaction no longer constituted a concentration. Where a notification is withdrawn, the Commission no longer has the power to adopt the decision and prohibit the concentration (Case T-310/00, *MCI v Commission*). Any withdrawn transaction may, however, still fall within the scope of national merger control regimes.

1.2.3.4 The Commission's decision

Where the Commission finds that the merger is not compatible with the common market, it may require divestiture of assets, or order any other action which it considers appropriate to restore conditions of "effective competition". For example, *Tetra Laval/Sidel* (Case M.2416) involved public bids for a French company which had closed before the Commission's decision was taken. The Commission prohibited the concentration and made orders for divestment.

1.2.3.5 Challenging the Commission's decision

The Commission decision to unconditionally clear, conditionally clear or prohibit a transaction may be the subject of an appeal to the Court of First Instance ("CFI"), and, from there, on points of law, to the European Court of Justice ("ECJ") by either the merging parties or third parties such as complainants (e.g., T-114/02, *BaByliss v Commission* [2003] ECR II-1279).

As introduced in 2001, any appellant may benefit from the use of expedited procedure to fast-track appeals before the CFI. The expedited procedure has succeeded in delivering judgments within approximately seven months (e.g., Case T-77/02, *Schneider Electric v Commission* and Case T-87/05, *EDP v Commission*) from the date of the application to appeal, while other appeals have taken considerably longer (e.g., 19 months in Case T-464/04, *Impala v Commission*). Due to the delays in the appeal process, there is an ongoing debate whether the expedited procedure should be revised or a specialist EU competition tribunal created.

Despite the length of the appeal process, in substantive terms, as demonstrated by two judgments in 2006 and 2007, it would appear that the CFI is carefully scrutinising the Commission's decisions.

In July 2006, the CFI annulled the Commission's decision to clear the Sony/BMG joint venture (Case T-464/04, *Impala* v *Commission*), following an appeal by the trade association Impala. Although the CFI had previously annulled prohibition and conditional clearance decisions, this was the first time that the CFI over-turned an unconditional clearance decision. The Commission had concluded, following an in-depth investigation, that it did not have sufficiently strong evidence to oppose the deal on the basis of collective dominance in the market for recorded music. However, the CFI criticised the Commission for failing to adequately reason the decision and ordered the Commission to re-examine the transaction. Sony and Bertelsmann have appealed the CFI's judgment to the ECJ (Case C-413/06, *Bertelsmann AG and Sony Corporation of America*), although on 13 December 2007, Advocate General Kokott recommended that the ECJ dismiss the appeal. Meanwhile, on 3 October 2007, the Commission announced that, after a further in depth investigation, it had again unconditionally approved the Sony/BMG merger.

In July 2007, the CFI ruled that the Commission must pay Schneider Electric partial compensation for losses sustained due to procedural flaws in the review of its bid for rival Legrand in 2001 (Case T-351/03, *Schneider Electric* v *Commission*). Although this is the first award of damages in relation to an unlawful prohibition of a merger, it adopts a relatively narrow interpretation of the Commission's liability. While procedural breaches are a good candidate for compensation, most substantive errors are unlikely to constitute a "manifest breach" given the margin of discretion available to the Commission in its application of the competition provisions. The Commission is appealing this judgment before the ECJ.

In addition to previous successful appeals to prohibition and conditional clearance decisions, the increased scrutiny of the Commission's decisions in these cases can be expected to further increase the burden on the Commission to fully justify all of its decisions and to follow appropriate procedures in order to respect rights of defence.

1.2.3.6 *The role of third parties*
Immediately following the notification of a concentration or the opening of a second-phase investigation, the Commission publishes a notice in the *Official Journal of the European Communities*, inviting third parties (customers and suppliers as well as competitors) to comment on the transaction (normally within 10 or 15 days from publication of the notice). In addition, where necessary, the Commission requests third parties to answer specific questions during the course of the investigation. Third parties may also submit comments to the Commission voluntarily at any stage of the proceedings and may apply to be heard by the Commission. Substantial criticism from third parties may trigger a second-phase investigation.

Third parties are often able to impact significantly the EU merger investigation process. It is increasingly the case that, if a merger is likely to be challenged by a deep-pocketed complainant and/or a considerable volume of negative third-party comment, it will be probed in considerable depth by the Commission. Indeed, as discussed above at 1.2.3.5, the Commission decision to clear the *Sony/BMG* joint venture was annulled by the CFI following an appeal from a third party. Even if the proposed transaction is not subjected to an in-depth investigation, in order to achieve clearance the notifying parties are required to produce more extensive evidence than has previously been the case, and particularly good evidence is required to dispel third-party complaints.

1.2.4   Compatibility with the common market

1.2.4.1   Significant impediment to effective competition
The Commission must determine whether a concentration significantly impedes effective competition in the common market, in particular, by creating or strengthening a dominant position. This substantive analysis also considers any unilateral effects in oligopolistic markets where the merged entity's market share falls below the traditional dominance threshold. Unilateral effects occur in relation to horizontal mergers which remove important competitive constraint on one or more sellers, such as the elimination of a price maverick.

In assessing a concentration's compatibility with the common market, the Commission initially considers the market share of the merged entity in the relevant product and geographic markets. The Commission must define these markets as part of its assessment, and guidance on this process is given in its Notice on the definition of the relevant market. A market share below 25 per cent is generally not liable to impede competition. High market shares (typically in excess of 40 per cent), whilst often triggering a second-phase investigation, will not necessarily lead to a finding of incompatibility as, for example, in *Danish Crown/Vestjyske Slagterier* (Case M.1313), market shares of 80 per cent were cleared.

Following the calculation of market shares, the Commission will assess the characteristics of the relevant market in order to determine whether the concentration creates any competition concerns. The Commission may rely on economic theories to articulate its competition concerns, such as:

(a)   portfolio effects – in *Guinness/Grand Metropolitan* (Case M.938), the Commission considered the inclusion of strong brands in a range of drinks belonging to separate markets, and found that their inclusion could give each of the brands in the portfolio greater strength on the market than if they were sold individually, thereby strengthening the competitive position of the portfolio's owner on several markets;

(b)   conglomerate effects – in *Tetra Laval/Sidel* (Case M.2416), the Commission concluded that Tetra Laval's dominance in one market could be leveraged into another distinct, but closely related, market, and blocked the merger. On appeal, the CFI did not dispute the economic theory but found that the Commission must adduce convincing evidence to support a finding (*see* also *GE/Honeywell* (Case M.2220) and *SEB/Moulinex* (Case M.2621)). It would appear from *GE/Amersham* (Case M.3304) that the Commission has taken seriously some of the CFI's criticisms by implementing a more rigorous economic and empirical approach;

(c)   network externalities – in *WorldCom/Sprint* (Case M.1741), the Commission found that the attraction of a network to its customers was a function of the number of other customers connected to the same network and would have enabled the merged entity to behave independently of its competitors and customers and to degrade the quality of internet-related services offered to its competitors (*see* also *WorldCom/MCI* (Case M.1069));

(d)   gatekeeper effect – in *Vodafone/Vivendi/Canal+* (Case JV.48), the Commission found that the merged entity would be able to control the emerging market of TV-based internet portals through proprietary technology (*see* also *Vivendi/Canal+/Seagram* (Case M.2050) and *Microsoft/Time Warner/ContentGuard* (Case M.3445)).

In assessing any competition concerns, as stated in its Horizontal Guidelines, the Commission must take into account factors such as:

(a)   strong evidence of potential new entrants;
(b)   low barriers to entry;
(c)   the availability of alternative (albeit not substitutable) products;
(d)   the existence of countervailing buying power;
(e)   a tendency to wider geographic markets; and
(f)   the limited impact of the concentration on the merged entity's market position.

Although typically reticent to accept any arguments based on post-merger efficiencies, the Commission has cleared the creation of a duopoly on the basis that the transaction would generate substantial merger-specific efficiencies that would be likely to be passed on to consumers (Case M.4057 *Korsnäs/Assidomän Cartonboard*).

The Commission has published guidelines on the assessment of non-horizontal mergers, the purpose of which is to consolidate and elaborate on the Commission's experience in this area. The guidelines note that non-horizontal mergers are generally less likely to create competition concerns than horizontal mergers for two reasons. First, unlike horizontal mergers, vertical or conglomerate mergers do not entail the loss of direct competition between the merging firms in the same relevant market. As a result, the main source of anti-competitive effect in horizontal mergers is absent from vertical and conglomerate mergers. Second, vertical and conglomerate mergers provide substantial scope for efficiencies. A characteristic of vertical mergers and certain conglomerate mergers is that the activities and/or the products of the companies involved are *complementary* to each other. The integration of complementary activities or products within a single firm may produce significant efficiencies and be pro-competitive.

1.2.4.2   *Joint dominance and oligopolies*

The Commission may prohibit concentrations which create or strengthen oligopolistic market structures, even if the merged entity on its own would not occupy a dominant position. In cases involving collective dominance, the Commission must ascertain "whether the concentration would have the direct and immediate effect of creating or strengthening a collective dominant position which is such as significantly and lastingly to impede competition in the relevant market" (Case T-342/99, *Airtours* v *Commission* [2002] ECR II-2585). In making this analysis the Commission takes into account a range of factors, such as transparency in the market, product homogeneity, market growth, innovation, barriers to entry, incentives to compete and possibilities for retaliation, as well as the position of smaller operators.

Although the CFI has confirmed the substantive test to be applied, it has been extremely critical of the way in which the Commission has applied the test to the facts of the case. As a result, the Commission would appear to be taking a more cautious approach in its review of mergers. Furthermore, in the wake of the CFI's decision in *Sony/BMG* (discussed above at 1.2.3.5), the Commission is likely to be even more thorough in its assessment and reasoning.

1.2.4.3   Full-function joint ventures

Full-function joint ventures that give rise to coordination of competitive behaviour between the parents (so-called cooperative joint ventures) will, in addition, be examined under Article 81 of the EC Treaty, which prohibits restrictive agreements and practices. These joint ventures are therefore subject to a double test: the establishment of the joint venture will be subject to the same test as for mergers and acquisitions, whereas the coordination between the parents will be assessed under Article 81 of the EC Treaty.

1.2.5   Interplay with national merger controls

There are a number of referral mechanisms whereby concentrations that do not have a Community dimension may be referred to the Commission and also, in an exception to the one-stop shop principle, concentrations with a Community dimension may be referred to the national competition authorities. In addition, there is scope for Member States to review concentrations with a Community dimension other than on competition grounds.

1.2.5.1   Pre-notification referrals to Member States

Parties may request that a concentration with a Community dimension be referred, in whole or in part, to a Member State on the basis that it affects competition in a market within that Member State which presents all of the characteristics of a distinct market. Unless that Member State disagrees within 15 working days, the Commission, where it considers that such a distinct market exists and that competition in that market may be significantly affected, may decide to refer the whole or part of the concentration to the Member State(s) concerned.

1.2.5.2   Post-notification referrals to Member States

The Commission may, at the request of a Member State, refer a notified concentration with a Community dimension, in whole or in part, to the relevant authority of the Member State concerned. It has a discretion as to whether to make such a referral when the concentration threatens to significantly affect competition in a distinct market within that Member State, unless the territory concerned does not form a substantial part of the common market, in which case the Commission is obliged to make the (partial) referral.

1.2.5.3   Legitimate interests

The Commission retains sole jurisdiction to investigate mergers on competition grounds, but the ECMR sets out other grounds on which Member States may carry out a parallel investigation if its "legitimate interests" are affected, such as "public security", "plurality of the media" and "prudential rules". Member States may rely on other legitimate interests as long as they are notified to the Commission. Other legitimate interests need only be notified by the Commission if they are aimed at the transaction as such (*EDF/London Electricity* decision (Case M.1346)).

However, the Commission remains competent to determine whether a Member State's legitimate interests are affected and may prevent a Member State from blocking a concentration falling within the scope of the ECMR.

There has been a resurgence of economic protectionism across a number of EC industry sectors (in particular, energy and financial services), with national regulators utilising special rights in relation to certain sectors to block an acquisition by a foreign entity or pass through an acquisition by another national company to prevent a foreign acquisition. In response to this protectionism, the Commission has taken action to ensure that its exclusive competence to assess the competitive impact of concentrations with a Community dimension is not infringed.

For example, in July 2007, the Commission unconditionally cleared the acquisition of joint control of Endesa by Enel and Acciona in the Spanish energy sector (Case M.4685 *Enel/Acciona/Endesa*). The CNE, the Spanish energy regulator, had previously imposed a number of conditions on the concentration. As these decisions were adopted without prior communication to, or approval by, the Commission, the Commission launched proceedings against Spain for violation of the ECMR. On 5 December 2007 the Commission announced that it had notified Spain of its provisional conclusion that the conditions imposed by the CNE breached Article 43 (freedom of establishment) and Article 56 (free movement of capital) of the EC Treaty. It also considered that one condition breached Articles 28 and 29 of the EC Treaty (free movement of goods). Although Spain subsequently modified the CNE conditions, following an appeal by Enel and Acciona, the Commission concluded (by a decision of 5 December 2007) that its concerns had not been fully addressed. It required Spain to withdraw the relevant conditions by 10 January 2008. At the time of writing, the Spanish authorities have not informed the Commission of any steps or measures taken in order to comply with the decision of 5 December 2007. As can be seen from *Enel/Acciona/Endesa*, the Commission's powers to enforce the ECMR coincides with its general powers to implement the basic freedoms guaranteed by the EU Treaty. For example, although the Commission cleared the acquisition of Antonveneta, an Italian bank, by ABN Amro, the governor of Italy's central bank, who at the time held a personal veto right over banking mergers, attempted to prevent this acquisition by favouring a rival bid by another Italian bank. Although ABN Amro eventually won the takeover battle, the Commission investigated the matter and initiated proceedings against Italy on the basis that the discriminatory exercise of the governor's veto rights violated EU rules on free movement of capital and freedom of establishment. The Italian legislators subsequently amended the legislation and the Commission dropped the proceedings.

1.2.5.4   Pre-notification referrals to the Commission

Parties may request that a concentration without Community dimension but which triggers the merger control laws of three Member States be referred to the Commission. Upon such a referral, each Member State, whose merger control is triggered, has 15 working days to express its disagreement. In the absence of any disagreement, the concentration shall be deemed to have a Community dimension and require a full-form notification.

1.2.5.5   Post-notification referrals to the Commission

A Member State, or several Member States acting together, may request the Commission to investigate a concentration that does not have a Community dimension, insofar as the concentration affects trade between Member States. Such a request must be made within 15 working days of the concentration being notified or otherwise made known to the Member States. The Commission will refuse to investigate a concentration unless it meets the criteria set out in the ECMR. For example, the Commission refused Portugal's and Italy's application for a referral of the *Gaz Natural/Endesa* merger from the Spanish competition authority, despite concerns that the transaction was being rushed through by the Spanish authorities in order to create a "national champion" and prevent an overseas company from gaining control of one of Spain's largest energy companies.

1.2.5.6   International cooperation

The increasing frequency of mergers with international or even global effects poses particular challenges in the field of competition enforcement, as they are often reviewed by a number of different agencies.

For instance, many international mergers will be reviewed by both the Commission and the US antitrust agencies (the US Federal Trade Commission and the Antitrust Division of the Department of Justice ("DOJ")). Following the divergent EU/US outcomes in *GE/Honeywell* in 2002 (Case M.2220), the Commission and the US antitrust agencies developed a set of best practices on cooperation in reviewing mergers that require approval on both sides of the Atlantic. The best practices put in place a more structured basis for cooperation in reviews of individual merger cases and recognise that cooperation is most effective when the investigation timetables of the reviewing agencies run more or less in parallel. Merging companies will therefore be offered the possibility of meeting at an early stage with the agencies to discuss timing issues. Companies are also encouraged to permit the agencies to exchange information which they have submitted during the course of an investigation and, where appropriate, to allow joint EU/US interviews of the companies concerned. The practices moreover designate key points in the respective EU and US merger investigations when it may be appropriate for direct contacts to occur between senior officials on both sides. In 2006, the Commission has worked closely with the DOJ in relation to *Inco/Falconbridge* (Case M.4000).

The Commission also has a number of other bilateral agreements, which include cooperation in the field of merger control, for example, with Canada (1999) and Japan (2003).

In addition to bilateral agreements, there is increasingly a trend towards involving a wider range of countries and agencies in a multilateral approach to addressing the issues. This is best illustrated by the development of the International Competition Network ("ICN"), which is a forum within which antitrust officials from developed and developing countries can work to address practical enforcement and policy issues of common concern. The network aims to facilitate procedural and substantive convergence in antitrust enforcement and develop non-binding recommendations for consideration by individual enforcement agencies.

The ICN's Merger Working Group has been focusing on the merger control process as it applies to multi-jurisdictional mergers. In particular, there are two sub-groups focused on merger notification and procedures, and merger investigational analysis.

1.2.6 Merger control and takeovers

Provided the takeover meets the requirements of being a concentration and has a Community dimension, the ECMR will apply. Particularly in transactions which involve companies in more than one Member State, it is usually preferable to fall within the ECMR and have the Commission handle the matter exclusively. With its mandatory timetable, the ECMR provides the companies with more legal certainty than some of the national merger control procedures. Competitive bids for the same target may be subject to different systems.

The initial 25 working day period during which the Commission must make its preliminary finding is unlikely to interfere with most bid timetables which usually require that an offer be open for a minimum three-week period. The consequences for a takeover bid of the Commission initiating proceedings vary between jurisdictions. At one extreme are France and Spain where an offer cannot be conditional on proceedings not being initiated; if proceedings are initiated the offeror must go ahead with the offer and take such action as may be required by the Commission at the end of its investigation. At the other extreme is the UK, where the offer must lapse if proceedings are initiated within a specified period after launch. In Belgium, Germany, Italy and the Netherlands, for example, the bid may be conditional.

1.3 The Takeover Directive

1.3.1 Background

After over 14 years of negotiations and redrafts, the European Directive on Takeover Bids (2004/25/EC) ("the Takeover Directive") finally was adopted in spring 2004. The Takeover Directive's aim was to introduce certain common rules for conducting takeover bids in the EU, in pursuance of the EU's fundamental objective to promote and achieve a single market in financial services to facilitate pan-European restructuring and help make Europe the most competitive economy in the world. It can be viewed within the context of the regulatory regime changes that have brought about the adoption and implementation of the Prospectus Directive, Market Abuse Directive, Transparency Directive and MiFID, among others. However, in contrast to such aims the Takeover Directive is essentially a compromise, not least owing to the difficulties encountered in reaching agreement between Member States. Moreover, as a "minimum-standards" rather than a "harmonisation" directive, the Takeover Directive has not been wholly successful in achieving a truly level playing field across the EU. The fact that Member States can opt out of some fundamental provisions of the Takeover Directive reduces still further its ability to standardise a regulatory approach to takeovers across Europe.

The Takeover Directive stipulated an implementation deadline of no later than 20 May 2006, by which time EU Member States were to have enacted the laws, regulations and administrative provisions necessary to comply with the Takeover Directive.

Every EU Member State has now implemented the Takeover Directive with the exception only of the Czech Republic, Denmark and Estonia.

The degree to which implementation of the Takeover Directive has (or will have) altered the law and impacted upon market practice in each of the EU Member States varies considerably. In some Member States such as the UK, the overall impact in practice has not been particularly significant. In contrast, Member States that previously had more lightly regulated or less mature takeovers markets have been more significantly affected. The following sections of this Chapter describe, in overview, some of these changes. For a fuller description of specific current regimes, *see* the later Chapters in this Guide.

1.3.2   Main features of the Takeover Directive

1.3.2.1   Scope and framework of general principles

The Takeover Directive applies to takeover bids for securities of companies governed by the laws of a Member State if all or some of the securities are admitted to trading on a regulated market in one or more Member States. The Takeover Directive does not apply to bids for central banks or open-ended investment companies or to targets which are non-EU issuers, even if such companies' securities are traded in the EU.

In the interests of maintaining a unified national takeover regime, many Member States have taken the approach of adopting Takeover Directive equivalent regulation in respect of bids for companies falling without the scope of the Takeover Directive. For example, in the UK, bids for UK companies admitted to trading on non-regulated UK markets (such as the London Stock Exchange's Alternative Investment Market ("AIM")) are subject to substantially the same regime as companies admitted to trading on the London Stock Exchange's Main Market (which is a "regulated market" for the purposes of the Takeover Directive).

Similarly and by way of further example, Spain has chosen to apply Takeover Directive equivalent provisions to its regulation of all bids for listed companies whose registered addresses are in Spain.

In Germany and the Netherlands, the Takeover Act applies only to companies whose securities are admitted to trading on an "organised", that is, "regulated" market. Therefore, takeover offers for companies whose securities are only admitted to trading on other markets (such as the open market) do not fall within the scope of the Dutch or German Takeover Act respectively.

In France, bids for French companies whose shares are admitted to trading on Alternext, a non-regulated market, are subject to a slightly less strict regime than companies admitted to trading on Eurolist Paris (which is a "regulated market" for the purposes of the Takeover Directive).

The Takeover Directive sets out a framework of general principles establishing minimum requirements which must be complied with by Member States when implementing the Takeover Directive. The six general principles, in summary, provide that:

(a)   target shareholders of the same class should be afforded equivalent treatment;
(b)   target shareholders should be given sufficient time and information to enable them to reach a properly informed decision on a bid and the target board should give its opinion on the effects of the bid on employment and locations of business;
(c)   the target board acts in the interests of the company as a whole;
(d)   no false markets should be created;
(e)   a bid should only be announced after a bidder is certain that it can fulfil any cash consideration; and
(f)   the target should not be hindered by a bid for longer than is reasonable.

As noted above, the Takeover Directive is a minimum-standards directive and thus Member States are permitted to impose their own additional and more stringent standards than the minimum. As a result, takeover rules across Member States continue to vary.

1.3.2.2   Supervisory authority
Under the Takeover Directive, Member States are required to designate an authority to supervise bids which can be a public or private body.

Since 1968 takeovers in the UK have been supervised by the Panel on Takeovers and Mergers ("the Panel"). Prior to the implementation of the Takeover Directive in the UK, the Panel was a non-statutory body without statutory enforcement powers. Its rules, as set out in the Code, similarly lacked the force of law. Despite this lack of statutory force prior to implementation of the Takeover Directive, the Panel still exerted much influence, and the courts were impressed by the Panel's ability to regulate the UK takeovers market.

Further to this, the Panel had various sanctions at its indirect disposal. For example, the Panel could request the FSA to take enforcement action against a firm that did not comply with the Code. One of the actions possible was the so-called "cold shoulder" rule. Under this rule, a firm could not act for any person in connection with a transaction governed by the Code if it had reason to believe the person for whom it was acting was not complying with the Code. The Panel would publish notices identifying specific persons or firms who, in its opinion, were not likely to have complied with the Code. In the UK market, the fear of censure or criticism, whether public or private, by the Panel was, and continues to be, a powerful deterrent for companies and their advisers. In implementation of the Takeovers Directive, the Panel was given a statutory footing, and the Code was given the force of law (in respect of bids for London Stock Exchange Main Market listed companies from 20 May 2006 and in respect of bids for most other listed companies from 6 April 2007). With its new status, the Panel has been granted a wide range of enforcement powers, including the power to require the disclosure of documents and information, the ability to require compensation to be paid to target shareholders, and the power to seek enforcement orders from the Courts.

In Spain, the body responsible for supervising and inspecting the Spanish securities markets and, in particular, responsible for authorising and controlling takeover bid procedures is the Spanish Securities Market Commission, Comisión Nacional del Mercado de Valores ("CNMV"), created by Law 24/1988. The implementation of the Takeover Directive has had little impact on the Commission's status or responsibilities.

In the Netherlands, whilst the Authority for the Financial Markets Autoriteit Financiële Markten ("AFM") remains the competent authority with respect to monitoring the procedural aspects of a takeover bid, the Enterprise Chamber of the Amsterdam Court of Appeal is competent in all company law matters, including, in particular, the determination as to whether a duty to make a mandatory bid has arisen. This effectively means that the supervision of the new rules that were introduced on implementation of the Takeover Directive is allocated between the AFM and the Enterprise Chamber.

1.3.2.3 Jurisdiction

Under the Takeover Directive, if a target has its registered office and its securities are admitted to trading on a regulated market in the same Member State, then the supervisory authority of such Member State has jurisdiction over all matters in connection with the takeover bid. If the securities of the target are not admitted to trading on a regulated market in the Member State in which such company's registered office is situated, jurisdiction lies with the supervisory authority in the Member State on whose regulated market the securities of the target are admitted to trading, but it shares responsibility with the supervisory authority where the target has its registered office.

Although the EU Member States that have implemented the Takeover Directive have generally enacted such jurisdiction provisions into the relevant laws, it is possible that complicated issues regarding shared supervisory jurisdiction will arise at some point. This is because the Directive does not set out a comprehensive list of those aspects of a bid which are to be governed by each authority, nor are any procedures for resolving disputes concerning shared jurisdiction provided for in the Directive.

Given the drive to open up regulated markets across the EU, it is likely to become increasingly common for a company's shares to be traded in a different country to that of its registered office and therefore the issues arising with shared supervisory jurisdiction are likely to have to be addressed in the future.

1.3.2.4 Mandatory bids

The Takeover Directive requires Member States to implement a mandatory bid requirement for the acquisition of shares above a certain threshold, at an equitable price. The threshold at which a bid must be made is left for Member States to determine.

In the UK, prior to the implementation of the Takeover Directive, Rule 9 of the Code already required a person to make a mandatory bid in cash for a company where such person and its concert parties acquired an interest in shares carrying 30 per cent or more of the voting rights of the company. As the minimum price for such mandatory bid was fixed by reference to the highest price such person or its concert parties had paid for shares in the company in the previous 12 months, Rule 9 was already Takeover Directive compliant.

Similarly, minimal changes were required in Member States such as France and Germany, whose regimes previously required mandatory bids set at thresholds, broadly, of 33.33 per cent and 30 per cent respectively of the target share capital.

This is in stark contrast to the position in, for example, Belgium, Spain and the Netherlands. Prior to implementation of the Takeover Directive, Belgian takeover law did not contain a set threshold triggering the obligation to launch a mandatory bid except where an absolute majority of over 50 per cent of voting rights was acquired. Instead, a case-by-case analysis was required, which led to varying stakes triggering mandatory bids in different circumstances.

Belgium implemented the Takeover Directive on 1 April 2007 and had to substantially alter its former regime. The new regime entered into force on 1 September 2007. It provides that, similarly to the situation in the UK and Germany, the threshold at which a bid must be made is 30 per cent. A "grand-fathering clause" allows shareholders, alone or acting in concert, not to launch a mandatory bid if they held more than 30 per cent prior to the entry into force of the new law on 1 September 2007 (provided that they had notified this situation to the company and the competent authority, the Belgian Banking Finance and Insurance Commission).

The pre-Takeovers Directive regime in Spain required a bidder to make a filing before it acquired the relevant shareholding in the target. A mandatory bid may have arisen, depending on the percentage of the share capital of the target that the bidder would have acquired, as well as on the number of directors of the target that the bidder would have been entitled to appoint as a result of the acquisition. The previous Spanish regulations provided not only for mandatory bids for 100 per cent of the target's securities, but also for mandatory partial takeover bids in certain circumstances.

Following implementation of the Takeover Directive in Spain, the historic regime has been replaced by a mandatory full takeover bid procedure pursuant to which the party acquiring control (broadly the acquisition of more than 30 per cent of the voting rights, or a smaller stake with the appointment of a majority of directors within 24 months following the acquisition) of a listed target company has to launch a bid for 100 per cent of such company at a reasonable price.

The implementation of the Takeover Directive introduced a mandatory bid in the Netherlands for the first time. The threshold triggering a mandatory bid is set at 30 per cent of the total amount of the shares or depositary receipts owned in a Dutch public company listed on a regulated market. The minimum price for such a mandatory bid is fixed by reference to the highest price that the mandatory bidder or its concert parties have paid for shares in the company in the previous 12 months, or, when the mandatory bidder or its concert parties did not acquire any shares in the company during the previous 12 months, the average share price during the same 12 months.

The 30 per cent threshold for mandatory bids has been fully implemented in a number of eastern European countries too, for example, in Hungary, Romania and Poland, although in these three countries the threshold is slightly higher at 33 per cent.

1.3.2.5   *Squeeze-out and sell-out rights*

The Takeover Directive requires Member States to enact provisions enabling a bidder to squeeze out minority shareholders at a fair price once it has obtained a percentage threshold (between 90 and 95 per cent, at the discretion of the Member State) of the target's voting share capital and to provide minority share-holders with a reciprocal right upon a bidder's shareholding reaching such threshold.

In the UK, such squeeze-out rights (and reciprocal minority sell-out rights), set at a threshold of 90 per cent of the shares to which an offer relates, already applied to UK takeovers prior to implementation of the Takeover Directive. Aside from a few procedural changes, these provisions have not materially changed.

Similarly, in France the threshold remains at 95 per cent of shares and voting rights in accordance with previous practice.

Dutch corporate law already provided for a squeeze-out procedure, with a 95 per cent threshold. This was augmented by the introduction of sell-out provisions contemplated by the Takeover Directive available in the context of a successful takeover bid. The implementation of the Takeover Directive in the Netherlands did introduce the possibility of a squeeze-out procedure in relation to a separate class of shares (if applicable to the target company), thus enabling the bidder only to squeeze-out holders of a certain class of shares, rather than having to squeeze-out all shareholders.

Prior to the implementation of the Takeover Directive, Belgian law already provided that a shareholder holding 95 per cent of the voting securities of a company following a successful offer had the right, but not the obligation, to buy out the remaining minority shareholders, provided such shareholder had been able to acquire at least 66 per cent of the securities he did not hold prior to launching the offer. This procedure remained unchanged following the implementation of the Takeover Directive, with a 95 per cent threshold require-ment, but the 66 per cent threshold was increased to 90 per cent. However, the requirement that a shareholder who holds 95 per cent of the voting securities following his bid should also have acquired 90 per cent of the securities he did not hold prior to launching the bid only applies if the bid was voluntary, and not if it was mandatory. Under the new rules, it will also be possible to offer shares as consideration in a squeeze-out offer following an exchange offer. Further, the Belgian rules have been supplemented by the sell-out procedures contemplated by the Takeover Directive.

A squeeze-out procedure existed in Germany prior to the implementation of the Takeover Directive, whereby with a 95 per cent holding in a company's share capital, no matter how that holding was acquired, or whether or not the company was listed, it was possible to request the squeeze-out of the minority shareholders. Following the implementation of the Takeover Directive, additional squeeze-out provisions as well as sell-out provisions have been introduced into the German Takeover Act. The thresholds for both procedures pursuant to the German Takeover Act amount to 95 per cent of the voting rights.

For many Member States, such as Spain, Greece, Luxembourg, Slovenia, Malta and Slovakia, the introduction of the squeeze-out provisions was a major development, as their previous regimes did not contemplate such provisions at all.

1.3.2.6 *Frustrating action and breakthrough provisions*

The Takeover Directive contains provisions which prohibit target companies taking action without shareholder approval, which might have the effect of frustrating or hindering a bid ("frustrating-action provisions").

The Takeover Directive also includes so-called "breakthrough provisions" which require that, once a bid has been made public, any restrictions on share transfers are to be suspended during the acceptance period, and any restrictions on voting rights, or weighted voting rights, are to be disapplied with respect to the passing of shareholder resolutions relating to defensive measures proposed by the directors. Under the breakthrough provisions, a bidder who has acquired 75 per cent of a target is entitled to "breakthrough" any restrictions on the transfer of securities contained in a target's constitutional documents and to override multiple voting rights. The Takeover Directive requires that equitable compensation be paid to shareholders suffering a loss as a result of the operation of the breakthrough provisions and bidders will therefore need to assess whether this will impact on the pricing of their bid.

The 14-year battle over the Takeover Directive focused principally on the frustrating action and breakthrough provisions, and illustrated the difficulties of establishing common ground between Member States. In order to reach agreement on the Directive, a compromise was reached which allows Member States to choose to opt out of the frustrating-action provisions and breakthrough provisions. However, where a Member State opts out of either or both of these provisions, companies in that Member State may nonetheless opt back in if they obtain shareholder approval.

The Takeover Directive also contained optional "reciprocity" provisions with the effect that if Member States choose not to opt out of the frustrating-action provisions and breakthrough provisions, they can permit companies in their jurisdiction to disapply such provisions if the bidder is not subject to the same restrictions.

This complex compromise recognises therefore that the playing fields for takeover bids in the EU may not be level. Indeed, this may lead to certain bidders being discriminated against (including non-EU bidders and private companies) which do not have the reciprocal benefit of these provisions.

The UK has opted in to the prohibition of frustrating-action provisions. This principal was already enshrined in the Code at Rule 21.

However, the UK has opted out of the breakthrough provisions, but has enacted the necessary provisions enabling companies to opt in with shareholder approval. Note that the restrictive provisions in companies' articles that the breakthrough provisions are intended to dismantle are not commonly found in UK listed companies. The UK has not opted in to the reciprocal provisions.

France has opted in to the provisions in Article 9 of the Takeover Directive on frustrating action. Under the previous regime, the Board was simply required to notify France's financial regulatory body, the Autorité des Marches Financiers ("AMF"), prior to any such action which was likely to deter an offeree from initiating any defensive action where this had not received the prior approval of the AMF.

France has not opted out of the breakthrough provisions. However, French law has been amended to mitigate the effects of existing legislation that allow the articles of association to limit the number of voting rights exercisable by a single shareholder. Such limitation is suspended at a first general meeting of share-holders that takes place following the closing of an offer where the bidder becomes holder of a stake that exceeds two-thirds of the share capital or total number of voting rights.

Germany has opted out of the frustrating-action provisions of the Takeover Directive. However, German rules already provided for extensive prohibition of frustrating action. In cases where German stock corporations do not opt in to the frustrating-action provisions of the Takeover Directive, they are nevertheless subject to frustrating-action provisions pursuant to the German Takeover Act and the German Stock Corporations Act. These frustrating-action provisions are not, however, as strict as those contained in the Takeover Directive.

Germany has also opted out of the breakthrough provisions. As required by the Takeover Directive, German companies may opt in to either the frustrating-action provisions or the breakthrough provisions, in which case they must submit their amended articles of association to the German Federal Financial Supervisory Authority (Bundesanstalt für Finanzdienstleistungsaufsicht).

In the Netherlands, a Dutch listed company may opt to become subject to the requirement that any proposed frustrating action be approved by the share-holders in general meeting, by voluntarily incorporating this into its articles of association. Furthermore, a company may provide that transfer restrictions that may frustrate a bid will not apply to shares being offered to the bidder.

The Netherlands has also opted out of the breakthrough provisions. However, it is still possible for a Dutch listed company to opt voluntarily for the breakthrough provisions of the Directive to apply by incorporating the necessary provisions in its articles of association, although it is expected that few Dutch listed companies will opt in. For those companies that do, the ability for a major shareholder to propose and adopt resolutions will be limited to resolutions appointing and dismissing directors. Furthermore, the breakthrough provisions will not affect the so-called large company rule, which applies to a significant number of Dutch companies. Under this rule, it is the supervisory board and, to a lesser extent, the relevant works councils, rather than the shareholders that can effectively control the composition of a company's board.

Belgium opted out of both the frustrating-action provisions and the breakthrough provisions. However, Belgian companies may voluntarily opt in by amending their articles of association. If a company decides to opt in, it may do so under condition of reciprocity (i.e., the bidder must also have opted in). The reciprocity condition must also be inserted in its articles and be renewed every 18 months (otherwise it lapses and may no longer be invoked against the bidder).

1.3.2.7 Litigation

Prior to the implementation of the Takeover Directive, there were concerns that there would be an increase in the amount of tactical litigation, as often seen in the course of US takeover battles, particularly since the creation of statutory frameworks and statutory bodies to govern bids would seem to invite a more legalistic and, therefore, more litigious approach to takeovers. In practice, however, the drafting of the Directive itself, and its implementation, has meant that there has been little or no takeover-related litigation resulting from the implementation of the Directive, although this cannot be ruled out in the future.

Traditionally in the UK, the courts have been reluctant to interfere with the Panel's de facto jurisdiction over UK takeovers; indeed, in the landmark 1980s *Datafin* and *Guinness* cases, the court expressly recognised that contemporary intervention by the court in the heat of a takeover battle would be impossible or contrary to the public interest, assisting to ensure that the courts have not become involved in the conduct of takeovers, which have instead been regulated by the Takeover Panel (the "Panel"), with its flexibility and ability to move rapidly. Article 4(5) of the Takeover Directive requires that the national supervisory authorities (such as the Panel) shall be vested with all the powers necessary for the purposes of carrying out their duties, including ensuring compliance with the rules introduced pursuant to the Takeover Directive. Article 4(5), therefore, by ensuring that the national supervisory bodies are in effect self-governing and legally self-sufficient, has arguably, in the UK at least, strengthened the position of the Panel.

1.3.3 Impact of the Takeover Directive

As seen above, the Takeover Directive has led to a significant degree of harmonisation of takeover law and practice in Europe, but it does not guarantee a totally level playing field, not least because of the opt-out provisions. Further, its impact has varied considerably between Member States. Implementation of the

Takeover Directive has, for example, involved few changes of substance in UK takeover law and practice. However, the Takeover Directive has introduced certain elements that, whilst familiar to markets such as the UK, were entirely new to other countries. For example, minority squeeze-out provisions were introduced into the jurisdictions of Greece, Spain, Luxembourg, Slovenia and Slovakia for the first time, and in Poland squeeze-out has been expanded to apply to listed and unlisted companies.

1.4 Market Abuse Directive

Takeover activity has always carried with it the spectre of market abuse in its various forms, in particular, insider dealing and market manipulation. Whilst many jurisdictions have over recent decades introduced national laws to combat such practices, the Directive on Insider Dealing and Market Manipulation (known as the Market Abuse Directive or "MAD") (2003/6/EC), adopted in December 2002, sought to address these issues on an EU-wide basis.

The MAD required only minimum harmonisation of rules relating to market abuse and, in many jurisdictions, MAD-compliant rules were already in force prior to the MAD's implementation date.

Some of the most important elements of the MAD are that it:

(a) applies to all transactions concerning shares, securities or other financial instruments that are admitted to trading on at least one regulated market within the EU. Whether the transaction is actually undertaken on a regulated market is irrelevant, and the Directive will apply;

(b) established transparency standards requiring people who advise on and recommend investments to the public to disclose their relevant interests. This would cover, for example, financial analysts and journalists who recommend investments to the public;

(c) introduced an obligation to report suspicious transactions;

(d) covers both insider dealing and market manipulation to ensure that the same framework is applied to both categories of market abuse; and

(e) requires each Member State to designate a single administrative regulatory and supervisory authority, with a common set of responsibilities, to deal with insider dealing and market abuse.

The MAD introduced new measures to help detect and prevent market abuse. Such measures include the introduction of "insider lists", requiring companies which have securities admitted, or which have requested admission, to trading on a regulated market to maintain lists containing names of all persons who have access to inside information. It also introduced provisions for "suspicious transactions reporting", which require professionals engaged in arranging transactions in financial instruments to notify to the competent authority transactions where there is a reasonable suspicion that market abuse might have taken place.

In the UK, the MAD amended Part VIII of the Financial Services and Markets Act 2000 ("FSMA 2000"). The UK regime prohibits behaviour amounting to insider dealing (including dealing with insider information and improper disclosure) and market manipulation (including disclosure of misleading information and failure to properly disclose information to the market). The regime also catches those who require or encourage others to breach the laws on market abuse and insider dealing.

Through its Code of Market Conduct, the FSA provides formal guidance on the UK market abuse regime and specifies certain types of behaviour that do not amount to market abuse, known as defences or safe harbours. In the context of takeovers, the regime allows for some forms of behaviour that may be considered to constitute market abuse to fall outside of the provisions of the FSMA 2000. For example, stakebuilding, seeking irrevocable undertakings or letters of intent should not amount to market abuse. The FSA has power either to impose unlimited financial penalties or to censure publicly a person that has engaged in market abuse, or that has required or encouraged another person to so do. The FSA can also make use of injunctions and restitution orders against any person. The market abuse regime supplements rather than replaces the criminal sanctions for market abuse and insider dealing that had previously existed under UK law.

In the Netherlands, most of the material provisions of the MAD were already enshrined in national regulation. However, the implementation of the MAD in the Netherlands also introduced new elements. These include broadening the scope of the definition of market manipulation, transferring the supervision of the publication of non-public price-sensitive information from Euronext Amsterdam to the AFM, together with provisions for suspicious transactions reporting and the obligation to ensure transparency when giving investment recommendations. The latter serves to protect investors by granting them the opportunity to verify the status and credibility of an investment recommendation.

In France, in particular, French securities regulations on insider trading have been aligned with the minimum provisions of the MAD. French law still provides for additional criminal sanctions and proceedings where the offences of disclosure of false information, market manipulation and insider trading occur, but these are applied less often than those sanctions enshrined in the MAD-compliant French securities regulation. The French securities regulator will probably continue to follow the same standards that were developed before the implementation of the MAD, meaning that it is likely that the MAD will not have a significant impact on the regulation of French securities.

In Germany, in 2005, the German Federal Financial Supervisory Authority (Bundesanstalt für Finanzdienstleistungsaufsicht) ("BaFin") published its *Issuer Guide* (*Emittentenleitfaden*). This provided practical advice to domestic and international issuers whose securities were admitted to trading on a Stock Exchange in Germany on how to deal with the change in regulations brought about by the implementation of the MAD. Although the guide did provide guidance on the MAD and its implementing regulations, it has not yet been amended to take into consideration the implementation of the Transparency Directive (*see* 1.5 below).

1.5 Impact of the Transparency Directive

1.5.1 Background

Directive 2004/109 (the Transparency Directive) was adopted on 17 December 2004 with the aim of harmonising requirements for disclosure of information about companies whose securities are admitted to trading on regulated markets across the EU ("issuers"). The deadline for implementation of the Transparency Directive by Member States was 20 January 2007. The Transparency Directive is a minimum harmonisation directive in that it sets out minimum standards upon which Member States may impose more stringent requirements.

1.5.1.1   Relevance to EU Takeovers

The key provisions of the Transparency Directive relate to periodic financial reporting by issuers and notification of major shareholdings. It is this latter requirement that is most significant in the context of takeovers, in that it restricts the ability of potential bidders from stakebuilding in an issuer undetected.

The Transparency Directive provides that each Member State must ensure that where a shareholder acquires or disposes of shares of an issuer, to which voting rights are attached, then such shareholder must notify the issuer of the proportion of voting rights that it holds as a result of such acquisition or disposal where that proportion reaches, exceeds or falls below the thresholds of 5, 10, 15, 20, 25, 30, 50 and 75 per cent. The Transparency Directive also provides that the Member State must ensure that once the company has received such notification, it must then inform the market of such acquisition or disposal.

1.5.1.2   Impact of implementation

Prior to implementation of the Transparency Directive in the UK, statutory disclosure requirements pursuant to the Companies Act 1985 already provided that when a person acquired or disposed of an interest in shares of a public limited company (whether listed or not) that took its holding of that class of shares in such company above or below 3 per cent (and every subsequent 1 per cent above 3 per cent) of the issued shares of that class in such company, such person was obliged to notify the company of such acquisition or disposal.

These statutory provisions were repealed when the Transparency Directive was implemented on 20 January 2007. Equivalent provisions were instead included in the UK Disclosure and Transparency Rules ("DTRs"). The DTRs kept the same threshold limits of 3 per cent and every 1 per cent above that, effectively "gold plating" the requirements of the Transparency Directive. Moreover, the DTRs apply these requirements to issuers other than those listed on the London Stock Exchange's Main Market (a "regulated market"). Significantly, in contrast to the previous UK statutory regime, the DTRs calculate such thresholds by reference to interests in voting rights in the target company, and not by reference to the broader concept of an "interest in shares".

No significant change resulted from the implementation of the Transparency Directive to the French practice of disclosure arising from the building of stakes in French listed issuers. However, at the same time as the implementation of the Takeover Directive, the French Parliament was influenced by the *Danone/Pepsi* case in the summer of 2005 to vote in March 2006 for a "put up or shut up" obligation. Under these rules, the AMF may require persons publicly to disclose their intentions within a set deadline if there are rumours and large swings or unusual trading volumes. A negative statement of intentions is binding for the following six months.

At the time of writing, the Transparency Directive had only partially been implemented in Belgium and the provisions of the Transparency Directive impacting upon disclosure of stakebuilding activity had not been brought into force. The standard notification threshold will still be set at 5 per cent or any multiple thereof. Under the current regime, the articles of association of the issuer may provide for a lower notification threshold at 3 per cent and multiples thereof (i.e., 6 per cent, 9 per cent, 12 per cent etc.). Under the new regime, the issuer may set lower thresholds of 1, 2, 3, 4 or 7.5 per cent in its articles of association. Most significantly, reaching, exceeding or falling below any such threshold will also require a notification when the change in percentage does not result from a positive action of the person who is obliged to notify (for instance, where there is a change in the securities in issue, such as a capital increase or share buy back, which would respectively entail a dilution or restoration/reinstatement of the notifying person's interest).

In Spain, the Transparency Directive was also implemented through Law 6/2007, which came into force on 13 August 2007.

The implementing legislation will require the notification by the entity holding a stake in a company whose securities are listed on the Spanish Stock Exchange of the acquisition or loss of significant stakes in capital with voting rights in the issuer's share capital or of financial instruments that provide the right to acquire such securities. This new legislation will lower the previous minimum threshold from 5 per cent to 3 per cent.

The German law implementing the Transparency Directive also sets the lowest disclosure threshold at 3 per cent of the voting rights in an issuer (as opposed to 5 per cent under the prior regime).

The Netherlands has not yet fully implemented the provisions of the Transparency Directive but has implemented those provisions relating to the notification of major shareholdings with little or no "gold plating", setting the minimum notification threshold at 5 per cent. Recently, it has been proposed by the Dutch Secretary of Finance to include a new, lower notification threshold of 3 per cent, thus forcing potential bidders to reveal their stake building in a target company even earlier.

1.6   Cross-Border Mergers Directive

The Cross-Border Mergers Directive (2005/56/EC) (the "Mergers Directive"), which was adopted on 26 October 2005 and whose purpose is to facilitate the carrying out of cross-border mergers between various types of limited liability company governed by the laws of different Member States, was to be implemented by Member States no later than 15 December 2007. A cross-border merger for the purpose of the Mergers Directive can take one of several specified forms and where a company transfers all of its assets and liabilities to another company in exchange for shares in the transferee company or to a parent company holding all its shares, the transferor company ceases to exist. Further, the company resulting from the cross-border merger is to be subject to the employee participation rules (if any) in force in the Member State in which that company has its registered office. In many Member States, this creates a new type of statutory merger.

Although the Mergers Directive will make available to companies different potential merger routes, for companies that currently do not have employee participation arrangements in place, it is unlikely these routes will be viewed as an attractive alternative to existing takeover transaction processes. Further, regulatory authorities have had to review whether existing takeover rules apply to cross-border mergers under the Mergers Directive. For example, in the UK, the Panel issued a Practice Statement in October 2007 confirming circumstances in which certain cross-border merger transactions would be subject to the Takeover Code.

1.7 Structural barriers to takeovers

1.7.1 Examination of barriers

1.7.1.1 The responsibilities of directors
The responsibilities of the directors of a company under the laws of the jurisdiction to which it is subject vary considerably throughout Europe, reflecting the diversity of cultures and social attitudes. This, in turn, translates into significant differences in the rules governing a target board's duties following receipt of an offer.

At one extreme is the UK, where the paramount responsibility of the directors has traditionally been to the owners of the company, the shareholders. Many potential defensive techniques or actions founder on the principle that it is contrary to the interests of shareholders for the directors of a company to restrict the means of their realising value from their shares. For this reason, many takeovers which are not initially welcomed by the target's board of directors may ultimately receive their recommendation if the terms are such that it is in the interests of shareholders to accept them.

In October 2007, the relevant sections of the UK Companies Act 2006 creating new laws relating to directors' duties and codifying in statute for the first time many previous common law and equitable duties were implemented. One of the most significant changes was the introduction of an overall duty for a director to "promote the success of the company for the benefit of its members as a whole".

The new Companies Act provisions introduced a non-exhaustive list of factors to which directors must have regard when exercising their duty to promote the success of the company for the benefits of its members as a whole. These factors include, amongst other things, a duty to have regard to the:

(a)   likely consequences in the long term;
(b)   interest of the company employees;
(c)   need to foster relationships with suppliers, customers and others; and
(d)   impact of the company's operation on the community and the environment; and
(e)   desirability of the company maintaining a reputation for high standards of business conduct.

However, it should be noted that the Government rejected the approach of extending directors' duties so that they are owed beyond the company and its members to third-party stakeholders.

It remains to be seen how the UK courts will interpret the new provisions, but as directors are only required to "have regard" to these factors, amongst others, it is difficult to see bids actually being frustrated by boards' compliance with these new requirements.

In many other Member States, directors and equivalent managers have long since owed duties to a wider range of stakeholders than shareholders alone. Often management may be entitled, or required, to give equal weight to the interests of employees, creditors and those of the business itself (including the continuation of the current management). For example, in the Netherlands and to a certain extent Germany, where large public companies typically have a supervisory board as well as a management board, and many of what would otherwise be shareholders' powers are vested in the supervisory board, both boards have a duty to consider the interests of the company as a whole, which comprises the interests of the employees, creditors, suppliers and customers and the public interest as well as the interests of shareholders.

In Germany, the duty of neutrality of the target management has been one of the most discussed aspects of the Takeover Act. The Takeover Act grants the management a certain amount of room for manoeuvre in terms of defending against an unwelcome offer, although shareholder approval is still needed in some circumstances depending on the nature of the frustrating action. The consent of the general meeting can be granted either after the takeover offer is launched or by way of an anticipatory resolution, which is an abstract resolution issued prior to a takeover situation authorising the management to frustrate unfriendly bids by specific measures and for a maximum time period of 18 months after the resolution.

In Italy, legislative decree number 58/98 (the *Testo Unico sulla Finanza*) and the regulations published by CONSOB (the state Stock Market Supervisory Authority) have introduced new rules in the field of directors' responsibilities. Whenever a bid is launched, the directors have to issue a statement providing relevant information, setting out their opinion and stating whether or not a general meeting will be held to consider defensive measures. At the shareholders' meeting, members representing more than 30 per cent of the share capital can authorise actions which might be considered prejudicial to the bid. Prior to the introduction of these rules, Italian boards were exclusively responsible for matters relating to the management of the company.

In Belgium, the board of directors of a target company does not have a general duty of neutrality and hence can take certain frustrating actions or preventative measures. The Takeover Directive has not required the limitations on the power of the board to frustrate or prevent a bid that existed prior to its implementation to be amended. The situation has thus remained unaltered and, as a matter of principle, the board of directors of a target company may carry out the frustrating actions or implement the preventative measures allowed to it by the target's articles of association and the Company Code. However, Belgian law offers the possibility for companies to opt in to the frustrating-action provisions (*see* 1.3.2.6 above). Following implementation of the Takeover Directive in Belgium, the process by which the target's board conveys its opinions on the bid has been amended. Under the new regime, in a first phase, the target's board must give an opinion in respect of missing elements or misleading information in the draft offer document within five business days. In a second phase, and within five business days from the receipt of the offer document as approved by the Banking Finance and Insurance Commission ("BFIC"), the target's board must provide the BFIC with a draft memorandum in reply setting out, *inter alia*, its remarks concerning the offer document, its views on the bidder's strategic plans and their impact on the target, the board's opinion on the offer, having regard to the interests of the company, all of its securities holders, its creditors and its employees.

1.7.1.2   *Ownership*

In many Member States, the widespread existence of cross-shareholdings, controlling family groupings and holdings by institutions with close relationships with the incumbent management have historically represented a key structural barrier impeding the achievement of a "level playing field". However, there are a number of developments which have lowered these barriers in a number of Member States.

The importance of the banks as investors in German companies is attributable to a number of factors. Post-war Germany was built on debt rather than equity financing. As a consequence, banks sought to protect their investments and had easy access to equity participation and seats on the supervisory boards. The banks were traditionally also large investors in listed companies. In their position as investor, adviser, lender and often with representation on the management and supervisory boards, the banks used to exercise considerable influence. Combined with an investment culture which looked to long-term development rather than short-term profit, this resulted in a relatively low level of market activity in Germany, particularly in relation to the size of its economy. However, recent years have seen a strong trend towards a much stronger equity culture, with many banks divesting their industrial holdings. This continuing trend, together with a considerably improved investment climate resulting from recent reforms, has led to increased takeover activity and is – despite the current credit crunch – expected to continue. This prospering market environment has, in particular, attracted financial investors to invest in the German market. However, in the months prior to the time of writing, German industrial companies had also increased their investment activities.

In an attempt to limit the constraints caused by cross-shareholdings in Italian companies, legislative decree number 58/98 (the *Testo Unico sulla Finanza*) has provided that where a cross-shareholding held by an Italian listed company exceeds 2 per cent of the share capital of another listed company (or 5 per cent if approved by both companies' shareholders in general meeting), the last shareholder purchasing the shares is prevented from exercising the voting rights which relate to the shares in excess of the threshold and must sell those shares within 12 months. This rule does not apply where the threshold is exceeded following the launch of a bid, the purpose of which is to acquire at least 60 per cent of the company's ordinary shares.

On the other hand, this barrier remains strong in a number of countries. For example, in Spain, the high percentage of shares in listed companies held by banks, institutional investors and family groups has also contributed in part to the low level of takeover activity to date. Further, in Belgium, the shareholding structure of listed companies is often characterised by the presence of one or more shareholders having either the absolute majority of the voting rights or a significant percentage of voting rights who, by effect of law or de facto, control the board of directors.

1.7.1.3 *Identifying and accessing shareholders*

One of the greatest obstacles to effecting a takeover is the difficulty of identifying and accessing the shareholders of the target company. Only in the UK and Sweden are quoted companies required to maintain a complete and up-to-date share register which is readily accessible to all, although in the UK the increasing use of derivatives (by hedge funds and others) to exercise de facto control over underlying shares means that the "ownership" picture can become harder to interpret during takeover situations.

In the UK, the increased significance of derivatives was recognised by the Panel and led to a series of changes being made to the Code during 2005 and 2006. In particular, Rule 8.3 of the Code, which provides for the disclosure of dealings in securities of a target by persons interested in 1 per cent or more of any class of relevant securities in a target during a takeover "offer period", was amended such that holdings and dealings in certain derivatives became captured by the definitions of interests in securities and dealings respectively. As testament perhaps to the significance of derivative dealings, according to a review by the Panel's Code Committee, the number of Rule 8.3 disclosures increased by 19.3 per cent over the period from 7 November 2005 to 31 May 2007.

With the increased use of registered shares in Germany since the Daimler–Chrysler merger in 1999, registers in Germany provide better information on the shareholder structure, though this is generally available only to the shareholders. In Member States where there is a register, to the extent that there is a register which is accessible to the public, nominee or custodian names will frequently obscure the identity of the real holders. In Germany, the share register frequently shows only a small percentage of the shareholders because many shareholders make use of nominee registrations. According to the draft Risk Limitation Act which aims, *inter alia*, at increasing transparency in relation to the true owners of registered shares, a stock corporation shall be entitled in its articles of association to stipulate the extent to which nominees can be registered. Furthermore, the stock corporation shall be entitled to request that the registered party provides information on the persons for whom it is holding the shares. This claim to information extends over the entire chain of intermediaries through to the true owner of the shares.

The use of bearer shares, particularly common in Austria, Belgium, France and the Netherlands, makes it very difficult to access shareholders. In Italy, only the company's own shareholders have a right to examine and obtain abstracts of the share register (however, listed companies or companies which hold, directly or indirectly, an interest in a listed company are required by CONSOB to publish details of any major shareholding). In France, shareholders have access to shareholder lists (not including the names of holders of bearer shares) prior to each shareholders meeting and, at any time, to the attendance sheets for all shareholders meetings held during the last three financial years.

Whether or not shareholder identification issues are an obstacle to making an offer or a problem encountered in carrying it through will depend very much on the attitude of the target company's board. If the board is supportive of the offer, then its cooperation will assist in identifying shareholders and gaining acceptances. If, on the other hand, the board rejects the offer, it may be almost impossible to identify shareholders to seek to persuade them of the merits of the offer and put pressure on the board to recommend it.

These difficulties have been alleviated in recent decades by the Directive on disclosure of major shareholdings (88/627/EEC), and of course, more recently, by the Transparency Directive (discussed above).

1.7.1.4   *Availability and reliability of information*
Historically, there has been a wide disparity between Member States in the information which companies are required to publish, and in the rigour with which filing requirements are enforced.

By the turn of the twentieth century, national accounting requirements based on the Fourth and Seventh Directives were seen increasingly as a barrier to EU companies' attempts to access global capital markets. In 2002, the Commission passed the EC Regulation on the application of international accounting standards (EC/1606/2002) which came into force on 12 September 2002 and changed the landscape of financial reporting in the EU by requiring that publicly listed companies governed by the law of an EU Member State must, with certain exceptions, prepare their consolidated financial statements in conformity with International Financial Reporting Standards ("IFRS"). The introduction of IFRS marked a significant development towards harmonising financial reporting across the EU.

1.8   Conclusion

After the lull in takeover activity at the turn of the century, following the burst of the "tech bubble", the last few years have proved an exciting time for European takeovers, with a significant increase in activity leading to some high-profile and ground-breaking bids, and the emergence or increased aggres-siveness of new, or less traditional, players, such as sovereign wealth funds, hedge funds and investors from the Gulf States and Asia. Similarly, private equity, which has been making major incursions into the takeover arena over recent years, has become a truly mainstream takeover participant. At the time of writing, however, these developments were inevitably overshadowed by the ongoing credit crunch and market volatility, and it is impossible to predict what the long-term effects of this crisis will be.

The years since the turn of the century have also proved significant from a legal perspective, with the implementation across most of the EU of the Takeovers Directive, the Transparency Directive and the MAD. Whilst these changes have meant relatively little change for certain jurisdictions such as the UK, they have necessitated significant overhauls of various other Member States' regulatory regimes, particularly those of the central and eastern European accession states.

Chapter 2

Austria

Stefan Köck

Partner
Freshfields Bruckhaus Deringer

2.1 Introduction

Since 1975 Austria has seen a tremendous increase in takeover activity and, at least since 1990, there has been a high level of takeover activity in the sense of changes of ownership in businesses. To a large extent at the time of writing, such takeovers have been cross-border investments by foreigners.

Although previously almost all takeovers resulted from privately negotiated deals between a very limited number of shareholders, the late 1990s saw an increasing number of public tender offers, including a few hostile tender offers. The occurrence of these public tender offers led the Austrian lawmakers to focus on the absence of Austrian takeover legislation regulating the conduct of such offers. In response to this void, and to address increasing concerns regarding the potentially abusive conduct of bidders and the protection of minority shareholders generally, the Austrian legislators introduced the Austrian Takeover Act (*Übernahmegesetz*) on 1 January 1999.

The Takeover Act provides a comprehensive framework for the initiation and the process of a public tender offer and, most significantly, introduces the concept of a "mandatory tender offer", whereby bidders for a controlling interest in a publicly held company are obliged to make a tender offer to the remaining shareholders of the company. Application and interpretation of the Takeover Act rests largely in the hands of the newly created Takeover Commission (*Übernahmekommission*), which has made great use of this opportunity, issuing and publishing (as of December 2007) more than 60 formal decisions and informal statements on the interpretation of the Act since 1999.

It has become quite clear that potential bidders for direct or indirect interests in publicly listed Austrian companies have to consider carefully both the structure and the potential consequences of their bids in light of the Takeover Act as the Takeover Commission imposes strict interpretation of the Act, putting special emphasis on compliance with formal requirements, financing and pricing rules in order to ensure protection of minority shareholders.

2.2 Acquisition targets

2.2.1 General

Austrian law offers a variety of types of business organisation. Virtually all of them resemble legal types of organisation that are also found in Germany. This is attributable to the fact that Austria and Germany have closely related commercial and corporate laws.

The most important forms of business organisation in Austria are the private limited liability company (*Gesellschaft mit beschränkter Haftung* ("GmbH")), the stock corporation (*Aktiengesellschaft* ("AG")), and various forms of partnership, with the number of the latter declining in comparison to the GmbH and the AG. Unlike in Germany, there is no limited partnership by shares (*Kommanditgesellschaft auf Aktien* ("KGaA")). Although the number of AGs is rising, and the AG is the only corporate form the shares of which can be publicly traded, the GmbHs by far outnumber the AGs (there are more than 90,000 GmbHs and approximately 1,500 AGs) since the GmbH requires lower initial capitalisation, is easier and less costly to administer, more flexible, and generally better attuned to the needs and interests of shareholders who want to hold and control a company closely.

The proportion of companies listed on the Vienna Stock Exchange is small due to the traditional preference of bank financing over equity financing and the slow development of capital markets in Austria. By the end of 2006, the shares of 113 companies were listed on the Vienna Stock Exchange, all of them AGs. Of those listings 89 were in the regulated markets of the first and second tier of the Vienna Stock Exchange (the *amtlicher Handel* and the *geregelter Freiverkehr*), and the rest were in the third tier (the *Dritter Markt*), which is essentially an unregulated, or only sparsely regulated, market.

In the 1980s, several companies went "public", not by having the operating company's shares listed on the Stock Exchange, but by listing the shares of a holding company which held only a minority interest in the operating company. This practice, increasingly considered as an abusive one, has virtually ceased. Nonetheless, a tender offer for listed shares would hardly ever be an offer for the control of a company: probably only a handful of the listed companies (other than the above-mentioned holding companies) have more than 50 per cent of their shares "floating", the rest are controlled by one or a very limited number of shareholders who often coordinate their behaviour through complex and elaborate shareholders agreements. Developments between 2000 and 2007 show that the number of companies that could theoretically become the target of a classic public takeover offer to an unlimited number of shareholders is decreasing rather than increasing, evidenced by the fact that Austria has seen more "going-privates" than initial public offerings ("IPOs") in past years.

2.2.2 The stock corporation (AG)

2.2.2.1 General
An AG, like a GmbH, is a legal entity. Its capital is divided into shares (stock). The shareholders are not liable for the corporation's debts once they have fully

paid in their contribution. It is the only legal vehicle available for companies who wish to offer shares publicly as investments.

The AG's management structure rests on the assumption that management ought to be independent from direct shareholder influence. Due to the specific management structure and the rules applicable thereto, an AG is therefore not an easy target for a hostile takeover: it may take time, a lot of money and possibly even litigation before a new majority shareholder can take control of the company's management.

2.2.2.2 Types of shares
The shares of an AG can be in the form of either par value shares (*Nennbetragsaktien*) or no par value shares (*Stückaktien*). An AG may have bearer shares, registered shares or both.

Bearer shares are the most common type of shares. Ownership is theoretically transferred by physically handing over the share in fulfilment of a contractual or other legal obligation, typically a purchase, although in practice share certificates hardly ever leave the banks' securities deposits (in fact all banks have the share certificates deposited with one particular bank, the *Österreichische Kontrollbank*, which acts as the clearing house for securities transactions). In the case of closely held AGs, share certificates usually do not exist. Typically, the company has no means of identifying the shareholders (but *see* 2.7.2 on the disclosure of shareholdings) unless it has issued interim certificates or registered shares, which is not very common. Listed shares are practically always bearer shares.

Registered shares are transferred by endorsement and physical transfer. The change of shareholders must be notified to the company, which maintains a share register. Transfer of registered shares can be restricted in the AG's articles of association so that the consent of the company (i.e., its management board) must be obtained (*vinkulierte Aktien*). Under existing case law the management board may withhold its consent to the transfer only for good reason (e.g., to avoid damage to the company, its shareholders or its creditors). The shares of certain corporations, notably investment and investment fund corporations, must be of this type.

2.2.2.3 Voting
Normally all shares carry (equal) voting rights. Only shares that carry a preferred (necessarily cumulative) dividend may be non-voting. Even then, if the higher ("preference") dividend is not paid out for one year and not paid out in the subsequent year together with the preference dividend of that year, the shares carry full voting rights until payment of all outstanding dividends has been made. The aggregate nominal amount of all non-voting preference shares is limited to one-third of the company's stated share capital.

Shares with multiple voting rights are not permitted in Austria. However, the company's articles of association may limit the number of votes that one single shareholder may exercise. Such a restriction is hardly ever used in practice.

Shareholders agreements governing the exercise of voting rights are frequent and often very concise and restrictive. They are largely permissible by law, and even to the extent they are not, they are often complied with nonetheless in practice.

2.2.2.4   Management structure

The organisation of an AG is regulated relatively strictly by law. The company's articles of association cannot change the prescribed structure to a large extent.

Unlike its Anglo-American counterpart, the Austrian AG has a two-tier management structure:

(a)   a management board that is appointed by the supervisory board for up to five years; and

(b)   a supervisory board that is appointed by the shareholders and must include employee representatives if the company's workforce is represented by a works council.

The management board is responsible for the day-to-day management of the company's business. The appointment of each member of the management board requires a resolution passed by a simple majority of the supervisory board and, in addition, when works council members are on the supervisory board, by a simple majority of the supervisory board members elected by the shareholders. Appointments last for a period of up to five years. Premature removal of a member of the management board is only possible when justified by good cause. The shareholders meeting cannot remove a member of the management board, although it can hand down a vote of no confidence in a board member, and that vote permits the supervisory board, if the vote is not entirely unjustified, to remove the respective person from office (although this will in practice often violate the employment contract of a management board member who may then be entitled to considerable compensation).

The supervisory board exercises merely a supervisory and guiding role, and it appoints and removes the members of the management board. The supervisory board does not normally participate in the management of the company, although for certain types of major transactions (such as the acquisition and sale of other companies or interests therein, the acquisition and sale of real estate, certain investments and the taking or granting of certain loans (the list can be enlarged by the company's articles of association)) the management board must obtain the supervisory board's prior consent.

The members of the supervisory board are elected by resolution at the shareholders meeting for a period of up to four years. Almost no rules for the representation of minority shareholders exist, which means that a majority shareholder can normally determine all members of the supervisory board (to the extent they are elected by the shareholders). As an exception, under certain circumstances a minority that holds at least 33 per cent of the stated share capital may elect a delegate to the supervisory board. In addition, one-third of the members of the supervisory board is elected by the company's works council (if such works council exists, which is usually the case). If the company has large subsidiaries the works councils of the subsidiaries will also participate in order to allow for proper representation of the group's workforce.

2.2.2.5 The shareholders meeting

Shareholders meetings are usually called by the management board. Any 5 per cent shareholder (or shareholders who together hold 5 per cent of the capital) may request that a meeting be called.

With few exceptions there is no quorum requirement.

The law contains detailed majority requirements, some of which can be changed in the company's articles of association and some of which cannot. A majority of the shares will usually suffice to adopt many resolutions, in particular to elect supervisory board members, but a 75 per cent majority will often be necessary to effect major changes. Such matters include the reduction of the share capital, the conversion into a limited liability company, a normal consolidation or merger, or an exclusion of shareholders' pre-emptive rights when new shares are issued. For other resolutions the 75 per cent majority will only be required if the articles of association do not stipulate a lower majority requirement (which is often the case), for example the premature revocation of members of the supervisory board, an ordinary capital increase, or general amendments to the AG's articles of association.

2.2.2.6 Conversion into a GmbH

An AG can easily be converted into a GmbH. Such a conversion requires a shareholders resolution approved by 75 per cent of the capital represented at the meeting (or a larger majority if so required by the company's articles of association). The principal problem of a conversion is the right of the company's creditors to ask for proper security for their claims (since creditor protection rules applicable to a GmbH are less strict than in the case of an AG), although this creditors' right is hardly ever exercised and therefore usually poses no problem in practice. According to a recent amendment, every shareholder now has an exit right in case of such conversion. In order to exercise such a right, the shareholder will have to file an objection to the shareholders resolution on the conversion and request the transfer of his/her shareholding to the company against an adequate cash compensation.

2.2.3 The private limited liability company (GmbH)

2.2.3.1 General

As the most common type of business organisation, the GmbH (or rather its shares), is the most frequent acquisition target in the context of privately negotiated deals. There are now more than 90,000 such private limited liability companies in Austria. A GmbH requires less initial capitalisation and is simpler to set up and to administer than an AG, and it is in many ways almost as flexible as a partnership. Management can be directly and closely controlled by the shareholders. In almost all circumstances (except where the articles of association contain very unusual rules) control can be established quickly and efficiently by a new majority shareholder.

2.2.3.2 Shares and votes

A GmbH is also a legal entity, with the shareholders generally not being liable for the company's debts once they have fully paid in their contributions. No share certificates may be issued. The articles of association must be in the form of a notarial deed, and all share transfers must be effected through such notarial deed (although a recording before a German public notary also suffices). The minimum stated capital stock of an Austrian limited liability company is €35,000. All shareholders are registered in the Commercial Register (*Firmenbuch, see* 2.7.1 below), which is open to public inspection.

Dividend rights usually follow the capital held by each shareholder, but alternative arrangements in the articles of association are permissible. Likewise, voting rights are usually allocated in relation to the capital held (e.g., one vote per €10 of nominal capital) but deviating arrangements (including multiple voting rights) are permissible as long as every shareholder has at least one vote.

Transfer restrictions are frequent, consisting either of a consent requirement of the company (i.e., the shareholders) or a right of first refusal, or a combination of such restrictions.

2.2.3.3   *Managing directors*
The company is managed by one or more managing directors (*Geschäftsführer*). A managing director also represents the company vis-à-vis third parties, either alone or jointly with another managing director, as determined by the shareholders. Managing directors are appointed and can be removed at any time by shareholders resolution, although employment contracts may contain rights under which an immediate removal without cause triggers certain compensation entitlements.

As opposed to the management board of an AG (*see* 2.2.3.1 above), managing directors of a limited liability company are subject to, and legally bound to comply with, the instructions given by shareholders resolution, even when such instructions relate to the day-to-day management of the company.

2.2.3.4   *Supervisory board*
Most limited liability companies are not required to have a supervisory board. Only where the articles of association so require or where the law specifically so mandates must a supervisory board be formed. Otherwise, a supervisory board is optional, and the option is hardly ever made use of since every existing supervisory board is open to employee representation. A legal requirement to establish a supervisory board exists only, roughly speaking, in companies with a particularly large number of shareholders (over 50), with a large number of employees (over 300), or in companies having a particular purpose as laid down by law (such as investment and investment fund companies).

The supervisory board of a GmbH has powers comparable to those of the supervisory board of an AG, although in a GmbH the key power to appoint and remove managing directors always rests with the shareholders.

2.2.3.5   *Shareholders meeting*
The shareholders meeting must take place in Austria. It is called by the managing directors. A shareholder, or a group of shareholders, holding 10 per cent of the stated share capital can ask that a meeting be called. Majority requirements are regulated by law, mostly in the same way as for an AG (*see* 2.2.2.5 above). The

articles of association can increase the majority requirements according to the needs of the shareholders for almost all issues.

2.2.4 Other types of business organisation

Other types of business organisation include the sole proprietorship and various forms of partnership-type organisations. First and foremost are the partnership (*offene Gesellschaft*) and the limited partnership (*Kommanditgesellschaft*), but there is also the civil law partnership (*Gesellschaft bürgerlichen Rechts*). All of these organisations have a very high degree of flexibility, which is not especially well suited to large businesses, although some larger companies do operate (traditionally for tax reasons) as limited partnerships with a GmbH being the unlimited partner.

There are also special forms of companies with limited liability in particular business sectors, in particular savings institutions (*Sparkassen*) and specific types of insurance companies (*Versicherungsverein auf Gegenseitigkeit*). The opportunity to organise savings institutions (*Sparkassen*) in the form of a private trust according to the Private Trust Act (*Privatstiftungsgesetz*) was recently made available.

2.3 Exchange and investment control

2.3.1 Introduction

Although the rather restrictive Austrian Foreign Exchange Act (*Devisengesetz*) is still in force, the Austrian National Bank (*Österreichische Nationalbank*) has made use of its powers under that Act and has practically waived all requirements of prior consent for any transaction covered by the Act. Only some reporting duties remain. However, these do not apply to the foreign investor.

Thus, in effect, foreign investment in Austria has been completely liberalised. No permission or consent will generally be necessary for a takeover in Austria (*see* 2.3.2 below for exceptions).

2.3.2 Regulated industries

Only in very few regulated industries does the nationality of the shareholder play a role. For example, a licence for an air service company in Austria can only be granted if the shares are at least majority-owned by citizens of Member States of the European Economic Area ("EEA"). If such a company is taken over by a foreign (i.e., non-EEA or non-EEA controlled) corporation, the concession could be revoked immediately.

Further, each of Austria's nine provinces (*Bundesländer*) has statutes regulating the acquisition of certain real-estate rights (primarily title to real estate; sometimes also long-term leases) by foreigners (i.e., foreign citizens, companies or foreign-controlled Austrian companies). Usually approval must be obtained for such a transfer. Many of the provinces attempt to prevent the circumvention of these rules by also requiring approval when control of a real-estate owning company is transferred to a foreigner or foreign-controlled entity. Compliance with EU rules in this respect is growing slowly.

The provinces' real-estate commissions will give, and will have to give, permission under certain circumstances. Usually there is no substantive problem with business premises (i.e., when the real estate concerned serves the business of the company), but obtaining permission is still a formality to be complied with.

Austrian regulatory law of the banking, insurance and gambling industries requires certain "fit and proper" tests applicable to significant shareholders, depending on the level of the shareholding (e.g., 20 per cent, 33 per cent and 50 per cent for banks). However, these rules apply in a non-discriminatory fashion to Austrian and foreign shareholders alike. To enforce such tests in the case of change of ownership, any acquisition will usually have to be notified in advance to the regulatory authority in charge, which may then be in a position to block the acquisition, although no prior clearance has to be obtained.

2.4　Merger control – Changes resulting from the *KartellG 2005*

2.4.1　General

Austrian merger control law is part of the Cartel Act 2005 (*Kartellgesetz 2005*) which entered into force on 1 January 2006. The Austrian merger control rules must be considered in the context of EU merger control rules and are – generally speaking – applicable only to the extent that the thresholds of the European Merger Regulation are not met and the concentration therefore does not have a "community dimension" or where the European Commission passes the case to the local Austrian authorities. However, regardless of their community dimension, media concentrations must always be notified under Austrian law.

Austrian merger control rules provide for an obligatory pre-merger notification.

If the requirements for such a pre-merger notification (*see* 2.4.2 below) are met but the concentration has not been cleared in advance, a transaction will be deemed void under civil law. Further, the Cartel Court may, upon the request of one of the statutory parties (*Amtsparteien*) (i.e., the Federal Competition Authority and the Federal Cartel Prosecutor) impose on each party that has intentionally or negligently violated the standstill obligation a fine of up to 10 per cent of the worldwide turnover of the last business year. (In a recent case, for instance, the Cartel Court imposed a fine of €1.5 million for implementation without pre-merger notification.)

All notifications must be made to the Federal Competition Authority (*Bundeswettbewerbsbehörde*).

2.4.2　Concentration

Under the definition of the Cartel Act the following transactions or measures constitute a concentration:

(a)   an undertaking (entrepreneur or company) acquires another undertaking (i.e., its assets) in full or in a substantial part;

(b)   an undertaking acquires certain rights to a plant of another under a contract for the lease or management of such plant;

(c)   an undertaking acquires, directly or indirectly, shares in another undertaking, and the acquisition leads to a 25 per cent interest or more, or to a 50 per cent interest or more in that undertaking;

(d)   a measure is taken that causes at least half of the positions on the executive bodies or supervisory boards of two or more undertakings to be held by the same individuals;

(e)   any other measure is taken that permits one undertaking to directly or indirectly control another undertaking; and

(f)   the formation of a joint venture that permanently fulfils all functions of an independent economic entity (full-function joint venture).

In addition, certain agreements between banks on mutual financial assistance in the event of a financial crisis, on common business activities, on a uniform market policy (in particular common planning, development, offering and marketing of banking services) as defined in the Banking Act require merger clearance (such agreements exist in the Austrian saving banks sector).

Intra-group transactions are not considered as concentrations.

Austrian merger control law also contains a bank exemption, according to which merger control rules do not apply if a bank temporarily acquires shares in an undertaking for the purpose of reselling them, for securing its claims against the undertaking, or in the context of a restructuring process in an insolvency scenario. The shares must be sold after one year, as soon as security is no longer required, or after completion of the restructuring process. The exemption also applies to the acquisition of shares by equity participation businesses, equity fund businesses and companies whose only purpose is the acquisition of shares in other enterprises and the administration and utilisation of these shares, without directly or indirectly interfering with the administration of the respective undertaking, provided that they do not exercise their voting rights to influence the competitive conduct of the undertaking.

2.4.3   Scope of Austrian merger control (thresholds, calculation of turnover)

The relevant requirements for pre-merger notification are essentially turnover thresholds. A pre-merger notification must be filed if in the last business year before the transaction:

(a)   the combined aggregate worldwide turnover of the undertakings concerned exceeded €300 million;

(b)   the combined Austrian turnover of the undertakings concerned exceeded €30 million; and

(c)   the individual worldwide turnover of at least two of the undertakings concerned each exceeded €5 million.

Even where these thresholds are met, mergers are exempt from the notification obligation where the Austrian turnover of only one of the undertakings concerned exceeded €5 million and where the worldwide combined turnover of the other undertakings concerned did not exceed €30 million (*de minimis* exception).

For calculating the turnover of an undertaking concerned (company involved) the turnover of the entire group is taken into account (to the exclusion of intra-group turnover). For the purpose of calculating such group turnover a group is essentially considered to include all companies that are connected in one of the ways that give rise to a concentration (in particular, by way of a shareholding of at least 25 per cent upstream or downstream).

When calculating the turnover of banks, the sum of interest and similar revenues, proceeds from shares and participations, commission income as well as income from financial transactions and other banking income has to be taken into account. With regard to insurance companies, the premium income is relevant.

Specific rules apply to media mergers, where the turnover of media undertakings and media service undertakings has to multiplied by a factor of 200; the turnover achieved by media support undertakings must be multiplied by a factor of 20.

2.4.4 Form of notification

The Cartel Act requires the parties to provide, in the notification, full and detailed information on all aspects that may cause or strengthen a dominant position in particular on:

(a)   ownership and the corporate structure of the undertakings concerned;
(b)   the turnover (in terms of quantity and value) achieved by each of the undertakings concerned in the relevant products or services;
(c)   the market share of each of the undertakings concerned in the relevant products or services;
(d)   the market structure.

In the case of media concentrations, the notification must contain precise and exhaustive information on all aspects that could also affect media plurality.

Individual notifications and joint notifications are permissible.

The Federal Competition Authority has published a merger form on its web page (www.bwb.gv.at) which should be used for the notification of a concentration in Austria.

2.4.5 Proceedings

Proposed concentrations must be notified to the Federal Competition Authority, which immediately forwards the notification to the Federal Cartel Prosecutor and publishes a short summary of the notification on its web page (www.bwb.gv.at).

Each of the statutory parties may request an in-depth investigation of the concentration within four weeks after receipt of the notification. Within 14 days after the mandatory public announcement of the concentration on the web page of the Federal Competition Authority, third parties are entitled to comment in writing on the proposed concentration. However, they do not have the status of a party to the procedure. In particular, they do not have the right to a particular treatment of their comments or a right of appeal.

A transaction that is subject to Austrian merger control must not be implemented until:

(a)   both statutory parties have waived their right to request an in-depth investigation by the Cartel Court; or

(b)   neither statutory party has requested the initiation of an in-depth investigation within four weeks after receipt of the notification; or

(c)   if an in-depth investigation has been initiated, the issuing of a final decision of the Cartel Court whereby these proceedings are terminated, the relevant request of a statutory party is held inadmissible, or the merger is approved.

If a request for an in-depth investigation is made, the Cartel Court reviews the competitive effects of the concentration. In such case, the Court has five months from the request to investigate the merits and either prohibit or clear the transaction (or declare that no concentration exists at all). Clearance may also be conditional upon pro-competitive remedies taken by the undertakings concerned.

The parties to the concentration and/or the statutory parties may appeal against the Court's decision within four weeks. The Austrian Supreme Court as Appellate Cartel Court (*Oberster Gerichtshof als Kartellobergericht*) then has two months to render its decision.

2.4.6   Relevant considerations

The Cartel Court will prohibit a consideration if it creates or strengthens a dominant position.

A dominant position is deemed to exist if an undertaking:

(a)   has no or only insubstantial competition;

(b)   has a superior market position in relation to its competitors, taking into account its financial strength, its links or relationships with other undertakings, and its access to suppliers and customers. Barriers to entry will also be taken into account; or

(c)   is in such a superior position in respect of its customers or suppliers that such parties must maintain their business relationship with the undertaking concerned as an economic necessity.

Moreover, the Austrian Cartel Act provides for a statutory presumption of dominance if the combined market share of the undertakings concerned exceeds 30 per cent. In such cases, the undertakings concerned will have to prove to the Cartel Court that the concentration would still not create or strengthen a dominant position.

The Cartel Court may clear a concentration despite the creation or strengthening of a dominant position, if the proposed concentration:

(a) leads to an improvement of competitive conditions that outweighs the disadvantages of market dominance, and

(b) is necessary to preserve or enhance the international competitiveness of the undertakings involved and is justified by economic considerations.

2.5 Regulation of the conduct of mergers and acquisitions

The Austrian Takeover Act regulates *public* tender offers for shares, options and other securities (securities with the right to participate to the company's profits) listed on the Vienna Stock Exchange. The application of the Takeover Act is limited to tender offers for the shares, options and securities of an AG whose corporate seat is in Austria and whose securities are traded on the official market (*amtlicher Handel*) or the semi-official market (*geregelter Freiverkehr*) of the Vienna Stock Exchange, provided, however, that certain (but not all) rules of the Austrian Takeover Act apply in case at least one of these two criteria is met. The Takeover Act provides for the creation of a Takeover Commission (*Übernahmekommission*), whose responsibilities include monitoring the process of takeovers that fall within the scope of the Act (*see* 2.6.5 below).

Transactions relating to non-listed companies are only subject to the generally applicable rules of Austrian civil law for the conclusion of a contract. Under these rules, offers are irrevocable for the period determined in the offer, otherwise for a reasonable period. An offer should therefore indicate the period during which the offeror regards himself as being obliged to honour the offer. The contract becomes binding at the time acceptance is received by the offeror.

The conclusion of the contract does not of itself transfer ownership of the shares to the offeror either under general civil law rules or under the Takeover Act. In order for shares to be transferred effectively the appropriate transfer mechanism must be complied with (*see* 2.2.2 and 2.2.3 above).

2.6 Methods of acquisition

2.6.1 General considerations

The acquisition of an Austrian target company will usually occur either as an asset or as a share transaction. Legal mergers are rarely used as an acquisition technique.

The decision on whether an asset or a share transaction will be entered into will usually be tax driven, whereby different considerations from both sides will come into play. It will also matter whether a party is a private individual or a business entity. A share deal is likely to be more attractive to a private seller, whereas an asset deal may have tax advantages for the purchaser. From a technical point of view, share transactions are somewhat easier to carry out, while asset transactions are better suited to limit the acquirer's risks, although both advantages are rather relative.

2.6.2　Legal mergers

More often than not, legal mergers are used for intra-group restructuring rather than for acquisition purposes. AGs or GmbHs can be merged in two ways:

(a)　either the target is merged into an AG, with the shareholders of the target receiving shares in the latter as compensation; or,

(b)　a new corporation can be established to which all the assets of two or more corporations are transferred, with the shareholders of all of these companies receiving shares of the newly formed corporation.

With respect to mergers involving both a GmbH and an AG (*rechtsformübergreifende Verschmelzung*), every shareholder in the discontinued corporation has an exit right. In order to exercise such right, the shareholder will have to file an objection to the shareholders resolution on the merger and request the transfer of his/her shareholding to the company against an adequate cash compensation.

Usually, a merger requires shareholders resolutions from all participating companies (usually with a 75 per cent majority, *see* 2.2.2 and 2.2.3 above). Shareholders with special rights will also need to give their consent if such rights will be restricted or eliminated as a consequence of the merger and a merger agreement concluded between the companies (negotiated by the management boards). A shareholders resolution in the surviving corporation will not be necessary when 90 per cent of the capital of the discontinued corporation is held by the surviving corporation or when the shares given in consideration for the merger do not exceed 10 per cent of the stated share capital of the surviving corporation.

Often a capital increase in the surviving corporation will be necessary to implement the merger. Cash payments to the shareholders of the discontinued corporation(s) are only permissible to a small extent and only for necessary equalisation purposes.

Shareholders of all participating companies (including the surviving corporation) have a special "appraisal right" entitling them to initiate a court review of the exchange ratio given for their shares. To commence such an action, the shareholders must hold (alone or in aggregate) a minimum of 1 per cent of the capital or a nominal capital of €70,000. The appraisal right has certain characteristics of a class action: the court decision on the exchange ratio of the shares applies to all shareholders of all participating companies (and also to shareholders who did not request a court review).

The merger becomes effective upon its entry in the Commercial Register. The initiation of an appraisal right proceeding will not block such an entry, but any other challenge to the shareholders resolution approving the merger may do so.

Creditors of all participating companies are protected by the right to demand security for their claims within six months of the merger. However, creditors must attest that their claims are endangered as a consequence of the merger.

2.6.3   Private share acquisition

The acquisition of shares in an Austrian company will virtually always be effected through a privately negotiated agreement between the seller and the acquirer. No regulation exists concerning such deals, as the scope of the Takeover Act is limited to public tender offers (in listed companies). However, the term "public tender offer" is not specifically defined, so the distinction between a public and private share acquisition is not always clear and must be made on a case-by-case basis (*see* 2.8.1 below).

As stated above, the Takeover Act only applies to the listed equity securities of an AG. In the case of a GmbH, no listing on any exchange is possible, and the legal regulations governing the transfer of the shares are deemed sufficient to protect shareholders' rights. Shares in a GmbH can only be transferred in the rather strict form of the notarial deed of an Austrian notary. Furthermore, the articles of association of a GmbH generally will require shareholder consent, or the consent of the managing directors, to a share transfer. The transfer is completed by its registration in the Commercial Register.

The transfer of shares in an AG is considerably easier and requires no specific formal agreement. The privately negotiated share transfer agreement will typically contain representations and warranties with respect to the target company's business, assets and financial condition that are in line with commercial practice. Transfer restrictions in an AG are less frequent (and only permissible in the case of registered shares), although they do exist where control of the company is exercised by a group of shareholders, who often have internal arrangements concerning voting and other matters.

2.6.4   Asset transactions

Asset transactions are always privately negotiated agreements. Only the sale of all or almost all assets is subject to regulation. A shareholders resolution on the seller's side will be required (usually 75 per cent, *see* 2.2.2 above). All other aspects of the transaction are unregulated (i.e., governed only by general civil and commercial law).

Usually third-party contracts will have to be specifically transferred to the acquirer by obtaining the consent of the third party. Only employees, certain insurance contracts, and certain tenancy rights will automatically pass over to the new owner (although the landlord will have the right to increase the rent to the current market value).

The restriction of the acquirer's liability to new debt, and the exclusion of liability for "old" debt, will only be partly possible. Usually, some liability for known, or visible, "old" liabilities will remain under general civil law rules (as well as special rules applicable to taxes and social security obligations), which is another reason for the acquirer to conduct a due diligence review even in the case of asset transactions.

2.6.5   *Public tender offers – background*

Until 1999, public tender offers for an AG were entirely unregulated in Austria. No recommendations or guidelines existed (although the intention to acquire a significant stake in a credit institution or an insurance company had to and still must be notified to the regulatory authority (*see* 2.3.2 above)). The terms of a tender offer were also unregulated. Even two-tier tender offers (tender offers launched in two steps with different purchase prices offered by the bidder) were possible, and no obligation existed to make an offer for 100 per cent of the shares. This situation changed with the implementation of the Takeover Act on 1 January 1999 (for details *see* 2.8 below). The introduction of legislation regulating the conduct of public tender offers was the subject of a protracted debate in Austria. The spectacular takeover of one of Austria's principal banks, Creditanstalt, by Bank Austria at the turn of 1997 highlighted the legislative shortcomings in this area and prompted Parliament to introduce rules to provide a structured arena for takeovers, and principally to protect the interests of minority shareholders. The legislators used the (then existing) proposal of the European Commission for the Thirteenth Directive on Company Law concerning Takeovers and other General Bids (COM [97] 565 final) as the principal model for the Takeover Act, although some features were borrowed from the UK City Code.

The Takeover Act was thus introduced to provide safeguards for the protection of minority shareholders' rights, and to ensure that public tender offers occur in a regulated context under supervision of a state agency, the newly created Takeover Commission (*Übernahmekommission*).

Given that many large Austrian companies are still state controlled, and that most small and medium-sized companies are closely held, the practical development of the application of the Takeover Act did not occur very fast. Further, as in Germany, banks exert a considerable influence on companies in Austria by way of their often large shareholdings, although banks have started to divest.

Lastly, to achieve control of the acquired company, the acquirer will usually replace the members of the management board. However, due to the two-tier management structure of AGs (*see* 2.2.2 above), any change in the management board may take considerable time and expense. The new majority shareholder will first have to remove the members of the supervisory board prematurely (which usually requires a 75 per cent majority). The new supervisory board will then want to remove the members of the management board, which either may not be possible at all prematurely, or may be expensive. This might be considered a structural impediment to the decision to engage in a public tender offer.

2.7   Preparation of an offer

2.7.1   *Available information*

Essential information on every company is recorded in the fully computerised Commercial Register (*Firmenbuch*). Such essential information includes the company's address, details of the management board and supervisory board (if applicable), stated share capital, balance sheet date, and some other information. Only in the case of the GmbH will the shareholders appear in the Commercial Register. The articles of an AG and the articles of association of a GmbH can be inspected (and copied) from the Commercial Register files.

It will often be difficult to gain access to shareholder information in the case of an AG. Where a shareholders register must exist (i.e., in the case of registered shares, which are not too common), such a register can be inspected by any shareholder, but even then the information may reveal little since beneficial ownership need not usually be (and often is not) disclosed. And where shares are bearer shares not even a shareholder will have a right to inspect any unofficial shareholders lists that the company may keep.

Certain other information on company assets can be obtained through other registers such as the computerised land register (*Grundbuch*), which contains entries for all land parcels (in particular their owners), and the likewise computerised patent and trade-mark register. However, both types of register are only partly useful for information-gathering purposes, since queries such as for all real property (or all trade marks) owned by a particular corporation anywhere in Austria will not generally be permitted or possible.

As to environmental matters, pursuant to a specific statute, anyone may request, without showing cause, certain environmental information from the competent authorities, in particular whether any proceedings are pending.

Certain companies must file their accounts with the Commercial Register where they become open to inspection. The extent of the filing requirement varies depending on the size of the company. There are three groups of companies: large, medium-sized and small ones. Small GmbHs must file their accounts only in a very abbreviated way: in particular they do not need to disclose earnings. All large and medium-sized GmbHs as well as all AGs must have audited annual accounts, but medium-sized GmbHs may file somewhat abbreviated accounts with the Commercial Register. Large AGs, which exceed at least two of the following criteria:

(a)   balance sheet total in excess of €14.6 million;
(b)   sales in excess of €29.2 million; and
(c)   more than 250 employees,

must also publish their audited financial statements (including information on when and in which court the financial statements were filed) in the official gazette, the *Amtsblatt zur Wiener Zeitung*. Medium-sized and small AGs, as well as all GmbHs, are under no obligation to publish annual accounts in such a manner; they need only file them with the Commercial Register.

Listed companies are required to publish additional information, including an interim report covering the first six months of each business year.

Certain additional information will be available in the case of newly listed companies due to the prospectus requirements under the Stock Exchange Act.

2.7.2   Disclosure of shareholdings

The Stock Exchange Act requires every individual or company acquiring or selling shares, as a result of which transaction the thresholds of 5, 10, 15, 20, 25, 30, 35, 40, 45, 50, 75, or 90 per cent of the voting rights in a listed company are either reached, exceeded or fallen short of, to notify the company and the executive committee of the Stock Exchange of the post-transaction level of the shareholding.

Every listed company must publish such information, as well as any other significant change in its shareholder structure, in the official gazette within two trading days of gaining knowledge of such a change.

The Stock Exchange Act contains detailed rules as to which voting rights must be added together in order to calculate the thresholds mentioned above. These rules attempt to ensure that whenever voting rights are controlled by one and the same source, such voting rights will have to be added together for disclosure purposes.

2.8   Conduct of a public offer

2.8.1   Background/scope of the Takeover Act

As stated above, the Austrian Takeover Act regulates public tender offers for shares, options and other securities (such as securities providing the right to participate in the company's profits) of AGs whose corporate seat is in Austria provided that such securities are listed on the official market (*amtlicher Handel*) or the semi-official market (*geregelter Freiverkehr*) of the Vienna Stock Exchange (provided, however, that certain (but not all) rules of the Austrian Takeover Act apply in case at least one of these two criteria – corporate seat in Austria and listing on the Vienna Stock Exchange – is met).

The Takeover Act does not set forth a specific definition of what constitutes a "public" tender offer. Based on the practice of the US Securities and Exchange Commission a flexible test for making such determination can be made. In order to qualify as "public", an offer does not need to meet all prongs of the test. In any event, the determination must be made on a case-by-case basis:

(a)   Does the bidder extend his offer to a large number of shareholders?

(b)   Does the bidder act with the intent of acquiring a meaningful amount of the securities of the target company?

(c)   Is the offered price per share higher than the price on the market/the Stock Exchange?

(d)   Is the offer unilateral and binding or are the terms of the offer negotiated in detail with the sellers?

(e)   Does the offer include customary provisions (i.e., the withdrawal of the offer in the event that a certain percentage of the shareholders does not accept the offer)?

(f)   Is the offer open for a limited time?

(g)   Are there any economic considerations that would put pressure on the shareholders of the target company to accept the offer?

(h)   Has the offer been publicly announced?

2.8.2   General principles

The Takeover Act defines the procedural requirements for the implementation of any public tender offer that falls within its scope, and also prescribes the conditions under which the acquirer of a direct or indirect "controlling interest" in a company's stock will be *required* to extend its tender offer to the target company's minority shareholders ("mandatory" tender offer). The Takeover Act provides that all public tender offers shall be governed by five fundamental principles:

(a)   equal treatment – all holders of securities of the target company must be treated equally, unless otherwise specified by the Takeover Act;

(b)   informed decision – the target company's securities holders must have sufficient time and information to make a considered decision with knowledge of all relevant facts;

(c)   board's duty of care – the managing board and the supervisory board of the target company must act in the interest of all shareholders, the employees, the creditors and in the public interest;

(d)   proper market – there shall be no market trading irregularities in the securities of the target company, the bidder or any other company affected by the tender offer; insider trading is prohibited; and

(e)   protection of target company – the tender offer process must be completed quickly and shall not affect or disrupt the operations of the target company beyond a reasonable time.

Even though market protection is a major concern of Austrian takeover regulations, other than in other European countries, dealing in the shares of the target company before the bid is publicly announced is not explicitly forbidden for the bidder. As long as the bidder complies with applicable insider dealing regulations (*see* 2.13 below) it may freely acquire shares in the target company in the preparatory phase of a bid.

2.8.3   General duties of the bidder

The Takeover Act provides that to avoid market irregularities, the bidder and the members of its executive board must keep the tender offer plans secret until the offer is made public. Naturally, the bidder may initiate negotiations with the target company. The bidder may be forced to make a public announcement of its intentions prior to the beginning of the offering period in the event of rumours and speculations about the tender offer.

The bidder shall make a tender offer only after careful consideration, especially with respect to the financing of the offer. As soon as the bidder has unsolicitedly made the decision to submit an offer, or becomes subject to the requirement to make a mandatory tender offer, the bidder shall make a public announcement of its intentions. Prior to such announcement, the bidder shall inform the board of the target company.

2.8.4   Tender offer procedure

Within 10 "market" days (defined as trading days at the Vienna Stock Exchange) from the date of public disclosure that the bidder is considering a public tender offer, the bidder must notify the Takeover Commission of the tender offer and submit to it for review the required tender offer documentation. The tender offer documentation consists of a description of the terms of the tender offer (including price and offer period), a description of the bidder and a statement of the bidder's future plans, particularly with respect to the target company's activities. Upon request, the Takeover Commission can prolong this 10-day period to a maximum of 40 trading days.

Between the twelfth and the fifteenth trading day following the notification to the Takeover Commission, the bidder must publish the tender offer documentation (in a brochure or in a newspaper of national circulation) unless the Takeover Commission has prohibited it from doing so. The management of the target company must comment publicly (while the supervisory board may comment publicly) on the tender offer within 10 trading days from such publication. The management and supervisory boards of the target company must remain strictly objective and refrain from taking any action restricting the target shareholders' possibility to render a free and informed decision, although they are allowed to voice an objective conclusion that the tender offer is unfavourable.

The bidder's documentation and the statement of the management board (and supervisory board, respectively) of the target company must be reviewed by independent expert advisers. Both the bidder and the target company must appoint their own expert adviser. A credit institution, a financial institution situated in Austria or in an EU Member State that offers services in Austria, a certified auditor or an auditing company can be appointed to serve as an expert adviser. In practice the Takeover Commission favours the appointment of national credit institutions or auditing companies.

The tender offer period must extend from two to a maximum of 10 weeks starting from the publication of the offer document. During such period the bidder has the option to improve or amend the terms of the offer, provided that any improvements will extend to shareholders who accepted the offer on its initial terms. Shareholders may object to other types of changes in the offer. In the event that a competing offer is made by another bidder, a shareholder who accepted the initial offer is allowed to withdraw such acceptance in order to accept the competing bid. As most takeovers are friendly, however, such a situation had not occurred at the time of writing. To the extent that the bidder makes a tender offer for a portion of the outstanding securities of the target company only, acceptances will be considered on a pro rata basis.

Upon expiration of the tender offer period, the bidder must publicly disclose the number of shareholders who accepted the tender offer. In the case of a mandatory tender offer or in case certain acceptance thresholds have been reached, the tender offer period will subsequently be prolonged for another three months from the publication of the results of the offer.

2.8.5   Voluntary offer and mandatory offer

The Takeover Act draws a distinction between "voluntary" tender offers and "mandatory" tender offers. The latter refers to a situation where a bidder is required to extend a tender offer to minority shareholders. Voluntary tender offers can be further divided into two groups, one of which includes voluntary tender offers which aim at the acquisition of a controlling interest (often also called "anticipatory" mandatory offer). Voluntary tender offers aiming at the acquisition of a controlling interest are largely subject to the same rules as mandatory tender offers. The key point is that in case of a mandatory offer the acquirer of a direct or indirect controlling interest in a target company must make a public tender offer for the outstanding equity securities of the target company. The purpose of this requirement is to ensure that minority shareholders are protected from being "squeezed out" by a new "controlling" shareholder on unfavourable terms. Mandatory tender offers apply to all forms of equity securities, whether common or preferred stock, options, or convertible securities. The Takeover Act does not limit the necessity for a mandatory tender offer to scenarios in which the controlling interest is acquired by stock purchases, but extends it to all situations in which the acquirer directly or indirectly (e.g., by acquisition of a holding company, by a merger, or through a capital increase) acquires a controlling interest.

Prior to the 2006 amendment, the Austrian Takeover Act contained a definition of "controlling" interest that focused mainly on the possibility of exerting a sufficient amount of influence over the target company and assigned significant discretion to the Austrian Takeover Commission to determine whether a person actually had such controlling influence. Now the Austrian Takeover Act as amended in 2006 provides for a strict threshold that determines whether a controlling interest exists. Under such new law, any shareholding exceeding 30 per cent of the voting rights in a company is classified as a controlling interest and results in the following obligations:

(a)   to notify the Austrian Takeover Commission; and
(b)   unless an exemption is available – to launch a mandatory offer.

In the case of indirect shareholdings, the 30 per cent threshold must be met on both levels if the direct shareholder is a listed company. If the direct shareholder is privately held or a limited liability company, the determination whether a controlling interest exists or not is, even under the new Austrian Takeover Act as amended in 2006, still to be made on the basis of all circumstances of the case, which may again give a certain amount of discretion to the Austrian Takeover Commission.

Furthermore, the Austrian Takeover Act stipulates that an acquirer who has acquired a controlling interest (but does not have the majority of the voting rights) in the target company is subject to the mandatory tender offer requirements each time the bidder acquires an additional 2 per cent or more of the targeted securities within the 12 months following the initial acquisition ("creeping in").

In addition to the threshold of 30 per cent of the voting rights, the Austrian Takeover Act as amended in 2006 now also foresees consequences in case another threshold is crossed. Any voting rights exceeding the threshold of 26 per cent cannot be exercised. Exemptions are available in case this shareholding was held prior to the entry into force of the relevant provisions of the Austrian Takeover Act on 20 May 2006 or in case of another shareholder holding a bigger stake in the target company.

The most important difference in the treatment under the Takeover Act of a voluntary tender offer on the one hand and a mandatory tender offer as well as a voluntary tender offer to acquire a controlling interest (or "anticipatory" mandatory offer) on the other is that in the latter case the proposed price per share is strictly regulated. The Takeover Act states that the price per share offered in a mandatory tender offer (or an anticipatory mandatory tender offer) must be a minimum of the average market price of the target's equity securities during the six-month period before the tender offer is publicly announced. The offer price must also reach the highest price which the bidder has paid for the target securities in the 12-month period preceding the tender offer. Furthermore, certain situations (e.g., an indirect acquisition of control or cases where the bidder granted shares as consideration for the acquisition of the controlling interest) require that the tender offer price for equity securities must reasonably reflect the value of the target company's stock. Further, in a mandatory offer, a cash consideration *must* be offered (shares might be offered as an alternative), while a voluntary tender offer can be structured as a sole share ("paper") offer. The Takeover Commission puts strong emphasis on these pricing rules.

The 2006 amendment of the Takeover Act has substantially changed the available exemptions from the obligations to make a mandatory tender offer. These exemptions can be categorised in scenarios where:

(a)   the shareholding does not provide its holder with a controlling interest; and

(b)   the influence, from an economic perspective, does not change substantially.

In line with this rationale, exemptions from the obligation to make a mandatory tender offer within the first category exist in case another shareholder or group of shareholders controls a larger stake in the target company, in case the outcome of shareholders' meetings demonstrate that the shareholding will not result in a majority of the voting rights or in case the voting rights are limited by means of the target company's articles of association. Under the second category, exemptions are available in case of mere restructuring measures within a group of companies, the transfers of shares to certain private trusts or certain changes within a group of controlling shareholders.

Finally, a third set of exemptions is available in the following cases which in fact do result in a change of control but nonetheless justify that an obligation to merely notify the facts of the case to the Takeover Commission is sufficient:

(a)   the indirect acquisition of control and the book value of the shareholding in the target company amounts to less than 25 per cent of the net asset value of the entity acquired by the bidder;

(b)   the number of voting rights needed to obtain a controlling interest is exceeded only slightly and temporarily or unintentionally;

(c)   shares are acquired only for recapitalisation purposes or in order to secure claims; or

(d)   shares are transferred between relatives by way of gift, succession or split of an estate following a divorce.

2.8.6   Sanctions

The Takeover Commission is responsible for ensuring compliance with the Takeover Act. The Takeover Commission also has exclusive jurisdiction over all matters regulated in the Takeover Act. The decisions of the Takeover Commission cannot be appealed before any administrative body, with the exception of decisions imposing administrative fines, which can be appealed before the Administrative Court (*Verwaltungsgerichtshof*). As a result, decisions of the Takeover Commission can only be appealed to the Constitutional Court (*Verfassungsgerichtshof*) on the basis of a claim for infringement of constitutional rights.

Failure to comply with the regulations of the Takeover Act may lead the Takeover Commission to impose the following sanctions:

(a)   suspension of voting rights;

(b)   suspension of other rights of the holder of equity securities and forfeiture of payments made to the bidder; or

(c)   granting to the seller of the securities the right to rescind the sale within a period of six months.

A breach of the Takeover Act is an administrative offence for which the Takeover Commission may impose a fine in the range of €5,000 to €50,000. A breach may also constitute a criminal offence.

2.9   Defences to a hostile offer

2.9.1   Background

At the time of writing, few hostile public offers had occurred in Austria and hostile offers in cases of a limited number of shareholders have also been very rare (to the extent they have become well known). The Takeover Act imposes a strict neutrality obligation on the board members of the target company allowing only such defence measures that are explicitly authorised by a shareholders meeting. Many of the typical anti-takeover strategies are therefore either unknown or have at least not been tested in practice, although some elements of such longer-term strategies have been employed in specific circumstances, for example in cases where majority shareholders have pledged their shares and feared that the lender would attempt to realise the pledge and take control of the company following a default, or in cases where companies are controlled by a group of shareholders in order to make it less attractive to violate shareholder agreements, in particular using rights of first refusal or other transfer restrictions.

2.9.2 *Protective measures*

It is useful to distinguish between protective measures of the shareholders, often taken long in advance in order to deter, or make impossible, a takeover attempt, and defensive measures of the management board, which are more likely to be taken when the danger of a hostile takeover arises or in direct response to an offer.

Shareholders are relatively free to engage in all sorts of protective strategies as long as they have the necessary votes to implement them. For example, providing for staggered terms of office for the supervisory board and the management board in order to make it more difficult for a potential buyer to establish effective control. It should be mentioned, however, that shareholders have no absolute freedom in this respect. Although much of the law is not yet settled, the principle is recognised that shareholders owe certain duties to each other and that a majority may make use of their rights only for a valid reason. It is not certain that deterring a potential buyer constitutes such a valid reason.

Further, larger individual shareholders often enter into shareholder agreements where all parties are restricted, for instance, from transferring their shares to outside shareholders without having offered them to the other parties first.

Some Austrian AGs issue non-voting preference stock to effect capital increases without a substantial change in majority interests. Only one-third of the total share capital may consist of non-voting preference shares. To impede the acquirer from taking control of the shareholders meeting too easily, the shareholders may also want to convert non-voting preference shares to voting shares. Non-voting preference shares become voting shares if the preferential right to dividends is eliminated, such elimination requiring a shareholders resolution as well as the additional and separate approval of the meeting of the holders of preference stock.

Whether a capital increase deters a potential buyer will depend on various factors. In the case of a regular capital increase, each shareholder will have a pre-emptive right which allows that shareholder to maintain its equity participation voting power, unless the shareholders meeting excludes such pre-emption right with a 75 per cent majority (or more, depending on the articles). In any event, new shares are only allocated to existing shareholders if they actually exercise their subscription right.

The articles of the AG (or an amendment thereto, which requires a 75 per cent majority) may authorise the management board to issue new shares up to a maximum value of half of the stated share capital at some later date, the latest date being five years after registration. If the articles do not define the terms and conditions of the capital increase, the management board itself can determine the conditions for the issuance of new shares. It may even decide to preclude subscription rights or fix the issue price of new stock. The management board could then decide whether to issue voting or non-voting preference shares. All conditions of the issuance of new stock have to be approved by the supervisory board. Clearly, such an existing authorisation has a deterrent effect on a potential buyer.

2.9.3   Management measures – defensive responses

2.9.3.1   Principles

The range of defensive responses available to the management is limited by the general legal rule that the management board as well as the supervisory board are legally bound to act in the best interests of the company.

It is one of the basic principles of the Takeover Act that, in the face of a tender offer, the managing board and the supervisory board of the target company must act in the best interest of all holders of the company's securities, and must also consider the interests of the employees, the creditors and the public. Therefore, the managing board and the supervisory board are obliged to refrain from taking any action to avoid the takeover. Furthermore, the executive bodies of the target company may not attempt to influence or exert control over the decision of the shareholders to accept or refuse the offer.

Consequently, the managing board can only take defensive measures at the time of a takeover attempt if the shareholders of the target company have agreed to do so pursuant to a shareholders resolution taken in advance to help deter a takeover. The only exception is in the context of capital increases made as a defensive measure. For such capital increases, the shareholders resolution cannot be adopted in advance, but must be voted on at the time of the takeover. The purpose of this limitation is to prevent abusive use by the management of pre-authorised capital increases.

2.9.3.2   Repurchase of shares

It is doubtful whether the repurchase of a company's own shares will ever be a workable defence strategy. Grounds for the permitted repurchase of shares have been broadened: an AG may *inter alia* acquire and own its own shares (treasury shares) generally only under certain, albeit still limited, circumstances such as:

(a)   where the acquisition of the treasury shares is necessary to ward off severe damage to the company; or

(b)   where shares are acquired either in order to be offered to employees or (under approval by shareholders resolution) to be offered to the management pursuant to a stock purchase or a stock option plan.

The aggregate nominal amount of a corporation's own shares so acquired may not usually exceed 10 per cent of the company's entire stated share capital.

In addition, publicly listed AGs may repurchase up to 10 per cent of their entire stated share capital upon an authorisation of the shareholders meeting. Such authorisation is valid for 18 months and must not necessarily state a specific reason for the repurchase. The Takeover Commission has decided that the rules for voluntary takeover offers set forth in the Takeover Act apply to share repurchases of listed companies.

These restrictions also apply to the purchase of shares of a parent corporation by its directly or indirectly owned subsidiary companies. To what extent cross-shareholdings are otherwise permissible is unclear.

Treasury shares are non-voting and carry no dividend rights.

A limited liability company may never purchase its own shares.

2.9.3.3 *Sale of assets*

The target company may consider selling, or granting an option to a third party to purchase, some valuable assets. In this respect the general principles (*see* 2.9.3.1 above) would apply. Certain transactions will also require the approval of the supervisory board, which must adhere to the same standard of care and loyalty to the company.

For a variety of reasons the management's decision to entirely or partially liquidate the target company would be even less practical than the sale of valuable assets. In particular, a shareholders resolution will be required. Also, the "aggressor" may halt the dissolution process and decide on a continuation of the company if he can muster a 75 per cent majority in the shareholders meeting.

2.9.3.4 *Other*

A "pac-man defence", where a tender offer for the aggressor's shares is launched, will seldom be practical in Austria in the case of an Austrian bidder, since such bidder will probably not be publicly owned. Otherwise, the management board may need the approval of the supervisory board and will have to show good business reasons for such an offer. It is unclear to what extent any resulting cross-shareholding would be permissible.

The management of the target company may seek to solicit a tender offer from a third company ("white knight") which it prefers to the aggressor. Austrian law does not restrict the target company's management from asking a friendly third party to launch an equally good or even better tender offer. Of course the feasibility of such a strategy could be highly increased by means of a "re"-authorised capital increase (*see* 2.9.2 above) with exclusion of the equity shareholders' subscription rights. But even then, the "white knight" would not usually be allowed to pay a lower price for the capital increase than that offered by the aggressor. The general limitation on the percentage of treasury shares also excludes an agreement with the "white knight" to the effect that his blocking stake of the target company's shares be resold to the target company at some later date.

2.10 Profit forecasts and asset valuation

Other than the requirements for the tender offer documentation (*see* 2.8.2 above), no specific rules exist concerning profit forecasts and asset valuations. This means that the offeror as well as the management of the target company would essentially be free to choose which information is given and by which documents such information is supported, in addition to the minimum required information.

In doing so, the management of the target company will have to comply with its duty of loyalty and standard of care vis-à-vis the shareholders. For the members of the management board as well as for the members of the supervisory board it would be a criminal offence if any misleading statements were made or any material information were omitted.

On the part of the offeror it would be risky to make incomplete or misleading statements for other reasons: this could give rise to a relevant mistake on the part of the sellers, who may then be entitled either to rescind any sales of their shares or to ask for an increased purchase price.

2.11 Documents from offeror and offeree board

Again, other than the documentary requirements set forth in the Takeover Act (*see* 2.8.2 above), no specific regulations exist with respect to documents from the offeror or from the target boards. Outside the Takeover Act, the relevant guiding principles could be gleaned only from general civil and corporate law. *See* 2.9 above, where these principles are set out.

2.12 Compulsory sale of minority shareholdings ("squeeze-out")

As indicated above (*see* 2.6.2), Austrian law provides the 90 per cent shareholder of a GmbH or an AG with the ability to squeeze out the minority shareholders (on the basis of the new Squeeze-out Act which entered into force simultaneously with the 2006 amendment of the Takeover Act).

The Squeeze-out Act (*Gesellschafter-Ausschlussgesetz*) generally (i.e., irrespective of a previous takeover) permits a 90 per cent shareholder ("the principal shareholder") of an AG or GmbH target to cause, by means of a shareholders resolution, that the minority shareholders' shares are transferred to the principal shareholder against adequate cash compensation.

Rules on shareholders' protection and information are essentially in line with the rules applying to normal legal mergers (*see* 2.6.2 above). The decision on such a squeeze-out must set forth explicitly the cash amount offered by the main shareholder to the minority shareholders. A balance sheet as of the transformation date must be set up and will be available to the minority shareholders for prior inspection. All minority shareholders are entitled to receive such cash compensation within two months of the registration of the squeeze-out. However, every shareholder can invoke an "appraisal right" along the same lines as described for normal legal mergers (*see* 2.6.2 above): every minority shareholder (here irrespective of the number of shares held) may ask the court to determine the appropriate amount of compensation, and the court's decision will apply to all minority shareholders.

The squeeze-out becomes effective with its entry into the Commercial Register.

2.13 Insider dealing and market manipulation

2.13.1 General

Austria has implemented the Market Abuse Directive (2003/6/EC) by adopting an amendment to the Stock Exchange Act (*Börsegesetz*), effective as of January

2005, setting forth certain rules against market manipulation, including insider dealing, the violation of which is punishable as a criminal offence. Austria has also created a financial market authority, an integral supervisory authority also responsible for market surveillance (*Finanzmarktaufsicht*) to help enforce insider dealing provisions among other things. Insider dealing cases relating to tender offers are also handled by the Takeover Commission.

The Takeover Act includes a cross-reference to these insider trading provisions. The bidder, the executive bodies of the target company and all independent expert advisers are subject to a confidentiality requirement and must refrain from taking advantage of inside information regarding the potential tender offer. The bidder is responsible for informing all involved persons of their confidentiality obligations and is required to take all other necessary measures to ensure confidentiality. The Takeover Commission can issue general ordinances supplementing the Takeover Act's information delivery requirements.

Although some apparent instances of insider trading have occurred on the Vienna Stock Exchange since these rules came into effect, very few related legal proceedings have been instituted and the most prominent insider trading case (*Causa Struzl*) was settled out of court. Another prominent case (dealing with alleged insider trading in connection with the takeover of an Austrian group of brewing companies by Heineken in 2003) has recently been concluded (with one conviction) in the first instance before the Criminal Court of Vienna. In any event, enforcement of these new provisions is expected to be enhanced due to increased integration efforts on a European level.

2.13.2　Inside information

Inside information to which the rules against insider trading apply is any information of a precise nature which has not been made public, relating, directly or indirectly, to one or more issuers of financial instruments or to one or more financial instruments which, if it were made public, would be likely to have a significant effect on the prices of those financial instruments or on the price of related derivative financial instruments. A reasonable investor can be expected to take this information into account when rendering his investment decision.

2.13.3　Market manipulation

Market manipulation under the Stock Exchange Act is defined as at least one of the following:

(a)　Transactions or orders to trade:
    (i)　which give, or are likely to give, false or misleading signals as to the supply of, or demand for or price of financial instruments; or
    (ii)　which secure, by a person, or persons acting in collaboration, the price of one or several financial instruments at an abnormal or artificial level,
unless the person who entered into the transactions or issued the order to trade establishes that his reasons for so doing are legitimate and that these transactions or orders to trade conform to accepted market practices on the regulated market concerned.

(b)   Transactions or orders to trade which are fictitious or any other form of deception or contravention.

(c)   Dissemination of information through the media, including the internet, or by any other means, which gives, or is likely to give, false or misleading signals as to financial instruments, including the dissemination of rumours and false or misleading news, where the person who made the dissemination knew, or ought to have known, that the information was false or misleading.

2.13.4   Insider

The new definition of insiders not only includes persons who have access to inside information due to their profession, occupation, duties or interest in the capital of the issuer, it also includes persons who have received inside information as a consequence of a criminal offence.

2.13.5   Forbidden actions

Insiders are prohibited from taking advantage of the inside information, if done with the intention of enrichment (of himself or others), by either:

(a)   buying, selling, offering or recommending an affected security; or

(b)   giving this inside information to a third party without obligation thereto.

In addition, other persons (non-insiders) are prohibited from taking advantage of the inside information which they have been informed about or which otherwise has come to their knowledge, if done with the intention of enrichment. It should be noted that under the Stock Exchange Act gross negligence is sufficient for the prohibition of actions as described above.

Finally, market manipulation as defined above is prohibited as a consequence of the amendment to the Stock Exchange Act.

2.13.6   Sanctions

Violation of the rules against misappropriation of inside information is a criminal offence. Such offences can be sanctioned by imprisonment for up to five years if the pecuniary advantage exceeds €50,000.

Market manipulation is considered an administrative offence, subject to an administrative fine to be imposed by the Financial Market Authority ("FMA") of up to €35,000.

2.13.7   Compliance

The Stock Exchange Act and related directives issued thereunder by the financial market authority contain some additional rules aimed at improving compliance with, and enforcement of, the rules against insider dealing. Credit institutions, insurance companies and pension funds as well as all issuers must inform employees about insider dealing rules, adopt internal guidelines for the internal passing-on of information and for enforcement of such guidelines, and adopt suitable organisational measures to impede violations of insider dealing rules.

Further, issuers must inform the public and the executive committee of the Stock Exchange of new facts that may have a significant impact on the share price. Certain important information listed in the Stock Exchange Act (e.g., a change in the rights attaching to shares) must be made public without undue delay, regardless of whether such an impact on prices can be assumed or not (although the executive committee of the Stock Exchange may grant an exemption in specific cases).

Finally, directors' dealings in securities of the issuer must be made public within five days of the transactions.

2.14 Financial assistance

Only in very limited circumstances is a GmbH or an AG permitted to repay capital to its shareholders. Repayment of capital is not only the actual disbursement of funds, but rather any favour granted because the shareholder is a shareholder. Generally, under Austrian law a target company is therefore prohibited from providing funds to a third party for the purchase of its own shares. The prevailing view holds that the same rule applies also to all sorts of collateral granted by the target – in other words, the target would not be permitted to grant a surety, guarantee or a pledge of its assets for such a purchase.

Chapter 3
Belgium

Chris Sunt

Partner
Freshfields Bruckhaus Deringer, Brussels

3.1 Introduction

In Belgium, the majority of takeovers take the form of private acquisitions (as opposed to acquisitions by way of public offer) of unlisted companies. Most of these companies are either family owned or are subsidiaries of multinational groups. Although the number of Belgian listed companies increased in the late 1990s, when Initial Public Offerings ("IPOs") were popular, their number has decreased since then, mostly as a result of public-to-private transactions. Some recent, often smaller, IPOs in 2006 and 2007 have not really changed this picture. A unique feature of the Belgian market is that a large percentage of listed companies are controlled by only a few shareholders. The first stage of most acquisitions of public companies is thus the private acquisition of a controlling interest in a public company, which is then followed by a bid for the shares that are held by the public. Since 2000 the number of both public and private acquisitions made by private equity houses has increased. Recently, private equity houses have started to resell certain of their Belgian portfolio companies.

Until the 1980s hostile mergers and acquisitions did not occur very often in Belgium. At that time only a few aggressive acquisitions had been recorded and the legal framework applicable to mergers and acquisitions was not well defined. The direct consequence was that when foreign companies started to launch bids for Belgian companies in the late 1980s, hardly any regulations applied. This is one of the reasons for the chaos that surrounded the unsuccessful hostile takeover bid for *Société Générale de Belgique/Generale Maatschappij van België*, then Belgium's largest company. Immediately afterwards, Parliament and the Government enacted detailed legislation to regulate these areas.

In addition, the powers of the Banking, Finance and Insurance Commission ("CBFA"), Belgium's main regulatory body for capital markets, credit institutions and insurance companies, have been broadened significantly.

Changes to Company Laws were also introduced, mainly to bring Belgian legislation in line with EU Directives. In particular, mergers and split-ups of companies (but also contributions of activities) became regulated. The Companies Code, which came into effect on 6 February 2001, and its implementing Royal Decree of 30 January 2001, brought together in one Code a number of separate pieces of legislation affecting corporate takeovers. They have already been amended on a number of occasions.

Belgium has implemented the EU Takeover Directive 2004/25/EU of 21 April 2004. As from 1 September 2007 public takeover bids have been regulated by the Law of 1 April 2007 on public takeover bids and by two Royal Decrees of 27 April 2007 on public takeover bids and public squeeze-out bids respectively. Furthermore, Belgium has implemented the Markets in Financial Instruments Directive ("MiFID") by way of two Royal Decrees of 27 April 2007 and 3 June 2007 respectively and has implemented the EU Transparency Directive (2004/109/EU of 15 December 2004) by way of a Law of 2 May 2007.

Concentrations may fall under the scope of Belgium's Competition Law, which requires large concentrations resulting from mergers and acquisitions to receive the approval of the Competition Council.

3.2   Acquisition targets

Belgian companies can be classified into three different categories:

(a)   listed companies (i.e., companies whose shares are listed on a regulated market (Article 4 Company Code));
(b)   public companies (i.e., companies, whether or not listed, that have issued securities publicly either in Belgium or abroad (cf. Article 438 Company Code)); and
(c)   all other (private) companies.

3.2.1   Listed companies

As in all other jurisdictions, companies listed on Euronext or a foreign Stock Exchange or other regulated market are heavily regulated. The acquisition of their shares is subject to detailed regulations.

3.2.2   Other public companies

Public companies are defined as companies making, or having made, an offer of securities (including shares) to the public in Belgium or abroad, by way of public subscription, a public offer of sale or a public offer of exchange and also include those listed on a regulated market. Every public company must indicate in its articles of association that it qualifies as a public company.

Public companies are subject to the rules applicable to all companies, except that some additional regulations apply, particularly with regard to corporate govern-ance and the protection of capital.

3.2.3   All other companies

Most Belgian companies are still privately owned and do not qualify as public companies. Acquisitions of such companies are therefore subject to the agreement of the controlling shareholders, who in most cases run the business (unless it is a subsidiary of another Belgian or foreign company).

3.3 Notification and authorisation

3.3.1 Exchange controls

Belgium used to have two foreign exchange markets and the flow of payments in these markets was controlled. The double exchange market was abolished in 1990, and there are no longer any exchange controls.

3.3.2 Controls on investment

As a rule, no foreign investment authorisation is required in Belgium. In exceptional cases, foreign investment from certain countries may (temporarily) be prohibited (e.g., Iraq and Kuwait, the former Yugoslavia, etc.). Investments in certain industries, particularly the financial sector, may require (prior) approval by the Banking, Finance and Insurance Commission, for Belgians and foreigners alike.

3.3.3 Disclosure of significant shareholdings

In 1989 Parliament introduced the obligation to disclose significant shareholdings in listed companies. Certain provisions of the law of 2 March 1989 were subsequently incorporated into the Companies Code (Articles 514–516). This obligation on the part of shareholders of listed companies is generally known as the "transparency obligation".

The Law of 2 March 1989 was subsequently replaced by the Law of 2 May 2007 on the publication of important shareholdings. The transparency law in principle only applies to Belgian issuers of shares which are traded on a regulated market. Any person acquiring directly or indirectly 5 per cent or more of the securities carrying voting rights (or of the voting rights) of a Belgian issuer must inform the issuer and the CBFA thereof. Notification is required each time another 5 per cent threshold is reached, e.g., 10 per cent, 15 per cent, 20 per cent, etc. An issuer can set out in its articles of association different thresholds: 1 per cent, 2 per cent, 3 per cent, 4 per cent and 7.5 per cent. Similarly, if the shareholding drops below any of these thresholds, a new transparency declaration is needed. The entering into, modification or termination of an agreement by which parties act in concert, must be notified in the same manner. Certain exemptions apply in view of clearing and settlement within three trading days, for depositaries, market makers, for trading portfolios of credit institutions, etc. The transparency declaration needs to be made as soon as possible and at the latest on the fourth trading day after the acquisition. The format of the transparency declaration is determined by Royal Decree. The issuer has to publish the transparency declaration within three days of its receipt. Moreover, the issuer's annual report must contain its shareholder structure based upon the transparency declarations received. Compliance with the transparency obligations is supervised by the CBFA. In case of non-compliance, the CBFA can impose administrative fines, and criminal sanctions are also provided for.

3.3.4   Notification to the Government

The Economic Expansion Law of 30 December 1970 (Article 36) states that the federal Ministers of Economic Affairs and Finance and the Regional Minister of Economic Affairs must be informed in advance of any transaction involving the sale of one-third or more of the equity of a company operating in Belgium. This regulation applies if the net assets of such company sold amount to at least €2.5 million. In the Flemish Region, this law was abolished by the Decree of 23 December 2005, with effect as from 1 January 2006. In the Walloon Region, this was abolished by the Decree of 11 March 2004, which had effect from 1 July 2004.

There are no sanctions for non-compliance with this provision and none of the Ministers have the authority to oppose or delay the transaction for failure to comply with this rule or otherwise. Therefore, in practice, it is often disregarded.

3.3.5   Information to and consultation of the workforce

In the case of a company conducting negotiations about a merger, concentration, takeover, closure or other major structural change, its works council must be informed thereof in due time and prior to the (actual) decision being made and any public announcement. The works council must be properly consulted, in advance, concerning such matters as the likely impact on the prospects of the employees, the organisation of work and employment in general (Article 11, Collective Labour Agreement No. 9 of 9 March 1972). In addition, each time an event occurs that could have a significant impact on the company, for example in the case of a takeover of the company, the works council must be informed and consulted (Article 25, Royal Decree 27 November 1973).

If there is no works council in the company, the trade union delegation must be informed and consulted. In the absence of a trade union delegation, there is only an obligation to inform the employees concerned in the case of a transfer of undertaking regulated by EC Directive 2001/23, as implemented in Belgium.

EC Directive 2001/23 of 12 March 2001 on the approximation of the laws of the Member States relating to the safeguarding of employees' rights in the event of transfer of undertakings, businesses or parts of undertakings or businesses (codified version of the original Directive 77/187 of 14 February 1977 as amended on various occasions) is implemented in Belgium by means of various acts and collective bargaining agreements. The most important piece of implementation legislation is Collective Bargaining Agreement No. 32bis of 7 June 1985 as amended on various occasions. This Collective Bargaining Agreement provides for, amongst other things, the automatic transfer of the employees concerned and joint liability of the transferor and the transferee for all outstanding liabilities, existing at the moment of transfer, that arise from the employment contracts of the transferring employees. It is therefore highly relevant in the case of assets and liabilities transactions.

Moreover, in the case of a public takeover bid, the law of 1 April 2007 on public takeover bids explicitly requires the bidder and the target company to inform the employee representatives, or in the absence thereof, the employees themselves, of the bid as soon as it is announced, and provide them with the draft prospectus. The works council of the target will formulate its views on the bid and may request the management of the bidder to present to them the bid and explain the industrial and financial policy of the bidder and the likely impact of its strategy on employment at the target (Articles 42–45 Law of 1 April 2007 on public takeover bids).

3.4 Merger control

On 1 October 2006, a new consolidated Belgian Competition Act entered into force, replacing the Competition Act of 1991. The law is in many respects modelled on the new EC Merger Regulation which came into force on 1 May 2004.

3.4.1 Thresholds for mandatory notification

The Competition Law sets out a mandatory merger notification process very similar to that in the EC Merger Regulation, applying only to concentrations meeting the following thresholds:

(a)   the aggregate turnover in Belgium of the companies involved in the concentration is higher than €100 million; and

(b)   each of at least two of the companies involved has a turnover in Belgium of more than €40 million.

The Belgian rules for the calculation of turnover of credit institutions and other financial institutions are the same as the EC Merger Regulation ("ECMR") rules.

For the purposes of the Competition Law, a concentration is deemed to arise when:

(a)   two (or more) previously independent companies merge;

(b)   an undertaking or a person already controlling an undertaking acquires control over the whole or part of another undertaking; or

(c)   two or more undertakings form a "full-function" joint venture.

If a given concentration falls within the scope of the EC Merger Regulation, the Belgian Competition Act does not apply.

3.4.2 Procedure

Concentrations falling within the scope of the Competition Act are subject to the prior consent of the Competition Council, which determines whether or not they may proceed. The criteria applied by the Competition Council in evaluating notified concentrations are similar to those of the 2004 EC Merger Regulation – that is, whether the concentration significantly impedes effective competition on the Belgian market or on a substantial part thereof, in particular as a result of the creation or strengthening of a dominant position (the so-called SIEC test).

Concentrations meeting the turnover thresholds must be notified to the competition auditors prior to their implementation. Draft agreements may be notified as well. The notification must be made jointly by the parties in the case of a merger which creates a new undertaking and by the parties or acquirers jointly in the case of an acquisition of joint control. In the case of an acquisition of sole control, the acquirer alone must notify. The notification package to be submitted to the competition auditors includes a large number of documents and requires extensive paperwork. Gathering the necessary information can take up to a month.

Concentrations may not be implemented until the Competition Council has cleared the transaction. The suspension obligation does not prevent the implementation of a public bid or of a series of transactions in securities provided that the concentration is notified without delay and the acquirer does not exercise the voting rights attached to the securities in question or does so only to maintain the full value of its investments based on a derogation granted by the Competition Council.

Within 40 working days from the date of notification, the Competition Council will decide whether or not the concentration falls within the application of the Competition Law. If it does, the Competition Council must further decide whether:

(a)   the concentration is admissible; or
(b)   there is serious doubt about the admissibility of the concentration and an in-depth (phase 2) investigation is needed.

If the Competition Council makes no decision within 40 working days, the concentration is deemed to have been cleared.

In the case of an in-depth (phase 2) investigation, the Competition Council must in principle decide within an additional 60 working-day period. If the parties offer commitments, the first phase will be extended by 15 working days and the second phase by 20 working days.

In the cases of those concentrations which do not raise any competition concerns and hence qualify for notification under a simplified procedure, the competition auditor will confirm this in a simple letter to the notifying parties within a time limit of 20 working days. The letter has the legal value of a Competition Council clearance decision.

In the event that the Competition Council establishes that the concentration cannot be allowed, it suggests, with a view to restoring effective competition, a split-up of the merged companies or businesses, the abandoning of joint control, or any other appropriate measure. Finally, Belgium's Council of Ministers may, at the request of one of the parties, allow a concentration that is otherwise considered to be unacceptable by the Competition Council if this is justified by the general good. The Council of Ministers may take into account the safety of the country, the competitive position of the relevant sector in the light of international competition, the interest of the consumer and employment.

3.4.3   Appeals

Decisions adopted by the Competition Council may be appealed to the Brussels Court of Appeals. An appeal may be lodged by the companies involved in the concentration within 30 days of notification of the decision to the parties. Third parties can appeal the decision within 30 days of publication in the *Belgian State Gazette*. An application for annulment of a decision of the Council of Ministers may be brought before the Council of State.

3.4.4 Sanctions

If, before having obtained the Competition Council's approval, the parties to the concentration have implemented it, the Council may impose fines of up to 10 per cent of the parties' annual turnover in the preceding financial year. In addition, it can impose periodic penalty payments not exceeding 5 per cent of the average daily turnover in the preceding financial year, per day. There are also fines for procedural infringements, including late notification.

3.5 Regulation of the conduct of mergers and acquisitions

The Banking, Finance and Insurance Commission is Belgium's main regulatory authority for the capital markets (including public takeover bids) and financial institutions. Founded in the 1930s, its powers were broadened as from the late 1980s to give it extensive regulatory powers over stock markets in general and public offers in particular. With effect from 1 January 2004 the Insurance Control Office merged with the Banking and Finance Commission to form the Banking, Finance and Insurance Commission.

The Banking, Finance and Insurance Commission is responsible for the supervision of public takeovers in Belgium and in general for the application of the takeover legislation (Articles 35–40, Law of 1 April 2007 on public takeover bids). In case of a violation of the rules, the Banking, Finance and Insurance Commission can impose administrative fines. The CBFA must approve all public takeover prospectuses before they are made public (Article 18, Law of 1 April 2007 on public takeover bids). However, the powers of the Commission do not pre-empt those of the courts. Appeals against decisions made by the Commission in public takeover matters and any other legal action in relation to the conduct of public takeovers may be brought before the Court of Appeals of Brussels.

The findings of the Commission are published in summary form in its annual report, which provides the minimum guidelines to be followed in the case of public offers. These guidelines relate in particular to the protection of the equality of shareholders, which is one of the principles that the Commission seeks to preserve.

The powers of the Banking, Finance and Insurance Commission are limited to public offers. Mergers and acquisitions of privately owned companies fall outside its remit.

3.6   Methods of acquisition

As elsewhere, methods of acquisition vary greatly in Belgium.

3.6.1   Private agreements

As a result of foreign influence and owing to internationalisation, most major acquisition agreements used in Belgium are modelled on US or UK purchase agreements, although it is fair to say that they are shorter than a typical Anglo-Saxon agreement. The representations and warranties usually contained in a share purchase agreement governed by Belgian law are quite similar to those contained in a UK or US agreement although less detailed, particularly with respect to pensions and taxation. Moreover, a distinction is increasingly made between representations and warranties on the one hand, and indemnities on the other. Under Belgian law, there is no need to make the distinction, but this practice is influenced by Anglo-Saxon legal considerations. With the increase of sales by private equity houses, very short share sale agreements, with locked-box mechanisms and no representation other than title to the shares, are also becoming more frequent in Belgium. Belgian law does not require the inter-vention of a Notary Public for the execution of a share purchase agreement. Nor does it make the application of Belgian law or the use of the Dutch or French language mandatory.

The main reason for following international practice is that, although Belgium is a civil law country with statutory protection to fall back on, the Civil Code offers very little protection for buyers of shares. The Belgian Civil Code does not specifically address the sale of shares, and share purchase agreements are governed by the general rules of the Belgian Civil Code on sale of goods contracts. The basic principles of the Civil Code can be summarised as follows:

(a)   the goods subject to sale (i.e., the shares) must be delivered by the seller to the buyer;

(b)   the seller must warrant peaceful possession (i.e., no claims by third parties relating to the goods, the goods are sold free of charges and encum-brances); and

(c)   the seller must provide the buyer with a guarantee against hidden defects.

These principles do not offer much protection to the buyer of shares. Case law has held that the guarantee against hidden defects only applies to the shares being sold and not to the underlying business. In practice, this means for instance that the seller guarantees that the shares are valid shares representing part of the capital of the company at hand. This does not imply that the buyer has any kind of guarantee in connection with the financial condition of the company whose shares are sold. Neither is there any guarantee as to the value of the shares.

Private share purchase agreements usually provide that the time limit during which claims for breach of warranty can be filed is between two and three years. For claims in connection with tax and social security, the time limit is longer and usually corresponds with the expiry date of the statute of limitations. Claims in connection with environmental matters are also usually subject to a longer time limit. In addition, the contracts contain the usual clauses regarding thresholds, *de minimis* and cap provisions.

3.6.2 Voluntary public offers

Belgian legislation contains provisions regarding voluntary public offers for companies. These provisions are explained at 3.8 below.

3.6.3 Mandatory public bids

Belgian legislation also contains provisions that trigger the mandatory launching of public offers for public companies in well-defined circumstances. These provisions are explained at 3.8.4 below.

3.6.4 Mergers and split-ups

In 1993 a new set of regulations was enacted dealing with the rules applicable to mergers and split-ups of commercial companies. The main feature of these regulations is that merging or splitting companies in Belgium requires strict compliance with procedural formalities. The main benefit of this legislation is that it makes the merger or split enforceable against all third parties, such as creditors, by the sole publication of certain notices in the official Belgian *State Gazette*. It is also worth noting that any failure to comply strictly with the procedural rules applicable to mergers has an indirect effect. Failure to comply indeed allows the tax administration to deny the companies concerned the benefit of the favourable tax-neutral regime of the operation.

Mergers are carried out by a simple decision of the shareholders to transfer all assets and liabilities of a given company to another (or to a new company), as a result of which the acquired company is dissolved and its shareholders receive shares in the acquiring company.

The regime applicable to mergers and splits is also applicable to the contribution by a company of either its entire business or a self-contained part thereof (a "branch of activity") to another company. In the case of the sale of the entire business or a branch of activity (as opposed to a contribution thereof) by a company, parties can voluntarily submit the sale to these legal provisions in order to benefit from the rules regarding enforceability vis-à-vis third parties.

3.6.5 Joint ventures

In most cases, the partners will decide to incorporate a new special-purpose vehicle. Joint ventures receive rather favourable legal treatment under Belgian law, as voting agreements between shareholders are allowed and are enforceable to the extent that they are limited in time and in the company's best interest. Also, as mentioned in 3.9.1 below, standstill clauses are allowed under the same conditions.

3.6.6   Asset transactions

Although this section does not address the issue of asset transactions and concentrates only on the sale and purchase of shares of companies, it should be mentioned that asset deals are common in Belgium. These transactions are usually more difficult to carry out from a technical standpoint. Real-estate matters (and consequently environmental matters) in particular demand great care and attention. It is also of paramount importance to assess the tax consequences of an asset transaction from different angles such as those of capital gains tax, VAT, registration duties and so on.

Transfers of assets between credit institutions, insurance companies and financial institutions may benefit from specific rules which allow the transfer to be deemed a universal succession enforceable vis-à-vis all third parties. *See* also 3.6.4 above with respect to the sale of an entire business or of a branch of activity.

Of some importance is Article 442bis Income Tax Code. It applies to a transfer of a branch of activity other than by way of a merger or other similar operation as described in 3.6.4 above. Such a transfer is only enforceable vis-à-vis the tax administration one month from the date on which it was notified of the transfer. During this one-month period, the tax administration can exercise its rights, deriving from unpaid taxes by the seller, on the assets sold. The purchaser is jointly and severally liable vis-à-vis the tax administration for the tax debts of the seller, up to the amount of the purchase price. The purchaser will normally protect himself against this risk by requiring the seller to deliver a certificate issued by the tax administration that no taxes are due. This regulation, applicable to income taxes, has also been made applicable to social security contributions for employees (Article 41 *quinquies* of the law of 27 June 1969 on employee social security), social security contributions for self-employed persons (Article 16 of the Royal Decree No. 38 regarding the social status of self-employed workers) and Value-Added-Tax (Article 93 *undeciesB* of the Belgian VAT Code).

3.7   Preparation of an offer

3.7.1   Preliminary steps and conduct of negotiations

The sale of private companies constitutes the core of mergers and acquisitions activity in Belgium. The form and structure can be very different from one acquisition to another. Sophisticated acquisition structures are relatively common in Belgium. Controlled auction procedures have become the norm. Acquisitions by private equity funds are also, in general, more complex given:

(a)   their aversion to risk; and
(b)   the fact that they are highly leveraged.

The whole acquisition process usually begins with informal contacts between prospective buyers and the seller, either directly or more often through an investment banker. Local investment bankers as well as foreign specialists are active on the Belgian market for mergers and acquisitions. The bankers of the seller will most often prepare an Information Memorandum about the target company.

The first written document is usually a confidentiality or non-disclosure agreement, which is valid under Belgian law. Breaches of confidentiality may result in compensatory damages. The non-disclosure agreements often also include undertakings not to hire personnel from the other party.

Letters of intent or non-binding offers are frequently used when the preliminary negotiations have reached a certain stage. The legal status of letters of intent or non-binding offers is imprecise as their enforceability mainly depends on the inclusion of provisions indicating whether or not the parties intend to be bound by the terms thereof. Under Belgian law, whenever two parties agree on the object to be sold and the price to be paid, legally binding obligations are created as the intent of the parties has been expressed. There is no need to enter into a written agreement. Courts have sometimes ordered the execution of sale contracts when a party was able to demonstrate that there was indeed an agreement on the object and the price. If preliminary documents are not intended to have any binding legal effect, in whole or in part, great attention should be paid to the drafting of the relevant clauses.

It should also be borne in mind that, during the process leading to an offer, the German-inspired *culpa in contrahendo* principle applies. Under Belgian law, parties are bound to negotiate in good faith and are liable in tort for sudden and unjustified termination of ongoing negotiations. Case law demonstrates that Belgian courts have granted damages to the party that alleges that its counterpart in negotiations was not acting in good faith, invoking the *culpa in contrahendo* principle.

3.7.2 Due diligence

When preparing an offer, the offeror will try to gather as much information as possible on the target company. Public records can provide substantial data, including financial statements (available from the National Bank of Belgium) and corporate documentation (available from the clerk of the Commercial Court of the district where the target company has its registered office and from the *Bijlagen tot het Belgisch Staatsblad/Annexes au Moniteur Belge*). Property information can be obtained from the Mortgage Registry (even if the property is not mortgaged).

Due diligence investigations are very common in Belgium. These are usually carried out by lawyers, except for areas falling outside their usual competence such as environmental audits, the analysis of the financial situation of targets, insurance coverage or funding of pension plans. Vendor due diligence or "VDD" is becoming common practice in auctioned sales. The fact that the target company is a listed company may in effect limit the scope and duration of the due diligence investigation. Indeed, due diligence with regard to listed companies remains an issue. First of all, the Board of Directors of the target company must decide that it is in the best interests of the company to allow such due diligence. They will normally require proof of the "seriousness" of the purchaser, such as an offer or letter of intent, and will often insist on a confidentiality and stand-still undertaking. The potential purchaser, on the other hand, will, once it gets access to the confidential information of the target, be subject to the rules prohibiting insider trading. The Banking, Finance and Insurance Commission may issue regulations specifying under which conditions due diligence of listed companies does not violate the rules regarding the prohibition on insider trading, but has not yet done so (Article 30, 2, Law of 2 August 2002).

The use of data rooms is widespread, especially in auction procedures.

3.7.3   Increasing shareholdings

When preparing an offer, the prospective buyer may gradually increase its shareholding in the target company. It thus acquires different rights, depending on the size of the shareholding.

The table below shows what powers are given by law to shareholders owning a specific number of shares. It also indicates some of the obligations imposed upon shareholders owning such quantities of shares. With respect to the obligation to disclose certain shareholdings, *see* 3.3.3 above.

Table 3.1   Powers of shareholders owning a specific number of shares

Per cent of shares or powers of shareholder voting rights in target	Effect
Any amount	Exit: may force other shareholders to buy its shares for "good cause" (Articles 642–643 Company Code) – applicable in case of dispute between shareholders.
1% or €1,250,000	May request the court to appoint one or more experts to audit the accounts and records of the company and the decisions made by the Board, if it is demonstrated that the interests of the company could be seriously at risk.
1% or €1,250,000	Possibility to initiate a minority shareholder action – derivative action – against the directors of the company.
20%	Power to requisition the Board of Directors to convene a general meeting of shareholders (Article 532 Company Code).
Over 20%	Power to block: (a) amendments to purpose clause of target (Article 559 Company Code); and (b) the delegation to the Board of Directors of the target of the power to repurchase its own shares (Article 620 Company Code).
Over 25%	Power to block any amendment to articles of association of target or merger/split thereof (Articles 558 and 699/736 Company Code).

Table 3.1   continued

30%	Power to ask a court to squeeze out a shareholder for good cause (Article 636 and following Company Code) – applicable in case of dispute between shareholders.
Over 50%	Legal control – power to pass resolutions at ordinary shareholders meeting and thus to appoint and remove directors and auditors.
75%	Power to pass resolutions at extraordinary shareholders meeting, including amendments to articles of association, mergers and splits.
80%	Power to pass any resolution at extraordinary shareholders meeting, including: (a) amendments to target's purpose clause; and (b) delegation to the Board of Directors of the authority to repurchase the company's shares.
95%	Power to acquire all shares in target – squeeze-out (Article 513 Company Code) in case of a public company.
100%	After one year of 100 per cent ownership, the sole shareholder becomes jointly liable with target (Article 646 Company Code).

3.8   Conduct of a public offer

Public offers are regulated by:

(a)   the law of 1 April 2007 on public takeover bids;
(b)   the Royal Decree of 27 April 2007 on public takeover bids; and
(c)   the Royal Decree of 27 April 2007 on public squeeze-out bids.

This section deals with the basic rules applicable to the conduct of voluntary public offers and with the procedure to be followed in cases where a mandatory public offer must be launched.

3.8.1   Notification to the Banking, Finance and Insurance Commission

Any person intending to launch a public offer for a company must notify the Banking, Finance and Insurance Commission thereof in advance. The notification must include the price, the terms and conditions of the offer, the draft prospectus and evidence to demonstrate that all the applicable rules will be complied with.

The Banking, Finance and Insurance Commission will then verify whether the proposed offer complies with all legal requirements applicable, such as:

(a)   the offer must relate to all the securities with voting rights or giving access thereto not yet owned by the offeror. It is nevertheless possible to make the offer conditional upon acquiring a minimum number of acceptances (e.g., 50 per cent of all the securities issued by the target) and to submit the bid to obtaining competition clearance;

(b)   the offeror must demonstrate that it has the necessary funds to carry out the public offer either in an account opened with a credit institution or in the form of an unconditional and irrevocable credit facility granted by a credit institution;

(c)   in the case of a bid offering shares, the offeror has to demonstrate either that it already possesses the shares offered or that it has secured the means of acquiring or producing them.

After receipt of the notification by the offeror, the Banking, Finance and Insurance Commission will publicly announce that it has received such notification. A copy of this announcement will be sent to the offeror, the target company and the management committee of the Stock Exchange where the shares of the target company are listed, if such is the case. Prior to this announcement, no one may make the offer public, but in view of the proper functioning of the markets the Commission can issue a "put-up or shut-up" order where a party has made certain statements that will leave the public in doubt whether or not a public bid will be launched.

3.8.2   Contents of the offer document

The offer document (commonly known in Belgium as the prospectus) aims to provide information to the shareholders of the target company in order to allow them to decide whether or not they should sell their shares. Detailed information must be supplied regarding the offeror, the target, the shares to be bought, the consideration and the terms and conditions of the offer. The required content of the prospectus is laid down in Schedule I to the Royal Decree of 27 April 2007. The prospectus must contain a summary.

Within a period of five days from receipt of the draft prospectus, the board of directors of the target may forward its remarks and comments regarding the draft offer document to the Banking, Finance and Insurance Commission and to the offeror. If the board of directors of the target company is of the opinion that the draft prospectus is incomplete or misleading, it must inform the offeror and the Banking, Finance and Insurance Commission thereof.

The board of directors of the target company must also prepare a statement ("Notice of Reply") regarding the offer itself. In formulating its statement, the board of directors must take into account the interests of the shareholders, the creditors and the employees of the target company. The statement must also indicate whether the directors of the company intend to sell their shares, if they hold any.

3.8.3   Publication of the prospectus and procedure for the offer

The prospectus may only be made public after it has been approved by the Banking, Finance and Insurance Commission. It will include a statement containing the formal approval by the Commission and the date of such approval.

A bidder can request the recognition in Belgium of a prospectus that has been approved by the competent authority of another EU Member State in accordance with Article 4 of the Directive 2004/25/EU. In addition to a possible translation, the Banking, Finance and Insurance Commission can request that the prospectus is supplemented by a document addressing Belgian specific issues, such as the tax treatment of the sale.

The prospectus is made freely available to the public through at least one Belgian credit institution. The fact that a prospectus has been issued must be published in one or more Belgian newspapers.

The period during which the public offer is open starts not earlier than the fifth business day after the approval of the prospectus, and must last at least two weeks, but no more than 10 weeks.

A counter offer may be made up to two days before the expiration of the original public offer. The counter bidder must propose a consideration at least 5 per cent higher than that proposed by the first offeror. The same procedure and requirements as apply to a public offer apply to any counter offer. In the event of a counter offer, the first offeror may in turn make a second counter bid, at least 5 per cent higher than the first counter offer, but is not required to submit a new notification or prospectus.

The results of the public offer must be made public at the latest on the fifth day following the closing of the offer. The purchase price needs to be paid no later than the tenth day after the publication of the results of the offer. The Banking, Finance and Insurance Commission must be informed of the total number of shares in the target company acquired and held by the offeror.

The bidder may not purchase securities of the target that were the subject of the public bid within one year from the close of the offer period at a price above the public bid price, unless the price difference is also paid to the shareholders who tendered their shares in the public bid.

3.8.4 Mandatory public offers

A mandatory public takeover bid must be launched when a person or a legal entity through acquisition by itself or by a party acting in concert, directly or indirectly, holds 30 per cent of the securities with voting rights of a Belgian company of which all or part of the securities are listed (Article 5, Law of 1 April 2007 on public takeover bids). Specific rules apply in case of persons acting in concert or using one or more intermediate holding companies. Certain exemptions exist, for example if another party holds more than 30 per cent of the same company, as a result of a rights issue, in case of merger, etc. The price of the mandatory bid is at least the higher of:

(a) the highest price paid by the bidder over the last 12 months; and
(b) the weighted average trading price on the market over the last 30 days.

3.9 Defence strategy in the face of a hostile offer

Major raids conducted in the 1980s and 1990s by (foreign) investors on Belgian companies have led the latter to develop defence strategies against hostile bids. At about the same time, new legislation was enacted to regulate public offers and the use of defensive measures against hostile bids. The most common defence strategies used by Belgian companies in the face of hostile offers are mentioned below.

3.9.1 Transfer-blocking clauses

Transfer-blocking clauses as such are allowed by the Companies Code to the extent that they are limited in time and are at all times in the interest of the company in question. However, these clauses are impractical for listed companies. Such clauses may either be inserted into the articles of association of companies or into private instruments such as shareholder agreements. If such a clause is inserted into the company's articles of association, it is binding upon all shareholders, whereas shareholder agreements only bind the parties thereto.

Most commonly such clauses restrict the free transfer of shares of companies by way of first-refusal clauses and approval clauses. In first-refusal clauses, the current shareholders of the company must be offered the shares to be sold prior to any sale at the same price and conditions as those proposed by a prospective buyer. This is, however, difficult to apply in the case of public companies unless the shares are registered shares, which is highly exceptional in Belgium. In approval clauses, the board of directors of the company whose shares are to be sold must give its approval to any share transfer. In this case, however, the share-holders willing to sell their shares to a prospective buyer must be given the opportunity by the board of directors to sell their shares in the company, under the same conditions, to another party having been presented by the board, and thus acceptable to it.

It should be noted that the procedure of the board's approval or of first refusal may not under any circumstances delay the share transfer for more than six months.

3.9.2 Authorised capital

The widely-used technique of "authorised capital" allows the board of directors (as opposed to the shareholders) to increase the company's capital and issue new securities in one or more stages, up to an amount defined in the articles of association of the company in question.

However, the Companies Code restricts the powers of the board of directors of a company subject to a public offer (from the time of notification of the public offer to the target company by the Banking, Finance and Insurance Commission until the close of the offer) to increase the capital of the company by cancelling the pre-emption rights of the existing shareholders. Although the powers of the board of directors with regard to capital increases are restricted during this period, they can still increase the capital by using the authorised capital technique if the authorisation to increase the capital was granted by the share-holders no more than three years before the notification of the offer and if the resolution was adopted at a meeting by a quorum of half of the shares issued and with a three-quarters majority. In addition, the newly issued shares must be fully paid up, the price of these shares must not be lower than the bid price and the number of shares thus issued may not exceed 10 per cent of the issued share capital prior to the new issue. Provided that the articles of association of the target company allow for such technique, the board of directors may use it to issue shares to third parties of its choice.

3.9.3   *Change of control provisions*

Many important contracts contain change of control provisions. They are subject to Article 556 Company Code, which states that the shareholders must formally approve any transaction whereby the company would grant a right to a third party contingent upon the launching of a public offer for the company in question or a change of the control over it. The minutes of the shareholders meeting deciding upon such a transaction must be filed with the clerk of the commercial court of the district where the company has its registered office.

3.9.4   *Crown jewel defence*

Crown jewel defence is not widespread in Belgium since, from the notification of the public offer by the Banking, Finance and Insurance Commission to the board of directors of the target company and until the expiry of the offer, the powers of the board of directors are restricted (Article 557 Company Code). In particular, the board of directors may not, without the approval of a shareholders meeting specially called for this purpose, make decisions or carry out trans-actions that could substantially modify the assets and liabilities of the target company, or assume obligations without appropriate consideration. Such trans-actions may not be conditional upon the success or failure of a takeover bid. The target company may nevertheless complete the transactions that were under-taken prior to the notification of the offer to the company by the Banking, Finance and Insurance Commission.

3.9.5   *Specific voluntary rules in case of a public bid*

The articles of association of a Belgian company may provide:

(a) that the management may not frustrate the public bid unless it is previ-ously authorised thereto by the general shareholders' meeting;
(b) that share transfer restrictions contained in agreements or in the articles of association do not apply in case of a public bid;
(c) that voting limitations will not apply in these circumstances; and
(d) that special voting arrangements with respect to the appointment of directors shall not apply.

The articles of association can furthermore contain a reciprocity provision under which the Belgian company would not be obliged to respect the above-mentioned rules if a foreign bidder does not have similar provisions in its articles of association.

3.10   Compulsory acquisitions of minorities

Compulsory buy-outs of minority shareholders of public companies are regulated by the Law of 1 April 2007 on public takeover bids and by the Royal Decree of 27 April 2007 on public squeeze-out bids, in the framework of voluntary and mandatory public offers. In addition, the Companies Code provides for special procedures dealing with squeeze-outs of minority share-holders of private companies and other buy-out schemes, in particular in case of disputes between shareholders.

3.10.1   Compulsory re-offers to minorities after a public offer

The Belgian regulations regarding public offers provide for a compulsory re-offer to minorities under certain conditions, after the close of the public offer. The offer must be re-opened within 10 business days from the date on which the results of the offer were made public.

If, after a successful public offer, the bidder owns more than 90 per cent of the securities issued by the target company, it must re-open the offer for a minimum of five and a maximum of 15 business days.

Moreover the offeror must re-open the offer for a minimum of five and a maximum of 15 business days if, within a three-month period from the close of the bid, the offeror wishes the shares of the target company to be withdrawn from the listing on the Stock Exchange.

Lastly, if the offeror wishes to proceed to a squeeze-out bid the offer must also be re-opened.

3.10.2   Compulsory acquisitions (sell-outs)

The Companies Code provides for a special procedure applicable to all limited liability companies, whereby a shareholder can request a court to force the other shareholders to buy his or her shares. The Companies Code allows a shareholder to sell his or her shares to the other shareholders provided it can be demonstrated that the selling shareholder has a just cause to request the court to force the other shareholders to buy the shares.

It is generally understood that this procedure is to be used in situations in which the behaviour of a shareholder or a group of shareholders prejudices a fellow shareholder. The simple fact of being a small minority shareholder facing a strong majority shareholder is not considered as a just cause triggering this provision of the Companies Code.

Any minority shareholder has the right to sell its securities to the bidder who, pursuant to a public takeover bid holds 95 per cent or more of the securities with voting rights of the target. The minority shareholders must notify their intention within three months from the close of the bid.

3.10.3   Compulsory sales (squeeze-outs)

The Companies Code only provides for an effective squeeze-out procedure applicable to public companies. Shareholders holding 95 per cent of the voting rights in a public company may squeeze out the other shareholders. The actual procedure differs depending on whether or not the squeeze-out follows a public offer for the same shares. In the case of private companies, the 5 per cent minority shareholders can be forced to convert their bearer shares into registered shares, but cannot be effectively squeezed out.

The Companies Code also sets out a special mechanism to resolve conflicts between shareholders. The shareholders of a company owning 30 per cent of the voting rights or capital may commence proceedings before the President of the Commercial Court to squeeze out another shareholder for just cause. The requirement of 30 per cent of the voting rights may be met either by one shareholder acting independently or by several shareholders filing the request jointly.

3.11   Insider trading

The office of the Public Prosecutor has a special division for financial matters, charged with detecting possible breaches of financial regulations carrying criminal sanctions, such as insider trading and market manipulation.

Anyone who knows or should not have been unaware of the fact that he/she is in possession of privileged information is prohibited from performing certain actions.

Privileged information is defined as any information relating to a publicly traded company which is specific, unknown to the public, and which, should it be made public, would have a material impact on the price of securities issued by the company in question.

The prohibition applies not only to information relating to companies listed on a Belgian Stock Exchange, regardless of whether or not trading transactions were carried out on a Stock Exchange, in Belgium or abroad, but also to information relating to companies listed on a foreign Stock Exchange, provided that the trading transaction is carried out in Belgium.

Persons in possession of privileged information are prohibited from performing the following actions:

(a)   buying or selling or trying to buy or sell the relevant securities, either directly or indirectly, for their own account or on behalf of another person;

(b)   disclosing inside information to a third party, except in the normal exercise of their profession or function; and

(c)   using inside information to advise a third party to buy or sell transferable securities.

3.12   Financial assistance

Some acquisitions of companies are structured as leveraged deals, in which a portion of the purchase price of the assets or the shares to be purchased is obtained through loan financing. In such a transaction, the buyer may intend to use the assets and cash flow of the acquired company to reimburse or secure the loan.

3.12.1   *Financial assistance by the target company*

Under Belgian law, financial assistance by the target company is in some instances prevented by the Companies Code, which provides that a company may not advance funds, grant loans or provide surety with a view to the acquisition by a third party of its own shares. Any breach of the Companies Code renders the transaction (i.e., the loan, the surety, etc.) null and void and may result in criminal sanctions and fines for the directors responsible for granting financial assistance.

3.12.2   *Intra-group financial assistance*

Another difficulty under Belgian law arises from the general corporate law principle which states that the board of directors of a company must always act in the best interests of that company. The giving of a guarantee by a company to secure the debts of an affiliated company or the granting of a low-interest loan to such a company are usually not seen per se as being in the company's best interests, as the concept of group companies is not legally recognised in Belgium. A company is not supposed to give a guarantee for the debts of another unless it can benefit or expect to benefit from the giving of such a guarantee.

Chapter 4

Bulgaria

Damian Simeonov and Peter Petrov

Partners
Borislav Boyanov & Co

4.1 Introduction

As in most central and eastern European countries, free-market mergers and acquisitions only emerged in Bulgaria in the early 1990s. Over the last seventeen years there has been unprecedented growth in mergers and acquisitions, initially in the context of privatisation of state-owned companies, and subsequently between privately owned companies.

While most state assets have been privatised, some are still to be offered for sale. These include *inter alia* the tobacco monopoly, major electricity generation utilities as well as the Bulgarian Maritime Fleet. Nonetheless, mergers and acquisitions which relate to the sale of state-owned or municipality owned stocks or assets have diminished in significance, and the primary deals with the state are concession agreements combined with asset leases or transfers, as well as various public–private partnership structures involving the state, municipalities and private interests.

In recent years, most mergers and acquisitions in Bulgaria have been private-to-private mergers. These mergers, range from secondary mergers of companies privatised earlier by management buy-out or by sale to strategic investors, to acquisitions of newly established businesses, and acquisition or divestment of holdings owned by investment funds (often to other investment funds).

The wave of private mergers and acquisitions is growing. These affect primarily undertakings privatised by local acquirers or local start-ups in need of investment to realise their potential. Such investment may not be forthcoming from their present owners. In these cases the owners are looking for strategic international investors capable of implementing a consistent investment policy. Usually deals result in either acquisition by an international investor or in the establishment, in one way or another, of joint control.

A significant trend of recent years is the increasing presence of investment funds, which are taking controlling stakes in a growing number of businesses and industries.

Since the latter part of the 1990s, Bulgaria has made significant efforts to introduce regulation on public offerings and issuers of securities, investment brokers and collective investment undertakings. The 1999 Public Offering of Securities Act (*State Gazette* Issue 114 of 1999, as amended) ("POSA") made an effort to transpose a large portion of the European Community Acquis in these areas, and even some preparatory acts of the Community. By 2007 the harmonisation process was virtually complete, following the adoption of the new Markets in Financial Instruments Act (*State Gazette* Issue 52 of 2007, as amended). Capital markets in Bulgaria have recently (over the last two to three years) seen strong growth in terms of volumes and assets traded, but can still be considered in their infancy, and although several dozen acquisitions have taken place on the Bulgarian Stock Exchange, Bulgaria still has not witnessed the first truly market-driven takeovers of public companies.

In the area of competition, in concert with the Europe-wide trend, with the 1998 Protection of Competition Act (*State Gazette* Issue 52 of 1998, as amended) Bulgaria accepted to a great extent the solutions and principles of the European Merger Control Regulation. Therefore, for many of the bigger mergers, competition regulators have a say, particularly with regard to creation or strengthening of dominant position.

4.2 Acquisition targets

The targets of acquisition in Bulgaria can be categorised in several groups, based on criteria material to the type and procedure of acquisition which may be followed with respect to them. These include the following.

4.2.1 *Public and private companies*

4.2.1.1 *Public companies*
According to the POSA, public companies are joint-stock companies which have issued stock in the context of an initial public offering, or have an issue of shares entered into the registries of the Bulgarian Financial Supervision Commission (Bulgaria's securities regulator) for the purposes of trade on regulated markets of securities, or had more than 10,000 shareholders on the last day of two consecutive calendar years. As in most countries, public companies are heavily regulated, and any mergers and acquisitions involving public companies are subject to specific regulatory requirements.

Of around 400 public companies in Bulgaria, most became public on the basis of the offering of their stock to the public in the so-called "mass privatisation" procedure via centralised public auctions.[1] However, an increasing number of private companies are going public these days, following initial or secondary public offerings of their stock. All public companies are listed on the Bulgarian Stock Exchange, which is the only regulated securities market currently licensed in Bulgaria.

4.2.1.2 *Private companies*
This category includes all companies which are not public.

---

[1] Under this procedure shares were offered to the public for vouchers, purchased or delivered free of charge to Bulgarian nationals.

The acquisitions of private companies are usually free from or have minimal regulatory intervention as it is generally left to the parties to fend for their interests and, in contrast to public companies, minority shareholders are afforded little protection.[2]

4.2.2 State-owned, municipally owned and privately owned companies

4.2.2.1 State- and municipally owned companies

According to the Bulgarian Privatisation and Post-privatisation Control Act (*State Gazette* Issue 26 of 2002, as amended), the sale of, among other things, shares owned by the State or by municipalities, or of self-contained parts of the property of companies with more than 50 per cent equity interest owned by the State or the municipalities, is regulated by a special procedure for privatisation, discussed at 4.6.3 below. The procedure is primarily aimed at transparency of privatisation, protection of the interests of the State and the municipalities, and providing equal treatment to potential investors.

4.2.2.2 Privately owned companies

The sale of shares not owned directly by the State or municipalities is not subject to the conduct of a procedure for privatisation. This includes also the sale of shares owned by a state- or municipally owned holding company.[3] Also excluded from the scope of the mandatory privatisation procedure are asset transactions, involving self-contained parts of companies, in which the State or the municipalities hold less than 50 per cent of the voting stock.

4.2.3 Joint stock companies, limited liability companies and other companies

4.2.3.1 Joint stock companies

Joint stock companies can be private or public. The shares in private joint stock companies are in the form of transferable securities, either in physical or non-physical form, which makes the transfer quick and easy. In private joint stock companies, in principle, there should be no restrictions and formalities for transfer of equity, including for attaining a controlling interest, unless the statutes of the company provide otherwise.

4.2.3.2 Limited liability companies

Limited liability companies can only be private. Due to the fact that Bulgarian law imposes no restrictions on the number of shareholders in such companies or on their aggregate assets, some of the biggest targets of mergers or acquisitions are limited liability companies. By contrast to joint stock companies, limited liability companies' shares are not securities. They are transferred by a procedure involving a written share transfer agreement with notarised signatures of the

---

[2] Recent years have seen increasing levels of protection for minority shareholders in private companies, including by giving powers to the shareholders meeting to resolve on transactions involving significant assets of the company.

[3] A notable example is Bulgartabac Holding AD, which while itself being owned by the state, holds the shares of more than 20 cigarette manufacturing and tobacco processing factories in Bulgaria.

parties and a subsequent registration of the transfer in the Commercial Register, preceded by a procedure for clearance of the transfer and admission of new shareholders by the shareholders meeting of the company.

4.2.3.3   Other companies

While Bulgarian law regulates several other types of companies, these forms are rarely used as they hold few advantages and some major handicaps. All of them are characterised by the fact that one or more of the members are generally liable for the obligations of the company. Such companies may only be private. Depending on the form, acquisition of effective control would include attaining membership as a general partner. Following Bulgaria's EU accession, the Community framework on the European Cooperative Society and the European company also applies in Bulgaria. However, Bulgaria is yet to see these types of companies emerging as potential acquisition targets, since they are still relatively unknown in local practice.

4.2.4   Companies and businesses

Sections 4.2.1 to 4.2.3 above relate to mergers and acquisitions of companies, but an alternative form of acquisition in Bulgaria is the acquisition of the business of a company as a going concern. As a matter of Bulgarian law, the business of a company is defined as a set of rights, obligations and factual relations, and may include, among other things, the trading name of the company. An acquisition target can be the entire going concern or only a part of the business of a company.

The reasons for using the transfer of a business as a method of acquisition are varied, and range from limitations of corporate organisation to regulatory hindrances against making an acquisition by purchase of stock.

Bulgarian law regulates a number of other types of mergers and acquisitions, including acquisition of the insurance portfolio of insurance companies, mergers of pension funds within pension companies or between pension companies etc. These mergers and acquisitions enjoy special regulation and until now have been practised rarely, if at all.

4.3   Exchange and investment controls

4.3.1   Exchange controls

Transfers of funds into the country, including in the context of mergers and acquisitions, is free.

Transactions which will lead to direct investment of a Bulgarian resident abroad, being *inter alia*:

(a)   the attaining in a company, which is a non-local resident, of the rights of a general partner or a shareholder having more than 10 per cent of the votes in the shareholders meeting of a company;

(b)   the creation of a company abroad;

(c)   the giving of a loan for the purposes of making a direct investment under (a) or (b) above, or relating to a profit sharing arrangement; as well as

(d)   investment additional to a direct investment under (a) and (b) above,

will require that the Bulgarian resident should submit a declaration within 15 days following the entry into the respective transaction.

Additional disclosure requirements may relate to the financing of a transaction, by means of foreign-to-local loans, as well as to the provision of collateral by local residents for debts between foreign residents or of local to foreign residents.

4.3.2   Controls on investments

No authorisations, specific to an investment of a foreign entity by way of acquisition or merger involving a Bulgarian undertaking, are required as a matter of Bulgarian law. Investments in and by certain establishments, including banking, investment firms, insurance, pension insurance, etc., may be subject to regulatory approvals, for both local and foreign investors.

Outside the declaration requirements discussed at 4.3.1 above, investments of local persons and entities abroad, involving mergers or acquisitions, are not subject to any approval or authorisation except for certain regulated entities, whose investments are subject to regulatory oversight. In certain cases, particularly in the context of sanctions imposed by the Bulgarian Government on foreign countries and territories, depending on the nature and scope of the sanctions, investments may be limited or prohibited.

4.3.3   Disclosure and approval of significant shareholdings

4.3.3.1   Public companies

The POSA requires a notification to be made to the public company, the Financial Supervision Commission and the regulated securities market, in which the shares of a company have been admitted to trading, about any person whose voting rights reach, exceed or fall below 5 per cent or a multiple thereof of the number of votes in the shareholders meeting of the company.

Notifications should be submitted independently by the person acquiring the voting rights and the Central Depository of Securities, which settles the transaction,[4] except in cases of indirect holding of voting rights, where only the acquiring person will be under an obligation to notify. There are a number of exceptions to the notification obligation, relating to shares acquired for the purposes of clearing and settlement, in custody etc. The notifications should be submitted immediately, but not later than four business days following the day on which the shareholder or the relevant person that has acquired indirect control of the voting rights has become aware of the acquisition or transfer, or of the ability to exercise the voting rights, or any other event that has led to the crossing of the disclosure threshold. The contents and the form of the notification

---

[4] All shares in public companies are mandatory in non-physical form and the settlement of their transfer is effected via the Bulgarian Central Depository of Securities.

have been determined by the Financial Supervision Commission. The POSA also provides for a disclosure obligation in respect of the direct or indirect holding of financial instruments which allow the holder to acquire at its own initiative and on the basis of a written agreement voting shares in a public company. The public company itself is under an obligation to disclose to the public the information received in respect of disclosure of significant shareholdings within three business days of receiving the notification.

Short of being qualified as a crime, failure to make timely disclosure of the above information constitutes an administrative offence, punishable by fines of between BGN2,000 and BGN5,000.

4.3.3.2 Banks

Any person or persons, local or foreign, require advance written permission from the Bulgarian National Bank to acquire, directly or indirectly, shares in a local bank, which entitle them directly or indirectly to a qualified holding, or a holding reaching or exceeding the thresholds of 20, 33, 50, 66, 75 or 100 per cent of the voting shares of such bank. A qualified holding is present where a person holds directly or indirectly 10 or more than 10 per cent of the capital or the voting rights in the shareholders meeting or where the holding of shares in the capital or voting rights in the shareholders meeting entitles it to exercise decisive influence over the management of the bank. Such a permission is also required whenever the bank becomes a subsidiary, that is, an entity controlled by another legal entity, directly or indirectly. Failure to obtain advance permission will lead to the invalidity of the acquisition by operation of law.

The permission of the Bulgarian National Bank is further required in cases where a shareholder, as part of a capital increase or via conversion of bonds into equity, acquires or retains 20, 33, 50, 66, 75 or 100 per cent of the voting shares in the increased capital. In cases of failure to obtain advance permission, the Bulgarian National Bank may mandate the shareholder to divest its shareholding entirely.

Whenever a shareholding is acquired in the context of a public offering on a Stock Exchange or another regulated securities market, no advance permission is required. However, if the permit triggers have been met, the voting rights under the shares cannot be exercised until a permit from the Bulgarian National Bank is received.

In addition the Central Depository (which acts as a depositary institution for all shares of Bulgarian banks, which have to be obligatorily dematerialised) has to notify the Bulgarian National Bank of the name and the seat/address of any person who has acquired 3 per cent or more than 3 per cent of its voting stock. The Bulgarian National Bank may require additional documents regarding such person. It may further require the relevant shareholder to divest its interest, where by its activity and influence on the making of decisions it can affect the reliability or security of the bank or its operations, or has made is contribution not using its own funds, or where the shareholder has disclosed untrue or incomplete data or has not disclosed information within the terms laid down by the Bulgarian National Bank.

Any person that intends to transfer a qualified shareholding, or a shareholding leading to its shares falling below 20, 33, 50, 66, 75 or 100 per cent of the shares of the capital of the bank, must notify the Bulgarian National Bank about the size of its holdings before and after such transfer. A notification must also be submitted where the bank will stop being a subsidiary to a person. The notification must be submitted not later than 10 days before the planned occurrence of the relevant event.

Banks themselves are under an obligation to notify the Bulgarian National Bank within seven days of becoming aware of the crossing of any of the thresholds requiring advance or subsequent permission by or notification to the Bulgarian National Bank.

4.3.3.3 *Insurance and pension companies and other institutional investors*
Any person that intends to acquire directly, together with or via affiliates, 10 per cent or more than 10 per cent of the votes in the shareholders meeting of an insurance company, or another shareholding which would allow it to control the insurance company, or which intends to acquire 20, 33, 50 or more than 50 per cent of the votes in the shareholders meeting of an insurance company has to give at least three months' notice of its intention to the Deputy Chairman of the Financial Supervision Commission responsible for insurance supervision. The notice of the acquisition must be accompanied by sufficient evidence that proves beyond doubt that the prospective direct or indirect acquirer corresponds to a number of requirements set under the law.

Within the three-month period the Deputy Chairman may object to the acquisition where the acquirer endangers the stability of the insurer or the interests of the insured's, or does not correspond to the requirements of the law. The Deputy Chairman may also approve the change and set a deadline within which it may be completed. Acquiring shares prior to the expiration of the notice period or in violation of an express prohibition by the Deputy Chairman will lead to the relevant person being deprived of its voting rights in the shareholders meeting of the insurance company. If the Deputy Chairman has not issued an express prohibition within the three-month period, an implied clearance is presumed.

Where the acquisition has resulted from trading on a Stock Exchange or another regulated market of securities, the notice should be submitted within 14 days of the entry into the trade. However, in this case the holder will not be entitled to exercise the voting rights in respect of its shares before the Deputy Chairman has ordered the entry of the change of the shareholding in the registers maintained by the Financial Supervision Commission.

Any person that decreases its interest in an insurance company below the above thresholds, or for any other reason ceases to exercise control in respect of a Bulgarian insurance company, also has to notify in advance the Deputy Chairman. The insurance company itself, as well as the Central Depository, the depositary institution which maintains in book-entry form the dematerialised shares of all insurance companies in Bulgaria, are also under an obligation to notify the Deputy Chairman of the Financial Supervision Commission responsible for insurance supervision within three days of becoming aware of any of the above thresholds being crossed.

Any person, acquiring initially 1 per cent or more than 1 per cent of the issued stock of an insurance company, or increasing its holding above 1 per cent, should identify itself to the Deputy Chairman within 14 days of the acquisition or increase and present evidence of the origin of the funds used to acquire such stock as well as information regarding its affiliates. The same evidence is to be presented whenever in the context of a capital increase a shareholder's contribution exceeds BGN30,000.

Any person that intends to acquire directly and/or through related parties 10 per cent or more than 10 per cent of the shares of a pension company or to increase subsequently its shareholding reaching or exceeding the thresholds of 20, 33, 50, 66, 75 or 100 per cent of the stock of a pension company, or a company for additional voluntary social security for unemployment and professional qualification, has to obtain the advance permission of the Deputy Chairman of the Financial Supervision Commission, responsible for social security supervision. Shareholders holding 10 per cent or more of the stock of a pension company or additional voluntary social security company, or who can exercise control over such company, have to comply with certain requirements, particularly relating to their current and historical good standing.

Any person that acquires individually or through related parties 10 per cent or more of the shares of a company providing private health cover is required, within 14 days following the acquisition, to notify the Deputy Chairman of the Financial Supervision Commission responsible for Insurance Supervision of the relevant shareholding. The Deputy Chairman has the power to order the divestment of such shareholdings.

Any person that intends to acquire or divest directly or indirectly 10 per cent or more than 10 per cent of the capital or the votes in the shareholders meeting of a Bulgarian investment intermediary or a participation which allows it to control the investment intermediary, or acquire a shareholding reaching or exceeding the thresholds of 20, 33 and 50 per cent of the capital or of the votes in the shareholders meeting of the investment intermediary, must notify the Financial Supervision Commission in advance. Within one month the Deputy Chairman of the Financial Supervision Commission responsible for investment supervision may issue a prohibition in respect of the acquisition or the divestment if he finds:

(a)   that the requirements of the law have not been met;
(b)   that the notifying party has submitted untrue documents or data with its notice;
(c)   that the stable management and the security of the investment intermediary have been endangered or otherwise the interests of the clients of the investment intermediary have not been protected.

If no prohibition is issued within the above period, clearance is implied and the Deputy Chairman may set a deadline within which the acquisition or divestment have to be completed. A person which has acquired shares in contravention of a prohibition issued by the Deputy Chairman is deprived of the right to exercise its voting rights in the shareholders meeting of the investment intermediary.

4.3.3.4 State-owned and municipal companies

In companies where there is an interest of the state or the municipalities, the decrease of this interest will be allowed only following the approval of the Privatisation Agency of the Republic of Bulgaria, respectively the Municipal Council, except in cases where the company has undergone privatisation and the obligations of the buyer under the privatisation transaction have been completed. Therefore, any equity investments, acquisitions included, realised by means of subscribing shares in a capital increase, which will have this effect, will need to be approved by the Privatisation Agency.

4.3.4 Acquiring control over a public company

Acquisitions of holdings of more than 50 per cent or two-thirds of the votes in the shareholders meeting of a public company, will lead to a requirement to register in the Financial Supervision Commission a tender offer to the other voting shareholders to purchase their shares or exchange their shares for shares to be issued by the offeror for this purpose, or transfer such number of shares so as to own less than 50 per cent of the votes, or less than two-thirds of the votes, whether directly or indirectly. A mandatory tender offer is required in cases where a person holding more than 50 per cent of the voting stock acquires with a period of one year more than 3 per cent of the votes in a public company. The tender offer requirements are reviewed in detail at 4.10 below.

4.3.5 Labour law considerations

Following the implementation of the provisions of EU Council Directive 2001/23/EC[5] into Bulgarian law, prior to a merger or an acquisition the incumbent employer is obliged to inform the employees or their representatives concerning the projected changes and the date or proposed date of the changes, the reasons for the changes, the possible legal, economic and social implications of the changes for the employees, as well as any measures envisaged in relation to the employees.

The notification should be accomplished not later than two months before the occurrence of the consequences relating to employment and conditions of work for the employees.

Where, in relation to the merger or acquisition, measures are envisaged in relation to the employees, the employer is under an obligation, prior to making the notification discussed above, to conduct consultations in good time with the representatives of the employees with regard to these measures.

Where applicable, consultations should be conducted within the framework of the procedures of information and consultation for a European Workers' Council, established in the relevant multinational company or group of companies.

---

[5] Council Directive 2001/23/EC of 12 March 2001 on the approximation of the laws of the Member States relating to the safeguarding of employees' rights in the event of transfers of undertakings, businesses or parts of undertakings or businesses (OJ L 082 22.03.2001).

4.4   Merger control

Bulgarian law follows closely the provisions of the former EU Council Regulation (EEC) No. 4064/89[6] in matters regarding the control over concentrations. The Bulgarian Protection of Competition Act applies also to undertakings established outside Bulgaria, to the extent their activity impacts competition in Bulgaria. The prevailing practice of the Bulgarian Commission for the Protection of Competition, holds that a merger or acquisition will be considered to have a competitive impact in Bulgaria, in all cases where the parties to such concentration have some form of presence/turnover in the Bulgarian market, through direct sales or through sales via a local establishment.

Therefore, any foreign-to-local, foreign-to-foreign or, as the case may be, local-to-foreign merger or acquisition, will be assessed for its competitive impact, subject to the notification thresholds.

4.4.1   Thresholds for mandatory notification

The Bulgarian Protection of Competition Act ("PCA") defines a concentration as:

(a)   the merger of two or more independent undertakings;[7] or

(b)   a case where one or more persons, already controlling one undertaking, acquire, whether by purchase of securities, shares or assets, by contract or by any other means, direct or indirect control of the whole or part of one or more undertakings; or

(c)   the creation of a joint venture performing on a lasting basis all the functions of an autonomous economic unit.

A concentration is not deemed to occur where:

(a)   banking or non-banking financial institutions or insurance companies, the normal activities of which include transactions with securities for their own account or for the account of others, hold on a temporary basis securities of a certain undertaking with a view to reselling them, provided that they do not exercise voting rights in respect of those securities with a view to determining the competitive behaviour of that undertaking, or provided that they exercise such voting rights only with a view to preparing the disposal of those securities, which should take place within one year of their date of acquisition; or

(b)   control is acquired by a person, which according to the applicable law discharges certain functions, related to the liquidation or the declaration of bankruptcy of the undertaking; or

(c)   the acquisition of control is carried out by financial holding companies, provided however that the control acquired by the holding is exercised

---

[6] Council Regulation (EEC) No 4064/89 of 21 December 1989 on the control of concentrations between undertakings (OJ L 395 30.12.1989), as last amended.

[7] An "undertaking" under the PCA will be considered any person, entity or association which engages in a business activity on a relevant market, regardless of its legal form.

only to maintain the full value of the capital invested, and not to determine directly or indirectly the competitive conduct of those undertakings in which the holding participates.

A concentration will be subject to mandatory advance notification to the Bulgarian Commission for the Protection of Competition, if the combined aggregate turnover for the previous year of the parties to the concentration in the relevant market in the territory of Bulgaria exceeds BGN15 million.

The Bulgarian Commission for the Protection of Competition has held that the turnover should consist of the net income from sales, excluding indirect taxes, discounts and intra-group sales. For undertakings, established outside the country, only the turnover of the products sold and services provided to customers in Bulgaria should be taken into consideration. Whenever the concentration relates to parts of an undertaking, only the turnover relating to such part should be taken into account. The calculation criteria are analogous to those used by the EU Merger Regulation.[8]

In cases of concentrations of banks and financial institutions, their aggregate income (following deduction of tax) as per the financial statements for the latest complete financial year are to be considered. As regards insurance companies, the gross insurance premiums written, following the deduction of all taxes, charges and imposts provided by law are to be considered.

4.4.2 Procedure

In all cases, where the relevant notification threshold is met, a notification should be submitted prior to the consummation of the transaction. The parties may submit a notification also in cases where they are not certain the transaction will constitute a notifiable concentration. There are no set periods for submission. However, in view of the applicable periods of investigation, the filing is advised at least 45 days prior to the consummation of the transaction.

The notification starts a suspension period where all legal and factual acts, relating to the planned concentration, are prohibited. The suspension period ends with the issuing of a clearance decision.

The notification should contain information about:

(a) the undertakings concerned;
(b) the nature and legal form of the concentration;
(c) the products and services to which the concentration relates;
(d) the undertakings controlled by the parties to the concentration;
(e) the combined market share and the aggregate turnover of the parties to the concentration;
(f) information with regard to the main competitors, suppliers and buyers.

---

[8] While there has been some ambiguity in the past over whether turnover should be calculated based on a single relevant (product and geographic) market, the current prevailing practice of the Commission for the Protection of Competition holds that the entire Bulgarian turnover will be relevant.

In its Methodology on Investigation and Determination of the Market Position of Undertakings on the Relevant Market, the Commission for the Protection of Competition has provided a form in which a notification should be made, and which requires certain additional information and documents.

Following submission of the notification and all additional documents, the Commission will conduct an investigation of the concentration within a period of one month. The period is not binding on the Commission, and the failure to pronounce within such period is not considered to constitute clearance of the concentration. Practice shows that in certain cases the investigation takes longer. During the investigation the Commission may require additional documents and information.

Following the investigation, the Commission for the Protection of Competition may:

(a)   find that the transaction is not subject to notification and clearance; or
(b)   permit the concentration; or
(c)   begin an extended three-month investigation; or
(d)   prohibit the concentration if it has found sufficient evidence that the transaction would lead to the creation or strengthening of a dominant position, which will significantly impede effective competition in the relevant market in Bulgaria.

If within the extended three-month period it is established that the concentration would lead to the creation or strengthening of a dominant position which will significantly impede effective competition, the Commission will issue a decision, mandating the parties to terminate immediately all actions relating to the concentration.

The concentration will be permitted in cases where it does not create or strengthen a dominant position, as a result of which effective competition would be significantly impeded in any relevant market in Bulgaria. A concentration may still be permitted by the Commission, even if it will create or strengthen a dominant position, if it aims at:

(a)   modernising production and the economy as a whole;
(b)   bettering market structures;
(c)   attracting investments;
(d)   creating positions of employment;
(e)   better satisfaction of the interests of consumers, and

the positive consequences predominate over the negative impact on competition on the relevant market.

Following the investigation, the parties will be allowed to review the collected materials. The concentration is reviewed in an open session, with the participation of the notifying parties. Following the hearing the decision is made in a closed session and enters into force immediately.

4.4.3   Appeals

The decisions of the Commission for the Protection of Competition, with which it declares that a concentration is not subject to notification and clearance or permits the concentration, are subject to publication in the Bulgarian *State Gazette* and can be appealed within 14 days following the publication by the parties to the proceedings, as well as by any interested third party. An interested third party is considered any person, undertaking or association whose interests may be affected by a violation of the law (i.e., competitors or organisations of competitors).

The decisions by which the Commission for the Protection of Competition prohibits a merger, or appoints an extended investigation, can be appealed by the parties to the proceedings within 14 days after receipt of the notice that the decision has been issued.

The appeals are heard by the Supreme Administrative Court in a three-member panel. The judgments of the three-member panel are appealed before the Supreme Administrative Court sitting in a five-member panel.

4.4.4 Sanctions

If the parties complete a concentration, which is subject to obligatory notification, without receiving the relevant permission from the Commission for the Protection of Competition, the Commission may impose on each of the undertakings involved sanctions amounting to between BGN5,000 and BGN300,000.

If the parties complete a concentration, or fail to accomplish the conditions attached to the completion of a concentration, in violation of a decision of the Commission, it may impose a fine of between BGN100,000 and BGN500,000. The same sanction can be applied in the case of a repeated violation.

Where a concentration, which is subject to obligatory notification, is completed without permission from the Commission for the Protection of Competition or in violation of a decision of the Commission, in addition to imposing the relevant fines, the Commission may order appropriate measures to restore the status of the undertakings in the relevant market prior to the concentration, including ordering the combined capital, shares of property to be divided and/or joint control to be terminated.

The lack of a permission may prevent any further actions, relating to the concentration, such as registration with a registrar court or another public body, which may be a precondition for the effectiveness of the transaction.

4.5 Regulation of the conduct of mergers and acquisitions

The primary regulator of the public offer of securities and mergers and acquisitions of public companies in Bulgaria is the Financial Supervision Commission. The Financial Supervision Commission was originally created in 1995 (under the then effective Securities, Stock Exchanges and Investment Companies Act (*State Gazette* Issue 63 of 1995, repealed). Currently, under the effective Public Offering of Securities Act, the Financial Supervision Commission Act (*State Gazette* Issue 8 of 2003, as amended), the Markets in Financial Instruments Act (*State Gazette* Issue 52 of 2007, as amended), the Insurance Code (*State Gazette* Issue 103 of 2005, as amended) and the Social Security Code (*State Gazette* Issue 110 of 1999, as amended) it has broad powers of supervision and regulation of the public offer and transfer of securities, public companies, open-ended and closed-ended investment companies, investment intermediaries, as well as insurance companies, pensions companies and social security companies. The address of the Commission is Financial Supervision Commission, Sofia 1303, 33 Shar Planina St. (Комисия за финансов надзор, гр. София 1303, ул. "Шар Планина" No. 33.)

The regulatory authority responsible for the assessment of matters of competition relating to mergers and acquisitions in Bulgaria is the Commission for the Protection of Competition. The address of the Commission is Commission for the Protection of Competition, Sofia 1000, 18 Vitosha Blvd. (Комисия за защита на конкуренцията, София 1000, 6ул. "Витоша" No. 18.)

Bulgaria's Central Bank (the Bulgarian National Bank) is entrusted with regulatory functions with respect to mergers and acquisitions relating to locally incorporated banks by virtue of the Bulgarian Banks Act (*State Gazette* Issue 52 of 1997, as amended). The regulatory powers are discharged by the Governor of the Bulgarian National Bank with the assistance of the Bank Supervision Division of the bank. The address of the Bulgarian National Bank is Bulgarian National Bank, Sofia 1000, 1 Alexander Batenberg Sq. (Българска народна банка, София 1000, пл. "Княз Александър Батенберг" No. 1.)

4.6   Methods of acquisition

4.6.1   Private agreements

Private mergers and acquisitions still prove to be the overwhelming majority of corporate reorganisations effected in Bulgaria at this time. This is understandable in view of the fact that only approximately 500 of the several hundred thousand commercial companies incorporated in Bulgaria are public. However, the number of public companies is increasing following a wave of initial and secondary public offerings. Many of the biggest industries are still organised as private (i.e. non-public) companies. A decreasing number of transactions are accomplished in the context of privatisation of state- and municipally owned enterprises – these types of acquisition are reviewed at 4.6.3 below.

The methods of acquisition of private companies can be divided broadly by the type of target.

4.6.1.1   Limited liability companies
Shares in a limited liability company established under Bulgarian law are transferred by way of a written agreement, with notarisation of the signatures of the parties. The agreement is only one element of the transfer. To make the transfer effective, it has to be approved and the new shareholder has to be admitted to the company by the other members (if he is not already a member) and the transfer has to be registered with the Commercial Register in respect of the target company. The decision for the admission of a new shareholder is taken by the shareholders meeting of the target, with a majority of 75 per cent of all shares in the capital of the company unless the articles of association provide for a higher

majority. The transfer is effective following registration with the Commercial Register.

A share in a limited liability company can be acquired jointly by several persons. In this case they can exercise the membership rights attached to such share only jointly.

A more specific method of acquisition could be the acquisition in the context of a capital increase, or more rarely a capital decrease.

In principle shareholders are entitled, in the context of a capital increase, to increase their share proportionally to their participation in the capital prior to the increase. This right can be waived by the articles of association or by the decision of the shareholders meeting which invoked the capital increase. Therefore, an acquisition can occur if, as part of a capital increase, a party acquires shares of a greater proportion than its previous participation in the capital, affording it control over the company. The decision for a capital increase should be taken unanimously by the shareholders. In companies where there exists a shareholding interest of the Bulgarian state or of the municipalities, the decrease of this interest (whether by dilution as a result of a capital increase, or as a result of capital decrease affecting this share) will be allowed only following the approval of the Privatisation Agency of the Republic of Bulgaria, respectively the Municipal Council, except in cases where the company has undergone privatisation and the obligations of the buyer under the privatisation transaction have been completed.

In the context of a capital decrease, an existing member's share may gain controlling powers when the decrease is either the result of a shareholder leaving the company or results in the decrease of another shareholder's share in a greater proportion than that of the shareholder which acquires control.

Table 4.1 reviews the powers afforded to key levels of shareholding in a Bulgarian limited liability company.

Table 4.1 Powers afforded to key levels of shareholding

Shareholding level	Powers
Any percentage	Block any decision on capital decrease or capital increase (100 per cent vote required).
10%	Require the convocation of the shareholders meeting.
20%	Request the termination of the company by the district court if there are material reasons therefor.
50%+[9]	Elect the manager, determine his remuneration and release him from responsibility. Approve the annual financial statement, distribute the profit and make a decision for its payment.

---

[9] The articles of association can determine a different majority.

Table 4.1 continued

Shareholding level	Powers
	Resolve on the opening and closing of branches and participation in other companies.
	Resolve on the acquisition and disposal of real estate and easements thereon.
	Resolve on other matters put within the province of the shareholders meeting for which a qualified majority is not required.
75%[10]	Amend the articles of association.
	Admit and discharge shareholders.
	Approve the transfer of shares to a new member.
	Resolve on mandatory shareholder loans.
	Resolve on termination of the company, including by way of merger.
100%	Resolve on a capital increase or capital decrease.

A limited liability company may be merged with or into any type of company, and any type of company can be merged into a limited liability company.

The merger process starts with the entry into a reorganisation (merger) agreement. Parties to the merger agreement will be all companies participating in the merger. The merger agreement will normally be entered into prior to the approval of the merger by the shareholders of the participating companies. Alternatively it may be entered after the approval of the shareholders, based on a draft approved by them. The merger agreement is entered into on behalf of the relevant participating company by the executives or by their management bodies.

As a minimum the merger agreement has to arrange:

(a) the legal form, trading name, unified identification code and seat of each of the participating and recipient companies;
(b) the exchange ratio for shares, determined as of a certain date;
(c) the amount of cash consideration which has to be paid to shareholders to achieve an equivalent ratio of exchange[11] as well as the deadlines for their payment;
(d) the description of the shares or membership rights that each partner or shareholder will acquire in any recipient or newly established company;

---

[10] The articles of association can determine a higher majority.
[11] Such cash consideration cannot exceed 10 per cent of the aggregate par value of the acquired shares.

(e)   any conditions regarding the distribution or delivery of the shares of the recipient or newly established companies;

(f)   the moment as of which a holding in the recipient or newly established company gives to its holder the right to distributions from the profits of the company, as well as any special conditions relating to such right;

(g)   the moment as of which the actions of the former companies are considered to have been effected for the account of the recipient or newly established companies for the purposes of accounting;

(h)   any special rights granted in the recipient or newly established companies to specific shareholders or to bondholders;

(i)   any benefits granted to the auditors, auditing the merger, to members of the management and supervisory bodies of participating companies.

The signatures of the parties to the merger agreement will have to be notarised.

The merger agreement is effective as of the day of its signing. However, it will be terminated if the shareholders or partners of any of the participating companies reject it. Prior to the approval of the shareholders/partners, the merger agreement may be terminated by the management of any of the participating companies. After shareholder/partner approval the merger agreement may be terminated by the relevant company only based on a new decision by the shareholders/partners.

The merger agreement has to be audited by an independent auditor appointed by the management body/managing partners of each participating company. It is admissible that the same auditor is appointed by all participating companies. The scope of the audit covers:

(a)   the methods used to determine the exchange ratio for the shares;

(b)   to what extent the use of these methods was appropriate in the specific case;

(c)   the values resulting from the application of each of the methods; and

(d)   any issues which have arisen in the process of valuation.

Where the resulting (recipient or newly established) company is a capital company, the amount of the capital cannot be higher than the net assets value of such company. The auditors have to confirm this fact in their report.

The management body of each participating company has to prepare a report to the shareholders of the relevant company which provides, among other things, a detailed statement of the legal and economic reasons behind the entry into the merger agreement and plan, especially in respect of the exchange ratios and the distribution of shares following the merger.

The merger agreement and the report of the management have to be submitted with respect to each company into the Commercial Register. With respect to limited liability companies, partnerships limited by shares and joint stock companies, the agreement of merger has to be presented to the Commercial Register not later than 30 days prior to the date for which a meeting of the shareholders/partners has been convened to approve the merger.

Prior to the meeting, the materials relating to the merger have to be made available to the shareholders/partners free of charge. This includes the merger agreement, the management report, the auditors' report, financial statements and draft by-laws of the resulting companies.

The shareholders/partners of each of the participating companies has to make a decision approving the merger, which approves, among other things, the merger agreement. In a limited liability company, approval is granted by a majority of 75 per cent of all voting shares. In order to take place, the merger has to be approved by the shareholders/partners of all participating companies.

The merger becomes effective as of the date of registration of the merger into the Commercial Register. The merger agreement may provide an earlier date as of which the acts of participating companies will be considered undertaken for the account of the recipient or newly established companies, provided that such date is not more than six months before the date of the merger agreement.

A substantially similar procedure has to be followed in the case of spin-off or partition of a company. However, in this case the merger agreement is replaced by a merger plan, approved by the shareholders/partners of the relevant company.

4.6.1.2   Joint stock companies

The mode of transfer of shares in a joint stock company will depend on the type of securities in which such shares are incorporated. If the shares are incorporated in physical securities, the transfer should be effected by endorsement, signed by the endorser on the back of the share/temporary certificate or on an allonge attached thereto. The transfer is effective with respect to the company, following its registration in the Book of Shareholders kept by the company.

If the shares are incorporated in non-physical securities, their transfer will be effected by means of registration with the Bulgarian Central Depository of Securities. The registration of the transfer has to be made via a member of the Central Depository, while both delivery versus payment and free delivery systems of settlement can be used.[12] For the non-physical securities of private companies the settlement will be effected on the same day.

Bulgarian law does not have any formal requirements regarding the contract of sale which regulates the transfer of the securities. Therefore, a wide variety of practices exists depending on the particular case, ranging from oral agreements to extensive written share purchase agreements.

A share in a joint stock company can be held jointly by several persons, in which case they will exercise their shareholder rights only jointly, through a proxy.

As with a limited liability company, outside the outright sale, acquisition of control can occur in the context of a capital increase, or more rarely a capital decrease. With respect to joint stock companies, Bulgarian law recognises the

---

[12] Provided that the transaction is not entered on the floor of the Bulgarian Stock Exchange, where only the delivery versus payment method is applied. This would be the case if the transaction is entered into outside the exchange floor but is only registered there (block transactions). Block transactions are permissible for packages exceeding 5 per cent of the relevant stock.

concept of the so-called "conditional capital increase". The shareholders meeting has the power, with a majority of two-thirds of the votes present, to waive the right of existing shareholders to subscribe to shares, in the context of a capital increase, pro rata to their existing participation in the capital. In this case the management board or the board of directors should present a report regarding the reasons for the waiver or the restriction of the rights of existing shareholders and arguments regarding the subscription value of the shares of the new issue. The decision for the capital increase and the waiver should be submitted to the Commercial Register. Such waiver may be a precondition for the increase of the capital provided that either:

(a)   the shares will be subscribed by specific persons at a specified price; or
(b)   the shares will be acquired by bondholders as a result of the conversion of bonds, previously issued by the company, into shares.

The requirement for governmental consent for the decrease of the actual percentage of the capital held by the Bulgarian state or the municipalities in companies where the Bulgarian state or municipalities have a shareholding, will apply accordingly.

Table 4.2 shows the powers afforded to key levels of shareholding in a Bulgarian joint stock company.

Table 4.2   Powers afforded to key levels of shareholding in a Bulgarian joint stock company

Shareholding level	Powers
5%	In a public company – file the company's claims against third parties in the case of inaction by the management which endangers the company's interests.
	Require the convocation of the shareholders meeting (provided the 5 per cent shareholding has been held for more than three months).
	Include additional items on the agenda of a shareholders meeting already convened (provided the 5 per cent shareholding has been held for more than three months).
10%	Initiate an action for damages, incurred by the company, as a result of actions or omissions of members of the supervisory or management board.
	Request from the shareholders meeting or the court the appointment of an auditor to audit the annual financial statement and report on his findings.
50%+[13]	Appoint and dismiss the members of the board of directors or the supervisory board.

[13] The statutes can determine a higher majority.

Table 4.2 continued

Shareholding level	Powers
	Approve directors' remuneration, including the right to receive any bonuses in relation to the company's profits.
	Release directors of responsibility.
	Appoint and dismiss auditors.
	Approve annual financial statements.
	Approve distribution of profits.
	Appoint liquidators.
	Approve the issuance of bonds.
	Give advance approval for: the transfer of the business of the company as a going concern; disposal of assets whose aggregate value exceeds half of the value of the assets according to the latest audited financial statements; undertaking of obligations or the giving of securities with respect to one person or related parties, whose value during the current year exceeds half of the assets value of the company according to the latest audited financial statements.[14]
	In a public company, approve transactions as a result of which the company will incur obligations to one person or to related parties, exceeding in aggregate one-third of the lowest of the value of assets according to the latest audited or the latest prepared financial statements, and if such person is an interested party 2 per cent of that value.
	In a public company, approve transactions as a result of which the company will become a creditor to one person or to related parties for claims, exceeding in aggregate one-third of the lowest value of the assets according to the latest audited or the latest prepared financial statements, and if such person is an interested party 10 per cent of that value.
66.67%[15]	Amend and supplement the statute of the company.
	Increase and decrease the capital.

---

[14] The statutes may provide that these decisions will be made by a unanimous resolution of the Board of Directors or the Management Board instead.
[15] The statutes can determine a higher majority.

Table 4.2   continued

Shareholding level	Powers
	Waive the rights of other shareholders to subscribe to a new issue, shares pro rata to their current holdings of the capital (or to give analogous powers of waiver to the board of directors or supervisory board of the company).
	Resolve on the redemption of shares.
	Resolve on winding up of the company.
75%	Increase the capital by capitalisation of the undistributed profit.
	In a public company, approve the acquisition, transfer, receipt or grant for use of or as a security in any form of long-term assets, having an aggregate value of (a) one-third of the lowest value of the assets according to the latest audited and the latest prepared financial statements, (b) 2 per cent of the lowest value of the assets according to the latest audited and the latest prepared financial statements. A shareholder that is an interested party in respect of the transaction may not vote on the issue, and therefore it may be decided with the votes of the remaining shareholders.

A private joint stock company may be merged with or into any type of company, and any type of company can be merged into a joint stock company. The considerations discussed above with respect to mergers of limited liability companies apply accordingly. The required majority is three-quarters of the votes present at the shareholders meeting of the joint stock company, provided that not less than 50 per cent of the voting shares are present.[16]

4.6.1.3   Other companies
In contrast to limited liability and joint stock companies, the acquisition of control over other types of companies in Bulgaria will involve attaining membership as a partner with unlimited liability. The control and distribution of powers between partners with unlimited liability largely depends on the articles of association or statutes of these companies. Due to the fact that these corporate vehicles are very rarely used and are usually quite small in scale, they represent a negligible proportion of targets for acquisitions and mergers in Bulgaria.

4.6.1.4   Businesses
The acquisition of the business of a company as a going concern, involves the signing of a written agreement. The signatures of the parties need to be notarised.

---

[16] The statutes can provide a higher quorum requirement.

The transfer of the business should be preceded by a decision of the share-holders/partners of the transferor and of the transferee, made with the same majority as for reorganisation. In particular with respect to a limited liability company this decision should be taken with a majority of three-quarters of all shares, and with respect to a joint stock company with a majority of three-quarters of the shares present at the relevant shareholders meeting, unless the statutes provide otherwise. The written and notarised agreement is sufficient to transfer all rights and obligations of the company, irrespective of the fact that for the transfer of some rights a special form would normally be required by law or that some of them will not, individually, be considered transferable (e.g., some licences, and rights under administrative acts).

The transfer of the business is effective following registration at the Commercial Register. Any resulting transfer of real estates which may be part of the business has to be recorded in the land registers.

The transferor has to notify the creditors and the debtors of the business about the transfer. Absent any agreement with the creditors to the contrary, the transferor is liable jointly and severally with the transferee for the obligations of the business, up to the value of the assets received. Within six months of the entry of the transfer of the business into the Commercial Register, the creditors of the transferor or of the transferee may require performance or collateral for the obligations which have occurred prior to the registration of the transfer of the business at the Commercial Register, and are unsecured. If the respective creditor does not obtain performance or collateral, it will have a priority with respect to the rights which have belonged to its debtor (transferor or transferee) prior to the transfer of the business. Within the six-month period the transferred business has to be managed separately from the business of the transferee.

4.6.2 Acquisitions in the context of insolvency

For companies and sole traders against which insolvency proceedings have been opened, instead of the declaration of bankruptcy and liquidation of the assets, the creditors can adopt a rehabilitation plan with the approval of the bankruptcy court. A rehabilitation plan can be adopted on a motion of, among other things, the debtor, the Trustee in Bankruptcy, creditors holding more than one-third of the secured claims, creditors holding more than one-third of the unsecured claims, shareholders holding more than one-third of the capital etc. The plan is obligatory for the debtor and for the creditors whose claims have arisen prior to the opening of the insolvency proceedings

The plan can provide for the transfer of the entire business or of part of the business of the debtor, or for the conversion of debt into equity. The plan usually simultaneously provides for a reduction of the claims of some or all creditors, and provides that, to disagreeing creditors, payment will be made up to the amount such creditors would have received from the liquidation of the property of the debtor.

The plan, which provides for the acquisition of the business of the insolvent debtor, should have attached to it a market valuation of the assets of the debtor, which should also be approved by the creditors' meeting. Whenever the plan provides for the conversion of debt into equity, a valuation of each individual claim has to be performed by court-appointed experts. When the plan involves the transfer of the whole or part of the business of the debtor, a draft agreement should be attached, signed by the prospective purchaser.

Acquisitions of this type are becoming more common. Apart from the fact that, following reduction of the debts, the business of the debtor can be quite attractive, the acquirer can obtain certain licences of the debtor (e.g., the banking licence, subject to following a special procedure to obtain a conditional licence for the purpose of the acquisition).

4.6.3 *Privatisation*

For the initial decade of Bulgaria's transition to a market economy, privatisation was the predominant type of acquisition practiced in Bulgaria. While its significance has now significantly decreased, since most of the possible targets are already in private hands, some major transactions are still expected (the maritime fleet and some energy generators).

The privatisation procedure reveals a number of specifics in contrast to the normal course of acquisitions of privately owned undertakings. The following are subject to a procedure for privatisation:

(a)   the acquisitions of shares owned by the state or the municipalities in joint stock companies or limited liability companies;
(b)   self-contained parts of the assets of companies in which more than 50 per cent of the equity interest is held by the state or the municipalities;
(c)   non-residential real estate, owned by the municipalities; and
(d)   unfinished construction sites which are not included in the assets of any undertaking.

The negotiating party on behalf of the state is the Privatisation Agency. On behalf of the municipalities, the negotiating party will be the municipal councils or bodies appointed by them.

The methods of privatisation of state and municipality owned targets are clearly set out and delineated. The following methods are applicable for the privatisation by purchase of shares in joint stock companies:

(a)   public offering of shares;
(b)   public auction;
(c)   publicly announced tender;
(d)   centralised public auction;
(e)   acceptance of a mandatory tender offer (*see* 4.6.6 below);
(f)   negotiations with the owner of the majority package.

There are two methods available for privatisation of shares in limited liability companies and self-contained parts of assets of companies:

(a)   public auction;
(b)   publicly announced tender.

For certain companies which are included in a special list to the Privatisation and Post-privatisation Control Act (*State Gazette* Issue 28 of 2002), the only available method for privatisation is a publicly announced tender.

Public auction and publicly announced tender are the principal methods of privatising controlling stakes in state-owned enterprises. In both cases, under current regulation a panel consisting of three or more members is appointed and conducts the procedure. All participants would normally be given the opportunity to make a due diligence investigation of the enterprise, to have visits and meetings with the management. In both cases a deposit would be required, which is to be refunded to the unsuccessful participants upon the decision which determines the winning bidder.

A public auction is the method by which the selection criterion is solely the offered price. The auction can be administered by open bidding (where at a bidding session the participants can increase their offered price) or by closed bidding, where the offer of the participant is made known only to the panel and cannot be changed. If there is only one participant, a winner can still be determined if the price offered is not lower than the fixed minimum price. Following the announcement of the winning participant, it has to conclude the contract which was included in the auction documents. No negotiations on the contract terms and conditions will be possible at that point.[17]

In a publicly announced tender the offers are rated on the basis of pre-announced criteria which have a predetermined weight. The panel assesses the offers on the basis of the pre-announced criteria and the tender should be won by the offer with the highest complex rating. In principle, changes to offers already submitted are not allowed. The tender can be validly conducted with only one participant. Irrespective of the number of participants, the privatising body may refuse to choose any of the participants if it considers than none of the offers meets the criteria for the tender to a sufficient degree.

Particularly in the case of publicly announced tenders, the privatisation agreement will normally regulate some post-closing obligations of the buyer, which may include:

(a)   commitments to retain the main object of activity;
(b)   retain or not reduce the average number of staff below a certain level;
(c)   implement an investment programme with strictly set milestones;
(d)   comply with obligations to the state and military reserves of the country etc.

A special procedure, included in an annex to the Privatisation and Post-privatisation Control Act, is applied with respect to certain companies which are considered to be of material importance for national security. This procedure is based on the publicly announced tender process. However, it is characterised by the fact that the most important decisions are made by the Bulgarian Council of Ministers and approved by the Parliament. In this procedure the possibilities for the parties to the privatisation process to launch appeals are very limited.

---

[17] The practice, however, demonstrates some exceptions from this principle.

The methods of transfer of the targets themselves are marginally different from those under the general procedure, and provide some preferences with regard to the form of the transactions.[18]

As part of the privatisation transaction, the target may receive a concession for the exploitation of natural resources or a licence, without the conduct of a separate tender or auction.

The Privatisation and Post-privatisation Control Act provides the opportunity for payment with so-called non-cash payment instruments. These include vouchers of the mass privatisation, and compensatory notes and bonds of the indemnification of former owners of nationalised properties, as well as sovereign securities issued for the covering of state debt. These instruments are offered by their current owners at a fraction of their nominal value but are used in privatisation at par.

4.6.4 Mergers involving a public company

Bulgarian public companies are organised in the form of a joint stock company. Therefore, in general their merger with or into other companies will involve the procedures and formalities applicable to a joint stock company. In addition to these, the POSA provides some additional conditions to such mergers.

In cases where at least one public company participates in a reorganisation, the resulting company will also become public following the merger. Therefore, the resulting company in a merger in which at least one public company participates can only be a joint stock company.

The process of merger with or into a public company is the same as the process with respect to general joint stock companies, with some additional requirements:

(a) The merger agreement or merger plan has to include, in addition to the items already discussed with respect to private joint stock companies:
   (i) information about the fair price of the shares of each of the participating companies and the exchange ratio for the shares of participating companies for shares of the recipient or newly established companies, determined as of a date which is not earlier than one month prior to the date of the merger agreement or merger plan;
   (ii) a justification of the above value based on generally accepted valuation methods;[19] and
   (iii) any other privileges offered to shareholders holding special rights, as well as to other security holders of the company, other than rights holders, if any.

---

[18] For example the transfer of physical shares does not need to be entered into the Book of Shareholders of the company to become effective, and in a case where a notarised agreement would normally be required simple written form is sufficient for the transfer.

[19] The requirements to the justification of the price are regulated by the Regulation Concerning the Requirements to the content of the justification of the price of shares of a public company, including the application of valuation methods in cases of reorganisation, joint-venture agreement or tender offer (*State Gazette* Issue 13 of 2003).

(b)   Auditors of the merger agreement/merger plan can be chosen only from a list approved by the deputy chairman of the Financial Supervision Commission responsible for investment supervision.

(c)   The merger agreement/merger plan, the management report and the auditors' report are to be approved by the deputy chairman before they are submitted for approval by the shareholders. The deputy chairman may refuse to grant approval if the documents are not compliant with the requirements of the law, if the information is not presented in a manner accessible to the shareholders or does not disclose correctly and completely the significant circumstances of the merger offer, or if in any other way the interests of the shareholders have been compromised.

4.6.5   Voluntary public offers

See 4.8.1 below.

4.6.6   Mandatory public bids

Pursuant to the POSA, any person or legal entity who acquires, directly or via affiliated persons, more than 50 per cent or two-thirds of the voting rights in a public company, is obliged within 14 days of the acquisition to either:

(a)   make a tender offer to the rest of the voting shareholders to buy all their shares in the company or exchange them for shares issued by the acquirer; or

(b)   transfer as many shares in the company as are necessary to ensure that he will hold, directly or via affiliated persons, less than 50 per cent (or, as the case may be, less than two-thirds) of the voting rights in the company.

The requirement to make a tender offer applies also to persons or entities holding jointly more than 50 per cent, respectively two-thirds of the voting rights in a public company if they have entered into an agreement to adopt a common policy towards the management of the company, as well as where third parties hold voting shares for the account of the acquirer and the shares held by the acquirer and such third parties represent jointly more than 50 per cent, respectively two-thirds of the voting rights in the company concerned. The same obligation applies to a person already holding (directly, through affiliated parties or indirectly) over 50 per cent of the voting stock of a public company where it desires to acquire more than 3 per cent of the voting stock in any one-year period. Where the relevant person acquires, within 14 consecutive days, control over more than 50 per cent and two-thirds of the votes in a public company, only one tender offer is to be made.

See 4.8.2 below regarding the contents and the procedure for conduct of a tender offer.

4.7   Preparation of an offer

Bulgarian law provides very limited protection to an entity acquiring or merging with another company with respect to the value of the business transferred. It is not uncommon for undisclosed liabilities or legal deficiencies to be found following the transfer. It is therefore very important that a proper and in-depth knowledge of the target is attained prior to any transaction, and that the common understanding of the parties to the transaction regarding the value of the business transferred is incorporated in the relevant representations and warranties, guarantees, penalties and other remedies as part of the transaction documents.

Bulgarian law recognises the concept of *culpa in contrahendo* and proclaims that when conducting negotiations the parties should act in good faith. Otherwise they will be liable for an indemnity. This principle is applied in privatisation procedures, where the bidding candidate will be required to make a deposit in the Privatisation Agency which will be retained if the bidder is chosen but fails to conclude a deal.

Private-to-private mergers and acquisitions are characterised by quite an informal precontractual relationship. Depending on the knowledge of the target, the acquisition or the merger will be preceded by either extensive or limited legal, financial, tax and technical due diligence, as appropriate in the specific circumstances. In some cases the transaction is concluded while providing for post-closing due diligence, usually with certain guarantee and escrow provisions. Privatisation transactions (particularly in the case of tenders) are usually preceded by an extensive procedure of investigation and negotiations. The privatising authority will conduct an internal due diligence and prepare an expert valuation and an Information Memorandum which will be distributed to the bidders. The bidders will then be allowed to make their own due diligence investigations. Following the investigation the bidders will either make an offer with respect only to the price (in the case of an auction) or with respect to the price and other conditions of the transaction (in the case of a tender). The deal is concluded based on a draft contract included in the tender or auction documents, which sometimes contain non-negotiable terms and conditions.

4.8   Conduct of a public offer

4.8.1   Voluntary public offers

Any person who holds at least 5 per cent of the shares in the shareholders meeting of a public company and intends to acquire directly, via affiliates or indirectly more than one-third of the votes in the shareholders meeting of such company can publish a voluntary tender offer for the purchase or exchange of shares to all shareholders following the registration and approval of the offer by the Financial Supervision Commission. The voluntary offer may be conditional upon being accepted by a certain percentage of the shareholders. It may further be limited up to a certain level of shareholding, and if it is accepted with respect to a greater number of shares, the shares will be acquired proportionately from all accepting shareholders.

Any person who has acquired directly, indirectly or through affiliates more than 90 per cent of the votes in the shareholders meeting of a public company has the right (but not the obligation) to register a new tender offer (a "closing tender offer") to purchase the shares of the remaining shareholders. If the person has not registered a voluntary tender offer within 14 days of the acquisition of 90 per cent of the voting rights, in order to make such a voluntary tender offer the person has to notify the shareholders of the public company, the Financial Supervision Commission and the regulated market on which its shares are traded at least three months in advance. A person who has acquired in the context of privatisation by way of public offering more than two-thirds of the voting stock of a public company, can also make a closing tender offer.

The procedure and requirements for the conduct of such offer are identical to the requirements for the conduct of a mandatory tender offer (*see* 4.8.2 below), with the exception that the inability to publish a tender offer does not block the voting rights of the shares held by the offeror, and that such subsequent closing tender offer cannot provide for the exchange of shares of the target for shares of the offeror instead of payment.

Following the successful completion of such closing tender offer, the offeror is entitled to require the target company to be delisted from the register of public companies and thus become a private company. The offeree shareholders are not mandated to accept the closing tender offer. The company will be delisted if no less than half of the total number of shares to which the closing tender offer was addressed have accepted the bid or the shareholders meeting of the company has resolved to delist the company with a majority of half of the capital present, provided that for the purposes of such majority only the shares to which the tender offer was addressed are taken into account, and the offeror can vote only with the shares it has acquired during or after the tender offer.

Any person who has already accomplished a tender offer, as a result of which it has acquired directly, via affiliates or indirectly at least 95 per cent of the votes in the shareholders meeting of the company has the right (but not the obligation) to register a new tender offer (a "squeeze-out tender offer") to purchase the shares of the remaining shareholders within three months of the end of the acceptance period for the previous tender offer. The addressee shareholders are obliged to tender their shares within one month, after the expiration of which all outstanding shares will be considered transferred to the offeror. Following the squeeze-out the company will stop being public and will be delisted.

4.8.2   *Mandatory public offers*

Subject to fulfilment of the criteria discussed at 4.6.5 above, the person acquiring directly or indirectly more than 50 per cent or two thirds of the voting stock of a public company is under an obligation to draw up and publish a tender offer to the other shareholders to purchase their shares or to exchange their shares for shares issued by the offeror.[20] The same obligation applies to a person already

---

[20] By way of derogation from the above mandatory tender offer requirements, no tender offer is to be made where the shares were acquired in the context of privatisation, or the shares are acquired in the context of a capital increase by way of the issue of rights, or the person has already made a tender offer within one year prior to reaching the two-thirds threshold.

holding more than 50 per cent of the voting stock of a public company where it desires to acquire more than 3 per cent of the voting stock in any year.[21]

The offer should be published in at least two central daily newspapers or magazines. The offer can be published only if the Financial Supervision Commission does not object to the bid within 14 working days following submission of the draft offer to it. The draft offer must be submitted at the same time to the management of the target company, to the employees or to their representatives and to the regulated market on which the target company is listed, noting that the Financial Supervision Commission has not ruled on the offer. The management of the offeree company may submit to the Financial Supervision Commission, to the offeror, to the employees or to their representatives an opinion on the offer within seven days following receipt of the draft offer. The opinion of the management is to be published along with the tender offer itself.

The tender offer must ensure that:

(a)   all shareholders of the offeree company, who are in the same position, are treated equally, and the remaining shareholders are protected when control is acquired;

(b)   the addressees of the bid have sufficient time and information to enable them to reach a properly informed decision on the bid;

(c)   the management of the offeree company acts in the interests of the company, and does not preclude its shareholders from making a decision in respect of the tender offer;

(d)   false markets are not created in the securities of the offeree company;

(e)   a tender offer is issued only after ensuring the ability of the offeror to pay fully, respectively, exchange fully the shares of the tendering shareholders;

(f)   the offeree company's business is not impeded for an unjustifiably long period of time.

The term for acceptance of the tender offer cannot be less than 28 days or more than 70 days following publication, except in the case of the publication of a competing tender offer, where the acceptance periods for all prior offers extend until the expiration of the latest competing tender offer.

After the receipt of the draft offer by the management of the offeree company it cannot undertake any acts (with the exception of soliciting a competing tender offer), whose main objective is to frustrate the acceptance of the tender offer, or to create significant obstacles or significant additional costs for the offeror, such as the issuance of shares, or the entry into transactions which would result in a significant change of the assets of the company, except where such actions are undertaken following the advance approval of the shareholders meeting of the offeree company.

---

[21] By way of derogation from this requirement, a tender offer will not be required where the acquirer has made a mandatory tender offer within one year prior to the latest acquisition. The requirements for the making of a tender offer apply to cases where the public company itself acquires as treasury stock more than 3 per cent of its shares.

The price/exchange ratio offered by the offeror in a mandatory tender offer upon exceeding 50 per cent or reaching two-thirds of the voting stock, or a closing tender offer, has to be justified by generally accepted valuation methods.[22] It cannot be lower than the highest of either:

(a)   the fair price per share indicated in the justification attached to the tender offer and determined according to generally accepted valuation methods; or

(b)   the average weighted market price of the shares during the last three months; or

(c)   the highest price paid by the offeror or its affiliates during the six months before the registration of the bid, and where the price of the shares cannot be determined in this way, then the higher among the latest subscription value and the most recent price paid by the offeror, will be taken into account.

With respect to a mandatory offer to acquire more than 3 per cent within one year, or a voluntary offer of a person holding more than 5 per cent of the voting stock, the offered price/exchange ratio cannot be lower than the average weighted market price of the shares for the last three months, or where this is not available the highest price paid by the offeror, or its affiliates during the six months prior to the registration of the offer. Alternatively, the above criteria applicable to the price in a mandatory tender offer upon exceeding 50 per cent or reaching two-thirds of the voting stock, can be used at the option of the offeror also in respect of a mandatory offer to acquire more than 3 per cent within one year, or a voluntary offer of a person holding more than 5 per cent of the voting stock.

In respect of a squeeze-out tender offer the offer price has to be at least equal to:

(a)   the price offered during the tender offer as a result of which the 95 per cent threshold was reached, where this was a mandatory tender offer;

(b)   the price offered during the tender offer as a result of which the 95 per cent threshold was reached, where this was a voluntary tender offer, but the offeror had acquired at least 90 per cent of the addressee shares in such tender offer; or

(c)   the limits set in respect of a mandatory tender offer upon exceeding 50 per cent or reaching two-thirds of the voting stock, or a closing tender offer.

If the Financial Supervision Commission does not prohibit the publication of the tender offer within the 14-day period after its receipt, the offer must be published (along with the opinion of the management of the offeree company) in at least two central daily newspapers within three days. After the publication the offer cannot be withdrawn by the offeror unless he cannot fulfil the offer due to reasons outside his control and only after approval by the Financial Supervision

---

[22] The requirements to the justification of the price are regulated by the Regulation Concerning the Requirements to the Content of the Justification of the Price of Shares of a Public Company, Including the Application of Valuation Methods in Cases of Reorganisation, Joint-venture Agreement or Tender Offer (*State Gazette* Issue 13 of 2003).

Commission. This does not apply to a voluntary tender offer which is not a closing or a squeeze-out tender offer.

The offer is accepted by an express written statement and by depositing the certificates of the shares in the investment broker organising the tender offer process or in the Central Depository, as well as by undertaking the other actions necessary for the transfer. The acceptance of the offer can be withdrawn until the expiry of the term of the offer. The transfer is deemed finalised with the expiry of the term of the offer – the offeror is mandated to purchase the shares for which the offer was accepted. Payment for the shares must be made within seven days of the expiry of the term of the offer.

The provisions of the POSA governing takeover bids do not apply to the buyers of shares under privatisation transactions.

4.9 Defences to a hostile offer

Due to the fact that Bulgarian equities markets are still in the early stages of development, Bulgaria is yet to witness a truly hostile takeover. Therefore, local practice has developed little in the way of defences against potential hostile bids.

Perhaps the major obstacle to a bidder acquiring control of a public company is the mandatory tender offer requirement, which in effect obligates the offeror to purchase or exchange the shares of minority shareholders at a price which is justified. The Financial Supervision Commission uses the justification of the offered price as a control against the offering of a price which is too low in the Commission's opinion. If the Financial Supervision Commission considers that the price is not sufficiently justified it will issue a prohibition against the publication of the tender offer. Failure to publish a mandatory tender offer has some quite severe consequences for the offeror – it is unable to exercise the voting rights attached to its shares until the offer is published.

As of 2003, securities regulations have provided the possibility of launching competitive tender offers in response to a voluntary tender offer which is not a closing tender offer. A competitive tender offer can be launched by any person who holds more than 5 per cent of the voting stock of a public company, and desires to acquire more than one-third of the votes in the shareholders meeting. It has to improve on the original voluntary tender offer, and be published not later than three days before the expiration of the term for the original tender offer. Prior to such a competitive offer being published, it has to be registered with the Financial Supervision Commission provided that Commission has not objected to the offer. In response to a competing offer the previous offer/s may be improved only once. The period for acceptance of all offers is extended until the expiration of the period for acceptance of the latest one.

The POSA provides some safeguards against frustrating the bid. These include the suspension of all transfer restrictions in respect of voting shares as regards the offeror, whether set in the company's statutes, in shareholders' agreements or in agreements between the company and shareholders. Any voting restrictions contained in the statutes of the company, in shareholders' agreements or in agreements between the company and shareholders will not apply to the adoption of resolutions which may frustrate the tender offer. Where the offeror has acquired more than 75 per cent of the votes in the shareholders meeting of the company the above restriction will continue to be suspended, and in addition any appointment and dismissal rights of individual shareholders in respect of members of the management bodies will not apply. The offeror will need to compensate the respective shareholders for the suspension of these rights. The restrictions in respect of voting rights will nonetheless apply where they have been compensated by additional dividend or other payments. The above safeguards will also not apply to special rights of the state under so-called "golden shares".

4.10   Profit forecast and asset valuation

In the context of a mandatory tender offer or a closing tender offer, the offeror has to present a justification of the offered price, containing a description of the criteria and methods of valuation used.

Although the offeror is required to state its intentions with respect to the future development of the target, it is not explicitly required to make a profit forecast. The public company itself is required to make a forecast, in its annual disclosure statement, of the profit during the next financial year.

4.11   Documents from the offeror and the offeree board

4.11.1   *The tender offer*

A tender offer has to contain:

(a)   Information about the offeror:
  (i)   full name and address for an individual, or for a legal entity the name, seat and address of management, telephone, fax, e-mail and website, if any, the objects of activity and information about any past changes in the name of the offeror, if any;
  (ii)   as regards the members of its management and supervisory board, respectively the board of directors – full name and address for an individual, including where the individual is acting on behalf of a legal entity which is a member of the board of the offeror;
  (iii)   for individuals who hold directly, or through affiliates, more than 5 per cent of the votes in the shareholders meeting of the offeror or who can exercise control over it, their full name and address; or for a legal entity the name, the seat and address of management, as well as the number of the voting shares owned and their percentage of the votes in the shareholders meeting of the offeror or the methods of control exercised with respect to it;
  (iv)   any voting agreements with respect to the shares of the offeror, to the extent that such exist and the offeror is aware thereof.

(b) Information about the investment broker, authorised by the offeror – its name, seat and address of management, the number and date of the investment brokerage licence, as well as telephone, fax, e-mail and website details, if any.

(c) Information about the target company – its name, seat and address of management, as well as telephone, fax, e-mail and website details, if any.

(d) Information about the participation of the offeror in the votes of the shareholders meeting of the target company:

(i) the number, type and rights attached to the securities owned, the manner of holding (directly or indirectly), the percentage of the total number of votes and the date of their acquisition;

(ii) the number, type and rights attached to the shares owned by the member of the management board, supervisory board or board of directors of the offeror and the manner of holding (directly or indirectly), the percentage of the total number of the votes and the date of acquisition;

(iii) the information under (a) above with respect to the person through which the offeror holds the shares (be it an affiliate or a nominee), if any;

(iv) the number of voting shares which the offeror does not hold and is required or wants to acquire.

(e) The price per share offered.

(f) The term for acceptance of the offer.

(g) The conditions of financing for the acquisition of the shares, including whether the offeror will use its own capital or borrowed funds.

(h) The intentions of the offeror with respect to the future activity of the target company, including:

(i) reorganisation or winding up of the company;

(ii) changes to the capital of the company within one year of entering into the transaction;

(iii) the main activity and the financial strategy of the company during the current financial year and the financial year immediately following;

(iv) changes to the membership of the management bodies, the personnel and the conditions under contracts of employment, if such are expected;

(v) the dividend distribution policy.

(i) The procedure for acceptance of the offer and the payment of the price, including information regarding:

(i) the place where accepting shareholders should submit the written statement of acceptance and deposit the certificates for the shares held;

(ii) the term and manner of payment of the price by the offeror.

(j) Information about the applicable formalities in case the tender offer is withdrawn by the offeror.

(k) Information about the possibility of an accepting shareholder withdrawing his acceptance, as well as the procedure for such withdrawal.

(l) The place where the annual financial statements of the offeror for the last three financial years are available to the shareholders of the target company, and where additional information can be received regarding the offeror and the offer.

(m)   The total amount of the expenses of the offeror for the realisation of the offer, outside the funds necessary for the purchase of the shares.

(n)   The two national dailies in which the offeror intends to publish the tender offer, the opinion of the managing body of the company regarding the acquisition if such an opinion is issued, and the results of the bid.

(o)   Other data and documents which in the judgement of the offeror are material to the accomplishment of the tender offer.

(p)   Information about the responsibility of the authorised investment broker, jointly and severally with the offeror, for the damages caused by untrue, misleading or incomplete data in the offer.

In the case of a voluntary tender offer which is not a closing tender offer, the offer should contain the above elements, with the exception of items (e) and (j) above, and should also contain:

(a)   information about the objectives of the acquisition;

(b)   the minimum number of shares which have to be tendered to make the offer binding;

(c)   information about the possibilities for the offeror to withdraw the offer;

(d)   the price per share offered.

Where the offeror has elected to provide a justification of the offer, it should be attached.

In the context of a voluntary closing tender offer, the offer should also contain an indication that, following the expiration of the term for acceptance of the tender offer, the company may stop being public, and an indication on whether the offeror intends to require the company to be written off the register of public companies kept by the Financial Supervision Commission.

To the tender offer should be attached:

(a)   a declaration by the offeror regarding compliance with the requirements for notification of the managing body of the target company and the regulated market on which the shares of the target company have been admitted to trading;

(b)   a certificate or another analogous document of corporate status for the offeror, issued not earlier than one month prior to the date of registration of the tender offer with the Financial Supervision Commission;

(c)   copies of documents evidencing the availability of funds to accomplish the tender offer;

(d)   form of acceptance statement as well as form for withdrawal of acceptance.

The signatures of the representatives of the offeror and the appointed investment broker, certifying that the offer is compliant with the requirements of the law, should be executed on the offer document.

If the tender offer will involve the exchange of shares of the target company for shares issued by the offeror, the offer should also contain:

(a)　additional information about the offeror;

(b)　an overview of the activity of the offeror during the last three financial years prior to the registration of the tender offer and information and forecasts about the current financial year and the financial year immediately following;

(c)　the major risks related to the activity of the offeror and the methods of their management;

(d)　information about the planned use of the accruing capital;

(e)　information about previous issues of securities issued by the offeror;

(f)　the regulated markets on which the securities issued by the offeror are being traded, including maximum, minimum and average weighted price, and volumes of trade during the last year;

(g)　information about the shares with which the exchange will be accomplished;

(h)　the exchange ratio;

(i)　the conditions of subscription of the exchanged shares etc.

4.11.2　Documents from the offeree board

Within seven days of receiving the tender offer, the management body of the target company may present to the Financial Supervision Commission, to the employees or to their representatives and to the offeror, an opinion regarding the proposed transaction, including concerning the consequences of accepting the offer in respect of the company, the employees and the management's opinion in respect of the strategic plans of the offeror, and their potential impact on the employees and the location of business. The opinion has further to contain information about the existence of possible voting agreements in the target company, to the extent the management body is aware of the existence of such agreements, as well as information about the number of shares of the company held by members of its management body and whether they themselves intend to accept the offer. Where, within the above seven-day period, the management has received an opinion from the representatives of the employees in respect of the tender offer's impact on the employees, it has to attach this opinion to its own opinion on the bid.

4.12　Compulsory acquisitions of minorities

Both in the context of a mandatory tender offer and a voluntary closing tender offer (after achieving over 90 per cent of the voting power in the public company) (*see* 4.8.1 and 4.8.2 above) the offeror is obliged to acquire the shares it does not own in the target company for which the offer was accepted. In the context of a voluntary tender offer, the offeror will be obliged to acquire only the shares which it has indicated in the offer that it intends to acquire, and provided that any minimum acceptance conditions are met.

However, irrespective of whether a voluntary closing tender offer is accomplished or not, any person, holding directly or indirectly more than 90 per cent of the votes in a public company, is obliged upon a request by any shareholder to purchase the shares of such shareholder until a closing tender offer is published and within 14 days following the end of its acceptance period. Where as a result of a tender offer the offeror, directly, indirectly or via affiliates has acquired at least 95 per cent of the votes in the shareholders meeting of the company, it is obliged to acquire any shares tendered to it within three months following the end of such tender offer.

4.13   Financial assistance

The primary source of financial assistance in acquisitions for players on the Bulgarian markets has been loan financing from banks.

4.13.1   Leveraged financing

Following the introduction of financial assistance rules in 2005, a Bulgarian joint stock company is precluded from providing loans or giving collateral securing the acquisition of its own shares by a third party. The restriction will not apply to transactions entered into by banks or financial institutions in the ordinary course of business, provided, following the relevant transaction, their net assets value continues to be at least equal to their registered capital along with any statutory reserves.

4.13.2   Exchange controls

Foreign-to-local and local-to-foreign loans, as well as the provision of collateral for the obligations to non-local residents or between non-local residents, are subject to declaration with the Bulgarian National Bank within 15 days following entry into the relevant transaction. The declaration is a precondition for the ability to repay such loans by way of bank transfers outside of Bulgaria.

4.13.3   Origin of the funds

Buyers in privatisation transactions are required to declare and possibly prove the origin of the funds with which they participate. Where a transaction is subject to regulatory clearance, disclosure of the origin of the funds will also normally be required. Money laundering and measures against terrorism legislation also require disclosure of sources of financing in various transactions.

Chapter 5

Cyprus

Elias Neocleous, Partner
Kyriacos Georgiades, Partner
Achilleas Malliotis, Associate

Andreas Neocleous & Co.

5.1 Introduction

Takeovers and mergers are a comparatively new development in the commercial life of Cyprus. The enactment of the Cyprus Securities and Stock Exchange Law in 1993 and its various amendments, the passing of regulations under it in 1995 and 1997, the inauguration of the official Cyprus Stock Exchange in 1996, the introduction of the Cyprus Securities and Exchange Commission in 2001, the Financial Services Law of 2002 and the amendments to the Companies Law with respect to mergers heralded a new era in the Cyprus securities industry and the associated activity of acquisitions generally.

On 1 May 2004, Cyprus joined the European Union ("EU") and, while the economic and cultural gaps between Cyprus and the EU were smaller than those of the other acceding states, many changes in the financial structure were required. Cyprus law is now harmonised with the *acquis communautaire* in all significant areas and Cyprus completed its integration into Europe with the adoption of the euro as its official currency on 1 January 2008 in place of the Cyprus pound. Since most laws have yet to be updated for the new currency, monetary amounts in this Chapter are shown both in Cyprus pounds ("CYP") and in euros.

Although there are currently some 200 public companies whose securities are listed on the Cyprus Stock Exchange, there are numerous important private companies whose activities should not be underestimated and which may be the target of local or foreign bids, leading to concentrations as in other European markets. In recent years the EU, influenced by the US policy on this matter, has been waging war against monopolies. Because of the small size of the domestic market, combined with Cyprus's unique market structure and financial history, much of Cyprus's economy, and particularly its infrastructure and public services, is based on monopolies. The field of telecommunications, in which the Cyprus Telecommunications Authority previously held a monopoly, has been opened to competition relatively successfully. However, in other areas new competitors have either not come forward or have failed.

5.2   Acquisition targets

5.2.1   *Cyprus companies and the law*

The primary statute governing the company as a separate legal entity is the Companies Law, Chapter 113 of the Laws of Cyprus ("the Companies Law"). It recognises and regulates a number of different corporate forms, namely companies limited by guarantee (most of which are non-profit making organisations) and companies limited by shares, which may be classified as exempt private companies, private limited companies, public limited companies and European public limited companies (usually known by the abbreviation "SE", which stands for Societas Europaea).

The original Companies Law dates back before independence and closely follows the UK Companies Act 1948, but it has been extensively amended and added to for the purposes of harmonisation with the relevant EU Directives. For example, Law 70(I) of 2003 introduces Sections 201 A–H, which adopt in their entirety the following relevant EU Directives:

(a)   77/91/EEC on the formation of public limited liability companies and the maintenance and alteration of their capital;
(b)   78/855/EEC on the merger of public limited liability companies;
(c)   82/891/EEC on the division of public limited liability companies;
(d)   89/666/EEC on the disclosure requirements in respect of branches opened in Member States by certain types of company governed by the law of another state;
(e)   68/151/EEC on the coordination of guarantees; and
(f)   89/667/EEC on single-member private limited liability companies.

Law 70(I) of 2003 defines the merger and division procedures in Cyprus and represents a major development in the area of mergers and takeovers. More recently, Cyprus has enacted legislation transposing the European Takeover Bids Directive (Directive 2004/25/EC) into domestic law in the form of the Law on Public Takeovers (Law no. 41(I) of 2007), which applies to public takeover bids for companies whose registered office is in the Republic of Cyprus and which are admitted to trading on a locally regulated market.

A key feature of the new law is the provision of a set of general principles governing public takeover bids, such as equal treatment of shareholders and shareholder protection. In addition, the law sets out the procedures to be followed before and after the announcement of the public takeover bid, the mechanics of a public takeover bid (such as the way in which information will be disseminated), restrictions on the offeror company after the announcement of the bid and the circumstances under which the initial public takeover bid can be revoked. The law also includes new "squeeze out" and "sell out" provisions.

5.2.1.1   *Private companies*
A private company is a company which by its articles of association specifically:

(a)   restricts the right to transfer its shares;
(b)   limits the number of its members to 50, excluding persons who are employed by the company and persons who, having been employed by

the company, were (while in that employment and after its determination have continued to be) members of the company;

(c)   prohibits any invitation to the public to subscribe for its shares or debentures;

(d)   prohibits the issue of bearer shares.

Under an amendment to the Companies Law enacted in 2000, it is now possible for a private company to have only one shareholder.

5.2.1.2   *Exempt companies*

As its name implies, an exempt company is not subject to certain provisions of the Companies Law, as follows:

(a)   it is not obliged to file financial statements with the annual return which it submits to the Registrar of Companies;

(b)   its auditors need not be qualified under Section 155 of the Companies Law;

(c)   it need not print special resolutions to be filed with the Registrar of Companies;

(d)   it may provide loans and guarantees to its directors.

In addition to meeting the requirements of a private company, to be classified as exempt a company must satisfy the following conditions:

(a)   no corporate body may hold any of its shares or debentures unless it is itself an exempt private company registered in Cyprus;

(b)   the number of debenture holders may not exceed 50;

(c)   no corporate body may be a director of the company;

(d)   nobody other than the holder may have any interest in any of its shares or debentures;

(e)   neither the company nor its directors may be privy to any agreement under which the policy of the company is determined by persons other than its shareholders and directors.

5.2.1.3   *Public companies*

A public company is a company which does not qualify as a private company and to which the following provisions also apply:

(a)   it must have at least seven members;

(b)   it must have at least two directors;

(c)   if directors are appointed by the articles of association, their consent must be filed on incorporation;

(d)   it must obtain a trading certificate from the Registrar of Companies before it commences business. To obtain such a certificate, and before it issues any of its shares or debentures to the public, the company must issue a prospectus or a statement in lieu of prospectus;

(e)   it must have a statutory meeting and its directors must make a statutory report to its members;

(f)   it has the power to issue share warrants;

(g)   its share capital must be at least CYP15,000 (€25,629).

5.2.1.4   Societas Europaea ("SE")

The Council of the European Union adopted the Regulation on the Statute for a European Company (SE) (Regulation 2157/2001, generally referred to as "the SE Regulation") in 2001. Its purpose was to allow the establishment of a transnational European public limited-liability company or Societas Europaea, able to merge or relocate across national frontiers without losing or altering its legal personality.

The aim of the SE regime is to allow companies incorporated in different Member States to avoid the legal and practical constraints arising from the existence of 15 different legal systems and to merge or form a holding company or joint subsidiary that is able to operate throughout the internal market and beyond. Incorporation as an SE can significantly reduce the costs for businesses operating in more than one Member State of the EU. Furthermore a business can restructure quickly and easily to exploit the advantages presented by the internal market.

However, due to Member States' reluctance to give up their national corporate laws, the SE Regulation does not go into detail but limits itself to general provisions and to setting out a framework of rules relating to key areas including formation, structure, accounts, insolvency and winding up. This means that there will not be a uniform type of SE across Europe, but a variety of SEs depending on the corporate laws of the Member States in which they are incorporated.

Cyprus enacted the legislation to allow SEs to be formed in August 2006. It is interesting to note that the Cyprus legislature followed the British and Irish route of adopting subsidiary legislation to implement the Regulation and the Directive rather than introducing a new "stand-alone" Companies Law. A Cyprus SE may be established by a merger of two or more public limited-liability companies located in different Member States, it can be set up as a holding company for European limited-liability companies or it can be formed as a subsidiary. Alternatively an existing Cyprus company may be converted into an SE. Existing companies from other Member States may be merged into an SE in Cyprus without any tax cost since Cyprus has fully implemented the EU Mergers Directive.

5.2.2   Taxation

Following the entry of Cyprus into the EU, there was a major overhaul of the Cyprus taxation system to align it with EU law. In particular, the Income Tax Law which came into force on 1 January 2003 ("the Law") brought about major changes to the Cyprus tax system as it affects companies, abolishing the distinction between local companies and international business companies ("IBCs") and providing for:

(a)   a single corporate tax rate of 10 per cent for all companies registered in Cyprus;

(b)   no geographical limitation on the exercise of any company's activities. Its income may be derived from any source including a Cyprus-based source;

(c)   no restriction on the ownership of a company's shares.

5.2.2.1 *Cyprus tax residence*

Taxation of company profits is based on worldwide income for resident companies and on Cyprus-source income for non-resident companies. In determining residence of companies, the Law adopts management and control as the key test. The test for residence is management and control. Mere registration or incorporation in Cyprus will not be sufficient to render a company liable to tax in Cyprus: for the company to be treated as resident, the locus of management and control must be in Cyprus. The Income Tax Law does not formally define the criteria for management and control, and determination of tax residence relies heavily on the management and control test established under pre-1960 English common law, which is directly applicable in Cyprus as part of its common law heritage.

It should be noted that the Law has introduced general anti-avoidance clauses and there is a growing attitude of the Cyprus tax authorities to screen and assess commercial transactions to ensure that there will be no abuse of tax laws and regulations. This is a point of much relevance to the issue as to whether the management and control of a company is exercised in Cyprus.

It is vital that all key management and commercial decisions that are necessary for the conduct of a company's business are actually made in Cyprus. To that end, the majority of the board meetings should be held in Cyprus and the directors must be adequately informed about the matters on which they are making decisions. A company should have economic substance in terms of staff, premises and equipment, and sufficient competence in Cyprus to make necessary business decisions.

5.2.2.2 *Resident companies*

The taxable income of companies, whether incorporated in Cyprus or not, which have their management and control exercised in Cyprus, is liable to corporation tax at the rate of 10 per cent, irrespective of whether the shareholders are residents of Cyprus or not. Corporation tax is charged on the following types of income:

(a) business profits;
(b) interest;
(c) rents from immovable property;
(d) royalties;
(e) profit from the sale of goodwill.

The profits of a resident Cyprus company, which are derived directly or indirectly from a permanent establishment outside Cyprus, are exempt from Cyprus tax. However, this exemption is not granted if the Controlled Foreign Company ("CFC") provisions apply, namely if:

(a) more than 50 per cent of the paying permanent establishment's activities results in investment income; and
(b) the foreign tax is significantly lower than the tax payable in Cyprus.

5.2.2.3 *Holding structure*

A Cyprus holding company is generally set up as an ordinary company resident in Cyprus which, besides participating in domestic or foreign companies (or both), may also have other functions such as trading, manufacturing or financing. There are no restrictions on its activities. It is taxable in Cyprus on its worldwide income, provided that it is managed and controlled in Cyprus.

5.2.2.4   Dividend income

From 1 January 2003, dividends are not subject to Cyprus income tax generally, but a 15 per cent special defence contribution ("SDC") tax is levied on the dividend income of a Cyprus resident company or individual subject to the following exemptions:

(a)   Exemption for dividends payable abroad: non-residents of Cyprus are not subject to SDC tax, and therefore dividends payable by a Cyprus-resident company to foreign shareholders, whether corporate or individual, do not attract any withholding taxes in Cyprus.

(b)   Exemption for intercompany dividends: dividends payable by a Cyprus-resident subsidiary to its Cyprus-resident parent are exempt from taxation and are not included in the taxable income of the recipient company, although deemed distribution rules will apply.

(c)   Exemption for dividends receivable from non-resident companies: dividends payable by non-resident companies to resident companies are exempt from SDC tax provided that the Cyprus-resident company receiving them owns at least 1 per cent of the company paying them (under the transposition of the EU Parent/Subsidiary Directive, which applies to all non-resident subsidiaries not only EU subsidiaries). The above exemption does not apply, however, if the CFC provisions are triggered.

5.2.2.5   Controlled Foreign Company legislation

Compared with many other jurisdictions, Cyprus's CFC legislation is limited, targeting only certain types of income that is not derived from real business activities to create a distinction between participation (active income) and investment (passive income). The CFC provisions will only be triggered if more than 50 per cent of the non-resident company's activities result directly or indirectly in investment income, and the foreign tax burden on the income of the non-resident company paying the dividend is substantially lower than the tax burden of the Cyprus-resident company which is receiving the dividend.

5.2.2.6   Capital gains tax

Any profits from the disposal of securities (shares, bonds, debentures, founder's shares and other company securities) are exempt from taxation under the Law and the Capital Gains Tax Law. The only gains subject to capital gains tax in Cyprus are gains on the disposal of immovable property in Cyprus or on the shares of unlisted companies owning immovable property in Cyprus.

Many of Cyprus's double taxation treaties provide for taxation of capital gains only in the country of residence of the person (company or individual) disposing of a capital asset. The above-mentioned provision could therefore lead to double non-taxation, as a capital gain made by a Cyprus-resident company from a sale of its foreign subsidiary's shares will be exempt from taxation both in Cyprus and in the country where the subsidiary (i.e., the capital asset) is located.

5.2.2.7 Group relief

Trading losses incurred by one group company may be set off against trading profits of another group company by way of group relief, provided that the losses and profits have occurred in the same year of assessment and both companies are resident in Cyprus and members of the same group for the whole of that year.

Companies are deemed to be members of a group if one is the 75 per cent subsidiary of the other or both are 75 per cent subsidiaries of a third company. "75 per cent subsidiary" means holding at least 75 per cent of the voting shares with beneficial entitlement to at least 75 per cent of the income and 75 per cent of the assets on liquidation.

5.2.2.8 Finance structure

Cyprus tax legislation does not contain any thin capitalisation rules, i.e., a debt to equity ratio requirement. However, there are certain indirect debt to equity restrictions.

Under the Law, any interest paid in the course of a company's normal trading activities is an allowable deduction, including any amount in relation to the acquisition of assets used in the business.

However, if a Cyprus company that pays interest makes advances to related parties at a zero rate of interest or at a rate lower than the rate it pays, interest equal to 9 per cent per annum on those advances, or the difference between the actual interest paid and received, will have to be added back, because such advances are not considered as expenses incurred for the purpose of producing income.

Cyprus holding companies are liable to 10 per cent SDC tax on interest income from any source, whether from Cyprus or abroad. The deduction is made at source if the interest is received from Cyprus, otherwise by assessment on the basis of returns.

However, SDC tax does not apply to "active" interest, that is, interest earned from or closely related to the taxpayer's main business (for example, interest earned by a bank or an insurance company), which is subject to income tax with no exemption available.

Any interest received by a Cyprus holding company which is deemed not to be from or closely related to its ordinary business activities will be subject to 10 per cent income tax on 50 per cent of the interest received and to 10 per cent SDC tax at 10 per cent on the whole amount of the interest received, thus giving an effective total tax burden of 15 per cent.

According to Income Tax Office Circular 003–8, interest earned in the ordinary course of business includes interest earned from banking and finance and hire purchase and leasing activities. Interest closely related to the ordinary course of business includes:

(a) interest received from trade debtors by companies engaged in the trading or development of land, and by traders of new or old cars or of any other vehicles or machines;

(b)   interest earned by insurance companies;
(c)   interest earned by banks on current accounts;
(d)   interest earned by a company acting as a vehicle to finance other group companies.

Interest earned from loans by a company to third parties and interest from savings and deposits are taxed under the SDC tax provisions, unless these fall within one of the above categories.

5.2.2.9   Royalty structure

The gross amount of any royalties derived from Cyprus is subject to income tax at 10 per cent. In cases where an intellectual or industrial property right is granted for use outside Cyprus, the royalty will not be deemed to be income derived from sources in Cyprus and will therefore be tax exempt. Accordingly, Cyprus companies can continue to be used advantageously as intermediary licensing vehicles for the routing of royalties out of countries with which Cyprus has concluded double taxation treaties.

Royalties paid in connection with the exploitation of any intellectual or industrial property right effectively connected with a permanent establishment in Cyprus will be considered as derived from Cyprus-based sources and will therefore be taxed in Cyprus.

5.2.2.10   New reorganisation rules

The new tax rules for the reorganisation of companies follow the rules set out in the EU Mergers Directive. Part V of the Law extends these rules to domestic reorganisations, to all cross-border reorganisations between member and non-member countries and to reorganisations abroad with tax implications in Cyprus. The types of reorganisation covered are mergers, divisions, transfers of assets and exchanges of shares. All these reorganisations do not lead to recognition of income at company and shareholder level and therefore any profits or gains made as a result of reorganisation fall outside the ambit of the Cyprus tax net. Book values have to be carried forward and losses are transferred to the absorbing company. Reorganisations are exempt from VAT, capital gains tax and stamp duty.

5.2.2.11   Double taxation relief

Section 34 of the Law provides for relief from double taxation in relation to income tax and any tax of a similar character that is imposed by the laws of another country. The Law distinguishes between the situation where there is a double taxation treaty in force between Cyprus and another country and the situation where there is no such treaty.

Section 35 of the Law applies where, under a treaty having effect under Section 34, tax payable in respect of any income in the treaty country is to be allowed as a credit against tax payable in Cyprus in respect of that income. The tax charge will be reduced by the amount of the credit. The Special Contribution for the Defence of the Republic Law (which, as mentioned above, imposes the payment of SDC tax on dividends, interest and rents) specifically states that the provisions of the Law relating to the application of double taxation treaties and the granting of credits will also apply to any tax or contribution payable under this law.

Under Section 36 of the Law, where income tax has been paid on income derived from a foreign country with which a double taxation treaty is not in force, and such income is subject to income tax under the Law, relief from tax payable under the Law will be granted in respect of such income, not exceeding the amount of tax paid in the foreign country in respect of such income, namely unilateral relief. Such relief is also granted in cases where SDC tax is payable.

5.3 Arrangements, amalgamations and takeover bids

The Companies Law provides distinct means by which the capital structure of a company may be reorganised – one in Section 198 and the other in Section 270. In addition, as stated at 5.2.1 above, Section 201A–H sets out in detail the merger and division procedure for public companies in Cyprus with the exception of publicly listed companies where reorganisations involve transactions undertaken via a stock exchange, such as the submission of a public takeover bid or offer for the acquisition of a listed company's shares.

Prior to 2007, Section 201 provided the sole means by which the shares of a minority of shareholders dissenting from a scheme or contract approved by the majority might be acquired. Following its accession to the European Union, Cyprus was obliged to align its legislation governing public company takeover bids with Directive 2004/25/EC ("the Takeover Directive"). The Takeover Directive was transposed into the Cyprus legal order by the Law on Public Takeovers (Law 41(I) of 2007) which was complemented by four directives issued by the Cyprus Securities and Exchange Commission ("CySEC"). The Law on Public Takeovers includes specific "squeeze-out" and "sell-out" provisions, which are elaborated upon at 5.3.5 below.

5.3.1 Arrangements under Section 198

Section 198 provides a method whereby a compromise or arrangement may be made between a company and:

(a)   its creditors or any class of them; or
(b)   its members or any class of them; or
(c)   any combination of the above.

A scheme under this Section requires the sanction of the court. It is applicable to both a going concern and a company in the process of winding up.

A "compromise" presupposes the existence of a dispute, whereas the meaning of an "arrangement" is not to be limited to something analogous to a compromise.

The usefulness of the Section may be seen principally in two instances. First, it enables a company to agree a compromise with a majority of its creditors which may then be imposed on all of its creditors (a "cramdown"). Secondly, it enables class rights to be varied where no provision otherwise exists to vary them, for example where such rights are contained in a memorandum of association which provides no procedure for their alteration.

The Section offers no assistance where the compromise or arrangement may be *ultra vires* the company. Clearly, a scheme cannot be sanctioned where it may usurp Cyprus law or be contrary to it, for example to convert issued ordinary shares into preference shares.

As indicated above, a scheme under Section 198 must be sanctioned by the court. Application is made by summons providing the information set out in Section 199 of the Companies Law. In deciding whether to exercise its jurisdiction and sanction a scheme, the court will normally need to be satisfied on three matters, as follows:

(a)   the provisions of the statute must have been complied with;
(b)   the class must have been fairly represented;
(c)   the arrangement must be such as a man of business would reasonably approve.

5.3.2   *Mergers and divisions of public companies under Section 201A–H*

Introduced in 2003, this Section supplements Sections 198–201 with respect to company reorganisations. Specifically it provides for:

(a)   a merger by absorption of one or more public companies by another public company;
(b)   the merging of public companies to create a new public company;
(c)   the division of public companies.

Furthermore this Section is a map of the merger and division procedure as follows:

(a)   It is stated in the Section that in cases of mergers the assets and the liabilities are transferred from the absorbed company to the absorbing company.
(b)   This Section sets out the steps that are necessary for mergers and divisions, namely:
  (i)   the directors of the participating companies are required to prepare a merger or division reorganisation plan, which should include the name, the form and the registered office of the company, the relationship of the transfer and exchange of the shares and the total of the merged amount in cash, how the shares will be distributed, the date after which the shares provide the right of participation in profits, the date after which the acts of the absorbed or divided company are considered to have been done on behalf of the absorbing or the benefited company, the rights that are guaranteed by the absorbed or the benefiting company and all the special privileges that are provided to the experts;
  (ii)   if the absorbing company already possesses less than 90 per cent of the shares of the absorbed company, this plan should be

accompanied by a detailed written report by the directors, which explains and justifies the plan financially, and this plan should be examined by independent experts who are appointed by the court;

(iii) the company should provide sufficient protection to all creditors.

5.3.3 *Amalgamations or reconstructions under Section 270*

This Section relates only to a members' voluntary winding up. It enables a company to be reconstructed by means of a sale or transfer of the whole or part of the business or assets of the transferor company to a transferee company in exchange for shares or other securities of the transferee company. In turn, the acquired shares or securities are distributed amongst the shareholders of the transferor company so that they become shareholders in the transferee company. The sale or transfer is carried out by the liquidator, who requires a special resolution of the shareholders of the transferor company as authority to proceed.

In effect, the assets and property of the transferor company have been absorbed by the transferee company; an amalgamation has taken place. The same principle applies where two or more companies are absorbed by another company incorporated for that purpose.

It should be noted that the transferee company need not be a company incorporated under the Companies Law. It may therefore be a foreign entity provided that it is defined as a company under the law of its place of origin.

Any sale or transfer pursuant to Section 270 is binding on all the members of the transferor company. However, members who do not vote in favour of the special resolution may within seven days of the resolution express their dissent by written notice addressed to the liquidator, requiring the liquidator either to abstain from carrying the special resolution into effect or to purchase their interests. If the liquidator proceeds with the scheme or proposes to do so, the shares of dissenting shareholders must be purchased before the company is dissolved. Accordingly, the liquidator will need to retain sufficient liquid reserves to discharge payment. The value of the shares of dissentients should be based on their value prior to the company's reconstruction.

Creditors of the transferor company remain its creditors. It is usually part of the amalgamation process under Section 270 for the transferee company to agree to meet the debts due to the creditors or for the transferor company to retain sufficient assets to satisfy them. However, statutory protection is, to a degree, afforded to creditors, providing, *inter alia*, that if within a year of the passing of the special resolution a winding up order is made by or subject to the supervision of the court, the special resolution will not be valid unless sanctioned by the court.

5.3.4 *Takeover bids under Section 201*

In simple terms this Section enables a company which has made what is commonly called a takeover bid for all the shares or a class of shares of a company and which has secured acceptance by 90 per cent or more of the holders of the target shares, to acquire the shares of dissenting members on the same terms, unless the dissenting shareholders succeed in persuading the court not to permit such acquisition.

This compulsory acquisition of shares must strictly follow the mechanism provided by Section 201.

5.3.5 Takeover bids under the 2007 Law on Public Takeovers

CySEC is designated as the competent authority to supervise the application of the new law and the related directives, which have significantly streamlined the takeover bid process and have entirely substituted and replaced the Cyprus Stock Exchange (Public Takeover Bids) Regulations of 1997–2006. The principal provisions of the law and its impact are set out below.

5.3.5.1   Article 36(1) "Squeeze out"

A bidder who has made an offer to all holders of the target company's securities for all of their securities has the right to require all the holders of any outstanding securities to sell him those securities if:

(a)   he holds securities representing at least 90 per cent of the capital carrying voting rights and at least 90 per cent of the voting rights in the target company; or

(b)   following acceptance of the bid, he has acquired or has firmly contracted to acquire securities representing at least 90 per cent of the target company's capital carrying voting rights and at least 90 per cent of the voting rights comprised in the bid.

In implementing Article 15(2) of the Takeover Directive, Cyprus chose not to avail itself of the option to set a higher threshold (up to 95 per cent) in the case referred to in (a) above.

The squeeze-out procedures under the new legal regime are much simpler than those available under Section 201 of the Companies Law. Once the offeror has acquired 90 per cent of the voting rights of the target company (including any shares in the target which it or its subsidiary held prior to the bid) it may exercise its right to squeeze out any remaining shareholders as soon as the offer period has expired (but in any event not later than three months thereafter).

The application to trigger the squeeze-out under the new law is made by the offeror to CySEC. If, *inter alia*, CySEC is satisfied that 90 per cent of the voting shares in the target have been attained by the offeror, it will authorise the offeror to proceed with the squeeze-out procedure to acquire the balance of the company's shares, subject of course to fulfilment by the offeror of certain conditions as to the payment to be made to the remaining shareholders. By contrast to Section 201, dissenting shareholders do not have the right to dispute the acquisition of their shares, although this does not preclude their right to take legal action to dispute the level of the consideration paid to them.

The procedural requirements to be followed to effect a transfer of shares under the squeeze-out provisions of the new law have not yet been finalised. Regulations to address this matter are currently in draft form and are expected to be issued by CySEC in the very near future.

5.3.5.2 Article 34(1) "Board neutrality"
Without the prior authorisation of a general meeting of shareholders, the board of a target company may not take any action which may result in the frustration of the bid, other than seeking alternative bids. This restriction applies from the time the board becomes aware of a possible takeover bid until the bid is withdrawn or annulled.

5.3.5.3 Article 35(1) "Breakthrough"
The Article gives a target company with a registered office in Cyprus the reversible option of dismantling any obstacles to being taken over, by decision of a general meeting of shareholders. These obstacles are set out in subparagraphs 2 to 6 of Article 35 and include restrictions on the transfer of shares, on voting rights and on multiple-vote securities. The decision of the general meeting must be immediately notified to CySEC and to the regulated markets in which the target company's securities have been or are intended to be traded.

5.3.5.4 Article 12(3) "Reciprocity"
The 2007 law allows reciprocity only for the breakthrough principle. Article 35(7) of the new bid law effectively reproduces Article 12(3) of the Takeover Directive and states that a company which respects the breakthrough rule may disapply that rule if it becomes the subject of an offer launched by another company which employs anti-takeover defences. That is subject to the authorisation of the general meeting of shareholders and applies only in relation to bids made 18 months after the relevant decision was made. The reciprocity rule is not applicable to cooperatives or to companies in which the Republic of Cyprus holds securities which confer special rights.

5.3.5.5 Article 13(1) "Mandatory bids"
Any person who, as a result of his own acquisition or the acquisition by persons acting in concert with him, holds securities of a company which, added to his existing holdings and those of persons acting in concert with him, directly or indirectly give him 30 per cent or more of voting rights in that company, is obliged to make a bid for the outstanding securities. Such a bid must be addressed immediately to all of the remaining shareholders for all of their securities at the "fair price" (*see* 5.3.5.7 below).

5.3.5.6 Article 37 "Sell-out right"
This provides protection for minority shareholders in a takeover situation. The sell-out right is exercisable under the same conditions as the squeeze-out right. If the bidder holds securities representing at least 90 per cent of the capital carrying voting rights and at least 90 per cent of the voting rights in the target company, or if, following acceptance of the bid, the bidder has acquired or has firmly contracted to acquire securities representing at least 90 per cent of the target company's capital carrying voting rights and at least 90 per cent of the voting rights comprised in the bid, the minority shareholders may require the bidder to buy their securities at the "fair price".

5.3.5.7   Article 18(1) "Fair price"

The fair price is set by CySEC. Article 18(1) stipulates that it must be not less than the highest price paid for the same securities by the bidder or by persons acting in concert with him during the 12 months before the announcement of the decision to launch the bid. CySEC may at its full discretion permit the payment of a lower price in case of voluntary takeover bids. However, the criteria for fixing that lower price are not identified in the law.

5.3.5.8   Funding of bids

Under the new law any public offer document must be accompanied by a "certain funds declaration" made by one or more Cyprus or other recognised European banking institutions.

5.4   Investment controls

The legal regime governing securities in Cyprus has been largely codified and harmonised with the relevant EU Directives. The principal items of legislation concerned are:

(a)   the Companies Law as amended;

(b)   the Cyprus Securities and Stock Exchange Laws of 1993–2000 ("the CSSE Law");

(c)   the Cyprus Securities and Stock Exchange Regulations of 1995 and 1997 ("the CSSE Regulations");

(d)   various regulations passed under the CSSE Law, including the Public Bids for Mergers and Acquisitions of Titles of Companies listed in the Cyprus Stock Exchange Regulations of 1997 ("the Mergers and Acquisitions Regulations");

(e)   the Cyprus Securities and Exchange Commission (Establishment and Responsibilities) Law of 2001, Section 5 of which established CySEC;

(f)   the Insider Dealing and Market Manipulation (Market Abuse) Law (Law 116(I) of 2005;

(g)   the Public Offers and Takeovers Law of 2007 (Law 41(I) of 2007);

(h)   the Cyprus Securities and Stock Exchange (Central Depository and Central Registry) Law of 1996;

(i)   the Trading Rules (Electronic System) 839/2003;

(j)   the Clearing and Settlement Rules 306/99;

(k)   the Cyprus Securities and Stock Exchange (Inserting, Trading and Settlement of Stocks) Law.

5.4.1   Disclosure of substantial holdings

5.4.1.1   Shareholders' and directors' duties

The CSSE Law, which has been considerably amended in the last few years, imposes an obligation on substantial shareholders, and those who by acting in concert have a substantial interest, in a quoted company to disclose their holdings and report subsequent transactions. This obligation applies where the relevant holdings have an aggregate value equal to or greater than 5 per cent of the company's securities. A person will be deemed to have a substantial holding in such securities as are held by a nominee, spouse or blood relative up to the second degree, or companies which he controls. To address the practice of "warehousing", there are "concert party" provisions under which persons will be regarded as acting in concert if there is an agreement or arrangement between them for the acquisition by any one or more of them of interests in securities of a particular public company. The disclosure requirement on acquisition of substantial holdings also extends to the company's board of directors, officers, auditors and any provident funds.

Deliberate or intentional non-compliance is a criminal offence punishable by imprisonment for up to two years, a fine of up to CYP5,000 (€8,550) or both.

The Mergers and Acquisitions Regulations contain additional disclosure and reporting requirements for substantial holdings.

5.4.1.2 *Companies' duties*
Under an amendment to the Companies Law enacted in 2000, a company may repurchase its own shares subject to the following conditions:

(a)   the purchase must have been authorised by a special resolution at an Annual General Meeting held not more than 12 months before the purchase;
(b)   the shares may not be held for more than two years;
(c)   where the shares are quoted on the Cyprus Stock Exchange, the acquisition price may not be more than 5 per cent above the average price of the shares during the last five days before the purchase.

Certain other conditions may also apply. However, none of the conditions applies to acquisitions made under a scheme of reduction of capital or under a court order for the protection of minority shareholders.

The amendment, originally enacted in order to enable public companies to repurchase their stock which was thought to be undervalued following the sudden slump in stock prices on the Cyprus Stock Exchange in 2000 and 2001, has not been as effective as was originally hoped. There are also legal gaps and uncertainties which have made it difficult to use this legislation, but elaboration of these points goes beyond the scope of this Guide.

A body corporate cannot be a member of a company which is its holding company, and any allotment or transfer of shares in a company to its subsidiary will be void. Moreover, it is illegal for a company, directly or indirectly, to give financial assistance for the acquisition of any of its shares or any shares in its holding company. It is therefore not possible for a company to acquire a substantial holding in itself. There is no "whitewash" procedure such as exists in the UK.

Under the CSSE Law, a company whose shares are listed on the Cyprus Stock Exchange is obliged to notify CySEC and the Council of the Stock Exchange of any commercial activity that it undertakes with its management or any other person with whom it is connected within seven days from the time that such activity is entered into where its value exceeds CYP50,000 (€85,500). This obligation is in addition to the provisions contained in the Companies Law relating to disclosure on the part of directors and certain other insiders, controlling such persons' involvement in substantial commercial transactions with the company and related companies and regulating the circumstances in which they may receive loans and other financial facilities.

The CSSE Law also imposes an obligation on a listed company to supply CySEC and the Council of the Stock Exchange immediately and on its own initiative with any information in its possession which may affect the value of its listed securities. A listed company which fails to comply with the disclosure requirements laid down in the CSSE Law may be delisted following a reasoned decision from the Council.

5.5   Foreign investment

In 2003, the Cyprus Government introduced the Movement of Capital Law, Law 115(I) of 2003. This effectively repealed the Exchange Control Law, and hence relaxed the restrictions on the movement of capital and payments between residents of Cyprus and other EU Member States and between residents of Cyprus and those of third countries. Restrictions on transactions in foreign currencies and gold within Cyprus were also reduced. Subject to limited exceptions, all such movements – including investments in immovable property, share transactions, loans and movement of personal capital – may be carried out without any restrictions.

5.5.1   *Investment from EU countries*

5.5.1.1   *Direct investment*
Except in a small number of areas (*see* 5.5.3 below) there are no restrictions on the amount of the investment made by EU investors in any kind of enterprise in Cyprus.

5.5.1.2   *Portfolio*
Up to 100 per cent of the share capital of a company listed on the Cyprus Stock Exchange may be acquired by investors from the EU. In the banking sector, the maximum non-resident participation, whether EU or not, is 50 per cent and no individual may own, directly or indirectly, more than 9 per cent of a bank's share capital without the approval of the Central Bank of Cyprus ("CBC").

5.5.2   *Investment from non-EU countries*

5.5.2.1   *Direct investment*
With effect from 1 October 2004 foreign direct investment in Cyprus from non-EU countries has been fully liberalised, and the minimum amounts of investment and the maximum percentages of participation have generally been abolished (*see* 5.5.3 below for exceptions), but licences may be still required for certain investment activities. There is no difference between companies carrying on business outside Cyprus (previously known as offshore or international business companies) and companies carrying on business inside Cyprus.

One of the practical effects of the liberalisation is that foreigners wishing to register companies in Cyprus or buy shares in existing Cyprus companies no longer need to seek approval from the CBC. Applications for such activities should be submitted directly to the Registrar of Companies. Applications for licences under the Movement of Capital Law should be made to the Ministry of Finance.

5.5.2.2 Portfolio

Up to 49 per cent of the share capital of a company listed on the Cyprus Stock Exchange may be acquired by non-EU investors. In the banking sector, the maximum equity participation is 50 per cent, as stated above, and no individual may own, directly or indirectly, more than 9 per cent of a bank's share capital without the Central Bank's approval.

5.5.3 Restricted investments

For nationals of both EU and non-EU countries, there are still restrictions on acquisitions in the areas of real estate, tertiary education, public utilities, radio and television stations, newspapers and magazines, and airlines. For nationals of non-EU countries there are also some restrictions on investment in the tourist sector. The current policy provides for participation of up to 49 per cent in projects such as hotels and tourist villages. For projects that enrich the tourist product, such as golf courses and theme parks, up to 100 per cent participation is permitted. Each restricted-investment application is considered on its merits.

5.5.4 Incentives

There are several incentives for locating a business in Cyprus, including:

(a) a favourable business environment, with highly educated personnel available at reasonable rates of pay and world-class infrastructure, support facilities and services;

(b) a virtual absence of exchange controls, allowing profits, interest and dividends from approved investments, capital invested and any capital gains from the disposal of shares in such investments to be freely remitted overseas;

(c) the accession of Cyprus to the EU on 1 May 2004 (and from 1 January 2008 the adoption of the euro as the currency of Cyprus), providing a base for the production and export of goods to the larger EU market;

(d) more than 40 double taxation treaties including many treaties with eastern European countries facilitating investment;

(e) a uniform low rate of corporation tax of 10 per cent applicable to all companies resident in Cyprus, as well as to resident branches of foreign companies. A company or a branch is considered resident if the locus of its control and management is in Cyprus, irrespective of the country of registration;

(f) industrial estates, and the Industrial Free Zone ("IFZ") near Larnaca close to the port and international airport, where industries can import their machinery, equipment and raw materials free of customs duty. Products manufactured in the IFZ may enter the Cyprus market on payment of the lowest preferential tariff;

(g)   bonded factories and warehouses, having the same customs status as the IFZ.

5.5.5   Recent developments

The Government of Cyprus has worked hard to ensure harmony between its domestic legislation and relevant EU directives. Significant legislative changes have included the following:

(a)   The Financial Services Firms Law, 148(I) of 2002, transposing the Investment Services Directive 93/22/EC, was enacted to regulate the licensing and supervision of financial and investment services in Cyprus, and to harmonise domestic legislation with EU law by introducing the free movement of investment services and reforming CySEC. This law regulates investment services provided by a Cyprus investment firm, a branch of a foreign investment firm and cross-border transactions within the EU, both on a freedom of services and a freedom of establishment basis, under the European Passport Benefit System with supervision by CySEC.

(b)   The adoption of the Prospectus Directive 2003/71, which regulates the laws in relation to the content and format of prospectuses. One of the major consequences of the Prospectus Directive has been the ability to raise capital in any of the EU Member States with the production of a single prospectus in the prescribed format. All prospectuses are now vetted and approved by a single competent authority.

(c)   Law 114(1) was introduced in 2005, concerning the admission of securities, the obligations of issuers and the information to be published in compliance with the above-mentioned Directive 2003/71.

(d)   Legislation to allow SEs to be formed was enacted in August 2006. Existing companies from other Member States may be merged into an SE in Cyprus without any tax cost, since Cyprus has fully implemented the EU Mergers Directive.

(e)   As stated at 5.3 above, Directive 2004/25 on takeover bids was implemented via the Law on Public Takeovers in 2007.

(f)   Directive 2004/39 on markets in financial instruments was transposed into Cyprus law by the Investment Services and Activities and Regulated Markets Law of 2007, Number 144(1) of 2007, which replaces the Investment Firms Law of 2002 with effect from 1 November 2007. As well as implementing MiFID the new law also harmonises domestic law with relevant European directives regarding investor compensation schemes; capital adequacy of investment firms and credit institutions; organisational requirements, operating conditions for investment firms and recordkeeping obligations for investment firms, transaction reporting, market transparency and admission of financial instruments to trading.

(g)   Council Directive 2001/86/EC of 8 October 2001 supplementing the statute for a European company with regard to the involvement of employees and Council Directive 94/45/EC of 22 September 1994 on the establishment of a European Works Council or a procedure in Community-scale undertakings and Community-scale groups of undertakings for the purposes of informing and consulting employees, as amended, have both been implemented with the enactment of Laws 227(I)/2004 and 68(I)/2002.

5.6 Merger control – general

Merger control is a relatively new area of law in Cyprus. The Merger Control Law, 22(I) of 1999, as amended by Law 107(I) of 1999 ("the Law"), came into effect in 2000. The Law is modelled on Council Regulation (EEC) 4064/89 as amended by Council Regulation (EC) 1310/97, adapted to conform with existing Cyprus competition rules and procedures. Another important development in the area of competition law (not merger control) was the adoption of the new Anti-Monopoly Directive 1/2003, which promotes healthy competition, since it gives an opportunity to companies to reach an agreement with the local Competition Committee.

5.6.1 *Jurisdictional thresholds*

Under Section 3 of the Merger Control Law a concentration of undertakings will be subject to the Law when:

(a)   the aggregate turnover of at least two of the undertakings exceeds CYP2 million (€3,440,000);
(b)   at least one of the undertakings has commercial activities within the Republic of Cyprus;
(c)   at least CYP2 million (€3,440,000) of the aggregate turnover of all the undertakings relates to the sale of goods or the offering of services within the Republic of Cyprus; or
(d)   the concentration is declared to be of major importance by the Minister of Commerce, Industry and Tourism under Section 8 of the Law.

The guidance provided by the Law in calculating the aggregate turnover makes no reference to whether it is limited to Cyprus or to the aggregate worldwide turnover. However, the threshold under Section 3(2)(a)(iii) of the Law specifically refers to an aggregate turnover of at least CYP2 million (€3,440,000) in the Republic of Cyprus, which would seem to suggest that the aggregate turnover referred to in Section 3(2)(a)(i) of the Law relates to the worldwide turnover of the participating undertakings. The Law does not define the term "commercial activities" under Section 3(2)(a)(ii), but the approach adopted seems to be narrow and conservative.

By virtue of Section 3(2)(b) of the Law, taken in conjunction with Section 8, the Minister of Commerce, Industry and Tourism has the power to bring a concentration within the ambit of the Law if it is considered to be of major importance, regardless of whether the concentration meets the criteria outlined in Section 3(2)(a). Section 36 of the Law provides some guidance as to what may amount to "a concentration of major importance" in that it refers to concentrations which will have an effect on economic or social development, technical progress, employment, or the supply of goods and services necessary for public safety in the Republic or part thereof.

5.6.2   Types of transactions

The requirements of the Law must be complied with where a takeover or merger involves undertakings established outside Cyprus if and to the extent that this arrangement creates or strengthens a dominant position in the affected market within the Republic of Cyprus (Section 10 of the Law). Section 2 of the Law defines a dominant position as:

> "a position of economic strength enjoyed by an undertaking which enables it to prevent effective competition in the relevant product or service market and to behave to an appreciable extent independently of its competitors and customers and ultimately its consumers."

The Law was silent as to the imposition of any requirement for foreign companies to have a physical presence in Cyprus to come within the scope of the Law. As stated above, the criterion for deciding whether a particular concentration may be given clearance or not is the extent to which this arrangement creates or strengthens a dominant position in the affected market within the Republic of Cyprus.

5.6.3   Mandatory nature of merger control rules

Notification of the concentration is mandatory, and the time limits are expressly set out in the Law. Concentrations which meet the criteria mentioned above must be notified to the Competition and Consumer Protection Service ("the Competition Authority") not more than a week after the date of the conclusion of an agreement, the announcement of a public bid or the acquisition of a controlling interest, whichever event occurs first.

Once a concentration has been notified and the relevant documentation filed, the Competition Authority has one month to carry out a preliminary examination of the compatibility of the concentration with competitive market requirements. The period of one month may be extended by 14 days, depending on the workload of the Competition Authority. At the end of its preliminary examination, the Competition Authority will send a reply to the Competition Committee. This is stage one.

If the Competition Committee decides that the concentration falls within the scope of the Law and that there are serious doubts about its compatibility with competitive market requirements, the Competition Committee refers the case back to the Competition Authority for full examination. This is stage two. In this event, the Competition Authority has three months from the date of the notification to it to report its findings to the Competition Committee. However, this period may be extended depending on any complications that may arise in the process.

5.6.4 *Suspension of concentrations prior to implementation*

Under Section 9 of the Law, a concentration cannot be implemented until clearance is given or is deemed to be given by reason of the relevant authorities failing to comply with the limits set out in the Law. In cases where the investigation of the concentration proceeds to stage two, the undertakings concerned may apply for temporary clearance. If the Competition Committee is satisfied that the undertakings would incur serious damage from delays in implementing the concentration, temporary conditional or unconditional clearance may be granted, without prejudice to the final decision of the Competition Committee.

5.6.5 *Exemptions*

Apart from threshold requirements that bring the provisions of the Law into effect, Section 4(5) of the Law provides for four specific instances where a concentration is deemed not to exist:

(a)   credit, finance, insurance or other organisations with similar activities that are involved in the trading of shares for themselves or third parties as part of their activities and have acquired a company for the purpose of holding their shares temporarily and disposing of them within one year. To fall within this exemption, the organisation in question must not exercise the voting rights that these shares may have in order to determine any issues that may affect the acquired company's competitive position;

(b)   control is exercised by a person empowered by legislative provisions involving the winding up or liquidation of the company in question;

(c)   the activities mentioned above are being exercised by portfolio management companies;

(d)   the shares have been acquired by inheritance.

5.6.6 *Penalties for non-compliance*

The Competition Authority may impose financial penalties of up to CYP50,000 (€85,500) for each breach of the Law, depending on the circumstances of each case, with an additional fine of CYP5,000 (€8,550) for each day that the breach continues, or a fine of up to 10 per cent of the total revenue of the concentration.

5.7   Merger control – listed companies

The Public Takeovers Law of 2007 applies to mergers and acquisitions of publicly listed companies. The Law is based on the relevant EU Directives, harmonising Cyprus law with the *acquis communautaire* in this area of law. The Law applies only to companies whose securities are listed and traded on the Cyprus Stock Exchange or another regulated market.

5.7.1 *Procedure*

CySEC is responsible for supervising the application and enforceability of the rules concerning mergers and acquisitions of publicly listed companies. These stipulate that any legal or natural person or group of investors acquiring more than 30 per cent of a target company's stock are generally obligated to submit a public offer for the acquisition of the entire stock or shares of the target company. Once this threshold is reached they must immediately notify both the target company's board of directors and CySEC and thereafter notify the public of the acquisition of such a stake and their intention to make a public offer.

The obligation for the submission of a public offer may be waived by CySEC where the acquirer already possessed in excess of 50 per cent of a listed company's shares or where the shares were acquired by way of gift, succession due to death, the sale of pledged shares, a declaration of trust or the issue of new shares under certain conditions.

5.7.2 *Timetable*

The following time frame is stipulated by the Public Takeovers Law of 2007:

(a) Within 12 working days of the announcement of the offeror's decision to make a public takeover bid, a document providing details of the bid together with a "certain funds" declaration must be submitted to CySEC and the board of directors of the target company and, once approved by CySEC the offeror must announce this fact and advertise CySEC's approval in at least two daily national newspapers as soon as possible.

(b) The Council is required to issue its decision as to its approval of the public offer document within eight working days of its filing, unless further information has been requested from the offeror. The deadline for acceptance of the relevant offer is specified by the offeror in the public bid document. This deadline must be not earlier than 30 days and not later than 55 days from the day on which the document was made available to the shareholders of the target company. In the event of a review of the bid, the stated deadline may be extended up to 70 days from the day on which the document was made available to the target shareholders or any greater period that CySEC determines.

(c) Any counter offer must be made prior to the beginning of the fourteenth day before the deadline set for acceptance of the initial public bid. Within 48 hours after the deadline for acceptance of the offer, the results of the public bids must be announced by the offeror to each of the following:
 (i)   the Cyprus Stock Exchange;
 (ii)   CySEC;
 (iii) on its own website (if it has one); and
 (iv)   the board of directors of the Target.
 On the day following the announcement, the offeror must publish the results in two national daily newspapers.

5.8   Directors' fiduciary duties

Directors owe fiduciary duties to shareholders in the course of a takeover bid when they are advising them whether to accept or reject a bid. These clearly include a duty to be honest and a duty not to mislead. In the case of *International*

Ltd v *Lord Grade (sub nom Re ACC)* (1983) BCLC 244 it was held that when directors have decided that it is in the best interests of their company that it should be taken over and when there are two or more bidders, the only duty they owe to the company is to obtain the best price. When they must decide between rival bidders, the interests of the company must be the interests of the current shareholders. The directors do not owe a duty to the successful bidder. In *Morgan Crucible Co. plc* v *Hill Samuel & Co. Ltd* (1991) 1 All ER 148 it was held that if during a takeover directors make representations to a bidder, they owe a duty to the bidder not to be inaccurate or negligent.

5.9   Transfer of shares

5.9.1   General

The articles of association of a company normally regulate the way in which its shares may be transferred.

5.9.2   Public companies

The Cyprus Companies Law defines a public company as a company which is not a private company. Since, as noted in 5.2 above, one of the fundamental characteristics of a private company is a restriction on members' ability to transfer their shares, it follows that public companies may not impose any restrictions on share transfers.

5.9.3   Private companies

The Companies Law provides that, unless excluded or modified by its articles, the regulations contained in Table A in the First Schedule to the Companies Law will control the transfer of the shares of a Cyprus company.

Table A does not include a right of pre-emption or a right of first refusal on a transfer of shares, but it is the normal practice for Cyprus companies to include such rights in their articles.

Part II of Table A empowers the directors of a company, in their absolute discretion and without giving any reason, to decline to register any transfer of shares.

5.10   Conclusion

Takeovers and mergers are becoming increasingly significant in Cyprus due to the island's continuing development as an international business centre and in view of the widespread use of Cyprus companies as intermediate holding and finance vehicles for the routing of investments to various countries.

It has therefore become necessary for Cyprus companies, in order to expand their activities, to seek either loan or equity finance in established financial markets and many of them have become takeover or merger targets of substantial overseas concerns. This important international element has been a significant driving factor for the development of a sound structure of corporate law in general and for takeovers and mergers in particular.

The fact that the legal system of Cyprus has a substantial common law element, largely inherited from English law, is extremely positive and advantageous because it enables banks and other financial institutions and foreign lawyers to understand the Cyprus system readily.

Significant factors contributing to the attraction of Cyprus as an international business centre are the fact that Cyprus company law is based on that of the UK, and that corporate financial legislation is constantly being amended or replaced as part of the Government's ongoing commitment to implement all relevant EU Directives. However, as always, more needs to be done. In particular there is a need for a comprehensive law on insolvency. Such developments, coupled with a clear policy of implementation by the regulators of all changes in the corporate sector, will play a large part in consolidating Cyprus's position as an international business centre in the area.

Chapter 6
Czech Republic

Ivo Bárta
Partner
White & Case[1]

6.1 Introduction

Until the early 1990s not only were there no mergers and acquisitions in the Czech Republic, there were no companies and no corporate or commercial law. Following the collapse of the Communist regime in 1989, the country began to build its entire commercial law system from scratch. The outcome was a mixture of pre-World War II Czechoslovakian law and present-day German and Austrian law.

The Commercial Code,[2] the main body of law concerned with corporations and commercial transactions, was adopted in 1991 and came into effect on 1 January 1992. It introduced a relatively simple and liberal regime, although often superficial and not always cohesive. What it lacked was a tradition of implementation including case law and experienced business people, lawyers and judges.

Simultaneously the country implemented a "large privatisation" programme, massive in scale, using coupons. During the early 1990s millions of Czechs invested their coupons in thousands of companies that were there for the taking. Somewhat unexpectedly, the vast majority of the coupons and, consequently, control of most of the companies in the privatisation process was amassed by newly established privatisation funds. After two waves of coupon privatisation the country had acquired, practically overnight, hundreds of privatisation (investment) funds, several thousand listed companies and millions of small shareholders.

The years that followed saw hard-fought battles for control of the privatised companies and the privatisation funds controlling them. In the absence of proper legal protection and enforcement, small investors, especially in the investment funds, were often mistreated. The capital market suffered heavily even before it had a chance to begin functioning properly.

In the second half of the 1990s Czech legislators reacted. The first major amendments to the Commercial Code and securities laws were seen in 1996, and in

---

[1] With thanks to Václav Jerman (partner), Irena Bílá, Eva Svobodová and Ivo Janda (associates) for their contributions.
[2] Act no. 513/1991 Coll., the Commercial Code, as amended.

1998 the Securities Commission was established. Further significant changes to corporate legislation, mostly related to the implementation of EU directives, followed after 2000 and more of them are in the pipeline. Protection of minority shareholders became a serious issue, although effective measures to enforce that protection were still lacking. In 2006, the Securities Commission was replaced by the Czech National Bank (the "CNB").

Due partly to the continued presence of thousands of small investors in most of the companies privatised during the 1990s and partly to lingering old liabilities, foreign investors often preferred to acquire assets or parts of a business rather than shares in a target company.

However, a number of the transactions that took place between 1990 and 2007 would be considered fair and standard by any criteria. The vast majority of transactions involving foreign investors were carried out in a manner more or less similar to that in western countries. Since the late 1990s certain high-profile and more sophisticated merger and acquisition schemes have developed, with the emphasis being on ethical conduct, transparency and fairness.

6.2   Acquisition targets

Czech companies attracting private investors can be divided into the following three categories:

(a)   companies listed on the Prague Stock Exchange or RM-System (the Czech regulated electronic stock trading system);
(b)   unlisted companies with a large number of shareholders owning small (non-controlling) numbers of shares (often delisted companies, formerly privatised through coupon schemes); and
(c)   all other (private) companies.

The Commercial Code distinguishes between the following corporate forms:

(a)   a joint stock company (*akciová společnost, akc. spol., a.s.*);
(b)   a limited liability company (*společnost s ručením omezeným, spol. s r.o., s.r.o.*);
(c)   a general commercial partnership (*veřejná obchodní společnost, veř. obch. spol., v.o.s.*);
(d)   a limited partnership (*komanditní společnost, kom. spol., k.s.*);
(e)   a European Company;[3] and
(f)   a European Economic Interest Grouping (EEIG).[4]

---

[3] Council Regulation no. 2157/2001 of 8 October 2001 on the Statute for a European Company. With effect as of December 2004, Act no. 627/2004 Coll. on the European Company implemented Council Directive 2001/86/EC of 8 October 2001, supplementing the Statute for a European Company with regard to the involvement of employees.
[4] With effect as of June 2004 (certain provisions since October 2004), Act no. 360/2004 Coll. on the European Economic Interest Grouping ("EEIG") implemented Council Directive 2137/85/EEC of 25 July 1985, on the EEIG.

Other types of legal entity also exist, such as a cooperative, a European Co-operative Society ("SCE"),[5] a state enterprise, an association and various entities established under separate laws. However, only a joint stock company and a European Company may have listed shares and a dispersed base of shareholders having only a few shares (so-called "small shareholders"). Unless stated otherwise, this Chapter refers only to joint stock companies.

6.2.1 Listed companies

Czech law does not use the term "public company". The term is often used to denote either a listed company or an unlisted company with a dispersed shareholder base. It is worth remembering that most Czech public companies only became "public" through coupon privatisation. The few true examples of initial public offerings of shares in the Czech Republic were done using Dutch or Luxembourg holding companies.

Companies that have shares listed on an official market in the Czech Republic are called "listed companies". There are two Czech official markets on which listed shares are traded: the Prague Stock Exchange and the RM-System. Listed companies are extensively regulated and acquisition of their shares is also subject to regulation.

In parallel with the strengthening of market regulation, the Czech official markets made efforts to delist companies that would not qualify for trading under normal circumstances, for example due to insufficient market capitalisation, thin trading or failure to comply with disclosure requirements. The number of listed companies is also steadily decreasing due to the delisting of shares initiated by the majority shareholders of certain companies formerly traded on the official markets.

6.2.2 Other companies with small shareholders

Companies that fall into the second category are usually those whose shares were once traded on the Czech public markets but were then excluded from trading by the relevant market itself or delisted following a decision of the company's majority shareholders.

Subject to certain exceptions (the most important of which is the duty to make a mandatory buy-out of minority shareholders by a shareholder acquiring a certain share of voting rights in a listed target company – *see* also 6.8.4 below), minority shareholders in both listed and unlisted companies benefit from substantially the same protections established by the Commercial Code. The same rules apply generally to all companies, regardless of whether or not they are listed or have minority shareholders, save for the fact that corporate

---

[5] With effect as of August 2006, Act no. 307/2006 Coll. on a European Cooperative Society ("SCE") implemented Council Regulation (EC) no. 1435/2003 of 22 July 2003, on the SCE and Council Directive 2003/72/EC of 22 July 2003, supplementing the Statute for a European Cooperative Society with regard to the involvement of employees.

governance regulation in unlisted companies is somewhat less stringent. Also, the level of the information obligation of listed companies is much higher.

6.2.3 All other companies

Joint stock companies form a minority of Czech companies. The main corporate form is the limited liability company. Most joint stock companies are not listed.

Historically, most acquisitions in the Czech corporate environment have required the prior approval of the controlling shareholders. Moreover, there have been no hostile takeovers so far, although battles for a majority interest in privatised companies during the 1990s sometimes produced similar results.

6.3   Foreign exchange and investment controls

6.3.1   Foreign exchange controls

The Czech Republic has been gradually phasing down its foreign exchange controls since the beginning of the 1990s. Only a few, relatively insignificant, burdens are now placed on a foreign investor investing in the Czech Republic or on a Czech company doing regular business abroad. The remaining restrictions concern, for example, the right of non-resident foreigners to acquire real estate; in the case of EU-resident foreigners this restriction applies only to agricultural and forest land in the Czech Republic. However, non-resident foreigners are not limited in setting up Czech entities which can, in turn, own any real estate in the Czech Republic.

6.3.2   Controls on investments

As a rule, no foreign investment authorisations are required in the Czech Republic. Investments in certain industries, particularly in the financial and insurance sectors, may require prior approval by the relevant supervisory authorities (e.g., the CNB in the case of banks and securities dealers), such approval being applicable to Czechs and foreigners alike. The advantageous EU rules on single passport apply to entities with the seat within the EU.

6.3.3   Disclosure of significant shareholdings

One of the changes introduced into Czech law during the late 1990s imposed an obligation to disclose significant shareholdings in listed companies (which, for these purposes, also include companies with shares listed on an official market in any EU Member State) and certain changes to those shareholdings.

This provision stipulates that any person who:

(a)   acquires any voting rights in a listed company having its seat in the Czech Republic, resulting in an increase of that shareholder's total percentage voting rights in the company to 5 per cent (or 3 per cent in the case of companies having a registered capital in excess of CZK100 million), 10, 15, 20, 25, 30, 40, 50 or 75 per cent; or

(b)   decreases their share of the voting rights in the target company below any of these thresholds,

must notify the target company and the CNB. The same obligation applies to any person holding at least 5 per cent of voting rights in a Czech target company when the company's shares are admitted for trading on an official market in the Czech Republic or any EU member state for the first time. The CNB then publishes that information.

However, no such notification is required if:

(a)   the shares being transferred are book-entry shares registered with the central depositary (the centralised register of book-entry securities in the Czech Republic);[6]

(b)   the acquiring person's share of the voting rights can be determined directly from the records of the central depositary; and

(c)   the acquiring person has concluded a contract with the central depositary, by which the latter undertakes to perform this reporting duty towards the target company and the CNB.

The notification is also not required from:

(a)   a person controlled by another person which fulfilled the reporting duty;

(b)   a securities broker (with a permit of the CNB); or

(c)   an owner of shares in an investment fund.

The disclosure statement must be presented to both designated recipients within three business days after the disclosing party discovers or should have discovered that the qualifying acquisition or disposal has occurred. It is sufficient if the disclosure statement is posted within this time period.

Should the disclosing party be late in fulfilling its notification duty, the acquisition or disposal will still be valid, but such party may not exercise any voting rights conferred by the newly acquired shares until the proper notification is given. The notification duty applies also to persons acting "in concert" when transferring shares amongst themselves, even if the aggregate shareholding of these persons did not change.

6.3.4   *Notification to the Government*

Apart from the approvals and notifications described at 6.3.2 and 6.3.3 above, Anti-Trust Office filings, notifications in connection with takeovers or squeeze-outs and certain reports of management trades under insider trading laws, if applicable, no other notifications need be made to the Government with respect to any transaction involving the acquisition of shares in a Czech company.

6.3.5   *Acquiring control over a listed company*

Any person who acquires control of a listed company must, within 60 days of acquiring such control, offer to purchase the remaining equity securities in that

---

[6] Until the creation of the central depositary, its functions are being performed by the Securities Centre.

company from the minority shareholders. In certain limited circumstances the CNB may grant the acquirer an exemption. The procedure regarding public offers is described at 6.8 below.

6.3.6 Labour law considerations

Under the Labour Code, prior to transferring labour law rights and obligations, both the acquiring and the disposing employer are obliged to inform and consult with the trade unions, employees' council or the respective employees about the timing, reasons and impact of the transfer and planned measures affecting the employees.

The Commercial Code and the Czech Labour Code both contain provisions similar in concept, pursuant to which all employees' labour law rights and obligations are transferred to the new (acquiring) employer in the event that the former employer transfers its business (enterprise) or part thereof as a going concern or in the case of reorganisation of companies (i.e., mergers and de-mergers). The Labour Code expands this principle to certain asset transactions similar in effect to transfers of business or part thereof as a going concern. The Czech Republic has already implemented EU Directive No. 77/187/EEC concerning the protection of the rights of employees in the case of merger transactions.

Under the Commercial Code, the board of directors of a target company is obliged to inform employees' representatives about the offeror's decision to launch a tender offer for the company's shares and to provide them with relevant documents together with the board of directors' statutory opinion on the tender offer.

6.4 Merger control

The legal framework for mergers is primarily contained in the Commercial Code. The competition element of mergers is regulated by the Competition Act,[7] which replaced its predecessor from 1991. The new Competition Act took effect on 1 July 2001 and was significantly amended in 2004 in order to harmonise Czech competition rules with EU Merger Control Regulations.

The Competition Act regulates competition on the products and services markets and protects those markets against:

(a)   agreements of competitors that may lead to the elimination or restriction of effective competition;
(b)   the misuse of dominant position;
(c)   concentrations of undertakings (competitors); and
(d)   transactions that have occurred abroad but which tend to distort or threaten to distort competition in the territory of the Czech Republic.

---

[7] Act no. 143/2001 Coll., on Protection of Economic Competition and on the Change of Certain Acts, as amended.

If a transaction has a community dimension, it will be subject to EU merger control rules.

6.4.1 Thresholds for mandatory notification

Under the Competition Act, the Anti-Trust Office must be notified of and approve any concentration of undertakings that exceeds the following thresholds:

(a) an aggregate net turnover of all undertakings concerned for the last accounting period in the Czech market in excess of CZK1.5 billion and at least two of the undertakings concerned having achieved a net turnover of at least CZK250 million each during the last accounting period in the Czech market; or

(b) a net turnover, achieved on the Czech market during the last accounting period, by:
   (i) a participant in the merger,
   (ii) the target enterprise,
   (iii) the target entity, or
   (iv) at least one of the establishers of a joint venture,
   in excess of CZK1.5 billion and an aggregate worldwide net turnover during the last accounting period of another participant in the concentration in excess of CZK1.5 billion.

Under the Competition Act, concentrations include:

(a) mergers;
(b) acquisitions of enterprises from other persons or substantial parts thereof;
(c) acquisitions of direct or indirect control over other persons by one or more persons; and
(d) joint ventures.

6.4.2 Procedure

Concentrations falling within the scope of the Competition Act are subject to the prior approval of the Anti-Trust Office. In coming to a decision, the Anti-Trust Office will consider whether the concentration would significantly impede competition on the relevant market (taking into account the necessity of preserving and further development of effective competition), the structure of all affected markets, the respective market shares of the parties to the concentration, and their respective economic and financial power.

If a proposed concentration meets the threshold requirements, the Anti-Trust Office must be notified of the transaction by:

(a) all parties intending to jointly implement the concentration by transformation or acquisition of an existing enterprise, or a part thereof, or by establishing a joint venture; or

(b) a single undertaking that is about to acquire control of another undertaking directly or indirectly.

Unlike the previous law, the current Competition Act does not provide for deadlines by which the transaction must be notified to the Anti-Trust Office. However, the transaction may not be implemented before it is approved. Undertakings may actually notify the Anti-Trust Office even before the agreement establishing the concentration is concluded.

The notification must cite the reasons for the concentration and all information relevant to the approval process, including specific documents evidencing certain facts concerning the concentration.

The Anti-Trust Office announces the commencement of concentration approval proceedings in the *Commercial Gazette* upon receipt of the complete notification ("the Commencement Day"). It also stipulates the period of time within which objections to the concentration may be filed. Upon receipt of the proposal, or otherwise if it deems it necessary, the Anti-Trust Office may order an oral hearing at which witnesses may be heard.

The Anti-Trust Office is obliged to decide whether a concentration is properly subject to its approval within 30 days of the Commencement Day. In the event that the Anti-Trust Office finds, within that time period, that the concentration is potentially liable to constitute a significant impediment to competition, it will provide the parties with a statement on its findings and continue with the proceedings. In this case, the Anti-Trust Office is obliged to issue its final decision on the concentration within five months of the Commencement Day.

The prohibition to implement the transaction does not apply to concentrations resulting from a tender offer or due to transactions with listed securities, provided that the approval proceedings are filed for immediately and the voting rights are not used. The Anti-Trust Office must decide, within 30 days, about the approval of an exception from the general prohibition to implement the transaction.

In all of the cases mentioned above, if the Anti-Trust Office fails to issue its decision within the prescribed period it is deemed to have approved the concentration.

Upon the request of the Anti-Trust Office, the parties or undertakings concerned are also obliged to provide additional information and documents and the deadline for the Anti-Trust Office to issue its decision is extended by the amount of time elapsing between the parties' or undertakings' receipt of the request for supplemental information and delivery of all the required documents to the full satisfaction of the Anti-Trust Office. Such extensions are not limited in number or in time and the Anti-Trust Office uses them frequently.

In its decision approving the transaction, the Anti-Trust Office may impose certain obligations on the parties or undertakings concerned, in the interests of preserving effective competition, provided, however, that such obligations were suggested by the parties before the commencement of or during the proceedings but not later than the deadlines set forth in the Competition Act.

The Anti-Trust Office may revoke its decision if its approval was based on false or incomplete information or because of a subsequent breach by the parties or undertakings of the obligations (conditions or restrictions) stipulated in the decision. The Anti-Trust Office may initiate revocation proceedings within one year of its discovery of such facts, but at the latest within five years of such events having occurred.

In the event that the parties or undertakings implement a concentration without the required notification to the Anti-Trust Office, the Anti-Trust Office may demand the sale of the business interest, the transfer of the business or any part thereof, the termination of the concentration agreement or any other action that may be deemed appropriate in order to restore conditions of effective competition.

6.4.3   Appeals

Any decision issued by the Anti-Trust Office may be appealed to the chairman of the Anti-Trust Office within 15 days of its delivery. The chairman renders a decision on the appeal on the basis of a proposal prepared by a special competition committee established for each individual appeal case. The chairman's final decision may be appealed to the Regional Court in Brno. This appeal must be made within two months of the delivery of the final decision of the Anti-Trust Office.

6.4.4   Sanctions

The Anti-Trust Office may impose fines of up to CZK10 million or up to 10 per cent of the net annual turnover of the parties or undertakings concerned if they are found to have breached the Competition Act. In addition, it can impose a fine of up to CZK1 million for failure to comply with an enforceable decision. The Anti-Trust Office is also entitled to impose fines on parties or undertakings providing incomplete, inaccurate or false information, failing to submit required documents or otherwise refusing to submit to investigation (up to CZK300,000) or on parties or undertakings which intentionally, or through negligence, fail to attend a scheduled oral hearing (up to CZK100,000).

6.5   Regulation of the conduct of mergers and acquisitions

Effective from 1 April 2006, the CNB was appointed to act as the independent administrative authority for the Czech capital market. Its predecessor was the Securities Commission, in existence since 1998. The CNB's main governing body is the Bank Board. The Board has seven members, including the governor and two vice-governors, all of whom are appointed by the President of the Czech Republic.

The tasks of the CNB in the supervision of the capital markets include the regulation of tender offers (applicable to both listed and unlisted shares) and the listing or issuance of listed shares or supervision of squeeze-outs. The CNB is authorised to impose penalties and use other means, including, for instance, the suspension of voting rights of an entity failing to comply with the tender offer regulations. The CNB is also empowered to issue generally binding regulations to implement certain provisions of the Capital Markets Act.[8]

The CNB may be contacted at the following address: Na Příkopě 28, 115 03 Prague 1, Czech Republic, telephone: +420 224 411 111 or +420 800 160 170, e-mail: info@cnb.cz or podatelna@cnb.cz (for electronic filing of documents).

6.6   Methods of acquisition

6.6.1   *Private agreements*

Despite the fact that Czech law has traditionally been continental in character, the documentation implementing the most important corporate transactions, such as mergers and acquisitions or securities transactions, tends to be Anglo-Saxon in style. This is due mainly to the London-trained investment bankers and the takeover of a substantial portion of the high-profile segment of the local legal market by US and UK law firms, which then rapidly spread their standard procedures and style of drafting across central and eastern Europe.

After 15 years of experience, the bigger and more sophisticated Czech law firms have also shifted towards traditional US- or UK-style purchase agreements, although usually simplifying them and combining them with standard Czech law document templates. The resulting product still depends, to a large extent, on the background of the specific lawyer preparing the document.

Another important reason for following the Anglo-Saxon style of documentation was the hope that this would compensate for the lack of express legal regulation under Czech law. The current Czech commercial, civil and securities laws still only inadequately reflect the requirements of modern corporate transactions. Without the proper contractual safeguards, a purchaser cannot be sure that he is protected not only against factual or legal defects concerning the acquired shares, but also against those that concern the underlying assets. Indeed, the acquisition of securities or assets as they stand, without effective guarantees as to their future adverse development, was long the tradition in the Czech environment.

Thanks to internationally experienced lawyers introducing representations and warranties, covenants and events of default clauses into the contractual documentation, transactions involving a foreign element tend to resemble those commonly used in the original Anglo-Saxon environment, although in an abridged form. Many of these Anglo-Saxon concepts have not been tested before the Czech courts, and it remains to be seen if they will indeed provide effective protection in judicial proceedings.

Private share purchase agreements usually provide that the time limit for claims to be brought for breach of warranty is up to four years (for breaches that are subject to the regular statute of limitations) whilst claims of a governmental nature, such as taxes or social security payments, may be subject to up to a

---

[8]   Act no. 256/2004 Coll., on Conducting Business on the Capital Markets, as amended.

10-year limitation period. In transactions involving privatisation, environmental or restitution (real estate) matters, it is not unusual to see provision for some claims unlimited in time.

Since the late 1990s there has been a tendency towards a more formalistic approach in Czech law supported by the practice of the Czech courts, which often focus on the formal elements of a case rather than its merits. Increasingly, a notary public is required for the execution of documents concerning real estate and corporate issues. The use of the Czech language in contracts is not mandatory, even among Czech individuals and corporate entities. However, Czech entities can choose a foreign governing law for their contracts only if they can sufficiently establish the presence of a foreign element in the transaction.

6.6.2 *Voluntary public offers*

Czech law contains provisions regarding voluntary public offers for companies. These provisions are explained at 6.8 below.

6.6.3 *Mandatory public offers*

Czech law also contains provisions that make it mandatory for certain shareholders of public companies to launch public offers in specific circumstances. These provisions are explained at 6.8.4 below.

6.6.4 *Mergers and split-ups*

Although basic rules concerning mergers and split-ups of companies were described in the Commercial Code from its inception in 1992, they were too cursory to constitute a comprehensive or adequate regulatory regime. This shortcoming was partially corrected in 1996 and then again by a series of amendments at the beginning of this decade. Now it could be said that the pendulum has swung too far in the other direction, resulting in a new set of rules too complex and burdensome to implement.

Legally, a merger or split-up becomes effective only as of the day when it is duly entered into the Commercial Register, while the application for the entry into the Commercial Register must be filed within nine months of the so-called "decisive day". The decisive day is determined by the parties involved, but it is usually the first day of the new financial year of the companies involved, in order to avoid the need to prepare another set of audited accounts.

In mergers and split-ups either the entire or a distinguishable part of assets and liabilities is transferred from one company to another. The transfer of all assets and liabilities is based on the principle of "dissolution without liquidation", the result of which is the dissolution of the predecessor company while its shareholders receive shares in the successor company. The exception is a so-called "spin-off de-merger", introduced into the Commercial Code by an amendment effective as of March 2006, in which the divided company does not cease to exist and only the selected part of its assets are transferred to an existing or a newly established successor company or companies.

As a rule, the decision to merge or split a company must be approved by the general meeting of each company concerned, such approvals generally requiring an affirmative vote of shareholders having at least three-quarters of all votes present at the general meeting. If a company has more classes of shares outstanding, a separate vote by each class of shares is required.

6.6.5 *Joint ventures*

Czech law does not contain any special legal regime or procedure for establishing joint ventures. Although joint ventures are not uncommon in the Czech environment, most foreign investors prefer a clear corporate governance structure, leaving no doubts as to who the ultimate decision-making shareholder is. This preference may be partially explained by the history of mistreatment of minority shareholders in Czech companies and the lack of confidence in enforcement of contractual obligations.

Despite the above, shareholders agreements are numerous. However, it is necessary to bear in mind that shareholders agreements are, to a large extent, an untested instrument in the Czech courts and that Czech law does not often recognise the equitable concept of "specific performance". Often only monetary damages are available to a party claiming breach of a shareholders agreement.

6.6.6 *Asset transactions*

Acquisition of assets is a legal structure that is often used in the Czech Republic, especially by investors who intend to:

(a)   "cherry pick" certain assets;
(b)   avoid unpredictable or potentially costly liabilities;
(c)   achieve different tax consequences for a transaction; or
(d)   avoid mandatory tender offers (in connection with the sale of shares).

Under Section 67a of the Commercial Code, in the event of a conclusion of an agreement on a transfer, lease or a pledge of a business (or a part thereof), it is necessary to obtain an approval of the participants or the general meeting of the company. In practice, it is therefore necessary to decide whether a transfer of certain assets amounts to the "transfer of a part of a business", which may, in certain cases, be difficult.

From the technical point of view, asset transactions are generally lengthier and require more preparatory work, but this may be outweighed in terms of reduced risks and liabilities for the client. An asset deal usually consists of a number of separate agreements concerning:

(a)   real estate, including easements, long-term leases and pre-emptive rights to real estate;
(b)   movable assets, including machinery, stock and work in progress;
(c)   assignments of receivables and assumption of liabilities, including the conclusion of new agreements with principal suppliers and customers;
(d)   registered intellectual property;

(e)   miscellaneous service agreements, usually with the seller keeping the assets that remain in the former large industrial unit; and

(f)   termination of old and the conclusion of new employment agreements with the employees who leave the old employer to join the new one.

Like mergers or sale of a business (or its part) as a going concern, asset transactions that produce similar effects may trigger the automatic transfer of employees. A potential obstacle to any asset deal is the limited transferability of certain governmental licences and permits (e.g., telecommunication or banking licences).

Needless to say, in addition to other legal considerations, such as assumption of unwanted liabilities, tax issues are often the driving force behind the choice of a specific transaction structure. The tax treatment of a share deal compared to an asset deal may differ substantially, and it is always advisable to get proper advice regarding Czech and foreign tax implications before entering into any deal.

6.7   Preparation of an offer

6.7.1   *Preliminary steps and conduct of negotiations*

In the current Czech environment, acquisitions vastly outnumber mergers. Also, private transactions by far outnumber transactions involving listed companies. The form of these transactions largely depends on the parties involved (especially where foreign investors are concerned), the experience of such parties and their choice of advisers. Although the Anglo-Saxon style of documents came to prevail in larger transactions or transactions involving a foreign element, traditional Czech-style documents still tend to be much shorter and simpler, relying to a large extent on implied provisions of the Commercial and Civil Codes. Acquisitions can be broadly divided between those that are organised as exclusive deals between specific parties, and those that are organised as tenders, regardless of whether the company is being sold privately or is government controlled. Government-run tenders tend to be overly formalistic and are governed by specific procedures, rules and practices. Private tenders are much more flexible.

For tender offers, the participation of financial advisers is almost inevitable. Depending on the value of the transaction, the financial adviser may be one of the London-based investment banks or one of the Czech "investment boutiques" that have emerged since the early 1990s. Direct deals are often run directly by the selling shareholder, with the occasional assistance of lawyers and/or a financing institution if the sale is the result of financial distress on the part of the seller.

Information memoranda are prepared in the most important transactions organised by sophisticated sellers (e.g., private equity funds) or tenders organised on behalf of the Government, especially if they take the form of an auction.

Following initial informal talks, parties usually sign a confidentiality agreement. Although this practice is common, the legal basis of the agreement is vague and there is little practical experience with its enforcement. It is advisable for the parties to agree on a contractual penalty in connection with a breach of confidentiality or exclusivity, although, in reality, such provisions are rarely seen in the agreements.

In the case of a tender and following the first round of preliminary non-binding or conditional offers, parties often conclude an exclusivity agreement. This agreement is often called a "memorandum of understanding", "letter of intent" or "heads of terms", although all these titles are imports from the Anglo-Saxon environment and do not have an established legal meaning or basis in Czech law. If there is no tender procedure, the confidentiality agreement and the exclusivity agreement are often combined into one document.

6.7.2   Due diligence

Due diligence is becoming increasingly common in Czech transactions, especially in relation to the major transactions involving clients, lawyers or financial advisers with western experience. Lawyers and financial advisers usually carry out important roles and are often accompanied by accountants/auditors and tax advisers for the financials. Where appropriate, the investor often hires a separate company to undertake environmental due diligence, especially if a local company with a long industrial history on a factory site is being acquired. Specialist advisers may also be called in to conduct due diligence in specific areas such as telecommunications or insurance companies, particularly if the purchaser is a financial (private equity) investor rather than the ultimate strategic investor.

Due diligence is more typical in sophisticated private deals or in public or private tenders. Vendors' due diligence is becoming increasingly popular in auction sales.

A due diligence exercise can be rather limited with respect to a listed company and even more so should the management refuse to cooperate. Even where there is a majority shareholder willing to facilitate the transaction, due diligence is often an issue of concern for the management of a target company since the rules concerning protection of business secrets, insider trading, disclosure of information that has an impact on the value of the shares on the market and non-discrimination of minority shareholders, require careful evaluation. It is not unusual for the management of the target company to resist attempts by the potential investor to obtain the most sensitive "confidential" information.

The investor can always utilise public sources concerning the target company to learn more about its business and health, including financial reports published in the Czech *Commercial Gazette*, filed with the Commercial Register (maintained by the respective regional court according to the address of the registered office of the company), the Cadastral Office (the real-estate register) and information from the public securities market. The Commercial Register should contain all basic corporate data and documents, and financial results (if required by law, audited), although companies do not always comply with their reporting duties.

6.7.3 Increasing shareholdings

Table 1 shows, in simplified form, certain important shareholding thresholds and includes a basic description of the corporate powers and duties that accompany such percentage shareholdings (and corresponding voting rights).

In practice, it is sometimes necessary to distinguish between thresholds relating to voting rights and those relating to share capital of the target company. Also, individual classes of shares may need to be voted on separately and certain shareholders may, in specific cases, be prohibited from voting (such as, for instance, in cases where a general meeting is required to decide whether the company should enter into a particular transaction which provides a benefit or advantage to a shareholder or any person affiliated therewith).

Table 6.1 Powers and obligations of shareholders and relevant thresholds

Percentage of shares or voting rights in the target	Rights granted to or obligations imposed on the holder of the shares
Any amount	Ability to claim the invalidity of any resolution of a general meeting within three months of its adoption.
	The right to attend the general meeting, to vote one's shares at the general meeting, to demand and obtain an explanation as to matters concerning the company (provided that such explanation is necessary for considering matters that are on the agenda of the general meeting) and to make proposals to the general meeting relating to matters put on the agenda of the general meeting.
	The pre-emptive right to subscribe pro rata for any newly issued shares, convertible bonds or bonds with pre-emptive rights.
	The right to file a petition to the court asking for the appointment of an expert to examine the report on the relationship between a controlled entity and related entities, if at least one of the specific conditions stipulated by the Commercial Code requiring such an examination is met.
3% or 5%*	Ability to ask the board of directors to call an extraordinary general meeting of the company or request that a particular matter be placed on the agenda of a general meeting.
	The right to file a lawsuit for damages on behalf of the company against members of its board of directors if the supervisory board fails to do so upon the shareholder's request.
	The right to file a petition to the court asking for the appointment of an expert to examine the report on the relationship between a controlled entity and related entities, if there are serious reasons requiring such an examination, even though the specific conditions stipulated by the Commercial Code are not met.

Table 6.1 continued

Percentage of shares or voting rights in the target	Rights granted to or obligations imposed on the holder of the shares
3% or 5%*	A shareholder acquiring 3 per cent or more of the voting rights in a listed company is generally required to disclose its shareholding to the CNB, the central depositary and the company itself (*see* 6.3.3 above).
10%	Power to block a "squeeze-out" in the form of a compulsory takeover of shares or assets by the principal shareholder (*see* below on 90 per cent majority). An entity is considered "interconnected" with another entity by the Commercial Code if the former owns at least 10 per cent of the basic capital of the latter.
25%	Power to block significant corporate actions, for example mergers and split-ups and an increase in the registered capital by in-kind contributions or conclusion of an agreement on control or an agreement on transfer of profit (*see* below on 75 per cent majority). Power to block delisting of the company's shares.
30%**	Thirty per cent of shareholders present form a quorum to decide at a regular shareholders meeting. (If the quorum has not been reached at the regular shareholders meeting, a substitute shareholders meeting can decide, irrespective of the number of shareholders present.)
33.34%	Power to block, for example, amendments to the articles of association, transfer, lease or pledge of a business (or a part thereof), dissolution of the company with its liquidation or increase or decrease in the registered capital (*see* below on 66.67 per cent majority).
40%	A shareholder acting alone or in concert with others controlling 40 per cent or more voting rights in a company is considered to be the controlling shareholder with respect to such company, unless another person controls the same number or more voting rights in the same company.
50%**	Legal control – power to pass ordinary resolutions at general meetings, including the appointment and removal of directors and the ultimate decision on the majority of issues submitted to the general meeting for approval.

Table 6.1 continued

Percentage of shares or voting rights in the target	Rights granted to or obligations imposed on the holder of the shares
66.67%**	Control of, for example, amendments to the articles of association, increase or decrease in the registered capital (other than through an in-kind contribution), the liquidation of the company, the issuance of preferred bonds or convertible bonds and the transfer, lease or pledge of business or part thereof.
75%**	Approval of a merger of the company. Approval of a split-up of the company provided that the proposed share exchange ratio is the same for all shareholders.
	Control over changes in the class or form of shares, changes to the rights attached to a specific class of shares, changes to the transferability of registered shares, delisting of shares, exclusion or limitation of preferred rights to acquire convertible or priority bonds, and exclusion or limitation of preferred rights to subscribe for new shares.
	Approval of the controlling agreement or the agreement on the transfer of profit and approval of any changes thereto (if the amount of compensation or indemnity is being decided a 75 per cent vote of present shareholders other than the controlling shareholder is also required).
	Approval of any increase in the registered capital of the company through in-kind contributions.
90%	Approval of a split-up of a company provided that the proposed share exchange ratio is not the same for all shareholders.
	A 90 per cent or more single majority shareholder (by share in capital or voting rights) may compulsorily squeeze out minority shareholders for fair compensation following a resolution of the general meeting at which it may exercise its vote. The company survives the squeeze-out and becomes a 100 per cent subsidiary of the former majority shareholder.
	A 90 per cent or more single majority shareholder may also effect a takeover of the assets (business) of a target company by resolution of the general meeting. This form of takeover results in the termination without liquidation of the target company.
95%	The 95 per cent shareholder or shareholders acting in concert may be ordered by the CNB, following a request from a minority shareholder, to make an offer to buy out the minority shareholders. This applies only to listed companies.

Table 6.1   continued

Percentage of shares or voting rights in the target	Rights granted to or obligations imposed on the holder of the shares
	The 95 per cent shareholder or shareholders acting in concert may also make an offer to buy out minority shareholders and, following such offer, delist the shares of the company. This applies only to listed companies.
100%	Ability to add issues to the agenda of the general meeting that were not included in the invitation thereto.

* The 5 per cent threshold applies to companies with a registered capital not exceeding CZK100 million

** These thresholds may be increased by an amendment to the articles of association of the company; such amendment generally requires a two-thirds majority of the votes of all shareholders present

6.8   Conduct of a public offer

Public offers are regulated by the Commercial Code, primarily by Sections 183a to 183g, which cover the following main topics:

(a)   tender offers;
(b)   mandatory tender offers;
(c)   competing tender offers; and
(d)   penalties in connection with tender offers.

There are also many other related provisions of the Commercial Code that should be taken into account in this respect, although, due to repeated legislative amendments that tend to be quite lengthy and technical, and the frequent use of cross-references, the Commercial Code is currently rather difficult to comprehend.

Certain provisions relating to tender offer are also set forth in the Capital Markets Act (Act no. 256/2004 Coll.), the Act on Supervision of Capital Markets (Act no. 15/1998 Coll.), the Act on Collective Investment (Act no. 189/2004 Coll.) and the Act on Protection of Economic Competition (Act no. 143/2001).

Currently, two important new laws are being prepared. The first one is the Act on Transformations of Companies which should replace the relevant sections of the Commercial Code, for example on mergers, split-ups, changes of legal form or taking over of assets of the target company. It should also implement the Directive 2005/56/EC of the European Parliament and of the Council of 26 October 2005, on cross-border mergers of limited liability companies. The second new law is the Act that will implement the Directive 2004/25/EC of the European Parliament and of the Council of 21 April 2004, on takeover bids.

6.8.1 Notification to the CNB and the target company

Once an offeror makes the decision to proceed with a tender offer, it is required, without delay, to inform the board of directors and the supervisory board of the target company of its intention. In the case of a tender offer for listed shares, the offeror must also:

(a) inform the CNB and publish the information without delay;
(b) prevent the premature or unequal dissemination of information about its intentions to make the tender offer; and
(c) adopt measures aimed at preventing insider trading. In this regard, it is necessary to distinguish between a proposal to make a tender offer and the actual tender offer itself.

In the case of an offer for listed shares, the offeror must submit the terms of the proposed tender offer to the CNB for approval within five days of the publication of its intention to make an offer. In the event that another state authority's approval is required in connection with this offer, the offeror must also present that approval to the CNB. If an expert opinion is required to verify the price offered or the fairness of the exchange ratio, that opinion must also be submitted. A foreign offeror is obliged to instruct a Czech securities dealer or a Czech advocate to act on its behalf before the CNB in connection with these proceedings.

6.8.2 Contents of the offer document

In the case of a tender offer for listed shares, the application form must be filed with the CNB by the offeror together with the requisite supporting documents and additional information. The information provided to the CNB must include a draft of the tender offer terms (*see* 6.11.1 below).

The CNB reviews the draft tender offer terms in order to confirm that they meet all material and formal requirements. Within eight business days of submission of the application, the CNB may order the offeror to amend the following terms of the draft offer within the time period prescribed by the CNB:

(a) the offer price or the exchange ratio of the offered securities, taking into account commonly accepted, objective valuation principles and the specific circumstances of the target company;
(b) the minimum number of acceptances required by the offeror for the offer to be consummated; and
(c) the class and number of the securities offered by the offeror in exchange for shares to be acquired in the tender offer.

The CNB can repeatedly recommence the running of the deadline by requesting the offeror to amend its draft tender offer. The CNB can also extend the deadline for its decision by an additional five business days.

The CNB can prohibit the offeror from making a tender offer if:

(a) the terms of the tender offer breach Czech law;
(b) the amendments to the tender offer that the CNB ordered have not been made; or

(c)   the offeror has not proved the source and sufficiency of its acquisition funds or failed to deposit the specified amount of funds with a bank following a request by the CNB.

If the CNB fails to decide or deliver its decision to the offeror within eight business days of the application, the proposed tender offer terms are deemed approved.

6.8.3   Publication of the tender offer

A tender offer for shares may not be published:

(a)   before the offeror obtains the opinion of the board of directors of the target company (unless the board fails to deliver its opinion in time); and
(b)   unless the offeror has, or at the time when the payment will fall due will have, sufficient funds to pay the purchase price.

The tender offer must be published in a manner prescribed by the Commercial Code and by the target company's articles of association for the convening of a general meeting, and in at least one nationwide distributed daily paper.

A tender offer for listed shares may not be published before it has been approved by the CNB. Once the CNB approves the offer, the offeror must publish it within 15 business days.

6.8.4   Mandatory public offers

Whereas an offeror's decision to acquire control or increase its participation in a listed target company is usually voluntary, under certain circumstances an existing shareholder or group of shareholders acting in concert is obliged to launch a mandatory tender offer. In such cases, specific rules apply in addition to those that apply to voluntary public tender offers.

Pursuant to the Commercial Code, any shareholder (together with all other persons acting in concert with that shareholder) acquiring sufficient voting rights in a Czech listed company to enable it to exercise control (*see* also 6.3.3 above) must make a tender offer for the shares of the remaining minority shareholders within 60 days following the day of reaching or exceeding the relevant threshold. The same obligation applies also to a person who exceeds a two-thirds or three-quarters majority of voting rights of a listed company. The obligation to make a tender offer for the shares of minority shareholders in a target company is also imposed upon any person who has acquired control over any entity already controlling the listed target company.

Although the obligation to make a mandatory tender offer is discharged once any of the entities acting in concert publishes the offer (assuming all such entities are mentioned in the offer), all such entities are jointly and severally liable for obligations arising under contracts concluded under the tender offer, even if they are not specifically mentioned in the offer documents.

A mandatory tender offer applies to all the remaining shares of the target company (by contrast, terms of a voluntary tender offer may stipulate a maximum or minimum number of shares to be purchased as a condition of such offer being consummated by the offeror). Special rules apply to the price offered for shares in a mandatory tender offer (*see* 6.11.1(b)(iii) and 6.9 below). The offer price must, in any event, be confirmed by appraisal. The deadline for the transfer of shares and payment of the purchase price is 60 days following the conclusion of each tender contract.

A mandatory tender offer may not be withdrawn and, once published, the offer may be modified only in a manner that would make it more advantageous to the offerees.

Failure to make a mandatory tender offer or breach of material provisions in connection therewith may result in the suspension of the respective person's voting rights in the target company as well as certain other administrative sanctions. In the event of a major violation of the law, the CNB may rule that the defaulting shareholder is no longer entitled to exercise the rights attaching to its shares. Apart from voting rights, other rights that may be suspended include the right to receive dividends, pre-emptive rights to acquire newly issued shares, etc. The level and degree of the penalty is dictated by the gravity of the breach.

6.8.5 *Obligations of the board of directors and supervisory board of the offeree*

Once notified of the offeror's intention to launch a tender offer, members of both the board of directors and the supervisory board of the target company are obliged to act not only in the interests of all the company's shareholders, but also in the interests of its employees and creditors.

Members of the board of directors and the supervisory board are also required to:

(a) refrain from adopting any measures which could deprive the target company's shareholders of the opportunity to make a free and fully informed decision;

(b) refrain from doing anything that could frustrate or complicate the offer, in particular they should refrain from authorising the issuance of securities which could prevent the offeror from gaining control of the target company (i.e., no "poison pills"), except when such action is approved by a resolution of the general meeting during the offer open period;

(c) prepare, within five business days of receipt of the proposal of the tender offer, a written opinion and, within two business days thereafter, deliver it to the offeror and publish it in the same manner as the offer, either as a part of the offer itself or as a separate document, but in any case no later than the date of publication of the tender offer.

In addition, the board of directors of the target company is required, without undue delay, to:

(a) inform the employee representatives about the offeror's voluntary decision to make the offer or the occurrence of the obligation to make a mandatory tender offer;

(b) present copies of documents received from the offeror to the employee representatives; and

(c)   present a copy of the opinion on the tender offer, prepared by the target company's board of directors and the supervisory board, to the employee representatives.

Members of both the board of directors and the supervisory board of the target company are also required to maintain the confidentiality of any information acquired from the offeror in connection with the tender offer until the information becomes public.

Like the offeror, the target company is also required to take measures necessary to prevent the premature or uneven dissemination of information about the offeror's plans to make a tender offer or any other intentions of the offeror that may give rise to a mandatory obligation to make a tender offer.

6.8.6   Competing offers

If, during the offer open period, another entity expresses its intention to launch a competing bid, the price offered must be at least 2 per cent higher than the price set in the original offer. Otherwise, the normal rules for a tender offer apply, as appropriate.

If the original offeror wishes to increase its offer price in response to the competing offer, the new price must be at least 2 per cent higher again. If the original offeror makes a new offer, it may not accept the competing offer selling thus the securities acquired under the terms of its original offer.

6.9   Defences to a hostile offer

So far, there has been only a very limited number of initial public offerings of shares in the Czech Republic. Moreover, there are relatively few companies with listed shares that do not have a dominant shareholder. A true hostile takeover of a listed company has yet to take place.

As a result, provisions specifically drafted to address hostile takeovers are usually nowhere to be found in a company's articles of association or by-laws, or in Czech law generally. Whatever provisions have been implemented for this or a similar purpose, at the time of writing they had not been tested in the Czech courts and there is little jurisprudence to draw upon on this subject.

However, Czech corporate law does recognise certain instruments that can be used as shields against hostile takeovers, including transfer-blocking clauses (e.g., pre-emption and approval clauses) and the power of a board of directors to propose an increase in the registered capital of the target company by a certain percentage. However, as previously noted, one of the Commercial Code amendments prohibits members of both the board of directors and the supervisory board of a target company from doing anything that may frustrate or complicate a third-party tender offer (*see* 6.8.5 above). The Commercial Code also explicitly prevents the target company's board from using any authorisations they may otherwise have to issue new equity securities if such action could frustrate the intention of an offeror to gain control of a target company, unless such issuance of new securities is approved by the general meeting of the target company during the offer open period.

Furthermore, the Commercial Code allows companies to adopt provisions in their articles of association that would limit or exclude altogether the right of an offeror to propose a tender offer price that is lower, by up to 15 per cent, than the premium price (*see* 6.11.1(b)(iii) below).

Provisions such as those mentioned above can be considered the nuclei of any defence against a hostile tender offer. However, it remains to be seen what practice and theory will contribute to this issue in the future.

6.10 Profit forecast and asset valuation

There is no strong tradition of profit forecasting among Czech companies and companies do not generally provide profit forecasts or valuations of their assets except on occasions required by law. Those that are voluntarily provided are read with some reservation unless there is a clear rationale underlying the forecast or valuation. Czech accounting rules normally rely on the historical cost of long-term assets rather than other forms of valuations. Only certain financial assets and derivatives are revalued to fair market value.

The Capital Markets Act imposes an obligation on Czech listed companies to publish annual and semi-annual accounts and reports. Such accounts and reports should provide investors with a true and fair view of the financial situation, business activities and economic results of the company over the previous year and should also include forecasts for its development in the next year or, possibly, over a longer period of time.

The Commercial Code requires a company to obtain an expert's opinion on the valuation of its net assets in the event of mergers, split-ups or transactions between related entities. In the event of a mandatory tender offer, the adequacy of the offer price must be confirmed by an expert's appraisal. A revaluation of assets carried out in accordance with Commercial Code requirements is usually also reflected in the accounting of the company.

Since the board of directors and the supervisory board of the target company (in the case of a public tender offer for its shares) are obliged to express their opinion on the offer, they can of course draw the attention of their shareholders to the hidden values of the company.

Czech corporate law relies to a large extent on the opinions of court-appointed experts. However, most of these experts are Czech professionals or entities.

6.11 Documents from the offeror and the offeree

6.11.1 *The tender offer*

A tender offer must take the form of a draft public agreement to buy securities and it must be processed and published in such a manner that all addressees are able to make a fully informed decision in due time.

The offer document must include at least the following information:

(a)   As regards the offeror:
- (i)   its identity, including its business name and registered office address; and
- (ii)   its existing participation in the shareholding or voting rights of the target company.

(b)   As regards the conditions of the tender offer:
- (i)   identification of the target shares, their class, form, type, nominal value and International Securities Identification Number ("ISIN");
- (ii)   identification of the maximum or minimum amount of shares that the offeror intends to acquire (only applicable in the case of a voluntary tender offer – this information needs to be published only if the offeror proposes such condition);
- (iii)   the price offered for the shares (if other securities are offered in exchange for the shares of the target company, the offer must include the class, form, type, nominal value and exchange ratio of such securities), as well as the method of determination of the price (or the exchange ratio of the offered securities), while the price (or the exchange ratio) must be the same for all holders of shares to which the same rights are attached.

     In the case of a tender offer for listed shares, the offer must also contain the average price of the target shares and the premium price for the target shares (if any). The average price is calculated as the weighted average of prices for the shares registered by the central depositary during the six months preceding the date of the occurrence of the obligation to make the offer. The premium price (being higher than the average price) is the price for which the offeror, or a person acting in concert with the offeror, acquired any of the target shares during the previous six months. For mandatory tender offers, the offer price or exchange ratio must adequately reflect the value of the target shares. When considering the adequacy of the offer, the average price and premium price mentioned above are both taken into account. If there is a basis for establishing a premium price, the offer price may not be lower than the premium price decreased by a maximum of 15 per cent, although never lower than the average price;
- (iv)   the required manner of acceptance of the offer or the designation of the regulated market (i.e., the Prague Stock Exchange or RM-System) where the transaction is to be consummated;
- (v)   the period of time during which the tender offer remains open (this period may not be less than four weeks or more than 10 weeks from the date of its publication unless the CNB permits a shorter period);
- (vi)   settlement and clearance procedure and payment terms (under a mandatory tender offer the settlement period may not be longer than 60 days; also the Prague Stock Exchange or RM-System may require alterations to the settlement terms, including the settlement period, in order to comply with their internal procedural rules);

(vii) rules for the withdrawal of acceptances of the tender offer by offerees;

(viii) sources and methods of financing the purchase price; and

(ix) in the case of a mandatory tender offer, the reasons for the offer.

(c) As regards the target company:

(i) the offeror's plans concerning the target company's future activities, its employees and members of its boards, including any planned changes to employment conditions.

6.11.2 Documents from the offeree

Members of both the board of directors and the supervisory board of the target company are obliged, within five business days of receipt of the offer terms, to prepare a written opinion on the offer (*see* also 6.8.5 above). The opinion must state whether the tender offer is in the interests of the target company's shareholders, employees and creditors. The opinion must be reasoned and include the facts that form the basis of the boards' opinion.

The boards must then, within two business days of its preparation, deliver the opinion to both the offeror and, in the case of listed securities, to the CNB, and publish it in the same manner as the offer, either as a part of the offer or as a separate document. The opinion may not be published later than the date of publication of the tender offer.

6.12 Compulsory acquisitions

The Commercial Code, within the framework of public offers, regulates the compulsory buy-out of minority shareholders and also provides special procedures for the squeeze-out of minority shareholders and other buy-out schemes.

6.12.1 Mandatory offers after change of control

The rules regarding mandatory public offers are explained at 6.8.4 above.

6.12.2 Compulsory re-offers to minorities after a public offer

The Commercial Code does not have provision for a compulsory re-offer to minority shareholders after the close of a public offer. However, if the controlling shareholder does not achieve a two-thirds or three-quarters majority of the voting rights of a listed company after its original offer, but exceeds such thresholds at a later date, it has to initiate a new mandatory tender offer.

6.12.3 Compulsory acquisitions outside the framework of a public offer

The CNB may, following a proposal from a minority shareholder, order the majority shareholder, or a group of shareholders acting in concert, to make an offer to purchase the remaining equity securities of the target company from the minority shareholders provided:

(a) the majority shareholder, or group of shareholders acting in concert, controls at least 95 per cent of the voting rights of the target company;
(b) the equity securities are listed;
(c) the requesting shareholder is not acting in concert with the controlling shareholder(s); and
(d) there are serious reasons to justify such an order. The term "serious reasons" is not defined in the Commercial Code.

6.12.4   Compulsory sales by minority shareholders (squeeze-outs)

In May 2005, the Czech Parliament approved an amendment to the Commercial Code, according to which the majority shareholder is allowed to force minority shareholders to sell their shares (a squeeze-out).

According to the amendment, a 90 per cent or more single majority shareholder (measured by its share of the registered capital or by its share of the voting rights) is allowed to squeeze out minority shareholders in a company for fair compensation following a resolution of the general meeting at which the majority shareholder may exercise its vote. Upon the proper exercise of the right, the shares of the minority shareholders are transferred by virtue of law to the majority shareholder. Any pledges over the minority shares cease to exist on the transfer of title.

The passing of the resolution of the general meeting is conditioned by a prior approval of the squeeze-out by the CNB. The fairness of the proposed compensation to minority shareholders has to be substantiated by an expert opinion, examined by the CNB.

Prior to the general meeting, the majority shareholder has to transfer a sufficient amount of money to a securities broker or a bank that will make the payment of the compensation to minority shareholders. The Board of Directors of the company opines on the fairness of the amount of the compensation.

Shareholders may contest the level of compensation in the courts, but a judgment on the adequacy of compensation does not invalidate the squeeze-out resolution itself. The squeeze-out right may be exercised only within three months following the acquisition of the 90 per cent stake.

In addition, the Commercial Code already provides the majority shareholder with an option, which has a somewhat similar effect to a squeeze-out. A majority shareholder may take over the assets (business) of a target company if it owns at least 90 per cent of the shares. This form of takeover results in the termination of the target company without liquidation and must be approved by the general meeting of the company. The majority shareholder is not excluded from voting on such a measure.

The existing provisions concerning squeeze-outs are likely also to be amended by the Act on Takeover Bids that is currently being prepared (*see* also 6.8 above).

6.13 Insider trading and market manipulation

6.13.1 *Insider trading*

Since the beginning of the 1990s, Czech law has included some relatively brief and broad provisions prohibiting insider trading and market manipulation. The law has been amended several times since 2000 to achieve harmonisation with the relevant EU directives. However, the enforcement of these rules has so far proved difficult.

6.13.1.1 *Prohibitions on the use of inside information*
The Capital Markets Act prohibits the use of inside information for the benefit of an insider or a third person. The insider:

(a)   may not acquire or dispose of or attempt to acquire or dispose of any financial instrument to which the inside information relates;

(b)   may not make any direct or indirect recommendation to any person regarding the acquisition or disposition of any financial instrument to which the inside information relates; and

(c)   must keep confidentiality of the inside information and must prevent third parties from accessing the inside information, except where the insider discloses the confidential information as part of his usual activity, obligation or employment. The confidentiality restriction survives even the termination of the insider's privileged position.

Information is considered to be "inside information" if it:

(a)   is not publicly known;

(b)   is precise and concerns directly or indirectly:

    (i)   a "financial instrument" (defined as an investment instrument or another instrument accepted for or applied for trading on a regulated market of any EU Member State),

    (ii)   another instrument not accepted for trading on a regulated market of any EU Member State and deriving its value from a financial instrument,

    (iii)   an issuer of those financial instruments, or

    (iv)   other facts significant for the determination of the market or other price of this financial instrument or its proceeds; and

(c)   could, after becoming publicly known, significantly affect the market or other price of this financial instrument or another instrument deriving its value from the financial instrument.

An insider is a person who has acquired inside information:

(a)   in connection with his employment, occupation or function, or in connection with his share in the capital or voting rights of an issuer;

(b)   in connection with the fulfilment of his obligations;

(c)   in relation to any crime; or

(d)   in any other manner, provided that he knows or may know that it is inside information.

Furthermore, the Capital Markets Act sets forth a number of preventive measures against insider trading. These include:

(a)   an obligation imposed upon issuers of all financial instruments to promptly make public and send to the CNB, in the electronic form, any inside information, directly relating to the issuer. In certain cases and if certain conditions are met, an issuer may delay the disclosure of inside information upon notification to the CNB;

(b)   an obligation imposed on issuers to maintain a list of individuals who have access to inside information and to make that list available to the CNB, upon request, without delay; and

(c)   an obligation imposed on:

   (i)   managers and members of the managing and supervisory bodies (and their relatives) of the issuer,

   (ii)   entities in which persons referred to in item (i) above are managers or members of the managing and supervisory bodies,

   (iii)   entities controlled by the above persons, or

   (iv)   economically interconnected entities,

to report to the CNB, within five days, all trades in the securities issued by the relevant issuer, or any financial instruments derived therefrom, carried out on their own account.

The Commercial Code sets out rules relating to insider trading specifically in connection with tender offers. The parties involved in a tender offer must ensure that the confidential information is not misused, and the capital markets are not distorted, during both the preparation and the making of the tender offer. These obligations extend to the offeror and its employees as well as both boards, the shareholders and employees of the target company.

In the case of a tender offer for listed shares, the offeror and the members of both boards must take appropriate measures to prevent the premature and uneven flow of information regarding the offeror's intentions to make a tender offer. These measures include:

(a)   instructing persons who are aware of those intentions about the prohibition on misuse of the confidential information;

(b)   taking appropriate organisational measures; and

(c)   monitoring whether there is any misuse of confidential information.

The offeror, as well as the members of both boards, must inform the CNB in writing without delay of the measures they have taken to protect the confidential information and of any suspicions they may have that confidential information is being misused.

6.13.1.2   Sanctions

Violation of the prohibition of insider trading may result in the imposition of fines under the Capital Markets Act (up to CZK10 million) and related regulations, civil liability for damages and, in the case of a serious breach, criminal prosecution. Insider trading and market manipulation can also fall within the scope of the Criminal Code, which recognises crimes such as "misuse of information in business dealings", "breach of obligatory rules in business dealings" or "fraud".

6.13.1.3 Conduct of investigations

Policing of the insider trading rules under the Capital Markets Act and Commercial Code is reserved to the CNB as the main authority supervising the capital markets. The CNB is not, however, entitled to enforce criminal laws. This authority is vested with the criminal law authorities (e.g., the offices of state attorneys, police and the criminal courts).

6.13.2 Market manipulation

The Capital Markets Act expressly prohibits market manipulation by any person.

Market manipulation is broadly defined in the Capital Markets Act as any conduct by any person that may mislead market participants with regard to the value, supply or demand of any financial instrument (*see* the definition in 6.13.1.1 above) or in another manner mislead the market price of any financial instrument. On the other hand, the Capital Markets Act carves out a number of activities which do not constitute market manipulation (e.g., execution of any transaction where the relevant party demonstrates that the transaction had a proper substance and was carried out by a practice generally recognised on regulated markets).

As for insider trading laws, violation of market manipulation laws may result in the imposition of fines under the Capital Markets Act (up to CZK20 million) and related regulations, civil liability for damages and, in the case of a serious breach, criminal prosecution.

6.14   Financial assistance

Certain company acquisitions are structured as leveraged deals. In these cases, the acquirer procures external financing in respect of a portion of the purchase price for the acquired shares, business or assets. Such external financing may be secured by the acquired shares, business or assets (the creation of a security concerning each of the above items has a different legal regime).

The law envisages different consequences for the different classes of security taken. Broadly speaking, the acquirer is free to pledge shares, ownership interests or assets that were acquired directly by the acquirer and are being pledged in the acquirer's own name. However, the law greatly limits the possibility of creating pledges over the business or assets of a subsidiary of the acquirer that are supposed to facilitate the acquisition.

6.14.1   Financial assistance by the target company

Under Czech law, financial assistance by the target company is prohibited under the Commercial Code. A company may not advance funds, grant loans or provide security for the purpose of or in connection with the acquisition by a third party of its own shares. Any such conduct carried out in violation of the Commercial Code is void and may result in liability for damages on the part of the directors responsible for granting the financial assistance.

6.14.2   Intra-group financial assistance

Intra-group financial assistance may also be a problem under Czech law, depending on the factual circumstances of each case, especially as regards the shareholder structure of the companies involved, the market availability of the specific financial instrument to the recipient of the assistance and the arm's-length price of such an instrument. In the past, cross-financing, cross-guarantees and transfers of assets among related companies were often misused to the detriment of controlled companies and their minority shareholders.

The law deals with the above restrictions in two ways:

(a)   it contains the general duty of the board of directors to act in the best interests of the company; and

(b)   it places certain legal restrictions on the acquisition of assets or the provision of financial assistance to the controlling company or its affiliates.

A company intending to provide or facilitate intra-group financial assistance may need to obtain either a prior evaluation of the transaction by an independent court-appointed expert or a favourable vote from its general meeting.

Generally speaking, it is important to mention that the Commercial Code also contains specific rules defining a controlling and controlled person/entity, a concern (holding) and a controlling agreement. There are provisions regulating the relationships of these persons/entities, in particular their corporate governance, intra-group dealings and protection of minority shareholders.

6.14.3   Other rules applicable to debt financing

Debt financing may be sourced from within the country or from abroad, and financing agreements may be governed by Czech or foreign law. Loan agreements are often governed by foreign (usually English) law.

Chapter 7

Denmark

Mikkel Baaring Lerche and Philip Risbjørn

Partners
Bech-Bruun Law Firm

7.1   Introduction

This Chapter covers the essence of the Danish takeover regulation, the most important corporate law rules in the context of a takeover and provides an outline of the Danish merger control rules.

The primary legal regime relevant for making a takeover in Denmark, be it a contested or an uncontested takeover, is the Danish Securities Trading Act Consolidated Act no. 479 of 1 June 2006, as amended, (the "Danish Securities Trading Act") as well as orders promulgated pursuant to this Act, most importantly Executive Order no. 712 of 21 June 2007 ("the Takeover Order"), which implements the Takeover Directive (2004/25/EC). Denmark has opted out of the "non frustration" regime and the "breakthrough" regime. The rules on prospectuses and listing of shares are relevant if share consideration is offered. Also, Danish company law, including the Danish Public Limited Companies Act (the "Danish Companies Act") contains certain limitations as to how a takeover or a defensive strategy may be structured. The Danish Financial Supervisory Authority (the "FSA") has been the supervisory authority in respect of takeovers in Denmark since 1 September 2006.

The Takeover Order applies to takeovers of Danish target companies which have securities admitted to trading on a regulated market (primarily OMX Nordic Exchange Copenhagen) or an alternative market place in Denmark (i.e., First North), and non-Danish companies with securities listed in Denmark. If the securities are also listed in another EU Member State (or EEA Member State), the Takeover Order applies to an offer if the initial listing took place in Denmark or if the securities were listed at the same time on different regulated markets and the FSA has been appointed as the competent supervisory authority by the target company.

At the end of 2007, there were 851 companies listed on OMX of which 211 were Danish companies.

In the last 10 years, takeovers have occurred frequently in Denmark. The largest takeover ever in the Nordic region took place in Denmark in 2006.

7.2   Acquisition targets

7.2.1   *Company with limited liability ("Aktieselskab")*

In order for a Danish company to be admitted to listing on OMX, it needs to be a limited liability company, a so-called *aktieselskab* (in abbreviated form, an "A/S").

There is one matter which is particularly worth noting in the takeover context, and that is the voting rights system that applies to limited liability companies in Denmark. The Danish Companies Act provides that all shares must carry voting rights. This means, for instance, that preference shares without votes are not permitted. Disparate voting rights are allowed, provided that no shares carry more than 10 times the voting value of any other shares of the same denomination.

A significant number of the Danish companies listed on OMX are "semi public" in the sense that only the low-vote class of shares (typically labelled "B shares") are listed, whereas the high-vote shares (typically labelled "A shares") remain in the hands of the founder, a holding company or a foundation. In most cases, the maximum permitted difference in votes of 10:1 is used.

In addition, as is shown in 7.9 below, the voting rights of a company may be further restricted by provisions in the company's articles of association providing for voting caps.

7.3   Exchange and investment control

With a few exceptions, there are no special rules for foreign buyers and no restrictions apply to foreign investment in Denmark. The acquisition of shareholdings of at least 10 per cent of the share capital or the voting rights in financial undertakings, such as companies within the insurance, banking and securities trading industry, is subject to the consent of the FSA. This applies whether or not the acquirer is Danish.

7.4   Merger control

7.4.1   *Introduction*

A merger control regime applies to concentrations in Denmark, but only if the concentration is not subject to the EC Merger Regulation.

The Danish merger control rules are to be interpreted in accordance with the principles of the EC Merger Regulation and the accompanying interpretative documents issued by the European Commission.

A general overview of these Danish rules is provided below.

7.4.2 Interpretation of the notion of a concentration

According to the Danish merger control rules, a concentration is deemed to arise where:

(a) two or more previously independent undertakings or parts of under-takings merge; or

(b) one or more persons already controlling at least one undertaking or one or more undertakings acquire, whether by purchase of securities or assets, by agreement, by contract or by any other means, direct or indirect control of the whole or parts of one or more other undertakings.

The creation of a joint venture also constitutes a concentration when performing on a lasting basis all the functions of an autonomous economic entity.

7.4.3 Thresholds

The Danish merger control rules apply to concentrations that meet the following thresholds and which are not subject to merger control under the EC Merger Regulation:

(a) the combined aggregate turnover in Denmark of all the undertakings concerned is at least DKK3.8 billion (approximately €510 million), and the aggregate turnover in Denmark of each of at least two of the undertakings concerned is a minimum of DKK300 million (€40.3 million); or

(b) the aggregate turnover in Denmark of at least one of the undertakings concerned is a minimum of DKK3.8 billion, and the aggregate worldwide turnover of at least one of the other undertakings concerned is a minimum of DKK3.8 billion.

7.4.4 Calculation of turnover

The Danish Minister for Economic and Business Affairs lays down the more detailed rules on the calculation of turnover.

According to the explanatory notes and the executive order issued by the Minister, an assessment of whether the turnover thresholds have been met is to be based on the net turnover on ordinary activities after deduction of VAT and other direct and indirect taxes directly related to turnover.

Turnover in Denmark comprises the sale of goods and the provision of services to customers who, at the time when the agreement is entered into, are resident in Denmark.

7.4.5 Substantive requirements for the approval of a reportable concentration

In connection with the Danish Competition Council's assessment of a concen-tration, the Council must apply the same competition law principles as set out in the EC Merger Regulation.

The basic substantive test is whether the concentration significantly impedes effective competition, in particular as a result of the creation or strengthening of a dominant position. If this is not the case, the Danish Competition Council must approve the concentration.

In its assessment of whether to approve the concentration, the Danish Competition Council must also assess the restraints of competition directly related and necessary to the implementation of the concentration – the so-called ancillary restraints – which could for instance be non-competition clauses, licences of know-how as well as purchase and supply agreements. The assessment of these restraints must be made in accordance with the European Commission's notice regarding restrictions ancillary to concentrations.

7.4.6   Procedure and timetable

Concentrations that meet the thresholds must be notified to the Danish Competition Authority prior to their implementation and following the conclusion of the agreement, the announcement of the public bid or the acquisition of a controlling interest. There is no formal notification deadline.

No later than four weeks after the receipt of a complete notification form, the Danish Competition Council must decide whether to allow the concentration or to start a separate investigation.

If the Danish Competition Council decides to initiate an investigation, the decision whether to allow or disallow the concentration must be made no later than three months after receipt of a complete notification form.

The concentration may not be implemented until the Danish Competition Council has made its final decision in the matter or the time limits have expired. However, this stand-still obligation does not prevent the implementation of a public bid or a series of transactions in securities, including those convertible into other securities admitted to trading on a market such as a stock exchange, by which control is acquired from various sellers, provided that the concentration is notified to the Danish Competition Authority without delay and that the acquirer does not exercise the voting rights attached to the securities in question or does so only to maintain the full value of his/her investments based on a derogation granted by the Danish Competition Council.

7.5   Regulation of the conduct of mergers and acquisitions

In the following, the term "takeover regulation" is used to describe the regulation of the takeover process itself (i.e., the acquisition of shares in a Danish listed company for the purpose of obtaining control) and the most typical rights and obligations of the target company including the room for defensive measures. Consequently, other types of regulation which may affect the possibilities of making a takeover (and other important issues, such as tax issues) are not dealt with.

7.6   Methods of acquisition

A takeover may in principle be structured on the basis of the fundamental principle of freedom of contract. However, the rules discussed below need to be observed and therefore constitute limitations in terms of flexibility.

A company may be acquired pursuant to a public offer (contested or not) which is or is not preceded by one or more privately negotiated transactions with certain shareholders.

Also, public offers can normally be preceded by a due diligence on the target company, subject to compliance with certain requirements which are discussed in 7.10.2 below.

A typical acquisition strategy is to make the public offer conditional upon acquisition of more than nine-tenths of the votes and the share capital, and to follow up such acquisition with an acquisition of the shares of the remaining shareholders pursuant to the rules on compulsory acquisition which the minority shareholders are subject to. Once compulsory acquisition procedures have been initiated, a delisting of the target company may be applied for.

These issues are discussed in more detail below.

7.7   Public offers

7.7.1   *The distinction between mandatory and non-mandatory bids*

When structuring a public bid transaction it is of key importance to know when the transaction falls within the mandatory bid rules.

7.7.1.1   *Mandatory bids*
Section 31 of the Danish Securities Trading Act and the Takeover Order sets out the rules on when a mandatory bid is required.

It follows from these rules that if a shareholding in a company which has one or several share classes listed on a stock exchange is transferred, directly or indirectly, to an acquirer or persons acting in concert with him, the acquirer must, no later than four weeks after the acquisition, allow all other shareholders of the company to dispose of their shares on identical terms if such transfer means that the acquirer:

(a)   will hold the majority of voting rights in the company;
(b)   becomes entitled to appoint or dismiss a majority of the company's members of the board of directors;
(c)   obtains the right to exercise a controlling influence over the company pursuant to the articles of association or pursuant to an agreement with the company;
(d)   pursuant to agreement with other shareholders, will come to control the majority of voting rights in the company; or
(e)   will be able to exercise a controlling influence over the company and will hold more than one-third of the voting rights.

The mandatory bid must be made as soon as possible and no later than four weeks after the occurrence of any one of the above situations.

The mandatory bid requirement is a requirement to make a public offer to the minority shareholders on "identical terms".

An acquirer often gains a controlling interest in a company through a series of share purchases in the market. The offer to the minority shareholders must in such cases be at least equal to the highest price paid by the acquirer (or by a person acting in concert with the acquirer) within the last six months prior to the publication of the offer ("the highest price principle"). The FSA may in special circumstances decide that the offer price is to be adjusted (upwards or downwards) in which case objective criteria for the adjustment must be used. If the offeror wishes to request such adjustment, he needs to make a request to the FSA immediately after having announced that he is going to make a mandatory offer.

The "identical terms" requirement gives rise to particular problems in connection with the existence of dual or multiple classes of shares. If the target company has several classes of shares, an offer price must be fixed for each class. The highest-price principle must be applied to the share classes in which the offeror has acquired shares. Where all share classes are listed, an offer price which, based on the stock market prices, is proportionately equal to the highest price in the share class or classes in which the offeror has acquired shares must be fixed for the share classes in which the offeror has not acquired shares. Where one or more of several share classes are listed, the price fixed for the unlisted share classes may not be more than 50 per cent higher than the price offered to the minority shareholders.

As to the form of consideration to be offered in mandatory offers, the offeror can offer voting shares, cash or a combination thereof. If the consideration offered does not consist of liquid shares listed on a stock exchange (or certain other markets), the offer must include a cash offer as an option for the offerees. Irrespective of what is stated in this paragraph, if the offeror or persons acting in concert with the offeror have acquired, for cash, shares in the target company which represent at least 5 per cent of the voting rights during a period of six months prior to the offer having been made and until expiry of the time allowed for acceptance of the offer, then cash must be offered at least as an alternative.

As a general guideline it should be noted that if a mandatory bid results in the bidder not acquiring the entire share capital, a subsequent acquisition of shares in the company (i.e., consolidation of control) will not trigger an additional mandatory bid.

7.7.1.2   Non-mandatory bids

A very important exception to the rules on mandatory offers applies to an offer made to all shareholders in the target company for all of their shares and which complies with certain information requirements.

Such offer is referred to herein as a non-mandatory bid or a voluntary offer.

Like mandatory bids, such offers need to comply with the requirements set forth in the Takeover Order (including the obligation to treat all shareholders within the same class equally) and must be made public pursuant to certain rules which are described below.

7.7.1.3 Announcement of public bids

Once an offeror has decided to make a voluntary offer, he must submit a stock exchange notification to OMX to that effect. OMX will then publish its receipt of such notification. An offer document must be published no later than four weeks after publication of the decision to make the voluntary offer.

Employee representatives of the target company and of the offeror or – if employee representation does not exist – the employees directly also need to be notified.

Once an acquirer has acquired a controlling stake and thereby triggered the mandatory acquisition obligation, the acquirer must submit a stock exchange notification to OMX to that effect (the actual mandatory offer must be made as soon as possible and no later than four weeks thereafter). OMX will then publish its receipt of such notification. Again, OMX publishes its receipt hereof, and the employee notification rules apply.

Before making any such stock exchange notification, the acquirer or offeror, as the case may be, must have ensured that he is able to fully meet the cash consideration requirements in respect of the offer (and, in case of another form of consideration, has taken all reasonable precautions to secure that such other consideration can be paid).

7.7.2 Offer rules and essential considerations before and after launching the offer

7.7.2.1 The formal offer rules

The offer document
Pursuant to the Takeover Order, a public offer document must include information on the financial terms of the offer and other terms and information necessary to enable the shareholders to make an informed assessment of the offer. The offer must as a minimum contain the following information:

(a) The name, address and registration number of the target company which is covered by the offer.
(b) The name, address and organisational structure of the offeror together with a list of the persons or companies which act in concert with the offeror, or, if possible, with the target company, and, if they are companies, their type, name and registered address and their relation to the offeror and, if possible, the target company.
(c) The name and address of the person or company responsible for conducting the offer on behalf of the offeror.
(d) The share of the voting rights or the extent of the controlling influence that the offeror has already acquired or has otherwise obtained, including information about any transfer agreement not yet completed and about

any special terms attaching to the voting rights acquired or the controlling influence obtained. Not yet completed transfer agreements include for instance convertible bonds, subscription rights, options or warrants.

(e)   The form of consideration, *see* Section 9 of the Takeover Order as regards mandatory offers.

(f)   The price offered, *see* Section 8 of the Takeover Order as regards mandatory offers.

(g)   The shares or the share class(es) comprised by the offer.

(h)   If applicable, compensation offered to the shareholders for any suspension of special shareholder rights (*see* 7.9.4 below).

(i)   How the offer is financed.

(j)   How the cash payment is made or, where shares in another company are offered, how the exchange ratio is fixed, or, if a combination of cash and shares is offered, how the combination is fixed.

(k)   When settlement will take place.

(l)   Where the consideration is shares, the date from which entitlement to dividends on the shares arises and the date from which the voting rights may be exercised.

(m)   In case of voluntary offers, the maximum and minimum quantity of shares expressed in per cent or number which the offeror is committing to acquire.

(n)   Any conditions attaching to the offer (if it is a voluntary offer), including the circumstances under which the offer may be withdrawn.

(o)   The period during which the offer is open, which must be at least four weeks and no more than 10 weeks from publication of the offer.

(p)   What the shareholders need to do in order to accept the offer.

(q)   Where and when the result of the offer will be announced, and whether conditions attaching to the offer are fulfilled.

(r)   The offeror's intentions with the target company and, if relevant, the offeror's future activities, including for example continued listing or trading of the company's shares on a stock exchange, employee and management retention, which includes any material changes in the employment terms. Also, the offeror must disclose his strategic plans for the target company and the offeror and the likely impact this will have on employment and operational sites.

(s)   Distribution of the target company's funds following the takeover (*see* below).

(t)   Any agreement with others concerning the exercise of the voting rights attaching to the target company's shares to the extent the offeror is a party to such agreement or has knowledge thereof.

(u)   Governing law and competent authorities.

(v)   Whether accepting shareholders are bound in case of a competing offer.

If the offeror contemplates having the target company distribute funds within a period of 12 months following the takeover, this must be stated in the offer document. Such information must include information about the type and size of the distribution. If this requirement has not been complied with, the offeror will not be allowed to make any distributions of funds in the target company during the said 12-month period unless it is based on specific circumstances which improve the financial situation of the target company and which were not foreseeable by the offeror when making the offer.

If, at the time of publication of the offer, the offeror has decided to enter into or seek to enter into agreements with individual shareholders or others regarding the purchase or sale of shares in a target company, this must be stated in the offer document (such trading can only take place if in compliance with the insider rules).

If shares are offered as consideration, this may trigger an obligation to distribute a prospectus or – at the choice of the offeror – to issue an equivalent document containing information similar to that of a prospectus. The "equivalent document" is often the preferred solution, as the disclosure can be included in the offer document, without necessarily being Prospectus Directive compliant. The information requirements for prospectuses are extensive and include detailed information regarding the business of the company and the share consideration offered. Also, extensive financial information accompanied by statements from the accountants must be included. The prospectus needs to be approved on a separate basis.

In the period from commencement of discussions with the target company and until such negotiations are terminated and/or the takeover has been completed, the offeror (and persons acting in concert with the offeror) and the target company's board of directors must not enter into agreements (or make changes to already existing agreements) regarding bonus and the like payable to the target company's board of directors or executive management.

In the event of material changes to the submitted information which cannot be considered terms as such and which are necessary to enable the shareholders to make an informed assessment of the offer, the offeror must as soon as possible make a public announcement to this effect.

If control over a listed company is achieved as a result of a voluntary offer which complies with the rules of the Takeover Order, the offeror is not obligated to subsequently summit a mandatory offer. This needs to be stated in the voluntary offer document.

Publication of the offer
Before any other publication of the offer is allowed (be it a mandatory or a voluntary offer), an advertisement announcing the offer and the offer document must be sent by the offeror to the FSA who will assess whether the advertisement and the offer document comply with the takeover rules. The advertisement must contain information on the deadline for acceptance, from what website the offer document can be obtained and where a shareholder is able to place a request for the offer document. Publication of mandatory bids is deemed to have been effected when the FSA has published its receipt of the advertisement announcing the offer. For planning purposes, the offeror and its advisers should allow up to four weeks from submitting the first draft offer documentation to the FSA and until the documentation is in its final form and ready to be published.

Immediately after publication, the offeror must submit a notification to OMX containing the offer and the advertisement. The target company is also under an obligation to immediately thereafter place the offer document on the above-referenced website and to insert the advertisement announcing the offer in a Danish daily national newspaper.

The target company must send the advertisement announcing the offer to the registered shareholders, and any costs associated with this are to be borne by the offeror. Also, the target company and the offeror must present the offer document to representatives of the target company's and the offeror's employees.

Mandatory statement by the target company's board of directors
The board of directors of the target company must draw up for the shareholders of the company a statement of the board of directors' position on the offer and its reasons for such position, including the board of directors' position on the consequences for all of the company's interested parties, in particular the employees, and the offeror's strategic plans for the target company and its likely consequences for the employees and the operational sites mentioned in the offer document. This obligation does not include an obligation to recommend or not recommend the offer. The statement must be published by the board of directors of the target company before the expiry of the first half of the offer period. The statement will be deemed to have been published when the FSA has published it. In addition, immediately after such publication, the target company must – for the account of the offeror – insert an advertisement in a Danish daily national newspaper containing the statement or excerpts therefrom and place the statement on a website. The advertisement must state the website on which the statement can be found, the contact information to be used to request having the full statement sent, and where it will be available for inspection by the public. Also, employee representatives or – if employee representation does not exist – the employees are to be informed directly, and the statement is to be placed on the website indicated in the advertisement. The advertisement must be sent to the FSA who will publish it. The target company must send the statement to the registered shareholders for the account of the offeror.

In recent years, a market practice has developed in Denmark pursuant to which, in offers that are not contested, the board of directors' recommendation of the offer is published as part of the offer document, or separately but simultaneously with the offer document.

7.7.2.2   *Essential issues to consider when preparing the offer*

Negotiation in secrecy
Negotiations with the target company (and/or shareholders) may be conducted in confidence, provided that the target company is able to maintain con-fidentiality. In 2007, the FSA issued guidelines containing a strict interpretation of the "inside information" concept, which has led to a more rigorous application of the rules on disclosure. Thus, rumours in the press (apart from pure speculations) regarding a possible takeover, e.g., detailed information on the intention to make an offer and the price to be offered and/or significant price

movements, are likely to require that an announcement be made by the target company.

The Takeover Order does not require a post-acquisition disclosure of the track of contacts between the target board and the offeror.

The offer and acceptance mechanism
Once the offer is published, it is binding on the offeror. Each shareholder of the target company can freely decide whether or not to accept a public offer. However, once a shareholder has accepted the offer, such acceptance may not be withdrawn unless otherwise provided for in the offer document.

Unless the offeror is entitled to revoke its offer (*see* further below), the offeror is obliged to keep the offer open throughout the entire offer period and will be bound by acceptances made by shareholders within the offer period, subject to the satisfaction of any conditions attached to the offer.

Once it is clear that conditions made in the offer, if any, have been fulfilled (or waived) and the offeror has made an announcement to that effect, the acquisition is binding.

Making the offer conditional
Non-mandatory offers can be made on a conditional basis, provided the fulfilment of a condition can be assessed objectively and provided fulfilment or non-fulfilment is beyond the offeror's control.

It is often advisable to make the offer conditional upon the offeror obtaining more than nine-tenths of the votes and the share capital of the target company in order to enable the offeror to subsequently squeeze out the outstanding minority (*see* 7.8.1 below).

Other typical conditions include:

(a) the absence of changes in the target company's capital structure or articles of association whilst the offer is open;

(b) the obtaining of antitrust clearances and other necessary approvals from public authorities;

(c) the absence of new legislation, court orders, etc. obstructing the offer;

(d) the absence of material adverse changes whilst the offer is open and that the target company does not itself in that period publish information of an adverse nature.

In addition to the above conditions, other conditions may be used, provided that they are reasonably objective. The offeror is entitled to waive or reduce conditions if this is provided for in the offer document. The offer document would ordinarily include such a right.

Mandatory bids cannot be made conditional, not even on antitrust clearances or other regulatory approvals.

Revocation of the offer
Pursuant to a previous takeover order, a non-mandatory offer could be revoked if:

(a)   a competing offer was made;
(b)   legal or administrative consents or approvals necessary for the takeover were not obtained, or were denied;
(c)   a condition included in the offer itself was not fulfilled; or
(d)   the target company had increased its share capital.

The existing Takeover Order does not contain such provisions, except that it is clear from the Takeover Order that – even without it being specified in the offer document – the offeror may withdraw his offer if a competing bid is made.

These revocation conditions are believed to be in compliance with Danish law. Other objective revocation conditions may also apply. A basic requirement for revocation to be permitted is that the specific revocation condition has been specified in the offer document.

7.7.2.3   Essential issues following submission of the offer

Deadline for publication of offer result
The result of the offer must be published no later that three trading days after the offer has lapsed.

Changed offer conditions
Until expiry of the period during which the offer is open, the offeror may change the terms of the offer if this constitutes an improvement of the terms offered to the shareholders. If the change is effected within the last two weeks of the offer period, the offer period must be extended to expire 14 days after the publication of the changed offer. The offeror is entitled to extend the offer period by 14 days at a time; the entire offer period is not to exceed 10 weeks from the date of publication of the offer. For purposes of obtaining antitrust clearances, the offeror is entitled to prolong the offer period beyond the 10-week limit, by four weeks at a time; however, not beyond four months from the date of publication of the offer.

If, following publication of the offer document and before expiry of the offer period, the offeror or a person acting in concert with the offeror contracts with shareholders or others regarding the purchase and sale of shares in the target company, the offeror must as a minimum increase its offer to the other shareholders correspondingly if such shares are included in the offer and if the agreements are entered into on terms and conditions more favourable than those which pursuant to the offer document are offered to the shareholders. Subject to the prohibition on insider trading, the offeror is free to make open market purchases throughout the offer period at a price not exceeding the offer price in the offer document.

In case of changes to the offer, the offeror must prepare an addendum to the offer document which must be published in the same way as the offer. The board of directors of the target company must, in the event of such changed offer, draw up and publish an additional statement for the shareholders of the target company on the changes. The statement must be published before the expiry of half of the remaining part of the offer period or, if the remaining part of the offer period is less than 14 days, within seven days after the publication of the changes. Publication of the additional statement must be made in the same manner as used in connection with the original statement by the board of directors.

Competing offers
A competing offer is defined as an offer made prior to the expiry of the longest deadline for acceptance of any offer already made. If the original offeror does not withdraw his offer, the period stipulated for acceptance of the original offer is automatically extended until expiry of the period stipulated for acceptance of the competing offer.

7.8   Compulsory acquisition of minority shareholdings

7.8.1   Squeeze-out of minority shareholders

7.8.1.1   Traditional squeeze-out of minority shareholders
The original and traditional way of compelling minority shareholders to dispose of their shares is dealt with in Section 20b of the Danish Companies Act.

Thus, if a shareholder holds more than 90 per cent of the share capital and the votes in a company, the shareholder may jointly with the target company's board of directors decide that the other shareholders are to be subjected to compulsory buy-out by the shareholder.

If an acquirer wishes to go down the Section 20b route, he must – observing the notice rules for the convening of a shareholders meeting – call for the minority shareholders to transfer their shares within four weeks. The next step is to summon any remaining shareholders to transfer their shares by an announcement in the Official Gazette. The notice period is three months.

The terms of the squeeze-out and the basis for fixing the squeeze-out price must be stated in the notice.

Furthermore, it must be stated that, in the case of disagreement on the squeeze-out price, the price must be fixed by expert valuers pursuant to certain rules in the Danish Companies Act (the decision made by such experts may be brought before the courts within three months).

If the price fixed by the expert (or subsequently by the courts) is higher than the squeeze-out price stated in the squeeze-out notice, such higher price must apply to all remaining minority shareholders.

In 2005, an independent new squeeze-out rule, Section 20e of the Danish Companies Act, was introduced in Danish law. This provision was introduced into Danish law in order to comply with the requirements in the Takeover Directive. Like Section 20b of the Danish Companies Act, it contains a compulsory acquisition provision, which provides that a shareholder who, in a mandatory tender offer (and arguably also a voluntary offer), acquires more than 90 per cent of the share capital and votes in a listed company may personally (i.e., without the board of directors' cooperation) effect a compulsory acquisition.

Since 1999 and until the so-called TDC decision of 8 March 2006 by the Danish Commerce and Companies Agency (the "DCCA"), the DCCA did accept another (faster) way of carrying out compulsory acquisition, namely pursuant to Section 79(2)(iii) of the Danish Companies Act. This method entailed the calling of a general meeting of shareholders at which it is resolved with nine-tenths of the votes cast and the voting share capital represented at the general meeting of shareholders (i.e., not of all votes and shares in the company) to insert a provision in the target company's articles of association pursuant to which the shareholder could require – upon giving notice to the minority shareholders – that the minority shareholders sell their shares to the majority shareholder in question (a so-called "articles-based squeeze-out").

The Danish High Court confirmed the DCCA's decision in its ruling on the matter in June 2007. The High Court ruling was not appealed. Hence, articles-based squeeze-outs are not currently permitted under Danish law.

As to minority shareholders' rights to be bought out, each individual minority shareholder of a company in which more than nine-tenths of the shares and the votes are owned by one shareholder is entitled to force the major shareholder to acquire the minority shareholders' shareholding. If the majority shareholder and the minority shareholder cannot agree on the price applicable to the buyout, an expert will have to be appointed.

7.8.2 Delisting

OMX can decide to delist a company's shares if it finds that the listing is no longer in the interest of the investors and in the general interests of the market.

If OMX receives an application for delisting in a situation where compulsory acquisition procedures regarding the minority shareholders' shares have been initiated in accordance with the Danish Companies Act, it is current practice that OMX will delist the shares.

7.9 Defences to a hostile takeover

7.9.1 Introduction

Denmark has only experienced a few hostile or contested takeovers, and practice and case law are scarce on this subject. Section 7.9.2 below deals with specific defensive devices and 7.9.3 below covers the basic rights and obligations of the directors of the target company.

7.9.2 Specific defensive devices

The focus here is on some of the main defensive devices that are sometimes inserted in the articles of association of a company. It should be noted, however, that rather than having defensive provisions inserted in the articles of association, the shareholders of a company may elect to enter into shareholders' agreements.

The right to amend the articles of association of a Danish company is vested in the general meeting of shareholders, whereas the board of directors, with very few exceptions, may not make any amendments on its own. This means that as a point of departure all amendments to a company's articles of association for defensive purposes must be submitted to the shareholders for approval. Amendments to the articles of association of a Danish company require a minimum two-thirds majority of the votes cast and of the voting share capital represented at a general meeting of shareholders. Certain categories of amendments, for instance those that restrict the negotiability of existing shares or those that reduce the shareholders' rights to dividends for the benefit of persons other than the shareholders and the employees, require the favourable votes of at least nine-tenths of both the votes cast and of the voting share capital represented at a general meeting.

7.9.2.1   A and B shares

As mentioned in 7.2.1 above, the share capital of many Danish listed companies is divided into different classes of shares, typically A shares and B shares, of which the A shares carry 10 times as many votes per share as the B shares. A classic scenario is that the original shareholders of a company decide that the company will issue B shares for listing on OMX while the A shares – that are not listed – remain in the hands of the original shareholders who thereby retain control of the company.

As the A shares carry 10 times as many votes per share as the B shares, 9.1 per cent of a company's share capital may hold the majority of the votes in the company as illustrated by the example in Table 7.1.

Table 7.1   Example of A-share control

Share capital	Percentage	Votes	Percentage
91 A shares of 10 votes each	9.1	910 votes	50.03
909 B shares of one vote each	90.9	909 votes	49.97
1,000 shares	1,000	1,819 votes	100.00

Thus, the division of a company's share capital into high-vote A shares and low-vote B shares represents one of the greatest obstacles to hostile or contested takeovers.

Another obstacle of equal importance is the fact that many Danish companies are controlled by foundations which under their constituent documents may be obliged to maintain control at all times.

7.9.2.2   Voting caps

The Danish Companies Act stipulates that the shareholders may, by a majority of nine-tenths of the votes cast and the voting share capital represented at a general meeting, decide that no shareholder may exercise voting rights attached to their own shares or those of others for more than a specific part of the voting share capital of the company. In this way, the articles of association will provide that the votes of any one shareholder are capped, irrespective of the size of the holding. It is even possible to limit the voting rights of the shareholders by limiting each shareholder's voting power to one vote, no matter how many shares the shareholder owns. In companies where the shares are spread among many small shareholders, this provision would give the board of directors a substantial influence over the company.

7.9.2.3   Consent to transfer

Restrictions on the negotiability of existing shares in a Danish company are valid only to the extent that such restrictions are adopted by a minimum of nine-tenths of the votes cast and the voting capital represented at a meeting of shareholders. If this majority can be obtained, provisions for approval of the transfer of shares, rights of first refusal or ownership limitations regarding the shares of the company may be inserted in the articles of association of the company.

For listed companies it follows from the Executive Order no. 172 of 23 February 2007 on the conditions for the admission of securities to stock exchange listing that listed shares must be "freely negotiable". However, it also appears from the order that the competent authorities may grant an exemption from this principle for provisions in the articles of association that approve the transfer of shares, provided, however, that the "use of the approval clause does not disturb the market". This guideline has given rise to some uncertainty as to how an approval clause is to be administered.

7.9.2.4   Issue of new shares

The share capital of a Danish company may be issued either as a bonus issue (*fondsaktieemission*) or as an issue by subscription for cash or contribution in kind.

The power to increase the share capital of the company is vested in the shareholders who can do so by a majority of two-thirds of the votes cast and the voting share capital represented at a general meeting. With the same majority, the shareholders may authorise the board of directors to issue new shares with or without pre-emptive rights for the shareholders. Based thereon (and subject to 7.9.3), the board of directors may effect a so-called directed issue and, for example, allocate the newly issued shares to one or more "friendly" investors. Such issue of new shares with or without pre-emptive rights for the shareholders against cash or against contribution in kind gives rise to various company law issues which are not dealt with here.

7.9.3   Basic rights and obligations of the directors in the target company

Except for the obligation of the board of directors to publish a statement regarding a public offer made (*see* 7.7.2.1 above) and its duty to disclose at some stage (*see* 7.7.2.2), there are no provisions in Danish statutory law or in Danish regulations setting forth the duties of the directors and the management of a company when faced with a hostile takeover attempt. Danish case law is extremely scarce on the subject.

The provisions of the Danish Companies Act dealing with directors and management liability are based on the general standard in Danish tort law being a rule of negligence. According to this rule, a person is liable for damages caused by him as a consequence of an act or omission that is based on his intent or negligence measured against what a prudent and reasonable person would have done in the circumstances. In that regard it is important to note that Danish company law also imposes on the target board a duty to act loyally towards all shareholders and in the short-term and long-term interest of all shareholders and thus prohibits the target board and the management from acting in a fashion that is clearly likely to provide certain shareholders or others with an undue advantage at the expense of other shareholders or the company. It is generally accepted that the target board need not only act in accordance with the collective shareholder interest. It can take other factors into consideration as well when considering how to address an offer situation, e.g., the impact on the employees. There is no bright line in Danish law between events where pursuit of interests other than that of the shareholders is permissible and where such pursuit violates the duties owed to the shareholders.

7.9.4 *Suspension of special shareholder rights*

Denmark has opted out of Article 9 ("the non-frustration regime") and Article 11 ("the breakthrough regime") of the EU Takeover Directive.

Thus, as regards for instance the breakthrough regime, pursuant to the rules in the Danish Companies Act implementing the Takeover Directive, the shareholders may resolve to introduce procedures ("opt-in") pursuant to which special shareholder rights (including without limitation voting caps and ownership caps) are suspended in the event of the company being faced with a takeover bid. In companies that may introduce such suspension of shareholder rights, if the takeover bid is completed, the offeror must pay compensation to those shareholders who may suffer a loss due to suspension of shareholder rights. As stated at 7.7.2.1 above, the offer document must include information on the compensation to such shareholders.

The shareholders are free to decide if they wish to introduce procedures regarding suspension of shareholder rights. However, if they introduce such measures, it will entail that, for example, pre-emptive rights on transfer of shares, ownership caps, etc. cannot be invoked against the offeror, and disparate voting rights may be dismantled in the takeover process. The suspension of special rights will, however, only apply if the offeror is a company within the EU (or EEA) that has introduced similar procedures on suspension of special rights.

It remains to be seen to what extent the shareholders of Danish listed companies will make use of the opportunity of introducing procedures suspending special shareholder rights.

7.10 Insider dealing and due diligence

7.10.1 Insider dealing and market manipulation

Denmark has implemented Directive 2003/6/EC on insider dealing and market manipulation (market abuse). The Danish Securities Trading Act includes a ban on insider dealing. Inside information means specific non-published information on issuers of securities, and securities or market conditions with respect to such securities which could be likely to have a noticeable effect on the price formation of one or more securities if such information were made public. In this respect, information must be considered made public once a general and relevant dissemination has been made to the market.

Purchase, sale or recommendation to buy or sell a given security must not be performed by any person with inside information which could be of importance to the relevant transaction. This ban, however, does not apply to the acquisition of securities which takes place as a necessary part of the completion of a public offer put forward to gain control of a listed company if the inside information has been obtained in connection with investigations (due diligence) of the company carried out for the purpose of submitting the public offer.

Any person with inside information is prohibited from disclosing such information to any other party unless such disclosure is made within the normal course of his employment, profession or duties.

The Danish Securities Trading Act also forbids market manipulation. It is important to note that the Danish rule is not a general fraud provision but a listing of various prohibited actions that are generally considered capable of causing the share price to deviate from the market price or to affect the demand for the securities.

Non-compliance with the provisions on insider trading and market manipulation may result in fines or imprisonment. The usual penalty for illegal insider trading has been imprisonment for three to five months as well as confiscation of the unjust enrichment and a fine. The penalty for illegal market manipulation has so far been set at a level of 30 days' imprisonment and a fine of DKK10,000.

7.10.2 Due diligence

Outside-in due diligence does not give as much insight as if the target were listed in the US. Thus, Danish securities law does not require listed companies to publish certain agreements. Outside-in due diligence will typically include the following. Announcements and financial statements published by the target company through OMX. Information memoranda/prospectuses used in share offerings by the target company will be available on the FSA's website. Corporate information and documents and annual accounts can be retrieved or requested from the DCCA.

If the board of directors of the target company is willing to give due diligence access it needs to observe the following:

The overriding rule is that due diligence (allowing a third party access to information which is not available to the market) is only allowed to the extent that it is in the target company's interest (and not only in its shareholders' or some of its shareholders' interests).

In addition to the "in the interest of the target company requirement", due diligence access will require that the third party in question (i.e., the potential acquirer and its advisers carrying out the due diligence):

(a)   signs a confidentiality undertaking; and
(b)   undertakes to refrain from trading in the share (other than pursuant to a public offer).

It has been very helpful to practitioners that Danish law has implemented the exception that the insider trading ban does not apply in relation to inside information which has been obtained in connection with a due diligence investigation carried out for the purpose of submitting a public offer.

Also, it should be noted that the target board is under an obligation to ensure that the period of time during which the due diligence is carried out is limited as much as possible.

7.11   Reporting obligations

Notification must be made to the target company:

(a)   when the voting right conferred on the shares represents at least 5 per cent of the share capital's voting rights or their nominal value accounts for at least 5 per cent of the share capital; or
(b)   when a change of a holding already notified entails that limits of 5, 10, 15, 20, 25, 50 or 90 per cent and also limits of one-third or two-thirds of the share capital's voting rights or nominal value are reached or the change entails that the limits stated in paragraph (a) are no longer reached.

Types of instruments to be included when calculating disclosable shareholdings are as follows (these rules follow Directive 2001/34/EC of the European Parliament and of the Council of 28 May 2001 – Article 92):

(a)   shares held by a natural or legal person;
(b)   shares held by a natural or legal person, but where the attaching voting rights may be exercised by another person;
(c)   shares where the attaching voting rights are controlled by the natural or legal person;
(d)   shares which are lodged as security, unless the holder of the security also has the attaching voting right and declares his intention to exercise it;
(e)   shares held by the natural or legal person as security where such natural or legal person also has the voting right and declares his intention to exercise it;
(f)   shares where the attaching voting rights are held by the natural or legal person;

(g)   shares where the natural or legal person under a written agreement has the right in his own discretion to acquire the attaching voting right;

(h)   shares which are deposited with the natural or legal person as security if the natural or legal person has the attaching voting right.

Simultaneously with the notification to the company, a notification with the same information must be submitted for the FSA. The company must publish the notification as soon as possible following receipt.

7.12   Financial assistance

7.12.1   Introduction

The Danish legal regime on financial assistance is divided into two sub-regimes, the first of which (the Section 115 Regime) reflects the implementation into Danish law of the Second Company Directive of the European Community, which sets out (on an objective basis) those persons and liabilities for which the provision of financial assistance by a Danish company is not permitted, and the second of which (the Section 54 Regime) reflects the limits within which the board of directors/management of a Danish company, in the specific circumstances, may provide financial assistance with due consideration of the risk of incurring personal liability.

Although there is no statutory or unified definition of the term "financial assistance", it may be argued that only the Section 115 Regime qualifies as a true financial assistance regime, whereas the Section 54 Regime essentially deals with rules and principles of good management practice and potential mismanagement with associated risks of personal liability.

For Danish law purposes, the two regimes are normally seen and applied such that, after deciding that a certain financial transaction would be compliant with the Section 115 Regime, a second assessment would be required to decide whether it would also be compliant with the Section 54 Regime.

7.12.2   The Section 115 Regime

Statutory rules exist in Section 115 and Section 115a of the Danish Companies Act restricting the right of a Danish limited liability company to provide financial assistance to certain persons and allowing financial assistance to other persons. The contents of the rules may be explained as follows:

(a)   Acquisition debt: an A/S company ("the Provider") is prohibited under Section 115(2) of the Danish Companies Act from lending to or providing security (including guarantees and indemnities) for any investor for the purpose of financing an acquisition or subscription of shares issued or to be issued by the Provider itself or by an EU parent company.

(b)   Other (i.e., non-acquisition) debt: a Provider is prohibited under Section 115(1) of the Danish Companies Act from lending to or providing security for the indebtedness of a shareholder (natural or corporate) in the Provider or in an EU parent company.

(c)   Exceptions for Group financing: the prohibition in respect of non-acquisition debt does not apply to the lending to or the provision of security for the indebtedness of an EU parent company. Furthermore, the lending to and provision of security for related companies of the Provider are not affected by the rules and are therefore permitted.

(d)   Abuse of the rules: structures in which the individual steps are in compliance with the rules, but the aggregate effect of which is that the above rules are being circumvented, are not allowed. Abuse might for instance be to lend or provide security to or in the interest of a person qualifying under the rules for the purpose of such person then passing on the benefit of the financial assistance to another person not qualifying to benefit from the financial assistance if provided directly to it. This would also include the interposition of a non-EU parent company for the purpose only of re-characterising a shareholder from being a shareholder in an EU parent company to being a shareholder in a non-EU parent company.

7.12.3   The Section 54 Regime

7.12.3.1   Statutory rules

Section 54 of the Danish Companies Act provides the statutory basis for the distribution of management responsibilities between the board of directors and the management board, and pursuant to Section 54(3) an obligation is imposed on the board of directors to "consider from time to time whether the financial position of the company is sound in the context of the company's operations".

The potential consequences of failure to observe the Section 54 rules are set out in Section 140 of the Danish Companies Act which reads as follows:

> "members of the board of directors ... who, in the performance of their duties have caused damage to the company due to wilful misconduct or negligence, shall be liable in damages. This consequence shall also apply where damage has been inflicted upon shareholders, creditors of the company or any third party in violation of the provisions of the Act or the articles of association."

7.12.3.2   Explanatory comments

The legal implications of the Section 54 rules in relation to providing financial assistance may be explained as follows:

The board of directors (and each director) must at all times consider whether the company is adequately capitalised to support its business plan and to meet its commercial and financial obligations, and, in connection with a proposed provision of financial assistance, the board of directors must consider whether the risk thereby assumed is proportionate to the financial capacity of the company.

In terms of risk-taking, it is primarily a financial and commercial decision, and the directors must take into account, *inter alia*:

(a)   the risk that the security will be enforced;

(b)   the credit risk associated with the beneficiary and with co-obligors;

(c)   the risk protection arrangements relating to the final distribution of losses among the Provider, the beneficiary and co-obligors;

(d)   the risk that enforcement of the security may adversely affect the company's business operations and financial conditions; and

(e)   the benefit obtained by the company in exchange for the provision of security.

The perspective from which the matter must be considered is the company's ability to discharge its commercial and financial obligations to its stakeholders (contractual parties, public authorities, employees and shareholders). The interests of shareholders may be considered secondary in circumstances where the assistance is provided at the request of (all of) the shareholders.

The directors' assessment must include an analysis based on the company's financial conditions at the time of provision of the assistance, but the assessment must also include a forward-looking analysis with reference to the company's strategic goals and business plans and its budgets and forecasts, and in such respect it bears resemblance to the directors' assessments made in relation to proposed substantial business investments.

For the avoidance of doubt in respect of item (e) above, "corporate benefit" on the part of the company is not an absolute requirement, but the existence of a corporate benefit is an argument in support of providing assistance. A reference to corporate benefit of the group as a whole without demonstration of any benefit attributable to the company in itself has no substantive merit.

7.12.4   Breach of the rules

7.12.4.1   Overall observations
The legal effects of a breach of the rules are significantly different depending on whether the breach relates to the Section115 Regime or the Section 54 Regime.

In the case of the Section 115 Regime, the affected security arrangements are held invalid and not enforceable, and any person who has taken part in the setting up of such arrangement may be held personally liable for any damage caused to the security provider and the beneficiary of the invalidated security interest.

In the case of the Section 54 Regime, the affected security arrangements are upheld, but the directors who have taken part in the setting up of such arrangements may be held personally liable for any damage caused to the security provider, the stakeholders of the security provider and the beneficiary of the security interest.

7.12.4.2   The Section 115 Regime

Non-criminal legal consequences of breach
The general rules in respect of criminal legal consequences of breach of the Section 115 Regime include a range of prioritised legal consequences and remedial actions.

First, the provision of financial assistance in breach of Section 115 is deemed invalid. This will have a direct effect on guarantees and security provided, which will not be enforceable by the assistance recipient ("the beneficiary") against the assistance provider and must be released. Indeed, there is an exception in case the beneficiary was acting in good faith and did not know that the provision was in breach of Section 115 (a situation which is unlikely to arise in connection with acquisition finance).

Second, if the beneficiary has already received amounts under the financial assistance arrangement, the beneficiary has an obligation to repay amounts received (and interest thereon) to the security provider.

Third, if a guarantee or security provided cannot be released or repayment from a beneficiary cannot be achieved, the persons (legal or natural) that have made, maintained or assisted in making and maintaining the provision of the financial assistance may be held jointly and severally liable for the resulting loss incurred by the security provider. Such persons may include directors, managers, shareholders, auditors, accounting and tax advisers, legal counsel, banks and bankers and others.

Criminal legal consequences of breach
The general rules in relation to criminal liability under the Section 115 Regime include a dual system of actions.

The Danish Companies Act contains penalty provisions under which fines can be levied on each natural person and the company as a legal person that has committed or assisted in the breach of the rules. The penalty provisions apply to a wide range of provisions in the Danish Companies Act, and there are no special provisions applicable to the Section 115 Regime.

The Danish Penal Code contains a range of penalty provisions in respect of various economic crimes, fraud, improper enrichment, etc.

Historically, actions for criminal liability in relation to financial assistance play no significant role. Ignoring cases of clear fraudulent behaviour and cases where a single investor holding the positions of shareholder and management would commingle corporate funds and private funds, it is hard to find any precedence at all.

7.12.5 Certain specific leverage buy-out-related issues regarding financial assistance

7.12.5.1 Distribution of post-acquisition dividends
The legal position on post-acquisition dividends is very clear in Denmark, especially since the Danish Supreme Court handed down its judgment in the so-called *Procuritas* case in October 2005. The *Procuritas* case involved an acquisition of all of the shares in a target company. The facts relied on by the court included that, to a very substantial degree, the buyer's financing of the acquisition was based on borrowed funds which, after completion of the transaction, would be repaid by share dividends distributed by the target company. The court ruled that:

> "Neither the wording of the Danish Companies Act nor the relevant preparatory work sufficiently supports the conclusion that such financing

scheme based on distributable reserves distributed in accordance with Section 110 of the Danish Companies Act (i.e., the dividend distribution rules) will constitute a breach of the financial assistance provisions of Section 115(2) of the Danish Companies Act."

Unrelated to the financial assistance position, distributions to shareholders in the past 12 months following a takeover require compliance with the information requirement discussed at 7.7.2.1 above.

7.12.5.2   Post-acquisition merger

The DCCA has established a practice according to which registration of a merger between an acquiring company (the investor) and the target company is rejected if the investor has funded the purchase of shares in the target company, and the target company's assets, by loans, and if, as a result of the merger, the target company's assets could be used directly to service and repay the investor's loan.

The DCCA's practice serves the purpose of preventing that investors evade the restrictions contained in the regulated capital distribution methods, by merging a debt financed investor and the target company, and thereby creating a possibility of using the target company's assets to service and repay the debt at the expense of the target company's creditors and stakeholders.

The DCCA's practice does, in the authors' view, not aim to introduce any additional limitations in the investor's right to transfer capital back to the investor through the regulated capital distribution methods. This is in accordance with Section 115(2) of the Danish Companies Act, the intention of which is, likewise, not to introduce additional limitations in the investor's right to transfer capital back to the investor in accordance with the provisions of the Danish Companies Act (this is confirmed in the Supreme Court judgment in the Procuritas Case). In its judgment, the Supreme Court established a narrow interpretation of the expression "make assets available" in Section 115(2) of the Danish Companies Act. Therefore, if the acquirer is not acquisition debt financed (i.e., it is equity capitalised) and the remaining acquisition debt is held by its parent company, a transaction entailing a post-closing merger between the acquirer and the target company followed by distribution of dividends by the merged entity to the parent company, which then repays the acquisition financing, is not, in the view of the authors, comprised by the above mentioned practice of the DCCA.

Chapter 8

Estonia

Raino Paron, Partner
Marina Tolmatšova, Associate Lawyer
Heili Haabu, Associate Lawyer
Raidla & Partners

8.1 Introduction

Since the beginning of the 1990s, Estonia has been experiencing a steady increase in the number of mergers and acquisitions. The growth started after Estonia regained its independence and was initially caused by the privatisation of state-owned property (including companies and land) and the transition to a market economy that facilitated Estonia's economic recovery and increased investment opportunities for foreign investors. The following have stimulated further growth in the mergers and acquisitions ("M&A") sector:

(a) the opening of the market to foreign investments;
(b) the rapid development of Estonia's legal system in accordance with developments in the European legal system; and
(c) Estonia's preparations to become a member of the European Union that resulted in Estonia's accession in 2004.

The principal legislative Acts that govern mergers and acquisitions of corporate entities in Estonia are:

(a) the Commercial Code of 1995 (*Äriseadustik*) that sets out general rules on the transfer of shares of companies registered in Estonia and contains regulation of mergers and separations (including break-ups); and
(b) the Competition Act of 2001 (*Konkurentsiseadus*) that establishes which merger and acquisition cases require the prior approval of the Competition Board.

The Estonian Central Register for Securities Act of 2000 (*Eesti väärtpaberite keskregistri seadus*) sets out rules for registration of transactions with securities of (mainly) Estonian public companies. The Securities' Market Act of 2001 (*Väärtpabrituru seadus*) provides the rules applicable to the public sale of securities in Estonia and requirements relating to activities of and acquisition of qualifying holdings in market participants.

In addition to the Commercial Code, the Competition Act, the Securities Market Act and the Estonian Central Register for Securities Act, certain companies (banks, investment funds, insurance companies, etc.) are subject to special laws that regulate their activities.

Furthermore, in the case of listed companies, issues related to mergers and acquisitions are also regulated by the Rules of the Tallinn Stock Exchange ("TSE"). The TSE is the only active Stock Exchange in Estonia and is the principal centre for public trading of securities in Estonia.

The function of supervision and enforcement of merger and acquisition regulation is carried out by the Competition Board (*Konkurentsiamet*), the Estonian Financial Supervisory Authority (*Finantsinspektsioon*), the Estonian Centre of Securities (*Väärtpaberikeskus*) and to a certain extent also by the Commercial Register (*Äriregister*). In the case of listed companies, their compliance is also monitored by the TSE.

8.2   Acquisition targets

8.2.1   General

Estonian companies can generally be divided into five categories:

(a)   general partnerships (*täisühingud*);
(b)   limited partnerships (*usaldusühingud*);
(c)   private limited companies (*osaühingud*);
(d)   public limited companies (joint stock companies) (*aktsiaseltsid*); and
(e)   commercial associations (*tulundusühistu*).

General and limited partnerships and commercial associations comprise only a small fraction of the companies registered with the Estonian Commercial Register and they are rarely chosen as target companies in M&A transactions.

Private limited companies make up the vast majority of registered companies, followed by public limited companies which constitute the second most-common category of registered business in Estonia. Private and public limited companies are the most common acquisition targets in M&A transactions in Estonia.

8.2.2   Private limited companies

A private limited company (*osaühing* or "OÜ") is a limited liability company with a minimum share capital of EEK40,000 and it is a separate legal entity that has a power to contract in its own name, sue and be sued, own and convey property. As in all limited liability companies, private limited companies offer their shareholders protection from personal liability, that is, the company's shareholders are not generally personally liable for the company's obligations and the company itself is liable for its debts and obligations to the extent of all its assets. Private limited companies tend to be closely-held businesses formed and managed by a relatively small group of people that share profits.

Shares in a private limited company (*osad*) are treated as belonging to a single class. However, the company's articles of incorporation may provide that certain rights or benefits attach to a particular individual's share. Shares are freely transferable to other shareholders of the company. Existing shareholders usually have a pre-emptive right to buy shares offered for sale to a third party. The whole shareholding of each shareholder in a private limited company is deemed as one share. However, the nominal values and numbers of corresponding votes of the shares of different shareholders may vary.

Private limited companies usually have a one-tier board structure and the shareholders have discretion to make decisions on all issues related to the business of the company.

Shareholder dividends need not be distributed pro rata, but the applicable rules of distribution must be stated in the articles of incorporation. A private limited company's share capital must be fully paid-up before the company may be incorporated through registration with the Commercial Register. Private limited companies are not required by law to register their shares with the Estonian Central Registry of Securities (*Eesti väärtpaberite keskregister*, the "ECRS"), Estonia's public register of securities, although they may choose to do so. In the case of private limited companies that are not registered with the ECRS, share transfer agreements must be verified by a notary public of Estonia.

8.2.3   Public limited companies

Like a private limited company, a public limited company (*aktsiaselts* or "AS") has powers attributable to a separate legal entity and offers its shareholders the advantage of limited liability. Public limited companies, however, are characterised by greater capital requirements and more numerous classes of shares than private limited companies, and are required to register with the ECRS and to submit to independent audits.

Public limited companies must have a minimum share capital of EEK 400,000 as opposed to the EEK 40,000 minimum applicable to private limited companies. The shares of a public limited company may be divided into different classes, each of which may be granted different rights. Shares of public limited companies (*aktsiad*) are freely transferable, unless the company's articles of incorporation confer a pre-emptive right on other shareholders.

Estonian public limited companies have a mandatory two-tier board structure consisting of a management board (*juhatus*) and supervisory board (*nõukogu*). The general shareholders meeting has the sole right to decide on certain corporate matters (e.g,. changes in the share capital and articles of incorporation, merger, split-up, transformation and winding-up of the company and election of the supervisory board), but may adopt resolutions on other matters related to the activities of the company only upon demand of the management board or supervisory board.

In public limited companies, dividends must be distributed to shareholders pro rata, based upon the nominal value of the shares of each shareholder. Where a public limited company has different classes of shares, owners may enjoy different rights, such as, for example, the right of preferred shareholders to receive dividends in a predetermined amount.

Unlike in the case of private limited companies, for whom registration with the ECRS is optional, ECRS registration is mandatory for public limited companies. The ECRS holds securities and records securities transactions, maintains ownership registration records and records of pledges, and processes and clears securities transactions. This information is accessible to the public through the ECRS register. All transactions executed on the TSE are cleared and settled through the ECRS, and therefore only those securities that are registered with the ECRS may be traded on the TSE.

8.3   Exchange and investment controls

8.3.1   Exchange control

Exchange control regulation has not been applicable since the introduction of the Estonian national currency, the "eesti kroon", in June 1992. The Estonian kroon has a fixed exchange rate against the euro whereby €1 equals EEK15.6466. Estonia has decided to accede to the European Monetary Union ("EMU") as soon as possible. While meeting the other Maastricht criteria required to accede to EMU is not problematic, the inflation rate has been above the applied limit in Estonia in the past years (which is mostly attributable to fast economic growth).

8.3.2   Investment control

To meet the requirements of acquis for EU accession, by the time of its accession to EU Estonia had abolished almost all investment restrictions, including restrictions relating to the acquisition of real estate and shareholdings in Estonian companies by nationals and companies of other Member States of the EU. However, according to the EU Accession Treaty, Estonia is entitled to maintain in force, for a transitional period of seven years as from the date of its accession to EU, restrictions regarding acquisition of agricultural land and forests by foreign persons, including nationals and companies of other Member States of the EU.

Investments in certain industries, particularly the financial sector (i.e., credit institutions, investment funds, brokerage firms, pension management companies, etc.), may be subject to prior notification or approval of the relevant supervisory authority. However, such rules apply to both Estonian and foreign persons alike.

In the financial sector, there are specific requirements for owning qualifying holdings, thresholds of which are established by the Credit Institutions Act (*Krediidiasutuste seadus*), Investment Funds Act (*Investeerimisfondide seadus*) and the Securities Market Act (*Väärtpaberituru seadus*). Under Estonian law a qualifying holding is deemed to be a holding which directly or indirectly represents 10 per cent or more of the share capital or votes in a company, or which grants dominant influence over the management of the relevant company in another manner.

The Securities Market Act, Credit Institutions Act and the Investment Funds Act provide that qualifying holdings in an investment firm, credit institution or management company may be held by persons who, in the opinion of the Financial Supervisory Authority, are able to ensure the sound and prudent management of the credit institution and whose business connections and ownership structure are transparent and do not prevent the exercise of supervision. Similar restrictions in respect of shareholding have also been established in the Pension Funds Act and in the Estonian Central Register of Securities Act (*Eesti väärtpaberite keskregistri seadus*).

Furthermore, Estonian law sets out certain notification obligations regarding the acquisition or change of the qualifying holding. The general rule that applies similarly to investment firms, credit institutions and management companies is that a person who intends to acquire a qualifying holding in such an entity or to increase a qualifying holding so that the proportion of the share capital or votes in the bank or investment firm held by such person exceeds respectively 20, 33 or 50 per cent, or to reduce the amount of its qualifying holding below the above-referred levels, is required to inform the Financial Supervisory Authority thereof. In cases provided by law the Financial Supervisory Authority may refuse to authorise acquisition of the qualifying holding.

8.3.3 Competition law restrictions

In certain merger and acquisition cases a notice of concentration must be submitted to and a respective approval obtained from the Estonian Competition Board, which has the right to prohibit a merger or acquisition if this might cause a dominant position in the market or strengthen such a position which substantially restricts competition on the market. Concentrations with a community dimension are subject to control under the EC Merger Regulation ("ECMR").

For further details on Estonian competition law concentration regulation issues, *see* 8.4 below.

8.3.4 Labour law considerations

Estonian law does not set forth labour-related restrictions on transfer of shares or on other important structural changes in companies. It should be mentioned, however, that pursuant to the Estonian Employment Contract Act (*Eesti Vabariigi töölepingu seadus*) the reorganisation or change of affiliation, or form of ownership of a company, agency or other organisation, or the transfer of an enterprise does not terminate employment contracts. In the case of transfer of an enterprise, employment contracts are transferred along with the enterprise and certain notification and consultation obligations must be complied with.

8.3.5 Share transfer regulation

Pursuant to the Estonian Central Registry of Securities Act, the shares of all Estonian public limited companies must be registered with the Estonian Centre for Securities ("ECS") in the book-entry (dematerialised) form. The ECS runs the main register of securities, the ECRS, and oversees the deposit of dematerialised securities, the registration of security ownership and pledges, and the processing and clearing of security transactions. Every investor intending to acquire shares registered with the ECRS must open a securities account in the ECRS in its own name. However, professional securities market participants (local and foreign) holding a licence have the right to open nominee accounts in the ECRS in order to hold the shares owned by their clients. The registration system in the ECRS provides an additional guarantee that the share transfers will be duly registered and the buyer will obtain a valid title to the purchased shares.

Securities accounts opened in the ECRS are accessed by account owners via account administrators authorised by the ECS. Currently there are 10 account administrators authorised by ECS, seven of which are Estonian credit institutions. The transactions with securities registered with the ECRS may be executed on terms of Free of Payment delivery ("FOP") or Delivery versus Payment ("DVP"). In the case of Free of Payment ("FOP") transactions, parties must submit to the ECS via their account administrators matching transaction orders for transfer and acceptance of securities, whereas payments for the transferred securities are not verified by the ECS and conducted by parties separately from the security transfer. In Delivery versus Payment transactions the payment of the purchase price is settled simultaneously with the share transfer and is supervised by the ECS, which ensures that the shares are not transferred without the transfer of the purchase price and vice versa. All Stock Exchange transactions are executed on terms of DVP and are settled on the third exchange day after the transaction date.

In order to operate on the regulated stock market, an investor has to cover various expenses, which, according to the character and content of the service, are divided into regular fees (e.g., for account maintenance) and single fees (e.g., transaction fees). Execution of the transactions by the ECRS also incurs certain fees which are payable by the investors. Neither the Tallinn Stock Exchange nor the ECRS prescribes for maximum transaction fees offered to investors by the account operators. Therefore, different financial institutions acting as account operators may have different fees.

The share transfer agreements of private limited companies whose shares are not registered with the ECRS must be executed in notarised form and the change of shareholders is registered in the share register of the company that is kept by the management board.

8.3.6   Requirements for disclosure of shareholdings

8.3.6.1   Disclosure of over 10 per cent shareholdings
According to the Commercial Code, once a year, along with submission of approved annual accounts, the board of directors of a private limited company must submit to the Commercial Register a list of shareholders who hold more than 10 per cent of votes determined by shares as of the date of the shareholders' annual general meeting. In the case of private limited companies, such list must contain details of all the shareholders. In the case of listed companies, a list of shareholders who hold at least 5 per cent of votes determined by shares must be disclosed in the annual accounts.

8.3.6.2   Mandatory notification in the case of limited liability companies
If one single shareholder acquires all the shares of a public limited company or a private limited company (and even if at the same time the shares of the public limited company are also owned by the company itself), the board of directors

shall immediately submit a written notice to the Commercial Register in that respect.

8.3.6.3 Disclosure of qualifying holding in listed companies

Everyone who has either directly or indirectly, individually or together with persons operating in concert, acquired a holding of 5 per cent in an Estonian company listed on the Tallinn Stock Exchange or admitted for trading on another regulated market, or has increased such holding to more than 10, 20, 33⅓, 50 or 66⅔ per cent of all votes represented by shares of such company, must immediately notify the respective company and the securities market supervision authority (the Financial Supervisory Authority ("FSA")). The same notification requirements also apply if the holding falls below the rates quoted above.

8.4 Concentration control

8.4.1 General

In Estonia, the competition law-related rules on concentrations are set out in the Competition Act. Concentrations with a community dimension are subject to control under the EC Merger Regulation ("ECMR"), and the Estonian Competition Board does not have authority to control concentrations controlled by the European Commission under the ECMR.

8.4.2 Concentration under Estonian competition rules

Pursuant to the Competition Act, a "concentration" is deemed to arise if:

(a) previously-independent undertakings merge within the meaning of the Commercial Code;
(b) an undertaking acquires control of the whole or part of another undertaking;
(c) undertakings jointly acquire control of the whole or part of a third undertaking;
(d) a natural person already controlling at least one undertaking acquires control of the whole or part of another undertaking;
(e) several natural persons already controlling at least one undertaking jointly acquire control of the whole or part of another undertaking.

The transactions described above are not deemed to be a concentration if the transactions are carried out as an internal restructuring of a group of companies.

The Competition Act defines "control" (or prevalent influence) as being the opportunity for one undertaking or several undertakings jointly or for a natural person, by purchasing shares or on the basis of a contract, transaction, articles of incorporation or by any other means, to exercise direct or indirect influence on another undertaking which may consist of a right to:

(a) exercise significant influence on the composition, work or decision-making of the management bodies of the other undertaking;

(b)   use and dispose of all or a significant proportion of the assets of the other undertaking.

8.4.3   Thresholds for mandatory notification

According to the Competition Act, a concentration shall be subject to control by the Competition Board if:

(a)   the aggregate turnover of the parties to the concentration in Estonia exceeded EEK100 million during the previous financial year; and

(b)   the turnover of each of at least two parties to the concentration in Estonia exceeded EEK30 million during the same period.

The turnover in Estonia of a party to a concentration is obtained as a result of sale of goods to buyers within the territory of Estonia. Therefore, also foreign-to-foreign acquisitions are subject to Estonian concentration control rules if all the above conditions are fulfilled.

8.4.4   Procedure

The Competition Board shall be notified of a concentration subject to control before the entry into force of the concentration and after entry into a merger agreement, performance of a transaction for acquisition of parts of the under-taking, performance of a transaction for acquisition of control or joint control or announcement of a public bid for securities.

Credit institutions, securities brokers and insurers shall give notification of a concentration after obtaining permission for the transfer from the Financial Supervisory Authority.

The relevant notification must be submitted jointly by the merging parties, or by a person or undertaking acquiring sole control, or jointly by persons or under-takings acquiring joint control. The list of documents and information to be submitted to the Competition Board must comply with the extensive require-ments of the Competition Act and the decrees adopted pursuant to the Competition Act. Detailed market information must be submitted if the parties to the concentration (or any of their group companies) operate on the same market or on connected markets and the concentration results in certain market shares. A state fee of EEK30,000 is payable for the processing of the concentra-tion notification.

The Competition Act stipulates that, within 30 calendar days from the sub-mission of the notification, the Competition Board must make one of the follow-ing decisions:

(a)   to grant permission to the concentration; or

(b)   to initiate supplementary proceedings if as a consequence of the trans-action competition might be significantly restricted in the goods market; or

(c)   to send a written notice informing that either the transaction does not constitute a concentration or the concentration is not subject to control; or

(d)   to terminate the proceedings if the parties to the concentration decide not to concentrate.

The supplementary proceedings may last for a maximum of four months and shall end with one of the following decisions by the Competition Board:

(a)   to grant permission to concentrate; or
(b)   to prohibit the concentration; or
(c)   to terminate the proceedings if the parties to the concentration decide not to go forward with the transaction(s) at issue.

A concentration is permitted if the Competition Board has not made at least one of the above-stated decisions within the specified time frame.

8.4.5   Substantive test for control and suspension of concentration

The Competition Act states that the Competition Board shall prohibit a concentration if it may create or strengthen a dominant position as a result of which competition would be significantly restricted in the goods market.

In order to avoid restriction of competition through creation or strengthening of a dominant position, the Director General of the Competition Board or his or her deputy may, on the basis of the proposals of the parties, attach certain additional conditions to the consent to concentration. Such conditions and obligations may take the form of divestments of or restrictions on certain business operations, etc.

Pursuant to the Competition Act, the parties to the concentration may not perform any acts directed at giving effect to the concentration or do anything that would hinder execution of a decision prohibiting the concentration, and all such acts (if performed) are void, until permission to concentrate has been obtained from the Competition Board unless concentration is deemed to be permitted under the Competition Act.

This means that the parties may sign the relevant agreements but they may not be implemented (e.g., the shares or assets (where relevant) may not be acquired) until permission to concentrate is granted by the Competition Board.

8.4.6   Appeals

The decisions of the Competition Board may be contested in the Administrative Court by the parties to the concentration or by any other persons whose rights or liberties have been violated through such decision. The complaint must be submitted within 30 days of the date of notification of the decision by the Competition Board.

8.4.7   Sanctions

The Competition Act sets forth penalties for non-notification of the concentration, the violation of the prohibition of concentration, and violation of conditions of a concentration. Repeated violation may bring about criminal liability of an infringing company and a pecuniary punishment of up to EEK250 million.

8.5   Methods of acquisition

8.5.1   Private agreements

Acquisition agreements used in Estonia vary considerably and depend on various circumstances, for example:

(a)   the size of the target company and the size of shareholding to be acquired;
(b)   whether the shares of private or public limited liability companies will be transferred; and
(c)   whether the acquirer has been offered an opportunity to conduct due diligence of the underlying company, etc.

It should be noted that private transfers of shares in Estonian companies are not highly regulated and are subject to general rules on sale contracts provided in the Law of Obligations Act (*Võlaõigusseadus*). However, Estonian law also recognises the principle of "freedom of contract" that allows the parties to agree on applicable terms and conditions of sale that differ from the provisions of law. In practice, such freedom is widely used by the parties and different specific price adjustment agreements, parties' covenants, and representations and warranties granted by the seller(s) of shares are common for the share transfer agreements.

The Commercial Code provides certain mandatory requirements in respect of the sale of shares. In the case of transfer of shares of the private limited company to third persons, other shareholders have a pre-emptive right to purchase such shares unless the articles of incorporation of the company provide otherwise. The shares of the listed companies are always freely transferable.

8.5.2   Mergers and split ups

The Commercial Code regulates the procedure for mergers of companies registered in Estonia. With the exception of commercial associations, the mergers of different types of companies are allowed (i.e., mergers between full and limited liability companies as well as mergers between private and public limited companies).

According to the Commercial Code a merger may be implemented in one of two ways:

(a)   the company A (the company being acquired) merges with company B (the acquiring company) and company A shall be considered dissolved as of the registration of the merger and without further liquidation procedure. Upon the merger, the assets of company A shall transfer to the acquiring company. The shareholders of company A will become shareholders of company B;
(b)   the merging companies form a new company. Upon formation of a new company, the assets of the merging companies shall transfer to it and the merging companies shall be considered dissolved. The shareholders of the merging companies will become the shareholders of the new company.

For the implementation of a merger, a time-consuming formal procedure must be followed. The representatives of the companies must conclude a merger agreement in which the merging companies shall, *inter alia* agree on the share exchange ratio, the terms of transfer of the shares and the consequences of merger for the employees of the company being acquired. The merger agreement shall be submitted to the auditors for their approval. The rights and obligations arising from the merger agreement will become effective upon the approval of the merger agreement by the shareholders general meetings of the merging companies where the merger resolution shall be adopted. The merger agreement has to be certified by a notary public. The assets of the companies absorbed shall pass to the acquiring company as of the registration of the merger with the Commercial Register.

Separations and break-ups have similar time-consuming and formal procedures. However, separations and break-ups are rare as more convenient tools are available (e.g., the establishment of a subsidiary and making a contribution in kind to the new company is much less time consuming).

8.5.3 Joint ventures

There is no special regulation of joint ventures in Estonia and the establishment of such ventures is not common.

8.5.4 Transfer of business enterprise

Pursuant to the Commercial Code, a business enterprise is an economic operating unit comprising things, rights and obligations designated for the activities of the enterprise. Upon the transfer of ownership or possession of things and rights belonging to an enterprise as a whole, all obligations related to the enterprise or to the organisationally independent part thereof shall be transferred to the transferee or recipient of possession. If executed, the agreements of the enterprise transfer are usually detailed and provide an extensive list of representations and warranties given by the seller(s).

8.6 Offers

8.6.1 Private offers

The definition of a "private offer of securities" is provided in the Securities Market Act ("SMA"). The SMA defines an offer of securities as private (or non-public) if the securities are offered only:

(a) to professional investors (the SMA sets out a specific list of persons that qualify as professional investors in the meaning of the SMA, and such list includes, *inter alia*, credit institutions, investment firms, insurance companies, foreign persons that are deemed to be professional investors under the laws of their jurisdiction, etc.); or

(b) to fewer than 99 persons per Contracting State, other than qualified investors; or

(c) to investors who acquire securities for a total consideration of at least €50,000 per investor, for each separate offer; or

(d)   for a nominal value of at least €50,000 per unit; or

(e)   for a total price of less than €100,000 in a period of 12 months.

For the purposes of the SMA an offer of securities is defined as any proposal to acquire securities, including an invitation to make an offer, the issue of securities, and offers under conditions whereof securities would be issued or transferred to investors by a third party.

In the case of a private offer of securities there is no requirement for the publication and registration of the prospectus with regard to the offering of securities with the Financial Supervisory Authority ("FSA"). Furthermore, no public announcement of the offering is required in the case of a private offer.

Private offers account for most of the mergers and acquisitions conducted in Estonia. During the 10 years to 2005, when a wide range of state-owned companies were privatised, the transfers were often made in the form of a public auction. However, most of the other acquisitions are still conducted by means of initial informal contacts between the potential buyers and the seller, followed by execution of a letter of intent and a non-disclosure agreement. Private sales include options to acquire all or a certain portion of the existing share capital or acquisition of newly issued shares of the company. Usually, the potential buyer conducts legal and financial due diligence of the company to be acquired and the share purchase agreement is negotiated and executed thereafter. However, on several occasions the parties to the transaction have first executed the share purchase agreement and made the final determination of purchase price and the closing of the deal dependent on the findings of the due diligence conducted in the company to be acquired.

8.6.2   Public offers

8.6.2.1   General

Pursuant to the SMA, each offer of securities shall be a "public offering" unless the offer falls into a category of a "private offer" as described at 8.6.1 above.

If the offering is classified as a public offering, publication and registration of the prospectus with regard to the offering of securities ("prospectus") with the FSA and public announcement of the offering are required as a rule. However, certain categories of public offerings which are specifically listed in the SMA (e.g., offering of securities of an issuer or of companies belonging to the same consolidated group companies with the issue solely to current or former employees and members of managing bodies of these companies, etc.) do not require publication and registration of the prospectus with the FSA. The SMA also sets out a specific procedure for public offering of securities of foreign issuers.

The Investment Funds Act ("IFA") sets out specific rules on public offering of units or shares of Estonian and foreign investment funds. In accordance with EU applicable rules, public offerings in Estonia of undertakings for the collective investment of transferable securities ("UCITS") funds which are registered for public sale in European Economic Area ("EEA") Member States and that comply with requirements of public offering of eurofunds set out in the IFA are not subject to prior approval by the FSA, but must be notified to the FSA in advance.

8.6.2.2   Contents of the offer documents

A prospectus must contain all significant information necessary to make an informed investment decision about the offer, the securities offered, the issuer, the economic situation and future prospects of the issuer, as well as other circumstances that influence or may influence the price of the securities offered. The detailed requirements in respect of the prospectus are established by the regulation adopted pursuant to the SMA.

The prospectus must be drafted in the Estonian language. In certain cases the prospectus or a part thereof may be presented in another language. Any circumstances that may affect the price of the securities, which become known after registration of the prospectus or during the period between publishing the prospectus and the beginning of the offer, must be immediately stated by the offeror in an annex to the prospectus.

If the offered securities will be listed on the TSE or traded through a regulated market, separate Listing Particulars (or Listing Prospectus) must be submitted to the TSE.

8.6.2.3   Notification and approval

Prior to its publication and announcement of the offer, a prospectus must be registered with the FSA. In order to register a prospectus a relevant application together with the prospectus and a set of additional documents must be filed with the FSA. In order to register a prospectus of a foreign issuer, certain additional documents may need to be submitted as established by the SMA.

The FSA shall, within 20 days of submission of the application, make a decision about registering or refusing to register the prospectus.

Notification requirements also exist in respect of offerings of securities issued by Estonian local governments or legal persons to persons residing or located in foreign countries.

8.6.2.4   Publication of the prospectus and procedure of the offer

The person arranging the offer of the securities of the issuer ("the offeror") is obliged to disclose a prospectus pertaining to the public offer of securities (unless the prospectus need not be made public pursuant to the exceptions provided in the SMA as detailed at 8.6.2.1 above).

The prospectus must be disclosed no later than the day that the public offer of securities is announced, and it must be accessible to the public (primarily to all investors and other interested parties) during the term of the offer. If the securities are intended to be listed on a Tallinn Stock Exchange, the Listing Particulars may be disclosed instead of the prospectus.

Prior to commencement of an offer, the offeror shall announce the offer by means of publishing the relevant announcement in at least one national newspaper. An offer can be advertised only after announcement of that offer.

The offeror is obliged to ensure that during the offer:

(a)   all potential investors receive information on an equal basis;

(b)   the printed prospectus is available to all investors free of charge.

The offeror must immediately inform the FSA of any significant changes that have occurred in information presented in the prospectus during the period of the offer and disclose such changes in at least the same national daily newspaper in which the announcement of the offer was published.

If the offeror changes the terms and conditions of the offer significantly during the period of the offer, it has the obligation upon request of the respective investor to cancel the subscription and return all funds received, or to redeem the securities from the investors provided that the respective claim has been submitted to the offeror during the term of offer.

8.6.2.5   *Mandatory public offers*

The shares which are traded on the regulated market are subject to mandatory public offers in the event that certain conditions have been met (*see* 8.6.4.1 below).

8.6.3   *Hostile offers and defences thereof*

Pursuant to general rules established by the Commercial Code, shares of public limited liability companies are freely transferable. An exception to this rule is a pre-emptive right of shareholders to purchase shares transferred to third persons. Pursuant to the Rules of the TSE, shares listed on the TSE must be free of any pre-emptive rights. Therefore, the transfer-blocking clauses may not effectively prevent transfer of shares under Estonian law. There are no rules on compulsory repurchase of shares under Estonian law.

The use of generally known anti-takeover devices (such as poison pills, classi-fied boards, etc.) is not sufficiently supported by Estonian law currently, but the situation is expected to be improved with the implementation of the directive on takeover bids, 2004/25/EC. Amendments to the Securities Market Act whereby directive no 2004/25/EC will be implemented are currently being processed by the Parliament.

8.6.4   *Compulsory acquisition of minorities*

8.6.4.1   *Protection of minority shareholders*

The law provides protection to minority shareholders in the event of mergers and takeovers in three ways:

(a)   the law sets forth the requirement that a merger may be only conducted on the basis of a decision of the general meeting of shareholders adopted by at least a two-thirds majority of the votes, and if a company has several classes of shares, the resolution must be adopted by at least a two-thirds majority of the holders of each class of shares (NB: even a higher majority requirement may be stipulated in the articles of incorporation of a company);

(b)   if the minority shareholders do not have a sufficient percentage of votes to reject merger, the rule of mandatory share repurchase will apply under the certain conditions. Namely, in the case of a merger of different types of companies (private limited and public limited companies), a shareholder of the company who opposes the merger may, within two months from the registration of the merger in the Commercial Register, demand that the acquiring company repurchase such shareholder's shares or may sell its shares regardless of any restrictions on disposal applicable pursuant to law or the articles of incorporation of the company. In the case of mandatory repurchase, the amount of compensation for the shares must be equal to the sum which the shareholder would have received from the distribution of the remaining assets if the company had been liquidated at the time of the adoption of the merger resolution;

(c)   the Securities Market Act sets forth the terms of mandatory takeover bids for the acquisition of the shares held by minority shareholders of the companies, the shares of which are traded on the regulated market.

Pursuant to the terms of the SMA, a person who has acquired control (or a dominant influence) over a company registered in Estonia ("the target company"), the shares of which are traded on the regulated market, either directly or in concert with other persons acting together, must, within 20 days of acquiring a dominant influence make a tender offer for all shares of the target company. The takeover bid must be valid for at least 28 days.

For the purpose of the SMA a control (or dominant influence) is acquired over a company by a person if the person:

(a)   owns half or more than half of the votes represented by shares; or
(b)   being a shareholder of the company, has the right to appoint or remove a majority of the members of the supervisory board or management board of the company; or
(c)   being a shareholder of the company, controls more than half of the votes represented by shares on the basis of an agreement entered into with other shareholders.

In certain cases listed in the SMA, the FSA may grant an exemption from the requirement of mandatory takeover bid on the basis of a relevant written application from the person that has acquired a dominant influence over a target company.

Competing bids are allowed under Estonian law. In the event that another offeror makes a tender offer for the shares which are the object of the tender offer (competitive tender offer), the target person will have the right to choose between the offers and, during the term of the original tender offer:

(a)   to withdraw from the proposal to transfer the shares made to the offeror within the framework of the original takeover bid; and
(b)   to withdraw from the share transfer agreement executed within the framework of the original takeover bid.

The Securities Market Act provides that the purchase price of a share, which serves as the object of a mandatory takeover bid, shall be a fair price. The shares may be acquired for cash or for securities which are listed or traded on the regulated market.

The Securities Market Act states that a takeover bid must be submitted for prior approval of the FSA. The FSA must decide on approval of the takeover bid or refuse to approve the takeover bid or grant the exception referred to above within 15 days of receiving a relevant written application from the offeror. The FSA must refuse to approve a takeover bid if it violates the requirements of applicable legal acts.

The offeror and a person operating in concert with it shall have no right to make a new takeover bid in respect of the same target company for six months from the expiration of the term of the takeover bid as determined by the offeror unless the FSA consents to such new bid in order to protect the investors or on some other justified grounds.

8.6.4.2   Squeeze-outs (compulsory sales by minority shareholders)
The rules on the "squeeze out" of minority shareholders are provided in the Commercial Code.

Pursuant to the Commercial Code, upon the application of a shareholder whose shares represent at least nine-tenths of the share capital of a public limited company (majority shareholder), the general meeting of shareholders of that company may decide that the shares belonging to the remaining shareholders of the public limited company (minority shareholders) be taken over by the majority shareholder for a fair monetary compensation to be paid to the minority shareholders. For the purpose of calculation of the majority shareholder's holding in a company, the shares of the majority shareholder are also deemed to include the shares of its parent undertaking or subsidiary, provided the parent undertaking or subsidiary has granted its consent to this effect.

The above takeover rules are generally known as "squeeze-outs" and they may be characterised as a technique by which a minority shareholding in a company may be eliminated, and 100 per cent of the shares of the company can be acquired by a sole shareholder or by majority shareholders who belong to the same group of companies.

Squeeze-out rules are applicable only to public limited companies. Squeeze-out is initiated by a majority shareholder at its discretion, and the majority shareholder does not have an obligation to submit a mandatory takeover bid, except upon acquisition of a majority shareholding in a listed company, in which case the rules on mandatory takeover bids set out in the SMA will apply (*see* 8.6.4.1 above).

8.6.4.3   Determination of the compensation payable
The amount of fair monetary compensation payable to minority shareholders will be determined by the majority shareholder and may be contested by minority shareholders if it does not objectively meet the criteria of "fair compensation". As a rule, the amount of compensation will be determined on the basis of the value of the shares to be taken over. The value is determined as of the date that is 10 days prior to the date on which the notice calling the general meeting

was sent out. The management board shall submit to the majority shareholder all the necessary data and documents and provide respective information to the majority shareholder.

However, if the person seeking to take over the shares belonging to minority shareholders has become a majority shareholder during the six months before the general meeting as a result of a takeover bid conducted pursuant to the Securities Market Act (*see* 8.6.4.1 above for the details), compensation may not be less than the takeover bid purchase price provided that the takeover bid was accepted by shareholders owning at least nine-tenths of the votes represented by shares.

8.6.4.4 *Procedure for conducting the takeover*
The following steps need to be taken for the takeover under the Commercial Code:

(a) Application for the decision of the general meeting. The majority share-holder must submit the application for the decision of the general meeting of shareholders to the management board of the company, who is required to call a general meeting to decide on the takeover of shares. The named application may not be withdrawn and its conditions may not be amended to the disadvantage of minority shareholders. The application must be appended with the takeover report explaining and justifying the conditions of taking over shares belonging to minority shareholders and the bases for determining the amount of compensation payable for the shares. The takeover report must be audited unless the amount of compensation is determined on the basis of the previous takeover bid made pursuant to the SMA.

(b) Decision of the general meeting on the takeover. A resolution on the takeover of shares belonging to minority shareholders shall be adopted if at least 95 per cent of the votes represented by shares are in favour of the decision. The minutes of a general meeting at which a decision is made on the takeover of shares belonging to minority shareholders shall be attested by a notary.

(c) Contesting the takeover decision. A minority shareholder may contest the resolution of the general meeting of shareholders approving the takeover in the court within one month as of the resolution being made, if the named resolution is in conflict with law and is submitted to the court. The takeover resolution may not be declared invalid on the basis that the compensation payable to minority shareholders is set too low. In such a case, however, the court may, upon the request of a minority shareholder, determine a fair rate of compensation and order the majority shareholder to pay such fair compensation. The compensation may not be contested if it was not lower than the price of the mandatory takeover bid made within six months prior to the squeeze-out.

(d) Conduct of the takeover. If the general meeting approves the takeover, the board of the company must submit an application to the ECS for transfer of the shares of minority shareholders to the majority shareholder. The named application must be filed within one month of the adoption of the resolution of the general meeting approving the takeover. The registrar of the ECRS shall arrange for the transfer of the shares to the account of the majority shareholder against payment, the size of which corresponds to the compensation payable for the shares.

(e)   Notifying the Commercial Register. Immediately after transfer of the shares to the account of the majority shareholder, the management board must submit a corresponding written notice to the Commercial Register.

Squeeze-out is used fairly often in Estonia and in several cases minority shareholders have contested in the court the amount of compensation offered by the majority shareholders.

8.7   Insider trading and market manipulation

8.7.1   *Insider trading*

Insider trading is forbidden under both the Securities Market Act and the Rules of the TSE, and is punishable under the Penal Code (*Karistusseadustik*). Restrictions established to stop the misuse of inside information also apply to financial instruments that are not admitted to trading in Estonia or in an EEA Member State but the value of which depends on a financial instrument that is admitted to trading in Estonia or in an EEA Member State.

Inside information is information of a precise nature which has not been made public, relating, directly or indirectly, to the financial instrument or its issuer and which, if it were made public, would be likely to have a significant effect on the price of the financial instrument or on the price of related derivative financial instruments. The law establishes additional conditions under which information may qualify as inside information.

An insider is a person who possesses inside information by virtue of being a partner in the issuer, or by virtue of his membership of the management or supervisory bodies of the issuer, or by virtue of his shareholding in the issuer, or by virtue of having access to the information through the exercise of his employment, profession or duties, or by virtue of his criminal activities. Third parties that have directly or indirectly received inside information from an insider are also treated as insiders if they knew or should have known that the information is inside information. The Rules of the TSE stipulate that persons who hold or control at least 10 per cent of shares in an issuer and certain officials of such shareholders are deemed to be insiders for the purpose of the Rules of the TSE.

Misuse of inside information comprises, among other things, trading on the basis of inside information, unauthorised disclosure of inside information, and the making of recommendations (on the basis of inside information) for the acquisition or disposal of financial instruments to which that information relates.

Misuse of inside information is a criminal offence, and may result in fines or imprisonment. Issuers of publicly traded securities and other individuals or entities that have regular access to inside information are required to establish internal rules and procedures to prevent the disclosure of such information.

In order to monitor compliance with the prohibition on insider trading, the operator of the Tallinn Stock Exchange has the right to receive from the ECS information on transactions involving an issuer's securities. In addition, the Estonian Financial Supervisory Authority ("EFSA") is obliged to monitor transactions involving an issuer's shares.

The Rules of the Exchange also restrict transactions involving an issuer's securities by certain officials of the issuer and by persons connected with such officials, to avoid them profiting from short-term price fluctuations of the issuer's securities and during restricted periods (in particular, after the end of a financial period but when the financial results of the issuer have not yet been made public). The Listing and Supervisory Committee of the Tallinn Stock Exchange has the right to make exemptions from this requirement.

8.7.2 Market manipulation

The Securities Market Act prohibits market manipulation. In addition, the Rules of the TSE impose obligations on relevant persons to avoid market manipulation.

The SMA provides a non-exhaustive list of acts that are deemed as manipulation of the market, including:

(a)   execution of transactions or transaction orders that create a misleading impression of the offer, demand or price of a financial instrument if the person that made the transaction or transaction order does not have sufficiently justified grounds for its actions or if the transaction or transaction order does not comply with the accepted market practices;

(b)   communication of misleading or possibly misleading information regarding a financial instrument by a person who knows or presumably knows that the information is incorrect, unclear, incomplete or inaccurate.

The manipulation of regulated securities markets may bring criminal or administrative sanctions.

Chapter 9
Finland

Tarja Wist, Partner
Tom Fagernäs, Associate
Waselius & Wist

9.1   Introduction

Takeovers of Finnish companies are regulated by a number of different laws and regulations. The applicable legislation in each case depends largely on whether the company in which shares are to be acquired (the target company) is listed in the European Economic Area ("EEA"). While takeover bids for shares of listed companies are regulated primarily in the Securities Market Act 1989 ("SMA 1989"), which is the main legal framework regulating issuance of securities to the public and public trade in securities, acquisitions of non-listed companies are mainly regulated by general contract law and company law.

In general, Finnish contract law regulates issues such as the binding effect of an offer, the right of withdrawal, acceptance of an offer, seller's liability etc. Company law sets forth the main legal framework for the method and structure to be chosen for the acquisition and regulates, *inter alia*, questions such as defences, financial assistance and compulsory acquisition of minority holdings in squeeze-out procedures. In addition, the provisions of Finnish commercial law, and certain established principles concerning the protection of title in relation to third party claims apply. Acquisitions meeting certain turnover-related criteria, but not falling within the remit of the EU Merger Control Regulation 2004, are subject to the national merger control regime.

In addition to the laws and regulations that apply to acquisitions and takeover bids generally, the articles of association of the target company may, in certain cases, affect the way in which an acquisition or a bid is to be structured. The articles of association of Finnish companies sometimes include, for instance, selling restrictions (however, not as regards listed shares), specific voting requirements, and provisions on compulsory offers to acquire minority holdings under more stringent conditions than those required by the SMA 1989.

The main supervisory authority is the Finnish Financial Supervision Authority ("FFSA"), which acts as a division of the Bank of Finland and has the authority to supervise compliance with the provisions of the SMA 1989 and to give guidance on their interpretation. The OMX Nordic Exchange Helsinki, which is part of the Swedish OMX Group, supervises, under its rules, the trading in publicly quoted securities in Finland. Compliance with national merger control regulations is, furthermore, supervised by the Finnish Competition Authority.

In September 2006, the new Panel on Takeovers and Mergers ("the Takeover Panel") was established under the Central Chamber of Commerce of Finland. The Takeover Panel was set up to promote good securities markets practice in Finland and to give recommendations and statements on good practice in connection with takeover bids. On 15 December 2006, the Takeover Panel issued its Recommendation on Procedures to be followed in Public Takeover Bids, the so-called Helsinki Takeover Code ("the Takeover Code"). The Takeover Panel also issues *in casu* recommendations on resolutions in specific cases at the request of the offeror, the target company or the FFSA.

Table 9.1   Public Bids in Finland during the past Year

Date	Target	Acquirer	Size (€ million)	Offer price	Price T – 1	T – 1	Premium 1 month	Premium 3 months
12/2006	Finnlines	Grimaldi	692	17.00	17.10	–1%	5%	5%
2/2007	FIM	Glitnir	341	8.00	6.17	30%	32%	43%
3/2007	Birka Line	Eckerö	142	17.00	13.00	31%	29%	37%
2/2007	Evox Rifa	Kemet	21	0.12	0.09	33%	38%	44%
5/2007[1]	Aldata	Sauna Acquisition	124	1.82	1.53	19%	14%	13%
5/2007	eQ	Straumur-Burdaras	256	7.60	5.10	50%	48%	42%
3/2007	Puuha-ryhmä	Aspro Ocio	38	95.00	65.12	46%	41%	67%
5/2007	Kemira GrowHow	Yara International	693	12.12	9.27	31%	34%	31%
8/2007	Perlos	Lite-On Technology	275	5.20	3.70	41%	20%	23%
9/2007	Salcomp	Nordstjernan	156	4.01	4.19	–4%	–7%	–10%
9/2007	Kasola	John Nurminen	15	6.80	3.50	94%	95%	87%
				Average premium		28%	26%	31%

[1] Sauna Acquisition did not complete its offer
Source: FFSA, press releases, Danske Markets Corporate Finance

9.2   Acquisition targets

9.2.1   Public and private companies

Limited companies are by far the most important form of business organisation in Finland, and the vast majority of businesses incorporated are organised as limited companies.

Under the Companies Act 2006 ("the Companies Act"), Finnish limited companies are divided into public limited companies (in Finnish *julkinen osakeyhtiö* or *Oyj*) and private limited companies (in Finnish *osakeyhtiö* or *Oy*). Only shares of public limited companies may be listed and traded on a Stock Exchange. Domestic or foreign securities not listed on a Stock Exchange in Finland may be traded on multilateral trading facilities in Finland, provided that sufficient information on the issuer and the securities is available to investors in Finland.

9.2.2 Share capital

Under the Companies Act, a private limited company must have a minimum share capital of €2,500, whereas a public limited company must have a minimum share capital of €80,000. A limited liability company must have at least one share.

9.2.3 Organisation of limited companies

The governing bodies of a limited company include the board of directors, the managing director and the general meeting of shareholders. In addition, a limited company may have a supervisory board.

Under the Companies Act, the board of directors of a limited company is responsible for all duties not delegated to another corporate body under the Companies Act, the articles of association of the company or implicitly through practice. The general duties of the board of directors include the management and the proper arrangement of the operations of the company as well as the outward representation of the company. The board of directors is, furthermore, responsible for the proper supervision of the company's bookkeeping and its financial matters. It is also responsible for appointing, discharging and supervising the managing director of the company.

The managing director is, under the Companies Act, in charge of the day-to-day management of the company in accordance with the instructions and orders given by the board of directors. Measures that, considering the scope and nature of the operations of the company, are unusual or extensive, may generally not be undertaken by the managing director unless authorised by the board of directors.

The responsibilities of the supervisory board include the supervision of the management of the company by the board of directors and the managing director. In addition, the company's articles of association may provide that the supervisory board elects the board of directors. In all other respects, the supervisory board can only undertake duties which are within the ambit of the authority of the board of directors and which are not, by virtue of the Companies Act, delegated to other corporate bodies.

Generally, the board of directors, the managing director and the supervisory board (if any) are bound by an obligation to act in the best interests of the company and all its shareholders. The best interests of the company are to be assessed on the basis of the company's purpose, which is assumed to be the generating of profit to the shareholders, unless otherwise designated under the articles of association. The governing bodies of a limited company may not undertake any act or measure that is likely to cause unjust benefit to a share-holder or a third party at the expense of the company or another shareholder.

9.2.4   Shareholders

A limited company can have one or more shareholders. The shareholders of a limited company are not personally liable for the obligations of the company.

Unless otherwise provided for in the company's articles of association, all shares in a limited company entitle their holders to equal voting rights, dividend rights and rights to other distributions from the company. However, it is not uncommon for Finnish limited companies to have different classes of shares. Different classes of shares may carry a different number of voting rights or different rights in relation to the distribution of the funds of the company. A limited company's articles of association may sometimes also include additional restrictions on the exercise of voting rights.

Generally, all shareholders in limited companies, except for holders of non-voting preference shares, are entitled to participate and vote at the shareholders meetings. Shareholders meetings are usually convened by the board of directors of the company or, if so provided in the articles of association, by the supervisory board. Shareholders holding not less than one-tenth of the share capital of the company or any smaller proportion specified in the articles of association are entitled to request that a shareholders meeting is convened. Any shareholder is entitled to request that a matter is included in the agenda for a general meeting of shareholders.

9.2.5   Voting requirements

At the shareholders meeting, resolutions are generally taken by a simple majority of the votes cast at the meeting. However, under the Companies Act, resolutions on, for example, share issues or sale of treasury shares without applying the shareholders' preferential right to subscribe, issuance of warrants or convertibles or other similar instruments, amendments to the company's articles of association, merger or liquidation of the company, decrease of the share capital and share buy-backs must generally be approved by a majority of two-thirds of both the votes cast and the number of shares represented at the meeting, or any higher majority specified in the articles of association. The same majority requirements apply where the shareholders meeting decides to authorise the board of directors to make decisions on issuances of shares or other equity instruments, sale of treasury shares or share buy-backs.

In addition, certain resolutions to amend the articles of association (generally amendments affecting the respective rights of the shareholders) must be approved by each share class or taken unanimously under the Companies Act.

9.2.6   The Finnish book-entry securities system

Physical share certificates for listed securities have been withdrawn from the Finnish securities market and replaced by computerised book entries. The book-entry securities system is mandatory for shares listed on the OMX Nordic Exchange Helsinki.

The central activities relating to the book-entry securities system are maintained by the Finnish Central Securities Depository (the "FCSD" or the "APK"). The FCSD acts as an account operator in the centralised book-entry system and it maintains a register on accounts of the shares and shareholders of each company participating in the book-entry securities system and keeps book-entry accounts for individual shareholders. The Finnish State, the Bank of Finland, the OMX Nordic Exchange Helsinki and many banks and investment firms that fulfil the requirements set out in the Act on Book-Entry Securities System 1991 act as book-entry account managers and may register transfers and enter other registrations in the book-entry securities system. Furthermore, account managers may have agent companies authorised to enter registrations on the book-entry accounts on their behalf.

In order to effect entries in the book-entry securities system, a shareholder must establish a book-entry account directly with the FCSD or through a licensed book-entry account manager. All transactions in securities registered in the book-entry securities system are executed as computerised transfers between book-entry accounts. Upon each transaction, corresponding information is automatically entered into the company's shareholders register, which is maintained by the FCSD.

Instead of opening an individual book-entry account, non-Finnish shareholders may register their shares on a custodial nominee account, which is managed by the account manager for the account of the shareholder. The name and other details of the account manager will in such case appear on the account entries and the company's register of shareholders, instead of the name of the shareholder. An owner of nominee registered shares is entitled to receive dividends and other distributions from the company and to exercise his preferential right to subscribe for new shares, but may not attend and vote at a general meeting of shareholders unless he has notified the company of his intentions to attend at least 10 days prior to the date of the meeting. The notification must include the shareholder's name, postal address, number of shares held and an identification code confirmed by the FCSD.

Upon request, the account manager of a custodial nominee account is required to inform the FFSA and the company of the identity of the owner of the nominee registered shares, where this is known, and of the number of shares owned by the person in question.

9.3 Exchange and investment control

9.3.1 Exchange control

The acquisition of shares in Finnish companies is not subject to any exchange control restrictions or authorisation requirements, nor are there any restrictions on repatriation of capital or profits from Finland.

9.3.2   Foreign investment control

Restrictions on the right of foreign investors to purchase and own shares in Finnish companies were generally abolished as of 1 January 1993.

However, investments from countries not belonging to the European Economic Area ("EEA") or the Organisation for Economic Co-operation and Development (the "OECD") that concern one-third or more of the voting participation in large Finnish limited companies or businesses remain subject to governmental control under the Act on Control of Foreigners' Acquisitions of Finnish Companies 1992 ("the Investment Control Act").

Large companies or businesses are defined in the Investment Control Act as companies or businesses with more than 1,000 employees, or with a balance sheet or an annual turnover exceeding approximately €168.2 million on a consolidated basis.

Companies and businesses operating in the defence industry are subject to investment control regardless of the above thresholds.

If an acquisition falls under the provisions on foreign investment control, an application for approval of the acquisition must be filed with the Ministry of Employment and the Economy (or with the Ministry of Defence for companies in the defence industry) either in advance or within one month from the acquisition. The approval may be refused if the acquisition is deemed to jeopardise important national interests.

9.3.3   Credit institutions, investment firms, stock and option exchanges and clearing houses

The acquisition of shares in a bank or another credit institution, an investment firm, stock and option exchange or clearing house leading to a direct or indirect qualifying holding (i.e., at least 10 per cent (5 per cent in respect of a clearing house)) of the share capital or the total number of votes pertaining to the share capital, is subject to a prior notification to the FFSA. A similar notification obligation applies for direct or indirect qualifying holdings in holding companies controlling any of the above entities.

The notification obligation also applies in case the holding reaches or falls below one of the thresholds of 20, 33 or 50 per cent (or 10 per cent in respect of clearing houses) of the share capital or the total voting rights, or where the acquisition results in the target company becoming a subsidiary of the acquirer. For the purposes of the above thresholds, the following holdings shall also be included in the acquirer's holdings:

(a)   shares held by an undertaking controlled by the acquirer;
(b)   shares held by a pension fund or foundation of the acquirer or of a controlled undertaking;
(c)   shares that the acquirer may vote, whether alone or together with a third party; and
(d)   shares that the acquirer may acquire pursuant to an existing agreement or other arrangement.

The FFSA may, within three months from the filing of the notification, oppose the acquisition where it finds it likely, based on an account on the reliability and fitness and propriety of the acquirer, that the acquisition would jeopardise the operations of the credit institution in accordance with diligent and sound business practices.

If the acquirer fails to notify the acquisition to the FFSA or completes the acquisition despite the FFSA's opposition the FFSA may, in respect of stock and option exchanges and clearing houses, prohibit the acquirer from exercising its voting rights in the exchange, and in respect of credit institutions and investment firms, prohibit the acquirer of the shares from registering its holding in the share register or shareholder register of the credit institution and investment firm.

Moreover, if the FFSA, after the acquisition of shares of a credit institution or investment firm has been completed, finds that the acquisition jeopardises operations of a credit institution, investment firm or the consolidation group of such entity, the FFSA may prohibit the acquirer of the shares from registering its holding in the share register or shareholder register of the credit institution or investment firm.

If the credit institution or investment firm, as a result of the acquisition of shares, becomes a subsidiary of another credit institution, investment firm or insurance company licensed in another EEA Member State or of the parent company of such, or if dominant control in the first-named credit institution is held by the same natural persons or entities who control the foreign regulated entity, the FFSA must, before making its decision, consult the competent authorities of such other EEA Member State.

Furthermore, the efficient supervision of a credit institution, stock or option exchange or an investment firm must not be obstructed by so-called close links or by the laws and regulations of a non-EEA state applicable to a party forming a close link to the credit institution, stock or option exchange or investment firm. A close link is considered to appear, *inter alia*, where:

(a)   a natural or legal person directly or indirectly owns at least 20 per cent of the shares in an entity;

(b)   a natural or legal person holds directly or indirectly at least 20 per cent of the voting rights attached to the shares in the company, where such voting rights derive from ownership, articles of association or similar rules and arrangements; or

(c)   a natural or legal person directly or indirectly has the right to appoint or remove at least one-fifth of the members of the board of directors or similar body of an entity, or the members of a body having this right of appointment or removal.

9.3.4   *Insurance companies*

Direct or indirect investments in the shares of an insurance company reaching or falling below one of the thresholds of 10, 20, 33 or 50 per cent of the share capital or the total voting rights pertaining to the share capital are subject to an advance notification to the Ministry of Social Affairs and Health. A similar notification obligation also applies when the insurance company becomes or ceases to be a subsidiary.

If the acquisition is made indirectly by purchasing shares of an insurance group or financial conglomerate as defined in the Act on the Supervision of Insurance Groups and Financial Conglomerates 2004, a similar notification shall be made to the FFSA or the Finnish Insurance Supervision Authority, as the case may be. The notification shall be made to the FFSA if the group parent is a credit institution, investment firm or investment fund, and to the Insurance Supervision Authority if the parent is an insurance company.

The Insurance Supervisory Authority may, within three months from the filing of the advance notification, oppose the investment if it finds it likely that the investment would jeopardise the sound development of the insurance business. The Insurance Supervisory Authority may, furthermore, set additional conditions for the exercise of shareholders' rights by the acquirer in order to secure the sound development of the insurance business.

If, after the acquisition has been completed, the Insurance Supervisory Authority finds that the acquisition seriously jeopardises the operations of the insurance company in accordance with sound and diligent business practices, it may prohibit the acquirer of the shares from exercising his voting rights in the insurance company. The same applies if the acquisition has been completed without the approval of the Insurance Supervisory Authority or despite the Insurance Supervisory Authority's opposition.

Prior to its decision regarding the approval of the acquisition, the Insurance Supervisory Authority may be obligated to consult the relevant authorities of another EEA Member State (as with credit institutions and investment firms; *see* 9.3.3 above).

9.4   Merger control

The Act on Competition Restrictions 1992 provides for national merger control regulation. Such regulation is aimed at concentrations that do not have a Community dimension and thus do not fall under the EC Merger Control Regulation.

The Act on Competition Restrictions is applicable to:

(a)   the acquisition of control of an undertaking;
(b)   the acquisition of the business operations of an undertaking or a part thereof;
(c)   a merger; and
(d)   the setting up of a full-function joint venture (i.e., a joint venture which, on a lasting basis, performs all of the functions of an autonomous economic unit),

(each referred to as a "concentration").

The Act on Competition Restrictions is applicable only where the concentration meets the following turnover requirements:

(a)   the aggregate annual worldwide turnover of all the parties exceeds €350 million; and

(b)   at least two of the parties each have an annual turnover accrued in Finland exceeding €20 million.

Specific rules apply to the calculation of the turnover of financial institutions and insurance companies.

Under the Act on Competition Restrictions, a notification of a corporate acquisition must be filed with the Finnish Competition Authority ("FCA") within one week from the signing of a binding agreement concerning a concentration or, in the case of a takeover bid, from the publishing of the bid. A concentration can be completed after it has been approved by the FCA or after one month has lapsed since the receipt of a complete notification by the FCA if the FCA does not initiate further investigations within this one-month period. If further investigations are initiated but the FCA does not clear the concentration unconditionally or conditionally or propose to prohibit the concentration within three months of initiating further investigations, the acquisition is considered approved. The Market Court can suspend the three-month period by a maximum of two months.

The Market Court may, upon the FCA's proposal, prohibit or set conditions upon a concentration or order a concentration to be dissolved if the concentration would lead to the creation or strengthening of a dominant market position that would significantly impede competition in the Finnish market or a substantial part thereof.

9.5   Regulations on the conduct of mergers and acquisitions

9.5.1   General contract law

An offer to acquire shares in a limited company is, as any other purchase offer, subject to the general rules of Finnish contract law relating to offer and acceptance. Under Finnish contract law, an offer is binding on the offeror and, as a rule, may not be withdrawn after it has been received, or duly accepted, by the offeree unless otherwise provided under the terms of the offer.

Under the Contracts Act 1929, an acceptance that arrives too late constitutes a new offer by the offeree to the original offeror. Also, an acceptance that includes an addition, limitation or condition that does not correspond to the terms of the offer, is considered as a rejection, containing, however, a new offer, which may be accepted or rejected by the original offeror.

The above applies equally to private purchase offers and takeover bids. Accordingly, once a takeover bid has been published, its terms may generally be amended only if such amendment is to the benefit of shareholders. Hence, amendments in favour of the shareholders to whom the offer is addressed are permitted (e.g., the price payable under the offer may be increased) provided that the requirement for equal treatment of the holders of the securities tendered for is observed.

9.5.2 Company law and the articles of association

Although the Companies Act does not specifically address acquisitions, it sets out the main legal framework to be observed when structuring an acquisition of a limited company.

Under a general principle of the Companies Act, all shares in limited companies must be free to be purchased or sold. The articles of association may, however, provide certain exceptions from this principle either with respect to all shares of a company or with respect to a specific class of shares. The articles of association often provide, for instance, that the holder of a certain proportion of the shares of a company must offer to purchase the remaining shares of the company for a specified price.

Provisions of the Companies Act that may be relevant for the structuring of a purchase offer include the provisions on voting (*see* 9.2.5 above) and minority protection, the prohibitions on financial assistance (*see* 9.14 below) and purchase by the company of its own shares, as well as the provisions concerning compulsory acquisition of minority holdings (*see* 9.12.2 below).

The Companies Act also includes provisions on mergers of limited companies, providing for the transfer of the assets of the merging company to the receiving company *ex lege* as well as the assumption by the receiving company of the liabilities of the merging company *ex lege*. The provisions on mergers in the Companies Act only apply to mergers between such Finnish limited companies that are not subject to specific legislation such as, *inter alia*, banks, investment firms and insurance companies.

9.5.3 Takeover bids under the SMA 1989

Finnish takeover legislation has undergone material changes in connection with the implementation of the Takeover Directive in 2006. Generally, a purchase offer falls under the provisions on takeover bids in the SMA 1989 if the offer is considered to be public and if it concerns shares listed on a stock exchange, or other securities (including convertible bonds, subscription rights and warrants) which entitle their holder to subscribe for listed shares.

Under the SMA 1989, if the target company's registered office is in another EEA Member State, many of the provisions in the SMA 1989 relating to takeover bids are not applicable. In such situations, for instance, the obligation to launch a mandatory bid, the conduct of a mandatory bid and the pricing of a bid are governed by the target company's home state regulations. The FFSA may grant further exemptions from the provisions of the SMA 1989 upon application.

An offer is considered public when it is published in a newspaper or released through other forms of media or is delivered in some other manner (for instance by mail) to a large number of holders of the securities concerned. A purchase offer in which all shareholders have an opportunity to actually negotiate the terms of the offer with the bidder does not usually constitute a takeover bid. As opposed to the definition of a takeover bid in the Takeover Directive, the definition under the SMA 1989 does not require that the bidder aims at the acquisition of control of the target company.

The provisions of the SMA 1989 on takeover bids are divided into provisions that apply to all takeover bids and provisions that apply only to mandatory bids.

The SMA 1989 does not draw a distinction between friendly and hostile takeover bids. Offers of both kinds are treated equally under the provisions of the SMA 1989. Actions by the target company are primarily addressed in the general principles of Finnish company law, including the requirement for equal treatment of shareholders and the observance of the best interest of the company.

9.5.4 Supplementary regulation

The provisions of the SMA 1989 on takeover bids are supplemented by a decree of the Ministry of Finance setting forth the content requirements for tender offer documents. Moreover, the FFSA has issued Standard 5.2c on the interpretation of the provisions of the SMA 1989 on takeover bids.

Furthermore, the Helsinki Takeover Code comprises 25 recommendations relating primarily to the responsibilities of the target company's board of directors, but also extending to certain issues concerning the preparation of a bid, due diligence, competing bids, holdings in the target company and the conditions of a takeover bid.

The rules of the OMX Nordic Exchange Helsinki apply to trading in securities on the Stock Exchange and the listing and delisting of securities. Transactions resulting from a takeover bid are usually effected on the OMX Nordic Exchange Helsinki and settled in the systems of the FCSD in accordance with its rules.

9.5.5 Other

In addition to the above laws and regulations, the acquisition of shares may in certain cases be subject to Finnish commercial law, including the Consumer Protection Act and the Unfair Business Practices Act 1978. Furthermore, the general principles established with respect to the protection of title in relation to third-party claims may in some cases become applicable.

In addition, the Act on Cooperation within Enterprises 2007 and other labour law implications may be relevant to mergers and acquisitions in Finland.

9.5.6 Offering of securities as consideration

In private transactions, any type of consideration, whether cash, securities or commodities, may be offered for the shares to be purchased.

In takeover bids, however, the consideration may include cash, securities or a combination of the two. A cash consideration is required at least as an alternative in all mandatory bids and in such voluntary bids that are made for all of the shares or equity securities in the target (and that, hence, are not followed by a mandatory bid, as explained below) if:

(a)   the securities offered as consideration are neither listed nor applied to be listed on a regulated marketplace in the EEA; or

(b)   the bidder has acquired or will acquire, against a cash consideration, securities of the target entitling to at least 5 per cent of the voting rights of the target within a period of time which begins six months prior to the publishing of the bid and ends at the close of the time allowed for the acceptance of the bid.

The offering of shares as consideration usually involves the issuance of new shares or the sale of treasury shares by the bidder. Where the bidder is a Finnish limited company, such decision must usually be made with a two-thirds majority in a shareholders meeting unless the board of directors has been authorised to make the decision (*see* 9.2.5 above).

9.6   Methods of acquisition

Shares of a listed Finnish company may be purchased by transactions on the Stock Exchange, by launching a takeover bid for all or part of the shares of the target company, or by purchasing shares through off-market transactions with the major owners of the target company. None of these methods is, as such, prohibited by Finnish law. Shares listed on the OMX Nordic Exchange Helsinki may be sold and purchased outside the OMX Nordic Exchange Helsinki, but are subject to a transfer tax at the rate of 1.6 per cent of the purchase price of the shares (except where neither the seller nor the buyer are generally liable to tax in Finland). The acquisition of shares by means other than a takeover bid, or the purchase of a business, does not require any specific form or procedure.

Except for the provisions on mandatory bids, there are no provisions requiring that shares be acquired only through a takeover bid. The bidder is generally allowed to acquire further shares privately. When considering private acquisitions in connection with a takeover bid, the bidder should, however, pay careful attention to the provisions prohibiting the use of inside information and to the requirement for equal treatment of shareholders. Acquisitions effected outside of the bid usually also affect the pricing of the bid.

Furthermore, where the bidder's holding exceeds three-tenths (30 per cent) or one-half (50 per cent) of the voting rights of a listed company, a mandatory takeover bid to purchase the remaining shares must be made (*see* 9.12 below). Since acquisitions through voluntary tender offers are usually exempted from the requirement to launch a subsequent mandatory offer (as explained below), the mandatory offer rules are applied primarily in situations where the holding exceeding the mandatory offer threshold is acquired through private transactions.

9.7   Preparation of an offer

9.7.1   Disclosure of the offer

Under the SMA 1989, a decision to launch a takeover bid for the securities of a listed company must be made public and disclosed to the target company, the relevant marketplace and the FFSA immediately after the decision has been made. The bidder is generally not required to disclose that a takeover bid is being prepared until it has made a formal decision to launch the bid. Until a formal decision has been made and disclosed to the market, information on the preparation of a takeover bid constitutes inside information. Before the bidder may disclose its intention to launch a takeover bid, it must ensure that it is able to pay the cash consideration for the tendered securities in full and take all reasonable measures to ensure that it will be able to deliver any other type of consideration offered.

Under the SMA 1989, when the bidder publishes the bid, the following information must be included:

(a) the number of securities tendered for;
(b) the term of the bid;
(c) the consideration offered;
(d) any conditions to the bid; and
(e) the procedure to be followed should the acceptances to the bid exceed the number of securities tendered for.

The target company must publish information on a bid for its shares without undue delay after it has learned about the bidder's decision to launch a bid. Furthermore, the target company may have an obligation to disclose the bid to the market before the bidder's decision if the target company enters into a combination agreement with the bidder or if information about the bid has leaked to the market. Furthermore, as soon as the bid has been disclosed, the target company's and the bidder's employees or employee representatives must be informed about the bid.

The Takeover Code contains further recommendations concerning the information to be published on the bid. In pursuit of providing the market with sufficient information essential in assessing the merits of the bid, the following information is recommended to be given in addition to the requirements of the SMA 1989:

(a) information about the bidder;
(b) information about the target company's securities held or otherwise controlled by the bidder;
(c) the essential terms and conditions of the bid, including the consideration, the premium offered in relation to the market value of the target company as well as the principles used for the calculation of the premium;
(d) information about the financing of the bid or other necessary arrangements with respect to the consideration;
(e) information about the material conditions set for the completion of the bid;
(f) information about any shareholders of the bidder who have announced their support to any actions that may be required for the completion of the bid in the general meeting of shareholders of the bidder;
(g) information about any target company's shareholders that have committed (conditionally or unconditionally) to accept the bid or otherwise announced their support for the bid;
(h) information about any other related arrangements between the bidder and the holders of the tendered securities;

(i)   information about the reasons for the bid;

(j)   where securities of the bidder are being offered as consideration, information about the effects of the bid and of the consideration paid on the business, results and financial condition of the bidder (calculated per share, if possible);

(k)   the estimated date of the publication of the offer document;

(l)   information about any necessary governmental approvals; and

(m)   estimate of the duration of the takeover bid process and the implementation of any related arrangements.

In addition, the bidder shall inform how it has ensured that it has the necessary financial means to complete the bid. In particular, any special elements of uncertainty relating to the completion of the bid shall be disclosed.

9.7.2   Negotiations with the target company

Typically, before a takeover bid is launched, the bidder would seek to approach the board of directors of the target company. According to the Takeover Code, the target company's board of directors should in each case evaluate whether the approach is to be considered serious in light of the reliability of the approach, the type and amount of the consideration offered, the likelihood of the bid being successful and other relevant circumstances. In order to achieve the best deal for the shareholders, any serious approaches should be examined in further detail and their merits should be assessed in comparison to other available options.

The Takeover Code acknowledges that the board of directors may initiate negotiations with the bidder and other interested parties, and that such negotiations may result in a combination agreement between the target company and the bidder. However, the Takeover Code recommends that any combination agreement should not restrict the ability of the board of directors to act upon a competing bid that would better serve the shareholders' interests. Whilst in some circumstances non-solicitation commitments, if limited by time, may be helpful in advancing an attractive transaction and, therefore, serve the interests of the shareholders, the Takeover Code finds exclusivity arrangements problematic and generally highlights the need of the board of directors to remain free to commence negotiations with a competing bidder.

9.7.3   Offer document

Before the commencement of the offer period, the bidder must prepare an offer document. The offer document must contain essential and sufficient information in order to enable the shareholders of the target company to make an informed assessment on the merits of the bid. The offer document must be submitted to the FFSA for approval before it is published. Within five business days of the date of filing, the FFSA must make a decision on whether the offer document may be published.

The Ministry of Finance has, by virtue of the SMA 1989, issued a detailed decree on the content requirements for an offer document and reciprocal approval of offer documents within the EEA. The decree regulates the contents of offer documents insofar as the Takeover Directive does not regulate such documents. According to the decree, the information contained in the offer document must be clearly provided and easy to analyse. The offer document must contain, *inter alia*:

(a) details of the target company, the bidder and the bidder's advisers;
(b) information on the bidder's future plans for the target company, its operations and strategy as well as the use of assets and the bid's effects on the management and employees;
(c) indication of any intention to apply for the delisting of the securities of the target company;
(d) details on any bonuses payable to the target company's management on completion of the bid;
(e) information on the financing of the bid;
(f) statement of the board of directors (which can be given later as a supplement) of the target company and any statement provided by the employee representative of the target company;
(g) details on the pricing of the bid;
(h) details on the performance of the target company's share;
(i) three-month volume weighted average price of target company's shares before the bid;
(j) conditions of the bid; and
(k) the latest annual and interim reports of the target company.

The FFSA has issued further guidelines relating to the contents of an offer document.

Where securities are offered as consideration, the offer document must also comply with the requirements set for the contents of prospectuses and include information on, for example, the grounds on which the exchange ratio between the securities tendered for and the securities offered as consideration has been determined.

In addition to the offer document, other marketing material may be used in connection with a takeover bid.

9.7.4 Due diligence

9.7.4.1 General
The offeror usually wishes to conduct a due diligence review of the target company before the launch of a takeover bid. A due diligence review in a listed company may, however, raise considerations under, *inter alia*, insider regulations (*see* 9.13 below), antitrust regulations and the requirements on the contents of the offer document.

The SMA 1989 does not require that the management of the target company disclose any unpublished information concerning the target company to the offeror. Accordingly, a request for due diligence access may be refused. In such cases, the offeror is entitled to rely on publicly available information when preparing the offer document.

The Takeover Code contains recommendations on the conduct of a due diligence review in the target company. According to the Takeover Code, the target company's board of directors shall consider and decide on a request for a due diligence review. In case a due diligence review is conducted, the board of directors must see to it that insider dealing and confidentiality issues are addressed appropriately. If inside information is obtained by the bidder, the bidder may not launch the bid before such information is disclosed to be public.

In addition, the Takeover Code addresses situations in which the consideration consists of the bidder's shares and recommends that the target company in such situations would request a due diligence review of the bidder in order for the target company's board of directors to be better positioned to assess the merits of the bid.

9.7.4.2   Public information

Public information on Finnish limited companies is available from a variety of official sources. Decisions and other matters that may materially affect the value of listed securities and information on major holdings should have been made public by the target company pursuant to the general provisions of the SMA 1989 and be available on the website of the OMX Nordic Exchange Helsinki (www.omxgroup.com/nordicexchange) and, under the corporate governance recommendations of the OMX Nordic Exchange Helsinki, the website of the target company.

The Trade Register of the National Board of Patents and Registration ("the Trade Register") keeps a public register of all businesses (including limited companies) engaged in business activities in Finland. In the case of limited companies, the Trade Register includes information on, *inter alia*:

(a)   the company's authorised and paid up share capital and classes of shares;
(b)   any convertible bonds or bonds linked with warrants issued by the company;
(c)   the directors;
(d)   any authorisation given to the board of directors to issue new shares; and
(e)   any pending merger or liquidation of the company.

In addition, copies of the articles of association of the company as well as any other documents filed with the Trade Register may be obtained.

All limited companies must file a copy of their annual accounts with the Trade Register within two months of the date when the annual general meeting of shareholders has adopted and approved the income statement and balance sheet. The annual accounts so filed are open to public inspection. Annual and interim accounts as well as the annual statements of listed companies are made public in accordance with the SMA 1989 and are available at the company's website.

A register of floating charges over movable assets is maintained by the National Board of Patents and Registrations. District courts keep registers of real-estate ownership and mortgages registered against real estate.

A list of all shareholders of the target company is available for inspection either at the company's head office or, if the shares of the company are entered into the book-entry securities system, at the FCSD. Listed companies are also required to maintain permanent insider registers in which the holdings of the members of the board of directors, the managing director and certain other statutory insiders are registered and to publish on their respective websites up-to-date information on the securities portfolios of such insiders and changes thereto during the preceding 12-month period.

9.8 Conduct of a takeover bid

9.8.1 *The single bid procedure and pricing*

The starting point in the Finnish takeover regime is a single-phase bid procedure including a voluntary bid with a bid period of three to 10 weeks (unless extended by the FFSA). The bidder is not obligated to make a subsequent mandatory bid notwithstanding that the mandatory bid threshold may be exceeded in the voluntary bid as long as the voluntary bid is made for all shares and securities entitling to shares in the target company. A mandatory bid obligation is, nevertheless, triggered, if the bidder's holding remains under the mandatory bid threshold after completing the voluntary bid, and the bidder later acquires additional shares on the market and thereby exceeds the threshold.

To ensure investor protection in this single bid procedure, voluntary bids for all shares and securities entitling to shares are in some respects treated in the same manner as mandatory bids. For example, if the bidder has purchased shares of the target company within a period of six months preceding the publishing of a voluntary bid, the pricing of the voluntary bid must follow the same rules as that of a mandatory bid and the price offered should match the highest price paid by the bidder for the shares during such six-month period. The price so determined may be adjusted for special reasons, such as material changes in the target company or in the market conditions or if the bidder has purchased large quantities of the target's shares shortly before the six-month period. In addition, if the bidder acquires shares in the target for a higher price during the bid or the nine months following the completion of the bid, the bidder must make an additional "top-up" payment to all shareholders who have accepted the bid, to equal the higher price so paid by the bidder.

In the absence of any such purchases during, after or prior to a voluntary bid, the bid may be freely priced by the bidder.

9.8.2 *Good securities market practice and the requirement for equal treatment*

Under a general rule of the SMA 1989, securities may not be marketed or acquired in business by giving false or misleading information or by applying procedures that are unfair or otherwise contrary to good practice. This so-called "general clause" applies equally to all kinds of marketing and acquisition of securities in business and will apply in parallel with the specific requirements of the SMA 1989 on takeover bids.

Under the SMA 1989, the holders of the securities tendered for in a takeover bid must be treated equally. A takeover bid must, therefore, be extended to all holders of the securities for which the offer is made. Furthermore, the terms and conditions of the offer, in particular the price and type of consideration offered, must be the same irrespective of the identity of the holder of securities.

The requirement for equal treatment has from time to time been tested in the case of partial offers where acceptances have exceeded the number of securities tendered for. Generally, it has been held that the terms of the bid in such situations must apply equally to all holders of the securities. More specifically, the terms of an offer may not favour Finnish shareholders over foreign shareholders or large shareholders over small shareholders or vice versa.

Furthermore, shares of different classes may carry different rights in the company and, accordingly, may be priced differently. However, the price offered for the shares of each class must be in a justifiable relation to the price offered for the shares of any other class.

The requirement for equal treatment is applied also in relation to private transactions concluded in connection with a takeover bid. Accordingly, whilst private transactions are as such allowed, their terms may not be more favourable than those of the takeover bid.

9.8.3   Conditional bids

Pursuant to the SMA 1989, voluntary takeover bids may concern all shares and other securities issued by the target company, or they may be limited to a certain class of securities or a specified maximum number of shares or other securities. Any limit to the bid must, nevertheless, be designed and applied in a non-discriminating manner to comply with the requirement for equal treatment.

The SMA 1989 does not specify the matters upon which a takeover bid may be conditional. However, under the FFSA's guidance the conditions of the bid must be sufficiently transparent, unambiguous and reasonable and, in order to comply with good securities market practice, the bidder should not invoke a condition unless the condition has significant importance to the contemplated transaction. The FFSA generally accepts conditions typically used on the financial markets, including a requirement that no material adverse changes take place on the market or in the target company.

A takeover bid is typically conditional upon merger clearances being obtained for the transaction. A conditional takeover bid is also often subject to the bid being accepted for at least a certain proportion of ownership or voting rights in the target company (usually 90 per cent, which is also the squeeze-out threshold for minority shareholdings). If the number of shares in respect of which acceptances from shareholders have been received is not sufficient to meet such a proportion, the bidder may withdraw from the bid. If the bidder has reserved the right to withdraw its offer, a shareholder accepting the offer should also have an equal opportunity to withdraw his acceptance during the offer period.

After the launch of the bid, the bidder can waive conditions or change conditions in favour of the holders of the tendered securities and otherwise as may be provided for in the terms and conditions of the bid. Any such waivers or changes will have to be disclosed without delay and included in a supplement to the offer document.

9.8.4 Competing bids

Pursuant to the Takeover Code, the board of directors should be open to discuss with any competing bidder if this serves the shareholders' best interests. Accordingly, any agreements that the target company may have entered into with another bidder should include appropriate conditions to allow the board of directors to reflect upon competing bids. Whenever a competing bid is published, the board of directors must, as soon as possible, publish a supplement to its opinion on the first bid.

Furthermore, under the SMA 1989, if a competing bid is launched during the term of another takeover bid (the first bid), the conditions of the first bid can be changed and its term lengthened to match the length of the competing bid, irrespective of the statutory maximum length of a bid period. Alternatively, the first bidder is entitled to withdraw the first bid. Also shareholders who have accepted the first bid may, under a specific provision of the SMA 1989, withdraw their acceptances to the first bid.

9.8.5 Disclosure

9.8.5.1 Disclosure of holdings in the course of a takeover bid
Under the SMA 1989, a shareholder of a Finnish listed company is required to notify the company and the FFSA without delay when its voting participation in or percentage ownership of the outstanding total number of shares reaches, exceeds, or thereafter falls below 5, 10, 15, 20, 25, 30, 50 or 66.67 per cent.

When calculating a shareholder's holding for the purposes of the above thresholds, the holding of the shareholder is deemed to include:

(a)   shares held by a controlled undertaking;
(b)   shares held by a pension fund or foundation of the shareholder or of a controlled undertaking; as well as
(c)   shares carrying voting rights, the exercise of which is dependent on a decision by the shareholder alone or together with a third party.

Disclosure in accordance with the above is furthermore required where the shareholder is party to an agreement or other arrangement that, when and if effected, would result in the shareholder's holding reaching, exceeding or falling below one of the above thresholds. Accordingly, a holding that may be acquired by exercising, for example, options or warrants or by converting convertible bonds, is to be disclosed if one of the above thresholds will be reached or exceeded by virtue of such exercise or conversion.

A company that has received a notification or that otherwise has learned about a change of holding such as referred to above must immediately disclose such information to the market in which its securities are traded as well as to the appropriate media. The Ministry of Finance has issued more detailed regulations as to the information to be included in a shareholder's notification and the disclosure by the target company, as well as the procedures to be followed. According to guidance issued by the FFSA, the above notification and disclosure requirements apply equally in the course of a public bid whenever the acceptances received give rise to one of the above thresholds being reached or exceeded, irrespective of the conditionality of the bid.

9.8.5.2   *Information at the close of the offer period*

After the close of the offer period, the bidder must, without delay, disclose the holding that he may acquire in the target company by acquiring the securities offered for sale in the bid and taking into account any securities that he may otherwise have acquired. If the bid has been conditional, the bidder must also indicate whether the conditions have been met or waived and whether the bid will be completed. This information must also be communicated to the target company, the relevant exchange and the FFSA.

The management of the target company shall communicate the notification to the employees or their representative.

9.9   Defences to a hostile offer

9.9.1   *Protective measures*

The articles of association are the primary instrument of a limited company for protection against hostile bids. The articles of association may, for example, include the following:

(a)   a pre-emption clause under which the existing shareholders have a right of first refusal; that is, existing shareholders are entitled to acquire shares transferred to a new shareholder for a (sometimes lower) price specified in the articles of association;

(b)   a consent clause providing that no shares in the company may be transferred without the consent of the board of directors of the company; or

(c)   clauses limiting the voting power of any one shareholder to a certain percentage of the total voting participation of the company, irrespective of the number of shares held by such a shareholder.

The transfer restrictions described in (a) and (b) above may not be included in a company's articles of association with respect to shares listed on the OMX Nordic Exchange Helsinki.

The articles of association of a limited company may also provide that certain decisions (e.g., concerning mergers, liquidation and amendments to the articles of association) must be made by the shareholders meeting with a super-majority of the votes cast and/or of shares represented at the meeting. Companies can, furthermore, develop "golden shares" by introducing in their articles of association a procedure for voting among each class of shares with specific majority requirements to be satisfied.

Also, cross-shareholdings between two or more companies may be used to protect a company against hostile takeovers. Since cross-shareholdings between two or more limited companies are allowed under Finnish law (but restricted in the case of entities with a parent–subsidiary relationship), a substantial percentage of the company's shares may be held by a friendly party in order to prevent a hostile takeover.

Finland has opted out from the "breakthrough rule" included in Article 11 of the Takeover Directive and, accordingly, super-majority requirements, voting limitations, share classes with multiple voting rights as well as shareholders' agreements will continue to have full force and effect in the course of a takeover bid.

9.9.2 *Defensive actions*

Article 9 of the Takeover Directive, which forbids actions purporting to frustrate a takeover bid, is deemed to be implemented in the basic principles of Finnish company law. Accordingly, the right of a limited company to take actions to defend itself against a takeover bid that is classified by the management of the target company as a hostile bid, is limited primarily by the general principles of Finnish company law.

Generally, the management of a limited company is required in all respects to act in accordance with good business practices and in the best interests of the company. Furthermore, all corporate actions must be of corporate benefit. Corporate benefit, on the other hand, is defined through the objective of the company, which is assumed to be the generation of profit to shareholders.

Members of the board of directors of the company and the managing director of the company are not entitled to take any actions to advance their personal interests at the expense of the company. Generally, decisions made by the board of directors or the shareholders meeting must maintain equality between all shareholders and may not confer upon any shareholder or other party unjustified benefit at the expense of the company or another shareholder.

Furthermore, issuance of new shares without regard to the existing shareholders' preferential right to subscribe is allowed only for weighed economic reasons. The explanatory notes of the Government Bill for the Companies Act states specifically that the intention to block a change of control does not qualify as such a weighed economic reason that would justify an issuance of new shares. The issuance of new shares to existing shareholders may also be deemed to breach the requirement for equal treatment if the sole purpose of the issuance is to increase the costs of a takeover by a shareholder.

Finally, in accordance with Article 9 of the Takeover Directive, the Helsinki Takeover Code recommends that any actions by the board of directors that would compromise the bid or its completion should always be approved by the shareholders meeting.

9.10 Profit forecasts and asset valuations

The offer document to be published by the bidder in connection with the bid must contain a statement on the future outlook of the target company if not already part of its latest financial report included in the offer document. However, no similar requirements apply for profit forecasts or asset valuations.

In practice, bidders or target companies have seldom published profit forecasts or asset valuations in order to enhance public takeover or as a defence against a bid. No specific rules apply to profit forecasts or asset valuations of the target company in connection with a bid.

The FFSA's view of profit forecasts is generally positive. Standard 5.2b, which addresses the disclosure obligation of listed companies and their shareholders in general, encourages listed companies to publish profit forecasts and thereby to provide additional information assisting investors in their valuation of the company and its securities. According to Standard 5.2b, however, to avoid any misconceptions when profit forecasts are published, particular attention should be paid to the reasoning of the profit forecasts, including any underlying assumptions and facts that such assumptions are based on, and to their presentation in an unambiguous, clear and consistent manner. Profit forecasts should only be provided with respect to such time periods that match the company's reporting periods.

9.11 Documents from the offeror and target boards

9.11.1 *The offeror*

Under the SMA 1989, before the offer period may begin, the bidder must prepare, publish and keep available during the offer period an offer document that includes all material and sufficient information to enable the shareholders of the target company to assess the merits of the offer, as detailed in the decree of the Ministry of Finance (*see* 9.7.3 above). The offer document must be submitted for approval by the FFSA and published before the commencement of the term of the takeover bid. The FFSA must approve or disapprove the offer document within five banking days from its filing.

In accordance with the Takeover Directive, an offer document that has been approved by a competent authority of another EEA Member State and that fulfils the minimum requirements set forth for an offer document must be approved by the FFSA to be used in Finland. However, the FFSA may require that such offer document would be translated into Finnish or Swedish or supplemented with information relevant for Finnish investors.

An offer document must be made available to the public and be obtainable, free of charge, from the offices of the bidder, the managers of the bid (i.e., the investment firms advising the bidder) and the marketplace on which the target company is listed (OMX Nordic Exchange Helsinki).

When published, the offer document must be delivered to the target company and the marketplace in which the securities are quoted (*see* 9.7.3 above). After the publication of the offer document, the target company must provide it to the employees or their representative.

The offer document must specify the persons who are responsible for the contents of the offer document and include a statement by such persons providing that, to the best of their knowledge, the information in the offer document is accurate and that the offer document does not omit to state any information that is likely to be relevant for the assessment of the merits of the bid. Where the bidder is a Finnish company, members of the board of directors and the managing director of the offeror are generally deemed responsible for the offer document.

9.11.2 The target company

The board of directors of the target company must publish its opinion on the bid and communicate it to the bidder and the FFSA. This should be done as soon as possible after the offer document has been provided to the target company, but at the latest five banking days prior to the close of the time allowed for the acceptance of the bid.

The opinion must consider:

(a)   the bid from the perspective of the target company and its shareholders; and
(b)   the strategic plans presented in the offer document and on their likely effects on the operations of and employment in the target company.

The board of directors' opinion must also be communicated to the employees of the target company or their representative. If the target company obtains from the employees' representative an opinion on the bid's effects on employment, this opinion must be attached to the opinion of the board of directors.

When evaluating a takeover bid and preparing its opinion, the board of directors of the target company may use external advisers and, for example, obtain a fairness opinion. According to the Takeover Code, a fairness opinion should be considered especially if the members of the board of directors or other members of the management of the target company participate in the making of the bid or have committed to accept it.

9.12   Compulsory acquisition of minorities

9.12.1 Mandatory bids under the SMA 1989

9.12.1.1   General
Under the SMA 1989, a shareholder whose proportion of the voting rights in a listed limited company exceeds 30 or 50 per cent is under an obligation to launch an unconditional takeover bid for the remaining shares of the company as well as other securities giving the holder the right to subscribe for such shares (i.e., convertibles, warrants and subscription rights). However, if the threshold of 30 or 50 per cent has been reached in the course of a voluntary takeover bid for all shares and securities entitling to shares in the target, no obligation to launch a mandatory bid will apply.

For the purposes of the above thresholds, the voting rights held by undertakings controlled by the shareholder and voting rights held by the shareholder together with a third party as well as voting rights held by parties acting in concert with the shareholder in order to exercise control of the target company are included in the shareholder's holding. If necessary, the FFSA will decide which of the above parties must launch the mandatory bid.

A shareholder who becomes obligated to launch a mandatory bid must immediately disclose such an obligation to the target company, the marketplace on which the securities are quoted and to the FFSA. The bid must then be launched within one month from the time when the obligation emerged.

9.12.1.2   Exemptions
The mandatory bid obligation does not apply to shareholders who already held at least 30 per cent of the voting rights in the company at the time the company was listed, unless the level of ownership after the listing exceeds the 50 per cent threshold or falls below and thereafter again exceeds the 30 per cent threshold. In addition, the shareholder is not under an obligation to make a mandatory bid if:

(a)   there is already another shareholder in the company whose voting proportion is greater;
(b)   the shareholder's proportion of voting rights exceeds a mandatory offer threshold solely as a result of actions taken by the company or another shareholder;
(c)   the FFSA, upon application, for a special reason grants a shareholder exemption from the mandatory offer rules.

9.12.1.3   Offer document
As in the case of a voluntary takeover bid, an offer document in respect of the offer to purchase minority holdings must be prepared, submitted to the FFSA's scrutiny, and published before the offer period commences (*see* 9.7.3 above). The FFSA must decide on the approval of the offer document within five banking days of its submission.

9.12.1.4   Consideration
A mandatory bid under the SMA 1989 must be made at an equitable price. A starting point for determining the equitable price is the highest price paid by the bidder for the shares in question during the six months preceding the obligation to make the mandatory bid. In the event the bidder has not made any purchases during that period but nevertheless exceeds the mandatory bid threshold (by, for example, having acquired a subsidiary holding shares in the target company), the equitable price is determined on the basis of the three-month volume weighted trading price of the shares. In both cases, such price may be deviated from for special reasons such as, for instance, a material change in the market or in the target company.

In a mandatory bid, a cash consideration must be offered at least as an alternative to another consideration consisting of securities.

9.12.2   Acquisition of minority holdings under the Companies Act

Under the Companies Act, a shareholder that holds more than 90 per cent of the shares and votes in a limited company (whether public or private) is entitled to purchase the remaining shares in the company at fair market value (a "squeeze-out"). This threshold also triggers an obligation for the shareholder to purchase the shares of any minority shareholder who so requests. For the purpose of the above 90 per cent threshold, the following holdings are also regarded as holdings of the shareholder:

(a)   shares in the target company held by a controlled entity; and
(b)   shares in the target company held jointly by the shareholder and a controlled entity.

Under the Companies Act, a limited company is deemed to have control over an entity when it has the majority of the voting rights in the relevant entity or the right to appoint the majority of the members of the board of directors or a corresponding body of such entity. When determining whether an entity is controlled by the shareholder, voting restrictions based on law, articles of association, shareholders agreements or corresponding arrangements relating to the relevant shares are not taken into account.

A shareholder that is entitled to purchase minority holdings is obligated to notify the target company without delay when its holding has reached or fallen below the 90 per cent threshold. The target company must file a notification without delay with the Trade Register.

According to the Companies Act, the squeeze-out price must be the fair market value of the shares before the commencement of any arbitration proceedings to implement the squeeze-out. If the obligation to acquire minority holdings has arisen from a voluntary or mandatory bid, the starting point for determining the squeeze-out price is the bid price unless there are special reasons to determine another price. The longer the time between the voluntary or mandatory bid and the acquisition of minority holdings, the less reason there is to follow the pricing of the bid. Moreover, emphasis is placed on the number of shareholders that have accepted the bid and thus considered its pricing fair.

Any disagreements regarding the acquisition of minority holdings, including disagreements on the acquisition price, are settled in arbitration proceedings, which the major shareholder would typically initiate to proceed with the squeeze-out in a swift manner. Upon a party's application, the Arbitration Board of the Central Chamber of Commerce appoints a sufficient number of independent and competent arbitrators, including a chairman. The arbitral award, once given, may be appealed against to a district court, and further to the Finnish Supreme Court, if admitted. The acquisition price for the minority holdings must be paid within one month from the arbitral award having legal effect. The arbitrators may request the major shareholder to provide a security for the payment of the squeeze-out price if they find that the prerequisites for the squeeze-out are met but that the acquisition price remains open.

9.13   Insider dealing and market manipulation

9.13.1   Definition of use of inside information

The Finnish provisions on use of inside information were revised with effect from 1 July 2005 by legislation implementing the Market Abuse Directive (2003/6/EC) in Finland. Under the SMA 1989 and the Criminal Code, use of inside information by dealing in financial instruments (insider dealing) and the provision of direct or indirect advice based on inside information (tipping) is prohibited. In addition, the SMA 1989 contains a prohibition against undue disclosure of inside information.

Inside information is defined as such information of a precise nature that has not been made public or otherwise been available on the market, that relates to publicly traded securities or derivatives with publicly traded securities as underlying and that may materially affect the value of the securities in question.

Not only information on the securities as such, but also so-called market information or information on a specific industry or line of business may qualify as inside information. Inside information typically includes undisclosed information on contemplated share issuance, major investments, mergers and acquisitions by the target company, as well as unpublished information on planned takeover bids or other major transactions concerning the securities in question.

Insider dealing and tipping may constitute criminal offences falling under the scope of the Criminal Code, when committed deliberately or by gross negligence and with the intention of obtaining financial benefit. A person who, on the basis of inside information, refrains from selling or buying securities does not breach the prohibition against use of inside information.

The Criminal Code specifically addresses aggravated misuse of inside information. Aggravated misuse of inside information means an act whereby the offender has attempted to obtain particularly large profits or considerable personal benefit, misused a position of responsibility or is deemed to have acted in a particularly premeditated manner.

When the misuse of inside information constitutes a criminal offence, the offender may be sentenced to fines or imprisonment for up to two years, or if the offence is considered to be aggravated, up to four years. For acts not falling under the scope of the Criminal Code, the prohibition against the use of inside information is enforced in administrative procedure by the FFSA and non-compliance is subject to administrative sanctions.

In order to prevent use of inside information, public registers are kept of the holdings of shares in listed companies and such securities that entitle the holder to subscribe for shares in listed companies by, *inter alia*, securities brokers as well as board members, managing directors, auditors and other persons closely related to the company.

9.13.2 Inside information in takeover bids

Until a decision to launch a takeover bid has been disclosed to the market, information concerning the preparation of a takeover bid is inside information. A listed company that is preparing a public takeover bid or that is a target to a takeover bid must compile and maintain a project-specific insider register of the persons who are not registered in the company's permanent insider register and who receive information on the bid.

According to the preambles of the Market Abuse Directive, having access to inside information relating to another company and using it in the context of a public takeover bid for the purpose of gaining control of that company should not in itself be deemed to constitute insider dealing. The use of such information in the ordinary trading in the securities will, however, qualify as misuse of inside information.

The Takeover Code specifies this by providing that the bidder is generally not deemed to be prohibited from acquiring shares of the target company only because the bidder is aware of its own intention to make a takeover bid of the target. According to the Takeover Code, the bidder's position may, however, be judged differently if the bidder possesses information on the target company's or its major shareholders' willingness to recommend or accept the bid or if the bidder has had access to inside information of the target company through, for example, a due diligence review. Furthermore, purchases of the target company's shares by other persons who are employed by the bidder or otherwise aware of the contemplated bid may in such circumstances constitute prohibited insider dealing.

Furthermore, as the offeror is obligated to include in the offer document all information relevant for the assessment of the merits of a takeover bid, the failure to make public and disclose such information may also constitute a breach of the provisions of the SMA 1989 concerning the contents of an offer document.

In 2006, the Finnish Supreme Court ruled (in case 2006:110) on trading in shares of a listed company by a party close to a potential bidder. In this case, the president of a Finnish company had been engaged in discussions regarding a suggested bid for a Finnish listed company. Pending these discussions, the president had acquired shares in the Finnish listed company on behalf of a member of his family and a company under his control. The negotiations on the possible bid were subsequently released to the Finnish press. In its ruling, the Supreme Court confirmed that also information which still is uncertain may be precise enough to qualify as inside information. In addition, the fact that the bidder was considering alternative approaches to the bid, depending on the development of the bid process, did not exclude such information from the scope of inside information. Whilst the events leading to the case in question took place at a time before the Market Abuse Directive was implemented, the principles established in the reasoning of the judgment are still deemed valid.

9.13.3 *Market manipulation*

Market manipulation is prohibited by the SMA 1989 and the Criminal Code, and is defined as:

(a) the making of a misleading purchase or sale offer, fictitious transaction and any other form of deception or contrivance in respect of publicly listed securities;

(b) transactions or other measures in respect of publicly listed securities which give, or are likely to give, false or misleading signals as to the supply of, demand for or price of the securities;

(c) transactions or other measures in respect of publicly listed securities which secure, by a person or persons acting in collaboration, the price of securities at an abnormal or artificial level; or

(d)   publication, or dissemination by any other means, of false or misleading information as to publicly listed securities, where the person who made the publication or dissemination knew, or ought to have known, that the information was false or misleading.

The provisions on market manipulation also apply to securities trading on a multilateral trading facility.

If committed deliberately, market manipulation may constitute a criminal offence falling under the scope of the Criminal Code. For the Criminal Code to apply, it is furthermore required that the offender had the intention to obtain financial benefit either for himself or for somebody else. The Criminal Code also includes provisions on aggravated market manipulation, which apply when the offender has caused extensive financial losses or when the offence may harm the confidence in the securities markets generally. When market manipulation constitutes a criminal offence, the offenders may be sentenced to fines or imprisonment for up to two years or, if the offence is considered aggravated, up to four years.

When not falling under the scope of the Criminal Code, the prohibition against market manipulation is enforced in administrative procedure by the FFSA and non-compliance is subject to administrative sanctions.

9.13.4   Disclosure offences

The Criminal Code defines a security markets information offence as:

(a)   the provision in the professional marketing or buying of securities of false or misleading information pertaining to the securities; or

(b)   the failure to provide appropriate information pertaining to listed securities, as required by the SMA 1989, which is conducive to essentially affecting the value of the securities, or the provision, when fulfilling the disclosure obligation provided in the SMA 1989, of false or misleading information pertaining to the securities.

The provisions on security markets information offences apply to listed companies and other entities that, under the SMA 1989, are obliged to publish information on their securities and financial status. In addition, the provisions in (a) above apply to persons engaged in professional marketing or acquisition of publicly traded securities.

A security markets information offence is a criminal offence for which offenders may be sentenced to fines or imprisonment for up to two years.

9.14   Financial assistance

Under the Companies Act, a Finnish limited liability company may not grant monetary loans or provide security for the purpose of financing the acquisition of the company's or any of its parent companies' shares. It is noteworthy that this prohibition does not extend to other group companies.

Under the Companies Act generally, the granting of a monetary loan by a limited liability company as well as the provision of security (or indeed, entering into any other agreement or undertaking by the company) requires that it serves a genuine business or commercial rationale of the company and is of corporate benefit to the company. Civil liability of the management towards the company granting the loan/providing the collateral may arise where the granting of the loan/provision of collateral does not serve such justified business rationale from the company's point of view.

Chapter 10

France

Thierry Vassogne, Marc Loy and Bertrand Cardi

Partners[1]
Linklaters (Paris)

10.1 Introduction

With a share market capitalisation of approximately €1,895 billion, the French stock markets ranked second in Europe after the UK markets in 2007. In 2007, 54 offers were completed.

Since November 2003 and the merger of the *Conseil des Marchés Financiers* ("CMF") and the *Commission des opérations de bourse* ("COB"), which put an end to a period of more than 30 years during which the stock market regulations emanated from, and were implemented by, two distinct authorities, the regulatory and controlling authority of the French stock markets is the *Autorité des marchés financiers* ("AMF"). The AMF powers consist in the control of the quality of information given to the markets, the protection of minority shareholders, as well as the regulation of the market and the takeover offer process.

When issuing its general regulation ("the General Regulation"), the AMF sets forth rules ensuring that offers are not frustrated by transactions which are contrary to interests of the target company shareholders and to provide for equality of treatment of such shareholders.

The General Regulation was amended further to the implementation in France by Law no. 2006–387 of 31 March 2006 ("the Implementing Law") of Directive 2004/25/EC adopted on 21 April 2004 by the European Parliament and the Council ("the Takeover Directive") to establish minimum guidelines for the conduct of takeovers involving the securities of companies listed on European Stock Exchange markets. The Takeover Directive aimed to facilitate cross-border takeovers or takeovers of companies listed on several markets as well as involving the offer of securities in several jurisdictions throughout the European Community.

In addition, 2007 saw the merger of the French Stock Exchange market, Euronext, with the New York Stock Exchange.

---

[1] The authors wish to thank Thomas Meli, Christophe Vinsonneau and Aurélien Veil for their help in preparing this article.

10.2   Acquisition targets

10.2.1   Listed companies and non-listed companies

Essentially, companies which become the subject of takeover offers in France are those listed on the regulated market (Eurolist; *see* 10.5.1.2 below) and, to a limited extent, to companies which used to be listed.

Companies the shares of which are not traded on any stock market may also be acquired by way of a takeover offer, which is the only practical way of gaining control of companies with a wide share ownership. Such takeover offers do not come within the jurisdiction of the AMF pursuant to provisions of the General Regulation applicable to takeovers. However, rules applicable to *appel public à l'épargne* or *solicitation* would certainly apply, especially in the case of exchange offers.

The French Commercial Code ("the Commercial Code") provides for a number of corporate forms, but only two may be listed: *sociétés anonymes* ("SA") and *sociétés en commandite par actions* ("SCA").

An SA is a public limited company similar to those known in other jurisdictions. An SCA is a form of limited partnership with limited partners, who hold shares in accordance with the rules applicable to SAs, and general partners (*associé(s) commandités*) whose shares in the SCA are not negotiable and who usually benefit, pursuant to the provisions of the articles of association, from veto rights on significant corporate decisions, such as the appointment or removal of the managers, amendments to the articles of association or the issue of new shares. Since the general partner(s) can oppose such decisions even against the will of all of the shareholders, the SCA constitutes an efficient takeover defence. Some significant French listed companies are incorporated under that form (e.g., Michelin, Euro-Disney, Lagardère Groupe, IDI). However, the authorities are increasingly reluctant to list an SCA, and very few SCAs have been listed since 1999 (e.g., Groupe Steria and Elior; the latter was delisted at the end of 2006). The financial valuation of the rights of the general partners is generally a key issue when structuring a transformation or merger of an SCA (e.g., in 1993 for the transformation of Yves Saint Laurent and more recently for the reorganisation of Maurel et Prom in 2004).

10.2.2   Form of French listed companies

10.2.2.1   Management
The Commercial Code provides for two alternative management structures for an SA:

(a)   a "classical" management structure, consisting of a board of directors (with a chairman) and a chief executive officer;[2] and

(b)   a "dual" board structure consisting of a board of management and a supervisory board.

---

[2] The chairman (*président du conseil d'administration*) may also be at the same time the chief executive officer.

The chief executive officer, in the "classical" management structure, and the management board (*directoire*), in the "dual" board structure, have the broadest powers to bind the company vis-à-vis third parties.

The members of the board of directors and the supervisory board members are directly appointed by resolution of the shareholders in general meeting and may be dismissed in the same manner, without notice, justification or indemnity payments (provided such dismissal is not "abusive" or "vexatious"), any provision in the articles of association or agreement to the contrary being void. In the "dual" board structure, the board of management members are appointed by the supervisory board, and may be dismissed, by a decision of the share-holders in general meeting or, if provided in the articles of association, by a decision of the supervisory board (if dismissed without "just cause", they may be entitled to indemnity payments).

As mentioned above, in the "classical" management structure, the board of directors may opt either to dissociate the jobs of chairman and chief executive officer or to appoint the same person to hold both positions. When he is not also the chairman of the board of directors, the chief executive officer (who is in charge of the day-to-day management and represents the company vis-à-vis third parties) is entitled to some indemnification if not dismissed for just cause (*juste motif*), whereas the chairman (who is in charge of the organisation and direction of the board's works, the smooth running of the bodies of the company and the provision to the shareholders' meeting of a report on the conditions of the preparation and organisation of the board's works and the internal control procedures) may be dismissed at any time without notice, justification or indemnity payments as any other officer. When the chairman is also chief executive officer, he combines the duties attached to both positions but loses the protection granted to the chief executive officer and may be dismissed at any time without notice, justification or indemnity payments.

Among the French companies within the 40 largest entities listed on the French market which form the CAC 40 index, seven have adopted the "dual" board structure, 14 have opted for the dissociation of the positions of chairman and CEO, and 16 have opted not to dissociate these positions. The most common governance structure is by far the traditional structure with a board of directors.

The managers (*gérants*) of an SCA may only be appointed or dismissed according to the provisions of the articles of association, which invariably grant the general partners a veto right.

10.2.2.2 Shares and voting rights

Whereas SAs and SCAs which are not listed may include provisions restricting the free transferability of shares in their articles of association, in particular requiring the prior consent of the management before transfer to a new share-holder, such provisions are not permitted in the articles of association of listed companies.

On the other hand, agreements between shareholders providing restrictions on the free transferability of shares (e.g., rights of first refusal) are permitted and extremely frequent. Their review and the assessment of their implications is often a key element in the takeover process. It must be noted that any clause in an agreement providing for preferential sale or purchase conditions, if it relates to shares admitted to trading on a regulated market which represent more than 0.5 per cent of the share capital or voting rights of the issuer, must be disclosed to the issuer and the AMF within five trading days of the signing of such agreement. Failing such disclosure, the effects of the clauses would be suspended during an offer period.

Shareholders are normally granted such number of voting rights as corresponds to the number of their shares. As an exception to this rule, the Commercial Code provides that companies may issue shares with particular rights (*actions de préférence*) (e.g., no voting rights, specific financial rights).

More significantly, the articles of association of a number of listed companies provide that shares obtain double voting rights when they have been registered under the name of the same shareholder for a minimum time period (which cannot be less than two years). Listed companies must disclose their total number of voting rights and shares at the end of each month when such numbers have changed compared to the last publicly disclosed numbers. Articles of association may further provide a general limitation on the number of votes of each shareholder at general meetings, to the extent they respect the breakthrough provisions proposed by the Takeover Directive.

Indeed, the Implementing Law and the General Regulation state that:

(a) any restriction regarding share transfers specified in the target's articles of association shall not apply to an offeror with respect to the shares tendered to the takeover offer; and

(b) any ceiling on voting rights provided for in the target's articles of association shall not apply to the first general meeting following the outcome of the offer, should the offeror (acting alone or in concert) hold more than two-thirds of the share capital or voting rights of the target.

In addition, companies may elect to amend their articles of association to provide that:

(a) During the offer period:
  (i) any restriction regarding share transfers specified in any agreement entered into after 21 April 2004 shall not apply to an offeror; or
  (ii) any restriction on voting rights specified in their articles of association or in any agreement entered into after 21 April 2004 shall not apply to any general meetings convened to consider any defensive measures.

(b) At the first general meeting following the outcome of an offer, should the offeror (acting alone or in concert) hold in excess of 50 per cent of the share capital and voting rights of the target:
  (i) any restriction on voting rights specified in the articles of association or in any agreement entered into after 21 April 2004; or
  (ii) any extraordinary right granted to any shareholders to appoint or revoke the members of the governing bodies,
  shall not apply.

However, the reciprocity exception has not been implemented under French law with respect to breakthrough rules. Consequently, the above-mentioned rules, which are favourable to an offeror, will apply whether such offeror is virtuous or not.

Besides, in addition to their voting rights, shareholders have various information rights of a permanent or occasional nature with regard to the company, the right to receive dividends and liquidation proceeds, as well as pre-emptive rights with regard to the issue of new shares and certain other securities. Groups of minority shareholders also have certain other rights, such as the rights (for a group holding more than 5 per cent of the share capital of the company or an association formed by shareholders holding their shares in registered form for more than two years who hold a certain number of shares (such number being dependent on the size of the share capital of the company)) to request the dismissal of the statutory auditors or to ask for a court-appointed expert to review the acts of management.

Moreover, pursuant to Article 452–2 of the French financial and monetary code, a duly authorised association may initiate an action in the interest of individual investors. The *Association de défense des actionnaires minoritaires* ("ADAM") or *Deminor*, for example, regularly file claims against decisions of the AMF or against companies which they consider have misled shareholders. However, the efficiency of such provision is generally considered limited because any such association must receive written instructions (*mandat*) from at least two claimants and, unlike class actions in the US, the association must identify each claimant.

10.2.2.3 *Voting*

The ordinary shareholder general meeting ("OGM"), which must be held at least once every year within six months of the end of the preceding financial year, makes all decisions which are not expressly reserved to the extraordinary shareholders meeting and more specifically with regard to all acts of management outside the scope of management's authority.

In particular, decisions falling within the exclusive authority of the OGM are the approval of the accounts, the allocation of profits and distribution of dividends, the appointment and/or dismissal of directors/supervisory board members. Provided the supervisory board has been empowered to do so by the articles of association, both the supervisory board and the OGM may dismiss members of the management board where there is a dual board structure.

The quorum at an OGM is at least one-fifth of the company's voting shares. If these quorum requirements are not met, the meeting must be adjourned and there will be no quorum requirements in respect of any such adjourned meeting. Decisions are made by simple majority vote of the shareholders present or represented.[3]

The extraordinary general meeting of shareholders ("EGM") has sole authority to decide, *inter alia*, on any amendments to the articles of association, which

---

[3] Under French law the abstention of a shareholder is therefore considered as a negative vote.

258 *A Practitioner's Guide to Takeovers and Mergers in the EU*

include, in particular, major corporate reorganisations, such as mergers or divestitures of essential corporate assets and the issuance of shares or any equity-related securities (for more details on the issuance of securities by a target company during the course of an offer *see* 10.9.2 below). It should be noted that in almost all listed companies the EGM has delegated to the management for a limited time period (up to a maximum of five years) the authority to issue new shares.

The quorum required for an EGM is at least one-fourth of the company's voting shares, or if such quorum is not met at the first such meeting at least one-fifth of the company's shares carrying voting rights at the adjourned meeting. Decisions are made by a majority of two-thirds of the votes of the shareholders present or represented.[4]

To convene a shareholders meeting in a listed company, whether ordinary or extraordinary, the board of directors or the management board is to issue:

(a)   at least 35 days before the meeting:
    (i)   a meeting notice to be published in the French legal newspaper ("the *BALO*"), together with
    (ii)   a press release to be posted on the company's website and published in a French nationwide financial newspaper; and
(b)   at least 15 days before the first meeting and six days before any following adjourned meeting:
    (i)   a convening notice to be published in the *BALO* and in a legal gazette, together with
    (ii)   a press release to be posted on the company's website and published in a French nationwide financial newspaper.

It is worth noticing that "pure" OGMs of listed companies hardly happen; most general meetings of shareholders mix ordinary and extraordinary resolutions.

10.2.2.4 *Disclosure of significant thresholds and concerted action*

Article L.233–7 of the Commercial Code provides that any person, whether acting alone or in concert, who crosses the thresholds of 5, 10, 15, 20, 25, 33.33, 50, 66.66, 90 or 95 per cent of the shareholding or the voting rights (either upwards or downwards) of a company listed on a regulated or on a financial instruments market must disclose this fact to the company in question and, where the shares are listed on a regulated market, to the AMF within five trading days. This information is then published by the AMF. The articles of association may provide for disclosure to the company at lower thresholds (as low as 0.5 per cent).

In addition, any person who crosses (directly, indirectly, alone or in concert) the thresholds of 10 per cent or 20 per cent of the shareholding or the voting rights of a listed company must, within 10 trading days, declare to the company in question and to the AMF its intentions over the next 12 months with regard to its shareholding in the company. This statement must indicate whether the

---

[4] As for votes in the OGM, the abstention of a shareholder in an EGM is therefore considered as a negative vote.

person is acting alone or in concert, whether they contemplate ceasing or continuing the purchase of shares, taking control of the company, or being appointed a member of the board of directors/supervisory board of the company. The shareholders concerned may subsequently modify their published intentions if they can justify that there have been "significant changes in the environment, the situation or the shareholding of the persons concerned", in which case they must publish a new declaration.

The following shares or voting rights are, pursuant to the Commercial Code, deemed to be held by a given shareholder when calculating the threshold of shareholdings or voting rights:

(a)   those held by other persons but for the account of the shareholder;
(b)   those held by companies under the control of the shareholder;
(c)   those held by persons acting in concert with the shareholder;
(d)   those that the shareholder may acquire at his own option;
(e)   those held in usufruct by the shareholder;
(f)   those held by a third party under an agreement providing for their temporary sale;
(g)   those deposited with the shareholder when he may vote as he thinks fit; and
(h)   those that the shareholder may exercise pursuant to a proxy without specific instructions.

It must also be noticed that, depending on the chosen structure, certain equity swaps may consequently have to be disclosed in application with the above-mentioned rules.

Persons are deemed to be acting in concert when they enter into agreements either:

(a)   relating to the acquisition of shares or voting rights (e.g., drag-along rights, but not mere rights of first refusal, since such rights do not enable their beneficiary to force the other party to sell its shares,[5] provided of course that such rights of first refusal are not mixed with cooperation, consultation or other obligations); or
(b)   relating to the exercise of their voting rights, in both cases in order to enforce a common policy towards a listed company (e.g., agreements providing for joint determination of the votes to be cast at an OGM or EGM).

In addition, the definition of concert has been extended in the course of a takeover offer to include:

(a)   persons who enter into an agreement with the offeror with a view to acquiring the control of the target; and
(b)   persons who enter into an agreement with the target with a view to frustrating the successful outcome of a takeover offer.

---

[5] *Club Méditerranée*, CBV, decision no. 90–1500 dated 17 May 1990.

Finally, any company and the chairman of its board, its executive directors, members of its management board (*directoire*), its managers (*gérants*), companies it controls, and companies under the same control are deemed by law to be acting in concert. Similarly shareholders of *sociétés par actions simplifiées* ("SASs") are deemed to act in concert vis-à-vis the companies that such SAS controls. It should be noted, however, that such presumption is simple and therefore rebuttable.

Concerts may be either written or oral, formal or tacit. However, it is generally considered difficult to prove the existence of a concert action in the absence of a written agreement (being in turn specified that the mere existence of a share-holders agreement does not necessarily imply the existence of a concert party between the parties). It must be noted that the decision of the AMF in the Eiffage/Sacyr situation[6] confirmed that an aggregation of facts can be considered as characterising a de facto concert action to the extent that they are sufficiently strong and converging.[7] However, at the time of writing, this decision was subject to an appeal before the Paris Court of Appeal, which will have to be followed closely: the hearing occurred in early February 2008 and the decision was expected in early April 2008. Another recent decision of the AMF in the Gecina situation[8] has confirmed the tougher stand taken by the AMF with respect to de facto concert, even when the parties have explicitly stated they were not acting in concert.[9] These decisions are particularly noteworthy considering

---

[6] *Eiffage*, AMF, decision no. 207C1202 dated 26 June 2007.

[7] In the Eiffage/Sacyr situation, the AMF referred mainly to:
  (a)   the relationships (either business or financial) between the suspected parties, their officers and their shareholders;
  (b)   the inadequacy of the link between the corporate purpose of the suspected parties and the business of the target;
  (c)   the high level of the price paid for the purchases of the shares of the target as compared to analysts' objectives for the market price of such shares (*objectifs de cours*);
  (d)   the limited financial capacity of the suspected parties as compared to the financial burden represented by the purchase of the shares; and
  (e)   the close date and rhythm of the shares purchases, to decide that there was a concert action.

[8] *Gecina*, AMF, decision no. 207C2792 dated 13 December 2007.

[9] In the Gecina situation, the majority shareholders of Metrovacesa, the Spanish parent company of Gecina, had entered into a separation agreement providing for the separation of the companies and the split of their control over the companies among them. The AMF considered that, even limited in time to the period required to proceed to the separation, the undertakings given in connection therewith were sufficient to demonstrate a common policy towards the company and therefore characterise the existence of a concert action between two of these majority shareholders (who owned respectively 17.80 per cent and 15.36 per cent of the share capital and voting rights of Gecina), even though these shareholders had expressly stated in their respective filings (threshold crossing statement and declaration of intent) that they were not acting in concert. Consequently, the AMF refused to give clearance to the buy-back offer filed by Gecina that would have resulted in these two majority shareholders holding in concert up to 42.70 per cent of the share capital and voting rights of Gecina, a situation that would require the filing of a mandatory offer. The majority shareholders have already lodged an appeal against the AMF decision, the outcome of which will have to be followed closely.

that this type of precedent used to be very rare. As far as the authors are aware, there have been only two previous precedents of de facto concert: the *Delmas–Vieljeux* case[10] in 1991 and the *Lagardère Groupe/Arjil Groupe* case[11] in 1993.

In the Eiffage decision, the qualification of concert triggered the following consequences: the voluntary exchange offer filed by the offeror was not approved by the AMF, which required the concerting parties to file a mandatory offer, necessarily including a cash option and restricting the possibilities for the offeror to freely set the offer price. By the same token, the decision of the AMF in the Gecina situation that a mandatory offer would have to be imposed on the majority shareholders if the buyback offer were to proceed would also prevent the offerors from freely setting the offer price.

10.3 Exchange and investment control and other regulatory restrictions

Direct foreign investment in France is now governed by the French Monetary and Financial Code as updated by Decree no. 2005–1739 of 30 December 2005.

In most cases, a transaction must simply be notified to the competent authorities "at the moment of the first operation materialising the agreement between the contracting parties", such as the signature of the agreement, the publication of the public offer or the acquisition of an asset constituting a direct investment in France. In addition, a number of investments, listed in Article R.152–5 of the Monetary and Financial Code, are exempted from the notification requirement.

However, prior authorisation is still required for the acquisition of shares in companies engaged in certain "sensitive" activities, such as public sector companies, businesses involved in:

(a) public security;
(b) defence industry; or
(c) research and development, retail or production of arms or explosives.

Furthermore, investments in certain other areas require the approval of specific authorities. For instance, this is the case in the banking, insurance, press, broadcasting and mining industries.

In particular, the opening of an offer for a credit institution is subject to the prior approval of the *Comité des établissements de crédit et des entreprises d'investissement* ("CECEI"). In addition, the governor of the *Banque de France* (president of the CECEI) must be informed eight business days prior to the filing or the announcement of an offer on a credit institution. A similar information obligation also

---

[10] *Delmas–Vieljeux*, CBV, press release dated 13 June 1991.
[11] *Lagardère Groupe*, CBV, decision no. 93–1068 dated 21 April 1993 where the CBV considered that the common goal of the concert actions between Arjil Groupe and GEC on the one hand and Arjil Groupe and Daimler Benz on the other hand (i.e., to ensure the control of Arjil Groupe over Lagardère Groupe) resulted in a global de facto concert action between Arjil Groupe, GEC and Daimler Benz.

applies to offers for insurance companies through a notification of the *Comité des entreprises d'assurance* but with a reduced delay of two business days in this case. Given the absence of an express penalty, however, the efficacy of such provisions may be questioned.

It must be kept in mind that a company subject to an offer has to convene its works council as soon as a public offer is filed with the AMF. At this meeting, the works council has to decide whether it wants to hear the offeror. If this is the case, the offeror must attend the next works council meeting to be held within a 15-day period following the publication of the offer document. If the offeror fails to appear, it will be deprived of its voting rights in the target until:

(a)   its interview by the works council; or
(b)   in the absence of a new convocation by the works council within a 15-day period following the first meeting to which the offeror was invited, the end of such 15-day period.

As an offer is irrevocable and generally completed within 25 trading days following its opening, both the opportunity and the practical interest of such provision can be questioned. In addition, the offer document must be sent by the offeror to the works council of the target within three days of its publication.

The offeror must also convene its works council within two days from the publication of the offer (i.e., in the authors' view, in principle from the filing of the offer rather than the announcement of the offer, but the appropriate solution should be checked on a case-by-case basis) and provide it with precise information with respect to the offer.

10.4   Merger control

10.4.1   New economic regulations

France first enacted legislation on mergers, acquisitions and business structures likely to inhibit competition (*Concentrations*) in 1977. Following an amendment in 1985, the anti-trust aspects of mergers and acquisitions in France were then governed by Ordinance no. 86–1242 of 1 December 1986 ("the 1986 Ordinance"). On 15 May 2001 the New Economic Regulations Act ("the 2001 NER Act") introduced a new system of merger control in France. This new regime came into force in May 2002, the 2001 NER Act having been supplemented by the implementing decree of 30 April 2002 ("the Decree"). Merger control in France is now governed by Articles L.430–1 to L.430–10 of the French Commercial Code.

The procedure of the 2001 NER Act is largely supervised by the Minister of the Economy ("the Minister"), assisted by the Competition Council (*Conseil de la Concurrence*).

The role of the French anti-trust procedures is to prevent transactions the anti-competitive effects of which would exceed their economic and social benefits to the French market.

10.4.2 Procedure

The pivotal innovation introduced by Article L.430–2, as modified by the 2001 NER Act, is that it has established a system of compulsory notification of concentrations which is triggered when certain turnover thresholds are reached, in contrast with the 1986 Ordinance which set out a voluntary system of notification. In this respect French merger control rules are similar to those in force at Community level and in most EU Member States.

Article L.430–4 requires parties to a concentration to suspend their transaction until express clearance has been granted or the time limits imposed by the Minister have expired.

Nevertheless, the parties can apply for a derogation enabling them to proceed with the closing of their transaction prior to clearance from the Minister. The parties must establish in a "duly reasoned" application that there is "a particular need" for such derogation. As the French competition authorities apply this provision quite strictly, the derogation is granted only in exceptional cases.

Besides this derogation, the Decree sets out a general exception to the suspension principle concerning public bids. Thus, French Merger control rules allow offers to close before they have been cleared by the Minister provided that the acquirer does not exercise the voting rights attached to the securities in question before such clearance. This is another similarity with the Merger Control Regulation (Article 7.4).

French merger control rules do not specify any compulsory time limit within which the notification must be made. Since December 2004, a concentration may be notified to the Minister on the basis of a "sufficiently advanced" draft agreement (e.g., letter of intent). It is therefore no longer necessary to have entered into a final agreement in order to be able to notify a concentration to the French competition authorities (Article L.430–3).

Amongst other sanctions, Article L.430–8 provides that fines may be imposed in cases where a concentration has not been duly notified, where implementation has occurred prior to clearance, where misleading or incorrect information has been given, or where information has been omitted. These fines, set out in the same Article L.430–8, may reach a maximum of 5 per cent of the net turnover achieved in France by the companies for the last complete financial year. This amount can be increased, if appropriate, by the net turnover in France of the acquired party during the same period.

10.4.3 Thresholds

In the absence of a change of control, there is no concentration and no obligation to notify. Article L.430–1 of the French Commercial Code sets out three instances of a change of control constituting a concentration. They are:

(a)   where two or more previously independent undertakings merge; or
(b)   where one or more undertakings or persons acquire, whether by purchase

of securities or assets, by contract or by any other means, direct or indirect control of the whole or parts of one or more other undertakings;[12] or

(c)　　where a joint venture is created which performs on a lasting basis all the functions of an autonomous economic undertaking.

Once it has been established that a transaction does in fact constitute a concentration, it must be ascertained whether the merger control thresholds set out in Article L.430–2 of the French Commercial Code are met.

Turnover is the sole criterion used in determining the Minister's merger control jurisdiction.

Henceforth, concentrations are to be notified to the French Minister where (Article L.430–2):

(a)　　the aggregate total worldwide turnover net of tax of all the parties to the concentration exceeds €150 million;

(b)　　the total turnover net of tax achieved in France by at least two of the parties to the concentration exceeds €50 million; and

(c)　　the European merger control thresholds are not met.

In addition, the European Commission may refer to the French Minister concentrations which meet the European merger control thresholds where each of the undertakings concerned achieves more than two-thirds of its aggregate Community-wide turnover in France.

10.4.4　Time frame

Once a notification is filed with the Minister, Article L.430–5 of the French Commercial Code requires him to respond within a Phase I period of five weeks (except in the case of commitments where Phase I may extend to a maximum of eight weeks). Time runs from the date the notification is declared complete. During this period the Minister may (Article L.430–5):

(a)　　declare that the transaction does not fall within the scope of French merger control; or

(b)　　issue a clearance decision, possibly subject to commitments by the parties; or

(c)　　refer the matter to the Competition Council if he is of the view that the transaction is such as to give rise to competition concerns and that any commitments put forward by the parties are not sufficient to remedy these concerns. This event triggers the Phase II procedure.

Upon a referral being made, the Competition Council has three months to decide whether the transaction referred gives rise to competition concerns, for example by creating or strengthening:

---

[12] Including the cases where one shareholder which previously exercised joint control over a given company acquires exclusive control over such company, or where the owner of an exclusive control transfers part of its shareholding to another entity to create a joint control over the target company.

(a)   a dominant position; or

(b)   buying power, placing suppliers in a position of economic dependence.

The Minister then has four weeks to adopt a final decision concerning the transaction (except in the case of commitments in Phase II which extend the procedure for three weeks).

Thus, in cases where Phase II proceedings are initiated, the time limit for the Minister and the Competition Council to examine a transaction will be a minimum of five months and one week and a maximum of six months and three weeks.

10.4.5   Substantive test

The French substantive test relates to the potential lessening of competition and therefore the Minister will have the power, in his assessment, to determine whether a transaction will result in economic progress of sufficient significance to compensate for its anti-competitive features. Furthermore, the Minister will also take into consideration the international competitiveness of the companies which are parties to the transaction in question.

10.4.6   Territorial jurisdiction

In the event of a cross-border transaction, the French authorities will have jurisdiction over the transaction, provided that the above-mentioned thresholds are fulfilled.

French merger control and EU merger control are mutually exclusive.

10.5   Regulation of the conduct of mergers and acquisitions

10.5.1   Stock market authorities

10.5.1.1   The AMF

The AMF is the French regulatory and controlling financial market authority. It was established by the Financial Security Act of 1 August 2003 through the merger of the COB (the market's external regulatory authority modelled on the US Securities and Exchange Commission) and the CMF (the market's self-regulatory authority). This merger came into effect in November 2003.

The AMF comprises the Board (*collège*) with 16 members and the Sanction Commission with 12 members (each including six members appointed by the finance minister after consultation with organisations representing main actors of the stock market).

The powers of the AMF include protecting investments in financial instruments, ensuring that investors are provided with relevant information, as well as regulating the markets and takeover offers.

In this respect, following the enactment of the Implementing Law, the AMF updated in September 2006 its General Regulation, which contains, *inter alia*, the principles applicable to issuers (in particular, principles applicable to takeovers), to service providers, to collective investment products and to regulated markets and the conditions to be met for markets to be recognised as regulated markets.

It is possible at any time, and in particular at the planning stage of a transaction, to consult the AMF on the interpretation of any one of its rules. Although this is very rare in practice, the AMF may give a written answer in the form of a *rescrit*, which is legally binding.

The AMF also issued several instructions and recommendations, in addition to the General Regulation, to clarify the applicable Stock Exchange regulations on specific matters.

In addition to its regulatory functions, the AMF has a supervisory role which consists, *inter alia*, of monitoring the entire procedure applicable to takeovers (decisions on the conformity or the prolonging of an offer, publication of the outcome of an offer, etc.) and reviewing information disclosed by companies raising capital from the public (*sociétés faisant appel public à l'épargne*).

Pursuant to the injunction powers it has been vested with by French law, the AMF also has the right:

(a)   to require companies to proceed with corrective publications in the case of inaccurate public disclosure. If the company fails to do this, the AMF may proceed itself with such corrective publications at the expense of the company in question; or

(b)   either directly, or indirectly through a court (in which case a penalty per day can be included), to order a person in breach of its obligations to regularise the situation, provided the AMF can prove that such non-compliance is an obstacle to the good functioning of the market or that it prejudices the protection of investors. Interestingly, this power is not used very frequently (since the mere threat of informing the market often leads to a "common understanding" and subsequent settlement of the issue) but is generally of interest to the AMF either in the case of obvious violations (e.g., where a company has crossed a threshold triggering a mandatory offer but refuses to implement such offer[13]) or in highly political cases;

(c)   to request courts to order that funds or shares held by a person who is sufficiently likely to have violated a regulation which may prejudice the interest of the investors or the good functioning of the market are put in escrow. This power has rarely been used for funds,[14] and as far as the

---

[13] Ord. réf. TGI Paris, 13 July 2005, R. Chamla; *see* also AMF communiqué no. 205C1980 dated 23 November 2005 relating to the decision of the Paris Court of Appeal dated 19 October 2005 confirming the decision dated 13 July 2005.

[14] Ord. req. TGI Paris, 8 November 2004, Y.Z. and Société AI Investment, *Bull. Joly Bourse* 2005.130; TGI Paris, 9 October 2003, Société Vivendi Universal and J-M. Messier, RTD Com. 2003, p. 775; Ord. réf. TGI Bordeaux, 21 January 2000, Conseil Finance, *Banque et Droit* March–April 2000, p.39.

authors are aware it has been exercised only once in relation to shares, and in very specific circumstances (which have finally given rise to a settlement agreement).[15]

In addition to its injunction powers, the AMF has been granted with sanction powers. Such monetary sanctions remain one of the AMF's most effective means of control since it can impose a fine of up to €1.5 million or up to 10 times the profit made by the offending person, bearing in mind that the sanction should be proportionate to the breach at stake. The maximum sanction has already been imposed by the former COB (e.g., around €1.5 million for the use of inside information: in 1992, a member of the board of directors of Delalande bought Delalande shares, being aware of the expected merger between that company and Synthelabo). However, the possibility for the AMF to grant its sanction powers an international efficacy is not always clearly assessed and may give rise to legal and practical issues.

The AMF also has a mediation power. The possibility of creating a settlement procedure is being considered, and that project raises several issues (in particular whether entering into a settlement with the AMF should be considered as a recognition of liability before a civil court).

The conformity decision (implying the delivery of the so-called "visa" on the offer documents) issued by the AMF in the context of an offer may be appealed before the Paris Court of Appeal. Other AMF decisions may be appealed before the Paris Court of Appeal or administrative courts depending on the nature of the decision.

10.5.1.2 The markets

In addition to the regulatory bodies, it should be noted that from a regulatory perspective three markets currently co-exist in France:

(a) Eurolist or the Paris Stock Exchange;
(b) the MONEP; and
(c) the MATIF.

The *Hors Cote* (unlisted market), where securities not traded on the other markets were traded, ceased to exist in July 1998 and has been replaced by the *Marché Libre* or OTC Market, which is not a regulated market. Public offer regulations do not apply to the *Marché Libre*.

---

[15] The shares of a French company listed in France which was the subject of an offer (Société Générale) had been traded abroad off market at a price which was higher than the offer price. The COB (predecessor of the AMF) had requested before the courts that such transaction be cancelled because it was contrary to French law and that in the meantime, such shares are put in escrow. No specific decision was made by the courts which only registered the settlement agreement entered into between the COB and the other parties: the COB agreed not to proceed with its request for cancellation in exchange for the shares being put in escrow and the voting rights being exercised by the escrow agent until the end of the offer (to avoid any interference with the offer): Ord. réf. TGI Paris, 3 August 1999, société CGU, *Banque et Droit* November–December 1999, p. 43 and COB 1999 Annual Report, p. 74.

On 21 February 2005, the First Market (*Premier Marché*), the Second Market (*Second Marché*) and the New Market (*Nouveau Marché*) were merged into one single market called Eurolist. Shares are now divided between three different sections of Eurolist (A, B and C) depending on the market capitalisation of the company in question. Although different disclosure rules previously existed for each market (e.g., specific rules for small companies listed on the *Nouveau Marché*), the same disclosure obligations now apply to all companies listed on Eurolist.

Finally, both the MONEP and the MATIF, which are managed by Euronext concurrently with the LIFFE in London, are derivative markets.

These markets are run by Euronext Paris S.A. the French subsidiary of Euronext NV.

In April 2005, Euronext launched Alternext, a non-regulated but organised market (*marché régulé*), for small and mid-cap companies. Public offer regulations do not apply to Alternext.

In 2007, the Euronext group merged with the New York Stock Exchange ("NYSE") under a holding company called NYSE Euronext, registered in New York.

Further to the implementation in France of Directive 2004/39/EC adopted on 21 April 2004 by the European Parliament and the Council ("the Markets in Financial Instruments Directive"), two types of markets have been designed in addition to Stock Exchange markets where financial instruments may now be traded in France:

(a)   multilateral trading facilities; and
(b)   systematic internaliser.

The creation of such new trading places may raise technical difficulties as to the determination of the subsequent share price of the listed company, difficulties which will have to be assessed in the context of the development of these new markets.

10.5.2   *Regulations applicable to public takeovers*

Apart from the Commercial Code, the main provisions applicable to public takeovers are set out in *Titre III Livre II* of the General Regulation.

10.6   Methods of acquisition

There are three main methods by which the control of a French listed company can be acquired. The takeover offer and the acquisition of a controlling interest followed by a mandatory offer are the most commonly used methods. Control can also be achieved by way of mergers or related transactions.

10.6.1 Takeover offer

A takeover offer is the method of acquisition generally employed when no group of shareholders holds a controlling shareholding. It is also used when the target company is controlled by one distinct shareholder, but either:

(a)   such controlling shareholder is reluctant to irrevocably commit to sell his shares to the offeror; or

(b)   the offeror wishes to make his offer conditional upon reaching a certain percentage of the capital and/or voting rights of the target company.

Finally, it is used whenever the bid is hostile.

The most significant distinguishing feature of a voluntary takeover offer as opposed to a mandatory offer is that, in the case of a voluntary offer, the offeror can make his offer conditional upon a certain level of acceptances (*see* 10.7.2 below) and that a competing offer may always be filed.

10.6.2 Acquisition of a controlling interest and mandatory offers

Since a significant number of French listed companies are controlled by a shareholder or group of shareholders, many takeovers are structured as the acquisition of a controlling block of shares followed by a mandatory offer.

10.6.2.1 Triggering a mandatory offer

The obligation to file an offer is imposed by Article 234–2 of the General Regulation on any person, acting alone or in concert, who crosses the threshold of one-third of the capital or of the voting rights of a listed company.

Article 234–4 of the General Regulation allows the AMF to grant an exemption from the mandatory bid requirement if the crossing of the above threshold does not exceed 3 per cent of the share capital and the voting rights and occurs over a period of less than six months. In addition, the shareholder must undertake not to exercise the voting rights in excess of this threshold during this period. Article 234–9 also permits the AMF to grant an exemption in circumstances where the relevant threshold has been crossed indirectly (*see* 10.6.2.2 below).

Pursuant to Article 234–5 of the General Regulation, the obligation to file an offer also applies to any person, acting alone or in concert, who holds, directly or indirectly, more than one-third but less than half of the capital or of the voting rights of a listed company and who increases his stake by 2 per cent or more of the capital or voting rights within 12 consecutive months.

In order to avoid circumvention of the obligation to file a mandatory offer through the constitution of holding companies, the same obligation applies when the relevant threshold is crossed indirectly. Article 234–3 of the General Regulation provides that, in the event that more than one-third of the share capital or the voting rights of a listed company is held by another company and such holding constitutes an essential part of the assets of the holding company, a mandatory offer is required when:

(a)   a person acquires control (as defined under regulations applicable to the company; i.e., if the company is French, control will be defined by Article L.233–3 of the Commercial Code) of the holding company;

(b)   a group of persons acting in concert acquires control of the holding company (as defined under regulations applicable to such company), without any of such persons having previously alone controlled the holding company and remaining predominant (in that latter case, the filing of an offer will not be required as long as the balance of the shareholdings is not modified). In this respect, the Commercial Code provides that one or several persons acting in concert are considered to control jointly another company if they de facto determine the decisions made by the shareholders at general meetings of that company.

Persons acting alone or in concert must also file a mandatory offer when they hold, as a result of a merger or contribution in kind, more than one-third of the share capital or the voting rights of a listed company where such holding constitutes an essential part of the assets of the merged or contributed company.

It should be noted that the trigger is exclusively the crossing of the relevant threshold irrespective of the reasons for which such threshold was crossed. Thus, the obligation to file an offer may not only result from share purchases but equally from subscription to new shares in cash or in consideration for assets contributed to the company, from a merger or even from a reduction of the total number of voting rights (subject to the possible exceptions identified at 10.6.2.2 below).

10.6.2.2   *Exemptions to the mandatory filing of a tender offer*
Pursuant to Article 234–7 of the General Regulation, the AMF may consider that a potential offeror who crosses the one-third threshold or the 2 per cent increase referred to in Articles 234–2 and 234–5 of the General Regulation (*see* 10.6.2.1 above) is exempt from filing a mandatory offer if this is due to the offeror:

(a)   creating a concert party with other shareholders who, alone or in concert, held the majority of the target company's share capital or voting rights prior to the triggering event, as long as the latter remain predominant in the company; or

(b)   creating a concert party with other shareholders who:
   (i)   held already, alone or in concert, between one-third and half of the share capital or voting rights of the company, and
   (ii)   continue to hold a greater stake than the person joining the concert party, and
   (iii)   do not cross either of the above one-third threshold or 2 per cent increase.[16]

---

[16] Although there is still some uncertainty as to the precise meaning of the General Regulation in this respect, it may be considered in this case that the AMF will analyse the evolution of the situation of each of the persons acting in concert rather than the evolution of the situation of the concert party taken as a whole. For instance, if an entity A (holding 40 per cent of the target) creates a concert action with an entity B (holding 5 per cent of the target), no mandatory offer should have to be filed even though the one-third threshold has been crossed by the global concert: entity B should indeed be considered as not having crossed (alone) the one-third threshold and entity A should be considered as not having increased (alone) its shareholding by more than 2 per cent.

Pursuant to Article 234–9 of the General Regulation, the AMF may grant an exemption to the obligation to file a mandatory offer where the acquisition of the shares of a listed company occurs in any of the following cases:

(a) transfer for nil consideration between individuals;

(b) distribution of assets made by a company to its shareholders in proportion of their equity;

(c) any subscription of shares in a company which is in recognised financial difficulties, provided such issuance is approved by the shareholders in general meeting;

(d) a merger or contribution in kind provided such transactions are approved by the shareholders in general meeting;

(e) the combination of:
  (i) a merger or a contribution in kind which is approved by the shareholders in general meeting, and
  (ii) the conclusion between the shareholders of the concerned companies of an agreement constituting a concert party;

(f) a decrease in the total number of shares or voting rights in the target company;

(g) holding of the majority of the voting rights of the company by the person requesting the exemption or by a third party, acting alone or in concert;

(h) any transfer of shares between companies or persons belonging to the same group.

Even if the crossing of a threshold is eligible for exemption under Article 234–9 of the General Regulation, the AMF may in its discretion refuse to grant the exemption requested.

As a general rule the AMF is likely to refuse the exemption if it considers that an actual change of control has taken place. This is particularly the case when the crossing of the threshold results from either a merger or a contribution in kind (*see* 10.6.3 below) where the necessary EGM resolutions have not been approved by a majority of the minority shareholders and would not have been passed but for the votes of the controlling shareholder. Moreover, the AMF reviews with extreme care any situation where the control of a listed company is held by shareholders acting in concert, especially if one of these shareholders was not originally the controlling shareholder of the company and subsequently becomes dominant in the concert, thus becoming the de facto controlling shareholder (this was typically the situation in the *Hyparlo* case[17]).

---

[17] Paris Court of Appeal, first chamber, section H, 13 September 2005, *ADAM/SA Hyparlo*, *Bull. Joly Bourse* 2005, p. 735. In this case, an agreement relating to their shareholdings in Hyparlo SA was entered into on 24 December 2004 between:
  (a) the controlling Arlaud family; and
  (b) the Carrefour Group, which mainly provided for:
    (i) a put option in favour of the Arlauds for a period of three years commencing 1 January 2012, and
    (ii) the reorganisation of the parties' interests in Hyparlo in the meantime, through the interposition of a new controlling holding company, Hofidis II, which was managed on a day-to-day basis by members of the Arlaud family.

Exemptions to the obligation to file an offer are published, whereas refusals to grant exemptions are usually not made public. In 2007 more than 50 such exemptions were granted by the AMF.

10.6.2.3   The mandatory offer

As soon as one of the above thresholds is crossed, the relevant shareholder must immediately file with the AMF an offer for all of the shares and other securities giving access to the capital or the voting rights of the listed company. Pursuant to Article 234–2 of the General Regulation, the offeror cannot make his offer conditional upon any level of acceptances.

The AMF reviews the price or other consideration offered, which in practice has to be at least equivalent to that paid to the sellers of the shares transferring control over the company (*see* 10.7.7 below).

In general, the offer follows the rules applicable to voluntary takeover offers. However, in certain cases (*see* below), the AMF may authorise the use of a more flexible acquisition procedure such as the simplified offer procedure (*offre publique simplifiée*) or the guaranteed price procedure (*garantie de cours*).

Compared with a normal takeover offer, the distinguishing features of these simplified procedures are that they are performed through direct purchases on the market (except in limited cases) at the price offered and that they remain open for a limited number of days only (at least 10 trading days, or 15 trading days if non-cash consideration is offered, as compared to 25 trading days for the normal takeover procedures).

The use of a simplified offer procedure may be authorised by the AMF in the following cases (Article 233–1 of the General Regulation):

(a)   an offer filed by a shareholder holding directly or indirectly, alone or in concert, the majority of the share capital and the voting rights of a listed company;

(b)   an offer filed by a shareholder who comes to hold, directly or indirectly, alone or in concert, the majority of the share capital and the voting rights of a listed company;

Whereas the Arlauds were granted the majority in the management board of the controlling holding company, major decisions involving Hyparlo had to be ratified by the supervisory board, which was evenly split between Carrefour and the Arlauds. Failing the approval of such major decisions by the supervisory board of Hofidis II, Carrefour was granted double voting rights in the following shareholders' meeting of Hofidis II, providing it *at that time only* the control of Hofidis II, and subsequently of Hyparlo. Considering the fact that:

(a)   the powers of the management board were finally limited by the necessary approval of the supervisory board and consequently of Carrefour; and

(b)   the possibility that Carrefour took control of Hyparlo at any time simply by opposing the Arlauds' decisions at the supervisory board,

the Paris Court of Appeal decided that even though the Arlauds and Carrefour were still acting in concert, the leadership of the concert had skipped from the Arlaud family to the joint control of Hyparlo, therefore preventing the application of the provisions of Article 234–7 of the General Regulation and triggering on the contrary the requirement to file a mandatory offer on the remaining shares of Hyparlo.

(c)   the purpose of the offer is to enable the offeror to acquire a maximum of 10 per cent of the share capital or the voting rights of a listed company;
(d)   an offer relating only to voting rights and to shares with no voting rights;
(e)   certain purchases by a listed company of its own shares, or other types of securities;
(f)   an offer whereby a listed company exchanges debt securities for securities representing share capital.

The guaranteed price procedure is applicable in cases where the offer is filed by a person, acting alone or in concert, who has acquired or has agreed to acquire a controlling interest giving such person, together with the shares and voting rights it already holds (together with persons acting in concert), more than half of the share capital or voting rights of a listed company (Article 235–1 of the General Regulation).

Under such procedure, the purchaser of the controlling interest undertakes to acquire during a minimum 10 trading-day period any shares offered for sale, at the same price as it purchased the controlling interest. However, a lower price may be authorised by the AMF if the purchase of the controlling interest contains warranties for specific clearly identified risks or deferred consideration.

Although eligible for the guaranteed price procedure, the AMF may decide that the following transactions should nevertheless be implemented within the usual takeover offer regime:

(a)   a transaction containing features likely to affect the equality between the price paid for the controlling interest and the price offered to the other shareholders;
(b)   a transaction whereby the acquisition of the controlling interest would be from persons who did not previously hold, in concert among themselves or with the offeror, the majority of the voting rights of the company.

10.6.3   Mergers and related transactions – delisting offers

Acquiring control of a company can be achieved by schemes which do not entail the purchase of shares, mainly by way of merger or contribution of businesses or assets, in exchange for shares.

10.6.3.1   Mergers

A French merger is an agreement between two companies whereby all of the assets and liabilities of one of the companies (the disappearing company) are transferred to the other (the surviving company). As consideration for the merger, all shareholders in the disappearing company receive shares in the surviving company in exchange for their shares in the disappearing company.

The exchange ratio is determined by the relative values of the companies which are parties to the transaction. The values of such companies are estimated using several criteria, taking into account, as appropriate, valuations resulting from the net assets, profits, stock market value or other relevant criteria for each of the companies. Although not provided for in regulations, this approach has been vigorously recommended by the COB since 1977 and the AMF in 2005 and is generally followed in practice.

The exchange ratio and other significant aspects of the merger are reviewed by a court-appointed independent financial expert (*Commissaire à la fusion*) who issues an opinion on the fairness of the exchange ratio to the shareholders of the companies concerned. For the merger to be completed, an EGM of each of the surviving and disappearing companies has to be held at which at least two-thirds of the shareholders present or represented vote in favour of the transaction. If one of the companies which is party to the transaction is a listed company, the shareholders must be provided with extensive information on the merger in the form of an appendix to a report of the board of directors. The information contained in this document, commonly known as *Document de fusion*, is at least as extensive as the information contained in a normal takeover document. A *Document de fusion* must be reviewed and registered by the AMF.

10.6.3.2 Contribution of business or assets

Control of a listed company can be gained by contributing all of the assets and liabilities of a business (*apport partiel d'actifs* or contribution of business) or assets, in the form, for example, of shares of another company (*apport en nature* or contribution of assets) in exchange for the issue of shares in the offeror.

A contribution of business follows exactly the same rules as a merger, whereas a contribution of assets differs in so far only as it is solely the EGM of the company receiving such assets that has to approve the contribution. However, if the assets contributed represent a significant part of the assets of the contributing company, the former COB strongly recommended that the transaction be structured in the form of a contribution of business, consequently requiring the approval of the shareholders of the contributing company as well as the shareholders of the offeror.

Both in the case of mergers and in the case of contributions of businesses or assets, if, upon completion, a shareholder crosses one of the relevant thresholds, he will be under an obligation to file an offer (*see* 10.6.2.1 above). In certain circumstances the obligation to file a delisting offer may also be imposed (*see* 10.6.3.4 below).

10.6.3.3 Other methods

Finally, control of the business of a listed company may be acquired independently of the purchase of shares of such a company by purchasing the shares of its significant subsidiaries or by purchasing its significant businesses. Although these methods of acquisition will not entail the obligation to file a mandatory bid since no threshold of the capital or voting rights has been crossed, it is likely that the AMF will oblige the controlling shareholder of the listed company (but not the purchaser of the assets of the business) to file a delisting offer (if conditions for such delisting offer are met) (*see* below).

10.6.3.4 Delisting offers (offres publiques de retrait or "OPR")

If it considers that the rights of the minority shareholders are affected by the contemplated changes, the AMF is likely to require controlling shareholders to launch an *offre publique de retrait* ("OPR") in the following cases (Article 236–6 of the General Regulation):

(a)   when these controlling shareholders have proposed to submit for approval to the other shareholders significant changes to the articles of association of the listed company (in particular in relation to the form of the company, to the conditions for the transfer of shares or the rights attached thereto);

(b)   when these controlling shareholders have decided to merge the company with its holding company, to sell or contribute to another company all or the principal assets of the company or have decided a change in its activity or a suspension of dividend payments for several accounting periods.

An OPR relating to shares (or respectively to investment certificates or to voting right certificates) may equally be initiated by shareholders holding, in concert, more than 95 per cent of the voting rights of a listed company either spontaneously or at the request of the AMF upon application by minority shareholders holding shares (or respectively investment certificates or voting rights certificates) (*see* 10.11 below). The OPR follows the same procedure as the simplified offer (*see* 10.6.2.3 above) and cannot be conditional upon reaching any level of acceptances.

Furthermore, when a listed company incorporated in the form of an SA resolves to change its form to an SCA, an obligation to file an OPR is imposed on the controlling shareholders or (if there is no controlling shareholder) on the general partners (*associés commandités*).

An OPR may be conducted in connection with both shares that are traded on a regulated market and shares that have ceased to be traded. In addition, any shares of a company that was once listed on the Hors-Cote (which ceased to exist in July 1998) may be subject to an OPR.

10.7   Preparation of an offer

10.7.1   *Filing of the offer*

A public offer requires a filing to be made with the AMF by one or more presenting banks (*banques présentatrices*) acting on behalf of the offeror.

The offer period, as well as the rules of conduct applicable throughout the offer, begins on the day the AMF makes the main terms of the draft offer public by issuing a receipt notice (*avis de dépôt*). The offer will actually only formally start after the AMF has declared the offer conform (*see* 10.7.7 below). The trading in the shares of the target company is not suspended automatically from the moment the filing with the AMF is made (as was the case previously), but at the AMF's discretion (Article 231–15 of the General Regulation). In practice, the AMF nearly always requires a suspension. Such a provision also applies to the shares of the other companies concerned by the proposed offer (in particular in the case of an exchange offer).

The AMF aims at preserving liquidity for investors and tends to minimise the duration of such suspension where companies with significant market capitalisations are involved.

The file submitted to the AMF, which is now publicly disclosed as a draft upon filing of the offer, must specify or contain:

(a)   the objectives and intentions of the offeror;

(b)   the number and type of shares of the target company that the offeror already holds, alone or in concert, or may at its option hold, as well as the date of acquisition and the terms thereof;

(c)   the proposed price or exchange parity proposed, the valuation methods retained therefor and the terms of the payment or the exchange;

(d)   the minimum number of shares or voting rights which must be tendered to the offer ("level of acceptances"), failing which the offeror must withdraw its offer (such acceptance condition being only permitted for voluntary offers). The offeror may make the outcome of an offer conditional on the outcome of another offer and vice versa. Indeed, Article 231–10 of the General Regulation authorises the filing of two offers on different targets and such conditions. However, it must be noted that this new text does not prevent the filing of two simultaneous independent offers, thus implying that a situation similar to BNP's double offer on Société Générale and Paribas could be repeated;

(e)   a copy of the notifications (or seizing – *saisine* – if such notifications are not ready at the time of the filing) to merger control authorities that have been made (if the offer is conditioned to merger control clearance);

(f)   a copy of the request for any prior authorisations from any governmental agencies (French or foreign) required to authorise the offer;

(g)   the draft offer document (which may be issued jointly by the offeror and the target in a friendly offer); and

(h)   the undertaking that an offer relating to the listed subsidiary representing an essential asset of the target will be filed, together with a copy of the draft offer prospectus.

The presenting banks have to guarantee the performance by the offeror of its obligations pursuant to the offer (*see* 10.7.2 below).

The offeror is required to make a detailed announcement in a French national financial newspaper describing the main terms and conditions of the draft offer. The target may, after the publication of the above-mentioned announcement, issue a press release stating the opinion of its board of directors prior to the publication of the draft defence document and the conclusions of any independent appraiser.

Immediately upon filing of the draft offer, the offeror must make the draft offer document publicly available at its registered office as well as at those of the sponsoring banks, or at the registered office of an appointed investment services provider in case their registered offices are not located in France. In the case of a joint draft offer document, the document shall also be made publicly available at the registered office of the target company as well as at the registered office of its financial institution. Such draft offer document shall also be published on the AMF's website, on the offeror's website and on the target's website if prepared jointly. If the offeror's or the sponsoring bank's registered office is not located in France, the draft offer document shall be made available at the registered office of a financial institution located in France.

Furthermore, as from the filing of the offer, any clause in an agreement which may frustrate the offer must be notified by the persons involved in such agreement to the persons involved in the offer as well as to the AMF and to the public. Any clause not so disclosed in the offer document must be disclosed by way of a press release (Article 231–5 of the General Regulation).

Under Article 232–4 of the General Regulation, if the offer has a successful outcome, it is automatically reopened within 10 trading days of the publication of the outcome of the initial offer for another 10 trading-day period. This permits the offeror to increase its stake in the target company without the offer having to be reviewed again by the AMF and it avoids the publication of a second offer document.

10.7.2 The offer is irrevocable

One of the key rules of French takeover regulations is that takeover offers may not be revoked by the offeror, except in the cases set out below.

However, the offeror may provide that the offer will be subject to one or more of the following conditions:

(a) A minimum level of acceptances: although not mentioned explicitly in the applicable regulations, the AMF will only accept a minimum level of acceptances which can be reasonably expected to be reached given the situation of the target and of the offeror. The AMF usually accepts acceptance thresholds up to 66.67 per cent of the share capital and voting rights. It should nevertheless be highlighted that in recent significant transactions the threshold retained was only 50 per cent of the share capital and voting rights on a fully diluted basis (Sagem–Snecma, Sanofi/Aventis, Alcan/Pechiney, Saica–Mondi–La Rochette) because the offeror considered it sufficient to achieve satisfactory control given the fact that majorities at French general meetings are calculated based on votes present or represented only (and not all voting rights) (Article 231–9 of the General Regulation).

(b) A minimum level of acceptances being reached in the context of an offer launched by the same offeror for another target (Article 231–10 of the General Regulation).[18]

(c) The authorisation to the offeror to make the offer given by its shareholders in general meeting (if required by its articles of association or applicable regulations) provided that the general meeting has already been convened (Article 231–12 of the General Regulation), which condition is used in practice by foreign companies.

---

[18] When the offers for the different targets are all subject to the jurisdiction of the AMF and the General Regulation, such inter-conditioning does not raise further question. However, if one of the offers is subject to foreign regulations authorising to submit this offer to conditions precedent which are not authorised by the AMF General Regulation, the validity of such inter-conditioning could be questioned. The authors believe this should be possible since the General Regulation does not restrict the scope of inter-conditioning, but this issue, for which there is no precedent as far as the authors are aware, should be treated carefully in any case.

(d) In the case of an exchange offer, the authorisation of the offeror's share-holders in general meeting to issue the securities to be given as a consideration under the offer, provided that the board of directors of the offeror has undertaken to convene such meeting (Article 231–12 of the General Regulation).

(e) Receipt of competition clearance from the:

    (i) European Commission;

    (ii) the French ministry of economy or other authority with jurisdiction over such matters in another Member State of the European Economic Area and/or any Member State of the US (i.e., receipt of a "Phase I" antitrust approval or any similar authorisation issued by the foreign state), provided the offeror provides the AMF with a copy of the *saisine* of the relevant competition authorities when filing its offer.

The offer automatically lapses if the envisaged transaction becomes subject to a "Phase II" investigation, to a referral to the French competition authority (in case of an initial EU filing) or if a similar procedure is undertaken by the competent authority of the foreign state (Article 231–11 of the General Regulation). It is not clear whether Article 231–11 of the AMF General Regulation, which authorises offerors to condition their offers upon the non-initiation of "Phase II" investigation by antitrust authorities, designates either that:

(a) official filings of the competition file with the competition authorities had to be made together with the filing of the offer; or

(b) the offeror only had to initiate contacts with the competition authorities and discuss the file with them first.

However, the fact that the latter interpretation has been retained in at least two precedents (offer of Alcan for Pechiney and of Sanofi-Synthélabo for Aventis) plus amendments in the applicable texts ("seizing" was replaced by "notification" and then finally reinstated) advocates the idea that AMF regulations do not actually require an official filing.

The presenting banks have to guarantee the obligations of the offeror, and consequently all appropriate financing arrangements must be unconditional at the time of the filing of the offer. If the offer is invalidly revoked by the offeror before payment to the accepting shareholders, the presenting banks will have to finance the transaction in the place of the offeror.

Finally, the offeror may withdraw its offer either:

(a) within five trading days of the publication of the timetable of a competing offer; or

(b) with the authorisation of the AMF:

    (i) if the offer becomes irrelevant (e.g., where competing offerors finally decide to launch a joint offer), or

    (ii) upon definitive changes to the substance of the target, whether such changes are implemented during the offer period or after the offer has been declared successful (Article 232–11 of the General Regulations).

10.7.3 Due diligence

A due diligence process used to be considered, in particular by the management of potential target companies, as inappropriate in takeover situations. The scope of a due diligence which can be effected in the case of a hostile offer is extremely narrow as it is limited to a review of publicly available information such as that filed by the target company with the trade and companies registry, annual reports, prospectuses published in connection with the issue of securities or corporate reorganisations and Euronext Paris SA notices disclosing the total number of voting rights, crossing of thresholds or shareholders agreements.

In the case of a recommended offer, there is absolutely no limit on the information which can be legally made available to the potential offeror. Whenever proceeding with a due diligence, and if the information provided could influence the trading price of the shares of the target company if made public, the offeror should refrain from any purchase of the shares on the market since such purchases might constitute insider dealing (*see* 10.12 below). This privileged information shall be disclosed in the offer document.

In a recommendation relating to the due diligence process with respect to listed companies issued in 2003, the COB confirmed the above analysis and recommended that access to a data room should be limited to persons having previously shown an interest (e.g., through a letter of intent) and having entered into a confidentiality agreement.

Also, the AMF insisted that great care be taken to comply with insider dealing prohibition rules and that access to the data room may have to be given to a competing offeror if certain conditions are met.

10.7.4 Secrecy

10.7.4.1 General disclosure obligation

When preparing an offer, secrecy is of the utmost importance since, particularly in the case of hostile offers, advance notice may enable the target company to prepare its defence more efficiently. Pursuant to Article 223–6 of the General Regulation, any person preparing a transaction that may have a significant influence on the trading price of a listed security must inform the public of this transaction as soon as possible. Such information may only be deferred if confidentiality is necessary for the preparation of the transaction (e.g., a proposed takeover), provided, however, that utmost secrecy can be maintained. Finally, the mere fact of communicating confidential information outside the scope of business purpose for which a person holds such confidential information, constitutes a criminal offence (*see* 10.12 below).

10.7.4.2 "Put-up or shut-up" mechanism

The "put-up or shut-up" procedure has been formalised in the context of improvement of the defence mechanisms available to French companies, and largely results from rumours of a possible unsolicited takeover of Danone by Pepsico during the summer of 2005. The aim of this procedure is to oblige a potential offeror, in certain circumstances, to anticipate the disclosure of its intent to launch an offer or not.

Triggering events

Under the put-up or shut-up procedure, the AMF may require persons to publicly disclose their intentions within a set deadline where there is reason to believe they are preparing a public offer on a company listed in France, and in particular if they perform preparatory work with a view to filing an offer (e.g., discussions with management, appointment of counsel, etc.).

The occurrence of unusual price swings or trading volume may, without being a necessary condition, enter into consideration in the AMF decision to use the procedure. It is at the AMF's discretion to decide whether to implement the put-up or shut-up procedure.

It is presently difficult, without a significant sample of precedents, to have a precise idea of what will be the AMF policy in implementing the put-up or shut-up mechanism. The few available precedents show that the AMF may refrain from triggering the procedure if the target does not consider itself under siege and does not put pressure on the AMF to let the target organise freely its own sale process.

Given the wide powers available to the AMF, a potential offeror should be as ready as possible before initiating contacts that may lead to leaks and the launch of such procedure.

Consequences of the request for disclosure

The request for a disclosure made by the AMF specifies the deadline by which the suspected offeror must disclose its intentions. Two situations may then arise:

(a)   either the suspected offeror confirms his intent to file an offer; or
(b)   he confirms that he has no such intent (or he does not answer and does not file an offer within the time period set by the AMF).

If the suspected offeror indicates that he intends to file an offer, the AMF then determines the deadline by which the main terms and conditions of such offer must be announced or, as the case may be, such draft offer must be filed (no mandatory or maximum deadline is set out in the General Regulation).

Note that at the time of writing, the AMF had not been satisfied by answers that did not give a clear view of the intentions of the potential offeror. In the Artemis/Suez situation, following the request of the AMF, Artemis merely mentioned that all options were open and that no decision had been made yet, and had confirmed to the AMF the existence of a very preliminary draft offer document. The AMF construed this announcement as a confirmation of its intention to file an offer and therefore set a deadline for Artemis to file an offer or announce the characteristics of its projected offer.

The AMF may, if they believe it is in the interests of the market, give the future offeror some time to finalise a draft offer. In the *Suez–Artemis* case, the deadline set was one month, bearing in mind that rumours had been ongoing for quite a long time. However, it may set a very short deadline for a suspected offeror to answer. In the case of the would-be "mysterious" attempt by the Swiss company Center-Tainment AG to launch a hostile takeover on Eurodisney, the AMF requested the company to confirm its intents in a very short period of time – less than a week.

Given the political or specific nature of the above cases, it cannot be excluded that this very restrictive position of the AMF could evolve in the future, and that a possible offeror may in futures cases be provided with more time to finalise its offer if there are legitimate reasons for this.

If the suspected offeror indicates that he does not have the intention to file an offer, or fails to file its offer within the deadline determined by the AMF, it must "shut-up" for a six-month period.

For example, the AMF has asked Saipem/ENI to confirm their intents regarding Technip following press-reported rumours of an unsolicited takeover. ENI and Saipem confirmed that they were not intending to file an offer on Technip shares. It is worth noting that ENI/Saipem's answer was not an express answer to the AMF's request since it was addressed to the Consob (the Italian regulator) but was logically regarded as such by the AMF in its decision to apply a shut-up.

10.7.5   Stake building

Often an offeror will seek to enhance the chances of success of his offer by purchasing shares of the target company in the market prior to making its offer. Subject to the provisions relating to insider dealing and market manipulation (*see* 10.12 below), it is generally considered that stake building is perfectly legal. This position was supported by former COB Regulation no. 90–04 which provided that prior to the filing of an offer, market orders by the parties to the transaction had to be in conformity with the objectives of such parties (i.e., the offeror shall not resell the shares on the market whilst still contemplating an offer). Although this provision has now been revoked, it is believed that the position of the stock market authorities will not change in this respect.

Any offeror effecting such purchases should take extreme care in complying with the disclosure obligations applicable to crossing the share capital or voting right thresholds which are extremely formalistic, including those provided for by the articles of association of the target company (*see* 10.2.2.4 above). If the offeror has purchased in cash, in the 12 months preceding the filing of the offer, securities giving more than 5 per cent of the shares or voting rights of the target, a cash option must be included in the offer. The offeror may also have to comply with possible regulatory formalities or antitrust notifications triggered by crossing that threshold.

10.7.6   Irrevocable undertakings

Whether or not irrevocable undertakings to accept an offer conform to French Stock Exchange regulations is a disputed issue. The debate is centred around Article 231–3 of the General Regulation which provides that a takeover offer shall be conducted in accordance with the principle of free competition (i.e., that a competing offer should always be possible). The COB has consistently considered that the principle of free competition should be read as a prohibition on irrevocable undertakings.

In the light of case law, the current situation can be summarised as follows:

(a)   irrevocable undertakings relating to shares which, aggregated with the shares already held by the offeror, represent less than 10–15 per cent of the target company, are most probably valid;

(b)   irrevocable undertakings which provide for break-up fees are also generally considered valid, provided that the level of the fee in question does not render impossible the filing of a competing offer. In the context of the offer carried out in 2002 by Accor Casinos for Compagnie Européenne de Casinos, shareholders of the target, holding 13.5 per cent of the share capital on a fully diluted basis (which, aggregated to the shares already held by the offeror, amounted to 31.2 per cent of the share capital on a fully diluted basis) undertook to indemnify the initial offeror up to the difference between the initial price and the competing price (this difference being capped to €5 per share, i.e., almost 10 per cent of the initial offer price) in the event that they would tender their shares to a competing offer.

Failing these two conditions, there is no certainty as to what position either the AMF or the Paris Court of Appeal will adopt. Consequently, the signature of irrevocable undertakings in a hostile situation is generally regarded as likely to provoke pressure from the AMF and litigation from a competing offeror. However, it may be thought that such irrevocable undertakings must be assimilated to clauses providing for preferential sale or purchase conditions, the validity of which is implicitly recognised by the 2001 NER Act. Indeed, it is estimated that the sanction of a suspension of the effects of such clauses during the offer period does not make sense if such clause is not held valid in the first place (*see* 10.2.2.2 above).

However, undertakings which can be revoked without the payment of a break-up fee by the shareholder giving the undertaking if a competing offer is filed are undisputedly valid.

10.7.7   *Conformity of the offer*

The AMF has a period of 10 trading days as from filing to approve the offer. Simultaneously with the review of the offer, the AMF reviews the draft offer document within the same 10 trading days from the date of filing. The AMF may request for the purpose of these reviews any justifications, guarantees and additional information that it considers appropriate (in which case that 10-day period may be extended until the AMF is satisfied). Where an independent appraiser must be appointed by the target (e.g., when there is a risk of potential conflict of interest or breach of the principle of equality of treatment for target shareholders), the clearance of the offer may not take place before five trading days following the filing of the defence document by the target.

The review by the AMF is mainly concentrated on the following:

(a)   the aims and intentions of the offeror;

(b)   where applicable, the type, listings and characteristics of and market for the shares proposed in exchange;

(c)   the conditions precedent stipulated by the offeror;

(d)   the information provided in the draft offer document; and
(e)   where an independent expert has been appointed, the financial terms of the offer, notably with respect to the independent expert's report or the reasoned opinion of the board of directors or supervisory board of the target.

As regards shares proposed in an exchange offer, it must be noted that the General Regulation requires that the offer contains a full cash option if the shares remitted in exchange are not listed on a European Community's Stock Exchange or are not liquid. Implicitly, this means that an offeror in a position to offer liquid shares listed on an European Community's Stock Exchange has no obligation to list the shares to be remitted in exchange on the French market as well. However, offerors will sometimes decide to list their shares on the Paris market for practical, political or strategic reasons.

During its review process, the AMF may ask the offeror to change the terms and conditions of the offer if it considers that the offer breaches the principles of equality of treatment for target shareholders, market transparency, fair trading or fair competition, although this is an extremely rare occurrence in voluntary offers.

Furthermore, the AMF must review the offer in light of applicable regulations, including the General Regulation and the principle of free competition. One of the two instances to date where an approval of the CMF was overruled by the Paris Court of Appeal relates to this issue of free competition. In the *OCP* case (Paris Court of Appeal, 27 April 1993), two major subsidiaries of OCP, the target company, were incorporated as SCAs, the entire share capital of which was held by OCP but whose general managers were exclusively controlled by members of OCP management. GEHE AG, the offeror, had obtained from the management of OCP an option to purchase the control of the general managers of the subsidiaries in the event its offer was successful. The CMF cleared the offer but its decision was appealed by minority shareholders to the Paris Court of Appeal on the grounds that the option granted to GEHE AG gave it a significant advantage since, unlike potential competitors, it was certain to obtain control over the management of the two principal subsidiaries of OCP if its offer was successful. The court overruled the decision of the CMF on that basis. OCP subsequently announced that the option granted to GEHE AG would be offered to any offeror.

The second example is the *ADAM/Schneider and Legrand* case (Paris Court of Appeal, first chamber H, 3 May 2001). Until that case it was generally considered that, in cases of voluntary offers, the Paris Court of Appeal, when reviewing decisions of the CMF, would limit its review to compliance with applicable regulations but would not second guess the CMF on the financial conditions of the offer. However, the Paris Court of Appeal (pursuant to a claim brought by certain Legrand preferred shareholders), in its decision of 3 May 2001, overruled the CMF decision on the Schneider exchange offer on Legrand on the grounds that the difference between the exchange ratios for the ordinary shares and the preferred shares was not sufficiently motivated, de facto inviting Schneider to revise the financial terms of its offer.

Although this case law relates to decisions of the CMF, it should be equally applicable to the AMF.

When the AMF declares an offer conform, its decision is published (*avis de conformité*) and trading in the securities of the target company resumes (if previously suspended) on the date decided by the AMF, which can be no later than the opening of the offer period.

The declaration of conformity provided by the AMF implies the delivery of an approval number (visa) on the offer document. The offer document is made available on the AMF's website and published within two trading days of the conformity decision in a French national financial daily newspaper. The offeror also has the opportunity to make the offer document available and publish a summary only. The offer starts on the day following the publication of the offer document, the defence offer document and the general information documents of the offeror and the target, provided that the regulatory authority authorisations have been obtained by such date.

In the particular case of an unsolicited offer with no joint offer document, the authors believe that the opening of the offer would occur after the issuance of the offeror's offer document and general information document. Article 231–32 of the General Regulation is unclear, but it could nonetheless be claimed that the opening of the offer cannot occur before the release of the target company's defence document. However, that position was not followed by the AMF in the only precedent of unsolicited offer since the amendment of the General Regulation further to the enactment of the Implementation Law.[19]

10.7.8 *Requirement to appoint an independent appraiser*

Pursuant to Article 261–1–II of the AMF General Regulation, the target shall appoint an independent appraiser to issue a fairness opinion as to the financial terms of the contemplated offer if the transaction is likely:

(a)   to cause conflicts of interest within the target's board of directors, which could impair the objectivity of the opinion to be included in the draft defence document; or

(b)   to impact the equality of treatment among the target's shareholders.

Although debatable for certain specific cases, the AMF estimates that an independent appraiser has to issue a fairness opinion when the offeror already controls the target company (whether such control has already been held for a long time or whether the offer is made immediately after a block purchase) or when the offeror and the target's controlling shareholders or managers have entered into an agreement likely to affect their independence prior to the filing of the offer. Such requirement may also apply if a squeeze-out is to be implemented.

The appraiser has at least 15 trading days to produce his report.

---

[19] *GFI Informatique*, AMF, decision no. 207C1090 dated 13 June 2007.

10.8 Conduct of the offer

10.8.1 Timing

The offer opens the day after the publication of either the joint offer document (for a recommended offer for which no independent expert is required), the offeror's offer document (in the case of a hostile offer where the offer document is by definition not jointly prepared) or the offer document in response issued by the target (if the offeror and the target did not have sufficient time to prepare a joint document or where an independent expert has been appointed). In total, the offer, in a normal offer procedure, must remain open for 25 trading days, such period being likely to be extended to a maximum of 35 trading days where no joint offer document has been filed. In case of competing offers or litigation, the AMF may however impose a longer offer period.

The critical dates in an unsolicited offer process are shown in Table 10.1.

Table 10.1   Critical dates in the unsolicited offer process

D1[20]	Filing of the proposed offer with the AMF (including the draft offer document) and publication of a filing notice by the AMF.
	At the option of the AMF, suspension of trading in the shares of the target company (may be extended to any other securities, e.g., convertible bonds).
	Public announcement of the filing and publication of the draft offer document.
D1 + 10 TD[21]	Conformity decision rendered by the AMF on the terms of the offer, including the delivery of the visa by the AMF on the offer document.[22, 23, 24]
	Public announcement of the conformity decision and fixing by the AMF of the date on which the trading in the securities of the target (or any other securities concerned) is to resume (if previously suspended).
D1 + 12 TD	Publication of the offer document (in final form) and the general information documents relating to the offeror.

---

[20] Day one.

[21] TD: trading day.

[22] The 10 trading-day period during which the AMF may render its conformity decision may be suspended in the event the AMF requests justifications, guarantees or additional information (which is very frequent in practice, in particular for the information on the offer document) or considers that the offer breaches the principles of equality of treatment for target shareholders, market transparency, fair trading or fair competition. It resumes upon receipt of such additional information or implementation of the changes requested.

[23] The conformity decision (including the delivery of the visa of the AMF on the offer document) may be challenged before the Paris Court of Appeal within 10 calendar days of the publication of the decision in the BALO.

[24] If an independent expert has been appointed in accordance with Article 261–1 of the General Regulation, the conformity decision is issued by the AMF no earlier than five trading days after the filing of the target's defence document.

Table 10.1   continued

D1 + 12 TD	Publication of the offer document (in final form) and the general information documents relating to the offeror.
D1 + 13 TD	Opening of the offer.[25]
D1 + 15 TD at the latest	Filing of the target company's draft defence document with the AMF and publication of the draft defence offer document.[26]
D1 + 20 TD	Delivery of the visa on the target company's defence document by the AMF and communication of this defence document to the offeror.[27]
D1 + 22 TD	Publication of the target company's defence document (in final form) and the general information documents relating to the target. Publication by the AMF of the offer timetable (e.g., closing date and date of results).
D1 + 42 TD	Deadline for the filing of a competing offer or an increased offer.
D1 + 47 TD	Closing of the offer.
D1 + 56 TD	Publication of the outcome of the offer.
D1 + 66 TD	Automatic reopening of the offer in case of successful outcome of the initial offer.
D1 + 76 TD	Closing of the reopened offer.
D1 + 85 TD	Publication of the outcome of the reopened offer.

The timetable shown in Table 10.1 is also applicable to a competing offer. In this case, the AMF will adjust the timetable of both offers according to the closing date of the competing offer. In addition, the AMF may fix a deadline for the filing of the various bids when more than 10 weeks have elapsed since the opening of the offer period.

---

[25] Article 231–32 of the General Regulation is unclear, but it could be considered that, in the case of an unsolicited offer with no joint offer document, the opening of the offer will not occur before the release of the target company's defence document. However, such position was not followed by the AMF in the only precedent of unsolicited offer since the amendment of the General Regulation further to the enactment of the Implementation Law.

[26] If an independent expert has been appointed in accordance with Article 261–1 of the General Regulation, the period for the target company to file its defence document is extended to 20 trading days following the filing of the proposed offer, following that the AMF has an additional period of at least five trading days to issue its conformity decision on both the offer and defence documents (as stated above).

[27] The five trading-day period during which the AMF may deliver its visa on the defence document may be suspended in the event the AMF requests additional information from the target, and it resumes upon receipt of such additional information.

Pursuant to Article 232–2 of the General Regulation, any order to tender securities to the offer may be cancelled at any time up to and including the offer's closing date.

10.8.2 Permitted dealings

Article 231–7 of the General Regulation provides that all dealings in the shares of the target company must be made on market, even though the implementation of the Markets in Financial Instruments Directive seems to have limited the scope of applicable sanctions to those that may be generally decided by the AMF for breach of its General Regulation.

Also, special restrictions apply to the offeror, and the persons acting in concert with it, who may not purchase any shares of the target company if:

(a)   either its offer is conditional upon a minimum level of acceptances (with respect to that offer or any other offer launched by the same offeror) or upon receipt of competition clearance; or

(b)   the offer is a share exchange offer. In this case, the offeror may also not trade in the shares offered in exchange. In this respect, Article 232–18 of the General Regulation extends this prohibition for the offeror (in the case of an exchange offer) to trade in the shares of the target or in the shares offered in exchange to any other person involved in the offer.

Furthermore, if the offeror purchases, between the date of the filing of the offer or the date on which the trading of the shares concerned by the offer has resumed (if previously suspended) and five trading days before the closing of the offer, any shares on the market at a price which is above the offer price, the offer price is automatically increased to the higher of such price and 102 per cent of the original offer price. As from the fifth trading day before the closing of the offer until the publication of the results, the offeror may not purchase any shares at a price higher than the offer price. Although other interested parties and, in particular, potential competitors of the offeror, are, in theory, authorised to purchase shares in the target company, if such purchases may eventually frustrate the ongoing offer, there is a question whether the AMF could require such a potential competitor either to file a competing offer or to stop any further purchases on the ground that, once an offer is launched, competition should take place through a competing offer only. However, HAL (a Dutch investment fund) succeeded in frustrating an offer by PAI for Grandvision in 2003 by purchasing close to one-third of Grandvision's share capital, which entailed the failure of the offer as it was conditional upon receiving two-thirds of the share capital.

Finally, Article 232–19 of the General Regulation provides that the above dealing rules apply to the offeror's advising institutions and to their group companies as well as to the target's advising institutions and to their group companies.

10.8.3 Disclosure of dealings

Articles 231–38 to 231–41 contain detailed provisions relating to disclosure of share dealings during the course of an offer.

Any dealings in the securities of the target company and of the offeror (in the case of an exchange offer) by any person involved in the offer, their directors, their advising institutions, any person holding 5 per cent or more of their capital or voting rights and persons acting in concert with them must be disclosed to the AMF on a daily basis. The same obligation applies to any person who, since the beginning of the offer period, has acquired 0.5 per cent or more of such securities. Such dealings (except those carried out by the advising institutions) are also disclosed to the public on a daily basis.

10.8.4   Competing offers

A competing offer must be filed at least five trading days before the closing of the original offer. If a cash offer, such offer must be at a price which is at least 2 per cent higher than that offered in the original offer. In any other case, the competing offer must be on terms that are considered significantly more favourable by the AMF. However, if the original offer is conditional upon a certain level of acceptances, the competing offer can be made at the same price but with no such condition. The competing offer is subject to the same conditions and reviewed by the AMF as any initial offer. If the competing offer is declared conform, it will have to remain open for at least 25 trading days. If the initial offeror maintains his offer, the timetable of the initial offer will be adjusted so as to close on the same date as the competing offer. In this respect, the powers of the AMF in terms of acceleration of the timing of an offer have been reinforced by the 2001 NER Act. The AMF has the right to fix a definitive closing date for all the offers on the same target when more than 10 weeks have elapsed since the filing of the offer. However, this provision does not solve the timing issues which may be raised by parallel offers launched by the same offeror on two different targets.

On the day the filing of a competing offer is announced, all acceptances of the prior offer automatically become null and void. The shares can then be tendered to another offer or retendered to the original offer.

The initial offeror must indicate to the AMF within five trading days after publication of the timetable of the competing offer whether he intends to maintain or revoke his offer.

10.8.5   Increased offers

Each offeror has the opportunity of increasing its offer. The regime for increased offers is substantially the same as that applicable to competing offers (*see* 10.8.4 above).

Any increased offer may be filed at any time from the opening of the offer but no later than five trading days before its closing.

10.9   Defences to a hostile offer

A variety of defences can be implemented by French companies to reduce their vulnerability to hostile takeovers. Even if the regime of anti-takeover defences has been widely modified by the Takeover Directive, the effectiveness of such defences, if not in place prior to the filing of an offer, seems to remain limited. However, the implementation of the Takeover Directive was used to implement in France a new defensive measure (the so-called *bons Breton*), the efficacy of which remains to be tested.

10.9.1 Defences prior to an unsolicited offer

The most efficient defence against a hostile takeover is the incorporation of the listed company as an SCA (*see* 10.2.1 above). Even if the offeror is successful in acquiring the majority of the shares, he will not acquire control over the management against the will of the general partners.

Another effective defence is when the by-laws provide that no shareholder may exercise more than a given percentage of the voting rights (e.g., the by-laws of Danone provide for a limit by shareholder of 6 per cent of the voting rights; until 1 June 2007, those of Alcatel-Lucent provided for an 8 per cent limit). However, the by-laws usually provide that such limit is no longer applicable if a shareholder holds more than two-thirds of the share capital. The Implementing Law also froze such limitations, since Article 231–43 of the General Regulation provides that any ceiling on voting rights provided for in the target's articles of association shall not apply to the first general meeting following the outcome of the offer should the offeror, acting alone or in concert, hold more than two-thirds of the share capital or voting rights of the target (*see* 10.2.2.2 on this and the other breakthrough provisions that may be applied by French listed companies).

It should also be noted that, if a listed company's articles of association are to be amended to change its corporate form into an SCA or to limit the exercise of the voting rights, it will render its controlling shareholder liable to file a delisting offer. Other measures of defence include cross-shareholdings and shareholders' agreements (e.g., rights of first refusal).

Defensive cross-shareholdings are quite common in France. A French company may not hold any shares of another French company when this second company already holds more than 10 per cent of sthe shares of the first company. However, this prohibition is frequently circumvented given that it does not apply if the shares are held indirectly through a subsidiary, and it is usually considered as not applying to shares held through a foreign entity. Such indirect cross-shareholdings are frequently supported by shareholders' agreements granting, in particular, rights of first refusal to one party if an offer is made for the other. Although valid, these measures are of a limited effectiveness when an offer is initiated due to the specific rules which are then applicable.

10.9.2 Defences during the course of an offer

10.9.2.1 General principles
Once an offer has been filed, the management of the target company is required to exercise special care in connection with any announcement or transaction.

Also, it is now very clear that, during an offer period, the board of directors (*conseil d'administration*), the supervisory board (*conseil de surveillance*), the management board (*directoire*), the general manager (*directeur général*) or one of the deputy general managers (*directeur général délégué*) of the target company must obtain the prior authorisation of the shareholders in general meeting before taking any action (other than seeking alternative offers or exercising their appointment rights, if any) which may result in the frustration of an offer.

Shareholder approval or confirmation must also be obtained with regard to any decisions taken prior to the offer period by any such corporate body if they:

(a)   are outside the ordinary course of business;
(b)   are not yet partly or fully implemented;[28] and
(c)   may result in the frustration of an offer.

However, these rules are different if the offeror is not reciprocal (*see* below for the specific regime then applicable). The Implementing Law also clearly provides that any delegation which may result in the frustration of a takeover offer (other than seeking alternative bids) previously granted by the shareholders in general meeting shall be suspended during an offer period.

In order to facilitate the convening of the general meeting for the purposes of approving a defensive measure during a takeover offer, the Commercial Code has been amended to reduce the convening period from 35 calendar days to 15 calendar days.

However, the approval of a defensive measure by the shareholders of the target company is not sufficient to ensure that the defensive measure complies with the general principles applicable to takeovers. An example of this occurred in 2004 in the context of the hostile bid by Sanofi-Synthélabo for Aventis. The supervisory board of Aventis had planned to submit to its shareholders a resolution authorising the issue of share warrants (*bons de souscription d'actions*) in order to protect Aventis shareholders (should the offer prove successful), against the consequences of the potential loss of the Plavix patent held by Sanofi-Synthélabo. The AMF decided that the issuance of these share warrants was not compatible with the general principles applicable to takeovers in France, and in particular with the principles of free competition between offers and increased offers and orderly development of the offers. Indeed, the AMF considered that the issuance of the share warrants was a method to unilaterally raise the offer price and that it interfered with the offeror's freedom to make an increased offer.

This is consistent with the fact that Article 231–3 of the General Regulation provides that in order to ensure that operations are in the best interests of investors and the market, all persons who are involved in a takeover must comply with the principles of free competition between offers and increased offers, equality of treatment between target shareholders, loyalty, transparency and integrity of the market.

Although drafted in very general terms, these principles have in effect considerably limited the opportunity for target companies to implement defensive measures during the course of an offer. On the basis of these rules, the courts

---

[28] The exact scope of the legal provision imposing that the decision is "not yet partly or fully implemented" is still debated among French scholars.

have for example frustrated attempts by target companies to transfer shares that they indirectly controlled to a friendly offeror or white knight competing with a hostile bid (e.g., *Télémécanique Electrique/Schneider* case, Paris Court of Appeal, third chamber, Section B, 18 March 1988 and *Demilac/Groupe Perrier* case, Paris Commercial Court, first chamber, 16 March 1992).

The general principles applicable to French takeovers finally include the requirement to comply with French corporate law, including the rules relating to corporate benefit (*intérêt social*). For the above reasons, defensive measures, even where approved by the shareholders of the target company, will also need to comply with this requirement. Although not defined under French law, it is generally accepted that this concept refers to the interests of the company as a whole and is distinct from that of its shareholders, employees or creditors.

Defensive measures available to French companies during the course of an offer are therefore generally considered as being limited in scope and effectiveness.

10.9.2.2 Reciprocity principle

The above-mentioned limitations may not be applicable in the event the offeror (or its controlling entity or the parties acting in concert with it) is not subject to the same or equivalent provisions, and the target shareholders have approved the decisions made by the management or board of directors within the 18-month period prior to the filing of the offer ("reciprocity principle").

Therefore, if the reciprocity test is not met by an offeror, a general meeting of the shareholders of the target would not be required to adopt a defensive measure during the offer period. Any defensive measure implemented must nonetheless have been specifically approved (as a decision that may be made in the course of an offer) by the target shareholders in general meeting no more than 18 months prior to the filing of the offer.

The AMF is the competent authority to decide whether or not any rules are equivalent to the French rules regarding the requirement for shareholders to approve defensive measures in case of challenge. To that effect, the General Regulation provides that in the case of a challenge, the target company must present its arguments within 10 trading days, and the AMF will render its decision within the following five trading days.

In addition, the application of the reciprocity test will inevitably raise a number of complex questions in practice.

Some French legal scholars had raised the question of its compliance with the EU Takeover Directive, on the basis that the reciprocity principle was only available where the implementation of the board neutrality rule was only optional for companies. Their objections were not taken into account by the French Parliament.

One of the most obvious questions will be the criteria to determine the equivalence of the rules. On the issue of whether the foreign rules are equivalent to the French rules or not, the major question, given the ambiguity of the term "equivalence", is whether only the restrictions on the powers of the board shall be studied or also the general legal background surrounding the offeror.

Furthermore, as understood by the French Parliament, the reciprocity principle would be applicable to any kind of entity or individuals. However, case law will probably have to determine whether the exception to board neutrality rules could be opposed systematically to non-listed companies, equity funds or individuals who by nature cannot be subject to a takeover offer.

10.9.2.3 Defensive warrants

The Implementing Law has specifically introduced the possibility for the target to issue warrants as a defensive measure. The shareholders of the target may in an extraordinary general meeting (the "GM") (but in accordance with the majority and quorum required in an ordinary general meeting) approve the issue and free allocation to all shareholders being shareholders before the expiration of the offer period of warrants giving the right to subscribe on preferential terms for shares of the company.

The conditions of exercise of such warrants (that must relate to the terms of the offer or of any competing offer) as well as the other characteristics of such warrants (including the exercise price or the way to determine such price) shall be determined by the target shareholders in GM or, as the case may be, by the board of directors or the managing board (in accordance with a delegation granted by the GM).

The GM may delegate this power to the target's board of directors or management board. However, it must determine the maximum share capital increase that can result from the exercise of all such warrants as well as the maximum number of warrants to be issued.

When granting this power to the target board of directors or management board, the GM may also determine the circumstances in which the board of directors or the management board shall proceed with, delay or abandon the warrant issue.

The company shall disclose its intention to proceed with the warrant issue before the end of the offer period.

Should the offer and any competing offer, fail for any reasons, the warrants shall automatically become null and void.

At the time of writing, no such warrants had been issued in the context of a takeover offer, but a number of major French companies had obtained delegation from their shareholders to issue such warrants. However, such delegations can only be used if the offeror does not meet the reciprocity test and if they have been granted less than 18 months prior to the filing of the offer. In all other cases a new shareholders meeting would be required in order to approve the issuance.

Those warrants may be mainly used as a threat to force the negotiation with the offeror. As mentioned above, any decision which would change the substance of the target would give a right to the offeror to withdraw his offer (the General Regulation has even been amended in this respect to include changes of the substance of the target company that have occurred once the offer has had a successful outcome in addition to changes that have occurred during the offer). Therefore, it is to be anticipated that a board of directors will be extremely cautious prior to making such a decision, since it would risk depriving share-holders of an existing offer. Also, although there is now a clear legal basis to issue such warrants, it remains to be tested whether they can be efficiently structured in practice without triggering criticism by the AMF, as in the *Plavix* case in 2004, on the ground of the general principles applicable to takeover offers (*see* 10.6.1 above).

10.10   Documents from the offeror and offeree

10.10.1   *The offer document*

Whereas the description of the offeror is provided for in a separate general information document (*see* 10.10.3 below), the offer document is focused on the description of the offer and must contain the following basic information:

(a)   The identity of the offeror.
(b)   The terms of the offer, including in particular:
    (i)   the proposed price or exchange ratio offered;
    (ii)   the number and type of shares that the offeror undertakes to purchase;
    (iii)   the number and type of target shares that the offeror already holds, directly or indirectly, alone or in concert, or may hold on its own initiative, as well as the date and terms on which such holdings were acquired in the last 12 months or may be acquired in the future;
    (iv)   where applicable, the conditions precedent to which the offer is subject;
    (v)   the planned timetable of the offer;
    (vi)   where applicable, the number and type of shares tendered in exchange by the offeror;
    (vii)   the terms of financing of the offer and the impact of those terms on the assets, activity and financial results of the companies involved.
(c)   The intentions of the offeror for the next 12 months with regard to the industrial and financial strategy involving the offeree and with regard to equity and equity-linked securities of the offeree.
(d)   The policy of the offeror with respect to employment (including in particular any foreseeable changes in the size and composition of the workforce).
(e)   The law applicable to contracts between the offeror and shareholders of the target following the offer, and the competent jurisdictions.
(f)   Any agreement entered into by the offeror in connection with the offer or which comes to its knowledge, as well as the identity and characteristics of the persons acting in concert with the offeror or the target.
(g)   If necessary and on a case-by-case basis, the reasoned opinion of the board of directors or supervisory board of the offeror on the merits of the offer or on its impact on the offeror, its shareholders or its employees. By which majority such opinion has been reached has to be specified and dissenting directors may require that the reasons for their opinion are inserted into the offer document.
(h)   Where applicable, the undertaking to file an irrevocable and fair draft offer relating to the listed subsidiary representing an essential asset of the target.

(i) Where applicable, the report by the independent appraiser mentioned in Article 261-3 of the General Regulation.

(j) The procedures for making available the general information document.

More precisely, the section of the offer document relating to the presentation of the offer must contain the following basic information:

(a) structure of the offer (including, if appropriate, agreements to which the offeror is a party);

(b) objectives and intentions of the offeror;

(c) elements of value of the offer: quoted value; net profit per share; net asset value per share;

(d) method of financing;

(e) tax regime;

(f) intermediaries' fees and commissions;

(g) impact of the offer on the accounts and the financial results of the offeror.

The offeror signs the offer document, guaranteeing the accuracy of the information disclosed.

The presenting banks countersign the offer document and guarantee the accuracy of the information relating to:

(a) the presentation of the offer; and

(b) the appraisal of the proposed price or exchange ratio only.

The information listed above is formatted and presented in a standardised form.

10.10.2   *The defence document*

If the offer document was not filed jointly by the offeror and the target, the latter has to publish a defence document.

As for the offeror, the description of the target is provided for in a separate general information document (*see* 10.10.3 below). Consequently, the defence document contains the following information:

(a) The agreements having an impact on the assessment of the offer or its outcome.

(b) The information relating to:

    (i) the structure of the capital of the target;

    (ii) the provisions limiting the exercise of voting rights or share transfers;

    (iii) the interests held directly or indirectly in the target which have been disclosed to such target;

    (iv) the list of the persons holding special control rights with respect to the target;

    (v) the agreements between shareholders providing for limits in the exercise of voting rights or share transfers;

    (vi) the rules applicable to:

        • the appointment and removal of the members of the board of directors or management board, and

        • the amendment of the articles of association;

> > (vii)   the powers of the board of directors or management board, in particular as regards the issuance of repurchase of shares;
> >
> > (viii) the agreements entered into by the target which would be modified or terminated in case of a change of control of the target;
> >
> > (ix)   the agreements providing for compensation at the benefit of the members of the board of directors or management board or employees if they resign, are dismissed or their job is terminated because of a public offer.
>
> (c)   The independent appraiser's report where the transaction is likely:
>
> > (i)   to cause conflicts of interest within the target's board of directors, which could impair the objectivity of the opinion to be included in the draft defence document; or
> >
> > (ii)   to challenge the equality of treatment among the target's shareholders.
>
> (d)   The reasoned opinion of the board of directors or supervisory board on the merits of the offer. By which majority such opinion has been reached has to be specified and dissenting directors may require that the reasons for their dissenting opinion are inserted into the defence document.
>
> (e)   If they are available and different from the opinion of the governing bodies mentioned above, comments by the works council.
>
> (f)   Whether members of the governing bodies intend to tender their shares to the offer.
>
> (g)   The procedures for making available the general information document.

The target signs the defence document guaranteeing the information disclosed.

10.10.3 *The general information documents*

General information documents incorporating the characteristics (notably legal, financial and accounting) of the offeror and the target have to be filed with the AMF and be made available to the public on the opening day of the offer at the latest. The content of such general information documents is defined by an instruction by the AMF.

The information relating to the offeror to be included in such document depends on whether the offer is a pure cash offer or whether it also has an exchange element. In the latter case, the offeror would have to establish a document which describes its situation by reference to the relevant Annex to the EC Regulation no. 809/2004 dated 29 April 2004 relating to Prospectuses. If a recent prospectus approved of by the AMF or by another competent authority and "passported" in France pursuant to the Prospectus Directive is available, the general information document relating to the offeror will refer to such document and only include an update if necessary.

In a pure cash offer, the information to be included regarding the offeror is less extensive (summary presentation of its articles of association and annual or consolidated accounts relating to the last accounting year, even if in practice offerors often provide the three last accounting years).

As regards the target, the information to be included in the general information document consists of a presentation of its legal situation, its assets and liabilities, its financial situation (including financial statements relating to the last two financial years). In practice, the general information document usually refers to the annual report filed with the AMF (*document de référence*) including sometimes an update.

Those documents are made available to the public under the same conditions and means as the offer document and the defence document.

Opinions of the statutory auditors of the offeror and target are included in their respective general information documents.

10.11   Mandatory acquisition of minority shareholdings ("squeeze-out")

The chance for a controlling shareholder to force minority shareholders to sell their shares was introduced in France by Article 16 of Law no. 93–1444 dated 31 December 1993. In 1998, the squeeze-out procedure was extended to investment certificates and voting rights certificates. In 2006, the scope of the squeeze-out was extended to any public offers,[29] provided that:

(a)   the offeror obtains in the framework of the offer at least 95 per cent of the share capital and voting rights of the target; and

(b)   the squeeze-out is implemented within the three-month period following the closing of the offer.

10.11.1   *Squeeze-out following an offer*

A squeeze-out procedure may be carried out within a three-month period after the closing of any public offer provided the offeror holds at least 95 per cent of the share capital and voting rights of the target[30] (Article 237–14 and *seq.* of the AMF General Regulation). The General Regulation provides that the consideration paid to the other shareholders by the offeror shall be equal to:

(a)   the price offered in the previous offer if the offer was made in cash and in accordance with the normal offer procedure (as opposed to the simplified procedure or the guaranteed price procedure), without the intervention of an independent expert; or

(b)   the price offered in the previous offer if the offer was made in cash and in accordance with the simplified procedure or the guaranteed price procedure, and if for the purpose of the clearance of such offer the AMF was provided with a multi-criteria valuation as well as a valuation procedure confirmed by an independent appraiser; or

---

[29] Until then, a squeeze-out could only be implemented after a successful buy-out offer.

[30] It is unclear whether such squeeze-out procedure can also be carried out when the 95 per cent threshold has been crossed further to additional purchases on the market after the closing of the offer, or whether the 95 per cent threshold has to be crossed as a result of the tenders to the offer.

(c)   in other cases to the price as determined on the basis of a multi-criteria valuation supported by a fairness opinion by an independent appraiser.

In addition, where the previous offer had an exchange component, the offeror can offer shares as an indemnification on the condition that a cash consideration is offered at least as an alternative to the other shareholders.

In the cases referred to in (a) and (b) above, the squeeze-out procedure will not be subject to a review by the AMF. The AMF will only publish the date of implementation of the squeeze-out and the offeror will publish a press release which indicates where the offer document relating to the previous offer is available. Therefore the implementation would be very fast.

As regards the hypothesis described in (c) above, the offer and the relating documentation will need to be cleared by the AMF. For those purposes, the same offer documents as those required in the context of an offer will need to be prepared, except that the offeror will not have to describe its intentions over the following 12 months. The clearance process will be the same as that described for voluntary offers. The minimum period of time to implement the squeeze-out would be approximately 25 calendar days.

10.11.2   *Squeeze-out following a buy-out offer*

The majority shareholder (or shareholders) who holds, alone or in concert, at least 95 per cent of the voting rights of a listed company can file a minority buy-out offer with the AMF on the shares that they do not hold (Article 236–3 of the AMF General Regulation). The minority buy-out offer must be cleared by the AMF in the same conditions as for any voluntary offers. The minority buy-out offers follow the rules of the simplified offer procedure, in particular the offer remains open for at least 10 trading days and gives rise to purchases that should, in principle, correspond to daily irrevocable transactions.

If, following such minority buy-out offer, the shareholder (or shareholders) holds, alone or in concert, at least 95 per cent of the voting rights and the share capital, they are entitled to receive the shares of the remaining minority shareholders.

If the offeror has not indicated in its minority buy-out offer that such offer will automatically be followed by a squeeze-out, it has 10 trading days following the closing of the offer to announce its decision to the AMF, which will publish the offeror's decision. The price for the squeeze-out must be at least equal to the price of the minority buy-out offer and subject to a report by an independent appraiser. In practice, the issue of the price fixation is usually sensitive, and challenges by minority shareholders of the AMF's decision to clear the minority buy-out offer followed by a compulsory squeeze-out are likely to arise on the grounds of an insufficient price.

In most cases, the decision to launch a squeeze-out is anticipated in the minority buy-out offer documentation, thus the implementation of the squeeze-out will occur on the day after the end of the minority buy-out offer period. If the decision to launch a squeeze-out has not been anticipated, it must be announced to the AMF within 10 trading days following the closing of the offer. It will not be implemented before the end of a 10-day period following the publication by the AMF of the offeror's decision.

10.12   Insider dealing and market manipulation

10.12.1   *Insider dealing*

10.12.1.1   *The offences*

Insider dealing is prohibited under two different sets of rules. Not only is it an offence under Article 465–1 of the Monetary and Financial Code (*Code Monétaire et Financier*), but it may equally result in administrative proceedings by the AMF and a fine under Articles 621–1 to 622–2 of the General Regulation. The offence is prosecuted in the courts and penalties on conviction may be up to two years' imprisonment and a fine of up to the greater of either €1.5 million or 10 times the profit made on the trading. Since it constitutes a violation of a provision of its General Regulation, the AMF may also initiate administrative proceedings and impose a fine of up to the greater of either €1.5 million or 10 times the profit made (Article 621–15 of the Monetary and Financial Code).

Criminal proceedings and proceedings being brought by the AMF are not mutually exclusive. As a matter of fact, after an initial investigation in suspected dealings, it is quite common for the AMF to simultaneously report its findings to the public prosecution office (*parquet*) and simultaneously initiate administrative proceedings. If the AMF decides that a violation of its regulations has been committed and imposes a fine, its decision can be appealed before the Paris Court of Appeal.

Despite some technical differences, the definition of insider dealing under both sets of rules is very similar. The offence is committed by any manager or director or any other person who:

(a)   comes into possession, by reason of his profession or position, of privileged information on the situation or prospects of an issuer or on the future prospects of a security; and

(b)   who carries out, or knowingly causes to carry out, directly or through an intermediary, one or several transactions before such information has been communicated to the public.

The mere fact that a person in possession of privileged information obtained in the course of his duties communicates such information to a third party outside the normal course of business equally constitutes an offence.

Privileged information is defined by Article 621–1 of the General Regulation as non-public and precise information that relates, directly or indirectly, to an issuer or to a security, which, if made public, could influence the price of such security. Whether information is public is essentially a question of fact. However, it should be noted that the release of information even to 300 financial analysts has been considered insufficient for that information to be deemed public. It is only considered to be public if the information is communicated by a public announcement of the company in accordance with the requirements of Articles 221–3 and 221–4 of the General Regulation, which provide, *inter alia*, that the issuer complies with its obligations when it makes all regulated information public by resorting to an information provider having specific characteristics.

As drafted, the rules impose an absolute duty on insiders not to trade without providing any defences. Originally the 1967 Ordinance provided that the offence was only committed if it could be proven that the transaction was effected only because of the possession of privileged information. The disappearance of the link between the possession of privileged information and the transaction raises certain practical issues in relation to takeovers which, to date, have not been completely resolved.

10.12.1.2 Some practical implications
The most critical issue raised by the prohibition of insider dealing in connection with acquisitions relates to stake building prior to a takeover.

Although the provisions relating to insider dealing are drafted in very general terms, the interpretation of which could cover the acquisition of shares prior to an offer, it is generally believed that stake building does not constitute a violation of those rules. This position was supported by former COB Regulation no. 90–04 which provided that, prior to a transaction relating to a controlling block of shares or the filing of an offer, market orders by the parties to the transaction had to be in conformity with the objectives of such parties (i.e., purchase orders for the purchaser and sales orders for the seller). By regulating such orders, the stock market authorities implicitly but necessarily recognised that stake building did not per se constitute insider dealing. Although this provision was revoked in November 2004, it is believed that the position of the stock market authorities will not change in this respect.

Some guidelines on this issue can be found in a decision rendered by the Paris Court of Appeal in the *Zodiac* case (Paris Court of Appeal, first chamber, COB Section, 15 November 1994, *SA Zodiac/Agent judiciaire du Trésor*). The court upheld a decision of the COB which had imposed a fine on an offeror for having acquired shares of the target company prior to initiating an offer. The court considered that the acquisition of shares prior to initiating an offer could be legal if such acquisition was motivated by the need to progressively build a stake in the target company or to enhance a position against a potential competing offer.

In the particular case, however, the court found that the shares had been purchased not for one of those motives but in order to reduce the overall cost of the acquisition, since at the time the purchases were made the acquirer knew that the offer price would be significantly higher than the then listed price. In rendering its decision, the court was probably influenced by the fact that at the time the trades were initiated, the acquirer had almost reached an agreement with the controlling shareholder of the target company and knew at what price he would have to fulfil his mandatory offer obligation.

This decision seems to confirm the current trend in the French courts to consider that, despite the fact that the provisions concerning insider dealing do not contain any statutory defences, no offence is committed if the dealings are made for legitimate reasons, which, in the case of acquisition of control, must be entirely independent from the desire to minimise the cost of acquisition.

Stake-building strategies have been used in recent tender offers in France. For instance, Groupe Partouche, prior to launching a tender offer for Compagnie Européenne de Casino which was also the subject of an offer by Accor Casinos, acquired from third parties or through purchases on the market up to 36.8 per cent of the share capital of such company (partly below and partly at the price of such competing offer).

10.12.2   Market manipulation

Like insider dealing, market manipulation is prohibited not only by Article L.465–2 of the Monetary and Financial Code but equally by Article 631–1 of the General Regulation. Maximum penalties on conviction are identical to those for insider dealing. The offence is committed when a person knowingly operates or attempts to operate on the market in order to disrupt its regular operation by misleading orders.

10.13   Financial assistance

Under Article L.225–216 of the Commercial Code, a company may not provide financial assistance in the form of advances, loans or security "with a view to the subscription or purchase of its own shares by a third party". Under this rule a target company may not finance or pledge any of its assets as security for loans extended to the acquiring company. Thus, the offeror will normally only be able to offer a pledge on the shares of the target company and not on its assets as security to its lenders. Violation of Article L.225–216 will make the managers and directors of the company liable to a fine of up to €9,000 and the loans or securities granted in breach of article L.225–16 may be sanctioned by nullity.

Article L.225–216 provides for two exceptions to the prohibition of financial assistance: one for loans made by banks in the normal course of their business when the funds lent are used to purchase shares issued by the bank, and the other for loans by a company to its employees in order to acquire its shares.

There are also possible alternatives to avoid falling foul of the prohibition on financial assistance – distribution of dividends, reduction of capital or even a merger in certain circumstances – which must be considered with care on a case-by-case basis.

In addition to the specific provisions prohibiting financial assistance, the refinancing by a company of the acquisition of its own shares by a third party may constitute an offence under Article L.242–6 of the Commercial Code as an abuse of corporate assets (*abus de biens sociaux*). Under this provision, which is widely prosecuted, it is an offence for any manager or director of a company to use in bad faith, in a way which would be contrary to the company's interest but in the furtherance of their own personal interest, the credit or assets of the company. Article L.242–6 is therefore an even stronger deterrent against financial assistance. Offending managers and directors are liable for up to five years' imprisonment and a fine of up to €375,000.

Chapter 11
Germany

Frank Burmeister and Georg Frowein

Partners
Hengeler Mueller

11.1 Introduction

Germany is a country with approximately 82 million inhabitants. It is the largest European country in terms of population and economic output. Its business environment comprises the following forms of undertakings:

(a)   about 70 per cent sole proprietorships;
(b)   about 9 per cent general partnerships ("OHGs" and "GbRs");
(c)   about 4 per cent limited partnerships ("KGs"), including KGs in which a company with limited liability is the (sole) general partner ("GmbH & Co. KGs");
(d)   about 15 per cent companies with limited liability ("GmbHs");
(e)   about 0.2 per cent stock corporations ("AGs");
(f)   there are very few partnerships limited by shares ("KGaAs");
(g)   the remainder are businesses with other legal forms.

(Source: Annual Report of the Federal Statistical Office on Value Added Tax, Series 14, Vol. 8, June 2007: www.destatis.de)

As far as sales are concerned the picture is entirely different: Whereas 83 per cent of all businesses generate sales of less than €500,000 per year and only 0.3 per cent of all businesses account for sales of more than €50 million, 11 per cent of all stock corporations generate sales of more than €50 million. Stock corporations generate approximately 20 per cent of the total sales, GmbHs approximately 35 per cent, and limited partnerships approximately 23 per cent, whereas sole proprietorships and partnerships account for 16 per cent (source: Annual Report of the Federal Statistical Office on Value Added Tax, Series 14, Vol. 8, June 2007).

The German mergers and acquisitions ("M&A") market represents roughly 3 per cent of the worldwide M&A market. The estimated purchase price paid for companies in Germany jumped steadily from about €34 billion in 1996 to the peak of €246 billion in the international M&A boom year 2000 (source: *Finance*, March 2001). A number of multi-billion transactions, some of them structured as mergers of equals, heavily contributed to this increase, including the Daimler Benz/Chrysler, Thyssen/Krupp-Hoesch and Allianz/Dresdner Bank mergers as well as the Vodafone/Mannesmann takeover.

The decline in transaction value that had emerged in the German market in line with global downward trend during the years 2001 to 2004 has reversed since

2005: $135 billion in 2001, $84 billion in 2002, $81 billion in 2003 and $76 billion in 2004, in comparison to $130 billion in 2005 and $158 billion in 2006 (source: *M&A Review*, 2/2002, 2/2003, 2/2004, 2/2005, 2/2006, 2/2007). The transaction volume during the first five months of 2007 confirm this steady upward trend: there were 20 per cent more transactions compared to the reference period of the preceding year (source: *M&A Review*, 7/2007). Even though the figures of the record boom year of 2000 have not yet been met, the German M&A market shows a positive picture. This is due to a heightened level of restructuring within German industry, the availability of high-quality assets, and an opportune investment window in the German economic cycle. In addition, the pressure on corporate management to divest non-core assets has risen. Recent large-scale transactions have been the sale of Siemens VDO Automotive to Continental, the UniCredit/HVB merger and the Allianz/AGF takeover. However, the vast majority of transactions to date have related to the acquisition of medium-sized, mostly family-owned businesses, which make up the bulk of active companies in Germany.

While in 2000, in one-third of all transactions a telecommunications or IT company was involved (source: *Finance*, March 2001, pp10, 13), in 2006 more than a quarter of all buyers came from the financial sector. Accordingly, the financial services sector headed the German transaction league tables by volume, followed by the general services and the chemicals/pharma sector. Telecommunications/IT was in fourth position (source: *M&A Review*, 2/2007). In terms of transaction volumes, the chemicals/pharma sector has been particularly significant in 2005 and 2006. Recent headline-making transactions in this sector have been the takeovers Bayer/Schering, Linde/BOC Group, Merck/Serono, Novartis/Hexal, UCB/Schwarz Pharma, BASF/Engelhard as well as the sales of Merck Generics to Mylan Laboratories and the pharmaceutical business of Altana to Nycomed.

The financial services sector in Germany was affected by the growing activity of private equity investors (being involved in more than 41 per cent of all transactions in the first half of 2007) (source: Ernst & Young, *German Private Equity Activity*, June 2007) such as the sale of Chrysler by DaimlerChrysler to Cerberus and the sale of the Haim Saban stake in ProSiebenSat1 Media AG to Permira and KKR (both in 2007). The market for secondary buyouts emerged further. For instance, Cinven and Apax sold the leading fashion company CBR to EQT, whereas CVC Capital Partners sold ista Deutschland, the global market leader in the consumption-dependent billing of energy, water and ancillary costs, to Charterhouse Capital Partners (both in 2007).

The year 2007 has also shown a trend to increasing multinational consortium deals. The share of merely domestic transactions has constantly declined. In 2007, more than half of the transactions involved foreign companies (source: *M&A Review*, 2/2007, 7/2007). With respect to investments in Germany in 2006, US companies were the strongest investors with 79 acquisitions, followed by Austrian investors with 49 deals and 42 British acquisitions. In 2006, German companies mainly invested in Austria and the US, followed by Switzerland, France, China and the UK (source: *M&A Review*, 2/2007). Prominent examples of transactions with a non-German target company include the takeovers of UGS and Diagnostic Products Corp. (both by Siemens) and the takeover of Swiss International Airlines by Lufthansa.

Prior to the famous takeover of Mannesmann by Vodafone in 2000, there were few hostile takeover attempts in Germany. The most prominent example was the takeover attempt of Thyssen by Krupp-Hoesch in 1991 which finally resulted in a friendly "merger of equals" (others have been AMB/AGF in 1998, Barilla/Kamps in 2002 and P&G/Wella in 2003). More recent attempts in 2006, for example the unsolicited bid of MAN to take over its Swedish competitor Scania and of Merck to take over Schering, failed.

While hostile takeovers have not been very successful in Germany so far, "friendly" public takeover activity has substantially increased over the last few years. In many cases, the public offer was preceded by agreements between the bidder and substantial shareholders through which the bidder ensured a base acceptance level in advance.

However, recent changes in the ownership structure of listed German stock corporations may allow for the prediction that hostile takeover bids could be more successful in the future. Disposals of shareholdings by most of the major financial services institutions may lead to termination of cross-shareholdings. Together with an increasingly widespread acceptance of hostile takeovers in the German business community, this will stimulate the German takeover market.

11.2 Acquisition targets and corporate governance

Potential targets for acquisitions include all forms of enterprises – sole proprietorships, general partnerships, limited partnerships, companies with limited liability, stock corporations (including the *Societas Europaea*) and partnerships limited by shares.

However, this Guide primarily addresses tender offers submitted to the shareholders of publicly held companies (i.e., stock corporations and partnerships limited by shares), as only such companies may be listed on a Stock Exchange. Since there are very few partnerships limited by shares, they will not be addressed here specifically.

Traditionally, there have been only a few takeover bids in Germany. The reasons are twofold. One reason was the limited number of truly publicly held corporations, but this has changed. By the end of December 2007, 754 companies were listed on the Frankfurt Stock Exchange in the regulated market.

The other reason for the traditionally low public takeover activity has been the rather complex legal organisation of German stock corporations which makes it difficult to take immediate control of a corporation after having acquired the majority of the shares. However, recent experience shows that the complex corporate structure does not represent a crucial factor:

(a)   Shareholders' influence in a German stock corporation is vested in the shareholders meeting. However, the shareholders meeting may not interfere with the management of the corporation unless requested by the management board (*Vorstand*) (Section 119, paragraph 2 of the Stock Corporation Act).

(b)   In all stock corporations employing 2,000 or more persons the shareholders meeting elects and dismisses half of the members of the supervisory board – subject to any rights of specific shareholders to appoint up to one-third of the supervisory board members to be appointed by the shareholders. The other half is elected by the corporation's labour force under the so-called Labour Codetermination Act. In a stock corporation with more than 500 but fewer than 2,000 employees, one-third of the supervisory board members must be appointed by the labour force. Members of the supervisory board normally serve for a period of five years; their terms of office may be staggered. The shareholders may only dismiss a member of the supervisory board prior to the expiration of its term of office with a 75 per cent majority of the votes cast (Section 103, paragraph 1 of the Stock Corporation Act). The articles of association may stipulate a higher or lower majority to include a simple majority of the votes. However, only some corporations provide for such provisions. The shareholders have no power to dismiss a labour representative on the supervisory board.

(c)   The management board manages the corporation independently (Section 76, paragraph 1 of the Stock Corporation Act). The management board is appointed by the supervisory board, normally for a period of five years; it cannot be appointed for a longer period of time (Section 84, paragraph 1 of the Stock Corporation Act). The term of office of the members of the management board is staggered in practically all cases. During the term of office a member of the management board can only be dismissed by the supervisory board for gross violation of duties, incompetence, or by a vote of no confidence resolved by the shareholders meeting, unless such vote is exercised for arbitrary reasons (Section 84, paragraph 3 of the Stock Corporation Act). The resolution of the supervisory board on the appointment or revocation of members of the management board of companies with more than 2,000 employees requires a two-thirds majority in the first ballot. If such majority is not reached, a conciliation committee consisting of members of the supervisory board, including the employees' representatives, must be consulted. At the next ballot only a simple majority is required. In case such majority is not met, the chairman of the supervisory board has a tie-breaking second vote at the next ballot (Section 31 of the Co-Determination Act).

Hence, it might be difficult for the acquirer of a majority stake in a German stock corporation to dismiss the members of its management board and to replace them with his people. Such replacement may only be accomplished through the supervisory board. However, members of the supervisory board who are appointed by the shareholders may only be replaced upon a 75 per cent vote of the shareholders. It is not possible for the shareholders to dismiss members of the supervisory board who are appointed by the labour force. Even if the buyer is in a position to replace all shareholders' representatives, it may be difficult to oust the management. The employees' members of the supervisory board might be hesitant with respect to measures to be taken in order to achieve synergies, or to close down or spin off certain departments which will result in lay-offs and therefore also to a new management which is supposed to take such steps. A veto of the employees' representatives in the supervisory board may at least delay corporate developments considerably. The German labour codetermination system has therefore often been labelled a very effective "poison pill".

(d)   Resolutions of the shareholders of a German stock corporation require, as a rule, only the simple majority of the votes cast (Section 133 of the Stock Corporation Act). The voting right is exercised pursuant to the nominal amount of the shares (Section 134 of the Stock Corporation Act). However, until 1 June 2003, the articles of association could deviate from this principle and provide for a limitation of voting rights to the effect that shareholders are prohibited from voting more than a certain percentage of the share capital. The existence of such maximum voting rights certainly made it much more difficult for a buyer to exercise control over the target company. It was not by coincidence that the first shareholders meeting of Mannesmann following the takeover by Vodafone took place just after the expiration of the voting right limitation contained in the articles of association of Mannesmann.

(e)   The articles of association of some corporations (in particular in the insurance sector) provide that there are only registered shares and that their transfer requires the consent of the management board or the supervisory board or the shareholders meeting (Section 68 of the Stock Corporation Act). These bodies have some discretion to decide whether they want to grant such consent. Warding off an unfriendly takeover attempt might be considered, depending on the case, as being in the interests of the corporation.

(f)   Section 53a of the Stock Corporation Act provides that all shareholders are to be treated equally. Such rule imposes the obligation on the management board not to grant any special favours to any shareholder, in particular to any buyer of its shares. This even means that any information which was given to one shareholder in its role as shareholder must also be given to all other shareholders in the general shareholders meeting upon their respective request (Section 131, paragraph 4 of the Stock Corporation Act).

(g)   A majority shareholder of a German stock corporation may not use its influence on the corporation to cause the company to engage in a transaction which is disadvantageous to such corporation or to take or to omit to take actions which are to its disadvantage, unless such disadvantages are compensated (Section 311 of the Stock Corporation Act). In other words, a majority shareholder must treat the corporation "at arm's length". To ensure such principle, the corporation is required to prepare each year a so-called dependency report listing the transactions between majority shareholder and corporation and stating whether the corporation has been disadvantaged by such transactions or not. The report will be audited by the corporation's auditors and examined by the supervisory board (Sections 312 and 313 of the Stock Corporation Act). Statements in such a report, which are intentionally incorrect, entail criminal liability of the members of the management board, the auditor and the members of the supervisory board (Sections 400 and 403 of the Stock Corporation Act). In addition, the majority shareholder and its management are liable for damages if they have not ensured compensation for any disadvantage caused to the corporation by exercising dominating influence (Section 317 of the Stock Corporation Act). However, such liability does not apply if a conscientious manager of an independent company would have acted in the same manner as the management of the dominated company.

(h) There are other provisions preventing shareholders from exercising influence on the corporation to the detriment of the company. For instance, Section 117 of the Stock Corporation Act provides that whoever influences a corporation and causes a member of its management board or its supervisory board or any other executive to act to the detriment of the corporation or its shareholders shall be liable for damages to the corporation. Such damage claim may also be raised by the corporation's creditors if they cannot obtain satisfaction from the corporation.

(i) A majority shareholder who intends to exercise its influence in such a way that the dominated company will not always be treated at arm's length may enter into a so-called "domination agreement" with the corporation. This permits the majority shareholder to issue even disadvantageous instructions to the corporation which the management is, generally speaking, obligated to comply with (Section 308 of the Stock Corporation Act). But this has its price. In such event, the dominating shareholder is obligated to absorb all losses of the corporation (Section 302 of the Stock Corporation Act). On the other hand, if there is a combined domination and profit and loss pooling agreement, which is typically the case in order to allow consolidation for tax purposes, the majority shareholder is also entitled to all the profits. The conclusion of such a domination and/or profit and loss pooling agreement requires a majority of 75 per cent of the share capital represented at the shareholders meeting of the dominated company and, generally speaking, also of the dominating company (Section 293 of the Stock Corporation Act). Further, the dominating shareholder is obliged to offer the minority shareholders a guaranteed dividend. In addition, upon request of the minority shareholders the dominating shareholder is obliged to offer to purchase their stocks against cash payment, to offer stocks in the dominating shareholder if such entity is an independent corporation with a seat in the EU or EEA, or to offer stocks in the parent company of a controlled dominating shareholder if such entity has its seat in the EU or EEA (Sections 304 and 305 of the Stock Corporation Act). The guaranteed dividend and the purchase prices for the shares shall be based on the profitability such corporation would have without the respective domination and/or profit and loss pooling agreement. In case of disputes, the amount of the dividend and/or purchase price is to be determined by the courts.

(j) German law provides for legal mechanisms to force minority shareholders to sell their shares to the majority shareholder ("squeeze-out") if the latter already holds or acquires 95 per cent of the share capital (Section 327a of the Stock Corporation Act, Section 39a of the Takeover Act, *see* 11.11 below for details).

(k) Section 71a of the Stock Corporation Act prevents the acquirer from using the funds of the target corporation to finance the acquisition of its shares (*see* 11.13 below).

(l)   Due to the relatively thin equity capital base of many German companies, and therefore their reliance on debt financing, banks traditionally have played a major role with respect to the financing and the structure of German companies. Such dominant role of the banks is strengthened by the fact that single shareholders of the free-float typically do not attend shareholders meetings but authorise their depositary banks to exercise their voting rights (Sections 128 and 135 of the Stock Corporation Act).

For these reasons, publicly held German stock corporations are rather difficult acquisition targets. However, obviously such difficulties may be overcome. The environment for takeovers has become substantially more friendly over the last few years.

11.3   Exchange and investment control

Germany has a liberal attitude towards investments by foreigners. There is no exchange control in Germany. However, the Foreign Trade Regulation (*Außen-wirtschaftsverordnung*) sets forth certain reporting requirements. Capital investments and cross-border payments exceeding certain thresholds must be reported to the Federal Reserve Bank (*Bundesbank*) through the competent State Central Bank (*Landeszentralbank*). Such reports merely serve statistical purposes and do not restrict foreign investments in any way.

Under the Aviation Act (*Luftverkehrsgesetz*), and subject to overriding provisions of European law, an aircraft may in general be registered in the German aircraft registry only if it is owned by German nationals or by a company which is domiciled in Germany and which is under the control, in terms of shareholding and management, of German nationals. Similar concepts apply to the operating permits of air carriers under EU law and under bilateral treaties.

The War Armaments Control Act (*Kriegswaffenkontrollgesetz*) provides that the licence necessary to manufacture or distribute armaments may be denied if the granting of such a licence would interfere with the interests of the German government in maintaining friendly relations with other countries or if a member of the management of the company applying for the licence is not a German national. In addition, the German government may restrict foreign investment in German companies producing or developing military weapons and other military equipment or encryptions systems. Apart from said exceptions, as opposed to for example in the US and France, discussions to enable the German government to control certain foreign investments under the label "national interests" have not yet been translated into legislation in Germany.

11.4   Merger control

11.4.1   Statistics

The number of completed transactions notified to the Federal Cartel Office (*Bundeskartellamt* – "BKartA") from 1990 to 2006 was 25,040 and since 1973 merely 164 concentrations have been prohibited (source: *Tätigkeitsbericht des BKartA 2005/2006, BT-Drucks 16/5710* pp14 and 223).

11.4.2 General

Merger control was introduced in Germany in 1973. It is governed by the Act Against Restraints of Competition (*Gesetz gegen Wettbewerbsbeschränkungen –* "GWB") which also covers the rules on horizontal and vertical restraints of competition, as well as the abuse of dominant positions. The GWB has been revised seven times since its entry into force. Its latest revision came into force in December 2007.

Merger control in Germany is governed by Section 35 et seq. of the GWB. Merger control will only apply where certain thresholds are exceeded (*see* below). If these tests are met, the parties have to file a pre-merger notification and must wait for clearance or the expiry of applicable waiting periods before they may consummate the transaction.

German merger control applies to all mergers which have an effect within Germany, regardless of where the merger will be implemented ("effects doctrine"). In practice this means that if the target has any business activities in Germany, German merger controls will apply. The ambit of German merger control may even go beyond this, for example if the target, although not being active in Germany, is in possession of know-how which may enhance the purchaser's German market position. It does not matter whether a party has a subsidiary, branch or sales office in Germany, or whether sales are made through agents or dealers. In practice, the "effect" on the market required to trigger the application of German merger control is extremely low.

The governmental authority in charge of merger control in Germany is the Federal Cartel Office (BKartA) in Bonn. Cases are handled by 10 divisions, and the allocation of a specific proposed transaction to one of those divisions is made in accordance with each division's responsibilities which follow lines of business. The divisions, in their decision making, enjoy a quasi-court position of independence and are not subject to instructions.

11.4.3 EC merger control regulation

German merger control does not apply where the transaction is subject to control pursuant to EC Regulation 139/2004 on the control of concentrations (Merger Control Regulation – "MCR") unless the case is referred back to the BKartA under the MCR.

The participants may apply to the EC Commission by means of a reasoned submission that the transaction should be examined by the EC Commission even though it genuinely falls within the jurisdiction of the BKartA if the transaction is capable of being reviewed under the national competition laws of at least three EC Member States. This application must be made prior to the notification to the BKartA. Objections to the referral of the case to the EC Commission may be raised by any EC Member State competent to examine the transaction.

11.4.4   Definition of concentration

Merger control only applies where a "concentration" (*Zusammenschluss*) has been or is proposed to be implemented. The GWB contains a list of transactions deemed to constitute a "concentration", namely:

(a)   the acquisition of all, or a substantial part of, the assets of the seller;
(b)   the acquisition of direct or indirect control of the whole or parts of one or more other undertakings;
(c)   the acquisition of 25 per cent or 50 per cent of the capital or the voting rights of another undertaking; and
(d)   any other transaction enabling one or several undertakings to directly or indirectly exercise "competitively significant influence" on another undertaking.

A combination of enterprises which once fulfilled the criteria for a "concentration" will still be subject to (additional) merger control if a new transaction again qualifies as a "concentration" (e.g., going up from 30 per cent of the voting rights to 60 per cent of the voting rights, or from "competitively significant influence" to "control") unless the new concentration does not result in a material strengthening of the existing affiliation.

It is important to note that the concept of concentration in German merger control law goes far beyond what is defined as concentration in the MCR (namely, the merger of independent undertakings or the acquisition of direct or indirect control). Accordingly, a transaction which due to its size would fall into the ambit of the European merger control regulation, but which does not qualify as a "concentration" under the MCR and is therefore not subject to European merger control, may still be subject to German merger control.

11.4.5   Pre-merger notification

In order to determine whether a merger notification has to be filed, the market position of the parties involved is irrelevant. Instead, the applicable thresholds refer to the size of the parties to the transaction and the size of the markets involved.

Where a transaction qualifies for merger control, the parties are prevented from completing the transaction (e.g., transfer of title to the assets or shares, but also from taking de facto control over the target) prior to having obtained clearance. Legal acts (i.e., the transfer of assets or shares) which have been implemented will be regarded as null and void except for defined cases where completion involves registration in a public register. Upon request of the parties, the BKartA may allow the parties to complete prior to clearance, in particular to prevent serious damage to a party to the transaction or a third party. The BKartA will only grant such release in extreme cases (*see* also 11.4.11 below).

Merger control will generally apply where:

(a)   all of the undertakings participating in the concentration had in the business year preceding the transaction a consolidated worldwide annual turnover of more than €500 million in the aggregate; and

(b)   at least one of the undertakings participating in the transaction had in the business year preceding the transaction a domestic consolidated turnover of at least €25 million.

The parties participating in the transaction will be the purchaser and the target company but, for purposes of calculating turnover thresholds, not the seller (however, in the case of an asset deal, the seller is considered participant as far as the sold assets are concerned). If two or more parties acquire simultaneously or successively at least 25 per cent of the shares, this will be deemed to be a concentration between all such parties holding 25 per cent or more, and all of them will be considered as participating in such a concentration. In cases of the acquisition of joint control, all of the parties sharing joint control will be considered participants.

For the purposes of calculating the thresholds, sales of trading groups are reduced by 25 per cent. For credit institutions, the reference to turnover is replaced by aggregate net income as defined in Section 38, paragraph 4 of the GWB, but for insurance companies by their premium income. For companies involved in certain electronic media or in the publication of newspapers or other periodicals, the turnover will be multiplied by 20.

11.4.6   De minimis

If, and to the extent that, the concentration concerns sales to a market in the preceding calendar year of less than €15 million, a transaction will not be controlled, provided such a market has existed for at least five years. Furthermore, a transaction will not be subject to merger control if a company merging with another undertaking is an independent company (as opposed to a group company) and if it had in the business year preceding the transaction a worldwide consolidated turnover of not more than €10 million.

11.4.7   Contents of a notification

The notification will have to state the following for all undertakings participating in the transaction, which will include for this purpose all companies affiliated with the undertakings directly participating:

(a)   name and place of the business or registered seat;
(b)   type of business;
(c)   turnover or other relevant threshold criteria in Germany, the EU and worldwide on a consolidated basis (*see* 11.4.5 above);
(d)   all areas where the participants have a domestic market share of 20 per cent or more;
(e)   in the case of the acquisition of shares, the size of the interest to be acquired and of the interest already held (if any); and
(f)   for each participant not being resident in Germany, an agent for service in Germany.

Furthermore, the BKartA can require the parties to make information available on the market conditions. Therefore, a notification should always contain at least some basic information on the markets involved and the market position of the parties. On the other hand, the BKartA normally does not insist on the submission of information which, although required in theory, obviously has no bearing on the transaction.

The BKartA can rely on more than 30 years' experience with mandatory merger control and is normally very flexible and cooperative in determining, together with the parties and their lawyers, what degree of information and investigation is needed for the filing. A filing may therefore consist of two or three pages, but in critical cases it may be a far more substantial document.

11.4.8 Periods

The BKartA must inform the parties within one month from receipt of the complete notification whether a formal investigation is to be opened, and must render its decision within four months of receipt of the complete filing. The vast majority of cases are cleared within the initial one-month period. For unproblematic cases, the typical period of time until clearance is one to three weeks (provided the filing contained sufficient data to enable the BKartA to form a view on the transaction).

In problematic cases, the BKartA will inform the parties within one month that it has opened an investigation. The BKartA will then (but possibly also during the initial one-month period) normally contact competitors, customers and suppliers, and will certainly also have additional discussions with the parties involved. Should the BKartA come to the conclusion that the transaction will have to be prohibited, it will issue a warning letter. Such warning letter is normally issued about one month prior to the expiration of the four-month period, to give the parties an opportunity to comment on the assessment of the BKartA, and try to convince it that the transaction should be cleared. At this stage (if not earlier), the parties may also commence discussions with the BKartA about removing clearance obstacles by way of divestitures or the like. A clearance decision or prohibition order issued after the opening of second-stage proceedings will be reasoned.

11.4.9 Substantive evaluation

The BKartA must prohibit a concentration if it is expected that the concentration will result in the creation or strengthening of a dominant market position, unless the undertakings participating in the concentration prove that the concentration will also lead to improvements of the conditions of competition, and that these improvements will outweigh the disadvantages of dominance (Section 36, paragraph 1 of the GWB).

In order to determine whether a dominant market position will be created or strengthened, the BKartA will evaluate all factors of the individual case but will consider in particular:

(a)   whether there is an increase in market share and what the resulting total market share is;
(b)   the size and market share of other market participants; and
(c)   the financial and technical resources of the market participants.

Normally a dominant market position will only be deemed to be created or strengthened if there is an increase in market share, but in some instances vertical integration, or the combination of the large financial resources of the purchaser, together with the existing strong market position of the target, may be considered as leading to or strengthening a dominant market position.

Should the BKartA come to the conclusion that the concentration will result in the strengthening of a dominant market position without improvements in competitive conditions, it is bound to prohibit the transaction. It may grant clearance subject to conditions and obligations which may, however, not aim at subjecting the conduct of the undertakings concerned to a continued control.

German law lays down a number of provisions defining certain market share criteria of a position of market dominance. These criteria will have to be considered carefully when making a notification. An undertaking is presumed to be market dominant if it has a market share of 33 per cent. Furthermore, the law contains certain oligopoly presumptions to the effect that if the three or fewer largest players have a joint market share of 50 per cent or more, or if the five or fewer largest players together have market shares of 66 per cent or more, all such undertakings taken together are presumed to be dominant. These presumptions can be rebutted. In practical terms they are often simply regarded as a checklist for an initial assessment as to whether there might be a merger control problem, although in some cases the BKartA has relied on the presumptions to prohibit a merger.

11.4.10   Involvement of third parties

Upon the request of third parties, the BKartA may determine that they are allowed to join in the proceedings if they have a significant business interest in the transaction. This will normally be the case for competitors. Such a third party has access to the files. The parties to the transaction may designate certain information as confidential but in this case may not rely on such confidential information to support their view that the transaction should be cleared.

11.4.11   Appeal

It is possible to appeal against a prohibition order of the BKartA. The decision rendered by the court may be subject to further appeal. However, delays in obtaining clearance may cause problems because the transaction cannot be completed until clearance has been granted. The Court of Appeals ("OLG") Düsseldorf has held that the courts cannot grant temporary relief from the prohibition to complete the transaction (OLG Düsseldorf, decision of 8 August 2007, Phonak/GN ReSound). However, the BKartA may at any time grant, upon application, exemptions from the prohibition of putting a concentration into effect if the undertakings concerned put forward important reasons for this (in particular to prevent serious damage to a participating undertaking or to a third party; *see* also 11.4.5 above). Since such exemptions are rarely granted, and although the rejection by the BKartA of an application for an exemption can be appealed to the courts, the BKartA is, in practice, often the one and only chance to decide on whether the transaction can go forward. Pursuant to a new decision by the German Federal Court of Justice ("BGH"), however, the designated buyer of an undertaking, the acquisition of which has been prohibited by the BKartA, may, in certain circumstances, have a considerable interest which entitles it to appeal to the courts for judicial review of the prohibition order even though the contemplated transaction has been abandoned in the meantime. This may be the case where the arguments on which the prohibition order was based may play a role for potential future acquisitions by the same buyer which are similar to the abandoned transaction (BGH, decision of 25 September 2007, KVR 30/06, Springer/ProSiebenSat1).

Prior to 1999, third parties, in practice, had no chance to challenge a clearance order by the BKartA because their appeal did not preclude the statutory waiting periods from expiring. While this continues to be the case, the law has changed in that the waiting periods will start running again upon a final court decision repealing a clearance order. The courts allow third parties to interfere if the clearance order negatively affects their economic interests (BGH, decision of 24 June 2003, WuW/E DE-R 1163, HABET/Lekkerland). The BGH has clarified that third parties whose economic interests are affected by a clearance order, and which were therefore eligible to be admitted as a party to the proceeding before the BKartA, may appeal against the clearance order even if, for reasons of "procedural convenience", the BKartA did not actually admit them to the administrative proceeding (BGH, decision of 7 November 2006, WuW/E DE-R 1857, pepcom; BGH, decision of 7 November 2006, WuW/E DE-R 2029, iesy/Ish). Third-party appeals against clearance decisions have been an area of specific interest over the last years in Germany, and an increasing number of cases have reached the courts (in addition to the cases cited above, *see* for example OLG Düsseldorf, decision of 6 September 2006, WuW/E DE-R 1835, Deutsche Börse/London Stock Exchange; OLG Düsseldorf, decision of 25 October 2005, WuW/E DE-R 1644, Werhahn; BGH, decision of 28 June 2005, WuW/E DE-R 1571, Ampere; BGH, decision of 22 February 2005, WuW/E DE-R 1544, Zeiss/Leica; OLG Düsseldorf, decision of 19 September 2001, WuW/E DE-R 759, NetCologne; Kammergericht, decision of 5 April 2000, WuW/E DE-R 641, tobaccoland).

Instead of, or in addition to, appealing to the courts the parties may apply to the Federal Minister of Economics to clear a transaction which was prohibited by the BKartA. The Federal Minister of Economics may in his decision take into account aspects of the economy as a whole which the BKartA is not allowed to do. However, this is a remedy of last resort.

11.4.12 *Sanctions*

Under German law it is unnecessary to enter into binding contracts in order to be able to file a notification, and there is no obligation to file within a certain period once binding contracts have been entered into. The "sanction" in such a case is simply that the transaction cannot be completed.

Completing a transaction prior to having obtained the required clearance is an administrative offence subject to fines of up to €1 million. If undertakings or associations of undertakings are fined, the administrative fine may, in addition to this amount, be up to 10 per cent of the total revenue of such undertaking or association of undertakings in the preceding business year.

Failure to file a required notification is also an administrative offence subject to fines of up to €100,000. Other offences include the making of false or incomplete statements.

11.4.13   *Informal contacts/confidentiality*

The BKartA is open to being approached informally on a confidential basis. This is unnecessary in standard cases but may be useful where the parties anticipate problems. Understandably, at these informal meetings the BKartA will not give more than a tentative indication of what its position might be.

Once a filing has been made, the investigations of the BKartA may result in third parties obtaining knowledge of the transaction.

11.5   Regulation of the conduct of mergers and acquisitions

11.5.1   *The Takeover Act*

The German Takeover Act applies to public bids targeted at a company in the legal form of a stock corporation ("AG") or *Societas Europaea* ("SE"), or a partnership limited by shares ("KGaA"), having its registered seat in Germany, or a company having its registered office in another Member State of the EEA; in each case provided that the shares of the target company are admitted for trading on a domestic Stock Exchange, or on an organised market in any other Member State of the EEA. With regard to takeover bids targeted at German companies that are not listed in Germany, the Takeover Act applies to takeover bids and mandatory offers to the extent only that it regulates the control, the obligation to make an offer, the information provided to the employees, the actions of a target company's board of management that might prevent the success of an offer, or other issues governed by corporate law.

The Takeover Act regulates "takeover bids" (bids aimed at acquiring control of the target) and all other public bids where the bidder intends to acquire only part of the shares (thereby not acquiring control), or where the bidder intends to enhance an existing controlling position.

Basic principles relating to public bids as laid out in the Takeover Act are the following:

(a)　the bidder shall treat equally all holders of securities of the target company belonging to the same class;

(b)　holders of securities of the target company shall have sufficient time and information to be able to decide on the offer on the basis of full knowledge of all relevant facts;

(c)　the management board and the supervisory board of the target company shall act in the best interests of the target company;

(d)   the bidder and the target company shall carry through the procedure in a timely manner and the target company must not be impeded in its business operations beyond a reasonable period of time;

(e)   no distortions of the relevant market shall be caused regarding the trade in securities of the target company, an offering company or another company affected by the offer.

11.5.2   *The Securities Trading Act*

The German Securities Trading Act (*Gesetz über den Wertpapierhandel*) came into force in 1994 and has been amended several times since then.

The BaFin issues non-authoritative interpretations of the Securities Trading Act (Issuer Guideline of July 2005 – "*Emittentenleitfaden*") in an attempt to set uniform standards. The Issuer Guideline is available both in German and English on the web page of the BaFin (www.bafin.de).

Section 21 of the Securities Trading Act provides that whoever reaches, exceeds or falls below the thresholds of 3, 5, 10, 15, 20, 25, 30, 50, or 75 per cent of the voting rights of a company for which Germany is the home country must report this fact forthwith (but in any event within four trading days) both to the corporation concerned and the BaFin. The company is then obligated to publish such notice without delay, at the latest within three trading days. In addition, the company has to notify the electronic company register. A company for which Germany is the home country in this context means any corporation whose shares are admitted to trading on an organised market in a Member State of the EU or EEA which has its domicile either in Germany or in a country which is neither a Member State of the EU or EEA provided that the company has to lodge its annual information with the BaFin.

To avoid circumventions, pursuant to Section 22 of the Securities Trading Act, for the calculation of the thresholds, the following voting rights from shares shall be equivalent to the voting rights of the party obligated to report:

(a)   voting rights of a subsidiary of the party obligated to report;

(b)   voting rights of a third party which are held for the account of the party obligated to report;

(c)   voting rights assigned by the party which is obligated to report to a third party as security, unless such third party is entitled to exercise the voting rights attached to the shares and declares its intention to do so independently of the notifying party's instructions;

(d)   voting rights in which a usufruct has been created in favour of the party required to report;

(e)   voting rights which the party which is obligated to report can acquire by exercising an option;

(f)   voting rights placed in custody with the party required to notify or shares whose voting rights can be exercised by such party as a proxy, in each case which have been entrusted for safekeeping to the party which is obligated to report provided that such party can exercise voting rights arising from such shares at its own discretion in the absence of specific instructions from the shareholders; and

(g)   shares belonging to a third party with whom the party which is obligated to report or an enterprise controlled by it coordinates its behaviour in respect of the listed company on the basis of an agreement or by any other means (except for agreements on the exercise of voting rights in individual cases).

Not added are voting rights held in the trading book that do not exceed 5 per cent and the company ensures that such voting rights are not exercised nor otherwise used to intervene in the management of the issuer.

Notification requirements with respect to 5, 10, 15, 20, 25, 30, 50 and 75 per cent thresholds also apply to persons who hold financial instruments that result in an entitlement to acquire, on such holder's own initiative alone, under a formal agreement, shares to which voting rights are attached, already issued, of an issuer whose shares are admitted to trading on a regulated market. The notification must also contain the name of the third party from which the voting shares may be acquired.

The issuer is required to disclose to the public the total number of voting rights and capital at the end of each calendar month during which an increase or decrease of such total number has occurred. In addition, after publication, the issuer is obliged to report this information to the electronic company register.

Failure to report, reporting inaccurately, incompletely, not in the required form or not in time is punishable as an administrative offence by fines (Section 39 of the Securities Trading Act). In addition, any rights resulting from such shares are, generally speaking, lost for the time during which the notification has not been made in violation of the aforementioned rules (Section 28 of the Securities Trading Act). The purpose of the provisions is to create more transparency in the securities market, and to prevent so-called "creeping in" (i.e., an acquisition of shares without the market being informed thereof).

In addition, the Securities Trading Act also addresses the target company itself. Pursuant to Section 15 of the Securities Trading Act it shall promptly publish all insider information ("ad hoc disclosure"). Also, after the publication, the company has to notify the company register about the insider information. "Insider information" is defined as any information of concrete nature which is not publicly available and which relates to the issuer or insider securities; further, in the view of a prudent investor, such information must be capable of having a significant impact on the market price of the respective security. Information is deemed to have significant effect on the price of securities in the event a prudent investor would take the information into account in making his investment decision. As a consequence of this definition, future developments (such as the intention to launch a takeover) may qualify as insider information if sufficiently likely to occur.

An issuer may – under its own responsibility – delay the ad hoc disclosure of insider information as long as:

(a)   its legitimate interests require so;
(b)   the delay is not likely to mislead the public; and
(c)   the issuer is able to ensure the confidentiality of the insider information.

However, the issuer has to accomplish the disclosure as soon as the above-mentioned prerequisites do not apply any more. Moreover, the issuer is obliged to notify the BaFin of the reasons for its decision to delay the immediate publication of the relevant insider information, and the point in time when the decision was made. If, for example, an issuer is awaiting the supervisory board's consent to a transaction, or is conducting negotiations on a corporate transaction, it may (as long as confidentiality is secured and the public is not being misled) be entitled to delay ad hoc disclosure as in such events an early disclosure could lead to negative consequences on the success of corporate developments.

It is important to note that:

(a) a decision needs to be made by the issuer not to publish at the time when the information first becomes notifiable;

(b) the exemption only applies for as long as confidentiality remains secured (i.e., a leak must promptly be followed by disclosure); and

(c) although the prevailing view of practitioners seems to be that the issuer will not have to guarantee confidentiality (which is practically impossible), it could be that accusations are raised of not having taken adequate measures to procure confidentiality, with potential liability risks.

Failure to comply with the obligation under Section 15 of the Securities Trading Act is punishable as an administrative offence. Intentional misrepresentations in ad hoc announcements may lead to personal liability of management board members vis-à-vis individual investors. Damaged investors are not only entitled to compensation in cash, but also to full restitution of purchase price against transfer of purchased shares.

11.6 Methods of acquisition under the Takeover Act

In the case of a takeover bid, the offeror seeks to acquire control of the target corporation, i.e., 30 per cent of the voting rights of the target company.

Given the relatively low number of shareholders present at shareholders meetings, a simple majority of votes at that meeting requires less than 50 per cent of all votes. The more critical threshold is not, however, 50 per cent of the votes but 75 per cent of the capital of a company represented at shareholders meetings. For instance, the conclusion of a domination and profit and/or loss pooling agreement and also decisions as to change of legal form and mergers require, generally speaking, a majority of 75 per cent of the capital which is represented at the vote. The number of shareholders present at the shareholders meeting determines how many shares are needed to acquire a 75 per cent majority of the capital present at the respective meetings; it could be less than 50 per cent.

The next critical threshold that in many instances an offeror wants to get over is the 95 per cent of share capital. This is needed in order to squeeze out minority shareholders or to integrate a company.

In lieu of acquiring shares it is sometimes also an option to acquire assets of a listed company, for instance one of its subsidiaries. Such an acquisition might be prepared by a hive down of assets into a newly formed subsidiary. Depending on the method by which this hive down is made and the value of the assets which are involved, it requires the approval of the shareholders of such company, typically with a majority of 75 per cent of the share capital present at the vote.

11.7   Preparation of an offer

11.7.1   Due diligence

Before giving any non-public information to a (prospective) offeror, the target company will generally insist on a strict confidentiality agreement, as otherwise the target's directors may be in breach of statutory fiduciary duties. Pre-takeover due diligence in Germany is usually limited in scope. In the case of a hostile offer, the due diligence exercise will be limited to a review of publicly available information. In the case of a friendly bid, the due diligence may be more extensive, although the target board will have to decide carefully how much information it is appropriate to disclose, taking into account its fiduciary duties. With regard to specific insider dealing problems in this regard, *see* 11.12.1 below. German law is silent as to whether information given to one offeror in a due diligence exercise must also be passed on to other (competing) offerors. Previously the majority opinion was that no such obligation existed, but this is now being disputed.

11.7.2   Standstill provisions

The target company may seek to include "standstill" provisions preventing the offeror from acquiring shares of the target for a specified period without the target's consent. While in principle this is permissible under German law, there may be problems if the standstill period is unduly long or if a payment is made to the potential offeror to enter into a standstill agreement. An acceptable period for a standstill agreement will vary from case to case, but it should not generally exceed the period during which the information provided is likely to cease being confidential and become public knowledge.

11.7.3   Stake building

An offeror may seek to enhance the chances of a successful offer by way of purchasing shares in the target company prior to the offer. This is allowed, provided that the disclosure obligations under the Securities Trading Act are complied with (*see* 11.5.2 above). Further, in an offer aiming at control of the target company (takeover bid) purchasing shares prior to an offer may influence the consideration payable as well as the price an offeror is obliged to pay in a takeover bid. If the bidder has acquired shares in the target company during a six-month period before launching the bid, the offer price must be at least equal to the highest price paid in such acquisition. For details, *see* 11.8.2 below.

11.7.4   Irrevocable undertakings

An offeror may further seek acceptance undertakings from target shareholders before making the offer. A shareholder who enters into such an undertaking but nevertheless accepts a competing offer would be liable to a damages claim from the offeror, unless the parties have agreed on a withdrawal right. If such an undertaking is entered into, this must be disclosed in the offer document. Such undertakings may, if expressly agreed between the parties, cease to apply in the event of a higher offer. Practice on this point is not yet established.

11.8 Conduct of a public offer

11.8.1 Timeline

Any "decision to make a public offer" must be published promptly. In advance of the publication, the bidder must notify the Stock Exchanges on which the securities of the bidder, the target company and other affected companies are listed or traded. Further, the bidder must notify the BaFin. The decision to launch a public bid must be published in German, either on the internet or via an electronic system widely accepted by certain financial institutions and financial services institutions which are, in particular, admitted to trading on one of the German Stock Exchanges. Directly after the publication of the decision to make a public offer, the bidder must inform the management board of the target company which in turn has to inform the target company's work council or its employees (in case no works council exists). Further, the bidder must inform its own works council or its employees (in case no works council exists).

Within four weeks after publication of the decision to launch a bid (or after the acquisition of "control" in the event of a mandatory offer (*see* below)), the bidder must file the offer document with the BaFin. Upon application by the bidder, this period may be extended by the BaFin up to an additional four weeks.

The offer document must be in German and has to contain all information which is necessary to enable the shareholders of the target company to make an informed decision whether to accept the bid or not. The content of the offer document is described in detail in the Takeover Act and a corresponding statutory ordinance (*WpÜG-Angebotsverordnung*). For details, *see* 11.10 below.

The Takeover Act imposes liability on the issuers of an offer document, and on those persons who assume responsibility for the offer document, for wrong, misleading, or incomplete statements made in the offer document which are material to evaluate the bid. If the defendant can prove that those who accepted the offer knew that the issued statements were wrong, misleading or incomplete, he can avoid liability.

The offer must be accompanied by the written confirmation of an independent financial institution that financing is secured. Should the bidder not be able to pay, the financial institution will be directly liable to the investors.

The acceptance period (offer period) can be not less than four weeks and generally not more than 10 weeks. The bidder has to publish the acceptance level on a weekly and, within the last week of the acceptance period, on a daily basis. The offer results must be published immediately after the end of the offer period.

In the event of a competing offer, shareholders who have already tendered their shares may rescind their acceptances so that they can accept the competing offer.

11.8.2   Takeover bid

The above rules apply to all offers including "takeover bids" (i.e., bids aimed at gaining control). Control in this context is defined as holding at least 30 per cent of the voting rights in the target company. For a calculation of the 30 per cent threshold, own voting rights and those voting rights which are attributed to the offeror according to the Takeover Act are relevant. For example, voting rights arising from shares owned by a subsidiary of the offeror, or by a third party for the account of the offeror, or which were assigned as security by the offeror to a third party, or in respect of which a usufruct has been created in favour of the offeror, or which the offeror may acquire by exercising options rights, are attributed to the offeror. Also, voting rights which have been entrusted to the offeror or which he may exercise by means of proxy voting are attributed to the offeror, provided that the offeror may exercise the voting rights attached to the shares at his own discretion in the absence of specific instructions of the shareholder. In addition, voting rights owned by third parties that are acting in concert with the offeror are taken into account when calculation the proportion of voting rights. Parties that intentionally coordinate their conduct in regard to the target company on the basis of an agreement or in any other manner may be deemed to act in concert.

In addition to the rules for all offers, the following rules specifically address takeover bids:

(a) takeover bids must be for all shares in the target; partial offers are not permitted;

(b) in the event of a takeover bid, the consideration has to be in cash or in "liquid stock" which is admitted to trading within a regulated market within the EEA. In principle, the bidder is free to choose whether it will offer cash or shares. However, the bidder is obliged to make a cash offer if, within the six months before the publication of the decision to launch a takeover bid until the end of the offer period, the bidder, persons acting in concert with him, or subsidiaries of the latter have purchased in return for a cash payment at least 5 per cent in aggregate of the shares or voting rights in the target company.

The consideration in a takeover bid has to be "adequate" on the basis of the average Stock Exchange price of the shares in the target, and stock purchases (if any) made by the bidder. The consideration for shares in a target, which are admitted to a domestic organised market, must be at least equal to the average weighted Stock Exchange price during the three-month period preceding the publication of the intention to launch a takeover bid. If the shares are admitted only to an organised market in another Member State of the EEA, the consideration must be at least equal to the average Stock Exchange price during the three-month period. If the bidder has acquired shares in the target company during the six-month period before launching the bid, the offer price must be at least equal to the highest price paid in such acquisition.

The bidder is under an obligation to increase the offer price if he acquires shares in the target company during the offer period and pays or agrees to pay a higher consideration than the one offered in the takeover offer. The same applies if shares are acquired at a higher price outside of an organised Stock Exchange during the first year after the end of the offer period.

After the end of the offer period in a takeover bid, the shareholders can still accept the offer within two weeks after the publication of the (successful) offer results ("grace period").

11.8.3 Mandatory offer

A shareholder must publish the fact that it has acquired control of the target (again, 30 per cent of the voting rights). Such publication must be made without delay and in any event no later than seven calendar days after the shareholder knew or should have known about the acquisition of a controlling interest. Additionally, within four weeks after such publication, the controlling shareholder is required to make a mandatory offer to the outstanding shareholders. The consideration to be offered in a mandatory offer generally equals the consideration payable in a takeover bid.

Under limited circumstances, exemptions from the obligation to make a mandatory offer may be granted by the BaFin.

If a bidder acquires control over a target company which itself controls a subsidiary, the bidder thereby also acquires indirect control over the subsidiary as the voting rights from the shares the target holds in its subsidiary are attributed to the bidder. Therefore, the bidder is, in principle, obliged to make a mandatory offer for all the shares in the subsidiary as well (provided that its shares are admitted to trading on an organised market). An exemption by the BaFin may be granted if the book value of the shareholdings in the subsidiary does not exceed 20 per cent of the book value of the assets of the target company.

11.8.4 Conditions

Only a voluntary offer can be made subject to a condition that it will lapse unless the offeror receives a certain level of acceptances. Acceptance level conditions are normally set at 50 or 75 per cent of the voting rights of the target.

11.8.5 Partial offers

As laid out above, partial offers are only permitted for offers which do not aim at gaining control. In the event of a partial offer, if more shares have been tendered than the bidder has promised to acquire, all acceptances will have to be on a pro-rata basis.

11.9 Defences to a hostile offer

11.9.1 Pre-bid defence tactics

As mentioned above, there have been few hostile takeover attempts in Germany, so consequently there is little practical experience of how to defend against such attempts. The various methods used, particularly in the US, have been much discussed by German legal writers but most of the methods are not available in takeover scenarios.

(a)　　Poison pills: these are illegal under German stock corporation law. As their characteristic feature involves the issuance of shares or other equity rights, contingent upon change of control over the company, to only some of the shareholders, they violate German stock corporation law.

(b)　　Restricted registered shares (*Vinkulierte Namensaktien*): the articles of association of a corporation can provide for registered shares (*Namensaktien*) the transfer of which requires the approval of the corporation (*vinkulierte Namensaktien*). The approval is granted by the management board unless the articles provide that the supervisory board or the shareholders meeting is to decide. If the original articles of the corporation do not already provide for restricted registered shares, it will be virtually impossible to create them at a later point in time because such a change requires the consent of each single shareholder affected. Moreover, restricted registered shares may be admitted to the official market (*Amtlicher Markt*) of a Stock Exchange only if their free negotiability is ensured by appropriate precautions. Accordingly, restricted registered shares are, with the exception of insurance companies, rarely seen in large public corporations.

(c)　　Limitation of voting rights (*Höchststimmrechte*) and multiple voting rights (*Mehrstimmrechte*): limitations to voting rights attributed to the shares of a single shareholder, regardless of the size of the interest held (*Höchststimmrechte*), may be imposed in the articles of non-listed companies only. For listed companies, since 1 June 2003 the creation of multiple voting rights has no longer been permissible. Existing multiple voting rights terminated on that date, unless the shareholders meeting had resolved with a 75 per cent majority that they be continued.

(d)　　Appointment rights and staggered supervisory board: the articles of association can provide that individual shareholders have the right to designate one or more members of the supervisory board. The number of designation rights is limited to one-third of the board members appointed by the shareholders. The term of office of the entire shareholders bench of the supervisory board is usually identical. All members are elected at the same time for the maximum statutory term (i.e., for about five years). It is legally possible, however, to provide for staggered terms for the shareholder board members. For example, with respect to a supervisory board having 20 members 10 of whom would be elected by the shareholders meeting, the articles of association could provide that at each annual shareholders meeting two members of the supervisory board are elected. Under these circumstances, an acquirer would be in the position to take control of the company only after a period of four to five years unless the majority necessary for the removal of members of the supervisory board (normally 75 per cent of the votes cast in the shareholders meeting) has been obtained.

It should be noted that staggered terms for shareholder members of the supervisory board are not very common in Germany. The employee members of the supervisory board would have the advantage of continuity because they are all elected at the same time for about five years. In addition, most companies want to avoid a discussion about the election of members of the supervisory board at each annual shareholders meeting.

11.9.2   Post-bid defensive tactics

Once the decision to launch a public bid has been published by the bidder, the Takeover Act does not, in principle, allow frustrating measures (i.e., measures which are capable of preventing the success of the takeover bid) to be taken by the management board of the target. However, this is subject to the following exceptions:

(a) measures which a prudent and conscientious manager of a company not affected by a takeover bid would have taken. This allows for carrying on with the day-to-day management of the business, as well as for exceptional transactions which could have been implemented in the absence of a bid;

(b) endeavours to find a competing offer (search for a white knight);

(c) measures which have been approved by the supervisory board of the target company;

(d) specific measures, which are approved by the shareholders meeting up to 18 months before a certain measure is taken, with at least a 75 per cent vote of the capital present. The measures must be approved for the purpose of frustrating a potential bid. Once a takeover bid has been launched, such measures require the approval of the supervisory board.

However, the articles of the target company may provide that the afore-mentioned rules do not apply and the target company instead opts in to the more restrictive rules set forth in the EC directive (Section 33a of the Takeover Act). Under this so-called "European Restriction on Frustrating Action", the manage-ment and the supervisory board of the target company are not allowed to conduct defensive measures, except for:

(a) actions to which the management and the supervisory board have been authorised by the shareholders meeting after the publication of the decision to make an offer;

(b) actions taken in the ordinary course of business;

(c) actions taken outside the ordinary course of business, to the extent that they serve the realisation of decisions that were made and partially realised prior to the decision to make an offer; and

(d) endeavours to find a competing offer (search for a white knight).

In addition, the articles of the target company may provide that it opts in to the following "European Breakthrough Rule" after the offer document has been published (Section 33b of the Takeover Act):

(a) during the offer period share transfer restrictions set forth in the articles or in contractual agreements between the target company and its share-holders or between shareholders shall not apply with regard to the bidder;

(b) during the offer period voting rights restrictions set forth in contractual agreements as well as multiple voting rights shall have no effect in the shareholders meeting that decides on defensive measures; and

(c)   voting rights restrictions set forth in contractual agreements, multiple voting rights and designation rights shall have no effect in the first shareholders meeting called by the bidder to amend the articles or remove or appoint members of the management board or the supervisory board, provided the bidder holds at least 75 per cent of the voting rights following the bid.

If shareholder rights are cancelled on the basis of the aforementioned European breakthrough rule, the bidder is obliged to pay an adequate compensation provided that the rights were established prior to the publication of the decision to launch a public bid and are known to the target company.

The shareholders meeting of a target company that has opted in to the European restriction on frustrating action and/or the European breakthrough rule may resolve that such European rules shall not apply and instead apply the statutory German rules pursuant to Section 33 of the Takeover Act if the bidder is not subject to equivalent provisions ("European Reciprocity Rule"). Such resolution expires 18 months after the date of the resolution.

The management board of the target company must promptly inform the BaFin and the supervisory authorities in any Member State of the EEA in which the target company's shares are admitted to trading on a regulated market that its articles provide for the application of the aforementioned European rules. The same applies if the target company's shareholders meeting resolves on the European reciprocity rule.

The most discussed tools to be used to implement a defence strategy after the decision to launch a bid has been made public are the following:

(a)   Disposal of crown jewels: the sale of important assets ("crown jewels") is typically no valid defence. In principle, the sale falls within the authority of the management board. However, due to several legal restrictions such measures do not work as a means of defence against a takeover. As mentioned above, transaction and restructuring measures of the target corporation which might result in the frustration of a takeover bid are prohibited under the Takeover Act except if the prohibition has been suspended (e.g., approval of the supervisory board). Even if this is the case, the management board must act in the best interests of the corporation. Only in exceptional circumstances will a sale of important business assets, or the implementation of break clauses, in each case motivated by the desire to avoid a change of control, be justifiable under such test. The management board faces the risk of personal liability for damages suffered by the corporation if its actions are found not to be in the corporation's best interests. In addition, the management board may be required to obtain prior approval of the shareholders meeting when major portions of the business or an entire division are being spun off.

(b)   Use of authorised capital (*Genehmigtes Kapital*): an increase in the share capital and the issuance of new shares to all shareholders or to a (friendly) third party may prevent an unfriendly acquirer from achieving the desired majority. Typically, however, this measure cannot be used as a valid defence. A regular capital increase is not feasible in a takeover situation.

Although the notice period to call a shareholders meeting may be reduced to two weeks in a takeover situation, the wide range of other formalities to be observed may make it impossible to act with the flexibility necessary in such situation. An alternative could be the more flexible so-called authorised capital. The management board can be authorised by the shareholders meeting for a maximum of five years to increase the capital up to a certain amount which may not exceed 50 per cent of the issued share capital. However, the Stock Corporation Act affords each shareholder the right to subscribe to such newly issued shares in proportion to its holding at the time of issuance of the new shares. This subscription right exists both for a regular capital increase and with respect to authorised capital. Therefore, authorised capital may serve as a real means of defence only if the new shares can be issued without such subscription rights for the present shareholders. The exclusion of these rights requires a shareholders' resolution. Such shareholders' resolution may either directly restrict the subscription rights or expressly delegate the power to do so on the management board when the new shares are issued. In either case, the restriction of subscription rights requires a number of conditions:

(i) the resolution of the shareholders meeting must be taken with a qualified majority of at least 75 per cent of the share capital represented at the vote;

(ii) a written report on the reasons for the restriction of the subscription rights must be submitted by the management board describing in general terms the purpose for which the management board is authorised to issue new shares;

(iii) the restriction of the subscription right must be in the best interest of the company. It is highly disputed to what extent a defence against a hostile takeover meets this requirement. Arguably this is the case if the objective of the bidder is the elimination of the company as a competitor or the liquidation of the target. Under the statute, the restriction is also deemed to be permissible if the amount of the increase is limited to 10 per cent of the share capital and if the issue price is close to the then applicable price payable at the Stock Exchange. In all other cases – that is if the 10 per cent threshold is exceeded – the objective of the authorised capital must be described precisely at least in an abstract form in the authorising shareholders' resolution.

Within the limits of Section 33 paragraph 1 of the Takeover Act (e.g., approval of the supervisory board) or – as the case may be – the European Restriction on Frustrating Action, the use of authorised capital could serve as a defensive measure for the target company's management.

(c) Acquisition of own shares: purchasing own shares by the target may increase the voting power of friendly shareholders and reduce the number of shares available for purchase by the potential acquirer. However, at the same time any existing shareholdings of the hostile bidder will be increased in their voting power as the shares repurchased are not vested with voting rights.

A stock corporation may acquire its own shares only under specific circumstances. The following authorisations under the Stock Corporation Act are discussed in this context:

(i) a purchase of own shares is possible if the acquisition is necessary in order to avert severe and imminent damage to the company. It is quite settled that this exception cannot be invoked to ward off an unwelcome acquirer. Some legal writers nevertheless suggest applying this exception in "extreme cases" of hostile offers, such as situations where the only objective of the acquirer is the liquidation of the target company, or the elimination of the target company as a competitor. However, it appears defensible to use this exception in this situation;

(ii) the shareholders meeting may have authorised the management board to acquire up to 10 per cent of the company's shares. The authorisation can be given for a period of up to 18 months and must specify the minimum and maximum price for the acquisition. When acquiring the shares, the management board must, however, observe the principle of equal treatment of the shareholders.

     Similar to the authorised capital, the acquisition or disposal of own shares in a takeover situation is only permitted within the limits of the Takeover Act (e.g., after approval of the supervisory board). However, even if this requirement is met, the acquisition and disposal of own shares provides only limited possibilities for a defence due to the 10 per cent threshold mentioned above. However, in combination with a capital increase from authorised capital, the target management may use this to successfully defend a hostile bid.

(d) Search for a competing bidder ("white knight"): the management of the target company may attempt to find a friendly purchaser. This is permitted under the Takeover Act as long as the management of the target company is not promised any monetary or other financial advantages to be paid out of the assets of the target company.

(e) "Winning the argument": Ultimately, the best defence may be to try to persuade the shareholders of the target corporation that the offer is not attractive and that the shareholders are better advised not to accept it. This defence will mostly depend on winning a battle of words and advertisement against the bidder. Vodafone and Mannesmann had engaged in large-scale investor relations and press battles in the hostile phase of the bid. The same was the case in the Barrilla/Kamps situation in the early hostile phase. In general, public campaigning is not prohibited in a takeover scenario as German law allows management to spend appropriate sums on communications and external advisers. However, the Takeover Act authorises the BaFin to issue cease and desist orders to prevent irregularities relating to advertisements or certain methods of advertisements.

11.10   Documents from the offeror and offeree board

The offer document to be published by the offeror must contain all information necessary to allow a reasonably informed decision to be made about the offer. It must be in German.

The offer document must include, *inter alia*:

(a)   details of the offer, such as the identity of the offeror and the target, the class of target securities which are the subject of the offer, the acceptance period and any conditions on which the effectiveness of the offer is dependent;

(b)   the consideration offered for the securities, the method of its determination, an explanation of why such consideration is adequate, and the consideration offered for the cancellation of certain shareholder rights during the offer period;

(c)   where offeror securities are being offered as consideration, all of the basic information required for an offer prospectus (unless such a prospectus/listing particulars has been published by the offeror within the 12 months preceding the bid, and such document is still freely available);

(d)   the financing of the bid, a description of the measures taken to ensure that the offeror has sufficient financing available and confirmation by an investment service provider that any cash consideration will be at the offeror's disposal when it is due as well as the expected consequences of a successful takeover on the financial condition and the results of operations of the bidder;

(e)   the plans of the offeror as to the future business of the target and – if affected by the bid – the bidder, including the expected impact on target employees and their representative bodies (e.g., plans for dismissals, transfer of the target's domicile or closing down of branches);

(f)   information on payments and other benefits granted or promised to members of the management board or supervisory board of the target;

(g)   information about regulatory clearance proceedings (in particular, merger clearances) required for the acquisition of securities in the target;

(h)   the number and amount of voting rights in the target already held by the offeror and its strategic affiliates (e.g., subsidiaries, entities with which the offeror has concluded a shareholders agreement, etc.) and information on previous acquisitions within the last three months prior to the publication of the decision to make an offer.

If shares are offered as consideration, there will be additional requirements as a prospectus needs to be published for the offering in line with EC Regulation 809/2004 and the corresponding domestic ordinance (*Angebotsverordnung*).

The managing board (*Vorstand*) of the target company has to pass on the offer document without delay to the competent works council (*Betriebsrat*) or, in case a works council does not exist, directly to the employees. The bidder must provide the offer document to its own works council or its employees (in case no works council exists). Further, the managing board and the supervisory board of the target company have to issue a statement evaluating the bid as soon as possible after publication of an offer. The statement shall consider in particular the consideration offered by the bidder, the impact of the bid on the interests of the company, including its employees and their representative bodies, and the aims of the bidder. Furthermore, both boards have to indicate whether any of their members intends to accept the bid.

11.11 Mandatory acquisition of minority shareholdings (squeeze-out)

Upon request of a majority shareholder holding at least 95 per cent of the share capital of a stock corporation, the shareholders meeting may resolve upon the transfer of all shares held by the minority shareholders to the majority shareholder (squeeze-out). Such squeeze-out is to be made against "adequate compensation in cash" (*angemessene Barabfindung*). Every minority shareholder who is subject to the squeeze-out may challenge the cash compensation in a special proceeding in court.

The majority shareholder is required to present a written report ("the Squeeze-out Report") to the shareholders meeting explaining the requirements for the squeeze-out and also the adequacy of the cash compensation. The cash compensation offered is to be audited by an expert auditor.

As the squeeze-out will be resolved upon in the shareholders meeting, it will become a topic on the agenda when the shareholders meeting is called. As from the day of calling the shareholders meeting, the following documents must be provided at the offices of the company for inspection by interested shareholders:

(a) draft of the shareholder resolution;
(b) annual accounts and business reports for the last three business years;
(c) the squeeze-out report; and
(d) the report of the expert auditor.

During the shareholders meeting, the management board of the company may give the majority shareholder the opportunity to explain the squeeze-out and the appropriateness of the cash compensation. The squeeze-out has to be filed with the commercial register and ownership in the minority shares will be transferred to the majority shareholder with effect as of the registration with the commercial register only.

To fulfil its obligation of the European Takeover Directive, the German legislator has also introduced a takeover squeeze-out and sell-out into the German Takeover Act. This new takeover squeeze-out represents an alternative to the traditional corporate squeeze-out described above and enables the offeror to require the minority shareholders to sell him all remaining securities if he has acquired at least 95 per cent of the share capital of the target company without a shareholders' resolution. Instead, following a takeover offer (including a mandatory offer), the bidder has to file an application with the District Court (*Landgericht*) Frankfurt am Main for the squeeze-out of minority shareholders (Sections 39a and 39b of the Takeover Act). The application must be filed within three months after the expiration of the offer period. If the consideration offered is adequate, the District Court must approve the squeeze-out and the minority voting shares transfer automatically to the bidder. Such court decision takes effect for and against all shareholders. The consideration offered is deemed to be adequate if it is the same as the consideration offered in the takeover bid and at least 90 per cent of the outstanding shares were tendered to the bidder. Potentially complex valuation issues can therefore be avoided if these two requirements are met. In the event of a share-for-share exchange offer, a cash consideration must always be offered as an alternative. Whether the offered consideration is adequate forms part of the ordinary proceeding before the District Court. The minority shareholders may also appeal against the decision of the District Court to the Court of Appeals (*Oberlandesgericht*) Frankfurt am Main. Such appeal suspends the effectiveness of the squeeze-out until the decision has been rendered.

Even if the bidder does not make use of his right to apply for a squeeze-out, shareholders who have not accepted the takeover offer during the offer period may accept the takeover offer within three months after the end of the offer period (sell-out right as defined in Section 39c of the Takeover Act).

11.12 Insider dealing and market manipulation

11.12.1 Insider dealing

Under the Securities Trading Act, any person is prohibited from:

(a) acquiring or disposing of (be it for its own account or for the account of a third party or on behalf of a third party) securities (insider securities) by using insider information;

(b) disclosing insider information to another person or making such information available to another person without justified reason; and

(c) recommending to, or otherwise inducing, a person to acquire or dispose of insider securities on the basis of insider information.

Until October 2004, a violation of the prohibition from insider dealing required that an insider exploited its knowledge of insider information for the acquisition or disposal of insider securities. The revised Securities Trading Act has replaced this subjective requirement by the more objective test of "using" insider information by acquiring or disposing of insider securities. A violation now also exists in case the acting person had motives other than taking economic advantage of the insider information. However, the "usage" of insider information still requires that relevant action was somehow influenced by the knowledge of insider information. This suggests that a violation of the insider trading rules does not exist when the respective action would have taken place in any event had the acting person not had insider information (e.g., when the acquisition or disposal of insider securities is carried out in performance of an obligation which has been created prior to the acting person having obtained knowledge of the relevant insider information). The BaFin has confirmed this view in its Issuer Guidelines for due diligences in the context of public M&A transactions in Germany: In the case of stakes acquired outside the Stock Exchange, where both the acquirer and the seller of the stake have identical information, the prohibition of insider trading is not infringed provided that the acquirer purchases the stake as planned prior to the due diligence process, even though inside information obtained in the course of the due diligence may be used. However, any alongside purchases, in addition to the stake originally planned, constitute a punishable use of insider information. Also, the prohibition of the use of insider information is generally applicable to takeover of companies or the acquisition of a controlling stake. The BaFin stresses that Consideration 29 to the EC Market Abuse Directive, according to which the use of insider information in the context of a public takeover offer should not be deemed in itself to constitute the use of insider information, does not represent an exemption. Target companies are authorised to disclose insider information to the bidder during the due diligence process. The bidder is also permitted to use such information to prepare his public offer. However, the submission of the public takeover offer in which the bidder uses insider information requires prior publication of an ad hoc disclosure. Companies considering a takeover should therefore always ensure comprehensive and detailed documentation, incorporating each step from the planning stage right through to implementing their corporate decision. The Securities Trading Act in connection with Regulation EC No. 2273/2003 provides for certain exceptions from the prohibition of insider dealing with regard to a stock corporations trading with their own shares within the scope of repurchase programmes as well as with regard to measures for the purpose of stabilising the price of financial instruments.

Further, in order to facilitate the monitoring of insider dealings, issuers have to maintain registers of those persons acting on their behalf (under a contract of employment or otherwise), who have access to insider information. This register must be updated immediately and submitted to the BaFin upon request. Moreover, investment firms, credit institutions and off-market operating companies are obliged to inform the BaFin of suspicious facts (blow the whistle).

Besides possible claims for damages against the insider, the violation of the prohibition of acquiring or disposing of insider securities is a criminal or administrative offence subject to fines or to imprisonment for up to five years. Under former law, a criminal offence always required intent of the acting person. Under the new regime, recklessness is also caught, with a somewhat reduced range of sanctions. The sanction is dependent on whether the offender acted as "primary or secondary" insider. A "primary insider" is a person having knowledge of insider information in its capacity as a member of the management board or supervisory board or as a general partner of the issuer or of a company affiliated with the issuer; due to its shareholdings in the capital of the issuer or a company affiliated with the issuer; as a result of its profession or its function or job or as a result of the preparation or commitment of a crime. The violation of the insider rules by a primary insider is regarded as criminal offence subject to imprisonment for up to five years or a fine. If the violation is committed by any other person ("secondary insider"), such violation is regarded as an administrative offence subject to an administrative fine of up to €200,000.

11.12.2 Market manipulation

The Securities Trading Act also contains a prohibition from making false or misleading statements about facts relevant for the evaluation of financial instruments, such as the earnings or sales generated by a listed company. Therefore, any issuer is also prohibited from making statements which are per se correct but which are – due to their presentation – likely to evoke a false impression of the respective issue. Unclear or ambivalent wordings in statements to the public which are capable of being misunderstood run the risk of being regarded as misleading and therefore have to be avoided. Important statements to the public should be made clearly and unambiguously.

In addition, the law contains a prohibition from carrying out transactions and from placing sale or purchase orders which might send false or misleading signals as to the supply of or the demand for financial instruments or as to the market or Stock Exchange price of such instruments or which might effect an artificial price level. However, this prohibition of misleading transactions and sale/purchase orders does not apply when the respective transaction or order conforms to the accepted market practice on the respective market and the acting person or entity has legitimate reasons for such a transaction or order. However, a practice is only deemed an accepted market practice when such practice is accepted by the BaFin and may reasonably be expected in the respective market. According to the legislative materials, legitimate reasons for a transaction will normally only be deemed not to exist when the acting person/entity has acted with fraudulent or manipulative intent.

In addition, the Securities Trading Act contains a prohibition of other acts of deception which may influence the Stock Exchange or market price of a Financial Instrument in Germany or its price on an organised market in another Member State of the EEA. Such act of deception does not have to be carried out with the intention of influencing the Stock Exchange or stock market price of the financial instrument. Rather, the ability of the act of deception to influence such price is sufficient.

In connection with Regulation No. 2273/2003 of the European Commission, the Securities Trading Act establishes a safe harbour for certain transactions, namely:

(a)   buy-back programmes; and
(b)   price stabilising measures of financial instruments.

11.13   Financial assistance

An offeror will often try to persuade the management of the target corporation to assist in the financing of the takeover. This is not permissible under German law. According to Section 71a of the Stock Corporation Act it is prohibited for a stock corporation to advance any funds, make any loans or to provide securities for the purpose of acquiring shares of such stock corporation.

Section 71a confirms the general principle laid down in Section 57 that the capital of the corporation may not be distributed to the shareholders, so that prior to the liquidation of the corporation (with the exception of repayments by way of a capital decrease and repayments of certain free reserves), the shareholders are only entitled to the profit shown in the corporation's balance sheet.

The assets of the target corporation can therefore only be used as collateral for any financing taken up by the offeror once the target corporation has been merged into the offeror or after it has been converted into another legal form to the extent that financial assistance is permitted for a company of this legal form. There are also restrictions, for instance, on companies with limited liabilities and for limited partnerships. However, these are not as strict as the restrictions on stock corporations.

Chapter 12

Greece

Katia Protopapa

Partner
T.J. Koutalidis

12.1 Introduction – acquisition targets

Having a long tradition in attracting foreign investments, a tradition that
stretches from the 18th century until today, the challenge for Greece in the post-
Olympics period was to create new investment incentives for foreign investors.
But this was not an easy challenge Having just completed a series of large
"concession projects" – one of the most favoured categories of foreign investments in Greece, all tailor-made for the needs of the Games or effectively
supporting the Games' successful organisation (e.g., Athens International
Airport, Athens Ring Road) – the odds for finding investment incentives after
the Games were not good.

The state, based on its years of experience in organising projects and requiring
resources from outside Greece, knows that one of the most significant risks that
an investor-friendly jurisdiction must tackle is the legal risk. Thus, acting as a
prudent full EU and EMU Member State, it saw that the "storm" of new EU
directives dealing with various financial markets and taxation issues was in due
time incorporated into Greek law. The long list of the new generation of EU
directives that preceded the enlargement and rendered almost useless any practitioner's knowledge about the previous legal framework, have now become
Greek law. Starting with the financial collateral, the prospectus, the market abuse
and transparency, and the take-over directives, and recently concluding with the
markets in financial instruments and the banking directives, Greece has kept
pace with all significant EU law developments, harmonising the respective
Greek law fields.

New tools for fund-raising were introduced into the Greek legal system. In June
2003, Law 3156/2003 was enacted which introduced the notion of private
securitisation of receivables and modernised the framework of issuance of bonds
by a Greek entity. This Law, by providing for tax reliefs and cost caps and limitations (e.g., notary fees, costs for registration with public registries) and by
deviating from rules of traditional legal notions, such as that of the assignment
of claims (e.g., announcement of the assignment of the claim, constituting the
subject matter of the securitisation, as of the registration of the assignment
agreement with a special registry – not as of the service thereof), set a safe legal
environment for the purposes of raising funds channelled to investments in
Greece. The result was that, as of the enactment of Law 3156/2003, almost any

and all investments made in Greece are brought into the safe environment of this Law.

Furthermore, the process was completed by modernising the Greek banking system. Greek banks, the traditional ally of foreign investors in Greece, now operate in a regulatory environment in line with the rules of the third-generation banking directives and the findings of Basel II. Also, in August 2007, a new framework has been introduced dealing with the issuance of covered bonds by Greek banks.

Another critical development in the field of finance was the legislation introducing into Greek Law the notion of Public Private Partnerships ("PPPs"). The new PPP Law aims to gradually minimise the State's participation in certain activities, maximise efficiency in the relevant sectors and enhance the country's economy in the post-Olympics era. It has to be noted that the concept of PPP is not altogether a *terra incognita* in Greece, as certain important projects, such as the Athens International Airport and the Rio-Antirrio Bridge, mentioned above, were fruits of partnerships between the state and private entities. Thus, the purpose of the PPP legislation is to extend this model, which has been proved to be successful, to smaller scale projects of value up to €200 million in a country where there is plenty of room for further infrastructure development.

During 2007, the legislation on the operation of Greek companies limited by shares was impressively modernised. New concepts at the level of equity financing, such as that of redeemable shares, have now been introduced, whilst legal issues – such as the Greek financial assistance rules – that were traditionally a "headache" for almost all investments through Greek vehicles have now been dealt with. Last but not least and always in the wider field of Greek company law, the Greek bankruptcy code was also reformed and modernised.

But legal certainty and new financing tools are not the only things needed. A safe and attractive tax framework has to be developed in order to persuade foreign investors.

The work of the state in this field also is considerable. Highlights undoubtedly include the reduction of the effective corporate tax rate at a competitive level (25 per cent); the application of a one-stop taxation system to the profits of corporations, distributed tax-free to the shareholders; the implementation of the dividend and interest directives for groups of companies; the exemption of tax residents and many others from Greek withholdings of interests payable under Greek bonds.

12.1.1　Types of business association

Greek law recognises the following basic partnership and corporate forms:

(a)　general partnership (*omorrythmi etairia*);
(b)　limited partnership (*eterorrythmi etairia*);
(c)　limited liability company (*etairia periorismenis efthynis*);
(d)　*société anonyme* or limited company by shares (*anonymos etairia*).

12.1.1.1 *General partnership*

General partnerships are governed by the provisions of the Greek Commercial Code, supplemented by the provisions of the Greek Civil Code.

A general partnership must be drawn up either by a private document or by a public deed which contains the statutes of the partnership. A ratified copy of the deed must be published in the Companies' Book of the First Instance Court of the area where the partnership has its registered office.

The partners in a general partnership may be either natural persons or legal entities. The partners' interest is not, in principle, transferable. Every partner is entitled to participate in the management of the partnership unless this authority has been delegated to one or more of the partners exclusively. Moreover, every partner is entitled to represent the partnership in dealing with third parties unless the articles provide that a particular partner or partners shall jointly represent the partnership. Such an exclusion or limitation of the power of individual representation must be published in the *Government Gazette*.

Greek law establishes the parallel liability of each of the partners for the obligations of the partnership – namely, all partners are simultaneously liable with their personal property, jointly and severally.

A partnership is dissolved if bankruptcy proceedings have been initiated against any partner, unless otherwise provided in the articles. Moreover, the death of any partner dissolves the partnership. It may, however, be agreed among the partners that the partnership will continue between the surviving partners or between them and the heirs of the deceased partner.

12.1.1.2 *Limited partnership*

A limited partnership is in essence a general partnership and thus it is subject to most of the same rules. The basic difference is that this form of partnership comprises two types of partners: at least one general partner who is individually without limitation liable for the partnership debts and obligations, and at least one limited partner whose liability is limited to the amount of their respective contribution. In order to avoid confusion and to protect third parties, the name of the limited partner does not appear in the name of the partnership.

12.1.1.3 *Limited liability (without shares) company*

The establishment and operation of a limited liability company is governed by Law 3190/55 as amended by Presidential Decree 419/86 (PD 419/86) which adapted national legislation with the first (68/151), the fourth (78/660) and partially the seventh (83/349) EEC Directives, PD 326/1994, PD 279/1993 and Laws 2065/1992, 2339/1995, 2579/1998, 2842/2000 and 2948/2001. This corporate form is quite common for smaller business and family enterprises. Similar to *sociétés anonymes*, the liability of each partner in a limited liability company is limited to the nominal value of his shareholding.

Establishment

The articles of association of a limited liability company must be signed before a notary public by one or more founders. A copy of the articles of association must be submitted within one month to the Court of First Instance of the place where the company has its registered office. Similarly to *sociétés anonymes*, an announcement of the establishment of the limited liability company together with details of its articles of association must be published in the "Bulletin of Sociétés Anonymes and Limited Liability Companies" of the *Government Gazette*.

Share capital

Pursuant to Law 2842/2000, as of 1 January 2002, the minimum company capital required for the establishment of a limited liability (without shares) company is €18,000, and the minimum nominal value of each part is set at €30 or multiples thereof. These parts are not negotiable instruments and can only be transferred by an act executed before a notary public.

Administration

By the articles of association or a decision of the meeting of partners, the administration of the company affairs and the representation of the company may be assigned to one or more partners or non-partners for a definite or indefinite period of time. The administrator(s) represents the company and carries out in its name every act relating to the scope of the company's business.

Meeting of the partners

The members' meeting is the "supreme body" of the company and is entitled to decide on any of the company's affairs. It is exclusively competent to decide on the following matters:

(a)   amendments to the articles of the company;
(b)   appointment of the administrators;
(c)   approval of the annual balance sheet;
(d)   initiation of an action against the administrators;
(e)   merger, prolongation or dissolution of the company; and
(f)   any other matter specified by law.

Meetings are ordinarily convened at least once a year and within three months from the end of the annual accounting period.

Resolutions are passed by a majority of more than one-half of the total number of members and a majority of more than one-half of the total capital. For some material decisions a greater majority or unanimity is required.

Taxation

The yearly net profits of a limited liability (without shares) company are subject to income tax at the following rates:

(a)   32 per cent for net profits in the financial year beginning after 1 January 2005;
(b)   29 per cent for net profits in the financial year beginning after 1 January 2006 and before 1 January 2007;
(c)   25 per cent for net profits in the financial year beginning after 1 January 2007.

The dividends paid by the limited liability (without shares) company to its shareholders or unit holders, respectively, are not subject to income tax since the relevant profits have been taxed in the name of the limited liability company.

12.1.1.4 *Société anonyme (limited liability company with shares)*

The establishment and operation of *sociétés anonymes* is governed by Law 2190/20, as recently amended by Law 3604/2007 and earlier by Law 3156/2003, PD 409/86, 419/86 and 498/87, which adapted Greek law to the Directives of the EEC Council on the harmonisation of national company law. The modification of Codified Law 2190/20 by Law 3604/2007 aims at:

(a)   the reduction of state interference in the establishment or operation of a *société anonyme* and simplification of the above procedures;
(b)   the reinforcement of the shareholders' and minority shareholders' position;
(c)   the increase of a *société anonyme's* flexibility and competitiveness through the inclusion of various provisions in the respective articles of association.

The basic characteristic of a *société anonyme* is that the liability of its shareholders is limited to the nominal value of the shares they hold.

Establishment

The articles of association of a *société anonyme* must be signed before a notary public by one or more founders. The establishment of a *société anonyme* with a share capital exceeding €3 million together with its articles must be approved by the competent administrative authority, namely by the Prefect of the area where the company has its registered office. The company becomes a legal entity upon registration in the relevant Limited Companies Register of the administrative decision for its establishment and the approval of its articles. The decision of the Prefect together with details of the articles must be published in the "Bulletin of Sociétés Anonymes and Limited Liability Companies" of the *Government Gazette*. For a *société anonyme* with a share capital not exceeding €3 million an approval by the competent administrative authority is not required. However, this does not apply in relation to companies with listed shares, banks, insurance companies and investment and mutual funds companies.

Share capital – shares

Pursuant to Law 2842/2000, as of 1 January 2002, the minimum share capital required for the establishment of a *société anonyme* is €60,000. However, due to the nature of their business, the minimum capital for certain corporations (i.e., banking institutions, insurance corporations, etc.), must exceed €60,000.

Within two months from the date of the company's establishment, the payment of the share capital must be certified by a resolution of the board of directors at a specially convened meeting.

The payment of the share capital may be in cash or in kind. In the latter case the value of the contributions in kind must be verified by an evaluation committee of the Ministry of Commerce or by independent chartered accountants.

The shares of a *société anonyme* may be either registered or bearer shares. In certain cases, issuing registered shares is compulsory by law. The shares of a *société anonyme* may be ordinary or preference. The right to issue preferred shares must be specified in the articles of association. The privileges of preference shares may consist of:

(a)   the right to collect partially or wholly the first dividend prior to the ordinary shares;

(b)   preferential payment prior to the ordinary shareholders' repayment of the capital, out of the liquidation proceeds of the corporation's assets, including preferential payment out of the capital paid above par value;

(c)   preferred payment of dividends for fiscal years with respect to which no dividends were distributed;

(d)   receipt of a permanent dividend or participation in part of the company's profits.

A *société anonyme* may not normally acquire its own shares either directly or by persons acting in their own name but on behalf of the company. Exceptionally, a *société anonyme* is permitted to acquire its own shares following approval of the General Meeting, which should provide the conditions of the acquisition, the maximum number of shares which can be acquired, the duration of the approval and, in the event of onerous transaction, the minimum and the maximum value of the shares. The board of directors is liable for the said acquisitions under certain conditions provided by the law. The above-mentioned conditions are not applied for:

(a)   shares acquired with the intention of decreasing share capital or as a result of redemption of shares;

(b)   acquisitions after a total transfer of property;

(c)   acquisitions of shares which have been fully paid off and gratuitously made or acquired by banks or other credit institutions as commission for acquisition;

(d)   acquisitions of shares which have been fully paid off by way of compulsory executions in satisfaction of the company's own claims;

(e)   acquisitions of shares following an obligation imposed by the law or by a court decision, with the purpose of protecting the minority shareholders, and acquisition of shares with the purpose of fulfilling an obligation of the company from a convertible bond loan.

It should be noted that, provided certain conditions are met, acquisitions made for the purpose of distribution of shares to the company personnel or to the personnel of a company connected therewith are also permitted. The distribution of these shares must be effected within 12 months of their acquisition.

Additionally, a *société anonyme* is not permitted to provide advance payments, loans or guarantees with the intention of its shares' acquisition by third parties. However, Law 2190/1920 on Sociétés Anonymes provides exceptions under special conditions following the resolution of the General Meeting.

Moreover, a *société anonyme* may not accept its own shares, or shares of its parent company, as liens or as a security for loans granted by it or for other claims. This prohibition does not apply to the current transactions of banks or other financial institutions.

Finally the articles of association may provide an increase in share capital by the issuance of redeemable shares under special conditions.

Administration

The board of directors manages a *société anonyme*. There must be at least three directors and they are appointed by the general assembly of the shareholders for periods not exceeding six years. Exceptionally, the term of office of the board of directors may be exceeded until the end of the time period in which the next General Assembly should be convened. The articles of association can provide that a certain shareholder or shareholders may appoint members of the board but never more than one-third of the total number of directors, and must stipulate the conditions under which this right is to be exercised. Additionally, the articles of association may provide that a legal entity can be a member of the board.

The board of directors is convened at the place where the company's registered office is situated at any time that the legislation, the articles of association or the needs of the company require it. Exceptionally, the articles of association may provide that the board of directors is legally convened in another place in Greece or abroad.

General assembly of the shareholders

The general assembly of the shareholders is the supreme body of a *société anonyme*. It meets at least once every fiscal year and within six months from the fiscal year end. It should be noted that the General Meeting can be conducted through a conference call or the shareholders can participate in the General Meeting or vote by distance even via the internet, on the premise that the articles of association provide for the above procedures. It is exclusively competent to resolve on:

(a)   amendments to the articles, including any increase or decrease of the share capital;
(b)   election of members of the board of directors and the auditors;
(c)   approval of the company's balance sheet;
(d)   disposition of the annual profits;
(e)   the merger, prolongation or dissolution of the company; and
(f)   the appointment of liquidators.

The following decisions are exempted from the above exclusivity of the general assembly:

(a)   any increase of the capital decided upon by the board of directors during the first five-year period from the establishment of the company (this power of the board of directors may be renewed by the general assembly for a period of time which cannot exceed five years for every renewal) as well as any increase imposed by the provisions of other laws;
(b)   amendments to the articles by the board of directors under the conditions provided by the Law;
(c)   the appointment, according to the articles, of the first board of directors;
(d)   the election, according to the articles of association, of provisional directors to replace, until the next general assembly is held, the directors who resigned, died or otherwise forfeited their office;

(e)   the absorption of a *société anonyme* by another *société anonyme* owning 100 per cent of its share capital;

(f)   disposition of the profits or optional reserves during the current fiscal year after the decision of the board of directors, only if the latter has been authorised by the ordinary General Meeting.

Unless the articles provide otherwise, resolutions of the general assembly require an absolute majority of the votes represented at the assembly. Resolutions on:

(a)   changing the company's nationality;

(b)   changing its object;

(c)   increasing share capital not provided for in the articles or imposed by provisions of laws or effected by capitalisation of reserves;

(d)   increasing shareholders' obligations;

(e)   decreasing share capital;

(f)   altering the mode of distribution of profits;

(g)   the merger, prolongation or dissolution of the company;

(h)   the granting or renewal of authority to the board of directors for an increase of the share capital,

can be adopted by a majority of two-thirds of the shareholders present at the relevant meeting, with a quorum of at least two-thirds of the shareholders of the company.

Taxation
The yearly net income of a listed or unlisted *société anonyme* from 1 January 2007 and onwards is taxed at the rate of 25 per cent.

The dividends paid by the *société anonyme* company to its shareholders or unit holders, respectively, are not subjected to income tax, since the relevant profits have been taxed in the name of the *société anonyme*.

Distribution of profits
Annually, at least one-twentieth of the net profits of a *société anonyme* must be set aside to form an ordinary reserve. This applies until the reserve reaches an amount equal to at least one-third of the share capital.

No distribution of profits is possible if by the closing date of the last fiscal year shown in the balance sheet the net worth of the company is, or will become after distribution, less than the share capital of the company plus reserves which may not be distributed under the law or the articles of association.

Moreover, the amounts distributed may not exceed the sum of profit and loss of the last fiscal year, increased by the profits of previous fiscal years and by any reserves which may, pursuant to the decision of the General Assembly, be distributed and reduced by the amount of loss of the previous financial years and the amounts due to be disposed of for the formation of reserves as provided by law and the articles of association.

The net profits of a *société anonyme* are distributed as follows:

(a)   an amount necessary for the formation of ordinary reserves must be deducted;

(b)   an amount for the payment of the first dividend equal to at least 6 per cent of the paid-up share capital must be retained; and

(c)   the balance shall be disposed of according to the provisions of the articles of association.

Under certain circumstances, the compulsory dividend must equal at least 35 per cent of the net profits after deducting the amount necessary for the formation of the ordinary reserves, provided this is higher than the 6 per cent mentioned above.

12.2   Investment and exchange controls

Several essential sectors are subject to statutory licensing and other controls. In certain cases, as set out below, it is necessary to obtain a licence from the central regulatory body for that particular sector. In some other cases, the acquisition of any substantial ownership by non-EU nationals is prohibited.

12.2.1   Banks

(a)   Pursuant to Law 3601/2007, any natural or legal person who intends to hold or cease to hold a holding representing, directly or indirectly, 5 per cent or more of the registered share capital or the voting rights in a bank which has been established in Greece, first notifies the Bank of Greece of the size of the new holding. The same obligation exists if:

    (i)   an already existing holding is increased or reduced, to the effect that the proportion of the voting rights held by a natural or legal person, directly or indirectly, results to the holding or cessation of holding of 5, 10, 20, 33 or 50 per cent of the total voting rights; or

    (ii)   a natural or legal person acquires the control or ceases to control, directly or indirectly, a credit institution.

(b)   The Bank of Greece has a maximum of three months from the date of the notification provided for above to approve or oppose such a plan by a reasoned decision if, in view of the need to ensure sound and prudent management of the credit institution, it is not satisfied as to the suitability of the person concerned.

(c)   If "Special Participation" is acquired, namely direct or indirect holding of at least 10 per cent of the registered share capital or the voting rights of a credit institution or exercise of significant influence over the management of the credit institution, by:

    (i)   another credit institution, insurance undertaking or investment firm authorised in another Member State, or

    (ii)   the parent undertaking of another credit institution, insurance undertaking or investment firm authorised in another Member State, or

    (iii)   a natural or legal person controlling another credit institution, insurance undertaking or investment firm authorised in another Member State, and if, as a result of that acquisition, the credit institution will become a subsidiary of the acquirer or will be subject to the control of the acquirer, the assessment of the acquisition shall be subject to the prior consultation provided for in Law 3601/2007.

(d) Subject to the obligations arising from international agreements concluded between the EU and third countries, concerning the taking up and pursuit of the business of credit institutions by legal or natural persons residents of said countries within the EU, the Bank of Greece may oppose the acquisition of participation by legal or natural persons resident in third countries in the share capital of credit institutions which have been established in Greece.

(e) In addition to the obligations mentioned in paragraph (a) above, the holders of a "special participation" must notify the Bank of Greece in advance of any increase exceeding their existing participation at an amount which corresponds to 5 per cent of the bank's share capital (the participation having been previously notified), until the total participation reaches 33 per cent.

(f) The credit institutions notify the Bank of Greece, by 15 of July of each year, of the names of the shareholders possessing a holding of more than 1 per cent, as well as the size of such holdings, as shown, for example, by the information received at the annual general meetings of the shareholders or as a result of compliance with the regulations relating to companies listed on Stock Exchanges.

In addition, credit institutions shall, within 10 working days having become aware of any acquisitions or disposals of holdings in their capital that cause holdings to exceed or fall below one of the thresholds referred to in paragraph (a) above, notify the Bank of Greece of those acquisitions or disposals.

(g) In case that participation is acquired or increased without previous notification or previous approval by the Bank of Greece, as required above, the notifying entity is automatically prohibited from exercising the voting rights arising from said participation. In addition the Bank of Greece may impose, cumulatively or alternatively, the following sanctions:

(i) a fine in favour of the Greek State amounting to up to 10 per cent of the value of the shares acquired by the notifying entity;

(ii) removal from the board of directors or any executive position in the credit institution for a definite or indefinite time in the case of natural persons.

Finally, it should be mentioned that Law 3606/2007 which has implemented the Markets in Financial Instruments Directive (2004/39/EC) into Greek Law, applies to credit institutions to the extent they provide investment services or exercise investment activities. The above Law came into effect as of 1 November 2007.

12.2.2 *Television*

According to Law 2328/95, as amended by Laws 3310/2005 and 3414/2005, on the legal status of private television and local radio and the regulation of special issues in the relevant market, TV licences are granted to concerns belonging to local government organisations, to *sociétés anonymes* controlled by Greek citizens or by citizens of EU Member States, and to companies which are established according to the legislation of a Member State of the EU and which have their establishment or central administration in a Member State of the EU.

The shares of the *sociétés anonymes* which apply for a TV licence must be registered until a natural person is identified as owner. If another *société anonyme* possesses, in whole or in part, the registered shares of the above companies, then the shares of said *société anonyme* must also be registered and must belong to natural persons. The contribution of foreign capital (outside the EU) cannot exceed 25 per cent of the entire share capital of the company having a TV licence. *Sociétés anonymes* legally operating according to the legislation of another country (within or outside the EU), are subject to the above obligation that shares be registered until a natural person is identified as owner, provided that such an obligation is imposed by the legislation of the country where these companies have their establishment. Companies listed on Stock Exchanges of EU or OECD Member States are not subject to the above obligation.

Every *société anonyme*, as well as every undertaking of a local government organisation, can possess only one TV licence or can participate in only one company possessing a licence. Any natural or legal person (including the administrators, the directors and the managing directors) can be a shareholder in only one company possessing a TV licence (holding up to 25 per cent of the share capital of the company), or in one company which participates in a company possessing such a licence and with the same percentage.

The following must be notified within 10 days to the National Council of Telecommunications:

(a) any transfer of a business holding a TV licence;
(b) any transfer, within or outside the Stock Exchange, of at least 1 per cent of the share capital of a company possessing a licence;
(c) any establishment of a new company in which an undertaking possessing a TV licence participates;
(d) any transformation of a company having a TV licence; and
(e) any amendment of its articles of association.

12.2.3 Radio

Pursuant to Law 2328/1995, as amended by Laws 3310/2005 and 3414/2005, on the legal status of private television and local radio and the regulation of special issues in the relevant market, the conditions for the granting of radio licences, and the conditions for operating a company to which a radio licence has been granted, are very similar to the rules for companies having a TV licence.

12.2.4 Mass media companies

According to Law 3310/2005, as amended by Law 3414/2005, the definition of a mass media company is the profit or non-profit making entity or company, under whatever legal form, the operation of which is subject to Greek law and which carries out an activity (exclusive or not) consisting of:

(a)   the publishing of newspapers or magazines, or papers of political or financial character, of any form whatsoever, including electronic form, which are published, or distributed; or

(b)   installing and operating or administrating a television channel, or transmitting a television signal, under whatever form or way, such as free, satellite, digital, wireless reception, in accordance with the Greek legislation in every case; or

(c)   installing and operating or administrating a radio channel or transmitting a radio signal under whatever form, in accordance with the Greek legislation in every case; or

(d)   the provision of audiovisual services via the internet, provided they have a news content.

A main shareholder is one of the following:

(a)   The person or the legal entity, which owns, either directly or indirectly through participation of a third person, an amount of shares or voting rights which correspond at least to 1 per cent of the total share capital or the total voting rights at the shareholders meeting of the company, or owned at least 1 per cent of the total share capital or held voting rights corresponding to at least 1 per cent of the total share capital represented, or exercised the voting right at the shareholders meeting which resolved upon the election or removal of the last board of directors of the company or the majority of its members, provided that, as of the publication of the relevant tender notice or issuance of the decision on the procurement procedure (with a view to concluding a public contract) until the completion of the inspection provided for in Article 5 of Law 3310/2005, as amended by Law 3414/2005, the following conditions are or were also met:

    (i)   he owns or owned, at the time period mentioned above, an amount of shares which rank or ranked him among the 10 major shareholders of the company; or

    (ii)   he holds or held, at the time period mentioned above, for any reason whatsoever, voting rights in the shareholders meeting, which rank or ranked him among the 10 major holders of voting rights in the company; or

    (iii)   he is or was entitled, at the time period mentioned above, either by the law or the articles of association or due to an assignment by other shareholders, to appoint or remove one member of the board of directors; or

    (iv)   he concludes or has concluded, directly or indirectly, at the time period mentioned above, contracts with the company, from which the company acquired income or other economic benefits, which correspond to at least one-tenth of the gross income in the last year.

(b)   The person or the legal entity which is a shareholder either directly in the company or in other legal entities which are shareholders in said company or shareholders in said legal entities or shareholders of their shareholders illimitably up to the last natural person, and which owns an amount of shares which correspond to at least 1 per cent of the total share capital of the company or holds voting rights which correspond to at least 1 per cent of the total voting rights in the shareholders meeting of the company, provided that the conditions of paragraph (a) above are met.

For the purposes of calculating the proportion of share capital or voting rights mentioned in (a) and (b) above, the following shall be taken into account:

(a)   shares or voting rights owned or held by:
  (i)   middlemen, or
  (ii)   companies controlled by the same shareholder or by their related companies in the meaning of Article 42e of Greek Law 2190/1920, as well as by other companies related to the latter, or
  (iii)   another shareholder with which the main shareholder has concluded an agreement for determining, through coordinated exercise of voting rights, a common lasting policy regarding the company's administration;
(b)   voting rights held by another shareholder by virtue of a pledge, agreement or a life interest; and
(c)   shares, the dividends of which the main shareholder is entitled to receive.

A person or a legal entity may not be, at the same time, a main shareholder in a mass media company and in a company which enters into agreements for the provision of services or supply of goods to the Greek State or to public entities, provided that conditions of para. 4 of Article 3, Law 3310/2005, as amended by Law 3414/2005, are met.

It is also prohibited for an offshore company to hold, directly or indirectly, a participation exceeding 1 per cent of the total share capital in a mass media company, provided that conditions of para. 6 of Article 2, Law 3310/2005, as amended by Law 3414/2005, are met.

Following the issuance of a condemnatory decision, having the force of *res judicata*, by which the crime of bribery is ascertained, in the meaning of Article 45 para. 1b) of the 2004/18/EC Directive of 31 March 2004, a fine may be imposed on the natural person related to a mass media company, in contravention of the above obligations of Law 3310/2005, as amended by Law 3414/2005, up to seven times (and in the case of recidivism up to 15 times) over the fine, as such is calculated in Article 7 of the above Law.

12.2.5   *Insurance*

(a)   Insurance corporations must issue registered shares and the majority of their board of directors must be Greek nationals or nationals of other EU Member States.
(b)   According to Law 400/1970, no one may hold, directly or indirectly, 10 per cent or more of the registered share capital or the voting rights in an insurance corporation, or exercise, in any other way, substantial influence on the management of an insurance corporation, established and operating in Greece (called hereafter "special participation"), without having notified to the Committee for the Supervision of the Private Insurance Sector of its

intention and the proportion of the participation to be acquired and received its approval in advance.

The same obligation exists if the special participation is to be increased resulting in the proportion of voting rights or of the share capital reaching or exceeding 20, 33 or 50 per cent of the total voting rights or share capital, or if the insurance corporation becomes a subsidiary of the notifying entity. If the special participation is acquired or is increased beyond the afore-mentioned thresholds, without previous notification or previous approval, the notifying entity is automatically prohibited from exercising the voting rights arising from said special participation. In addition the Committee for the Supervision of the Private Insurance Sector may impose, cumula-tively or alternatively, the following sanctions:

(i)   a fine amounting to up to 10 per cent of the value of shares trans-ferred without previous notification or approval;

(ii)   removal from the board of directors or any executive position.

(c)   Furthermore, holders of special participation shall notify beforehand to the Committee for the Supervision of the Private Insurance Sector any increase of their participation, exceeding the participation which has been previ-ously notified by an amount corresponding to 2 per cent of the share capital, until the total participation reaches 33 per cent.

(d)   Any person intending to cease holding, directly or indirectly, a special participation shall notify beforehand to the Committee for the Supervision of the Private Insurance Sector its intention and the size of holding which it intends to maintain.

The same obligation applies to any person intending to reduce its special participation resulting in the proportion of voting rights or of share capital held by the said person falling below 20, 33 and 50 per cent, or if the insurance corporation ceases to be a subsidiary of that person.

The same announcement obligation applies to persons who cease to control legal entities which hold a special participation in an insurance corporation.

In the case of breach of the above obligations, the Committee for the Super-vision of the Private Insurance Sector may impose a fine amounting to up to 5 per cent of the value of the shares which have been transferred without previous notification.

12.2.6 Shipping

Pursuant to Law 959/1979, which is the basic law for maritime companies, citizens or legal entities of states which are not members of the European Union or do not belong to the European Economic Area can only acquire shares of up to 49 per cent of the share capital of a Greek shipping company.

Furthermore, according to Law 3182/2003 regarding maritime companies of leisure vessels, citizens or legal entities of states which are not members of the European Union or do not belong to the European Economic Area can only acquire real rights on shares which represent in total up to 49 per cent of the share capital of a Greek maritime company of leisure vessels.

12.2.7 Air transport

According to the Greek Aviation Code, an aircraft is considered Greek if it belongs to nationals of EEA Member States (owning more than 50 per cent), or to Greek legal entities by the same percentage provided that certain additional conditions are met.

12.2.8 Brokerage companies

According to Law 1806/1988, the approval of the Capital Market Committee is required for the transfer for any reason whatsoever (other than inheritance or parental gift) of the shares of a brokerage company. Any transfer that contravenes this law is void unless the acquirer receives less than 10 per cent. To grant approval, the Capital Market Committee examines the suitability of the potential acquirer to ensure the proper management of the company.

Any transfer of shares for which no prior approval is required must be notified to the Capital Market Committee which can ask the new shareholders to provide any information it considers necessary if it is thought that they may directly or indirectly affect the management of the brokerage company.

Legal entities, except for credit institutions, insurance companies and companies providing investment services having a paid-up share capital equivalent to the share capital required by law for credit institutions, cannot acquire more than 40 per cent of the shares of a brokerage company. Shares of brokerage companies that are listed on the main market of the Stock Exchange are exempt.

Legal entities which violate these requirements will have their voting rights at the general assemblies suspended. The Capital Market Committee orders the suspension.

Furthermore, pursuant to the same Law, a previous approval by the Capital Market Committee is required for the acquisition of shares issued by a brokerage company listed on the Athens Exchange if the said acquisition results in a person or a legal entity holding a proportion of the total share capital exceeding 10, 20, 33, 50 or 66 per cent of the share capital. If the above approval has not been obtained, the voting rights attaching to the shares, which have been transferred, may not be exercised.

A person or legal entity intending to dispose of its shares in a brokerage company and as a result of the said disposal its participation in the total share capital or in the total voting rights falls below 10, 20, 33, 50 or 66 per cent must notify the Capital Market Committee of such intention at the latest one month prior to the disposal. If that obligation is not observed, the Capital Market Committee may impose a fine amounting to between €293.47 and €146,735.14.

Note: The above Law 1806/1988 is extensively amended by Law 3606/2007, which incorporates the Markets in Financial Instruments Directive (2004/39/EC) and came into force as of 1 November 2007.

12.2.9 Foreign exchange control

Greece has traditionally imposed severe restrictions on the movement of foreign exchange. Some of these restrictions were relaxed by PD 207/87 which incorporated into Greek law the EU provisions on the free movement of capital.

Capital movements have been liberalised further by PD 96/93 as amended by PD 104/94 which adapted Greek law to the provisions of EEC Directives 86/361 and 92/122 on capital movement.

The types of capital movement which have been liberalised, and which are of interest to a foreigner who wishes to acquire a Greek company, are the following:

(a)   direct investments and the proceeds of liquidation of these investments;
(b)   investments in real estate and repatriation of the proceeds of liquidation of these investments;
(c)   acquisitions of securities dealt on the Stock Exchange and repatriation of the proceeds of liquidation of these securities;
(d)   transactions in current accounts and deposits in credit institutions;
(e)   granting and repayment of loans and other credits;
(f)   guarantees, pledges or similar securities;
(g)   rights over intellectual property.

The Bank of Greece and the other credit institutions operating in Greece and authorised to conduct foreign exchange transactions will, following an application by the interested party, provide the foreign exchange required to realise and enforce these transactions.

12.3   Merger control

12.3.1 The legislation

In 1977, Law 703/77 on the protection of competition established rules equivalent to Articles 85 and 86 of the Treaty of Rome. This legal framework to protect free competition has been supplemented by Laws 1934/91, 2000/91 and 2296/95 the provisions of which are intended to harmonise Greek law with the letter and spirit of Council Regulation 4064/89, Law 2741/1999 and more recently Law 2837/2000.

Furthermore, in 2005 the Greek Parliament passed the new Law 3371/2005, by which several provisions of Law 703/77 were amended with the intention of harmonising the provisions of Greek law with the letter and spirit of Council Regulations 1/2003 and 139/2004. Law 3371/2005 brought back the obligation for post-merger notification. Moreover, in the case of pre-merger notification the market share criterion has been lifted and only the turnover criterion now applies.

Law 703/77 applies to Greek enterprises and to foreign ones established in Greece. It also applies to a foreign enterprise which is involved in an agreement or which abuses its dominant position with the result that competition in the Greek market is or may be affected.

12.3.2   Restrictions and prohibitions

Article 1 of Law 703/77 prohibits any restrictive practices of competition, and indicates certain special cases which exemplify the general rule.

12.3.3   Abuse of dominant position or of economic dependence

Law 703/77 prohibits establishments from abusing their dominant position within a relevant market, and from abusively exploiting the economic dependence of another. Abusive exploitation of economic dependence may take the form of either terminating existing trading relations (refusal of sale) or imposing arbitrary terms of trade.

12.3.4   Concentration of undertakings

12.3.4.1   The legislative view

To protect free competition, the law takes an interest in the concentration of undertakings when the concentration creates a dominant position, strengthens an existing one, or generally when effective competition is significantly impeded.

12.3.4.2   What constitutes concentration?

The crucial point is the meaning of the term "concentration". Law 703/77 provides that a concentration shall be deemed to exist where:

(a)   two or more previously independent undertakings merge; or
(b)   one or more persons already controlling at least one or more undertakings acquire, whether by purchase of securities or assets, by contract or by any other means, direct or indirect control of the whole or parts of one or more other undertakings.

In view of this provision, it is clear that the most important factor is the possibility of exercising a decisive influence on the undertakings' activity. The existence of such a possibility depends on the conditions of each specific case. Therefore, it must be determined whether achieving control enables the acquiring entity to influence the competitive behaviour of the undertaking in the relevant market and thus to limit or prevent effective competition. Acquiring decisive control, expressed in percentages, depends on the specific corporate type and concentration. Thus, minority rights in a capital company may fall within the meaning of "concentration". It all depends on the degree of the shares' dispersion.

12.3.4.3   Notification of concentrations

According to Article 4a of Law 703/1977, as amended by Law 3371/2005, all concentrations of enterprises must be notified to the Competition Commission ("CC") within a month from completion when:

(a)   the relevant market share of goods or services represents at least 10 per cent of the domestic market; or
(b)   the entire turnover of the parties in the domestic market amounts to at least €15 million.

12.3.4.4　Pre-merger notification

Law 1934/91 introduced pre-merger control which until 8 March 1991 was unknown in Greece. According to this law, the Ministers of National Economy and Commerce could, by joint Ministerial Decision, specify which concentrations of similar enterprises should be notified. This could be decided on the grounds that such concentrations concern sectors in which an increase in the degree of concentration might lead to the prevention, restriction or distortion of competition in general or in certain parts of the domestic market, creating or reinforcing a dominant position. But as this Ministerial Decision has never been issued, until the introduction of Law 2296/95 pre-merger notification had never been applied in Greece.

Pursuant to the requirements of pre-merger notification, a concentration must be notified to the CC within 10 working days from the conclusion of the agreement, or the announcement of the bid or the acquisition of the controlling interest, when the aggregate international-wide turnover of the undertakings participating in the concentration amounts to at least €150 million and at least two of the undertakings achieve, separately, in the domestic market an entire turnover exceeding €15 million.

In the case of failure to notify, the CC imposes on each of the notifying entities a fine of at least €15,000, which [fine] however cannot exceed 7 per cent of the aggregate turnover.

12.3.4.5　Procedure of the pre-merger inquiry

The CC examines the pre-concentration notification as soon as it is received. If it concludes that the concentration does not fall within the scope of Law 703/77, the president of the CC shall record that finding by means of a decision that shall be issued within one month of notification. If it finds that the concentration notified, although it falls within the scope of Law 703/77, cannot significantly restrict competition, it records that finding in a decision that must be issued within one month from the notification.

On the other hand, where the CC finds that the concentration is not compatible with the operational requirements of competition, it issues a decision within one month of the notification, by which the case is held for further examination and the undertakings concerned are notified without delay. Following the examination of the case by the CC, a decision is issued, within 90 days of the notification, by which the CC either prohibits or allows the concentration. The lapse of the above 90-day time limit without the issuance of a decision by which the concentration is prohibited, means that the concentration is approved by the CC.

Following the decision by which the CC prohibits the concentration, and within one month from its notification, the companies concerned can file an application to the Ministers of Economy and Finance and Development. The Ministers may approve the concentration if they consider that it presents financial benefits or that it is indispensable on the grounds of overriding public and general social interest.

It should be noted that the Supreme Administrative Court has ruled that the time limits set by the laws are not legally binding upon the Administration and the Administration may exceed the time limits set by the laws.

12.3.4.6 Suspension of concentrations

Law 703/77 provides that concentrations for which a prior notification is required shall not be put into effect until the issue of any of the decisions mentioned above. This also applies to concentrations which fall under the obligation but have not been notified. In cases of failure to comply with the prohibition, the CC imposes a fine of at least €30,000 and up to 15 per cent of the aggregate turnover.

The CC may, on request, grant an exemption from the suspension, in order to prevent serious damage to one or more undertakings in a concentration or to a third party.

Where the concentration has already entered into effect, the CC may require the undertakings brought together to be separated or all the shares or assets acquired to be disposed, in order to restore the situation existing before the concentration entered into effect.

If there is a failure to comply, the CC imposes a fine of up to 15 per cent of the turnover of all the companies concerned and a fine of €10,000 for every day of delay in complying.

12.3.4.7 Appeals

The parties may lodge an appeal with the Court of Administrative Appeals against the decision of the Ministers of Economy and Finance and Development or of the CC.

The appeal must be filed with the Court within 60 days from the date of notification of the decision to the party concerned. Filing the appeal does not by itself suspend the decision of the CC. Should there be substantial reasons justifying a suspension, then, on the application of the party concerned, the Chairman of the Court may suspend, in whole or in part, the enforcement of the appealed decision. The appeal must be heard within three months and only one postponement of the hearing is permitted as long as there are serious reasons for it. Unfortunately, due to the large backlog at the Court the time limits are often exceeded.

The decision of the Court of Administrative Appeals is subject to further appeal to the Supreme Administrative Court. The provisions on the suspension of the appealed decision and the time of hearing are also applicable to such appeals.

12.3.4.8 Fees

All notifications required to be made to the CC must be accompanied by a collection certificate showing prepayment of €1,050.

All documents filed with either of the courts referred to above must be stamped.

12.4 Regulation of mergers

Merger is the financial act whereby one or more undertakings are dissolved with the purpose of creating a new financial unit. Liquidation procedures are not applicable to the dissolved companies since their property is not distributed to their shareholders. Instead it is transferred to the undertaking resulting from the merger. A merger can be brought about in the following ways:

(a)   by the formation of a new company;
(b)   by the absorption of one or more companies into another.

Under Greek law, the transfer by one or more companies, not liquidated, of all their assets and liabilities to another company in exchange for cash and not for shares is also considered and regulated as a merger.

The only types of merger which have been subject to direct regulation by Greek law are mergers between companies limited by shares (*sociétés anonymes*) and mergers between limited liability companies. In all other cases the same procedure applies *mutatis mutandis*.

12.4.1 Companies limited by shares (sociétés anonymes)

Law 2190/1920 on corporations, as amended by PD 498/1987 and Law 3604/2007, recognises two types of merger:

(a)   merger by the absorption of one or more companies by another;
(b)   merger by the formation of a new company.

12.4.1.1 Merger by absorption

Absorption is the operation whereby one or more companies which have been dissolved without going into liquidation transfer to another all their assets and liabilities in exchange for issuing, to the shareholders of the company(ies) being acquired, shares in the acquiring company and a cash payment, if any, not exceeding 10 per cent of the nominal value of the shares to be issued.

According to Article 69 of Law 2190/1920, the board of directors of the merging companies must prepare a draft merger agreement which must contain the following:

(a)   the type, name, registered office and registration number of each of the merging companies;
(b)   the share exchange ratio and the amount of any supplementary cash payment;
(c)   the formalities relating to the delivery of the new shares that will be issued by the absorbing company;
(d)   the dates from when the shares entitle the holders to participate in profits and any special conditions affecting that entitlement;
(e)   the date from which the transactions of the company being acquired shall be treated for accounting purposes as being those of the acquired company, and the treatment of the financial results of the acquired company which will occur from that date until the completion of the merger;

(f)   the rights conferred by the acquiring company on the shareholders who have special rights in the absorbed company(ies), and on the holders of securities other than shares, or the measures proposed for them;

(g)   all the special benefits which may be granted to the members of the board of directors and the auditors of the merging companies.

The board of directors of each merging company must also draw up a detailed written report explaining the draft terms of the merger and setting out the legal and economic grounds for them, in particular the share exchange ratio. In addition the report must describe any special valuation difficulties which may have arisen.

Under Article 7b of Law 2190/1920, the draft merger agreement as well as the board of directors' report are entered in the appropriate Register of Limited Companies at the district of each company's registered office. Moreover, notice of the registration must be published in the *Government Gazette*. A summary of the draft merger agreement must also be published in a daily financial newspaper.

The assets of the merging companies are evaluated either by a specialist committee or the committee of para. 1 of Article 9 of Law 2190/1920 or two auditor members of the chartered accountants' body pursuant to para. 4 of Article 9 of Law 2190/1920. Said persons are appointed through a joint application or agreement of the merging companies to the Ministry of Development in this respect. The specialist committee of para. 1 of Article 9, Law 2190/1920 is constituted by three members, one or two of whom must be government officials who are university graduates with at least three years' service with the Government, or one or two auditor members of the chartered accountants' body, and one specialist representing the appropriate chamber of commerce. The above persons request from the merging companies any information or document considered useful for the accomplishment of their task and carry out all the necessary investigations and controls. Their report is submitted to the general assemblies of the merging companies.

According to Article 72 of Law 2190/1920, the final decision for the merger is taken by the general assemblies of the merging companies with increased quorum and majority. The general assembly of the acquiring company must also decide on the increase of capital and any other amendments to the articles of association.

The final merger agreement, when drawn up, is based upon the draft merger agreement and the resolution of the general assemblies. The final agreement must take the form of a notarial deed.

The notarial deed, together with the general assembly's resolutions on the merger and any amendments of the articles, are submitted to the competent Prefecture for approval. A relevant announcement is subsequently published in the *Government Gazette*.

Results of the merger

(a)   Merger procedure and merging companies – a merger entails the automatic and simultaneous transfer to the acquiring company of all the assets and liabilities of the company being acquired.

According to Greek law, the transfer of these rights and liabilities is similar to a succession right and, therefore, no special act is necessary in connection with the transfer of each right and liability. However, it is also clearly stated by Greek law that the formalities imposed by current legislation regarding the transfer of certain specific assets must also be complied with in this case. Thus, the transfer of real estate requires a notarised transfer document and subsequent registration at the Land Registry. The transfer of a motorcar requires an amendment to the relevant licence. The transfer of a vessel requires registration at the relevant Registry, etc.

Any pending legal actions are continued *ipso jure* by the absorbing company without the necessity of any act by transfer.

(b)   Merger procedure and shareholders – the shareholders of the acquired company become shareholders of the acquirer and the former ceases to exist. Every shareholder of the absorbed company must deliver his shares which are cancelled and take shares of the absorbing company according to the share price ratio specified in the merger agreement.

According to Article 72 of Law 2190/1920, if there is more than one class of shares, the resolution of the general assembly approving the merger becomes effective with the approval of the holders of each class of shares whose rights are adversely affected by the merger.

According to Article 73 of Law 2190/1920, at least one month before the general assembly which is convened to approve the draft merger agreement, every shareholder has the right to receive notice, at the company's registered office, of the following documents:

(a)   draft of the merger agreement;
(b)   the annual financial reports, as well as the management reports of the board of directors of the merging companies concerning the last three financial years;
(c)   temporary financial statements of the merging companies drafted no earlier than three months before the date of the draft merger agreement provided that the end of the last fiscal year occurs at least six months before the date of the draft merger agreement;
(d)   the board of directors' reports on the merger.

Article 76 of Law 2190/1920 provides that each member of the board of directors of the absorbed company, as well as each member of the specialists' committee, is accountable and responsible to the shareholders of the acquired company in respect of any error made during the course of preparing and effecting the merger and in respect of any other error made during the course of carrying out their related tasks.

Finally, according to Article 39 of Law 2190/1920, shareholders representing one-twentieth of the company's paid-up capital have the right to demand the adjournment of the general assembly for the approval of the merger agreement, also setting the date when a new general assembly is requested, which must not be more than 30 days after the date of the adjourned general assembly.

Merger procedure and third parties

(a)   Creditors – from the completion of the merger procedure the creditors of the absorbed company(ies) become creditors of the absorbing one. After the acquisition of new assets and the increase of the share capital, the absorbing company becomes financially stronger, thus the position of the creditors is improved. As this is not, however, always the case, Article 70 of Law 2190/1920 provides that within a month from the publication of the summary of the draft terms of the merger as mentioned above, any creditors of the merging companies whose claims arose before the date of the publication, and have not fallen due at that date, have the right to demand adequate safeguards, if the financial condition of the merging companies makes such protection necessary and if safeguards have not already been granted. If the creditors are not satisfied with the securities granted to them, they have the right to submit written objections during the course of the merger within the specified time period of one month mentioned above. The submission of these objections prevents the merger from being completed.

The law, however, gives the right to the absorbing companies to request, from the First Instance Court in the area of the registered office of any of the applicant companies, permission to proceed with the merger notwithstanding the objections. The relevant application may be filed by one or more of the merging companies, and is heard according to the procedure of injunctive relief measures; it is not subject to appeal. The Court will permit the merger if it finds that the financial condition of the merging companies, or the securities received by the creditors or offered to them, do not justify their opposition, making their objections unreasonable. The Court may also allow the merger on condition that adequate security is granted to the creditor or creditors opposing the merger.

If there are debenture creditors, then the decision for the merger must be approved by them. However, if they oppose the merger, the law gives the right to the merged companies to request the Court to permit the merger.

(b)   Debtors – the debtors of the absorbed company(ies) become debtors of the absorbing one.

(c)   Employees – Greek legislation and case law protects the rights of employees of the merging companies. In particular, Article 6, paragraph 1 of Law 2112/20 provides that a change in the person of an employer, however caused, has no effect on the application of the provisions of this law which are in favour of the employees. The new employer automatically assumes all the obligations of the previous employer towards the employees.

Moreover, PD 178/2002 (the provisions of which are intended to harmonise Greek law with the letter and spirit of Council Regulation 98/50) stipulates even more clearly that in a transfer of an undertaking (by sale, contribution, transformation, merger, etc.) the transferor's rights and obligations stemming from a contract of employment, or from an employment relationship existing on the date of the transfer, shall, by reason of such transfer, be transferred to the acquirer. Thus, the personnel of an absorbed company continue the employment relationship with the new employer, namely the absorbing company, and previous employment periods counted in the salary increase the compensation if the employment contract is terminated by the absorbing company. Therefore, it is clear that a merger does not constitute a reason to terminate an employment contract. This does not apply, however, for dismissals that may take place for technical, economic or organisational reasons, as long as appropriate compensation is paid.

12.4.1.2   *Merger by the formation of a new company*
Merger by the formation of a new company is a merger whereby two or more companies, which are dissolved but not liquidated, transfer to a newly formed company all their assets and liabilities in exchange for issuing to their shareholders shares in the new company and a cash payment, if any, not exceeding 10 per cent of the nominal value of the shares so issued.

According to Article 80 of Law 2190/1920, the provisions for a merger by absorption also apply to a merger involving the formation of a new company. Since, however, this type of merger involves the incorporation of a new company, the provisions for the establishment of a new company must also be complied with.

12.4.1.3   *Mergers where a parent company acquires its wholly owned subsidiary*
Article 78 of Law 2190/1920 provides that the action by one or more companies, which are dissolved but not liquidated, to transfer their total assets to another company which holds all their shares, either directly or through nominees, is subject to the provisions regarding merger by absorption, with certain differences.

Thus, in such a case, no specialist committee valuation is required, and no decision of the general assemblies is necessary. Since the shares of the acquired company which are held by the acquiring company cannot be exchanged for shares in the acquiring company as a company is not allowed to acquire its own shares, the consideration corresponding to these shares is placed in special reserves.

12.4.2   **Limited liability (without shares) companies**

Law 3190/55 recognises two types of merger:

(a)   merger by the formation of a new limited liability company;
(b)   merger by absorption of one or more limited liability companies by another.

The merger procedure is much simpler than the procedure for *sociétés anonymes*. It consists of the procedures described below.

12.4.2.1   *Decision of the meetings of the members of the limited liability companies*
The members' meeting of each limited liability company involved in a merger agreement approves the merger either by the formation of a new company or by absorption. The resolution of the members' meeting will be based on a report prepared by the administrators containing all the preceding negotiations and

agreements of the merging companies, together with the reasons which dictate and render the merger indispensable. The resolutions of the members' meetings must be adopted by at least a three-quarters majority of the members who represent not less than three-quarters of the company's capital. If a new company is formed apart from the merger, the members' meetings must also approve the articles of the new limited liability company. In cases of absorption, the members' meeting of the absorbing company must also approve the increase of its capital.

12.4.2.2   Valuation of the assets of the merging companies
The absorbed company's assets or the assets of the merging companies, in cases of the formation of a new company, are valued by the specialist committee referred to at 12.4.1.1 above.

12.4.2.3   Publication requirements
A summary of the resolution of the members' meeting of each company must be published once in the *Government Gazette* and twice in a daily newspaper. The merger procedure cannot be completed until after two months from the last publication if no written objections to the merger have been submitted by the creditors.

12.4.2.4   Notarial deed
The merger agreement must take the form of a notarial deed.

12.4.2.5   Publication requirements in relation to the merger agreement
These requirements include the submission of the agreement within one month of its execution to the Secretary of the First Instance Court of the district of the merging companies, entry in the Register of Limited Liability Companies, and publication of a notice regarding the entry in the *Government Gazette*.

Once these formalities are complied with, the merger is concluded. However, when there is a merger through the formation of a new company, it is also necessary to comply with the requirements relating to the formation of a limited liability company.

12.4.3   Results of the merger

Once the publication requirements have been fulfilled, the acquirer of the new company takes on the rights and liabilities of the acquired or merged company. According to Greek law, the transfer of these rights and liabilities is similar to succession. Any pending legal actions are continued *ipso jure* by the absorbing company without the need for any action to be taken.

The members of the acquired company become members of the acquirer as stipulated in the merger agreement.

12.4.3.1   Merger procedure and partners of the limited liability company
In contrast to the *sociétés anonymes*, there are no special provisions for the protection of the partners of a merged limited liability company. The reason for their absence is justified by the nature of a limited liability company, which is much more personalised than that of a *société anonyme*.

Therefore, only the general provisions concerning the protection of partners apply here. Thus, in cases of serious breach of duty or incapacity for administration, the administrative authority granted to one or more partners or to third parties can be recalled by a decision of the multi-member court of the district where the company has its registered office, following a resolution of the partners' meeting. Moreover, each partner may claim compensation from the responsible administrators who are liable for any breach of any legal provision of the articles of association or any fault in the exercise of the administration. The right to bring such a claim is recognised only if the partners' meeting has rejected a proposal to bring a civil action on behalf of the company or if the partners' meeting failed to decide the issue within a reasonable period of time. Finally, every partner has the right, within 10 days of the expiry of each three-month calendar period, to be informed either personally or by a representative, of the progress of the company's affairs and to examine the company's books and documents.

12.4.3.2   Merger procedure and creditors
As mentioned above, creditors have the right to submit written objections to the merger within two months from the latest publication of the summary of resolutions (in daily newspapers) adopted by the partners' meetings of the merging limited liability companies published in the district of the companies' registered offices. This action prevents the merger from being completed. However, the law gives the merging companies the right to request from the First Instance Court in the area of the registered office of any of the applicant companies permission to proceed with the merger notwithstanding the objections. The relevant application may be filed by one or more of the merging companies, and is heard according to the procedure of injunctive relief measures. The Court will only permit the merger if it finds that the creditors are granted sufficient security.

Moreover, as mentioned above, each creditor has the right to take civil action for damages against the administrators of the merging limited liability company if the merger contravenes the law and the articles of association.

12.5   Division

With the introduction of PD 498/1987, the concept of division of companies was introduced for the first time in Greece. A division may be a first step towards a subsequent merger or acquisition. There are two methods of division:

(a)   division by acquisition;
(b)   division by the formation of a new company.

Division is the operation whereby a *société anonyme*, which is dissolved but not liquidated, transfers its total assets and liabilities to other *sociétés anonymes* which are either already in existence or which were established at the same time, in return for granting to its shareholders newly issued shares and perhaps a cash payment corresponding to the value of the shares to which they are entitled.

The procedure followed for divisions is very similar to that for mergers.

12.6 Regulation and methods of acquisition

Shares or parts of a company or a business in its entirety are acquired by a sale and purchase agreement which is negotiated and executed between the seller and the purchaser.

12.6.1 Acquisition of a société anonyme

A party interested in acquiring a *société anonyme* may purchase existing shares, or new shares issued further to an increase of capital, or bonds convertible into shares.

12.6.1.1 Sale of existing shares
The sale of existing shares is effected by an agreement between the existing shareholder-vendor and the purchaser. Every *société anonyme* has the right to issue either bearer or registered shares. In certain cases, however, the issue of registered shares is compulsory by law. Thus, partially paid-up shares, as well as shares in banking, insurance, air and railway companies, companies engaged in the production of gas, the generation and distribution of electricity, the installation and operation of water and drainage, and companies engaged in telecommunications, radio-broadcasting or producing war materials must be registered. Also, the shares of football companies, brokerage and venture capital companies, companies managing mutual funds, factoring and forfeiting companies, companies which own newspapers and magazines must be registered. According to Law 3310/2005 as amended and currently in force, the shares of Greek *sociétés anonymes* which participate in projects of, or supplies to, the Greek state or of legal entities of the public sector, amounting to more than €1 million, must also be registered. If a shareholder of the latter companies with a participation of more than 1 per cent is a société anonyme, then its shares must also be registered.

Transfer of bearer and registered shares
The transfer of shares entails the following steps:

(a)   tax registration of the selling entity in case the latter does not have a tax registration number in Greece;
(b)   filing of a Transfer Tax Return with the tax office which is competent for the Greek company, the shares of which are transferred;
(c)   execution of agreement between the purchaser and the seller of the shares. According to para. 4 of Article 79, Law 2238/1994 (as amended by Law 2459/1997) shares, registered or bearer shares, not listed on the Athens Stock Exchange, may be transferred by a private agreement or by a notarial deed, otherwise the transfer is considered null and void. If a private agreement is opted for, it has to be subsequently authenticated, that is, stamped by the tax authority which is competent for the seller of the shares, within 10 days from the date of signing.

In the case of transfer of registered shares, there are certain additional formalities to be observed, the aim of which is to give notice to the company. Thus, according to Article 8b of Law 2190/20, to transfer registered shares an entry in the shareholder's register is required, dated and signed by both the transferor and the transferee or by their representatives. Upon the transfer, a new title is issued, or the effected transfer is mentioned by the company in the existing title, together with the names, addresses, occupations and nationalities of the transferor and the transferee. If these formalities are not observed, the transfer is invalid.

Transfer of shares in a book entry form (dematerialised) listed on the Stock Exchange
Transfer of ownership of dematerialised shares may be effected in two ways:

(a)   transfer may be effected by an "on market" transaction through the Athens Stock Exchange and the Depositary of Titles Company ("CSD") by registration of the transaction in the CSD's records. The securities accounts of the investors are credited and debited by the account operators after each transaction;

(b)   the requirements and restrictions regarding "off exchange" transactions that existed under the Law 3632/1928 were abolished by Law 3606/2007 which has implemented the Markets in Financial Instruments Directive (2004/39/EC) into Greek law and came into effect as of 1 November 2007. The said law provides for the issuance of a series of regulatory Acts by the competent supervisory bodies, such as the Bank of Greece ("BoG") and the Capital Markets Commission ("CMC"), which have not yet been issued.

Law 3556/2007 implemented into Greek law Council Directive 2004/109 EC "on the harmonisation of transparency requirements in relation to information about issuers whose securities are admitted to trading on a regulated market and amending Directive 2001/34/EC". According to that Law, when, as a result of a transfer of registered shares listed on the Athens Stock Exchange, a person acquires or assigns a participation in a listed company and due to this acquisition or assignment the percentage of the voting rights that he holds reaches or exceeds the limits of 5, 10, 20, 33.3, 50 and 66.6 per cent of the total of the voting rights or falls below these limits, the holder is, pursuant to the provisions of Law 3556/2007 (EU Directive 2004/109 EC), required to notify such company within three days as to the percentage of the voting rights held by this person after the acquisition or assignment. The same obligation is also triggered by corporate events that result in a change in the distribution of voting rights. The law provides for exceptions to that obligation in specific cases, such as:

(a)   when shares are acquired for the sole purpose of clearing and settling within the usual short settlement cycle (set at three days maximum by CMC Decision No. 1/434/3.7.2007);

(b)   when shares are held by custodians in their custodian capacity provided such custodians can only exercise the voting rights attached to such shares under instructions given in writing or by electronic means;

(c)   when a major holding reaching or crossing the 5 per cent threshold is acquired or disposed by a market maker acting in its capacity of a market maker, provided that:

(i)   it is authorised by its home Member State under Directive 2004/39/EC, and

(ii)   it neither intervenes in the management of the issuer concerned nor exerts any influence on the issuer to buy such shares or back the share price.

The above notification requirements also apply to a natural person or legal entity to the extent it is entitled to acquire, to dispose of, or to exercise voting rights in any of the following cases or a combination of them:

(a)   voting rights held by a third party with whom that person or entity has concluded an agreement, which obliges them to adopt, by concerted exercise of the voting rights they hold, a lasting common policy towards the management of the issuer in question;

(b)   voting rights held by a third party under an agreement concluded with that person or entity providing for the temporary transfer for consideration of the voting rights in question;

(c)   voting rights attaching to shares which are lodged as collateral with that person or entity, provided the person or entity controls the voting rights and declares its intention of exercising them;

(d)   voting rights attaching to shares in which that person or entity has the life interest;

(e)   voting rights which are held, or may be exercised within the meaning of points (a) to (d), by an undertaking controlled by that person or entity;

(f)   voting rights attaching to shares deposited with that person or entity which the person or entity can exercise at its discretion in the absence of specific instructions from the shareholders;

(g)   voting rights held by a third party in its own name on behalf of that person or entity;

(h)   voting rights which that person or entity may exercise as a proxy where the person or entity can exercise the voting rights at its discretion in the absence of specific instructions from the shareholders.

Any person owning or indirectly controlling more than 10 per cent of the voting rights of the company is required to proceed to the above notifications if the percentage of his or her voting rights is modified equally to or in excess of 3 per cent of the total of the voting rights of the company.

According to Law 3461/2006 implementing into Greek law the EC Directive 2004/25 on takeover bids, if by a share purchase on the market, a person exceeds, due to this acquisition, the limit of 33.3 per cent of the total of the voting rights of a listed company, he or she is obliged to make a mandatory offer for 100 per cent of the company's shares within 20 days from the share purchase. An Offering Circular prepared by the investor has to be approved by the Capital Market Commission within 10 days from the day of the submission to the Capital Markets Commission ("CMC") of the draft of the Offering Circular.

Pursuant to the recent modification of the basic law on *sociétés anonymes* 2190/1920, a sell-out and a squeeze-out right against and in favour of the holder of 95 per cent of the share capital of a company respectively has been established.

12.6.2   Increase of share capital

The general assembly of the shareholders of a *société anonyme* can decide on an increase of the share capital by a resolution adopted with increased quorum and majority. However, the Articles of a *société anonyme* may also provide that:

(a)   during the first five years from the establishment of the *société anonyme* or within five years from the relevant decision of the general assembly of the shareholders, the board of directors by a majority of two-thirds of all its members shall have the right to increase the share capital by issuing new shares. The share capital increase may not exceed the amount of the initial share capital. Such power may be extended by the general assembly of the shareholders for a period which cannot exceed five years for each extension;

(b)   during the first five years from the establishment of the *société anonyme*, the general assembly by a resolution adopted by simple majority shall have the right to increase the share capital by issuing new shares equal to fivefold the initial capital.

The above-mentioned power of the board of directors to decide the increase of the share capital may be also granted to it by the general assembly (i.e., without the need for a relevant provision in the articles of association), in which case the share capital increase may not exceed the amount of the then paid up capital. Such power may also be extended in the above-mentioned manner. In an attempt to facilitate book building, recent amendments have allowed the general assembly to authorise the board of directors to determine the price at which any new shares may be offered. It has also been made possible for the articles of association to provide for an increase in the share capital through the issuance of redeemable shares.

It must be noted that the above restrictions to the amount of the share capital increase do not apply to banking *sociétés anonymes* (Article 55 of Law 1961/1991).

The above increases of the share capital do not constitute an amendment of the articles of association, but a resolution of the general assembly of shareholders adopted with increased quorum and majority is always required when the reserves of a *société anonyme* exceed one-fourth of the paid-up share capital.

In every case of increase of the share capital, which is not effected by means of a contribution in kind or the issuance of bonds with the right of their conversion into shares, pre-emption rights are provided in favour of existing shareholders according to the proportion of share capital they hold. After the time set for the exercise of the pre-emption right has expired (it is set by the body deciding the increase and may not be shorter than a month or 15 days for listed shares), any shares which have not been subscribed as above shall be freely disposed of by the board of directors. The invitation to exercise the pre-emption right must be published in the *Government Gazette*. If, however, all the shares are registered, the invitation to exercise the pre-emption right may be carried out by sending registered letters to the shareholders.

The pre-emption rights in favour of existing shareholders may be cancelled or restricted by a decision of the general assembly taken with increased quorum and majority. Any such decision is valid only if the board of directors submits a written report explaining the reasons for the cancellation or restriction of the shareholders' pre-emption rights and justifying the suggested price. The relevant decision of the general assembly must be duly published.

Further to the recent amendments of the applicable law, an increase of the share capital of only one class of shares may take place with the relevant pre-emption rights existing in principal only for shareholders of that class.

12.6.3   Bonds convertible into shares

A decision to issue bonds convertible into shares is adopted by the general assembly of the shareholders with an increased quorum and majority or by the board of directors by a majority of two-thirds of all its members and for an amount that does not exceed the amount of the paid-up capital. The publication requirements for any increase of the share capital also apply.

If there are several classes of shares, every decision of the general assembly of the shareholders pertaining to the issue of bonds convertible into shares or the granting of a relevant power to the board of directors must be approved by the classes of shareholders whose rights are affected by those decisions.

The corporate body which decides to issue bonds must also determine the time and the manner of exercising the right of conversion as well as the conversion rate.

12.6.4   Acquisition of a limited liability company

A limited liability company can be acquired either by purchasing existing company parts from a partner or partners of the limited liability company or by purchasing new parts if there is an increase of the company's capital.

12.6.4.1   Purchase of existing company parts

The parts of a limited liability company are freely transferable and inheritable. However, the free transferability of the parts may be restricted by provisions of the articles of association requiring the consent of the other members, or further conditions, in particular a right of first refusal of the other members to purchase the portions.

The transfer of parts is effected by a contract in notarial form containing the name, profession, address and nationality of the acquirer. The notarial deed must be entered in the Book of Partners. This requires an application by the transferor or the transferee and submission of the notarial deed.

Publication requirements also apply. Thus, the notarial deed shall be filed with the Secretary of the First Instance Court of the district where the company has its registered offices by any member, company officer or notary public, and it shall be entered in the Register of Limited Liability Companies. A notice of the entry shall be published in the *Government Gazette*.

12.6.4.2 Increase of the company's capital

The increase of the capital of a limited liability company can be effected as follows:

(a) the decision for the increase is adopted by the members' meeting with an increased majority and is subject to the publicity formalities mentioned at (e) below. In the absence of any provision in the articles of association to the contrary, every member has a preferential right to the new portions according to his/her participation;

(b) the new portions are taken by the interested parties (members or third parties) by a written declaration addressed to the company, within 20 days from the relevant decision for the increase of the company's capital;

(c) within 10 days from the expiry of the above time limit, a notarial instrument shall be drafted between the administrators of the company and the new members. All the portions shall be fully paid up. Contributions in kind are valued by the specialist committee of Law 2190/20 on *sociétés anonymes*;

(d) entry in the Book of Members;

(e) the notarial deed shall be filed with the secretary of the First Instance Court of the district where the company has its registered offices by any member, company officer or notary public, and it shall be entered in the Register of Limited Liability Companies. A notice of the entry shall be published in the *Government Gazette*.

12.6.4.3 Sale of shares or parts and third-party consents

If there is a transfer of shares or parts by sale or otherwise, there is no change in the legal status of the company so there is no need to obtain the consent of third parties who may have contractual relationships with the said company. However, some contracts (i.e., distribution agreements, lease agreements) provide that they are subject to termination if there is any change in the actual ownership or control of the company with which they have entered into the agreement, so that the other contracting party will always be fully aware of any such changes. Other contracts may also provide that the prior written approval of the other contracting party is required for any such changes.

Since the transfer of shares of parts of a company does not involve any change in the legal status of the employer-company, any rights and obligations of the employees are not affected. Moreover, in the absence of a specific agreement to the contrary, no consultation or agreement with the employees is required.

12.6.5 Sale of business

A sale of business involves the transfer from the seller to the purchaser of all the assets and liabilities of the seller. With the exception of mergers between *sociétés anonymes* and limited liability companies under Law 2190/1920 and Law 3190/55, a transfer of a business can be effected through the separate transfer of all the assets and liabilities of the company provided that all the formalities set out by Greek law are followed. Thus, according to Greek law, to transfer the ownership of immovable property, an agreement which shall take the form of a notarial deed is required between the owner and the acquirer. The notarial instrument shall also be duly registered at the Land Register. On the other hand, to transfer the ownership of movable property, the actual transmission of the possession thereof by the owner to the acquirer is required and the agreement of both to the effect that ownership has been transferred. A special procedure may be provided for certain movables, such as vehicles, the transfer of which is effected with the issue of a new vehicle circulation licence by the Ministry of Transport & Communications further to relevant certification by the tax inspector. Rights and obligations are also transferred. However, certain contracts (i.e., leases and distribution agreements) can be transferred only with the consent of the other party, otherwise they are subject to termination.

According to Article 479 of the Greek Civil Code, if a business is sold in its entirety, the acquirer shall be liable to a creditor for the debts burdening the business to the extent of the value of the assets transferred. The responsibility of the transferor shall be maintained. Any agreement to the contrary between the contracting parties that is to the detriment of the creditors is void.

In view of the above, if in the sale of a business the obligations are transferred without the prior consent of the creditors, they may turn against both the original debtor – the seller – and against the acquirer, who becomes jointly liable with the seller.

Moreover, under Article 455 of the Greek Civil Code the seller may, by contract, transfer to the acquirer his rights stemming from a contract, without the consent of the debtor (assignment). In this case, however, in order to acquire any right against the debtor and any third parties, the acquirer (assignee) or the assignor must notify the assignment to the debtor. This notification is not subject to any particular form but it is usually served by a court bailiff.

12.6.6   Tender offer

As mentioned above, Law 3461/2006 has implemented into Greek Law the EC Directive 2004/25 on takeover bids. Specific related issues are regulated by Decision no. 17/427/9.5.2007 of the CMC.

12.7   Special issues

12.7.1   Tax considerations

12.7.1.1   Tax incentives for mergers and conversions of companies

To encourage the creation of larger economic units through mergers which are competent to meet the various problems arising from speedy technical and financial progress, Legislative Decree 1297/72 and Law 2166/93 introduced special tax incentives.

LD 1297/72

The provisions of LD 1297/72 apply to mergers or conversions of undertakings of any legal type into a *société anonyme* or a limited liability company as long as the merger or the conversion is completed before 31 December 2005.

The incentives provided are the following:

(a)   At the time of the merger or conversion there is no obligation to pay income tax on the surplus value arising thereon. The surplus value is ascertained after an evaluation of assets and liabilities of the undertakings to be merged or converted and appears in a special account of the company which will result from the merger and will be subject to income tax when the company is eventually dissolved.

(b)   The following are all exempt from any tax, stamp duty or any other duty or charge in favour of the state or any third person:

   (i)   the merger or conversion agreement;
   (ii)   the contribution and transfer of assets and liabilities of the companies to be merged or converted;
   (iii)   any relevant act or agreement pertaining to the contribution or transfer of assets, liabilities and rights;
   (iv)   any title;
   (v)   the decisions of the statutory bodies of the undertakings under merger or transformation;
   (vi)   any other agreement or act necessary for the merger, conversion and formation of the new company;
   (vii)   the publication thereof in the *Government Gazette* and the registration of related acts.

   However, the company resulting from the merger or conversion is subject to tax on concentration of capital equal to 1 per cent. In a merger by acquisition or absorption, this tax will be calculated on the amount whereby the share capital of the acquiring company has been increased; while in a merger by the creation of a new company, it will be calculated on the share capital of the new company after deducting the sum of the nominal share capital of the merging entities, plus reserves and non-distributed profits;

(c)   Real estate owned and used by the undertakings under merger or conversion is exempt from property transfer tax on the condition that the property thus contributed to the merged or newly formed company shall be used for the needs of the company for a period of at least five years starting from the date of merger or conversion.

During this five-year period, the merged or newly formed company, on condition that the principal activity of the "new" company shall not change, is allowed:

(a)   to lease the property contributed;

(b)   to sell the property contributed provided that the proceeds from the sale shall be used during the next two years for the acquisition of real estate or other new fixed assets intended for the operational needs of the company or for the settlement of debts existing at the time of sale from bank loans and credits or from tax liabilities towards the state and social security contributions.

The above exemptions and facilities are subject to the following prerequisites:

(a)   the capital of the company created as a result of the merger or conversion must be, for a *société anonyme*, at least €293,470 fully paid up and for a limited liability company €146,735;

(b)   the shares of the "new" *société anonyme* corresponding to the value of the contributed capital must be registered and 75 per cent thereof must be non-transferable for a period of five years from the year of the merger or conversion, except for shares corresponding to the value of the capital contributed from another *société anonyme* whose shares are bearer shares. Moreover, in the case of a limited liability company, the parts corresponding to the value of the contributed capital of the merged or converted company must be non-transferable by a percentage of 75 per cent for a period of five years from the merger or conversion.

If the merging or the newly formed company is dissolved before five years have elapsed after the merger or conversion, it must pay the income tax on the surplus value from which it had been exempted by reason of the said provisions. The tax is calculated on the basis of the surplus value at the time of the dissolution of the company and is payable as determined by the income tax provisions in force at the relevant time. Thus, *sociétés anonymes* are taxed on their value prior to distribution, and limited liability companies and partnerships are taxed on income received during the year in which the companies were dissolved. All other taxes, duties and dues from which exemptions had been claimed are payable on the basis of the rates applicable at the time when the merger, conversion, etc. was carried out.

These taxes are paid to the state without any penalties as long as the tax declaration is filed by the responsible company with the competent tax office within two months of the company's dissolution.

However, the benefits of LD 1297/72 are applicable if the company claiming the benefits is dissolved prior to the expiry of the five-year period with the purpose of:

(a)   merging with another undertaking;
(b)   establishing one or more other *sociétés anonymes* by dividing the initial one;
(c)   seceding a sector and contributing the assets and liabilities of the sector to another operating or newly established *société anonyme*.

Law 2166/93
The provisions of Law 2166/93 apply in the following cases:

(a)   conversion or merger of undertakings of any type located in Greece into a domestic *société anonyme* or a limited liability company;
(b)   absorption of undertakings of any type by an existing or newly established domestic *société anonyme* or limited liability company;
(c)   merger of *sociétés anonymes* within the meaning of Law 2190/20 (regulating *sociétés anonymes*).
(d)   dissolution of *sociétés anonymes* provided that the so dissolved companies are absorbed by existing *sociétés anonymes*.
(e)   contribution by a company of one or more sectors or parts to an existing *société anonyme*.

In order to fall within the scope of the law, companies under transformation must keep third-class books (double-entry bookkeeping system) under the Code of Fiscal Books and Records and must have drawn up at least one balance sheet for a 12-month fiscal period or longer.

Since the introduction of Law 2166/93, it is possible for the first time in Greece for the branches of foreign limited companies which are established in Greece to convert or merge into a Greek *société anonyme* or limited liability company.

According to Law 2166/93, the transformation is effected contrary to the relevant provisions of Law 2190/20 and Law 3190/55 (regulating limited liability companies) by consolidating the assets and liabilities reflected in the balance sheets of the companies under transformation, which are transferred to the company resulting from the transformation, hereinafter called the "new company". The registered capital of the undertaking or the sum of registered capitals of undertakings under transformation is considered as capital contributed to the new company. If the undertakings to be transformed have losses suffered during the current or previous accounting year's operation, these losses must appear in a specific account in their balance sheet and in the balance sheet of the "new company".

The capital participation ratios in the new company are determined by the partners' meeting or by the General Assembly of shareholders of the companies under transformation. The capital of the new company cannot be less than €293,470 for *sociétés anonymes* and €146,735 for limited liability companies.

Any transactions carried out by the undertakings under transformation subsequent to the date of the balance sheet drawn up for the purpose of transformation are considered as carried out on behalf of the new company and the relevant account balances are transferred to its books.

The tax exemptions and benefits provided by Law 2166/93 are the following:

(a) the merger agreement, the contribution and transfer of assets and liabilities of companies under transformation, any relevant act or deed, the decisions of statutory bodies, the capital participation ratio, any other agreement or act necessary for the transformation or establishment of the new company, the publication thereof in the *Government Gazette* and the registration of related acts are exempted from any tax, stamp duty or any other duty in favour of the state or any third party;

(b) in order to facilitate the transformation, the undertakings involved can apply to the competent tax office for a tax inspection according to the applicable provisions. In this case, the reports, etc. resulting from the inspection must be served on the applicant within a three-month period from the date of application. This period can be extended for three months by the head tax officer on the grounds of exceptional circumstances relating to the size of the company or the inspection procedures required. The income tax reports of tax experts which are drawn up for each company under transformation shall include a special Chapter referring to the accounting value of assets and liabilities. If the companies do not apply for a tax inspection, the accounting value of the assets and liabilities of the companies involved is ascertained by a chartered accountant;

(c)   in cases of transformation of undertakings pursuant to the provisions of this law, the tax incentives extended to them by virtue of other investment laws apply also to the new companies to the extent that the undertakings under transformation have not made use of these benefits;

(d)   special tax-free deductions or reserves created out of profits of companies involved are not subject to tax at the time of transformation provided they are transferred and shown separately in special accounts.

The enforcement of this law is not incompatible with the provisions of Law 2190/20 regulating the legal status of *sociétés anonymes*. As mentioned above, LD 1297/72 shall remain in force up to 31 December 2005. As long as LD 1297/72 remains in force, the undertakings to be transformed may choose to follow the procedures of this LD or of this Law.

12.7.1.2   Sale of shares

Law 2753/1999 imposed a 5 per cent tax on transfer of shares of companies not listed on the Athens Stock Exchange which tax is assessed on real value of shares. Capital gains from the sale of listed securities earned by natural persons without obligation to maintain double-entry accounting records (Greek or foreign residents) and companies domiciled in Greece without obligation to maintain double-entry accounting records are exempt from taxation without the need to comply with any requirements. It should be noted that the 5 per cent tax is currently treated by the Greek Ministry of Finance as income tax, though there is a contradictory opinion of the State law council, treating the 5 per cent tax as transfer tax. Such opinion is not yet accepted by the Greek Ministry of Finance. Accordingly, in the event that the seller in the transaction is a foreign company, exemption from the said tax can be obtained by application of the relevant treaty provisions and as long as the requirements set forth by the treaty are met.

By virtue of Law 2579/1998 (as amended and in force), a tax is imposed on Athens Stock Exchange securities listed transactions at the rate of 0.15 per cent of the purchase price. The tax is borne by the seller and is charged by the Depositary of Titles Company to brokerage firms, who then in turn charge their clients. In addition, a levy is charged by the Athens Stock Exchange to cover settlement costs.

12.7.1.3   Sale of parts

The sale of parts of limited liability companies is not subject to any tax or stamp duty. However, since the portions of a limited liability company can be transferred only by an act executed before a notary public, the sale of portions is subject to notarial and other charges amounting to approximately 3–3.5 per cent of the purchase price, plus publication expenses in the *Government Gazette*. Moreover, any profit made from the sale of parts is taxed independently at a rate of 20 per cent.

12.7.1.4   Sale of business

The sale of business involves the separate transfer of all the assets of the company for a certain price. Any profits derived from the sale of the company assets will be subject to tax according to certain basic rules:

(a)   immovables are primarily subject to property transfer tax which is paid by the buyer. Any profits made by a *société anonyme* or a limited liability company from the sale of immovables are subject to income tax;

(b)   any profits made from the sale of fixed assets used in the business other than immovables are considered to be income, and taxed as such. In addition such transactions are subject to VAT;

(c)   pursuant to Law 2238/94 (as amended and in force) profits arising from the transfer (sale) of an entire business are subject to 20 per cent tax. The sale of a "significant" shareholding in a Greek *société anonyme* may be subject to the provisions of this law should the tax authorities construe, or argue successfully, that such a sale constitutes a transfer of an entire business. Moreover, according to the same law any benefit derived from the transfer of any right or privilege (e.g., leases, patents, etc.) is also taxed separately at a rate of 30 per cent and is subject to VAT.

12.7.2   Insider dealing and market manipulation

Recently, Greek Law 3340/2005 implemented Council Directive 2003/6 regarding insider dealing and market manipulation.

According to Law 3340/2005, any person who possesses inside information:

(a)   by virtue of his membership of the administrative, management or supervisory bodies of the issuer; or

(b)   by virtue of his holding in the capital of the issuer; or

(c)   by virtue of his having access to the information through the exercise of his employment, profession or duties; or

(d)   by virtue of his criminal activities,

is prohibited from using that information by acquiring or disposing of, or by trying to acquire or dispose of, for his own account or for the account of a third party, either directly or indirectly, financial instruments to which that information relates.

Where the said person is a legal person, the above prohibition shall also apply to the natural persons who take part in the decision to carry out the transaction for the account of the legal person concerned.

In addition, any person subject to the above prohibition is prohibited from:

(a)   disclosing inside information to any other person, unless such disclosure is made in the normal course of the exercise of his employment, profession or duties;

(b)   recommending or inducing another person, on the basis of inside information, to acquire or dispose of financial instruments to which that information relates.

The aforementioned prohibitions also apply to any person who possesses inside information, while that person knows, or ought to have known, that it is inside information.

According to same Law, "inside information" means information of a precise nature which has not been made public, relating, directly or indirectly, to one or more issuers of financial instruments or to one or more financial instruments and which, if it were made public, would be likely to have a significant effect on the prices of those financial instruments or on the price of related derivative financial instruments.

Moreover, Law 3340/2005 prohibits any person from engaging in market manipulation. "Market manipulation" means:

(a)   transactions or orders to trade which give, or are likely to give, false or misleading signals as to the supply of, demand for or price of financial instruments, or which secure, by a person or persons acting in collaboration, the price of one or several financial instruments at an abnormal or artificial level;

(b)   transactions or orders to trade which employ fictitious devices or any other form of deception or contrivance;

(c)   dissemination of information through the media, including the internet, or by any other means, which gives or is likely to give false or misleading signals as to financial instruments, including the dissemination of rumours and false or misleading news, where the person who made the dissemination knew, or ought to have known, that the information was false or misleading.

In breaches of the above provisions of Law 3340/2005, the Capital Market Committee is competent to impose, other than administrative sanctions, a fine up to €2 million. The maximum limit may triple in the case of a relapse.

In addition, any person who, with the aim of acquiring, either himself or through a third party, property profit, knowingly uses inside information to acquire or dispose of, either himself or through a third party, financial instruments to which that information relates, is penalised by imprisonment.

Similarly, any person who, with the aim of manipulating the price or marketability of financial instruments in order to acquire, either himself or through a third party, property profit:

(a)   carries out transactions, using knowingly fictitious devices or deceitful means; or

(b)   knowingly disseminates, through the media, internet or by any other means, misleading or false information, news or rumours,

is penalised by imprisonment.

The implementation of the above-mentioned provisions is further specified in the CMC Decisions nos. 1–4/347/12.7.2005.

12.7.3   *Financial assistance*

12.7.3.1   *Banks*
Banks operating in Greece can financially assist Greek companies to acquire the shares of another company. Prior to the deregulation of the banking system in Greece, banks were not allowed to finance more than 50 per cent of the purchase price of the shares in question. Nowadays the banking market is free to establish its own rules for the acquisition of shares or of another company. Terms and

conditions are fixed on the basis of the credibility of the specific buyer between him and his bankers.

12.7.3.2 *Foreign interests*

Foreign interests, when acquiring a Greek enterprise, do not usually obtain financial assistance from the local money market. Usually they are financially assisted through bankers operating abroad under terms and conditions that are neither announced nor reported to any regulatory body, there being no such obligation.

12.8 Conclusions

Due to the fundamental changes in the Greek economy that have occurred since 1995, the country has enjoyed steady growth and joined the Economic Monetary Union at the beginning of 2001. The economy is now functioning more efficiently. Business initiative is also increasing. These factors in combination with the removal of exchange rate risk and low interest rates have contributed to a more stable environment promoting consumption and private investment.

In August 2004, Athens hosted the 28th Olympic Games and the 12th Paralympic Games. High levels of private and government investment have significantly improved the infrastructure around Athens. While there may be some deceleration of growth following the Olympic and Paralympic Games, Greece is expected to have sustained growth for several years provided that fiscal consolidation accelerates and bureaucratic blockages are eliminated.

Chapter 13

Hungary

Konrád Siegler, Partner
Gábor Zoltán Szabó, Senior Associate
Siegler Law Office Weil, Gotshal & Manges[1]

13.1   Introduction

Hungary first introduced legislation regulating takeovers of public companies in 1998. Prior to 1998 most mergers and acquisitions ("M&A") activity in Hungary involved privatisations, joint ventures and, to a limited extent, greenfield investments. Only one public takeover, that by Bristol Myers-Squibb of Pharmavit (a pharmaceutical manufacturer), occurred before the enactment of Act CXLIV of 1997 on Economic Associations ("the old Companies Act"), which came into effect on 16 June 1998, amending Act CXI of 1996 on the Offering of Securities, Investment Services and on the Stock Exchange ("the Securities Act"). The amended Securities Act contained provisions that, for the first time in the Hungarian legal history, regulated public takeovers.

Since 1998 more takeovers of public companies have been attempted and completed in Hungary. Among the completed transactions that have occurred under the 1998 legislation are the successful takeovers of:

(a)   Cofinec, a packaging company;
(b)   TVK, a chemicals manufacturing conglomerate;
(c)   Kékkúti Ásványvíz, a mineral water producer; and
(d)   Eravis, a hotel company.

The 1998 legislation sought to protect minority shareholders from the devaluation of their shares as a result of a takeover. However, that legislation was seen as inadequately regulating many aspects of takeovers; it is generally perceived that apparent circumvention of the takeover laws then in effect enabled a blue-chip Hungarian company to be taken over in early 2001 without the occurrence of a public purchase offer (takeover offer), which generated heavy eco-political pressure to amend the takeover laws.

Hungary's new capital markets legislation, Act CXX of 2001 on Capital Markets ("the Capital Markets Act") came into effect on 1 January 2002. The Capital Markets Act basically copied the new takeover regulations which came into effect on 18 July 2001 as a result of the amendment of the Securities Act, since the adoption of the new takeover legislation was accelerated separately from the

---

[1] With thanks to László Nagy (senior associate) and Dániel Dózsa (associate) for their contributions.

drafting of the Capital Markets Act. Compared to earlier laws, the revised legislation was strict and detailed, seeking to address all possible takeover scenarios and to impede circumvention of the law.

The Capital Markets Act has been amended several times and significant changes came into force:

(a)   on 1 July 2005 due to the implementation of the Directive 2003/71/EC on the prospectus to be published when securities are offered to the public or admitted to trading and amending Directive 2001/34/EC ("Prospectus Directive") and Directive 2003/6/EC on insider dealing and market manipulation ("Market Abuse Directive");

(b)   on 1 January 2006 due to the implementation of the new regulation on private equity funds;

(c)   on 20 May 2006 due to the implementation of Directive 2004/25/EC on takeover bids ("the Takeover Directive");

(d)   on 1 July 2007 due to the implementation of Directive 2006/49/EC on the capital adequacy of investment firms and credit institutions;

(e)   on 24 October 2007 as a result of the adoption of Act CXVI of 2007 on amending various acts affecting strategic companies engaged in the provision of public utilities ("the Strategic Companies Act"); and

(f)   on 1 December 2007 due to the implementation of Directive 2004/39/EC on markets in financial instruments amending Council Directives 85/611/EEC and 93/6/EEC and Directive 2000/12/EC and repealing Council Directive 93/22/EEC ("the MiFID Directive").

As a result of the implementation of the MiFID Directive, not only was the Capital Markets Act amended but Act CXXXVIII of 2007 on investment enterprises, commodity exchange brokers and their services was adopted as well.

Following the adoption of the new takeover legislation in 2001, several takeovers were completed or commenced, for example the takeover of:

(a)   Graboplast (a plastics manufacturer);

(b)   Brau Union Hungária (a brewery company);

(c)   DÉDÁSZ, TITÁSZ, ÉDÁSZ (all electricity companies);

(d)   Zalakerámia (a tile and sanitaryware manufacturer);

(e)   Pick (a food manufacturer);

(f)   MKB, Erste Bank Hungary and Postabank (all credit institutions);

(g)   Antenna Hungária (broadcasting and telecommunication company);

(h)   Danubius (a hotel company);

(i)   Borsodchem (a chemical company);

(j)   Graphisoft (a software company).

In the context of these transactions, the Hungarian Financial Supervisory Authority ("the Supervisory Authority"), as regulator of Hungary's capital markets and financial and insurance sector, was asked to interpret certain provisions of the takeover legislation. In connection with various takeovers, the Hungarian courts (including arbitration courts) have been called upon to provide such interpretation. However, Hungary does not have an extensive court practice or precedents relating to takeover issues. Thus practice relating to the interpretation of the new takeover legislation is still underdeveloped.

On balance, the takeover legislation is potentially of importance to a relatively small number of companies which impact a comparatively large portion of the Hungarian economy. Due to privatisations and greenfield investments, many Hungarian companies are subsidiaries of foreign multinationals and are operated as private rather than public companies. These privately owned subsidiaries represent a significant number of companies existing in Hungary. However, several of the blue-chip Hungarian companies with significant annual turnover are public and listed on the Budapest Stock Exchange ("BSE") as well as foreign exchanges. Trends in capital markets indicate that a significant increase in the number of blue-chip Hungarian public companies cannot reasonably be expected.

Unlike the Capital Markets Act, the interpretation of, and the related court practice regarding, Act IV of 2006 on economic associations ("the Companies Act") is significantly more developed. Essentially following the German company law model, the Companies Act was first enacted in 1988 and has been amended several times since (most significantly in 1997 by the old Companies Act and in 2006 by the new Companies Act) in an effort to incorporate the latest experiences, to respond to the new challenges and to harmonise the Hungarian companies law with that of the European Union ("EU law"). The Companies Act regulates, among other things, mergers and demergers (spin offs), and imposes certain reporting obligations upon the acquisition of a significant ownership interest, even in a privately held company.

Significant acquisitions – of companies and lines of business – resulting from M&A transactions may require Competition Office approval in accordance with the provisions of Act LVII of 1996 on the Prohibition of Unfair and Restrictive Market Practices, as amended ("the Competition Act"), if the turnover thresholds of the transaction participants meet the minima established by the Competition Act. The Capital Markets Act shall apply to an acquisition of influence in target companies with shares which are either listed on a Hungarian-regulated market or not listed but were offered publicly in Hungary. The Capital Markets Act shall not apply to an acquisition of influence in:

(a)   collective investment vehicles operating in the form of a company under its own law; or

(b)   the central banks of EU Member States.

If the target company's shares are admitted to trading on regulated markets in more than one EU Member State, the competent supervisory authority for the public purchase offer shall be from the EU Member State on the regulated market of which the securities were first admitted to trading. If the target company's shares were first admitted to trading on regulated markets in more than one EU Member State simultaneously, the target company shall determine which supervisory authority of those EU Member States shall be competent to supervise the public purchase offer by notifying those regulated markets and their respective supervisory authority on the first day of trading.

If the Supervisory Authority is competent to supervise the public purchase offer of the target company, and the target company has its registered office in an EU Member State other than Hungary:

(a)   the level and calculation method of the acquisition of influence triggering the obligation to make a public purchase offer;

(b)   the disclosure of information to the employees; and

(c)   the performance of an exceptional nature by the target company's board of directors following its initial awareness of the public purchase offer (i.e., actions to frustrate the public purchase offer),

shall be governed by the laws of the EU Member State in which the target company has its registered office.

If the target company's shares are admitted to trading on regulated markets in more than one EU Member State, the Supervisory Authority shall communicate its decisions concerning any acquisition of influence or public purchase offer to the supervisory authorities of the EU Member States affected within two working days from the date the resolutions are adopted. At the request of the competent supervisory authorities of such EU Member States, the Supervisory Authority shall forward the information requested concerning any particular acquisition of influence. Where the Supervisory Authority is convinced that any actual or alleged breaches of the rules governing the acquisition of influence are being or have been committed in another EU Member State, the Supervisory Authority shall notify the competent supervisory authority in such EU Member State.

13.2   Acquisition targets

Hungarian companies may be classified into three main categories:

(a)   partnerships (unlimited partnership, limited partnership) which are always private;

(b)   limited liability companies ("Kft") which are always private; and

(c)   companies limited by shares ("Rt"), which may be either private or public.

A private Rt is one which has never made a share issuance to the general public. A public Rt is one which has made a share issuance to the public; it might be listed on a Stock Exchange, but this is not a requirement.

Companies conducting certain types of business activities, such as banking services, are required to be established in the form of an Rt (and may require advance regulatory approval).

13.2.1   Private companies

Many Hungarian companies are privately owned and do not qualify as public companies. Acquisitions of such companies occur under the purchase agreement among the shareholders and the purchasers. Such agreements are regulated by Act IV of 1959 on the Civil Code, as amended ("the Civil Code") and the Companies Act provisions, but generally are not impacted by the Capital Markets Act. There are also certain reporting and publication requirements related to share acquisitions in a private company and an obligation to register the shareholding of registered shares into the shareholders' registry in order to ensure the exercising of shareholders' rights vis-à-vis the company.

The Civil Code and the Companies Act do not contain specific regulations applicable to share purchase agreements. Thus, in the absence of the parties' express agreement concerning particular issues, only the Civil Code's rules generally applicable to contracts would apply. Certain aspects of the transfer of shares in an Rt or quotas in a Kft are regulated in the Companies Act and the Capital Markets Act. Accordingly, the printed registered shares must be endorsed to the purchaser, while the dematerialised shares must be transferred to the purchaser's securities account.

13.2.2 Public and public listed companies

Generally, the acquisition of shares of a public Rt, whether listed or unlisted, is governed not only by the Civil Code and the Companies Act, but the Capital Markets Act as well and other relevant (e.g., industry specific) legislation.

Shares of a public company, whether listed or not, may be purchased through a simple share purchase transaction if the acquirer does not exceed the takeover thresholds established by the Capital Markets Act, or the acquisition occurs after a successful public purchase offer in which the acquirer has obtained influence above the respective takeover thresholds. However, such acquisition could trigger certain reporting and publication requirements both by the acquirer and the target company.

13.2.3 The BSE's rules apply to public listed companies

Public Rts listed on the BSE are also governed by the BSE's regulations which regulate, amongst other things, the delisting process that typically occurs following the completion of a takeover. Delisting generally requires an application to the BSE and a delisting offer must also be performed. However, if the public purchase offer fulfils certain simple conditions, the public purchase offer can be accepted by the BSE as a delisting offer as well. If the offeror exercises its squeeze-out right following a public purchase offer, the BSE will automatically delist the shares.

The Capital Markets Act authorises the BSE to adopt further rules regarding the acquisition by way of a public purchase offer of a listed company's shares. Such BSE regulations must be approved by the Supervisory Authority. At the time of writing, the BSE did not have such regulations.

13.3 Exchange and investment controls

13.3.1 Exchange controls

Foreign exchange controls were effectively abolished on 16 June 2001, when Government Decree 88/2001 (VI. 15.) concerning the implementation of Act XCV of 1995 on Foreign Exchange entered into force. As part of the completion of this legislation procedure, Act XCV of 1995 on Foreign Exchange which contained certain restrictions on the convertibility of the Hungarian legal tender, has been set aside as well by Act XCIII of 2001 on the Termination of Foreign Exchange

Controls, effective as of 1 January 2002. As a result of the new legislation, the Hungarian forint ("HUF") became fully convertible. Prior to that, transactions of Hungarian persons – whether inside or outside Hungary – and of foreign persons in Hungary in foreign currency and in other pecuniary values were regulated. Following the foreign exchange market's liberalisation, the establishment and operation of Hungarian companies is free of exchange controls. However, in the case of economic difficulties caused by a significant decrease of the Hungarian foreign reserve or if it appears that such difficulties are imminent, the Hungarian Government has the right to restrict international money transfers temporarily.

13.3.2   Controls on investment

Act XXIV of 1988 on the Investments of Foreigners in Hungary, as amended, states that the investments of foreigners in Hungary enjoy full protection and security. Hungary is party to several investment protection accords with various countries.

Hungarian legislation permits a Hungarian registered company to be wholly owned by foreign natural or legal persons. Under "national treatment" principles, such a company is subject to the same laws as a company which is wholly or mainly owned by Hungarian natural or legal persons.

Since Hungary is an EU Member State, the EU law which protects the freedom of capital movement and cross-border investment for EU Member States is directly applicable in Hungary as well.

Investment in certain industries, such as the media, energy and financial services sectors, may require the relevant supervisory agency's prior approval, generally regardless of whether Hungarian or foreign investors are involved. In certain limited industry sectors, such as media, certain Hungarian ownership requirements apply. Absent a sector-specific regulation, generally there are no investment restrictions applicable specifically to foreign investors' purchase of securities in Hungary.

13.4   Labour law considerations

If a workers' representative body (e.g., workers' representative, workers' council or labour union) exists, it must be informed and consulted concerning important measures which the management intends to introduce in respect of the company and concerning the possible legal succession of the employer. The public purchase offer and the offeror's operational plan, as discussed at 13.11.1.2 below, which must be enclosed with the public purchase offer relating to the future operations of the target company, is required to describe the effect of the acquisition of influence on the target company's employees. It is not entirely clear whether the management's awareness of the pendency of a takeover triggers the requirement to consult with the workers' representative body. However, such a requirement would be detrimental to the secrecy of the transaction and, therefore, it can be argued that it is inapplicable in a takeover.

13.5   Disclosure of significant shareholding

13.5.1   *Disclosure of significant shareholdings – general requirements*

The Companies Act requires a notification to the competent Court of Registration if the acquirer directly or indirectly acquires more than 75 per cent of the votes ("qualified interest"). Pursuant to Act V of 2006 on public company information, company registration and winding-up proceedings ("the Company Registration Act"), the target companies must notify the Court of Registration if one person has acquired more than 50 per cent of the votes or has acquired a qualified interest in a Kft or a private Rt. The Court of Registration shall publish a notice regarding such acquisition in the official journal of companies (*Companies Gazette (Cégközlöny)*).

13.5.2   *Definition of influence – disclosure of an acquisition of voting rights or voting shares*

13.5.2.1   *Definition of influence*
The Capital Markets Act implemented the definition of "influence" which must be used when calculating the takeover thresholds. Pursuant to the Capital Markets Act, the acquisition of influence means, in connection with a public Rt, that the acquisition of voting rights enables the acquirer to participate in the decision-making process at the shareholders meeting of the public Rt. An acquisition of influence includes the exercise of call options, repurchase rights or forward purchase rights of voting shares, and the exercise of the voting rights on the basis of the rights of use and of usufruct. Acquisition of influence also includes the indirect acquisition of influence through means other than the direct conduct of the party acquiring the influence, such as legal succession or any resolutions of the public Rt amending voting proportions and/or affecting the voting rights of the shareholders, or where the recovery of the voting rights may result in the acquisition of influence or an acquisition of influence may occur as a result of the cooperation of persons acting in concert. Pursuant to the Capital Markets Act, "persons acting in concert" shall mean natural or legal persons, or organisations without legal personality, who cooperate on the basis of an agreement aimed either at the acquisition of influence in the target company or acquiring control of the offeree company or at frustrating the successful outcome of a public purchase offer. Companies belonging to the same corporate group shall qualify as persons acting in concert without respect to their goals.

To determine the occurrence and the extent of the acquisition of influence, the direct and indirect acquisition of influence, the influence of the persons acting in concert and, in the case of natural persons, the extent of the influence exercised by close relatives must be aggregated.

If a third party exercises voting rights in its own name but on behalf of a shareholder, said rights must be deemed as the shareholder's voting rights, unless the public Rt's shareholders register indicates the nominee as a shareholder and not as a nominee. If the shares were provided as collateral, the obligee of such collateral must be considered as the person exercising voting rights unless the parties' agreement states otherwise.

The exercise of indirect ownership or indirect influence in a target company (public Rt) is also regulated by the Capital Markets Act. An indirect ownership/influence means the exercise of the ownership proportion and/or the voting rights in a target company (public Rt), through the ownership proportion and/or voting rights of another undertaking (intermediary company) holding a direct stake and/or having direct voting rights in the target company (public Rt). In order to establish the ratio of the indirect ownership/influence, the direct voting rights or the direct ownership proportion in the intermediary company is multiplied by the greater of the voting proportion or the ownership proportion which the intermediary company holds in the target company (public Rt). If the voting rights or the ownership proportion of the indirect owners in the intermediary company exceed 50 per cent then the influence of the indirect owner (the owner of the intermediary company) in the target company (public Rt) is deemed to be equal to the direct ownership/influence of the intermediary company in the target company (public Rt).

13.5.2.2 Notification and publication requirements

Under the Capital Markets Act, a person directly or indirectly acquiring or disposing of voting shares or voting rights exceeding 5 per cent (and every multiple of 5 per cent up to 50 per cent, then 75, 80, 85 and 90 per cent, and then every further 1 per cent) in a public Rt, must, without delay, but not later than within two calendar days after the acquisition or disposal, submit a notification to the Supervisory Authority and the board of directors of the target company. For the calculation of the voting rights, all shares to which voting rights pertain must be taken into consideration, even if the exercise of such voting rights is suspended. However, the day following the date on which the acquiring or disposing party becomes aware (or should have become aware) of the acquisition or disposal crossing the notification thresholds, must be deemed the first day for the purposes of the notification obligations. Therefore, it seems that the actual deadline to make the notification is three days from the date of the acquisition or disposal.

Persons who are entitled to acquire, dispose of or exercise voting rights:

(a)   on the basis of an agreement enabling the concerted exercise of voting rights (with the purpose of applying a joint long-term policy vis-à-vis the target company);
(b)   on the basis of an agreement on the temporary transfer of voting rights against consideration;
(c)   in respect of voting rights pertaining to shares provided as a security deposit on the basis of an agreement enabling the exercise of the voting rights by the beneficiary of the deposit;
(d)   on the basis of a right of usufruct; or
(e)   as a proxy if, without any voting instructions from the shareholders, such proxy may exercise the voting rights within its discretion,

must be also taken into account when calculating the notification thresholds.

Further, persons who are directly or indirectly in possession of financial instruments under which a party is able to acquire voting rights over the shares of the target company (including forward and option agreements) must be taken into account when calculating the notification thresholds.

Also, when calculating the notification thresholds, an investor does not need to take into consideration the following:

(a)   the holding of shares, when such shares are purchased for the sole purpose of mutual set-off or settlement during a customarily short settlement period;

(b)   the holding of shares by depositories in their capacity as depository, provided that such depositories may only exercise the voting rights pertaining to the shares subject to instructions received in writing or via electronic means; or

(c)   the purchase or sale by a market maker, provided that it has the licence from its country of registration and it does not intervene in the management of nor exercise any influence with respect to the target company.

When calculating the notification thresholds, the shares held by the shareholder and, among others, its parent company shall be taken into consideration. The parent company directly or indirectly controlling the shareholder or the person holding the voting rights may make the notification on behalf of the direct shareholder.

The above disclosure and notification obligations are not applicable in respect of a parent company whose subsidiary (being an investment enterprise or a credit institution):

(a)   holds a portfolio management licence;

(b)   may only exercise voting rights subject to instructions or if it ensures that it carries out its individual portfolio management services separately from all other services; and

(c)   if it exercises the voting rights independently from its parent company.

The parent company of a fund management company does not have to consolidate its securities portfolio with the securities portfolio managed by the fund management company if the fund management company exercises its voting rights independently from its parent company. However, if and to the extent that the voting rights are exercised directly or indirectly over the securities held at the fund management subsidiary by the parent company or an entity controlled by the parent company, such voting rights must be consolidated.

If the issuer purchases or disposes of treasury shares and as a result the amount of the treasury share exceeds or falls below the respective notification thresholds, the issuer shall publish this information within two days.

In addition to this, no shareholders' right can be exercised until the acquirer complies with its notification obligations.

Following the receipt of the notification, the issuer shall be responsible for publishing the information as an extraordinary announcement.

The Minister of Finance has received authorisation to regulate the details of the notification and publication obligation in its decree. As of the end of December 2007, no such decree had been published.

13.6　Merger control

13.6.1　Concentrations

Hungary first enacted merger control legislation in 1990; the 1990 law was replaced by the 1996 competition legislation which came into force on 1 January 1997 and which is the basis of the current Competition Act, the last major amendment of which came into force on 1 November 2005.

The Competition Act applies when two or more previously independent undertakings consolidate or an undertaking is merged with and/or into another, as well as when part of an undertaking becomes part of a previously unrelated undertaking ("the concentration"). A concentration is also deemed to exist if one or more undertakings acquire control over the whole or part of a previously independent undertaking. The acquisition of the majority of the voting shares of a company – the end result of the takeover of a public company – qualifies as a concentration.

The Competition Act's provisions also apply to acquisitions of the other types of control (i.e., through agreements or by the right to appoint, elect or recall the majority of the target company's executive officers). Further, control may also be acquired where, without owning more than 50 per cent of the voting rights in a company, one or more undertakings are jointly able to exercise decisive influence over the target company. Consistent with the relevant European laws, this type of control occurs *inter alia* when the largest minority shareholder of a public company may exercise de facto control over it, for example if:

(a)　the second-largest shareholder has a shareholding which is much smaller than that of the largest shareholder; and

(b)　the ownership of the target company's shares is widely dispersed. This implies only the possibility of control, the actual existence of which must be established on a case-by-case basis.

The Competition Act excludes from the definition of concentration the acquisition of control by those types of undertakings which generally purchase and sell undertakings or the shares or other securities of undertakings or their assets. Thus, the following does not qualify as a concentration: if a credit institution, an insurance institution, a financial holding company, a mixed-activity holding company, an investment company or the asset management organisation of the state (the holding company of the state-owned undertakings) acquires temporary control (for a maximum of one year, which time period may be extended by the Competition Office upon request) over an undertaking or assets, provided that the purpose of such acquisition is to prepare said undertaking or assets for resale, and the acquirer does not exercise its controlling rights, or exercises such rights only to the extent necessary for the preparation of the resale.

13.6.2　Turnover thresholds and calculation methodology

Generally, Competition Office approval must be requested if, in the year preceding the year in which the concentration occurs:

(a) the aggregate net turnover of the relevant parties to the concentration exceeded HUF15 billion (approximately €60 million); and

(b) there are at least two undertaking groups (participating in the concentration) whose net turnover in the preceding business year, together with the net turnover of undertakings jointly controlled by such undertaking groups and third parties, exceeded HUF500 million (approximately €2 million).

Based on the foregoing rules, the acquisition of a Hungarian undertaking with a HUF16 billion (approximately €64 million) turnover by a non-Hungarian undertaking with no revenues in Hungary, does not require Competition Office approval.

However, Competition Office approval must be obtained if the net turnover of the undertaking(s) coming under control is under HUF500 million but the acquiring undertaking or another undertaking which is non-independent therefrom has conducted concentrations in the previous two years and the aggregate net turnover of the undertakings acquired during the previous two years, together with the undertaking coming under control in the given concentration, exceeds HUF500 million.

For the purposes of the two-year rule, only those prior acquisitions of the acquiring undertaking group made during the previous two years will be taken into consideration where the seller was in the same undertaking group. Consequently, acquisitions of smaller undertakings (i.e., undertakings with annual net revenues below HUF500 million) within a period of two years will add up only if the seller in each case is the member of the same undertaking group.

The Competition Act broadly defines concentration participants to include all direct and indirect participants (i.e., the parent, affiliate and subsidiary companies of the companies participating in the concentration). However, the company losing its respective controlling rights over the target company – typically the seller of the shares – is not considered a participant.

Generally, when calculating turnover figures, trade among the concentration participants must be excluded, and, in the case of foreign companies, only sales made in Hungary by such companies during the year preceding the concentration must be taken into account. Special rules apply to the calculation of the turnover of banks, insurance companies and investment service providers and for the controlling rights over companies owned by the state and municipalities.

13.6.3 Procedures

Generally, if a concentration occurred and the turnover thresholds are met, Competition Office approval must be sought within 30 days of the following (whichever is the earlier to occur):

(a) the date of the signing of the agreement giving effect to the concentration;

(b) the publication of the public purchase offer; or

(c) the actual acquisition of control over the target company.

Without Competition Office approval for the concentration, the agreement is deemed not to have been entered into.

The Competition Office examines the merits of the case, particularly the effects of the concentration on the relevant market, and then approves, prohibits or establishes conditions or obligations in respect of the concentration. The Competition Office must adopt its final decision within:

(a)   45 days if:
     (i)   the transaction is not subject to the Competition Office's approval; or
     (ii)   the granting of the approval obviously cannot be refused; or
(b)   120 days in all other merger control cases.

The above deadlines may be extended once, by 60 days. If the Competition Office does not render a decision within that period, the Competition Office is deemed by law to have approved the concentration.

13.7   Methods of acquisition

13.7.1   Regulation of the conduct of mergers and acquisition

The Supervisory Authority administers and regulates public takeovers. Following the mandatory notice of the offeror concerning the proposed takeover, the Supervisory Authority may prohibit the transaction if the content of the public purchase offer does not comply with the provisions of the Capital Markets Act. The role of the Supervisory Authority in the public takeover regulation process is further detailed at 13.9 below. The Supervisory Authority can be contacted at the following address: Pénzügyi Szervezetek Állami Felügyelete, 1013 Budapest, Krisztina Krt. 39, Hungary; telephone +361 489 9100; fax: +361 489 9102; website: www.pszaf.hu.

As in other European countries, mergers and acquisitions generally not regulated by the Capital Markets Act take the various forms as described at 13.7.2–13.7.8 below.

13.7.2   Private agreements

Due to foreign influence on Hungary's business culture, acquisition agreements used in Hungary (at least in the case of acquisition agreements which are used in connection with huge, complex deals) tend to be modelled to a large extent on the US or UK form of purchase agreements, with certain alterations stemming from the fact that Hungary is a civil law country.

Where a "foreign element" exists, the acquisition agreement is not required to be governed by Hungarian law. Generally, such a "foreign element" can be found to exist if either the seller or purchaser of the shares is a foreign company, regardless of whether the target is a Hungarian company. Advice should be taken concerning choice of law and choice of forum clauses to facilitate enforcement of the agreement's provisions in case of a dispute. Regardless of the law governing the interpretation of the acquisition agreement, the applicable provisions of

Hungarian law, such as the various notification and reporting requirements summarised in this Chapter, apply to the acquisition.

Acquisition agreements typically limit the time period during which the purchaser may recover from the seller for a breach of a warranty. Generally, that time period should be such that it permits the acquirer to close at least two consecutive years' worth of the target company's financials. Sellers typically resist permitting representations and warranties to survive for, and indemnification claims to be made during, longer periods. The statute of limitations is generally five years. Provisions containing thresholds and basket minima and maxima in respect of a potential recovery are typically included.

The acquisition agreement need not be signed before a notary or in compliance with formalities other than general compliance with the signature authority established under each participating company's corporate documents.

The signing of a valid agreement only creates the proper legal title necessary to acquire the given shares, but the purchaser acquires ownership of the shares if the printed bearer shares were handed over to him or the printed registered shares were endorsed to the purchaser or, in the case of a blank endorsement, the shares must also be handed over or the dematerialised shares are credited to the purchaser's securities account.

13.7.3   Mandatory public purchase offers

The Capital Markets Act requires a mandatory public purchase offer for the shares of a public Rt to be launched in the circumstances described at 13.9 below.

13.7.4   Voluntary purchase offers

The Capital Markets Act regulates voluntary purchase offers for the shares of a public Rt. The relevant provisions are summarised at 13.9 below.

13.7.5   Mergers and demergers

The Companies Act permits the merger and demerger – or spin off of a part – of companies. Mergers may take one of two forms:

(a)   the acquisition merger, in which one company merges with and into another, with the latter surviving the merger; or

(b)   the consolidation merger, in which two companies merge with and into a third which survives the merger as the general legal successor.

The company surviving a merger or demerger is the general legal successor of the companies participating in that process.

The procedural rules for consolidations, mergers and demergers are similar, and the procedures are more constrained by the preparation of the required financial and accounting documentation than by the corporate law formalities relating to the process.

13.7.6   *Joint venture*

Initially popular in the late 1980s and early 1990s, joint ventures were displaced by the greenfield investment model in the middle and late 1990s. Recently, the joint venture model, under which two or more persons form a new, special-purpose company usually in the form of a Kft or an Rt through which to conduct their common business activities, is becoming more used in the local market.

13.7.7   *Voting agreement*

Generally, Hungarian legislation does not prohibit entering into voting agreements among the shareholders of an Rt and the members of a Kft. The Companies Act permits classes of shares or quotas with particular voting rights to be established, within the scope of the variations permitted by the Companies Act. However, voting agreements between shareholders are not specifically enforceable under Hungarian law unless the voting agreement's provisions are mirrored in the company's establishment documents. The Courts of Registration generally interpret the Companies Act such that not all voting agreement provisions can be included in the said establishment documents. If such provisions are not mirrored in such establishment documents, action for damages is the only recourse for breach of a voting agreement to the extent that the damages incurred as a result of the breach may be quantified.

Technically, a voting agreement may state that its interpretation is governed by a foreign law if one or more of the shareholders is a foreign company. However, because the Companies Act's provisions deeply impact the relationship of the shareholders, the recent tendency is to agree to Hungarian governing law in respect of such agreements, with disputes to be settled by arbitration in Hungary.

13.7.8   *Asset transactions*

Besides share deals, asset transactions are a common method of selling all or part of a business. Hungarian law generally does not contain specific rules regarding the sale of a division of a business; such sales are treated as asset transactions. The Hungarian labour law regulates the case of "legal succession" of the employer, which requires the transfer of employees to the purchaser of the assets when, for example, a line of business or department is sold.

Asset sales are complex and technical procedures, particularly where real estate is involved. The tax, stamp duty, value added tax and accounting consequences of an asset sale should be carefully considered in advance.

13.8   Preparation of a public purchase offer

13.8.1   *Conduct of negotiation*

Acquisitions of private Hungarian companies occur under share purchase agreements. The shares in a public company may also be acquired under such an agreement if the share acquisition does not trigger the Capital Markets Act requirement to make a public purchase offer for the target's shares.

Negotiations typically involve the signing of a confidentiality agreement – which may or may not contain a standstill clause under which the parties agree to negotiate exclusively with one another for a stated time. Although used in larger transactions, letters of intent are not uniformly used in acquisitions in Hungary.

Generally, the mere negotiation of a share purchase does not seem to give rise to any reporting obligation prior to the conclusion of the contract, although the practice of the Supervisory Authority is continuously developing in this regard.

The Civil Code requires the parties to cooperate during the negotiation and to respect each other's legitimate interests, as well as to inform each other regarding all essential circumstances in relation to the proposed contract before its conclusion. Payment of damages may be the consequence of the violation of this obligation. The Civil Code also permits a court to award damages if a party wholly or in part, through its wilful conduct, explicitly induced another bona fide person to act in a manner that caused damage to the latter through no fault of its own. These "loss of expectation" damages might be applicable, for example, where the parties negotiate the principal contract terms, and one party then unexpectedly interrupts the negotiation without concluding the contract, causing the other to suffer damages as a result.

13.8.2   Due diligence

Due diligence exercises are common in Hungary and are typically conducted by a team of lawyers, financial advisers and commercial representatives of the potential acquirer, with specialist support, such as that of environmental consultants.

13.8.3   Public information

There are several sources of public information which a purchaser may use in preparing for an acquisition.

The trade registry administered by the Court of Registration contains the main corporate details of companies, which are required by the Companies Act to be maintained in that registry. In respect of an Rt, those include, among other things:

(a)   the company's registered capital;
(b)   the name and address of its board of directors and supervisory board members;
(c)   the names of the person(s) authorised to sign on behalf of the company; and
(d)   (except for a public Rt.) those shareholders owning more than 50 or 75 per cent of the votes.

A company's trade registry file at the Court of Registration may be accessed by any third party.

A company's annual financial report or, as the case may be, the consolidated annual financial report must also be submitted to the Company Information Service each year. Those reports are also available to the public upon request at the Court of Registration as well as the Company Information Service.

Prior to the adoption of the Strategic Companies Act, it was possible to obtain information as to the identification of the owner, managing directors and members of the board of directors/supervisory board etc. of a given company provided this information was registered by the trade registry (the shareholders of an Rt are not registered in the trade registry). However, access to information regarding ownership interests or positions of specific persons registered in the Hungarian trade registry was restricted. Following the adoption of the Strategic Companies Act, such access is now allowed.

Under the Capital Markets Act, public companies must regularly disclose to the public information concerning the main data relating to their financial and income position and operations in annual and biannual flash reports, annual reports and periodical management reports.

The issuer shall publish its annual report within four months following the end of the relevant business year and its biannual flash report within two months following the end of the relevant half year and the issuer must ensure that these reports are available for the public for an additional five years. Under the BSE rules, BSE listed companies also must prepare and file biannual or quarterly flash reports (depending on the BSE listing classification of their shares) as well as their annual reports prepared in accordance with the BSE rules. Listed companies generally provide reports which satisfy the requirements of both the Capital Markets Act and the BSE rules. BSE listed companies must also publish their annual reports, biannual or quarterly flash reports by posting them on the BSE's official website. Public companies must publish a periodical management report following the end of the first 10 weeks and before the beginning of the last six weeks of the given half year regarding the period between the commencement of the half year and the publication of the periodical management report if they do not prepare a quarterly flash report under the rules of the given regulated market or on their own initiative.

The Capital Markets Act also requires a public company – whether or not BSE listed – to notify the Supervisory Authority and the public the occurrence of an extraordinary business event within one business day of its occurrence and to publish it. Such an event is one which is likely to directly or indirectly affect the value or return of the company's securities. Similarly, the BSE rules require the issuer to notify the BSE within 30 minutes of becoming aware of information regarding its operation or financial situation which directly or indirectly affects the value or return of its securities, if it occurs between 8 a.m. and the close of BSE opening hours or by 8.30 a.m. on the next trading day if the information was obtained after the close of the BSE. Such information must also be posted on the BSE's website. The issuer must send all information published pursuant to its reporting obligation to the official information storage system. All information that the Supervisory Authority receives pursuant to the issuers' reporting obligation shall be published on a website operated by the Supervisory Authority. As of 1 December 2007, the rules regulating the reporting obligation changed significantly and the detailed rules of the Capital Markets Act regulating the reporting obligation were repealed. Simultaneously, the Minister of Finance received the authorisation to regulate the reporting obligations in detail in its decree but as at 31 December 2007 such decree had not entered into force.

13.8.4 Information from the target company

The Companies Act requires an Rt to keep a shareholders register containing at least the name of the shareholder(s) and the number of the shares held by them. The shareholder may exercise the rights incorporated into the acquired shares only after he has registered himself in the shareholders register and the acquisition of shares becomes effective vis-á-vis the company after the registration. Any shareholder, including one owning a single share, may inspect the shareholders register. Although the relevant legislation is not clear on this point, a shareholder may probably also make notes on the contents of the said register. A third party may also inspect the shareholders register if he can prove a legitimate interest in so doing. In any case, the shareholders register reveals only the target's then current ownership structure (and the shareholders register includes only those shareholders who have registered themselves).

The previous effective takeover legislation required that, prior to the announcement of the public purchase offer, the target company's board of directors had to provide the potential buyer, upon its request, with information concerning the target's operations, which were necessary to establish the terms and conditions of the public purchase offer. Under the new legislation, upon the offeror's request, the board of directors may, but is not required to, disclose such information. The legislation further requires that if said information is released, the offeror, its agent and the investment service provider managing the public purchase offer must treat the information as a business secret, and that the securities-related secrecy obligations apply to said information, as do the prohibitions on insider dealing.

Pursuant to the general rules of the Capital Markets Act, the issuer must publish all insider information which relates to the issuer. Nevertheless, the issuers, in order to protect their legitimate interests, shall be permitted to delay public disclosure of inside information at their own risk, if:

(a)   the delay does not result in misleading the public;
(b)   the issuer notifies the Supervisory Authority concerning the delay immediately; and
(c)   the issuer ensures that the insider information in question is kept confidential.

13.8.5 Increasing shareholding

Hungarian legislation does not regulate the timetable for the building up of a stake in a target company; the stakebuilding process may thus occur gradually. The articles of association of a public Rt may not include restrictions on the acquisition of the company's shares by certain persons, or in any manner contrary to that of a private company. However, a public Rt's articles of association may prescribe the maximum voting rights which may be exercised by an individual shareholder or a shareholder group. The Strategic Companies Act has invalidated the provision of the Companies Act which prescribed that any restriction of voting rights under the articles of association of a public Rt shall cease by virtue of the law upon closing an public purchase offer, if in consequence of the public purchase offer, the offeror acquires influence exceeding 75 per cent.

(However, this invalidated rule should not be applicable until 31 December 2009 if the target company's articles of association contained the voting restriction on 18 July 2001.) If a public Rt has acquired more than 25 per cent of voting rights in an Rt or a Kft, this Rt or Kft may not acquire any shares in the public Rt and must sell its shareholding in the public Rt within 60 days after the acquisition of influence in the public Rt. If the Rt or Kft does not comply with its obligation, they may not exercise any of their voting rights at the shareholders meeting of the public Rt.

13.8.6   *Consequences of achieving various levels of investment in a public Rt*

The Capital Markets Act and the Companies Act focus on ownership percentages and the proportion of influence exercised. Various levels of ownership or influence trigger different reporting rights of the acquirer and vest the minority shareholders with various special rights.

Table 13.1   Powers and obligations of shareholders and relevant thresholds in a public Rt

Percentage threshold	Rights granted to or obligations imposed on the holder of the shares
1%	In the case of a public Rt, the shareholders of at least 1 per cent of the votes may exercise the following minority rights: (a) require the modification of the agenda of a shareholders meeting; and (b) require the review by an independent expert as to whether the payment to the shareholders does not violate the payment restrictions of the Companies Act.
5%	The owners of at least 5 per cent of the votes may exercise minority rights provided that the articles of associations of a company do not set lower thresholds. Minority rights mean the rights to: (a) initiate the convening of a shareholders meeting; (b) require the modification of the agenda of a shareholders meeting (in the case of a Kft, any quota holder may add additional items to the agenda of the quota holders meeting and in the case of a partnership, the members may regulate this issue in the articles of association); (c) require the review by an independent auditor of the company's last annual financial report or any other event which has occurred during the last two years of the company's operation; and (d) enforce a claim of the company against the shareholders or officers of the company; and (e) in the case of an Rt, require the review by an independent expert as to whether the payment to the shareholders does not violate the payment restrictions of the Companies Act.

Table 13.1   continued

Percentage threshold	Rights granted to or obligations imposed on the holder of the shares
	(In the case of a recognised corporate group, the minority owners of at least 5 per cent of the votes may have additional rights under the Companies Act.)
	As mentioned at 13.5.2 above, the Capital Markets Act requires the acquirer to notify the Supervisory Authority and the board of directors of a public Rt of an acquisition of voting rights equal to or exceeding 5 per cent and then of each additional acquisition of voting rights breaking the thresholds prescribed by the Capital Markets Act within two calendar days of the acquisitions. The notification obligation also applies in respect of a decrease of voting rights breaking the given thresholds.
	The BSE rules provide for an extraordinary disclosure requirement to be made by the public Rt in case of a registration of voting rights in the shareholders register breaking the 5 per cent threshold or any integral multiple thereof.
10%	Any person directly or indirectly having at least 10 per cent ownership interest or 10 per cent of the voting rights in a public Rt shall qualify as an inside person and must report any further transaction with such shares to the Supervisory Authority.
	The Strategic Companies Act invalidated the previous 10 per cent maximum for treasury shares of the registered capital. However, no voting rights may be exercised with treasury shares.
25%	The owner of more than 25 per cent of the voting rights in a company may block those actions which require the affirmative vote of a qualified majority of the shareholders. Those are, for example:
	(a) the transformation or winding up of the company without legal successor;
	(b) the transformation of the company into a private company;
	(c) the amendment of the company's articles of association;
	(d) a change in the rights attached to a series of shares;
	(e) the reduction of the registered capital; and
	(f) such other matters as are specified in the Companies Act or in the company's articles of association as requiring a qualified majority vote.
	Where a public Rt acquires 25 per cent or more of the voting rights in another Rt or Kft, henceforward, the other Rt or Kft shall not be entitled to acquire the shares of the public Rt, and shall be required to alienate any shares previously obtained within 60 days following the acquisition of the public Rt. In the event the other Rt or Kft fails to comply with this obligation, it shall not be

Table 13.1 continued

Percentage threshold	Rights granted to or obligations imposed on the holder of the shares
	entitled to exercise shareholders' rights attached to these shares in question. In certain cases a mandatory public purchase offer must be made to acquire influence in excess of 25 per cent in a public Rt, as described at 13.9 below. As explained at 13.5.2.1 above, influence is a broader concept than mere ownership.
33%	This level of influence is the general threshold for the making of a mandatory public purchase offer, absent other circumstances mandating that said public purchase offer occur when a 25 per cent influence is achieved (namely if no shareholder other than the offeror exercises more than 10 per cent influence in the target company).
50%	A shareholder having more than 50 per cent of the voting rights in a company may adopt a resolution not requiring a qualified majority (i.e., 75 per cent) of the votes. The target company must notify the Court of Registration if the shareholders' voting rights exceed 50 per cent in a Kft or a private Rt. The Court of Registration shall publish a notice regarding such acquisition in the official journal of companies (*Companies Gazette (Cégközlöny)*). If a parent company is obliged to prepare consolidated financial statements (amongst others, the parent company is obliged to prepare consolidated financial statements if it has more than 50 per cent of the voting rights in its subsidiary), the parent company and its subsidiaries may conclude a control contract (in Hungarian: *uralmi szerződés*) to create a recognised corporate group. The autonomy of the controlled companies of the recognised corporate group may be restricted in the manner and to the extent specified in the Companies Act and in the control contract, as may be necessary with a view to maintain the interest of the recognised corporate group as a whole. The control contract shall contain provisions for the protection of the rights of the members (shareholders) of controlled companies and for the protection of creditors' interests.
75%	Generally, a 75 per cent shareholder may adopt all resolutions. The Companies Act requires the notification to the competent Court of Registration if the acquirer directly or indirectly acquires more than 75 per cent of the votes (a "qualified interest"). The target companies must notify the Court of Registration if one person has acquired a qualified interest in a Kft or a private Rt. The Court of Registration shall publish a notice regarding such

Table 13.1 continued

Percentage threshold	Rights granted to or obligations imposed on the holder of the shares
	acquisition in the official journal of companies (*Companies Gazette* (*Cégközlöny*)).
90%	An offeror who has an influence equal to or in excess of 90 per cent within three months following the closure of its successful mandatory or voluntary public purchase offer has the option to acquire the balance of the target company's shares: *see* 13.12 below. Also, if the offeror's influence in the target company exceeds 90 per cent at the closing of the public purchase offer, any remaining shareholders may request that the offeror purchases their shares within 90 days of the publication of the acquisition exceeding 90 per cent.
100%	If all of the shares of a public Rt are acquired by one person, it becomes a private company. Thus, it must, among other things, be delisted from the BSE.

13.9 Conduct of a public purchase offer and defences to a hostile public purchase offer

13.9.1 *Hostile and recommended public purchase offers*

The Capital Markets Act does not distinguish between hostile and recommended public purchase offers. The rules of the Capital Markets Act apply without regard to whether the public purchase offer is hostile or friendly.

13.9.2 *Mandatory takeover*

The acquisition of influence exceeding 33 per cent in a public Rt must be made via a public purchase offer, which is approved by the Supervisory Authority in advance. However, where none of the other shareholders of the public Rt holds either directly or indirectly more than 10 per cent of its voting rights, then an acquisition of influence exceeding 25 per cent triggers the requirement to make a public purchase offer.

Further, the acquirer must notify the target's board of directors and the Supervisory Authority if the acquisition of influence exceeding 33 per cent or 25 per cent, as the case may be, was implemented:

(a) not as a result of the direct conduct of the party acquiring the influence; or

(b) through the exercise of a call option, repurchase right, or based on the performance of a forward contract; or

(c)   within the framework of proceedings governed by law and conducted by a state property management organisation (i.e., a privatisation); or

(d)   as a result of the cooperation of persons acting in concert.

This notification is due within two days of the acquisition exceeding said thresholds. The acquirer must simultaneously arrange to publish a notification concerning said acquisition of influence. In such a case the public purchase offer must be made at the latest within 15 days of the notification.

When persons acting in concert acquire influence, all parties to the agreement of such persons are liable for making the public purchase offer. However, they may agree that one of them shall make the public purchase offer. Such an agreement does not exempt the other parties from their responsibility for the making of the public purchase offer.

The offeror must hire a Hungarian investment service provider having the necessary licence to manage the implementation of the public purchase offer.

If, through the public purchase offer the offeror does not acquire all of the target company's shares, it may later increase its influence over the target company without complying with the takeovers rules, provided that it has initially acquired more than 33 per cent or 25 per cent, as the case may be, of the target company's shares. Otherwise, the acquisition of influence in excess of said thresholds may occur only through another public purchase offer.

The takeover rules of the Capital Markets Act are mandatory, and the articles of association of a public Rt may not deviate from said rules except if the Capital Markets Act explicitly allows such deviation. In a particular lawsuit, the court of first instance declared that if an acquirer has acquired influence exceeding the takeover threshold without making a public purchase offer in advance, contrary to the previous practice of the Supervisory Authority, the offeror may not rectify the wrongdoing by making a subsequent public purchase offer. The Supreme Court has overruled this decision on a procedural basis and annulled the decision of the court of first instance (the Supreme Court has declared that the shareholders of the target company have no right to challenge the approval of the Supervisory Authority). However, since the Supreme Court has not decided on the merits of the case, it is not entirely clear at this stage what the practice of the Supervisory Authority and the courts will be in the event a public purchase offer is made following an illegal acquisition of influence exceeding the takeover threshold.

13.9.3   *Terms of the public purchase offer*

The Capital Markets Act contains detailed rules regarding the public purchase offer and its enclosures. Those are described at 13.11 below.

The public purchase offer must be made for all of the shares, and to all of the shareholders holding shares representing voting rights.

The public purchase offer may not contain any conditions which violate the principles of equal treatment of shareholders in connection with their acceptance declaration.

It is a general practice that the offerors exclude US shareholders (or other shareholders residing in a country in which securities law might be applicable, if the citizens or other entities of the given country are not excluded) to avoid the application of US (or another country's) securities law to the public purchase offer. Although it seems that this practice is contrary to the literal meaning of the above-mentioned anti-discrimination rules of the takeover rules, it appears that it is accepted by the Supervisory Authority.

The Capital Markets Act regulates the method for establishing the price to be offered for the target company's shares. In the case of listed companies, the offered price must exceed the higher of:

(a)   the weighted average price of the shares on the Stock Exchange during the 180-day period immediately preceding the submission of the public purchase offer to the Supervisory Authority; or

(b)   the highest price to be paid by the offeror or affiliated persons for the target company's shares under a share purchase agreement concerning such shares, entered into during the above 180-day period; or

(c)   the weighted average price of the shares on the Stock Exchange during the 360-day period immediately preceding the submission of the public purchase offer to the Supervisory Authority; or

(d)   if an option or a repurchase right was stipulated or exercised during the above 180-day period by the offeror or affiliated persons, the cumulative option price and option fees; or

(e)   if the related agreement was concluded within the above 180-day period, any consideration received by the offeror or its affiliated persons for cooperation or concerted action in relation to the exercise of its voting rights; or

(f)   the equity per share.

In the case of non-listed shares, the same rules apply except that the average price for 360 days shall not be taken into consideration when calculating the minimum price.

If less than 36 transactions occurred within the above 180-day period, the weighted average price should not be taken into consideration when calculating the minimum price. Nevertheless, the weighted average price and the highest price paid by the offeror or affiliated persons for the target company's shares must be taken into consideration if more than 90 days but less than 180 days elapsed prior to the submission of the public purchase offer at the Supervisory Authority. If the shares of the target company are listed on more than one regulated market, the highest price from the average prices calculated for each regulated market shall be taken into consideration and the official exchange rate of the Hungarian National Bank in effect on the day of the transaction shall be used.

When calculating the minimum price, the equity indicated in the last audited financial statement or consolidated financial statements (if the target company is obliged to prepare a consolidated financial statement) must be used. If the target company has still not prepared an audited financial statement, the equity which was indicated in the annual or biannual flash reports must be used.

In addition to the public purchase offer, an offeror must prepare an operational plan for the target company's future operation, and if the offeror is a business organisation for the purposes of the Companies Act, it must also prepare a report of its business activities. The offeror and the investment service provider are jointly and severally liable for damages resulting from the lack of truthfulness, accuracy or completeness of the written report concerning the offeror's business activities.

The consideration for the public purchase offer may consist of:

(a)   cash;
(b)   government securities issued by EU Member States or other Organisation for Economic Co-Operation and Development ("OECD") Member States; or
(c)   bank guarantee issued by a credit institution resident in the EU or in another OECD Member State.

No funds are required with respect to those shares which are held by persons acting in concert if they provide a statement declaring that they will not accept the public purchase offer and that they will not alienate their shares during the period to which the bid pertains and for the following two years, nor will they enter into an agreement therefor. Although this restriction is quite logical during the acceptance period, this additional two-year selling restriction seems to be completely nonsensical.

13.9.4   *Public purchase offer timetable*

13.9.4.1   Notification to the board and to the Supervisory Authority
The offeror must submit the public purchase offer to the Supervisory Authority for approval and simultaneously the public purchase offer must be:

(a)   sent to the target company's board of directors; and
(b)   published.

The announcement concerning the public purchase offer must highlight that the Supervisory Authority has not yet approved the public purchase offer and the commencement of the Competition Office proceedings, if any, is required.

Within 15 days from its receipt of the public purchase offer, the Supervisory Authority must decide concerning the public purchase offer. The Supervisory Authority may request additional information and data regarding the public purchase offer and/or its enclosures within five days. The Supervisory Authority must decide on the supplemented offer within five days. The Supervisory Authority must approve the public purchase offer if it and its enclosures satisfy the requirements of the Capital Markets Act. If the Supervisory Authority fails to either approve or reject the public purchase offer within the statutory deadlines, the public purchase offer is deemed to have been approved.

If the Supervisory Authority prohibits a takeover, there is no statutory provision preventing the offeror at any time after such prohibition from preparing another public purchase offer, in compliance with the legislative requirements, to attempt to (re)commence the transaction.

Upon receipt of the public purchase offer, the board of directors of the target company shall immediately forward it to the representatives of the company's employees.

13.9.4.2 *Acceptance period for the public purchase offer*

Before the start of the acceptance period, the board of directors must inform the shareholders of its opinion concerning the public purchase offer and make the opinion available for shareholder review at the place of the inspection of the operational plan and the business activity report. If the Supervisory Authority has approved the public purchase offer with amendments, the board of directors may revise its opinion concerning the public purchase offer. The board of directors must appoint, at the target company's cost, an independent financial adviser to evaluate the public purchase offer. The board of directors must make the adviser's report accessible to the shareholders in the same manner used to disclose the board's opinion concerning the public purchase offer.

Immediately after receiving the Supervisory Authority's decision concerning the public purchase offer, the offeror must arrange to publish the Supervisory Authority's decision and the public purchase offer, indicating its commencement date and the acceptance expiration deadline.

The acceptance period must be at least 30 days but not more than 65 days (including the potential extension). The first day of the acceptance period may not be earlier than the second day nor later than the fifth day after the date of publication of the announcement regarding the Supervisory Authority's approval of the public purchase offer.

The offeror and the persons acting in concert with the offeror, and the close relatives of the offeror and the persons acting in concert with the offeror having influence in the target company provided that the offeror is a natural person, and the affiliated companies (as defined in the Capital Markets Act) of the above mentioned (altogether "the affiliated persons") may not engage in any transaction concerning the transfer, alienation or encumbrance of the shares to which the public purchase offer pertains, until the last day of the acceptance period, unless said transactions are pursuant to a share transfer contract concluded under the public purchase offer. The investment service provider managing the public purchase offer may not engage in any transaction for his own account concerning the shares to which the public purchase offer pertains – except share transfers conducted pursuant to the public purchase offer – until the last day of the acceptance period.

Upon the offeror's justified request to do so, the Supervisory Authority may extend the acceptance period by up to 15 days. Such extension must be published before the expiry of the original acceptance period.

Until the closing date of the acceptance period, the offeror may modify the purchase price stated in the public purchase offer if the modified price represents a higher value, calculated in HUF, than the original consideration. The offeror must publish the new price. Once published, the modified price applies also to acceptances filed before its publication date.

13.9.4.3   Outcome of the public purchase offer

Generally, the offeror must purchase all the shares referred to in acceptance declarations. If the offeror failed to acquire influence exceeding 50 per cent in the target company, and the public purchase offer was expressly conditional thereon, then the purchase obligation will not be triggered. In purchasing the shares, the offeror may not violate the principle of equal treatment of shareholders in connection with their exercising rights in the course of the acceptance of the public purchase offer. Declaration of acceptance may not be rescinded unless the offeror fails to pay for the shares within 30 days after the last date on which payment for the shares was due.

The contract between the offeror and each shareholder that has submitted a declaration of acceptance comes into existence on the last day of the acceptance period, unless the required Competition Office proceeding is not completed by that date. In the latter case, the contract comes into existence on the date the Competition Office's approval of the acquisition is granted.

The offeror must pay the purchase price within five days of the last day of the acceptance period. If a Competition Office proceeding is pending, said deadline runs from the date on which the Competition Office's approval is granted. The Competition Office's decision to reject the transaction cancels the takeover.

If the consideration for the shares is a blend of cash and other instruments, or exclusively other instruments, the shareholders filing acceptance declarations may require payment in cash upon their filing of the acceptance declaration rather than the payment with other instruments.

The offeror must pay default interest if it is late in paying the consideration for the tendered shares. If the offeror has not paid for the tendered shares within 30 days of the purchase price becoming due, the shareholders may rescind their declarations of acceptance. The offeror must report such rescission to the Supervisory Authority within two days of its occurrence. The payment of the default interest or the rescission does not exempt the offeror from fines which the Supervisory Authority may impose on the offeror for the failure to make payment.

As mentioned above, the offeror may rescind its public purchase offer if the offeror failed to acquire influence exceeding 50 per cent in the target company or if the Competition Office failed to approve the transaction. In the case of a financial institution or a gas distributor (or other gas-related company), the approval of a relevant authority is also needed for an acquisition of influence above a certain level. Nevertheless, the Capital Markets Act fails to mention that if the above referred approval is not granted the takeover shall be cancelled.[2]

---

[2] The authors also believe that the Capital Markets Act might be seen as generally illogical and fundamentally wrong in restricting the offeror's right to make the public purchase offer subject to any conditions the fulfilment of which is independent from the offeror. Assuming that the law would allow the offeror to stipulate conditions and if the offeror has, for example, 5 per cent influence in the target company and the offeror's conditions are not fulfilled, in such a case the public purchase offer would not succeed; accordingly the offeror's influence would remain at 5 per cent. The authors believe that there is no reason to compel the offeror to make a public purchase offer in such circumstances.

13.9.4.4 *Publication of the takeover's result*

The offeror or its investment services provider must notify the Supervisory Authority of the result of the takeover within two days of the expiry of the acceptance period, and must simultaneously publish said notification. The offeror must notify the Supervisory Authority concerning the payment of the consideration for the shares (or, if it has failed to occur, of the reasons for said failure) within two days of the expiry of the payment deadline.

13.9.5 *Competing offers*

The rules governing a public purchase offer also apply to a competing offer.

A competing offer may be launched up until the fifteenth day before the expiry of the acceptance period. The competing offer must be published and have been approved by the Supervisory Authority if its terms and conditions are better for the target company's shareholders. A competing offer – and any competing offers issued in response to it – is deemed to be better than the original or the previous public purchase offer if at least a 5 per cent higher purchase price (in HUF) is offered. If a subsequent competing offer differs from the previous offer or competing offer only in terms of purchase price, the Supervisory Authority must approve such subsequent competing offer within three days.

The Supervisory Authority's approval of a competing offer and its publication renders any acceptances issued in respect of all prior offers out of force.

13.9.6 *Acquisition of influence through a Voluntary Purchase Offer*

The offeror may make an offer even if it is not required to do so (a "Voluntary Purchase Offer"). The Voluntary Purchase Offer may be made if the acquirer's influence would not, as a result of the proposed purchase, hit the 25 or 33 per cent takeover thresholds or if the offeror has acquired influence exceeding the 25 or 33 per cent takeover thresholds as a result of the public purchase offer but the offeror has not acquired all shares of the target company. The takeover rules applicable to public purchase offers apply also to a Voluntary Purchase Offer.

In addition to this, sometimes it is critical for the offeror to acquire influence exceeding 75 per cent (to have a qualified majority at the shareholders meeting) or 90 per cent (to exercise the squeeze-out) and, under the current rules, the offeror cannot avoid the obligation to purchase the offered shares even if the acquired influence after the closing of the public purchase offer does not exceed the intended 75 per cent or 90 per cent thresholds (but it exceeds 50 per cent). As mentioned at 13.9.2 above, in certain specific cases it is possible to exceed the respective takeover thresholds (i.e., 25 or 33 per cent) without making a public purchase offer, but the acquirer must make a public purchase offer within 15 days following the acquisition of influence exceeding the takeover threshold. Since in such event the offeror has already exceeded the takeover threshold, the offeror should not be able to make a public purchase offer subject to conditions other than the approval of the Competition Office or other relevant authorities. However, as mentioned above, if the offeror's influence does not exceed the respective takeover thresholds (i.e., 25 or 33 per cent) at the time of launching its public purchase offer, the authors believe that the offeror should be able to make the public purchase offer subject to any conditions the fulfilment of which is independent from the offeror.

However, the offeror may stipulate the maximum amount of shares it is willing to purchase, and no competing offer may be issued in response to a Voluntary Purchase Offer. Also, the target's board of directors is not required to form a view regarding a Voluntary Purchase Offer and the board of directors is not obliged to retain an independent expert to give an opinion about the Voluntary Purchase Offer either. If the shares offered in the declarations of acceptance exceed the maximum amount of the shares stipulated for purchase in the Voluntary Purchase Offer, the shares must be purchased proportionately with the nominal value of the shares in respect of which acceptances were issued. No Voluntary Purchase Offer may be submitted between the date of the publication of a mandatory public purchase offer and the last day of its acceptance period. A new provision in the Capital Markets Act, which was implemented by the Strategic Companies Act, prohibits the offeror from launching a Voluntary Purchase Offer within six months of another Voluntary Purchase Offer being launched (i.e., in order to avoid that an offeror makes several Voluntary Purchase Offers, thus paralysing the operation of the target company).

13.9.7 *The consequences of violating the takeover rules and sanctions*

If influence in a public Rt was acquired in violation of the relevant regulations of the Capital Markets Act, the shareholders' rights arising from such influence may not be exercised towards the target company. The acquirer must alienate those shares which were acquired by circumvention of the takeover rules, within 60 days of the day of its acquisition of the shares, or from the date of the resolution of the Supervisory Authority determining the consequences of the unlawful acquisition of influence in a public Rt. Even the rights vested in shares not affected by the compulsory alienation requirement may be exercised only after the alienation has occurred. In practice, if the illegal acquisition occurred indirectly through the acquisition of a foreign shareholder (foreign intermediary) of the target company, the prohibition or suspension of the exercise of the shareholders' right and the alienation obligation is likely not applicable. The reason for this is that the exercise of the shareholders' right of the direct owner (the foreign shareholder) cannot be prohibited or suspended since such direct owner did not commit any violation of the law and the Hungarian Supervisory Authority has no power to prohibit or suspend the exercise of shareholders' rights in a foreign company (i.e., in the intermediary company) having an influence in the Hungarian target company.

Upon the Supervisory Authority's or the Rt's request, any person (i.e., a nominee) exercising shareholders' rights on behalf of a third party (shareholder) must identify said party or, at the request of the company or the Supervisory Authority, must certify his appointment to exercise the shareholders' rights on behalf of the third party (shareholder). In addition to this, the Supervisory Authority may request in writing that copies of the related documents be submitted by the nominee. A third party, if it can prove that it might have an interest, can obtain the data of the shareholder represented by the nominee from the Supervisory Authority. In its investigation procedures, the Supervisory Authority may require compliance with the takeover rules, it may suspend the acquisition of influence through a public purchase offer (i.e., the takeover process), and it may suspend the exercise of the shareholders' rights. The Supervisory Authority may also impose fines of between HUF500,000 and HUF100 million (approximately €2,000 and €400,000) in the case of a violation of the takeover rules.

13.9.8 Failed public purchase offers

The consequences of a failed public purchase offer are not statutorily regulated. However, if due to a failed public purchase offer the offeror's influence does not exceed 33 or 25 per cent, respectively, and the offeror wishes to acquire an influence exceeding said thresholds, then the offeror must launch a new public purchase offer.

13.9.9 Target company's response and defences to a hostile public purchase offer and the Strategic Companies Act

In the summer of 2007, OMV, the Austrian oil company, made an attempt to acquire MOL, the Hungarian oil company, without the support of MOL's management (OMV did not make any formal public purchase offer until the end of 2007). This move triggered the Hungarian Parliament to adopt the Strategic Companies Act. Certain provisions of the Strategic Companies Act are to be applied only for strategic companies, but the Act has also amended the Capital Markets Act, the Companies Act and the Company Registration Act, which amendments are applicable for all companies beyond the strategic companies.

According to the new definitions in the Strategic Companies Act, undertakings operating in the water and energy sectors may be defined as strategic companies. Strategic companies (or their parent or subsidiary) in the energy sector are defined as electricity and gas undertakings operating a transmission or distribution system, owning such strategic assets, or having public service obligations in the field of electricity or gas supply. Strategic assets are defined as assets without which the strategic company cannot pursue its main activity. A strategic company's strategic assets may not be alienated without the approval of the shareholders meeting of the company. In the event of a public purchase offer for the shares issued by a strategic company, the business report of the offeror shall be approved by the shareholders meeting of the offeror prior to launching the public purchase offer. In the case of strategic companies, a recall of the board of directors or supervisory board members requires a three-quarters majority decision by the shareholders unless the articles of association provide otherwise.

Under Act XLII of 2003 on the supply of natural gas and Act LXXXVI of 2007 on electricity, the authority regulating the electricity and gas sectors shall delegate one member each to the board of directors and the supervisory board of strategic companies operating in the electricity or gas sectors. The delegates have no decision-making right. The Strategic Companies Act provides more detailed rules regarding the obligations and liabilities of these delegates.

Prior to the adoption of the Strategic Companies Act, the corporate actions of the target company's board of directors were limited between the date of receipt of the public purchase offer and the last date of the acceptance period (or, if the target company's board of directors was informed concerning the intent to make a public purchase offer before the public purchase offer was issued, then the restrictions on the board of directors' activities commence on the date it received said information). The board of directors was not allowed to adopt any decision that could frustrate the public purchase offer and in particular, the board of directors may not resolve on a capital increase (under the Companies Act the shareholders meeting may under certain circumstances authorise the board of directors to increase the share capital without any further approval from the shareholders meeting) or on the purchase by the target company of its shares. The Strategic Companies Act changed the relevant provisions, and in the absence of restrictions set out in the public Rt's articles of association the board of directors may implement measures which may result in the frustration of the public purchase offer. (Articles 9 and 12 of the Takeover Directive allow an EU Member State to select this option.) However, the potential restrictions of the articles of associations are not applicable if the shareholders meeting of the target company authorised the board of directors to implement measures to intervene in the public purchase offer. The potential restrictions of the articles of associations shall not apply where the public purchase offer for the acquisition of influence in the target company is launched:

(a)   by a company that does not apply similar regulations when it is itself being the target of a public purchase offer; or

(b)   by a company that is controlled, directly or indirectly, by the company referred to in (a) above.

Pre-emption or option rights in respect of the target company's shares may be used as a defence against a takeover. However, such rights are enforceable against third parties only if the dematerialised shares issued by the public Rt are placed into a blocked account.

The Companies Act permits the articles of association to prescribe the maximum voting rights of a single shareholder. The Strategic Companies Act allowed the application of the voting restriction for a group of shareholders and not only a single shareholder. (Prior to the adoption of the Strategic Companies Act, several public Rt's articles of association restricted the voting rights of a group of shareholders, and although the Court of Registration has accepted such restrictions, the legality of the restrictions was not entirely clear since the Companies Act only allowed the restriction of the voting rights of a single shareholder and not of a group of shareholders.) This poison pill appears to be an effective takeover defence.

In addition to this, the Strategic Companies Act repealed certain other provisions of the Companies Act, namely:

(a)   the restriction concerning the maximum number of treasury shares;

(b)   the prohibition that the articles of association of a public Rt may not stipulate a higher majority than a simple majority regarding a decision on the withdrawal of members of the board of directors; and

(c)   the provision stating that it is within the shareholders meeting's competence to decide on the acceptance of a public purchase offer in respect of the treasury shares.

13.9.10 *Breakthrough rules*

The articles of association of the target company may prescribe that, during the time allowed for accepting a public purchase offer:

(a)   any restrictions on the transfer of shares provided for in the articles of association of the target company shall not apply vis-á-vis the offeror; and

(b)   any restrictions on the transfer of shares provided for in contractual agreements between the target company and its shareholders, or in contractual agreements between shareholders of the target company entered into after the adoption of the amendment of the articles of association shall accordingly not apply vis-á-vis the offeror.

The articles of association of the target company may prescribe that, at the shareholders meeting which decides on any defensive measures (i.e., measures that may frustrate the public purchase offer):

(a)   restrictions on voting rights provided for in the articles of association of the target company shall not have effect unless the restrictions on voting rights are compensated by specific pecuniary advantages;

(b)   restrictions on voting rights provided for in contractual agreements between the target company and its shareholders or in contractual agreements between the shareholders of the target company entered into after the amendment of the articles of association shall accordingly not have effect unless the restrictions on voting rights are compensated by specific pecuniary advantages; or

(c)   multiple-vote securities shall carry only one vote each unless they are provided as equitable compensation for any loss suffered by the shareholders of such shares.

If the shareholders meeting so resolves, the provisions of the articles of association of the target company adopted pursuant to the above-mentioned rules shall not apply after the public purchase offer for the acquisition of influence in the target company is launched:

(a)   to a company that does not apply similar regulations when it is itself the target of a public purchase offer; or

(b)   to a company that is controlled, directly or indirectly, by the company referred to in the point (a) above provided that the authorisation was adopted within 18 moths prior to the launching of the public purchase offer.

The articles of association of the target company may prescribe that if the offeror holds 75 per cent or more of the voting rights following a public purchase offer, the offeror shall have the right to convene a shareholders meeting of the target company in order to amend the articles of association or to remove or appoint board members and supervisory board members. In such shareholders meeting:

(a)   the voting restrictions mentioned above or any extraordinary rights of shareholders concerning the appointment or removal of board of directors and supervisory board members shall not apply; and

(b)   multiple-vote shares shall carry only one vote each, unless they are pro-
        vided as equitable compensation for any loss suffered by the holders of
        some other rights.

In compensation for the loss of rights in the event that the offeror holds 75 per
cent or more of the voting rights following a public purchase offer, the remaining
shareholders shall have the right to sell their shares vis-á-vis the offeror, which
may be exercised within 90 days from the date of publication of the acquisition
of at least 75 per cent of the voting rights. The shareholders exercising their right
to sell shall offer their shares at the price quoted in the public purchase offer. If
the offeror convening the shareholders meeting has purchased any shares during
the past period at a higher price, the shares of the remaining shareholders shall
be purchased by the offeror at that price. These provisions shall not apply where
the public purchase offer for the acquisition of influence in the target company
is launched:

(a)   by a company, or a company acting in concert, that does not apply similar
        regulations when it is itself the target of a public purchase offer; or
(b)   by a company that is controlled, directly or indirectly, by the company
        referred to in (a) above.

Where a holder of preference shares with prior voting rights did not have or
could not have had knowledge of the potential restriction of the articles of
associations implemented under the breakthrough rules regarding the voting
rights carried by such shares at the time the shares were acquired, and the
shareholder suffered any consequential loss, the offeror or the person or body
carrying out the breakthrough shall be liable to pay compensation to the affected
shareholder. The minimum amount of compensation shall be fixed in the articles
of association of the target company, which may not exceed the value of the
target company's equity multiplied by the number of voting rights that the
preference share carries. The compensation shall be paid by the offeror in cash,
not later than by the eighth working day preceding the date of the given shareholders meeting.

The breakthrough rules shall not apply if the Hungarian state has a preference
share in the target company. (This amendment was implemented by the Strategic
Companies Act and Article 11(7) of the Takeover Directive which allows an EU
Member State to select this option.)

13.9.11   BSE rules

As already discussed at 13.2.3 above, the BSE rules permit a listed company to
delist its securities following the making of a so-called delisting offer. However,
if the public purchase offer fulfils certain simple conditions, the public purchase
offer can be accepted by the BSE as a delisting offer as well. If the offeror exercises
its squeeze-out right following a public purchase offer, the BSE shall automatically delist the shares. Pursuant to the BSE rules approved by the Supervisory
Authority, the delisting offer is not to be approved by the Supervisory Authority.
However, it is not entirely clear whether the delisting offer qualifies as a
Voluntary Purchase Offer, which would otherwise require an approval from the
Supervisory Authority.

13.10   Profit forecasts and asset valuation

Hungarian law neither requires nor prohibits the disclosure by a company of its profit forecasts. However, the Capital Markets Act requires public companies to reveal their operational plan and significant risk factors; to evaluate their market position; and to list their investments in their annual reports, which may imply certain future forecasts. In the biannual flash report, a listed company must disclose to the greatest extent possible, the expected developments at the company in the given year.

Further, BSE listed companies issue biannual or quarterly flash reports, depending on their BSE listing classification.

Also, as noted at 13.11.2 below, the board of directors must inform the shareholders of its opinion concerning the public purchase offer. In that opinion the board of directors should indicate whether in its view, based on the value of the target company's assets, its market position and potential, the public purchase offer is adequate or not.

13.11   Documents from the offeror and the target company

13.11.1   *Documents from the offeror*

In the takeover process – regardless of whether the public purchase offer is hostile or recommended – the target company's shareholders have the right to inspect the following documents:

(a)   the public purchase offer;
(b)   the operational plan for the target company's future operations; and
(c)   a report concerning the offeror's business activities (if the offeror is a Hungarian or foreign business organisation).

The public purchase offer must include at least the following:

(a)   the name and domicile (registered office) of the offeror;
(b)   the number and series of shares which the offeror, all persons acting in concert with the offeror and the close relatives of the offeror, directly or indirectly hold in the target company;
(c)   the amount and type of the consideration offered for the shares (e.g., a ratio of cash to securities, description of securities, if any offered), and the method of the purchase price calculation, as well as the proposed payment terms and the description of the rules of the Capital Markets Act regulating the payment of the consideration;
(d)   the acceptance period;
(e)   the designated place and method for accepting the public purchase offer and the conditions under which an agent or an intermediary may be involved;
(f)   the name and the registered office of the investment service provider managing the public purchase offer;

(g)   the place at which the operational plan for the target company's future operation and the report of the offeror's business activities may be accessed;

(h)   if the public purchase offer is submitted jointly, the ratio of distribution of the shares among the offerors;

(i)   reservation of the right to rescind the public purchase offer if the declarations of acceptance indicate that the influence to be acquired would be less than 50 per cent;

(j)   a description of the offeror's relation to the target company;

(k)   the compensation offered for the rights which may be removed as a result of the breakthrough rules (*see* 13.9.10 above), with the description of how the compensation was calculated and how it will be paid;

(l)   the likely repercussions on employment;

(m)   the stipulation of the governing law and the competent court in connection with any legal dispute between the offeror and the accepting shareholder regarding the share purchase agreement concluded upon the acceptance of the offer; and

(n)   all other important conditions which may affect the public purchase offer.

13.11.1.1   *The offeror and the investment service provider*

The offeror's (and its investment service provider's) application for approval of the public purchase offer must include:

(a)   the operational plan and the report of the offeror's business operations;

(b)   proof that the offeror has sufficient funds available for the shares to which the public purchase offer pertains;

(c)   if the public purchase offer is submitted by one person acting in concert with others and it is not submitted by the parties jointly, the agreement that stipulates the party empowered to submit the public purchase offer;

(d)   the document containing the terms of the share purchase, if the public purchase offer results from a futures contract or the exercise of a call option or a repurchase right; and

(e)   a declaration regarding the exercise of the squeeze-out, if the public purchase offer was made for an acquisition of influence of at least 90 per cent or more.

13.11.1.2   *The operational plan and the business activity report*

These documents must include at least the following general data:

(a)   the offeror's name and domicile (registered office);

(b)   identification data of persons acting in concert;

(c)   the target company's name and registered office;

(d)   the name and registered office of the investment service provider managing the public purchase offer;

(e)   the place of the publication of the public purchase offer;

(f)   details of any existing interest of the offeror, and of persons acting in concert with the offeror, in the target company;

(g)   the time allowed for acceptance of the public purchase offer;

(h)   information concerning the financing for the public purchase offer;

(i)   where the consideration offered by the offeror includes securities of any kind, information concerning those securities, including:

    (i)   information concerning the last 12 months' trading (minimum price, maximum price, average price, volume) if the security is listed on a Stock Exchange; and

    (ii)   the price and the calculation formula of the security as included in the consideration.

The operational plan must include at least the following:

(a)   a description of the business policy proposed for future operations of the target company;

(b)   the offeror's intentions with regard to the future business of the target company and, in so far as it is affected by the public purchase offer, the offeror company;

(c)   provisions on safeguarding the jobs of the employees and management, including any material change in the conditions of employment at the target company;

(d)   the offeror's operational plans for the offeror and the target company;

(e)   the likely repercussions on employment;

(f)   the likely repercussions on the locations of the companies' places of business.

The offeror's report concerning its business activities must include at least the following:

(a)   the offeror's name and domicile (registered office);

(b)   the target company's name and registered office;

(c)   a short summary of the offeror's history and business activity;

(d)   a short introduction of the offeror's management and supervisory board;

(e)   a summary of any agreement between the offeror or persons having influence in the offeror and the target company or any persons having influence in the target company, if said agreement might impact the evaluation of the public purchase offer;

(f)   a summary of any agreement between the offeror or any persons having influence in the offeror and the target company, any persons having influence in the target company, or members of the target company's board of directors, if such agreement might impact the evaluation of the public purchase offer;

(g)   analyses regarding the financial situation of the offeror, and any changes that may have occurred thereto;

(h)   the offeror's statement regarding the availability of the funds necessary to perform the payment obligations under the public purchase offer and disclosure concerning the sources of said funds;

(i)   the undertaking of liability for the authenticity of the data and information in the public purchase offer and in the report concerning the offeror's previous business activities.

13.11.2   Documents from the target company

As mentioned at 13.9 above, the target company's board of directors must present the shareholders with its opinion concerning the public purchase offer. The board of directors, at the target company's cost, must hire an independent financial adviser to evaluate the public purchase offer except if the public purchase offer was triggered by an acquisition of influence which:

(a)   occurred within the framework of proceedings governed by law and conducted by a state property management organisation (i.e., a privatisation); or

(b)   resulted in persons acting in concert; or

(c)   occurred in the event of a Voluntary Purchase Offer.

The opinion of the employees of the target company shall be included with the opinion of the board of directors (if the opinion of the employees is available).

The board of directors' opinion regarding the public purchase offer must include at least the following:

(a)   the target company's name (company) and its registered seat;

(b)   a summary of the public purchase offer, detailing its most important aspects – consideration, acceptance period, method of payment;

(c)   a declaration of whether any board member has any position with or influence in the offeror, or other entities having an influence in the offeror, or any other relationship with the offeror or a person having influence in the offeror;

(d)   the ownership structure of the target company, disclosing the identity of each person having at least a 5 per cent influence, including the number of their shares and votes;

(e)   an opinion regarding the effect of the acquisition of influence on the target company's employees;

(f)   a recommendation to accept or reject the public purchase offer with detailed reasoning and an indication of whether any board member dissented from the majority's view or abstained from voting and his or her reasoning;

(g)   the name of the independent financial adviser appointed by the board of directors and a statement of the adviser that there is no conflict of interest which may influence the adviser's ability to give an impartial evaluation of the public purchase offer; and

(h)   the opinion of the employees regarding the public purchase offer.

13.12   Compulsory acquisition of minorities

13.12.1   Compulsory sales to the offeror after a public purchase offer

If the offeror:

(a)   declared that it wants to exercise its call option (squeeze-out) rights in its request to the Supervisory Authority for approval of its mandatory or voluntary public purchase offer;

(b)   has an influence in the target company equal to or in excess of 90 per cent within three months following the closure of its successful mandatory or voluntary public purchase offer, and

(c)   is able to verify that it has sufficient financial means to cover the purchase of the shares to which its call option pertains,

the offeror may exercise an option (squeeze-out) to purchase within three months from the date of closure of its mandatory or voluntary public purchase offer the remaining shares of the target company. The offeror shall notify the Supervisory Authority within this three-month period and shall simultaneously publish a notice of its intention to exercise the call option (squeeze-out). The notification and the announcement shall indicate:

(a)   the place, time and procedure for the delivery of the shares;

(b)   the consideration; and

(c)   the time and conditions of payment.

At the time of giving notification of its intention to exercise the call option (squeeze-out), the offeror shall deposit the funds to cover the consideration in an account opened at a credit institution with a registered office in an EU Member State for the benefit of the shareholders of the target company. The price payable for the shares obtained by way of exercising the call option (squeeze-out) shall be the price paid in the mandatory or voluntary public purchase offer or the amount of equity per share, whichever is higher. Equity means the amount shown in the last audited annual financial statements, with the exception that if the issuer is required to prepare consolidated annual financial statements in accordance with the Accounting Act, equity means the consolidated equity. The target company shall invalidate the shares which were not delivered in due time, and shall issue new shares to the offeror in lieu of such invalidated shares due to the exercise of the call option (squeeze-out).

Under the Companies Act, an Rt may issue employee shares up to 15 per cent of its registered capital and the employee shares entitle their holders to exercise voting rights. The employee shares may be transferred to other employees or some other person who is authorised to acquire the employee shares, pursuant to the articles of association, as a result of their previous employment at the Rt. This could mean that the employee shares may not be offered during a public purchase offer and if the target company has issued employee shares which represent more than 10 per cent of the voting rights, it is impossible for the offeror to acquire influence equal to or in excess of 90 per cent.

13.12.2   *Compulsory acquisition after a public purchase offer*

If the offeror's influence in the target company exceeds 90 per cent at the closing of the public purchase offer, any remaining shareholders may request the offeror to purchase their shares within 90 days of the publication of the acquisition exceeding 90 per cent. The consideration payable for such shares may not be less than the consideration payable in a squeeze-out. As discussed at 13.9.10 above, the breakthrough rules may trigger the obligation of the offeror to purchase all shares of the target company offered by other shareholders.

13.13   Insider dealing and market manipulation

13.13.1   Insider dealing

The rules of the Capital Markets Act apply if the insider trading has occurred in Hungary or, in the case of a foreign transaction, such insider trading could have an effect in Hungary. The Capital Markets Act prohibits insider dealing. Under the Capital Markets Act, insider dealing occurs when an insider:

(a)   using inside information, directly or indirectly trades with financial instruments or entrusts another person to trade in such financial instruments to which the inside information relates;

(b)   reveals the inside information to third parties; or

(c)   suggests to another person that he trades in the financial instruments to which the inside information relates.

The activity of any person described in points (a)–(c) qualifies as insider dealing if this person knew or should have known that the information used is inside information.

Pursuant to the definition of the Capital Markets Act, inside information shall mean material information which has not been made public, and which relates, directly or indirectly, to an issuer of financial instruments or to financial instruments and which, if it were made public, would be likely to have a significant effect on the prices of such financial instruments. In addition to that mentioned above, for persons charged with the execution of orders concerning financial instruments, "inside information" shall also mean information conveyed by a client and related to the client's pending orders.

An inside person means, for example:

(a)   the members of the board of directors and the supervisory board of an issuer;

(b)   any legal person or unincorporated business association if it holds, directly or indirectly, an interest or voting rights of 10 per cent or more in an issuer; or any executive officer, managing director, or member of the board of directors or supervisory board of such an entity;

(c)   any natural person or legal person holding an interest, directly or indirectly, of 10 per cent or more in the registered capital of an issuer;

(d)   any person obtaining inside information as part of his of her job or when discharging his or her usual duties in an official capacity, or in any other way relating to work performed under contract of employment or otherwise.

The Capital Markets Act requires that certain inside persons (e.g., members of the board of directors and supervisory board or the issuer or those persons having more than a 10 per cent interest or voting right in the issuer and in certain cases their related persons as well) must immediately notify the Supervisory Authority of any securities transaction he or she concluded (i.e., it means that if a legal person has more than 10 per cent of the shares or the voting rights in the issuer, all transactions must be reported to the Supervisory Authority regarding the issuer's shares). With limited exceptions, the members of the board of directors or the supervisory board must publish this notice as well.

Any person who provides an investment service must notify the Supervisory Authority if any data, fact or circumstance indicates insider dealing. The Supervisory Authority shall disclose all data regarding insider dealing required by the competent authority of another EU Member State.

The Capital Markets Act empowers the Supervisory Authority to fine any person who committed insider dealing. The amount of the fine may be HUF2 million–HUF100 million (approximately €8,000–€400,000) or a maximum of 400 per cent of the pecuniary benefit realised from the transaction, provided that the exact amount of the benefit is discovered.

Under Act IV of 1978 on the Criminal Code ("the Criminal Code"), as amended, an individual who uses inside information when dealing in transactions relating to financial instruments, commits an offence punishable by imprisonment of up to three years. Further, a person holding inside information who, on the basis of such inside information, entrusts another person to deal in a transaction relating to financial instruments, or hands over inside information to an unauthorised person in order to gain profit, commits a criminal offence punishable by imprisonment of up to three years.

Although individuals or officers of entities owning, directly or indirectly, at least 10 per cent of an issuer are regarded as insiders, such persons are only committing insider dealing if they use inside information in trading the securities issued by the issuer.

Trades concluded pursuant to a share buy-back programme or for the purpose of stabilising the market price of the given financial instrument do not qualify as an insider trade if they occur as prescribed by the Commission Regulation (EC) 2273/2003.

13.13.2   *Unfair manipulation of market price*

The rules of the Capital Markets Act apply if the market manipulation has occurred in Hungary or, in the case of a foreign transaction, such market manipulation could have an effect in Hungary. The Capital Markets Act prohibits market manipulation. Under the Capital Markets Act, market manipulation means:

(a)   transactions or orders to trade which give, or are likely to give, false or misleading signals as to the supply of, demand for or price of financial instruments;

(b)   transactions or orders to trade which secure the price of the given financial instrument at an abnormal or artificial level;

(c)   transactions or orders to trade which employ fictitious devices or any other form of deception or contrivance;

(d)   the dissemination or publication of rumours and false or misleading news, where the person who made the dissemination knew, or ought to have known, that the information was false or misleading.

The activities described in points (a) and (b) shall not qualify as a market manipulation if the person who entered into the transactions or issued the orders to trade establishes that his reasons for doing so are legitimate and that these transactions or orders to trade conform to accepted market practices in the regulated market in question.

Any person who provides an investment service must notify to the Supervisory Authority if any data, fact or circumstance indicates market manipulation. The Supervisory Authority shall disclose all data regarding market manipulation required by the competent authority of another EU Member State.

The Supervisory Authority may impose fines between HUF2 million and HUF100 million (approximately €8,000–€400,000) or a maximum of 400 per cent of the pecuniary benefit realised from the transaction for market manipulation, provided that the exact amount of the benefit is discovered.

Trades concluded pursuant to a share buy-back programme or for the purpose of stabilising the market price of the given financial instrument do not qualify as a market manipulation if they occur as prescribed by the Commission Regulation (EC) 2273/2003. The BSE may also impose sanctions on its members for violations of the rules regarding insider dealing and unfair manipulation of market price.

13.14 Financial assistance

The Companies Act prohibits any financial assistance by a target company limited by shares, including the granting of a loan, provision of a security, or performance of any of its financial obligations before their maturity, for the purpose of assisting the acquisition of the target company's shares by a third party. Any transaction violating this rule shall be null and void.

Generally, only the shares of the target company obtained by the offeror may be offered as a security for a loan. However, nothing in Hungarian law expressly prohibits a merger between the acquirer and the target company. In the absence of court practice and based on market practice, it appears a merger between the offeror and the target company following the acquisition does not qualify as financial assistance because in this structure, the target company will not provide a loan or security, or will not fulfil its obligations prematurely for the acquisition of the shares, and in any case this is a post-acquisition scenario.

The Companies Act requires that the shareholders meeting of each company approve the merger with 75 per cent of the votes. Shareholders not wishing to own a stake in the merged company may quit the company surviving the merger. In such a case, the leaving shareholder can claim adequate consideration for his stake in the merging companies which equals the proportionate part of the relevant company's equity capital. The said amount may be higher than the purchase price offered by the offeror. The requirement that the offeror prepare an operational plan for the target company's future operations may be interpreted to imply that plans to merge the target with the offeror must be disclosed.

Chapter 14

Ireland

Eithne FitzGerald

Partner
A&L Goodbody, Dublin

14.1 Introduction

The vast majority of companies incorporated in Ireland are private companies limited by shares, the takeover of which is most frequently achieved by a negotiated share purchase agreement. Companies that are the subject of takeover offers in Ireland are usually public companies limited by shares. Due to the relatively small number of Irish incorporated public companies, takeover bids targeting such companies are reasonably infrequent.

The level of reported takeover activity in Ireland continues to increase on the domestic and international front. Particularly active areas in terms of takeover activity include the financial services sector, healthcare and food and drink.

14.2 Acquisition targets

The most common form of business entity for medium to large-scale business operations in Ireland is the company. The operation of companies is governed by the Companies Acts 1963 to 2006. Irish company law is similar in a number of respects to English company law, but the English Companies Act 2006 has introduced a number of changes which are not currently reflected in Irish Company Law, (for example, the codification of directors' duties). It is anticipated however that some provisions similar to these changes will be reflected in a Companies Consolidation and Reform Bill which is expected to be published in the second half of 2008 – *see* further paragraph 14.13.8 below.

Although there are various types of company which can be incorporated in Ireland, the overwhelming majority of companies are private companies limited by shares. Irish incorporated public companies limited by shares are the other principal form of investment vehicle.

A private company must have a minimum of one member and a maximum of 99 members (excluding current or former employees). Its articles of association must contain a restriction on the transferability of shares, that is, the shares in a private company cannot be freely or publicly traded. There must also be a prohibition on any invitation to the public to subscribe for shares or debentures in a private company, subject to a number of exceptions introduced by the Investment Funds, Companies and Miscellaneous Provisions Act 2006 which permit a private company to offer debentures (and, in more limited circumstances, shares) to specific classes of persons without breaching Irish securities laws.

A public limited company is any company which is not a private one. It must have a minimum of seven members, but there is no maximum number and its shares are freely transferable. The shares of public limited companies frequently have a listing on a recognised Stock Exchange. The shares of a number of Irish technology companies are dealt in on NASDAQ.

Businesses in Ireland can also be conducted through companies limited by guarantee, unlimited liability, public and private companies, investment companies with variable capital, cooperatives, sole traders or partnerships. The nature of the acquisition target determines to a large extent the means by which a takeover of that target is effected and regulated.

14.3   Exchange and investment control

There are no exchange controls currently in force in Ireland save for in the limited circumstances provided for in the Financial Transfers Act 1992. This Act empowers the Minister for Finance to make orders restricting financial transfers between Ireland and other countries. At present, orders are in place in respect of Liberia, Zimbabwe, Myanmar, Iraq, the Federal Republic of Yugoslavia, the Democratic Republic of Congo, Belarus, Iran, Ivory Coast, North Korea, Lebanon, Sudan and Uzbekistan as well as a number of individuals, groups and entities associated with terrorism or criminality. The orders preclude any financial transfer (including a transfer on acquisition of an existing Irish business) to, or by the order of, or on behalf of, a resident of any of these countries. The definition of a "resident" covers a person living in the country to which the order relates, or a body corporate or entity operating from that country, and includes any person acting on behalf of such person. Certain transactions and payments involving the government of any country which is the subject of United Nations sanctions or regulations made in Ireland implementing Council Regulations of the European Communities in relation to sanctions may also be subject to restrictions.

Other investment controls can arise where various merger regulation provisions apply (*see* 14.4 below) and where third-party consents to a takeover (e.g., the consent of banks or the Irish Industrial Development Authority ("IDA")) are required.

Certain businesses and activities are subject to specific regulatory regimes, usually established by statute, which may be of relevance where a takeover of an entity engaged in such activity is proposed. Examples of such businesses include banks, building societies, insurance undertakings and cooperative societies.

14.4 Merger control

14.4.1 *Introduction*

Ireland has a "compulsory notification" regime in terms of the competition law control of mergers and takeovers. This means that, as a matter of Irish law, transactions which fall within the scope of Ireland's Competition Act 2002 ("CA 2002" or "the Act") must be notified to the Competition Authority ("the Authority") and must be cleared by the Authority before they may be implemented. Ireland also has a voluntary regime (which is not often used) which means that parties to a merger or takeover which falls below the thresholds for compulsory notification may nonetheless notify the deal to the Authority for approval.

The Irish regime is primarily embodied in CA 2002. It is modelled on, but far from identical to, the EC regime in Regulation 139/2004. There are significant differences between the EC and Irish regime and therefore local advice is required.

The regime is administered by the Authority with two exceptions: the Minister for Enterprise, Trade and Employment is involved in (a) proposing legislation and policy, and (b) the decision-making process in so-called "media mergers" (*see* 14.4.6 below).

If a concentration (e.g., a merger or acquisition) is subject to the EC's Merger Control Regulation (Regulation 139/2004) then Irish competition law may not apply so there is no need for, nor is it possible for, a notification to be made to the Competition Authority under Part III of the Competition Act 2002. The Irish Competition Authority may still be involved in a transaction which has been notified to the Commission under Regulation 139/2004 where the proposed transaction has been referred to Ireland under Article 9 of Regulation 139/2004.

14.4.2 *Transactions regulated by CA 2002*

14.4.2.1 *Nature of transaction*
The CA 2002 applies to mergers, acquisitions and full-function joint ventures.

In more specific terms, three types of transaction are notifiable to the Authority under the Act:

(a) a merger – this involves two or more undertakings, previously independent of one another, merging;
(b) acquisitions – this occurs where a purchaser acquires direct or indirect control of the whole or part of another undertaking, thereby replacing or substantially replacing that undertaking in the relevant business;
(c) full-function joint ventures – this occurs whenever a joint venture is created to perform, on an indefinite basis, all the functions of an autonomous economic entity.

Before a transaction is subject to the notification requirement under the Act, it is necessary to determine whether "control" is being acquired. If control is not being acquired then the Act does not apply. For the purpose of the Act, control is regarded as existing where "decisive influence is capable of being exercised" over the undertaking being acquired or, in the case of a full-function joint venture, the entity being created. In more specific terms, "decisive influence" is regarded as existing when the acquisition of ownership of, or the right to use all or part of, the assets of an undertaking, or rights or contracts occurs which enables decisive influence to be exercised with regard to the composition, voting or decisions of an undertaking.

Some transactions fall outside the scope of the Act. They include:

(a)   intra-group transfers;
(b)   mergers where a financial undertaking acquires control over another undertaking on a temporary basis (where any exercise of voting rights is for disposal purposes and the undertaking is disposed of within one year);
(c)   acquisitions by receivers, liquidators, underwriters and jobbers; and
(d)   acquisitions arising from testamentary dispositions, intestacy or the right of survivorship under a joint tenancy.

14.4.2.2   Turnover thresholds

The Act provides for certain financial thresholds which must be met before a transaction. A transaction must be notified to the Authority if:

(a)   the worldwide turnover of at least two of the undertakings involved is not less than €40 million;
(b)   at least two of the undertakings carry on business in any part of the island of Ireland (i.e., the Republic of Ireland and Northern Ireland); and
(c)   the turnover in the State (i.e., the Republic of Ireland) of at least one of the undertakings involved in the transaction is not less than €40.

The term "undertakings involved" excludes the vendor of the business being sold. The term "carry on business in any part of the island of Ireland" is interpreted widely and includes sales of goods or supply of services into the island of Ireland without having a physical presence in the island.

Apart from these "compulsory" notifications, there can also be voluntary notifications. If a transaction falls below the thresholds then it may still be the subject of a notification to the Authority either:

(a)   because the parties voluntarily notify it to the Authority; or
(b)   the Minister for Enterprise, Trade and Employment has decided that transactions in that particular sector must be notifiable irrespective of the turnover of the parties. This has only occurred in respect of certain "media mergers" (e.g., the purchase of newspapers) and, in the context of those transactions, notification is compulsory irrespective of the turnover of the parties (*see* 14.4.6 below).

Parties would make a voluntary notification where they believe that the transaction could give rise to competition law concerns such as where it would prevent, restrict or distort competition or amount to an abuse of a dominant position. (However, such voluntary filings are very rare).

Apart from the general "compulsory" and "voluntary" notifications, the Minister for Enterprise, Trade and Employment may decide, because competition concerns in a particular industry or the exigencies of the common good require it, that all transactions in a particular sector are notified irrespective of whether the thresholds are met. To date, as mentioned above, only transactions in the media sector are subject to this regime.

14.4.2.3   *Foreign to foreign transactions*
The Act makes no special provision or exemption for foreign to foreign trans-actions. This means that even though the purchaser and vendor are both non-Irish, the Act applies to transactions falling within its scope where the thresholds in the Act are met.

14.4.3   **Test for approval**

The test to be used by the Authority in deciding whether to approve a notified transaction is whether or not the proposed transaction would "substantially lessen competition in markets for goods or services" in Ireland. This is the so-called "SLC" test. There are additional criteria in the case of media transactions (*see* 14.4.6 below).

The Authority would pay attention to:

(a)   the relevant markets;
(b)   the effect of the proposed transaction on market structure;
(c)   the effect on rivalry;
(d)   the possible entry into the market by a new competitor;
(e)   the pro-competitive benefits of the transaction; and
(f)   whether in all circumstances it would substantially lessen competition.

14.4.4   **Timetable**

The notification must be made within one month of the conclusion of an agree-ment or, in the case of a public bid, the making of the public bid. The Authority must clear the transaction or initiate a full investigation (i.e., open a so-called Phase II investigation) within one month of the notification (or of the receipt of further information in response to formal questions after the notification). No exception is made in this regard for public holidays or weekends. If the Authority finds that the proposed transaction would not substantially lessen competition then the Authority adopts and publishes a "determination" (subject to any business secret being omitted) and the transaction may proceed.

The parties to a proposed transaction may offer commitments to the Authority to assuage any competition concern of the Authority about the proposed trans-action. If the parties have offered commitments then the Authority must either allow the transaction to proceed or initiate within 45 days (i.e., not the usual "one month") of the notification (or of the receipt of further information in response to formal questions after notification) a Phase II investigation.

If the Authority believes that there is a risk that the transaction would substan-tially lessen competition then the Authority will open a Phase II investigation. During Phase II, the Authority may issue a statement of objections, granting notifying parties some level of access to the file, conduct an oral hearing and receive additional submissions. Interestingly, the Authority may also compel executives and others to attend before the Authority to explain the proposed transaction, the market and other related issues.

If the parties have not offered commitments then the Authority has four months from the date of notification (or of the receipt of further information after notification in respect of formal question) in which to consider the transaction.

14.4.5   Practical matters

The fee payable to the Authority for notifications is €8,000 per notification. No additional fee is required for a Phase II notification.

There is a specific form which is used for notification. The form is in eight parts:

(a)   the first requires general information about the transaction;

(b)   the notifying parties are asked to give a detailed description of the proposed transaction;

(c)   details are asked about the undertakings involved;

(d)   a description of any horizontal or vertical overlaps in products or services produced, supplied or distributed by the undertakings involved in the island of Ireland and related information;

(e)   the views of the undertaking involved are sought;

(f)   information is required on ancillary restraints (if any);

(g)   further information and supporting documentation is sought; and

(h)   the final part includes a declaration, signature and power of attorney.

It is possible, and sometimes advisable, to have an informal discussion with the Authority in advance, but the guidance given, if any, will be non-binding.

The determination is a relatively short document which sets out the views of the Authority.

14.4.6   Media transactions

A special regime applies in the case of "media mergers". A media merger is a transaction in which any of the undertakings involved carries on a media business in Ireland. A media business is defined as:

(a)   the publication of newspaper or periodicals consisting substantially of news and comment and current affairs;

(b)   a business providing a broadcasting service; or

(c)   a business providing a broadcasting services platform (e.g., a cable television network).

Media transactions are notified to the Competition Authority which considers the matter in respect of whether there is a substantial lessening of competition. The proposed decision of the Authority is then sent to the Minister for Enterprise, Trade and Employment for his or her consideration.

The Minister applies certain public interest criteria. These criteria are whether or not the transaction will have an effect on:

(a) the strength and competitiveness of the media business indigenous to Ireland;
(b) the extent to which ownership or control of media businesses in Ireland is spread among individuals and other undertakings;
(c) the extent to which ownership and control of particular types of media businesses in Ireland is spread among individuals and other undertakings;
(d) the extent to which diversity of views prevalent in Irish society is reflected through the activities of various media businesses in Ireland; and
(e) the market share in Ireland of one or more of the types of business activity falling within the definition of "media business" that is held by any of the undertakings involved in the media merger concerned or by any individual or other undertaking who or which has an interest in such an undertaking.

14.4.7 Appeal against decisions to the Court

It is possible for the parties which were involved in the notification to appeal the decisions of the Authority to the High Court in certain circumstances. The Act provides for an expedited procedure.

14.4.8 Involvement of the public

A transaction which is notified to the Authority ordinarily becomes known to the public through the Authority's website within seven days of the receipt of the notification. Third parties are invited to make submissions and must do so within ten days of the publication of the notice. The notification itself is not published or made available to third parties and relatively limited details are published, such as names of the parties, the sector involved and the date by which submissions must be made.

14.4.9 Overall

The regime works well and relatively few transactions are referred to "Phase II". The new regime came into force on 1 January 2003 and there were 47 notifications that year with no prohibitions. During 2004, there were 81 notifications and one prohibition. During 2005 and 2006, there were 84 and 98 notifications respectively. As of 20 November 2007, there had been 62 notifications.

14.5 Regulation of the conduct of mergers and acquisitions

14.5.1 Introduction

The conduct of mergers and takeovers of private companies and public companies whose shares are not listed or dealt on any recognised Stock Exchange is not regulated, as such, in Ireland. A takeover of a private company and, in some cases, a public company having a small number of members, is most commonly achieved by way of an individually negotiated share purchase contract executed by the sellers and the purchaser. Alternatively, the business of such companies may be sold by way of an individually negotiated asset sale agreement between the target and the purchaser. The position is different for Irish incorporated public limited companies or other bodies corporate incorporated in Ireland whose securities (other than debentures, bonds or other similar securities that do not confer voting rights in the company or body corporate) are authorised (or have been so authorised within the preceding five years) for trading on a market regulated by a recognised Stock Exchange (the Irish Stock Exchange has been prescribed as such) or on one or more of the markets operated by the London Stock Exchange, on the New York Stock Exchange, or on NASDAQ. The conduct of mergers and takeovers of such companies is regulated by the European Communities (Takeover Bids) (Directive 2004/25/EC) Regulations 2006 ("the Takeover Regulations"), as regards takeover bids to which the Takeover Directive applies (*see* paragraph 14.5.2 below) and/or by the Irish Takeover Panel Act 1997 (as amended) ("the 1997 Act") and takeover rules made thereunder (the "Takeover Rules") by the Irish Takeover Panel ("the Panel"). The Panel is a company limited by guarantee whose members are appointed by various bodies connected with the securities industry.

14.5.2   *The Takeover Rules and substantial acquisitions of securities ("SARs")*

On 20 May 2006, the Takeover Regulations implementing the Takeover Directive came into effect in Ireland. The Takeover Directive ("the Directive") sets down minimum EU-wide rules concerning the regulation of takeovers of companies whose securities are admitted to trading on a regulated market. Following the making of the Takeover Regulations, further amendments were made to the 1997 Act which is the primary legislation regulating the conduct of all takeovers in Ireland, and a relatively complex takeover regime is now in existence.

The Directive and the Takeover Regulations apply to companies admitted to trading on a "regulated market" (e.g., the Official List of the Irish Stock Exchange in Ireland) and only to takeover bids. The 1997 Act applies to a wider cohort of public companies, for example, an Irish-incorporated public limited company whose shares are traded only on the Irish Enterprise Exchange (IEX) operated by the Irish Stock Exchange and/or on the Alternative Investment Market ("AIM") of the UK. The 1997 Act and the Takeover Rules made by the Panel also contain provisions governing substantial acquisitions of shares and other methods of takeover such as takeovers effected by a scheme of arrangement under the Companies Act 1963 (as opposed to a takeover bid). There are also special rules applicable in the case of takeover bids made for so-called "shared jurisdiction" companies, namely companies with registered offices in an EU/EEA Member State which have one or more listings on regulated markets in one or more other EU/EEA Member States.

As a result of the Directive and the Takeover Regulations, there are now two main categories of companies, takeovers of which are regulated by the Panel – described by the Panel as "Directive Companies" and "non-Directive Companies" the latter of which can be Directive Relevant Companies and Non-Directive Relevant Companies.

"Relevant Companies", are public limited companies whose securities are admitted to trading on a market regulated by a recognised stock exchange such as Official List of the Irish Stock Exchange, the London Stock Exchange, NASDAQ and the New York Stock Exchange.

For the purposes of this chapter, references to the Takeover Rules will be primarily to those applying to a takeover of a Directive Company by means of a takeover bid. A commentary on the other regimes mentioned would require more in-depth legal analysis on a case-by-case basis and is outside the scope of this chapter.

The Takeover Regulations and the 1997 Act prescribe certain general principles to be adhered to in the conduct of a takeover. The Takeover Rules lay down rules which are intended to provide an orderly framework within which takeovers are conducted, and also set out notes, the aim of which is to provide an indication as to some of the considerations which the Panel may take into account in applying the Takeover Rules. The Takeover Rules are similar in many respects to the UK City Code on Takeovers and Mergers although some differences do exist. The Takeover Rules are founded in statute with the Panel having statutory power to issue rulings and to give directions and the power to apply for an order of the High Court to facilitate enforcement, if it considers that a ruling or direction has not been complied with or is unlikely to be complied with. Failure to comply with such an order would constitute contempt of court.

The Panel also administers the Rules governing substantial acquisitions of securities ("SARs" *see* 14.7.4 below).

The fundamental objectives underlying the general principles can be summarised as follows:

(a) to ensure equal treatment of shareholders of the same class;
(b) to ensure that due and responsible consideration is given before an offer is made and that the offeror is satisfied it can implement the offer;
(c) to provide adequate and timely information and advice upon which shareholders can reach a properly informed decision on the merits of an offer;
(d) to ensure a fair market in the shares of companies which are involved in takeovers;
(e) to prevent the boards of directors of target companies from taking action without shareholder approval, which would frustrate an offer, and to oblige them to act in disregard of their personal interests; and
(f) to prescribe a timeframe for takeovers and substantial acquisitions.

In cases where the Takeover Regulations apply, parties will only be acting in concert if they either seek to acquire control of the target or are seeking to frustrate the successful outcome of the bid. Under the 1997 Act in respect of non-Directive Companies, parties can be acting in concert if they actively cooperate in acquiring securities in the target company. They do not need to be doing this for the purposes of acquiring *control* (at least 30 per cent of the voting rights), although this will also constitute acting in concert under that Act.

14.5.3   *The Listing Rules and rules of other markets*

The rules of the Irish Stock Exchange are set out in the Irish Listing Rules which are broadly aligned with the Listing Rules of the London Stock Exchange and are relevant if the offeror is listed on the Irish Stock Exchange or the London Stock Exchange. Depending on the size of the offer relative to the size of the offeror, the offeror may have to dispatch to its shareholders an explanatory circular and be required to obtain the approval of its shareholders to implement the offer, which can affect timing in the conduct of an offer. Also, where the proposed offer is to be made to a related party, as defined in the Listing Rules (which includes a substantial shareholder or a director or shadow director of the offeror but which, with effect from the specified commencement dates of the revised Irish Listing Rules published on 1 November 2007, excludes a 50/50 joint venture partner), a circular and the prior approval of the shareholders of the offeror in general meeting will generally be required.

Agreements or arrangements under which a listed company agrees to discharge any exceptional liabilities, losses or expenses of another party, which exceed certain limits may also require shareholder approval.

In certain cases, for example where the consideration comprises shares in the offeror, the offeror will have to publish a prospectus complying with the requirements of the Prospectus Directive unless a document containing information which is considered "equivalent" to that of a prospectus is available.

14.5.4   *Industry-specific regulations*

Additional regulations apply to certain companies and industries including banks and building societies, insurance undertakings, media companies, airlines, telecommunications operators and pharmaceutical companies.

14.6   Methods of acquisition

14.6.1   *Introduction*

Takeovers of Irish companies can be effected in a variety of ways, the method of acquisition often being determined by whether a partial or 100 per cent takeover is proposed. Tax considerations also often influence to a considerable degree the structure adopted. It is not uncommon for a variety of consideration options to be offered to sellers including cash, loan notes or debentures and/or shares in the acquiring company in exchange for the vendor's shares in the target company. The primary methods adopted in Ireland for effecting a takeover are described briefly below.

14.6.2   *Share purchase agreement*

Due to the preponderance of private companies in Ireland, by far the most usual means of effecting a takeover is by a privately negotiated share purchase agreement executed by all the shareholders of the target company and the purchaser. All shareholders agree to waive their pre-emption rights and such agreements frequently contain extensive warranties and indemnities given by the sellers relating to the business, taxation and other affairs of the target company, permitting a purchaser to recover in the event of loss. It is common for the purchaser to be given access to considerable amounts of information in relation to the target's business in advance of the execution of any agreement, with a view to enabling it to have a clearer picture of what it is buying.

14.6.3   Asset purchase agreement

It is possible, instead of buying the entire issued share capital of a company, to purchase its business and assets alone. Such purchase is usually effected by means of a privately negotiated asset purchase agreement between the target company and the purchaser. This can be an attractive option if the purchaser is unwilling to take on, or is unsure about, the extent of the liabilities of the target. However, such acquisitions are usually more complex than share acquisitions, involve notifications to employees or their representatives in advance of a sale and can result in significant tax disadvantages. In particular, the transfer of certain assets can attract *ad valorem* stamp duty on a sliding scale of between 0 per cent and 9 per cent, whereas share sales only attract *ad valorem* stamp duty at a rate of 1 per cent.

Asset purchase agreements also often contain warranties and indemnities from the seller to the purchaser in relation to the business being bought, enabling the purchaser to recover in the event of loss.

14.6.4   General offer

Takeovers of public limited companies whose shares are listed on, or are dealt on, a Stock Exchange and companies having a large number of shareholders, often with disparate interests, are usually effected by way of a general offer made by an offeror to purchase all the shares of the target company. Acceptance of the offer is achieved by each member completing a form of acceptance and sending it back to the offeror.

Potential offerors normally seek the recommendation of the target company's board of directors before making the offer and an opportunity to conduct due diligence in relation to the target. However, if an approach is unwelcome the potential purchaser will usually have to rely primarily on publicly available information, such as that published in listing particulars and annual and interim financial reports.

A general offer is usually made conditional upon the offeror receiving a stated percentage of acceptances. In the case of an offer governed by the Takeover Rules this cannot be less than 50 per cent except in exceptional circumstances agreed by the Panel. More usually, except in the case of a mandatory offer, the acceptance level is 90 per cent or 80 per cent, depending on the compulsory acquisition provisions applicable.

As referred to above, the making and conduct of an offer to shareholders of companies whose shares are authorised for trading on a market regulated by the Irish Stock Exchange, the London Stock Exchange, the New York Stock

Exchange, NASDAQ, or have been so authorised within the preceding five years, is subject to the Takeover Rules and the 1997 Act and may be subject to the Takeover Regulations as regards takeover bids to which the Takeover Directive applies (*see* 14.5.1 and 14.5.2).

14.6.5   Schemes of arrangement

Takeovers can also be effected by use of amalgamation and reconstruction provisions contained in the Companies Act 1963. An acquisition effected in this manner can result in stamp duty savings and can be attractive in that there is no need to go through compulsory acquisition procedures and get to 90 per cent (or 80 per cent in certain instances) relevant acceptances in order to achieve 100 per cent ownership of a target (*see* paragraph 14.12). Typically, the provisions can be used to effect an amalgamation by way of a share-for-share exchange. Accordingly, the target company becomes a subsidiary of another company (for example, ABC Co.). All shares in the target company other than those held by ABC Co. are cancelled. The shareholders in the target company are issued shares in ABC Co. to compensate them for loss of the cancelled shares. The reserve created from the cancellation of the target company's shares is capitalised to enable the target company to pay up and issue extra shares to ABC Co., equal to the shares cancelled. The provisions can also be used to effect an amalgamation by way of a transfer of assets.

Takeovers in Ireland are increasingly being effected by means of schemes of arrangement. This means of acquisition was used in the First Active plc takeover by the Royal Bank of Scotland in 2003, in the 2006 takeover by Australian investment firm Babcock & Brown of eircom plc and in the recent acquisition by Hypo Real Estate Holding AG of Depfa Bank plc in 2007. It was also intended to be used in the recent high-profile battle during 2007 for ICG Group plc between the rival consortia Aella plc and Moonduster.

A significant difference exists between takeovers which fall under the Takeover Regulations and takeovers effected by means of schemes of arrangement. Schemes of arrangement are takeovers governed by the different processes of the Companies Acts, and they must be approved by the High Court. The approval of a majority of the shareholders, representing 75 per cent in value of the shareholders present and voting at the meeting, is required (as opposed to a 90 per cent or 80 per cent threshold). This lower acceptance threshold enabling an acquisition of 100 per cent of the target, combined with certain other advantages, such as the possible elimination of 1 per cent stamp duty for the purchaser and the avoidance of the application of the compulsory acquisition procedure applicable under the Takeover Regulations or Irish Companies Acts, in the case of a conventional takeover offer has, in practice, resulted in the scheme of arrangement becoming an increasingly popular means of acquisition in Ireland. This is likely to remain the case for the foreseeable future.

A takeover effected by Scheme is, however, a less flexible procedure, as it needs High Court approval procedures and it cannot be used for a hostile offer, as it requires the cooperation of the target company.

In the light of recent experience the Irish Panel has considered it inappropriate for timing requirements which apply to takeover offers not to apply to takeover schemes as well, and so is proposing a change in the Takeover Rules with the objective of putting the offeree shareholder considering a takeover scheme in a more analogous position to the offeree shareholder considering an offer.

14.6.6 European Communities (Mergers and Divisions of Companies) Regulations 1987

The European Communities (Mergers and Divisions of Companies) Regulations 1987 implement Council Directives 78/855/EEC and 82/891/EEC to enable mergers by way of acquisition of all the assets and liabilities of the target in exchange for the issue of shares to the target's shareholders, with a view to dissolution of the target. The Regulations are rarely used in practice as the procedures involved are somewhat cumbersome. The existing regime is due for a measure of reform in the relatively near future – *see* further paragraph 14.13.6 below.

14.7 Preparation of an offer

14.7.1 Investigation of the offeree target

In preparing to make a public general offer to all the shareholders of a target company it is obviously important to gather as much information as possible in relation to the target and its shareholders in advance of the making of the offer. The potential offeror, together with its advisers, will want to collect and examine all publicly available information relating to the target. Copies of annual returns (annexing the annual accounts of a target), constitutional documents, particulars of charges and details of directors in relation to an Irish incorporated target company can be obtained from the Companies Office in Dublin. Analysis of all such information will assist in determining the structure and pricing of an offer. Depending on whether the offer is a recommended or a hostile one, it may also be possible to conduct due diligence on the target. In a recommended bid a considerable amount of non-publicly available information is normally requested by an offeror before making an offer. Target companies will usually only supply this on receipt of confidentiality undertakings and possibly a standstill agreement not to buy shares or launch a hostile offer. Target companies may be reluctant to supply full information due to the requirement in Rule 20.2 of the Takeover Rules that such information must also be provided to a competing offeror if requested, even though that offeror is not favoured.

It is important in preparing for an offer to be aware of Irish market abuse laws and other regulations prohibiting insider dealing. Market abuse regulations provide that having access to inside information relating to another company and using it in the context of a public takeover made in conformity with the Takeover Rules does not, of itself, constitute market abuse. However, Rule 4.2(b) of the Takeover Rules provides that neither an offeror or any person acting in concert with it may deal in securities of the offeree before the announcement of an offer, if the offeree has supplied confidential information to the offeror or its associates. Any pre-bid buying should therefore take place prior to any access to due diligence information.

14.7.2   Timing

Consideration should be given to the timing of an offer and, in particular, to the possibility of a leak of the potential offeror's plans or of a competing offeror pre-empting the offeror if the announcement of the offer is delayed. The offeror should also bear in mind when the offeror and offeree are due to report on their financial results.

14.7.3   Stake building

In advance of making a full offer, the potential offeror might decide to purchase some of the potential offeree's shares in the open market. By building up its stake in the offeree in this way, the offeror increases its chances of success with the subsequent offer as it will require less acceptances to acquire control of the offeree. Furthermore, in the event that a successful competing bid is subsequently made by another offeror, the gain realised from the sale of these shares to the competing offeror might cover the offeror's costs incurred in making its offer.

There are a number of matters which may affect a potential offeror's decision, such as whether there are restrictions which would prevent it from acquiring shares and also the timing restrictions and disclosure obligations to which a stake building exercise can give rise. Any offeror thinking of acquiring a stake in a proposed target needs to check that doing so would not contravene any laws on insider dealing (*see* paragraph 14.13 below). As mentioned earlier at 14.7.1, the Takeover Rules also preclude persons, other than the offeror, who are privy to price-sensitive information concerning an offer or contemplated offer, from acquiring the target's shares at any time when there is reason to suppose an offer is contemplated and before the offer is announced.

Stake building is subject to compliance with the rules governing substantial acquisitions of securities ("SARs"), the Takeover Rules, the Companies Act 1990 (as amended) and transparency laws implementing the Transparency Directive. Stake building may also require clearance from the Competition Authority.

Financial advisers and stockbrokers (and any person controlling or controlled by them) to a target group or its associates are prohibited from acquiring interest in the target groups shares either on their own accounts or on behalf of discretionary clients (*see* Rule 4.4 of the Takeover Rules).

The Transparency (Directive 2004/109/EC) Regulations 2007, which implemented the Transparency Directive in Ireland and the Transparency Rules made by IFSRA require a person to notify an Irish listed company and IFSRA each time its percentage of voting rights in the company (held directly or indirectly or by a combination of both) reaches or crosses (on the way up or down) 3 per cent to 10 per cent and every 1 per cent threshold after that.

Once these thresholds have been reached or crossed, notification to the company and IFSRA must be made within two trading days where the target is an Irish incorporated company, and the company itself must notify the Irish Stock Exchange by the end of the next trading day. Accordingly, these provisions impact on the ability of an offeror (or persons acting in concert with it) to quickly acquire a significant stake in an Irish incorporated company listed on the Official List of the Irish Stock Exchange without making disclosure of this fact.

Irish company law and, normally, a public limited company's articles of association provide that the company can require any person to disclose their interest in the company held at any time in the previous three years. Articles of Association often complement this power by giving the directors the power to require a person to disclose interests held in the company at any earlier time.

14.7.4 The rules governing substantial acquisitions of securities

The SARs are issued and administered by the Panel. They essentially restrict the speed with which a person (and its concert parties) may increase a holding of, or rights over, voting securities in an Irish incorporated company the shares of which are authorised for trading on a market regulated by a recognised stock exchange, or were so authorised at any time within the preceding five years, the London Stock Exchange, New York Stock Exchange or NASDAQ between 15 per cent and 30 per cent. Subject to certain exceptions, the SARs preclude a person, within a period of seven days, from acquiring securities carrying voting rights or rights over such securities in a company representing 10 per cent or more of the voting rights if, as a result, that person would hold securities or rights over securities carrying between 15 and 30 per cent of the voting rights of that company. Acquisitions of securities or rights over securities from a single shareholder, if it is the only such acquisition made within such seven-day period and substantial acquisitions made pursuant to a tender offer where the offer does not involve an acquisition of securities carrying more than 30 per cent of voting rights, is not precluded. Neither are substantial acquisitions immediately before the announcement of a firm intention to make an offer which will be recommended (or which are made with the agreement of the offeree board) provided that the acquisition is conditional upon the announcement of the offer, nor after the acquirer has announced a firm intention to make an offer which is not subject to a pre-condition. Acquisition by concert parties is aggregated.

The SARs also require accelerated disclosure to the target, the Irish Stock Exchange and the Panel of acquisitions of shares or rights over shares relating to such holdings. They do not apply to an acquisition by a person who has announced a firm intention to make an offer for a company to which the Takeover Rules apply, provided that the making of the offer is not subject to a precondition or immediately before a person announces a firm intention to make an approved or recommended offer. Neither do they apply to an acquisition resulting in a holding of 30 per cent or more of the voting rights of a company. In such an event the Takeover Rules will apply. Notably, the SARs were abolished in the UK in May 2006 at the time of the implementation of the Takeover Directive.

14.7.5 The Takeover Rules

The Takeover Rules contain further restrictions on stake building and prohibit, subject to certain specified exceptions, a potential offeror, and persons acting in concert with it, from acquiring shares carrying voting rights, or rights over such shares in the target which would increase the holdings of such persons in the target to 30 per cent or more. This is on the basis that such a holding effectively gives control of a company and a breach of these provisions may have serious consequences.

If an offeror and its concert parties hold less than 30 per cent of the voting rights in the target it may not acquire shares which would bring it above 30 per cent of voting rights.

A person holding 30 per cent or more, but less than 50 per cent, of shares carrying voting rights may not acquire in a 12-month period shares carrying more than 0.05 per cent of voting rights. The exceptions to these Rules include where:

(a)   the acquisition is from a single shareholder, provided that it is the only such acquisition within any seven-day period and no announcement of a firm, unconditional intention to make an offer has been made;

(b)   the acquisition takes place immediately before the announcement by the acquirer of a firm intention to make a full offer which is recommended by or made with the agreement of the board of the target and is conditional on the announcement of the offer;

(c)   an announcement of a firm intention to make an offer has been made and certain other specified conditions are met; or

(d)   the acquisition is by way of acceptance of the offer made in accordance with the Takeover Rules (*see* Rules 5.1 and 5.2).

Where the offeror (or any person acting in concert) has acquired shares in the target within a period of three months prior to the announcement of the offer (or such longer period as the Panel may prescribe), the terms of the offer will have to be on at least as favourable terms.

Where shares are acquired under one of the above exceptions, the acquirer will, except with the consent of the Panel, be required to make a mandatory offer under Rule 9 of the Takeover Rules. Rule 9 provides that where a person acquires shares which, when added to the shares held or acquired by persons acting in concert with it, give it 30 per cent or more of the voting rights of the target, unless the Panel otherwise agrees, it must make a "mandatory offer" for all the equity share voting capital of the target company, whether it carries voting rights, and each other class of transferable securities carrying voting rights. Similarly, where a person which, with persons acting in concert with it, already holds between 30 per cent and 50 per cent, increases its holding by more than 0.05 per cent of the voting rights in the target in any 12 months, it must, unless the Panel otherwise agrees, make a mandatory offer. That offer must be made at the highest price per share paid by the offeror or any person acting in concert with it for shares in the target of that class in the 12 months prior to the announcement by the offeror of a firm intention to make an offer and ending on the date on which the offer closes for acceptance. It must also be in cash or accompanied by a cash alternative offer.

In certain circumstances, the Panel may, having regard to the General Principles, decide that the highest price, calculated by this method, may be adjusted. Rule 9.4 of the Takeover Rules states that when assessing this, the Panel may take into account factors such as the size and timing of the relevant purchases, the attitude of the offeree board, whether an offer is required to rescue a company in serious financial difficulty and the pattern and number of securities purchased in the preceding 12 months.

No conditions can attach to a mandatory offer save for a 50 per cent acceptance condition and a competition condition (*see* Rule 9.2(b)).

A mandatory offer is not required where control of a target is acquired as a result of a voluntary offer made in accordance with the Takeover Rules.

The Panel may also require that a mandatory offer is made where a person or any person acting in concert with it acquires 30 per cent or more of the voting rights of a target as a result of the target purchasing or redeeming its own shares or holding between 30 per cent and 50 per cent if by virtue of such redemption or purchase the aggregate percentage they hold is increased by more than 0.05 per cent in any 12-month period (*see* Rule 37).

14.7.6 *Disclosure of shareholdings*

As indicated previously, the Transparency Regulations 2007 and the Transparency Rules made by IFSRA contain disclosure requirements for companies whose securities are admitted to trading on a regulated market. Importantly, they require a person to notify an Irish public company whose shares are listed on the Official List of the Irish Stock Exchange (the "ISE"), and IFSRA, each time his percentage of voting rights in the company (held directly or indirectly or by a combination of both) reaches or crosses (on the way up or down) 3 per cent to 10 per cent and every 1 per cent threshold after that.

Once these thresholds have been reached or crossed, notification to the company and IFSRA must be made within two trading days and the company itself must notify the ISE by the end of the next trading day. The notification requirements also extend to persons holding directly, or indirectly, financial instruments which result in an entitlement to acquire already-issued shares carrying voting rights.

The Market Abuse Directive was implemented in Ireland in 2005 and disclosure obligations arise under this regime also for companies whose securities are admitted to listing on a regulated market. "Persons discharging managerial responsibilities" (such as directors or senior executives) in a company are subject to notification obligations contained in the Market Abuse (Directive 2003/6/EC) Regulations 2005 (the "Market Abuse Regulations") and the Market Abuse Rules made by IFSRA. They must notify the company in writing within four days of any dealing by them in the company's shares. The company must, in turn, notify IFSRA.

The relationship between the disclosure obligations arising under the Transparency Rules and the regime established by the Companies Acts and Market Abuse law is complex but some streamlining has been undertaken. For example, the Transparency Regulations provide that if a requirement arises to notify an acquisition or disposal of shares under the Transparency Regulations and Rules, the overlapping disclosure obligations contained in the Companies Act 1990 do not apply. In addition, there is no longer any need to separately notify the ISE if a person acquires or disposes of 10 per cent, 25 per cent, 50 per cent or 75 per cent of the company's share capital, following the repeal of Sections 89 to 96 of the Companies Act 1990 by the European Communities (Admission to Listing and Miscellaneous Provisions) Regulations 2007.

The obligation on a director or secretary to notify interests in shares or debentures in his or her company set out in the Companies Act 1990 remains in force.

The Takeover Rules also contain detailed disclosure requirements in respect of dealings by an offeror or offeree, or their associates and holders of 1 per cent or more of relevant securities. Disclosure has to be made no later than 12 noon on the business day following the date of the transaction (*see* Rule 8 Takeover Rules).

14.7.7   The Listing Rules

The Listing Rules also contain disclosure obligations for companies subject to its provisions, over and above those prescribed under legislation. They also limit the amount of a listed company's assets which can be used in buying shares in a target without the consent of, or the giving of notice to, its shareholders and, depending on the structure of an offer, certain other relevant restrictions on the making of announcements.

14.7.8   Information, announcements and secrecy

The "absolute secrecy" obligations in respect of the offer or contemplated offer under Rule 2 of the Takeover Rules need to be continually borne in mind in the preparation of an offer. Every person who has access to confidential and, particularly, price-sensitive information must control access to that information and minimise the possibility of accidental leaks.

Rule 2.2 prescribes the circumstances in which an announcement concerning an offer or a possible offer must be made unless the Panel directs otherwise and include circumstances where the target is the subject of rumour and speculation or there is an anomalous movement in its share price. Before the target board is approached, the responsibility for making an announcement is on the offeror which needs to carefully monitor the target's share price. After an approach to the target board has been made, which may or may not lead to an offer, the primary responsibility for making an announcement normally rests with the target board.

Sometimes an announcement will only be to the effect that discussions are taking place which may or may not lead to an announcement of a firm intention to make an offer.

Rule 2.5(a) of the Takeover Rules provides that an offeror should only announce an offer after it and its financial adviser are satisfied after careful and responsible consideration that the offeror can and will continue to be able to implement the offer.

Promptly after the commencement of an offer period the target must send a copy of the relevant announcement, or a circular summarising the terms and conditions of the offer, to each of its shareholders and the Panel. After the publication of a Rule 2.5 announcement the offeror and target must let the employees' representatives, or where there are none, the employees themselves know (Rule 2.6(c) Takeover Rules).

Rule 2.5 of the Takeover Rules prescribes the contents of any Rule 2.5 announcement which must include the terms of the offer and all conditions to which the offer is subject.

An offeror is obliged to proceed with an offer once there has been an announcement of a firm intention to make an offer except in the very limited circumstances set out in Rule 2.7 of the Takeover Rules.

14.7.9 Obligation to notify target's board

Rule 1 of the Takeover Rules requires an offeror to inform the board of directors of the target or its advisers of its intention to make an offer before making an announcement. The target's board is entitled to be satisfied that the offeror is, or will be, in a position to implement the offer in full. In practice this comfort will take the form of an assurance from the offeror's financial adviser. Where the offeror expects the target board to be hostile to the bid it will inform the target board only shortly before it announces its intention to make an offer.

14.8 Conduct of a public offer

The essential function of the Takeover Rules is to regulate the conduct of public offers to which the Takeover Rules apply to ensure fair and equal treatment of all shareholders. In circumstances where the Takeover Rules apply to a public offer most of the Takeover Rules will have an impact.

Most importantly, the Takeover Rules require adherence to a strict timetable of events, prescribing matters such as the date of posting of the offer document after the announcement of the offer, the period for which the offer should be left open, the making of revised offers and the latest date for satisfaction of conditions and for receipt of acceptances. The timetable is likely to be extended in the event of competing offers for the same target.

Section 14.11 below refers to the detailed requirements in the Takeover Rules relating to the issue of documents from the offeror and target boards.

The Takeover Rules also contain provisions on other issues affecting the conduct of an offer such as:

(a)   the publication of advertisements;
(b)   radio or television interviews and debates during the course of a bid;
(c)   telephone campaigns directed at shareholders of the target;

(d)   meetings with shareholders, analysts, stockbrokers or others engaged in investment management or advice;

(e)   action taken to frustrate an offer (*see* 14.9 below); and

(f)   equality of information to competing offerors.

14.8.1   Restrictions following offers

The Takeover Rules prohibit an offeror whose bid has failed to become wholly unconditional from making another bid for a period of time except with the consent of the Panel. They also prohibit persons acting in concert with such offeror from making a fresh offer within 12 months from the date on which the original offer was withdrawn or lapsed. Furthermore, the offeror or concert parties cannot acquire shares sufficient in number to give rise to the need to make a mandatory bid under Rule 9 of the Takeover Rules within the 12-month period. The offeror or concert parties cannot acquire shares within the 12-month period if they hold shares carrying over 49.95 per cent but not over 50 per cent of the voting rights of the offeree.

14.9   Defences to a hostile offer

14.9.1   Introduction

The Takeover Rules impose considerable restraints on the actions of directors in defending their company from a hostile offer. Directors must observe their fiduciary duties to the company and act in the best interests of the company. As a matter of law they can also have regard to the interests of employees and share-holders. Directors of companies not subject to the Takeover Rules may have more flexibility, but they are also obliged to act in the interests of the company as a whole and not to use their powers for an improper purpose and, if the company has a listing on the Irish or London Stock Exchange, to comply with the require-ments of the Listing Rules. Private companies frequently impose restrictions on transfers of shares in their articles of association, which can frustrate an offer.

Due to the Takeover Rules restrictions, which apply when an offer is believed to be imminent or has been made, it is better to try and set up defences such as long-term directors' service contracts or other long-term "poison pill" contracts well in advance of any offer.

14.9.2   Conflict of interests

Bids are often unwelcome to the target's board of directors as a successful bid often results in the target's board losing its independence or, in more extreme cases, the members of the board being replaced. Consequently the interests of the directors of the target might conflict with the interests of the target's share-holders and the company as a whole. It is because of this potential conflict of interest that the Takeover Rules, the principal object of which is the protection of the target shareholder's interests, restrict the ability of the board to take unilat-eral action in relation to a hostile bid.

14.9.3 *The Takeover Rules*

General Principle 3, set out in the Schedule to the 1997 Act, restricts the ability of the board of the target, to take action in relation to the affairs of the target which could effectively result in the shareholders being denied an opportunity to decide on the merits of an offer.

Rule 21 of the Takeover Rules elaborates further on General Principle 3 and provides that, subject to a number of exceptions, (such as where the offeree's shareholders have given their consent in general meeting, or, with the Panel's consent in pursuance of a contract entered into earlier), during the course of an offer or at any earlier time at which the offeree board has reason to believe that the making of an offer is or may be imminent, the board of the target must not take frustrating action. Frustrating action includes action to allot or issue any authorised but unissued shares, grant options, conversion rights, or subscription rights in respect of the target's shares, or purchase or sell assets of a material amount (as defined by the Takeover Rules). The offeree board is also prohibited from entering into contracts other than in the ordinary course of business and generally from taking any action regarding the conduct of its affairs (other than seeking alternative offers), which may result in frustration of the making or implementation of an offer or in the target shareholders being denied the opportunity to decide on the merits of such an offer or possible offer.

The notes to Rule 21 indicate that an amendment to or entry into of a service contract with a director may be regarded by the Panel as the entry into of a contract other than in the ordinary course of business if the new or amended contract constitutes an abnormal increase in emoluments or a significant improvement in terms of service. The Rule may also apply to proposals affecting the target's pension scheme arrangements.

Rule 22 obliges the target's board to ensure that transfers are promptly registered during an offer to enable the offeror to exercise its voting rights.

General Principle 3 also, *inter alia*, provides that the directors of the target owe a duty to the target and to the shareholders of the target to act in the interests of the company as a whole, for example, when giving advice and providing information in relation to the offer.

14.9.4 *Potential defences*

Although potential defences are quite limited, the following strategies may be adopted.

14.9.4.1 *Documents from the target's board*

The target's board, through documents circulated to shareholders and announcements, may seek to convince the shareholders that the offer is commercially unattractive for the company and its shareholders and will seek, generally within the constraints of the Takeover Rules, if applicable, to discredit the offer. Where a hostile bid has been made, the offeree board will frequently allege that the offer seriously undervalues the target. The offeree board might take the opportunity to disclose favourable information in relation to the target or, if shares in the offeror are offered by way of consideration, to show that it is worth less than it appears. It may also appeal to the shareholders' loyalty or patriotism and might argue that redundancies will follow the takeover. Rule 25.2(a) of the Takeover Rules requires the offeree board to include, in its written opinion on the offer, its views on the effects of implementation of the offer on all the company's interests, including, specifically, employment and the offeror's strategic plans for the offeree and their likely repercussions on employment and on the locations of the offeree's places of business. Rule 30.3(b) further requires that the offeree board append to the first response circular a separate opinion from the representatives of its employees on the effects of the offer on employment, provided the opinion is received in good time before the circular is dispatched.

Directors of companies subject to the Takeover Rules will have to be careful not to issue statements which, while not factually inaccurate, may mislead share-holders and the market or may create uncertainty. Also, any profit forecasts or asset valuations will have to comply with Rules 28 and 29 of the Takeover Rules (*see* 14.10 below).

14.9.4.2 White knights
In the face of a hostile offer the target's board may seek to solicit a competing offer from another potential offeror which is more acceptable to the target's board. This may also have the benefit of increasing the price payable to share-holders. However, the Panel can be censorious of attempts by the target's board to circulate rumours of another interested party. Where, in the Panel's view, such rumours create uncertainty amongst shareholders at a critical stage and this prejudices the offeror, it may extend the time limits relating to the offer.

14.9.4.3 Purchasing shares in the market or exercising options
The directors of the target may seek to procure that persons or companies friendly to the board acquire sufficient shares in the market to defeat the bid or seek to have friendly option holders exercise their options. Such a course of action can, however, be fraught with difficulties. For example, if the directors and their associates acquire 30 per cent or more of the voting rights of the company, these individuals might be viewed by the Panel as acting in concert and consequently will be obliged to make a bid for the whole company pursuant to Rule 9 of the Takeover Rules (*see* 14.7.5 above). Market abuse and insider dealing prohibitions may also be relevant.

14.9.4.4 Litigation
Recourse to the courts (e.g., to obtain an injunction prohibiting a proposed takeover due, for example, to some element of illegality) is a relatively rare defence to a hostile takeover and is frowned upon by the Panel, which has expressed the view that where litigation might have the effect of frustrating an offer, shareholder approval to such litigation should first be obtained. The Panel has stated that it would expect to be consulted before any legal proceedings are initiated.

14.9.4.5 Increased dividends
The directors might announce increased dividends and/or a capitalisation issue with a view to increasing the market value of the target, although such action

may not have a significant impact on the outcome of an offer. It may also be possible to announce proposals for a buy-back of shares if the offer fails, although any such buy-back is likely to require shareholder approval.

14.9.4.6 *Appeal to regulatory authorities*
If the hostile offer is subject to the Competition Act (*see* 14.4 above), the target's board may seek to have the Competition Authority make an order prohibiting the takeover or permitting it subject to conditions likely to be unattractive to the offeror. There may also be occasions on which appeal can be made to other regulatory authorities, for example, whose approval is required if the target is a bank or insurance company, or to the European Commission on competition law grounds, to stop completion of the offer.

14.9.5 *"Pre-bid defences" or "breakthrough provisions"*

Part 3 of the Takeover Regulations (entitled "breakthrough provisions") enable an Irish registered company to which the Takeover Regulations apply to opt in or opt out by special resolution of the breakthrough provisions of that part of the Regulations.

The background to these provisions is that they represent an attempt by the EU to impose a uniform requirement that where a bid has been made public, pre-bid defences, known as "breakthrough provisions", such as differential share structures, limitations on share ownership and restrictions on transfers of shares set out in the company's articles or in contractual agreements, will not apply to restrict the ability of the offeror to take over the target company. Under the Takeover Directive, Member States had the right to permit such companies to have such restrictions set out in the company's articles or in contractual agreements either between the members or between the members and the company. Such restrictive provisions are very unusual in Irish companies the shares of which are dealt in on a stock exchange. However, if Member States made use of this option and permitted these restrictions, they were required to grant companies a reversible option and make such restrictions invalid.

The Takeover Regulations implement this by giving companies which satisfy certain conditions the right by special resolution to opt in to the breakthrough provisions and thereby ensure that where a bid is made for the company, any pre-bid defensive measures that have been put in place will be invalid. Where a company opts in, it becomes an "opted in company", and where a takeover bid is made for such a company (assuming its shares are admitted to trading on a regulated market) then, in broad terms, agreements between shareholders, or entered into between shareholders and the company (for example, contained in a "standstill" or similar agreement) are invalid if they restrict:

(i)   the transfer of shares in the target to the offeror or its nominees during the offer period, or

(ii)   the transfer of shares to any person at a time during the offer period, when the offeror holds 75 per cent or more in nominal value of all the voting securities of the Company, or

(iii) rights to vote at a general meeting of the company that decide whether to take any action that might result in the frustration of the bid, or

(iv)   rights to vote at general meetings after a time when the offeror holds not less than 75 per cent in value of all the securities of the company.

Persons who are parties to these agreements and who suffer loss as a result of a breach of them are entitled to apply to the High Court to seek compensation from the other party or parties to them.

A company can only "opt in" if certain conditions are met, namely that its securities are admitted to trading on a regulated market, that its articles of association must not contain restrictions such as loaded voting rights, limits on share ownership and restrictions on share transfers and that there must be no securities conferring special rights on the company held by the Government, and no rights exercisable by the Government under any enactment.

A company can revoke an opting in resolution by a further "opting out" special resolution of the shareholders.

14.10   Profit forecasts and asset valuations

14.10.1   Introduction

Either the offeror or the target may make a profit forecast or publish an asset valuation in connection with an offer. It can readily be appreciated how such forecasts and valuations, giving new and important information about the target or made by the offeror to support its own share price if its shares are being offered by way of consideration, might be significant factors in determining whether the target's shareholders will accept the offer or not. Where the Takeover Rules apply to a takeover of an Irish company, Rules 28 and 29 of the Takeover Rules contain detailed provisions regulating such matters and essentially seek to protect shareholders from misleading or excessively optimistic forecasts and valuations.

Whilst any profit forecast or asset valuation given in connection with an offer is the sole responsibility of the directors of the target or the offeror, as the case may be, the Takeover Rules require it to be examined and reported on by appropriate independent advisers or valuers (other than in the case of a forecast made by an offeror offering cash only).

14.10.2   Profit forecasts

The Takeover Rules warn that certain forms of words, even though not mentioning a particular figure, may constitute a profit forecast. Any statement, however published, issued by or on behalf of an offeror or target, which puts a minimum or maximum figure on its likely profits or losses or which contains the data to calculate an approximate figure for profit or losses, is deemed for the purposes of the Takeover Rules to be a profit forecast (*see* Rule 28.6). For example, a chairman's statement that the current year's results will be better than the previous year's would be regarded by the Panel as a forecast. Care needs to be taken when talking to the media since relatively minor changes in wording can result in a phrase which constitutes a profit forecast being printed. Profit projections, where a company calculates the possible future profits which could arise given differing assumptions as to future circumstances, are not allowed under the Takeover Rules. In cases of doubt the Panel should be consulted in advance.

The Panel is concerned to ensure that any forecasts by parties to an offer constitute the best objective assessment that can reasonably be made of the outcome of the event forecast and that such forecasts are formally supported by independent experts' reports and are presented to all shareholders. It is a requirement of the Takeover Rules that the advisers' reports are published in an offer document. The Takeover Rules require the assumptions (including the commercial assumptions) which have been made when arriving at a forecast to be stated in order to enable shareholders to form a view as to the reasonableness and reliability of the forecast. The financial advisers to the offeror or, as the case may be, the target are obliged to discuss with the company the assumptions on which the profit forecast is based and to satisfy themselves that the forecast has been made in the manner required by Rule 28.1. The auditors and financial consultants also must be satisfied that the forecast has been properly compiled on the basis of the assumptions made and advise the company accordingly.

Rule 28.5 of the Takeover Rules requires that once a forecast has been made in an offer document, each subsequent document published in connection with the offer must, except with the consent of the Panel, confirm its continued validity and that the advisers have not objected to their reports continuing.

14.10.3   Asset valuations

Directors of a target company may look to revalue its assets in order to defend the company or seek a price increase. Asset valuations given in connection with an offer governed by the Takeover Rules must be supported by a named independent valuer unconnected with the other parties to the transaction. The Takeover Rules describe what qualifications a valuer should have, although, in relation to assets other than land, buildings, plant and machinery, a valuer with "appropriate qualifications, experience and knowledge" is treated as being qualified. The basis of the valuation is also prescribed by the Takeover Rules in relation to companies to which the Takeover Rules apply, and the basis used needs to be clearly stated. In certain cases, for example, where there is a shortage of time and a large quantity of assets or properties to be valued, valuations by the independent valuer based on representative samples which are then extrapolated out by the directors to give a full value for the portfolio as a whole, may be acceptable to the Panel.

Potential tax liabilities which could arise on a sale of assets at the valuation amount have to be given in connection with an offer and also a comment made as to the likelihood of any such liability crystallising.

An asset valuation must state the effective date at which the assets were valued, and where the valuation is not sufficiently current it cannot be used unless the independent valuer states that he is satisfied that a valuation at the current date would not be materially different (*see* Rule 29).

14.11   Documents from the offeror and offeree board

14.11.1   *General*

In circumstances where the Takeover Rules apply to a takeover of an Irish company the obligations of the offeror and target boards to post certain documents and the detailed contents of such documents are regulated by the Takeover Rules and, where shares are listed, to a lesser extent, the Listing Rules. Where the Takeover Rules do not apply to a takeover, for example where the target is a private company, there is no specific obligation on the boards of either the offeror or target to post or circulate communications. Quite apart from the obligations under the Takeover Rules and the Listing Rules, there can be legal consequences where statements included in documents relating to the offer are inaccurate. For example, an action for damages in respect of a negligent misstatement may be maintainable.

The Takeover Rules require that the offeror gives sufficient information, and the target's board gives sufficient information and advice, to shareholders to allow them to reach a properly informed decision as to the merits or demerits of an offer. Care must be taken to ensure documents do not contain statements which, whilst not factually inaccurate, may mislead shareholders and the market or may create uncertainty. Apart from such general obligations, the Takeover Rules have detailed provisions as to the content of documents produced by the offeror and the target boards' circulars. The Takeover Rules also prescribe the timetable for the issue of relevant documents and the conduct of an offer.

The Takeover Rules contain a general Rule 19.2 that companies issuing documents or certain advertisements in the course of a bid must have their directors expressly accept responsibility for the information contained in such a document or advertisement and confirm that, to the best of their knowledge and belief (having taken all reasonable care to ensure that such is the case), the information contained in the document or advertisement is in accordance with the facts and, where appropriate, that it does not omit anything likely to affect the import of such information.

Given the standards of care with regard to documents and advertisements required by the Takeover Rules, the good practice has evolved of the directors and their advisers undertaking a detailed verification exercise, formally checking all facts and the bases and assumptions for statements of opinion or belief contained in documents relating to an offer.

At the time that documents, announcements or advertisements relating to an offer are released, copies must be lodged with the Panel and the advisers to all other parties to the offer.

The following is a list of the principal documents which are typically issued by the offeror and target boards in the course of a takeover bid:

(a)   announcement;
(b)   offeree board circular;
(c)   offer document; and
(d)   defence document (where the bid is hostile).

14.11.2   Announcement and target board's circular

Promptly after the announcement of a firm intention to make an offer (which should contain a number of details specified in Rule 2.5(b) of the Takeover Rules including the terms of the offer and conditions attaching to it), a copy of the press announcement containing the detailed terms and conditions of the offer, or a circular summarising the terms and conditions of the offer, must be sent by the target's board to its shareholders and to the Panel together, where necessary, with the board's explanation of the implications of the announcement. This document is often accompanied by the target board's preliminary views on the offer.

14.11.3   Offer document

The offer document normally sets out the commercial arguments and rationale for the offer, its terms, the offer timetable and information about the consideration offered to shareholders. It must normally be issued within 28 days of the announcement of a firm intention to make an offer. A list of conditions upon which the offer is dependent will be set out in the appendix to the document including, for example, the required acceptance levels, time of announcements, rights of withdrawal, anti-trust and other regulatory consents needed, there being no material adverse change and no material undisclosed litigation. The conditions of the offer must not be based on the subjective judgments of the directors of the offeror or solely within the offeror's control (*see* Rule 13.1). If the offer is supported by the board of the target company, a letter of recommendation of the offer will usually be contained in the offer document.

Specific requirements as to the contents of offer documents are set out in Rule 24 of the Takeover Rules.

A form of acceptance is issued with the offer document whereby shareholders of the target can accept the offer.

The target's shareholders may be resident in certain jurisdictions to which an offer document cannot be sent.

If the offeror is borrowing monies to enable it to fund a takeover it will need to have an unconditional loan agreement available to it at the time the offer is announced. The offeror's financial adviser has to confirm that an offeror has sufficient resources to enable payment should the offer be accepted in full (*see* Rule 24.7). Rule 31.8 of the Takeover Rules requires settlement of the consideration within 21 days of the first closing date or, if later, the date on which the offer becomes wholly unconditional.

14.11.4   Target board's document

Under the terms of the Takeover Rules, usually within 14 days of the posting of the offer document, the target must send to its shareholders a document containing its views, and those of its independent financial advisers, on the offer. In a hostile takeover the document will seek to refute the arguments and the commercial logic of the bid put forward by the offeror. The Takeover Rules set out (in Rule 25) the specific content requirements for the first major circular from the target's board of directors and these substantially reflect the information requirements imposed on the offeror. Also, as indicated at paragraph 14.9.4.1 above, Rule 25.2(a) of the Takeover Rules requires the target board to include, in its written opinion of the offer, its views on the implementation of the offer on employment and the offeror's strategic plans for the target and their likely repercussions on employment and the locations of the target's places of business, Rule 30.3(b) adds a further requirement to append a separate opinion from the target's employee representatives on the effects of the offer on employment (if received in time before the circular is posted).

14.11.5   Other documents

In a hostile takeover, after the initial offer and defence documents have been issued, further documents are frequently issued from the offeror and target containing further arguments and further information. Such documents must contain details of any material changes in information previously published by or on behalf of the offeror or target during the offer period. If there have been no such changes, this must be stated. Advertisements relating to an offer are essentially limited to statements of fact and, in most cases, will have to include the directors' responsibility statement and be cleared by the Panel in advance.

Offerors are permitted to revise their offers up to day 46 after the offer document is posted save where they have stated that the offer will not be increased. There are certain exceptions to this Rule especially in the event that there is a competing bid.

If the consideration for the offer comprises shares or debentures in the offer or which are to be listed, a prospectus may have to be prepared (*see* 14.11.6 below).

14.11.6   The Listing Rules

The Listing Rules impose yet further requirements on the contents of offer documents published by an offeror listed company or where the target is a listed company. These requirements supplement, and in some respects overlap with, the detailed requirements of the Takeover Rules in relation to offer documents. Proofs of offer documents relating to listed companies must be submitted to the Stock Exchange for approval, quite apart from any requirement to comply with Takeover Rules.

In some cases where the offeror is listed on the Stock Exchange, documents will have to be sent to the offeror's shareholders. This will be necessary where the offer is sufficiently large relative to the size of the offeror. For example, if the takeover offer is classified as a Class 1 transaction under the formula set down in the Listing Rules, the offeror must dispatch to its shareholders an explanatory circular complying with detailed content requirements laid down in the Listing Rules and obtain prior approval of its shareholders in general meeting. Upon the announcement of a reverse takeover which has been agreed, or is in contemplation, the Stock Exchange will suspend listing of the company's securities. The company is also required to produce a Class 1 Circular and obtain shareholder approval of the transaction. Also, where the proposed offer is to be made to a related party, a circular and the prior approval of the company in general meeting will usually be required.

A listed offeror may, in certain circumstances, for example where it is offering new securities which are to be listed or which will increase the number of a class of its existing securities in issue by 10 per cent or more, have to prepare and publish a prospectus in accordance with the Prospectus Directive (Directive 2003/71/EC) and the regulations which implemented this into Irish law in 2005 if it is offering its own securities as consideration. *See* also paragraph 14.11.8 below.

14.11.7   Companies Act 1963

Where a payment is to be made to a director by way of compensation for loss of office, or as consideration for loss of office in connection with the transfer of any shares as a result of an offer, the director must take all reasonable steps to ensure the offer document contains details of the proposed payment. Shareholder approval is also required before any such payment is made.

Section 204 of the Companies Act 1963 provides a mechanism by which an offeror who has obtained an 80 per cent acceptance level pursuant to an offer may compulsorily acquire the remaining shares. Where the offeror makes use of this facility a notice document will be sent to the remaining shareholders in the form prescribed by regulations (*see* 14.12 below).

14.11.8   Potential applicability of the Prospectus Regulations to a takeover offer

In circumstances where the consideration being offered by an offeror in the context of a takeover offer consists either wholly or partly of shares or other securities of the offeror, an analysis will need to be carried out to assess whether or not the Prospectus (Directive 2003/71/EC) Regulations 2005 (the "Prospectus Regulations") would apply. The Prospectus Regulations implement into Irish law the provisions of the EU Prospectus Directive of 2003 and provide that any offer of securities to the public in Ireland must be the subject of a prospectus drawn up in accordance with the Prospectus Directive and implementing regulations and approved by IFSRA, in circumstances where Ireland is the home Member State for the company issuing the securities in question or, where Ireland is the host Member State for the public offer, approved by the competent authority of the home Member State of the company making the offer. There are exemptions from the need to publish a prospectus where securities are offered in connection with a takeover by means of an exchange offer or in connection with a merger provided that a document is available containing information which is regarded by IFSRA as being equivalent to that of a prospectus, taking into account any EC legislation.

14.11.9   Additional rules relating to offer terms

If purchases of the target's shares have been made by an offeror before an offer period, except with the consent of the Panel, any subsequent offer must be on no less favourable terms (*see* Rule 6.1).

If after the start of the offer period, but before the offer closes for acceptance, the offeror or its concert parties purchase the target's shares at above the offer price, the offeror's offer must be increased to the highest price paid. Rule 11.1 of the Takeover Rules also prescribes the circumstances in which offers for shares in the target have to be made in cash. Favourable deals can also not, except with the consent of the Panel, be done with some shareholders or persons interested in shares in the target carrying voting rights to the exclusion of others. Exceptions are sometimes made in the case of management buy-outs provided that the risks as well as the rewards associated with an equity shareholding apply to the management's retained interest (*see* Rule 16).

14.12   Compulsory acquisition of minorities

When a takeover has the overwhelming support of the shareholders of a target company, an offeror company can compulsorily acquire the shares of a dissenting minority of shareholders in that Irish incorporated target company who have not accepted a general offer to purchase their shares, provided that there is strict adherence to statutory time limits and prescribed procedures.

Compulsory acquisition provisions are also valuable in circumstances where a general offer has been made to a diverse range of shareholders in a public company who cannot all be relied upon to respond, let alone accept.

The Takeover Regulations contain compulsory acquisition provisions which only apply in the case of companies to which the Takeover Regulations apply e.g., if the target is incorporated in Ireland and its securities are traded on a regulated market in Ireland. In this case, a bidder is only entitled to compulsorily acquire the shares of dissenting holders if it has acquired (or unconditionally contracted to acquire) not less than 90 per cent in nominal value of the shares carrying voting rights which are comprised in the bid. This is to be contrasted with the 80 per cent threshold contained in Section 204 of the Companies Act 1963, which still applies to non-Directive Company bids, and which differs in a number of respects from the compulsory acquisition provisions contained in the Takeover Regulations.

The bidder has three months, beginning with the day after the last day on which the offer can be accepted, to give notice to dissenting shareholders that it wishes to acquire the beneficial ownership of their shares. When such notice is given the offeror is entitled and bound to acquire the beneficial ownership of the shares on the same terms as the bid. The compulsory acquisition rules are subject to a right of appeal to the High Court by a dissenting shareholder.

As mentioned above, it is open to any dissenting minority shareholder to apply to court to avoid compulsory acquisition. Such application must be made within 21 days (in the case of takeovers governed by the Takeover Regulations) or one month (in the case of takeovers governed by the 1997 Act and Section 204 of the Companies Act 1963) of the date on which the notice of compulsory acquisition from the offeror was given. In cases taken in the past under the compulsory acquisition procedure set out in Section 204 of the Companies Act 1963, the courts have tended to give weight to the fact that a considerable majority have accepted the offer. Provided that the offer is at market value, an offer governed by Section 204 will not be regarded as unfair only because it could be improved upon, even if the dissenting shareholders are thereby at a loss. The grounds for appeal against compulsory acquisition under the Takeover Regulations would appear to be more tightly circumscribed than under the equivalent provisions of Section 204 of the Companies Act 1963. The compulsory acquisition provisions under the Takeover Regulations provide that a dissenting shareholder is entitled to seek a declaration that the conditions specified in the relevant regulation for the giving of the notice have not been satisfied, or that the terms on which the offeror proposes, on foot of the notice, to acquire the dissentient's shares do not comply with that Regulation (e.g., the terms are not the same).

14.13   Insider dealing and market manipulation

14.13.1   Insider dealing

Takeovers and mergers have often been considered to provide opportunities for insider dealing and the misuse of price-sensitive information. The Market Abuse Directive has been implemented in Ireland by the Market Abuse (Directive 2003/6/EC) Regulations, 2005 (the "Market Abuse Regulations") and Part 4 of the Investment Funds, Companies and Miscellaneous Provisions Act 2005.

IFSRA is the competent authority for the purposes of the Market Abuse Regulations. However, the Irish Stock Exchange also has a role as delegate authority under the Market Abuse Regulations.

The Market Abuse Regulations prohibit market abuse, the two central concepts of which are insider dealing and market manipulation. Persons who possess information which is of a precise nature relating directly or indirectly to an issuer of securities which has not been made public, but if it were, would be likely to have a significant effect on the price of those securities, are prohibited from using that information by acquiring or disposing of those securities to which the information relates. They are also precluded from disclosing that information to third parties or recommending, on the basis of such information, acquisition or disposal of securities.

Market manipulation is the actual manipulation of the market by, for example, providing false information or engaging in fictitious transactions, or where someone seeks to distort the price of financial instruments by giving misleading information about their value.

The Market Abuse Regulations prohibit insider dealing and market manipulation in respect of securities admitted to trading on a regulated market. The prohibition also applies in respect of securities for which a request for admission to trading on a regulated market has been sought.

The Market Abuse Regulations also include specific obligations requiring persons professionally arranging transactions to notify suspicious transactions to IFSRA. Obligations also exist for listed companies which issue securities to publicly disclose inside information without delay and to draw up lists of persons with access to inside information.

IFSRA has issued Market Abuse Rules which set out procedural and administrative requirements and guidance in respect of the Market Abuse Regulations. Companies falling within the scope of the Market Abuse Rules should also have regard to the Guidance and Information of the Common Operation of the Market Abuse Directive issued by the Committee of European Securities Regulators (CESR).

Persons obliged to make disclosures or notifications to IFSRA under the Market Abuse Regulations, such as persons discharging managerial responsibility, must do so in accordance with the Market Abuse Rules (*see* also 14.7.6).

Market abuse is a criminal offence, with the maximum sanction being a fine of €10,000,000 and/or imprisonment for a term of up to 10 years. IFRSA imposes a sanctioning regime for less serious breaches.

The Market Abuse Regulations replaced Part V of the Companies Act 1990, in respect of Irish companies listed on the Official List of the ISE. However, Part V, which contains provisions on insider dealing, still applies to Irish companies whose securities are listed on other exchanges which are operated by the ISE, such as the Irish Enterprise Exchange (IEX), and may also apply to Irish companies whose securities are listed on markets such as AIM in the United Kingdom. The ISE remains responsible for the investigation of activities relating to Part V.

The ISE is obliged to report any market abuse identified on any of its markets (including IEX) to IFSRA.

The Market Abuse Regulations provide for a number of exceptions and "safe harbours" from the market abuse prohibition. Having access to inside information relating to another company and using it in the context of a public takeover offer for the purpose of gaining control of that company or proposing a merger in conformity with the Takeover Rules does not, of itself, constitute market abuse. Nor do actions taken in compliance with the Takeover Rules of themselves constitute market abuse, provided that the general principles under the Takeover Panel Act 1997 (as amended) are also complied with.

There is also a price stabilisation regime for Irish companies to which the provisions of Part V of the Companies Act 1990 continue to apply, and this is contained in the Companies (Amendment) Act 1999. It is broadly similar to the price stabilisation regime applying under the Market Abuse Regulations.

14.13.2   *Irrevocable undertakings*

In a recommended bid, the offeror may seek irrevocable undertakings to accept the offer from major shareholders and from the target's directors who are also shareholders. In a hostile bid, irrevocable undertakings may be sought from major shareholders. Such undertakings can also extend to precluding any action which could prejudice the outcome of an offer.

Where the provisions of Part V of the Companies Act 1990 on insider dealing, rather than the provisions of the Market Abuse Regulations, apply, for example, where there is a takeover offer for an Irish public limited company whose shares are traded on the IEX, the gathering of irrevocable undertakings is likely to be first subject to an announcement that, subject to satisfaction of a precondition that irrevocable undertakings to accept the offer are received from a stated percentage of shareholders of the target company by a certain period of time (often no more than 24 hours), an offer would be made for the entire issued share capital of the target company. This is because the wide definition of insider dealing contained in the 1990 Act precludes the seeking or execution of an irrevocable undertaking before such an announcement is made.

Rule 4.3 of the Takeover Rules requires any person who proposes to contact a holder of securities who is not a professional investor with a view to seeking an irrevocable undertaking to consult the Panel in advance.

14.13.3 The Listing Rules

The Listing Rules require that companies subject to its rules adopt by board resolution and take all proper and reasonable steps to ensure compliance with a code no less exacting than its Model Code for securities transactions by directors of listed companies. The Model Code refers to the provisions of the Market Abuse Regulations and Market Abuse Rules but goes further in its prohibitions in circumstances where it would be undesirable for a director to deal in his company's securities. The Listing Rules also contain provisions requiring the timely release of price-sensitive information and maintenance of standards of the strictest confidentiality in relation to information, prior to its release.

14.13.4 The Takeover Rules

The Takeover Rules contain a number of provisions aimed at combating insider dealing in the lead-up to takeover bids for a company. In particular, the importance of absolute secrecy before the announcement of a bid is emphasised and the circumstances in which an announcement is required are prescribed. In addition, Rule 4.1 of the Takeover Rules provides that no dealings of any kind in securities of the target company by any person, not being the offeror, who is privy to confidential price-sensitive information concerning an offer or contemplated offer, may take place between the time when there is reason to suppose that an approach or offer is contemplated and the announcement of the offer or approach or the termination of the discussions. No person who is privy to such information may make any recommendation to any other person as to dealings in the relevant securities. No such dealings may take place in securities of the offeror except where the proposed offer is not price-sensitive in relation to such securities.

During an offer period the offeror and persons acting in concert with it must not sell any securities in the target company except with the prior consent of the Panel and following 24 hours' public notice that such sales might be made.

14.13.5 Market practice

The Irish Association of Investment Managers has also laid down a code of best practice for participants in the stock market based on Part V of the 1990 Act and this is aimed at combating dealing on the basis of unpublished price-sensitive information.

The guidance is still in use as a general indication as a code of best practice, although it is based on Part V of the 1990 Act which does not apply to companies caught by the Market Abuse Regulations.

Transactions which potentially constitute "market manipulation" may escape the prohibition on such activity contained in the Market Abuse Regulations on the grounds that the reason for entering into the transaction was legitimate and was in conformity with "accepted market practice" in the regulated market concerned, as permitted under those Regulations.

Accepted market practices ("AMP's") are practices that are reasonably expected in one or more Financial Markets and are accepted by IFSRA in accordance with certain criteria as specified in Schedule 1 of the Market Abuse Regulations. IFSRA would be required to consult with relevant bodies such as issuers, financial service providers, consumers, other authorities and market operators before issuing a decision as to whether or not to accept an AMP.

To date no AMP's have been accepted by IFSRA in relation to the Main Market (Official List) of the Irish Stock Exchange, so it is not possible to give any guidance on what IFSRA might deem to be acceptable market practice. However, it is possible that the guidance provided by the FSA in the UK would be relevant in this regard, bearing in mind the similarities between the Irish and UK market abuse regimes.

14.13.6 *Future developments in Europe*

The EC (Cross-Border Mergers) Directive (Directive 2005/56/EC) is due to be implemented in Ireland in 2008. It applies to limited liability companies and aims to simplify the legislative framework surrounding cross–border mergers. Under this Directive, Member States must allow the cross-border merger of a national limited liability company with a limited liability company from another Member State, if the national law of the relevant Member States permits mergers between such types of company.

Additionally, Directive 2007/63/EC has recently been published by the European Commission ("EC"). This Directive provides that public limited liability companies undertaking a merger or division may dispense with the requirement for an independent expert's report on the merger or division, following approval by all the shareholders. It amends Directives No. 78/855/EEC and No. 82/891/EEC, which were implemented in Ireland by the European Communities (Mergers and Divisions of Companies) Regulations 1987. The rationale behind this new Directive is recognition by the EC of the importance of reducing the administrative burdens faced by companies from existing legislation. It must be implemented by Member States by 31 December 2008.

14.13.7 Future domestic developments

An ambitious project, aimed at consolidating the entire body of Irish company law, is underway in Ireland, and a preliminary Companies Consolidation and Reform Bill is expected in the latter half of 2008.

The proposed Bill aims to simplify and consolidate the current law, with the European Communities (Mergers and Divisions of Companies) Regulations 1987 being incorporated into primary legislation. Of interest in the context of takeovers and mergers is the proposal to enable the directors of a company to convene a meeting to approve a scheme of arrangement without the need to apply to court for permission to do so, although the court's discretion to convene a meeting on the application of the company or a member is retained. Another interesting development is the proposal that all companies, and not just public limited companies, will be able to effect a merger modelled on the mergers at present available for public limited companies under the European Communities (Mergers and Divisions of Companies) Regulations. It is also proposed to establish new forms of company called "designated activity companies", or DACs, and a new form of model company known as a "CLS" or company limited by shares. The purpose of these changes is to facilitate corporate activity. It is thought unlikely, however, that these new corporate forms will have a significant impact on the way in which mergers and acquisitions are conducted in Ireland in the foreseeable future.

14.14 Financial assistance

14.14.1 General prohibition

Irish law, in common with the laws of many jurisdictions, prohibits the giving of financial assistance by a company in connection with the purchase of, or subscription for, its shares except in certain specific circumstances. The prohibition is contained in Section 60 of the Companies Act 1963 (as amended).

Section 60(1) provides, as a general rule, that it is unlawful for a company to give, whether directly or indirectly, and whether by means of a loan, guarantee, the provision of security or otherwise, any financial assistance for the purpose of, or in connection with, a purchase or subscription made or to be made by any person of, or for any shares in, the company or, where the company is a subsidiary company, in its holding company.

Section 60(1) aims to prevent a company financing its own takeover. Thus, the repayment by a recently acquired company of bank borrowings incurred by the acquirer to enable it to purchase the target company's shares or the granting by the target company of a guarantee or a mortgage or charge over its assets to secure indebtedness incurred by the acquirer to enable it to purchase or subscribe for the target shares come within the terms of the prohibition. This Section is wide-reaching in its terms and can catch financial assistance given for the benefit of the seller as well as the purchaser of shares.

However, Section 60 does not prohibit the payment of a dividend by a company, the discharge of a liability lawfully incurred by it or the lending of money by a company in the ordinary course of its business, where the lending of money is part of its ordinary business. Nor does it preclude:

(a) the reimbursement by an offeree company or its subsidiary of the expenses of an offeror pursuant to an agreement approved by the Panel;

(b) the incurring by a company of expenses to enable compliance by the company or its holding company with the 1997 Act or the Takeover Directive; and

(c) the payment by a company of fees or expenses of the advisers of any subscriber for shares in the company.

Also permissible is the provision by a company, in accordance with an employee share scheme, of money for the purchase of, or subscription for, fully paid shares in the company or its holding company, where the shares are to be held by or for the benefit of employees or former employees of the company (or of any subsidiary of the company). A further exception is the making by a company of loans to persons (other than directors) bona fide in the employment of the company, or any subsidiary of the company, to enable them to purchase or subscribe for fully paid shares in the company (or its holding company) to be held by themselves as beneficial owners.

Section 60 does not apply either to the acquisition by a company of shares in its holding company or to investment companies with variable capital.

14.14.2   *Exceptions for private companies*

Notwithstanding the above general prohibition, private companies can give financial assistance in connection with the purchase of, or subscription for, their own shares if they comply with certain procedures laid down in Section 60(2) to (7) of the 1963 Act referred to below. This facility is not available to public limited companies which may only provide financial assistance if such assistance comes within the permitted exceptions some of which are referred to above and, even then, they can only lend money, provide money for employees to acquire their shares, and make loans to employees (other than directors) to enable them to acquire shares, as aforesaid, if the company's net assets are not thereby reduced or, to the extent that they are, the assistance is provided out of profits available for dividend. Private companies are also precluded from going through the validation procedures if they have as a director a person who is the subject of a restriction issued pursuant to Section 150 of the 1990 Act.

It is particularly common in management buy-out transactions for companies to go through the Section 60 procedures to enable financing of the buy-out.

The prohibition in Section 60(1) will not apply to the giving of financial assistance by private companies if:

(a) such financial assistance is given under the authority of a special resolution of the members of the company passed not more than 12 months previously;

(b) the company has forwarded with each notice of the meeting at which the special resolution is to be considered, a copy of a director's statutory declaration complying with Section 60(3) and Section 60(4) (*see* 14.14.3

below), and also delivers, within 21 days after the date on which the financial assistance was given, a copy of the declaration to the Registrar of Companies in Dublin for registration.

14.14.3   The statutory declaration

The statutory declaration must be made at a meeting of the directors held not more than 24 days before the meeting at which the special resolution is to be considered and must be made by all the directors if there are only two, or if there are more than two by a majority of the directors. The statutory declaration must state:

(a)   the form such assistance is to take;
(b)   the persons to whom it is to be given;
(c)   the purpose for which the company intends those persons to use such assistance; and
(d)   that the declarants have made a full inquiry into the affairs of the company and that, having done so, they have formed the opinion that the company, having carried out the transaction whereby such assistance is to be given, will be able to pay its debts in full as they become due.

If the Company is wound up within 12 months after the making of the declaration and its debts are not paid or provided for in full within 12 months after the commencement of the winding up, there is a presumption that a director making the declaration did not have reasonable grounds for his opinion.

14.14.4   The special resolution

The special resolution must be passed by not less than three-quarters of the votes cast by members who being entitled to vote in person do so (or, where proxies are allowed, do so by proxy). Every member of the company has a right to receive notice of and attend the meeting at which the special resolution is to be proposed, notwithstanding anything in its articles of association. Unless all of the members of the company entitled to vote at general meetings of the company vote in favour of the special resolution, assistance must not be given before the expiry of 30 days after the special resolution has been passed or, if an application by dissentient shareholders for cancellation of the special resolution under Section 60(8) has been made, until such application has been disposed of by the High Court.

Holders of not less than 10 per cent in the nominal value of the company's issued share capital or any class thereof who have not voted in favour of the special resolution can apply to court within 28 days after the date on which the special resolution was passed to cancel the special resolution. Section 60(8) provides that if application is made to the High Court for cancellation, the special resolution will not have effect except to the extent to which it is confirmed by the High Court.

It is possible for a company (if permitted by its articles of association) to pass such a special resolution by way of a resolution in writing signed by all the members for the time being entitled to attend and vote on such resolutions at a general meeting.

14.14.5   Consequences of breach and penalties

Any transaction in breach of Section 60 is voidable at the instance of the company against any person (whether a party to the transaction or not) who had notice of the facts which constitute such breach. There is case law which provides that "notice" means actual rather than constructive notice. The giving of financial assistance in breach of Section 60 cannot be retrospectively validated.

If a company contravenes Section 60, every officer of the company who is in default is liable to fines or imprisonment, or both.

Any director making a declaration of solvency referred to above without having reasonable grounds for his opinion that, having given the assistance, the company will be able to pay its debts in full as they become due, is liable to imprisonment or to a fine, or both.

Chapter 15

Italy

Nicolò Juvara, Partner
Rocco Santarelli, Associate
Norton Rose, Milan

15.1   Introduction

15.1.1   *Economic trends and stock markets*

In Italy, the Gross Domestic Product ("GDP") (*Prodotto Interno Lordo*) growth rate in 2006 and in 2007 was positive (around 2 per cent/year), as compared to near-zero growth rates for 2004 and 2005. Although significant, this positive trend, due mainly to increased investment, family consumption and exports, was inferior to the GDP growth rates of other countries in the Euro zone.

The favourable economic scenario contributed to a good framework for the growth of the Italian stock market.

At the close of 2006, financial analysts were positive in their evaluation of listed Italian companies. At that time, over half of the companies listed on a Borsa Italiana S.p.A. (the Italian Stock Exchange management company's index called S&P/Mib) were in the "buy" category (about the same as the prior year); many companies in the "underperforming" category moved up to the "hold" category; and, the percentage of companies which received the highest rating increased from 60 to 75 per cent (as compared to the prior year). Moreover, although the number of listed Italian companies did not grow significantly in 2006 (there were 25 new listings, including 21 Initial Public Offerings ("IPOs"), and 16 revocations), the composition of companies in the "buy" category was richly modified by the entrance of companies with higher capitalisation.

During the last few years, the Italian market has reported an increase in the number of listed companies: 315 in 2007 compared to the 284 of 2006 and the 275 of 2005. With reference to the takeover market, it has registered a sharp decrease from 2005 to the present time: in 2005 the turnover was €19.840 million, in 2006 €7.074 million and finally in 2007 €5.625 million.

During 2007, 31 new companies listed on the Italian stock exchange and share trading exchange values reached a new historical high of €1,572 billion, but the performance of Borsa Italiana S.p.A.'s indices was down. The Mibtel (the major index used by Borsa Italiana S.p.A.) closed down 8 per cent from 2006, S&P/Mib down 7.0 per cent, Midex down 13.8 per cent, AllStars down 15.2 per cent, and Expandi down 12.7 per cent.

From a legal point of view, after the termination of a legislative process which developed during the 1990s, by way of Law no. 58 of 14 February 1998 (the "Financial Services Act 1998" or "FSA") and by way of the consequent implementation of rules issued by the *Commisione Nazionale per le Società e la Borsa* (the Italian Stock Exchange Authority, "CONSOB"), some of the principles contained in European Directives and concerning corporate matters and financial services were finally implemented in Italy. In addition, Law no. 6 of 17 January 2003, effective from 1 January 2004, has introduced a new legal framework for Italian companies (the "Reform"). The Reform substantially redefines a number of features and the corporate governance rules of the two main types of companies in Italy, that is, limited liability companies (*società a responsabilità limitata*) and joint stock companies (*società per azioni*), as well as cooperative companies.

More recently, the Italian Parliament recently implemented EU Directive 2003/6/EC on insider trading and market manipulation, by way of Law no. 62 of 18 April 2005, and EU Directive 2004/25/EC on takeover bids, by way of Legislative Decree no. 229 of 19 November 2007 (the "Takeover Act").

15.2   Acquisition targets

15.2.1   *Listed and unlisted companies*

Companies which can be taken over in Italy, irrespective of whether or not they are listed, are essentially those governed by the Italian Civil Code, and precisely:

(a)   partnerships, divided into non-commercial partnerships, unlimited partnerships and limited partnerships;

(b)   stock companies, divided into joint stock companies, limited liability companies and unlimited partnerships with share capital;

(c)   cooperative companies, within the limits in which a cooperative structure (based on the principles of single vote, irrespective of the number of shares owned, and a limit on the possession of shares) renders feasible the transfer of interests in share capital for the purpose of changing the controlling interest in the company.

Normally, these companies and the business concerns that they manage are acquired through the execution of purchase and sale agreements (of shares, quotas or of business concerns directly) following negotiations with controlling shareholders.

In some cases (which are relevant in the context of this Guide), the acquisition of a controlling or minority interest in a company can only be realised through the launch of a public purchase and/or exchange offer (takeover bid) on the market. These other cases only concern companies with listed shares and companies with unlisted shares which are already widely distributed with the public. Pursuant to Rules approved by way of CONSOB resolution no. 11971 of 14 May 1999, as further amended and supplemented (the *Regolamento degli Emittenti*), offers concerning securities distributed among the public are those targeted at more than 100 investors which concern securities for an overall amount equal to or in excess of €2,500,000.

Companies with listed securities or securities distributed among the public can only be *società per azioni* (joint stock companies or "SPA"), *società in accomandita per azioni* (unlimited partnerships with shares or "SAPA") and cooperative companies to the extent that their share capital is represented by shares.

SPA are companies whose share capital is represented by shares and whose shareholders are not personally liable for company undertakings, in that they are only answerable within the limits of the subscribed and paid-up shares.

SPA have a structure similar to that recognised in other jurisdictions and are designated as the most appropriate form of business organisations for wide enterprises.

SAPA are companies characterised by the presence of two different types of partners:

(a)   acting partners who are liable without limits for the corporate undertakings and are directors of the company by law; and

(b)   silent partners who are only liable within the limits of the subscribed and paid-up shares and who cannot take on any managerial roles within the company.

The share capital is represented by shares, which are easily transferable. However, due to the liability which acting partners can have, SAPA are not very common and are traditionally used to establish family holdings which control some important Italian industrial groups (for example, FIAT and Pirelli).

As already stated above, the governance regulations for SPA and SAPA, provides for, together with the traditional management and supervisory bodies (i.e., the Board of Directors or sole director and the Board of Auditors (*Collegio Sindacale*)), two additional alternative governance regimes: the so-called single model and the dual model. Governance regulations provide also that various classes of shares can be issued by SPA, such as shares with full voting rights, shares with limited voting rights and shares with no voting rights, as well as the possibility to issue debt securities carrying economic and administrative rights (except for voting rights).

15.2.2   Listed companies

SPA, SAPA and cooperative companies can be listed in Italy on markets organised and managed by Borsa Italiana S.p.A., a private company which since 2007 belongs to the London Stock Exchange Group plc.

The main markets on which Italian companies can be listed are:

(a)   *Mercato Telematico Azionario* (the "MTA"), which is the standard equity share market on which blue-chip and consolidated companies are listed. It is divided into the following three segments:

   (i)   Blue Chip, for companies with a market capitalisation above €1,000 million,

   (ii)   High Standard Mid-Cap (*segmento titoli con alti requisiti* ("STAR")), for companies with a market capitalisation lower than €1,000 million complying with specific requirements in relation to transparency, corporate governance and liquidity, and

(iii)   Ordinary Market Segment (*segmento ordinario*), for companies with a market capitalisation lower than €800 million, that undertake to comply with ordinary standards of corporate governance;

(b)   MTAX Market ("MTAX") where companies with high growth are listed; and

(c)   *Mercato Expandi* ("EM") primarily designed for small companies with a consolidated position in their relevant market and a track record of positive financial results. EM started its operation on 1 December 2003 when it replaced the existing *Mercato Ristretto*;

(d)   alternative capital market ("MAC"): the alternative trading system dedicated to small enterprises, which does not require drafting a prospectus since it is reserved to professional investors.

In 2006 a new segment was introduced on the MTA market, called MTA International, reserved for foreign regulated companies which have already been quoted on another European market for more than 18 months, 21 companies were admitted to negotiate on MTA International.

The Trading After Hours Market is only used for trading in listed shares after the regular trading market is closed (i.e., until 8.30 p.m.).

Companies listed on the MTA, the MTAX and the EM are not only governed by the rules of the Italian Civil Code, but also by the rules of the FSA and by the *Regolamento degli Emittenti* issued by CONSOB. These various rules are principally intended to guarantee:

(a)   increased transparent and efficient management of the company;

(b)   increased saleability of the company; and

(c)   improved protection of minority shareholders.

The main differences in listed companies compared to unlisted companies are described below.

15.2.2.1   *CONSOB controls*

Listed companies are subject to regulation and control by CONSOB. It is the authority responsible for:

(a)   ensuring transparency and correct behaviour by securities market participants;

(b)   complete and accurate disclosure of information to the investing public from listed companies;

(c)   accuracy of facts described in prospectuses relating to the offering of securities to the investing public; and

(d)   compliance with regulatory provisions;

In this respect, CONSOB requires listed companies to transmit to the market and to CONSOB itself documents and records, mainly concerning facts and transactions carried out by such companies and which may be price sensitive. Transparency is also ensured by systematic compliance with reporting requirements by listed companies and their controlling entities. Such requirements essentially concern the management of the company and are satisfied by disclosing to the market, without delay, information regarding accounts, annual financial statements, and semi-annual and quarterly reports. To check whether information is complete and accurate, CONSOB may carry out inspections and require directors and officers to provide further information and clarifications. Moreover, following the implementation of EU Directive 2003/6/EC on insider trading and market manipulation, CONSOB has been given wide investigatory powers (*see also* 15.12 below).

15.2.2.2 Notification of material shareholdings

Furthermore, to ensure complete and accurate disclosure to the investing public, the shareholding structure of listed companies must also be notified to CONSOB and the market.

In fact, CONSOB must receive notice of all shareholdings of 2 per cent or more in the capital of a company listed on either the MTA, the MTAX and the EM. For the purposes of the application of this provision, only shares that benefit from voting rights will be taken into account. The notice must be served within five trading days of the date on which the acquisition has become effective and CONSOB shall publish such information within three trading days of receipt of the relevant information. The percentage rises to 10 per cent if the shareholder is a listed company with shares in a company that is not listed. Failure to comply with these requirements causes suspension of the voting rights pertaining to the listed shares. In the event of non-compliance, CONSOB may challenge resolutions where the required majority would not have been reached without the votes of the above-mentioned shares.

In the event of cross-shareholdings, the shareholder that was the last to exceed one of these limits (2 per cent or 10 per cent) may not exercise the voting rights on those shares it owns above the set limits and must dispose of them within 12 months of the date on which it exceeded the limit. In the event of failure to dispose the shares within such a time period, the suspension of the voting rights applies to the entire shareholding. Where it is not possible to ascertain which of the two companies was the last to exceed the limit, the suspension of voting rights and the disposal requirements apply to both companies unless they have agreed otherwise.

Where a person owns a shareholding that exceeds 2 per cent of a listed company, the company itself or whoever controls it may not acquire a shareholding in excess of that amount in a listed company controlled by that person. In the event of non-compliance, the voting rights pertaining to the listed shares are suspended. Where it is not possible to ascertain which of the two companies was the last to exceed the limit, the suspension of the voting rights and the disposal requirements apply to both corporations unless they have agreed otherwise.

The above requirements do not apply where the limits of 2 or 10 per cent are exceeded following a public purchase offer ("OPA") aimed at the acquisition of at least 60 per cent of the ordinary shares (*see* 15.6.2.2 below).

15.2.2.3   Shareholders agreements

CONSOB must be notified of any shareholders agreements (*patti parasociali*) concerning the exercise of voting rights in companies with listed shares or companies which control listed companies within five days of the execution of such shareholders agreements. The agreements must also be published in summary form (as provided for by the *Regolamento degli Emittenti*) in the daily press within 10 days and filed with the Company Register of the place where the company has its registered office within 15 days of the execution of the agreement. Under the *Regolamento degli Emittenti*, evidence of complete fulfilment of such requirements shall be transmitted without delay to CONSOB.

Failure to comply with these requirements will cause the shareholders agreement to be null and void and the right to vote pertaining to the listed shares referred to in the shareholders agreement will be suspended and cannot be exercised.

These rules also apply in the case of amendments made to the published shareholders agreements.

A shareholders agreement may not be entered into for a fixed term lasting more than three years (and if such an agreement were to exceed this duration, it is automatically reduced to three years) for listed companies or companies which control listed companies and of five years for any other companies, but it can be renewed upon expiry. If the agreement is concluded for an indefinite period, any contracting party may withdraw at any time with six months' prior notice and upon the same public notice required for the stipulation of the agreement. In the event of a public purchase offer or takeover bid towards listed companies, any party intending to adhere thereto may withdraw any shareholders agreements (including those for a definite period) following prior notice.

Agreements providing for the exercise of a right to vote in listed companies (and their controlling companies), as well as so-called "consultation agreements" and agreements that limit the transfer of shares or financial instruments attributing the right to purchase or to subscribe to the same, or that involve the purchase of shares or financial instruments or the joint exercise of a dominant influence on listed corporations (or their controlling companies) are all subject to the above requirements. According to CONSOB's resolutions, the above-mentioned provisions relating to shareholders agreements do not apply to "lock-up agreements"(entered into in the context of an Initial Public Offering), "put and call options" or to preliminary agreements, where these contracts contain specific clauses that may qualify as customary for shareholders agreements (for example, clauses limiting transfer of shares or consultation clauses).

15.2.2.4   Minority rights

In the Italian market, which is characterised by companies having a restricted shareholding, issues relating to potential conflicts of interests between controlling shareholders and minority shareholders have to be considered primarily. For this purpose, and in order to promote investments by small investors in listed companies, the FSA increased protection of minority interests by reducing the shareholding required for certain actions (which may be further reduced by provisions of the corporate by-laws). For example, shareholders having as little as 2.5 per cent of the issued share capital may appoint at least one member to the Board of Directors and one Statutory Auditor (who will be the Chairman) and one Alternative Auditor to the Board of Auditors. In addition:

(a)   the shareholders holding at least 10 per cent may call a meeting, unless the by-laws require a lesser percentage (the so-called "call of the shareholders meeting at the request of minority shareholders");

(b)   to pass resolutions at special shareholders meetings the affirmative vote of holders of two-thirds of the capital represented is necessary, unless the by-laws require a higher percentage;

(c)   to bring to the Board of Statutory Auditors' attention facts or acts which are deemed wrongful only 2 per cent of the shareholders need make the complaint rather than the 5 per cent required for unlisted companies;

(d)   if there is a basis for suspicion of "serious irregularities" in the discharge of directors' duties, shareholders representing 5 per cent (or more) of the shareholders can file a complaint with the courts (as compared to 10 per cent required for unlisted companies);

(e)   the company action for liability against the directors can be brought by shareholders representing at least 2.5 per cent (or more) of the shareholders (as compared to 20 per cent for unlisted companies).

Furthermore, the by-laws may provide that votes also be cast by post in shareholders meetings. The aim of this provision is to encourage the direct and indirect participation of the shareholders to the decision process within the company. Other provisions aimed at protecting small investors require equal treatment of shareholders with respect to the purchase of treasury shares and shares of the parent company.

Under the Reform, most of the provisions relating to the protection of minority shareholders have been taken from the FSA and inserted in the Italian Civil Code.

15.2.2.5   *Proxy solicitation and collection*

An opportunity to actively participate in the decision-making process within a listed company is granted to minority shareholders through proxies solicitation and collection. Only in such companies it is legal to solicit voting proxies even if forbidden by the corporate by-laws. As a matter of fact, provisions relating to proxy solicitation and collection contained in the FSA are different to the general rules concerning shareholders representation contained in the Italian Civil Code which apply to unlisted companies. Under the FSA there are two ways for using proxies: the solicitation and the collection.

Solicitation can be undertaken by a "promoter" who must be a shareholder owning at least 1 per cent, and must have been listed in the shareholders register for at least six months. A lower percentage (0.5 per cent) is fixed for companies with high capitalisation and a particularly broad shareholding. The promoter must use an approved intermediary, which may be an investment company, a bank, a financial adviser, an open-ended investment company (*società di investimento a capitale variabile* ("SICAV")) or a company whose sole purpose is the solicitation of proxies and the representation of shareholders. The intermediary must supply a prospectus and proxy form, the contents of which are established by CONSOB. The expenses of solicitation are borne by the promoter.

The proxy shall be exercised by the promoter or, upon delegation of the soliciting intermediary, by others, who may not further delegate the performance of this task.

Collection of proxies is carried out by shareholders' associations exclusively among their members, provided that such associations have been created by way of a notarial deed, they do not engage in any entrepreneurial activity and have at least 50 individual members each of whom are shareholders exceeding 0.1 per cent of the voting capital.

15.2.2.6   Supervisory Bodies

After the Reform, SPA have the opportunity to choose between three corporate governance models. The new provisions specifically allow three alternative auditing models.

The by-laws of a listed company must establish the number of auditors (no less than three), the number of alternatives (no less than two), the criteria and procedures for appointing the chairman, and limits on the accumulation of positions. The by-laws must also contain the clauses necessary to ensure that one of the auditors is elected by the minority shareholders. Where the board consists of more than three auditors, the number of auditors elected by minority shareholders may not be fewer than two. As opposed to unlisted companies, the auditors of companies listed on a Stock Exchange need not be chosen from among auditors registered in the Registry of Professional Chartered Accountants.

For listed companies, the principal duty of the statutory auditor or, in case of application of the dual model, of the Supervisory Board, is:

(a)   to check compliance with statutory legislation and the company's by-laws;
(b)   to follow the principles of correct administration;
(c)   to maintain the adequacy of the company's organisational structure, its internal control system and its administrative and accounting systems; and
(d)   to check the adequacy of the instructions imparted by the company to its subsidiaries.

The duty under (d) above is the only one applicable to the Internal Control Committee in case of implementation of the single model.

The statutory auditors must attend the shareholders meetings and the meetings of the Board of Directors and the executive committee, if appointed.

The managing directors must promptly advise the Board of Statutory Auditors at least once every three months with respect to business, financial and economic operations of the company and its controlled companies, with particular attention to operations that may involve conflicts of interest. The statutory auditors, or any one of them, may ask the directors for further information and may at any time inspect or review the business. These obligations are fulfilled in the so-called dual model by the Board of Management reporting to the Supervisory Board and in the so-called single model by the bodies with delegated powers reporting to the Internal Control Committee.

In the event that statutory auditors find irregularities they must:

(a)   report them to the shareholders meeting;
(b)   advise CONSOB;
(c)   provide the information to the external auditing firm and develop proposals to resolve the problems with such firm;
(d)   call a meeting of the executive committee, the Board of Directors or the shareholders and make proposals; or
(e)   report the facts to the courts, in the event of serious irregularities.

15.2.2.7   External auditing firms

For listed companies, verification of the accounts and financial statements is the exclusive duty of external accountants that must be enrolled in the special register of auditing firms. Enrolment in this register is made only after CONSOB has verified compliance with certain specific requirements. The external auditors can also report to CONSOB or to the Board of Statutory Auditors concerning any matters that they believe merit criticism.

CONSOB is responsible for keeping a special register of auditing firms and for overseeing auditing firms that are registered therein to examine listed companies. The auditing firm has the duty to express in its report a "judgment" on the profit and loss statement and on the financial statement (consolidated where appropriate). The auditors must inform CONSOB of a negative opinion or if they find it impossible to express an opinion. CONSOB is responsible for supervising the activities of such auditing firms by requiring them to periodically communicate data and information and through inspections and recommendations of principles and methods to be adopted in the auditing activity.

A shareholders' resolution approving the balance sheet (containing the judgment of the auditing firm) can be challenged by shareholders representing at least 5 per cent of the corporate capital who contend that the resolution is not in conformity with the rules, as opposed to the majority of shareholders required pursuant to the Civil Code.

The same number may petition the court to assess whether the consolidated balance sheet has been properly prepared. These same initiatives may be undertaken by CONSOB within six months of filing of the annual accounts in the Company Register.

In the event of a capital increase with exclusion or limitation of the right of first refusal of existing shareholders, the auditing firm is required to give its opinion as to the adequacy of the issue price. In the event of a capital increase by contribution in kind, the auditing firm must review the values established by appointed experts.

15.2.2.8   Corporate governance

Under new Italian corporate rules, SPA are now able to adopt one of the three alternative corporate governance models:

(a)   a traditional model, providing for a Board of Directors and a Board of Statutory Auditors;

(b)   a dual model with a Board of Management (*Consiglio di Gestione*) and a Supervisory Board (*Consiglio di Sorveglianza*); and

(c)   a single model with a Board of Directors and an Internal Control Committee (*Comitato per il Controllo sulla gestione*).

All such corporate governance models set out a separation between management and audit functions.

The corporate governance provisions applying to listed companies are also supplemented by a Code of Self-Discipline issued by Borsa Italiana SpA (the so-called *Codice Preda*).

This Code of Self-Discipline contains principles of corporate governance which should, ideally, be adopted by all listed companies. These principles mainly involve the appointment of independent directors to the Board of Directors and the institution of certain special committees with the task of establishing remuneration of directors (in order that no one director can influence his or her own fee and in order that there is sufficient transparency and disclosure of such matters) and the implementation of a sound internal control system for company activities. While compliance is not mandatory (save for the companies listed in the STAR segment), listed companies are nonetheless expected to adopt the Code of Self-Discipline.

15.2.3   Banks

15.2.3.1   *Authorisation to acquire material shareholdings*
If the object of the acquisition is a bank (or its controlling entity is a bank), the special rules provided in Legislative Decree no. 385 of 1 September 1993 ("the Italian Banking Act 1993") apply together with the Supervisory Instructions for Banks issued by the Bank of Italy on 21 April 1999 as subsequently amended.

Pursuant to such rules, parties who intend to acquire, directly or indirectly and for any reason, an interest in the corporate capital of a bank which, taking into account shares already owned, would give rise to:

(a)   a shareholding in excess of 5 per cent or in excess of the limits of 10, 15, 20, 33 or 50 per cent of the share capital; or

(b)   a controlling interest in the bank, irrespective of the size of the shareholding,

must request prior authorisation from the Bank of Italy. This prior authorisation is also necessary in order to promote a public purchase and/or exchange offer (takeover bid) which would result in the above-mentioned percentages being exceeded.

Authorisation is issued by the Bank of Italy within 60 days of the application, once the Bank of Italy has verified that:

(a)   the individual person and, in the case of legal entities, the directors and general manager of such legal entity which intend to acquire an interest in the share capital of a bank, are in possession of certain requirements of good repute (essentially aimed at avoiding that such purchaser has been sentenced for offences related to banking activities or which involved imprisonment for prolonged periods of time); and

(b) the acquisition takes place according to conditions which guarantee the prudent and sound management of the bank (therefore, both the financial situation of the purchaser and the method according to which the acquisitions will be financed are verified).

If authorisation is not issued or has been suspended or withdrawn by the Bank of Italy, the voting rights pertaining to the shares that are the object of the acquisition cannot be exercised. In the case of non-compliance, the Bank of Italy may challenge resolutions of the shareholders meeting where the required majority would not have been reached without the votes of the above-mentioned shares.

If the person who intends to acquire the control of an Italian bank is an EU bank or an entity that controls an EU bank, the Bank of Italy needs to consult with the corresponding competent regulator. The term for granting the relevant authorisation is thus suspended accordingly.

15.2.3.2 *Prohibition on acquisition of material shareholdings*
In any case, acquisitions of shareholdings in excess of 15 per cent of the capital of a bank (or of a company which controls a bank) or which involve the control of a bank by parties who carry out significant business activities in a non-banking, financial or insurance sector, cannot be authorised. Non-banking, financial or insurance activities are considered as carried out in a material manner in the event that they exceed 15 per cent of all activities directly carried out by such party. This rule represents one of the fundamental principles established by the Italian Banking Act 1993 which is that of the separation of banking and industrial activities.

15.2.4 *Insurance*

Similar provisions are made for the acquisition of shareholdings in insurance companies.

Pursuant to Law no. 20 of 9 January 1991, whomsoever directly or indirectly effects the acquisition of a shareholding in an insurance company which results in a shareholding of 5 per cent or more, taking into account shares already owned, must notify the *Istituto per la Vigilanza delle Assicurazioni Private e di Interesse Collettivo* ("ISVAP" – the Italian Insurance Supervisory Authority) within 30 days of exceeding such threshold.

In the event that the acquisition results in the acquiring party owning more than 10 per cent of the corporate capital of the company or of voting rights in the shareholders meeting ("qualified shareholding") or results in the transfer of control of the insurance company or of the body which controls the insurance company, the ISVAP must receive prior notification. The ISVAP grants its authorisation within five months of receiving the application and there may be a suspension of such term if further information is requested. An entity must inform the ISVAP within 30 days of the date on which it ceases to have the relevant requisites for authorisation.

If authorisation is not issued or has been suspended or withdrawn by the ISVAP, the voting rights pertaining to the shares acquired may not be exercised. In cases of non-compliance, the ISVAP may challenge resolutions of the shareholders meeting where the required majority would not have been reached without the votes of the above-mentioned shares.

Pecuniary sanctions may also be applied to any party which fails to make or delays in making the required notifications.

Similar rules are expected to be issued by ISVAP pursuant to Law no. 200 of 7 September 2005, the so-called Insurance Code, which in an organised way now regulates any matter concerning insurance companies, intermediaries and products.

15.2.5   *Financial conglomerates*

Law no. 142 of 30 May 2005, which implemented EU Directive 2002/87/CE, applies the acquisition of a controlling share of "financial conglomerates", and states that the Italian authority which may authorise said acquisition may be either the Bank of Italy or ISVAP, depending on whether the activity of the target is primarily "banking activity" or "insurance activity".

15.2.6   *Privatisation of state-owned companies*

Some specific rules have been established for acquisitions of companies directly or indirectly controlled by the Italian state or by public bodies, which can be sold as part of the process for the privatisation of state-owned companies.

In particular, for state-owned companies operating in sectors which are considered of significance for the national economy (defence, transport, energy, telecommunications, banks and insurance companies) it is provided that:

(a)   the by-laws or the privatisation process can establish limits on the possession of shares by each shareholder or by shareholders controlled by public bodies;

(b)   the acquisition can be conditional upon approval by the competent government authority;

(c)   in the event the sale is only partial, the state can exercise a right of veto with respect to the adoption by the shareholders meeting of some material resolutions for the company life (such as, for example, resolutions for winding up the company, transfer of going concerns, mergers and de-mergers, change of corporate object etc.);

(d)   in the event that the transfer is only partial, the state has the right to appoint a director or a number of directors which does not exceed one-quarter of the members of the Board of Directors.

In addition, in the context of the privatisation process, the purchaser is frequently requested to make certain commitments vis-à-vis the competent government authority and specific trade unions, concerning maintenance of employment levels in the privatised enterprise and waiver of the right to make collective dismissals or to provide for labour mobility (*mobilità*) for a certain period of time.

Sometimes, the purchaser is also required to represent and warrant that it is not a state-owned entity as per definition of the EU Directive 93/38 and that state-owned entities do not hold, jointly or severally, more than a certain percentage of the purchaser share capital.

15.3   Exchange and investment control

Corporate finance transactions of an extraordinary nature and, in particular, merger and acquisition transactions, are subject to exchange, investment and anti-money laundering laws.

Commencing from 1988, Presidential Decree no. 148 of 10 May 1988 (the "Italian Exchange Act 1988") liberalised foreign economic and financial relations, from an exchange control law point of view. Consequently, any resident in Italy can, *inter alia*, receive and effect payments in Italy and outside of Italy, and any non-resident abroad can effect investments in Italy using foreign or Italian currency or through a contribution of assets or rights.

However, limits and controls provided for in anti-money laundering laws remain in full force and effect.

The most important rules which govern these matters in the Italian legal system are contained in Law no. 55 of 19 March 1990, in Law no. 197 of 5 July 1991 and Law no. 227 of 4 August 1990, in various regulations issued by the *Ufficio Italiano Cambi* (the Italian Exchange Authority, which supervises the application of laws), and by the Bank of Italy which has intervened on many occasions in order to simplify the interpretation of law for parties subject to controls.

Recently enacted, Law no. 231 of 21 November 2007 implemented EU Directive 2005/60/EC regarding money laundering and established a new division within the Bank of Italy, the *"Unità di Informazione Finanziaria"*, to serve as the Italian Money Laundering Authority, replacing the *Ufficio Italiano Cambi*.

The principle upon which all of the above-mentioned legislation is based is that whereby all transactions involving the transfer of substantial sums of money or of bearer securities must be effected through authorised intermediaries (or other controlled parties) and must always be ascribable to the party who actually carried them out.

Therefore, any financial transactions (including corporate transactions) which result in the need to effect a transfer, within Italy or outside Italy, of sums of money for an amount – in one or in more transactions – in excess of €15,000, must be effected through an authorised intermediary (such as a bank, financial intermediary, investment company, insurance company etc.). The intermediary, in turn, must identify the party to the transaction and must register and keep the relevant data in a special archive (the so-called *"Archivio Unico Informatico"*), so that the Italian *Unità di Informazione Finanziaria* has the information necessary to monitor the transaction.

Furthermore, authorised intermediaries also have a general obligation to notify the supervisory authorities of any financial transactions, however devised, which give rise to a grounded suspicion that they are aimed at the laundering of money of illegal origin or connected to the financing terrorism. Identification duties also apply when a series of transactions, even if individually lower than €15,000, is ordered to be processed by the same person and may be reasonably deemed part of a single transaction (the so-called "fractioned transactions").

15.4 Merger control

15.4.1 Introduction

EU Member States' antitrust provisions normally establish that EU or domestic competition law is applicable if anti-competitive effects would arise within the domestic market or at European Union level.

Law no. 287 of 10 October 1990 ("Law no. 287/90" or the "Italian Competition Act 1990") only covers issues not governed by EU competition law. Law no. 287/90 applies to any:

> "agreements, abuses of dominant position and concentrations of enterprises which do not fall within the scope of application of (Articles 65 and 66 of the Treaty establishing the European Coal and Steel Community), Article 85 and 86 of the Treaty establishing the European Economic Community, EU regulations, or other provisions having similar regulatory effects".

With regard to restriction or distortion of competition and abuse of a dominant position. Law no. 287/90 mirrors, on a national level, the principles of Articles 85 and 86 of the Treaty. It also reflects the contents and purposes of EU Directive 4064/89, repealed by the EU Regulation 139/2004 (the "EU Merger Control Regulation").

The Italian Competition Act also provides for a regulatory body called the *Autorità Garante della Concorrenza e del Mercato* (the "Italian Antitrust Authority"), which is responsible for monitoring compliance with, and enforcement of, competition law.

15.4.2 Concentrations

Under Law no. 287/90, a concentration is deemed to exist under the following circumstances:

(a) two or more undertakings merge;
(b) one or more persons or entities already controlling at least one undertaking, or one or more undertakings, acquire directly or indirectly, whether by purchase of securities or assets, by contract or other means, control of the whole or parts of one or more undertakings; or
(c) two or more undertakings establish a new company to be used as a full-function "concentrative" joint venture. A full-function "concentrative" joint venture with the goal of coordinating the competitive behaviour of independent undertakings does not constitute a concentration under this provision.

On the contrary, notification is not required when:

(a)　the transaction falls within the scope of the EU Merger Control Regulation;

(b)　a bank or a financial institution effects a temporary transaction of shares without exercising the voting rights attached to those shares and then sells the relevant participation within 24 months from its acquisition;

(c)　the outcome of the operation is the creation of a cooperative joint venture (i.e., a joint venture which gives rise to a co-ordination of competitive behaviour between the parent companies);

(d)　the parties involved do not carry out an economic activity;

(e)　the operation is carried out by undertakings controlled by a single firm (infragroup merger).

15.4.3　Notification of concentrations

A concentration must be notified to the Italian Antitrust Authority before its completion:

(a)　when the combined aggregate domestic turnover of all the undertakings concerned, in the last fiscal year, exceeds €440 million (as revised on May 2007); or

(b)　when the domestic turnover of the undertaking to be acquired, in the last fiscal year, exceeds €44 million (as revised on May 2007).

Such thresholds are increased on an annual basis by an amount equal to the increases in the GDP deflator index (*Indice del deflattore di prezzi del prodotto interno lordo*).

"Domestic turnover" means revenue from the sale of all products and all services supplied on the Italian market during the last fiscal year net of the relevant returns, discounts, and taxes directly connected to the sale of products and the supply of services.

When calculating "domestic turnover" for companies based outside of Italy, figures in foreign currencies are converted into euro according to the average exchange rate during the concerned fiscal year.

Unlike EU antitrust provisions, the two above conditions are alternative: if one of the two is met, the concentration must be pre-notified to the Italian Antitrust Authority.

The transaction must be notified prior to the concentration having taken place but after the parties have reached a binding agreement on the relevant terms and conditions. For example, a transaction involving the establishment of a joint venture must be notified before the joint venture deed of incorporation has been filed with the competent Company Register. Where a concentration is carried out by means of a share and purchase agreement, the operation must be notified in advance if the execution of such agreement is conditional upon the clearance of the Italian Antitrust Authority. Finally, a merger must be notified prior the execution of the deed of merger.

15.4.4   The clearance

Under Law no. 287/90, concentrations notified to the Italian Antitrust Authority are cleared if they do not "entail the creation or the strengthening of a dominant position in the domestic market so as to substantially eliminate or reduce competition in a substantial manner". In such a case the Italian Antitrust Authority would forbid the concentration or, if the concentration has already taken place, it may take measures to restore effective competition (*see* 15.4.5 below).

To determine whether or not the concentration should be cleared, the Italian Antitrust Authority evaluates all alternatives for suppliers and customers, the market position of the undertakings involved, their access to sources of supply or market outlets, the structure of the markets, competition within the relevant domestic market, barriers to entry for competitors, and trends in demand for and supply of the products or services.

The interpretation of these broad concepts as they relate to the specific circumstances of each case is largely up to the discretion of the Italian Antitrust Authority itself. The "dominant position" concept was first defined by the EU Court as follows:

> "*A dominant position . . . relates to a position of economic strength enjoyed by an undertaking which enables it to prevent effective competition in the relevant market by giving it the power to behave to an appreciable extent independently of its competitors, customers, and ultimately, its consumers.*"

Ancillary restrictions must also be pre-notified to the Italian Antitrust Authority which ascertains and evaluates their ancillary nature. Ancillary restrictions include any restrictions and/or agreements, such as non-competition covenants and exclusive supply agreements, which are necessary for, and directly related to, the completion of a concentration.

15.4.5   The procedure

Within 30 days of receiving notification of a concentration, the Italian Antitrust Authority must notify the companies involved in the concentration and the Minister of Trade and Industry of its decision to either clear the concentration or commence an investigation procedure (if the concentration has been considered subject to the prohibition under Law no. 287/90). In the absence of notification by the Italian Antitrust Authority, the concentration is deemed tacitly cleared. If the notification which the Italian Antitrust Authority is examining lacks substantial data and information, a new 30-day period commences from the date on which the companies involved provide the Authority with all missing data and information.

Should the Italian Antitrust Authority notify its decision to commence an investigation procedure, it must notify the companies involved in the concentration and the Minister of Trade and Industry of its conclusions within 45 days of such commencement. This period may be extended during the course of the investigation for an additional period of up to 30 days if the undertakings fail to supply information requested by the authorities.

The Italian Antitrust Authority may suspend the completion of the concentration during the investigation procedure. However, the completion of a takeover bid which was notified to the Italian Antitrust Authority cannot be suspended provided the purchaser does not exercise the voting rights vested with the relevant securities.

If the concentration has already been completed, the Italian Antitrust Authority may prescribe the measures necessary to restore the *status quo ante*.

15.4.6 Fines

Law no. 287/90 also provides for:

(a) the imposition of a fine in the event that the companies involved complete a concentration prohibited by the Italian Antitrust Authority or without fulfilling the conditions provided by the Italian Antitrust Authority (this fine should be no less than 1 per cent and no more than 10 per cent of the turnover relating to the business activities concerned by the concentration); and

(b) the imposition of a fine in the event that the companies involved fail to comply with the pre-notification obligation provided for under Law no. 287/90; this fine should be no more than 1 per cent of the turnover for the fiscal year preceding the one in which the Italian Antitrust Authority is notified of the breach of the pre-notification obligation, and may be imposed in addition to the fine provided for under (a) above.

Under Italian law the Italian Antitrust Authority's power to impose such fines is subject to a statutory limitation period of five years from the date of the violation (i.e., completion of the concentration concerned). Additionally, a forfeiture term is provided for under Italian law, as the Italian Antitrust Authority must contest, with the party concerned, such party's violation of the concentration pre-notification obligation within 90 days from the date on which the Authority actually became aware of such violation.

15.5 Regulation of the conduct of mergers and acquisitions

As mentioned above (*see* 15.2), the acquisition of a company in Italy can be carried out:

(a) through agreements negotiated directly with the controlling shareholders of such company; or

(b) through public purchase and/or exchange offers (takeover bids) concerning the shares of listed and unlisted companies (with shares distributed amongst the public).

Whilst in the first event the acquisition follows private negotiations, in the second, the offer (as we will see):

(a)   must be communicated to CONSOB and authorised thereby in the case of a non-mandatory offer; and

(b)   must be carried out in accordance with applicable laws and regulations in force.

15.5.1   CONSOB

CONSOB, as specified above (*see* also 15.2.2.1), is the Italian Stock Exchange Authority. It was incorporated in 1974 with the specific tasks, principally but not solely, of guaranteeing the regular operation of the Stock Exchange and the completeness and accuracy of information disclosed to the investing public.

CONSOB is a public law entity which has full regulatory independence in respect of matters reserved to it and within the limits of the law. In order to guarantee the independence and impartiality of the entity, it is provided that CONSOB must be composed of a president and four government-appointed members who hold office for four years and may be re-elected once only. Various public and private offices are considered incompatible with appointment as a member of CONSOB.

With the introduction of the FSA, the functions and powers of CONSOB were significantly increased. In particular CONSOB has the task of regulating:

(a)   the institution, organisation and operation of the stock markets;

(b)   the organisation and activities of intermediaries authorised to operate on such markets and in general to solicit investments; and

(c)   disclosure obligations of issuing companies in respect of the investing public.

Further, CONSOB must authorise public offers for the sale of financial instruments (including the so-called "IPO" (Initial Public Offering)), public purchase and/or exchange offers in respect of listed and unlisted securities and, in general, any form of solicitation to buy in respect of the investing public.

15.5.2   *Rules relating to public purchase and/or exchange offers (takeover bids)*

Public purchase and/or exchange offers are governed by the following applicable laws and rules ("the Rules"):

(a)   the FSA, which reformed and simplified rules under the previous Law no. 149/1992, incorporating them in the context of general rules governing financial services, as amended by the Reform and more recently by the Takeover Act which implemented the European Directive 2004/25/EC on takeover bids). This law represented the first Italian set of rules for takeover bids issued with the aim of providing certain protection for minority shareholders in transactions for the acquisition of controlling shareholdings, although the protection is limited with respect to companies listed on the stock exchange market. Prior to 1992 the only requirement was the preparation and distribution of a prospectus ("Offering Circular") and there were no particular requirements as to form and content;

(b)   the CONSOB Regulation no. 11971/99 as further amended and supplemented (the *"Regolamento degli Emittenti"*), which implements and enacts the general rules of the FSA. By the end of June 2008, CONSOB is required, under the Takeover Act, to update the *"Regolamento degli Emittenti"*. Therefore, the provisions of the *Regolamento degli Emittenti* as set out below might be amended.

CONSOB's communications and measures on the occasion of specific offers or following questions asked by companies or other interested parties must also be given due consideration, in that, although they do not have mandatory force, they provide an authentic interpretation of the above-mentioned legislation and regulations.

15.6   Methods of acquisition

According to the type of acquisition, there are various different methods which can be utilised in Italy to acquire the control of a company.

15.6.1   Private agreements

The execution of private purchase and sale agreements for the majority shareholding with the controlling shareholders of the target company constitutes a method for the acquisition of an unlisted company of small to medium size.

It is now common practice for any purchase agreement to be preceded, during negotiation phases, by the execution of a non-binding letter of intent, containing, amongst other things, confidentiality agreements, and by the execution by the purchaser of a due diligence exercise in respect of activities and assets of the target company. The agreement also often contains representations and warranties prepared according to international practice, by which the seller warrants, *inter alia*, the net worth and profit results of the target company as well as the absence of contingent liabilities to the target.

The content of a purchase and sale agreement for shares can vary significantly, according to the parties' requirements, and is often influenced by the fiscal impact of the transaction.

15.6.2   Takeover bids

If parties wish to acquire a company with listed shares or shares distributed amongst the public (i.e., with shareholders numbering in excess of 200), they must launch a public purchase and/or exchange offer (takeover bid). The offer can provide that:

(a)   the price for the target shares will be paid in cash; in such cases the offer is defined as a Public Purchase Offer ("OPA");

(b)   the price for the target shares will be paid partly in cash, and partly by way of the transfer of other shares; in this case the offer is defined as a Public Purchase and Exchange Offer ("OPAS"); or

(c)   the price for the target shares will be made up of shares transferred as payment; in this case it is defined as a Public Exchange Offer ("OPS").

15.6.2.1   Mandatory bids

In some cases the purchaser of a shareholding in a listed company is obliged to launch a takeover bid (the so-called mandatory bid). More precisely, the Rules provide for four different occasions on which mandatory bids must be made, all of which follow the purchase of a material shareholding in the capital of a target company:

(a)   a universal or *totalitaria* bid;
(b)   a so-called "waterfall/multi-stage" bid ("*a cascata*");
(c)   an incremental bid; or
(d)   residual bid; or
(e)   a sell-out right bid.

Universal or totalitaria

Under the FSA, any individual or entity acquiring a participation of more than 30 per cent of the securities carrying voting rights which are listed on a regulated market must launch a mandatory bid for all the remaining securities of the same nature. In order to establish the percentage shareholding, ordinary shares indirectly held through fiduciary companies (*società fiduciarie*) or through an intermediary are also calculated. For the purpose of establishing the overall amount of relevant securities, in reference to which the shareholding percentage is determined, relevant securities of the company owned by the target company are also calculated. In the context of mandatory bids, voting shares are considered those that entitle their holders to vote in a shareholders meeting resolving upon the appointment, removal or liability of the members of the Board of Directors or, where the dual model has been implemented, members of the Supervisory Board.

The obligation to launch the bid arises at the moment when the 30 per cent threshold is exceeded, on the assumption that this gives rise to de facto control of the issuing company.

The offer must be launched for each category of securities within 20 days from the date on which the 30 per cent threshold is achieved. The price of the offer must be the highest price paid for the same category of securities by the offeror, or by the person acting together with the offeror, over a period of 12 months preceding the notice of the offer to CONSOB. In the event that no securities of the relevant category have been purchased in that period, the price of the offer must be the average weighted market price for the preceding 12 months (or the shorter available period).

Chain principle bid ("a cascata")

In compliance with the regulatory powers allocated by the FSA to CONSOB (and which CONSOB must exercise in order to protect investors and guarantee market efficiency and transparency), the *Regolamento degli Emittenti* provides for two occurrences on which the 30 per cent threshold can be deemed as achieved giving rise to the obligation to make a universal bid.

The first case is that of the "chain principle" bid which can be the result of an indirect acquisition. This occurs when the acquisition:

(a)   of a shareholding in excess of 30 per cent of the securities carrying voting rights of a listed holding; or

(b)   of control of an unlisted holding,

results in the acquisition of an indirect shareholding in excess of 30 per cent of the securities carrying voting rights issued by the target listed company, provided that the tangible asset of the holding is mainly constituted of shares of the target company. For such purpose, a shareholding is material where:

(a)   it constitutes the major asset of the holding with a book value which is in excess of one-third of the entire tangible assets of the holding; or

(b)   it constitutes the principal component of the price paid for the shareholding in the holding.

In the event that these conditions are met, the purchaser is obliged to launch a bid both for the relevant securities of the holding company (if listed) and, once the first offer has been successfully concluded, for the relevant securities of the company controlled by the holding (and this is why it is called a "chain principle" bid). Finally, it should be noted that neither the FSA nor the *Regolamento degli Emittenti* expressly set out the criteria for determining the offer price relating to downstream offers. However, in certain communications CONSOB has stated that the criterion indicated in relation to universal bids must also be used for the purposes of determining the offer price relating to *chain principle bids*.

Incremental bid

The second case provided for by the *Regolamento degli Emittenti* is that of the incremental bid. This occurs when those parties who already hold a shareholding in excess of 30 per cent of the securities carrying voting rights issued of the target company, but do not hold the majority of voting rights in shareholders meetings, acquire, including indirectly, more than 3 per cent of the ordinary shares of the target company for consideration or by way of subscription of such securities or conversion of convertible bonds, during the previous 12 months. In such case, the parties concerned must launch a mandatory universal bid (i.e., in respect of 100 per cent of the relevant securities of the target company). On the contrary, if the shareholder, directly or indirectly, already holds more than 50 per cent of the securities carrying voting rights issued, any increase of such shareholding does not trigger the requirement to launch a mandatory offer, except if such shareholding exceeds 90 per cent of the securities listed on a regulated market. In this case, a residual bid must be launched (*see* below).

The *Regolamento degli Emittenti*, concerning the incremental bid, does not indicate any criteria whatsoever for the determination of the offer price. Nevertheless, provided that the incremental bid is commonly regarded as a particular kind of mandatory offer, the provision which applies to mandatory offers should also be extended thereto. As a consequence, the offer price must be the highest price paid for the same securities by the offeror, or by the person acting together with him/her over a period of twelve months before the bid.

Sell-out right

The sell-out right occurs when, following a universal bid, there is a shareholder with 95 per cent (or more) of the securities carrying voting rights of a listed company. When this occurs, this majority shareholder is obliged to purchase the securities from the remaining shareholders who make a request for it. Where more than one category of securities has been issued, this obligation applies only to the category of securities for which the threshold has been reached.

Notwithstanding the above, when there is a shareholder with more than 90 per cent of the securities carrying voting rights of a listed company, that shareholder must purchase all the remaining securities from the other shareholders, unless such shareholder restores floating stock within four months so as to ensure a regular trading of the relevant securities on the market. Where more than one category of securities has been issued, this obligation applies only to the category of securities for which the threshold has been reached.

In the above-mentioned circumstance, the price must be equal to the price offered in the mandatory bid (provided that, following a voluntary bid, the offeror has acquired securities representing at least 90 per cent of the securities with voting rights comprised in the bid). In other cases, the price is determined by CONSOB, taking into consideration:

(a)   the price paid in any prior takeover;
(b)   the average weighted market price over the last six-month period preceding the offer.

In the event that the above-mentioned percentages have been achieved through a universal bid, the price shall be equal to the same form as that offered in the bid, but the holder of the securities may require that the price shall be in cash.

The Takeover Act provides a *squeeze-out right* which allows the offeror – who holds 95 per cent (or more) of the securities carrying voting rights of a listed company following a takeover bid – to purchase the remaining securities no later than three months from the end of the period of the offer and provided that this was stated in the offering document. Where more than one category of securities has been issued, this obligation applies only to the category of securities for which the threshold has been reached. The price is determined in the same manner as the previously mentioned *sell-out right*.

The aim of the *squeeze-out right* and *sell-out right* is clearly to favour the delisting of companies in respect of which the regular trading of shares cannot be guaranteed due to excessive accumulation of shares in the hands of one party, where the conditions for official revocation by Borsa Italiana S.p.A., as the company managing the Italian stock markets, are not fulfilled.

Essentially, all of the above events aim to:

(a)   protect the right of minority shareholders to dispose of the whole of their shareholding in the target company in case of a change of control at conditions which are no worse than market conditions;
(b)   guarantee equal treatment of all shareholders of the target company, distributing the so-called majority premium paid by the purchaser, in order to acquire control of the target, amongst minority shareholders also.

For listed companies, the majority premium is defined as the difference between the price paid per share for the transfer of the controlling stake of a listed company and the market price of the same shares;

(c)   benefit the saleability of the control of the target company.

15.6.2.2   *Parties operating in concert*

The obligation to launch a universal bid or the corresponding obligation of a sell-out right is also provided in respect of parties acting "in concert" who acquire a shareholding which exceeds the relevant thresholds, unless the above-mentioned percentages: (i) are achieved by entering into a shareholders' agreement (even though void) and (ii) the relating securities have been purchased more than 12 months before.

For these purposes, a person is deemed to be acting "in concert" with another person when he cooperates with such other person on the basis of an agreement, whether express or tacit, either oral or written, aimed either at acquiring control of the target company or at creating obstacles to the successful outcome of a bid launched by others.

15.6.2.3   *Exemption from mandatory bids*

Pursuant to the Rules, however, the following events of acquisition of a material shareholding in listed companies do not give rise to an obligation to make a universal bid (as described at 15.6.2.1 above).

Preliminary offer

It is not mandatory to launch a subsequent universal bid when 30 per cent of the ordinary shares are acquired following a preliminary public purchase and/or exchange offer.

This preliminary offer is voluntary and constitutes a way of acquiring more than 30 per cent of the securities carrying voting rights issued by the target company without giving rise to a mandatory universal bid. However, the preliminary offer must be directed at the acquisition of at least 60 per cent of the relevant category of securities of the target company and provided that all of the following requirements (justified by the consideration that in such a case no way out is guaranteed for all minority shareholders) are met and verified by CONSOB:

(a)   the offer cannot be preceded by acquisitions of ordinary shares effected by the offeror or by parties operating in concert with the offeror (*see* 15.6.2.2 above) in the 12 months prior to the offer or during the offer, for an amount in excess of 1 per cent of the ordinary shares of the target company;

(b)   the approval of the offer by a number of shareholders of the target company which holds the majority of the relevant securities. Any relevant securities held by the offeror or by the majority shareholders (where they hold a shareholding in excess of 10 per cent of the capital of the target company) or by parties operating in concert with the offeror are not included in the calculation.

Furthermore, the preliminary offer must not be followed, in the 12 months after the closing:

(a)   by acquisitions of the relevant securities in excess of 1 per cent of the ordinary shares of the target company;

(b)   by merger or spin-off transactions resolved upon by the target company.

Universal preliminary bid

Without prejudice to the provisions relating to the preliminary offer above, it is not mandatory to promote a subsequent universal bid when the 30 per cent threshold of securities carrying voting rights issued by the target company is acquired following a universal public purchase and/or exchange offer, aimed at the acquisition of the totality of such securities and provided that, in the event of an exchange offer, securities listed in a regulated market of an EU Member State or cash are offered.

Other exemptions

It is not obligatory to promote a universal offer when the 30 per cent threshold of securities carrying voting rights issued by the target company is exceeded if:

(a)   at the time of the acquisition one or more other shareholders hold the majority of voting rights which may be exercised in shareholders meetings of the target company and therefore they also hold the legal control of such company. This exemption is valid provided that no agreements have been entered into by the offeror and the controlling shareholders concerning future changes of control and aimed at derogating from the obligation to launch a public offer. For this purpose, CONSOB requires the offeror to render a declaration both to CONSOB itself and to the market stating that the relevant acquisition is not accompanied by agreements with the controlling shareholders;

(b)   the acquisition was carried out through the subscription of newly issued securities deriving from a share capital increase resolved in the context of a rescue plan for a listed company in economic and financial crisis aimed at avoiding the target's insolvency, and such plan has been notified to CONSOB and to the market;

(c)   the acquisition was realised in the context of intergroup transactions (i.e., between controlled and controlling companies or between companies controlled by the same party). For such purpose, control means the availability of the majority of voting rights in shareholders meetings. The exemption aims to create a regime favouring transactions for the reorganisation of shareholdings which do not involve an effective change in control from an economic point of view;

(d)   the acquisition follows the exercise of pre-emption rights, subscription rights or conversion rights originally due (i.e., allocated to the shareholder following capital transactions in the target company which have resulted in the allocation of such rights to the shareholder, for example in the case of bonus capital increases);

(e)   the acquisition follows transactions of a temporary nature, in which the 30 per cent threshold is exceed by no more than 3 per cent and the purchaser undertakes to sell the excess on the market within 12 months and in the meantime not to exercise the voting rights pertaining to the relevant securities held in excess;

(f)   the acquisition follows a merger or spin-off due to effective and motivated business needs to be evaluated by CONSOB at its own discretion. Such exemption is justified by the consideration that the mergers and spin-offs proceedings already protect minority and creditors' interests as this kind of transaction is subject to the approval of the shareholders meeting (*see* 15.6.3.2 below).

15.6.3   Merger

15.6.3.1   Introduction

A merger is another method for acquiring a company, whether listed or unlisted. If the target company is listed, however, the merger can involve an obligation to launch a universal bid for the securities carrying voting rights of this company unless:

(a)   once the merger has been effected the shareholder who has obtained the relevant securities under the merger does not hold 30 per cent or more of the securities carrying voting rights of the listed company; and

(b)   the merger is justified by real business needs (*see* 15.6.2.3 above).

It is highly probable that the latter requirement is not satisfied in the case of mergers effected in the context of leveraged buy-out or financing acquisition transactions, where frequently the business aspect of the transaction is of secondary importance compared to the aim of achieving sufficient resources to finance the acquisition price (*see* 15.13 below).

Mergers are regulated in Italy by Law no. 22 of 16 January 1991, which implemented EU Directive 78/855/EC on mergers and EU Directive 82/891/EC on spin-offs. In accordance with this new law, the relevant articles of Italian Civil Code were amended.

A merger is defined under Italian law as the consolidation of two or more undertakings to form a larger undertaking. Italian regulation of mergers allows different types of companies to be merged, even though EU Directive 78/855/EC only covers the merging of joint stock companies. Spin-offs follow a procedure similar to the process for mergers described below.

Italian Civil Code provides for the following ways of carrying out a merger:

(a)   consolidating one or more companies into a new one (*fusione propria*); or

(b)   consolidating one or more companies into an existing one (*fusione per incorporazione*).

The Italian Parliament has not yet enacted laws and regulations to implement the provisions contained in EU Directive 2005/56/EC regarding cross-border mergers. This is expected to occur by the end of spring 2008, after which CONSOB will be required to issue secondary implementing regulations.

Mergers involving a company undergoing a procedure for the conciliation of creditors or liquidation are prohibited. With regard to companies under liquidation, this prohibition applies if the liquidation of assets has already begun.

15.6.3.2 Merger procedure

The procedure provided by law for the completion of a merger is particularly complex in that it is essentially aimed at protecting the positions of minority shareholders, creditors and noteholders of the companies involved in the merger.

The main phases which must be effected in order to perfect a merger are the following:

(a) preparation of a merger project (by the directors of the companies participating) which must include, *inter alia*, the date commencing from which the merger will take effect and an indication of the exchange ratio and any other cash adjustment (which may not exceed 10 per cent of the nominal value of the shares resulting from the merger);

(b) filing with the companies participating in the merger and filing with the Company Register the merger project, the directors' report (which illustrates the economic reasons for the merger project and the criteria utilised to establish the exchange ratio) and a report prepared by an expert appointed by the president of the competent court (which confirms the suitability of the exchange ratio illustrating the criteria utilised to establish the ratio and the values resulting from their application, and any valuation difficulties);

(c) adoption of resolutions for approval of the merger project by the shareholders meetings of the companies involved in the merger and their filing in the Company Register;

(d) no opposition (or express approval) by the creditors of the companies involved in the merger. The owners of convertible shares must in any case be given the opportunity to exercise their conversion rights for a certain period of time prior to approval of the merger project;

(e) stipulation of the notarised merger deed and its filing with the Company Register with which each of the companies which has participated in the merger is registered and where the new company resulting from the merger will be registered. The merger is complete once the last of the above filings has been completed. Claims and liabilities are then passed from each of the participating companies to the new company (or to the incorporating company).

Moreover the by-laws may attribute to the competence of the management body the resolutions relating to the merger of a wholly owned company or to a company which is 90 per cent owned (this rule is also applicable to listed companies).

Listed companies are also required to comply with specific information duties towards the public and CONSOB. The company shall provide CONSOB with the merger project drafted by the directors at least 30 days before the shareholders meeting called to approve the merger. Such documentation shall also be made available to the public at the corporate registered office and to Borsa Italiana S.p.A. Furthermore, if the merger has the dimensional characteristics established by CONSOB, the companies involved in the transaction shall provide to the public and Borsa Italiana S.p.A. an information document providing the information requested by the *Regolamento degli Emittenti* at least 10 days before the shareholders meeting. After the resolution approving the merger, the company shall transmit to CONSOB:

(a) the minutes of the shareholders meeting and the merger resolution within 30 days of the day of the meeting;
(b) a copy of the merger deed (with the indication of the date of its entry in the competent Company Register) within 10 days of the filing;
(c) the deed of incorporation of the company, as amended, within 30 days of being filed with the Company Register.

If, following the merger, the company's capital has been changed, the company shall notify the amount of the share capital and the number and classes of shares into which the capital is divided to CONSOB and Borsa Italiana S.p.A. The latter entities shall make the information available to the public no later than the next day. This notification must be carried out at latest by the day following the date on which the merger produces its effects (i.e., when the filing described under (e) above has been made).

The Italian Government chose not to implement Article 22 of EU Directive 78/855/EC, which contains a detailed list of cases when a merger is void or voidable. Instead, it introduced a very narrow provision within the Italian Civil Code, which states that a merger is not voidable once all deeds of merger filings have been completed. However, a shareholder or a third party may sue for damages suffered as a consequence of the merger.

In practice, completion of the merger procedure takes four to six months. In the case of mergers involving a bank, this term can be shorter in that the term within which creditors may oppose the merger is only 15 days as compared to two months normally required under the Italian Civil Code as amended by Law no. 22 of 16 February 1991.

15.6.4   *Transfer of business*

Finally, the transfer of control of the business of a company (even if it is listed) may be executed independently of the purchase of the shares of such companies by purchasing the shares of its significant subsidiaries or by purchasing its significant business. In this case, even if the company is listed, there is no provision for an obligation to launch a public purchase and/or exchange offer in respect of the ordinary shares of such company.

Often, a purchaser prefers to conclude an asset acquisition rather than a share acquisition, in order to avoid having full responsibility (including fiscal responsibility) for the company transferred to the purchaser. However, such an acquisition involves some specific legal issues which must be complied with. Furthermore, the transaction may take a little longer than the simple transfer of shares.

In case of the purchase of assets of an Italian company, Italian law provides that, irrespective of the governing law of the purchase agreement chosen by the parties, such agreement must be executed by notarised deed before a notary public. Within 30 days from such execution, the deed must be filed with the Company Register as well as with the Land Registry (in relation to real estate property) in order to render the purchase of assets effective vis-à-vis third parties.

In addition, in relation to commercial agreements and commercial debts and receivables transferred as part of a going concern, the following should be noted:

(a)   Notwithstanding a general principle that no agreement may be assigned without the consent of the counterparty, Italian law provides for an automatic assignment of commercial agreements connected to the business from the seller to the buyer of a going concern. In such case, no specific authorisation or consent of the counterparty is required, but this principle is subject to contrary agreements between the seller and the buyer of the going concern. Further, it does not apply to contracts or agreements based on *intuitus personae* or to agreements which expressly state that they shall not be assigned without the consent of the counterparty.

In the case of automatic assignment of the agreement, the assigned party cannot oppose it, but has the right to rescind the agreement within three months of the date of notification of the assignment if a just cause exists. Under consolidated Italian case law, just cause is considered to exist when, for instance, the buyer's organisation appears not to be able to fulfil the seller's obligations under the agreement.

(b)   Similarly, commercial receivables relating to the business are automatically assigned to the buyer, although, if the assignment is not notified to the relevant debtors, the bona fide payment to the seller may free the debtors from their obligations. As far as debts are concerned, the transfer of the going concern does not release the seller from debts incurred in the operation of the business prior to the transfer, unless it may prove that the relevant creditors have expressed their consent to such release. In any case, the transferee is also jointly liable for such debts provided that they have been duly recorded in the seller's accounting books relating to the business.

In addition, Italian law provides for rules which forbid the seller to start up and run any business which may compete with the transferred going concern for a period of five years following the transfer.

With reference to the transfer of employees, it should be noted that Italian Labour Law provides for a general rule, under which the labour relationship continues in spite of the change of employer. The main consequence is that employees of a transferred enterprise continue to enjoy the seniority acquired prior to the transfer. Accordingly, the new owner of the enterprise is liable for all employee benefits, in the event the former was aware of them at the time of the transfer or if they were evident from the books of the enterprise or from the labour documents of employees. The same rule is also applicable where only part of an enterprise is assigned (i.e., a business unit).

The transfer of the whole or a part of an enterprise is also subject to a procedure of previous disclosure to and consultation of trade unions. Accordingly, both the purchaser and the seller interested in the transfer must inform the relevant trade unions 25 days before the completion of acquisition operations. The communication to be delivered to the trade unions must contain information concerning:

(a)   reasons for the transfer;
(b)   consequences for employees;
(c)   remedies provided for the same employees.

On request by the trade unions, the purchaser and the seller are required to jointly examine matters concerning the transfer in order to reach an agreement on issues deriving from such transfer.

15.7   Preparation of an offer

15.7.1   *Communication of the offer*

Pursuant to the FSA, whoever effects a public purchase and/or exchange offer (takeover bid) must give notice thereof to CONSOB and, simultaneously, to the public by providing the information requested by the *Regolamento degli Emittenti*. As soon as the bid has been made public, the Boards of the target company and of the offeror shall inform the representatives of their employees or, where there are no such representatives, the employees themselves. Not later than 20 days after the communication to the public, the offeror has to launch the offer by filing with CONSOB an offering document (the offering circular) containing the information necessary to allow the offerees to make an informed evaluation of the offer. In the event that the offer is not launched within the above-mentioned term, the offeror cannot launch an offer on securities of the target company for the next 12 months. The launch of the offer is followed by a period (of 20 trading days or 30 in the case of companies having securities distributed among the public) during which time CONSOB examines the document and can request further information or clarifications from the offeror. In the event CONSOB requires additional information, the above-mentioned term is suspended (but only once), until the requested information is received. CONSOB can also require the offeror to provide additional guarantees to secure the payment of the offer and it can also establish that the offering circular be published in a certain form. Following such period, the document can be published and the actual offer begins. In the event that a request for authorisation has been sent to the other competent authorities (for example, Italian Antitrust Authority which must be notified of any material concentration transactions (*see* 15.4 above), or the Bank of Italy or ISVAP, for transactions which require their authorisations (*see* 15.2.3.1 and 15.2.4 above), then CONSOB will approve the offering document within five days after the other competent authority has issued its authorisation.

The *Regolamento degli Emittenti* further sets out the obligations of an offeror as regards the preparation of the offer, providing for communication of the intention to launch an offer both to CONSOB and, simultaneously, to the market (with a press release containing the information required by the Rules).

The first version of the *Regolamento degli Emittenti* provided for a pre-notification which gave rise to commencement of the period during which CONSOB examined the offer from the date on which a draft of the offer document was also provided. This provision was interpreted in the sense that the offeror could give notice to CONSOB (and to the market and the issuer) without depositing the draft offer document at the same time. A practice therefore developed whereby whoever intended to launch a takeover bid effected the pre-notification and postponed preparation of the offer document. Through this tactic, the offeror achieved two benefits:

(a)   it increased the duration of the offer at its will, often for the time necessary to raise the funds required to finance the acquisition; and above all

(b)   the target company was immediately subject to the total disclosure obligations and to a prohibition on taking any anti-takeover action as provided by the Law (*see* 15.8.4.1 and 15.9 below).

The offer document must contain the following information:

(a)   The essential elements of the offer, including:
    (i)   the amount of shares object of the offer;
    (ii)   the price of the offer; and
    (iii)   the date from which the duration of the offer will presumably commence, to be agreed with Borsa Italiana S.p.A. or, if the shares are not listed, with CONSOB.

(b)   The purposes of the transaction, or rather information concerning the future plans of the offeror;

(c)   Guarantees given with the offer and possible means of financing; in this respect CONSOB has specified that it is not necessary for the guarantees to be given at the time of pre-notification (as at this phase a statement of commitment by the offeror is sufficient) provided that such guarantees are given at the date of commencement of the acceptance period;

(d)   Possible conditions of the offer (*see* 15.8.1.1 below);

(e)   Any interests already held by the offeror in the target company or which the offeror could acquire;

(f)   The names of the banks and financial advisers for the transaction.

The offer document must also indicate that:

(a)   any applications for necessary authorisations for the acquisition have been sent to the competent authorities (essentially the Italian Antitrust Authority which must be notified of any material concentration transactions (*see* 15.4 above) but also the Bank of Italy and ISVAP for transactions which require their previous authorisation (*see* 15.2.3.1 and 15.2.4 above)); and

(b)   a shareholders meeting has been called for the issue of securities to be offered as consideration in the case of an OPAS or OPS (there is no need to have the relevant securities already issued at the time of the filing of the document with CONSOB, but they must be issued on the settlement day).

In addition, an acceptance and acknowledgment form (*modulo di adesione*), which must comply with the form contained in the *Regolamento degli Emittenti*, must be attached to the notification to CONSOB.

As regards voluntary offers, the notice of intention to effect a takeover bid must be given by the offeror without delay, that is, immediately after a Board of Directors' resolution authorising the launch of the offer. In case of mandatory bids, the relevant offer must be launched within 30 days by filing the Offer document with CONSOB from the triggering of the requirement which made the offer compulsory.

15.7.2 *Acquisitions prior to the offer*

The question of whether the offeror can acquire securities of the target company prior to the launch of the offer is connected to the issue of identification of the time from which the obligation to give communication of the intention to launch a takeover bid applies.

The question is of relevance for two reasons:

(a) as regards insider dealing (a matter which is dealt with at 15.12 below); and

(b) as regards the applicable Rules.

In respect of this latter point, it should be noted that formally an obligation to launch the offer for listed companies only comes into play once the offeror has acquired a 30 per cent or more shareholding. Therefore, until this threshold has been exceeded the acquisition of shares on the market is perfectly lawful.

It is also clear that once the Board of Directors of the offeror has authorised the final decision to launch the takeover bid, the offeror is obliged to make public the decision (*see* 15.7.1 above).

15.7.3 *The offer document*

The offer document is the offering circular which must be made public no later than 20 days after the communication from the offeror of its intention to launch an offer and, once approved by CONSOB, it must be published and made available to the public to whom the offer is directed.

It must contain all of the information relating to the offer and to the purchase of the securities that are the target of the offer, the purchase of which will be stipulated by way of simple acceptance by the offerees.

For this reason it must be prepared according to scheme drafts prepared by CONSOB. An analytical description of the content of the Offer document is set out at 15.10.1 below.

15.7.4 *CONSOB's previous proceedings*

The offer and publication of the offer document must be authorised by CONSOB which carries out a previous check for the main purpose of verifying fulfilment of the conditions of absolute transparency for the market and suitability of the information contained in the offer document in satisfaction of disclosure requirements in respect of the public concerning the content of the offer.

For such purpose CONSOB can request that further data or information be inserted in the offer document or that significant deeds or information in respect of the offer are transmitted to the public.

Under no circumstances can CONSOB evaluate the suitability or the merits of the offer. In the context of protection of the market, however, CONSOB has the power to request that the offeror issue suitable guarantees or further guarantees for the fulfilment of payment obligations in respect of the price for the offer.

The term for previous proceedings effected by CONSOB is 15 trading days (30 in cases where the offer concerns, or will be paid by way of, unlisted shares), following which the offer document may be published without any further requirements. This term can be suspended, only once, in cases where CONSOB requires further information and data. CONSOB can also require a specific method of publication and additional guarantees to be provided by the offeror.

However, in practice the offer document is only published following express authorisation for such publication from CONSOB, known as *nulla-osta* approval. This is due to the fact that in the absence of such *nulla-osta* approval, once the offer document is published, CONSOB could suspend the offer in the case of suspected breach of the Rules or it could declare the offer cancelled in the case of a verified breach thereof.

15.7.5 Publication of the offer document

Following the term for the previous proceedings effected by CONSOB and once *nulla-osta* approval has been achieved, the offer document must be sent to the target company (issuer of the shares the object of the offer) and published.

The *Regolamento degli Emittenti* provides for three different means of publication:

(a)   full publication in newspapers with adequate circulation (e.g., national newspapers);
(b)   delivery of the document to the banks and other authorised intermediaries, and simultaneous publication of a press announcement of such delivery in newspapers with adequate circulation (e.g., national newspapers);
(c)   other forms of publication in agreement with (or imposed by) CONSOB provided that knowledge of the fundamental elements of the offer and access to the documentation is guaranteed (for example through the internet).

The method described under point (b) is the method most commonly used in practice.

There is no term provided within which the offeror must publish the offer document. However, it is held that publication should take place within a few days of the date of expiry of the previous proceedings effected by CONSOB and of the issue of *nulla-osta* approval. In practice, the date of publication of the offer document is agreed with CONSOB and with Borsa Italiana S.p.A., as the company which manages the market.

15.8   Conduct of the offer

15.8.1 Principles which govern the conduct of the offer

15.8.1.1 Irrevocability of the offer and conditions
One of the principles established by the Rules which govern the realisation of an offer is that of the irrevocability of the offer. This is a principle which is considered as essential and absolute without exceptions. The offer cannot be withdrawn even in the event that a competing offer is launched.

Before the approval of the Takeover Act, there was some debate regarding the time from which the offer can be considered irrevocable. Now, it appears reasonable to confirm that the offer is irrevocable from the time at which the communication of intention to launch such offer has been effected. In order to mitigate the consequences of the irrevocability of the offer for the offeror, the effectiveness thereof can be conditional upon the occurrence of certain conditions. Following amendments made to the Rules by CONSOB by way of resolution no. 12475 of 6 April 2000, this possibility has now been expressly confirmed (*see* 15.7.1 above).

Obviously no conditions can be imposed in a mandatory offer (*see* 15.6.2.1 above).

In compliance with a general principle provided by the Italian legal system, no so-called potestative conditions can be imposed (i.e., conditions whose occurrence depends exclusively on the will of the offeror). More specifically, the *Regolamento degli Emittenti* states that "the effectiveness of an offer cannot be subject to conditions whose occurrence depends solely on the will of the offeror". CONSOB confirmed such interpretation with communication no. 2047014 dated 4 July 2002, whereby it stated that public offers conditional on the occurrence of a future and uncertain event are commonly admitted, provided that the event does not merely depend on the discretion of the offeror. For example, the most common conditions inserted in the Offer document relating to a voluntary takeover offer can be summarised as follows:

(a) amendments to the by-laws of the target company which eliminate limits on the possession of shares;
(b) transformation of the target from a cooperative bank to a *società per azioni* (joint stock company);
(c) no increase in net indebtedness of the target company beyond a certain threshold;
(d) adoption by the target company of new by-laws;
(e) realisation by the target company of a share capital increase;
(f) absence of events which would have a negative impact or events of legislative or regulatory nature, either domestic or international, that may substantially affect the assets and liabilities and the economic and financial position of the company with respect to the figures contained in its financial statements.

Once the offer has expired as a consequence of the event contemplated in the condition, such occurrence must be published in a national newspaper and notified to CONSOB.

Furthermore, the offer document often includes a condition which renders the effectiveness of the offer conditional upon achievement of a minimum amount of acceptances.

As these conditions are imposed in the interest of the offeror (so-called unilateral conditions), it is possible for the offeror to waive such conditions and decide to consider the offer effective and binding, including in the case of failed fulfilment of one or more of the conditions imposed. In any event, it is necessary for the offeror to indicate in the offer document a term within which such conditions must occur and, according to CONSOB orientation, this term cannot be extended by the offeror. Any extension to the term in fact results in a change to the offer and as such is subject to the same rules provided for the realisation of changes to the offer (*see* 15.8.5 below).

15.8.1.2   Equal treatment

A further fundamental principle which the offeror must respect in carrying out the offer is that of equal treatment of all offerees.

As regards equal treatment, the following applies:

(a)   the principle is applied for identical categories of securities the target of the offer. Therefore, the offeror may offer a different price to holders of ordinary shares and holders of saving shares, in cases where the offer concerns these classes of securities;

(b)   the principle only applies in the context of public purchase and/or exchange offers; consequently the offeror may acquire securities on the market prior to the launch of the offer at different conditions;

(c)   the principle does not take into account the particular conditions of the offerees: what matters is that the offer is an unique offer containing the same conditions to be addressed to the public.

15.8.2   The duration of the offer

15.8.2.1   Terms

Once the offer document has been published the true offer is commenced.

The offer must have a term of between:

(a)   a minimum of 25 and a maximum of 40 trading days for preliminary offers (*see* 15.6.2.3 above);

(b)   a minimum of 15 and a maximum of 25 trading days for any other kind of takeover bid.

The actual duration of the offer is agreed with:

(a)   Borsa Italiana S.p.A., as the company which manages the market, in cases where the offer concerns listed securities (in order to coordinate the duration with the stock market calendar); or

(b)   CONSOB, in cases where the offer concerns unlisted securities.

In any event, the offer cannot commence before:

(a)   at least five trading days have passed since the publication of the offer document. This term is provided in order to permit the target company to issue its press announcement evaluating the offer (*see* 15.10.2 below);

(b)   authorisation provided for the acquisition of an interest in the share capital of a bank has been issued (*see* 15.2.3.1 above);

(c)   the shareholders meeting has resolved to issue new securities to be exchanged with those securities which are the target of the offer, as the price of the transaction in the case of an OPS or OPAS.

15.8.2.2 *Extensions*

The Rules also provide that the offer may be extended in the following events:

(a) following a justified measure issued by CONSOB for up to a maximum of 55 trading days, when requirements for market protection and the correct realisation of the offer so dictate;

(b) automatically for a further 10 trading days in cases where the shareholders meeting of the target company is called in the 10 final days of the offer in order to resolve the adoption of defensive measures in respect of the takeover effected through the offer (*see* 15.9 below);

(c) automatically in the case of competing offers, in order that the duration of the former offer is aligned with the duration of the competing offer.

In addition, it is held that the offer can be extended at the initiative of the offeror on the following conditions alone:

(a) the offeror has reserved the right to do so in the offer document; and

(b) if it is a change to the offer, it is notified to the market within the same term and according to the same methods provided for offer changes.

15.8.3 *Acceptance*

Acceptances of the offer take place during the offer period (*see* 15.8.2.1 above) by way of compilation of the acceptance form held by the offeror or by the authorised intermediaries.

Although the Rules are not clear on this matter, in practice the offeror specifies in the offer document that acceptances cannot be withdrawn.

It is, however, expressly provided that acceptances can be withdrawn in the case of competing offers or higher bids in order to permit the holder of the securities that are the object of the offer to accept the competing offer or the higher bid. However, it is clear that the withdrawal is only permitted provided that the offeree accepts the new and higher bid.

15.8.4 **Action permitted in realising the offer**

15.8.4.1 *Transparency obligations and proper conduct rules*

The Rules provide that, commencing from the date of communication to CONSOB and of the intention to launch a public purchase and/or exchange offer (takeover bid) up until the date of closing of the offer, interested parties are subject to particular transparency obligations for the purpose of promptly informing the market of the offer performance and any other information which could influence the same. In particular:

(a) any information concerning the issuer and the offer must be communicated to the market (through transmission to two press agencies) only in the form of a press release and simultaneously transmitted to CONSOB;

(b) any purchases and sales of securities that are the object of the offer must be notified to the market and to CONSOB on the day on which they are effected, together with an indication of the price;

(c)   data concerning acceptance trends must be circulated daily in the case of listed securities or weekly in the case of unlisted securities;

(d)   any advertising and promotional messages relating to the offer must be recognisable as such and the information contained therein must be clear, correct and consistent with the content of the offer document and of the target company's statement (*see* 15.10 below).

Pursuant to the *Regolamento degli Emittenti*, "interested parties" are considered:

(a)   the offeror;

(b)   the target company;

(c)   persons connected to parties under (a) and (b) by relationships of control;

(d)   companies subject to their common control and affiliated companies;

(e)   directors, members of the Board of Statutory Auditors and general managers of the companies under (a) and (b) above; and

(f)   the shareholders of the offeror or offeree company participating in a share-holders agreement.

Moreover, the *Regolamento degli Emittenti* requires that the offeror and other interested parties abide by the following prescriptions:

(a)   adherence to principles of proper conduct and equal treatment of those to whom the offer is addressed;

(b)   abstaining from carrying out transactions on the market with a view to influencing acceptances of the offer; and

(c)   abstaining from carrying out actions and executing agreements aimed at altering circumstances affecting the conditions precedent to a mandatory public offer to buy.

15.8.4.2   *Acquisitions by the offeror*

In the period between the date of the communication of the intention to launch a public offer and the settlement date, there is a possibility of trading the securities which are the subject of the public offer. However, should offerors acquire, directly or indirectly or through nominees, such securities or be granted the right to acquire them, even at a later date, at prices higher than those set out in the offer document, they are required to realign the latter with the highest price paid.

15.8.5   *Changes to the offer*

The offeror may unilaterally change the content of the offer, through an increase in the price or through changes to other elements. Unlike previous rules, in fact, the *Regolamento degli Emittenti* today expressly provides that the offer can be changed more than once, without limitations, provided that such changes occur during the offer period.

This rule is intended to favour the success of the venture, to the extent possible, as it permits the offeror to increase the offer in case of a negative market response in respect of the original content of the offer.

Changes must be notified to CONSOB, the market (outside trading hours in order to avoid any market disruption) and to the issuer, and must be published in the same manner provided for the original offer (*see* 15.7.1 and 15.7.5 above). There is no term provided for publication of the offer following notification, which in theory can take place immediately after the notification. In practice, however, the date of publication is agreed with CONSOB.

The offer can be changed for up to three trading days prior to the forecast closing date for the offer period. In any event, any possible increase in the offer price cannot be for less than 2 per cent of the global price.

Clearly any change made to the offer during the offer period also automatically extends in favour of parties who have accepted the offer, who are not required to make a new acceptance. In any case, reductions in the quantity requested are not permitted.

15.8.6 *Competing offers*

Competing public purchase and/or exchange offers are offers concerning the same securities that are the object of the original offer, published according to the terms and conditions of the Rules.

The purpose of competing offers is to assure the best benefit possible for the market in general and for shareholders of the target company in particular. The Rules, as amended by CONSOB resolution no. 13086 of 18 April 2001, therefore tend to favour competing offers, providing that the original offeror and the competing offeror can effect more than one higher bid.

However, it is required that:

(a)   the competing offer and any higher bids are not admitted if:
    (i)   they do not contain an increase to the global offer price, or
    (ii)   they do not involve the elimination of a condition;
(b)   the precise time limits within which it is possible to launch a competing offer and higher bids must be respected in full in order to avoid the target company's activities being restricted for an excessive period of time (*see* 15.9 below). In particular:
    (i)   the competing offer must be notified and published at least five trading days prior to the forecast closing date for the original offer (in order that, taking into account that the competing offer cannot commence until five days after such publication, the original offer and the competing offer are both effective at the same time for at least one day),
    (ii)   possible higher bids made by the original offeror or by the competing offeror are effected within five trading days of the date of publication of the previous higher bid and no later than 10 trading days prior to the forecast closing date for the last competing offer,
    (iii)   on the last possible day, each offeror may launch a final higher bid, following prior notice to CONSOB.

15.9 Defences to a hostile offer

15.9.1 Introduction

Rules applicable to anti-offer acts and transactions constitute one of the most important novelties introduced to the Italian legal system by the FSA and, in particular, by the Takeover Act. Whilst the previous legislation imposed a complete prohibition on the target company carrying out transactions which could impede the offer (the so-called "passivity rule"), the current Rules permit the shareholders meeting of the target company, by way of the favourable vote of shareholders representing at least 30 per cent of the share capital, to authorise directors to initiate acts and transactions (poison pills) which impede the takeover by the offeror. In this way, the takeover is de facto authorised by the offerees themselves.

15.9.2 Preventive defence techniques

No restriction is imposed by Italian law on so-called preventive defence techniques, or rather ventures carried out by listed companies in the absence of any offer, in order to render a takeover, and therefore the transfer of control of the company, more difficult.

Provided that, in any case, in the absence of a specific regulation, the legitimacy and applicability of the pre-bid defences must be determined on a case-by-case basis, the most common preventive defence techniques are the following:

(a) the acquisition of treasury securities by the target company, within the limits and according to the terms and conditions of applicable law: within the limits of the distributable profits and available reserves resulting from the most recently approved financial statement and for no more than 10 per cent of the share capital, through a public purchase and/or exchange offer or by way of methods approved by Borsa Italiana S.p.A. in the case of listed companies;

(b) the realisation of stock option plans, to favour the distribution of the relevant securities amongst employees of the target company;

(c) an increase in cross-shareholdings between parent company and subsidiary, within the limits provided by applicable provisions of law (a subsidiary can only acquire shareholdings in the parent company within the same limits provided for the acquisition of treasury shareholdings), which are even more stringent in the case of listed companies;

(d) realisation of a management buy-out which favours the delisting of a company;

(e) an increase in the share capital resolved by the directors (under Italian law, the by-laws can grant the power to the directors to increase the share capital one or more times up to a specified amount and for the maximum period of five years from the date of registration of the company in the competent Company Register);

(f) golden parachutes (i.e., the agreements entered into by a company and its top executives under which the company agrees to pay amounts in excess of the executives' usual compensation in the event that the control of the company changes or there is a change in the ownership of a substantial portion of the company's assets).

Other defensive actions might take the guise of issuance of warrants by the target company, which might make the existing shareholders more loyal and give them an incentive to keep their shareholdings and abstain from adhering to the proposed offer.

The role of the stock option plans as a preventive defence technique will also probably increase, given that the Reform has introduced the possibility for the extraordinary meeting to resolve upon the attribution of profits (through the issuance of special categories of securities) also to the employees of subsidiaries.

Preventive defence techniques based on shareholders agreements which limit shareholders' voting rights are no longer admitted. As seen, in case of a public purchase and/or exchange offer, any shareholder who is party to a shareholder agreement can terminate this agreement without notice (*see* 15.2.2.3 above).

15.9.3   Defence pending an offer

As already mentioned (*see* 15.9.1 above), once an offer has been launched, the directors of a target company can only execute acts or transactions which oppose the objectives of the offer with the authorisation of the shareholders meeting of such target company, by way of the favourable vote of shareholders representing at least 30 per cent of the share capital (the so-called "Passivity Rule"). This quorum is applicable irrespective of there having been a first, second or third call. Italian companies with securities listed on regulated markets in Italy or other EU Member State may issue securities with voting rights subordinated to an offer being made only if, for the condition to be satisfied, there has been an authorisation by the shareholders meeting as above described.

The Passivity Rule applies from the time the decision to launch an offer has been made public and communicated to CONSOB by the offeror until the result of the bid is made public or the bid lapses. With regard to decisions made before the beginning of the above-mentioned period and not yet partly or fully implemented, the shareholders at the shareholders meeting shall approve or confirm any decision which does not form part of the normal course of the company's business. The implementation of this decision may result in creating obstacles to the success of the bid. The search for other offers is not considered as being "against the purpose of the offer".

According to CONSOB, in the scope of the Rules:

(a)   offer objectives are considered to be the acquisition, as the case may be, of:
  (i)   a certain percentage of the share capital,
  (ii)   control, or
  (iii)   the business concern of the target company;
(b)   consequently acts or transactions that can oppose such objectives are, as the case may be:
  (i)   acts aimed at increasing the cost of achieving the shareholding desired by the offeror (i.e., share capital increase transactions and conversion of bonds into shares), as all these actions involve an

increase of the expenditure to be borne by the offeror for completing the takeover;

(ii) acts aimed at changing the net equity of the target company (i.e., transfers of material assets to a third party, mergers, de-mergers, spin-offs as well as any act which may cause a significant increase of the financial indebtedness), as all these transactions involve a substantial decrease of a company's assets and therefore the target company would lose its attractiveness; or

(iii) disruptive actions (i.e., launch of public purchase and/or exchange offers in respect of the offeror's shares, acquisition of new businesses carried out by the target company), which could make it more difficult to obtain clearance from the Antitrust Authority.

The prohibition on performing such acts and transactions in the absence of approval by the shareholders of the target company, by way of the favourable vote of shareholders entitled to vote and holding at least 30 per cent of the share capital, operates from the date on which the offeror effects the preliminary notification to CONSOB and to the market containing its intention to launch the offer. Directors of listed companies who carry out transactions in breach of the relevant obligation to abstain from carrying out actions in order to frustrate the proposed bid shall be punished with a pecuniary administrative fine up to €515,000.

15.9.4 Breakthrough rule

In addition, following the Takeover Act and the subsequent amendments to the Rules in compliance with the EU Directive 2004/25/EC, the so called "breakthrough rule" was been enacted in Italy. In essence, during the time period for acceptance of the bid: (i) no restrictions on the transfer of the securities provided for in the by-laws shall apply to the offeror; and (ii) no restrictions on voting rights provided for in the by-laws and in the shareholders' agreement shall apply to the shareholder meeting, which decides on any defensive measures.

Where, following a bid, the offeror holds 75 per cent or more of the securities carrying voting rights in the resolutions concerning the appointment or the removal of board members, in the first shareholders meeting held after the bid called to amend the by-laws or remove or appoint board members, no restrictions on the voting rights provided for in the by-laws or in shareholders' agreement, nor extraordinary rights of shareholders concerning the appointment or removal of board members provided for in the articles of association, shall apply.

Where the rights above are removed and the offer has been successfully carried out, equitable compensation shall be provided for any loss suffered by the holders of the relevant rights. The latter shall apply for compensation no later than 90 days from the closure of the bid and the offeror shall grant the payment within 30 days from the request. If an agreement regarding the size of the compensation is not reached, then a court of law shall decide, taking into account the difference in the average market price of the relevant securities before and after the bid.

15.9.5   *Reciprocity rule*

The Takeover Act exempts any company from applying the passivity rule and breakthrough rule (with the exception of the provision regarding the equitable compensation), if it becomes subject to an offer launched by a company (or a company controlled, directly or indirectly, by the latter) which does not apply the same or equivalent regulation, also with reference to the shareholders' resolution.

In the event that the bid is launched by parties operating "in concert", each participant shall comply with the relevant regulation. No later than 60 days from the request, CONSOB will determine whether or not the regulation applied to the offeror is equivalent to that of the target company.

However, the decision to make use of the above reciprocity rule shall be subject to the approval of the shareholders at a shareholders meeting of the target company, which must be passed no later than 18 months before the bid was made public.

This approval must be communicated to the public "without delay".

15.10   Documents from the Board of Directors of the offeror and offeree

15.10.1   *Offer document*

As mentioned above (*see* 15.7.3 above), the offering document is the offering circular prepared by the offeror and filed with CONSOB not later than 20 days after the communication to the latter and to the market, which, once approved by CONSOB, will be published and made available to the offerees.

The offering document must be prepared according to the template prepared by CONSOB and attached (Schedule 2A) to the *Regolamento degli Emittenti*. These templates indicate in detail the required content of the offering document and vary according to the type of offer (OPA, OPAS or OPS) and the type of the shares (listed or unlisted) which are being offered.

The offering document must contain certain basic information, including:

(a)   the terms of the bid;
(b)   the identity of the offeror and, where the offeror is a company, the type, name and registered office of that company;
(c)   the securities or, where appropriate, the class or classes of securities for which the bid is made;
(d)   the consideration offered for each security or class of securities and, in the case of a mandatory bid, the method employed in determining it, with particulars of the way in which that consideration is to be paid;
(e)   the compensation offered for the rights which might be removed as a result of the breakthrough rule (*see* 15.9.4 above), with particular indication of the way in which that compensation was determined and the way that it is to be paid;

(f)   the maximum and minimum percentages or quantities of securities which the offeror undertakes to acquire;

(g)   details of any existing holdings of the offeror, and of persons acting "in concert" with him/her, in the offeree company;

(h)   all the conditions to which the bid is subject;

(i)   the offeror's intentions with regard to the future business of the offeree company and, in so far as it is affected by the bid, including intentions to safeguard the jobs of the current employees and management (describing any material change in the conditions of employment, and in particular the offeror's strategic plans for the two companies and the likely reper-cussions on employment and the locations of the companies' places of business);

(j)   the time allowed for acceptance of the bid;

(k)   where the consideration offered by the offeror includes securities of any kind, information concerning those securities;

(l)   information concerning the financing for the bid;

(m)   the identity of persons acting "in concert" with the offeror or with the offeree company and, in the case of companies, their types, names, regis-tered offices and relationships with the offeror and, where possible, with the target company;

(n)   the national law which will govern contracts concluded between the offeror and the holders of the offeree company's securities as a result of the bid and the competent courts.

Although there is no legal requirement to have a risk factors section in the offer document, nevertheless CONSOB may require the offeror to insert such a specific section in the offer document. The offer document must also contain a statement of responsibility (drafted in accordance with the pattern established by CONSOB) from the offeror, in relation to the completeness and fairness of the document itself. Once authorised by CONSOB, the offer document must be published in a national newspaper and transmitted to CONSOB by electronic means.

15.10.2   Issuer's statement

In the context of protection of transparency of market conditions and the offerees' right to information, the Board of Directors (or, in case of a dual corporate governance, both the management body and the supervisory body) of the target company must prepare a statement containing its opinion in respect of the offer in order that shareholders of the target company have access to any useful data for reaching an informed decision in respect of acceptance of the offer. The press statement, which also includes the board's view on the effects of implementation of the bid on all the company's interests and specifically employment and places of business, is therefore of fundamental importance in that the majority of the information relating to the current situation and future prospects of the issuer are only known to the directors of the issuer itself and therefore cannot be found in the offer document prepared by a party who is extraneous to the issuer company.

Following the 15 days necessary for CONSOB to carry out its previous proceedings (*see* 15.7.4 above), the offer document, together with any possible supplements in light of requests made by CONSOB, is transmitted to the target company which, commencing from this moment, has an extremely brief period of time to prepare the statement.

Once prepared, the statement is sent to CONSOB at least two days prior to the date provided for commencement of the offer. In the context of its previous proceedings CONSOB may once again request clarifications, information or further explanations from the target company, it remaining understood that in case of silent consent (no request from CONSOB) the statement can be published in its original form after two days.

In the case of a friendly offer (in agreement with the offeror) the Rules provide that the statement can be attached to the offer document and, in such cases, the offer can commence from the day following publication. In the case of a hostile offer, the offer can only commence five trading days from the date of publication of the offer document in order to permit the target company to issue its statement.

As with the offer document, CONSOB is not responsible for exercising control over the merits or suitability of the content of the statement, but rather for controlling, in the context of market protection, the clarity of the information contained therein for the purposes of evaluating the offer. Once supplemented in line with any possible requests from CONSOB, the statement must be disclosed to the market on the first day of the acceptance period at the latest.

It is up to the Board of Directors (or, in case of a dual corporate governance, both the management body and the supervisory body) of the target company to prepare the statement. In preparing such a statement, the board's or other body's members are obliged to act in a diligent and regular manner, in the interests of the target company, and are liable vis-à-vis shareholders of the target company who may be directly damaged by information contained in the statement, and vis-à-vis the offeror where they have acted with negligence or bad faith in providing justifications in support of their evaluation. The board's or other body's members are obliged to remain impartial despite their knowledge that, if the hostile offer succeeds, the new controlling shareholder will appoint new board's or other body's members, whilst in the case of a friendly offer, agreements will have already been reached with the new offeror concerning the future of the board's or other body's members.

The *Regolamento Emittenti* provides that the statement must contain the following information:

(a) any data which assists the shareholders of the target company in evaluating the offer, and a motivated evaluation by the directors of the target company of the offer itself;

(b) a possible decision to call the shareholders meeting for authorisation to carry out anti-takeover acts or transactions (*see* 15.9 above);

(c) indications and updates concerning the fees received by or resolved in favour of the board's or other body's members, auditors and general managers of the target company;

(d)   information concerning direct or indirect possession of the securities of the offeror company by the target company or by the board's or other body's members, including those of parent companies or subsidiaries, and concerning shareholders' agreements relative to securities of the target company;

(e)   disclosure of material facts which were not indicated in the most recent financial statement or in the most recently published half-yearly statement.

15.11 Compulsory acquisition of minorities

A further important novelty introduced to the Italian legal system by the FSA is the right of the offeror to acquire residual shares on the market following completion of the offer (the so-called squeeze-out right).

In fact, following a universal offer (preliminary, mandatory or residual – *see* 15.6.2.1 and 15.6.2.2 above), whomsoever holds more than 95 per cent of the securities of the target company, can exercise the right of squeeze-out within three months of the close of the offer, provided that the offeror has indicated its intention to proceed with a subsequent compulsory offer in the offer document relative to the previous universal offer.

When the target company has issued more than one class of securities, the squeeze-out right can be exercised only in the class for which the threshold has been reached.

It is debatable whether this expression of intention, which aims to render the minority (who do not wish to accept the offer) aware that they could be subject to a compulsory offer if the original offer succeeds, binds the offeror to exercise the right of squeeze-out in the event that the offer results in acquisition of more than 95 per cent of securities of the target company.

The price must be established according to criteria set out for the sell-out right (*see* 15.6.2.1 above).

The compulsory transfer shall take place by operation of the law in the event that the offeror has notified the target company of the deposit of the purchase price with a bank. The target company will thereafter proceed to annotate the shareholders register with the transfer, and the transfer will be automatic and will not require an expression of intent or other formality.

15.12 Insider dealing and market manipulation

As already mentioned (*see* 15.7.2 above), in principle the offeror can acquire shares of the target company prior to the launch of the offer. However, any such acquisition must be made strictly in accordance with statutory and regulatory provisions regarding takeovers in Italy as well as with the insider dealing regulations.

With reference to Italian rules concerning insider trading offences, the FSA contains specific Articles describing in detail the unauthorised use of internal confidential information and stating the relevant applicable sanctions.

Law no. 62 of 18 April 2005 (the so-called *Legge Comunitaria 2004*) which deals, *inter alia*, with market abuse (i.e., the misuse of privileged information and market manipulation) implemented in Italy the principles set out in EU Directive 2002/6/EC (as integrated by the Commission Directives 2003/124/EC and 2004/72/EC). These principles have now been incorporated in the FSA. In this regard, CONSOB has been given broad investigatory powers, such as the ability to:

(a) carry out inspections with the joint collaboration of the Italian Tax Police (*Guardia di Finanza*);
(b) order seizures;
(c) carry out investigations on bank accounts and telephone communications.

15.12.1 *Misuse of privileged information (insider trading)*

The new provisions incorporated in the FSA are based on the principles of transparency and equal treatment of market participants and are aimed at reinforcing protection against insider trading and market manipulation. If privileged information is disclosed, either voluntarily or unintentionally, to a third party who is not bound by a duty of confidentiality, then such information shall also be "promptly" rendered public.

For this purpose, "privileged information" means any specific information the contents of which are unknown to the indistinct public, concerning securities or their issuers, and which, if made available to the market, could affect the market price of such securities.

Under the FSA, criminal sanctions (i.e., imprisonment for up to six years plus a fine ranging from €20,000 to €3 million) may be imposed upon any person who, being in possession of "privileged information" concerning securities either by virtue of his status as a shareholder or because of his position:

(a) buys or sells securities or undertakes other securities transactions, either directly or indirectly, taking advantage of such privileged information; or
(b) discloses privileged information to any other person unless such disclosure is made in the normal course of his employment, business or duties;
(c) advises or induces another person, on the basis of privileged information, to acquire or dispose of financial instruments to which that information relates.

15.12.2 *Market manipulation*

Pursuant to the FSA, dissemination of information through the media, including the internet, or by any other means, which gives or is likely to give false or misleading signals as to financial instruments, including the dissemination of rumours and false or misleading news, shall be punished with imprisonment from one to six years and a fine ranging from €20,000 to €5 million.

15.12.3   *Information concerning takeover*

Any and all information concerning the offeror's intention to launch an offer on listed securities, if disclosed to the market, would obviously have an impact on the market price of said securities. However, if the offeror itself proceeds to purchase securities in the market prior to the obligation arising for it to give notice to the market of the intention to launch a takeover on the same securities (this obligation does not arise until there is a resolution of the Board of Directors authorising the offer), it could be argued that such a purchase does not fall within the ambit of insider dealing regulations. Indeed, the offeror's intention to make the bid is not "privileged information" for the offeror itself but only for third parties (including, of course, the offeror's directors, officers and employees who do not act on behalf of the offeror).

Therefore, only if a third party takes advantage of such privileged information and buys or sells securities is a crime committed under insider trading regulations.

15.13   Financial assistance

Before the Reform, many authors were of the opinion that leveraged buy-out transactions were not allowed under Italian law on the grounds that they constituted a violation of the provisions of Article 2358 of the Italian Civil Code on financial assistance. In certain limited cases, leveraged buy-outs were considered null and void by Italian courts. This was due to Article 2358 of the Italian Civil Code, which states that: "A company cannot grant loans or give guarantees for the purchase of or subscription to its own shares." Therefore, under the previous regulations, in case of acquisition of the shares of the target company, in no circumstances could lenders provide financing to the purchaser against security over the assets of the target company. Investors in the proposed leveraged acquisition could therefore only seek to finance the transaction by:

(a)   entering into a pledge agreement on the shares of the target once these have been duly acquired by the investors; and/or

(b)   granting other forms of corporate guarantees from them or, should the acquisition be carried out through a specific vehicle which is an existing operating company, from such acquisition vehicle.

Given these financing constraints, the typical leveraged acquisition on an Italian company often involved a post-acquisition merger of the target company with the acquisition vehicle.

The new Article 2501-bis of the Italian Civil Code, introduced by the Reform, allows, subject to the condition that the merger is part of a broader economically justifiable business plan (together with the performance of other reporting and registration requirements), the merger of a target company with the acquiring company whereby the assets of the target company are used as a "general security" for the reimbursement of the acquisition finance, thus providing for an Italian-style "white-wash procedure" in respect of such transactions.

In particular, the Board of Directors of both buyer and target must disclose:

(a)   information on the funding;
(b)   the source of the funding;
(c)   reasons for and objectives of the proposed transaction.

Moreover, an independent expert must confirm the reasonableness of the information presented in the merger plan.

As Article 2501-bis of the Italian Civil Code is a new provision and there is no case law on this aspect, it is still unclear to what extent a leveraged buy-out transaction, structured through a merger between the target company and the acquiring vehicle, can be completed without violating (directly or indirectly) the provisions on financial assistance stated by Article 2358 of the Italian Civil Code. However, it is doubtful that the creation of "upstream collateral" guarantees is permitted.

In short, the Reform authorises a purchasing company to incorporate the target and to repay the acquisition finance debts with the cash flow originated by the former target's business (or by means of the sale of assets previously belonging to the target company).

Chapter 16

Latvia[1]

Liga Hartmane, Partner
Martins Gailis, Associate
Klavins & Slaidins LAWIN

16.1   Introduction

Mergers and acquisitions in Latvia became subject to special regulation in the latter half of the 1990s. Until then these activities were subject to the general legislative Acts enacted by the Latvian Parliament to ensure the functioning of a free-market economy after Latvia regained its independence in 1991. As a result of Latvia's decision to make joining the EU its main foreign policy objective, during the 1990s Latvian laws began to be harmonised with the legal requirements of EU legislation. This process has continued, and consequently Latvian legislative requirements with regard to mergers and acquisitions have become more comprehensive.

The Competition Council ("the Council") was established in 1998 to supervise the Latvian marketplace. The Competition Council's role is as follows:

(a)   to monitor the observance of prohibitions against the abuse of dominant position, unfair competition and agreements by undertakings, other regulatory enactments and international agreements;
(b)   to monitor the observance of the Advertisement Law;
(c)   to examine notices submitted regarding agreements of undertakings and decisions made in respect of them;
(d)   to control market concentration by making decisions in relation to mergers of undertakings; and
(e)   to cooperate with relevant foreign institutions.

In 1995 the Securities Market Commission was established. Its functions included:

(a)   regulating the issuance of and compliance with regulations and directives to be observed by participants in the financial and capital market;
(b)   the collection and analysis of information (data) relating to the financial and capital market participants.

On 1 July 2001 the Securities Market Commission was replaced by the Financial and Capital Market Commission.

---

[1] The Latvian Chapter reflects the law as at 2 April 2008.

The work of both the Competition Council and the Financial and Capital Market Commission has become more intense due to the growth and globalisation of the markets. The Competition Council in particular has played a considerable role in shaping the current market and regulating the performance of local and foreign companies operating in Latvia.

Latvian company and competition legislation is quite new. In both areas (company law and competition law) new legislation, which is in line with EU guidelines and requirements, came into force on 1 January 2002. In company law, however, there has been a transition period of three years during which both the old and the new legislation has been in force. The transition period ended on 1 January 2005.

16.2   Acquisition targets

In general, Latvian companies fall into one of the following categories:

(a)   public companies;
(b)   private companies.

16.2.1   Public companies

Public companies in Latvia are those that have registered issues of their shares with the Finance and Capital Market Commission. There are various legal Acts that regulate performance of public companies in Latvia including:

(a)   Commercial Law;
(b)   Law on the Financial Instruments Market;
(c)   Credit Institutions Law;
(d)   Law on Insurance Companies and their Supervision;
(e)   several other subordinate legislative Acts.

Since the early 1990s the framework of laws regulating the performance of public companies has become more complete and has introduced a considerable number of restrictive requirements with regard to the acquiring of shares in public companies.

16.2.2   Private companies

The majority of Latvian companies are classified as private. The acquisition of shares or takeovers of such companies is regulated by the Commercial Law, Civil Law, Competition Law and subordinate legislation.

16.3   Regulation of the conduct of mergers and acquisitions

The main regulatory authority for transactions resulting in mergers and acquisitions in Latvia is the Competition Council. The Competition Council was established in 1998, replacing the former state antitrust authority. The Council is a state institution which is financed from the state budget. The Council is composed of five members who are appointed by the Cabinet of Ministers on the nomination of the Minister of Economics for a five-year period. Its chairman, who is also appointed to the position by the Cabinet of Ministers for a five-year period, guides the work of the Council. The chairman is a member of the Council.

The powers of the Competition Council cover transactions involving private as well as public companies.

16.4　Merger control

Mergers in Latvia have been controlled since 1998 when the first Competition Law came into force. Since 1 January 2002 a new, amended and updated law has been in effect. The Competition Law has been amended twice, first, on 1 May 2004 and more recently on 16 April 2008. The latest amendments have, among other things, revised the merger notification thresholds and the notification procedure, as well as providing for a new definition of a dominant position. The Latvian Competition Law, particularly in the area of merger control, largely follows the same principles as the provisions of EU Competition Law.

16.4.1　Thresholds for mandatory notification

As defined by the Latvian Competition Law, a merger is performed if one of the following occurs:

(a)　two (or several) independent undertakings merge for the purpose of becoming a single undertaking (concentration);
(b)　acquisition of an undertaking by another undertaking (accession);
(c)　circumstances where one or several market participants acquire all or any part of the assets of another market participant/participants or the right to use such assets or any portion thereof, or direct or indirect decisive influence (control) over another market participant/participants (acquisition of control);
(d)　circumstances when two or more natural persons together, or a natural person simultaneously, acquires all or any part of the assets, of two or several market participants or the rights to use them, or acquire decisive influence (control) over two or several market participants.

Pursuant to the latest wording of the Competition Law, market participants who desire to merge in the manner described above must submit a notification to the Competition Council if the total turnover of merger participants in the last financial year in the territory of Latvia has exceeded LVL25 million.

Where the above threshold is not met, mergers do not require any notification or filing in Latvia. Due to their lack of significant effect on competition (*de minimis* rule), they do not fall under any merger control in Latvia.

The total turnover of any party to the merger is calculated as the aggregate income derived from products sold or services provided by that party's business activities in the relevant market during the last year less sales discounts, value added tax and other taxes directly related to the turnover. Turnover must be stated by the merging parties based on the annual accounts for the previous financial year. The calculation of total turnover does not include transactions among the immediate parties to the merger and their affiliated companies. However, the aggregate turnover of all affiliates is considered when determining the total turnover of the merging parties. For such purposes, affiliates are defined as either:

(a) companies over which the parties to the merger have a decisive influence, as defined by the Law;

(b) companies that have decisive influence on the immediate parties to the merger; or

(c) companies that have joint decisive influence.

In accordance with the current wording of the Competition Law, the total turnover of the undertakings is calculated within the Latvian jurisdiction. However, if any of the merging parties are not registered in Latvia, also included in the calculation is the amount of overseas sales of the particular foreign company (its branch, affiliate, etc.) which directly sells products or provides services in Latvia.

The notification is mandatory if the notification threshold described above is met. However, there is no mandatory waiting period enforced by the Competition Council with regard to mergers. Parties to a merger have the practical right to elect whether they will submit a merger notification, exercising their own judgment as to whether the threshold requiring merger notification is applicable in the particular circumstances. However, the Competition Council has the right to initiate its own review of a merger at any time notwithstanding the failure by the market participants to submit a merger notification.

Pre-notification contacts such as correspondence or meetings with the Competition Council are advisable in circumstances where the parties have doubts about whether the merger must be notified under the Latvian Competition Law.

16.4.2 *Procedure*

The Cabinet of Ministers has adopted the Regulations on Procedure of Submission and Review of Merger Notifications of Market Participants ("the Regulations"). According to the latest amendments to the Competition Law, these Regulations shall be replaced by new Regulations by 1 October 2008. According to the Regulations in force at the time of writing, the merger notification must be submitted by the market participants directly involved in a merger, or by the acquirer in the case of acquisition of control.

The amendments to the Competition Law provide for the possibility to file a short-form notification (as an alternative to a full-form notification) where either of the following is satisfied:

(1) the parties to the concentration are not present in the same or vertically related relevant markets;

(2) the combined market share of the parties to the concentration does not exceed 15 per cent in a relevant market.

However, since at the time of writing new Regulations have not been enacted and the current Regulations on the Procedure for Submission and Review of Merger Notifications of the Market Participants only cover the information and documents to be submitted to the Competition Council in a full-form notification, it will not be possible to file a short-form notification until the new Regulations are enacted.

In order to examine a proposed concentration, the Latvian Competition Law provides for a two-phase procedure.

16.4.2.1 First phase

After receipt of notification the Competition Council evaluates whether the notification and information contained therein is complete.

In accordance with the Regulations, if the information contained in the notification is not complete then the Competition Council informs the applicant to that effect and states the terms within which the full information must be submitted. Incorrect or misleading information is deemed to be incomplete information.

After receipt of a complete notification (whether full-form or short-form), within one month the Competition Council will adopt one of the following decisions:

(a)   to prohibit the merger;
(b)   to permit the merger on certain conditions;
(c)   to permit the merger; or
(d)   to commence in-depth investigation.

16.4.2.2 Second phase

If the Competition Council has decided to commence an in-depth investigation, its final decision shall be adopted within four months from the date of submission of the complete full-form notification or within three months from the date of submission of the complete short-form notification. If within four months after receipt of a complete notification (or within three months if a short-form notification has been submitted) the Competition Council has not adopted a decision on permission, prohibition or permission with conditions, then the relevant merger is deemed to be permitted.

The Competition Law does not provide for any circumstances in which the Competition Council is to carry out an expedited review of a merger notification in a period shorter than those described above.

According to the current Regulations, the (full-form) merger notification should contain:

(a)   a description of the parties participating in the merger;
(b)   an overview of the legal and financial aspects of the merger;
(c)   a description of the specific markets which may be affected as a result of the merger; and
(d)   the statement of purpose for the planned merger transaction.

The Council recommends that the following supplementary information is included in the merger notification:

(a) the purpose of the merger agreement;
(b) specific provisions contained in the agreement which may prohibit, limit or distort competition;
(c) any adverse consequences which may affect competition; and
(d) the positive effects arising from the merger.

In accordance with the Regulations, information regarding specific markets should also be included in the merger notification. This should state:

(a) the relevant product markets in respect of which the merger analysis should be based;
(b) related enterprises which operate in each such market or operate in the markets that are closely related to the market;
(c) the market share of each party to the merger; and
(d) the five main competitors of the parties to the merger agreement, their market share and five main clients in those specific markets in which the total market share of all parties to the merger exceeds 15 per cent.

The notification should describe any provisions of the agreement which limit the rights of the parties to the agreement to independently adopt commercial decisions relating, for example, to the following:

(a) sale or purchase prices, discounts or other commercial provisions;
(b) quantity of goods manufactured or sold, or amount of services offered;
(c) technical development or investments;
(d) choice of markets or supply sources;
(e) transactions with third parties; or
(f) application of identical or different conditions to the supply of goods or rendering of services, or simultaneous offering of identical or different services.

Any change of information which is known or which ought to be known to the applicants in connection with the merger notification should be forwarded to the Council without delay. There may be cases when certain essential data or indices are not known to the applicant when the notification is prepared, but it is possible to clarify such information. This must be indicated in the notification by stating the specific date when the information will be submitted to the Council. If the persons submitting the notification do not have certain details, the source of acquisition of such information must be stated.

The Latvian Competition Law mandates the responsibility of officials and employees of the Competition Council to observe confidentiality, and the Law further provides for compensation of damages to the market participants caused as a result of any unlawful acts of Competition Council officials and employees.

The Council officials have the following rights during the review process:

(a) to examine documents and other records relating to the party's business activities;
(b) to obtain copies of, and excerpts from, documents and other records relating to the party's performance;
(c) to request written or oral comments from the executive officials and other employees of the merging parties; and
(d) to perform other investigative activities.

The objective of the provisions on merger control in the Competition Law is to ensure competition in the Latvian economy by preventing the creation or strengthening of a dominant position or the reduction of competition in any relevant market. The Competition Council prohibits mergers as a result of which a dominant position is created or strengthened or where competition in any relevant market may be reduced considerably.

Each notification submitted by the parties to a merger is evaluated by the Competition Council, taking into account a range of factors such as the following:

(a)　the necessity to maintain and develop competition within the Latvian market, the analysis of the specific market structure, as well as the present or potential competition caused by Latvian or foreign parties;

(b)　the economic and financial position of the parties involved in the merger process, the availability of alternative markets to suppliers and consumers, the administrative or other barriers hindering entry to the specific market, trends of demand for and supply of the specific products, interests of intermediaries and consumers, development of technical and economic progress and possible obstacles to competition;

(c)　the position of the parties to the merger in the international market and the export potential of their products; and

(d)　the potential benefit for consumers and Latvian society in general.

Cases where, after the merger, the market participant will be subject to joint decisive influence (establishment of joint venture) and the consequence or purpose of creation of such market participant subject to joint decisive influence (joint venture) is or could be coordination of activities of the market participants, are evaluated by the Competition Council based on the provisions on prohibited agreements.

When reviewing cases of establishment of joint ventures, the Competition Council specifically considers:

(a)　whether the market participants acquiring joint decisive influence are engaged in significant business activity in the same market where the joint venture operates or will operate as well as the markets related to this market;

(b)　whether coordination of competing activity which could be a direct result of creation of a market participant subject to joint decisive influence will provide an opportunity to liquidate competition in a considerable part of the relevant market.

The principles developed with regard to the European merger control are usually applied by the Competition Council when investigating mergers.

16.4.3　Appeals

Parties to a merger may appeal a decision of the Council to the Administrative Regional Court according to the laws of administrative procedure within one month of the Competition Council decision coming into force. There is no appeal process at the Council following a final decision.

16.4.4   Sanctions

A merger that has taken place without a merger notification having been submitted, and which is at any time discovered to have been subject to the requirement of notification pursuant to the Competition Law, is illegal. In accordance with the Competition Law, failure to submit a merger notification, or consummation of a merger contrary to any decision of the Competition Council, may result in a penalty of up to LVL1,000 per day and retroactive to the date by which notification should have been made. The penalty shall be assessed against the new market participant or against the market participant (it might be a natural person) which acquired control in another market participant, as the case may be. Payment of the penalty does not excuse the market participant from the obligation to fulfil the provisions of the Competition Law and the decisions of the Competition Council.

16.5   Exchange and investment controls

16.5.1   Exchange controls

There are no restrictions in Latvia on the convertibility of cash and there are no ceilings in respect of the amount which can be converted. Profits can be repatriated provided that all relevant taxes, claims of creditors and withholding taxes, where applicable, have been paid.

With regard to the securities market, the Riga Stock Exchange is the only regulated secondary securities market in Latvia which brings together investors who have spare funds, the companies which need to raise capital, and Stock Exchange members acting as intermediaries. Only licensed Riga Stock Exchange members – banks and brokerage companies – may trade on the Riga Stock Exchange. Nevertheless, there is an opportunity for a Member State bank or investment company to provide services in Latvia by way of freedom to provide services.

16.5.2   Controls on investments

Foreign investments in Latvia are controlled mainly in the financial services sector. When entering the Latvian financial market, prior consent from the corresponding state authority – the Financial and Capital Market Commission – is required for banks, insurance companies and other financial companies established for the purpose of granting credits and other financial services.

16.5.3   Disclosure of significant shareholdings

The principle of disclosure and transparency of significant shareholdings has been introduced in the main legal Acts regulating performance of financial and public companies.

According to the Law on Financial Instruments Market, an investor who acquires ownership of shares put into public circulation (regulated market) in such an amount that it provides the investor with at least 5, 10, 15, 20, 25, 30, 50 or 75 per cent of all votes of the meeting of shareholders, shall notify the Financial and Capital Market Commission and the corresponding company about that fact within five working days of the acquisition of the shares. The company shall without delay, but not later than one working day from the date on which it received the notification, make the relevant information publicly available in the central storage of regulated information (i.e., the database of public traded financial instruments in the regulated market in the Republic of Latvia) and each Member State in the regulated markets of which the stocks of this stock company are included, in such a way that provides an opportunity for all stockholders to become acquainted with this information. Moreover, the market organiser shall without delay place the information on the home page of their website.

If the investor fails to notify the company in the above-stipulated acquisition cases, he is not entitled to use the voting rights arising from direct or indirect ownership of shares. Resolutions of the general meeting of shareholders which are adopted by means of unlawful use of voting rights are not valid.

With regard to insurance companies and credit institutions, the Laws on Credit Institutions and on Insurance Companies and their Supervision provide that if the investor (either an individual or legal person) wishes to acquire directly or indirectly 10 per cent or more of the share capital or shares with voting rights, it must receive the prior consent of the Financial and Capital Market Commission.

16.6   Labour law considerations

According to the Labour Law which came into effect on 1 June 2002 (as amended), employee representatives (who are either elected from the amongst the employees or the labour union) while performing their duties have a right to receive information and consult with the employer before the employer makes decisions which may affect the interests of employees. This applies particularly to decisions that may substantially affect work remuneration, working conditions and employment in the undertaking. Within the meaning of this Law, consultation is the exchange of views and dialogue between employee representatives and the employer. With regard to mergers, acquisitions or concentrations of companies, both the transferor of an undertaking and the acquirer of an undertaking have a duty to inform their employee representatives (or if such do not exist, their employees) regarding:

(a)   the date of transfer of the undertaking or the expected date of transfer;
(b)   the reasons for the transfer of the undertaking;
(c)   the legal, economic and social consequences of the transfer; and
(d)   the measures which will be taken with respect to employees.

The transferor of an undertaking shall perform this duty not later than one month before the transfer of the undertaking. The acquirer of an undertaking must perform the duty not later than one month before the transfer of the undertaking starts to directly affect the working conditions and employment provisions of his employees. The transferor or the acquirer of an undertaking, who in connection with the transfer intends to take organisational, technological or social measures with respect to employees, has a duty (not later than three weeks in advance) to commence consultations with his employee representatives in order to reach agreement on such measures and their procedures. The above provisions will apply irrespective of whether the decision on the transfer of an undertaking is made by the employer or the employer as a dominant undertaking of a dependant company. An objection that the failure to fulfil the duty of information and consultations is related to the fact that the dominant undertaking has not provided the necessary information is not permitted.

16.7   Methods of acquisition

16.7.1   *Mandatory public bids*

It is mandatory that an offer, addressed to other shareholders in a company included in the regulated market, to redeem the shares belonging to them be expressed by a person who:

(a)   directly or indirectly acquires the voting rights arising from the shares in such an amount that the voting rights of such person at the meeting of shareholders comprises or exceeds half of the total number of votes; and

(b)   at the meeting of shareholders has voted in favour of the matter regarding the exclusion of the shares from a regulated market. Such a vote may not be a closed vote.

A person may not exercise any voting rights arising from the shares belonging to them or any indirectly acquired voting rights, if such person:

(a)   within the time periods and in accordance with the procedures specified in the Law on Financial Instruments Market fails to express the compulsory offer to redeem the shares;

(b)   expresses an offer to redeem the shares which does not comply with the requirements of the Law; and

(c)   in accordance with the procedures specified by the Law has not operated accounts with the investors who have accepted the offer to redeem the shares.

Decisions of the meeting of shareholders which have been made through the exercise of voting rights contrary to the above provisions shall be void, and no entries in any type of public register may be requested on the basis of such decisions.

16.7.2   *Voluntary public bids*

A person is entitled to express a voluntary share redemption offer if the purpose thereof is to obtain shares in an amount which ensures not less than 10 per cent of the number of voting rights in a company. Such person expressing a voluntary offer to redeem shares shall set the minimum or maximum number of shares that it is offering to redeem.

Chapter 17

Lithuania

Dovilė Burgienė

Partner
Lideika, Petrauskas, Valiūnas ir partneriai LAWIN

17.1   Introduction

After regaining its independence in 1990, Lithuania needed to reform its economy and adjust it to the market conditions. This required enormous effort in creating the necessary legal rules. The Lithuanian legal system developed gradually, starting with the basic provision of the laws allowing establishment of companies, setting up of the securities market, creating competition law and reforming the major codified areas of law such as civil, labour, administrative and criminal law.

Another significant event was the country's accession to the EU in 2004. Until that time all existing rules had to be adjusted to the EU law (*acquis communautaire*). The current legal measures relating to European Community law include implementation of the Takeover Bids Directive and the Markets in Financial Instruments Directive ("MiFID"), enforcement of national regulations necessary for the establishment and operation of European companies (*Societas Europeae*), while the implementation of the Cross-border Mergers and Amendments to the Capital Maintenance Directives is in progress. Recent trends also include the introduction in 2006 of the Corporate Governance Code of the Vilnius Stock Exchange which includes the "comply or explain" principle.

In Lithuania, private companies are more common and because of that they are often the target of M&A activity. There are around 40 companies listing shares on the Vilnius Stock Exchange. Recent years showed both several delistings and new IPOs which means that there has been little change to the number of listed companies. Also the Vilnius Stock Exchange gained attention due to the merger of its operator, OMX, with the NASDAQ. This may raise liquidity in the market and attract more foreign investors. Further trends may include falling ownership concentration in companies because of increasing activity of investment, including private equity. Companies are further encouraged to search for equity investors due to rising costs of debt capital. If this process continues, the takeover market may change and become more sophisticated in the future. For the companies that are still not eligible for listing on the lists of the regulated market, OMX offers an alternative non-regulated market, First North, where trading is organised with a less complicated set of rules within the framework of a multilateral trading facility.

It is important to note that in the past many acquisitions occurred as a result of the privatisation process of the state- and municipally-owned assets. However, the privatisation process is practically over and private M&A transactions are becoming more important due to the growth of the Lithuanian economy. The M&A market has been increasingly active over the past few years. As it was mostly a sellers' market, a growing number of auctions were organised.

17.2   Acquisition targets

Lithuanian companies that participate in takeovers or mergers may be classified under two different categories:

(a)   public companies;
(b)   private companies.

Also there is a certain amount of interest in agricultural companies by investors seeking to indirectly acquire agricultural land either to create larger agricultural businesses or to change the use of the land and to develop greenfield projects. Certain rules described in this Chapter (e.g., competition law requirements) apply to public and private companies as well as to other types of enterprise such as personal enterprises or partnerships. However, this Chapter focuses on the regulation of stock companies participating in takeovers and mergers, since those entities are the most common types of business entities and thus the most frequent participants in such transactions.

17.2.1   *Public companies*

Public companies which are the issuers[1] are more heavily regulated than private companies or public companies which are not the issuers. Additional regulations apply to the public companies that are listed on the Vilnius Stock Exchange of Lithuania.

17.2.2   *Private companies*

Most Lithuanian companies are privately owned and do not qualify as public companies. In many instances, even in the case of listed public companies, only a very small proportion of shares is traded on the Stock Exchange. Acquisitions of private companies and certain public companies are therefore subject to the agreement of the controlling shareholders who, in most cases, run the business (unless it is a subsidiary of another Lithuanian or foreign company). It is

---

[1] Under the Law on Securities a legal person incorporated in the Republic of Lithuania is considered an issuer:
   (a)   where its securities have been admitted to trading on a regulated market in an EU/EEA Member State;
   (b)   where a prospectus of the securities issued after 12 July 2005 has been approved by the Securities Commission and the securities issued on the basis thereof have been publicly offered or admitted to trading on a regulated market; or
   (c)   where its securities are offered publicly.

therefore important to consider the issue of the post-acquisition future of the management team, as that team often holds the shares or is closely linked to the shareholders.

17.3 Exchange and investment controls

17.3.1 Exchange controls

According to the Law on Reliability of Litas, the official currency of Lithuania has been pegged to the euro since 1 February 2002. The official exchange rate is LTL3.4528 = €1. Foreign investments in Lithuania may be made in litas as well as in foreign currencies. However, accounting of Lithuanian companies must be done in litas. Payments within Lithuania are generally required by law to be carried out in litas (Law on Foreign Currency in the Republic of Lithuania). However, foreign currency may be used for non-cash payments and settlements upon the agreement of the parties, while euros may also be used for cash payments (upon agreement of the parties).

17.3.2 Controls on investments

As a rule, foreign investment is encouraged in Lithuania. The Law on Investments provides a list of areas where foreign investment is not allowed. Those areas include state defence and security (except when such investment originates from the EU, NATO or OECD countries and is approved by the State Defence Council). Investments in certain industries (such as the financial sector, activities employing potentially dangerous equipment, etc.) may require prior approval by the supervisory authority and/or the obtaining of a licence. Such requirements bind both local and foreign-owned entities. Incorporation of a company or acquisition of shares in a local company by a foreign entity is considered an investment for the purposes of Lithuanian law. Foreign investments are granted additional protection by virtue of bilateral or multilateral treaties executed between Lithuania and other countries (e.g., 18 March 1965 Washington Convention on the Settlement of Investment Disputes between States and Nationals of Other States). Since EU accession, investments from EU Member States have benefited from the EU freedom of establishment, free movement of capital and other protection granted by EU law.

17.3.3 Disclosure of significant shareholdings

The Law on Securities imposes a requirement to disclose shareholdings that grant five, 10, 15, 20, 25, 30, 50, 75 or 95 per cent of all votes in the issuer's[2] shareholders meeting. The notification is to be made upon reaching the respective threshold in the case of an increase or decrease of the shareholding in the issuer's company. The aggregate shareholdings of several related persons are also subject to such notification requirements. Related persons are controlled persons, persons with whom agreements on coordinated voting or transfer of voting

---

[2] *See* footnote 1.

rights are concluded, spouses or proxy holders of those persons, and others defined in the law. Any acquisition or sale that reaches the above-mentioned threshold triggers the obligation to disclose, whether the shares are acquired directly or indirectly. Acquisition of securities exchangeable to shares of the issuer must be notified in the same manner. The latter requirement of the Law on Securities firstly relates to the holders of type of convertible bonds or futures; however, in practice it is sometimes interpreted widely as also requiring the disclosure of contractual call/put option rights which raise uncertainties.

The notification must be given to the Securities Commission and the target company in the pre-approved form not later than four trading days after the person becomes or should have become aware that the threshold has been reached (the person is considered to be aware that the threshold has been reached not later than two trading days after the transaction).

The consequences of failure to notify are significant. A person who has failed to submit the required notification in due time will, for two years, be deprived of all votes which he acquired in addition to the percentage of votes which he duly notified. Furthermore, before the due notification of acquisition of the respective percentage of votes, an acquiring person should not attempt to replace the managers of the target company or adopt decisions which could violate rights of other shareholders. Such decisions, if adopted prior to notification, may be declared invalid.

17.3.4   Acquiring control over a public company

Any person intending to acquire control of a public company employing the public offer procedure must follow the rules established by the Securities Commission. The procedure regarding public offers (both voluntary and mandatory) is described at 17.8 below.

17.3.5   Labour law considerations

Investors are strongly advised to analyse labour relations in the target company. Complicated and expensive procedures for dismissing employees, collective agreement benefits, lifetime compensations for labour accidents and other financial liabilities that the company may have in respect of employees may all increase the expected business costs considerably. Pension schemes should not worry the purchaser of a target company since internal pension schemes are not widely used in Lithuania due to the fact that, traditionally, the social protection system was state owned. Since 2004, however, more private pension funds were set up as the necessary legislation was enacted. However, the system does not involve internal company pension funds or obligations to make additional contributions by the employer other than statutory payments made to State Social Security. Nor is it common to include such clauses in the collective or individual employment agreements, although theoretically this is possible through various schemes such as life insurance schemes. Another important issue concerns the retention of key employees, since if they leave to work for competitors this may devalue the business purchased.

Generally, labour law requirements in the event of an M&A transaction are in line with EC Council Directive of 12 March 2001 on the Approximation of the Laws of the Member States Relating to Safeguarding of Employees' Rights in the Event of Transfers of Undertakings, Businesses or Parts of Business (2001/23/EC). The degree to which employees' rights are protected when a business is purchased needs to be discussed according to the method by which the purchase takes place.

(a)   Article 138 of the Labour Code states that changes of the owner of a company, the subordination, founder or name thereof, any merger by forming a new company, or division by forming a new company, division by acquisition, or merger by acquisition may not be a legitimate reason to terminate employment relations. Evidently, in the case of acquisition of a target company's shares, as well as in the case of merger, division, realignment or change of the company type, the employer remains unchanged even though there have been certain alterations within the company as an employer. In all these cases, labour law guarantees are to remain in force to their full extent with respect to employees of the company. This includes the validity of employment contracts, the applicability of a collective agreement on the same terms, the company's financial obligations against employees, etc. Thus, a takeover does not in itself constitute grounds for dismissal of employees unless subsequent changes in work organisation of the company (i.e., structural changes) necessitate a reduction in the number of employees. Moreover, in this case employees have the right to information and consultation on issues relating to the current and future activities of the company and its economic and financial condition, current state and structure of labour relations, and potential changes in employment and other matters.

(b)   Business acquisition as an assets purchase transaction (*see* 17.6.6 below) does not explicitly fall under the scope of Article 138 of the Labour Code. However, the case law of the Supreme Court of Lithuania fills this gap in the law to a certain extent. The Court held that the assignment of part of the functions of a company to a new legal entity, together with the property required for fulfilment of the functions of the enterprise, may be considered a change of ownership of part of the property of the enterprise and equals a reorganisation of the company according to the meaning of labour law, thus making the interpretation of the Lithuanian Labour Code resemble the provisions of the Directive.

Most privatisation transactions (*see* 17.6.7 below) for big Lithuanian companies provide for additional employment guarantees. The privatisation laws require, and respective agreements signed at privatisation usually stipulate, that an investor is obliged to maintain a certain number (percentage) of jobs in a privatised company for a specified period of time. Such companies frequently have an excessive number of employees, and investors are well advised to explore the said restrictions on staff reduction.

In conclusion, legal investigation of the employment sphere prior to investing is recommended in most cases. Business takeovers take place in several different ways, and this may have decisive implications for employment relations.

17.4   Concentration control

Lithuanian competition law has emerged as a new area of law since 1992 when the first Law on Competition ("the Competition Law") was adopted on 15 September 1992. The major amendments were introduced in 1999 and 2004. They addressed, among other things, the area of concentration control. Lithuanian competition rules are based on the same principles as the European Community competition law.

Lithuanian competition rules are applicable to "undertakings", defined as enterprises, their formations (associations, amalgamations, consortiums, etc.), institutions or organisations or any other legal or natural persons who perform or may perform economic activities in Lithuania, or whose actions affect, or whose intentions, if they were realised, could affect economic activity in Lithuania. They also apply to the activities of undertakings registered beyond the territory of Lithuania if such activities restrict competition in the domestic market of Lithuania. By virtue of operation of Articles 81 and 82 of the EC Treaty, those anti-competitive practices which affect competition in Lithuania but also have an effect on trade between Lithuania and any other Member State of the European Union shall be assessed in the light of EU competition law.

17.4.1   Thresholds for mandatory notification

The Competition Law sets out a mandatory merger notification process, applying only to concentrations meeting both of the following thresholds:

(a)   the combined aggregate turnover of the undertakings concerned was more than LTL30 million (approximately €8.7 million) in the last financial year prior to concentration; and

(b)   the aggregate turnover of each of at least two undertakings concerned was more than LTL5 million (approximately €1.5 million) in the financial year prior to concentration.

If a participant of concentration is an undertaking of a foreign country, its aggregate turnover is calculated as the sum of income received from the sale of its products in the Lithuanian market.

Under the Competition Law, concentration is deemed to have arisen in case of:

(a)   the merger when one or more undertakings, which terminate their activity as independent undertakings, are joined to the undertaking that continues its operations, or when a new undertaking is established from two or more undertakings that terminate their activity as independent undertakings; or

(b)   the acquisition of control, when the same natural person or persons that exercise control over one or more undertakings, or an undertaking or several undertakings, acting on the basis of an agreement, jointly create a new undertaking or gain control over another undertaking by acquiring an enterprise or a part thereof, or all or a part of the assets of an undertaking, or shares or other securities, voting rights, or by concluding contracts, or in any other manner.

17.4.2 Procedure

Concentrations falling within the scope of the Competition Law are subject to the prior consent of the Competition Council which determines whether or not they may proceed. The Competition Council is a body consisting of five members (including the chairman) appointed by the President of Lithuania upon recommendation of the Prime Minister of Lithuania, and it is responsible for implementation of the Competition Law.

In evaluating notified concentrations, the Competition Council has to decide whether the concentration creates or strengthens a dominant position or substantially restricts competition in a relevant market. The relevant market is determined as a particular product market in a certain geographic territory which may cover the whole or part of Lithuania. The Competition Law establishes the extraterritorial application of Lithuanian competition rules to the activities of undertakings registered beyond the territory of Lithuania if such activities restrict competition in the domestic market of Lithuania.

Concentrations meeting both of the thresholds indicated above must be notified to the Competition Council through its administration. Notification must be submitted in the form approved by the Competition Council prior to the implementation of the concentration. The notification shall be made after:

(a) the submission of the proposal to conclude the agreement, or to acquire the shares or assets;
(b) an instruction to conclude an agreement;
(c) conclusion of the agreement;
(d) acquisition of the right of ownership or the right to dispose of certain assets.

The undertakings or controlling persons participating in the concentration which is subject to notification have no right to implement concentration until the resolution of the Competition Council is passed. Any transactions and actions of the undertakings and controlling persons performed prior to receiving permission for concentration are considered to be invalid, with no legal force and effect. However, upon justified request of the undertaking participating in the concentration or of the controlling person, the Competition Council, taking into account the consequences of the suspension of concentration on the persons concerned and the projected influence of the concentration on competition, may permit the exercise of individual actions of concentration. The permission of the Competition Council to implement individual actions of concentration may be issued subject to certain conditions and obligations necessary to ensure effective competition.

When the concentration is a merger, all the parties involved must make the notification jointly. When the concentration is the acquisition of control, the acquiring party must make the notification on its own. The notification package includes a large number of documents and involves to a great deal of paperwork. It is advisable to start gathering the necessary information ahead of time.

Having received notification of concentration, the Competition Council publishes a notice in *Valstybes zinios* (the Lithuanian *Official Gazette*), indicating the nature of concentration and identifying the parties concerned.

The Competition Council must examine the notification of concentration within four months of receipt of notification conforming to the established requirements. The Competition Council immediately notifies the parties in writing if the notification of concentration does not comply with the established requirements, and may request additional information.

The Competition Law establishes two phases of examination of the concentration. The initial examination period may not last more than one month. Thus, within one month of receipt of a proper notification of concentration, the Competition Council either permits the concentration (unconditionally or subject to certain commitments) or adopts a decision for further examination of the concentration. Such further examination may last up to three additional months. However, the Competition Council, intending to pass a decision on conditional permission of concentration, upon a duly grounded request of the person notifying the concentration may extend the initial examination period of the concentration by one month.

The persons having submitted the notification are informed in writing of any decisions of the Competition Council. If, after the date of receipt of a proper notification, the Competition Council does not issue a decision, or if the persons having provided such notification are not informed of the decision within four months after the date of receipt of a proper notification by the Competition Council, the undertakings or controlling persons have the right to exercise the concentration according to the conditions indicated in their notification.

Moreover, the Competition Council may obligate the undertakings to submit *ex post* notifications on concentration and *mutatis mutandis* apply the concentration control procedure, even though the mentioned thresholds are not exceeded, where it becomes probable that concentration will result in the creation or strengthening of the dominant position, or a significant restriction of competition in the relevant market. The Competition Council may pass an individual decision to apply the concentration control procedure only in cases where no more than 12 months have passed from the implementation of concentration in question. Recent practice of the Competition Council shows that entities, knowing that *ex post* control is likely to be applied to them, may voluntarily notify and have clear their intended concentration *ex ante*.

The Competition Council examines the notifications in its hearings based on the written material presented to it. The parties to the concentration may also argue their case orally. In cases of lack of information, the Competition Council may decide to request additional information from the parties concerned as well as from state institutions possessing useful information.

Having completed examination of a notification, the Competition Council will make one of the following decisions:

(a)   to permit concentration as described in the notification;
(b)   to permit concentration by establishing conditions and commitments for the undertakings or controlling persons participating in the concentration in order to prevent the creation or strengthening of a dominant position; or

(c)   to refuse to grant permission to exercise concentration by imposing commitments on the undertakings or controlling persons concerned to undertake actions to restore the previous situation or remove the consequences of concentration in the time periods and under the conditions determined by the Competition Council (which commitments may include full or partial divestment obligations, obligations to sell the assets or part thereof, requirements to amend or terminate the contracts, etc.).

The decisions of the Competition Council are published in *Valstybes zinios*.

Finally, it must be noted that there are certain exceptions provided in the Competition Law when notification of concentration and the Competition Council's consent is not required. Those exceptions include:

(a)   the acquisition of securities by financial institutions for a period not exceeding 12 months with the aim of transferring them, provided that voting rights granted by those shares are not used and that information on acquisition is given to the Competition Council;

(b)   taking over control of undertakings that are under bankruptcy proceedings by the state institutions;

(c)   acquisitions within the groups of companies;

(d)   acquisition by an undertaking, that has obtained consent from the Competition Council, of more shares of the target company than the number of shares notified, provided that acquisition of such increased number of shares does not confer more control rights of the target company than the number of shares notified.

17.4.3   Appeals

Decisions adopted by the Competition Council may be appealed against to the Vilnius District Administrative Court. An appeal may be lodged by the companies involved in the concentration or by other plaintiffs. The appeal must be brought within 20 days of the publication of the Competition Council's decision in *Valstybes zinios* or from the date of notification to the parties concerned. The Court may decide whether the implementation of the Competition Council decision should be suspended.

17.4.4   Investigation and sanctions

The Competition Council may, upon its own initiative or upon the initiative of the parties concerned, state institutions or non-governmental organisations, commence investigations on concentrations that:

(a)   have not been notified;

(b)   have been notified but made without obtaining the Competition Council's approval;

(c)   are carried out not in accordance with the conditions and commitments imposed; and

(d)   are carried out without regard to the temporary suspension.

The time periods and procedures of investigation are established in Competition Law. As a result of investigation, the decision is made by the Competition

Council in a hearing where all parties concerned have a right to be heard. If the existence of infringements of the Competition Law is established, the Competition Council may decide to apply sanctions. Those sanctions include fines on companies which can be up to 10 per cent of their annual turnover. In addition, it can impose daily lump-sum damages in the case of non-compliance with its decisions and failure to fulfil certain commitments within the fixed time periods. There are also fines for procedural infringements, including in the case of late notification or presenting of incomplete information.

17.4.5   *EU merger control*

The following concentrations are deemed to have a Community dimension and are subject to notification to the European Commission.

(a)   Where:
    (i)   the aggregate worldwide turnover of the parties exceeds €5 billion; and
    (ii)   the Community-wide turnover of each of at least two parties exceeds €250 million; unless
    (iii)   each of the parties achieves more than two-thirds of its aggregate Community-wide turnover in one and the same Member State.

(b)   Where:
    (i)   the aggregate worldwide turnover of the parties exceeds €2.5 billion; and
    (ii)   the Community-wide turnover of each of at least two parties exceeds €100 million; and
    (iii)   in each of at least three Member States, the aggregate turnover of all the parties exceeds €100 million; and
    (iv)   in each of at least three of the above-mentioned Member States, the turnover of each of at least two parties exceeds €25 million; unless
    (v)   each of the parties achieves more than two-thirds of its aggregate Community-wide turnover in one and the same Member State.

(c)   With regard to concentrations which do not fall under (a) and (b) above, and which are capable of being reviewed under the national competition laws of at least three Member States, the concentrations, before any notification to the competent authorities, may be informed to the Commission by means of a reasoned submission that the concentration should be examined by the Commission.

Following the "one-stop shop" principle, such concentrations need not be notified to any national competition authority.

17.5   Regulation of the conduct of mergers and acquisitions of public companies

Regulation of the conduct of mergers and acquisitions in Lithuania was created gradually, starting with the enactment of the first Company Law in 1990 and the creation of the securities market. The need for a securities market arose as a result of the initial wave of privatisation which created a vast number of individual owners of mostly small shareholdings in privatised state enterprises which were reorganised to public companies. The Government adopted resolutions establishing the underlying concepts and fundamental principles of Lithuanian securities regulation. In 1992, the Government provided for the establishment of the National Stock Exchange of Lithuania (now called the Vilnius Stock Exchange) and created the Securities Commission, which acts as a supervisory authority over the Lithuanian securities market. The legal and structural form of the Central Securities Depository was also established, laying out its operational procedures and main functions, as well as accounting principles of securities and their trade and circulation.

The Stock Exchange is already fully privatised and the Central Securities Depository is jointly owned by the private shareholder and the state.

The Securities Commission is Lithuania's main regulatory authority for the capital markets, including the regulation of public offers. The Securities Commission is composed of five members (including the chairman) appointed by the *Seimas* upon the recommendation of the President of Lithuania. The powers of the Securities Commission are, however, limited to mergers and acquisitions of public companies which are issuers.[3] Mergers and acquisitions of privately owned companies and public companies which are non-issuers fall outside the scope of its competence.

17.6   Methods of acquisition

There are several methods of acquisition commonly used in Lithuania, and these are described below. It is important to note that a great number of the acquisitions occurred during the privatisation process of the state- and municipally-owned assets. However, the privatisation process is coming to an end and private M&A transactions are becoming more important. As well as describing the acquisition methods, the peculiarities of the privatisation process are also addressed below.

17.6.1   *Private agreements*

Some major acquisition agreements used in Lithuania are either governed by or their content is strongly influenced by foreign law. This is because Lithuanian companies are often targeted for acquisition by foreign companies. In other cases (smaller acquisitions, local transactions, transactions involving a strong local player) agreements for acquisitions by foreign companies are governed by Lithuanian law. The agreements commonly used even by local entities acquiring shares in Lithuanian companies are governed by Lithuanian law and have become more sophisticated than before, in most cases based on the same principles as the major acquisitions. Lithuania is a civil law country. Therefore, in drafting the agreements lawyers often rely on the regulation by law and the

---

[3] *See* footnote 1.

statutory protection granted to parties. However, numerous legal provisions are rather new and in many cases judicial precedents have not been developed. Furthermore, recent developments of the case law show that parties to the share transaction may expect only very limited statutory protection, while many specific legal aspects of the asset deals have still not been developed. Therefore, it is advisable to define the clauses clearly, especially those that cover obligations of the parties, representations and warranties, and liability clauses, in order to avoid conflicts in the future. The agreements are becoming longer and more sophisticated as business people gain experience in M&As.

The representations and warranties usually contained in a share purchase agreement governed by Lithuanian law are quite extensive but not too detailed. Lithuanian law does not require the intervention of a notary public for the execution of a share purchase agreement. Intervention of a notary public is sometimes preferred in cases of acquisition agreements between private persons.

Lithuanian private international law rules do not make the application of Lithuanian law to a share purchase agreement mandatory. Use of the Lithuanian language, however, is mandatory in cases where one of the parties, the seller or the acquirer, is a Lithuanian entity and thus is subject to the Law on State Language. Use of foreign language in addition is allowed and such foreign language may prevail in the case of inadequacies, depending on which language the parties choose as governing the agreement.

The Lithuanian Civil Code does not specifically address the sale of shares. Certain specific provisions are contained in the Company Law, but they relate more to the formal requirements of share purchase agreements than to their content. The general rules of the Lithuanian Civil Code on sale of goods contracts, which are applicable to the share purchase agreements, provide for the following basic protections:

(a)   the goods subject to sale must be delivered by the seller to the purchaser, including transfer of the documents evidencing ownership right to the goods;

(b)   the seller must warrant peaceful possession (i.e., no claims by third parties relating to the shares, the shares are sold free of charges and encumbrances); and

(c)   the seller must provide the purchaser with a guarantee against hidden defects of the goods.

These principles do not offer much protection to the purchaser of shares. Moreover, even inclusion of such statements in the Civil Code does not deny that in case of a dispute, the court will apply the *caveat emptor* principle (stating that without a warranty the purchaser takes the risk as to the condition of the shares and the company). Though court practice is still scarce in this sphere, the tendency is that the statutory warranties cover the status of shares and not the status of assets, rights and liabilities of the target company. Therefore, it is advisable to provide more extensive representations and warranties as well as other obligations of the parties in the share purchase agreements. It seems that the purchaser of shares under the usual guarantees of the Civil Code can claim hardly anything from the seller even if the target company has serious undisclosed problems. For example, it may be indicated that a sample list of representations given by the state or municipality to the purchaser of shares covers:

(a)   a company's financial condition;
(b)   title to or right to use the property (assets);
(c)   loans granted by the company;
(d)   encumbrances created on a company's assets;
(e)   capitalisation;
(f)   financial liabilities;
(g)   off-balance sheet liabilities;
(h)   benefits granted to or liabilities towards employees;
(i)   claims and actions against the company;
(j)   licences and permits;
(k)   investments made by the company into other persons, etc.

Private share purchase agreements usually provide for the time limit during which claims can be made by virtue of a breach of a warranty. For claims in connection with tax and social security, the time limit usually corresponds with the expiry date of the statute of limitations. Claims in connection with environmental matters are also usually subject to a longer time limit. However, the time limits to claim for breach of warranty must be tailored carefully since Lithuanian laws do not allow the revision of terms of statute of limitations in a contract. Therefore the clause must be drafted so that it does not limit the statute of limitations, but establishes the period during which the claims can be made and breaches established. In addition, the contracts often contain the usual clauses on thresholds, *de minimis* and cap provisions. For example, the law limits the liability of the state for undisclosed liabilities of the sold companies in allowing the state institution charged with privatisation to enter into the share purchase agreements only under the following terms:

(a)   the time limit for claims related to undisclosed liabilities must be presented within one year of the date of the privatisation transaction; and
(b)   the amount of the claim must exceed 5 per cent of the purchase price or nominal value of the acquired shares, whichever is higher.

Again the cap clause must be drafted with due care so that all possible remedies are caught. For instance, where only the amount of liability for damage is capped, the seller may try to ask for a reduction in the purchase price (*actio quantum minoris*) which should be considered as a separate remedy from the right to damages and thus should be capped separately in the agreement.

The Lithuanian law, court practice or legal doctrine do not differentiate between "representations" and "warranties". Both terms are used interchangeably.

17.6.2   *Voluntary public offers*

Lithuanian legislation contains provisions regarding voluntary public offers on public companies. These provisions are explained at 17.8 below.

17.6.3   Mandatory public bids

Lithuanian legislation also contains provisions that trigger the mandatory launching of public offers for public companies issuers[4] in certain circumstances. These provisions are explained at 17.8.4 below.

17.6.4   Mergers and split ups

Mergers (by way of merger of several companies that are dissolved into one new company, or by way of merger of one or several companies that are dissolved into another company that continues its operations) and split ups (by way of split up into several new companies, or by way of split up into parts and merger of those parts into several existing companies) are regulated by the provisions of Civil Code and the Company Law. These regulations establish rather lengthy and burdensome procedural formalities. The most important procedural element of reorganisation is the publicity requirement (reorganisation must be notified several times in the media) and the rights of all creditors and shareholders to familiarise themselves with the documents prepared for reorganisation.

The Civil Code offers extensive protection to the shareholders and creditors of the companies undergoing reorganisation. Each creditor of the company being reorganised may either require early performance of the obligations owed by such company (and such obligations then become due) or additional guarantees of fulfilment of the obligations after reorganisation where the creditor is able to show that the reorganisation may encumber the fulfilment of the obligation. However, in practice the notion is rarely used as creditors such as banks usually rely on contractual safeguards, for example establishing a requirement for prior approval of the reorganisation scheme by the bank.

Any reorganisation is defined as "dissolution without liquidation". Therefore, reorganisation is carried out by a decision of the general meeting of shareholders which is required to be passed by a qualified majority (two-thirds) of the votes. During the reorganisation the companies must observe certain restrictions which do not allow deterioration of the company's value. In addition, certain reporting requirements must be followed by the reorganised company's managing bodies during the reorganisation. The boards of the companies being reorganised prepare the terms of reorganisation, indicating the structure, timetable and share exchange ratio, and providing other information about the reorganisation. The terms of reorganisation are evaluated by an independent auditor. The fact of preparation of terms of reorganisation must be publicly notified three times with 30 days intervals (but without individual notification to the creditors) or one time, however in combination with a separate written notification to all the creditors. The general meeting of shareholders must approve the terms of reorganisation not earlier than 30 days after the public notification. Shareholders and creditors have access to the terms of reorganisation. Certain simplified procedure applies in the case of merger of the wholly-owned subsidiaries into their parent companies.

---

[4] *See* footnote 1.

It is important to note that any failure to comply strictly with the procedural rules applicable to reorganisation may lead to a challenge of the validity of reorganisation in court. Such invalidity actions may be brought to the court up to six months after the cessation of activity of the reorganised company.

The Civil Code also provides for a transaction referred to as "acquisition of an enterprise". This transaction is understood as purchase of the enterprise as a complex of assets, rights and liabilities with all their ancillary elements. Since the respective provisions of the Civil Code are new to the Lithuanian legal system, the procedure is not often applied in practice. This procedure can be conveniently applied for acquisition of enterprises with unlimited liability (unlike companies discussed here) by companies or other persons, since the merger of unlimited liability enterprises into companies is not allowed. Following introduction of the "acquisition of an enterprise" transaction, there was legal uncertainty as to whether enterprises may be acquired through "asset deals" (*see* 17.6.6 below) as it is a much less burdensome alternative compared to reorganisation and the "acquisition of the enterprise" transaction. Practice shows that asset deals are very popular but they are carried out ensuring the protection of interested parties such as creditors and employees, to avoid illegality claims due to failure to apply the "acquisition of an enterprise" or reorganisation procedure.

17.6.5   *Joint ventures*

It is quite common for two or more parties to join forces to gain control over a company combining the required experience and finances necessary to qualify as potential purchasers or to sell a stake in a fully controlled company to exercise the joint control for the same purposes. Joint ventures (incorporated as separate companies) are often used as a vehicle not only to acquire but also to operate a joint business. Lithuanian law provides for favourable legal treatment for joint ventures. Shareholders' agreements are allowed and their clauses relating to voting are enforceable. However, the situation regarding clauses related to deadlock (call and put options, Russian roulette, etc.) or contractual priority rights is not clear and court practice does not give any guidance to date. It is recommended that these provisions are combined with the arbitration clause. The resolutions of the shareholders meeting passed contrary to the provisions of the shareholders' agreements may be declared invalid in court upon the actions of one of the parties when voting in breach of the agreement had an impact on the results of voting. Standstill clauses and other restrictions on transfers of shares are also allowed between the shareholders. However, they may not be made mandatory to all shareholders (i.e., those not parties to the agreements establishing this) if they are more restrictive than the law allows (*see* 17.9.1 below).

17.6.6   *Asset transactions*

It should be mentioned that so-called "asset deals" are very common in Lithuania. These transactions may seem to be difficult to carry out from a technical standpoint, but they are less burdensome procedurally than the reorganisation. However, other aspects, such as the tax consequences of an asset transaction, examined from different angles (profit tax, VAT, registration duties and so on) or special permits and licences granted to a target company (which may be both difficult and costly to obtain) may lead to a different choice of procedure.

17.6.7   *Acquisition through privatisation*

The transactions concluded in the process of privatisation are often similar to private transactions since they are governed by the general provisions of the Civil Code, the Company Law, the Law on Securities Market, etc. However, the Law on Privatisation of State-Owned and Municipal Property ("Privatisation Law") establishes certain specific conditions or restrictions. It also defines the limits of competence of the state institutions conducting privatisation in agreeing on certain conditions of the privatisation transactions which limits may not be exceeded. In addition, Privatisation Law defines in what cases and how the different privatisation methods may be applied. Each of the privatisation methods that may be used for the acquisition of shares is described below.

(a)   Public sale of shares is a method of selling the shares of public companies, which belong by the right of ownership to the state or municipality, on the national and (or) foreign Stock Exchanges (or outside the Exchanges), and where the sale price is determined by market-based supply-demand principles. If the shares of public companies are privatised by selling them on the Vilnius Stock Exchange, then the rules regulating the activity of this Stock Exchange shall be applied. The shares subject to privatisation may be replaced by Global Depository Receipts or other financial instruments.

(b)   Public auction is a method used in order to obtain the highest sale price for the privatised shares of public or private companies. The purchaser is the bidder who has offered the highest price and no limitation is placed on the number of potential bidders.

(c)   Public tender is a method used for the sale of shares of public or private companies to the purchasers who, in response to a tender, are judged to have provided the best written price and investment proposal, including a discussion of investments in the privatised company and the increase of the authorised capital of such company to finance the investments through equity. Also, the conditions on retaining the minimum number of employees are usually included in the tender. Negotiations to improve the offered conditions must be held with the potential purchaser who has presented the best proposal or with several potential purchasers whose proposals do not differ by more than 10 per cent. When privatising the companies through public tender, the employees of the company may be given the opportunity to purchase up to 5 per cent of state or municipally owned shares at a nominal price.

(d)   Direct negotiation is a method used for the privatisation of companies with specific features that may limit the number of potential interested purchasers (e.g., when certain qualifications are expected from the potential investor). Potential investors in this case are known as strategic investors, and are chosen by applying special qualification criteria and their list is approved by the Government. As a result of direct negotiations with potential investors, the shares are sold to the strategic investor judged to have presented the best proposal evaluated in the same way as in the case of a public tender. The same opportunity to sell up to 5 per cent of the shares to employees also applies in the case of direct negotiations.

(e) Transfer of control in state- or municipally-controlled enterprises is a method applied for the sale of shares in companies only if the shares of such companies were not successfully privatised on previous occasions, or if more than 50 per cent of the state- or municipally-owned shares in such a company have already been privatised by applying other privatisation methods and only the remaining minority shareholding is to be sold. The method of privatisation through transfer of control involves the issuance of the new shares or convertible bonds through additional capital contributions, as a result of which the shareholding of the state or municipality in the company falls below the two-thirds, half or one-third levels of votes granted by the shares in the general meeting of shareholders of the company. Transfer of control is executed through transfer by the state or municipality of its right of first refusal to acquire newly issued shares or convertible bonds to a privatising purchaser.

A combination of privatisation methods may be applied in cases of privatisation of state-controlled companies that are deemed to be important entities in the country's overall infrastructure, or entities holding a dominant position in certain branches of the economy. Depending upon the established privatisation objectives, qualifications applicable to potential investors and the specifics of the company under privatisation, a combination of the following may be used:

(a) public tender with a transfer of control; or
(b) direct negotiations with a transfer of control; or
(c) public tender and public sale of shares (in such case there are two tranches – strategic investor tranche privatised in public tender and the tranche sold through public sale of shares); or
(d) direct negotiations and public sale of shares.

Other combinations can be used.

It is important to note that such process of privatisation of the important infrastructure or dominant entities includes a pre-selection of bidders (strategic investors) and presenting the initial and final tender proposals.

17.7 Preparation of an offer

17.7.1 *Preliminary steps and conduct of negotiations*

Apart from privatisation transactions, the sale of private companies constitutes the core of mergers and acquisitions activity in Lithuania. The form and structure can be very different from one acquisition to another. Sophisticated acquisition structures were relatively common in Lithuania in the privatisation of state- or municipally-owned companies. However, private acquisitions are becoming more prevalent. In addition, extensive preparatory work is often carried out by foreign acquirers who are sometimes not familiar with the local business practices and lack trust in the Lithuanian sellers or partners. Often sales of businesses are carried out through auctions. This is due to the still rising activism of financial investors (which are ready to invest in companies involved in different activities, in contrast to the strategic investors) competing for the same targets.

The whole acquisition process usually begins with informal contacts between prospective purchasers and the seller directly. Investment banks (consultants) are increasingly active in the market. When investment banks (consultants) are involved, they usually prepare for the seller a Selling Memorandum about the target company. In many cases investment banks find the target for the acquirer or the investor for the target, whichever is the case.

Letters of intent (preliminary agreements) are frequently used when the preliminary negotiations have reached a certain stage. They are often complemented by a confidentiality agreement (if not signed earlier in the negotiations) which is valid under Lithuanian law. Breaches of confidentiality may result in compensatory damages. Lump-sum indemnities may also be provided for and are recommended. Letters of intent must be time limited. If the letter of intent does not contain a term of validity, it is valid for one year. Letters of intent are enforceable through damages, which may be claimed from the party that unreasonably refuses or avoids executing the final binding agreement under the conditions of the letter of intent (i.e., breaches the obligations under the letter of intent). Therefore, if the parties are willing to limit the enforceability of the letters of intent and eliminate the liability through damages, such letters of intent should be drafted with great attention. The liability in damages may also arise from a breach of a general obligation of the parties to act honestly and fairly and to conduct negotiations in good faith. Another caveat in drafting the letters of intent is that the seller should not undertake lengthy obligations to negotiate exclusively with a particular potential purchaser since auction sales are occurring more often even in situations where such auctions were not initially planned. Under Lithuanian law, however, preliminary agreements must be executed in writing. Therefore, oral agreements cannot produce legal effects such as the written preliminary agreements. It is important to note that advance payment of the purchase price, under Lithuanian law and court practice, is one of the factors (but not the single factor) indicating that the final and not preliminary agreement is concluded (despite the heading of the agreement being "preliminary" or "letter of intent"), allowing one of the parties to try to force another party in judicial procedure to consummate the sale and purchase transaction. Meanwhile under genuine preliminary agreement (letter of intent) only damages and contractual penalties claims are available as remedies.

17.7.2 Due diligence

When preparing an offer, the offeror will in most cases try to gather as much information as possible on the target company. Public registers can provide certain data, including financial statements of both public and private companies and corporate documentation (the information is available with the Register of Legal Persons).

Financial and legal due diligence investigations are very common in Lithuania. These are usually carried out by auditors and lawyers, respectively, except for areas falling outside their usual competence such as environmental and other technical audits. In cases of privatisation, due diligence is usually organised through data rooms that are open to the bidders for a certain number of days. Such practice is also sometimes implemented in private acquisitions. Of course, the use of data rooms limits the scope of the investigations of the potential purchaser.

17.7.3 Increasing shareholdings

When preparing an offer it might be the case that the prospective purchaser gradually increases its shareholding in the target company. It therefore acquires different rights depending on the size of the shareholding.

Table 1 shows what powers are given by law to shareholders owning a specific portion of shares. It also indicates some of the obligations imposed upon shareholders owning such portion of shares.

It is important to note that the Company Law provides for cumulative voting in electing the supervisory council of the company or the board if the supervisory council is not formed (neither the supervisory council nor the board is mandatory for public and private companies, solely the CEO may be appointed). Rules on such voting provide that upon election of the supervisory council members, the shareholders have a number of votes equal to a regular number of votes conferred by their shares multiplied by the number of members of the supervisory council (or the board if a supervisory council is not formed) subject to election. Then the shareholder may distribute the votes for one or several candidates. This cumulative voting ensures minority shareholder representation in the supervisory council (or the board). However, in the event that both the board and supervisory council are formed, the latter elects the board by a simple majority vote and consequently the majority shareholder(s) still control the entire board. Note that the shareholders willing to control the entire supervisory council (or the board if supervisory council is not formed) should have the percentage of shares exceeding the following percentage:

$A = N/(N + 1) \times 100\%$

where:

A is the required percentage

N is the number of the supervisory council (or the board, respectively) members.

Table 17.1   Powers and obligations of shareholders and relevant thresholds

Percentage threshold	Rights granted to or obligations imposed on the holder of the shares
Any number of shares	• May force the other shareholder to purchase the shares of the public company issuer[5] that are held thereby in a mandatory tender offer • May be squeezed out by the holder of more than one-third of all shares in a private company if such holder applies to court for mandatory sale of shares by a shareholder that is acting contrary to the objectives of the company • In public company issuer, may be squeezed out by a majority shareholder (or shareholders) holding 95 per cent of all votes, or may sell out his shares to such shareholder • Right to familiarise with the articles of association, list of shareholders, board or supervisory council members, financial statements, annual reports, audit findings, all minutes of the general meetings of shareholders and also minutes of the supervisory council and the board which do not contain confidential information • May request court to order to convene an annual general meeting if it has not been convened within four months after the end of the financial year • General rights (to receive dividend, to receive shares without payment if the authorised capital is increased out of the company funds, to have the pre-emption right in acquiring shares issued by the company, to lend to the company in the manner prescribed by law, to attend and vote in the general meetings of the shareholders, to file a claim with the court for reparation of damage resulting from non-feasance or malfeasance by the company CEO and board members of their obligations, to receive funds of the company where the authorised capital is decreased with the purpose of paying out such sums) • In private companies – a pre-emption right to purchase all the shares sold by other shareholders, unless the articles of association provide otherwise
5%	• Acquisition of this threshold in a public company issuer must be notified to the Securities Commission and the issuer
10%	• Acquisition of this threshold in a public company issuer must be notified to the Securities Commission and the issuer • Right to request the board, CEO or the court to convene a general meeting (including extraordinary) • Right to supplement agenda of the general meeting

---

[5] *See* footnote 1.

Table 17.1 continued

Percentage threshold	Rights granted to or obligations imposed on the holder of the shares
	• Right to propose new draft decisions on the items put on the agenda, nominate additional candidates to members of the company's bodies and audit firm • Right to request the court to order to initiate inspection of company's activity by court-appointed experts
15%	• Acquisition of this threshold in a public company issuer must be notified to the Securities Commission and the issuer
20%	• Acquisition of this threshold in a public company issuer must be notified to the Securities Commission and the issuer
25%	• Acquisition of this threshold in a public company issuer must be notified to the Securities Commission and the issuer • More than 25 per cent is required to block the decision for revoking of the pre-emptive right to acquire newly issued shares – articles of association may provide for a smaller blocking stake/greater majority required
30%	• Acquisition of this threshold in a public company issuer must be notified to the Securities Commission and the issuer
33.33%	• More than 33.33 per cent is required to block major decisions at the general meeting of a company (including increase of the authorised capital, reorganisation, etc.) – articles of association may provide for a smaller blocking stake/greater majority required • May apply to court to squeeze out the shareholder(s) of a private company that is/are acting contrary to the objectives of the company • May apply to court to force the other shareholder(s) to purchase the private company's shares held by them if such other shareholder(s) acts contrary to the objectives of the company and impedes the exercise of the rights by the selling shareholder
40%	• Acquisition of this threshold in a public company issuer triggers mandatory tender offer requirements with certain exemptions defined at 17.8.4 below
50%	• Acquisition of this threshold in a public company issuer must be notified to the Securities Commission and the issuer • Right to convene a general meeting (when the managing bodies refuse to do that) • General meeting quorum threshold

Table 17.1   continued

Percentage threshold	Rights granted to or obligations imposed on the holder of the shares
	• Majority sufficient to adopt resolutions at the general meeting except when qualified majority (two-thirds, three-quarters or higher) is required (to approve annual financial statements, buy-back shares, etc.) • Right to familiarise (subject to confidentiality undertaking) with all the documents of the company
66.66%	• Majority sufficient to adopt all major resolutions unilaterally (to amend articles of association, distribute profit, increase or decrease authorised capital, reorganise the company, etc.), except for revoking of pre-emptive right to acquire newly issued shares, decision to delist the company from the Stock Exchange and when articles of association establish other higher thresholds
75%	• Acquisition of this threshold in a public company issuer must be notified to the Securities Commission and the issuer • Majority sufficient to adopt all resolutions at the general meeting unilaterally, except when articles of association establish higher thresholds
95%	• Acquisition of this threshold in public companies must be notified to the Securities Commission • In public company issuers may squeeze out minority shareholders while minority shareholders may sell out their shares to such shareholder

17.8   Conduct of a public offer

Public offers are regulated by the Law on Securities, the regulations adopted by the Securities Commission and by the Rules of Vilnius Stock Exchange. These regulations are applicable to voluntary and mandatory public offers. This part deals with the basic rules applicable to the conduct of public offers (also referred to as bids) in accordance with the provisions of the above regulations.

The Law on Securities establishes certain general principles that apply to public offers:

(a)   equal treatment of the shareholders and protection of minority shareholders;

(b)   transparency and integrity of the securities market;

(c)   the shareholders must have sufficient time and information to decide on the merits of the offer;

(d) the management bodies of the target company must give their views on the workplaces, conditions of employment and the locations of the company's places of business;

(e) the management bodies of the target company must act in the interests of the company as a whole and must not deny the shareholders the opportunity to decide on the merits of the offer;

(f) false (i.e., artificial) markets must not be created in the shares of the target and bidder companies or other companies related to the bid;

(g) an offeror must announce the offer only after ensuring that it can fulfil in full the offered consideration;

(h) the target company must not be hindered in the conduct of its affairs for longer than is reasonable.

Notably, the information to be provided by the public company issuers[6] has been substantially expanded. In their annual reports, public companies which are issuers must disclose extensive information about their shares and status and any obstacles that a potential bidder may face, including:

(a) all restrictions applicable upon the transfer of shares (e.g., restrictions applicable to blocks of shares, or the requirement to obtain the approval of the holders of the company's and other securities);

(b) shareholders (total number of shareholders; shareholders holding more than 5 per cent shares);

(c) shareholders having special control rights and the description of such rights;

(d) all restrictions imposed upon the voting rights;

(e) all of the agreements concluded between the shareholders of which the issuer was aware and due to which the share transfer and/or voting rights may be restricted;

(f) members of management, data on the participation in the authorised capital of the issuer, information on the amounts designated to them by the issuer, other assets transferred and the guarantees granted to such persons;

(g) all material agreements to which the issuer is a party and which would come into effect, be amended or terminated in case of a change in the issuer's control (e.g., which contain "anti-merger covenants");

(h) all agreements of the issuer and the members of its management bodies or the employees providing for compensation in case of resignation or in case they are dismissed without a due reason or their employment is terminated in view of the change of the control of the issuer (e.g., golden parachutes);

(i) information on the major related parties' transactions while specifying the amounts of the transactions, the nature of the relations between the parties concerned and other information about the transactions necessary for the understanding of the financial status of the company where the transactions were material or were concluded under unusual market conditions.

---

[6] *See* footnote 1.

17.8.1   Registration of the public offer with the Securities Commission

Any person that has decided to launch a public offer for a company must notify publicly of the decision within seven days and within 20 days after such notification must submit the offer document to the Securities Commission. The following documents shall be presented to the Securities Commission for registration of the public offer:

(a)   a request for registration of the public offer;

(b)   a copy of the decision of the offeror to launch an offer;

(c)   the offer document (circular);

(d)   written agreement between several parties presenting the public offer jointly (if such agreement is concluded);

(e)   permission of the Competition Council (concentration clearance), if required, for acquisition of the target company and any other governmental authorisation if such authorisation is necessary;

(f)   documents evidencing the title to the target company's shares owned by the offeror or held as security by the offeror (if any);

(g)   documents evidencing the price paid for the shares of the target company already acquired (if any);

(h)   documents evidencing that the offeror has enough funds and/or securities (where these are offered as consideration) to implement the offer (bank guarantee, extract from the intermediary's account on the funds held therein by the offeror, etc.);

(i)   information about the offeror (including shareholders holding more than 5 per cent of the offeror, management of the offeror, including their shareholdings with the target company);

(j)   documents evidencing payment of a stamp duty.

The Securities Commission shall make the decision on registration of the public offer within seven business days of all necessary documents being presented to it by the offeror.

Where the Securities Commission approves the offer document, it must be submitted to the target company and abstract of the offer document must be made public through a newspaper.

The offer may relate to all or part of the shares (or other securities) not yet owned by the offeror. It is also possible to make the offer conditional upon acquiring a minimum number of acceptances (e.g., 50 per cent of all the securities issued by the target). The Law on Securities is somewhat vague when it comes to possible forms of consideration. The law establishes that the offeror, in the case of a voluntary offer, may pay for the shares acquired through the public offer in cash, in securities listed on the regulated market of the EU, or by way of a combination of cash and securities. However, then it is stated that where securities are offered as consideration, cash must be offered as an alternative. Seemingly "all share deals" according to the wording of the law are not possible under Lithuanian law. For the mandatory offer it is clear that only cash or a cash/securities alternative are possible forms of consideration.

Notably, the offer document approved by the competent authority of the other EU Member State is recognised in Lithuania under the operation of the "single passport" principle. Accordingly, the offer document approved by the Lithuanian Securities Commission must be recognised in other EU Member States.[7]

17.8.2 Contents and valuation of the offer document

The offer document (referred to as the circular) must be drafted according to the provisions of the regulations adopted by the Securities Commission. The circular aims to provide information to the shareholders of the target company in order to allow them to decide whether or not they should sell their shares. Detailed information that must be provided in the offer document is listed at 17.11.1 below.

The board of directors of the target company must prepare and publish in the newspaper and on the company's website a statement regarding the public offer within 10 days after the date of publication of the offer document. In formulating its statement, the board of directors must take into account the possible effects of the implementation of the offer on the whole company's interests and specifically conditions of employment and number of employees, on the offeror's strategic plans for the target company and likely repercussions to the number of employees and the job positions. However, it is not clear if the recommendation of the board to the shareholders to accept or to reject the bid must be based only on the price offered or also on all enumerated aspects of the offer.

The content of the statement is specified at 17.11.2 below.

Where the opinion of the employee representatives on possible repercussions to employment places is available in advance, it must also be published on the target company's website.

Additionally, the board's and employee representatives' position must be submitted to the Securities Commission.

17.8.3 Publication of the circular and procedure for the offer

Within three business days after having received the decision of the Securities Commission to register the public offer, the offeror must announce publicly (in the media indicated in the circular and additionally in other media if required by the Securities Commission) the key data of the public offer contained in the circular and submit the offer document to the target company.

The implementation of the public offer starts on the fourth business day after the decision of the Securities Commission to register the circular. The public offer is open from the date when implementation thereof is commenced and it must remain open for at least 14 but no more than 70 days.

---

[7] However, pursuant to the Article 6(2) of the Directive 2004/25/EC on Takeover Bids authorities of the other EU Member States may require the inclusion of additional information in the offer document where such information is specific to the market of a Member State or Member States on which the offeree company's securities are admitted to trading and relates to the formalities to be complied with to accept the bid and to receive the consideration as well as to the tax arrangements to which the consideration will be subject.

The offer is implemented in the regulated market. Target shareholders and employees of both the target and offeror companies must have efficient and equal access to information about the offer.

The Securities Commission as supervisory authority has the right to suspend the implementation of the offer where infringements are established or new essential information emerges. The implementation is continued where the problems indicated by the Securities Commission are solved; where they are not, the approval of the offer document may be cancelled.

Where the offer was made only for some of the shares and there were more acceptances than shares tendered, the sale is distributed pro rata to the shares accepted.

The tender for all the shares of the target company releases such offeror from the obligation to make a mandatory offer, therefore takeover offers normally take the form of full bids rather than partial offers.

The offer document may be modified during the offer upon approval of the Securities Commission. However, the form of consideration (cash or cash/securities) may not be changed. Further, the Securities Commission may refuse to approve such modifications where:

(a) the modification is to the detriment of the target company's shareholders;
(b) the conditions of the offer are substantively modified;
(c) less than 10 days would be left from the approval of the modified offer document until the date of expiry of the offer;
(d) the modifications are not in line with the provisions of the applicable laws.

The regulations do not stipulate verbatim that the initial offer document must contain the reservation that it may be modified later where the company contemplates it. However, it is advisable to do so, for example where the bidder is making a conditional bid he should reserve the right to make his offer unconditional.

Where the modifications are approved, the offeror must within three working days publish the abstract of the modifications in the newspaper and submit these modifications to the target company and regulated market operator and also to any person requesting them (until the expiry of the offer).

The modified offer is applicable to all of the shareholders including those who had already accepted the offer. Any orders to sell the shares are annulled.

A counter offer can be either a voluntary or a mandatory public offer. A counter offer must be registered during the term of implementation of the first public offer.

The procedures applicable to the ordinary public offer also apply to the counter offer. Since the modifications of the circular are permitted during the implementation of the offer with the consent of the Securities Commission, in the event of a counter offer, the first offeror may in turn increase the price offered for the target company's shares and for that it is not required to submit a new circular. However, in many cases the initial bidder will be interested in submitting a brand new offer with the new conditions. There are no specific restraints to do so.

The operator of the regulated market during the offer period submits the information on key aspects of the offer through its website. On the last day of the offer the operator announces the results of the implementation of the offer, including the number of shares and percentage of approved orders.

Not later than five working days following the settlement between the offeror and the target company's shareholders who accepted the bid, the offeror must file with the Securities Commission and the target company a report on the execution of the offer, indicating the shares purchased during the bid.

17.8.4 *Mandatory public offers*

The Law on Securities states that, where exclusive or joint control of a public company which is issuer[8] is acquired, the purchaser of the controlling stake of the shares which grant more than 40 per cent of all votes must offer to purchase all of the shares of the remaining shareholders of the target company or transfer the shares below the indicated threshold.

The person or persons who exceed the threshold must, within seven days from learning the fact, announce in the national daily paper and inform the Securities Commission and the operator of the regulated market of the acquisition of shares exceeding the threshold. They must also make known their intention to:

(a)   make the mandatory bid; or
(b)   transfer the shares below 40 per cent threshold.

Where the latter option is chosen they must notify also of the fact of getting back below the 40 per cent threshold.

Where they opt to make a mandatory offer, they must submit the offer document to the Securities Commission within 20 days from the public announcement of their intentions.

In order to induce the person to make the mandatory bid or sell below the 40 per cent threshold, the law establishes that all voting rights relating to those shares are suspended from the moment of exceeding the threshold referred until:

(a)   the Securities Commission approves the circular of the mandatory bid; or
(b)   the shares are transferred below the 40 per cent threshold of and the fact is notified or for other reasons the holding is reduced below the threshold.

However, the person who exceeds the indicated threshold is not obligated to make a mandatory bid where:

(a)   the threshold of shares was exceeded during the voluntary full bid;
(b)   he acts in concert with another person in respect of whom the obligation arises individually;
(c)   the threshold is exceeded in the reorganisation, spin-off or statutory restructuring procedure (in all cases under certain conditions);

---

[8] *See* footnote 1.

(d)   the acquisition is made within group of companies by the group companies;

(e)   the threshold is exceeded individually by the person who had already made the mandatory offer with other persons.

The price to be paid for the shares in the mandatory bid may not be less than the highest price paid for shares within 12 months prior to exceeding the threshold and not less than the average weighted market price in six months prior to exceeding the threshold when the shares are floated.

Where under any of the indicated criteria the price may not be established, the price is stipulated by the certified property valuer approved by the Securities Commission.

However, the Securities Commission has a right to interfere in the establishment of the price where:

(a)   the price used to set the price for the mandatory bid was established on the basis of an agreement between the purchaser and the seller;

(b)   the price of the tendered shares was manipulated;

(c)   the market price of the shares has been affected by exceptional occurrences.

The Securities Commission further has a right to allow adjustment of the price of the mandatory bid in order to enable a company incurring financial losses to be rescued.

Where the offeror from the date of exceeding the threshold and as long as the mandatory bid is open acquires the shares at a higher price than the mandatory offer price, the latter price must be increased accordingly. The same adjustment applies where the offeror acquires the shares at the higher price within one year after the end of the mandatory bid – the difference then must be paid to those who accepted the mandatory bid.

Shareholders of the target company may challenge the mandatory bid price in court.

The mandatory offer in general terms is implemented in the same procedure as the voluntary offer with certain exceptions. For instance, the mandatory offer may not contain any additional conditions other than those expressly provided by the laws.

According to the recent case law, even a single minority shareholder may request the court to obligate the person who exceeded the threshold to make a mandatory bid where the majority shareholder failed to do so within the time period indicated above. Such order by the court may be made even where the respondent sells his shares and holds less than the threshold at the moment the ruling of the court is passed. This remedy is available to the minority shareholders in addition to the suspension of the voting rights of the majority shareholder defined above. Therefore, currently case law seems to favour the minority shareholders.

17.9 Defences to a hostile offer

Defensive measures against hostile bids for the public companies' shares are rarely used. However, in certain cases defensive measures have been used with the aim of achieving a higher price for the shares. There have been no genuinely hostile takeovers, though there were several cases where bidders faced opposing boards of target companies being in conflict of interest. Notably, Lithuania was one of very few countries to implement board neutrality and breakthrough provisions of the Takeover Bids Directive to the full extent. As a result, legal regulation favours hostile bidders. However, the ownership concentration in the listed companies is still high with one or several majority shareholders having a controlling stake. Consequently, the practice of acquisitions is such that the bidders agree with the majority shareholders prior to making any movements and boards of such companies with concentrated ownership are loyal to the majority shareholder(s), thus not attempting to encumber the bids. The defences discussed below were and are sometimes used in practice; however, the situation is changing due to the current implementation of the Takeover Bids Directive.

17.9.1 Transfer-blocking clauses

Transfer-blocking clauses as such are allowed in public companies by the Company Law and the Civil Code only to the extent that they are established in the shareholders' agreements (private instruments) which are signed by the shareholders and not established in the articles of association. It is therefore possible that a certain group of shareholders has agreed to the transfer-blocking clauses that could block a hostile bidder from acquiring their shares; however, the structure of such agreements must be carefully tailored.

As mentioned above, Lithuania opted for implementation of the breakthrough provision of the Takeover Bids Directive. As a result, under the Law on Securities any restrictions on the transfer of shares or voting rights provided for in the articles of association of the target company, agreements between the target company and its shareholders or agreements between the shareholders of the target company do not apply in respect of the offeror during the time of the implementation of the bid. Since the court practice had prohibited share transfer restrictions in the articles of association long ago, and transfer-blocking clauses in the agreements between the company and its shareholders (e.g., share subscription agreements) are not used in practice, the major impact of the provision of the Law on Securities is upon shareholders' agreements. The law established that transfer-blocking clauses and voting restrictions are not applicable during the public offers where these agreements were entered into after 21 April 2004.

Because of the defined breakthrough provision, where persons want to acquire shares in public companies acting jointly and retain transfer-blocking clauses and voting restrictions to the full extent, they must incorporate a holding special-purpose vehicle ("SPV" – a private company) and make the shareholders' agreement at the SPV level, while later the SPV will become a shareholder of the relevant public company. Then potential bidders will only be able to acquire shares held by the SPV and the decision of the SPV whether to sell shares of the target company will depend on the internal SPV's shareholders' agreement.

This Chapter also deals with most common features of the shareholders' agreements; however, the defined structure of holding must be remembered.

Most commonly, these clauses restrict the free transfer of shares of the company by way of first-refusal clauses and approval clauses. In first-refusal clauses, the current shareholders of the company that are party to the same shareholders' agreement must be offered the shares to be sold, prior to any sale and at the same price and conditions as those proposed by a prospective purchaser. In approval clauses, the other shareholders that are party to the same shareholders' agreement must give their approval to any share transfer to a person that is not a party to the shareholders' agreement.

It is quite common for a group of shareholders to agree on a joint sale of their shares. This is an effective way to block the transfer. In such cases, the group of shareholders grant, for a certain period of time, the irrevocable powers to one or several persons to sell their shares as a block for a price not lower than an agreed sum.

17.9.2   Authorised capital

The increase of the target company's authorised capital and the issue of new securities in one or more steps (i.e., poison pill) may only be used as an effective defence to a hostile bid by the board of directors upon approval of the general meeting of the shareholders. The Law on Securities establishes a neutrality rule, requiring the board (and supervisory council) not to take any measures which would frustrate the offer (the only exception is defined at 17.9.3 below). Moreover, only the general meeting of the shareholders can decide to authorise the increase of the share capital under the Company Law. The general meeting for this purpose may be called upon with 15 days notice and must resolve the issue by two-thirds majority vote of the participating shareholders.

Where the capital increase was decided by the shareholders meeting before the announcement of the bid, the board is still prohibited from commencing the implementation of the capital increase without the approval of the shareholders meeting held during the bid.

Where, however, the general meeting approves the issue of capital, it may be an effective way to frustrate the bid. The existing shareholders have pre-emptive rights to subscribe for the new shares which can be recalled by three-quarters majority vote, indicating a specific third person (if known) who will subscribe for shares. Therefore, such an increase of capital may be coordinated with the "white knight" defence.

17.9.3   Alternative bids

The only defence which the board of the target company may use against a hostile bidder, on its own initiative and without prior approval of the general shareholders' meeting, is seeking alternative bidders (known as "white knight", "grey knight" and "white squire" defences). As the Law on Securities does not allow "all share deals", this defence tactic loses part of its appeal since it makes share swaps with the "white knights" (making the transaction as a merger rather than an acquisition) harder to achieve. However, the takeover market currently is predominantly a sellers' market. Investors/acquirers are very active, and there are many deals involving auctions for target companies. Therefore, searching for alternative bids may be an effective defence tactic.

17.9.4 Other defences

Implementing the Takeover Bids Directive, the Law on Securities introduced a general prohibition of defence tactics against hostile bids. In particular the board is prohibited from taking any action that may frustrate a bid (except for searching for alternative bids) without prior approval of the general shareholders meeting. Another novelty of the law was the introduction of the breakthrough provision, allowing a hostile bidder to overcome potential barriers to a successful bid.

Pursuant to the breakthrough provision, the following clauses in the articles of association of the target company, agreements between the target company and its shareholders, and also the shareholders' agreements are not applicable:

(a)   the limitation on the voting rights or vice versa – multiple voting rights – when deciding whether to allow the board to undertake defensive measures and frustrate the bid;
(b)   restriction on a transfer of shares.

Furthermore, the Law on Securities establishes that where, following a bid, the bidder holds 75 per cent or more of the shares carrying voting rights, the following provisions will not be applicable:

(a)   restrictions on the transfer of shares or on voting rights referred to in the articles of association of the target company, company-shareholders' agreements and shareholders' agreements;
(b)   any extraordinary rights of shareholders concerning the appointment or removal of board members provided for in the articles of association of the target;
(c)   multiple-vote securities (they will carry only one vote each).

The bidder has a right to convene a general meeting of shareholders to amend the articles of association of the target company and/or to elect the new board members upon 15 days' prior notice (this is a bidder-favourable clause since in other cases 30 days' prior notice applies).

It is important to note that these aspects of the breakthrough rule apply to the target company level agreements but not holding SPV level agreements (as indicated above).

Interestingly, the Law on Securities requires a bidder to provide the holders of rights which are removed by operation of the breakthrough provision with equitable compensation. The manner of the compensation must be established in the offer document, but the law does not contain any further guidance, leaving the offeror in a situation of great uncertainty.

Finally, the two key ideas brought to Lithuanian law by the Takeover Bids Directive – board neutrality and breakthrough – do not guarantee that the offerors will not face any obstacles to making their bids. Generally, rights of third parties (such as creditors), contingent upon change of control, are allowed and justifiable from the standpoint of protection of their rights. For instance, it is usual for the banks to require their prior approval for the takeover of the debtor company, otherwise they are entitled to accelerate repayment credits of the target company ("anti-merger covenants").

## 17.10	Profit forecast and asset valuation

Lithuanian companies do not generally provide for a valuation of their assets other than as contained in their annual accounts. Since the board of directors of the target company, in the case of a public bid for its shares, must express its opinion on the bid it can of course draw the attention of the shareholders to the value of the company's assets or shares. There is no verbatim requirement to consult with professional advisers when adopting the opinion; however, it is advisable for the board to do so in order to ensure that it follows the requirement to act with due care.

Lithuanian public and private companies must prepare their annual reports and submit them to the Register of Legal Persons (such reports are publicly available). Companies listed on the Vilnius Stock Exchange need to publish, in addition to their annual accounts, quarterly accounts and semi-annual accounts.

## 17.11	Documents from the offeror and the offeree board

### 17.11.1	The circular

The offer document should contain the following information:

(a)	conditions of the bid;
(b)	contact details of the target company;
(c)	contact details of the offeror and his representative;
(d)	details about the consultant of the offeror;
(e)	the period of the execution of the bid;
(f)	the number of the target company's outstanding shares according to type and class, ISIN code, their par value and the number of own shares held;
(g)	information about admission of the target company's shares to trading lists of the Stock Exchange;
(h)	the minimum and maximum number of the target company's shares intended for purchase by type, class, ISIN code; the number of shares upon acquisition of which the bid is made conditional;
(i)	the number of the target company's outstanding shares according to type, class and ISIN codes (specifying the number of votes (per cent) attaching to these shares) which:

(i) were/are held by the offeror at the time the threshold of 40 per cent of votes was exceeded, and on the day of signing the circular (to be reported in case of a mandatory bid); are held by the offeror on the day of signing the circular (to be reported in case of a voluntary bid);

(ii) were/are held by each of the persons acting in concert at the time the threshold of 40 per cent of votes was exceeded and on the day of signing the circular (to be reported in the case of a mandatory bid); are held by each of the persons acting in concert on the day of signing the circular (to be reported in the case of a voluntary bid);

(iii) may be acquired by persons referred to in items (i) and (ii) by the right to acquire them at their initiative according to the effective agreements;

(iv) are deposited by the third persons with persons referred to in items (i) and (ii) and the latter have the right to exercise the voting rights attaching to these securities at their discretion;

(j) shares (and votes) issued by the offeror held by the target company;

(k) consideration for shares offered to purchase;

(l) price or exchange rate into securities and cash alternative for the shares offered to purchase;

(m) methodology of establishing the amount of consideration for the target company's shares, the price substantiation;

(n) information on the securities offered for exchange;

(o) information about the sources of financing for the bid (including financing and security providers);

(p) compensation offered for all losses of the rightholders arising from the operation of the breakthrough provision (the method of the establishment of the compensation, and the method of payment);

(q) circumstances which do not directly depend on the offeror but which influence the success of the bid;

(r) the offeror's plans and intentions towards the target company if the bid is successful:

(i) continuity of the target company's business activities;

(ii) restructuring (change of management structure), reorganisation, change of legal form or liquidation of the target company;

(iii) employment policy;

(iv) policy in respect of the management of the target company;

(v) capital-raising policy;

(vi) dividend policy;

(vii) intended amendments in the target company's articles of association;

(viii) special bonuses, incentive schemes, etc. provided to the management of the target company;

(s) a written agreement providing for the rights and/or mutual obligations and liability of persons acting in concert, and their liability for failure to abide by the regulations of preparation, approval of the circular of the offer and execution of the offer;

(t) written agreements with other persons concerning voting at the general shareholders meetings of the target company;

(u)   law applicable to acceptances and competent courts to resolve disputes;

(v)   data about the offeror:

      (i)   whether or not the offeror (a natural person) has been, in the course of the last five years, subject to administrative penalties for violations of acts regulating the securities markets;

      (ii)   whether the offeror (a natural person) is still under criminal conviction for violations against property, economic order or finance;

(w)   information about pending disputes that have or may have a substantial effect on the offeror's activities and financial status;

(x)   the daily newspaper and other additional means of information wherein the offeror intends to publish the information on the offer and its execution;

(y)   other data at the offeror's discretion;

(z)   confirmation of the persons who prepared the circular and are responsible for the information disclosed, that the information disclosed in the circular is true and that there are no material omissions which may have an impact on the shareholders' opinion regarding the offer.

17.11.2   *Documents from the offeree board*

As indicated at 17.8.2 above, the board of the target company must prepare a statement which contains the following information:

(a)   opinion of the board regarding the offer;

(b)   opinion of the board about the plans and intentions of the offeror in respect of the target company:

      (i)   possible impact of the implementation of the offer upon the interests of the company;

      (ii)   impact upon the employment situation;

      (iii)   impact upon the number of staff;

      (iv)   opinion concerning the strategic plans of the offeror and the impact thereof on employment and the locations of the company's places of business;

(c)   opinion of the board on the price of the offer;

(d)   motivated recommendation of the board to the shareholders to accept or reject the bid or reasons why the board does not provide recommendation;

(e)   information of existence of a written agreement between the board (its members) and the offeror concerning the execution of the offer;

(f)   information of existence of a written agreement between the board (its members) and the offeror concerning the joint management policy in respect of the target company;

(g)   the number of voting shares and votes held by the target company in the general shareholders meeting of the offeror;

(h)   the number of voting shares and votes held by the target company's management in the general shareholders meeting of the offeror;

(i)   number of members of the board and the results of voting;

(j)   other information at the discretion of the board.

17.12 Compulsory acquisitions of minorities

Squeeze-out of minority shareholders in listed public companies was introduced in 2004. The list of public companies eligible for squeeze-out has increased slightly and squeeze-out may be implemented in all public companies issuers.[9]

Following the introduction of squeeze-out referred to above, it is possible for squeeze-out to occur under the provisions of the Civil Code which provide for a special procedure applicable to all private companies, whereby a holder of more than one-third of all the shares is able to request a court to force the other shareholders to sell their shares to him if such other shareholders act contrary to the objectives of the company. The Civil Code also allows a holder of more than one-third of all the shares to force by the judicial order to sell his shares to the other shareholders in a situation where the selling shareholder's rights are obstructed by the other shareholders that act contrary to the company's objectives.

This procedure should be used in situations in which the behaviour of a shareholder or a group of shareholders prejudices a fellow shareholder and is applicable in private companies only.

The "genuine" squeeze-out procedure in listed public companies in Lithuania was introduced in 2004 (it is currently available in all public companies which are issuers), as noted above. In order to exercise the squeeze-out, the following conditions must be met:

(a)   the public company must be issuer in terms of the Law on Securities;
(b)   a shareholder (or a group of shareholders jointly) intending to acquire shares through such mechanism must have at least 95 per cent of all votes at the general meeting of shareholders of that company.

Attention should be paid to the fact that in certain cases when one of the shareholders acquires shares in the company or agrees with the other shareholders to act in concert in implementing the compulsory sale of shares, an obligation emerges to announce the mandatory tender offer before the squeeze-out itself (these provisions are explained at 17.8.4 above).

Establishment of price is one of the most important steps determining successful completion of the procedure of mandatory sale of shares. When calculating the price, it is necessary to comply with the following rules:

(a)   the price is fixed at what was paid for the company's shares during the tender offer if:
   (i)   the 95 per cent threshold of shares was acquired during the mandatory offer;
   (ii)   the 95 per cent threshold of shares was acquired during the voluntary offer and holders of at least 90 per cent of all the shares tendered accepted the bid;

---

[9] *See* footnote 1.

  (iii) not more than three months have passed from the end of the offer indicated in (i) or (ii) until the notification of the squeeze-out of the shares (so that it is clear that the price is still actual);

(b) in the absence of at least one of the conditions stipulated above, the fair price for the shares to be squeezed out is to be established by the person buying them up, upon a prior approval of the price by the Securities Commission. The latter has the right to reasonably order the change of the price proposed by the potential acquirer.

Only cash may be used as a consideration. The Law on Securities grants the right to minority shareholders to dispute in court the proposed squeeze-out price in order that the price would not infringe the principle of fairness. The court may suspend the squeeze-out procedure until the date of coming into effect of the court ruling regarding the establishment of the fair price.

Upon establishing the acquisition price of the shares, the shareholder or shareholders intending to buy up all the shares in the company have to provide a notification to the company regarding the squeeze-out of the shares indicating therein the information stipulated in law and attaching the required documents.

Upon receipt of the notification regarding the squeeze-out of the shares, the public company must notify each shareholder of the company, the Securities Commission and the Stock Exchange, and publish a notice in the daily newspaper in which notifications of the company are published.

Minority shareholders have to sell their shares within 90 days following the date of announcement of such notification. Should the minority shareholders fail to fulfil this obligation, the shareholder (or shareholders) intending to squeeze out the shares have the right to pay the proposed price to the depository account and apply to court for an order to intermediaries to make necessary entries in the securities accounts of transfer of the title to shares to the shareholder (or shareholders) buying the shares.

Notably, the minority shareholders have a mirror right: they may require the majority shareholder (or shareholders) holding not less than 95 per cent of votes in the general meeting of shareholders of the public company issuer to purchase their shares (sell-out). In such event, rules of the squeeze-out procedure apply *mutatis mutandis*. Where the majority shareholder fails to fulfil its obligation to mandatorily buy the shares and does not contest the price of the shares, he is obligated to pay the 10 per cent annual interest in respect of the amount overdue.

17.13 Insider trading and market manipulation

17.13.1 *Insider trading*

Under the Law on Markets in Financial Instruments, insider trading is prohibited.

17.13.1.1   *Prohibition from using inside information*

Persons who are in possession of inside information[10] by virtue of being the company's management employees, members of supervisory or management bodies, or have access to such information by virtue of their office, profession or because they are shareholders of the company or have obtained such information by virtue of their criminal activities, are prohibited from directly or indirectly attempting to conclude or concluding deals with shares to which the information relates on their own account or the account of a third party until the information is publicly disclosed. If the person is a legal person, such prohibition also applies to the natural person who takes part in the decision to carry out the transaction for the account or on behalf of the legal person concerned.

Such persons are also prohibited from:

(a)   disclosing directly or indirectly inside information to other persons, except when information is disclosed by virtue of their office or in the course of executing their professional duties;

(b)   on the basis of the inside information, recommending, soliciting or offering other parties to enter into transactions in respect of the financial instruments to which the information concerned is related.

Such prohibitions are also imposed on any person possessing inside information who is aware or should be aware that such information is not publicly disclosed.

Managers of the issuer[11] company and persons closely related to such managers (the exact list is established by the Securities Commission) must notify of the transactions concluded on their own account in respect of the shares of that company or derivatives or other linked financial instruments. Such information is made public.

The company which is issuer or the person acting on the account and on behalf of the company, while disclosing the inside information to any third person in normal exercise of his employment, profession or duties, must at the same time (or in case of non-intentional disclosure – promptly after such disclosure), make complete and effective public disclosure of such information. This requirement does not apply where the person who has come into possession of such information owes a duty of confidentiality arising from legal acts, the articles of association or a contract. The company which is issuer and persons acting on behalf of or on the account of the company must furnish to the Securities Commission the data on persons entitled to have access to inside information by virtue of the employment contract or on any other basis, and on persons related to the company.

---

[10]   Article 3(40) defines inside information as information of a precise nature relating to issuer(s) on the material events that have already or are planned to take place, which, if they were made public, would be likely to have a significant effect on the price of those financial instruments and where such information has not yet been made public.

[11]   *See* footnote 1.

An intermediary, while performing his duties, who reasonably suspects that the transaction would be effected in violation of prohibitions on insider trading or market manipulation, must forthwith notify the Securities Commission thereof.

17.13.1.2   Sanctions

The breach of insider trading and/or market manipulation prohibitions is subject to administrative fines to be imposed by the Securities Commission which for the legal person may reach up to approximately €29,000 or up to the amount of unlawfully received proceeds multiplied three times where the proceeds constitute more than €29,000. The Commission is competent to conduct investigations and impose sanctions. If insider trading and/ or market manipulation are considered to constitute a serious violation of the laws regulating the securities market, criminal sanctions may also be imposed (including fines, restriction of freedom or imprisonment). Criminal sanctions may only be imposed by a court. In such a case the prosecution is carried out by the prosecutors' office.

17.13.2   Market manipulation

In addition to the legislation on insider trading, the Law on Markets in Financial Instruments prohibits market manipulation. Pursuant to the law, persons are prohibited from:

(a)   concluding purchase/sale transactions or placing purchase/ sale orders in respect of financial instruments where these transactions or orders form a misleading impression about the demand, supply or price of the financial instruments, also where the person or person acting in concert thus maintain an unusual or artificial price of one or several financial instruments. This prohibition does not apply where the person who entered into the transaction or issued the orders to trade establishes that his reasons for doing so are legitimate and that these transactions or orders to trade conform to accepted market practices on the regulated market concerned, approved by a supervisory authority;

(b)   concluding transactions or placing orders to trade which employ fictitious devices or any other form of deception or contrivance;

(c)   dissemination of information through the media, or by any other means, which gives or is likely to give, false or misleading signals as to the financial instruments, where the person who made the dissemination knew or ought to have known that the information was false or misleading.

The prohibited actions of market manipulation are those that take any of the following forms:

(a)   conduct by a person or persons acting in concert to secure a dominant position over the supply or demand of financial instruments which has the effect of fixing, directly or indirectly, the purchase or sale price or creating other unfair trading conditions;

(b)   buying or selling of the financial instruments at the close of the market with the effect of misleading investors acting on the basis of closing prices;

(c)   taking advantage of occasional or regular access to the mass media by expressing opinion about financial instruments (or directly about their issuer) while having previously taken positions on those financial instruments and profiting subsequently from the impact of the opinion expressed on the price of the financial instruments, without having simultaneously disclosed that conflict of interest to the public in a proper and effective way;

(d)   in other forms the model list of which is compiled by the Securities Commission.

17.14   Financial assistance

Some acquisitions of companies are structured as leveraged deals in which a portion of the purchase price for the assets or for the shares to be purchased is obtained through loan financing. In such a transaction, the purchaser may intend to use the shares or the assets of the acquired company to secure the loan.

17.14.1   *Financial assistance by the target company*

Under Lithuanian Company Law, the target company is prohibited from granting any financial assistance (by advancing funds, lending funds or providing credit support or security) in cases when such financial assistance is intended for acquisition of such company's shares. Consequences of breach of this Company Law provision are not finally clear as there are no cases in practice were such assistance would be challenged. However, the most likely remedy would be nullification of the transaction (i.e., the loan, the surety, etc.) upon request of the creditors. Theoretically, breach of company law could result in criminal sanctions and fines for the company and directors responsible for granting such financial assistance.

It is therefore quite difficult to structure a leveraged deal under Lithuanian law where the purchaser practically can only offer the acquired shares as a security.

The merger between the purchased company and the purchasing company is used from time to time as a method of avoiding the prohibition set forth in the Company Law.

The rules for financial assistance will probably be eased with the implementation of Directive 2006/68/EC amending the Capital Maintenance Directive.

17.14.2   *Intra-group financial assistance*

The general corporate law principle under Lithuanian law states that the board of directors of a company must always act in the best interests of that company. The concept of group companies is not legally recognised in Lithuania (however, consolidated financial accounts and consolidated annual reports are). Thus, the giving of a guarantee by a company to secure the debts of an affiliated company may be seen as not being in the company's best interests. Furthermore, with the aim of protecting the third-party creditors' rights, the law introduces a cap on the interest that a shareholder creditor may derive from the subsidiary (in particular, the interest rate may not be higher than the average rate charged by banks) and prohibits the company from pledging its assets for the benefit of the shareholder.

17.14.3   *Other rules applicable to debt financing*

Debt financing may come from within the country or abroad and financing agreements may be governed by Lithuanian or foreign law.

It is important to note that statute of limitations for periodic payments under loans is shortened (the general statute of limitations is 10 years):

(a)   the Civil Code provides that a creditor may not claim default interest (or other default payments) if such default payments have accrued over a period of more than six months;

(b)   the Civil Code provides that a creditor may not claim interest (or other periodic payments) if such periodic payments have accrued over a period of more than five years.

Lithuanian law requirements established for financing and related transactions should be examined before the financing is structured.

Chapter 18

Luxembourg

Guy Harles, Partner
Katia Gauzès, Senior Associate
Arendt & Medernach

18.1   Introduction

In the past, Luxembourg differed from other European Member States in that it lacked a regulatory structure for mergers and acquisitions. Takeover bids were not well regulated and Luxembourg law was characterised by an absence of domestic merger control.

In recent years, a number of companies listed on the Luxembourg regulated market have witnessed a change in their shareholding structure. The absence of protection for minority shareholders became a matter of political discussion and, at the same time, majority shareholders regretted the absence of squeeze-out provisions.

In response to these concerns, a number of EU directives were implemented in Luxembourg, namely:

(a)   the Law of 9 May 2006 on market abuse ("the Law of 9 May 2006");

(b)   the Law of 19 May 2006 implementing Directive 2004/25/EC of the European Parliament and of the Council of 21 April 2004 on takeover bids ("the Law of 19 May 2006");

(c)   the Law of 23 March 2007 modifying the Law of 10 August 1915 ("the Law of 23 March 2007");

(d)   the Law of 11 January 2008 concerning transparency (*Cette loi ne se rapporte pas à ce qui est dit dans l'introduction*) obligations for issuers of securities admitted to trading on a regulated market ("the Law of 11 January 2008").

These laws have provided a structured legal framework for the treatment of takeovers and mergers in Luxembourg.

In 1990, the Exchange Supervisory Commission was set up to ensure compliance with the rules and regulations of the Luxembourg Stock Exchange ("LSE") by financial sector professionals. Then in the late 1990s, the Law of 23 December 1998 merged the Exchange Supervisory Commission with the banking supervisory authority to form the *Commission de Surveillance du Secteur Financier* (the Commission for the Supervision of the Financial Sector or "CSSF"). The CSSF is an independent and impartial body and its employees are bound by the rules of professional secrecy. Under the above-mentioned legal innovations, the CSSF plays a central role in the regulation of takeovers governed by the Law of 19 May 2006 in Luxembourg, generally serving as the competent supervisory authority in such matters.

18.2   Acquisition targets

Luxembourg companies can be divided into two main categories: private companies and public companies.

18.2.1   Private companies

One of the main characteristics of private companies is the importance given to the *intuitu personae* (person or personality) of the shareholders. As a consequence, the partnership shares or shares of interest of a general partnership are generally not transferable without the agreement of a shareholder meeting representing at least three-quarters of the capital stock. The transfer of shares of an unlimited partnership requires either the unanimous consent of the other partners or it may be provided for in the articles of association under certain conditions (e.g., on the condition that the majority of shareholders agree to such a share transfer or that a pre-emption right is given to all existing shareholders over those shares to be transferred).

18.2.2   Public companies

The shares of a public company (i.e., a public limited company and a partnership limited by shares) are generally freely transferable and, thus, their transfer does not require the consent of the other shareholders. The public sale or offer of shares is, however, subject to a number of formalities for both listed and non-listed public companies.

However, some restrictions to the free transferability of shares may possibly apply even if the company is not listed on the LSE. Approval clauses or pre-emption clauses, for example, may also limit the free transfer of a listed company's shares (*see* 18.10.1 below). The articles of association of a listed company may limit the ownership of shares.

18.3   Exchange and investment control

In the Grand-Duchy of Luxembourg, foreign investors are not required to receive prior authorisation before investing. Additionally, Luxembourg has abolished all exchange controls and the disclosure of important shareholdings is not required for non-listed companies.

However, a notification requirement for major holdings does exist with respect to Luxembourg companies whose shares are listed on an exchange located in a Member State. Where the proportion of the voting rights held by a person acquiring or disposing of a holding in a listed company reaches, exceeds or falls below 5, 10, 15, 20, 25, 33.33, 50 or 66.66 per cent of the total voting rights existing in the company, the person in question must concurrently notify the company and the CSSF of the proportion of voting rights it holds following the acquisition or disposal (*see* Article 8(1) of the Law of 11 January 2008 concerning transparency obligations for securities issuers). This notification must occur within seven calendar days of reaching the threshold percentage. However, the requirement does not apply if the target company is an open-ended undertaking for collective investments (i.e., a collective investment undertaking whose units are, at the holder's request, repurchased or redeemed, directly or indirectly, out of the assets of this undertaking).

Additional rules apply to insurance companies, banks and credit institutions pursuant to the implementation into Luxembourg law of the relevant European Directives.

18.4 Merger control

The Luxembourg legal system does not include a law on domestic merger control per se, and instead merger control in Luxembourg is, in practice, governed from a competition law perspective by the Law of 17 May 2004 concerning competition law (hereafter the "Law of 17 May 2004") and by the Law of 19 May 2006, with respect to takeover bids.

The Law of 17 May 2004, which repealed and replaced the Law of 17 June 1970 on restrictive commercial practices, is unlike the domestic competition legislation of other EU Member States in that it does not set forth rules relating to pre-merger control. However, the relevant authorities may exercise merger control by using the Law of 17 May 2004 and the Council Regulation 1/2003 of 16 December 2002 on the implementation of rules on competition laid down in Articles 81 and 82 of the EC Treaty.

The Law of 17 May 2004 established the *Conseil de la Concurrence* (the Competition Authority) and the *Inspection de la Concurrence* (the Competition Inspectorate) which enforce and oversee the application of Luxembourg competition law. The Competition Authority is an independent administrative agency, composed of three members, that has the competence to enforce the Law of 17 May 2004 and Articles 81 and 82 of the EC Treaty. It has exclusive jurisdiction to hear competition law cases in Luxembourg, except for in those instances where inter-community commerce would be affected by the outcome of the case. Cases come before the Competition Authority either upon the request of persons, either moral or physical, the Minister for the Economy and Foreign Trade or the Competition Inspectorate. The Competition Authority may not act on its own initiative to hear a case. Individuals may appeal a decision made by the Competition Authority to an administrative court within the applicable two months statute of limitations.

The Competition Inspectorate is an administrative body within the Ministry of the Economy and Foreign Trade that serves a role on the Luxembourg level parallel to that of the European Commission on the EU level. With powers of investigation similar to those of the European Commission, the Competition Inspectorate receives complaints and investigates possible competition law infringements taking into account the Law of 17 May 2004 and Articles 81 and 82 of the EC Treaty.

Both the Competition Authority and the Competition Inspectorate are the competent national authorities in Luxembourg under Council Regulation (EC)

No. 139/2004 of 20 January 2004 on the control of concentration between undertakings. Furthermore, the Competition Authority represents Luxembourg within
the network of European competition authorities instituted by Council Regulation (EC) No. 1/2003 of 16 December 2002 on the implementation of the rules
on competition laid down in Articles 81 and 82 of the Treaty.

18.5   Regulation of the conduct of mergers and acquisitions

18.5.1   *Mergers*

Mergers are regulated by the Law of 23 March 2007 which modifies Articles 257
to 283 of the Law of 10 August 1915 on commercial companies, as amended ("the
Law of 10 August 1915"). Articles 257 to 283 were first introduced by the Law
of 7 September 1987 and originally applied only to Luxembourg public limited
companies (*sociétés anonymes*). The Law of 23 March 2007 expands the application
of these articles to all companies having legal personality by virtue of the Law
of 10 August 1915, as well as economic interest groupings ("EIGs"); it should be
noted that while the following discussion on mergers refers solely to companies,
it applies equally to EIGs. The Law of 23 March 2007 also extends the scope of
the merger provisions to include cross-border mergers as long as the laws of the
other country involved do not prohibit such a merger.

Under Luxembourg law, a merger is a transaction whereby one or more
companies may transfer their assets and liabilities to an existing company (*fusion
par absorption*) or a newly founded company (*fusion par constitution d'une nouvelle
société*). Although the law distinguishes between these two types of merger, the
rules applicable to them are largely the same. These rules may be summarised
as follows.

The Law of 23 March 2007 sets out a preparatory phase in which the managerial
bodies of the merging companies must create a detailed written report on the
draft terms of the merger. The draft merger terms must include:

(a)   the form, corporate denomination and registered office of the merging
        companies or the companies which will cease to exist (in the case of the
        establishment of a European company ("*Societas Europaea*" or "SE") by way
        of merger, the merger document must also include the location envisioned
        for the to-be-formed SE);
(b)   the share ratio and, where appropriate, the amount of cash payment;
(c)   the terms for the delivery of the shares or corporate units in the acquiring
        company or the newly formed company;
(d)   the date from which time the shares or corporate units shall carry the right
        to participate in the profits, and any special conditions regarding this right;
(e)   the date from which time the operations of the acquired company shall be
        treated for accounting purposes as being carried out on behalf of the
        acquiring company or the newly formed company;
(f)   the rights conferred by the acquiring company or the newly formed com-
        pany to members having special rights and to the holders of securities

other than shares or corporate units, or the measure proposed concerning them;

(g) any special advantages granted to experts, board members or managers, and statutory auditors of the merging companies; and

(h) if an SE is formed by way of merger, the report must also include the articles of association of the SE, as well as information regarding the effect the formation of the SE will have on company employees.

The draft merger terms must be published in the official gazette (*Mémorial*) in conformity with Article 9 of the Law of 10 August 1915 and for cross-border mergers, the draft merger terms must be published as well in the national bulletins of the other Member States involved in the merger. After publication of draft merger terms, the shareholders meetings or, where appropriate, the holders of securities other than shares or corporate units of the concerned companies will express their opinions of the envisaged merger. The draft merger terms shall also be examined by independent experts whose task it is to guarantee that the exchange value of the shares is reasonable and pertinent. A written report must be produced based upon these findings and submitted to the members. A second report shall be drafted by the managerial bodies of the merging companies, explaining and justifying the merger from both legal and economic standpoints.

Subject to a few exceptions, the merger must be approved by the members of each of the concerned companies. The law sets out a number of provisions in order to ensure that the members have all of the necessary information in order to make an informed decision on the merger.

A cross-border merger becomes effective once each company has adopted the terms of the merger. However, it is not effective vis-à-vis third parties until the decision to merge is published pursuant to Article 9 of the Law of 10 August 1915 in the official gazette (*Mémorial*).

Non-compliance with the above-mentioned legal requirements may lead to the individual or joint liability of the companies' managers or directors and/or their advisers. Under certain circumstances, the merger may also be declared null and void by judicial decision.

18.5.2 *Transfers of assets, transfers of branches of activity and all assets and liabilities transfers*

Under the Law of 23 March 2007, commercial companies and EIGs may transfer assets, branches of activities or all of their assets and liabilities to another entity without such transfers resulting in the winding-up of the contributor. A branch of activity is defined in Article 308bis-3 of the Law of 10 August 1915 as being a "division which, from a technical and organisational point of view, exercises an independent activity and is capable of functioning by its own means".

In general such transfers involve one contributor and one beneficiary. However, in the case of transfers of all of an entity's assets and liabilities, there may be more than one beneficiary.

Transfers of assets, branches of activities and all of the assets and liabilities in an entity may take the form of contributions in kind for shares in the beneficiary or may take place without consideration in return. The parties involved in such transfers may decide to submit the transfers to the procedures for divisions set forth in Articles 285 to 308, with the exception of Article 303, of the Law of 10 August 1915.

Transfers involving non-Luxembourg entities similar to commercial companies and EIGs are also permissible under the Law of 10 August 1915 so long as the foreign law governing these entities also permits such transfers.

18.5.3   *Acquisitions*

In contrast to other European countries that have provided for acquisitions regulations for many years, Luxembourg provisions in respect of acquisitions has emerged only recently with new legislation and a more structured system being built.

Before proceeding it is necessary to distinguish between the two forms of acquisition under Luxembourg law – takeover bids and tender offers:

(a)   Takeover bids (*offres publiques d'achat* or "OPAs") are regulated in Luxembourg by the Law of 19 May 2006. With the introduction of the Law of 19 May 2006, a person who takes control of a certain percentage of shares in a listed company in Luxembourg must make a takeover bid for all of the capital of the company (*see* 18.14 below).

(b)   Acquisitions by exchange of shares, that is, tender offers (*offres publiques d'échange* or "OPEs") are subject to a number of formalities. The Law of 10 July 2005 on the offer and sale of transferable securities are also applicable to tender offers (see 18.7 and 18.8 below).

18.6   Methods of acquisition

A distinction may be made between those acquisitions which are the result of a public offer and those which imply an agreement between the companies involved.

Acquisitions which are the result of a public offer include hostile takeovers. According to the Law of 19 May 2006, public offers may be either voluntary or mandatory.

As regards acquisitions which imply an agreement between the companies involved, mergers and divisions are also methods of acquisition. The procedure observed in respect of divisions is similar to the one relating to mergers (*see* 18.5.1 above).

Voluntary acquisitions may also result from private agreements. Although the Civil Code provides a guarantee against hidden defects and the guarantee of the buyer's peaceful possession of the shares, this protection does not guarantee the value of the shares. A private agreement thus may supplement the legal provisions by inserting representations, warranties and guarantees.

18.7 Preparation of an offer

A company which has taken a decision to make a bid and is subject to the Law of 9 May 2006 is required by such law to make this decision public without delay and to inform the supervisory authority of this intention.

A company intending to launch a public offer generally contacts the main shareholder or the board of the target company, in the case of an agreed bid, in order to start informal negotiations.

Negotiations are not binding upon the parties. However, if the fault of one or more of the parties causes the negotiations to end, such a termination may give rise to damages to the party not at fault. It should also be noted that according to Article 1583 of the Civil Code, an agreement on the price to be paid and the object to be sold is sufficient to conclude a sale. Thus, if a precise offer is made, its acceptance by a shareholder is binding on the offeror.

An offeror usually seeks to obtain information about the target company and thus a due diligence procedure conducted with the help of lawyers and auditors usually precedes the public offer. The Luxembourg trade and companies register or the official gazette (*Mémorial*) may also provide useful information about the target company.

In order to ensure the equal treatment of all shareholders, the LSE and the supervisory authorities require that the offeror informs the target company's shareholders of the bid and offers them identical conditions of sale. If the offeror does not comply with this obligation, the sanction could be the withdrawal of its shares from the LSE.

In relation to tender bids, it should be noted that the company intending to launch the public offer must ensure that it complies with all of the applicable legal provisions. If a non-Luxembourg company is involved in the tender bid, it must make sure that the bid also conforms to the laws of the company's country of origin. For example, if it intends to offer its own shares as consideration for the shares of the target company, it must verify that its national law allows such a transaction.

If the consideration for the shares of the target company consists of shares or bonds to be issued by the offeror, a meeting of its shareholders must approve the increase of share capital, while the issue of bonds may be decided by its board.

18.8 Conduct of a public offer

18.8.1 OPE (exchange offer)

If a public exchange offer is made for a Luxembourg company, the party launching the OPE must prepare a prospectus and submit it – along with a summary of the risks associated with the offer, characteristics of the securities and supporting documents referred to in the prospectus – for approval in compliance with the Law of 10 July 2005 on prospectuses for securities implementing

Directive 2003/71/EC of the European Parliament and of the Council dated 4 November 2003 ("the Law of 10 July 2005"). Prospectuses must include all relevant information required to properly inform the investors of the OPE. (*See* 18.13.1 below for a detailed explanation and description of prospectuses.)

The Law of 10 July 2005 names the CSSF as the competent authority to review and approve prospectuses in view of making public offers on the Luxembourg territory.

The prospectus must be made available to the public. The prospectus should be published on the day that it is approved or shortly thereafter.

18.8.2   OPA (takeover bid)

Pursuant to the Law of 19 May 2006, once a person decides to launch an OPA it must notify the CSSF of its decision and make its decision known to the public. Within 10 days of publication, the person launching the OPA ("the offeror") must submit an offer document to the CSSF for approval (*see* 18.13.2 for a detailed description of the offer document). The CSSF reviews the offer document from the standpoint of whether it conforms to the Law of 19 May 2006 and not in terms of the solvency of the offeror or the economic implications of the OPA. The CSSF has 30 days upon receipt to review and approve or reject the offer document. The CSSF may require the offeror to supplement or revise the offer document if it has good reason to believe that the offer document is incomplete.

Once the CSSF has approved the offer document, this document must be published in a manner determined by the CSSF and that will ensure that all security holders in Member States, upon whose regulated markets the company's securities are admitted to trading, are able to make an informed assessment of the offer document.

After publication of the approved offer document, security holders of the offeree company have between two and 10 weeks to make a decision on the OPA. The CSSF may permit an extension of the acceptance period, but nevertheless the period must not exceed a total of six months. If the offeror gains control of the offeree company before the end of the acceptance period, any securities holders who have not yet accepted the bid are given 15 days to accept the bid.

During the bid process, the offeror must adhere to the principles of equitable price and equal treatment of the shareholders. Therefore, the offeror must offer shareholders of the same class of securities identical conditions of sale. Accordingly, if the offeror increases the amount of consideration offered to some shareholders before the end of the acceptance period, those securities holders who have already accepted the bid must also benefit from the increase in consideration.

In the event that the obligations and procedures set forth by the Law of 19 May 2006 are not followed, the OPA will be deemed null and void. The CSSF may impose a fine (*amende d'ordre*) ranging from €125 to €12,500 for non-compliance. Criminal sanctions may apply where the offeror failed to inform the CSSF of the bid, did not comply with the CSSF's request for supplementary information to the offer document or where either the offeror or the offeree company failed to provide their personnel representatives, or employees, with the offer document for review. Such criminal sanctions may take the form of imprisonment for eight days to five years and a fine of between €251 and €125,000.

18.9 Method of calculating the acquisition of control

Article 5 of the Law of 19 May 2006 sets at 33.33 the percentage of voting rights which confers control of a company situated in Luxembourg. The calculation of this percentage takes into account every security carrying a voting right except for those which grant voting rights only in the exceptional circumstances listed in Articles 44(2) and 46 of the Law of 10 August 1915. According to the Luxembourg Chamber of Deputies' (*"Chambre des Députés"*) commentary on the bill leading to the Law of 19 May 2006, the threshold was set at 33.33 per cent because this is the threshold commonly used by other Member States and because, as mentioned at 18.3 above, this percentage corresponds to one of the thresholds already employed by Luxembourg company law in Article 67–1 of the Law of 10 August 1915.

18.10 Defences to a hostile offer

Among the defences to a hostile offer, the following are the ones which may be used in Luxembourg:

18.10.1 Restriction to the free transfer of shares

Public companies may limit the free transfer of their shares provided that the corresponding clauses are inserted in the articles of association of the company in question. The most common type of inserted clauses are approval clauses or pre-emption clauses.

18.10.1.1 Approval clauses

Approval clauses make the transfer of shares subject to the authorisation of either the shareholders meeting or company's managerial body, thus preventing a hostile raider from acquiring the company's shares.

Luxembourg company law does not directly regulate approval clauses. However, according to legal scholars, such clauses are allowed provided that they do not completely block the transfer of shares.

However, one obstacle to the use of approval clauses is a requirement found in the Rules and Regulations of the Luxembourg Stock Exchange (Part I, Chapter 5, Item 502 and Part I, Chapter 6, Item 602), which states that listed shares must be freely transferable. However, the Rules and Regulations of the Luxembourg Stock Exchange include a caveat whereby approval clauses will not prevent shares from being listed as long as the clauses do not disrupt the stock market (Part I, Chapter 5, Item 503 referring to Chapter V, Article 35() of Regulation (EC) No 1287/2006 and Part I, Chapter 6, Item 602).

18.10.1.2 Pre-emption clauses

Pre-emption clauses require that a shareholder give preference to the company or to other shareholders when transferring its shares. During a certain period of time the beneficiaries of the pre-emption right may buy the shares under the same conditions as proposed in the sale to third parties, or at a fixed price determined by the articles of association.

Pre-emption clauses are valid in Luxembourg provided that they do not obstruct the free transferability of shares in situations where pre-emption rights are not exercised and that they do not despoil the transferor. As with approval clauses, pre-emption clauses may also present an obstacle to the admission of the company's securities to the LSE.

18.10.2   Regrouping of voting rights

By the creation of "shareholder blocs" achieved through voting agreements, fiduciary agreements or the incorporation of an intermediate company, shareholders may discourage a hostile raider from acquiring shares of the company.

Voting agreements have the disadvantages (i) that they may be invoked only against shareholders and not against the company itself and (ii) above all that those working in concert must notify the CSSF of their voting agreement and may be required to make a public offer for the shares in the company if the relevant conditions are met. Non-compliance with the voting agreement will thus not have an effect on the validity of the resolutions made at a shareholders meeting.

Fiduciary agreements are governed by the Law of 27 July 2003 concerning the Convention of The Hague of 1 July 1985, as modified by the Law of 22 March 2004. The fiduciary in such agreements in Luxembourg is usually a credit institution, to which all of the shares of the company are transferred and which will exercise the voting rights attached to the shares in accordance with the fiduciary agreement.

Shareholders may also decide to create a holding company to which they will transfer their shares. In order to unify their votes, the shareholders give appropriate instructions to the management boards of the holding company with regard to the transferred shares.

18.10.3   Poison pills

Luxembourg law also permits the defensive strategy known as the "poison pill". The Law of 24 April 1983 modifying the Law of 10 August 1915, which itself is modified by the Law of 4 May 1984, introduced into Luxembourg company law the concept of authorised capital. The articles of association of a company or its shareholders meeting may authorise the board to increase, in one or more steps, the company's capital up to a certain amount with or without reserving to the existing shareholders a pre-emptive right to subscribe for the new shares. By issuing new shares the board of directors may thus dilute the participation of a hostile raider.

The authorisation given by the articles of association or adopted by a share-holders meeting, by a quorum of half of the shares issued and with a two-thirds majority, has a limited validity of five years from the publication of the authoris-ation in the official gazette (*Mémorial*), but may be renewed (*see* Articles 67–1(2) and 35(5) of the Law of 10 August 1915). Shares issued in respect of a contri-bution in kind must be fully paid up within a period of five years (*see* Article 32–1(5) of the Law of 10 August 1915).

However, as the "poison pill" strategy often implies a restriction or a cancellation of the pre-emptive rights of current shareholders and thus an unequal treatment of shareholders, a company listed on the LSE might, by adopting this strategy, violate the Rules and Regulations of the Luxembourg Stock Exchange. Indeed, one of the conditions for admission to official LSE listing is the undertaking by the issuer of securities to assure the equal treatment of all shareholders subject to identical conditions.

18.10.4   Other defences

Finally there are other defences such as putting the company in question in debt, for instance by bond issues or other means, stock redemption or a counter-offer to buy the hostile raider's shares.

18.11   Breakthrough rules

Directive 2004/25/EC of the European Parliament and of the Council of 21 April 2004, which the Law of 19 May 2006 implements into Luxembourg law, gives Member States the option of whether their implementations of the Directive will require companies to adhere to the board neutrality provisions of the Directive's breakthrough rules. If, however, a Member State "opts out" and chooses not to make these provisions mandatory, then the Member State must permit com-panies to "opt in" and voluntarily apply these provisions. Luxembourg, in its transposition of Directive 2004/25/EC, has chosen to "opt out" and thus the Law of 19 May 2006 allows companies to "opt in" by way of a reversible decision made by the general shareholders meeting.

Under the Luxembourg breakthrough rules (Article 12 of the Law of 19 May 2006) to which companies may "opt in", provisions in the companies' articles of association that restrict the transfer of securities are without force during the takeover bid process. If the company has entered into contractual agreements with security holders which include restrictions on the free transferability of securities, these provisions also will not apply during the takeover period. Such constraints included in contracts between security holders similarly will not apply if the contracts were entered into after 21 April 2004.

These breakthrough rules also apply to restrictions placed on voting rights that are either in the articles of association or contained in contractual agreements. In the case of voting rights, the restrictions will not apply when the shareholders' general meeting deliberates on any defensive measures to the takeover bid. The breakthrough rules also limit multiple voting rights to one vote during such general shareholders meetings.

The breakthrough rule also applies if the offeror holds 75 per cent or more of the share capital carrying voting rights following a bid. In such cases, restrictions on voting rights or the transferability of securities, or any extraordinary rights of shareholders concerning the appointment or removal of board members will not apply. Multiple voting rights will also only carry a single vote at the first general shareholders meeting convened by the offeror to amend the articles of association or remove or appoint board members.

18.12   Profit forecasts and asset valuations

Profit forecasts and asset valuations are conducted in accordance with the accounting principles generally accepted in Luxembourg (also referred to as LUX GAAP). Companies having securities listed and admitted to trading on an EU regulated market and companies falling within the scope of application of the law of 16 March 2006 *relative à l'introduction des normes comptables internationales pour les établissements de crédit* will in any cases have to draw up their financial information in accordance with IFRS.

18.13   Documents from the offeror

18.13.1   *Public offer prospectus (in the context of an OPE)*

A person launching an OPE must prepare and submit a prospectus to either the CSSF or the LSE (*see* 18.8.1). The mandatory contents of a prospectus, as described in the annexes of the Law of 10 July 2005, are the following:

(a)   summary of the principal information included in the prospectus;
(b)   identity of the directors, senior management, advisers and auditors, as well as all company representatives and other interested persons;
(c)   key information regarding the offer and important dates relating to the offer;
(d)   background information concerning the offeror company's financial status, capital stock and risk factors;
(e)   information regarding the offeror's business operations, the products it makes or the services it provides, as well as the factors that affect these operations;
(f)   the management's explanation of factors that have affected the offeror's financial condition and the outcome of operations included in financial statements, and the management's assessment of factors and trends which are expected to have a material effect on the offeror's financial condition and that may affect the future operations of the company;
(g)   information concerning the offeror's directors and managers that will allow investors to assess their experience, qualifications and levels of remuneration, as well as their relationship to the company, and information relating to the company's employees and shareholders;

(h)   information regarding major shareholders and others persons who control, or who could have an influence on, the offeror;

(i)   financial information;

(j)   information regarding the offer or the admission to trading of the securities, the plan for distribution of the securities and related matters; and

(k)   supplementary information such as nominal capital, expert opinions, etc.

The prospectus should be drafted in Luxembourgish, French, German or English. Depending upon where the OPE is made or on which Member State's market the securities are to be admitted, a prospectus might have to be drawn up in another language.

18.13.2   *Offer document (in the context of an OPA)*

According to the Law of 19 May 2006, the submission of an offer document to the CSSF is a prerequisite for an OPA. Article 6 of the law states that an offer document must include at least the following information:

(a)   terms of the bid;

(b)   identity of the offeror and, if the offeror is a company, its type, name and registered office;

(c)   the securities or, where appropriate, the class or classes of securities for which the bid is made;

(d)   the consideration offered for each security or class of securities and, in the case of a mandatory bid, the method used to determine the consideration and the means of payment of the consideration;

(e)   the compensation offered for the rights which might be removed as a result of the breakthrough rule described in Article 12(4) of the Law of 19 May 2006, specifying the way in which the compensation is to be paid and the method employed in calculating the compensation (*see* 18.11 for more information on the breakthrough rule);

(f)   the maximum and minimum percentages or quantities of securities which the offeror undertakes to acquire;

(g)   details of any existing holdings of the offeror, and of persons acting in concert with him, in the offeree company;

(h)   all of the conditions to which the bid is subject;

(i)   the offeror's intentions regarding the future business of the offeree company and, in so far as it is affected by the bid, any material change in the conditions of employment, the offeror's strategic plans for the two companies and the likely repercussions on employment and the locations of the companies' places of business;

(j)   the time allowed for acceptance of the bid;

(k)   information concerning securities offered as consideration, if applicable;

(l)   the financing of the bid;

(m)   the identity of individuals or companies acting in concert with the offeror or the offeree company and, where companies are acting in concert, their types, names, registered offices and relationships to the offeror and, where applicable, with the offeree company; and

(n)   the national law which will govern the contracts concluded between the offeror and the security holders of the offeree company as a result of the bid, and an indication of the competent jurisdictions.

The offer document should be drafted in Luxembourgish, French, German, English or in another language accepted by the CSSF.

Depending upon where the OPA is made or on which EU Member State's market the securities are to be admitted, a prospectus might have to be drawn up in another language.

18.14   Compulsory acquisitions of minorities

According to the Law of 19 May 2006, if a person, either on his own or through an acquisition by someone with whom he is working in concert, acquires securities in the offeree company granting him 33.33 per cent of the voting rights in the offeree, he must make a mandatory bid at a fair equitable price to buy the remaining shares of the minority shareholders. As explained in greater detail at 18.9 above, this threshold percentage is calculated by taking into account all of the securities of the offeree company, with the exclusion of those securities that confer voting rights only in specific situations.

The aforementioned fair equitable price is determined to be the highest price paid for the same securities by the offeror, or by persons acting in concert with him, over a period of 12 months before the mandatory bid. If, during the interim between the publication of the mandatory bid and the expiration of the acceptance period, the offeror or someone acting in concert with him purchases securities for a price higher than the fair equitable price of the mandatory bid, he must compensate the minority shareholders to ensure that the amount that they received for their securities is not less than the highest price offered for the same class of securities.

18.15   Insider dealing and market manipulation

18.15.1   Insider dealing

Insider dealing is currently governed in Luxembourg by the Law of 9 May 2006 concerning market abuse ("the Law of 9 May 2006"). The Law of 9 May 2006 repealed the previous law on insider dealing (the Law of 3 May 1991 relating to insider dealing, "the Law of 3 May 1991") and implements several EU Council Directives relating to insider dealing and market abuse. The Law of 9 May 2006 has introduced a number of significant changes to Luxembourg's treatment of insider dealing. For example, the Law of 9 May 2006 has substantially broadened the scope of the prohibition on insider dealing.

18.15.1.1   The scope of the prohibition on insider dealing
The prohibition on insider dealing set forth by the Law of 9 May 2006 extends to all financial instruments admitted to trading, or that are the subject of a request for admission to trading, on a regulated market or a multilateral trading facility

("MTF"). The mere intent to engage in insider dealing is sufficient to trigger the application of this law.

Definition of insider dealing

The Law of 9 May 2006 (Articles 8 and 9) states that insider dealing occurs when a person who is in possession of inside information:

(a) uses the inside information to acquire, or dispose of, or to try to acquire or dispose of, for his own account or for the account of a third party, either directly or indirectly, financial instruments to which the information relates;

(b) discloses the inside information to any other person, unless such a disclosure is made in the normal course of his employment, profession or duties; or

(c) recommends or induces another person, on the basis of the inside information, to acquire or dispose of financial instruments to which the information relates.

Inside information

"Inside information" is:

(a) information of a precise nature;

(b) which has not been made public;

(c) which relates, directly or indirectly, to one or more issuers of financial instruments or to one or more financial instruments; and

(d) which if it were made public, would likely have a significant effect on the prices of the financial instruments or on the price of derivative financial instruments.

Insiders

The Law of 9 May 2006 has broadened the definition of insiders, and distinguishes between "primary" and "secondary" insiders.

Article 8 of the Law of 9 May 2006 defines a "primary insider" as any person, physical or legal, who possesses inside information:

(a) by virtue of being a member of the administrative, management or supervisory body of the issuer; or

(b) by virtue of holding an interest in the capital of the issuer; or

(c) through the exercise of his employment, profession or duties; or

(d) as a result of his criminal activities.

A "secondary" insider is defined by Article 10 as being any person, other than a primary insider, who possesses inside information and who knows, or ought to have known, that it is inside information.

Financial instruments

Financial instruments are:

(a) transferable securities;

(b) units in collective investment undertakings;

(c) money-market instruments;

(d)   financial futures contracts, including equivalent cash-settled instruments;

(e)   forward interest-rate agreements;

(f)   interest-rate, currency and equity swaps;

(g)   options to acquire or dispose of any instrument falling into one of the above-mentioned categories, including equivalent cash-settled instruments and, in particular, options on currency and on interest rates;

(h)   derivatives on commodities; or

(i)   any other instrument admitted, or the subject of a request for admission, to trading on a regulated market.

Transactions covered by the Law of 9 May 2006

The Law of 9 May 2006 applies to transactions carried out either in Luxembourg or abroad concerning securities that are admitted to trading, or that are the subject of a request for admission to trading, on a regulated market or MTF located in Luxembourg and transactions carried out in Luxembourg relating to securities admitted to trading, or the subject of a request for admission to trading, on a regulated market outside of Luxembourg.

Transactions concerning financial instruments admitted to trading on, or that are the subject of a request for admission on, a foreign MTF are not within the purview of the Law of 9 May 2006. The Law of 9 May 2006 also does not apply to transactions carried out in pursuit of monetary, exchange-rate or public-debt management policies of a Member State or a country outside of the EU, the Central Banks of Europe, national central banks, any officially designated institutions or any person working on their behalf. The prohibitions on insider dealing also do not apply to buy-back programmes or financial instrument stabilisation measures if these measures are taken pursuant to Commission Regulation (EC) No. 2273/2003 of 22 December 2003 implementing Directive 2003/6/EC of the European Parliament and of the Council.

Mens rea

In order to prove insider dealing, it is insufficient to only demonstrate that a person has used inside information in a prohibited manner. The penalties provided for by the Law of 9 May 2006, in particular Article 32, apply only to insiders who took advantage of inside information with full knowledge of the facts and deliberately violated the provisions set forth by the law. Not only must knowledge of the inside information be proven in order to convict such a person, but also his intention to avoid a loss or to make a profit must be shown. Whether the transaction has actually benefited the inside dealer is irrelevant.

18.15.1.2   Sanctions

Criminal sanctions

Penalties of three months' to two years' imprisonment and/or a fine ranging from €125 to €1.5 million may be levied by a criminal court against a primary insider who deliberately used inside information in violation of the Law of 9 May 2006. Secondary insiders who deliberately used insider information in violation the law may be imprisoned for between eight days and one year and/or fined €125 to €1.5 million.

In the event that the insider did not use the inside information for his own personal gain or for that of a third party, but instead recommended or disclosed the information to others, a criminal sanction of imprisonment for between eight days and one year and/or a fine of €125 to €25,000 may be imposed. Attempted insider dealing carries the same criminal sanctions as the actual act of insider dealing.

In all of these situations, it is within the criminal court's discretion to increase the fine up to 10 times the amount of the proceeds of the offence.

Public law sanctions
Additionally, the CSSF may impose public law sanctions, including the temporary suspension of a person's professional licence. The period of such a suspension must not exceed five years.

Civil sanctions
An inside trader may also incur civil liability. A person who sold or transferred his securities at a very low price to an inside dealer may pursue a civil action against the dealer for any loss suffered as a result of the latter's illegal behaviour. The same applies to the issuer of the securities in question who may have suffered a loss due to the insider dealing. In addition, as insider dealing infringes the public economic order, the transaction should be declared null and void. However, practical considerations may make it difficult to carry out these civil sanctions.

18.15.1.3 *Administrative supervision and investigation*
The Law of 9 May 2006 designates the CSSF as the administrative authority competent to ensure that professionals comply with the law's provisions (*see* Article 28 and following of the Law of 9 May 2006). As mentioned above at 18.1, the CSSF is an independent, impartial body and its staff is bound by professional secrecy sanctioned by Article 458 of the Criminal Code. The CSSF may proceed with an investigation of alleged insider dealing either on its own initiative or upon request. Such a request may come from a foreign authority with which the CSSF collaborates. Pursuant to the law, the CSSF has wide investigative powers and has the power to impose sanctions (*see* 18.15.1.2 above). Decisions made by the CSSF may be appealed before the administrative courts.

18.15.2 *Market manipulation*

The Law of 9 May 2006 has introduced into Luxembourg law a working definition of the term "market manipulation". According to Article 1(2) of the Law of 9 May 2006, market manipulations include the following:

(a)   the act of carrying out an operation or ordering an operation that gives or makes available false or misleading information concerning the offer, demand or rate of financial instruments, or that fixes, by the action of one of more persons acting in concert, the rate of one or more financial instruments at an abnormal or artificial level;

(b)   the act of carrying out operations or ordering an operation that resorts to fictional behaviour or any other form of trickery or deceit;

(c)   the act of spreading information, either by way of the media or by any other means, gives or is capable of giving false or misleading information relating to financial instruments, including the act of spreading rumours, where the person spreading the information knows or should have known that the information was false or misleading.

The Law of 9 May 2006 prohibits all persons from taking part in market manipulations (*see* Article 11 of the Law of 9 May 2006) and provides for sanctions of three months' to two years' imprisonment and/or a fine of €125 to €1.5 million.

18.16   Transposition of the Transparency Directive

Directive 2004/109/EC of the European Parliament and of the Council of 15 December 2004 on the harmonisation of transparency requirements in relation to information about issuers whose securities are admitted to trading on a regulated market, part of the Financial Services Action Plan of the European Union, imposes a 20 January 2007 deadline by which Member States need to have taken the necessary measures to transpose the Directive into their national laws. Luxembourg has taken steps to implement the Directive and, on 11 January 2008, it adopted the law concerning the transparency requirements in relation to information about issuers whose securities are admitted to trading on a regulated market ("the Law of 11 January 2008") which transposes the aforementioned Directive into Luxembourg law. In transposing the Directive, Luxembourg has chosen not to take advantage of the option presented in Article 3 of the Directive whereby Member States may submit issuers to requirements stricter than those laid out in the Directive and, accordingly, the Law of 11 January 2008 faithfully reproduces, with a few variations, the provisions set forth by the Directive.

Luxembourg's transparency requirements used to be found in the Law of 4 December 1992 which largely reflected the dispositions laid out in Directive 2001/34/EC of the European Parliament and of the Council of 28 May 2001 on the admission of securities to official Stock Exchange listing and on information to be published on those securities. The Law of 11 January 2008 abolishes the Law of 4 December 1992 and parallels the construction and content of Directive 2004/109/EC, introducing a number of requirements and obligations which will affect the operations of investors and issuers in Luxembourg.

These requirements include *inter alia* periodic reporting (annual and half-yearly financial reports to be prepared by the issuer, as well as interim management declarations) and the publication and filing of regulated information. The Law of 11 January 2008 requires that the issuers of securities admitted to trading on a regulated market must publish regulated information, make it available to an officially appointed mechanism ("OAM"), which remains to be designated, and file it with the CSSF, the competent authority for such matters in Luxembourg.

The Law of 11 January 2008 also requires CSSF notification if an acquisition or disposal of major holdings results in the proportion of voting rights reaching, exceeding or falling below 5, 10, 15, 20, 25, 33.33, 50 or 66.66 per cent of the company's total voting rights. The Law of 11 January 2008 also combines other provisions from the Law of 4 December 1992 with those set forth in Directive 2004/109/EC. These references to the previous law are primarily with regard to administrative concerns and sanctions.

18.17 Financial assistance

Takeover bids or tender offers may be financed through bond issues or other credit instruments such as bills of exchange or letters of credit.

With regard to loan financing, it should be noted that Article 49–6 of the Law of 10 August 1915, as amended, prohibits a company from granting loans or guarantees, or advancing funds with a view to the acquisition of its shares by a third party. However, this prohibition does not apply to transactions made in the normal course of business of a bank or other financial institution, nor does it apply to transactions undertaken for the acquisition of shares by or for the staff of the company or for the acquisition of shares issued by an investment company with fixed capital and acquired at the investor's request by that company or by a person acting in his own name, but on the behalf of the company.

As a consequence of the dispositions laid out in Article 49–6 of the Law of 10 August 1915, a takeover bid or tender offer may not be financed through assets of the target company. This prohibition is sanctioned, pursuant to Article 168 of the Law of 10 August 1915, by imprisonment of one month to two years and/or fines of €5,000 to €125,000. Such sanctions may be imposed on any persons who, as directors, statutory auditors, managers or supervisory board members knowingly made such loans or advances in violation of Article 49–6. A decision by the company's shareholders meeting may not waive the criminal proceedings or criminal sanctions prescribed by Articles 49–6 and 168 of the Law of 10 August 1915.

Furthermore, although there is no case law directly relating to the matter, it has been theorised that Article 49–6 also prohibits similar financial assistance for the acquisition of shares in a parent company or affiliated companies, unless the assisting company has a direct interest in the granting of such a guarantee or loan.

Chapter 19

Malta

Nicolai Vella Falzon

Partner
Fenech & Fenech Advocates

19.1   Introduction

There has been considerable M&A activity in Malta since the last update of this publication in 2005, most notably as a result of the Government's continuing privatisation drive but also within the private sector. The more notable privatisations during this period were the Government's disposal of its stake in the national telecoms provider (Maltacom plc) in 2006 and more recently in 2007 the disposal of its minority stake in OilTanking Malta Limited (a subsidiary of OilTanking AG, a division of German Marquard & Bahls AG) and of a 25 per cent stake in Maltapost plc (the national mail service provider) with its remaining 40 per cent shareholding being offered to the public on the Stock Exchange. Notably, in the private sector in 2007, the majority shareholder in Melita plc (owner of the only television and data cable infrastructure on this island) transferred its shares in the company to GMT Communications Partners, a European independent private equity group focused exclusively on the communications sector.

More importantly, there has been considerable legislative activity between 2005 and 2007 in so far as laws and regulations relevant to mergers and acquisitions are concerned. In November 2005, the Listing Rules issued by the Malta Financial Services Authority for companies listed on the Malta Stock Exchange were relaunched with a view to introducing amendments necessary for the implementation of the EC Prospectus Directive (Directive 2003/71/EC) transposed into Maltese law in November 2005, by virtue of a legal notice entitled "Companies Act (The Prospectus) Regulations, 2005".

In 2006 there was more intensive legislative activity, most notably the transposition of the Takeover Bids Directive 2004/25/EC of the European Parliament and of the Council of 21 April 2004 into the Listing Rules with the addition of a new Chapter 18 effective as of June 2006. During the same time, a revised version of the Code of Principles of Good Corporate Governance applicable to listed companies was also brought into effect.

More recently, in February 2007, the Listing Rules were amended again following the transposition of the EC Transparency Directive (2004/109/EC) the scope of which is to harmonise the transparency requirements to disclose information about issuers whose securities are admitted to trading on a regulated market.

With effect from 13 March 2007, the local merger control regulations entitled "Control of Concentrations Regulations" issued pursuant to the Competition Act 1995, were amended with the principal aim of increasing the thresholds for notification. It is also expected that before the end of 2007 Malta will have implemented the Tenth Company Law Directive (No. 2005/56/EG) of 26 October 2005 on cross-border mergers of public limited companies as Member States have until 15 December 2007 to transpose the merger Directive into national law.

Notably, Malta adopted the euro as its national currency with effect from 1 January 2008 and accordingly by operation of law all figures appearing in any laws became denominated in euro on the basis of the irrevocably fixed conversion rate of 0.4293. Figures mentioned in this Chapter are shown in euro with the Maltese lira equivalent.

19.2   Acquisition targets

Most Maltese companies are still private companies, although there has been a wave of initial public offerings ("IPOs") since the early 1990s and an increasing number of public listings over the 10 years between 1997 and 2007. At the time of writing, there were 17 listed companies (one of which was listed on the Second-Tier Market) on the Malta Stock Exchange together with a number of corporate bonds, closed-ended collective investment schemes and government stocks.

Limited liability companies can be constituted as private or public companies. Once constituted, private companies can be converted into public companies and vice versa in accordance with the procedures laid down in Part VII of the Companies Act 1995.

As far as the constitution of limited liability companies is concerned, the law requires that the management and administration of the company is vested in a single board of directors generally appointed (and removed) by a simple majority of the shareholders in general meeting. Matters not concerning the ordinary administration of the company and affecting its constitution (such as changes to the memorandum and articles of association, increases in share capital and changes to the constitution of the board of directors) are reserved for the shareholders in general meeting.

19.2.1   *Private companies*

Private companies are mandatorily required through their memorandum and articles of association to:

(a)   limit the number of their shareholders to 50;
(b)   restrict the right to transfer their shares; and
(c)   prohibit any invitations to the public to subscribe for any shares or debentures in the company.

Offers for the sale of shares in private companies to the public are prohibited. Acquisitions of such companies are not regulated and are left to the discretion of the shareholders, whilst amalgamations (mergers) with other companies are subject to the rules laid down in Part VIII of the Companies Act 1995.

19.2.2   Public companies

Public companies must indicate in their memorandum and articles of association that the company is constituted as a public company and they must be set up with a minimum issued share capital of €46,587.47 (equivalent to LM20,000) subscribed to by at least two persons. As such, non-listed public companies are subject to the same rules regulating private limited liability companies in general, with the exception of special rules regulating capital issues by public companies. Public companies must issue a prospectus when issuing applications for their shares to the public. The matters to be specified therein and the reports to be set out by the company when making such an offer are set out in detail in the Second Schedule to the Companies Act 1995.

Listed companies are more heavily regulated and, in addition to the provisions of the Companies Act 1995, are subject to the Listing Rules issued by the Listing Authority (currently the Malta Financial Services Authority ("MFSA")) which include *inter alia* provisions regulating amalgamations (mergers) of listed companies, transactions involving substantial shareholdings (Chapter 8, Rules 8.142 to 8.152 of the Listing Rules) and (further to recent amendments) the provisions of the EC Prospective Directive and the EC Takeover Directive.

19.2.3   The regulatory authorities

The Malta Financial Services Authority is the single regulator for banking, investment and insurance business in Malta and also houses the country's Companies Registry. The MFSA supervises all licensed financial businesses, issues guidance notes, monitors local and international developments, works with relevant parties on legislative matters and plays a major role in training. Its responsibilities include the regulation, monitoring and control of *inter alia* :

(a)   banking and financial institutions;
(b)   investment funds and investment services providers;
(c)   insurance companies; and
(d)   insurance intermediaries.

As stated, the MFSA incorporates the Registry of Companies monitoring compliance of all companies, private and public, with the companies' legislation. As far as public listed companies are concerned, the MFSA is also the Listing Authority in terms of the Financial Markets Act 2002 (formerly the Malta Stock Exchange Act 1990), replacing the Council of the Malta Stock Exchange previously entrusted with the monitoring of such companies for compliance with *inter alia* the Listing Rules.

19.3   Exchange and investment control

In view of Malta's EU membership, exchange control laws have been abolished and the former Exchange Control Act 1972 has been renamed and replaced, with effect from 1 January 2004, by the External Transactions Act 2003. The aim is to provide the necessary infrastructure for full liberalisation of external transactions, whilst giving the Minister of Finance authority to introduce measures and controls when that would be critical for the balance of payments.

Some of the relevant restrictions that have been retained in terms of the External Transactions Act 2003 and the External Transactions Regulations 2003 are the following:

(a)   foreign currency holdings (the maximum limit on foreign currency holdings (cash/cheques) that a resident is exempted from surrendering to an institution licensed to carry on the business of foreign exchange is the equivalent of €116,468.67 (equivalent to LM50,000);

(b)   foreign currency current accounts with local credit institutions (the holding of foreign currency current accounts by natural persons and companies with local credit institutions is permitted subject to certain conditions);

(c)   foreign portfolio investments (while foreign portfolio investments are not subject to any quantitative limit, residents are not permitted to place funds in portfolio assets with a maturity period of less than six months);

(d)   financial loans by residents to non-residents (residents are not permitted to extend financial loans to non-residents for periods of less than six months);

(e)   financial loans to residents in foreign currency (residents are not permitted to borrow in foreign currencies from resident or non-resident sources for periods of less than six months);

(f)   investments by local fund investment schemes (fund investment schemes which collect funds in Maltese lira from residents with the specific aim of investing such funds in Maltese lira-denominated assets are not permitted to maintain foreign currency assets in excess of 15 per cent of their shareholders' funds);

(g)   spot/forward currency transactions (institutions licensed to carry on the business of foreign exchange are not permitted to enter into spot/forward contracts relating to capital account transactions where funds in Maltese lira borrowed by the resident or non-resident counterpart are used in the transaction);

(h)   repatriation of export receipts (residents involved in export transactions are not permitted to retain export proceeds in accounts with foreign credit institutions, as mentioned above, but they are permitted to deposit such proceeds in foreign currency accounts with local credit institutions);

(i)   the issue, acquisition, sale and redemption of securities not listed on the Malta Stock Exchange and registered in Malta – non-residents (applications by non-residents for the issue, acquisition, sale and redemption of securities not listed on the Malta Stock Exchange in local companies established, or to be established, in Malta have to be cleared by the Registrar of Companies of the Malta Financial Services Authority – with the exception of international holding/trading companies and companies which own a vessel registered under the Merchant Shipping Act 1973, Cap. 234, and where the resident participation does not exceed 20 per cent).

19.4   Merger control

On 1 January 2003 Parliament gave effect to Malta's first merger control regulations entitled "Control of Concentrations Regulations 2002" ("the Regulations"). The Regulations were amended with effect from 13 March 2007 principally with a view to increasing notification thresholds.

19.4.1   Applicability of the Regulations

In terms of the Regulations, a "concentration" arises in cases of:

(a)   a merger of two or more undertakings that were previously independent of each other;

(b)   an acquisition by one or more undertakings or by one or more persons already controlling at least one undertaking, whether by purchase of securities or assets, of direct or indirect control of the whole or parts of one or more undertakings; or

(c)   the creation of a "full-function joint venture" that performs on a lasting basis all the functions of an autonomous economic entity. The term "joint venture" is not defined,

subject to a threshold for qualification (*see* 19.4.2 below).

It should be noted that some activities are expressly deemed not to give rise to concentrations. These relate to:

(a)   temporary holdings by financial institutions or insurance companies;

(b)   liquidation, winding up, etc.;

(c)   the acquisition of holdings without being involved in the management.

The concept of "Control" is defined to mean the possibility of exercising a decisive influence on an undertaking, in particular:

(a)   through the ownership or the right to use all or part of the assets of an undertaking; or

(b)   through rights or contracts which confer "decisive influence" on the composition, voting or decisions of the organs of an undertaking,

provided that even persons or undertakings not holding such rights or entitled to such rights under the contract concerned are deemed to have acquired control if they have the power to exercise the rights deriving therefrom. The meaning of "decisive influence" is the same as under the EC Merger Regulation.

19.4.2   Qualification thresholds

A merger or acquisition qualifies as a "concentration" only if the combined aggregate turnover in Malta of all of the undertakings concerned in the preceding financial year exceeded €2,329,373.40 (equivalent to LM1 million) and each of the undertakings concerned had a turnover in Malta equivalent to at least 10 per cent of the combined aggregate turnover of the undertakings concerned. The Regulations state how the turnover should be calculated in various circumstances, but it is interesting to note that by virtue of the recent amendments to the Regulations, where a concentration consists in the acquisition of a part or parts of an undertaking or undertakings, it is only the turnover relating to the part or parts which are the subject of the transaction that ought to be taken into account with regard to the turnover of the seller or sellers. This also effectively increases notification thresholds in comparison to the position before the 2007 amendments.

As a general rule, aggregate turnover comprises the amounts derived by each of the undertakings concerned in the preceding financial year from the sale of products and the provision of services to other undertakings or consumers falling under the undertakings' ordinary activities after deduction of sales rebates and of value added tax and other taxes directly related to turnover. Intra-group sales of goods and services are generally excluded.

19.4.3   Applicability to foreign mergers

The Regulations are applicable to concentrations even in the case where the concentration takes place outside Malta, but only if the undertakings concerned have turnover in Malta that exceeds the statutory threshold.

19.4.4   Notification

Concentrations as defined in the Regulations must be notified to the Office for Fair Competition ("OFC"). Notification is mandatory. In the case of an acquisition of sole control, the notification must be made by the person or undertaking acquiring control. In the case of an acquisition of joint control, the parties acquiring joint control make a joint notification. In the case of a true merger, joint notification by the parties to the merger is required.

The effects of the transaction must be suspended until clearance is obtained. Where the OFC has not made a decision within the procedural time limits, the transaction is deemed to have been given clearance. A public bid may nevertheless be implemented subject to certain restrictions and conditions. Derogation is possible, upon a reasoned request to the OFC made before notification. The OFC will take into account, *inter alia* , the effects of the suspension and the threat to competition posed by the concentration. The derogation may be made subject to conditions.

19.4.5   The substantive test for clearance

Unlike the European Community in its Merger Regulation (4064/89 (1989) OJ L395/1), Malta has chosen to apply the Substantial Lessening of Competition Test ("SLC") in its merger regulations. The OFC will therefore not be concerned with whether or not the concentration might create or increase dominance in the market per se, but will examine the question as to whether or not the concentration might substantially lessen competition in the relevant market, irrespective of whether or not it might also create a dominant position. Potentially, the test applied by the OFC is a broader test than that applied by the EU Commission and the majority of Member States that apply the dominance test, but it is submitted that this is the more economically logical test as the real concern is not whether dominance will be created or strengthened but whether or not competition will ultimately suffer substantially as a result of the concentration.

19.4.6 Notification procedure

Within six weeks from receipt of complete notification the OFC is obliged either:

(a)   to issue a declaration stating that the Regulations do not apply to the concentration; or
(b)   to clear the concentration with or without conditions or restrictions; or
(c)   commence investigative proceedings if it is of the view that the concentration may have a significant impact on competition.

This first-stage period may be extended to eight weeks if the undertakings concerned submit commitments to the OFC in order that the concentration may be cleared without investigative proceedings, and may be extended further up to 12 weeks if the undertakings concerned have requested the OFC to discuss a new or substantially revised commitment proposal.

If investigative proceedings are commenced, the OFC must complete such proceedings within 16 weeks from the date of commencement. This period may be extended, at the request of the undertakings concerned, if they have in the meantime submitted commitments to the OFC. It may also be extended by the OFC in cases of incomplete information or other specified grounds.

There is a simplified procedure for specified categories of concentrations. The time limit in such cases is four weeks. The simplified procedure applies to the following categories of concentrations, as long as they are not deemed to raise serious doubts about their legality in terms of the Regulations:

(a)   where two or more undertakings acquire joint control of a joint venture where the joint venture has negligible actual or foreseen activities in Malta because the turnover of the joint venture in Malta is less than €698,812 (equivalent to LM300,000) and the total value of assets transferred to the joint venture in Malta is less than €698,812 (equivalent to LM300,000);
(b)   two or more undertakings merge, or one or more undertakings acquire sole or joint control of another undertaking, provided that none of the parties to the concentration are engaged in business activities in the same product and geographical market, or in a product market which is upstream or downstream of a product market in which any other party to the concentration is engaged;
(c)   two or more undertakings merge, or one or more undertakings acquire sole or joint control of another undertaking and two or more of the parties to the concentration are engaged in business activities either in the same product and geographical market and their combined market share is less than 15 per cent or in a product market which is upstream or downstream of a product market in which any other party to the concentration is engaged and their combined market share is less than 25 per cent.

19.4.7 Sanctions for non-compliance

Various sanctions, including fines and even imprisonment in certain cases, apply in cases where persons, undertakings or associations of undertakings intentionally or negligently:

(a)   fail to notify a qualifying concentration;
(b)   supply incorrect or misleading information to the OFC;
(c)   produce incomplete records or books required by the OFC during investigations;
(d)   refuse to submit to an investigation ordered by the OFC;
(e)   fail to comply with a decision of the OFC;
(f)   put into effect a concentration which has not been notified and cleared by the OFC;
(g)   put into effect a concentration that has been declared unlawful.

The validity of any such transaction giving rise to the concentration will also be at stake depending on the decision of the OFC at the first-stage proceedings. Therefore, if the OFC finds that it does not have any serious doubts about the lawfulness of the concentration, or the OFC does not make a decision within the statutory time limits, the transaction will be valid. On the other hand, should the OFC find that it has serious doubts, and commences investigative proceedings, the transaction will not be valid.

19.5   Regulation of the conduct of mergers and acquisitions

Unlisted companies are not subject to any particular legislation other than the rules relating to amalgamation of companies within the Companies Act 1995, as described 19.6.2 below. On the other hand amalgamations and mergers involving listed companies and transactions involving substantial shareholdings are regulated under paragraphs 8.142 to 8.152 of the Listing Rules discussed at 19.8 below. Public listed companies are now also subject to the rules of the Takeover Directive as transposed into Chapter 18 of the Listing Rules.

19.5.1 The Takeover Rules for listed companies

Where a person acquires a controlling interest in a listed company he must make a bid as a means of protecting the minority shareholders of that company. "Controlling Interest" is defined as an acquisition which gives the acquiring person, directly or indirectly, 50 per cent plus one of the voting rights of the company. Accordingly a bid must be made within a reasonable time for the acquisition of the shares of the holders of all other securities in the company at an equitable price. This obligation does not arise where the acquisition of the controlling interest was the outcome of a voluntary bid made to all the holders of all the securities in the company.

The person acquiring the controlling interest or "offeror" of the mandatory bid must inform the Listing Authority of the bid and must announce his decision to launch the bid within seven days of acquiring a controlling interest. The bid must be announced only after the offeror ensures that he can fulfil in full any cash consideration, if such is offered, and after taking all reasonable measures to secure the implementation of any other type of consideration. By way of consideration the offeror may offer securities, cash or a combination of both although a cash consideration must be offered as an alternative in all cases.

The offeror is obliged to draw up and make public (not later than 21 calendar days from announcing his decision to launch a bid) an offer document containing the information necessary to enable the holders of the offeree company's securities to reach a properly informed decision on the bid, which offer document shall be communicated to the Listing Authority prior to it being made available to the public. The Listing Rules include a detailed list of what the offer document itself must contain, but there must also be appended with the offer document a report on the consideration offered, drawn up by one or more experts who are independent of the offeror. The expert's report must confirm that the offeror has sufficient resources to meet the consideration to be provided on full acceptance of the offer and to pay any debts incurred in connection with the offer. Offerees must be given at least four weeks in order to make a decision whether to accept the bid or not and there are certain obligations imposed on the directors of the listed company to give advice to offerees and to publish an opinion on the effects of the implementation of the bid on the company's interests. During the term within which a bid is open for consideration, the directors of the company are prohibited from making any decisions that may result in the frustration of the bid without the prior consent of the shareholders in general meeting.

The purchase price for securities that are the object of a mandatory bid must be an equitable price determined in accordance with certain criteria laid down in the Listing Rules. Generally speaking the price offered for the security should not be below the weighted average price of the security made on a Recognised Investment Exchange during the previous six months; it should not be below the highest price paid for the security by the offeror during the previous six months; it should not be below the weighted average price paid for the security by the offeror during the previous six months; and it should not be lower than 10 per cent below the weighted average price of the security within the previous 10 trading days.

19.5.1.1 *Squeeze-out rights*
Where, following acceptance of the bid, the offeror has acquired or has firmly contracted to acquire securities representing not less than 90 per cent of the listed company's capital carrying voting rights and 90 per cent of the voting rights comprised in the bid, the offeror has the right (exercisable within three months of the end of the time allowed for acceptance of the bid) to require all the holders of the remaining securities to sell him those securities at a fair price and shall take the same form as the consideration offered in the bid or, alternatively, in cash. In order to establish a fair price the offeror must appoint an independent expert to draw up a report determining the price considered to be a fair and reasonable value of those securities, which price must however be equivalent to or higher than the equitable price determined as aforesaid.

19.5.1.2   Sell-out rights

At any time following a bid made to all the holders of a listed company's securities for all of their securities, the holder of remaining securities may require the offeror to buy his securities from him at a fair price under the same circumstances as provided for in the case of the exercise of a squeeze-out right. In order to establish a fair price, the holders of the remaining securities must appoint an independent expert to draw up a report determining the price considered to be a fair and reasonable value of those securities, which price must however be equivalent to or more than the equitable price determined as aforesaid.

19.5.1.3   Opting in and opting out

The Listing Rules contain further provisions allowing the holders of securities of listed companies, in certain circumstances, to opt in or opt out of the restrictions imposed in terms of the rules relating to takeover bids.

19.6   Methods of acquisition

Corporate law and commercial practice in Malta have been greatly influenced by UK law and practice and, also due to the language factor, major acquisition agreements used in Malta are modelled on UK purchase agreements modified and adapted in order to cater for the civil law implications of such share purchase agreements. Normally, however, the standard representations and warranties commonly found in UK share purchase agreements are almost entirely adopted to afford protection to the purchasers of shares since under civil law principles applying in Malta, purchasers of movable things (including shares in companies) are only given a warranty in so far as peaceful possession is concerned and are only afforded protection against "latent" (hidden) defects.

19.6.1   Private share purchase agreement

The most straightforward method of acquisition is by purchasing the whole or the controlling shareholding in the target company. Share purchase agreements are normally constituted as private agreements and the intervention of a Notary Public is not normally required.

It should be noted that, as of January 2005, the procedure for transfers of shares has been affected by new rules regulating Capital Gains computations in terms of the Income Tax Act 1949. The chargeable gain will now be computed not simply in relation to the price, but in relation to the higher of the transfer price or the market value of the shares transferred, where the shares being transferred constitute a "controlling interest" (less the cost of acquisition of the shares in question). "Controlling interest" is defined to include a situation where the shares being transferred represent at least 25 per cent of the nominal value of the issued share capital of the company or of the voting rights attaching to the company's shares.

The implication of this is that, prior to registering a share transfer, the parties to a share transfer agreement must submit to the Commissioner of Inland Revenue (Capital Transfer Duty Department) a statement issued by a certified public auditor in Malta with regard to the value of the shares transferred – at this stage, Provisional Tax will have to be paid. The statement must also state whether the transfer is a transfer of a controlling interest or not and indicate the grounds on which this statement is based.

Where the transfer is of a controlling interest, the statement will include a tax computation of the market value of the shares transferred and this must be accompanied by an architect's valuation of the market value of any immovable property taken into account in determining the value of the shares. There are detailed rules to be followed by the auditor in computing the market value of the shares, but essentially the method is based on the adjustment of the net asset value of the company in question.

Only once the provisional tax has been assessed and paid can the share transfer be submitted for registration to the Registry of Companies in order to be given legal effect.

As far as share transfers in private companies are concerned, the only formality that would apply, other than the capital gains rules described above, is that the share transfer agreement and the requisite forms giving notice of such share transfer together with any amendments to the memorandum and articles of association of the company must be registered with the Registry of Companies within the time frame provided by law.

As far as public listed companies are concerned, certain additional requirements are provided in the Companies Act 1995 and in the Listing Rules.

19.6.2   Amalgamation

Title II of Part VIII of the Companies Act 1995 deals with the amalgamation of limited liability companies. It distinguishes between two types of amalgamation, namely:

(a)   merger by acquisition; and
(b)   merger by formation of a new company.

19.6.2.1   Merger by acquisition
Merger by acquisition is the operation whereby a company ("the acquiring company") acquires the assets and liabilities of another company ("the target company") in exchange for the issue to shareholders of the target company of shares in the acquiring company and (possibly) a cash payment (provided this does not exceed 10 per cent of the nominal value of the shares so issued).

19.6.2.2   Merger by formation of a new company
This type of merger is the operation whereby two or more companies ("the merging companies") deliver to a company which they set up ("the new company") all their assets and liabilities in exchange for the issue to the shareholders of the merging companies of shares in the new company and (possibly) a cash payment (provided this does not exceed 10 per cent of the nominal value of the shares so issued).

In addition to the rules laid down in Sections 343 *et seq.* of the Companies Act 1995 dealing with amalgamation of companies, public listed companies are also bound by the provisions of paragraphs 8.142 to 8.152 of the Listing Rules which deal with amalgamations of listed companies and transactions involving substantial shareholdings.

19.7 Preparation of an offer

There are no rules or regulations in Malta dealing with the manner in which offers are to be prepared, made or announced, whether in relation to takeovers of private or public companies. As far as listed companies are concerned, a company announcement in English or Maltese must be made "without delay" through the relevant Exchange where it is listed in the event that any resolution for the merger or amalgamation of the listed company has been passed or any agreement entered into in connection with any acquisition or realisation of assets or any transaction outside the ordinary course of business of the company which is likely to affect the price of the shares of that company (Listing Rule 8.6.5). Similarly a listed company must make a company announcement in respect of any notice of changes in the shareholdings of 5 per cent or more of the equity share capital of the company (Listing Rule 8.6.6).

Most mergers and acquisitions activity in Malta has in the past concerned the sale of private companies, the bulk of which are small to medium-sized enterprises. Therefore, the takeover is neither complicated nor cumbersome and is usually achieved by virtue of a simple share transfer agreement as discussed above.

Larger takeovers have so far been rare and almost invariably involved acquisitions of government-owned entities as part of the ongoing privatisation process. In the absence of local rules regulating offers, offerors are allowed considerable freedom as far as the preparation and conduct of the offer is concerned.

Following consultations and informal contacts between the buyer and seller, whether directly or through investment banks or other intermediaries, successful preliminary negotiations commonly lead to the signature of a letter of intent or memorandum of agreement or similar preliminary contract. It is important that the parties are clear about whether they intend such letters of intent to be binding between them or whether they are merely declaratory of their intentions. The legal status of such preliminary contracts is not clear and should be well defined in the letter or memorandum itself. Under Maltese civil law the sale of a movable (and shares are considered to be movables) is complete as soon as there is agreement over the object and the price, even though delivery has not yet taken place (Section 1347, Civil Code). Promises of sale are also subject to specific performance and letters of intent should take into account the provisions of the Civil Code in this respect if they do not intend such letters to be binding between them.

Almost invariably an offeror will conduct a due diligence exercise to assess the commercial, legal and financial status of the target company. Due diligence exercises are normally carried out by lawyers who assess whether the affairs of the company are legally compliant, whilst auditors and accountants assess the financial state of the company. Publicly available information is that recorded at the public registry (concerning any immovable property owned by the company) and at the Registry of Companies (the M&A of the company, annual accounts, annual returns, changes to the board of directors, share transfers, etc.). Other information is normally accessed at the target company's premises and the use of data rooms is not uncommon for this purpose. Of course the target company would normally require that a confidentiality agreement is signed before the due diligence procedure takes place.

19.8   Conduct of public offer

So-called company amalgamations are regulated under Title II of Part VIII (Sections 344 et seq.) of the Companies Act 1995, and Rules 8.142 to 8.152 of the Listing Rules provide additional rules in relation to listed companies involved in an amalgamation or transaction concerning a substantial shareholding.

19.8.1   The Listing Rules – amalgamations

All listed companies are required to adhere to the provisions of the Companies Act 1995 dealing with amalgamations (discussed below) and Chapter 8 of the Listing Rules provides a number of general rules relating to acquisitions of listed companies by unlisted offerors and the offer documents.

19.8.1.1   General rules for acquisition of listed target
The general rules laid down by the Listing Rules in relation to the acquisition of a listed target are as follows:

(a)   Maintenance of secrecy. Where the directors of a listed company are having discussions with a company, person or group which may lead to an offer being made, everyone concerned must maintain secrecy in order to avoid disturbances in the price level of the shares.

(b)   Notification of offer. Where a listed company receives a notice of intention to make an amalgamation offer, the directors must advise each Exchange on which the company's securities are quoted of such notice. The target company must also send to all holders of other classes of shares and convertible notes in the company (whether or not such securities are covered by the amalgamation offer) a copy of all documents which it is required by law to send to the holders of the shares subject to the amalgamation offer (*see* 19.8.1.2 below). If the offeror extends the time for acceptance of the offer he must at the same time announce the percentage of shares accepted at that date.

(c)   Takeover of listed company by unlisted company. If, in the opinion of the Listing Authority, a company which is on a Recognised List has amalgamated or formed an association with an unlisted company and as a result the unlisted company has thereby acquired control of the listed company, the listed company must immediately lodge with the Listing Authority all information and documents required from any company seeking admission to the Recognised List .

(d) Acceptance of offer in excess of 90 per cent of shares. Where an amalgamation offer is made for the acquisition of 90 per cent or more of a listed company's securities, upon the announcement by the offeror that acceptances have been received from the holders of at least 90 per cent of such securities, all such securities will be removed from the Recognised List.

(e) Obligations on acceptance of 50 per cent of shares in listed target. Where an unlisted company, person or group submits an amalgamation offer for the acquisition of a listed company's securities, upon the announcement by the offeror that he has obtained sufficient acceptances and that he holds directly or indirectly more than 50 per cent of the target company's securities, the offeror shall disclose immediately to the Listing Authority its plans and intentions with regard to the target company and any other information that the Listing Authority considers necessary.

Where the offeror is also a listed company the requirements of the Listing Rules relating to amalgamations must be complied with.

19.8.1.2   *The offer documents*
In addition to complying with Title II (Amalgamation of Companies) Companies Act 1995, all offer documents must contain the following particulars:

(a) The date of the document, the name and address of the offeror and, if appropriate, of the person or company making the offer on behalf of the offeror.

(b) Precise particulars of the securities for which the offer is made; whether they will be transferred with or without any dividend or interest payment; the total consideration payable for the purchase; the period within which and the method by which any cash consideration will be paid; how any securities issued will rank for dividends or interest, capital and redemption; when and how the document of title will be issued and how any such offer may be accepted and within what period.

(c) A statement of all conditions attached to acceptances and in particular whether the offer is conditional upon acceptances being received in respect of a minimum number of securities and, if that is so, that minimum number and the last date on which the offer can be made unconditional. No offer may be conditional upon the payment of compensation for loss of office. If any such payment is proposed, full particulars must be given. A partial offer must be on a pro rata basis and the reason for the failure to make a full offer must be given.

(d) A statement as to whether the offeror or its directors or any person acting in concert has any beneficial interest – whether direct or indirect – in any of the securities for which the offer is made, giving full particulars. If there is no such interest, a statement should be made to this effect. Details, including dates and costs, must be given of any transactions in the securities for which the offer is made, entered into by any of these persons during the period commencing 12 months prior to the announcement of the offer and ending with the latest practicable date prior to the posting of the offer documents, or an appropriate negative statement made.

(e) A statement as to whether or not any securities acquired in pursuance of the offer will be transferred to any other person, together with the names of the parties to any such agreement and particulars of all securities in the offeree company held by such person, or a statement that no such securities are held.

(f)   A statement as to whether or not any agreement or arrangement exists between the offeror and any of the directors of the offeree company having any connection with or dependence upon the offer, and full particulars of any such agreement or arrangement.

(g)   The market quotation, if any, for any securities to be offered in exchange for and in addition to the securities to be acquired, which quotations in the case of listed securities should be taken from the Recognised List.

(h)   The intentions of the purchaser regarding its policy:

(i)   for the continuance of the business of the target company, explaining any major changes intended to be introduced in the business, including the redeployment of fixed assets of the target and setting out the long-term commercial justification for the proposed offer; and

(ii)   for the continued employment of the existing employees of the target company, setting out the extent of any steps to be taken towards terminating such employment.

(i)   Particulars of all documents required to be lodged for valid acceptance. If the offer lapses all such documents must be returned within 14 days of the closing date of the offer.

(j)   If the offer is for cash and is made on behalf of the offeror, a statement in the offer document as to what steps have been taken to ensure that the offer will be implemented if all the offerees accept.

(k)   If the offer is for the exchange of securities, the offer document must state:

(i)   the nature and particulars of the offeror company's business;

(ii)   its net profit before and after tax and rate per cent of dividends on the securities offered and the total amount absorbed thereby for the past three years;

(iii)   whether any financial advantage is expected to accrue to an acceptor;

(iv)   whether the issue of the new securities requires the passing of a resolution;

(v)   the first dividend in which they will participate; and

(vi)   particulars of all material changes in the offeror company since the date of its last published audited accounts together with a statement of the assets and liabilities stated in those accounts.

If the new securities are not to be identical in all respects to an existing listed security, all points of difference, full particulars of the voting rights attaching thereto and whether application for listing thereof has been or will be made to any Stock Exchange must be stated.

(l)   If the offer contains no recommendation by the target company's directors, the offer document must state particulars of any known material change in the target company's financial position since the publication of the last balance sheet.

(m)   If the total emoluments receivable by the directors of the offeror will be varied in consequence of the acquisition, full particulars of the variation; if there is no variation a statement to that effect.

(n)   If the offer document or any circular sent out in connection therewith, whether by or on behalf of the offeror company or the offeree company, includes expressly or by implication a recommendation by a financial adviser or other expert for or against acceptance of the offer, the Exchange may require the document, unless issued by the expert in question, to include a statement that the expert has given and not withdrawn his written consent to the issue of the document and the inclusion therein of his recommendation in the form and context in which it is included.

(o)   If the offer is recommended by the directors the offer documents must state the directors' recommendations regarding acceptance; the number, description and amount of securities held by or on behalf of the directors of the target company in that company and in the offeror company; and their intentions relating to such holdings as regards acceptance and otherwise as may be relevant. Full particulars of any material change in the financial position or prospects of the target company since the date of the last audited accounts must be stated.

(p)   The memorandum and articles of association, the audited accounts for the last three complete financial years of the offeror, any professional valuation of assets referred to in the offer document and all material contracts must be made available for inspection at the Exchange for the duration of the offer.

19.8.2   *The Listing Rules – transactions involving substantial shareholdings*

For the purposes of the Listing Rules, a "substantial shareholding" means:

(a)   the entitlement to exercise or control;

(b)   the exercise of 10 per cent or more of the votes able to be cast at general meetings; or

(c)   the entitlement to appoint a majority of directors on the board of directors of an issuer.

Any transactions involving a substantial shareholding must abide by the following rules:

(a)   All parties to an offer for an acquisition or disposal of a substantial share-holding in a listed company as well as the listed company itself must use every endeavour to prevent the creation of a false market in the securities of the listed company and must take care that statements are not made which may mislead shareholders or the market.

(b)   A listed company must promptly make a company announcement:

   (i)   when the board of directors of the listed company is advised or otherwise becomes aware that a purchaser is being sought for a substantial shareholding in the company;

   (ii)   when the listed company is the subject of rumour and speculation;

   (iii)   when the board of directors of the listed company is advised or otherwise becomes aware of a firm intention to acquire or dispose of a substantial shareholding in the company;

(iv) when the board of directors of the listed company is advised or otherwise becomes aware that an offer has been made to acquire or dispose of a substantial shareholding in the company.

(c) Without prejudice to any applicable privacy or secrecy obligations in terms of law, a listed company may furnish in confidence to a bona fide offeror and the corresponding bona fide transferor such information including unpublished price-sensitive information as may be necessary to enable the bona fide offeror, the bona fide transferor and their advisers to make, confirm, withdraw or modify the offer, provided that such disclosure of information may only be furnished subject to certain conditions including the express consent of the company in general meeting, the signing of a confidentiality agreement signed by the prospective transferor and the prospective offeror(s), an undertaking from the prospective offeror(s) whereby they bind themselves not to deal in the listed company's shares or any derivative instrument relating thereto, whether directly or indirectly, for a period of one year following completion of the transaction or termination thereof or discontinuance or withdrawal, other than to complete the transaction and an undertaking from the prospective transferor that it acknowledges that the information received from the listed company cannot be used or communicated other than for the purposes of a transaction in the shares that are the subject of the offer and that it cannot deal in other shares of the listed company for a period of one year following completion of the transaction or termination thereof or discontinuance or withdrawal.

(d) When the transaction is completed, or is not completed and the listed company is advised or otherwise becomes aware of such non-completion, the listed company must make a company announcement disclosing the outcome of negotiations. In case of a completion the announcement must include the price at which the substantial shareholding was acquired or disposed of.

(e) In the event that the transaction is completed, a purchaser which has had access to information in confidence in terms of this Listing Rule will be prohibited from acquiring further securities in the listed company or from disposing of securities in the company, whether directly or indirectly, for a period of one year from the date of acquisition.

(f) Similarly in the event that the transaction is not completed, a bona fide offeror which has had access to information in confidence in terms of this Listing Rule will be prohibited from acquiring securities in the listed company, whether directly or indirectly, for a period of one year following termination thereof or discontinuance or withdrawal, other than to complete the transaction that prompted the disclosure of information hereunder.

(g) Regardless of the outcome of the transaction, the purchaser or the bona fide offeror, as the case may be, shall, immediately following completion of the transaction or termination thereof or discontinuance or withdrawal, notify the listed company to that effect and return all the information furnished by the company and shall take prompt action to cancel, delete or destroy such information furnished by the company that cannot be returned.

19.8.3 *Acquisition procedure under the Companies Act 1995*

The directors of the acquiring company and of the company being acquired ("the amalgamating companies") must draw up draft terms of merger in writing. The draft terms of merger must specify:

(a) the status, name and registered office of each of the amalgamating companies;

(b) the share exchange ratio and the amount of any cash payment;

(c) the terms relating to the allotment of shares in the acquiring company;

(d) the date from which the holding of such shares entitles the holders to participate in profits and any special conditions affecting that entitlement;

(e) the date from which the transactions of the company being acquired shall be treated for accounting purposes as being those of the acquiring company;

(f) the rights conferred by the acquiring company on the holders of shares to which special rights are attached and on the holders of debentures or other securities, or the measures proposed concerning them; and

(g) any special advantage granted to the experts acting on behalf of each of the amalgamating companies authorised to examine the draft terms of merger and to draw up a written report to the shareholders, and to the directors of each of the amalgamating companies.

The draft terms of merger, duly completed, must be signed by at least one director and the company secretary of each of the amalgamating companies, and forwarded to the Registrar of Companies for registration.

A merger by acquisition can only be made if it has been approved by an extraordinary resolution of each of the amalgamating companies at least one month after the publication of the draft terms of merger and not later than three months thereafter. The shares held by the dissenting members must be redeemed by the companies participating in the acquisition if they so request. The extraordinary resolution taken by each of the amalgamating companies must cover both the approval of the draft terms of merger and any alterations and additions to the M&A necessitated by the amalgamation.

The directors of each of the amalgamating companies must draw up a detailed written report explaining the draft terms of the merger and setting out the legal and economic grounds for them, in particular the share exchange ratio, and they must describe any special valuation difficulties which may have arisen.

One or more experts acting on behalf of each of the amalgamating companies but independent of them and approved by the Registrar will examine the draft terms of the merger and draw up a written report to the shareholders. This report must specify whether the share exchange ratio is fair and reasonable, describing any special valuation difficulties which may have arisen.

All shareholders of every amalgamating company are entitled to inspect various documents at the registered office of each company at least one month before the date fixed for the general meeting which is to decide on the draft terms of merger, including:

(a)   the draft terms of merger;

(b)   the annual accounts and the directors' reports of the amalgamating companies for the preceding three accounting periods as well as updated interim accounts;

(c)   the reports of the directors of the amalgamating companies relating to the amalgamation; and

(d)   the reports of the experts relating to the amalgamation.

The law provides for an element of protection of creditors of companies involved in an acquisition and in fact the amalgamation of two or more companies will not take effect until three months after the date of publication of a notice of the proposed amalgamation in the Government gazette and in a daily newspaper. During this period of three months any creditor of any of the amalgamating companies whose debt existed prior to the publication of the draft terms of merger may by writ of summons object to the amalgamation.

The law also protects the holders of securities, other than shares, in the companies being acquired, to which special rights are attached. It requires that they are given rights against the acquiring company in accordance with the draft terms of merger at least equivalent to those they possessed in the companies being acquired, unless:

(a)   the holders of those securities individually agree to the alteration of their rights; or

(b)   the alteration has been approved by a meeting of the holders of those securities called specifically for the purpose, at which meeting all the holders of such securities shall signify their consent; or

(c)   the holders of those securities are entitled to have their securities repurchased by the acquiring company.

19.9   Defences to a hostile offer

Until the implementation of the Takeover Directive there were no specific rules regulating defences against hostile offers and general principles of company law applied in the sense that directors of a company are bound to act in good faith and in the best interests of the company. In this respect, the Maltese courts have traditionally applied normal civil law principles when discussing the duties of directors, principally the rules of mandate and agency, although they have also been influenced strongly by English judgments in this respect. In 2003, however, amendments to the Companies Act 1995 were introduced and the specific duties of directors towards the company were laid down in a new Article 136A.

Further to the transposition of the Takeover Directive and the addition of a new Chapter 18 to the Listing Rules, these rules now contain provisions prohibiting defensive tactics in the face of a takeover or potential takeover of a listed company. If a target company has received a takeover notice or has reason to believe that a bona fide offer is imminent, the board of directors of the company is prohibited from taking or permitting any action in relation to the affairs of the target company that could effectively result in the offer being frustrated or the holders of securities of the target company being denied an opportunity to decide on the merits of an offer. Provided, however, that the board of directors of a target company may take or permit the kind of action referred to above if the action has been approved by an ordinary resolution of the target company (subject to certain mandatory requirements in relation to the notice of the meeting at which such resolution is going to be proposed) or the action is taken or permitted under a contractual obligation entered into by the target company, or in the implementation of proposals approved by the board of directors of the target company, and the obligations were entered into, or the proposals were approved, before the target company received the takeover notice or became aware that the offer was imminent. Of course the prohibition will not apply either in the event that the action is taken or permitted for reasons unrelated to the offer with the prior approval of the Listing Authority.

It is also interesting to note that in the context of company amalgamations generally the Companies Act 1995 affords shareholders individually a right of action for damages against the directors of any of the amalgamating companies personally in the event that any such shareholder suffers a loss as a result of the directors' wilful or negligent misconduct in the preparation and the implementation of the amalgamation. Admittedly this provision would not cater for the eventuality where a takeover is prevented by the directors of the target company. It is merely intended to ensure that the takeover is carried out in a manner which is not prejudicial to the shareholders.

Similarly, experts responsible for drawing up, on behalf of any of the amalgamating companies, the report on the draft terms of the merger are also answerable for wilful or negligent misconduct in the performance of their duties and may be liable for damages occasioned to any shareholder of any of the amalgamating companies (Section 355).

19.10   Profit forecasts and asset valuations

There is no legal requirement as such for the conduct of a profit forecast prior to an amalgamation whether of a listed or unlisted company, although the target company or the offeror will normally be expected to make a profit forecast in the course of a takeover.

In so far as listed companies are concerned there are various rules relating to profit forecasts, but generally these apply where a prospectus is issued. There is an indirect reference to such forecasts in the context of an amalgamation of listed companies in clause 8.152.14 of the Listing Rules which states that if an offer document includes a recommendation by a financial adviser or other expert, the Listing Authority may require that document to include a statement that the expert has given his consent (and has not withdrawn it) to the issue of the document and the inclusion therein of his recommendation in the form and content in which it is included.

There is no specific requirement for a valuation of assets other than as contained in the annual accounts which all companies are required to submit to the Registrar of Companies after approval of the same at the annual general meeting of the company. Private and public companies must publish their reports and audited accounts in accordance with the regulations in the Third Schedule to the Companies Act 1995, whilst the Listing Rules require listed companies to audit their accounts in accordance with the International Auditing Guidelines in force at the end of each financial year. Listed companies are also required to file with the Listing Authority half-yearly reports on the activities and profits and losses for the first six months of each financial year.

The Listing Rules require listed companies involved in an amalgamation, as part of the offer documents listed under 19.8.1.2 above, to submit to the Listing Authority the audited accounts for the last three complete financial years of the offeror together with any professional valuation of assets that may be referred to in the offer document. These documents must be submitted to the Listing Authority and made available for inspection by all shareholders for the duration of the offer. Therefore, although not mandatorily required, in the event that a valuation of assets other than in the accounts of the company is prepared, this must be submitted to the Listing Authority for inspection.

19.11 Documents from the offeror and offeree board

See 19.8.1.2 and 19.8.2 above.

19.12 Compulsory acquisition of minorities

Apart from the squeeze-out rights mentioned in relation to listed companies and discussed at 19.5.1.1 above, compulsory acquisition of the shares of minority shareholders is also provided for in the Companies Act 1995 in the context of an acquisition of one company by another which holds 90 per cent or more of its shares, regulated under Chapter III of Title II of Part VIII of the Companies Act 1995.

The procedure to be followed in such acquisitions is largely similar to that described above in relation to mergers by acquisition (*see* 19.6.2.1 and 19.8.3 above) but, as expected, requires less formality in view of the fact that the acquiring company already owns 90 per cent or more of the shares of the target company.

In fact, in such instances the general meeting of the acquiring company need not approve the acquisition provided the following conditions are fulfilled:

(a)   the draft terms of the acquisition as regards the acquiring company are delivered to the Registrar for registration and are published by him at least three months before the date fixed for the general meeting of the target company which is to decide on the draft terms of the acquisition;

(b)   within the period mentioned in (a), all shareholders of the acquiring company are entitled to inspect the draft terms of merger, the annual accounts and directors' reports of the amalgamating companies for the preceding three accounting periods, and an accounting statement up to no more than three months from the issue of the draft terms of merger.

All the other provisions relating to merger by acquisition apply to such transactions. However, as far as compulsory acquisitions are concerned, Section 359(2) states that the provisions regarding the drawing up of a report on the draft terms of the merger by the directors and by the experts (*see* 19.8.3 above) and the right of all shareholders to inspect the documents mentioned above shall not apply as long as the dissenting minority shareholders of the target company have the right to have their shares purchased by the acquiring company for a consideration corresponding to the fair value of their shares, the fair value of such consideration to be determined by the court in the event of disagreement.

This right of compulsory acquisition in terms of the Companies Act, therefore, is a right competent to the shareholders of the target company and it is not a procedure by virtue of which the minority can be squeezed out.

19.13   Insider dealing

The first ever rules on insider dealing were introduced by the Malta Stock Exchange Act in 1990 (now the Financial Markets Act 2002). The establishment of the Exchange and a regulatory framework for the listing and trading of shares would have been incomplete without clear rules prohibiting and punishing insider dealing. Under the 1990 Act, the principal function of the former Malta Stock Exchange Tribunal ("MSET") set up under the Act was to investigate allegations or suspicions of insider dealing or other "irregular practices in Exchange dealings" on the Malta Stock Exchange. Today, the functions of the MSET have been largely absorbed by the Financial Services Tribunal set up under the arm of the MFSA. In fact the Malta Stock Exchange Council and the Malta Stock Exchange has gradually lost its regulatory role and has become almost exclusively an exchange operator.

In 1994 the Insider Dealing Act was enacted as part of the package of laws dealing with financial services in Malta being introduced at the time. The Act has recently been replaced by the Prevention of Financial Markets Abuse Act 2005, which came into force on 22 March 2005. When originally introduced, the Insider Dealing Act 1994 only caught and punished wrongdoing that can be brought within the meaning of insider dealing given in the Act. New market abuse and market manipulation offences have now been included in the Prevention of Financial Markets Abuse Act 2005, a development that was long overdue. Market abuse is defined as including both "the prohibited use of inside information" (as defined) and "the practice of market manipulation". This Act transposes into Maltese law the Market Abuse Directive (2003/6/EC) of the European Parliament and of the Council of 28 January 2003 on insider dealing and market manipulation including all implementing measures issued thereunder. The purpose of the Prevention of Financial Markets Abuse Act 2005 is to safeguard the integrity of Maltese and Community financial markets and to enhance investor confidence in them. The Act applies principally to financial instruments admitted to trading on a regulated market in Malta or in any other Member State or EEA state or for which a request for admission to trading on such a market has been made. The new Act has widened considerably the definition of "market abuse" to include:

(a) prohibited use of inside information to trade in any financial instrument admitted to a regulated market; and

(b) market manipulation through dissemination of false, exaggerated or misleading information, spreading of false rumours or putting into effect simulated or artificial operations or transactions or orders.

The provisions of the Act affect the following categories:

(a) issuers and their managers and other insiders;
(b) financial intermediaries;
(c) ordinary investors;
(d) journalists, researchers and disseminators of financial recommendations;
(e) national statistics bodies;
(f) competent authorities in Malta and abroad; and
(g) operators of recognised investment exchanges.

An innovative feature of the Act is the provision for two separate sanctions and procedures against market abuse. Provision is made for administrative sanctions by the competent authority as well as for criminal sanctions imposed by the criminal courts.

Powers of investigation and enforcement have also been widened considerably and the Act introduces the concept of "freezing of funds" whereby the criminal court, upon a request by the Attorney General, may issue an order whereby the assets of any person charged with a criminal or administrative offence under the Act are frozen, whether they are in the hands of third parties or otherwise, until a final determination of the criminal or administrative proceedings instituted against the person charged. The "freezing order" includes an injunction prohibiting the person charged from transferring, charging or otherwise disposing of any assets.

19.14 Financial assistance

The rules controlling financial assistance are contained in Section 110 of the Companies Act 1995 which states that it shall be unlawful for an undertaking to:

(a) subscribe for, hold, acquire or otherwise deal in shares in a company which is its holding company; or

(b) to give, whether directly or indirectly, and whether by means of a loan, guarantee, the provision of security or otherwise, any financial assistance for the purpose of or in connection with an acquisition or subscription made or to be made by any person of or for any shares in the company or its parent company.

These financial assistance provisions are of relevance in the context of mergers and acquisitions and are intended, in particular, to prevent unlawful share price manipulation practices by offerors who would have an interest in inflating the value of their shares prior to or during the offer. The financial assistance provisions, particularly paragraph (b) above is drafted in very wide terms and prohibits the giving of financial assistance whether directly or indirectly and irrespective of the manner in which it is given. These provisions would therefore successfully prevent various unlawful practices including:

(a)   lending, or otherwise making available, funds to buy shares in the company (pre-acquisition assistance);
(b)   loans to shareholders who have bought shares with bank finance, the loan being used to pay off the bank finance (post acquisition assistance);
(c)   releasing debtors from liability to the company in order to assist such debtors to buy shares in the company;
(d)   guaranteeing or providing security for a bank loan to be used by someone to buy shares in a company; or
(e)   buying assets from prospective shareholders at an overvalue to enable them to buy shares in the company.

The prohibition of financial assistance does not only apply where assistance is given by the company whose shares have been acquired but also where the assistance is given by any subsidiary of such company.

The only exception to the prohibition in Section 110(1) above is that contained in subsection (2) of the same Section which states that the prohibition does not apply to transactions effected with a view to the acquisition of shares by or for the company's employees or the employees of a group company provided, however, that such transactions do not have the effect of reducing the net assets of the company below the amount of issued share capital of the company plus undistributable reserves.

Chapter 20

The Netherlands

Weero Koster

Partner
Norton Rose, Amsterdam

20.1   Introduction

20.1.1   *The legal definition of a takeover*

The topic of this Guide, and thus this Chapter relating to the Netherlands, covers a vast area of the law as it relates to the many conceivable means of effecting a business combination. As a consequence, it covers as much legal ground as possible without making an attempt at completeness. Private equity transactions and strategic business combinations form a large part of the Dutch corporate finance landscape. Many of these transactions do not involve listed companies. Therefore, a considerable amount of attention is given in this Chapter to transactions in unlisted companies.

In the Netherlands, it is not possible to find the rules and practices related to takeovers, mergers, acquisitions and other business combinations logically compiled in one of the statute books. Dutch corporate law defines a "merger" only in connection with the "statutory merger" (Section 2:309 Civil Code ("CC")), which is often used as a technical means of combining businesses without actually having to transfer the individual assets and liabilities. Other rules on mergers in the Netherlands are spread out over numerous Acts and Decrees. These range from the Act on Public Offers and its Decree, to the code-termination rules in the Works Council Act, the employee protection provisions in the Civil Code, the SER Merger Code, the Act on Financial Supervision and the competition law aspects in the Competition Act.

There have been many changes in recent years. A number of attempts have been made to modernise and internationalise Dutch corporate law. Many of the improvements will benefit private equity and venture capital transactions. The Dutch listing rules were overhauled completely, introducing among other things the mandatory offer and certain funds rule in the Netherlands.

This Chapter has been substantially updated, and summarises some of the main rules to be observed in the process of effecting a business combination, takeover or merger in the Netherlands.

20.1.2   *Parties/stakeholders*

The process of negotiating a business combination in the Netherlands may be complicated by the substantial amount of employee and labour organisation involvement in the early stages of the negotiations and to some degree by the two-tier governance system required for larger companies (which may be relaxed in the near future by allowing one-tier boards). Thus, merger processes require the active and early involvement of a number of quite diverse parties and stakeholders. This in turn calls for careful project planning and early consultation of various advisers.

20.1.3   Legal review/due diligence

Most major corporate transactions in the Netherlands are preceded by a legal due diligence review. Generally, such a review is conducted contemporaneously with the financial, technical, environmental and tax due diligence, and assists in signalling major issues or deal breakers, in structuring and planning the transaction, and, overall, in putting the parties to a transaction in a position such that they can make informed decisions. It should be noted that, in Dutch law, in many cases a duty to investigate is assumed, and thus there is a necessity to conduct a legal review. The extent and scope of such a duty varies with the factual surroundings of the transaction. Significant factors in determining whether or not a duty to investigate exists are the nature and complexity of the transaction, the existence of specialised knowledge amongst the parties concerned and the feasibility of an investigation and the relationship based on trust between the parties concerned (High Court NJ 1986, 570; NJ 1991, 254; NJ 1996, 300 and NJ 2001, 559).

An action to rescind an agreement for mistake may be barred in the case that the party instituting such an action was under a duty to investigate (Section 6:228 (2) CC) but failed to do so or has decided not to obtain full information or further guarantees (High Court 10 October 2003, C02/149 HR). Dutch law deviates from certain common law systems in that it does not apply a strict "caveat emptor" or "*periculum est emptoris*" rule. Although duty-bound to investigate, a party in negotiations may rely on the correctness of statements and disclosures made by the other party (Court Den Bosh NJ 1993, 462). In private transactions, recurring issues during the review are the accuracy and completeness of disclosures made, and the relationship between such disclosures and the representations and warranties or indemnities that may subsequently be sought from the parties to the transaction.

20.1.4   Good faith negotiations

In Dutch case law, a doctrine of negotiation in good faith has developed which may create a duty to compensate the other party to negotiations in the event that the negotiations are prematurely terminated by one party. This duty is not a statutory one, but has been confirmed by law. The overriding principle is that parties to negotiations are under a duty to take into account each other's justifiable interests. Several stages of contract negotiation are generally distinguished on the basis of this principle, during the last of which the termination of the negotiations is deemed to be contrary to the doctrine of good faith or "reasonableness and fairness", as the Dutch refer to it. In such event, a court may make an order to continue negotiations or pay compensation or damages (which, in exceptional cases, may include compensation for lost profits).

20.1.5   Contract construction

Case law has underlined the importance of elaborate contractual provisions, clearly setting out the consequences of a default in respect of any of the provisions of a share purchase agreement or an agreement in respect of a sale of a business. Although under Dutch contract law, generally, in the case of a breach of a contractual duty, the remedies of rescission, damages and specific performance are available to the plaintiff (Section 6:265 CC, 6:74 et seq. CC, and 3:296 CC), case law has suggested that indemnification or hold harmless clauses are to be construed narrowly and in light of the reasonable expectations of the parties (High Court NJ 1996, 300 and NJ 2001, 559). Moreover, the High Court has held that while damage sustained by a company for which it is not compensated diminishes the value of the shares of such a company (High Court NJ 1995, 288), it has also suggested that – failing agreements stating otherwise – the damage sustained by a shareholder due to a loss incurred by the company of which he has purchased shares is in principle limited to the purchase price of such shares (High Court NJ 1995, 288 and NJ 1997, 662 and NJ 2001, 573).

20.2   Acquisition targets

20.2.1   Types of business organisations

Several types of business organisations can be distinguished. Limited liability companies can be either private (*besloten vennootschap met beperkte aansprakelijkheid* or "BV") or public (*naamloze vennootschap* or "NV"). Their common feature is that their capital is divided into transferable shares. Their main difference is the closed character of the private company, as opposed to the more open character of its public counterpart. As a result the first is required (under mandatory provisions of law) to have pre-emptive rights contained in its articles of association and may only issue registered shares (Section 2:175 CC) while the latter is under no such duty and may have freely negotiable bearer shares. There is also a difference in the minimum required issued capital. For the private limited company this is less than that of its public counterpart (€18,000 as opposed to €40,000). However, both amounts remain modest, so this cannot be viewed as a great distinguishing feature. Dutch corporate law recognises the need to organise corporate groups of companies and defines:

(a)   subsidiaries (related to sole or joint control) (Section 2:24a CC);
(b)   participations (related to the furnishing of capital) (Section 2:24c CC); and
(c)   groups (related to economic unity and joint organisation) (Section 2:24b CC).

A company forming part of a group is exempted from a number of requirements related to the organisation and publication of its annual accounts, on the condition that the consolidating parent files a statement of joint and several liability in respect of such a group company (Section 2:403 (1)(f) CC). Also, tax-transparent groups may be formed between parents and their wholly-owned subsidiaries through the formation of fiscal unities. In the case of a merger or acquisition of a group company, these group ties have to be untangled (in the case of group liability, through publication in the trade register (Section 2:404 CC)).

General Partnerships (*Vennootschap onder Firma*) and Limited Partnerships (*Commanditaire Vennootschap*) are types of business organisations commonly employed. Often, these partnerships are used as joint venture – project finance – or structured finance vehicles, for example in the form of a partnership between special-purpose private limited companies formed by the joint venturers, or in the form of a limited partnership of the joint venturers and one or more general partners (in the form of special-purpose private limited companies in which the joint venturers participate, too). Partnerships are not considered to be legal entities. General partnerships have a capital distinct from that of the partners that participate in them. However, if a general partnership is unable to meet its debts, the partners are jointly and severally liable for the deficit. In limited partnerships, the liability of each limited partner is limited to his capital contribution.

To some extent, recently, mainly for tax consideration, the use of Dutch co-operatives ("*Cooperatie*") (Section 2:53 et seq. CC) has become fashionable in structuring acquisitions and investments. Without diminishing the value of such considerations, it should also be considered that the statutory scope and object of Dutch cooperatives is rather narrowly defined, which may lead to risks of dissolution or compulsory conversion for failure to comply with mandatory law or acting outside the cooperative's object. Because of the statutory peculiarities of the cooperative, it also creates a number of challenges related to allocation and distribution of profits, transfer and encumbrance of membership interests, expulsion and withdrawal.

Dutch law does not contain specific rules for businesses in the form of sole proprietorships or in the form of a branch office. However, general rules of law which apply to business organisations and undertakings, such as the need to register at the trade register, do apply. There is a 1997 Act designed to curb the use of legal entities incorporated under the laws of a foreign state which conduct substantially all their business in the Netherlands and have no genuine link to their state of incorporation. Such entities were used in increasing numbers to avoid Dutch capital protection statutes and the review of incorporators of private or public companies. Pursuant to a decision of the European Court of Justice, the statute is no longer fully applicable to legal entities incorporated under the laws of one of the Member States of the European Union or the European Economic Area.

20.2.2 Corporate governance

For public and private companies, the Dutch system of corporate governance consists of a two-tier management system. In this system, the management board performs an executive function (Section 2:129/239 CC) and the supervisory board renders advice to, and supervises, the management board (Section 2:140/250 CC). Each board has powers and duties distinct from the other and from the powers of the general meeting of shareholders (High Court NJ 1959, 43). The general meeting of shareholders holds all residual powers (Section 2:107 CC). To a considerable degree, flexibility exists to tilt the balance of power in favour of either one of these corporate bodies by inserting appropriate provisions in the company's articles of association or by adopting by-laws specifically tailored to meet the requirements of the envisaged governance structure. Other corporate bodies may also be created, such as meetings of holders of certain classes of shares or shareholder committees. For non-corporate business entities, such as partnerships, an even greater amount of flexibility exists in crafting an appropriate corporate organisation and hierarchy.

On 1 January 2004, a code of proper corporate governance and best practice (the *Code-Tabaksblat*) came into force. This Code is applicable to all companies:

(a)   that have their corporate seat in the Netherlands; and
(b)   that have shares listed on a government-recognised Stock Exchange located either in the Netherlands or abroad.

Listed investment institutions that can be considered as mere "financial products" are exempted from the Code. The Code is based on the concept of "comply or explain". Under this regime, listed companies are required to apply the regulatory framework of the Code, or otherwise disclose and explain to shareholders in their annual report why certain best-practice provisions have not been adopted. The Code contains a number of principles summarising generally accepted modern concepts of proper corporate governance and a large number of best-practice provisions for stakeholders (such as managing directors, supervisory directors, shareholders and institutional investors), that may also be used as reporting guidelines for annual reports of listed companies.

In 2007, corporate governance formed a large part of the public debate through significant public takeover battles around major Dutch corporates, such as Stork, VNU, Petroplus and ABN AMRO. The most significant event took place in June 2007, when the Dutch Supreme Court partially overturned a landmark decision by the Amsterdam Enterprise Chamber, thus clearing the way for the sale by takeover target ABN AMRO of its major US subsidiary, LaSalle. Many viewed ABN's sale of LaSalle as a "poison pill" takeover defence. The ruling focused on the question of whether the Board of Directors of ABN AMRO was allowed to sell LaSalle without prior approval by ABN AMRO's general meeting of shareholders. This sale took place while the board of directors was involved in exclusive merger negotiations with Barclays. Before the sale of LaSalle, however, a Consortium of three banks (Royal Bank of Scotland, Santander and Fortis) had announced its intention to acquire the shares in ABN AMRO. That Consortium aimed at the acquisition of ABN AMRO including LaSalle, but eventually only succeeded in getting ABN AMRO and not its subsidiary. In brief, the Supreme Court ruled that the sale of LaSalle to Bank of America was not an unlawful anti-takeover device by ABN AMRO Holding. Also, Section 2:107(a)(1) CC did not confer to the shareholders a right of approval with regard to the sale of LaSalle, nor did such a right of approval arise from special circumstances and it is not required by the principles of proper corporate governance.

20.2.3 *Large company regime* (Structuurregime)

Since the 1970s, a special corporate regime has applied to public and private limited companies that are considered to be large. A large company is under a duty to register as such with the commercial register; three years of uninterrupted registration lead to a duty to amend the articles of association of the company (Section 2:154/264 CC).

The main changes to the ordinary governance regime applicable to large companies is that, by mandatory provisions of the law, a considerable amount of influence is shifted from the management and shareholders to the supervisory board, which is turned into the nucleus of corporate power. In addition to its supervisory task (Section 2:140/250 CC), the board of supervisory directors is accorded the power to:

(a)   appoint and remove directors (Section 2:162/272 CC);
(b)   adopt the annual accounts (Section 2:163/273 CC); and
(c)   approve the number of major corporate decisions (Section 2:158/268 CC).

In 2004, the legislation with respect to the large-company regime was amended considerably, enhancing the rights of shareholders in Dutch large companies. As a result, key elements of the large company regime have been amended as follows.

Power of the general meeting of shareholders:

(a)   the general meeting of shareholders adopts the annual accounts; and
(b)   prior approval of the general meeting of shareholders is required for certain important decisions of the management board involving the *identity or the character of the company or its business*. This concept is not clearly defined, but it includes the following:

    (i)   a disposal of all or substantially all of the company's business,

    (ii)   the entering into or the terminating by the company or a subsidiary of a long-term cooperation arrangement (notably a joint venture), if the arrangement is of fundamental significance to the company, or

    (iii)   an acquisition or disposal of an interest in the capital of another company by the company or a subsidiary equal in value to at least one-third of the value of the company's own assets (according to its latest consolidated balance sheet).

Power of the supervisory board:

(a)   the supervisory board must prepare a profile concerning its preferred composition taking into account the nature of the company, its activities and the desired expertise and background of each supervisory board member, and the profile will be discussed at the general meeting of share-holders and with the Works Council;
(b)   all supervisory board members will be appointed by the general meeting of shareholders upon nomination of the supervisory board;
(c)   prior to such nomination, the general meeting of shareholders and the Works Council can recommend persons to be nominated by the super-visory board. The Works Council has the right to nominate one-third of the supervisory board members; and
(d)   the general meeting of shareholders has the power to dismiss the super-visory board in its entirety if it has no further confidence in this corporate body.

20.2.4 Types of shares

The most commonly used types of shares are registered shares and bearer shares. There are also other types of (customised) securities such as redeemable, cumulative, convertible and profit-sharing preferred shares, founders' shares and bonus shares. Particular to the Netherlands are priority shares (*prioriteit-saandelen*) and the widely used depository receipts (*certificaten van aandelen*).

Priority shares are shares to which special voting rights attach, such as the right to render binding nominations in respect of the appointment of managing or supervisory directors, approve amendments to the articles of association or approve dissolution of the company.

Depository receipts are securities commonly used by both listed and unlisted companies. They are securities issued by an administration office (*adminis-tratiekantoor*), usually in the form of a foundation, representing certain shares held by such an office. In most cases, the conditions issued by the administration office stipulate that distributions of the shares made by the company to the administration office (often after deduction of certain administration costs) flow to the holders of the depository receipts. The voting rights, however, remain exclusively with the administration office and are not conferred on the holders of the receipts. Therefore, by applying this mechanism, an effective separation is made between the financial or economic rights attached to the shares, and the voting rights attached thereto. This system is commonly applied in the Netherlands as non-voting stock currently does not exist under Dutch law (but this will soon change; *see* section 20.2.6.1 below). With certain exceptions, the holders of depository receipts can only exercise rights against the issuing entity (i.e., the administration office).

20.2.5 Transfer of equity interests

The manner in which equity interests are transferred is dependent on the character of the issuing entity (corporate or non-corporate), the type of security (bearer or registered) and whether or not the security is listed.

One of the chief features of corporate entities is that their capital is divided into shares, which constitute negotiable instruments (albeit subject to certain restrictive clauses that may be inserted in the articles of association of such entities). Conversely, entities lacking corporate status – such as partnerships and sole proprietorships – do not generally issue shares to raise capital. Consequently, the business interests held by the participating parties are not transferable without transferring a property interest in respect of the underlying assets of the venture (as well as assigning part of its debt).

In practice, the complexities of such transfers or assignments may be prevented, for example by participating in such business entities through a wholly-owned special-purpose company (and subsequently transferring the shares in such an entity), or by providing that one of the partners shall act as the legal owner of the property interests in the assets and that the other partners shall hold only beneficial interests in such assets. This has led to the use of transfer of "*economic ownership*" mainly in respect of registered property. In such transactions the full economic risk is transferred, while legal ownership remains with the transferor. Since legislation in a number of cases has caused the transfer of economic ownership in registered property to be a taxable event, the popularity of this type of transfer in general has dwindled. In special sectors, however, transfer of economic ownership of registered property is commonplace and even compulsory. The Dutch Electricity Act and Gas Act, for example, contain definitions of the "economic ownership" concept and require transfer of such type of ownership in grids to specially regulated grid operators.

Public limited companies may issue both bearer and registered shares (Section 2:82 CC). Transfer of bearer shares is effected through transfer of possession of a share certificate (Section 3:93 CC). The issue and transfer of registered shares can only be effected by means of a deed of transfer executed in the presence of a Dutch civil-law notary. In practice, such a deed of transfer is drafted by the notary in whose presence it will be executed. This is connected with the notary's duty to research as described at 20.6.2 below. However, the rights attached to the registered shares transferred cannot be enforced against the issuing company until either the company has acknowledged the transfer or the deed of transfer has been served upon the company (Section 2:86a/196a CC).

Public limited companies may insert in their articles of association restrictive clauses in respect of the transfer and issuance of shares (Section 2:87 CC and 2:96a CC). For private limited companies such clauses are required by mandatory provisions of law (both on transfer (Section 2:195 CC) and on issue (Section 2:206a CC) of shares). These restrictive clauses may grant to the other shareholders either approval rights, rights of pre-emption of a combination of both (Section 2:87/195 CC).

20.2.6 Flexibilisation and modernisation initiatives

Recently, a number of legal initiatives have been undertaken to render Dutch company and partnership law more flexible, modern and international; all with the aim of enhancing the Dutch investment climate. These initiatives include the 2006 legislative proposal to simplify and enhance the flexibility of the Dutch private company (*besloten vennootschap met beperkte aansprakelijkheid* or "BV"), the 2007 Bill on Partnerships, and the announcement that "one-tier" boards will be allowed and the powers and role of the Dutch Enterprise Chamber will be reviewed.

20.2.6.1   The 2006 legislative proposal to simplify and enhance the flexibility of the Dutch private company

In 2006, the Dutch Cabinet agreed upon legislation through which the BV will attain a character more distinct from the other Dutch main corporate entity, the NV. The changes proposed in this legislation create more possibilities to adapt the constitution of the BV to the nature of the business it will develop and to the cooperation between the shareholders. Thus, it will make the BV an excellent vehicle for collaborative and investment structures, such as joint ventures and private equity investments. The increased flexibility is also of assistance in creating corporate groups. The main features of the proposal are greater flexibility in the internal organisation of the BV, protection of minority shareholders and a more balanced system of protection of creditors. Many of the issues that arise in creating corporate joint ventures under present legislation have been addressed. This includes that:

(a)   the minimum capital of €18,000 is no longer required and the requirement of an authorised capital is deleted;
(b)   the capital can be denominated in another currency than euro;
(c)   contributions in kind are made less bureaucratic (which makes business combinations easier);
(d)   protection of creditors is achieved through a test on distributions coupled with management and shareholder liability sanctions;
(e)   joint venture management arrangements are facilitated, as each shareholder can appoint its "own" member of the management board;
(f)   non-voting and non-profit sharing shares can be created;
(g)   a restriction on transfer of shares (through pre-emptive rights or approval rights) is no longer mandatory;
(h)   shares can be rendered non-transferable for a certain period of time;
(i)   more flexibility is created in the valuation of shares upon transfer/exit;
(j)   violation of contractual obligations (e.g., arising under the shareholders agreement or other ancillary agreements) can suspend voting and financial rights;
(k)   resolving outside of meetings is made easier; and
(l)   dispute resolution (e.g., through buy-out in case of a shareholder conflict) is enhanced.

20.2.6.2   Implementation of the 2005 Bill on Partnerships

In 2007, the implementation Bill regarding the 2005 Bill on Partnerships (*personenvennootschappen*) was presented to the Dutch Parliament. This Bill provides an overview of changes that need to be made in a number of laws due to the implementation of new legislation on partnerships which will be incorporated in the Dutch Civil Code. At the time of writing, it had not been decided when the Bill would enter into force. It contains a number of amendments to the Bill on Partnerships, as well as transitory provisions.

The new partnership rules will provide the practitioner with three main advantages:

(a)   the possibility for the partnership to own its assets;
(b)   enhanced possibilities to convert the partnership into a private limited company (which itself will be rendered much more flexible) and vice versa; and
(c)   greater flexibility in the admission of, and withdrawal by, partners, making it easier to transfer partnership interests.

The most remarkable change in respect of the partnership legislation regards the possibility to opt for legal personality. The implications thereof mostly relate to the ownership aspect of a partnership: its right to legally own its assets. Currently, a partnership does not qualify as a legal entity under Dutch law. As a consequence, it cannot own its assets. There are only exceptions to this rule in bankruptcy. Instead practitioners resort mainly to two structures:

(a)   legal title to the assets is generally held by the partners jointly, propor-
        tionate to their respective interest; and
(b)   mainly in limited partnerships, one general partner holds legal title to the
        assets on behalf of the other (limited) partners who have beneficial
        interests.

A disadvantage of the first structure is that if a new partner is admitted to the
partnership or a partner wishes to withdraw from the partnership, legal title of
each of the assets of the partnership has to be transferred to the new partner or
the remaining partners. The same issue arises where new assets are purchased
by the partnership.

By introducing the possibility to opt for legal personality, the Bill on Partnerships facilitates ownership of assets by a partnership itself. Some other important
aspects of the Bill on Partnerships are as follows:

(a)   The Bill distinguishes between two types of partnerships:
        (i)   a "public partnership" (*"openbare vennootschap"*) with or without
                legal personality, and
        (ii)   a "silent partnership" (*"stille vennootschap"*, often referred to as a
                "maatschap"). The "limited partnership" (*"commanditaire vennoot-
                schap"*) is considered a special type of public partnership.
(b)   The silent partnership is merely defined as "not being a public partner-
        ship". It is not registered with the Chamber of Commerce. The partners do
        not act under a joint name and are not authorised to represent the part-
        nership without a power of attorney by the other partner(s). The partners
        are each pro rata entitled to profits and liability for losses.
(c)   The public partnership conducts an enterprise or a profession. Its partners
        act under a common name and on behalf of, and in name of, the partner-
        ship.
(d)   The incorporation of a public partnership with legal personality requires
        a notarial deed. In the case of legal personality the partnership name needs
        to include the words "public partnership with legal personality"(*"openbare
        vennootschap met rechtspersoonlijkheid"*).
(e)   In order to create flexibility the Bill on Partnerships contains extensive
        provisions on obtaining and waiving legal personality and the conversion
        of a public partnership with legal personality into a private company with
        limited liability (*"besloten vennootschap"*) and vice versa.
(f)   The new legislation facilitates the admission of new partners to the part-
        nership and the continuation of the partnership by the remaining partners,
        for example in the event that a partner dies or goes bankrupt.
(g)   Upon the death of a partner his partnership interest can pass to his heirs.
(h)   In line with the changes proposed in respect of dissolution and continu-
        ation of the partnership, more flexibility is created in respect of liquidation
        and winding up. As indicated above, the "limited partnership" (*"comman-
        ditaire vennootschap"*) is considered a special type of public partnership. As
        such a limited partnership can have legal personality under the new legis-
        lation. The name of a limited partnership with legal personality needs to
        include the words "limited public partnership with legal personality"
        (*"commanditaire vennootschap met rechtspersoonlijkheid"*).

20.2.6.3   Further initiatives, one-tier boards, enquiries, social companies, etc.
Also in 2007, the Dutch Ministry of Justice announced further initiatives to modernise company law.

(a)   One-tier boards: one of the main features of the modernisation of company law will be the organisation of large undertakings. The Ministry of Justice is preparing a bill that will allow a one-tier board which brings together managing and supervisory directors into one board. The same bill will also provide for an arrangement in case of a conflict between the interests of managing or supervising directors and the interests of the company. A central question still to be resolved will be whether, and if so which, large undertakings should be legally required to have supervision.

(b)   Enquiry procedures: the Ministry will review the kinds of conflicts referred to the Enterprises Division of the Amsterdam Court of Appeal in the framework of an enquiry into the management of a company (*"enquête"*) as well as the kinds of interim measures imposed in such enquiries. There is no denying that recent high-profile cases, such as those relating to Stork and ABN AMRO (*see* 20.2.2 above) have fuelled the debate. Although the enquiry procedure is relatively fast, recently several objections have been voiced against it. Some argue that a number of conflicts could easily be dealt with by an ordinary court. Some say that the procedural guarantees are less than in other legal procedures and that an enquiry often results in an interim measure without actually having the enquiry for which it was requested. Some even argue that there is insufficient legal basis for the measures that the Enterprises Division sometimes orders.

(c)   Company with a social objective: a draft bill is in the making with regard to the "company with a social objective" (*"maatschappelijke onderneming"*), a legal entity which could be used by schools, organisations that provide for medical care, housing corporations and other institutions in the semi-public sector. This corporate form is based on the idea that on the one hand in these areas the state should intervene as little as possible, but that on the other the importance of these institutions is so great that they need guarantees for a qualified management and a greater form of account-ability. Consultations have already taken place and a bill is expected to be read in 2008. It may or may not fit the energy and infrastructure sectors.

(d)   In addition to the above, there is a host of further legislative activities in the field of company law. These activities concern draft bills with regard to the implementation of the following Directives:
(i)   2005/56/EC on cross-border mergers of limited liability companies;
(ii)   78/855/EEC and 82/891/EEC concerning the division and merger of public limited liability companies;
(iii)   2006/68/EC concerning the formation of public limited liability companies and the maintenance and alteration of their capital;
(iv)   2007/36/EC on the exercise of certain rights of shareholders in listed companies;
(v)   2006/46/EC which, *inter alia*, entails the obligation for companies to publish information concerning corporate governance and trans-actions with related parties and "off balance sheet arrangements";
(vi)   2006/43/EC on statutory audits of annual accounts and consoli-dated accounts.

They also concern harmonisation of the annual accounts and of the declaration for the purpose of corporate income tax; repressive (ex post) supervision instead of preventive (ex ante) supervision of legal entities; a shareholder's right concerning inclusion of issues on the agenda of the general meeting and introduction of the LLP in the Netherlands.

20.3   Exchange and investment control

No generic restrictions exist on the acquisition of ownership or control by foreign parties of business entities residing in the Netherlands. However, for certain industry sectors (e.g., energy, aviation, banking and insurance) through various means, specific rules may apply restricting the extent of foreign investment or control. Also, certain requirements exist in respect of notification to the Dutch Central Bank for statistical purposes.

20.4   Merger control

20.4.1   European merger control

If a concentration (i.e., a merger or an acquisition of sole or joint control) has a Community dimension as defined by the EC Merger Control Regulation (Council Regulation No. 139/2004), it must be notified to the European Commission and may not be implemented before the Commission has granted its approval. The Commission may grant an exemption from the obligation to suspend the transaction in certain circumstances. Moreover, in the case of a public bid, the EC Merger Regulation provides that the suspension obligation does not prevent its implementation, provided it has been duly notified without delay and that the acquirer does not exercise the voting rights attached to the securities. A merger will be cleared if it does not lead to "a significant impediment of effective competition in the Common Market or part of it, in particular as a result of the creation or strengthening of a dominant position" ("the SIEC test").

Ancillary agreements or undertakings entered into in connection with a concentration may be caught by the general prohibition of agreements and concerted practices in restraint of trade contained in Article 81 of the EC Treaty if restrictions are involved that are not directly related to, and necessary for, the successful implementation of the concentration. Therefore, careful analysis of such ancillary restraints is essential to make sure that they are objectively necessary and proportional.

20.4.2   National merger control

Since its entry into force on 1 January 1998, the Dutch Competition Act also provides for a merger control mechanism at national level. The national merger rules will apply to all concentrations that have no Community dimension under the EC Merger Regulation, and where the combined aggregate worldwide turnover of the undertakings concerned in the preceding calendar year exceeded

€113,450,000, and where at least two of the undertakings concerned individually achieve a turnover of at least €30 million in the Netherlands (Article 29, Competition Act).

The calculation of turnover under the Competition Act is roughly identical to the method used under the EC Merger Regulation (Article 30, Competition Act). The definition of a "concentration" under the Competition Act is in essence identical to the definition under the EC Merger Regulation. Article 27 of the Competition Act defines a merger as:

(a) the merging of two or more previously independent undertakings;
(b) direct or indirect acquisition of control over undertakings; and
(c) the setting up of a joint venture performing on a lasting basis all of the functions of an autonomous economic entity ("full-function" joint venture).

Excluded from the scope of concentration control are certain temporary acquisitions of shares by financial institutions, the acquisition of control by the trustee in bankruptcy of a company, and the acquisition of control by a financial holding company provided it does not exercise any voting rights to determine the commercial behaviour of the target (Article 28, Competition Act). However, in general, private equity transactions are notified because the investors will normally obtain rights to determine the "commercial behaviour" of the target. As mentioned above, also excluded from the scope of Dutch merger control are mergers falling within the scope of the EC Merger Regulation.

The procedural stage of Dutch merger control is divided into two phases. The first phase concerns the notification of any intention to establish a concentration to the director general of the Competition Authority ("NMa") (Article 34, Competition Act), which is announced in the *State Gazette (Staatscourant)* (Article 36, Competition Act). Notification is already possible on the basis of a good-faith intention that is sufficiently concrete, for example on the basis of a letter of intent (Case 988 Quality Bakers).

Within the first four weeks following the notification, the intended concentration is not permitted to be put into effect (Article 34, Competition Act). Before the end of this standstill period the Competition Authority informs the notifying parties whether or not a licence is required for the concentration (Article 37, Competition Act). As from 29 December 2006 a fee of €15,000 is charged after a first-phase decision.

A licence is required when reasons exist to assume that the concentration will lead to a significant impediment of effective competition on the Dutch market or a part thereof, in particular as a result of the creation or strengthening of a dominant position (Article 37(2), Competition Act). Expiration of the standstill period without a decision of the Competition Authority automatically means that the concentration does not require a licence and can be implemented. Alternatively, at the moment the parties are informed that no licence is required, the standstill period ends and the concentration is deemed to have received the go ahead (Article 37(6), Competition Act).

The second phase starts if the Competition Authority decides that a licence is required. A concentration rarely gets to the second phase in practice, and is even less likely to get there since the Competition Authority has the power to impose conditions on clearing mergers in the first phase to solve possible objections (e.g., the parties can agree with the Competition Authority to divest certain production facilities to obtain first-phase clearance). The standstill period is then extended until the imposed conditions are fulfilled (Article 37(6), Competition Act). To obtain a licence, a request has to be submitted which is separate from the original notification (Article 42, Competition Act). The request for a licence is also published in the *State Gazette* (*Staatscourant*) (Article 42(5), Competition Act). The Competition Authority has to decide on the request for a licence within 13 weeks after receipt of the request. As from 29 December 2006 a fee of €30,000 is charged after a second-phase decision.

Upon expiration of this time period without a decision from the Competition Authority, a licence is automatically deemed to have been granted (Article 44, Competition Act). A licence is refused when the effect of the proposed concentration would lead to a significant impediment of effective competition on the Dutch market or a part thereof, in particular as a result of the creation or strengthening of a dominant position (Article 41(2), Competition Act). A special provision is made for undertakings entrusted with the provision of services of general economic interest. If at least one of the undertakings concerned is entrusted with the provision of such services by law or by an administrative body, a licence can only be refused if this does not obstruct the performance of the particular tasks assigned to them (Article 41(3), Competition Act).

Failure to comply with the standstill period in any phase may result in administrative enforcement action by the Competition Authority and/or imposition of fines (Case 1774 Verkerk/Horn). A maximum fine of 10 per cent of annual turnover can be imposed (Article 74, Competition Act). Also, the concentration may be partly or wholly void (Case 811 Vendex Food Group – De Boer Unigro).

In relation to ancillary restraints, principles similar to those applicable under the EC Merger Regulation also apply to the merger provisions under the Competition Act. Careful analysis of such ancillary restraints is essential to make sure that they are objectively necessary and proportional.

It is advisable to include competition law specialists at an early stage in the transaction and to involve them into the structuring to ensure that competition issues can be avoided. Especially, issues on "control" of the target undertaking and the "undertakings concerned" are sometimes difficult to determine under competition rules.

If rights are acquired that could in any way determine the commercial behaviour of the target undertaking or target investment (e.g., in the shareholders agreement but also in loan documentation or other rights in relation to the target's commercial policy in any form) "control" can be deemed to exist. The competition authorities take a very wide approach to the notion of "undertakings concerned".

20.5 Regulation of the conduct of mergers and acquisitions

20.5.1 SER merger code

The procedural aspects of mergers and acquisitions in the Netherlands with regard to the protection of the interests of employees are, next to the codetermination rights, mostly regulated by the decree of the Dutch Social Economic Council ("SER") in 2000, entitled the SER Merger Code of Conduct (*SER-besluit Fusiegedragsregels*) or SER Merger Code.[18] The SER Merger Code is not a statute and, therefore, does not have force of law. As its name rightly suggests, it is a code of conduct. The powers of the body ensuring compliance, the SER Merger Committee, are limited to issuing a public notification or reprimand. It is arguable that a transgression of the SER Merger Code might be actionable in tort, and general law would thus be providing an indirect sanction. Even though the legal remedies in the case of infringement are limited, generally, the rules contained in the SER Merger Code are observed when takeovers having a sufficiently close connection with the Netherlands are conducted.

The SER Merger Code seeks to protect employee interests and provides that the labour organisations involved in the takeover as well as the Secretary of the SER Merger Committee should be notified before an agreement with regard to a merger is reached. The notifications are usually conducted simultaneously with the consultation process with the labour organisation and the works council. This may require involvement of the trade unions at a relatively early stage of the merger negotiations, as the SER Merger Committee has made clear that this requirement may be triggered by the execution of letters of intent or other agreements in principle. The above notification requirement also covers the granting of push-button options.

A merger is broadly defined as the acquisition or transfer of direct or indirect control over an enterprise or part thereof. This is obviously a very broad definition. The scope of the definition may, however, be restricted to a degree by the SER Merger Committee's position that such control should be durable in nature. It has also indicated that, in making its determination whether a merger has taken place, it will let substance rule over form and examine the totality of the transaction transferring control.

The rules contained in this chapter should be observed if:

(a) the merger involves at least one enterprise residing in the Netherlands regularly employing 50 or more persons; or

(b) an undertaking involved in the merger forms part of a group of companies, and the Dutch resident companies of that group together regularly employ 50 or more persons (Section 2(1), Merger Code).

It should be noted that in a number of collective labour agreements the scope of these provisions of the SER Merger Code have been widened (Section 2(2), Merger Code). Exempted from these rules are mergers of group companies, mergers through inheritance or marriage, and mergers outside the jurisdiction of the Netherlands (Section 2(3), Merger Code). This last exemption takes into account that, even though in some cases the stated 50 employees test may be met, the territorial application of the SER Merger Code requires that mergers of two or more largely foreign concerns controlled by foreigners do not fall within the ambit of the SER Merger Code. This would, however, be different in the event that the merger solely or principally applied to the Dutch entities of the concern.

The labour organisations are under a duty to maintain confidentiality in respect of the notification itself (Section 7, Merger Code). However, in addition to the notification, certain additional information must be provided to – and meetings held with – certain organisations. The information to be furnished relates to the motives of the merger, the business policies to implement the same, the anticipated social, economic and legal consequences of the merger and the measures planned to be taken in connection therewith. Confidentiality in respect of this information needs to be requested from the labour organisation by registered letter and in advance of the submission of such information. Such confidential treatment may be refused by the labour organisations. If such confidential treatment is refused, evidently, the information does not need to be furnished to the labour organisations.

The SER Merger Code contemplates that the consultations with the labour organisations also relate to the consultations with the works council(s), as required by the Works Council Act. The Code stipulates that the works council(s) concerned should be able to take the opinion of the labour organisations on the envisaged merger into account before rendering their advice.

20.5.2   Works Council Act

Pursuant to the Works Council Act (*Wet op de Ondernemingsraden*), an enterprise regularly employing more than 50 persons is under a duty to institute a works council. The works council will be granted the opportunity to render advice in connection with any intended decision by or attributed to management dealing with one of a number of topics enumerated in the Act.

The decisions covered by this provision of the Act include:

(a)   transfer of control over its own enterprise, or a part thereof, or over another enterprise;
(b)   entering into, or substantially amending or terminating, a long-term cooperation with another enterprise;
(c)   terminating the activities of the enterprise, or a substantial part thereof;
(d)   materially reducing, expanding or in another way changing the activities of the enterprise, etc.

The advice should be requested at a time such that it may have a substantial influence on the intended decision. This may even be prior to the execution of a statement of intent, as such a statement may entail a definitive choice from a number of possible future merger partners (Enterprise Chamber Court of Amsterdam, 10 July 1997, NJ 1997, 669). Although not immediately apparent from the text of the statute, in Dutch case law decisions were handed down holding that not only the works council of the acquiring company has a right to render advice, but, in most cases, the works council of the target too (Court of Amsterdam 27 July 1989, NJ 1990, 734).

Together with the request for advice, the works council must be provided with particulars of the reasons underlying the decision, the expected consequences for the employees of the enterprise and the measures intended to be taken in connection with such consequences. At least one consultative meeting should be held with the works council to discuss any intended decisions on which the works council's advice is requested.

To the extent that the works council has not yet rendered advice regarding the way in which the decision will be implemented, the works council will also have a right of advice in respect of such implementation. In many cases, a clear distinction between the decision and the manner in which it is implemented can hardly be made. Therefore, it is common practice to agree with the works council in advance on the subjects, manner and timing of the consultation process.

If the management makes a decision after having sought the advice of the works council, it is under a duty to inform the works council promptly of such a decision. If the decision deviates, wholly or partially, from the advice given, the reasons for this will have to be notified to the works council. Unless the decision fully complies with the advice, management is under a duty to suspend implementation of its decision for a period of one month from the date on which the works council was informed of the decision. This period is intended to enable the works council to file an appeal against the decision. The appeal can only be based on the grounds that the company could not reasonably have made the decision, taking into account all interests concerned.

The Act contains a "jurisdiction clause" (Section 25(1), last paragraph), stating in general terms that no advice needs to be sought from the works council where the target company is a foreign resident and it is not to be expected that the decision of the management of the Dutch company will lead to a decision subject to advice in respect of the Dutch part of such a company.

At the time of writing, the current Act was under review. It is expected that a new Act will not significantly amend the rights and obligations as already prescribed under the Act. It mainly intends to reorganise the current Act, as it was deemed to have become exceedingly complicated and inaccessible by the amendments made to it over the years.

20.5.3 Act on Notification of Collective Redundancies

If a takeover leads to an integration of the target into the business of the acquiring company, this may require substantial restructuring and rationalisation. In such a case, the intention of the employer to terminate the employment of at least 20 employees within the region of one Centre for Work and Income ("CWI"), within a period of three months, will trigger a duty to notify, and consult with, the labour organisations under the Act on Notification of Collective Redundancies (*Wet Melding Collectief Ontslag*). The consultation with the labour organisations should at least deal with the possibility of preventing collective lay-offs or reducing the number of employees affected by them, as well as other ways of reducing the consequences, by preparing what is referred to as a "social plan". Such a social plan should set out the terms and conditions under which the company will make redundancies. In its notification, the employer is under a duty to set out the reasons underlying its intention to make a large number of employees redundant, as well as particulars of the redundancies (e.g., number of affected employees, job descriptions, ages, seniority and date of termination).

In addition to notifying the labour organisations, the CWI should be notified and permission requested to terminate the employment of the affected employees. Such a centre will not rule on the matter until one month after the filing of the notification, and until consultation with the works council has taken place and the labour organisations have been invited to participate in consultations.

20.6   Methods of acquisition

20.6.1   General

Apart from the public offer, described at 20.7 below, the methods of acquisition most commonly applied are:

(a)   the acquisition of (a voting majority of) the entire issued share capital of the target company;

(b)   the sale by the target company of its entire business or all of its assets (or substantially all of its business or assets); and

(c)   the statutory merger.

Also, the business effect of an acquisition may be realised through the creation of corporate alliances by means of interlocking directorates. Clearly, these methods may be, and in many cases are, used in combination.

20.6.2   Share transactions

By far the most commonly used manner of takeover is to acquire a controlling interest in the equity of a company through the acquisition of its shares.

As stated above, in most cases, the transfer of title to registered shares is effected by means of a deed of transfer executed in the presence of a Dutch civil law notary. In an attempt to limit the possibility of abusing the corporate persona of limited companies, a duty has been created for the notary executing the deed to conduct an investigation into the validity of previous transfers of title (Section 2:195(2) CC). In practice, defects in such transfers or the authority of the previous transferors are frequently found. In order not to unduly frustrate otherwise perfectly valid transactions, a number of rules were created to remedy such past defects.

This notarial review, however, is limited in scope and is not a substitute for a legal review dealing with a great number of corporate legal issues. Also, this practice does not derogate from the need to incorporate appropriate representations and warranties in the documentation required to complete the transaction. In fact such representations and warranties, the related provisions on the computation of damages (and eventual limitations to the recoverable amount thereof) and disclosures by the seller, make up a substantial part of such documentation. Frequently, the right to rescind the acquisition agreement for breach of contract (Section 6:265 CC) is waived in transactions dealing with transfer of corporate control. Although such a rescission would not have a retroactive effect, it would create a duty to negate all actions rendered under the agreement (Section 6:271 CC). In general, such an approach is not considered to be feasible, practical or appropriate in such transactions. For much the same reason, the right to cancel for mistake (Section 6:228 CC) is often waived. If not waived, such a cancellation could be effected by simple notice (Section 3:49 and 50 CC) and would have retroactive effect.

20.6.3 Sale of a business

This way of transferring a business is commonly used as it grants the purchaser advantage in obtaining a greater degree of certainty as to the assets and liabilities that are employed in such a business. Much of what is stated in respect of the transfer of interests in non-corporate business entities in 20.2.4 above applies *mutatis mutandis*. Such a transfer may be a laborious process as it can only be put into effect by duly observing the rules of the law relating to the conveyance of property. For example, for transfer of tangible, non-registered property, transfer of possession suffices (Section 3:90 CC); for immovables and other registered property, a notarial deed of transfer and registration is prescribed (Section 4:89 CC). Transfer of contractual rights and claims may only be effected through a tripartite agreement (between the transferor, the transferee and the contract party/debtor) or a deed of transfer and notification to the contract party or debtor (Section 3:93/94 CC). Intangibles are transferred in the manner prescribed in legislation pertinent to each specific intangible asset (Section 3:95 CC). In addition, the transfer of immovable property is subject to taxation. Therefore, in the documentation of the transaction more elaborate provisions may be necessary, including those required to regulate the conduct of the business while the legal transfer of all rights and duties is being completed.

As in other EU Member States, special protection is granted to the employees in a business through an automatic transfer of most of their legal rights to the acquirer of the business. However, this protection does not extend to certain types of pension rights of such employees (Section 7:662–666 CC). In respect of the transferring entity, care should be taken that a sale of most of the assets and liabilities is beyond the powers of the management board and subject to the prior consent of the general meeting of shareholders.

20.6.4 Statutory mergers

The Civil Code defines a statutory merger as a legal act between two or more legal entities whereby one acquires the estate of the other, or whereby a new legal person is established by such persons through the said legal act and acquires their estate under general title. A statutory merger is only possible between legal entities which have the same legal form (e.g., between companies or between foundations). With the exception of the acquiring entity, the merging legal entities dissolve through the execution of the merger. With a number of exceptions, the members or shareholders of the dissolving legal entities become members or shareholders respectively of:

(a)   the acquiring legal entity (Section 2:311 CC); or
(b)   one of its group companies (Section 2:334 CC).

The merger procedure commences with a preparatory phase during which:

(a)   the management board of the merging companies prepares a merger proposal (Section 2:312 and 326 CC) (which includes an explanatory memorandum (Section 2:313 and 327 CC));
(b)   the accountants prepare reports related to the companies and, where applicable, the share exchange ratio (Section 2:328 CC); and
(c)   the proposal and reports are made available to the public (Section 2:314 and 328 CC).

Creditors may object to the merger and require that adequate security is provided to them for their outstanding claims (Section 2:316 CC).

After the completion of the preparatory activities, the general meeting of shareholders of the dissolving company and the general meeting of shareholders of the acquiring company (or – to the extent permitted by the articles of association of such a company – the management board of the acquiring company), both by special majority, resolve to merge their companies (Section 2:317 CC). The statutory merger is effected through a notarial deed.

20.6.5   Triangular mergers

Dutch statute provides for a statutory triangular merger by allowing the shareholders of a disappearing company in a statutory merger to become the shareholders of a group company of the acquiring company (Section 2: 334 CC). Such a merger is permitted only if such a group company, the shares of which will be provided to the shareholders of the disappearing company, itself or together with other group companies, holds the entire issued share capital of the acquiring company and has resolved to effect such a merger in conformity with the rules applicable to the issue of shares. This provision is invoked in cases where the acquiring company uses an operating company to act as surviving entity in a statutory merger. In this case it may be considered appropriate to provide the shareholders of the disappearing entity with shares in the capital of the holding company of the group of which the surviving entity forms a part. The statutory triangular merger is used as a mechanism for corporate restructuring, possibly in connection with, preceding or following, a takeover and as a "squeeze-out" mechanism (*see* 20.8 below).

20.6.6   Cross-border statutory mergers

A draft Act on cross-border mergers was presented to Parliament early in 2007. Currently, there is only legislation related to the cross-border mergers of the *Societas Europeana* ("SE") and European Cooperative ("SCE") and the jurisprudence of the European Court of Justice in *Re Sevic* (ECJ 13 December 2005, C-411/03). The draft Act provides for mergers between NVs, BVs or SCEs with companies and cooperatives under the laws of another EU or EEA Member State. The Act contains minority protection provisions for shareholders who have voted against a merger in which shares in a foreign company will be allotted to them. Such shareholders have a right to withdraw and be indemnified. It is not yet certain when the Act will enter into force.

20.6.7 *Interlocking directorates/corporate alliances*

The objective of a merger or takeover is to operate what once were several distinct sets of business operations under different groups of managers, under the ultimate control of one, single group of managers in a consolidated chain of control. Real decision-making power over major business issues will need to be consolidated.

In addition to share and asset transactions and statutory mergers, therefore, the functional equivalent of combinations can be brought about by creating such consolidated decision-making power through interlocking directorates. Dutch statute takes these ways of exercising joint control into account by defining a subsidiary (Section 2:24(a) CC), a large company (Section 2:153/263(3)(d) CC) and consolidated accounts (Section 2:409 CC).

Cross-border asset transactions can lead to a number of legal and tax complications. In practice, statutory mergers are mostly used for purely national corporate restructuring, and not for cross-border transactions. International business combinations through share transactions in most countries can be effected in a fairly straightforward manner but beg the question of who acquires control over whom. In other words, to use 1980s phraseology, "Who is predator and who is prey?" For these reasons, in a number of truly international deals where equality of the merger partners played an important role, combinations were brought about by retaining more than one listed company and, in addition to shareholder relationships, employing contractual means and interlocking directorates. Well-known Anglo/Dutch examples are Unilever Plc/Unilever NV, Shell Transport & Trading Plc/Koninklijke Nederlandse Petroleum Maatschappij NV, AMEV/AG, and Reed International Plc/Elsevier NV. The structures used in creating these combinations involve cross-participations, interlocking directorates at various sub-holding and holding levels, as well as contractual arrangements as to profit equalisation.

Also, more in a 1990s frame of mind, instead of creating market clout and market share by acquiring new businesses, corporations seek to reinvent themselves and focus on accumulation of core competencies. Alliances are created giving access to (local) markets, customer interfaces, or other, non-core, competencies. These alliances do not need to take the form of a fully-fledged merger or takeover, but often consist of minority cross-participations, contractual arrangements and interlocking directorates (i.e., vertical integration is replaced by virtual integration). Clearly, these arrangements rely to a greater extent on contractual means, so the remedies available in the case of non-performance will be those arising in contract or under general law for breach of contract.

20.6.8 Statutory demergers

Often in conjunction with mergers, statutory demergers are effected to transfer part of the assets of a company under general title (Section 2:334(a) CC). This avoids the laborious process of a transfer of assets and liabilities as described at 20.6.3 above. Statutory demergers can take the form of either a pure demerger or a partial demerger. In the former form two new companies are created, while in the latter the demerging entity will continue to exist and only one new company is created. This allows for variations in the form of hybrid demergers, demergers at the shareholder level and triangular demergers, but only applies to purely Dutch demergers. If this device is used in conjunction with a business combination, it is important to be aware of the special rules of joint and several liability between the demerging and demerged entities (Section 2: 334t CC).

20.7   Preparation of a public offer

20.7.1 Act on Financial Supervision/Decree on Public Offers

In 2007, the Decree on Public Offers ("Decree") entered into force. The Decree implements the 2004 EU Takeover Directive and is nothing less than a complete overhaul of the Dutch rules on public offers. The Decree is based on the 2006 Act on Financial Supervision ("Act"). It follows less drastic reviews in previous years when the takeover rules were compiled in various codes:

(a)   the 1995 Decree on securities supervision,
(b)   the Dutch financial supervisor, AFM's Temporary Exemption for Takeover offers and the Policy Rules on Offering Memoranda; and
(c)   Attachment X to the General Rules Euronext Amsterdam Stock Market, Euronext Rule Book, Book II.

The Decree replaces all these rules and thus provides an improved and more transparent set of rules for Dutch takeovers, be they friendly or hostile. After the public controversy over control battles around major Dutch companies like Stork, VNU, Petroplus and ABN AMRO (*see* also 20.2.2 above), considerable political pressure arose to streamline the regulatory regime around Dutch public offers. This is now achieved by the Decree. The one important feature that is still part of the public debate but is not in the Dutch rulebook is the creation of a specific takeover panel. Supervision of Dutch public takeovers is left to the Netherlands Authority for the Financial Markets, AFM, and the Enterprise Chamber of the Amsterdam Court.

20.7.2 General application

The Decree applies to public offers for shares in Dutch listed companies. The supervisory authority under the Act is the AFM. Non-compliance with the rules on public offers contained in the Act and the Decree may result in the AFM imposing administrative fines and penalties or even criminal prosecution by the public prosecutor. Non-compliance may, under certain circumstances, be tortious vis-à-vis third parties or the target and lead to civil liability.

It requires that the offer process commences with the announcement of a public offer. The Decree sets out in which circumstances an offer must be announced. After its announcement, a public offer must, within a term of 12 weeks, be officially posted by publishing an offering memorandum. Absent competing offers, the entire bidding process should be completed in 35 weeks.

The Decree sets out the various terms that apply to, for example, posting and publishing of the offer and acceptance by shareholders. There is a maximum term for acceptance to prevent the bidding process from dragging on. The AFM supervises compliance with these terms. The Decree also regulates the information flow to the market, shareholders and employees.

The Decree implements the 2004 EU Takeover Directive by, *inter alia*:

(a) implementing the "certain funds" rule;
(b) requiring a mandatory offer with an offering memorandum in case over 30 per cent of the voting shares are acquired;
(c) requiring that the offering memorandum is approved by the AFM; and
(d) prescribing a minimum and maximum term for acceptance of the offer.

20.7.3 Some specific features

The Decree has a number of new features:

(a) There is a new test for the moment on which a bid must be announced. The previous test of the moment on which there is "the justified expectation that agreement will be reached" was replaced by the moment on which conditional agreement is reached.
(b) The term within which a bidder must submit a request for approval of an offering memorandum is extended, to allow more time for preparation of complex offers. However, to create transparency in the market the bidder is under an obligation to publicly announce at which time the request will be made. There is also the obligation to disclose the manner in which the bid will be financed at the time of the request for approval of the offering memorandum.
(c) In addition to detailed specific requirements (including information on compensation paid to management and supervisory board members in connection to the offer), there are the general requirements that the offering memorandum must contain all information to allow a shareholder to take a "responsible decision" and that information in it should be clear and consistent.
(d) Information on the bid must be submitted to the employees of the target. The bidder must provide the offering memorandum to such employees. The offering memorandum should contain more information on the intentions of the offeror in respect of the employees and working locations. The target must also furnish its written statement to shareholders to the target's employees. Rules contained in other employee co-determination legislation remain applicable (e.g., Works Council Act and SER Merger Code).
(e) In case of a competing offer, the first offeror has the option to synchronise the timing of the bids and the offeror may increase the price of his offer

once. The target is under a duty to inform shareholders in writing of its position regarding the competing offers.

(f)   A hostile offer will have to be announced earlier, because the seven-day waiting period no longer applies and the offer is deemed announced in case the bidder makes statements regarding his offer, for example on price.

(g)   There are rules on pricing of a mandatory offer and the possibility is created to request the Enterprise Chamber of the Amsterdam Court for a price revision.

(h)   The Decree holds rules on a European passport for offering memoranda.

(i)   The rules on the way information on the bid should be published is harmonised with the rules aimed at preventing insider trading.

20.7.4   Definition of public offer and types of offers

The Act defines a public offer as:

> "an offer for securities made by means of a public announcement outside a restricted circle or a solicitation to make an offer for securities outside a restricted circle with the intent to acquire these securities."

The definition of securities in the Act is rather broad and includes shares, bonds, options, warrants, convertible rights, etc.

Four types of public offer are distinguished under the Decree:

(a)   a firm offer;
(b)   a partial offer;
(c)   a tender offer; and
(d)   a mandatory offer.

A firm offer is an offer made for 100 per cent of the issued class of securities, whereas a partial offer is an offer made for only a part of the issued class of securities. A tender offer is an offer under which holders of securities are invited to state the price at which they are prepared to sell their securities. An offer is mandatory if the total amount of securities represents more than 30 per cent of the votes in the general meeting of shareholders or if the offer is mandatory under the laws of another Member State. However, a public offer is not mandatory if the general meeting of shareholders has approved with 95 per cent of the remaining votes that the threshold of 30 per cent may be exceeded.

20.7.5   Procedure and timing

The Decree sets out in reasonable detail the procedure and the timing of an offer. From the perspective of the party making a firm offer, this procedure can be summarised as follows:

(a)   Announcement: the prospective offeror and the target are under an obligation to make an announcement of the offer, at the latest, on the moment that (conditional) agreement has been reached. The announcement contains the names of the offeror and the target company and, if possible, the proposed price or exchange rate and all conditions already agreed upon with regard to the issuing or compliance with the public offer. An offer also has to be announced if the offeror published specific details without there being (conditional) agreement, such as a proposed price, exchange rate or specific time schedule for the public offer. After its announcement, the Offer Memorandum must be filed for approval with the AFM within 12 weeks. The Offer Memorandum must be submitted to the competent competition authority as soon as possible. The whole procedure (i.e., from the announcement of the offer until the moment that the offeror announces whether the offer will be honoured or not) will take place within 35 weeks, at the most.

(b) Request for approval of the Offer Memorandum: within four weeks from the public announcement referred to above having been made, the offeror will have to either:

    (i) announce that it will submit a request for approval of the Offer Memorandum with the AFM, thereby indicating the time period in which it will do so; or

    (ii) announce the decision not to make the offer.

(c) Certain funds/information Offer Memorandum: at the latest at the moment of filing the request, the offeror has to confirm to be able to pay the price indicated in the offer or to have taken all reasonable measures to provide for an alternative form of compensation ("certain funds"). The AFM will only approve of the Offer Memorandum if it contains all of the information which is relevant for a "reasonably informed and conscientiously acting person" for making a well-considered decision on the public offer, including, *inter alia*:

    (i) the name of the offeror;

    (ii) the price or exchange ratio of the offer;

    (iii) a statement as to whether or not discussions with the target have taken place and if such discussions have led to agreement;

    (iv) a statement that the offer is directed to all holders of the type of securities which are the subject of the offer;

    (v) a statement that the terms and conditions of the offer are equal for all holders of the same type of securities;

    (vi) the compensation offered to shareholders of the target company for the loss of their special statutory rights with regard to a decision on the nomination or dismissal of a managing or supervisory director in case the articles of association enable a shareholder who has become a majority shareholder ($\geq$75 per cent of the shares) due to a public offer to, shortly after expiry of the acceptance period, convene all shareholders to an extraordinary meeting;

    (vii) the minimum number of securities ("acceptance level") which must be tendered within the acceptance period on which the offer is conditional;

    (viii) any other conditions to which the (honouring of the) offer is subject;

    (ix) the motivation of the offer price or exchange ratio and the means of financing if the offer is made wholly or partly in cash;

    (x) the terms with respect to delivery of shares tendered and payment;

    (xi) the tender period within which holders must have tendered their shares;

(xii)   to the extent the offeror is able, clear data on the assets and the results of the target over the past three years and over the last financial year, to be accompanied by the explanatory notes and available data relating to the current financial year if more than four months of the period between the moment of making the Offer Memorandum publicly available and the last working day of the past six months have elapsed;

(xiii) any intentions to amend the target's articles of association after completion of the offer;

(xiv)   a statement about the intentions as to the policy to be pursued in respect of the target and its business;

(xv)   any intentions to change the composition of the target's management board and supervisory board after completion of the offer;

(xvi)   the total of all compensation offered to be paid to the members of the offeror's management board and supervisory board;

(xvii) the total of all compensation offered to be paid to the resigning members of the target's management board and supervisory board;

(xviii) information regarding the direct or indirect mutual participations in the capital of the offeror and the target as at the date of publication of the Offer Memorandum;

(xix)   if applicable, any previous commitments of existing holders to tender their securities which are the subject of the offer;

(xx)   a statement whether the offeror, any of its group companies, or any insider of either the offeror or the target company (if the Offer Memorandum was jointly framed) has acquired any securities issued by the target in the period of one year prior to the announcement of the availability of the Offer Memorandum or will acquire pursuant to pre-existing agreements concluded during such period, together with certain terms and conditions in respect thereof;

(xxi)   a statement of the number and category or class of securities issued by the target company which are held – at the time of filing of the request – by the offeror and the target as well as by members of their management board and supervisory board, their spouses, minor children or any legal entity which these persons control;

(xxii) a statement as to how the interests of the target's employees are taken into account;

(xxiii) the names and functions of the persons or legal entities responsible for (parts of) the Offer Memorandum together with a statement from such persons or legal entities that the information provided in the (relevant part of) the Offer Memorandum is, to the best of their knowledge, true and complete;

(xxiv) in the case of a securities exchange offer, additional information must be included in the Offer Memorandum with respect to the company issuing such securities (in compliance with Section 8(2) of the Decree).

(d)   Approval Offer Memorandum: within 10 days after the AFM receives the request it will make its decision with regard to the approval known to the offeror and, within six days after notice of approval, the offeror either has to announce its offer by making the approved Offer Memorandum generally available or announce that it will not make a public offer.

(e) Opening for acceptance: not earlier than on the first trading day after the publication of the approved Offer Memorandum, the offer may be opened for acceptance and should remain open for at least at least four weeks and not longer than 10 weeks. Up until three days after the end of this period, the offeror can decide to extend the term for acceptance for a period of at least two weeks and at most 10 weeks. The extension starts at the end of the previous period.

(f) Extraordinary general meeting: after announcement of the availability of the Offer Memorandum but at least six trading days before the expiry of the acceptance period, the target (if it is a resident of The Netherlands) is to convene an extraordinary general meeting of shareholders to discuss the offer, and ultimately four days prior to such meeting management of the target should make available to its shareholders a report (to the extent that such information is not already included in the Offer Memorandum), containing, *inter alia*:

   (i) the reasoned position of the target's management vis-à-vis the proposed offer;

   (ii) data on the assets and results of the target, including data relating to the current financial year if more than three months thereof has elapsed, necessary for the shareholders to form a reasoned judgement of the proposed offer; and

   (iii) other information deemed relevant.

(g) Public announcement: on the third trading day after expiry of the acceptance period, at the latest, the offeror should announce publicly whether the offer will be honoured or not. If the offeror announces that it will not honour the offer, it will publicly state the reason thereof. The offeror states the total amount, the number and the corresponding percentage of the shares that have been presented in accordance with the offer as well as the total amount, the number and the corresponding percentage of the shares that the offeror has in possession after the acceptance period.

(h) Second opportunity: within three trading days after announcing to those who did not accept the offer that the offer will be honoured, the offeror can decide to give these shareholders the opportunity to offer their shares on the same terms and conditions as those provided for under the public offer. For this purpose, the offeror must publicly announce:

   (i) the reason for offering this opportunity;

   (ii) the term for offering these shares (two weeks at the most); and

   (iii) the applicability of the initial Offer Memorandum.

The shareholders may freely acquire shares and dispose of their shares during the acceptance period, provided they have not yet accepted the offer. By acceptance, a shareholder assumes the obligation to transfer the shares upon the offer becoming unconditional. However, shareholders who have accepted the offer during the acceptance period may freely withdraw their offer during a possible extension of the acceptance period by the offeror. The offeror may reserve the right to waive conditions which are not fulfilled and honour the offer nevertheless. Potestative conditions (conditions, the fulfilment of which depend on the offeror's own intent) are not allowed.

20.7.6 *Trading by the offeror*

The rules relating to public offers do not in any way limit the possibility of the offeror acquiring securities in the open market or by way of private transactions with shareholders. However, it is customary that a standstill agreement is entered into with the target, which may limit or preclude such transactions and agreements. However, once a public announcement has been made relating to a public offer (*see* 20.7.5(a) above), any subsequent (direct or indirect) transaction in securities which is the subject of the offer or in securities that are offered in exchange should forthwith be reported to the AFM, with the exception of transactions in securities which take place on financial markets on a regular basis. Both the offeror and the target company are allowed to conduct open-market transactions in securities related to the target or in securities that are offered in exchange during the period between the publication of the approved Offer Memorandum and the moment that the offeror announces that the offer will be honoured. However, with the exception of transactions in securities which take place on financial markets on a regular basis, a public announcement must be made with regard to these transactions. If the offeror has honoured its offer, for a period of one year after the approved Offer Memorandum was made publicly available the offeror it is not allowed to acquire, directly or indirectly, securities of the kind to which the offer relates on terms more favourable for the holder of such securities than those of the public offer.

20.7.7 *Disclosure of major holdings*

Under the Act of Financial Supervision 2006, anyone who knows or should know that they hold a major holding in a company incorporated under Dutch law listed on an officially recognised Stock Exchange within the EU, has a duty to notify that percentage of capital interest and/or voting rights to the AFM.

A notification is to be made, if – as a result of any acquisition or disposal of shares – the shareholdings would transgress certain thresholds (either upwards or downwards). These thresholds are set at 5, 10, 15, 20, 25, 30, 40, 50, 60, 75 and 95 per cent.

Notices received by the AFM are published in the registry on the website of the AFM. The notice includes:

(a)   name and place of residence of the (legal) person subject to notification duty;
(b)   name of the company;
(c)   percentage of shares in the capital and percentage of votes that can be exercised in respect of the issued capital which the person subject to notification has at his disposal;
(d)   the composition of the percentages referred to under (c); and
(e)   the date on which the notification duty arose.

20.8 Squeeze out

Where the offeror acquires more than 95 per cent of the shares, the offeror has the right pursuant to the Dutch Civil Code to enter into proceedings against the minority shareholders for the transfer of their shares. In such proceedings, the consideration due for the shares is determined by the court. The relevant section of the Civil Code provides for the possibility of the court to appoint either one or three experts to determine that consideration.

Alternatively, if the offeror acquires less than 95 per cent of the outstanding share capital, the issue of new shares to the offeror may be made under any authority to issue shares without regard to the pre-emptive rights of other shareholders (which it is common for a public company to have) which may dilute the shareholding of the minority unwilling to tender their shares under the offer to a percentage below 5 per cent. Subsequently, the buy-out procedure referred to in the paragraph above can be followed.

Under Dutch law, a legal merger can be used to a limited extent to squeeze out shareholders unwilling to tender their shares under the offer, provided that the offeror has acquired at least 70 per cent of the outstanding share capital of the target. The legal merger can take different forms. Mergers can take place between and among NVs and BVs. When the target is merged upstream into a Dutch acquisition vehicle (usually a BV), the minority shareholders unwilling to tender their shares under the offer are issued shares of a particular class in the acquisition vehicle in exchange for their shares in the target. That particular class of shares may then be redeemed in exchange for cash, thus squeezing out those shareholders unwilling to tender their shares under the offer. This scenario may be followed if the public offer does not lead to a 95 per cent shareholding.

20.9 Statutory dispute resolution

These measures can and should be taken against all remaining shareholders. If there is a single obstructive shareholder in a private limited company, the statutory dispute resolution provisions may apply, which include the possibility of expelling or buying out a minority shareholder, withdrawing the shareholder from the company and effecting a compulsory transfer of voting rights.

20.10 Financial assistance

In conformity with the requirements of the Second EC Directive, the Netherlands have promulgated statutory rules rendering it unlawful for a public or private limited company, or any of its subsidiaries, to give financial assistance in respect of the subscription for, or the acquisition of, shares issued by such company or depository receipts in respect of such shares, by a third party. The applicable statute describes financial assistance as the granting of a security, price guarantee or other guarantee, the acceptance of joint and several liability, or the acceptance in any other way of liability together with another person or in another person's place.

Financial assistance through loans is treated differently from the assistance mentioned above. In respect of such assistance – which forms an important element of any leveraged buy-out – a distinction is made between the treatment of public and private limited companies. For public limited companies, the prohibition extends to all financial assistance by way of a loan. However, private limited companies may grant loans for subscription for, or acquisition of, their shares or depository receipts issued in respect thereof, but only up to an amount equal to the distributable reserves of such company. Distributable reserves are reserves which are not prescribed by statute or by the articles of association. An example is a reserve comprising payments of share surplus or premium. In the event that the company (or its subsidiary) extends financial assistance by way of a loan, it is under a statutory duty to create a statutory reserve.

It is noteworthy that the wording of the statutory prohibition does not include loans provided by the company's subsidiaries. In legal doctrine this is generally considered to be a legislative omission; the statute is therefore construed so as to prohibit loans of this type, too. It should further be noted that, in order for the loan to be caught by the prohibition, it should also pass the hurdle of the restrictive statutory wording that it be granted "in view of" the subscription for, or the acquisition of, shares. This would appear to mean that it should be established in evidence that such subscription or acquisition was the objective of the assistance, and that a mere causal relationship would not suffice.

The circumstance that a loan should be regarded as permissible under the statutory provisions regulating financial assistance does not detract from the general requirement that such a loan should be in the interests of the company (Section 2:9 CC). Granting such a loan either to an uncreditworthy person or under manifestly unfavourable conditions to the company may subject the company's directors to personal, joint and several liability.

Chapter 21
Poland

Konrad Konarski
Partner
Baker & McKenzie, Warsaw

21.1 Introduction

Mergers and acquisitions of both listed and unlisted companies are becoming increasingly common in Poland. The development of capital markets and consequently the market for corporate acquisitions has been driven by the privatisation programme carried out in Poland since the introduction of the market economy in 1989. Most notable merger and acquisition ("M&A") transactions in Poland to date have been acquisitions of formerly state-owned enterprises by Polish and foreign private investors. Takeovers of publicly traded companies are quite common although they usually take the form of a friendly acquisition preceded by negotiations between the seller and the purchaser followed by a tender offer to all other shareholders. Several hostile takeovers have been attempted in Poland but they were ultimately unsuccessful.

The enactment of the Code of Commercial Companies ("CCC") and changes to the securities regulations in 2001 gave minority shareholders a number of instruments to protect their position in listed companies and, as a result, Poland has experienced a tide of minority shareholders' activism and raised interest in corporate governance issues. A voluntary corporate governance code was proposed by the Warsaw Stock Exchange in 2002 and subsequently revised in 2005 and 2007, and was accepted, either in full or with certain exceptions, by almost all listed companies. The pension reform in 2001 created around a dozen pension funds supplied by a steady flow of pension money and actively investing on the capital market. In addition, a decision to tax bank deposits has resulted in the shift of large amounts of capital to formerly less-popular investment funds. All this contributed to strengthening the position of minority shareholders and the greater influence of institutional investors whose interests must now be taken into account by any potential acquirer.

The Code of Commercial Companies of 15 September 2000 provided a new regulatory framework for M&A activity in Poland. The CCC is to a large extent based on the former Commercial Code enacted in 1934 although it contains a number of new provisions long awaited by legal practitioners. In particular, with respect to M&A activity, the CCC allows for mergers of different types of companies, clarifies different issues on the merger procedure and allows for division and spin-offs of companies.

The CCC, like its predecessor the 1934 Commercial Code, is based on the continental corporate model including two types of corporations (limited liability company and joint stock company) and two-tier boards (management board and supervisory board; supervisory board is optional in limited liability companies). The limited liability company (*spolka z ograniczona odpowiedzialnoscia*, "sp. zoo") closely resembles a German GmbH or a French sarl, while the joint stock company (*spolka akcyjna*, "SA") is the equivalent of a German AG or a French SA. Only shares in a joint stock company may be admitted to public trading and listed.

Merger and acquisition activity on the capital market, as well as corporate issues with respect to listed companies, is regulated by the Law on Public Offerings and Listings of Financial Instruments on Regulated Market and on Public Companies of 29 July 2005 (commonly referred to as the "Public Offerings Act"). The Public Offerings Act has not yet fully implemented the EU Directive on Takeover Bids. At the time of writing, amendments to the Public Offerings Act were being considered in the Polish Parliament. The amendment is expected to be adopted in mid-2008 and is to implement the EU Takeover Directive. However, it seems from the current draft of the amendments that, even after the amendments are adopted, the takeover regulation in Poland will continue to have certain national peculiarities. The new regulations are described in this chapter as the "Draft Takeover Regulations".

The market for corporate control is supervised by several government agencies. Tender offers for listed companies are supervised by *Komisja Nadzoru Finansowego* ("KNF", the Financial Supervisory Commission), the Polish financial markets authority. All transactions which may have an effect on competition must be notified and are reviewed by the Polish competition authority, the Office for Protection of Competition and Consumers ("OPCC"). Foreigners (including foreign-controlled companies) must obtain a permit for acquisition of real property in Poland as well as for acquisition of control over a company which holds real property. However, no such permit is required for acquisition of control over listed companies. Also, no permit is required for acquisition of unlisted companies by investors from EU countries except where such companies hold agricultural land. M&A transactions having a value exceeding €50,000 involving government agencies or companies wholly owned by the State Treasury need to be cleared by the Minister of the State Treasury. Furthermore, approval of relevant government agencies is required for the acquisition of large shareholdings in companies operating in regulated industries (banking, insurance, investment funds, securities brokerage, broadcasting).

Except for the permit for acquisition of real property, foreign purchasers are treated in the same way as Polish investors and no special approvals are required for merger and acquisition transactions by such purchasers.

21.2   Acquisition targets

The methods and procedures for the acquisition of companies differs substantially depending on whether the target is a listed or unlisted company.

21.2.1 Listed companies

The acquisition of public companies, that is, companies which have been admitted to public trading in Poland by the Securities and Exchange Commission, is subject to the regulation of the Securities Law. The regulations of the Warsaw Stock Exchange do not require any approval of the Stock Exchange for the acquisition of listed companies.

Poland has a two-tier system for listing companies, similar to that in the US. An issuer who intends to offer its securities by way of a public offering needs to obtain approval from the Securities and Exchange Commission, the government agency responsible for supervision of capital markets in Poland. In order to be able to trade the securities on a Stock Exchange, the securities also need to be approved for listing on the Warsaw Stock Exchange or on CeTO, the over-the-counter market in Poland. Therefore, a public company may not necessarily be a listed company. In fact, several companies have been admitted to public trading by the KNF but were not able to obtain listing, as they did not comply with the listing requirements. As a practical matter, a company admitted to public trading would at the same time be a company listed on the Warsaw Stock Exchange. This is supported by the requirement of the Public Offerings Act that shares in a company admitted to public trading may only (with limited exceptions) be traded on a Stock Exchange.

The legal framework for takeovers of listed companies in Poland will be, in general terms, familiar to any western European or US securities lawyer. Polish law provides detailed rules on notification of large shareholdings, acquisition of major holdings and mandatory tender offers if one shareholder or a group of affiliated shareholders acquires a majority stake in a company. An interesting peculiarity of the Polish system is the requirement that any acquisition of shares in a listed company representing 10 per cent or more of the votes may only take place through a tender offer addressed to all shareholders. Such requirement is described in more detail below. Therefore, privately negotiated acquisitions of large shareholdings in listed companies may be problematic.

21.2.2 Unlisted companies

There are no specific regulations on the acquisition of majority positions in unlisted companies, although such acquisition must be publicly disclosed (*see* 21.3.3 below). Except for the general fact that unlisted companies are not subject to the disclosure, approval and tender offer requirements of the Public Offerings Act, the other main differences in acquiring an unlisted company are as follows:

(a) acquisition of shares in unlisted companies holding real property in Poland by investors from outside the EU requires a permit from the Minister of Interior Affairs. Such permit is not required for the acquisition of shares in listed companies;

(b) share transfer restrictions are possible and in fact quite commonly imposed on unlisted shares;

(c) squeeze-out procedure is allowed in unlisted companies.

21.3 Exchange and investment controls

21.3.1 Exchange controls

The convertibility of the Polish zloty is regulated by the Foreign Exchange Law 1998. Generally, residents of Poland and residents of EU or OECD countries may engage in foreign exchange transactions and hold foreign currency or Polish zloty without special permits.

With some exceptions, all payments and transfers abroad involving foreign exchange transactions must be made through a bank authorised to make such transfers if the value of the transfer exceeds €10,000. Prior to transferring abroad any non-resident income (such as dividends, interest, etc.), a bank generally must be furnished with documents evidencing title for the payment and confirming that such transfer does not require a foreign exchange permit, as well as with a certificate issued by the relevant Polish tax authorities confirming that any taxes due in connection with such transfer have been paid.

21.3.2 Investment control

In principle, any Polish or foreign entity is allowed, on equal terms, to freely undertake and conduct business activity subject to fulfilment of the conditions defined by the provisions of law. There are at present no foreign investment approvals necessary in order to acquire interests in Polish companies.

21.3.2.1 Licences and permits

Certain types of business activity require a licence or a permit. The main difference is that a licence is granted at the discretion of a competent authority, whereas a permit must be granted if the applying entity meets all of the conditions provided by the law with regard to such permit.

Under Polish regulations, licences may be required for the following types of business activity of special importance for national security or other important public interests:

(a)   certain activities within the mining sector;
(b)   production of and trading in explosives, arms and ammunition, as well as products and technologies for military or police use;
(c)   production, processing, storage, delivery, distribution of and trading in fuel and energy;
(d)   security services;
(e)   radio and television broadcasting;
(f)   air transport.

Licences are issued for a specified period of time between five and 50 years. The licensing authority may refuse to grant a licence in any of the following cases:

(a)   the business entity does not meet the conditions specified in the law or specific requirements imposed by the licensing authority;
(b)   national safety or security are endangered;
(c)   for other important public interests;
(d)   the licence has been granted to other entities.

Any refusal to grant a licence may be appealed to the court.

In addition, certain business activities require a permit. Unlike a licence, a permit is granted to every entity that fulfils criteria set out in the law. The following business activities, among others, require a permit:

(a)   production and sale of liquors;
(b)   production of tobacco products;
(c)   casinos and gaming;
(d)   telecommunication services;
(e)   operation in special economic zones;
(f)   wholesale trade of medicines and pharmaceutical raw materials;
(g)   operating pharmacies;
(h)   airport management;
(i)   postal services;
(j)   ground transportation.

Permits are issued for an indefinite period of time.

Generally, acquisition of shares in companies holding licences or permits does not require the approval of the agencies who issued the permit or licence.

Special approvals are required by the laws regulating special industries, in particular financial services. Approvals are required in order to undertake the following types of financial services:

(a)   banking;
(b)   insurance;
(c)   securities and commodity brokerage;
(d)   operating securities and commodity exchanges;
(e)   investment funds;
(f)   pension funds.

In principle, acquisition of a substantial shareholding in companies operating in such financial services requires a permit from the relevant regulatory agency.

21.3.2.2   Restrictions on foreign investment
Restrictions on foreign ownership have generally been lifted. However, there are permit requirements for the acquisition by foreigners of real properties and of shares in companies holding real properties. Investors from EU countries do not require permits unless they acquire agricultural land.

21.3.3   Disclosure of significant shareholdings

Extensive provisions on disclosure of significant shareholdings are contained in the Public Offerings Act and apply to shareholdings in listed companies. In addition, both listed and unlisted companies are subject to the disclosure obligations when control over a Polish company is obtained.

21.3.3.1   Disclosure of acquiring control
The CCC requires that a company ("the dominant company") which acquires control over another company ("subsidiary") must notify the subsidiary of that

fact within two weeks. The notification must also be published in an official journal.

Pursuant to the CCC, control over a company is acquired when:

(a) the dominant company holds directly or indirectly the majority of votes at the general meeting of shareholders of the subsidiary (including votes held as pledgee, usufructuary or pursuant to agreements with other entities);

(b) the dominant company holds directly or indirectly the majority of votes in the management board of the subsidiary (including votes held pursuant to agreements with other entities);

(c) the dominant company is authorised to appoint or remove the majority of management board members of the subsidiary (including appointment or removal pursuant to agreements with other entities);

(d) the dominant company is authorised to appoint or remove the majority of the supervisory board members of the subsidiary (including appointment or removal pursuant to agreements with other entities);

(e) more than half of the total number of members of the management board of the dominant company are at the same time members of the management board of the subsidiary;

(f) the dominant company exercises decisive influence over the business of the subsidiary, in particular through management agreements.

If the dominant company fails to make the notification, it may not exercise more than 33 per cent of the votes in the subsidiary.

The above requirement applies equally to unlisted and listed companies. Despite somewhat ambiguous wording of the law, it seems that the requirement applies also to foreign companies acquiring control over Polish companies.

21.3.3.2 *Disclosure of substantial shareholdings in listed companies*

Disclosure of substantial shareholdings in listed companies is regulated by the Public Offerings Act. Any investor whose shareholding in a listed company reaches or exceeds 5 per cent or 10 per cent of the total votes must notify the KNF and the listed company within four days of the acquisition of shares. Such notification must also be made by any investor who has held at least 5 per cent or 10 per cent of the total votes in a listed company and sells such number of shares that as a result of a sale its shareholding is reduced to not more than 5 per cent or 10 per cent of total votes, respectively. Any investor who has more than 10 per cent of the votes at the general meeting of the company must also give notice of purchases or sales which change the number of votes by at least 2 per cent up or down, either in a single transaction or in a series of transactions. Any investor who has more than 33 per cent of the votes must give notice of purchases or sales which change the number of votes by at least 1 per cent. In addition, crossing the thresholds of 20, 25, 33, 50 and 75 per cent of votes in a listed company must be disclosed.

A notification of acquisition of 10 per cent of the votes or more in a listed company must also contain a description of an investor's plans to increase its shareholding in the company within the next 12 months and the objective of such increase.

For the purpose of all the large shareholding obligations, including large shareholding disclosures, approvals for acquisition of large shareholdings and tender offer requirements, the shareholdings of affiliated companies, parties acting in concert and parties acting for the account of the acquirer are aggregated. Also, shareholdings of investment funds managed by the same management company and shareholdings of relatives are aggregated.

Affiliated companies include companies directly or indirectly dominant, or who are direct or indirect subsidiaries of the acquirer. Parties acting in concert are defined as parties bound by a written or oral agreement regarding joint acquisition of shares, joint voting on the general meetings of the target or joint exercise of common lasting management policy in the listed company. Parties acting for the account of the acquirer include any third parties who acquire shares acting on their own behalf but on mandate or to the benefit of the acquirer. In particular, the term includes any financial institutions with whom the shares are "parked" on a temporary basis.

When the threshold triggering a certain obligation is crossed as a result of aggregation of shareholdings of several entities, such obligation is fulfilled by one of such entities jointly designated by all of them.

In addition, for the purposes of the disclosure obligations, holders of depositary receipts (American Depositary Receipts ("ADRs") or Global Depositary Receipts ("GDRs")) issued in connection with shares in a listed company are treated as direct holders of such shares, and therefore holders of depositary receipts must comply with the requirements described above.

The shareholder may not exercise any voting rights from shares with respect to which the notification has not been made. There are also substantial monetary penalties for breach of the notification requirement.

The above obligations apply in the case of purchase or sale of shares, but also if the change of the level of shareholding resulted from indirect acquisitions, for example acquisition of control over a company holding shares in the listed company, or from events which were beyond the control of the shareholder, for example redemption of other shares in the company.

The Draft Takeover Regulations will introduce two additional notification thresholds of 15 per cent and 90 per cent. It will be possible to prepare the notification in English.

21.3.4 Acquiring control over a listed company

Since 2005, the approval of the KNF has not been required in order to purchase a majority stake in a listed company. However, the acquirer must comply with the tender offer regulations (*see* 21.6.2 and 21.6.3 below).

21.3.5 Acquiring control over a company holding real property

The acquisition of real property in Poland by a foreign person requires a permit from the Minister of Internal Affairs. The following entities are defined as foreign persons:

(a) an individual who is not a Polish citizen;
(b) a body corporate with its seat outside Poland;
(c) a partnership including persons described in (a) or (b) above registered outside Poland and formed according to the law of foreign countries;
(d) a body corporate or partnership registered in Poland which is, directly or indirectly, controlled by persons or a corporation described in (a), (b) or (c) above.

For the definition of control *see* 21.3.3.1 above.

A foreign person must also obtain a permit for acquisition of shares in a Polish company holding real property in the following circumstances:

(a) as a result of the acquisition of shares the foreign person would acquire control over a company which so far has been Polish controlled;
(b) if the foreign person acquires any shares in a foreign-controlled company of which it is not already a shareholder.

The above permit requirement does not apply to the acquisition of shares in listed companies. Also, the permit requirement does not apply to individuals and companies resident in EU countries. However, until 2011, the permit is nevertheless required for the acquisition of agricultural land.

The procedure to obtain the permit from the Minister of Internal Affairs is quite time-consuming and may take several months.

21.3.6 Acquiring large shareholdings in companies operating in regulated industries

Special permits from regulatory agencies may be required when large shareholdings are purchased in companies operating in regulated industries like banking, insurance or investment funds. Usually the thresholds triggering the permit requirements are 25, 33, 50 and 66 per cent of votes. Obtaining the permit of the regulatory agencies may take several months, so the timetable for acquisition should allow for such delay.

21.3.7 Labour law considerations

21.3.7.1 Share sales
Share sales do not create any particular legal problems because the legal identity of the target company as employer is not affected.

21.3.7.2 Mergers and asset sales
The Polish labour law provides that where a business is acquired, all existing employment contracts relating to the acquired business or to any organised part of the business are transferred by operation of law to the buyer and no new employment contracts need to be signed. As a general rule, such an automatic transfer does not take place if the transaction merely involves selected assets of the target company which do not constitute a separate business.

The current employer is obliged to inform its employees of the forthcoming transfer. The employee has the right to terminate his employment on seven days' notice if he does not wish to work for the new employer. This notice must be served within one month of the employee being informed of the transfer of business. The labour code treats the termination of the contract of employment in these circumstances as a termination by the employer, although there is no obligation to pay severance payments.

The current and the new employer are obliged to notify all of the trade unions operating in the target company that a transfer of business is forthcoming and provide information on reasons for the transfer as well as legal, economic and social consequences which such a transfer will have for the employees and their employment.

If assets of the target company acquired by the buyer do not form an organised business unit then the employment contracts are not transferred with the assets but remain with the original employer. In such event, if the employees are not offered new employment by the buyer, the seller may terminate the employees' employment contracts but must pay severance pay. The amount of severance pay depends on the length of an employee's period of employment (which includes periods of employment with previous employers).

21.4   Merger control

Merger control in Poland is governed by the Act on Protection of Competition and Consumers dated 16 February 2007 ("the Anti-monopoly Act") and is within the jurisdiction of the Office for Protection of Competition and Consumers ("OPCC"). Potentially, any major concentration of companies (including concentrations between two or more foreign companies) may be subject to merger control by the OPCC if such concentration has, or may have, an effect on the Polish market. This may particularly be the case if the foreign companies involved in the concentration have subsidiaries or make sales in Poland. The OPCC takes the position that any foreign transaction between two non-Polish entities, which have any type of presence in Poland, are required to notify a concentration provided that the quantitative criteria are met and the transaction does not qualify for statutory exemptions (*see* 21.4.1 below).

The Anti-monopoly Act requires that the OPCC is notified of a planned concentration and approval of the OPCC must be gained prior to completion of the concentration. The mere intent to carry out a concentration is already subject to notification.

21.4.1   Thresholds for mandatory notification

The following concentrations are subject to merger control, provided that the total annual worldwide turnover of the undertakings concerned (including their parent companies and subsidiaries) exceeded €1 billion, or their total annual turnover in Poland exceeded €50 million, in the year preceding the year of the notification:

(a)   merger;
(b)   creation of a joint venture;

(c)   taking a direct or indirect control, by way of acquiring shares or in any other manner, of another undertaking or a part of it; or

(d)   acquisition of assets of an undertaking if such assets generated in Poland turnover of at least €10 million in any of the two years preceding the concentration.

Within the meaning of the Anti-monopoly Act, control is defined as the opportunity to exercise decisive influence over an undertaking, by way of holding shares, having rights, entering into contracts, or in any other way, and in particular by:

(a)   ownership of the right to use all or part of the assets of an undertaking; or

(b)   holding rights or contracts which confer decisive influence on the composition, voting or decisions of the governing bodies of the undertaking.

However, certain concentrations are exempt from the merger control regulations and in the following circumstances no notification needs to be filed with the OPCC:

(a)   the sales of the target company in Poland did not exceed €10 million in any of the two calendar years preceding the year of the notification (this exemption applies only to concentrations that take the form of taking control over another company);

(b)   the undertakings concerned are controlled, directly or indirectly, by the same entity; or

(c)   in the case of acquisitions by financial institutions, the acquired securities are sold within a year of the acquisition and no rights from securities (except the right to dividend) are exercised, or such rights are exercised solely with a view to resale of the undertaking concerned, or its part, or its assets, or the securities acquired; or

(d)   the shares are acquired on a temporary basis as collateral securing payment of a debt and the creditor does not exercise any voting rights except to the right to resell the shares; or

(e)   control of the target is taken as a result of acquisition of shares as part of bankruptcy proceedings of the target company except when the acquirer is a competitor of the target company or an affiliate of a competitor.

21.4.2   Notification procedure

The notification to the OPCC is a pre-merger notification (i.e., it has to be made before the concentration is effected). The concentrations may be effected only if the OPCC has been notified of the concentration and has approved the transaction.

The notification to the OPCC must be filed by the management body of the acquirer. In the case of a merger or creation of a joint venture, the notification obligation is imposed on all parties to the transaction.

The OPCC has to review the concentration within two months of the notification. Within that time the OPCC may clear the concentration, or, if the merger would result in the creation or strengthening of a dominant position on the market that may lead to significant impairment of competition, the OPCC may prohibit the transaction or impose conditions upon which the transaction may be completed. Under the Anti-monopoly Act, an undertaking is generally deemed to have a dominant position if its market share exceeds 40 per cent.

The notification has a standstill effect and concentrations may not be completed before the OPCC issues a clearance or the two-month time limit for issuing a decision prohibiting the merger lapses. If no objection is voiced within two months, the concentration may proceed. In practice, the OPCC usually requests additional documents or information about the transaction or on the under-takings involved and expiry of the two-month period is suspended until the missing documents or information are delivered.

A special exemption is available to the takeover of listed companies by way of a tender offer. In such cases, the takeover may proceed without prior approval of the OPCC provided that:

(a)   a notification to the OPCC has been filed prior to the takeover;
(b)   until the OPCC grants the approval the acquirer may not exercise any voting rights from acquired shares unless such exercise is necessary to protect the investment made by the acquirer or to prevent other material loss to companies participating in the takeover.

21.4.3   Appeals

A decision of the OPCC may be appealed to the Anti-monopoly Court within 14 days from the date of receipt of the decision. If the Anti-monopoly Court finds the appeal justified, it may change the decision in whole or in part and clear the concentration.

21.4.4   Sanctions

Companies which fail to notify a concentration, or which proceed with the concentration prior to lapse of the period for review of notification, may be fined up to 10 per cent of the annual revenue of the company obliged to notify the concentration. In addition, members of the management of such companies may be fined up to 50 times the average monthly salary in Poland.

Furthermore, the registration court may refuse to register any concentration which requires court registration (e.g., the issue of new shares or merger) if the court is not satisfied that the concentration has been cleared by the OPCC. As a result, such concentration would not be legally effective.

21.5   Regulation of the conduct of mergers and acquisitions

The Financial Supervision Commission (KNF) was established in 2006 as an integrated financial services supervisory authority and took over the duties of the former Securities and Exchange Commission established in 1991. The Financial Supervisory Commission is the main regulatory authority responsible for the supervision of financial markets, including capital markets in Poland. The KNF consists of the chairman, two vice-chairmen and four members.

The chairman and vice-chairman of the KNF are appointed by the Prime Minister. Members of the KNF are appointed by each of the President, the Minister of Finance, the Minister of Labour and Social Policy and the President of the National Bank of Poland.

As regards the capital market, the powers of the KNF include, *inter alia*:

(a) licensing and day-to-day supervision of entities and individuals providing investment services;
(b) supervision of Stock Exchanges;
(c) approval of prospectuses made in connection with offerings of securities or listings on Stock Exchanges;
(d) review of conduct of tender offers for listed companies;
(e) supervision of securities markets, including preventing and combating insider trading;
(f) imposing fines for violations of securities regulations;
(g) initiating civil actions in matters relating to trading in securities; and
(h) protecting rights of investors in listed companies.

The KNF supervises the securities markets and acquisitions of listed companies only. Mergers and acquisitions of privately owned companies are not within its jurisdiction.

The role of the Polish KNF is limited to interpretation and enforcement of the Public Offerings Act and other applicable laws. Unlike in certain other jurisdictions, the KNF does not have any rule-making power and does not have any discretion in, for example, granting exemptions from requirements set out in the Public Offerings Act. However, the KNF has discretion in relation to the application of penalties for violation of provisions of the Public Offerings Act.

At the request of a party concerned, the KNF staff may issue an interpretation of a particular provision of the Public Offerings Act. Such interpretations are not in the nature of legal rulings or administrative decisions based on the exercise of discretionary powers, but rather are simply a statement by the KNF staff as to how they interpret certain aspects of the Public Offerings Act that may be somewhat ambiguous or unclear in some circumstances. Although such rulings have no specific legal status, they are customarily treated as specific statements of policy of the KNF staff which can be relied upon by the recipient. Thus, when a recipient receives a letter from the KNF that an action is permissible, the letter is somewhat akin to "no action letters" as are customarily issued by the US Securities and Exchange Commission. Although such letters have no specific legal status, there have nevertheless been judicial decisions in which courts have confirmed that a person who obtained an interpretation of the law from an administrative agency must not bear any negative consequences in relying on such interpretation.

In the context of a public takeover, the authority of the KNF is evidenced by the ability of the KNF to request the acquirer to make changes to the tender offer document or to provide explanations regarding the tender offer. The tender offer is suspended until such changes or explanations are provided. However, the KNF does not have authority to approve or disapprove the merits of the tender offer.

The powers of the KNF do not pre-empt the powers of the courts. Even if the KNF does not have objections to the tender offer, any shareholder who claims that a public takeover was carried out in violation of the law may bring a private court action against the acquirer.

The KNF may be contacted at the following address:

Komisja Nadzoru Finansowego
Plac Powstancow Warszawy 1
00–950 Warsaw, Poland
Tel: (+48 22) 33 26 600
Fax: (+48 22) 33 26 602
email: knf@knf.gov.pl
website: www.knf.gov.pl

21.6   Methods of acquisition

21.6.1   Private agreements

Acquisition agreements have tended to follow the Anglo-Saxon model, with a large number of representations and warranties, although legally bearer shares in a joint stock company may be transferred even by way of an oral agreement. Customarily, parties to a private agreement would execute a long-form share purchase agreement in which the closing and actual transfer of shares would be conditional upon fulfilment of various conditions precedent, in particular the obtaining of all necessary regulatory approvals. After such conditions are fulfilled the parties would execute a short share transfer agreement which would effectively transfer the shares. A similar procedure would be used if assets rather than shares were to be transferred. Parties sometimes use various escrow arrangements under which the purchase price would be deposited with a bank or a broker at the signing of the long-form share purchase agreement and released upon closing and satisfaction of conditions precedent.

Private agreement between a Polish and foreign party may be subject to foreign law provided that such law has any connection to the transaction (e.g., it is the law of the country of the other party). Such agreements may provide for arbitration of disputes before a foreign arbitration court.

Contracts with Polish entities may be executed in a foreign language, except for contracts with consumers or employment agreements.

21.6.1.1   Form of transfer of assets

Transfer of real property, as well as an agreement to transfer a real property, requires a notarial deed. Agreement for transfer of an enterprise or an organised part of a business must be in written form with the signatures of the parties confirmed by a notary. Agreements which do not have the proper form are invalid. Agreements for transfer of other assets may be effected even by way of an oral agreement. In practice, any transfer of assets, except for minor day-to-day transactions, is evidenced by a written agreement or invoice due to tax reasons.

21.6.1.2   Form of transfer of unlisted shares

The share purchase agreement which does not actually transfer the shares does not need to be notarised. Transfer of shares in a limited liability company requires a written agreement with signatures of parties confirmed by a notary. Transfer of registered shares in a joint stock company requires delivery of share certificates and endorsement by the transferor on the share certificate or in a separate document. Transfer of bearer shares in a joint stock company requires delivery of share certificates.

In a joint stock company, the purchaser of registered shares may request that he is entered into the shareholders register. The transfer of registered shares is valid upon signing the agreement. However, any corporate rights from such shares may be exercised vis-à-vis the company only after the purchaser is entered in the shareholders register. Transfer of bearer shares does not need to be registered with the company. Corporate rights are exercised upon presenting the share certificate to the company.

In a limited liability company, the purchaser should notify the company of the acquisition of shares and deliver a copy of the share transfer agreement (which is an additional argument for using a separate short-form share transfer agreement). Until such notification, the transfer is deemed ineffective against the company.

The company's articles of association may restrict the transferability of unlisted registered shares, for example by requiring that each transfer is approved by the company or by granting right of first refusal to certain shareholders or third parties. Restrictions in the articles of association may be for an unlimited period of time. Agreements restricting transferability of shares are also valid but must be limited in time. Agreements containing restrictions on transfer are valid if the restriction is effective for not more than five years from the date of the agreement. Agreements granting rights of first refusal are valid provided that the right is effective for not more than 10 years after the date of the agreement.

21.6.1.3   Form of transfer of listed shares

In Poland all listed securities are dematerialised and exist only as book entries in the Polish central securities clearing system, the National Deposit of Securities. Transfer of shares is effected by way of appropriate entries made on the accounts kept by the National Deposit of Securities and on the accounts of brokerage houses and banks maintaining individual securities accounts for their clients. Transfer of listed shares is legally effective upon settlement of the transaction in the National Deposit of Securities.

The Public Offerings Act provides that, in principle, except for several limited exemptions, listed shares may only be traded on the Stock Exchange and therefore may not be transferred outside the Warsaw Stock Exchange by way of a private transaction. Also, such transfer would not be technically possible due to dematerialisation of unlisted shares. In practice, privately negotiated transfers of shares between an identified seller and an identified purchaser are effected as block trades through the facilities of the Warsaw Stock Exchange but off the ordinary Stock Exchange sessions. The rules of the Warsaw Stock Exchange provide that the price of securities sold in a block trade may differ by not more than 40 per cent up or down from the average trading price of such securities on the last session of the Warsaw Stock Exchange. The board of the Warsaw Stock Exchange may authorise a transaction at a price outside that bracket provided that the transferred shares would represent at least 5 per cent of the total votes in the target company.

21.6.2 Voluntary tender offers

21.6.2.1 Acquisition of 10 per cent of votes

Under Article 72 of the Public Offerings Act, the acquisition, either in one trans-action or in a series of transactions over a 60-day period, of a block of shares in a public company representing 10 per cent or more of the votes at the general meeting, may only be made through a tender offer addressed to all shareholders. For a shareholder holding 33 per cent or more of the votes in the company, the tender offer requirement applies in case of acquisition of additional shares repre-senting 5 per cent or more over a 12-month period. Therefore, as a general rule, in the absence of an exemption, privately negotiated acquisitions of listed companies are possible only if less than a 10 per cent stake in the company (or 5 per cent in the case of largest shareholders) is being acquired. If the stake is larger (which is usually the case in takeover attempts), the purchaser cannot buy shares directly from an individually identified seller but must announce a tender offer to purchase the shares on the market. The purchases made by affiliated companies or companies acting in concert are aggregated for the purpose of calculating the 5 per cent/10 per cent limit.

The tender offer to acquire shares representing 5 per cent/10 per cent or more of the votes is referred to here as a voluntary tender offer in order to distinguish it from the mandatory tender offer upon obtaining control in a listed company (*see* 21.6.3.1 below). However, in fact such tender offer is also compulsory and the "voluntary" element applies only to the acquirer's decision to purchase 5 per cent/10 per cent or more of the shares. Once the decision is made, such purchase must be effected only by way of a tender offer addressed to all shareholders. However, the tender offer must be not for all of the shares in the company but only for the amount of shares that the acquirer wishes to purchase.

21.6.2.2 Exemptions from the tender offer requirement

Certain acquisitions of large blocks of shares do not trigger the tender offer requirement. Acquisitions of newly issued shares or in a privatisation transaction are exempt. Transfer of shares between affiliated companies, transfer of shares in the course of bankruptcy or enforcement proceedings, or in-kind contribution of shares in order to pay for newly issued shares, or transfers in connection with a merger or spin-off are also possible outside the framework of a tender offer. In addition, Article 72 does not apply to indirect acquisitions where an investor purchases shares in a unlisted company which holds shares in a listed company. Since the 5 per cent/10 per cent threshold triggering the mandatory tender offer requirement applies to an acquisition of shares in one transaction or in a series of transactions over a 12-month/60-day period, then, for example, a 19.9 per cent block of shares may be purchased without triggering the tender offer requirement if the purchase is split into two separate transactions for an equal number of shares, one 61 or more days after the other.

21.6.3   *Mandatory tender offers*

Unlike in most other jurisdictions, under Polish law there are two separate thresholds which trigger the requirement to launch a mandatory tender offer.

21.6.3.1   *Crossing the threshold of 33 per cent or 66 per cent of the votes in a listed company*

A mandatory tender offer for shares representing 66 per cent of votes in a listed company must be launched if an acquirer intends to cross the threshold of 33 per cent of votes in the company. For example, if a shareholder who holds 30 per cent intends to purchase an additional stake of 10 per cent in that company, the shareholder must launch a tender offer for 36 per cent of the company (the difference between 66 per cent and the 30 per cent already held by the shareholder).

If an acquirer intends to cross the threshold of 66 per cent of the votes in a listed company, the mandatory tender offer must be launched for all outstanding shares in the company.

The mandatory tender offer obligation arises regardless of the method in which the acquirer intends to cross the threshold of 33 per cent or 66 per cent of votes. Therefore, the investor may become inadvertently obliged to announce a tender offer even if it has not purchased any shares but has crossed the 33 per cent or 66 per cent threshold as a result of, for example, redemption of shares held by other shareholders or as a result of conversion of other shareholders' shares with preferential voting rights into ordinary shares.

21.6.3.2   *Avoiding the mandatory tender offer requirement*

If a shareholder has crossed the 33 per cent or 66 per cent threshold by way of a transaction other than purchasing shares on the secondary market (i.e., by way of subscribing to new shares, by receiving the shares as in-kind contribution, by merger, by acquisition of control over a parent of the listed company or by change of articles of association) the shareholder has the option of either:

(a)   launching a tender offer for that number of shares that would represent 66 per cent or 100 per cent of the votes, respectively; or

(b)   decreasing its shareholding to less than 33 per cent, or 66 per cent, respectively.

The tender offer must be launched, or the shareholding must be decreased, within three months after the respective threshold has been crossed. The shareholding may be decreased by disposing of certain shares on the market, but also, e.g., by increasing the share capital or changing the articles of association of the target. Until the tender offer is launched or the shareholding is decreased, the shareholder may not exercise voting rights from shares acquired without the tender offer (or – in case of crossing the threshold of 66 per cent – from all shares held by such shareholder).

The option to dispose of the excess shares may be difficult to implement if the market liquidity of shares is low. When the 33/66 per cent threshold has been exceeded substantially, the market may not be able to absorb the excess shares sold by the acquirer. Such acquirer may then consider selling the excess over 33/66 per cent to an individually agreed purchaser. However, care should be taken that such purchaser is not in any way affiliated with the acquirer and is not deemed to be a party acting in concert. If the acquirer and such purchaser are affiliates or are deemed to be acting in concert then their shareholdings would be aggregated and would again be in excess of the thresholds triggering the tender offer requirement.

21.6.4 Mergers and split-ups

21.6.4.1 Forms of merger
Under the CCC, companies may merge either by:

(a)   transferring all of the assets of the company being taken over ("the target company") to another company ("the acquiring company") in exchange for the issue of shares in the acquiring company to the shareholders of the target company (merger by fusion); or
(b)   creating a new company to which the assets of the merging companies are contributed in exchange for the issue of shares in the new company to shareholders of the merging companies (merger by incorporation).

In a merger by fusion the acquiring company usually increases its share capital unless it holds its own shares which may be issued to shareholders of the target company.

21.6.4.2 Companies which may merge
Corporations may merge not only with another corporation of the same type (e.g., a joint stock company with another joint stock company) but also with other types of corporations (e.g., a joint stock company with a limited liability company) or with a partnership. However, a partnership may not be an acquiring company or a newly formed company. Partnerships may merge with one another only through the formation of a corporation. Mergers of three or more parties are possible. A company in liquidation which has begun to distribute assets, as well as a bankrupt company, may not merge.

21.6.4.3 Merger plan
A merger is carried out in accordance with an agreement entered into by the merging companies (the merger plan). The merger plan must stipulate at least:

(a)   basic information regarding the merging companies (type, business name, seat), the method of merging and, in the case of a merger through the formation of a new company, basic information regarding the newly formed company;

(b)   the ratio of exchange of the shares of the target company or companies merging by the formation of a new company for shares of the acquiring company or the newly formed company;

(c)   the amount by which the share capital of the acquiring company will be increased as a result of the merger (such increase is not obligatory if a subsidiary is acquired by its parent company);

(d)   rules of allocating shares of the acquiring or the newly formed company (not obligatory if a subsidiary is acquired by its parent company);

(e)   the dividend entitlement date (date as of which the new shares in the acquiring or newly formed company give the right to dividends (not obligatory if a subsidiary is acquired by its parent company));

(f)   special rights in the acquiring company or the newly formed company granted to shareholders or other persons enjoying special rights in the target company or in companies merging by the formation of a new company, if any;

(g)   special benefits for members of the governing bodies of the merging companies and other persons involved in the merger, if any.

The following documents should be attached to the merger plan:

(a)   draft resolutions of the shareholders meetings of merging companies on approval of the proposed merger;

(b)   draft amendments to the articles of association of the acquiring company or draft articles of association of the newly formed company;

(c)   valuation of assets of the subject company or of companies merging by the formation of a new company;

(d)   financial statement of the subject company or of companies merging by the formation of a new company.

21.6.4.4   Merger procedure

The merger plan is published not later than six weeks prior to the date of adoption of the first merger resolution by the shareholders of any of the merging companies, and filed with the registration court for each of the merging companies.

The merger plan should be examined by an expert auditor appointed by the court. The management board of each merging company should prepare a management report describing the legal and economic grounds of the merger and in particular the share exchange ratio.

Once the merger plan is examined and approved by the expert auditor, management boards of each of the merging companies shall twice notify the shareholders of their intention to merge. These notifications have to be at least two weeks apart and no later than six weeks prior to the proposed date for adopting the resolutions on merger.

The merger needs to be approved by general meetings of shareholders of the merging companies by way of a resolution taken by a majority of 75 per cent of the votes, representing at least half of the share capital. In listed companies, the resolution must be taken by a majority of two-thirds of the votes. The articles of association of merging companies may provide for a higher majority.

The merger is completed when the shareholders' resolutions are registered by the court.

The merger procedure is simpler in the case of the merger of two or more companies from the same group.

21.6.4.5   Effect of merger

The effective merger date is the date on which the relevant courts register the merger. On that date the target company, or companies merging by the formation of a new company, are automatically dissolved without going through the liquidation process.

As of the merger date, the acquiring company or the newly formed company enters into all rights and obligations of the target company or companies merging by the formation of a new company, including, in particular, permits, concessions and exemptions unless the law or conditions of such permit, etc. provide otherwise.

Within six months from the date of public announcement of the merger, creditors of the merging companies may request that their debt be paid regardless of whether that debt is due. Until such creditors are paid or receive adequate security, the assets of each of the merged companies must be managed separately. Separate management of assets means, in practice, keeping separate accounting records. During such period the creditors of each company have priority in satisfaction of their debts from separately managed assets over creditors of the other company. Members of the management board of the acquiring company or the newly formed company are jointly and severally liable for separate management of assets.

21.6.4.6   Divisions

The new CCC allows for different forms of dividing a company or spin-off of certain assets of a company. Division may be effected by:

(a)   transferring all of the assets of the divided company to two or more other companies ("the acquiring companies") in exchange for the issue of shares in the acquiring companies to the shareholders of the divided company (division by acquisition);

(b)   establishing two or more new companies to which all of the assets of the divided company are contributed in exchange for the issue of shares in the new companies (division by incorporation);

(c)   transferring all of the assets of the divided company to one or more existing companies and to one or more newly established companies (division by acquisition and incorporation); or

(d)   transferring part of the assets of the divided company to an existing company or to a newly established company (spin-off).

The procedure for division is generally identical to the merger procedure.

21.6.5   Joint ventures

A joint venture may be established either as a special-purpose corporate entity or as an unincorporated association bound by a contract. No prior authorisation of any governmental authority is required to establish either form of joint venture, although an anti-monopoly clearance may be required if the joint venture is established by competitors. Voting agreements and non-competition covenants are permissible in Poland.

21.6.6   Asset transactions

21.6.6.1   Assets versus shares

If a merger in accordance with the CCC is not undertaken, the acquisition of the target company may be achieved by acquiring either the shares or the assets of the target company. The main differences between the two options are summarised below.

Asset sale

(a)   The parties need not transfer the whole business but are free to select the assets and liabilities they wish to transfer.

(b)   In general, the purchaser will be liable only for those obligations of the acquired company which it expressly assumes. However, if the entire business is transferred the purchaser will be jointly and severally liable with the seller for liabilities of the acquired business, up to the value of the business assets.

(c)   An asset sale is a more complex transaction than a share sale since the assets and liabilities have to be specified in the purchase agreement in order to be included in the sale. Real property may only be transferred by a notarial deed and certain intellectual property rights have to be transferred separately.

(d)   The seller will not automatically be released from its liabilities by transferring them to the purchaser; the consent of creditors is required for the seller effectively to be replaced by the purchaser as the new debtor.

(e)   The transfer of the name of the business is often difficult and is generally only possible with a transfer of the whole business.

(f)   As a general rule, public law licences and permits cannot be transferred.

(g)   The tax position may be more complicated than on a share sale, but in general an asset sale is subject to VAT.

Share sale

(a)   A share sale is simpler and involves less documentation than an asset sale as individual transfers of title to the company assets are not required.

(b)   The company's name would be automatically acquired.

(c)   Normally public law licences and permits are not affected by a share transaction although the new shareholders may have to obtain a permit to acquire shares in the target from the body granting a permit to the target to conduct certain activities.

(d)   All of the company's liabilities are transferred.

(e)   No VAT is payable, but transfer tax equal to 1 per cent of the purchase price is payable.

21.6.6.2   Major tax considerations

The choice between a share sale and an asset sale will, in the absence of any other deciding factor, to a large extent depend on the tax considerations of the buyer and seller.

Income tax
Generally, the taxation of capital gains of the seller will be similar in the share sale or asset sale.

There is no separate capital gains tax in Poland. For corporate taxpayers, capital gains are aggregated with the taxpayer's other taxable income or losses, and are subject to the standard tax rate of 19 per cent. The income is calculated as the difference between the sale price and the historical acquisition costs. For individuals, capital gains are generally subject to the flat tax rate of 19 per cent and are not aggregated with other taxable revenues of the individual (which are subject to progressive tax rates of up to 40 per cent). However, in the case of sale of shares in a foreign company the capital gains are taxed at the progressive tax rates. Also, if the individual is an entrepreneur the capital gains are aggregated with other business income of that individual.

Transfer taxes
Sale or exchange of shares is subject to tax on civil transactions ("TCT"). The TCT rate is 1 per cent of the market value of shares. TCT is also due in the case of any increase of share capital, including the issue of new shares in connection with a merger or a split-up.

Sale of assets is generally subject to 22 per cent VAT. However, sale of business as a going concern is exempt from VAT but is subject to TCT.

21.7   Preparation of an offer

21.7.1   Preliminary steps and conduct of negotiations

The acquisition process is initiated either by the seller wishing to exit its investment or the buyer looking for a business opportunity. It becomes increasingly popular to appoint an investment banker to identify the other side of the transaction and to provide guidance over the entire acquisition process. If the acquisition is to take place by way of a tender offer the acquirer must appoint a brokerage house to launch the tender offer on behalf of the acquirer.

21.7.1.1   Confidentiality undertakings

In transactions involving unlisted companies, the investment banker acting on behalf of the seller may prepare an information memorandum to be delivered to prospective purchasers upon execution by such purchaser of a confidentiality undertaking. A breach of the confidentiality undertaking may expose the purchaser to civil liability. The liability is limited to the amount of losses which the other party to the confidentiality undertaking sustained as a result of the breach. Since proving such losses may be difficult, the confidentiality agreement usually provides for lump-sum damages which are payable irrespective of the amount of loss.

21.7.1.2   Letter of intent

After parties have expressed their preliminary interest in the transaction, they may wish to enter into a letter of intent. The binding effect of letters of intent depends on their wording. Unless they include express commitments, the letters of intent are deemed not to create any valid legal obligations. In fact, parties often include an express statement to the effect that the letter of intent is not binding except for the provisions on confidentiality and, possibly, on exclusivity of negotiations, and provide specific remedies for breach of such provisions.

21.7.1.3   Non-competition covenants

The buyer is usually keen to ensure that the seller does not compete in the future with the business acquired from the seller. Non-competition covenants are commonly included in the sale and purchase agreements. In principle, such non-competition covenants are enforceable provided that the clause has a limited duration (usually not exceeding several years).

Under Polish labour law it is possible to conclude non-competition agreements with key employees which prevent the employees from working for a competitor after termination of the employment agreement. The agreement must be in writing, must specify the period of non-competition and describe the prohibited activity. Throughout the period of non-competition, the employee must be paid a non-compete indemnity amounting to not less than 25 per cent of the salary he received before the termination of his employment.

21.7.1.4   Applying for required approvals

In the case of privately negotiated transactions, the approvals are usually sought after the parties sign a share purchase agreement. As a result the closing of the transaction and transfer of shares is conditional upon receiving the necessary approvals. In acquisition of public companies by way of tender offers, the approvals are usually obtained prior to announcing the tender offer although such approvals may also be obtained after announcing the offer but before commencement of the acceptance period for tendering shares. There have been several instances when purchasers decided to announce the tender offer without waiting for the approvals. In some of these cases the purchasers failed to obtain the necessary approvals within the assumed timetable and the whole tender offer had to be cancelled.

21.7.1.5   Negotiations with the State Treasury

Purchase agreements with the State Treasury in respect of the acquisition of privatised companies leave little room for negotiation and contain few representations and warranties. The purchaser is normally required to maintain employment at a certain level and normally has to commit to substantial capital investment in the company being acquired. In some cases the acquisition of further shares in the company is dependent upon the purchaser meeting the investment commitments.

21.7.2   Due diligence

Information on the target company may be obtained from public sources as well as directly from the seller and/or the target company. The Companies Register kept by the courts provides corporate information including articles of association, shareholders resolutions, names of members of governing bodies and shareholdings (in limited liability companies). In addition, companies are obliged to publish their corporate data in an official journal, *Monitor Sadowy i Gospodarczy* ("Court and Business Monitor"). Although that obligation is not strictly enforced and many companies disregard it, the official journal is an important source of information on companies. The official journal is available in printed form as well as through online legal databases accessible through commercial providers. Financial statements are obliged to be published in another official journal, *Monitor Polski B*. That official journal is also available in printed form and online.

In a privately negotiated transaction, and in particular in auction sales, the seller will usually organise a data room containing most important documents on the target company. The target company would also make available its employers and officers to answer questions raised by the due diligence team.

In acquisitions of listed companies the due diligence process may be difficult owing to the prohibition of selective disclosure. The Public Offerings Act interprets very strictly the rule of equal access to information on the capital market and strongly discourages selective disclosure of information on a listed company. Any material information on the public company should be disclosed publicly by the company within 24 hours. According to a long-standing interpretation of the KNF, before such disclosure, material information cannot be transferred even to a strategic shareholder. As regards the right to information, such shareholder is treated similarly to every other shareholder. Therefore, the listed company or a major seller of shares in a listed company cannot make available to the purchaser any information on the target company which has not been previously publicly available. However, the Public Offerings Act provides an exemption under which material non-public information on a public company may be disclosed, *inter alia*, to advisers to the listed company, who advise the company on financial, economic, tax or legal matters, or to parties with whom the public company negotiates an agreement. The potential acquirer may therefore be given access to non-public information on the target company if such target becomes a party to the acquisition agreement. The acquirer would be obliged to keep confidential any information received from the listed company and must sign an appropriate commitment to that effect.

In practice, information on a listed company is obtained primarily from public disclosures made by the company pursuant to the above-described obligation to disclose publicly any price-sensitive information. Listed companies are also obliged to provide information on each change of the articles of association, members of the governing bodies, major acquisitions or disposals, issues of securities, resolutions of the general meeting of shareholders, etc. Prospectuses issued by the listed company in the past in connection with the issue of securities are also a common, although not necessarily up-to-date, source of information on the listed company. Financial information is obtained from obligatory quarterly, semi-annual and annual financial statements published by listed companies. Some companies also voluntarily provide highlights of monthly results. Information on major shareholders is obtained from obligatory large shareholding notifications, which must be filed by each shareholder after such shareholder crosses the threshold of 5 per cent of votes. After each general meeting of shareholders, the listed company is also obliged to publish lists of major shareholders taking part in the general meeting and the number of votes they exercised.

Proper due diligence and identification of risks and liabilities is important also in asset sales. The Polish Civil Code provides that where an entire business is transferred, the purchaser by operation of law acquires not only assets but also liabilities of that business, in so far as they relate to the transferred business. The purchaser's liability in this case is limited to those liabilities of which he was aware at the time of the purchase having made appropriate enquiries. Thus, appropriate due diligence allows the limitation of the purchaser's liability.

21.7.3   Increasing shareholdings

21.7.3.1   Disclosure of stake building

Stake building in unlisted companies does not require any disclosures except for the requirement to notify the acquisition of control over the target (*see* 21.3.3.1 above). In a limited liability company, the purchaser should notify the company of the acquisition of shares. Until such notification the transfer is deemed ineffective against the company.

Stake building in listed companies must be disclosed by notifying the KNF and the company. The initial notification must be filed if the shareholder (together with affiliates) acquired 5 per cent or more of the total number of votes (*see* 21.3.3.2 above).

A notification of acquisition of 10 per cent or more of the votes in a listed company must also contain a description of an investor's plans to increase its shareholding in the company within the next 12 months and the objective of such increase. Thus, not later than at crossing the 10 per cent level the acquirer must disclose its intention to obtain control over the company.

21.7.3.2   Consequences of achieving different levels of shareholding

The consequences of achieving different levels of shareholding may be that:

(a)   the acquirer may achieve minority rights in the target company;
(b)   the acquirer may achieve voting power allowing it to block or pass certain shareholders' resolutions;
(c)   the acquirer may cross various thresholds which may trigger permit or tender offer requirements; and
(d)   the acquirer may become subject to disclosure obligations.

The majorities of votes necessary to block or pass shareholders' resolutions depend on the legal form of the company concerned and, to a certain extent, on its articles of association. Generally, all shareholders' resolutions are taken by ordinary (50 per cent) majority of votes unless the CCC or the company's articles of association provide otherwise. In particular, appointment of the supervisory board (which in turn appoints the management board) requires a resolution taken by a 50 per cent majority of the votes. Therefore, absent special provisions in the company's articles of association, obtaining 50 per cent of the votes usually yields control over the management of the target. The CCC provides that several important matters in the company (including a new issue of shares or amendment of the articles of association) must be decided by super-majority of votes which is 66.66 per cent in the limited liability company and 75 per cent in the joint stock company. The articles of association may also provide for higher majorities or require super-majority for resolutions on other matters not provided for in the CCC or lower minimum thresholds for certain rights of minority shareholders.

The general consequences of achieving different levels of investment are set out below. Unless indicated otherwise, the percentages in Table 1 are percentages of voting rights rather than percentages of share in share capital (because multiple voting shares or non-voting shares are possible, percentages of voting rights may differ from percentages of share in share capital).

Table 21.1   Powers and obligations of shareholders and relevant thresholds

Percentage threshold	Rights granted to or obligations imposed on the holder of the shares
One share	(a) All of the rights of a shareholder, as provided for in the Polish Code of Commercial Companies and the company's articles of association, including the right: (i) to participate and vote at shareholders meetings; (ii) to receive dividends; (iii) to receive proceeds from the liquidation of the company; (iv) to obtain information from the company and to request copies of the company's annual financial statements; (v) to subscribe to newly issued shares prior to any third party, in proportion to his current stake in the share capital of the company, if the share capital of the company is increased; (vi) to object to a resolution of the shareholders meeting (in order to have the resolution reviewed and potentially cancelled by a court) if the resolution is contrary to law, to the provisions of the company's articles, to good commercial practice, is detrimental to the interests of the company or is aimed at harming a shareholder; and (vii) to veto resolutions on amendments of the company's articles if the amendments increase the shareholder's obligations or reduce rights granted personally to such shareholder. (b) The right to demand that the shares are purchased by other shareholders in the event that the object of the company's business as stated in the articles of association is substantially amended (joint stock company).

Table 21.1   continued

Percentage threshold	Rights granted to or obligations imposed on the holder of the shares
5%	(a) The right to propose a resolution at a shareholders meeting to appoint a special auditor to investigate a particular matter regarding the company's business. The auditor must be a chartered accountant or an entity with the appropriate qualifications. The resolution must specify the subject and scope of the investigation, the documents that the company must make available to the auditor and the position taken by the management as to the requested investigation (listed companies). (b) The obligation to disclose that the threshold of 5 per cent was crossed, up or down (listed company).
10%	(a) The right to demand that a shareholders meeting is convened and the right to demand that a particular item is placed on the agenda of the earliest shareholders meeting. (b) The right to demand an inspection of the attendance register of a shareholders meeting by a special committee and the right to appoint one member of such committee (joint stock company). (c) The obligation to disclose that the threshold of 10 per cent was crossed (up or down) and to provide information on the intention and objective to increase its stake in the target company (listed company).
10%+	The obligation to disclose each change in shareholding by more than 2 per cent, up or down (listed company).
20%	(a) The right to appoint members of the supervisory board in such number which is in proportion to the percentage of share in the share capital – block voting procedure (joint stock company). (b) The power to block a resolution on removing the pre-emption rights of existing shareholders (joint stock company). (c) The power to block a resolution on delisting (listed company). (d) The obligation to disclose that the threshold of 25 per cent was crossed, up or down (listed company).
25%	The obligation to disclose that the threshold of 25 per cent was crossed, up or down (listed company).
25% + 1	(a) The power to block resolutions on change of the articles of association, issue of convertible bonds or bonds with pre-emption rights to subscribe for shares, redemption of shares, reduction of share capital, sale of the business or an

Table 21.1 continued

Percentage threshold	Rights granted to or obligations imposed on the holder of the shares
	organised unit of it, merger, division or liquidation (joint stock company). (b) The power to block resolution on transforming a joint stock company into a limited liability company and vice versa. (c) The power to block a resolution on merger or material change of the company's object of business (limited liability company).
33%	(a) The obligation to disclose that the threshold of 33 per cent was crossed, up or down (listed company). (b) The obligation to launch a mandatory tender offer for shares representing 66 per cent of votes (listed company).
33%+	The obligation to disclose each change in shareholding by more than 1 per cent, up or down (listed company).
33.33% + 1	(a) Power to block a resolution on the change of the company's object of business (joint stock company). (b) Power to block a resolution on amendment of the articles of association, sale of business or an organised unit of business or liquidation (limited liability company).
50%	(a) The obligation to obtain a permit from the Minister of Interior Affairs if the acquirer is a foreigner from a non-EU country and the target holds real estate in Poland (unlisted companies). (b) The obligation to notify the Office for Protection of Competition and Consumers due to acquisition of control over the target company. (c) The obligation to notify the target company and publicly disclose that control over the target company was obtained (both listed and unlisted company). (d) The obligation to disclose that the threshold of 50 per cent was crossed, up or down (listed company). (e) Power to block ordinary resolutions at a general meeting of shareholders.
50%+	(a) Power to pass ordinary resolutions at the general meeting of shareholders including appointment of all directors of the company (unless directors are individually appointed by the shareholders or the block voting procedure is used). (b) The ability and obligation to consolidate financial statements.
66%	The obligation to launch a mandatory tender offer for all outstanding shares in the company (listed companies).

Table 21.1   continued

Percentage threshold	Rights granted to or obligations imposed on the holder of the shares
66.66%	(a) Power to pass a resolution on change of the company's object of business (joint stock company). (b) Power to pass a resolution on amendment of the articles of association, sale of business or an organised unit of business or liquidation (limited liability company).
75%	(a) Power to pass resolutions on change of the articles of association, issue of convertible bonds or bonds with pre-emption rights to subscribe for shares, redemption of shares, reduction of share capital, sale of the business or an organised unit of business or liquidation (joint stock company). (b) Power to pass (with a minimum quorum of 50 per cent of the share capital) a resolution on merger, division or transformation into limited liability company (joint stock company). (c) Power to pass a resolution on merger or material change of the company's object of business (limited liability company). (d) Power to pass (with a minimum quorum of 50 per cent of the share capital) a resolution on transformation into joint stock company (limited liability company). (e) The obligation to disclose that the threshold of 75 per cent was crossed, up or down (listed company).
80%	(a) Power to pass a resolution removing the pre-emption rights of existing shareholders (joint stock company). (b) Power to pass a resolution on delisting (with a minimum quorum of 50 per cent of the share capital) (listed companies).
90%	(a) The right to squeeze out minority shareholders holding less than 10 per cent in the share capital in the joint stock company (listed company). (b) Obligation to buy out minority shareholders holding less than 5 per cent in the share capital of a joint stock company, at the request of such shareholders (listed company).
95%	The right to squeeze out minority shareholders holding less than 5 per cent of the share capital in the joint stock company (unlisted company).
100%	The right to pass resolutions without the convening of a formal shareholders meeting and the right to pass resolutions on matters not included in the agenda of the shareholders meeting.

21.7.3.3 Acquisition of depositary receipts

A number of Polish listed companies have in the past established depositary receipt programmes under which foreign investors, instead of trading directly in shares in Polish companies, may trade in depositary receipts issued by a foreign depositary bank and based on shares in Polish companies held directly by such depositary bank. Although depositary receipts are no longer popular and there have been no new issues of depositary receipts in the last several years, certain Polish companies still maintain depositary receipts programmes. The depositary receipts are listed on the Stock Exchanges or on over-the-counter markets in the US (American Depositary Receipts ("ADRs")) or in Europe (London, Frankfurt, Luxembourg – Global Depositary Receipts ("GDRs")). The depositary receipts may be exchanged for shares at the request of their holder. A foreign acquirer may therefore build the initial stake by purchasing depositary receipts on foreign markets. Acquisition of depositary receipts is subject to the same disclosure and tender offer requirements as direct acquisition of shares.

21.8　Conduct of a tender offer

Tender offers are regulated by the Public Offerings Act and the Regulation of the Minister of Finance dated 19 October 2005. The Public Offerings Act contains the general obligation to announce tender offers, it regulates the minimum price to be offered and imposes sanctions for failing to announce a tender offer. The Regulation on tender offers includes detailed provisions on the procedure of announcing, implementing and settling a tender offer. The Regulation also contains forms of tender offer documents.

The acquirer is obliged to use a licensed brokerage house to launch and complete the tender offer. The broker acts as an agent of the acquirer throughout the tender offer process and accepts bids from shareholders responding to the tender offer.

A tender offer may also be announced by a few acquirers acting jointly, in which case the shares would be acquired by them in proportions specified in the tender offer document.

In principle, no permit from the KNF is required to announce a tender offer although the KNF may request the acquirer to provide additional information or change the tender offer document and for such purpose the KNF may suspend the tender offer. Such request can be made not later than three business days prior to commencement of the acceptance period.

21.8.1　Tender offer notification

The tender offer is commenced by delivery of a tender offer document to the KNF and to the Warsaw Stock Exchange. The Warsaw Stock Exchange suspends trading in the relevant shares on the next trading day and, if the notification was delivered during a trading session, on the date of notification.

21.8.2 *Contents and publication of the tender offer document*

After filing the tender offer notification with the KNF and the Stock Exchange, the brokerage house delivers the tender offer document to the Polish Press Agency for publication. The document should also be published in one newspaper of nationwide circulation.

The tender offer document, the form of which has been prescribed by the KNF, is a document that is several pages long and contains basic information on the terms of the tender offer, the target company, the acquirer and its intentions towards the target. There is neither a legal obligation nor established practice to prepare a full prospectus for the tender offer. The tender offer document is not subject to any prior approval of the KNF, but if the document fails to comply with the legal requirements the KNF may require the acquirer to amend or augment the tender offer document. The content of the tender offer document is described at 21.11.1 below.

21.8.3 *Price in the tender offer*

The shares may be purchased for cash or exchanged for other securities, in particular equity or debt of the acquirer or its affiliates. However, since the tender offer is addressed to an unspecified addressee, issuance of the acquirer's securities to shareholders of the target would constitute public trading and therefore usually the acquirer would be required to prepare, approve and publish a prospectus.

The minimum price proposed in the tender offer is determined by the acquirer but may not be lower than the minimum price determined by the law. The minimum price determined by the law is the higher of:

(a)   the average market price of target company's shares during the six months before the date of the tender offer; and

(b)   the highest price which was paid for the target company's shares in target in the 12 months before the tender offer by either:

    (i)   the acquirer, or

    (ii)   entities directly or indirectly dominant, or who are direct or indirect subsidiaries of the acquirer, or

    (iii)   parties who are acting in concert with the acquirer.

In addition, in the mandatory tender offer for all shares in the company launched in connection with crossing the threshold of 66 per cent of votes, the minimum price may not be lower than the average market price of the target company's shares during the three months before the date of the tender offer.

Under the Draft Takeover Regulations the acquirer will be able to request the KNF for an exemption from the minimum price requirement in order to establish the tender offer price below the level normally required by law. Such exemption would be available if the acquirer is able to demonstrate that the fair value of the target's shares is at levels substantially lower than the minimum price required by law.

If there are different classes of shares in the target company, the acquirer may set different prices for each class of shares. If the shares, which are subject to the tender offer, are not traded and therefore no average market price can be established, the issue price of the shares on the primary market (i.e., at subscription) or in an initial public offering should instead be used for determining the minimum price. If none of the above methods can be used to determine the minimum price (in particular if there is no market for the shares), the price in the tender offer may not be lower than the fair value of shares to be acquired.

The price of shares purchased in the tender offer must be identical to all shareholders who respond to the tender offer. However, a shareholder selling at least 5 per cent of all shares in the company, may agree with the acquirer to receive a lower price, even if such price is lower than the minimum price required by law.

If the acquirer purchases any shares in the target within six months after completion of the mandatory tender offer and the purchase price is higher than the price in the tender offer, the acquirer is obliged to pay the difference to all shareholders who responded to the mandatory tender offer.

The acquirer may change the offered price throughout the period of the tender offer, but not more than once every five working days. This limitation does not apply where another entity announced a competing offer. If the price is increased, then the acquirer is obliged to pay the increased price to every shareholder who responded to the offer, regardless of when the shares were tendered. If the new price is lower than the previous price, then the acquirer should pay the previous, higher price to the shareholders who tendered their shares before the change of price, but can pay a lower price to those who tendered their shares after the announcement of a new price.

Before announcing the tender offer the purchaser should provide a deposit in cash, securities or other collateral equal to 100 per cent of the value of the shares to be purchased. A certificate of a bank or another institution confirming that the collateral has been provided must be attached to the tender offer document filed with the KNF and the Stock Exchange.

21.8.4 *Procedure for the tender offer*

The voluntary tender offer may be for a specified number of shares or for all of the company's shares. If the tender offer is for a specified maximum level and the total number of tendered shares exceeds that level, then the number of shares tendered by each investor is reduced proportionally. The tender may also be conditional upon acquiring a certain specified percentage of shares (e.g., not less than 50 per cent).

The mandatory tender offers must be for the number of shares required by law, that is, for shares representing 66 per cent of votes in the case of crossing the threshold of 33 per cent, and for all outstanding shares in the case of crossing the threshold of 66 per cent.

The period for tendering shares by shareholders may commence not earlier than the seventh day and not later than the thirtieth day after the notification is filed with the KNF. The period for tendering shares may not be less than 14 days (for voluntary tender offers) or 30 days (for mandatory tender offers) and not longer than 70 days. The period may be extended up to 120 days if the conditions of the tender offer have not been fulfilled before expiry of the original period (in particular the required permits have not been obtained).

The tender offer cannot be conditional except for the conditions that:

(a)   all required regulatory approvals are obtained;
(b)   a minimum number of shares specified in the tender offer document is achieved;
(c)   the general meeting of shareholders or supervisory board of the target takes a specified resolution;
(d)   the target enters into a specified agreement; or
(e)   a concurrent tender offer for another company from the same group of companies is successfully completed.

Paradoxically, the acquirer does not have the obligation to notify the management of the target that a tender offer has been launched, although it must notify employees of the target. In practice, the acquirer notifies at the same time the management and employees of the target.

During the offer the acquirer may not purchase any shares in the target outside the framework of the tender offer and may not sell any shares or enter into agreements obliging it to sell shares in the target during the period of the tender offer.

The acquirer may not withdraw from the tender offer unless a competing tender offer has been announced. Also, a shareholder who tendered its shares in response to the tender offer may not withdraw unless a competing offer has been announced, provided that the shares have not yet been transferred to the acquirer (because partial transfers of shares during the acceptance period are possible).

The transfer of title to shares takes place upon settlement of the transaction at the National Deposit of Securities but in any case not later than six days after the closing of the tender offer.

21.8.5   *Sanctions for breaching the tender offer regulation*

If the acquirer fails to announce the voluntary tender offer and yet it acquired, in less than 90 days, shares representing 10 per cent or more of share capital of the target company (or, for a shareholder already holding over 33 per cent in the target, shares representing 5 per cent or more, in less than 12 months), any shares so acquired would lose their voting rights.

If the acquirer fails to announce the mandatory tender offer in connection with crossing the threshold of 33 per cent or 66 per cent of votes in a listed company, the acquirer would lose voting rights from all of the shares that it holds in the target company.

Also, officers of the acquirer may be subject to criminal sanctions (involving a fine of up to PLN1 million).

21.9 Defences to a hostile offer

Although takeovers of listed companies are quite common in Poland, a sophisticated takeover market and associated defensive strategies have yet to develop. Most takeovers of listed companies in Poland to date have been privately negotiated purchases of a major (in some cases – majority) holding of shares followed by a tender offer addressed to the remaining shareholders. There have been several unsuccessful attempts at hostile tender offers. Although post-bid takeover defences are not yet developed and tested in practice, Polish law allows for a number of effective pre-bid defences.

21.9.1 Classes of shares

The most popular method of retaining control over a company is to create two or more classes of shares with different voting rights and transfer restrictions. Polish law currently allows the issue of preference shares with double voting rights although no such preference shares are allowed in listed companies. However, the previous Commercial Code (which was replaced by the CCC in 2001) allowed the issue of shares with up to five votes and such shares still exist in many listed companies. It is therefore possible to hold less than 17 per cent of share capital in preference shares holding five votes and yet have the majority of votes on the general meeting of shareholders. Preference shares may not be listed, although usually they may be converted into listed ordinary shares. In such cases, the preferential voting rights expire. The preference shares are transferable and therefore it is possible to transfer control over a company by transferring just the preference shares. However, in a number of companies the articles of association restrict the transferability of preference shares and provide that, for example, the preferential voting rights expire upon transfer of shares, or that approval of the management board is required to transfer the shares.

21.9.2 Limited free float

A popular method of going public yet at the same time retaining control over a company and making it immune to a possible hostile offer is to float only a small part of the company's shares. A majority of shares and therefore control over the company is held by the founders and usually transfer of founders' shares is restricted by pre-emption rights of other shareholders and/or transfer approval by the company or by other shareholders. In such cases, a hostile offer which results even in acquisition of all the listed shares would not give control over the company.

21.9.3 Transfer restrictions

Statutory transfer restrictions are very common in limited liability companies and unlisted joint stock companies, but they are not possible with respect to listed shares. However, it is possible to restrict the transfer of shares by contract. Such contracts are enforceable provided that the period of limitation is not more than five years from the date of the agreement. A shareholder may also contractually grant a right of first refusal or another form of option provided that the period of such right does not exceed 10 years. A transfer of shares in breach of the agreement would be legally valid, but the shareholder transferring shares may be civilly liable for damages to the other party of the agreement.

21.9.4   Super-majority voting

In principle, the entire supervisory board (which in turn appoints the management board) is appointed by 50 per cent majority of votes. However, the articles of association may provide that super-majority of votes (e.g., 75 per cent) is required in order to appoint the supervisory board. In such cases, obtaining the majority of votes at the general meeting would not give control over the management of the listed company.

21.9.5   Individual designation of supervisory board members

As a general rule, members of the supervisory board are appointed by the general meeting of shareholders. However, the articles of association may provide for a different method of appointment. In many companies, several or even all members of the supervisory board are individually appointed by shareholders or third parties indicated in the articles of association.

Nevertheless, even if the articles of association provide for individual designation, a shareholder or a group of shareholders holding at least 20 per cent of share capital may request that the supervisory board is appointed by shareholders through the so-called group voting procedure. Under the group voting procedure, a shareholder or shareholders acting together as a "group" will be permitted to select one member of the supervisory board without the approval of the other shareholders. A "group" may be created by a shareholder or shareholders holding such number of shares which will be the result of dividing the number of all shares represented at the general meeting by the number of seats on the supervisory board. Shareholders may establish one or more "groups" but each shareholder may belong to only one group. Seats on the supervisory board for which members have not been elected by the "groups" are appointed by all other shareholders who do not belong to any such "group". The effect of this complicated procedure is that the composition of the supervisory board more or less reflects the proportion of votes held by different groups of shareholders at the general meeting of shareholders.

21.9.6   Limitation on maximum voting power

The articles of association may limit the voting power of a shareholder holding over 20 per cent of votes in a company. The articles may, for example, provide that each shareholder holding more than 50 per cent of the total number of votes may exercise not more than 25 per cent of the total number of votes. The articles may also provide that the restrictions on voting apply only to specified matters listed in the articles of association.

21.9.7 Non-voting shares

The CCC allows for the issue of shares with increased divided rights but without any voting power. As far as the author is aware, at the time of writing no listed company had issued such shares.

21.9.8 Purchase of own shares

As a rule, a company may not acquire its own shares. Also, shares may not be purchased by a subsidiary or by any person acting for the account of the company or for the account of its subsidiary. There are a few exceptions: a company may defend a takeover and purchase up to 10 per cent of its own shares if the purchase is to prevent material damage directly threatening the company. At the next general meeting following the acquisition, the management board should inform the shareholders of the reason for the purchase, the number of shares purchased and the consideration paid by the company for the purchase. A company may also buy back its own shares if authorised by the general meeting of shareholders. A company may not exercise any voting rights from its own shares.

21.9.9 Crown jewel defence

Many listed companies in Poland are organised as holding companies where the actual business is carried, and assets are held, by subsidiaries of the listed company. Since subsidiaries usually are not listed, a number of arrangements restricting transfer of shares or giving third parties pre-emption rights to shares in subsidiaries are possible. Therefore, even if control over the listed company is acquired, it does not guarantee that control over the subsidiary would be automatically obtained.

Due to the required three weeks' advance notice of any general meeting of shareholders, it usually takes at least a month between the acquisition of a majority stake in a company and control over management being obtained. Therefore, during the month after the acquirer obtains a majority stake in the target company, the management of the target may be able to dispose of its assets held directly or in the subsidiaries or at least include appropriate change-of-control restrictions in the articles of association of its subsidiaries. On the other hand, the management of the target company has a fiduciary duty to act in the best interests of the company and may be held liable for any action against the interests of the target company.

21.9.10 Poison pills

Although shareholder's rights plans are legally possible in Poland the author is not aware of any listed companies in which such plans have been implemented.

21.9.11 Post-bid defences

Polish law does not specifically address or forbid any defences to takeover bids. However, any defensive actions taken by the management of the target company will be subject to two limitations stemming from general principles of corporate law:

(a)   the management of a company has a general duty to act in the best interests of the company; and

(b)   all shareholders should be treated equally in the same circumstances.

As explained above, the management of the target is obliged to issue an opinion on a takeover bid, but such opinion is just a recommendation and does not have any influence on the legal position of the acquirer.

Under the Draft Takeover Regulations, any frustrating actions undertaken by the management during the tender offer would have to be approved by the general meeting of shareholders of the target, if so provided in the articles of association of the target.

21.10   Profit forecast and asset valuation

All Polish joint stock companies, as well as large limited liability companies fulfilling certain criteria set out by the accounting regulations, are required to audit and publish their annual financial statements in an official journal, *Monitor Polski B*. The financial statements are publicly available in printed form as well as through online legal databases provided by commercial providers.

In addition, listed companies are required to publish their annual, semi-annual and quarterly financial statements.

The law requires that an asset valuation by an expert auditor is prepared in connection with a merger, a division or issue of new shares by way of in-kind contribution in joint stock companies. In major transactions it has also become common to request a fairness opinion issued by an investment bank.

21.11   Documents from the offeror and the offeree board

The offeror is not required to publish a full prospectus in connection with a tender offer. Rather, it prepares a several-page tender offer document containing basic information on the offer, the offeror and its intentions with respect to the target company.

21.11.1   *Tender offer document*

The content of the tender offer documents is prescribed by law and includes:

•   information on shares which are subject to the tender offer, their type and issuer;

•   name and registered seat of the entity announcing the tender ("offeror");

•   name and registered seat of the entity purchasing the shares ("purchaser", which may be different from the offeror);

- name, registered seat, address, telephone and fax numbers and email address of the broker acting on behalf of the purchaser;
- number of shares that the purchaser intends to purchase as a result of the tender and the number of votes represented by such shares;
- number of shares that the purchaser intends to achieve as a result of the tender and the number of votes represented by such shares;
- information on actual number of shares to be purchased by each entity purchasing the shares – if the shares are to be purchased by more than one entity;
- price at which shares covered by the tender are to be purchased;
- minimum price determined in accordance with the Public Offerings Act, with information on what basis the minimum price was calculated (the price at which the shares are to be purchased cannot be lower than the minimum price);
- date of launching the tender, dates of the subscription period, an indication whether and under what conditions the subscription period may be shortened;
- name of the dominant entity of the offeror;
- name of the dominant entity of the purchaser;
- number of shares in the target company, and number of votes represented by such shares, held by the offeror together with its dominant entity and subsidiaries;
- number of shares in the target company, and number of votes represented by such shares, held by the purchaser together with its dominant entity and subsidiaries;
- number of shares in the target company, and number of votes represented by such shares, that the offeror together with its dominant entity and subsidiaries intends to achieve after completion of the offer;
- number of shares in the target company, and number of votes represented by such shares, that the purchaser together with its dominant entity and subsidiaries intends to achieve after completion of the offer;
- description of the relationship between the offeror and the purchaser;
- places where subscriptions for shares would be accepted;
- dates on which the offered shares are to be purchased by the purchaser during the tender offer;
- procedure and manner of payment by the offeror for purchased shares – in the case of shares not admitted to public trading;
- information and description of whether the offeror is a dominant entity or subsidiary of the target company;
- information and description of whether the purchaser is a dominant entity or subsidiary of the target company;
- statement of the purchaser regarding lack of administrative objections to the purchase of shares or a decision of an appropriate authority, granting permission for the purchase of shares, or an indication that the tender is being announced subject to the condition of receiving appropriate decisions or notices;
- detailed intentions of the offeror with respect to the company which shares are subject to the tender offer;

- detailed intentions of the purchaser with respect to the company which shares are subject to the tender offer;
- other information that the offeror deems appropriate to provide, in particular information on procedure for responding to the tender and information on settlement of sales of shares in the tender offer;
- signatures of the offeror, the purchaser and the broker;
- date of the tender offer document.

The content and form of the tender offer document is prescribed in detail by the Regulation of the Minister of Finance.

21.11.2   Opinion of the offeree board

Management of the target company is obliged to issue an opinion on the tender offer. The opinion should be issued not later than two days before commencement of the acceptance period. The law does not stipulate what the content of the opinion should be. In practice, the opinions are very brief and include a general indication whether the management of the target considers the acquisition of shares by the acquirer to be favourable or unfavourable to the target company. A positive or negative opinion is merely an expression of the view of the management of the target and does not have any legal consequences for the acquirer or for the shareholders of the target company.

Management of the board is not obliged to seek a fairness opinion of an independent expert regarding price in the tender offer. However, if such opinion is obtained, the board must make it available to the public.

21.12   Compulsory acquisition of minorities

21.12.1   Mandatory tender offer after change of control

Any investor who intends to acquire shares in a listed company representing 66 per cent or more of the total number of votes is obliged to announce a mandatory tender offer for all of the outstanding shares in the company, or sell some of its shares so that his shareholding falls below 66 per cent, before exercising any voting rights. The mandatory tender offer after crossing the threshold of 66 per cent of votes is described at 21.6.3 above.

21.12.2   Tender offer in connection with delisting

Tender offers are also obligatory in connection with delisting of a public company. A proposal to delist a company may be put forward solely by a shareholder or a group of shareholders holding at least 10 per cent of the company's share capital. Such shareholder or shareholders acting jointly should:

(a)   announce a tender offer in which they would allow any other shareholders in the public company to sell their shares;

(b)   request the management board of the public company to convene a general meeting of shareholders at which the proposal to delist the company would be voted on;

(c)   propose to the general meeting of shareholders that they should make a resolution on delisting; such resolution needs to be taken by 80 per cent majority of votes in the presence of shareholders representing at least one-half of the company's share capital.

After the general meeting of shareholders approves the delisting, the management of the company should obtain a permit from the KNF for delisting the company.

It should be noted that the KNF discourages delisting of companies from the Warsaw Stock Exchange. The KNF believes that it is in the interest of the Polish capital market to maintain the largest possible capitalisation and number of companies listed on the Warsaw Stock Exchange and insists on keeping listed such companies for which the free float or trading liquidity is very low. In the application proceedings for approval of acquisition of large shareholdings in listed companies, the KNF usually requires that the applicant undertakes not to delist such companies for a specified period of time. However, the KNF does not oppose delisting of companies wholly-owned by one shareholder following a compulsory squeeze-out of minorities.

21.12.3   Compulsory acquisition of shares by majority shareholder

If a shareholder or a group of shareholders acting in concert hold shares representing at least 90 per cent of votes in a listed company, minority shareholders in such companies may request that the majority shareholder buys out the shares held by the minority shareholder. The price of shares may not be lower than the minimum price for the purposes of a tender offer (*see* 21.8.3 above) and the purchase should take place within 30 days after the request is made.

Under the Draft Takeover Regulation the request could be made within three months after a shareholder reaches the threshold of 90 per cent.

The above procedure is not available in unlisted companies. However, a similar procedure is provided if the general meeting of shareholders of a joint stock company makes a resolution on material change of the company's object of business as set out in the articles of association. In such cases shareholders who voted against the resolution or shareholders who were not present at the general meeting may request that their shares be purchased by the company for the account of the shareholders remaining in the company. The purchase price of the shares is established by an expert auditor appointed in the resolution of the general meeting. If such auditor is not appointed by the general meeting, he will be appointed by the registration court.

21.12.4   Compulsory sales of shares by minority shareholders (squeeze-out)

A shareholder or a group of shareholders acting in concert holding shares representing at least 90 per cent of votes in a listed company may involuntarily buy out minority shareholders in that company. The minimum price at which shares are to be acquired in the squeeze-out is established in the same way as for the purposes of a tender offer (*see* 21.8.3 above). The squeeze-out is launched by sending a squeeze-out notification to the KNF. The majority shareholder must be represented by a brokerage house. Shares of minority shareholders are automatically transferred to the majority shareholder upon settlement of the squeeze-out.

Under the Draft Takeover Regulation the request could be made within three months after a shareholder reaches the threshold of 90 per cent.

In an unlisted joint stock company, a shareholder or a group of shareholders together holding less than 5 per cent of the share capital may be squeezed out by way of an involuntary purchase of their shares by a shareholder or a group of not more than five shareholders holding together not less than 95 per cent of the share capital. The squeeze-out must be approved by a resolution of the general meeting of shareholders taken by a 95 per cent majority of the votes present at the meeting. The purchase price of the shares is established by an expert auditor appointed in the resolution of the general meeting. If such auditor is not appointed by the general meeting, he will be appointed by the registration court.

A shareholder in a limited liability company may be squeezed out for important reasons by a decision of the court in response to a petition made by all other shareholders representing at least 50 per cent of the company's share capital. The shares of the squeezed out shareholder may be purchased by other shareholders or by third parties. The purchase price is determined by the court and should be equal to the fair value of the shares on the date of filing the petition for squeeze-out.

21.13   Insider trading and market manipulation

21.13.1   *Insider trading*

Polish securities regulations fully implement the EU Market Abuse Directive 2003/6/EC.

Dealing on the basis of insider information as well as illegal disclosure of confidential inside information is illegal and is subject to penalties. Insiders face a fine and up to three years' imprisonment (with respect to the disclosure of the information) or five years' imprisonment (with respect to the using of the information). The user of inside information may also be held civilly liable for losses sustained by third parties as a result of using that information.

"Inside information" is defined in Polish law similarly as in other jurisdictions and means any information of a precise nature which has not been made public, relating, directly or indirectly, to one or more issuers or to securities and which, if it were made public, would be likely to have a significant effect on the prices of those securities or on the price of related derivative financial instruments.

An insider is defined as any person who possesses inside information by virtue of:

(a)   membership of the governing bodies of a listed company;
(b)   holding in the capital of a listed company;

(c)   having access to the information through the exercise of his/her employ-
        ment, profession (including brokers and investment advisers) or duties;
(d)   criminal activities,

or any other person who knows or should know that it possesses inside information.

This definition complies with Articles 2 and 4 the EU Market Abuse Directive
(2003/6/EC).

An insider may not use that information to acquire, dispose of or take other
actions for his/her own account or for the account of a third party, either directly
or indirectly, with respect to securities to which that information relates or any
derivative instrument based on such securities. Moreover, the insider may not
recommend or take other actions so that another person enters into the transactions referred to above.

The above prohibition on the use of inside information does not apply to:

(a)   stabilisation activities;
(b)   buy-back programmes; or
(c)   acquisition of financial instruments pursuant to an agreement providing
        for an obligation to acquire such instruments if the agreement has been
        made before the inside information was obtained.

Inside information may not be disclosed to any person except:

(a)   when disclosure is made between insiders in the normal course of the
        exercise of the insider's employment, profession or duties;
(b)   disclosure to financial, business, tax or legal advisers, provided that such
        advisers maintain confidentiality; or
(c)   to parties with whom the issuer is in negotiations, provided that such party
        maintains confidentiality.

The insider trading prohibition applies only to material non-public information.
Therefore, there are no restrictions on disclosure and usage of information which:

(a)   has already been released to the public; or
(b)   is not material, that is, if disclosed, would not materially influence the price
        of securities.

However, it should be noted that in certain circumstances a mix of non-material
information could create material information for the recipient.

Brokerage houses and other financial institutions operating on the securities
market are obliged to implement and enforce compliance procedures preventing the use of inside information.

Enforcement of insider trading regulations is within the jurisdiction of the KNF.
However, the criminal and civil sanctions may be imposed only by the court.
Pursuant to agreements with securities regulators in other countries the KNF
may provide to, and request from, such regulators, assistance in policing and
enforcement of insider trading regulations.

Use of inside information is a crime and is subject to a fine of up to PLN5 million, or imprisonment for up to five years, or both.

Unauthorised disclosure of inside information is subject to a fine of up to PLN2 million, or imprisonment of up to three years, or both.

21.13.2   *Reporting of transactions by insiders*

Directors, officers and other senior executives of a listed company who have regular access to inside information are obliged to notify the KNF of any material acquisitions or disposals of shares in that company or derivatives based on such shares. Such information is subsequently disclosed by the KNF to the public. The obligations apply also to transactions made by relatives and affiliates of directors and officers. This requirement complies with the EU Commission Directive 2004/72/EC implementing Article 6(4) of the EU Market Abuse Directive.

Directors and officers may not engage in transactions in shares (or derivatives based on such shares) during a closed period. A "closed period" is defined as a period:

(a)   until inside information is publicly disclosed;
(b)   in the case of the annual report, two months prior to publication of the report;
(c)   in the case of a semi-annual report, two months prior to publication of such report; and
(d)   in the case of quarterly reports, one month prior to the publication of such report.

An insider who breached the obligation to report an insider transaction may be subject to an administrative penalty imposed by the KNF of up to PLN100,000. However, there is no breach if:

(a)   the transaction was undertaken on behalf of the insider by a broker who is mandated to manage the portfolio of securities of the insider without disclosing to the insider any information of transactions ("blind portfolio"); or
(b)   the insider reasonably could not know or learn of the transaction.

21.13.3   *Prevention of disclosure of inside information*

A listed company is obliged to immediately publish any inside information disclosed to a third party and to prepare a list of persons having access to inside information. The issuer is obliged to immediately notify the Polish KNF, the Warsaw Stock Exchange and to publish the inside information if any such information has been voluntarily or involuntarily disclosed to a third and unauthorised party unless such party is obliged by agreement or by articles of association to maintain the confidentiality of such information. If the disclosure to the third party is voluntary, the publication should be made concurrently. If the disclosure is involuntary, the publication should be made as soon as possible. This requirement complies with Article 6.3 of the EU Market Abuse Directive (2003/6/EC).

The issuer is obliged to prepare and update a list of individuals acting as employee, agent or representative of the issuer, or any entity acting on behalf or for the account of the issuer, who has access to inside information. The issuer is obliged to provide such list to the Polish KNF at each request of the KNF.

21.13.4 Market manipulation

Market manipulation is a criminal offence in Poland punishable by imprisonment for up to three years and fines. Market manipulation is defined as:

(a) effecting an artificial increase or reduction in the price of securities, acting alone or in collaboration with other parties; or

(b) conspiracy, the objective of which is to effect the artificial increase or reduction in the price of securities.

A special exemption is provided for stabilisation activities.

21.14 Financial assistance

21.14.1 Financial assistance by the target company

Polish law prohibits any form of financial assistance by a joint stock company. There are no restrictions on financial assistance provided by limited liability companies. Pursuant to Article 345 of the CCC, a joint stock company may not give loans, provide security, advance payments or otherwise in any manner directly or indirectly provide financial assistance in connection with the purchase or subscription of shares issued by that company.

The prohibition does not apply to financial institutions acting within the ordinary course of its business and to assistance provided to employees of the company or its subsidiaries in order to allow them to purchase or subscribe for shares issued by the company.

If the prohibition is violated, the legal transaction by which financial assistance was provided (i.e., giving a loan, providing security, etc.) is null and void. Therefore, leveraged buy-outs in which assets of the target company are used as security for loan financing arranged for the acquisition may not be possible in Poland.

The Polish government has recently proposed changes to the CCC under which financial assistance would be allowed, provided that such financing is approved by the company's general meeting of shareholders.

21.14.2 Intra-group financial assistance

The law does not directly prohibit subsidiaries from providing financial assistance in connection with the purchase or subscription of shares issued by the parent company. Thus, prima facie, it seems that intra-group financial assistance is possible. However, there is a risk that such structure may be deemed to be established with the intention of circumventing the prohibition on direct financial assistance and therefore could be considered illegal by the court. In addition, the management board of the subsidiary is obliged to act in the best interests of the company. Providing security without any consideration or granting loans at below-market interest rates may not be regarded as acting in the subsidiary's best interests and may expose the management to liability.

21.14.3   Other rules applicable to debt financing

Issuance of bonds is regulated by the Bonds Act 1995. The Bonds Act allows for issuance of interest-bearing bonds, zero coupon bonds, convertible bonds, bonds that have the right to participate in the issuer's profits, and bonds that give the bondholder the pre-emptive right to acquire any newly issued share of the issuer. It is possible to issue bonds both in certificated and uncertificated form. Bonds may be issued by any corporation doing business in Poland, partnerships limited by shares and municipalities.

As a rule, the issuer is liable with all of its assets for payment of liabilities resulting from the bonds. The Bonds Act imposes an obligation on the issuer to supply investors with the minimum information required to evaluate the financial situation of the issuer and risks of the investment. Public offerings of bonds are governed by the Public Offerings Act, which requires the issuer to prepare, approve and publish a prospectus. In line with the EU Prospectus Directive, the offering of bonds issued in large denominations or available only to institutional investors is exempt from the prospectus requirement. In non-public issues, the issuer must provide investors with an abridged memorandum, which must include the information on the purpose of the issue, the size of the issue, the terms of repayment and interest on the bonds, and basic information on the issuer as well as a profit forecast. Bonds may be either secured or unsecured. Providing security is optional and may take the form of pledge, mortgage or guarantee issued by the State Treasury, a bank or another financial institution.

The interests of the bondholders may be protected through the use of a representative bank, the purpose of which is to perform the function of the statutory bondholders' representative in relations with the issuer. Appointment of the representative bank is optional unless the bonds are guaranteed by the State Treasury. Duties of the representative bank include monitoring the financial situation of the issuer and informing bondholders of any threats to the fulfilment of obligations under the bonds. In the event of default, the representative bank is obliged to take legal action against the issuer.

Chapter 22

Portugal

Nuno de Brito Lopes

Partner
PLMJ – Law Firm
(AM Pereira, Sáragga Leal, Oliveira Martins, Jùdice e Associados –
Sociedade de Advogados, RL)

22.1   Introduction

The Portuguese securities market is ruled by the 2000 Securities Code ("the Code") (which came into force in March 2000, replacing the 1991 Securities Market Code) and by the Securities Market Commission Regulations ("Commission Regulations"), the latter detailing the Code matters.

The main objectives of the Code are:

(a)   to create more clear and generic legal text;
(b)   to implement EU Directives on insider trading and public offers;
(c)   to provide a modern framework for takeovers regulation; and
(d)   to take into account recent developments, such as placing and trading of securities over the internet and placement of foreign securities in Portugal.

In November 2006, relevant modifications were made to the Code to implement the Takeovers Directive[1] and some aspects of the Transparency Directive.[2] Modifications include new provisions concerning the aggregation of voting rights, competing offers, breakthrough and information to be disclosed.

In 2006, due to national competition clearances two unsuccessful large takeover bids – Portugal Telecom and BPI – were under intense daily media scrutiny which lasted for over a year. This resulted in the approval of shorter deadlines for the Portuguese Competition Authority intervention. In 2007, the Companies Code underwent a major revision to reduce bureaucracy and to increase corporate governance for major companies.

Overseeing the market is the Securities Market Commission ("the Commission" – in Portuguese, "*Comissão do Mercado de Valores Mobiliários*") – *see* 22.5.2 below.

---

[1] Directive 2004/25/EC of the European Parliament and of the Council of 21 April 2004 on takeover bids (text with EEA relevance).
[2] Directive 2004/109/EC of the European Parliament and of the Council of 15 December 2004 on the harmonisation of transparency requirements in relation to information about issuers whose securities are admitted to trading on a regulated market and amending Directive 2001/34/EC.

22.2   Acquisition targets

22.2.1   *Company law background*

Under Portuguese law there are two types of company that represent almost all Portuguese companies: the *quotas* ("Lda.") companies and the share ("SA") companies; capital is represented by *quotas* and by shares respectively.

The quota companies account for over 90 per cent of Portuguese companies. They have a more closed holding structure, with legal pre-emptive rights in the transfer of *quotas* to third parties. The transfer of *quotas* is now made by a written document followed by registration in any Commercial Register office. A three-quarters majority is required for main corporate decisions in the General Meeting of quota-holders.

The share companies account for over 80 per cent of the total companies' stock capital and financial and economic assets, and they have a more elaborate corporate structure. The transfer of shares is generally free, this rule being mandatory to listed companies. However, the by-laws may enforce some limitations, in which case the shares must be name shares (as opposed to bearer shares). Issuance of non-voting shares, bonds giving a right to subscription to shares or convertible into shares, as well as the trading of subscription rights within a stock capital increase are allowed.

Within share companies, rights are attached to given percentages of voting shares such as:

(a)   1 per cent – right to information;
(b)   5 per cent – right to written information;
(c)   10 per cent – right to appoint a director (usually only applicable to one director, regardless of the number of shareholders holding more than 10 per cent);
(d)   one-third plus one share – blocking minority of main corporate decisions;
(e)   50 per cent plus one share – simple majority, giving control of the company for legal purposes;
(f)   two-thirds plus one share – qualified majority for main corporate decisions;
(g)   75 per cent plus one share – allows holder to prevent distribution of at least half of the distributable profits;
(h)   90 per cent – owned directly or indirectly, gives the right to the compulsory purchase of minority shareholders (*see* 22.13 below).

Although it is not common, the by-laws may also establish higher majorities for some or all decisions or voting limitations. Therefore it is imperative to consult them as part of the preparation of your takeover strategy .

22.2.2   *Securities law background*

The Code applies to the following types of public share companies ("open" companies):

(a)   companies incorporated through a subscription offer made specifically to persons residing or companies established in Portugal;

(b)   issuers of shares (or securities convertible into shares or giving the right to subscribe to shares) who make a subscription offer specifically to persons residing or companies established in Portugal;

(c)   issuers of shares (or securities convertible into shares or giving the right to subscribe to shares) who are or have been listed on a Portuguese market;

(d)   issuers of shares that have been traded in a sale or exchange offer amounting to over 10 per cent of its capital with persons residing or companies established in Portugal;

(e)   companies resulting from the demerger of an open company;

(f)   companies resulting from a merger with an open company.

The Code covers a broad range of matters, including organised markets, public offers, information duties, insider trading, market manipulation, etc. Sanctions for non-compliance also vary according to the type of action, ranging from a mere written warning to imprisonment.

The Code also revised the main Companies Code rules concerning securities (shares and bonds), evidencing a clear preference of the legislator for book-entry form securities. However, the concern for detail on this matter resulted in a number of different and complex processes and situations for transfer of shares (whether listed or not).

The Code provisions are complemented by Regulations and Recommendations enacted by the Commission as well as some Ministry Decrees (in Portuguese, "*Portarias*") on specific matters.

22.2.3   "Relevant holding" concept

As in most jurisdictions, the relevant holding for the purposes of the Code and obligations thereof, including mandatory full takeovers, comprises more than the shares held directly by the person or entity in question. The Takeovers Directive gives each Member Sate the prerogative to determine by means of its national rules the method of calculation of the percentage of voting rights which confers control for the purposes of requiring a person or entity to make a bid. Making use of this prerogative the already broad Portuguese legal concept has been further detailed and extended in 2006.

Currently all of the voting rights within the following situations are considered to be offeror's voting rights and they all add up to the directly held voting rights in order to determine the "relevant holding" for legal purposes:

(a)   of which the offeror has the usufruct;

(b)   held by third parties in their own name but in the offeror's account;

(c)   held by companies in a group or control relationship with the offeror (*see* 22.7.2 below);

(d)   held by third parties with a voting agreement with the offeror (except if the offeror is also bound to vote according to the third-party's directions);

(e)   held by the board of directors' members or audit board members if the offeror is a company;

(f)   that the offeror may purchase due to an agreement with its holders;

(g)   attached to shares lodged as collateral to, or managed by or deposited with, the holder, if the voting rights have been attributed to the holder;

(h)   concerning which the holder was granted exercise at its discretion;

(i)   held by anyone who as entered into an agreement with a holder aiming to acquire control or frustrating a change in control of the relevant company or which, in any other way, consists of an instrument of concerted exercise of influence upon the relevant company (*see* below);

(j)   those held by all persons or entities mentioned above through use of any of the above criteria.

Within item (i) above there is a legal assumption that all "agreements concerning the transferability of shares representing the share capital of the relevant company" are deemed by law to be an "instrument of concerted exercise of influence". However, such assumption may be refuted before the Commission if evidence is offered that the relationship with the holder is independent from any actual or potential influence over the relevant company.

Furthermore, the 2006 modification has also dealt with an issue that has been raised since the Code came into force in 1999 concerning the aggregation of voting rights by:

(a)   controlling companies of managing companies of:
    (i)   investment funds,
    (ii)   pension funds, and
    (iii)   venture capital funds;

(b)   financial intermediaries authorised to carry out individual portfolio management on behalf of third parties;

(c)   companies associated with pension funds.

A new (2006) provision states that, provided that the relevant managing company or financial intermediary exercises the voting rights attached to shares included in funds or managed portfolios in an "independent manner" from the controlling or associated company, such votes shall not be aggregated to the latter's votes in the relevant company. This generic concept is further detailed in the Code pursuant to which the controlling companies will only benefit from such derogation to the aggregation of voting rights provided that:

(a)   they do not interfere with the exercise of the voting rights attached to the shares in the funds or portfolios;

(b)   the managing company or financial intermediary evidence an autonomous decision process;

(c)   they send to the Commission:
    (i)   the updated list of all managing companies and financial intermediaries under their control. Foreign entities must also include the name of the respective local supervising authorities to whom information concerning qualified holdings must be reported;
    (ii)   a grounded statement concerning each managing entity or financial intermediary detailing how it fulfils the above requirements.

To benefit from a similar derogation concerning the aggregation of voting rights with its controlling company, the managing companies or financial intermediaries also have to send a grounded statement to the Commission stating that they fulfil their autonomy and independency obligations.

If at any time the Commission deems that the independence of a managing entity or financial intermediary involving a qualified holding in an open company is not evidenced, it will inform the market and the relevant corporate bodies of the company and also the Insurances Supervision Institute if it concerns a pension fund. The Commission's declaration will imply the immediate aggregation of the voting rights in the funds or portfolios until such time as the managing company or the financial intermediary company independence is duly evidenced again. All relevant legal consequences and sanctions shall be applicable and the managing company or financial intermediary clients shall be informed.

All percentages or holdings mentioned in this Section fall within this concept and must be interpreted as such.

22.3 Exchange and investment control

Since Portugal joined the European Union in 1986, the tendency of Portuguese law has been to liberalise international economic relations, although some controls and limitations still persist.

Usually, the "financial adviser" is in charge of preparing and implementing the offer and all acts pertaining to these controls together with a law firm (*see* 22.8 below).

22.3.1 Exchange control

As a general rule, any capital transactions, which include the acquisition by non-residents of national securities, may be freely undertaken. National securities are those issued by a company with its main office in Portugal.

However, the Portuguese Central Bank may verify any transaction or transfer, in its role as the exchange authority.

In cases of difficulties in the balance of payments, of or disturbance in the monetary or capital markets, capital transactions may be restricted or forbidden, including the acquisition of national securities by non-residents.

Under extraordinary circumstances, restrictions on capital transactions with non-EU countries may be imposed, but always in compliance with the international rules applicable to Portugal.

All exchange operations concerning capital transactions must be made through an entity authorised to carry out these activities. These entities cannot execute the exchange operations until their legal requirements are fulfilled.

As a general rule, the exportation of Portuguese securities is free.

Fines, based on the value of the operation, may be imposed by the Portuguese Central Bank for breach of any of the obligations set out for exchange control.

22.3.2 Investment control

Any investment in Portugal that implies the acquisition of equity by non-residents of over 20 per cent of the share capital is subject to a special registration. The registration is made in API-ICEP, the Portuguese entity that oversees foreign investment, in the 30 days following the operation.

Nowadays, the registration in API-ICEP seldom becomes more than a declaration for statistical purposes. However, failure to register may result in heavy fines.

22.4 Merger control and authorisations

22.4.1 Merger control

Besides the European Rules on merger control, Law 18/2003 which came into force in July 2003 comprises the usual rules on agreements, concerted practices, the abusive exploitation of dominant position and, among other things, a new merger control system.

Prior notification of all planned concentrations is required whereby one of the following requirements is fulfilled:

(a)   a market share of more than 30 per cent in the national market or in a substantial part of it is either created or strengthened as a result of the concentration;

(b)   the combined aggregate turnover of all the undertakings concerned in Portugal exceeds €150 million in the preceding financial year net of taxes directly related to turnover and provided that the individual turnover of at least two of those undertakings in Portugal is over €2 million.

Notification should take place up to the announcement of an offer. Competition law does not specify if this announcement is the preliminary announcement or the definitive announcement, but the notification should not occur prior to the preliminary announcement to ensure confidentiality.

The notification will be analysed over a 30-day period after which the Competition Authority may decide:

(a)   that the notice obligation is not applicable to the operation;

(b)   not to oppose the operation;

(c)   to undertake a full-scale investigation during the following 90 days.

The offer may proceed during the time that the analysis of the merger control is being made provided the purchaser does not exercise its voting rights or only does so under an authorisation from the Competition Authority. Until the 2006 provisions the Competition Authority's investigation deadline would be suspended each time a request for information was made. This led to investigations lasting several months, which was not compatible with a takeover process and caused severe limitations on the target company's management powers for an extended period of time.

Under the 2006 provisions the notification to the Competition Authority must be made in the seven working days following the preliminary announcement. The Competition Authority has 90 days to carry out additional investigations, and suspensions for additional information may not exceed 10 working days in concentration operations.

The Competition Authority may also undertake a prior assessment of projected concentration operations and the respective procedure will be established by the Authority.

However, if the Competition Authority opposes the concentration the outcome of the offer and the acquisitions arising from it will be considered null and void.

It is thus advisable to include the Competition Authority approval in the preliminary announcement as one of the offer conditions.

This merger control system is also applicable to credit institutions and insurance companies. Notwithstanding and as mentioned below, the acquisition of "relevant participations" as well as the merger of credit institutions is subject to the prior authorisation of the Portuguese Central Bank.

22.4.2 *Authorisation from competent authorities*

In some cases, an authorisation from a competent authority is required.

Under the General Regime of Banking and Financial Companies (approved by Decree Law 298/92 of 31 December 1992), any acquisition of a "qualified participation" that is over 5, 10, 20, 33 or 50 per cent of a banking or financial company is subject to a decision of non-opposition by the Portuguese Central Bank. An acquisition of at least 2 per cent must also be reported to the Portuguese Central Bank who may decide to consider it as a "qualified holding".

The intended acquisition, whether or not through a takeover, must be notified to the Portuguese Central Bank which has three months to declare its opposition to the intended purchase. If the Portuguese Central Bank does not declare its opposition by the end of that period it is understood that it does not oppose the acquisition.

In a takeover context it is considered (although not ruled and thus subject to change) that the three-month period does not prevent the implementation of the offer, in order to not over-extend the process of the offer.

However, if the Central Bank declares its opposition the takeover must be stopped and all acts pertaining to it are considered null and void.

22.5　Regulation of the conduct of mergers and acquisitions

22.5.1　Legal rules

The legal framework for mergers is within the Companies Code, and is described briefly below (*see* 22.6.2 below). The acquisition of *quotas* or shares by means other than a public takeover is made through private deals whose formalities and contents vary according to the *quotas* or the type of shares.

The main legal framework on takeovers is included in the Code. The first Chapter is applicable to all public offers, another Chapter is specifically about public offers of purchase and/or exchange, and there is a separate sub-Chapter for mandatory takeovers.

The 2006 provisions have made some modifications to the takeover process as well as upgrading the competing offer rules from the Regulations to the Code. As mentioned, a takeover may be subject to exchange and investment control rules (*see* 22.3 above) or merger control rules and authorisations (*see* 22.4 above).

22.5.2   *The role of the Commission*

The Commission is an administrative and public body, but independent from the Ministry of Finance in whose tutelage it is included. Its members are nominated for three-year terms and can only be replaced after the end of their term except in the case of disability, resignation or compulsory dismissal due to a grave fault or dereliction of duties.

In general the Commission has powers to regulate, supervise and oversee the Portuguese securities market, and is obliged to promote the market and inter-national cooperation. The Commission may enforce its powers through various sanctions, including fines, suspension of authorisations to operate in the securities market or prohibiting an individual being a member of a corporate body in a company operating in the securities market.

The 2006 provisions have consolidated the powers of the Commission through the implementation of Article 4 of the Takeovers Directive. So, besides issuing regulations, the Commission oversees the whole process of the takeover, not in relation to the merits of the offer but with regard to its compliance with the legal rules and principles set forth in the Code and in the Commission Regulations.

In order to ensure this compliance, the offer must be registered with the Commission before its definitive implementation. The Commission has powers to impose a course of action or disciplinary sanctions on any of the parties involved in the offer.

22.6   Methods of acquisition

22.6.1   *Checklist – are you free to choose the method of acquisition?*

When considering the purchase of a company, a number of Portuguese law issues should be considered in order to determine if the purchaser may find himself subject to a mandatory takeover.

The following is a short form checklist giving the first steps when considering an acquisition. The checklist must also be applied to an indirect holding, that is to all companies in which, through the acquisition of the intended target, a direct and/or an indirect holding will be purchased or increased. *See* 22.2.3 above on the "relevant holding" concept, since all percentages and holdings mentioned in this Section fall within this concept and must be interpreted as such.

22.6.1.1 *Checklist*

(a) Is the company's head office in Portugal?
If YES, go to (b);
If NO, go to (c).

(b) Is it a "Quota – Lda" or a "Share – SA" company?
If QUOTA, takeover rules are not applicable (either voluntary or mandatory). Merger control or other authorisations may be applicable (*see* 22.3 and 22.4 above);
If SHARE, go to (c).

(c) Is it an "open" company (*see* 22.2.2 above)?
If YES go to (d);
If NO, mandatory takeover rules will not apply and you may choose the form of acquisition. Should you choose a voluntary public offer/takeover (minimum 5 per cent), most of the takeover rules are applicable. Merger control or other authorisations may be applicable (*see* 22.3 and 22.4 above).

(d) Which percentage/control do I want as a final result OR how much direct and indirect voting percentage will I hold in "open" companies other than the direct target? (*see* 22.2.1 above – majorities – and check the company's by-laws for higher majorities).
If below one-third – mandatory takeover rules will not apply and you may choose the form of acquisition. Should you choose a voluntary public offer/takeover (minimum 5 per cent), most of the takeover rules are applicable. Merger control or other authorisations may be applicable (*see* 22.3 and 22.4 above). Notices to the public on purchases may also be applicable (*see* (e) below);
If over one-third and below 50 per cent – mandatory takeover rules *may* be applicable (*see* 22.7.2 below and go to (e)). Merger control or other authorisations may be applicable (*see* 22.3 and 22.4 above);
If over 50 per cent – mandatory takeover rules are applicable. Go to (e). Merger control or other authorisations may be applicable (*see* 22.3 and 22.4 above);
If 100 per cent – mandatory takeover rules are applicable and you must try to ensure acquisition of at least 90 per cent (*see* 22.13 below). Merger control or other authorisations may be applicable (*see* 22.3 and 22.4 above). Go to (e).

(e) Do I want to build a stake on the target before making a full takeover?
If YES, *see* 22.6.4 below with special attention;
If NOT, keep reading this Section.

If the outcome is that you either must take over, or want or are considering a takeover (public offer of purchase and/or exchange), this Section will provide you with additional information.

22.6.2 Mergers – a brief overview

Currently in economic and financial news, "merger" is a term used mostly on "de facto" or "economic" mergers, rather than in an actual "merger" in the legal sense of the term. In the latter sense, there are two forms of merger under Portuguese law:

(a)   merger-absorption (or "amalgamation"), in which all of a company's assets, debts, rights and duties are incorporated in an already existing company;

(b)   merger winding-up (or "consolidation"), in which a new company is incorporated through the global transfer of the merged companies' assets, debts, rights and duties.

In 2007, the merger process underwent a major revision eliminating the need for a notarial deed (except if real-estate assets are involved) and limiting the role of the Commercial Register office. The process now comprises the following main steps:

(a)   approval of the merger project by the board of directors;

(b)   Audit Board and independent public chartered accountant reports on the merger project;

(c)   registration of the merger project with the Commercial Register;

(d)   publication of the Merger Project registration, General Meeting summoning and Notice to Creditors;

(e)   a 30-day period for creditors to oppose the merger or ask for additional guaranties;

(f)   a General Meeting for approval of the Merger Project – at least 30 days after the last summoning;

(g)   execution of Merger Act;

(h)   registration with the local Commercial Register of the Merger Act.

The Portuguese law merger concepts allow the involved companies to use such process in various ways, for example as a downstream or upstream merger.

22.6.3 Takeovers

In its most general sense, the term "takeover" relates to the action of taking control of a company. Thus there are a wide range of processes – acquisition of shares, shareholders agreements, voting agreements, etc. An analysis of all of these processes is outside the scope of this chapter (although some features are analysed in other chapters).

In a more restricted sense, under Portuguese law a "takeover" is a "public offer of purchase and/or exchange". This is the sense which will be used for the purposes of this chapter (henceforth it will be referred to as a "takeover" or "offer"; *see* 22.7 below).

22.6.4 Stake building

Since the Code only foresees mandatory subsequent takeovers, a potential offeror may, as a way of increasing its chances of success, choose to purchase holdings before making a takeover. A one-third holding is important to prevent "poison pill" defences being approved by the target's General Meeting (*see* 22.9.4 below).

A notice to the public, the Commission, the target and the managing entities of the markets where the target shares are listed must be made whenever the acquirer purchases or passes (upwards or downwards) the following thresholds of voting rights in an "open" company – 10 per cent, 20 per cent, one-third, half, two-thirds and 90 per cent. Similar notices must be made when 2 per cent and 5 per cent in a listed company are passed (upwards or downwards). All notices must be made within three days.

However, such purchases must be made in compliance with pre-takeover secrecy rules and insider trading rules, and they will be paramount in determining the offer consideration (*see* 22.7.3 below).

22.7 Takeover offers

22.7.1 *Overview*

For purposes of this chapter, a takeover is deemed as an offer made to the public for purchase of securities issued by a given company.

The offers may be divided according to consideration, which may be in cash, securities or both. The consideration in securities may comprise existing securities or securities yet to be issued, either from the offeror or from a company belonging to the offeror's group. Whenever a securities consideration exists, the offer may also be called a "Public Offer of Exchange".

A takeover may be mandatory or voluntary. The latter means that the purchaser chooses to make a public offer although he is not bound and will not be bound as a result of such offer by mandatory takeover rules. After a complex system of mandatory takeovers (including both partial and full and also both previous and subsequent offers) foreseen in the previous Securities Market Code, the new Code was drawn up from a tabula rasa and foresaw only mandatory, full, subsequent takeover situations applicable to open companies, as described at 22.7.2 below.

Full offers must include all issued shares and "potential shares" (i.e., all bonds giving right to the subscription of shares or convertible into shares).

The same procedures are applicable to voluntary and mandatory offers, and legal rules and formalities are the same.

The only difference is that in a voluntary takeover (whether partial of full) the offeror may subject the offer to the condition of purchasing a given minimum (direct and indirect) shareholding as a result of the offer. Understandably, conditions on minimum purchases are not applicable on full mandatory takeovers (the offeror must buy whatever is sold). However, in both cases the offer may be subject to some conditions, namely the necessary authorisations from public authorities.

22.7.2 Mandatory takeovers

The Code approach to this matter is inspired by the UK City Code. A mandatory full offer must be made when a person or entity (individually or through a "relevant holding"):

(a) acquires (as a result of one or more transactions over any period of time) shares in an open company that carry a minimum of one-third plus one share or 50 per cent plus one share of voting rights (direct acquisition);

(b) acquires legal control of a company (public or private) that in turn holds a controlling interest in an open company representing the same minimum voting rights (indirect acquisition).

In both cases, the preliminary advertisement of a mandatory full offer must be made immediately after the fact that triggered the obligation. The holding entity or some other person or entity in its place may fulfil such obligation.

The 33.3 per cent threshold will not trigger a mandatory offer if the holding entity is able to prove that, notwithstanding its holding, it is not in a dominant position or group relationship with the target. A company is considered to be in a dominant position (also called a "control relationship") if it holds more than half of the target votes, whether directly or through a shareholders agreement, or has the power to appoint or remove the majority of the board of directors or the fiscal board.

In this case, the holding entity must inform the Commission of any change of voting rights over 1 per cent and make a full mandatory offer whenever it is in the position of having a "control influence" over the target.

The obligation to make an offer does not apply if the threshold is reached by means of a general offer made with no maximum limit under a company recovery plan or through a merger. The company's general meeting resolution must clearly state that the obligation would be applicable.

The obligation may also be suspended provided the potential bidder informs the Commission in the following five days and undertakes to end the situation that triggered such obligation within 120 days. In this period, such shares must be sold to persons or entities that fall outside the "relevant holding" perimeter.

The mandatory offer must include all the shares issued by the company (whether voting shares or not), as well as any "potential shares" – that is, other securities issued by the company that are convertible into shares or that give a right of subscription of shares.

22.7.3 Consideration

In a voluntary offer, the offeror is free to determine its consideration. However, should the voluntary offer be made to purchase or give the offeror the opportunity of purchasing a holding over the mandatory offer threshold in an open company, the Commission is likely to consider that mandatory takeover consideration rules are applicable.

In the case of a full mandatory offer, the consideration may be all-cash, all-securities, cash with a securities alternative and, although not used to date, a "mixed" consideration, i.e., cash plus securities.

The cash consideration or its securities equivalent must be equitable. They are deemed to be "non-equitable" in the following circumstances:

(a)   if the price was defined by the purchaser and seller through a private negotiation;
(b)   due to reduced liquidity of the securities; or
(c)   if the price is a result of exceptional events. In a voluntary offer the Commission may consider the alternative to be non-equitable as a result of transactions during the course of the offer.

The cash alternative cannot be lower than the highest of the following values:

(a)   the securities alternative, if it exists;
(b)   the highest price paid by the offeror, or any person within the "relevant holding" perimeter for the purchase of securities of the same type and class in the six months prior to the preliminary announcement;
(c)   the weighted average listing price of such securities in the six months prior to the preliminary announcement;
(d)   if the securities are not listed, or if it is not possible to determine the weighted average listing price, or if the Commission feels that the consideration is not fair or not justified, the value determined by an independent expert appointed by the Commission at the expense of the offeror.

The all-securities mandatory bid consideration must be composed of securities of the category of the target company securities and enjoy a high liquidity in a regulated market. Furthermore this is only possible if the offeror and all people acting in concert have not paid in cash any acquisition of the target shares in the six months prior to the preliminary announcement

22.7.4 Sanctions

Besides fines, the offeror will have its voting rights in the company frozen through a Commission decision, but not its obligations or its liability for any damages caused to the sellers of such securities or to the holders of securities that would be the object of the offer.

This freezing of the voting rights is applicable to all the shares acquired over the limits described above and within the "relevant holding" perimeter. Furthermore, all decisions that would not be taken if it were not for such votes may be judicially challenged and all dividends relating to the frozen shares will revert to the company.

The freezing lasts for five years from the date that the offer should have been made, and at the end of this time it automatically ceases.

The voting rights may be re-established before the end of the five years if the shares over such limits are sold to a third party or, if it is the case, a subsequent full offer is made by the offeror.

The purchaser may react and apply for an immediate judicial suspension of the effects of a Commission decision while challenging the decision itself in Court – the latter being a more lengthy process.

22.7.5 Breakthrough provisions

The provisions of Article 11 of the Takeovers Directive have been implemented in Portuguese Law, but they are not mandatory for companies – thus making use of the possibility given to the Member States by Article 12.1 of the Directive.

The offeror is responsible for any loss suffered due to the suspension of shareholders agreements made public up to the date of the preliminary announcement. However, no compensation has to be paid by the offeror to the shareholders who voted in favour of the resolution for inclusion of the breakthrough provisions in the company by-laws.

22.8 Preparation of an offer

22.8.1 "Internal phase"

One of the studies on takeovers in Portugal distinguishes between the "internal phase" and the "external phase" of the offer process. The latter also comprises three sub-phases – preliminary, offer and purchases.

The offer is prepared during the "internal phase", this being regulated by Portuguese law in some aspects. The internal phase ends with the publishing of the preliminary announcement.

As a general rule, all parties involved in the preparation of the offer or that have knowledge of the potential offer due to their functions, are required to keep this information confidential until an announcement is made.

During this phase the offeror must choose the "financial adviser" who will act as its representative during the whole offer and who has the function of preparing, announcing and implementing the offer. The financial adviser must be a bank, either retail or merchant, or a brokerage company.

All studies that usually precede an offer are subject to the confidentiality duty mentioned above.

If the Commission has reason to believe that an offer may be undergoing a preparation process, it may instruct the potential offeror to announce the offer or to publish a denial statement.

Therefore, when providing legal assistance in the preparation of an offer, legal counsel must bring to the attention of all those involved the confidentiality duty and draft the announcement with the utmost care. When preparing the offer, the financial intermediary and the target usually sign an agreement concerning the intermediary duties. In order to avoid immediately triggering the obligation to publish the preliminary advertisement, the agreement must clearly state that the offer is still being prepared and that the financial intermediary role is, at this stage, to assist the potential offeror in making its decision on the offer.

Once the preliminary announcement of a hostile takeover is published, the legal counsel of the target is sure to analyse every word of it in order to find some deficiencies or contradictions that may prevent the offer from taking place even before it actually starts. Moreover, the Commission is likely to ask for additional documents which may include documents made during the "internal phase".

22.8.2 Preliminary announcement

Portuguese law has a dual announcement system. The offeror is bound to publish a preliminary announcement of the offer as soon as it has reached the definite decision to make the offer or immediately after the mandatory takeover obligation is triggered. If the decision of the offeror is subject to any condition, the obligation to publish the announcement only arises after the condition is fulfilled. Until this moment, the confidentiality duty must be rigorously fulfilled.

The announcement must be published at the Stock Exchange Bulletin and in a major national newspaper. Prior to the publication of the preliminary announcement, the offeror must deliver a copy of this announcement to the Commission, to the board of directors of the target company and, if the shares are listed, to the Stock Exchange where those shares are listed. The target may, in the following eight days, deliver its comments on the offer to the Commission and the offeror.

Usually this communication is made the day before the announcement is published, that is, at the same time as the announcement is delivered to the Stock Exchange Bulletin and the newspaper for publication on the following day.

The announcement must provide information on the offeror, the target, the financial adviser, the objectives of the offer, the conditions of the offer (namely the minimum and/or maximum purchase limit), the consideration of the offer and the offeror's "relevant holding", and must be signed by the offeror and the financial adviser.

The preliminary announcement of the offeror must also include a summary of the offeror's goals (namely as to the target company's future) as well as his standing concerning the breakthrough provisions and the limitation of powers of the target's management.

After the announcement, the offeror is bound to:

(a) make the offer in conditions no less favourable than those of the preliminary announcement;
(b) request the registration of the offer within a 20-day deadline. The Commission may extend this deadline if it finds just cause to do so.

If the offeror does not comply with these obligations it may be subject to penal and contravention sanctions and will become responsible before the shareholders, the target and any third parties for all damages incurred by these.

The Commission may notify the offeror to correct the preliminary announcement, and to publish the amendment, if it finds it not in accordance with the applicable rules or unclear as to any of its information. Should the offeror not comply with this obligation, it may be subject to fines between €25,000 and €2,500,000.

22.9 Conduct during a public offer

22.9.1 Phases of the offer

The "external" process of the offer has the following phases, as mentioned before:

(a) preliminary phase – between the publishing of the preliminary announcement and the publishing of the definitive announcement;
(b) offer phase – between the definitive announcement and the closing date of the offer;
(c) purchase phase – when the transactions of shares and other securities actually take place.

There some general rules of conduct that apply to all phases.

22.9.2 General principles of conduct

The regulation of takeovers is based mainly on the following principles:

(a) freedom to launch an offer, that is, not subject to an administrative authorisation on matters other than legal matters (except in the case of a mandatory offer);
(b) equal treatment of shareholders in the same situations (e.g., the holders of the same category of shares or securities);
(c) adequate, true and timely information to the shareholders;
(d) the offer must be made at the same time to all bearers of the securities included in the offer.

All information must be subject to the Commission's approval before being published. Any person or entity related to the offer producing any information is responsible for the contents of such information.

22.9.3 Transaction of securities by the offeror

After making his final decision to make the offer, the offeror and all persons and entities within the "relevant holding" perimeter must, until the closing date, refrain from purchasing outside of regulated markets any shares or other securities of the target or companies belonging to the target group, as well as any securities included in the consideration without the Commission's prior authorisation. They must inform the Commission on a daily basis of such transactions.

The Commission's authorisation is given after prior consultation of the target company. The financial advisers are bound by the same obligation from the moment that they have knowledge of the final decision to make the offer.

If any acquisition of shares or securities of the target is made by the offeror or any persons acting in concert with him at a price over the proposed consideration, this will result in the breach of the principle regarding the equal treatment of the shareholders, unless the offer is immediately revised.

22.9.4 Duties of the target company

After the communication of the preliminary announcement and until the result of the offer is announced, the target company must:

(a) inform the Commission on a daily basis of all transactions on its securities;

(b) give to the Commission all information requested;

(c) inform its workers of the offer document's contents;

(d) act in good faith, namely concerning the accuracy of information and fair behaviour.

Furthermore, the target company may not make use of a "poison pill" defence, except in some very limited cases. Under Portuguese law this means that from the moment the target company's board of directors has knowledge of the offer and up until its closing date, it may not engage in any action that may cause a relevant change to the assets situation of the company, insofar as such acts:

(a) are not current management acts;

(b) may significantly harm the offeror's goals;

(c) do not result from previously undertaken obligations;

(d) were not allowed by general meeting expressly summoned for that purpose during the course of the offer.

A "relevant change to the assets situation of the company" would be the issuance of any shares or "potential shares' securities" and entering into contracts for sale of relevant assets.

Also during this period, the majority for by-laws modification (usually a two-thirds majority) is required for the general meeting decisions mentioned above and for decisions on distribution of profits. The Commission usually imposes on the target an obligation to publish an announcement describing the operation and its grounds.

Since the 2006 modifications, the limitation of powers has been extended to the execution of decisions taken prior to the knowledge of a takeover, thus suppressing one important takeover defence. However, management may now actively seek a "white knight" (competing offer) and general meetings may be summoned in half the usual time – a 15-day period instead of 30 days – thus allowing more swift decisions in possible takeover defences.

22.9.5 Information

All the information to be provided to the shareholders, either by the offeror or the target, is subject to a strict set of principles and rules, whose compliance is ensured by the Commission. Besides the information to be included in the documents of the offeror and the target, the Code regulates other aspects such as the responsibility for the contents of the documents (*see* 22.12 below).

Furthermore, any publicity or advertisements for the offer must follow the rules and care equivalent to those required in the preparation of the documents for the offer. Any publicity is subject to the prior approval of the Commission. Therefore, any publicity acts or campaigns, whether in the media or by telephone or mail or by any other means available, should be subject to prior clearance by the Commission.

If publicity is made without the Commission clearance the advertiser is liable to penal and contravention sanctions. Ultimately, the Commission may suspend, impose immediate withdrawal of or forbid any offer based on inadequate information or on the use of non-authorised publicity material.

Legal counsel must always pay special attention to any declarations made to the press and any direct or indirect publicity and advertisements, either from the offeror or the target, their subsidiaries or the members of their boards. Whenever possible, any press releases or advertisements must be subject to analysis by the legal counsel before being made public.

The 2006 modifications extended the information to be included in the prospectus and introduced the obligation to inform the workers' representatives and to include in the company's annual report a separate Chapter with the information listed in Article 10 of the Takeovers Directive (capital, securities, shareholdings, corporate bodies, significant agreements, etc.).

22.9.6 *Preliminary phase*

This phase begins with the preliminary announcement and ends with the definitive announcement and disclosure of the offer documents.

During this period, although the offer has already been made public, little information is given to shareholders since the offeror is engaged in preparing the application for registration of the offer before the Commission.

After the application, the Commission must assess the documents and may ask for any clarification or changes. The Commission is particularly strict on information concerning the offeror's "relevant holding", the offeror's objectives and, of course, the consideration and its justification.

Final registration only means that the Commission found the offer to be in accordance with the applicable rules and does not involve any assurance that the information provided is true or any judgment as to the merits of the operation.

Experience shows that even with the aforementioned restrictions, during this period the parties to a hostile takeover immediately start a more or less "covert" press campaign, either by providing grounds for economic news or by choosing to launch new products, services, actions or endorsements to improve their image.

On the side of the offeror, legal counsel must take special care in preparing the documents of the offer. After receiving the draft offer announcement, the target board is likely to scrutinise every word of the offer documents and make all sorts of comments on their report, even at the risk that the Commission later asks for the suppression of those comments when it finds the offer to be in accordance with the legal rules.

After registration of the offer all statements by the target commenting on possible illegalities of the offer must be avoided or at least made in terms that do not allow for penalties by the Commission.

Since the Commission is a public administrative body, its decisions are subject to an appeal to an administrative court, namely applying for suspension of the Commission's decision, such as to register the offer.

Although discussed as a possibility in some cases, no judicial measure of this kind has ever been filed. The filing of an appeal would pose delicate problems since the administrative courts are not used to dealing with company and securities market law. Furthermore, any decision by the courts on the matter would be bound to take some months, thus being published and enforced probably after the end of the offer or causing the offer process to be suspended for an indefinite (but very long) period.

If the court found for the target this could cause the offer to be null and void long after its completion, and if a new offer was allowed the market conditions might well be completely different.

Simultaneously, the directors of the target could find themselves restricted to the ordinary management of the target during the whole judicial process. If the court later found for the offeror, such directors could become responsible for any actions that caused damage to the value of the target.

Basically, the source of disturbance would arise from the different paces of the market, the offer and of the judicial procedure, the latter being much lengthier.

22.9.7 Offer phase

This phase begins with the definitive announcement and disclosure of the offer documents up until the closing date of the offer. This stage may last between two and 10 weeks or be further extended due to competing offers or upon request to the Commission.

During this phase the parties may make public their standing and arguments subject to clearance by the Commission. Daily information on the acceptance of the offer by the shareholders is given to the financial adviser of the offeror. This information must be disclosed to the Commission whenever requested. The Commission may impose on the offeror an obligation to advertise such information.

As in other jurisdictions, the offer may be subject to revision or to a competing offer during this phase.

22.9.7.1 Revision of the offer
The offeror may revise the offer once up to five days before the closing date if it results in more favourable conditions to the shareholders. The request for the revision, duly grounded, must be submitted to the Commission. The shareholders may withdraw their acceptance of it.

Revision will only be allowed if the revised consideration is at least 2 per cent higher.

22.9.7.2 *Competing offers*

A competing offer may be announced at any time until the fifth day before the closing date. The competing offer's preliminary announcement must be published so as to enable the launching of the offer, that is, the final announcement, up to the fifth day prior to the end of the initial offer deadline. Should CMVM consider that, taking into consideration the date of application for registration of the offer, this deadline may not be met, it may refuse to grant such registration. Therefore, special care must be taken when deciding to launch a competing offer process if the supervision authorities or other entities must intervene before registration is granted.

The target securities minimum and maximum thresholds may not be lower or the conditions less favourable than those of the already existing offer(s).

The competing offer may not be made by any person or entity within the offeror's "relevant holding" perimeter except upon authorisation from the Commission.

Whenever a competing offer is launched, the other offerors may choose (i) to revise their offers (even if they have already revised the offer once) but without lowering the minimum acceptance threshold; or (ii) withdraw their offers in the four days following the advertisement of the competing offer.

The closing date of the last offer to be launched becomes the closing date of all offers still standing.

22.9.8 **Purchase phase**

The outcome of the offer may be processed by a financial intermediary or through a special Stock Exchange session that must take place within the shortest delay possible after the closing date. The outcome of the offer must be published at the expense of the offeror.

If the number of acceptances/selling orders exceeds the number of securities the offeror proposes to acquire, a pro rata acquisition will take place. The result of the offer may also be subject to a minimum amount of securities being sold.

After the special session the liquidation of the transactions will take place. If the consideration is composed of securities to be issued, they must be delivered to the shareholders in the following 45 days.

22.10   Defences to a hostile takeover

22.10.1   *Overall considerations*

As in other jurisdictions, there are two classes of defence:

(a)   preventive measures (i.e., measures taken to discourage the implementation of any offer and make the possible target an unattractive acquisition target);

(b)   defensive measures (i.e., applied during the course of a takeover).

Portuguese corporate and securities market law allows some preventive measures, but restricts most of the defensive measures usually applicable in other countries. Legal counsel to the offeror must, in the selection process of an acquisition target, search for any preventive measures that the possible target has taken, these measures usually being included in its by-laws. In preparing the offer or during the course of the offer, the offeror must take special care in preparing the documents of the offer, submitting and publishing these documents by the deadlines imposed and not making any unauthorised transaction of shares.

Legal counsel for a possible acquisition target must propose the setting up of preventive measures and possible instruments for defensive measures. During the course of the offer, besides advising on any actions of the target, counsel must take special care in analysing the actions and documents of the offeror and any person acting in concert with him, and report possible illegalities to the Commission.

22.10.2   *Preventive measures*

Portuguese corporate law allows the by-laws of a company to restrict the amount of votes held by one single shareholder to a fixed percentage, regardless of the number of shares it holds.

This way, if by means of an offer the offeror purchased a majority percentage of the share capital, its actual percentage of votes would never surpass the percentage fixed in the by-laws.

The by-laws may also establish that the resolutions of the general meeting need to be approved by a qualified majority over 51 per cent (e.g., 70 per cent). Therefore, if the offeror is not sure that it may acquire the minimum number of shares required to gain control of the company, it may not make the offer.

A shareholders agreement may also prevent an offer, if the shareholders agree on staying together and not selling. However, in Portugal this has already proved not be an efficient defence on some occasions.

Promissory agreements for the sale of valuable assets of the company ("crown jewels") may be signed in order to later circumvent the limitation of powers of the board of directors on "poison pill" defences (*see* 22.9.4 above). Notwithstanding this, the Commission may come to consider the actual sale of the assets as an unlawful use of powers by the board of directors.

Agreements for "white knight" defences may be established. However, the Commission may not allow the implementation of a "white knight" competing offer, or it may prove to be difficult since it must be in more favourable terms (*see* 22.9.7.2 above).

Mandatory full takeover rules also apply to indirect acquisitions of the target's subsidiaries, creating an obligation on the offeror to purchase the remaining capital of such subsidiaries. Thus, the ultimate price to be paid by the offeror may be much higher than originally estimated.

"Golden parachute" defences (i.e., high compensation for target companies' directors whose duties have been terminated) may also be established, and they are becoming increasingly common in Portugal.

22.10.3   *Defensive measures*

The main and first defensive measure against a takeover is found in the bureaucracy of the offer process. In fact if the offeror or any of its actions or documents do not meet all requirements or give grounds to contradictions that may affect the shareholders, the Commission will not register the offer, thus preventing it.

This is also applicable when the offer is subject to the approval of other entities such as the Portuguese Central Bank, the Ministry of Finance, or to regulations, such as merger control and exchange control. Nowadays almost all companies also engage a corporate communication adviser.

In a hostile takeover, legal counsel for the target is expected to analyse every word and action of the offeror. In 2006 there was unprecedented hostile takeover activity in Portugal, and the experience gained means that there will be fewer mistakes by future offerors provided they are well advised. Even so, counsel to the target must make sure the Commission does not unintentionally overlook such errors made by the offeror.

Another line of defence may be established in the interpretation of some aspects of the law. However, there is a growing number of works on the matter and the last word usually belongs to the Commission, since no judicial procedure is likely to be filed.

Competing offers, such as "white knight" offers may, as mentioned, prove to be difficult since they must be in more favourable terms than the first offer.

The implementation of a "Pac-man" offer may only be achieved through a resolution of a general meeting expressly summoned for that purpose. Note that the general meeting *must* be called by an advertisement published 15 days before. This delay may cause the general meeting to take place after the registration of the offer, thus causing great divisions among the shareholders.

The "self takeover" (i.e., the target implementing an offer for its own shares) is virtually impossible under Portuguese law because a company may only acquire up to 10 per cent of its own shares.

However, within these limits the target may propose a share repurchase programme as a deterrent to the sale.

In Portugal, although an offer may be made for as little as 5 per cent of the target's shares, it is usually made for over one-third of the shares (the percentage that determines, under certain conditions, the launching of a mandatory takeover). Such an offer has to be resolved at a general meeting summoned for this purpose.

Regarding other types of defence, namely economical, financial and psychological defences, legal counsel for the target must always make sure that they do not violate the main three basic rules:

(a)   the limitation of powers of the board of directors – considering that most economic and financial defences must be executed by this body;

(b)   the rules applicable to information to be provided and advertised – since those defences, especially the psychological defences, are mainly based on information to the shareholders;

(c)   the limitations imposed on the transactions of shares by the target, the companies belonging to the same group as the target, the members of their boards, and any other person or entity acting in concert with the target.

22.11   Profit forecasts and asset valuations

These types of information may be provided by the offeror and included in its Information Note together with the report on which they were based.

Contrary to other foreign codes, the Portuguese Code only establishes the basic rules to be observed apart from the general rules applicable to all the information to be provided during the course of the offer.

Any study or report on these matters made by a party independent from the offeror may only be quoted or made public in the documents of the offer with the express written consent of its authors.

All profit forecasts, either regarding the offeror, the target or any companies related to these, must specify the facts, data and criteria used by its authors.

Any appraisal of assets of the offeror, the target or any companies related to these must state the name and professional qualifications of the evaluator, date of appraisal and criteria used.

The profit forecasts and the asset valuations may only be quoted, included or attached to the documents of the offer that are made public simultaneously with the definitive announcement of the offer. Any further information may only be disclosed subject to the clearance of the Commission.

The companies involved in the two largest takeover attempts in the Portuguese Market – BCP Millennium over BPI and Sonae Telecom over Portugal Telecom – made extensive use of valuations, analysis, profits forecasts and additional dividends programmes, present with straightforward slogans aimed at the media and shareholders.

22.12   Documents from the offeror and the target board

As mentioned before, Portuguese takeover rules are very detailed and comprehensive in the requirements of the documents of the offer, regulating their principles, contents, structure and formal aspects.

Providing a complete and comprehensive list of the documents and requirements of these documents is beyond the scope of this publication and it would never replace consultation of the applicable law when drafting such documents. Therefore, set out below is a short summary of such documents.

On both hostile and recommended offers, offerors must make an application for registration of the offer and publish or make available to shareholders the same set of documents. These documents are:

(a)   the preliminary announcement;

(b)   the final announcement. This states the main information relating to the offer, including the amount and characteristics of the offer securities, price, global amount and price range, form of consideration, conditions of payment, offer timetable, pro rata ratio and any other offer conditions;

(c)   the offer prospectus. This contains more detailed information on the bidder and its relationship with the target and third parties, the basis for determining the consideration, the purposes of the acquisition and, if securities consideration is being offered, all the information required for an offer for sale or a subscription offer.

The registration application must also include several documents concerning both the offeror and the offer itself (e.g., the financial intermediary agreement).

Both advertisements must be published in a major national newspaper and at the Stock Exchange Bulletin. The prospectus may be published with the final advertisement or made available at the offeror's and financial intermediary's offices.

The Commission can also require the offeror to publish additional information on any matter it considers necessary to keep the public informed and on any purchases made after the preliminary advertisement. It will also require a complementary prospectus or addendum to be issued if important information arises that relates to the content of the prospectus.

On both hostile and recommended bids, the target board of directors will issue a report either recommending or opposing the bid after receiving the draft final advertisement. On a hostile bid, this will constitute the main defence document. As the bid progresses, the board of directors may then issue further documents to counter information issued by the offeror, through advertisements or press releases. The Commission must previously approve such information and will only do so if it considers the details to be relevant to shareholders and the market.

22.13   Compulsory acquisition of minorities

22.13.1   *"Open" companies*

The Code foresees a compulsory purchase of minorities mechanism specifically applicable to "open" companies. For non "open" companies *see* 22.13.2 below.

If, as a result of a full takeover, the offeror owns 90 per cent of the voting rights, it may, in the following six months, purchase the outstanding shares. Consideration for these shares will be determined on the same terms as the mandatory offer consideration.

The offeror must immediately publish an announcement and send it to the Commission for registration. Simultaneously it must deposit the full consideration in a credit institution, at the order of the outstanding shareholders.

After publication of the Commission's registration, the acquisition is fully effective and the Commission will send the necessary orders to the securities clearing house or the securities register entity. Following this purchase, securities will be delisted and may not be listed again for a period of two years.

If the offeror does not exercise his compulsive acquisition right, within 30 days following the above six-month period any outstanding shareholder may "invite" the offeror to purchase his shares. Should the offeror not accept such "invitation", the outstanding shareholder may trigger a compulsory purchase mechanism before the Commission.

The compulsory purchase will be effective upon notice of the Commission to the offeror.

22.13.2 Non "open" companies (Article 490, Companies Code)

A company that, either by itself or together with its subsidiaries, acquires title to 90 per cent or more of the stock capital of another company, either a share company or a quota company, must report this fact to the latter in the 30 days following the occurrence of such fact.

In the six months following such communication, the dominant company may make an offer to the remaining shareholders. As mentioned before, this offer is not subject to the takeover rules described above, but to the following rules:

- the consideration may be in cash or in the dominant company's own *quotas*, shares or obligations. The consideration must be supported by a report of an independent Chartered Public Accountant (*"Revisor Oficial de Contas"*). This report must be deposited in the Commercial Register and be available for consultation by any interested party.

If the company so declares in the proposal, it may make a compulsory purchase of the shares of the remaining shareholders. The compulsory acquisition is subject to registration in the Commercial Register and publication in the Official Publications Website.

In order for registration to be executed, the consideration for remaining shares/quotas must be placed on deposit.

If the above-described offer is not made by the deadline, any remaining shareholder can require the dominant company to make him an offer in a deadline of no less than 30 days.

The consideration may also be in cash or in shares or *quotas* of the dominant company.

If the offer is not made or if the shareholder finds the consideration unfair, he may apply to the court in the following 30 days to set the terms for the acquisition and declare the shares/quotas as purchased as of the date of application.

Following a Supreme Court decision on the matter, the constitutionality of this compulsory acquisition mechanism has been subject to the Constitutional Court who upheld its constitutionality so far.

22.14 Insider dealing and market manipulation

The Code treats both insider dealing and market manipulation as crimes, punishable by fine and imprisonment.

The crime of insider dealing is also applicable to all those who breach the confidentiality duty applicable before the preliminary advert is published.

The Code also includes ancillary penalties such as the interdiction, for up to five years, of performing any activities or having any profession related to brokerage in the securities market, and the publishing of such a sentence.

22.14.1 *Insider dealing*

The Code defines "privileged information" as non-public information that, having a precise nature, is bound, if made public, to strongly influence the listing price or the price of securities in the market.

The Code foresees two kinds of insider dealing. The first is applicable to all those, that due to their functions or profession, or to any work done for a company, or due to their public duties, have knowledge of privileged information and know such information to be privileged.

In these cases, insider dealing occurs if the bearer of such information tries to make gains by trading, directly or indirectly in those securities, or if he gives such information to a third party not within his duties or activity, or if he recommends or orders a third party to deal in the same securities.

The insider dealer may be punished by imprisonment for up to three years or a fine.

The second category is applicable to all persons that are not included in the above description, but who have knowledge of privileged information whose direct or indirect source can only be one of such persons and who are aware that such information is privileged.

If these persons attempt to make gains based on such information, they can be subject to a term of imprisonment of up to two years or a fine.

22.14.2 *Market manipulation*

The Code considers this crime to occur when someone publicises false or misleading information, or takes part in any other fraudulent activities with the purpose of artificially disrupting the activities of the securities market.

Such persons are liable to a term of imprisonment of up to three years or a fine.

Members of the board of directors of the issuing company who, having knowledge of such actions, do not act with due diligence to prevent their effects, may be punished with a prison term of up to two years or a fine.

22.15   Financial assistance

As mentioned above, the offer must be organised and implemented by a financial adviser. It is usually this financial adviser who provides the offeror with all the financial assistance necessary, including the setting up of the financial operation to fund the purchase.

Other forms of financial assistance may be given through the studies and reports, including profit forecasts and asset evaluations, to be quoted or included in the documents of the offer.

Chapter 23

Romania

Neil McGregor
Managing partner
McGregor & Partners

23.1 Introduction

Romania's commercial legislation generally developed along the lines of the Italian Commercial Code of 1882, but this development was interrupted in 1948 by legislation of the Communist era. Since 1989 Romania has made efforts to modernise its legislation in general as part of the process of accession to the European Union ("EU").

Romania became a member of the EU on 1 January 2007 and EU legislation now applies in Romania as it does elsewhere in the EU. This is the major change since the publication of the last edition of this Guide, and the description of Romanian legislation in this chapter should be read bearing in mind that the doctrine of the primacy of EU legislation over national legislation now applies in Romania. Whilst this should make it considerably easier to do business in Romania, it is however expected that a degree of unfamiliarity with the application and requirements of EU legislation may still be encountered from time to time. For example, at the time of writing there were reports that the EU Commission was looking into the level of state aid given to certain businesses in Romania.

Romania has not yet adopted the euro and the national currency is the leu (plural lei). The leu has been redenominated on the basis of 10,000 old lei ("ROL") to one new leu ("RON"). In many cases transactions are required to be made in lei, although calculation of the amount to be paid may be made in other currencies.

The Romanian revolution of 1989 found most Romanian industry organised as state-owned enterprises, leaving the new Government with the huge task of establishing a framework for the operation of commercial companies and of privatising the economy. Although the Romanian Commercial Code came back into use following the revolution, new legislation in this field has been enacted. In 1990, Law 31/1990 on Commercial Companies ("the Company Law") was enacted and this, with amendments, was the governing law for Romanian companies at the time of writing. Although the Company Law envisaged the creation of a number of types of commercial companies, the two which are most relevant for this chapter are limited liability companies (*Societăţi cu răspundere limitată* or "Srl" – referred to in this chapter as "Srl companies") and joint stock companies (*Societăţi pe acţiuni* or "SA" – referred to in this chapter as "SA companies").

SA companies must have at least two shareholders, but there is no maximum number. At the time of writing, the minimum share capital of an SA company was RON90,000 (approx. €26,920). Srl companies can have a single shareholder but cannot have more than 50 shareholders. Their shares are more properly described as "social parts" and are not negotiable securities. At the time of writing, the minimum share capital of an Srl company was RON200 (approx. €59).

Progress in privatising the Romanian economy was not particularly rapid and many sectors have retained some degree of state participation until recently. The privatisation process has been an important political issue which has, for instance, led to legislation providing for the distribution of shares to the Romanian public and the giving of assistance to associations of employees to acquire shares in their respective companies.

The private ownership funds which were created as part of the former mass privatisation programme have since become financial investment companies (*Societăţi de investiţii financiare"* ("SIFs")), whilst other investors in the Romanian economy include both foreign strategic and financial investors.

Typical contractual provisions of privatisation contracts required investors to make agreed investments in the target companies and to undertake not to reduce staffing levels or make structural changes to the target businesses, in each case for a period of years after privatisation. Where such privatised companies were sold on, it was necessary for agreement to be reached in respect of these contractual post-privatisation obligations of the original purchaser. Not all privatisations have been wholly successful and some loss-making companies remained in public ownership whilst efforts were made to find suitable buyers, as the social costs of closure appear to be too severe for liquidation to be contemplated. It remains to be seen how the restrictions on state aid which apply following Romania's accession to the EU will change the economy, and at the time of writing there were a number of reports of concerns in the EU about this.

Due to the difficulties experienced in privatising the Romanian economy as it existed in 1990, the establishment of so-called greenfield operations has been encouraged. However, many greenfield operations in Romania have been established as subsidiaries by multinational institutional investors. There are also now some examples of new independent companies that have developed to the point where a listing on the capital markets is considered.

The Romanian capital markets themselves were another creation of the privatisation process. Shares in state-owned companies and, later, the SIFs were distributed to the public under the "mass privatisation programme". It might be argued that the capital markets were created more as a means of allowing the public to trade in these shares than as an institution allowing businesses to raise new capital. No person may hold alone or with other people acting together, more than 1 per cent of the shares in a single SIF.

The only regulated capital market is the Bucharest Stock Exchange ("the Exchange") which absorbed the over-the-counter market operated by the Romanian Association of Securities Dealers (generally known as "RASDAQ") at the end of 2005. The RASDAQ over-the-counter market continues to operate, so the regulated capital markets still consist of the two trading tiers of the Exchange and the RASDAQ over-the-counter market. SA companies whose shares were subject to the mass privatisation programme or had otherwise been the subject of a public offer were required to be listed. Admission to either of the tiers of the Exchange is optional and depends upon satisfaction of the respective listing requirements and continuing obligations. Such SA companies whose shares were not listed on the Exchange were supposed to be automatically listed on RASDAQ unless they went through the procedure to become unlisted or "closed". In practice, problems arose because the managements of some SA companies whose shares were listed on RASDAQ had no interest in their shares being so listed and consequently in complying with the relevant listing requirements and continuing obligations. Disputes arose over the rights and the alleged abuse of minority shareholders by majority shareholders, and the consequent political debate resulted in a number of amendments being made to legislation in respect of listed companies and minority shareholders' rights. It is hoped that this issue has been resolved, for the time being at least, by Law 297/2004 ("the Securities Law") which abrogated the relevant former legislation.

The Securities Law seeks to harmonise Romanian capital market legislation with that in the European Community and envisages that further subordinate legislation would be issued to clarify and regulate its detailed implementation (at the time of writing this had not been completed).

The National Securities Commission or *Comisia Naţională a Valorilor Mobiliare* ("CNVM") established under the old legislation continues to exist under the Securities Law and is responsible for the application of the Securities Law. The CNVM may issue formal opinions interpreting the legislation and assessments in respect of various issues covered by the Securities Law ex officio or at the request of an interested person. Such opinions (or the refusal of the CNVM to issue them) may be challenged by any interested party in administrative contentious procedure at the Court of Appeal in Bucharest.

23.2 Acquisition targets

Leaving aside privatisation projects (which are governed by special procedures), the following Romanian categories of companies are of interest for this Chapter:

(a) SA companies which are public companies under the Securities Law;
(b) SA companies which are closed-type companies under the Securities Law; and
(c) Srl companies.

These are described in more detail below. It should be noted that for Romanian companies, a "board of directors" is normally referred to as a "council of administration", and "directors" are referred to as "administrators".

23.2.1 *Public companies: listing and general conduct requirements*

Pursuant to the Securities Law a company must comply with certain legal conditions to become a public company. These conditions refer to the issuer (the company) itself and to its shares:

(a)   The following conditions relate to the issuer:

    (i)   the company must be established and carrying out its activity in a lawful manner;

    (ii)   the company must have a foreseeable capitalisation of at least the equivalent in lei of €1 million or, to the extent to which its capitalisation cannot be estimated, the company's capital and reserves, including profit or loss from the last financial year, must be at least the equivalent in lei of €1 million, calculated according to the reference rate announced by the National Bank of Romania on the date of the application for admission to listing on a regulated market;

    (iii)   the company must have a trading history of at least three years prior to its request for admission of its shares for listing on a regulated market and must have prepared and communicated its financial statements for the said period in accordance with the legal provisions.

(b)   The shares in respect of which listing is sought must be freely negotiable and fully paid up.

Where a public issue precedes admission to listing on a regulated market, such listing may take place only after the end of the subscription period.

A sufficient number of shares must be in the hands of the public if a company's shares are to be admitted to listing on a regulated market. This number is either at least 25 per cent of the subscribed capital represented by the relevant category of shares, or a smaller percentage where a large number of such shares are held by members of the public.

Admission to listing is on the basis of a prospectus approved by the CNVM and thereafter published, detailed provisions in this respect being contained in the CNVM's regulations. The Securities Law also contains specific conditions for admission to listing on a regulated market of bonds issued by companies, public authorities and public international bodies. Administrators (directors) of a listed company may be appointed by cumulative vote. However, it is compulsory for this method of appointment to be used where a significant shareholder so requests.

In general, any increase in the share capital must be authorised by an extraordinary general meeting of shareholders. However, either a general meeting of shareholders or the company's constitutive document may authorise the increase in share capital up to a maximum level, so allowing the administrators (directors) to resolve the increase of the share capital up to such authorised maximum. This power is exercisable by the administrators (directors) for a maximum period of one year and may be renewed by the general meeting for further periods, in each case not exceeding one year.

Where a resolution to pay a dividend is passed by the general meeting of a company, this must be notified to the Commercial Registry within 15 days for registration and published in the Official Gazette of Romania, Part IV. The relevant resolution is issued as a writ of execution based on which shareholders may enforce payment of the declared dividend by the company.

Increases of capital by contributions in kind must be approved by an extraordinary general meeting ("EGM") of shareholders attended by members holding at least three-quarters of the share capital. The support of members holding at least 75 per cent of the voting rights represented at such an EGM is required to adopt such a resolution.

Certain significant transactions also require the prior approval of an extraordinary general meeting of shareholders. Such significant transactions include the acquisition, sale, exchange or establishment of guarantees over immovable assets the value of which exceeds, either individually or in aggregate, 20 per cent of the total immovable assets of the company, less any claims, during a financial year. Such prior approval of an EGM is also required for any lease for a period of longer than a year of any tangible assets having a value which exceeds, either individually or in aggregate, 20 per cent of the total value of the tangible assets of the company, less any claims, on the date when the relevant legal document is concluded. Similarly, prior approval of an EGM is also required for the establishment of any association with a third party for a period of longer than a year and having a value which exceeds, either individually or in aggregate, 20 per cent of the total value of the tangible assets of the company, less any claims, on the date when the relevant association agreement was concluded. Transactions with the same third party or parties acting together are cumulated for the purpose of assessing whether these criteria are met.

23.2.2   *SA companies which are closed-type companies*

Not all SA companies satisfy the Securities Law's definition of public companies. In consequence, their shares may not be listed on a regulated exchange but such companies are exempt from the detailed regulatory regime instituted by the Securities Law.

23.2.3   *Srl companies*

Srl companies have been described briefly above. It is possible to convert an Srl company into an SA company (and vice versa) but, as the shares in an Srl company cannot be negotiable securities, it follows that an Srl company cannot be a public company. Whilst as closed-type companies Srl companies are exempt from the detailed controls and regulation of the Securities Law, they may be subject to restrictions contained in their own constitutive documents and they are excluded by law from undertaking certain particular activities (e.g., banking and insurance).

23.3   Exchange and investment controls; disclosure requirements

23.3.1   *Exchange controls*

Since 1990, legislation intended to encourage foreign investment has included certain repatriation guarantees, but such legislation has been subject to frequent change. Romania's accession to the EU and the consequent freedom of movement of capital in the EU is a welcome development. At the time of writing the exchange rate between the leu and other currencies was determined by the market, and in general there were no restrictions on the exchange of Romanian and foreign currency.

23.3.2 Controls on investments

Particularly following Romania's accession to the EU, generally there have been no restrictions on who may invest in Romania. However, from time to time particular investment restrictions may be applied (e.g., to enforce international sanctions).

23.3.3 Disclosure requirements

23.3.3.1 General disclosure (transparency) requirements

Listed companies are subject to specific disclosure requirements pursuant to the Securities Law and subordinate legislation. A non-exhaustive summary of the more important disclosure requirements is given below:

(a) Listed companies must register themselves with the CNVM and comply with the reporting requirements established by the CNVM regulations and by the regulated markets where their securities are admitted to listing.

(b) Listed companies must also ensure the availability of all the necessary facilities and information to enable shareholders to exercise their rights. Each listed company must, in particular:

　(i) inform shareholders about the holding of general meetings and enable them to exercise their voting rights there;

　(ii) inform the public of the allocation and payment of dividends, the issue of new shares, including allotment, subscription, renunciation and conversion arrangements; and

　(iii) appoint a financial institution as its agent, through which shareholders may exercise their financial rights (unless the issuer itself provides financial services).

(c) Furthermore, a listed company planning an amendment to its constitutive document must send a draft to the CNVM and to the regulated market before the date of the calling of the general meeting which is to consider the proposed amendment.

(d) A listed company must also inform the public, without delay and in any event within no more than 48 hours, of any major new developments in its sphere of activity which are not public knowledge and which may, by virtue of their effect on its assets and liabilities or financial position or on the general course of its business, lead to substantial movements in the price of its shares.

(e) If an issuer (or a person who acts on its behalf) discloses any inside information to a third party during its normal course of business, it must make that information public, simultaneously in the case of an intentional disclosure and promptly in the case of an unintentional disclosure.

(f) Listed companies are required to prepare, make available to the public and send to the CNVM and the relevant market operator quarterly, half-yearly and annual reports. Listed companies are also required to issue a press release in a national daily newspaper informing investors that such reports are available. Such reports must be submitted for publication no later than five days from the date on which they were approved.

(g)   The CNVM's regulations contain specific requirements for financial reports, but these must include any significant information to allow investors to make an informed assessment of the activity of the company and of its profits and losses, showing any exceptional factor that has influenced these activities and including the figures for the same period in the previous financial year to allow comparisons to be drawn.

23.3.3.2   *Disclosure of significant shareholdings*

The Securities Law requires the shareholdings in public companies of individual shareholders or of groups of shareholders to be reported in certain circumstances.

Where, consequent on the sale or purchase of shares, a person's shareholding with voting rights in a public company reaches or exceeds any of a number of thresholds, such person must inform concurrently the relevant public company, the CNVM and the regulated market within three business days. The relevant thresholds are 5, 10, 20, 33, 50, 75 and 90 per cent of the total shares of the company concerned.

When any of these thresholds is reached by a subsidiary of a parent undertaking, such subsidiary is exempted from the obligation to inform if this obligation has been discharged by its parent undertaking.

23.4   Merger control

Economic concentrations which are not subject to the approval of the European Commission fall under the national merger control which is governed by the Competition Law and related subordinate legislation. The Competition Council or *Consiliul Concurenţei* is responsible for the investigation and authorisation of economic concentrations which are not within the jurisdiction of the European Commission. Details of the Romanian merger control regime are given below.

23.4.1   *Thresholds for mandatory notification*

An economic concentration is deemed to arise in relation to Romanian companies through transactions where:

(a)   two or more previously independent companies merge; or

(b)   one or more persons that already control at least one company acquire, directly or indirectly, control of one or more other companies or a part thereof, either by participation in the share capital, or by purchase of assets, or by creating a situation of economic dependence (through long- or medium-term contracts of supply combined with structural links) or by other means.

Acquisitions of businesses or of business assets may also constitute economic concentrations.

A mandatory merger notification and approval process applies to transactions where the worldwide turnover of the undertakings concerned and their groups exceeds the equivalent in lei of €10 million and there are at least two undertakings concerned in the operation, each of which achieves turnover in Romania which exceeds the equivalent in lei of €4 million. Turnover is considered to be the amount obtained by the undertakings concerned and the members of their groups (if after the concentration such companies remain or become members of the group) from the sale of products and performance of services in the financial year preceding the year when the economic concentration occurs, as registered in the balance sheet of the undertakings concerned minus the value of excises and exports. The legislation contains detailed provisions concerning the calculation of the turnover for each type of concentration (i.e., achieved by merger, acquisition of sole/joint control, acquisition of assets).

23.4.2   *Procedure*

Notifiable economic concentrations are subject to the consent of the Competition Council and consequently no steps which are irreversible or which substantially modify the structure of the market may be taken before such consent is obtained. The Competition Council will evaluate economic concentrations on the basis of whether they will create or strengthen a dominant position or limit, remove or significantly hinder competition in all or part of the Romanian market.

Economic concentrations effected by agreements must be notified by all the participants to a merger by the party that acquires sole control, or by the parties that acquire joint control and by the parties to the joint venture. The notification must be lodged with the Competition Council within 30 calendar days of the date of the merger agreement/signature of the agreement by which sole/joint control is acquired.

A notification fee must be paid when lodging a notification with the Competition Council (at the time of writing this was approximately €800). The form and content of notifications follow a standard notification form but, depending upon the turnover of the undertakings concerned, the Competition Council may allow a more simplified notification form to be used (a "short-form notification").

The Competition Council must issue a decision within 30 days of the notification becoming effective – this is the date when the Competition Council considers that all documents and data required have been provided to it. It is not uncommon for the Competition Council to require further information and documents after a notification has been lodged. The notification will not be regarded as effective until these are provided.

The Competition Council will determine whether a notifiable economic concentration:

(a)   is admissible; or
(b)   requires investigation due to serious concern about its effects on the relevant market.

In the latter case, the parties have the opportunity to be heard by the Competition Council, which must make a final decision not later than five months after the decision to open an investigation. Such final decision may be:

(a)   to refuse approval; or
(b)   to give conditional approval; or
(c)   to give unconditional approval.

The Competition Council may ask the undertakings concerned to make certain modifications to the terms and conditions of the economic concentration (intended to make it compliant with a normal competitive environment) as a condition of approval.

An authorisation tax is payable where notifiable economic concentrations are admissible or are approved. This is 0.1 per cent of the aggregate turnover of the undertakings concerned, based upon the turnover in the year prior to the decision of the Competition Council in respect of the notified concentration. The legislation contains detailed provisions as to the calculation of this authorisation tax.

The Romanian Government may exceptionally, if justified by the general interest, permit an economic concentration that is otherwise considered to be unacceptable by the Competition Council.

23.4.3   Appeals

Decisions of the Competition Council in respect of an economic concentration submitted for its attention may be challenged in the administrative disputes section of the Court of Appeal of Bucharest within 30 days of the date of communication of such decision.

23.4.4   Penalties

Failure to comply with the Competition Law or with the decisions of the Competition Council may result in fines which can equal up to 10 per cent of annual turnover. In addition, daily penalties may be imposed for continued non-compliance.

23.5   Regulation of the conduct of mergers and acquisitions

Mergers and acquisitions of public companies are more heavily regulated than those involving closed-type SA companies and Srl companies.

23.6   Methods of acquisition

Various methods of acquisition should be considered as described below.

23.6.1   Private agreements

Many Romanian companies have been privatised through the sale of majority shareholdings by direct negotiations culminating in private agreements. However, these have generally been based on a standard prescribed form of contract drafted according to Romanian (civil) law principles. As Romania has both Civil and Commercial Codes, Romanian practice has therefore historically been to rely on these for general principles with only specific matters being set out expressly in contracts. Such matters may be permitted derogations or amplifications of general principles from the Codes. In consequence, such contracts in the civil law style are likely to be shorter and to contain fewer specific vendor's warranties than equivalent contracts drafted in the Anglo-Saxon style. However, the Anglo-Saxon style of detailed and lengthy contracts is becoming more common as the mergers and acquisitions ("M&A") market develops.

It is compulsory for privatisation contracts to be governed by Romanian law and for the governing language to be Romanian. Prospective foreign investors faced with only limited warranties in such circumstances are well advised to conduct full due diligence enquiries, since the protective provisions implied by law can be summed up as offering guarantees:

(a)   of delivery of the subjects of sale;
(b)   of peaceful ownership and possession; and
(c)   that no hidden defects exist.

It is doubtful that such concepts extend beyond the shares themselves to the company in which shares are sold, so prudent purchasers will seek to protect themselves with proper due diligence and appropriate, detailed and specific contractual warranties and indemnities.

The use of private agreements in the Anglo-Saxon style in transactions which do not involve privatisation is permitted and is becoming more common, particularly where foreign investors are concerned. There is freedom to conclude such agreements under laws other than Romanian law and in languages other than Romanian, although the practicalities of enforcing such contracts should be considered carefully and the formalities of transferring ownership of shares in a Romanian company are governed by Romanian law. Extensive contractual warranties and indemnities should not be regarded as a substitute for proper due diligence.

A written share purchase contract will need to be produced to the Commercial Registry for the purpose of registering share transfers. For this reason it is not uncommon for a short-form share sale agreement in Romanian to be executed for registration purposes in addition to a full share sale agreement in Anglo-Saxon style, although obviously the latter should govern the transaction and the price stated in the two contracts should not be different.

23.6.2   Public offers

The Securities Law regulates the following types of public offers: public sale offers, public purchase offers, voluntary takeover offers, mandatory takeover offers and competitive public offers. In general, all of these types of public offer have in common, in terms of legal procedural requirements, the requirement for the CNVM's approval and notification of the issuer, the regulated market where the securities are listed and the public (by publication of the prospectus in the press) of the existence and the various stages of the procedure as described in detail at 23.8 below.

23.6.3 Public sale offers

As a general rule, a public sale offer cannot be carried out in absence of an offer prospectus. Public sale offers must be carried out through an intermediary authorised to provide investment services.

The obligation to publish a prospectus does not apply:

(a)   to offers addressed solely to qualified investors;
(b)   to offers addressed to fewer than 100 investors, natural or legal persons, who are not qualified investors;
(c)   where the total amount of the offer, the issuing price of the securities and the minimum subscription made by an investor in the offer are at least equal to the amounts established by the CNVM's regulations;
(d)   to securities offered, allotted or to be allotted in connection with a merger when an offer document is provided containing information that is regarded by the CNVM as being equivalent to that of the prospectus, taking into account the requirements of EU legislation;
(e)   to securities offered, allotted or to be allotted free of charge to existing shareholders and when dividends are paid by issuing new shares of the same class as the shares in respect of which such dividends are paid, provided that a document is made available containing information on the number and nature of the shares and the reasons for any details of the issue; and
(f)   to shares issued in substitution for shares of the same class which are already issued, if the issue of such new shares does not involve any increase in the share capital.

An offer prospectus must contain all of the information which, according to the particular nature of the issuer and of the securities offered to the public, is necessary to enable investors to make an informed assessment of the assets and the liabilities, financial position, profit and loss, and prospects of the issuer and (where relevant) of any guarantor of the fulfilment of the obligations undertaken by the issuer, and of the rights attaching to such securities.

An offer prospectus approved by the CNVM is valid for 12 months after its publication and may be used for several issues of securities during this period, provided that the information contained therein is duly updated. A prospectus must also contain a summary of the information included therein.

A prospectus may be drawn up as a single document or as several separate documents, namely:

(a)   a registration document, containing information related to the issuer;
(b)   a securities note regarding the features of the securities offered or to be admitted to official listing; and
(c)   a summary note of the prospectus.

The CNVM will decide on the approval of the prospectus within 10 working days from the registration of the request. This deadline is extended to 20 working days if the securities are issued by an issuer which applies for admission to trading on a regulated market for the first time or which has not previously offered securities to the public. Any request for additional information or for the modification of the information already presented in the prospectus, by the CNVM or by the offeror, will interrupt these terms which will recommence from the date when the said information or modifications are provided.

Where prices and quantities of securities which are offered to the public cannot be included in the prospectus as approved, such prospectus must contain:

(a)　the criteria and/or conditions in accordance with which the price and the amount of the securities which shall be offered to the public shall be determined, and in the case of price, the maximum price; or

(b)　notification of the right to withdraw the subscriptions made within at least two working days from the date when the final price and the amount of securities offered has been registered with the CNVM and published.

Investors who have already agreed to subscribe for the securities before the supplement to the prospectus is published shall have the right to withdraw their acceptances within three working days after the publication of the supplement. Prices are fixed according to the legislation and the CNVM's regulations. Requests for confirmation of the investment intentions of third parties are allowed in order to assess the success of a future offer, in compliance with the conditions established by the CNVM. The CNVM issues regulations regarding cross-border public offers made in the EU by issuers with their registered office in Romania, or by non-residents in Romania, in accordance with the applicable EU legislation.

23.6.4　Public purchase offers

A public purchase offer is an offer by a person to purchase securities, addressed to all their holders, circulated by mass media or communicated by other means. A public purchase offer must be made through an intermediary authorised to provide investment services, and such public purchase offer price is established pursuant to secondary legislation enacted by the CNVM.

The CNVM will decide on the approval of the offer document within 10 working days from the registration of the request.

Any request for supplementary information or for the modification of the information originally provided in the offer document, by the CNVM or by the offeror, shall suspend this term, which recommences from the date when the said information is provided or the modification is implemented.

23.6.5　Voluntary takeover offers

A voluntary takeover offer is a public purchase offer addressed to all shareholders, for all their holdings, launched by a person who does not have the legal obligation to launch such an offer, and is made with the purpose of acquiring more than 33 per cent of the voting rights of the issuer.

The administrators (directors) of the issuer are entitled by law to express their collective opinion of the offer to the CNVM, the offeror and the regulated market where the securities are listed. In principle, as of the moment when the preliminary announcement is received, the council of administration (board of directors) of the issuer can make no resolution which may affect the asset position of the issuer or the objectives of the takeover, excepting current management activities. The publication of the preliminary announcement binds the offeror to submit to the CNVM, within 30 days at the most, the documentation underlying the takeover bid, including terms at least as favourable as the ones provided by the preliminary offer.

The CNVM will issue a decision on the approval of the offer document within 10 days of the registration of the application. The prices offered within voluntary takeover bids are established by express secondary legislation enacted by the CNVM.

The offeror or the persons acting in concert are prohibited from launching, within one year of the closing of the prior takeover bid, another takeover bid for the securities of the same issuer.

23.6.6 *Mandatory public offers*

A person who, as a result of his own purchase or that of persons acting in concert with him, holds more than 33 per cent of the voting rights in an undertaking must launch a public offer addressed to all securities holders for all of their holdings as soon as possible, but no later than two months from reaching such holding position. Until the public offer is made, all the rights related to the securities which exceed 33 per cent of the voting rights in the issuer are suspended and the said shareholder and the persons acting in concert may no longer purchase, by other operations, further shares in the same issuer.

However, the foregoing provisions do not apply to persons who have acquired more than 33 per cent of the voting rights in compliance with the legal provisions applicable at the time of such acquisition where the acquisition took place before the entry into force of the Securities Law. A mandatory takeover bid must be made in accordance with the provisions laid down in the first paragraph of this Section if, following the entry into force of the Securities Law, such persons increase their holdings to 50 per cent or more of the voting rights of the issuer. Until the public bid is made, the rights attaching to the shares purchased which exceed 50 per cent of the total voting share capital are suspended and the holder of such shares and any persons acting jointly with such holder may not purchase, by other operations, further shares in the same issuer.

The offer price must be at least equal to the highest price paid by the offeror or by the persons with whom he acts jointly within the period of 12 months prior to the offer. Failing this, the offer price will be determined in accordance with the CNVM's provisions, taking into account at least the following criteria:

(a) the weighted average trading price during the last 12 months prior to the offer being made;

(b) the value of the company's net assets according to the latest audited financial statements; and

(c)   the value of the shares, as established by valuation made by an independent auditor, in accordance with the international valuation standards.

However, it should be noted that the above provisions do not apply when the holding position accounting for more than 33 per cent of the voting rights in the issuer has been obtained as a result of an excepted transaction. For the purposes of the Securities Law, an excepted transaction is the acquisition of this position:

(a)   through the privatisation process;

(b)   by share acquisition from the Ministry of Public Finance or from other entities legally enabled within the budget claims collection procedures;

(c)   following the transfer of shares between the parent undertaking and its subsidiaries or between the subsidiaries of the same parent undertaking; and/or

(d)   following a voluntary takeover public bid addressed to all the holders of those securities and for all their holdings.

If the acquisition of the holding position accounting for more than 33 per cent of the voting rights in the issuer is made unintentionally (e.g., due to a reduction of capital through redemption by the company of its own shares; or as a result of exercising pre-emption rights or the subscription or conversion of the rights originally allotted as well as the conversion of preferred shares into common shares; merger/spin-off or succession), the holder of such a holding position has certain alternative obligations required by law and which must be fulfilled within three months from the acquisition of that holding position. These obligations are:

(a)   to launch a public offer according to the conditions and prices laid down in Article 203 of the Securities Law; or

(b)   to sell such number of shares as will result in the seller ceasing to hold the relevant unintentionally acquired position.

23.6.7   *Judicial mergers and divisions of companies*

Mergers of companies may be effected by the absorption of one by another or by the amalgamation of two or more companies in order to create a single new company. Companies may also be divided. This will result in the dissolution of the original company where all of its property is divided between successor companies, but it is not compulsory for all of the property of the original company to be so transferred and for the original company to be dissolved.

In addition to corporate consent for a judicial merger or division, such operation must be approved by the delegate judge at the relevant Commercial Registry and creditors of the relevant companies have an opportunity to object. Existing property, rights and liabilities will pass to the successor companies as determined by the approved merger or division plan or as prescribed by law.

23.6.8   *Joint ventures*

Joint ventures are common and are particularly useful where a foreign investor wishes to involve a Romanian partner in a business venture. Shareholders agreements are used, but it is important to ensure that the provisions of the joint venture company's constitutive document do not conflict with those of the shareholders agreement as the constitutive document will prevail in the event of a discrepancy. A further issue to be borne in mind is that the Company Law forbids "voting conventions", so careful thought needs to be given to how control is to be exercised in a joint venture company.

23.6.9 *Asset transactions*

Asset transactions are very common, particularly where a business is being sold by a liquidator. Care needs to be taken in dealing with the various classes of asset being transferred, including assessing the taxation consequences.

These consequences are not limited to VAT considerations since, according to fiscal legislation enacted in June 2005, income resulting from the transfer of ownership of buildings and corresponding land which are sold within three years after acquisition, and income resulting from the transfer of ownership of land without buildings acquired after 1 January 1990, are taxable.

If the proceeds of sale of real estate located in Romania exceed the base value of such real estate in the circumstances set out above, profit tax is payable at a special rate of 16 per cent of the difference between the gain and any fiscal losses incurred. Real-estate transactions require the participation of a notary, who is responsible for the calculation and collection of such taxes.

However, this 16 per cent tax is not applicable to contributions in kind of land and buildings to the social capital of commercial companies and to the sale of land and buildings previously recovered by their owners through the restitution process (i.e., the restitution of properties nationalised or otherwise abusively taken by the Communist regime between 1947 and 1989).

Certain assets may have been acquired by the selling company under one of various fiscal incentive regimes operated in Romania since 1990, such as exemptions from customs duties. Disposal of such assets before the expiry of certain periods established by law may, under certain conditions, trigger the clawback of any exemptions.

Until Romania acceded to the EU, the Romanian Constitution restricted the right of ownership of Romanian land to Romanian citizens and to Romanian companies and other legal entities. The only exception to this rule was that a non-Romanian might own Romanian land which had been inherited through the intestacy laws, that is, not through a will. The use by non-Romanians of Romanian companies as vehicles to hold land was therefore normal.

Following Romania's accession to the EU, citizens of other EU countries, stateless persons domiciled in Romania or in another EU country and legal entities existing under the laws of other EU countries may own Romanian land, subject to some exceptions, on the same terms as Romanian citizens and legal entities.

One such exception to the right to own Romanian land relates to the ownership of agricultural lands and forests. This exception will continue until 1 January 2014. However, this restriction on the right of ownership of Romanian land does not apply to independent farmers who:

(a)   are citizens of other EU countries or stateless persons domiciled in other EU countries who take up residence in Romania; or

(b)   are stateless persons domiciled in Romania.

Further such exceptions to the right of ownership of Romanian land relate to the acquisition of land for secondary residences by citizens of other EU countries and stateless persons domiciled in other EU countries who are not resident in Romania, and the acquisition of land for secondary premises by legal entities of other EU countries. These exceptions will last until 1 January 2012.

For other persons and legal entities, the restrictions under the Romanian constitution continue to apply unless and until relaxed on the basis of a treaty of reciprocity between the particular non-EU country and Romania.

In the meantime, it is possible to invest in Romanian land by using a Romanian limited liability company as the owning vehicle – there is no restriction on foreign ownership of such companies. Quite apart from legal restrictions on the ownership of Romanian land, commercial reasons often dictate the use of companies as special-purpose vehicles to own real estate.

It is also possible for non-Romanians to have rights of use of Romanian land which fall short of full ownership. Such rights include usufruct (where the user obtains ownership of the "fruits" of the land), servitude (easement) and concession.

23.7   Preliminary matters

23.7.1   Initial contacts

The sale of companies by private agreement is a particularly significant element of Romanian M&A activity, whether on privatisation or on sale by ordinary investors. Initial contacts leading to such transactions may come from a variety of sources. Privatisations will be initiated by the State authorities, but likely bidders may already have indicated their potential interest to them. Some companies which are to be privatised may have had existing business co-operation with potential purchasers. The same may be true of other sales, particularly where a foreign company moves to take over joint venture or other business partners. Existing business contact with or knowledge of a target company may be very helpful, as explained at 23.7.2 below.

23.7.2   Due diligence

Due diligence is fundamental to the acquisition of a Romanian company. As mentioned at 23.6.1 above, the practice in privatisation is to offer only very limited warranties. Institutional investors, if properly advised, will similarly give only limited warranties as to the shares that they are seeking to sell, leaving a purchaser dependent upon taking detailed warranties from the shareholders who have been active in the management of the target company. Even if detailed and extensive warranties and indemnities are obtained from vendors, enforcing them in the event of a breach is unlikely to be easy. A prospective purchaser will therefore be well advised to conduct careful due diligence enquiries to be quite sure of what he is buying. Due diligence enquiries carried out by prospective strategic investors generally involve business and technical teams, who will usually be the staff of the future purchaser. The enquiries will be supplemented by:

(a)   a legal due diligence carried out by lawyers;
(b)   a financial due diligence carried out by accountants; and
(c)   an environmental due diligence carried out by specialist consultants.

Other specialists may also be used if the circumstances so require. Existing knowledge of the target company, whether from a current business relationship or from market knowledge, is of course an advantage. It is also possible to check some information provided by the target company against public records, such as those held by the Commercial Registry. In some privatisations and in sales involving public offers or auctions, data rooms may be used.

It is normal for prospective vendors and the target company to require prospective purchasers to enter into confidentiality agreements before giving them access to the target for due diligence purposes. These obligations of confidentiality may be reciprocal, particularly where the potential purchaser or its holding company is a public company. "Lock-out" provisions may also be included to give the prospective purchaser time to investigate the target and to negotiate the acquisition, although these are most likely to be of relevance to acquisitions of private companies where the purchaser has incurred considerable expense in conducting due diligence enquiries. It is common for such agreements, governed by Romanian law, to contain contractual penalties as the remedy for breaches.

23.7.3   Precontractual liability

Under Romanian law, certain types of immovable assets such as land can only be sold using formal written and notarised contracts (*see* 23.6.9 above). Shares and other securities are movable assets and so can be sold without formalities, although in practice a form of transfer document is required for registration of transfers of registered shares and other securities. Therefore, it is important during initial negotiations and due diligence that care is taken to establish clearly the status of the potential transaction.

Further, under the general law, parties are required to conduct negotiations in good faith and may be liable in delict (equivalent to tort in common-law countries) should such negotiations be broken off without good reason.

Therefore, it is advisable for the status of the negotiations and the intended progress to a deal to be clearly established, including confirmation that negotiations and any eventual deal are subject to such matters as:

(a)   completion of satisfactory due diligence;
(b)   negotiation and execution of a formal contract;
(c)   main board approval, etc.

This can be combined with the confidentiality and lock-out agreement and should clearly set out the rights of either party to break off the negotiations without liability to the other, if this is the basis of the negotiations.

In privatisations and in other sale procedures where bids are used, such as in sales of assets by liquidators, it is normal for bidders to be required to lodge a tender guarantee. The winning bidder will be expected to negotiate and conclude a formal contract for the acquisition of the shares or assets concerned. If he fails to do so, or if he does so but fails to pay the balance of the purchase price when required, the tender guarantee will be forfeited.

23.8 General provisions concerning the conduct of public offers

All types of public offer are regulated by the Securities Law which contains basic procedural rules for all such offers, and these are described in detail for each type of offer at 23.6.3–23.6.6 above. Certain supplementary procedural details in this respect are also contained in the CNVM's regulations. However, all types of public offer share certain common procedural legal requirements described here.

The general rule is that any person who wishes to make a public offer must submit to the CNVM an application for the approval of the prospectus in the case of a public sale offer, or of the offer document in the case of a public purchase offer, accompanied by an announcement in accordance with the regulations issued by the CNVM. Once approved, the prospectus or offer document must be made available to the public no later than the beginning of the offer to the public.

Public offers made without the approval of the CNVM are null and void and render the makers liable to the sanctions set out in the Securities Law.

The public offer announcement may be made at any time after the CNVM has issued the decision to approve the prospectus or offer document and must be published in at least two national daily newspapers or in electronic form on the offeror's website and on the intermediary's website or on the CNVM's website. Information contained in the announcement must be consistent with the information contained in the prospectus/offer document.

The period during which the offer is valid must be stated in the announcement and in the prospectus or the offer document, but may not exceed the terms established by the CNVM's regulations.

Any significant modification of the original information contained in the prospectus or offer document during the time when the offer is valid and which is capable of affecting an investment decision must be included in a supplement. Such amendment shall be approved by the CNVM within a maximum of seven working days and must be made available to the public by an announcement.

The CNVM may make various types of decision described in detail by the Securities Law relating to an application of approval of a prospectus/offer document.

In general, the CNVM will require the offeror to include in the prospectus/offer document supplementary information or may suspend an offer, whenever it is considered necessary, for a maximum of 10 working days on any single occasion, if it has reasonable grounds for suspecting that the applicable legal provisions have been infringed. The CNVM may also prohibit or suspend advertisements relating to a public offer for a maximum of 10 working days on any single occasion.

Suspension of a public offer results in such offer becoming invalid. When suspension is withdrawn or ceases, the public offer becomes valid again.

Cancellation of a decision to approve the document/prospectus will annul the effects of the transactions carried out prior to the date of such annulment and will result in the return of the securities or payments made. Such unwinding may be voluntary or enforced through a court decision.

The following persons may be liable for failing to comply with the legal provisions regarding the truthfulness, accuracy and completeness of the information in a prospectus/offer document and in an announcement:

(a)   the offeror;
(b)   members of the board or the sole manager of the offeror;
(c)   the issuer;
(d)   members of the board of the issuer;
(e)   the founders, in the case of public subscription;
(f)   the financial auditor who certified the financial statements, information from which has been inserted in the prospectus;
(g)   the offeror's intermediaries;
(h)   any other entity which has accepted responsibility for any information, survey or assessment inserted or mentioned in the prospectus.

23.8.1   Counter offer

Subject to the following conditions, any person may launch a counter offer for the same securities:

(a)   the counter offer must be for the same amount of securities as the original offer or must be aimed at obtaining not less than the same level of shareholding that the original offer was intended to achieve;
(b)   the counter offer offers a price that is at least 5 per cent higher than the first offer.

A counter offer may be launched by submitting the required documentation to the CNVM within a maximum of 10 working days from the date when the first offer was made available to the public.

In making a decision to authorise counter offers, the CNVM must set the same closing term for all the offers, and a deadline for the submission for approval of increases in offer prices. Such single term for closing counter offers may not be later than 60 working days from the date when the first offer was made.

23.8.2   Withdrawal of shareholders, squeeze-outs

In one of the following situations after a public purchase offer made to all share-holders for their entire shareholdings in the relevant company, an offeror may require shareholders who have not accepted such offer to sell their shares at a "fair price":

(a)   the offeror holds shares accounting for more than 95 per cent of the share capital;

(b)   the offeror has acquired shares accounting for more than 90 per cent of those targeted by the public purchase offer addressed to all shareholders for all their respective shareholdings in the relevant company.

The CNVM's regulations contain detailed mechanisms by which such a squeeze-out is actually implemented, which are considered to work well in practice.

If a company has issued more than one class of shares, these provisions are applied separately for each class.

Prices offered in mandatory takeover offers and in voluntary takeover offers which have been accepted by holders of more than 90 per cent of the shares which are the subject of the offer are considered to be "fair prices" for the purpose of the exercise of squeeze-out rights within three months from the closing of the relevant offer. Failing this, the "fair price" is determined by an independent expert in accordance with international valuation standards. Such determined fair price is made available to the public through the market where the relevant shares are traded, by publication in the CNVM's official journal, on the CNVM website and in two national daily newspapers, within five days from the drawing up of the valuation report.

Conversely, following a public purchase offer to all holders and for all of their shareholdings in a particular company, a minority shareholder has the right to require the offeror holding more than 95 per cent of the share capital to buy its shares at a "fair price".

23.9   Defences to a hostile offer

At the time of writing, hostile takeover bids were not a feature of the Romanian capital market, but such bids may be expected in the future as the capital market and the companies listed on it develop.

As described above, there are considerable restrictions on what can be done once an offer has been announced. It remains to be seen to what extent Romanian companies will prepare for potential future hostile offers, but (subject to the specific restrictions once a hostile offer has been announced) possible defences might include the following.

23.9.1   Transfer blocking and similar clauses in the constitutive document

The constitutive documents of SA companies may contain provisions which restrict the free transfer of shares in them. In general, such clauses are not practical in a public company whose shares are traded on a regulated exchange, although limitations on the number of shares that may be held by a single investor may be acceptable. However, there is no reason why such provisions may not be used in the constitutive documents of closed-type companies or of Srl companies. The Company Law even provides that share transfers in Srl companies to non-shareholders will require the consent of shareholders representing not less than 75 per cent of the capital. Such provisions, possibly combined with shareholders' agreements, could therefore be a method of controlling changes in shareholders in private companies. The Romanian state has previously been able to hold a "golden share" in certain companies which were formed out of the former state-owned autonomous corporations or *regii autonome*". However, this right was abolished in 2005.

The Company Law provides that all shares are to grant equal rights to their owners, save that limited numbers of non-voting preference shares may be issued by SA companies (*see* 23.9.2 below). However, the Company Law also provides that the constitutive document of a company may limit the number of votes of shareholders who hold more than one share.

23.9.2 Capital manipulation

As mentioned above, non-voting preference shares may be issued by SA companies. These may be converted to and from ordinary voting shares by a resolution of an extraordinary general meeting of shareholders. There may therefore be scope for adjusting the balance of voting shares, although it should be noted that such non-voting preference shares may not exceed one-quarter of the company's share capital and that certain persons (i.e., the administrators (directors), members of the management and members of the council of administration (board of directors)) may not hold non-voting preference shares.

The Company Law does not generally allow a company to acquire its own shares, either directly or through third parties, unless this has been approved in detail by an extraordinary general meeting of shareholders and complies with various other conditions. These include requirements that the relevant company cannot hold its own shares with a nominal value exceeding 10 per cent of its share capital and that such shares be paid up in full.

Exceptions to this general prohibition also include price-adjustment operations approved by the CNVM.

The Company Law also prohibits a company from granting loans or giving security in order for its own shares to be acquired by a third party.

23.9.3 Poison pills and other contractual defences

The ability of the council of administration of a Romanian company to enter into contracts whereby, for example, certain adverse consequences will follow in the event of a change of control or whereby important assets of the company are sold, are limited by the powers delegated to it by the constitutive document of the company and should be checked in each case. It should also be remembered that the Company Law requires the council of administration and the management to obtain the consent of a general meeting of shareholders to be able to enter into agreements to acquire, dispose of, lease, exchange or constitute guarantees over assets of the company which have a value of more than half of the company's book value.

This has been reinforced by the Securities Law which requires general meeting approval for any acquisition, disposal or pledge of any asset of a public company whose value individually or collectively exceeds 20 per cent of the overall tangible assets during a whole financial year less the outstanding debts as at the date when the relevant contract was concluded. Similar restrictions apply to leases granted over the property of public companies.

23.9.4 General investor protection obligations

Any proposed action intended to counter a hostile bid should be carefully considered in the light of the general investor protection provisions contained in the Securities Law. In general, holders of securities issued by public companies must exercise the rights attaching thereto in good faith whilst observing the legitimate rights and interests of other shareholders and the priority interests of the issuer of the securities itself. Further, the positions of shareholders, members of the council of administration (board of directors) and employees of public companies may not be used abusively or fraudulently to impair rights attaching to securities or to cause prejudice to the holders thereof. The effect of these requirements upon the ability of shareholders and management of public companies to mount defences against hostile takeover bids remains to be seen.

23.10   Financial information

Romanian companies have historically been audited by the committee of censors, who are either accountants or shareholders and have various statutory powers of inspection and responsibilities to bring their findings to the attention of the shareholders. However, the use of external accountants and auditors is becoming more common. Similarly, Romanian accounting practice is being brought into conformity with international accounting standards: public companies are being given priority for the preparation of accounts which have been prepared to international accounting standards and the Securities Law contains provisions empowering the CNVM to issue regulations for the preparation of financial and accounting statements of public companies and for the audit thereof by special auditors. Financial information concerning public companies should therefore be brought into line with international accounting standards.

Although it is normal for a Romanian company to prepare accounts on an annual basis, the Securities Law allows shareholders who individually hold at least 5 per cent of the shares in a public company (or at least 10 per cent jointly) to require the managers or the censors to provide interim financial reports. The council of administration must prepare reports which may be checked by the censors before being given to the shareholders who requested them.

23.11 Market abuse

Insider trading and market manipulation are jointly addressed by the Securities Law which transposes the European Market Abuse Directive into national legislation.

"Inside information" is defined as information of a precise nature, which has not been made public, relating directly or indirectly to one or more issuers of financial instruments, or to one or more financial instruments and which, if it were made public, would be likely to have a significant effect on the prices of those financial instruments or on the price of related derivative financial instruments.

Any person who possesses inside information shall be prohibited from using that information by acquiring or disposing of, or by trying to acquire or dispose of, for his own account or for the account of a third party, directly or indirectly, financial instruments to which the information relates.

The above-mentioned provisions apply to any person who possesses inside information:

(a) by virtue of his membership of the administrative, management or supervisory bodies of the issuer;
(b) by virtue of his holding in the capital of the issuer;
(c) by virtue of exercising his employment, profession or duties;
(d) by virtue of his criminal activities.

Any person professionally arranging transactions in financial instruments who reasonably suspects that a transaction might constitute insider dealing or market manipulation is required to notify the CNVM without delay. Public institutions which disseminate statistics which may have a significant effect on financial markets must do so in a manner which is fair and transparent.

However, the prohibitions on insider dealing do not apply to transactions in a company's own shares as part of a buy-back programme or in stabilisation procedures provided that such trading is carried out in compliance with the CNVM regulations.

The prohibitions relating to market abuse apply to:

(a) operations carried out in Romania or abroad concerning financial instruments that are admitted to trading on a regulated market situated or operating in Romania or for which a request for admission to such market has been made;
(b) operations carried out in Romania concerning financial instruments that are admitted to trading on a regulated market in Romania or in a Member State or for which a request for admission to such market has been made.

The Securities Law further forbids market manipulation, which is defined as:

(a) Transactions or orders to trade:
    (i) which give, or are likely to give, false or misleading signals as to the supply of, demand for or price of financial instruments;
    (ii) which secure, by a person or persons acting in collaboration, the price of one or several financial instruments at an abnormal or artificial level.

(b)   Transactions or orders to trade which employ fictitious devices or any other form of deception or contrivance.

(c)   Dissemination of information through the media, including the internet, or by any other means, which gives, or is likely to give, false or misleading signals as to financial instruments, including the dissemination of rumours and false or misleading news, where the person who made the dissemination knew, or ought to have known, that the information was false or misleading. In respect of journalists when they act in their professional capacity, such dissemination of information is to be assessed taking into account the rules governing their profession, unless those persons derive, directly or indirectly, an advantage or profits from the dissemination of the information in question.

The CNVM is the competent authority in charge of the supervision and application of the legal provisions concerning market abuse. The CNVM may exercise its supervisory and investigation powers either alone or in collaboration with other market undertakings or the Parquet of the Supreme Court of Justice, the Commercial Registry and the police.

23.12   Financial assistance

As previously mentioned, the Company Law prohibits the giving of loans or guarantees by a company in order for its shares to be subscribed for or acquired by a third party. The only exceptions are for day-to-day operations of banks and credit companies or for employee share schemes, but such exceptions are subject to certain conditions being met.

23.13   Penalties

Breaches of the Company Law and the Securities Law are generally punishable by fines and/or imprisonment in serious cases. Liability for payment of damages may also arise in certain circumstances.

23.14   Warning

Romanian law and practice continue to change and develop. Whilst the information in this chapter is believed to have been correct at the time of writing, it should be noted in particular that the CNVM had not then issued all of the regulations to apply the Securities Law, although such regulations are expected and may have a significant effect upon law and practice. Such a situation is not uncommon in Romania and it is hoped that such regulations will be issued shortly. Consequently, and apart from the fact that a work such as this is not intended to be comprehensive and is not a substitute for specific professional advice (which should be taken before any proposed investment is made or other action taken), it is particularly important for readers to make enquiries as to whether such regulations have in fact been issued and the effect of these.

Chapter 24

Slovak Republic

Andrew Sandor, Michal Luknár and Peter Šuba

Squire Sanders sro[1]

24.1   Introduction

The Slovak Republic recorded the second highest rate of growth in Central and Eastern Europe in 2006 in terms of volume of mergers and acquisitions transactions with 103 deals being publicly announced, versus 81 in 2005. At the same time, according to PricewaterhouseCoopers, the average value of those transactions dropped from approximately €63 million to just under €32 million, perhaps indicating that the market is broadening and maturing and depending less on privatisations for growth. A good thing, too, given the current government's aversion to further privatisation.

As in previous years, in-bound investors were highly concentrated, with 63 per cent being from UK, Austria or the Czech Republic. Key sectors in 2006 included services, food and drinks and manufacturing, though in the authors' experience real estate is also an extremely active sector. While Slovak companies are just beginning to go further abroad in their investments (the authors are aware of at least a few who are seeking investment opportunities in Russia, for example), most outbound deals are focused on immediate neighbours, the Czech Republic and Hungary.[2]

The continuing strength of mergers and acquisitions trends in Slovakia is probably attributable to the country's relatively high growth rate, its business-friendly tax regime and low-wage environment, and to follow-on investments in the automotive sector. (The Slovak Republic is now the largest producer of automobiles, per capita, in the world.) One of the clouds on the horizon though is a labour market squeeze, especially in the western part of the country. Some companies have even resorted to importing labour from non-EU countries such as the Ukraine.

Almost all of the mergers and acquisitions in the Slovak Republic are the result of direct investment. The Slovak Republic does have a securities exchange

---

[1] This chapter represents the collaborative efforts of the firm's Bratislava office. Michal Luknár and Andrew Sandor were the primary authors and Tomáš Surgoš provided research assistance. The chapter is written based on Slovak law as at 1 September 2007. Subsequent amendments to the law may affect the analysis. This chapter does not constitute legal advice and should not be relied upon when making decisions.

[2] Statistics in this chapter on mergers and acquisitions activity in the Slovak Republic and in central and eastern Europe are derived from *CEE M&A Survey 2006*, a PricewaterhouseCoopers publication.

centred in Bratislava, but only a limited number of Slovak companies are listed. Indeed, in the first half of 2007 as in 2006 there were no new primary or secondary issuances of shares on the exchange, all issuances were for mortgage, bank, corporate and government bonds. Indeed, trading in equity securities accounted for only 0.15 per cent of overall financial volume in the first half of 2007. According to the exchange, total traded financial volume decreased by 18.27 per cent for the first six months of 2007 over the same period of 2006, though the number of actual transactions rose by 1.74 per cent over the same period. During the same period, market capitalisation increased by 5.5 per cent.

Although privatisations and private deals have been relatively commonplace in Slovakia, mergers and acquisitions in the Slovak Republic have become more sophisticated as the economy develops. Transactions involving special-purpose vehicles, restructurings and asset purchases as well as transactions with complicated financing structures and foreign legal elements are becoming more and more common.

As of 1 May 2007, Act no. 566/2001 Coll. on securities and investment services and on amendments of certain laws as amended ("the Securities Act") was significantly amended by Act no. 209/2007 Coll., especially with respect to squeeze-outs and mandatory public offers. This amendment has impacted the way mergers and acquisitions happen in the Slovak Republic and it is reflected here.

24.2   Acquisition targets

In the Slovak Republic there are three types of target for mergers and acquisitions: private entities, public entities and privatised state enterprises.

24.2.1   Private entities

Most companies in the Slovak Republic are privately owned and are not listed on the Bratislava Stock Exchange. Pursuant to the Commercial Code,[3] private business entities can take the form of general commercial partnerships (*verejná obchodná spoločnos*), limited partnerships (*komanditná spoločnos*), limited liability companies (*spoločnos s ručením obmedzeným*) or joint stock companies (*akciová spoločnos*).[4] Mergers with and acquisitions of such types of entities are subject to agreement with or among the controlling shareholders. Typically, for limited liability companies and joint stock companies, a proposal for a merger or acquisition will need to be approved by a resolution of the general meeting of the target entity.

---

[3] Commercial Code, Section 56.
[4] The focus of this chapter is on mergers and acquisitions affecting limited liability companies and joint stock companies only. These are described collectively as "private companies".

24.2.2 Public entities

Only a joint stock company may be deemed a public entity. The public joint stock company is a relatively new concept in the Slovak Republic. Such entities became effective on 1 January 2002 and made obsolete the previous "publicly-tradable company".[5] Pursuant to Section 154(3) of the Commercial Code, a public joint stock company is a company that issued all of its shares or part of its shares through a public call for subscription of shares[6] (a "public company"), or the shares of such company were accepted by the Bratislava Stock Exchange for trading in the securities market (a "publicly listed company"). The transfer of shares of publicly listed companies in the securities market is regulated by the Securities Act or Act no. 429/2002 Coll. on the securities exchange, as amended ("the Stock Exchange Act"). Shares may be offered to the public through a public offer[7] only after meeting certain conditions described in Section 120 of the Securities Act.[8]

24.2.3 Privatised state enterprises

As a method of increasing foreign direct investment and raising capital, the government privatised many formerly state-owned entities. Act no. 92/1991 Coll. on the terms for the transfer of state property to other persons, as amended ("the Privatisation Act"), governs the privatisation of certain large state-controlled companies.

For certain privatisations there are restrictions on the sale of the Slovak Republic's ownership interest of a state-owned enterprise. For example, Section 10(3) of the Privatisation Act states what cannot be the subject of privatisation. Pursuant to the Section 10(4), in the previous language which was effective until 1 January 2004, the Privatisation Act limited the percentage ownership of certain state-owned companies that could be sold by the Slovak Republic through the National Property Fund[9] and required that the Slovak Republic maintain majority control. In accordance with later amendments, such limitation became obsolete and the state or the National Property Fund is now only entitled to preserve certain not explicitly qualified shares. For privatisations (whether more

---

[5] Publicly tradable companies were companies for which shares were granted through an approval for the issuance of publicly tradable shares by the Ministry of Finance of the Slovak Republic.

[6] As defined in Section 154(5) of the Commercial Code, a public call for subscription means: "a call for subscription of shares made by any published means to a person not determined in advance of such publication".

[7] The public offer of shares is regulated by Sections 120 et seq. of the Securities Act. The public offer of securities under the Securities Act means any notice to a wider circle of persons in any form and any means which contains sufficient information about conditions for the public offer of securities and about the offered securities which enable the investor to purchase or subscribe for such securities as well as any placement of securities in the above manner through a trader in securities.

[8] For further information on the public offer of securities, *see* 24.8 below.

[9] The National Property Fund of the Slovak Republic ("the National Property Fund") typically acts as the vehicle to privatise a state-owned enterprise. *See*, generally, the Privatisation Act.

or less than majority ownership is transferred), acquisitions usually include the transfer of management control of the former state enterprise through management agreements and/or shareholder agreements.

24.2.4   *Participation in the acquisition targets*

Non-residents may participate in the establishment of a Slovak company or its operations and have the same rights and obligations as Slovak citizens.[10] Accordingly, non-residents can participate in any acquisition of a Slovak limited liability company or joint stock company.

24.3   Exchange and investment control

24.3.1   *Exchange controls*

Certain types of mergers and acquisitions require the participants to obtain the permission of and/or report to the foreign exchange authority, that is, the National Bank of Slovakia.[11] Mergers and acquisitions involving banks and certain types of financial institutions require such approval.[12]

Companies may trade in foreign currencies or provide foreign currency services only to the extent specified in a bank permit or in a foreign currency licence or in a permit to pursue such activity under a special law, unless the Foreign Exchange Act provides otherwise. A person authorised, as part of doing business

---

[10] Commercial Code, Section 24.

[11] Act no. 202/1995 Coll., Foreign Exchange Act, amending Act no. 372/1990 Coll. on violations, as amended ("the Foreign Exchange Act"), Section 4(1); Act no. 566/1992 Coll., on National Bank of Slovakia, as amended, Section 37.

[12] Section 28(1) of the Banking Act requires approval of the National Bank of Slovakia for:

  (a)   an acquisition or a series of related acquisition transactions of an interest in the registered capital of a bank or financial institution or in the voting rights in a bank to the extent of 5, 10, 20, 33, 50 or 66 per cent of the registered capital or voting rights;

  (b)   a merger, amalgamation or spin-off of a bank or financial institution or increase of the basic capital;

  (c)   a dissolution of a bank or a financial institution for a reason other than according to (b) or a change of its legal form;

  (d)   the sale of a bank, branch of a foreign bank or a part thereof;

  (e)   for a bank to become a subsidiary;

  (f)   for using of securities issued by the bank as a subject of securing the obligations of the security owner or other person excluding the situation when the subjects of securing are securities in the amount of 5 per cent or less of the registered capital share in one or more operations directly or acting in concert; or

  (g)   an acquisition or a series of related acquisition transactions of an interest in the registered capital of a foreign bank or financial institution or in the voting rights in a foreign bank or financial institution to the extent of 5, 10, 20, 33, 50 or 66 per cent of the registered capital or voting rights.

  Note that the threshholds provided in the Banking Act no longer correspond to threshholds stated in the Stock Exchange Act since the latter has been amended.

under a special law, to consummate certain transactions in foreign currencies or to provide certain foreign currency services may consummate such transactions or provide certain foreign currency services without a foreign currency licence only to the extent allowed under a special law.[13]

24.3.2 Controls on investment

Generally, for acquisitions of or mergers with private companies or public companies there are no restrictions on investment other than compliance with anti-monopoly requirements.[14]

Although there are no restrictions on investment in private or public companies, there are controls over investment in privatised state enterprises. Before its repeal, Act no. 192/1995 Coll. of the Slovak Republic on Ensuring the Interests of the State During the Privatisation of Strategically Important State Enterprises and Joint Ventures listed several state enterprises and categorised several strategic areas as ones that could not be sold or transferred to private entities. With the repeal, regulation of the privatisation of the bulk of those enterprises and strategic areas was moved over to the Privatisation Act, with investment controls remaining only on a few areas, such as forests and bodies of water.

24.3.3 Disclosure of significant shareholdings

Details of shareholdings of private companies are generally available for the public in the relevant commercial register (with the exception of shareholdings of joint stock companies, which are not listed in the relevant commercial register unless they have only one shareholder).

A public company must prepare a prospectus of securities for public offer, as described at 24.8.2 below, and submit it to the National Bank of Slovakia for approval. No disclosure of significant shareholding is required in the prospectus of securities for public offer.

Section 41 et seq. of the Stock Exchange Act governs the disclosure rules for publicly listed companies. A shareholder that acquired or transferred a certain threshold of shares of a publicly listed company must disclose such a purchase in writing to the issuer of the shares and the National Bank of Slovakia[15] without undue delay – no later than within four business days of purchasing the shares.[16] The relevant threshold levels are 5, 10, 15, 20, 25, 30, 50 and 75 per cent of the voting rights of the issuer attached to the shares admitted for trading on a regulated market.[17] Written notification must be sent after reaching, exceeding

---

[13] Foreign Exchange Act, Section 13(1) and (2).

[14] *See* 24.4 below for anti-monopoly rules. In addition, certain specific Acts restrict acquisitions of some entities, for example banks under the Banking Act, or insurance companies under Act no. 95/2002 Coll., as amended, of the Slovak Republic on insurance companies.

[15] Stock Exchange Act, Section 45(3).

[16] Stock Exchange Act, Section 41(11) and (13).

[17] Ibid, Section 41(1) and (2).

or dropping below any one of those thresholds. The threshold levels also apply to legal or natural persons acting in concert[18] and also, unless the Stock Exchange Act stipulates otherwise, to a person to the extent that such a person is entitled to acquire, transfer or exercise voting rights:

(a)   held by a third party with which such person concluded a written agreement that binds them to adopt a permanent common procedure with respect to the control of the respective issuer, through acting in concert with respect to their voting rights;

(b)   held by a third party based on a written agreement which temporarily provides for the transfer of a voting right in favour of such person for consideration;

(c)   attached to shares provided as security to such person on the condition that such person holds voting rights and announces its intention to exercise the rights;

(d)   attached to shares to which such person has a life right of use;

(e)   which are held or which can be exercised under (a) to (d) above by a person controlled by such person;

(f)   attached to shares deposited with such person which can be exercised by such person at its discretion, unless a shareholder gives special instructions;

(g)   held by a third party in its own name but for the account of such person;

(h)   which can be exercised by such person as an authorised representative at its discretion, unless shareholders give special instructions.[19]

A publicly listed company with shareholdings that reach, exceed or drop below one of the thresholds described above must submit in the notification the following information on:

(a)   a shareholder, even if the shareholder is not entitled to exercise the above-described voting rights, and on a person entitled to exercise voting rights on behalf of the shareholder, specifically:

   (i)   the trade name, seat and identification number, if a legal person,

   (ii)   the name and surname, permanent address and birth number, if a natural person; and if a foreign person, the date of birth shall be indicated instead of a birth number;

(b)   the final share of the persons under point (a) (above) in the voting rights;

---

[18] Ibid, Section 41(3). According to Section 66b of the Commercial Code, acting in concert is defined as actions leading to the achievement of the same goal and taken between:

   (a)   a legal entity and its partners, members or shareholders, its statutory body, members of its statutory body, members of its supervisory body, staff of the legal entity who are directly controlled by the statutory body or a member thereof, procurator, liquidator, trustee in bankruptcy, arrangement trustee of such a legal entity and parties related thereto, or between any two of the parties above;

   (b)   parties which enter into an agreement to uniformly exercise voting rights in one company in any matters concerning the management thereof; or a controlling party and a controlled party or between parties controlled directly or indirectly by the same controlling party.

[19] Ibid, Section 41(9).

(c)   the structure of the controlled legal persons' stakes through which the voting rights are actually held, if such legal persons exist,

(d)   the date of reaching, exceeding and falling below the limits.[20]

The issuer must, within three business days of delivery of the notification, publish the data contained in the notification (except for any birth certificate number or date of birth)[21] and submit them to the National Bank of Slovakia[22] (unless published by the National Bank of Slovakia itself within the mentioned period).[23] The means of publication include a newspaper with a nationwide circulation for the Member State where the issuer's securities were admitted for trading on a regulated market, or a generally accepted information system publishing official price data for securities and other financial market instruments.[24] If the issuer decides to publish the data via its web page, such data must also be published by one of the other listed means of publication.[25]

24.3.4   Notification to the Government

Generally there are no mandatory notification requirements to governmental entities when private companies seek to merge or enter into purchase and sale agreements. However, if the thresholds described at 24.4 below are met, the Anti-Monopoly Office must be notified of any contemplated merger or acquisition. As described above, with certain types of merger and acquisition there are notification requirements to National Bank of Slovakia.

Unless stated otherwise by the Securities Act, public companies may publicly offer their shares only if a prospectus for such shares, approved by the National Bank of Slovakia, has been published.[26]

For publicly listed companies involved in a merger or acquisition, notification is required when certain control thresholds are met, as described above.[27]

For privatisations, the National Property Fund must work together with the Ministry of Economy and the relevant ministry with statutory oversight over the state-owned enterprise that will be corporatised and privatised.

24.3.5   Acquiring control over publicly listed companies

There are no restrictions on purchasing shares of public companies and publicly listed companies. However, if the plan is to reach a certain threshold when purchasing shares of a publicly listed company (*see* 24.3.3 above and 24.6.3

---

[20] Ibid, Section 41(10).

[21] Ibid, Section 42(11).

[22] Ibid, Section 45(1).

[23] Ibid, Section 42(12).

[24] Ibid, Section 47(4).

[25] Ibid, Section 47(5).

[26] Securities Act, Section 120(1).

[27] The notification duty according to Section 41 of the Stock Exchange Act is described at 24.3.3 below.

below), the acquirer may have to make a mandatory public offer, subjecting the acquirer to approval by the National Bank of Slovakia.

24.3.6   Labour law considerations

As of 1 April 2002, a new labour code (codified under Act no. 311/2001 Coll., Labour Code, as amended on 1 September 2007 by Act no. 348/2007 Coll. ("the Labour Code")) came into effect and replaced Act. no. 65/1965 Coll., Labour Code, as amended. The new Labour Code is based on European Union Directives on the same subject.

The new Code requires the target company to notify its employees regarding any merger or acquisition (or sale of an enterprise or part of an enterprise, *see* 24.6.6 below) or any transfer of rights relating to its employees.[28] The former Labour Code did not have such a requirement. Section 29 of the new Labour Code states that the employer is obligated, no later than one month prior to the transfer of the rights and obligations arising out of the employment relationship, to inform the relevant trade unions in writing about the following:

(a)   the date or proposed date of the transfer;
(b)   the reasons for such transfer;
(c)   employment, economic and social consequences to the employees as a result of the transfer; and
(d)   any other contemplated items that relate to the employees as a result of the merger or acquisition.[29]

If there is no trade union, the employer still has a duty to inform its employees of the above. In addition, the acquirer, as the new employer, has a duty to inform the employees of any changes as described above.[30] However, it is interesting to note that the Labour Code does not provide for any penalties or sanctions if an employer or an acquirer does not notify the employees or relevant trade unions of the acquisition or merger. Prior to this most recent amendment, the Labour Code did not address the situation where an employee or trade union objected to a proposed merger or acquisition that would have an effect on the target company's employment obligations. Pursuant to the amendment which came into effect on 1 September 2007, however, if an acquisition alters the working conditions agreed under the employment agreement and an employee objects to such alteration, the employer terminates such employment due to redundancy or may conclude a termination agreement on the same grounds.[31]

Generally, with a merger or acquisition, the old employer's obligations to its employees transfer directly to the new employer.[32]

---

[28] Labour Code, Section 29.
[29] Ibid, Section 29.
[30] Ibid, Section 29(3).
[31] Ibid, Section 29a.
[32] Ibid, Sections 27, 28 and 31.

24.4 Merger control

In the case of any merger or acquisition, thought must be given to Slovakia's law on protection of economic competition.[33] The Anti-Monopoly Act prohibits concerted anti-competitive activity (e.g., price fixing, etc.)[34] and abuse of a dominant market position,[35] and provides for the approval of mergers and acquisitions meeting specific concentration thresholds.[36] The Slovak Republic is a notice jurisdiction with a somewhat broad definition of the types of transactions that fall within its control of any "concentration". Where certain target levels are reached, the parties to the concentration must notify the Anti-Monopoly Office of the Slovak Republic. The Anti-Monopoly Office has the power to prohibit a concentration,[37] to require adherence to certain conditions,[38] to decline jurisdiction for activities that would not adversely affect competition,[39] or to approve the concentration where there is no restriction on effective competition.[40]

The definition of a "concentration" is inclusive and may encompass primary concentration activities (*inter alia*, mergers and acquisitions) that take place in the Slovak Republic and those that take place abroad, provided that they lead or may lead to a restriction of competition in the domestic market (i.e., where there is some participation in an enterprise located in the Slovak Republic). The Anti-Monopoly Act states:

"A concentration shall be a process of an economic combining through:
(i)   merger or amalgamation of two or more previously independent undertakings; or
(ii)   the acquisition of direct or indirect control by one undertaking or more undertakings over another undertaking or undertakings, or over its part."[41]

Control includes the ability to exercise decisive influence over the activities of the target, especially through the exercise of property rights, voting rights or contractual agreement.[42] The definition of a concentration is also broad enough to include joint ventures.[43]

---

[33] Act no. 136/2001 Coll., as amended, on Protection of Competition and on Amendment of Act of the Slovak National Council No. 347/ 1990 Coll., as amended, on Organisation of Ministries and Other Central State Administrative Bodies of the Slovak Republic ("the Anti-Monopoly Act").
[34] Ibid, Section 4(1).
[35] Ibid, Section 8(6).
[36] Ibid, Section 10(1).
[37] Ibid, Section 12(6, 7).
[38] Ibid, Section 12(3).
[39] Ibid, Section 2(6).
[40] Ibid, Section 12(1, 2).
[41] Ibid, Section 9(1).
[42] Ibid, Section 9(4).
[43] Ibid, Section 9(5). *See* 24.6.5 of this Chapter for a description of joint ventures in the Slovak Republic.

24.4.1 Thresholds for mandatory notification

Not every potential concentration leads to an exercise of authority by the Anti-Monopoly Office. Only certain thresholds require notification and trigger Anti-Monopoly Office jurisdiction. There are two thresholds for determining whether the Anti-Monopoly Office has the duty to decide whether a merger or acquisition is subject to its review.[44]

The Anti-Monopoly Office has jurisdiction over a merger or acquisition in the following circumstances:

(a)   if the combined worldwide turnover of all parties concerned in the concentration is at least SKK1.2 billion and at least two of the parties concerned had an aggregate turnover in the Slovak Republic of at least SKK360 million for the accounting period prior to the establishment of the concentration; or

(b)   if at least one of the parties concerned had a total turnover in the Slovak Republic of more than SKK500 million in the prior accounting period, and at least one other party reached an aggregate worldwide turnover of SKK1.2 billion.[45]

Combined turnover is defined in the Anti-Monopoly Act as the total turnover of each of the following:

(a)   the participants to the concentration;

(b)   entrepreneurs, in which the participant of the concentration directly or indirectly:

    (i)   has a share in the basic capital that exceeds one half,

    (ii)   has more than one half of the voting rights,

    (iii) has the right to nominate more than one half of body members of the enterprise, or

    (iv) has the right to control the enterprise;

(c)   companies that have the same control rights as described under (b) in the participants to the concentration;

(d)   all other companies in which the companies referred to under (c) have similar control rights as described under (b) above; and

(e)   entrepreneurs out of which two or more mentioned under (a)–(d) jointly have the rights mentioned under (b) above.[46]

Turnover for the purposes of this test is the total revenues, yields or income from the sale of goods or services of the relevant companies. Financial aid granted to the relevant companies is also considered as part of the turnover.[47]

24.4.2 Procedure

In the case of an acquisition, the acquiring party of the requisite control level has a duty to notify the Anti-Monopoly Office.[48] The Anti-Monopoly Office may also

---

[44] Ibid, Section 10.
[45] Ibid, Section 10(1).
[46] Ibid, Section 10(2).
[47] Ibid, Section 10(3).
[48] Ibid, Section 10(11).

start a review process of its own accord.[49] Parties to a proposed merger or acquisition may also seek a non-binding opinion from the Anti-Monopoly Office before reaching the stage in the process where notification is required.[50]

A concentration subject to the control of the Anti-Monopoly Office must be reported to the Anti-Monopoly Office within 30 days of:

(a)   the conclusion of an agreement giving rise to the concentration;
(b)   the announcement of an acceptance of a bid in a public tender;
(c)   the day a decision of a state body has been delivered regarding an undertaking;
(d)   the announcement of the European Commission about acting in this matter; or
(e)   the date when the new fact arose which caused the concentration.[51]

Among other things, the notification must contain information regarding the parties to the concentration, the agreements giving rise to the concentration, and descriptions of the expected impact on the market and competition as a result of the proposed concentration.[52]

The Anti-Monopoly Office will review the proposed concentration and issue a decision regarding such merger or acquisition within 60 days of receipt of the complete required notification, unless this is extended by the chairman of the Anti-Monopoly Office. The chairman may extend the issuance of a decision to a maximum of 90 days. The periods for reviewing and issuing a decision may be delayed or interrupted if the required information regarding the proposed concentration is incomplete.[53]

24.4.3 Appeals

A party to a concentration may appeal a decision of the Anti-Monopoly Office within 15 days of the issuance of that decision.[54] Any appeal will be decided by the Anti-Monopoly Office. The office will review appeals within the time periods set out above.

24.4.4 Sanctions

The Anti-Monopoly Office also has the power to levy fines[55] which, depending on the significance of the violation, can be as high as 10 per cent of a violator's turnover for the previous accounting period, or up to SKK10 million where it is not possible to calculate turnover (or there is no turnover, or turnover is less than SKK10,000).[56] The Anti-Monopoly Office may levy a fine of up to SKK5 million if a party to a concentration fails to submit documents or information needed

---

[49] Ibid, Section 25(1) and (2).
[50] Ibid, Section 10(10).
[51] Ibid, Section 10(9).
[52] Ibid, Section 10(12).
[53] Ibid, Section 11.
[54] Ibid, Section 34(1).
[55] Ibid, Section 38.
[56] Ibid, Section 38(1).

within the requisite time period, or submits incorrect or incomplete documentation.[57]

Generally, the Anti-Monopoly Office has broad powers of investigation[58] and the authority to publish its notifications and decisions.[59] However, when issuing such public notifications and decisions, the Anti-Monopoly Office must consider the entrepreneur's right to protect its business secrets and confidential information. There is also a provision permitting civil litigation by private parties who can claim violation of consumer rights or unlawful restriction on competition, and penalties under the Civil Code are permissible.[60] There has been little civil litigation in Slovak courts, but the potential risk of such litigation and fines imposed by the Anti-Monopoly Office itself underscores the importance, especially in years to come, of securing an undisputed anti-monopoly clearance.

24.5   Regulation of the conduct of mergers and acquisitions

24.5.1   Private companies

Once a decision has been made by a private party to acquire another private entity, generally there are no special regulations that affect the conduct of the parties as they proceed to complete the acquisition. As discussed above, the Anti-Monopoly Office may place conditions on an acquisition, and as a result of such a decision the parties' conduct with respect to the transaction may be altered.

There are more issues related to a merger or amalgamation transaction than to an acquisition between private parties. Besides any conditions that may be imposed by the Anti-Monopoly Office pursuant to the Anti-Monopoly Act, amendments to the Commercial Code have introduced new provisions which relate to mergers and amalgamations of companies that may affect the parties' conduct.

Draft contracts regarding mergers and amalgamations must be reviewed not only by the relevant statutory bodies of each of the companies being merged or subject to the amalgamation, but also by an independent auditor.[61] The statutory bodies of the parties subject to the transaction must propose an independent auditor to the relevant Registry Court.[62] The Registry Court will then approve

---

[57] Ibid, Section 38(5).

[58] Ibid, Section 22(1) (general provisions); Section 22(2)(a)–(b) (access to business records, legal documents, and the right to require oral or written explanation "on the spot"); Section 22(3) (the right to enter premises, land or means of transportation on the basis of a special authorisation); and Section 22(4) (inspection of the office by the employees).

[59] Ibid, Section 24(1)–(3).

[60] Ibid, Section 42.

[61] Commercial Code, Section 218(a)(2).

[62] A Registry Court is a court maintaining a commercial register. Pursuant to the Commercial Code, Section 27(1), a commercial register is a public register containing data prescribed by law on various types of entities. For the matters related to the Commercial Register, a new Act was adopted, Act no. 530/2003 on Commercial Register, as amended, effective as of 1 February 2004 ("the Act on Commercial Register").

the independent auditor, who will have access to the relevant entities involved in the merger or amalgamation and the proposed documentation. After completing its evaluation, the independent auditor must submit its report to the shareholders of the contracting parties as well as to the Registry Court. If the shareholders approve the draft contract (generally through a general meeting of each of the merging companies), the contract and the evaluation of the independent auditor will be placed in the commercial register by the Registry Court. Given that any merger or amalgamation contract will be available for public inspection, private entities may seek to put as little information into the document as possible to avoid disseminating too much information to competitors.

With respect to mergers and amalgamations, the Commercial Code requires, unless otherwise provided, that the company being dissolved and the company receiving the transferred assets of such company have the same legal form.[63]

24.5.2 Public companies

To accomplish a merger or acquisition of a public company, a proponent must follow the procedure described in 24.8.3 below to acquire the requisite approval of the National Bank of Slovakia before publishing the public offer to the shareholders.

24.5.3 Publicly listed companies

If there is a voluntary public offer for acceptance or mandatory public offer for acceptance regarding a publicly listed company, the proponent must present a written proposal of the offer to the National Bank of Slovakia,[64] which may accept or reject the written proposal before it is published for prospective shareholders.[65] This regulation of the offer proposals forces proponents to make a transparent arm's-length bid and seeks to discourage a deceptive or lower-than-market offer.[66]

24.5.4 Privatised state enterprises

The Privatisation Act describes natural monopolies and specifically references certain state enterprises as natural monopolies.[67] The Slovak Government, after discussing the goals and procedures for privatisation with the National Council of the Slovak Republic (the Parliament), is the only entity that can decide to privatise a natural monopoly. Amendment no. 253/1999 Coll. to the Privatisation Act limited the amount of share capital of a monopoly company that might be offered for privatisation. In the past, only 49 per cent of the shares of such

---

[63] Commercial Code, Section 69(2).
[64] Securities Act, Section 115(1).
[65] Ibid, Section 117.
[66] For a detailed explanation of the voluntary and mandatory public offers for acceptance, *see* 24.6.2 and 24.6.3 below.
[67] Privatisation Act, Section 10(2).

monopolies could be sold to a private investor. Amendment no. 564/2003 effective as of 1 January 2004 amended that Section. Based on the resolution of the Government, the state or the National Property Fund may now sell majority ownership in the legal entities mentioned in the Privatisation Act.

Pursuant to the Privatisation Act, before a privatisation is approved the potential target company must develop a proposal describing the financial position of the state enterprise and the expected privatisation procedure.[68] The Privatisation Act details the prerequisites for any such proposal as well as the requirements for corporatisation of a state enterprise set for privatisation and the transfer of property from a state enterprise entity to its corporatised successor.[69] Draft privatisation proposals are mainly produced by the state enterprises set for privatisation; however, this is not a set rule. The Ministry of Economy coordinates and oversees the process, approves any proposal and may require the state enterprise set for privatisation to provide a more detailed proposal.[70]

After the Ministry of Economy approves the project and the Slovak Government has issued a decision approving the transaction, the relevant ministry, as the original founder of the state enterprise set to be privatised, will issue a resolution on dissolution without liquidation of the enterprise. The dissolution will be effective as of the date specified by the National Property Fund which overseas the corporatisation of the relevant state enterprise. The corporatisation usually takes the form of a joint stock company, and the successor joint stock company will be established on the day following the dissolution of the state enterprise.

The National Property Fund assists and cooperates with the Ministry of Economy and the founding ministry of the entity to be privatised throughout the whole process. Prior to the establishment of the new corporatised entity, the National Property Fund acts as the auditor for the state enterprise company and reconciles, with the approval of the Ministry of Economy, the accounts of that company with the statements listed in the privatisation project.[71]

On the day of dissolution, the property of the state enterprise is usually transferred to the National Property Fund, and the National Property Fund acts as the sole shareholder of the newly established joint stock company. However, with natural monopolies, the Privatisation Act provides that the relevant ministry (the founder of the original state enterprise) act as the shareholder of the corporatised entity and have the ability to exercise shareholder's rights over such newly created entity.[72]

The Privatisation Act does not specify any deadlines for the issuance of any of the above resolutions or decisions. The privatisation process is coordinated and conducted by the relevant authorities and it is within their discretion to set the deadlines for the relevant steps to be taken.

---

[68] Ibid, Section 6.
[69] Ibid, Section 6.
[70] Ibid, Section 7(3).
[71] Ibid, Section 29(2).
[72] Ibid, Section 47d(1).

After the state enterprise is corporatised, the National Property Fund will proceed with a tender to receive bids for the sale of a certain portion of the shares of the newly created entity, and, after selecting a winning bidder, the National Property Fund will proceed with the sale. The Privatisation Act does not specify any conditions related to the structure or the contents of the tender rules. Pursuant to the Privatisation Act, the rules must comply with the Slovak Government's privatisation decision and must specify criteria for the selection of the bidders.[73]

24.6 Methods of acquisition

The methods employed for mergers and acquisitions vary greatly depending on the characteristics of the acquirer and the target or the two merging entities. Generally, a merger or acquisition will occur through private agreement between the acquirer and the target company or the two merging entities. Public companies may be the subject of a public offer only when the prospectus of securities for public offer has been approved by the National Bank of Slovakia and published in compliance with the provisions of the Securities Act. Mergers and acquisitions for publicly listed companies can take place through voluntary public offers for acceptance or mandatory public offers for acceptance. For privatised state enterprises, acquisitions usually occur through a tender process.

24.6.1 Private agreements

The use of private agreements is the most common form of merger or acquisition.[74] Most private agreements are in Slovak and are governed by Slovak law. However, if there is a foreign entity involved, the agreements will often be in another language and governed by a foreign law, usually English. Generally, agreements concluded in another language and/or governed by a foreign law are accepted and enforceable in the Slovak Republic provided at least one of the parties thereto is non-Slovak or there is another non-Slovak element.

The typical agreements employed in an acquisition are as follows:

(a) a share purchase agreement, transfer of ownership interest agreement, or sale of enterprise agreement;
(b) a shareholders agreement or ownership agreement;
(c) an escrow agreement; and
(d) amended articles of association or amended articles of organisation.

---

[73] Ibid, Section 10a(3).
[74] The Commercial Code provides in Section 69 only for general legal regulation of merger or amalgamation of companies. In contrast, an amalgamation is where two or more companies wind up without liquidation and a new company is established from the wound-up companies, while a merger is where one company (to be dissolved) is merged into another company. In the event of an amalgamation, the business assets of the dissolved companies pass to the successor company resulting from the amalgamation. In the case of a merger, the business assets of the dissolved company pass to the company into which the dissolved company is merged.

While a share purchase agreement is the common type of agreement used in acquisitions of joint stock companies, in acquisitions of limited liability companies a transfer of ownership interest agreement is used.

Transfer of ownership interest agreements are governed by the Commercial Code. The Commercial Code distinguishes between the transfer of ownership between members and the transfer of ownership to a third person.[75] Transfers of ownership interests among members are generally allowed with the consent of the general meeting of the limited liability company unless the memorandum of association of the limited liability company states otherwise. On the other hand, transfers of ownership interests to third persons are generally not allowed unless the memorandum of association of the relevant limited liability company states otherwise. In the transfer of ownership interests to a third person, the member transferring its ownership will guarantee the payment of a contribution by a transferee.

24.6.2 *Voluntary public offers for acceptance*

Pursuant to the Securities Act, voluntary public offers for acceptance may be made for publicly listed companies (shares of which have been accepted for trading on a regulated securities market).[76] Voluntary public offers for acceptance may be made for a portion, or all, of the shares issued by a publicly listed company.[77]

Once a decision has been made to make a voluntary public offer for acceptance, the decision must be published and reported, in writing, to the board of directors of the target company and the National Bank of Slovakia without undue delay. Within 10 business days of the publication, the proponent must submit for approval the written form of the proposal for public offer for acceptance accompanied by the documents proving the publication to the National Bank of Slovakia.[78] The National Bank of Slovakia must subsequently approve or reject the proposal within 10 business days, or it may within five business days ask the proponent to qualify (supplement or rectify) the information submitted.[79] The decision of the National Bank of Slovakia may not be appealed.[80] The bid proposal may be published and submitted to the target company's board of directors only after the National Bank of Slovakia has approved the voluntary public offer proposal.[81]

The voluntary public offer proposal must be equal for all owners of substitutable equity securities of the target company.[82] Data specified in the proposal of the takeover bid must be complete and true, prepared with professional care, it may

---

[75] Commercial Code, Section 115.
[76] Securities Act, Section 114.
[77] Ibid, Section 114(1).
[78] Ibid, Section115(1).
[79] Ibid, Section 117(1).
[80] Ibid, Section 117(4).
[81] Ibid, Section 116(6).
[82] Ibid, Section 116(4).

not be deceptive or misleading, and it must provide to shareholders of an offeree company, well in advance, all available information so that shareholders can adopt an informal decision on the takeover bid. The legal or natural person making the offer shall be responsible for the accuracy of this data.[83] The proponent must also disclose the current concentration amount of its shareholding in the target company. Other types of information that must be published with the price per share are described at 24.11.1 below.

A voluntary public offer for acceptance may be revoked or modified only if it is expressly stated in the proposal that revocation is an option. However, the voluntary public offer for acceptance may not be revoked if it has already been accepted by an interested party.[84] Any revocation or modification of a voluntary public offer for acceptance after its publication is subject to the consent of the National Bank of Slovakia.[85] Once a voluntary public offer expires, the legal or natural person making the offer must publicly announce the results in the same manner in which the proposal was published.[86]

24.6.3 *Mandatory public offers for acceptance*

If a legal person or natural person, by itself or together with persons acting in concert with it, obtains shares of a publicly listed company in an amount sufficient to control at least 33 per cent of the voting shares of the publicly listed company, then the controller or controllers of such shares must make an offer for acceptance of all the shares of the listed company.[87] These mandatory public offer obligations do not apply to:

(a)   any natural person or legal person which has acquired controlling shares in a publicly listed company as a result of a public offer for acceptance in accordance with Securities Act.;

(b)   any legal successor entering into all rights and obligations of a shareholder of a publicly listed company if such shareholder has fulfilled the obligation under Securities Act or if legal succession does not result in an increase of such shareholder's shares in the voting rights in the publicly listed company;

(c)   any natural person or legal person acquiring a publicly listed company's shares by the purchase of an enterprise or part thereof by the procedure laid down in special law if this does not result in an increase of their shares in the voting rights in the publicly listed company; and

(d)   any natural person or legal person acting in concert with another natural or legal person if their total shares in the voting rights in the publicly listed company together with persons acting in concert is not changed and only changes to the internal structure of such shareholdings are made.[88]

---

[83] Ibid, Section 116(5).
[84] Ibid, Section 118a(1).
[85] Ibid, Section 118a(3).
[86] Ibid, Section 118(4).
[87] Ibid, Section 118g(1).
[88] Ibid, Section 118g(2).

The price offered for shares in a mandatory public offer for acceptance must be fair when compared to the value of a publicly listed company's shares. The fact that consideration is fair must be proved by an expert opinion. It may not be less than the highest price provided by an offeror or a person acting in concert with the offeror for a publicly listed company's shares for the last 12 months prior to creation of the obligation to announce the mandatory public offer for acceptance, and at the same time it is not lower than the consideration determined by an expert opinion and at the same time cannot be lower than the value of net equity including the value of intangible assets of an enterprise per share according to the last financial statements audited prior to the creation of the obligation to announce the mandatory public offer for acceptance. As for listed shares, fair consideration may not be also lower than an average price of such shares reached on the Stock Exchange during the 12 months prior to the creation of the obligation to announce the mandatory public offer for acceptance.[89] Once made, the mandatory public offer for acceptance may not be withdrawn.[90]

The procedure for making the mandatory public offer for acceptance is the same as for the voluntary public offers for acceptance described at 24.6.2 above. In the same manner, the National Bank of Slovakia must approve the mandatory public offer proposal, and the proposal must be published and reported to the issuer of the shares.[91]

24.6.4   Participation in tenders

As described above, for some privatisations the process of acquisition is achieved through participation in tenders. There are no set rules as to how a tender must be handled. Pursuant to the Privatisation Act, tender rules must be in compliance with the privatisation decision of the Slovak Government and must specify criteria for the selection of the bidders.[92] Throughout the tender process the Slovak Government should strive to create a competitive and transparent atmosphere.

24.6.5   Joint ventures and associations

A joint venture is not recognised under the Commercial Code as a distinct legal entity. However, joint ventures can take many forms, including joint stock companies and limited liability companies. A joint venture is considered to be a contractual arrangement between two or more parties to achieve a particular goal. Generally, the joint venture is regulated by the cooperation agreement entered into by the parties.

A cooperative action may not necessarily take the statutory form of a business entity, and such a joint venture may be regulated as an association. Generally, associations are governed by Act no. 40/1964 Coll., Civil Code, as amended ("the

---

[89] Ibid, Section 118g(5)–(6).
[90] Ibid, Section 118g(13).
[91] Ibid, Section 118g(10).
[92] Privatisation Act, Section 10a(3).

Civil Code"). Article 829 and following of the Civil Code defines an association as:

(a)   a non-legal entity;
(b)   a membership to achieve a common goal; and
(c)   a membership where each member is obligated to conduct activities to achieve established goals in a manner set forth in an agreement and is obligated to refrain from activities that would hinder such goal.[93]

Each member of an association is deemed to have an equal interest in the assets of the association unless the association agreement provides otherwise,[94] and all assets acquired by the joint activity of the association are co-owned by each member.[95]

Associations are normally not used, primarily because all members of an association have joint and several liability with respect to third parties.[96] Even after the termination of a member's participation, that member is liable for any obligations incurred up to the date of the termination.[97]

24.6.6   Asset transactions

As many Slovak joint stock companies and limited liability companies are riddled with debt, many foreign investors prefer asset acquisitions to an acquisition of the entire company and its debt obligations. There are numerous methods of structuring an asset transaction in the Slovak Republic, and most involve negotiations with the secured creditors of the company holding the target assets.

In addition to straight asset sales, Slovak law makes provision for so-called sale of an enterprise or sale of part of an enterprise. These constructs combine the tax features of asset sales with certain features of a stock or ownership interest sale, namely the transfer by operation of law of liabilities and employees.

24.6.7   Increasing shareholdings

One method of acquisition or merger is acquisition through subscription, or the increase of shares in the target company in consideration for an investor's contribution of certain tangible or intangible assets. Often, subscription will be regulated by the corporate statutes of a company or through an existing shareholders agreement.

By law, for limited liability companies and joint stock companies, the existing members or shareholders, as the case may be, have a pre-emption right over any subscription for shares.[98] This pre-emption right is irrespective of any such rights

---

[93] Civil Code, Sections 829 and 830.
[94] Ibid, Section 835(1).
[95] Ibid, Section 834.
[96] Ibid, Section 835(2).
[97] Ibid, Section 840.
[98] Commercial Code, Sections 143(1) and 204a.

mentioned in a shareholders agreement. Such a pre-emption right can be restricted in the memorandum of association of a limited liability company;[99] however, such rights cannot be restricted or excluded in the articles of association of a joint stock company.[100] Thus, if a merger or acquisition takes place through a subscription for shares, the pre-emption rights of the existing owners of interests must be taken into account.

24.7   Preparation of an offer

24.7.1   *Preliminary steps and conduct of negotiations*

There is usually an informal approach to begin acquisitions of, or mergers with, private companies in the Slovak Republic, followed by due diligence. Letters of intent and confidentiality agreements are becoming more common in merger and acquisition transactions, particularly when a foreign entity is involved. When these devices are used, the binding provisions of letters of intent are usually governed by foreign laws.

For the acquisition of or merger with a public company, due diligence is also conducted as a preliminary step. Offers may follow through a public call or takeover announcement.

For most privatisations, a tender is announced by the Slovak Government. Interested parties will then submit bids pursuant to the tender rules. Normally, due diligence on the target and management interviews are allowed before binding bids are submitted.

24.7.2   *Due diligence*

An acquirer or merger partner will want to learn as much as possible about the target company and will often require access to the target's business and financial information before submitting an offer to the target company. The Commercial Code has been amended so that more information about a company can be discovered through public means. However, the acquirer or merger partner must rely more often upon private disclosure gained through its due diligence.

Due diligence investigations are common with respect to large transactions in the Slovak Republic. The length and the scope of a due diligence investigation depends on the nature of the contemplated transaction, the risk aversion of the investor and the characteristics of the target.

24.7.3   *Commercial extract*

The primary source of information relating to any Slovak company is the Commercial Register or Collection of Deeds (as described below). After paying

---

[99] Ibid, Section 143(1).
[100] Ibid, Section 204a(5). The pre-emption right may only be restricted or excluded by a resolution of the general meeting if there is "serious interest" on the part of the company to have such a restriction.

an administrative fee, anyone may obtain an extract from the Commercial Register,[101] which must contain the following data:

(a) the business name and the registered office (in the case of legal entities) or the name, if different from the business name, the date of birth, the birth certificate number, the residence and the place of business, if different (in the case of individuals);

(b) the identification number;

(c) the scope of business or the scope of activities;

(d) the corporate form (in the case of legal entities);

(e) the name, the residence, the date of birth and the birth certificate number (if any) of the individual who was appointed as statutory body or its member, together with details concerning the conduct on behalf of the legal entity and the date of his appointment or, as appropriate, removal. If a legal entity is appointed as a statutory body, its business name, registered office and identification number (if any) shall be recorded, together with the name, residence, the date of birth and the birth certificate number (if any) of the individual who was appointed as its statutory body;

(f) the designation, address and scope of business or scope of activities of a branch or another organisational unit of the enterprise, and the name, residence, the date of birth and the birth certificate number (if any) of its director, the date of his appointment or, as appropriate, removal;

(g) the name, the residence, the date of birth and the birth certificate number (if any) of the procurist(s), together with details concerning the conduct on behalf of the entrepreneur, the date of his appointment or, as appropriate, removal;

(h) the name, the residence, the date of birth and the birth certificate number (if any) of the individual who was appointed as member of a supervisory body, together with the date of his appointment or removal, as appropriate, in case the registered party has a supervisory body;

(i) termination of the legal entity and the reason for its termination;

(j) date of the beginning and the end of the liquidation;

(k) the name and the residence, date of birth, birth certificate number of the individual or business name, the seat and identification number of the legal entity who was appointed liquidator, together with details concerning the conduct on behalf of the legal entity, the date of his appointment or removal, as appropriate;

(l) decision of the court on invalidity of the legal entity;

(m) information on announcement and the end of the bankruptcy;

(n) the name, mark and office address of the individual registered in the Commercial Register as a trustee appointed for a bankruptcy proceeding, restructuring proceeding or composition proceeding. If a legal entity is appointed as a trustee, its business name, mark and the office address shall be recorded;

(o) date of the issuance of the restructuring decision or composition decision and date of the end of these proceedings;

---

[101] A non-authoritative copy of the extract may be downloaded from the internet at www.orsr.sk.

(p) starting of official conservatorship;

(q) name, address, date of birth and birth certificate number, if any, of individual, or business name, seat and identification number, if any, of legal entity appointed as a trustee for execution of official conservatorship and its representative;

(r) the legal grounds for the deletion of the company; and

(s) other facts required by special laws.[102]

Each business form also has specific requirements for Commercial Register entries:

(a) with regard to limited liability companies – names and residences of members or, as appropriate, business names (designations) and registered offices of the legal entities; which are members; the amount of the pledged and paid-up registered capital; the individual amounts of each member's pledged and paid-up contributions;

(b) with regard to joint stock companies – the amount of a joint stock company's subscribed and paid-up registered capital; number, class, form, type and nominal value of its shares, and any restrictions of the transferability of such registered shares. If there is a sole shareholder, the name and residence or the business name (designation) and registered office of such a shareholder;

(c) with regard to cooperatives – the amount of a cooperative's reference capital plus amounts of the basic members' contributions; and

(d) with regard to state-owned enterprises – the name of the founder of a state-owned enterprise and the basic capital of the enterprise concerned.[103]

The Act on Commercial Register regulates the Collection of Deeds, an institution that is an integral part of the Commercial Register ("the Collection of Deeds"). A company is obliged to file the following documents with the Collection of Deeds within 30 days of issuance:

(a) the memorandum of association; establishment deed or founders' deed of a company or establishment agreement; any power of attorney authorising the execution of the above or, as appropriate, a notarial deed containing minutes from the constituent general meeting of a joint stock company or a decision of founders of the joint stock company to establish the same; a notarial deed containing the decision to establish a cooperative; together with the respective annexes and the articles of association, if any; with respect to legal entities other than the above, their incorporation documents to the extent prescribed by special legislation;

(b) any amendment to the memorandum of association, establishment deed or founders' deed of a partnership or company, or to the articles of association of a joint stock company, including the decision on the change of legal form; with respect to legal entities other than the above, any amendment to their incorporation documents;

---

[102] Act on Commercial Register, Section 2(1).
[103] Ibid, Section 2(2).

(c)   the full version of the documents referred to in (a) above incorporating any amendment referred to in (b) above;

(d)   trade licence;

(e)   a deed containing the name, surname, residence, date of birth and birth number of a natural person (if any), proving the appointment to the office or expiration of the office of: persons who are a statutory body or members of the statutory body; procurist; the head of enterprise or head of branch of enterprise registered in the Commercial Register; liquidator; bankruptcy trustee; restructuring trustee or arrangement trustee; compulsory receiver and deputy compulsory receiver; together with their specimen signatures;

(f)   a document showing the name, residence, date of birth and the birth certificate number, if any, of the individual, proving the appointment and removal from the position of the member of supervisory board;

(g)   ordinary financial statements and extraordinary financial statements, consolidated financial statement, preliminary financial statements and annual reports of the registered party, together with the auditor's report, as appropriate, and the name and residence of the auditor or the business name, registered office and identification number of the legal entity which was appointed as auditor, together with the number of the entry of the auditor in the register of auditors;

(h)   any decision of a court ordering a liquidation; the final report from a liquidation including the date of termination of the liquidation;

(i)   any decision of a court ordering the winding up of a registered party without liquidation;

(j)   any decision of a court on invalidity of the registered party;

(k)   any bankruptcy order made by a court, restructuring decision or composition decision made by court; any decision of a court to terminate the proceedings expressed above; any decisions of the court amending or overriding the types of decisions expressed above or any decision of the court to replace the bankruptcy trustee, restructuring trustee or composition trustee;

(l)   the official appraisal;

(m)   announcement of deposit trustee;

(n)   any merger agreement or split-up agreement of a company;

(o)   agreement on transfer of the entity or its part; and

(p)   other documents specifically prescribed by special law.[104]

Finally, in the case of a non-resident company that does business in Slovakia, the following documents (officially translated into Slovak) must be filed in the Collection of Deeds:

(a)   financial statements prepared and published by the non-resident party pursuant to its governing law (branches of foreign banks are exempt from this duty);

(b)   the establishment deed of the non-resident party and its articles of association, if any, together with any amendments thereto;

---

[104] Ibid, Section 3(1).

(c)   the certificate of registration of the non-resident party for the Commercial Register or other register if such a registration is required pursuant to the governing law;

(d)   the Trade Licence;

(e)   deed of proof of any encumbrance on property in the territory of the Slovak Republic owned by the non-resident party if the effectiveness of such security depends on publication;

(f)   specimen signature of the head of enterprise of a foreign person or head of branch of enterprise of a foreign person;

(g)   deed of proof that bankruptcy has been declared; that restructuring, arrangement or commencement of other similar proceedings has been permitted, if it relates to a foreign person, and termination of such proceedings;

(h)   deed of proof of the winding-up of a foreign person; and

(i)   other documents specifically prescribed by special law.[105]

Pursuant to the Commercial Code,[106] joint stock companies, limited liability companies, cooperatives and state-owned enterprises must file their financial statements with the Collection of Deeds after their approval by the respective statutory body.

Each company has to file the required documents within 30 days of their issuance. Pursuant to Section 27 of the Commercial Code, the Commercial Register and the Collection of Deeds is a public list of data.

The information available in the Commercial Register and the Collection of Deeds is significant and is available for public inspection (after the payment of an administrative fee). There is a wealth of information that can be used in the preliminary stages of any merger or acquisition.

24.8   Conduct of a public offer[107]

24.8.1   *Notice to the National Bank of Slovakia and the Bratislava Stock Exchange*

In the case of public companies and publicly listed companies, certain notification obligations merit mention. In short, transactions such as mergers and acquisitions involving public companies require notification to the National Bank of Slovakia by the shares issuer.[108] Transactions such as mergers and acquisitions involving publicly listed companies require notification both to the National Bank of Slovakia and the Bratislava Stock Exchange.[109]

---

[105] Ibid, Section 3(2).

[106] Commercial Register, Section 40.

[107] For detailed information regarding the conduct of a voluntary or mandatory public offer for acceptance, *see* 24.6.2 and 24.6.3 above.

[108] Stock Exchange Act, Section 132b

[109] *See* the Stock Exchange Act. The Bratislava Stock Exchange is a privately held joint stock company, although the state continues to hold a percentage of the equity. The rules of the Bratislava Stock Exchange are amended periodically and interested persons are directed to seek the current version.

As of 1 May 2007, the Securities Act no longer expressly defines the types of changes that require special notification to the National Bank of Slovakia by a publicly listed company through a public offer for acceptance. However, the issuer of shares must notify the National Bank of Slovakia on all issuer-related confidential information,[110] which is, *inter alia*, the information likely to affect the exchange rate or the price of these shares.[111]

The Stock Exchange Act imposes some additional requirements for publicly listed companies. The shares issued by publicly listed companies may only be accepted by the regulated market of the Stock Exchange if:

(a)   such security is an investment tool;
(b)   it is a substitutable security;
(c)   its transferability is not restricted;
(d)   such security is a book-entered security;
(e)   any foreign security is issued pursuant to the laws of the country of the issuer's registered office;
(f)   the Stock Exchange is not aware of any facts that would, in case the security is accepted for trading on the regulated market, lead to damage incurred by investors or to a serious threat;
(g)   prospectus of a security has been prepared and published;
(h)   the subscription price of shares was paid out;
(i)   its subscription was successfully concluded on the basis of the public offer or if the deadline for accepting the request to subscribe for shares has elapsed; and
(j)   other requirements in accordance with the Act are met.[112]

A publicly listed company must file an application with the relevant Stock Exchange market. The application must contain the prospectus of a security. An application for the admission of a security on the market in listed securities must relate to all securities of the same type and form issued by the same issuer, to which the same rights are attached. If the terms and conditions prescribed by generally binding legal regulations and Stock Exchange rules have been met, the Stock Exchange shall admit a security onto the market on the basis of the application filed by the issuer within 60 days from the delivery thereof.[113]

The Stock Exchange also requires notification of important changes to publicly listed companies, which are set out in Section 36 of the Stock Exchange Act and also in the Stock Exchange Regulations of the Bratislava Stock Exchange. Publicly listed companies must publish all the information mentioned in Sections 34 to 36, Section 37d and Section 41 of the Stock Exchange Act and in other legal regulations.

In addition to its financial statement, a publicly listed company must also publish its consolidated financial statements, if it has prepared any.[114] A publicly listed

---

[110] Stock Exchange Act, Section 132b.
[111] The prohibition on the use of confidential information for gain (insider trading) is addressed in Sections 132 and 134 of the Securities Act (confidentiality obligation), and at 24.13.1 below.
[112] Stock Exchange Act, Section 29.
[113] Ibid, Section 26(1)–(6).
[114] Ibid, Section 34(1) and (3).

company must promptly notify the Stock Exchange of, and publish, if required, any information requested by the Stock Regulations in order to verify whether the issuer is following the conditions laid down by the Stock Exchange Act and to ensure that the regulated market with securities works properly. If the issuer does not publish such information, it might be published by the Stock Exchange subsequent to a discussion with the issuer.[115] A publicly listed company must also send a proposal for any change in its memorandum of association, or founder's deed, to the Stock Exchange no later than the convening date of the company general meeting that is to make a decision concerning such proposed change.[116]

If a publicly listed company issues new shares admitted for trading on a listed market of the securities, it must request their listing within six months of the issuance.[117]

24.8.2   *Public companies: contents of the prospectus for securities for public offer*

As discussed in this Chapter, a public company may publicly offer shares only if the prospectus of securities for public offer has been approved by the National Bank of Slovakia and published accordingly.

24.8.3   *Contents of the prospectus for public offer for acceptance*

For publicly listed companies, a prospectus for public offer for acceptance must contain the data set out in Section 121 of the Securities Act. The prospectus must be approved by the National Bank of Slovakia on the request of the issuer, the announcer of a public offer of securities or a person requesting to be admitted for trading on a regulated market.[118]

The prospectus must contain all data which is necessary, pursuant to the specific nature of an issuer and securities which are being offered in a public offer or admitted for trading on a regulated market, to allow investors to properly assess the issuer, its assets and liabilities, financial condition, profit and loss and perspectives and persons which accepted guarantees for the repayment of securities or proceeds and rights attached to such securities. The prospectus must also contain data about the issuer, data about the securities which are being offered in a public offer or admitted for trading on a regulated market, and a summary of the prospectus ("the summary"), which will briefly and clearly specify basic data about the issuer, security, a person which accepted a guarantee for the repayment of securities or proceeds and risks attached thereto. The summary must also contain a note that:

(a)   it represents an introduction to the prospectus;
(b)   any decision of an investor to invest into securities should follow from the assessment of the prospectus as a whole;

---

[115] Ibid, Section 37d(1).
[116] Ibid, Section 37b(4).
[117] Ibid, Section 37d(2).
[118] Securities Act, Section 125(2).

(c) in the event of filing a court petition related to data contained in the prospectus, an investor – the plaintiff – may be obliged to bear the translation costs of the prospectus prior to the commencement of judicial proceedings in the relevant Member State;

(d) if damage occurred as a result of the fact that the summary contained misleading or incorrect information and such information was in discrepancy with other parts of the prospectus, liability for damage shall be borne by the responsible persons.[119]

The issuer, or its statutory body, governing body or supervisory body, one who makes a public offer of securities, a person requesting to be admitted for trading on a regulated market or a person which accepted a guarantee for the repayment of securities or proceeds, or a person which prepared a prospectus, is responsible for the data specified in it. Responsible persons must be clearly designated in the prospectus: for physical persons this includes their name, surname and title, and for legal persons it includes trade name or name and seat. The prospectus must also contain a representation of such persons, that to their best knowledge, the data contained in the prospectus reflect the issuer's factual status and that nothing has been omitted in the prospectus which could affect its significance for the correct assessment of an issuer or securities which are being offered in a public offer or admitted for trading on a regulated market. If a person responsible for the data specified in the prospectus has provided incorrect or untrue data, such a person shall be held liable for damage caused thereby. A person responsible for the summary or the translation thereof shall be responsible for damage incurred as a result of the fact that the summary contained misleading or incorrect data or such data was in discrepancy with other parts of the prospectus.[120]

24.8.4 *Publication of the prospectus and procedure for the offer*

An issuer, one who makes a public offer of securities or a person requesting to be admitted for trading on a regulated market, shall be obliged to publish the prospectus reasonably well in advance of making a public offer of securities or admitting for trading on a regulated market, but no later than on the day of the beginning of the public offer of securities or the beginning of trading with the relevant securities on a regulated market. In the case of the first public offer of securities, which have not been admitted for trading on a regulated market and which are to be admitted for trading for the first time, the prospectus must be published no less than six business days before the end of such offer.[121] The publication of the prospectus means:

(a) publication in a nationwide daily for Member States, in which the public offer is made or a request is made for admitting for trading on a regulated market;

(b) a written disclosure statement available free of charge in the operational premises of a regulated market on which the securities are being admitted for trading or in the seat of an issuer, in the operational premises of

---

[119] Securities Act, Section 121(1) and (2).
[120] Securities Act, Section 121(12) and (13).
[121] Ibid, Section 125a(1).

financial institutions placing or selling securities and in the operational premises of persons which ensure the repayment of the nominal value of securities and the payment of proceeds from securities;

(c)   disclosure in an electronic form on the website of the issuer, on the website of financial institutions placing or selling securities and on the website of persons which ensure the repayment of the nominal value of securities and the payment of proceeds from securities;

(d)   disclosure in an electronic form on the website of the regulated market on which admission for trading is requested; or

(e)   disclosure in an electronic form on the website of the National Bank of Slovakia if the National Bank of Slovakia has decided to provide such service.[122]

24.9   Defences to a hostile offer

Under Slovak law there are very few protections against hostile offers. Aside from the ultimate right to accept or reject an offer, Slovak companies generally have the instruments described below, which may be used as protection against unwelcome offers.

24.9.1   *Transfer-blocking clauses*

It is possible in the Slovak Republic to restrict and condition the transferability of registered shares by the company's consent, but only for private companies. Such a manoeuvre requires careful drafting of the statutes of the private company. If a private joint stock company issues registered shares it may secure protection against a hostile offer by placing transferability restrictions on such shares. For instance, the statutes may stipulate that the transfer occur subject to consent. The Commercial Code allows the private company to restrict, although not to prohibit, transfers of shares.[123]

Limited liability companies are protected against hostile bids by the fact that the transfer of an ownership interest to a third person is possible only where a memorandum of association permits such action. The consent of the general meeting to such a transfer may be required by the memorandum of association.[124]

Where a joint stock company is a public company or a publicly listed company, there is no effective means of protecting against, or even restricting, a hostile offer.[125]

24.9.2   *Authorised capital*

It is also possible to manipulate the authorised capital of the company. For a limited liability company, the memorandum of association generally contains the

---

[122] Ibid, Section 125a(2).
[123] Commercial Code, Section 156(9).
[124] Commercial Code, Section 115(2).
[125] Securities Act, Section 19(2).

preferential right of current members to assume the obligations for new contributions to the limited liability company. For a joint stock company, current shareholders generally have pre-emption rights for the subscription of newly issued shares in the joint stock company in the event of an increase in the registered capital of such companies.

Specifically for limited liability companies, the device to increase the registered capital may protect against a hostile offer by securing the rights of current partners to preferentially assume an obligation for new contributions within a period specified in the memorandum of association.[126] In cases where current members do not use their preferential right, the law provides the company with another level of protection in that a new member of the company must declare that it accedes to the limited liability company's memorandum of association.[127] This pre-emptive right preserves the shareholder's right to maintain his interest in the company.

For joint stock companies, one basic protection against a hostile offer is the current shareholders' right to preferential acquisition of any bonds (which do not increase the registered capital) issued by a company.[128] Where there is an increase in the registered capital, current shareholders have the right to preferential subscription of the shares increasing the registered capital pro rata to the nominal value of their shares to the amount of the existing registered capital.[129] This right cannot be excluded by the statutes of the joint stock company, but it can be acted on by the General Meeting based on important interests of the joint stock company.[130]

24.9.3 Poison pills

Another technique is to prepare the memorandum of association of a (private) limited liability company or the statutes of a private joint stock company so that it contains the requirement for the approval by the general meeting of any transfer of an ownership interest or shareholding to a third party. As noted above, for public companies, any decision related to the ownership structure of the company must be promptly reported in writing to the National Bank of Slovakia. For publicly listed companies, any decision related to the ownership structure of the company must be promptly reported in writing to the National Bank of Slovakia and the Stock Exchange.

24.9.4 Private limited liability companies

For private limited liability companies and joint stock companies, their protection against hostile offers comes from their very nature. Because they are private, these companies can simply reject any offer for the purchase of their shares or assets.

---

126 Commercial Code, Section 143(1).
127 Ibid, Section 143(3).
128 Ibid, Section 160(1) and (5).
129 Ibid, Section 204a(1).
130 Ibid, Section 204a(5).

Merger or amalgamation requires the consent of all members of the dissolving companies and the successor companies, unless the memorandum of association or law states otherwise.[131] The separate approval of any amendments to the memorandum of association for any successor company is required, in addition to approval of the transfer documents themselves.[132]

Slovak law provides some further statutory protection for the limited liability company. Any contract for amalgamation or merger must be approved by the general meetings of all companies that are being dissolved and by the General Meeting of any successor company in a merger.[133]

Executives of companies participating in a merger or amalgamation must convene a general meeting and deliver to all members of the dissolving companies invitations and deeds that contain detailed information and descriptions of the transaction.[134] If requested by a member of a company being amalgamated or merged, a draft contract on amalgamation or merger for each of the companies involved must be investigated by an auditor, who should then prepare a written report on the results of the investigation.

24.9.5   *Protection for joint stock companies*

Provisions regarding merger and amalgamation apply to private as well as to public joint stock companies.[135] The law requires that, upon the proposal of the board of directors, a court-appointed independent auditor should investigate each company to be merged or amalgamated.[136] The board is further obligated to prepare a detailed written report justifying the legal and economic grounds for amalgamation or merger, and including the share exchange ratio. The report is to be reviewed by the Supervisory Board who will submit to the general meeting its position to the intended amalgamation or merger.[137] The transfer must be approved by two-thirds majority of the votes of shares of the present shareholders upon the proposal of the directors, after a 30-day notice and review period. Slovak law precisely specifies numerous documents in the Commercial Code which are required to enable the shareholders to make an informed decision regarding the intended transaction.[138]

Again, the successor company to any merger or amalgamation must approve any changes to the statutes of the company together with the transaction details. The shareholders of a successor company who do not agree with a contract on amalgamation or merger are entitled, under certain circumstances, to require the successor company to purchase their shares acquired in the exchange.[139]

---

[131] Ibid, Section 69(7).

[132] Ibid, Section 69(10).

[133] Ibid, Section 152a(2) and (3).

[134] Ibid, Section 152a(4).

[135] As described at 24.2.1 and 24.2.2 above, a joint stock company may be a private company, a public company or a publicly listed company.

[136] Commercial Code, Section 218a(2) and (3).

[137] Ibid, Section 218b(1) and (2).

[138] Ibid, Section 218c(1) and (2).

[139] Ibid, Section 218j(1).

There is no effective means of protecting against a hostile offer for a public or publicly listed joint stock company. The company cannot restrict the transfer-ability of its shares or the decision-making capacity of its shareholders regarding an offer for securities. The publishing and notice provisions requiring approval prior to publishing by the National Bank of Slovakia are the only possible protection.[140]

24.9.6 State enterprise (privatised company)

As privatisation is the only way of acquiring control over a state enterprise, this Section covers only the process of privatisation. The Privatisation Act provides no effective means of protecting a state enterprise against a hostile offer since it cannot in any way affect a decision concerning which company shall privatise such state enterprise. The state authority adopting a decision on the privatisation (i.e., the Government or Ministry of Economy) is responsible for the selection of the investor.

Pursuant to Section 10(11) of the Privatisation Act:

> "a decision with regard to privatisation is not a public procedure. All privatisation proposals submitted for properties or interest in the business of another legal entity that are submitted with the prescribed period are taken into consideration, as well as all other proposals received in accordance with Section 8(4). The privatisation decision shall be put in writing and delivered to the entity which elaborated the privatisation proposal or submitted the Section 8(4) proposal, depending on which proposal was selected for implementation."

A more detailed description of the privatisation process is given at 24.5.4 above.

24.10 Profit forecasts and asset valuations

24.10.1 Private companies

Private companies in the Slovak Republic are not required to prepare special valuations. Often, however, a potential investor in a target will want access to a company's books and financial statements, particularly any fiscal reports, and will want the target company to allow the investor's auditors or evaluators to have access to information to generate forecasts and valuations.

Pursuant to the Commercial Code, joint stock companies (including private joint stock companies) must prepare annual reports and an auditor must verify any annual report or extraordinary financial statements.

Pursuant to the Act no. 431/2002 Coll., as amended, of the Slovak Republic on Accounting ("the Accounting Act"), under certain conditions the financial

---

[140] Securities Act, Section 114, regulating voluntary public offers for acceptance; *see* also 24.6.2 above. Securities Act, Sections 118g and 119, regulating mandatory public offers for acceptance; *see* also 24.6.3 above.

statements of limited liability companies must be verified by an auditor.[141] Typically the executives of a limited liability company or the board of directors of a joint stock company are responsible for the preparation of the financial statements for that company. Financial statements and annual reports must be filed with the appropriate commercial register within 30 days of their approval by the General Meeting of a limited liability or joint stock company. An annual report must include information mentioned in Section 20 of the Accounting Act.

For any merger or acquisition, such financial statements and audited reports will be a focal point for the transaction.

24.10.2   *Public companies and publicly listed companies*

Public companies and publicly listed companies must include all relevant information about their financial status in their prospectus of a security for public offer.[142]

However, in addition, public companies and publicly listed companies are subject to the notification duty in Section 132b of the Securities Act. For publicly listed companies Sections 34 to 36, Section 37d and Section 41 of the Stock Exchange Act also apply.

24.10.3   *State enterprises*

Financial evaluations of a state enterprise form an integral part of determining whether such state enterprise will be corporatised and privatised. The financial evaluations contain part of the privatisation proposals which are submitted to the relevant Ministry governing a state enterprise ("the Founder's Ministry"), and the Founder's Ministry will use the information in determining whether the state enterprise will be privatised. Slovak law requires detailed information to be included in the privatisation proposal, including:

---

[141] Section 19(1) of the Accounting Act requires that each accounting unit must have its financial statements audited by an auditor if:

   (a)   it is a corporation for which creation of registered capital is compulsory; or

   (b)   it is a corporation which in the preceding financial year met at least two of the three following criteria:

       (i)   the total amount of business assets exceeded SKK20 million;

      (ii)   the net turnover exceeded SKK40 million (whereas the net turnover for this purpose means the revenues from the sale of products or goods or from the provision of services); or

     (iii)   the average number of employees exceeded 20.

[142] A prospectus of a security for public offer must contain all of the data which is necessary, pursuant to the specific nature of an issuer and securities which are being offered in a public offer or admitted for trading on a regulated market, to allow investors to properly assess the issuer, its assets and liabilities, financial condition, profit and loss and perspectives and persons which accepted guarantees for the repayment of securities or proceeds and rights attached to such securities. (Securities Act, Section 121(1).)

(a)   the designation of an enterprise and specifications of assets to be privatised under such project;
(b)   a list of real property being privatised, information about the manner in which the state acquired such property and specifications of any claim for the delivery thereof;
(c)   specifications of part of assets not usable for business purposes and the manner of disposal of such assets;
(d)   the evaluation of privatised assets;
(e)   the manner of a transfer of privatised assets including the settlement of claims of eligible persons;
(f)   in the establishment of a trading company, the specifications of its legal form;
(g)   in the establishment of a joint stock company, the manner of share allocation, the interests thereof, or types, if any, as well as data on the scope of the use, if any, of investment vouchers;
(h)   in a sale, the manner thereof, a proposal for the price, payment terms and conditions as well as a proposal for investments and other terms of the sale which may be considered in negotiating the purchase price or as a reason for reduction of part of the purchase price;
(i)   the distribution of privatised assets among individual assignees (output privatised units);
(j)   the determination of a legal successor to the rights and obligations related to privatised assets, including unknown ones; and
(k)   the manner of a transfer of intellectual property rights discussed with the Industrial Property Office of the Slovak Republic if such rights are the property of an enterprise.[143]

24.11   Documents from the offeror and offeree boards

24.11.1   *Proposals for voluntary and mandatory public offers for acceptance*

Slovak law makes no requirement for proposals between private companies. Public companies do not issue proposals for public offers as their required information is contained in the prospectus of securities for public offer.

The proposal for a voluntary public offer for acceptance regarding the acquisition of shares of publicly listed companies must contain the following data:

(a)   trade name or name, seat and legal form of an offeror, if legal person; or name, surname, residence and date of birth of an offeror, if natural person; if the offeror acts in its own name but for the account of another person, also a trade name or name and seat of the legal person, or name, surname, residence and date of birth of a natural person, for the account of which the offeror is acting;
(b)   trade name and seat of an offeree company;
(c)   trade name and seat of a trader in securities or a foreign trader in securities who shall organise for an offeror the acquisition of securities of an

---

[143] Privatisation Act, Section 6(1).

offeree company based on a takeover bid and that shall ensure acts necessary for its realisation;

(d) period of validity of a takeover bid, which cannot be less than 30 calendar days or more than 70 calendar days, unless this Act stipulates otherwise; commencing on the day of publishing of the takeover bid;

(e) the specification of a number, class, type, nominal value and ISIN of shares to which the takeover bid relates;

(f) the specification of a number, class, type, nominal value of shares of an offeree company, to which voting rights are attached, which are owned by an offeror or by persons acting in concert with the offeror, including data on the time of their acquisition and acquisition price and data on the sale of shares of the offeree company by such persons for the last 12 months;

(g) the specification of the number (quantity) of securities that an offeror undertakes to acquire, including data as to whether the bid relates to the acquisition of all or only some of the shares of an offeree company ("partial takeover bid");

(h) the specification whether an offeror asserts a condition for a minimum number of shares which it undertakes to acquire; in such a case an offeror shall specify also the manner and period within which it shall notify the persons, who have accepted the takeover bid, whether the condition has been met or not;

(i) the consideration offered for the shares of an offeree company; in case of a proposal to purchase shares of an offeree company, it shall indicate the price offered per share of the same class and nature; for a proposal to exchange shares of an offeree company for other securities, it shall indicate the number, class, nature, type and nominal value of such securities and exchange rate for the shares of the offeree company; the price or exchange rate for substitutable securities must be determined in the same manner for all persons to whom the takeover bid is addressed;

(j) methods used to determine the purchase price or exchange rate under point (i) above including the specification of whether the method used reflects proceeds of an offeree company and the value of the assets, including immovable assets of the offeree company, and whether the value of the assets and the proceeds of the offeree company were calculated on a pro rata basis for each share of the offeree company according to proportional percentage of the share in the registered capital of the offeree company;

(k) data on the resources and manner of financing of liabilities of an offeror resulting from the takeover bid and data on any assumed indebtedness of an offeror relating to the performance of these liabilities;

(l) manner in which a takeover bid may be accepted, including procedure and manner of the conclusion of the share purchase agreement or agreement on exchange of shares for other securities; the manner, conditions and procedure in the payment of the purchase price or exchange of the securities;

(m) rules for withdrawal of the acceptance of a takeover bid or withdrawal from the share purchase agreement for other securities concluded as a result of the acceptance of a takeover bid;

(n)   targets and intentions of an offeror in relation to an offeree company; at each time it shall indicate those targets and intentions which relate to the future use of assets of an offeree company, the preservation of activities of such company, reorganisation of the offeree company and companies controlled by the offeree company; changes in the statutory and supervisory authorities of the offeree company, changes in the number of employees, and employment conditions, and the participation of employees in the profit or management;

(o)   compensation offered for non-assertion of rights, if the regime of non-assertion does not apply to an offeree company, including the data on the method used to determine its amount, and on the manner, conditions and procedure of the provision of the compensation;

(p)   name, surname and residence of a person acting in concert with an offeror or with an offeree company, if natural person, or trade name or name, seat and legal form of such person, if legal person; in the case of legal persons, also their relationship with the offeror and the offeree company shall be indicated;

(q)   the specification of the law of the state which shall govern the share purchase agreements or agreements on exchange of shares for other securities concluded in relation to the takeover bid between an offeror and shareholders of an offeree company, and the specification of the court of jurisdiction which shall resolve disputes out of the takeover bid;

(r)   other information and facts which may have an effect on a decision of shareholders of an offeree company regarding the takeover bid.[144]

The proposal for a mandatory public offer for a publicly listed company must contain all of the preceding data as well as the date the obligation to announce a takeover bid arose, the reasons for announcement of such bid, and description of methods applied to determine an amount of consideration. In addition to the proposal for a mandatory takeover bid, an offeror shall be obliged to also submit to the National Bank of Slovakia documents proving an amount of consideration provided by the offeror or persons acting in concert with the offeror over the 12 months prior to the creation of the obligation to announce the mandatory takeover bid.[145]

24.11.2   *Documents from the offeree board*

There is no requirement for the offeree to produce any documentation.

24.12   Squeeze-out right and sell-out right

24.12.1   *Squeeze-out right*

An offeror who has made an offer for acceptance that was not partial or conditional has the right to demand that all remaining shareholders of the offeree

---

[144] Securities Act, Section 116(2).
[145] Ibid, Section 118g(12).

company transfer to it their shares for adequate consideration ("the squeeze-out right") if the offeror is a holder of shares with the total nominal value of not less than 95 per cent of the registered capital of the offeree company carrying voting rights and also carrying not less than 95 per cent of voting rights in the offeree company.[146] The squeeze-out right may be exercised by an offeror not later than within three months from the expiration of the validity period of an offer for acceptance; otherwise such right shall cease to exist.[147] An offeror who has decided to exercise the squeeze-out right is obliged to notify without undue delay the offeree company, the National Bank of Slovakia and all the remaining shareholders of the offeree company and also specify the facts based on which it has become entitled to such right. For this purpose, the Central Depository shall provide to the offeror, at its written request, a list of shareholders of the respective issuer and their pledgees.[148] The squeeze-out right shall be effective vis-à-vis affected shareholders only upon consent granted by the National Bank of Slovakia. The National Bank of Slovakia shall grant consent to an offeror only if the conditions for the exercise of this right are met. Simultaneously with the filing of the request for consent, the offeror may exercise the squeeze-out right vis-à-vis shareholders. Simultaneously with the sending of the draft share purchase agreement and, if the exchange for other securities is offered, also a draft agreement on the exchange of shares for other securities, the offeror must send them a notice that this right is subject to the consent of the National Bank of Slovakia.[149]

An obligor shall accept a draft agreement within the time limit set out in the draft agreement, otherwise within the time limit of 10 business days from the granting of consent from the National Bank of Slovakia. If the obligor does not accept such a draft agreement within the time limit, the offeror may, not later than three months from the lapse of the mentioned time limit, apply to the court for specific performance, otherwise such right shall cease to exist.[150]

As to the content of the draft agreement, the offeror shall specify mainly the following:

(a)   the amount of consideration including the grounds for the amount of consideration;
(b)   time allowed for acceptance of the draft agreement;
(c)   time and procedure for realisation of the securities transfer.[151]

The consideration for the exercise of the squeeze-out right must be adequate when compared to the value of shares of an offeree company and may be in the form of cash consideration, securities or a combination of these two forms. If an offeror offers at least part of the consideration in the form of securities, it must offer also cash consideration as an alternative.[152]

---

[146] Ibid, Section 118i(1).
[147] Ibid, Section 118i(5).
[148] Ibid, Section 118i(3).
[149] Ibid, Section 118i(4).
[150] Ibid, Section 118i(8) and (9).
[151] Ibid, Section 118i(5).
[152] Ibid, Section 118i(6) and (7).

24.12.2 Sell-out right

The provisions applying to the squeeze-out right, as discussed at 24.12.1 above, also apply mutatis mutandis to the sell-out right.[153] A shareholder owning the remaining shares of an offeree company shall be entitled to request from an offeror who has made an offer for acceptance that was not partial or conditional to acquire from such a shareholder its shares for adequate consideration ("the sell-out right") if the offeror becomes a holder of shares with the total nominal value of not less than 95 per cent of the registered capital of the offeree company carrying voting rights and also carrying not less than 95 per cent of voting rights in the offeree company.[154] Such a remaining shareholder may exercise the sell-out right not later than three months from the lapse of the term of an offer for acceptance, otherwise such a right shall cease to exist. The remaining shareholder shall exercise such right by sending a draft share purchase agreement. It shall primarily specify in the draft agreement:

(a)   the required adequate cash consideration or adequate consideration in the form of securities;
(b)   a time limit for acceptance of the draft agreement;
(c)   a time limit and procedure for the transfer of securities.[155]

The obligor, that is, the offeror, must accept the draft agreement in a period specified in the proposal, otherwise in the period of 10 business days from its delivery. If the obligor does not accept the draft agreement in such period, the obligee may, not later than three months from the expiration of the mentioned period, apply to the court for specific performance, otherwise the right shall cease to exist.[156]

24.13   Insider dealing and market manipulation

An issuer of shares has an affirmative duty not to disclose untrue or misleading information or to withhold information important for an investor to make a determination whether to purchase the issuer's shares.[157] Providing false information or not providing vital information that could impact purchasing or selling decisions is considered market manipulation and an issuer may be liable for such acts or non-acts.

24.13.1 Insider trading

The Securities Act specifies certain information as confidential information of investment tools accepted for the business at the Stock Exchange which might bring any benefit to its owner or other physical or legal person. Confidential information is considered to be:

---

153 Ibid, Section 118j(5).
154 Ibid, Section 118j(1).
155 Ibid, Section 118j(2).
156 Ibid, Section 118j(3).
157 Ibid, Section 112.

(a)   non-published information;
(b)   information regarding one or more issuers of one or more investment tools accepted for the business at the Stock Exchange or other fact that is important for development of the exchange rate or the price of one or more investment tools; and
(c)   information that can affect the exchange rate or the price of listed shares of an issuer.[158]

Any legal or physical person who has a participation in the registered capital of the issuer, or who on the basis of their employment or position obtains confidential information, is prohibited from:

(a)   using such information to his benefit or to another person's benefit;
(b)   disclosing or giving access to such confidential information, unless properly authorised; or
(c)   advising anyone to buy or sell securities based on such confidential information.[159]

Such bans or prohibitions apply equally to individuals obtaining confidential information from employees or insiders with access to such confidential information.

24.13.2   *Market manipulation*

The Securities Act also prohibits market manipulation,[160] which it defines as:

(a)   a transaction or instruction to conduct a transaction ("instruction"), which gives or is capable of giving untrue, false or misleading signals on an offer, demand or prices of financial instruments ("false signals"), or which will cause the achievement or maintaining of the price of the financial instrument at an unnatural or artificial level; market manipulation does not occur if such transaction or instruction is based on a legal ground and is conducted in accordance with Stock Exchange rules or common market practice;
(b)   a transaction or instruction conducted by using fraudulent acts or machinations; or
(c)   dissemination of information capable of giving false signals, including spreading false or misleading news (subject to legal exceptions).

Market manipulation, as described above, primarily involves:

(a)   ensuring a dominant position, price fixing or creation of other unfair business terms and conditions;
(b)   purchasing or selling financial instruments in the final stage of a business day on the regulated market for the purpose of misleading investors acting on the basis of/pursuant to the closing prices; or

---

[158] Ibid, Section 132(1).
[159] Ibid, Section 132(9).
[160] Ibid, Section 131a(4).

(c)   abusing access to the means of publication in order to express an opinion influencing the market and subsequently benefiting from it without disclosing an existing personal conflict of interests.

This list of activities is not exhaustive – there are further factors laid down by the Securities Act which must be considered when assessing whether other activities may be market manipulation. The most important factors are:

(a)   the share of the transactions in the daily volume of transactions;
(b)   the extent of ability to cause a significant change in prices, exchange rates or valuations; and
(c)   a combination of transactions or instructions with dissemination of false information.

In addition, the National Bank of Slovakia is entitled to issue legal regulations providing further details about what market manipulation means and the criteria for assessing whether certain conduct may be viewed as market manipulation.

The National Bank of Slovakia, *inter alia*, is the regulatory body that controls the securities market and has the ability to impose various types of fines and sanctions if it discovers insider dealing or market manipulation. The sanction or penalty imposed depends on the degree of the transgression.

24.13.3   *Sanctions under criminal law*

In addition to the sanctions imposed under the Securities Act, criminal sanctions may be imposed for insider dealing and market manipulation. Pursuant to Act no. 300/2005 Coll. of the Slovak Republic, as amended ("the Criminal Code"), a person found guilty of misrepresenting information in such a manner that it affects the price of securities will be sentenced to between six months and three years in prison, or alternatively they could be sentenced to community service, fined or prohibited from taking certain actions in the future.[161] The length of the prison term may be extended to up to 12 years if greater damage or certain circumstances occur.

In addition, according to the Criminal Code, anyone found guilty of insider trading or an employee procuring a benefit for himself or another through the use of non-public information gained through employment with a company may be sentenced to up to three years in prison, sentenced to community service, fined or prohibited from taking certain actions in the future. If the benefit is considered to be large, the sentence can be between seven and 12 years in prison.[162]

24.14   Financial assistance

There are no requirements or procedures for financing a merger or acquisition in the Slovak Republic, but a foreign exchange permission from the National

---

[161] Criminal Code, Sections 259, 54, 56 and 61.
[162] Ibid, Sections 265, 54, 56 and 61.

Bank of Slovakia need no longer be secured before the payment of a portion of the purchase price with foreign securities (although there are certain notice provisions).

Any type of financing method may be employed for an acquisition or merger, including stock-for-stock transactions, contribution of assets in lieu of cash and delayed payment schemes. Some acquisitions or takeovers are structured as leveraged transactions in which debt financing is secured in order to complete the purchase of assets or shares. However, Section 161(e) of the Commercial Code prohibits leveraged buyouts, whereby the target itself lends the financing necessary for the takeover, or the assets or shares of the target are pledged to secure such financing.

Chapter 25

Slovenia

Srečo Jadek
Partner
Jadek & Pensa

25.1 Introduction

Since the early 1990s, Slovenia has dismantled the old economy and set up a new one. The former socially owned companies have been almost entirely privatised. The legal framework applicable to mergers and takeovers was defined in 1993 when the first Companies Act came into force. Based around the Companies Act, several other pieces of legislation and secondary legislation have been passed through the Parliament. Changes in the Companies Act were also introduced, mainly to make Slovenian legislation conform with EU Directives. In particular, mergers and takeovers (as well as split-ups) of companies are now strictly regulated. The new legislation regulates the power of different supervisory institutions and has significantly broadened it.

Mergers and takeovers in Slovenia are now regulated by two main laws: the Companies Act – 1 (the latest substantial changes came into force in May 2006) and the Takeover Act – 1, which was adopted pursuant to Directive 2004/25/EC that came into force in August 2006. There is also some other secondary legislation, mainly adopted by the Securities Market Agency, which has to be taken into account.

The Companies Act – 1 is the most important Act and it applies to commercial companies and regulates all necessary corporate issues related to the carrying out of their business. One part of the Act regulates mergers and transformation of the companies (i.e., the rules and merger procedure). The Takeover Act – 1 is the basic law which regulates the procedure for acquiring a qualifying holding (i.e., takeover) of stakes.

The Securities Market Agency issued 30 authorisations for takeover bids in 2004; in 2005 they issued 16; and in 2006 they issued 23 authorisations.

In Slovenia there is only one regulated official market where shares of listed companies are traded, that is the Ljubljana Stock Exchange. In September 2007, the market capitalisation on the Ljubljana Stock Exchange was €26.6 billion and shares of listed public limited companies represented 74 per cent of the market capitalisation.

25.2   Acquisition targets

From the M&A regulations point of view Slovenian companies may be divided into the following two categories:

(a)   companies for which the Takeover Act – 1 applies. These are listed companies and public limited companies not publicly traded which have at least 250 shareholders and at least €4,172,962 share capital as of 31 December of the year preceding the year that is relevant for the purpose of assessment of the application of the Takeover Act – 1; and

(b)   all other unlisted companies for which the Takeover Act – 1 does not apply.

The Companies Act – 1 defines the following corporate forms of company with share capital:

(a)   a limited liability company;
(b)   a public limited company;
(c)   a limited partnership with share capital; and
(d)   a European public limited company.

Only shares of public limited companies may be listed on the Ljubljana Stock Exchange. The majority of Slovenian companies are limited liability companies. The majority of Slovenian public limited companies are not listed.

There are companies (limited liability companies and public limited companies) in which the Republic of Slovenia has a shareholding. If the Republic of Slovenia's shareholding represents a majority shareholding in a particular company and if the value of the shareholding is more then €600,000, the following regulate the acquisition procedure:

(a)   the Public Financial Act;
(b)   the Decree on the sale and other forms of disposing of financial assets of state and municipalities; and
(c)   the individual programme of sale adopted by the Slovenian Government.

25.3   Foreign exchange and investment controls

In general, the acquisition by foreign investors of shares issued by Slovenian companies is not subject to any foreign exchange control restrictions or authorisation requirement. For some specific companies (i.e., banks, insurance companies, brokerage companies, etc.) some other pieces of legislation, which define specific requirements for their business, also have to be observed. In principle, foreign individuals and foreign legal persons are allowed to invest in Slovenia without any limitation, although some areas are still restricted.

Foreign participation is limited in the following sectors:

(a)   the field of production and trade with military equipment (the approval of the Slovenian Government is required);
(b)   media (maximum 20 per cent);
(c)   banks (10, 20, 33 and 50 per cent or more of shares is subject to approval by the Bank of Slovenia);

(d)   management companies (10, 20, 33 and 50 per cent or more of shares is subject to the approval of the Securities Market Agency);

(e)   insurance (10, 20, 33 and 50 per cent or more of shares is subject to approval by the Insurance Supervision Agency).

Shareholders acquiring or alienating any voting right in companies for which the Takeover Act – 1 applies, resulting in achieving, exceeding or ceasing to exceed a 5, 10, 15, 20 and 25 per cent, 1/3, 50 and 75 per cent share of voting rights, shall notify thereof the company and the Securities Market Agency in four working days.

Besides notification requirements described above and if certain thresholds are met, acquisition of shares must be notified according to the Prevention of the Restriction of Competition Act ("PRCA") (*see* 25.4 below).

25.4   Merger control

The competition aspect of mergers is regulated by the Prevention of the Restriction of Competition Act which came in force in 1999 and was amended in 2004 (to implement Council Regulation (EC) No. 1/2003) and again in 2007.

Merger control applies to concentrations when:

(a)   two or more independent undertakings merge;

(b)   one or more persons already controlling at least one undertaking, or one or more undertakings acquire whether by purchase of securities or assets, by contract or by any other means, direct or indirect control of the whole or parts of one or more other undertakings;

(c)   two or more undertakings create a joint venture performing on a lasting basis all of the functions of an autonomous economic entity.

Thresholds for mandatory notification are defined in the PRCA and a concentration must be notified if:

(a)   the combined aggregate annual turnover of all companies concerned, including affiliated companies, exceeds €33.3 million before tax in the Slovenian market in each of the last two years; or

(b)   all of the companies concerned, including affiliated companies, jointly achieve more than a 40 per cent market share in Slovenia, or a substantial part of it, with goods or services which are the subject of the transaction, or with their substitutes.

The party acquiring the control over the other undertaking has to notify the Competition Protection Office ("CPO") within one week of the signing of an agreement or the announcement of a public bid or the acquisition of a controlling interest, whichever occurs first. Until the CPO issues a decision following the first stage of concentration assessment, parties to a concentration are not allowed to exercise any rights acquired by the concentration.

Within 30 days of receipt of the notification the CPO has to issue either:

(a) a decision declaring that the proposed concentration does not fall within the scope of the PRCA;

(b) a decision that it will not oppose the concentration and that the concentration is compatible with the competition rules; or

(c) an order commencing the second-stage assessment of the concentration, because it raises serious doubts as to its compatibility with the competition rules.

If the CPO decides to enter into substantive assessment of the concentration, it has 90 days to either:

(a) approve the proposed concentration (subject to conditions if necessary); or

(b) oppose the proposed concentration and to order measures to eliminate any effects of the prohibited concentration that have already occurred.

A legal entity failing to notify a concentration, or failing to do so within the time limit can be penalised with fines from €25,000 to €83,400.

25.5 Merger of public limited companies

25.5.1 *General*

Two or more public limited companies may merge by:

(a) a merger by acquisition that shall be carried out by the transfer of all the assets of one or more public companies (company being acquired) to another public limited company (acquiring company) in exchange for the provision of shares of the acquiring company;

(b) a merger by formation of a new public limited company (acquiring company) to which all of the assets of the merging companies (company being acquired) are transferred in exchange for the provision of shares of the acquiring company.

The form of the merger according to the Companies Act has to be decided by the management board and, if required by the by-laws, the prior approval of the respective supervisory board has to be given. The general meeting of shareholders decides on the merger. Prior to that, certain documentation has to be drafted, also to be voted on at the general meeting of shareholders, and certain authorisations must be acquired, if necessary. What follows is a brief outline of the required documentation.

25.5.2 *Agreement on merger*

Agreement on merger is an important document which has to be prepared by the management board and approved by the shareholders of two or more public limited companies which merge. According to the law it must have the following elements:

(a) firms and registered offices of the merging companies;

(b) agreement on the transfer of assets of the acquired company in exchange for the shares of the acquiring company;

(c)   specification of the share exchange ratio;

(d)   in case of any cash payments:

      (i)   the amount of the cash payment, which must be expressed in a monetary amount per whole share in the company being acquired,

      (ii)   the statement to the effect that the cash payment will be provided by the acquiring company;

(e)   a description of the procedures in connection with the transfer of the shares in the acquiring company and the cash payment;

(f)   the date from which the shares will participate in the profit of the acquiring company;

(g)   the date from which the actions of the company being acquired shall be treated as being carried out for the account of the acquiring company;

(h)   measures taken for the exercise of the rights of holders of special rights;

(i)   all of the special benefits that will be provided to members of management and supervisory bodies.

25.5.3 Report on merger

The report on merger is an obligatory legal, economic and organisational analysis explaining the grounds of the merger agreement, criteria for the evaluation of assets and the calculation on which the share exchange ratio is based. It has to be made out separately by each management board of the two or more public limited companies and must contain an explanation of and grounds for the merger agreement and the share exchange ratio. It must also state criteria for the evaluation of assets used as a basis for determining the share exchange ratio.

25.5.4 Appointment of merger auditors

The merger auditor for a particular company shall be appointed by the court. If the management boards of all companies participating in the same merger agree, they may jointly propose to the court to appoint one or more auditors to audit all merging companies. By law the auditors are obliged to produce a written report which must contain the grounds for the proposed share exchange ratio with the following specifications:

(a)   methods applied in calculating the proposed share exchange ratio;

(b)   arguments proving the adequacy of the applied methods;

(c)   what share exchange ratios would be arrived at by applying different methods;

(d)   when more than one evaluation method is applied simultaneously, the weight attached to each.

25.5.5 Review of a merger by supervisory board

The supervisory boards of each of the companies participating in the merger have to review an intended merger on the basis of the report on the merger by the management and the report on the audit. The supervisory board shall draw up a written report on its review.

25.5.6 General meetings of shareholders of the merging companies

At least one month prior to the session of the general meeting that is to decide on consent for a merger, the following important documents shall be made available to the shareholders:

(a)   the merger contract;
(b)   the annual reports of all companies for the past three years;
(c)   if the last annual report refers to a financial year which ended more than six months prior to the concluding of the merger, interim balance sheets of these companies;
(d)   the reports of the management;
(e)   the auditors' reports on the merger; and
(f)   the supervisory boards' reports on the merger.

A general meeting resolution giving consent to a merger shall require a majority of at least three-quarters of the subscribed capital represented in the voting. A general meeting may give its consent either before or after a merger contract is entered into.

25.5.7 Execution of the merger agreement

A merger agreement has to be entered into in writing in the form of notarial record.

25.5.8 Appointing the representative

Each of the companies being acquired has to appoint a representative to receive the shares of the acquiring company which have to be provided to the shareholders of the company being acquired and any cash payments.

25.5.9 Registration and legal consequences of a merger

Merger shall be registered by the commercial court register competent for the acquiring company. If the acquiring company increased the subscribed capital for the purpose of the merger, the increase shall be entered in the register at the same time as the merger.

The entry of the merger in the register shall have the following legal consequences:

(a)   the assets of the companies being acquired shall be transferred to the acquiring company together with their liabilities;
(b)   the companies being acquired shall be wound up;
(c)   the shareholders of the companies being acquired shall become shareholders of the acquiring company.

25.5.10 Actions that shareholders may take in case of controversy

The general meeting resolution giving consent to the merger may be contested for general reasons but cannot be contested for the following reasons:

(a)   because the exchange ratio determined in the merger contract or cash payments are not appropriate;
(b)   because the amount of the monetary compensation is not appropriate;
(c)   because the explanation of the exchange ratio and potential cash payments in the reports are not in accordance with the law.

In these cases a shareholder may demand settlement in the form of an additional cash payment from the acquiring company by lodging a proposal for a court test of the exchange ratio.

25.5.11   *Labour law considerations*

According to the Law on Workers Participation on Management which came in force in August 1993, the workers' council (if it exists) or workers (if there is no workers' council) should be informed about important corporate issues 30 days before a decision is reached. Thereafter, in the next 15 days the workers' council has to be consulted.

25.6   Takeovers

25.6.1   *Introduction*

The Slovenian Takeover Act – 1 applies to:

(a)   listed securities;
(b)   securities traded in an organised market;
(c)   securities of a target company having registered capital in amount of at least €4,172,926 and at least 250 shareholders.

The term "securities" is used for voting shares and call options. In determining the proportion of voting rights of a person in the company for the purpose of the Takeover Act – 1, account shall be taken of the voting rights derived from:

(a)   securities whose rightful holder is this person on its own behalf and for its own account;
(b)   securities whose rightful holder is another person on its own behalf and for the account of such person;
(c)   voting shares which give this person the right to exercise its voting rights at its sole discretion on the basis of a power of attorney conferred on it by the rightful holder unless the rightful holder gives it voting instructions; and
(d)   call options held by this person on its own behalf and for its own account or by another person for its account, which are not included in the securities from point (b) above but arise from another legal transaction.

The takeover threshold is set at 25 per cent of voting shares in a target company. A person reaching such threshold is obliged to launch a public bid for all securities in the target company. Further, the public bid is mandatory also when a person who has already acquired less than 75 per cent of securities by means of a successful takeover bid under the Takeover Act acquires an additional 10 per cent of such securities after the completion of its takeover bid.

The most important rules are as follows:

(a)   the public takeover bid must be addressed to all holders of securities of the target company, with the same terms and conditions of the takeover bid applying to all;

(b)   the bidder is allowed to set a minimum acceptance threshold;

(c)   prior to the announcement of the takeover bid the bidder must deposit a sum of money, necessary for the payment of all securities of the target company not already held by the bidder or submit an adequate bank guarantee;

(d)   the bidder may offer:

   (i)   full payment in cash,

   (ii)   exchange for securities, complying with specific provisions of the Takeover Act ("consideration securities"),

   (iii) partial payment in cash and partial payment in consideration securities, and

   (iv)   an option to the holder of securities to select between payment in cash and by consideration securities ("alternative offer");

(e)   the offered price should not be lower then the highest price paid by the bidder for the target securities within the last 12 months before the launch of the public bid; if the bidder purchases target securities within one year of the successful takeover bid at a higher purchase price than offered in the public bid, then the bidder is obliged to pay the difference in price to all shareholders that accepted its public takeover bid;

(f)   the bidder may include in his offer as consideration securities:

   (i)   bidder's or bidder's parent's issued securities which are traded in an organised stock market,

   (ii)   additional new shares to be issued by the bidder or bidder's parent and from the same class of shares as aforementioned securities,

   (iii) in the case of alternative offer or offer for shares of non-public companies, the consideration securities need not to be securities traded in an organised stock market;

(g)   the period in which the target's shareholders may accept the offer shall not be shorter than 28 days and not longer than 60 days from the publication of the bid;

(h)   during the process of takeover, securities are freely traded on the Stock Exchange, but the bidder is not allowed to purchase them outside of the public bid procedure; trading may be stopped temporarily only in the event that the target company violates the rules of the Stock Exchange;

(i)   the bidder must conclude with a bank or a stockbroking company an agreement authorising the latter to prepare all of the required documents (the takeover prospectus, takeover bid, etc.) and to carry out the entire takeover procedure;

(j)   10 days prior to the expiration of the deadline for the acceptance of the takeover bid at the latest (but not later than 28 days prior to expiration of 60 days from the launch of the first bid), a third party (which must not act in concert with the offeror who made the first takeover bid and which must not be the authorised member that made the first takeover bid on behalf and for the account of the offeror) may address a competing takeover bid to all securities holders.

25.6.2 Takeover bid procedure

The important steps in the takeover procedure are:

(a) notification and publication of intended takeover (by the potential bidder; by the management of the target);
(b) drafting of the takeover prospectus;
(c) preparation of the takeover bid;
(d) agreement with the Central Clearing and Depository Corporation ("CCDC");
(e) depositing the sum of money or a bank guarantee;
(f) obtaining a permit from the Securities Market Agency ("SMA");
(g) publishing of the takeover bid and the extract from the takeover prospectus;
(h) opinion of the target company's management about the takeover bid;
(i) acceptance of the takeover bid;
(j) transfer of shares and purchase price.

25.6.3 Notification of intended takeover

25.6.3.1 Notification to the SMA
The potential bidder shall notify the SMA, the management of the target and the CPO of its intention to launch a takeover bid, and publish such notification on the same day. If its intention is later withdrawn or the bid is not launched within 30 days of the notification, the potential bidder is not allowed to launch the bid within one year, unless an approval for withdrawing of intention is obtained from the SMA.

The bid should be published not earlier than 10 days and not later than 30 days after the notification of intention.

The management of the target company must immediately notify the employees on the intended takeover. Within two business days of the notification on intended takeover, the management of the target company shall notify the SMA of any agreements or negotiations with the bidder.

25.6.3.2 Effects of the notification to the management of the target company
Following the receipt or publication of the notification of the intended takeover, the management of the target company must not without an approval of the general meeting of shareholders (which may be called with 14 days' notice) adopted with 75 per cent majority of votes cast:

(a) increase its authorised capital;
(b) enter into arrangements outside the company's regular operations;
(c) carry out transactions that might seriously jeopardise the company's operations;
(d) acquire treasury shares;
(e) perform activities whose purpose is to obstruct the procedure of the takeover bid.

25.6.4 Agreement with the CCDC

According to this agreement, the CCDC undertakes to perform all legal acts related to the fulfilment of obligations arising from the acceptance of the offer (i.e., acceptance of the deposited sum of money or bank guarantee for payment of the purchase price; securities account maintenance; after successful takeover, payment of the purchase price to the holders who accepted the offer, transfer of securities to the bidder).

25.6.5 Depositing the sum of money or a bank guarantee

The CCDC accepts a sum of money equalling the purchase price of all of the securities which are the subject of the takeover bid (all of target's shares not owned by the bidder). If securities are offered as the consideration for the target's securities, the CCDC makes an entry preventing their free disposal.

Instead of making a cash deposit, the bidder may provide the CCDC with a guarantee, issued by a bank with a registered office in a member country of the European Union, by which the bank irrevocably undertakes to pay to the CCDC on its first demand the amount, required for the fulfilment of the payment obligation, into a special account of the CCDC.

25.6.6 Obtaining a permit from the SMA

The takeover bid must be announced not later than 30 days after the notification of the intent, subject to the approval of the SMA.

The SMA grants its approval after it has established that:

(a) the takeover prospectus has been drafted in accordance with the law;
(b) the bid has been made (i.e., defined in accordance with the law);
(c) the bidder has deposited monies with the bank or obtained a bank guarantee;
(d) the bidder offering securities has deposited them;
(e) such securities meet the terms and conditions determined by the law;
(f) the bidder has entered into an agreement with the CCDC;
(g) the bidder has proved that it has not directly or indirectly pledged or promised to pledge securities issued by the target or assets of the target to acquire funds for payment of securities.

The SMA must review the application submitted by the bidder within three days of the receipt and can request changes or clarification, or submission of missing documents during that time. After the application is complete, the SMA shall decide on the application for approval of the takeover bid within five days; if the SMA fails to do so, it is deemed that it has granted its approval.

25.6.7 Launching of the takeover bid and the extract from the takeover prospectus

The takeover prospectus must be published in the form of an extract containing the essential information on the bidder, the target, the bid and the purpose or the intention of the bidder after a successful takeover. It must be published together with the takeover bid in a national daily newspaper covering the entire country.

The bidder shall send the takeover prospectus to the management of the target company, the CPO, the Ljubljana Stock Exchange, the CCDC and all stock-broking companies. The target company's staff must also be made familiar with the contents of the takeover prospectus in an appropriate manner.

The takeover bid when published becomes binding upon the bidder. He may recall the bid only if circumstances have changed or he may modify it only by offering a higher purchase price or a lower threshold for acceptance. The takeover bid must be addressed to all securities holders, meaning that all securities holders have the right to accept the bid. All holders must be offered equal purchase terms and conditions, (i.e., equal price or exchange ratio).

25.6.8 Notification to the CPO

The bidder must notify the CPO on the concentration within one week after the takeover bid has been published or the controlling stake acquired (whichever is the earlier).

25.6.9 Opinion of the target company's management about the takeover bid

Within 10 days of publishing the takeover bid, the target's management is obliged to publish its opinion specifying the following:

(a)   assessment of effects of a successful takeover bid on target company's interests and assessment of the effects of the bidder's strategic plans on the target company and especially on employment in the target company;
(b)   the existence of any agreement between the management of the target company and the bidder;
(c)   the existence of any agreement on the exercise of voting rights between the target company's management and the bidder;
(d)   a statement as to whether the management of the target company intends to accept the offer;
(e)   data on the last audited annual report and on the book value of securities.

25.6.10 Acceptance of the takeover bid

In order to carry out the takeover, the bidder must conclude a special agreement on the provision of services relating to the takeover with a stockbroking company. Based on this agreement the engaged stockbroking company performs the following services for the bidder:

(a)   prepares the takeover bid and its announcement;
(b)   drafts a takeover prospectus;
(c)   files an application with the SMA for approval of the takeover bid;
(d)   accepts from the securities holders written statements of acceptance;
(e)   establishes and announces the outcome of the takeover bid.

Holders of the target company's securities accept the offer by means of a written statement sent to the stockbroking company which performs services for the bidder relating to the takeover. At the same time they must deposit securities in a special account with the CCDC and order the CCDC to make entries denying the right of disposal of deposited securities.

The written statement (special form) must include the essential information prescribed by the law. The takeover bid is deemed accepted on the date the securities are deposited with the CCDC.

25.6.11 Announcement of the outcome of the takeover bid

The bidder must announce within three days of the expiration of the deadline for the acceptance of the bid:

(a)   the number of securities holders that have accepted the bid, the number of securities for which the bid was accepted and the percentage of represented securities for which the bid was accepted in the total number of the target's securities (by each class of securities);

(b)   whether the bid was successful,

(c)   if the bid was not successful – a statement of reasons for the failure of the bid.

The information on the outcome of the takeover bid must be submitted to the SMA and the CPO.

25.6.12 The SMA's declaratory decision about the success or failure of the takeover bid

The SMA must issue a declaratory decision about the success or failure of the takeover bid no later than three days after it has been notified about the outcome of the bid. This decision will also be sent to the CCDC, the target company and the Ljubljana Stock Exchange.

25.6.13 Official announcement of the outcome of the takeover bid

Within three days of receiving the decision from the SMA that the takeover bid was successful, the management of the target company must announce the outcome of the bid in a newspaper.

25.6.14 Title transfers made by the CCDC and paying of the consideration

Within eight days of receiving the decision by the SMA on the success of the bid, the CCDC enters the securities into the bidder's securities account, pays consideration to the sellers and returns any surplus amounts to the bidder.

25.6.15 Obtaining approval from the CPO

See 25.4 above.

Chapter 26

Spain

Carlos de Cárdenas Smith
Partner
Uría Menéndez

Alex Bircham
Secondee from Slaughter and May at Uría Menéndez

26.1 The takeover regime in Spain – background

26.1.1 Prior regulations

Takeover offers were regulated in Spain for the first time by Royal Decree 1848/1980 of 5 September 1980 which followed to a great extent the French regulation on takeover offers of 1970. Royal Decree 1848/1980 was repealed by Royal Decree 279/1984 of 25 January 1984, which introduced significant changes in the takeover offer regime by establishing tighter information requirements and regulating competing takeover offers for the first time. Royal Decree 279/1984 was amended by Royal Decree 726/1989 of 25 June 1989 in order to incorporate some provisions of Law 24/1988 of 28 July 1988 on the Securities Market ("the Securities Market Act") which created a completely new legal framework for the Spanish securities markets and for takeover offers in particular. Among the most significant changes introduced by Royal Decree 726/1989 was the substitution of the old supervising authorities by the Spanish Securities and Exchange Commission (the *Comisión Nacional del Mercado de Valores* or "CNMV").

However, the emergency changes introduced by Royal Decree 726/1989 were not sufficient to comply fully with the new Securities Market Act. It was necessary to introduce very profound changes in the takeover offer statute, taking into account the experience acquired from the application of the former regulations and, to a great extent, the provisions of the amended proposal of the Thirteenth Directive of 14 September 1990 which was being discussed at the time. This led the Spanish Council of Ministers to approve Royal Decree 1197/1991 of 26 July 1991 on takeover offers for securities ("RD 1197/1991") which repealed Royal Decree 279/1984 and introduced very significant changes to the takeover offer regime. The new statute was based on the principle of equal treatment: all shareholders and holders of certain other securities in a listed company were entitled to receive equal treatment in the event that any third party or existing shareholder intended to acquire a "significant shareholding" in such a company. Unlike the regulations of other EU Member States, RD 1197/1991 required the acquirer to launch an offer before the offeror acquired a "significant shareholding" (i.e., 25 per cent or more, 6 per cent or more during any 12-month period when the acquirer held between 25 per cent and 50 per cent, and 50 per cent or more of the capital) or appointed a certain proportion of the directors on the board of the target, and allowed for partial offers except when the bidder intended to acquire 50 per cent or more of the capital or appoint more than half of the members of the board.

RD 1197/1991 was amended a number of times following its approval, reflecting the main objection consistently raised against it: its rigidity, which was exacerbated by strict, defined rules that rarely afforded the CNMV the opportunity to apply its rules in a flexible manner, taking into account the particularities of each case.

26.1.2   *The Takeover Directive and current regulation*

The approval of Directive 2004/25/EC of 21 April 2004 on takeover bids ("the Directive") is the result of a tortuous legislative process that started in the mid-1980s. Its declared purpose is:

> "to create Community-wide clarity and transparency in respect of legal issues to be settled in the event of takeover bids and to prevent patterns of corporate restructuring within the Community from being distorted by arbitrary differences in governance and management cultures".

In summary, its purpose is to create a level playing field. The answer as to whether the Directive has achieved this objective is doubtful to say the least. The long legislative process that led to the approval of the Directive underlines the political difficulties in agreeing to common rules applicable to takeover bids. The only possible way to approve the Directive was to give up on any provisions that were controversial, or through opt-in and opt-out provisions that, in practical terms, give discretion to each Member State to decide whether or not to adopt provisions that are crucial in a takeover battle and essential to ensure a level playing field. The result is a "framework directive" which lays out certain "common principles and a limited number of general requirements which Member States must implement through more detailed rules in accordance with their national systems and their cultural contexts". Therefore, political consensus was reached at the expense of real harmonisation.

The Directive provides that Member States must enact the necessary laws and regulations in order to implement its provisions by 20 May 2006. To this effect but with considerable delay, Spain approved Act 6/2007 of 12 April 2007 ("Act 6/2007"), amending the Securities Market Act, providing for the reform of the rules on takeover bids, and Royal Decree 1066/2007 of 27 July 2007 ("the Royal Decree"), on the rules applicable to takeover bids, further developing Act 6/2007. The introduction of this new legislation is one of the major developments in Spanish commercial law in recent years.

Following the dictates of the Directive, Act 6/2007 and the Royal Decree introduce three major structural changes to the offer process:

(a)   The old regime under RD 1197/1991 established a system whereby the intent to exceed any of the then relevant thresholds triggered the obligation to make a mandatory bid. This prevented offerors from acquiring shares without first launching a takeover bid. In contrast, under the new regime, the obligation to make a takeover bid does not arise based on the intention of the offeror to exceed the established control threshold, but specifically because such threshold is reached.

(b) The old rules permitting partial bids have been removed. Now, whenever the obligation to make a takeover bid arises as a result of the acquisition of control of a listed company, the takeover bid must be directed to the acquisition of all the securities of the offeree.

(c) The old rules allowed an offeror to make a takeover bid at any price. Under the new regime mandatory bids must be made at an equitable price, which is equal to the highest price that the offeror, or persons acting in concert therewith, paid or agreed to pay for the same securities during the 12 months prior to the announcement of the takeover bid.

The new regime also introduces, amongst other things, rules governing squeeze-outs and sell-outs, break-up fees and neutralisation (breakthrough) measures.

26.2   Application of the takeover regime

Article 1 of the Royal Decree states that its rules apply to all individuals or legal entities that make or are required to make a takeover bid for the shares or other securities carrying the right to the acquisition or subscription of such shares of a listed company. A listed company for these purposes is deemed to be any company whose shares are admitted to trading on a Spanish official secondary market and which has its registered office in Spain. It is also possible that the new regime will apply to bids for companies that have their registered office in another Member State of the European Union, provided that the company's securities are listed on a Spanish official secondary market.

The new regime will not apply to bids for open-ended investment companies (*sociedades de inversión de capital variable*) or to bids for the shares of the Central Banks of Member States.

26.3   Types of offer

The new regime envisages two basic categories of takeover bids: mandatory bids (26.3.1 through 26.3.4) and voluntary bids (26.3.6).

26.3.1   *Mandatory bid where control is reached*

26.3.1.1   *The general rule*
Article 3.1 of the Royal Decree states that any individual or legal entity that obtains control (now set at 30 per cent of the voting share capital or the appointment of more than one-half of the members of the board, *see* 26.3.1.3 below) of a listed company by any of the means contemplated in that Article must make a takeover bid for all of the securities of the offeree at an equitable price (*see* 26.4 below). The bid must be submitted within one month of control of the listed

company having been obtained (three months in the case of indirect and un-expected takeovers, *see* 26.3.2 below).

26.3.1.2   *Offerees*

Article 3.2 of the Royal Decree provides that the bid must be made to all holders of:

(a)   shares with voting rights (including those holders of non-voting shares that at the time of the authorisation of the bid are entitled to vote); and

(b)   share subscription rights, if any, as well as holders of bonds that are convertible into or exchangeable for shares.

The bid may or may not be made to all of the holders of warrants or other securities or financial instruments carrying the option to acquire or subscribe for shares, except for those mentioned in (b), whether issued or to be issued. If made to them, the takeover bid must be made to all persons holding any such warrants, securities or financial instruments.

26.3.1.3   *The concept of control and control thresholds*

Control is defined in Article 4 of the Royal Decree. An individual or legal entity will be deemed to control a company where, individually or acting in concert with others, it:

(a)   directly or indirectly reaches a percentage of voting rights equal to or greater than 30 per cent; or

(b)   holds an interest carrying less than 30 per cent of the voting rights but appoints (together with those directors already appointed by it, if any) more than one half of the board of directors within 24 months of the acqui-sition of such lesser percentage (*see* 26.3.1.6 below for a more detailed discussion).

Control of a listed company may be obtained through the acquisition of shares carrying voting rights, through certain shareholders agreements (discussed at 26.3.1.4 below) or through indirect or unexpected takeovers (discussed at 26.3.2 below).

The CNMV shall waive the mandatory bid requirement where, even though a shareholder has reached the 30 per cent trigger percentage, another person or entity holds an equal or greater percentage of the voting rights, as effective control will not have been obtained in this scenario (*see* 26.3.5.2).

There are also special rules for those who, as at 13 August 2007, directly or indi-rectly held an interest carrying 30 per cent or more, but less than 50 per cent, of the voting rights of a listed company. In such case, the shareholder must make a mandatory bid in any of the following circumstances:

(a)   if it acquires shares of the company that increase its interest by at least 5 per cent over a 12-month period;

(b)   if it obtains a percentage of votes that is equal to or greater than 50 per cent; or

(c)   if it acquires an additional interest and, within 24 months following such acquisition, appoints a number of directors which, together with those previously appointed by it, if any, represent more than half of the members of the board of directors of the company.

26.3.1.4 *Acting in concert*

Parties will be deemed to be acting in concert where, pursuant to an agreement (which may be express, implicit, oral or written), they cooperate to obtain control of a listed company. Under Article 5, the Royal Decree presumes that concert exists when the persons in question have entered into a shareholders agreement mentioned in Article 112 of the Securities Market Act (i.e., agreements which restrict or condition the transfer of the shares or which regulate the exercise of the voting rights at general meetings), as long as such agreement is intended to establish a common policy as to the management of the company or is aimed at exercising significant influence thereon. The parties to an agreement that, while having the same purpose, governs voting rights on the board of directors or executive committee of the company are also presumed to be acting in concert. Under Article 3.3 of the Royal Decree, if parties are deemed to be acting in concert, the actual bid must be made by the party holding the greatest percentage, directly or indirectly, and jointly if the percentage is the same.

26.3.1.5 *Calculation of voting rights for control thresholds*

Under Article 5 of the Royal Decree, the percentage of voting rights relevant for the purposes of takeover bids must be calculated taking into account:

(a)   all shares carrying voting rights, even if such rights have been suspended;
(b)   non-voting shares shall only be computed if they carry voting rights under current law (for example, in the event of non-payment of preferred dividends); and
(c)   shares which, in accordance with the information available on the date of calculation, are owned directly or indirectly by the offeree and will therefore be excluded from the calculation basis (e.g., in a company where 5 per cent of voting capital is represented by treasury shares, the threshold for takeover bids will be reached upon the acquisition of 30 per cent of 95 per cent, that is, 28.5 per cent of the entire share capital).

Whilst the voting rights that are relevant for these purposes are generally those held by the shareholder in question (either through actual ownership or through usufruct, pledge or any other contractual arrangement), there are situations in which voting rights held by third parties will be attributed to the shareholder. These include:

(a)   the voting rights held by other companies of the same group (pursuant to the definition of group provided by Article 4 of the Securities Market Act);
(b)   the voting rights held by the members of the board of the shareholder and of the boards of companies of the same group, unless evidence is provided to the contrary;
(c)   the voting rights held by a third party when they can be exercised freely and permanently by the shareholder under a specific power of attorney in the absence of express instructions;
(d)   the voting rights of shares held by a nominee (the Royal Decree defines a nominee as a third party whom the person required to make a bid totally

or partially covers against the risks inherent to the acquisition or transfer of the shares or the possession thereof). Included in this section will be the voting rights of shares that constitute the underlying instruments or the subject matter of financial contracts or swaps when such contracts or swaps cover, in whole or in part, against the risks inherent to the ownership of the securities and have, as a result, an effect similar to that of holding shares through a nominee; and

(e)   the voting rights held, directly or indirectly, by persons acting in their own name but for the account of, or in concert with, the shareholder.

26.3.1.6   *Determination of directors' appointment for control thresholds*

Article 6 of the Royal Decree establishes certain rebuttable presumptions that the holder of the equity interest in question has appointed the members of the offeree board. Such presumptions are relevant to determine whether control has been acquired and a takeover bid is mandatory. The presumptions are as follows:

(a)   when the board member has been appointed by the holder of the equity interest, or by a company belonging to the same group as the holder, in the exercise of its right of proportional representation under the Spanish Companies Act (*Ley de Sociedades Anónimas*);

(b)   when the board member is or has been over the 12 months prior to his appointment a director, senior manager, employee of, or non-sporadic provider of services to, the holder of the equity interest or of companies belonging to the same group as such holder;

(c)   when the appointment resolution could not have been approved without the affirmative votes cast by the holder of the equity interest – or by companies belonging to the same group as such holder – or by the board members previously appointed by such holder;

(d)   when the person appointed is itself the holder of the equity interest in question or a company belonging to the same group as such holder; and

(e)   when in the corporate documents (minutes, notarial instruments, etc.) or the publicly available information of the company or of the holder of the equity interest, the latter asserts that the director has been appointed by such holder, or that he represents it or that he is a proprietary director of the offeree by reason of his relationship with such holder.

A shareholder will not be deemed to have appointed board members that are classified as independent directors or as proprietary directors representing other shareholders that do not act in concert with the holder of the equity interest.

26.3.2   *Mandatory bid in the case of indirect or unexpected takeovers*

Article 7 of the Royal Decree lists five cases of "indirect or unexpected takeovers" of listed companies that may render the making of a takeover bid mandatory. In each case, the bid must be made within three months of the event that gave rise to the obligation to make the mandatory offer, unless:

(a)   the CNMV grants a waiver because a third party has the same or a greater percentage of voting rights; or

(b)   within three months of the occurrence of the event that gave rise to the obligation to make the mandatory bid, there is a transfer of the number of securities required to reduce the excess of voting rights over the relevant control threshold, provided that in this latter case the voting rights corresponding to the excess over such threshold are not exercised in the meantime.

A notice making public the occurrence of the event triggering the obligation to make the unexpected takeover bid shall be published and specify whether the bid will be made or whether the option of reducing the interest below the threshold that triggers such obligation will be exercised.

In all five cases the bid must be made at the equitable price established in Article 9 of the Royal Decree.

26.3.2.1 Merger or takeover of another company or entity ("Shareholding Entity") that holds a direct or indirect interest in a listed company ("Listed Company")

If control of the Shareholding Entity (which need not be a listed company itself or be domiciled in Spain) is acquired, or if the Shareholding Entity is merged such that, as a result of such takeover or merger, at least 30 per cent of the voting rights in the Listed Company are obtained, a takeover bid, directed to the entire share capital, must be made within three months of the date of the merger or takeover.

26.3.2.2 Capital reduction of a listed company

When, as a result of a capital reduction of a listed company, a shareholder obtains not less than 30 per cent of the voting rights of the company, the shareholder in question must make a takeover bid directed to the entire share capital. Although the Royal Decree does not expressly provide it, it seems reasonable to apply the same rule to those shareholders who, as of the entry into force of the Royal Decree, hold an interest of between 30 per cent and 50 per cent and, as a result of the reduction, reach or exceed 50 per cent of the voting rights.

26.3.2.3 Conversion or exchange of securities

When shares of a listed company are acquired through the conversion or exchange of other securities or financial instruments and, as a result thereof, a shareholder obtains at least 30 per cent of the voting rights of the company, the shareholder in question must make a takeover bid directed to the entire share capital of the company.

26.3.2.4 Changes in treasury stock

When, as a result of changes in treasury stock, a shareholder obtains not less than 30 per cent of the voting rights of the company (for example, a shareholder holds 28.5 per cent of the capital in a company that subsequently acquires 5 per cent of its capital as treasury stock), the shareholder in question must make a takeover bid directed to the entire share capital of the company.

26.3.2.5 Commitment to underwrite issuances

Financial institutions and any other person that, in compliance with an underwriting agreement, reach not less than 30 per cent of voting rights of the company must make a takeover bid directed to the entire share capital of the company.

26.3.3   *Mandatory bid due to a capital reduction through the acquisition of a company's own shares*

Article 12 of the Royal Decree provides that, when the capital reduction of a listed company is made through the purchase of its own shares for redemption, without prejudice to the minimum requirements laid down in Article 170 of the Spanish Companies Act, a takeover bid must be made. This type of bid enables the company to carry out the purchase of its own shares by observing the principle of equal treatment of all its shareholders. However, where the buy back is made pursuant to Commission Regulation (EC) No. 2273/2003 of 22 December 2003 and the number of shares acquired does not exceed 10 per cent of the voting capital, a takeover bid shall not be required.

26.3.4   *Mandatory bid to delist a company*

26.3.4.1   *General rule*

Under Article 10 of the Royal Decree it is necessary to make a takeover bid to delist a company. Article 11 of the Royal Decree provides certain exceptions to this rule (discussed in more detail at 26.3.4.3 below). The delisting offer may be submitted by the issuer of the securities to be delisted or by a third party that has obtained the approval of the shareholders of the company to be delisted at a general meeting. If the offer is submitted by the issuer of the securities to be delisted, the securities acquired under the offer must be cancelled or transferred unless such cancellation or transfer is not necessary because the limitations and requirements established in Article 75 of the Spanish Companies Act for treasury shares are satisfied. For such purposes, the limit on the acquisition of a company's own shares will be 10 per cent of the share capital.

26.3.4.2   *Price for the delisting offer*

The price of the bid, which must be fully paid in cash and approved by the shareholders acting at a general meeting shall not be less than the higher of:

(a)   the equitable price; and
(b)   the price resulting from taking into account, collectively and based on a rationale for the respective relevance thereof, the valuation methods listed in Article 10.5 of the Royal Decree. These valuation methods are:
    (i)   the underlying book value of the company;
    (ii)   the break-up value of the company;
    (iii)   the average weighted price of the securities over the six-month period immediately prior to the announcement of the delisting proposal;
    (iv)   the value of the consideration previously offered in any takeover bid made in the immediately preceding year; and
    (v)   any other valuation methods applicable to the specific case and generally accepted by the international financial community, such as discounted cash flows, company multiples and comparable transactions, among others.

The directors of the issuer of the securities to be delisted must prepare a report for the shareholders on the delisting and its price, which should be made available at the time of the general meeting for the adoption of the resolution regarding the delisting, the offer and the price. The intention to delist must be stated in the offer document.

26.3.4.3 *Exceptions to the obligation to make a listing offer*
Under Article 11 of the Royal Decree, no delisting offer shall be required in the following cases:

(a) when the requirements for carrying out squeeze-outs and sell-outs as set forth in Article 47 of the Royal Decree are satisfied (discussed at 26.13.2 below);

(b) when the delisting is unanimously agreed and the requirement to make a takeover bid is waived by all affected offeree shareholders;

(c) when the company is terminated as a result of a corporate transaction whereby the shareholders of the terminated company become shareholders of another listed company;

(d) when a takeover bid has previously been made for the entire capital of the offeree where the offeror has expressed its intention to delist the shares, the price is justified by a valuation report as described at 26.3.4.2 above, and the sale of all of the securities is facilitated by means of an order to purchase such securities, at the same price as that in the prior bid, during at least one month over the six-month period subsequent to the end of the preceding bid; or

(e) when the shareholders and, if applicable, the bondholders of the issuer of the securities to be delisted approve a procedure that in the opinion of the CNMV is equivalent to a takeover bid as it ensures the protection of the holders of the securities to be delisted.

26.3.5 *Exclusions and waivable instances*

26.3.5.1 *Excluded instances*
Article 8 of the Royal Decree contains a number of excluded instances whereby, even though the circumstances set forth in the Royal Decree creating the obligation to make a takeover bid are present, the Royal Decree itself automatically exempts the recipient from the obligation to make it. A takeover bid shall not be mandatory in the following cases:

(a) Where shares of listed companies are acquired by Funds for the Insurance of Deposits in Banking Entities (*Fondos de Garantía de Depósitos en Establecimientos Bancarios*), Savings Associations (*Cajas de Ahorro*) or Credit Co-operatives (*Cooperativas de Crédito*), the Investment Guarantee Fund (*Fondo de Garantía de Inversiones*), the Insurance Compensation Consortium (*Consorcio de Compensación de Seguros*), and other legally established institutions of a similar nature, as well as acquisitions consisting of allotments approved by these bodies.

(b) Acquisitions or other transactions made pursuant to the Compulsory Purchase Act (*Ley de Expropiación Forzosa*).

(c)   When the offeree shareholders unanimously agree to sell or exchange all or a part of their shares, or agree to waive the requirement to make a takeover bid.

(d)   Acquisitions or other transactions resulting from the conversion or capitalisation of claims into shares of listed companies, where that company is experiencing severe financial difficulty (even if it is not undergoing formal bankruptcy proceedings) and the transaction in question is intended to ensure the company's long-term financial recovery. The CNMV has the discretion to grant this exclusion.

(e)   *Mortis causa* gratuitous acquisitions.

(f)   *Inter vivos* gratuitous acquisitions, provided that the recipient of such shares has not acquired offeree shares in the previous 12 months, and there is no agreement or concert with the transferor.

(g)   When control has been obtained after a voluntary bid for all of the securities, if either:

    (i)   the bid has been made at an equitable price, or

    (ii)   the bid has been accepted by holders of securities representing at least 50 per cent of the voting rights to which the bid was directed (excluding the offeror's shareholding and irrevocable undertakings).

(h)   When, as a result of a merger, a shareholder of the offeree companies directly or indirectly obtains a control threshold in the resulting listed company, provided that:

    (i)   such shareholder does not vote in favour of the merger at the relevant general meeting of shareholders of the offeree, and

    (ii)   it can be shown that the primary purpose of the transaction is not the takeover but an industrial or corporate purpose.

The CNMV shall have discretion to grant this exclusion.

26.3.5.2   CNMV waiver

Pursuant to Article of 4.2 the Royal Decree, the CNMV shall waive the obligation to make a takeover bid if the recipient company reaches or exceeds 30 per cent of the voting rights in the offeree in the event that another entity holds, individually or collectively with persons acting in concert, a voting percentage in the offeree equal to or greater than that held by the party required to make the bid. This waiver shall also apply in the case of a mandatory bid due to an indirect or unexpected acquisition.

However, the waiver shall be conditional upon the person or entity not reducing its shareholding below that held by the shareholder that has been the beneficiary of the waiver or upon the latter not appointing more than one-half of the members of the board. If this happens or if the interested party does not obtain the waiver, then a takeover bid must be submitted unless within a period of three months the excess of voting rights over the aforementioned percentage is transferred, and provided that the voting rights corresponding to the excess are not exercised in the meantime.

The waiver must be requested by the interested party, who shall at the same time give notice thereof to the offeree. Once the request for a waiver has been submitted, the offeree shall have a period of three business days within which to file allegations with the CNMV. Within 10 business days of the request, or of the date of registration of such documents and information as may be required, the CNMV shall give notice of its reasoned decision to the interested party and to the offeree and shall make it public on its website.

26.3.6 Voluntary bids

26.3.6.1 General rule
Takeover bids may be made voluntarily under Article 13 of the Royal Decree. Whoever does not hold control of a listed company and seeks to acquire it, or, while already possessing a controlling interest, wishes to increase its interest in the offeree, may make a voluntary bid. If, as a result of a voluntary bid, an offeror acquires a controlling interest in the offeree, that offeror will then be required to make a mandatory bid unless the offeror can benefit from the exemption described at 26.3.6.3 below.

26.3.6.2 Special provisions for voluntary bids
Voluntary bids are subject to the same rules as mandatory bids, with certain special provisions:

(a)   voluntary bids may be subject to certain conditions provided that the fulfil-ment or non-fulfilment thereof may be verified at the end of the accept-ance period for the bid (*see* 26.5.2 below);
(b)   voluntary bids need not be made at an equitable price;
(c)   in the event that the voluntary bid is structured as an exchange of securi-ties, a cash consideration or price that is at least financially equivalent to the exchange offered need not be included as an alternative; and
(d)   a voluntary bid for less than the total number of securities may be made (partial voluntary bids are allowed) by a party that, as a result thereof, will not acquire a controlling interest or by a party that already holds a control-ling interest and is free to increase its shareholdings in the offeree.

26.3.6.3 Exclusion from the obligation to make a mandatory bid
Article 8 of the Royal Decree states that the offeror will not be obliged to make a mandatory bid where control is obtained following a voluntary bid for all the securities of the offeree if either:

(a)   the bid has been made at an equitable price; or
(b)   the bid has been accepted by holders of securities representing at least 50 per cent of the voting rights to which the bid was directed (excluding the offeror's shareholding and irrevocable undertakings).

26.4   Equitable price and consideration for the offer

26.4.1 Equitable price

26.4.1.1 Calculation of the equitable price
In the case of mandatory bids due to control having been reached, Article 9 of the Royal Decree requires the bid to be made at the "equitable price". This

equitable price may not be less than the highest price that the offeror, or persons acting in concert with it, have paid or agreed to pay for the same securities over the 12 months prior to the announcement of the bid. When the acquisition includes any compensation in addition to the price paid or agreed, or when deferred payment has been agreed upon, the equitable price shall take into account such compensation or deferred payment. The Royal Decree contains special rules to calculate the equitable price in the cases where the shares of the offeree were acquired through the exercise of call or put options, derivatives and exchange or conversion of other securities.

If the offeror did not make any acquisitions in the 12 months prior to the announcement of the takeover bid, the equitable price may not be less than the price calculated pursuant to the valuation rules for delisting offers set forth in Article 10.5 of the Royal Decree (*see* 26.3.4.2(b) above).

26.4.1.2 *Exceptions to the obligation to make a mandatory bid at the equitable price*

The CNMV has the discretion to modify the equitable price upon the occurrence of any of the following exceptional circumstances:

(a) the listing price of the securities of the offeree during the reference period has been affected by the payment of dividends, a corporate transaction or any extraordinary event that warrants an objective correction of the equitable price;

(b) the listing price of the securities of the offeree during the reference period shows reasonable signs of manipulation, as a result of which a sanction proceeding has been commenced by the CNMV;

(c) the equitable price was lower than the trading range for the securities on the date of the acquisition when such price was determined, in which case the bid price shall not be less than the lower price in such range;

(d) the equitable price corresponds to an acquisition for a volume that is not significant in relative terms and provided that it was carried out at the listing price, in which case the applicable price shall be the highest price paid or agreed upon under the other acquisitions during the reference period;

(e) the acquisitions during the reference period include any compensation in addition to the price paid or agreed upon, in which case the bid price shall not be less than the highest price that results after including the amount of such compensation; or

(f) the offeree can be shown to be undergoing serious financial difficulties.

In all of the preceding cases, the CNMV may direct the offeror to submit a report on the valuation methods and criteria used to determine the equitable price. Such criteria may include, among other things:

(a) the average market value over a particular period;

(b) the break-up value of the company;

(c) the value of the consideration paid by the offeror for the same securities over the 12 months prior to the announcement of the bid;

(d) the underlying book value of the company;

(e) other generally accepted objective valuation criteria which ensure the protection of shareholders' rights.

26.4.2 *Consideration and payment*

The consideration in the bid may consist of cash (in which case it will be a purchase and sale), securities (in which case it will be a swap or exchange) or a combination of both.

26.4.2.1 *Obligation to offer a cash alternative to offers in which shares are offered as consideration*

Under Article 14 of the Royal Decree, such bids must include, at least as an alternative, cash consideration that is at least financially equivalent to the value of the exchange in the following circumstances:

(a) when the offeror, or the persons with whom it acts in concert, have acquired in cash, during the 12 months prior to the announcement of the bid, securities carrying not less than 5 per cent of the voting rights in the offeree;

(b) in the case of mandatory bids where control is reached, including bids triggered by indirect or unexpected acquisitions; and

(c) in the event of a swap, unless the securities offered in exchange are subject to one or more of the exceptions contained in Article 14c of the Royal Decree.

26.4.2.2 *Where shares offered as consideration have yet to be issued*

Where shares offered as consideration have yet to be issued by the offeror, the Royal Decree imposes certain procedural obligations on the offeror, for example to resolve to convene a general meeting of shareholders to decide on the issuance of the securities offered as consideration.

26.4.3 *Guaranteeing the consideration*

Offerors are required to provide evidence to the CNMV that guarantees have been put in place to secure compliance with their obligations in relation to the bid.

Where the consideration for the offer consists of cash, the offeror must provide a bank guarantee or documents showing that a cash deposit has been made to secure the cash consideration.

Where the consideration is securities that have already been issued, the offeror must provide evidence demonstrating that the securities are available and earmarked towards the result of the bid.

Where the consideration offered consists of securities to be issued by the offeror, the board members must act in a manner that is not inconsistent with the decision to make the bid. The CNMV may take action if it believes that the board of the offeror is not approaching the bid with the necessary degree of earnestness.

26.4.4   Modification of the offer price

The price may be modified at any time prior to the five calendar days preceding the expiration of the acceptance period of the bid (*see* 26.11.1).

26.4.5   Purchases of offeree shares outside the bid during the bid process

Under Article 32, the offeror, or persons acting in concert, may acquire offeree shares outside the bid during the bid process. However, this will have the following consequences:

(a)   when the bid is conditional upon obtaining a minimum number of acceptances, the acquisition will entail the removal of that and any other condition;

(b)   when the consideration offered consists in whole or in part of securities, the acquisition will create the obligation to offer an alternative consideration in cash of equal value; and

(c)   when the consideration for the bid consists solely of cash, the acquisition for a price higher than that offered in the takeover bid shall automatically result in the price offered being raised to equal the highest price paid.

26.5   Conditional offers

26.5.1   Conditional offers in the context of mandatory bids

With the exception of the condition that the bid be subject to the authorisation of the competition authorities, a mandatory bid may not be subject to any conditions.

26.5.2   Conditional offers in the context of voluntary bids

Voluntary bids, by contrast, may be subject to certain conditions provided that they can be verified at the end of the acceptance period of the bid. The following conditions are permitted by the Royal Decree:

(a)   the approval of amendments to the articles of association or of structural amendments (such as, for instance, a merger or split-off), or the adoption of other resolutions at a general meeting of shareholders of the offeree;

(b)   acceptance of the bid by a certain minimum number of securities of the offeree;

(c)   approval of the bid at a general meeting of shareholders of the offeror; and

(d)   any other condition that the CNMV deems acceptable under the law.

26.5.3   Waiver of conditions

In the event of voluntary bids being made subject to certain conditions, offerors may waive the conditions to which a bid is subject and acquire the securities to which that bid is directed. A conditional voluntary bid will be rendered void if the acceptance period expires and the conditions have not been complied with or waived.

26.5.4 *Making competition authorities' or other regulatory bodies' approval a condition of the offer*

26.5.4.1 Competition authorities

Under Article 26 of the Royal Decree, both mandatory and voluntary bids may be made contingent upon securing the authorisation or non-opposition of the appropriate competition authorities. This applies not only to the Spanish competition authorities (as was the case under the previous regime) but also to authorisation by the European Commission or by the competition authorities of third countries. The inclusion of this type of condition will have the following consequences:

(a)   if, before the expiration of the acceptance period, the competition authorities authorise or do not oppose the concentration transaction, the bid shall be fully effective;

(b)   if, before the expiration of the acceptance period, the competition authorities declare that the proposed transaction is inadmissible, the offeror must withdraw the bid; and

(c)   if, before the expiration of the acceptance period, no express or implied decision is made by the competition authorities, or those authorities establish that their authorisation is subject to a condition, the offeror may withdraw the bid.

In the event that the bid that is made subject to the authorisation of the competition authorities is a mandatory bid, the offeror may not, while the relevant decision is pending, exercise the voting rights corresponding to the excess of its shareholding over the threshold that created the obligation to make the mandatory bid. In addition, if the offeror withdraws the bid pursuant to (b) or (c) above, it must reduce its holding of voting rights below the control threshold within three months.

26.5.4.2 Other administrative authorisations

The Royal Decree provides that bids requiring other regulatory authorisations may be submitted without such authorisation having been previously secured. However, the CNMV shall not authorise the bid, and the acceptance period will thus not begin, until evidence is provided that the authorisation has been secured. The specific provisions in Article 26 regulating the offeror's conduct as described above (i.e., prohibition on the exercise of voting rights while the decision is pending and the reduction below the control threshold should the authorisation not be forthcoming) also apply in this context.

26.6   Preparation of offer: due diligence, break-up fees, irrevocable undertakings, etc.

26.6.1   *Due diligence*

26.6.1.1 Equality of information

The offeror may conduct a due diligence review of the offeree prior to any takeover bid. Article 46 of the Royal Decree lays down a general principle of "equality of information" so that all offerors are on a level playing field as regards information. The offeree must ensure that all potential good faith offerors receive the same information. The offeree must make this information available only if:

(a)   the information is specifically requested by the existing or potential offeror;
(b)   such information has been previously provided to other existing or potential offerors;
(c)   the recipient of the information duly ensures the confidentiality thereof, and that such information will be used for the sole purpose of making a takeover bid; and
(d)   the information is necessary to make the bid.

26.6.1.2   The offeror and offeree shareholders

If it has carried out a due diligence review of the offeree, the offeror, when making the bid, will most likely have information that the offeree shareholders lack. This imbalance of information raises a number of potential issues. On the one hand, pursuant to Article 82 of the Securities Market Act, the offeree should promptly disclose to the market all information that could materially affect the share price (it should, therefore, not have any material information, and, if it does, it should certainly not disclose it to third parties). On the other hand, if an offeror receives privileged information under Article 81.1 of the Securities Market Act it must abstain from buying securities or making the bid until such information becomes public.

Due diligence reviews prior to takeover bids are necessary and customary: by agreeing to provide more information on the offeree, the offeree board can encourage offerors to express an interest in bidding for the company, as offerors know that they will get an opportunity to produce a reasonably accurate valuation of the company from the information provided. This will eventually benefit the offeree shareholders by ensuring that not only are offers for their shares more likely to be received, but that they also receive the best possible price for their shares in the circumstances.

26.6.2   Break-up fees

Article 42.4 of the Royal Decree expressly allows for the possibility of the offeree and the first offeror agreeing on a break-up fee – or inducement fee – payable to the first offeror in compensation for the expenses incurred in preparing the bid in the event that it is not successful due to competing offers. Formerly, only the shareholders of the offeree, rather than the company itself, were allowed to enter into this kind of agreement. Such break-up fee agreements are subject to the following conditions:

(a)   that the fee does not exceed 1 per cent of the total amount of the bid;
(b)   that the fee is approved by the board of directors of the offeree with a favourable report from the financial advisers of the offeree; and
(c)   that the fee is described in the offer document.

26.6.3 *Agreements between the offeror and the offeree*

In Spanish practice, aside from the express regulation of break-up fees and confidentiality agreements, it is not customary for the offeree and the future offeror to enter into any agreements in preparation for the takeover bid. However, leaving aside financial assistance rules and the principle of "equal amount of information for competing offerors" established in the Royal Decree, there is nothing to prevent the execution of such preparatory agreements.

26.6.4 *Irrevocable commitments*

Under RD 1197/1991, irrevocable commitments were very common in Spanish practice. However, now that it is the actual exceeding of the thresholds, rather than the intent to do so, that triggers the mandatory bid, part of the reason for the execution of irrevocable commitments has disappeared, as the future offeror is now free to acquire shares in the offeree before making its bid.

However, irrevocable commitments are still useful in a number of ways. For example, if the shareholdings sought to be acquired prior to making the bid determine that the offeror will exceed the threshold of 30 per cent of the voting capital of the offeree, the future bid will be mandatory and, accordingly, may not be subject to conditions and must be made at an equitable price. Carrying out the purchase and sale of the shareholdings through an irrevocable commitment will make it possible, in some instances, to make the subsequent bid as a voluntary bid and, therefore, make it subject to conditions or to make it at a price other than the equitable price. Irrevocable commitments may also be an instrument used to facilitate the subsequent squeeze-out or, in general, to ensure the success of the takeover bid.

26.6.5 *Offeror protection*

There is nothing in the new regime to prevent the offeror seeking representations and warranties from the significant shareholders of the offeree to protect itself from potential contingencies. However, this is not standard practice.

26.6.6 *Acquisition of shares in the offeree by the offeror before the offer has commenced*

Under the new regime the future offeror is free to acquire offeree shares before making the bid. However, this may have the following consequences:

(a) if prior acquisitions result in the offeror reaching any of the control thresholds set out in the Royal Decree, a mandatory bid will be triggered, requiring the bid to be made at the equitable price (if this is the case, such purchases will also have an impact on the calculation of the equitable price) and to be free from conditions; and

(b) if securities carrying 5 per cent or more of the voting rights of the offeree are acquired in cash and the bid is announced within 12 months following the acquisition, the consideration offered in the takeover bid must at least include a cash alternative.

26.6.7 Obligations of the offeror should the offer become public before it is filed

If the bid is leaked to the market, the CNMV will normally require the offeree to confirm or deny the information. The CNMV may also require the potential offeror to publish a "significant event" (*hecho relevante*) regarding the matter.

26.7 Announcement and authorisation of the offer, documentation and directors' report

26.7.1 Announcement of the bid to the public and to employees

Article 16 of the Royal Decree regulates the announcement of bids. In the case of a voluntary bid, the decision to make a takeover bid must be announced as soon as it is adopted and the offeror has ensured that it can afford the consideration for the bid in full. Although the rules do not clearly specify what degree of certainty will suffice for such purposes, cash consideration for which the offeror needs external financing will most likely require the offeror to have at least signed a mandate letter with its financiers. However, most offerors will prefer to have signed a facilities agreement containing a "certain funds" clause. Regarding other types of consideration, the regulations merely provide that the offeror shall have adopted all reasonable measures to guarantee the satisfaction thereof.

In the case of mandatory bids, the obligation to make a takeover bid must be made public and announced to the market immediately. The communication must specify, if applicable, whether the person or entity intends to request a waiver and, in the case of indirect or unexpected takeovers, whether such person or entity intends to make a takeover bid or to reduce its shareholdings below the threshold that triggers the obligation to submit a bid. If a waiver is denied, the offeror shall make public and disseminate the decision to make the bid.

Once a takeover bid has been made public, the boards of both the offeror and the offeree must inform their respective employees' representatives, and deliver the offer document to them once it has been published (or to the employees themselves, in the absence of representatives).

In all cases, the communication to the market must be made in the same manner as in the case of a "significant event" (*hecho relevante*), and should therefore be sent to the CNMV at the same time that it is disseminated by any other means. The content of the communication must be true, clear and complete, such that it is not misleading or deceptive.

26.7.2 Request for authorisation

26.7.2.1 Time period for submission

Under Article 17.2 of the Royal Decree a request for authorisation of a takeover bid must be submitted to the CNMV within the following periods:

(a)   in the case of voluntary and mandatory bids, within one month following the date on which the decision to make the bid has been made public and within one month following the date on which the obligation to make the bid arises, respectively; and

(b)   in the case of unexpected or indirect takeovers, within three months of the date on which control is acquired.

26.7.2.2   *Form of authorisation request*

The request for authorisation must be in writing, contain the main characteristics of the bid, and be prepared in accordance with the form, if any, established by the CNMV by means of a circular. It should also be accompanied by documents evidencing the adoption of the resolution or decision to make the takeover bid, as well as the offer document, signed on all pages thereof by the person identified as responsible thereunder. In the case of a voluntary bid, it must be stated whether the decision to make the takeover bid is subject to approval by the offeror shareholders and, if applicable, the corresponding documents must be submitted as soon as such approval is obtained.

The CNMV will also require, within seven business days after the submission of the written request, the submission of various additional documents listed in Article 20 of the Royal Decree. These include:

(a)   documents evidencing the guarantee for the bid as provided in Article 15 of the Royal Decree;

(b)   if required, a request for administrative authorisation or, if applicable, documents evidencing that such authorisation has been obtained;

(c)   documents evidencing the price of the bid and valuation reports, if required;

(d)   certificates evidencing the blocking of the securities of the offeree, if required;

(e)   specimen form of the announcements to be published as provided in Article 22 of the Royal Decree and a certificate evidencing any other form of publicity or dissemination of the bid;

(f)   a certificate providing evidence of the creation of the offeror company and of the current articles of association thereof, unless already filed with the CNMV;

(g)   audited financial statements of the offeror company and, if applicable, of the group to which it belongs, for at least the fiscal year most recently ended or approved, unless already filed with the CNMV; and

(h)   where the consideration for the bid consists of shares issued by a company other than the offeror, audited financial statements of that issuer and, if applicable, of the group to which it belongs.

26.7.3   *Authorisation and dissemination of the bid*

The CNMV will review the request for authorisation and the documents filed and, if applicable, shall declare, within seven business days after any remaining documents have been submitted, that the request is admitted for processing.

The CNMV will then adopt a resolution granting or denying authorisation for the bid within 20 business days of the receipt of the request. However, this period must be calculated from the date on which any additional documentation that is required by the CNMV is registered or submitted.

Under Article 22 of the Royal Decree, once the offeror has been given notice of the authorisation by the CNMV, it must disseminate the bid and make it generally known to the public within five days through the Listing Bulletin (*Boletín de Cotización*) of the Stock Exchange where the securities are admitted to trading and in a newspaper of national circulation. In addition, the offer document and the supplemental documents must be made available to the public when published. The offeror may choose to do this by making printed copies available free of charge at the appropriate Stock Exchanges or by placing electronic copies on its website or on that of the CNMV. If the offeror elects to use electronic form for dissemination, it must also deliver a printed copy, free of charge, to any shareholder that requests it.

26.7.4 Documentation

26.7.4.1 The offer document

The content of the offer document is established in Article 18 and in the Annex to the Royal Decree. The offer document must be worded in a manner such that the content thereof may be readily analysed and understood. The offer document may also contain any other information that the offeror deems it advisable to include in order for the addressees thereof to be able to make an informed assessment of the bid. The CNMV may require the offeror to include in the offer document any additional information it deems necessary and to submit any supplemental documents that it deems appropriate. In addition, the CNMV may include in the offer document warnings and considerations that facilitate its analysis and comprehension. The CNMV can also relieve the offeror of the obligation to include in the offer document any information when such information is not available to the offeror, provided that it does not involve facts or circumstances that are essential to make an informed assessment of the bid.

In the event that, after the offer document has been published, any circumstance occurs which requires the inclusion of additional information or data, the offeror may provide it in the form of a supplement.

The Royal Decree requires the information in the offer document to be structured in five chapters, the content of which is broadly as follows:

(a) Chapter I: information regarding the persons responsible for the offer document; resolutions relating to the bid and applicable law; basic information regarding the offeree; information regarding the offeror and its group; description of any agreements regarding the bid between the offeror and the shareholders, directors or members of management of the offeree; information on securities of the offeree which are held by the offeror; information regarding transactions in securities of the offeree carried out by the offeror and persons acting in concert therewith over the 12 months preceding the announcement of the bid; information regarding the activities and financial position of the offeror.

(b)   Chapter II: information regarding the securities to which the bid is directed, the consideration offered, the conditions to which the bid is subject, and the guarantees for and financing of the bid.
(c)   Chapter III: procedure for acceptance and settlement of the bid.
(d)   Chapter IV: information regarding the purpose of the transaction, including strategic plans and intentions concerning the future activities of the offeree, the employees and managers thereof, the disposition of assets and the dividend policy.
(e)   Chapter V: authorisations and other information, including information regarding the application of the Defence of Competition Act (*Ley de Defensa de la Competencia*), and detailed description of the administrative authorisations required.

If the consideration consists of securities, the offer document must contain such additional information as is equivalent to the information contained in the prospectus for a public offer of securities, unless there is a registration document or prospectus of the issuer of the securities delivered in exchange that is valid under the provisions of the applicable regulations.

26.7.4.2   *The offeree directors' report*
The board of the offeree must prepare a detailed and reasoned report on the takeover bid, which must contain an outline of the board's position, whether in favour of or against the bid. It must also contain a variety of other information. Article 24 of the Royal Decree provides that the report must:

(a)   state whether any agreement exists between the offeree and the offeror, its managers or shareholders, or between any of these and the members of the board of the offeree, and state whether the direct or indirect holders of any shares affected by such agreements intend to accept or reject the bid;
(b)   set forth the possible repercussions of the bid and the strategic plans of the offeror that are included in the offer document in respect of various aspects of the offeree's business;
(c)   state whether a board member is subject to a conflict of interest, and, if this is the case, describe the nature of such conflict;
(d)   include the opinions of members who are in a minority in the event that the members of the board take differing positions in connection with the bid;
(e)   include details of any securities of the offeror that are directly or indirectly held by the offeree or by the persons with whom it acts in concert;
(f)   include details of any securities of the offeree that are directly or indirectly held or represented by the members of the board of the offeree; and
(g)   include details of any securities that the members of the board of the offeree hold in the offeror.

The report must be made public by the offeree itself by any of the means contemplated for the announcement of the bid within a maximum period of 10 calendar days after the start of the acceptance period of the bid and must also be submitted to the CNMV and to the representatives of the employees of the offeree.

26.8   Acceptance

26.8.1   *Accepting the offer*

Under Article 34 of the Royal Decree, statements of acceptance of the bid must be made as provided in the offer document, but will be invalid if subject to conditions. However, if there are competing offers, multiple statements of acceptance may be made as long as the order of preference among them is indicated and the statements are submitted to the various competing offerors.

Statements of acceptance may be revoked at any time before the last day of the acceptance period.

26.8.2   *Acceptance period*

26.8.2.1   *General rule*

Under Article 23 of the Royal Decree, the acceptance period of the bid must be established by the offeror in the offer document, and may not be less than 15 nor greater than 70 calendar days from the trading day immediately following the date of publication of the first announcement of the bid.

26.8.2.2   *Extension*

The acceptance period of the bid may be extended in the following circumstances:

(a)   the offeror may extend the acceptance period provided that the aforementioned maximum length of 70 days is not exceeded and the extension is announced at least three calendar days prior to the expiration of the original period;

(b)   the acceptance period shall be automatically extended, where applicable, such that at least 15 calendar days elapse between the date of holding of the general meeting at which the issuance of the securities offered as consideration must be approved or at which a decision must be made regarding the conditions to which the bid has been subjected and the last day of the acceptance period;

(c)   the CNMV may extend the acceptance period when a supplement to the offer document is published and it is so required by the significance of the information contained therein (e.g., as a consequence of the amendment of the terms of the bid);

(d)   in the case of competing offers, the periods for acceptance of prior bids shall automatically be lengthened such that all offers expire on the same day; and

(e)   the CNMV may, by means of a reasoned resolution, approve an extension of the acceptance period in all other cases in which it may be necessary to ensure the adequate protection of the addressees of the bid.

26.9   Defensive measures and neutralisation

26.9.1   Most common defensive measures

From a legal viewpoint, the preventive measures that may be adopted by a listed company in the event of a possible hostile takeover bid are basically of two kinds: measures contemplated in the articles of association, and contractual measures.

The offeree's articles of association may contain a number of measures designed to prevent hostile takeovers. The principal and most effective preventive measure of this type admissible in Spain is the limitation on the number of votes that may be cast by a single shareholder or by all shareholders belonging to the same group. The articles of association may also provide for qualified quorums or voting majorities for the approval of certain resolutions (e.g., capital increases, issuances of debentures, mergers and split-offs). While the latter measures may favour the creation of a blocking minority that hinders the future plans of a possible hostile acquirer, they may also affect the day-to-day management of the company. The articles of association may also establish special requirements to be appointed director (such as, for example, to have been a shareholder of the company over a minimum period of time prior to the appointment) or to serve in key positions (chairman, chief executive officer) on the board of directors (such as, for example, a particular length of service as director of the company). This measure may hinder the access of a hostile acquirer to the company's board of directors, but it could not apply to the appointment of directors in the exercise of a shareholder's right of proportional representation.

26.9.2   Offeror's knowledge of the offeree's defensive measures

The articles of association of listed companies, as well as shareholders agreements executed by their shareholders which regulate the exercise of voting rights at general meetings or which restrict or condition the free transfer of shares, may be inspected at the Commercial Registry where the issuer is registered, as well as on the websites that issuers must have in compliance with the duties of information and transparency. The detailed content thereof is regulated by Circular 1/2004, of 17 March, of the CNMV. Shareholders agreements are also available on the website of the CNMV (www.cnmv.es).

In addition, the management report prepared annually by listed companies at the time of submission of their annual accounts must contain information regarding, *inter alia*:

(a)   all significant agreements that the company has executed and which become effective, are amended or end in the event of a change of control at the company as a consequence of a takeover bid, as well as the effects of such agreements, except when the dissemination thereof is seriously detrimental to the company (which exception shall not apply when the company is obligated by law to make such information public); and

(b)   all agreements between the company and persons serving in management positions or employees, which provide for compensation payments when such persons or employees resign or are wrongfully dismissed or if the employment relationship ends as a consequence of a takeover bid.

26.9.3　Neutralisation of defensive measures

The new regime allows the establishment of an optional regime that companies may impose upon themselves in order to neutralise some of their own preventive measures.

26.9.3.1　Neutralisation measures

Under Article 29 of the Royal Decree, listed companies that have preventive measures in place may decide that one or more of the following neutralisation (breakthrough) measures apply in the event that the company is the target of a takeover bid:

(a)　the ineffectiveness of any restrictions on the free transfer of securities established in shareholders agreements in relation to the offeree during the acceptance period of the bid;

(b)　the ineffectiveness, at the general meeting of shareholders of the offeree at which decisions are made on the possible adoption of preventive measures, of any restrictions on the voting rights contemplated in the articles of association of the company and in shareholders agreements relating to such company; and

(c)　the ineffectiveness of the restrictions contemplated in (a) and (b) when, after a takeover bid, the offeror has reached a percentage equal to or greater than 75 per cent of the voting capital.

26.9.3.2　Approval of neutralisation measures

The decision to apply the neutralisation to the above measures must be adopted at the general meeting of shareholders of the company in compliance with the qualified quorum and majority requirements referred to in Article 103 of the Spanish Companies Act. For such purpose, the board of directors of the company must prepare a report under Article 29.2 of the Royal Decree containing:

(a)　a description of the restrictions in the articles and in shareholders agreements which are intended to be neutralised;

(b)　the neutralisation measures that the board seeks to apply;

(c)　the agreements executed or being negotiated by the company or third parties with potential offerors of which the company is aware;

(d)　the reasons why the directors propose the adoption of such neutralisation measures; and

(e)　the direction of the vote cast by each director on the approval of the report.

Such report must be made available to the shareholders from the time the general meeting is convened.

When a company decides to apply neutralisation measures, it must compensate the holders of the neutralised rights for the loss that they suffer. In addition, shareholders that have previously approved the application of neutralisation measures may revoke such decision with the same qualified quorum requirement and voting majority as apply to approval. The adoption and revocation of neutralisation measures must be reported to the CNMV.

26.9.3.3   *Exclusion of neutralisation measures in the event of a lack of reciprocity*

Listed companies that have opted to apply neutralisation measures to themselves may decide, by means of a resolution adopted within a maximum period of 18 months prior to the takeover bid in question being made public, that such measures do not come into play and that, accordingly, the preventive measures contemplated in their articles of association and shareholders agreements will be maintained when the bid is made by an entity or group that has not adopted equivalent neutralisation measures.

26.10   Offeree board's duty of passivity

26.10.1   *The passivity rule*

26.10.1.1   *General rule*

Under Article 28 of the Royal Decree, the board of directors of the offeree, any executive body of such board or any body receiving powers therefrom, their respective members, as well as the companies belonging to the group of which the offeree is a member, and any other company that may act in concert with any of the foregoing, may not take any action that may hinder the success of the bid without first obtaining the prior approval of the offeree shareholders at a general meeting granted in compliance with the qualified quorum and majority requirements referred to in Article 103 of the Spanish Companies Act. This restriction applies from the public announcement of a takeover bid on the company until the publication of the result of the bid. In addition and without prejudice to the general limitation described above, offeree shareholder approval shall be specifically required:

(a)   to approve or commence any issue of securities that may hinder the success of the bid;

(b)   to carry out or promote, directly or indirectly, transactions that may hinder the success of the bid involving the securities covered by the bid or any other securities, including actions intended to promote the purchase of such securities;

(c)   to dispose of, encumber or lease real property or other corporate assets when such transactions may hinder the success of the bid; or

(d)   to pay extraordinary dividends or give any other kind of compensation that is not consistent with the customary policy for payment of dividends of the offeree, unless the corresponding corporate resolutions have been adopted and made public by a competent decision-making body before making the bid.

It should be noted that any measures designed to prevent a takeover bid that the directors may implement following specific shareholder approval must still be fully lawful and legitimate in and of themselves; for example, they cannot go against the corporate interest of the offeree.

26.10.1.2   *Prior decisions*

With respect to decisions adopted prior to the announcement of a bid which may hinder the success of the bid and which have not yet been carried out, the shareholders must approve or confirm any resolution that is not within the ordinary course of business of the offeree.

26.10.1.3   Board of directors' report

The offeree board of directors must prepare a report, to be made available to the shareholders from the time the general meeting is convened, containing a detailed description of and the rationale for the actions which require share-holder approval and setting out whether each director approved the report. The notice of the meeting must set out the measures to be decided on in that meeting, and the meeting shall be held specifically for this purpose.

26.10.1.4   Exceptions

As an exception to the passivity rule:

(a)   the offeree board may seek offers that compete with the original bid, as this is consistent with the board's fiduciary duty to maximise the value of the offeree for the benefit of the shareholders; and

(b)   the rule applies to the directors of the offeree but not to the shareholders who may put in place any measure by resolution passed at a general meeting.

26.10.2   Exclusion of the duty of passivity in the event of a lack of reciprocity

The offeree shareholders may opt, through successive resolutions with an effective period of 18 months each, to release the board of directors from its duty of passivity if the company is the offeree of a takeover bid made by a foreign entity which does not have its registered office in Spain and which is not subject to the same or comparable provisions. Such decision shall require the approval of the shareholders at a general meeting, as prescribed in Article 103 of the Spanish Companies Act.

The directors of the company must prepare a detailed written report containing the rationale for the resolution to be adopted. Such report must set forth the direction of the vote cast by each director. The report must be made available to the shareholders from the time the general meeting is convened. The call of the meeting must clearly set forth the decision proposed to the shareholders.

26.11   Modification and withdrawal of the offer

26.11.1   Conditions for modifying an offer

Under Article 31 of the Royal Decree, the offeror may freely revise the terms of its bid one or more times from the time it is submitted until any time prior to the last five calendar days of the acceptance period. Any revision must comply with the rule of equality of treatment and must result in more favourable treatment of the shareholders. This will generally be achieved as follows:

(a)   in any bid by increasing the consideration offered;

(b)   in a partial voluntary bid by extending the bid to a greater number of securities; or

(c)   in a voluntary bid by eliminating or lessening any conditions to which the bid may be subject.

The offeror may also modify its bid by acting in association or concert with third parties. In these cases the Royal Decree requires such offeror and third parties to assume joint and several liability for the revised bid.

26.11.2   Procedure for the modification of an offer

26.11.2.1   Offer document supplement
Once it has adopted the corporate resolutions required to modify its bid, the offeror must then prepare and submit for approval by the CNMV a supplement to the offer document containing a description of the changes to the bid. The CNMV must then make a decision within three business days of receipt of the request, during which period the acceptance period is suspended. Once approved by the CNMV, the changes must be published by the offeror on the business day immediately following the approval, and the offeree board of directors must issue a report on the revised bid within five calendar days after the revised bid is published.

26.11.2.2   Acceptance of revised offers
The CNMV may extend the original acceptance period of the bid if it deems it necessary for the purpose of better analysis of the proposed changes. Unless an express statement to the contrary is made, it shall be deemed that the addressees of the bid that have accepted it prior to the changes consent to the improved bid.

26.11.3   Withdrawal of an offer

The general rule under Article 30 of the Royal Decree is that bids are irrevocable once they have been announced. However, the Royal Decree does envisage under Article 33 certain circumstances in which the offeror may withdraw its bid. The instances in which withdrawal is permitted naturally vary depending on whether the bid is voluntary or mandatory.

26.11.3.1   Mandatory bids
Mandatory bids may be withdrawn in the following circumstances:

(a)   when the bid is subject to approval by the competition authorities and, before the expiration of the acceptance period, the transaction is prohibited, or the transaction is authorised subject to conditions by such authorities, or no decision is made by such authorities regarding the authorisation of the bid;

(b)   when, due to exceptional circumstances beyond the control of the offeror, the bid may not be carried out or is manifestly unfeasible, provided that the CNMV authorises the withdrawal; and

(c)   when an unconditional competing offer which contains better terms is maintained.

26.11.3.2   Voluntary bids

Voluntary bids may be withdrawn, in addition to the circumstances outlined above for mandatory bids, in the following circumstances:

(a)   when a competing offer is authorised; or

(b)   when the offeree shareholders (or the board of directors, if it has been released from the duty of passivity) approve a preventive measure against the bid which, in the opinion of the offeror, prevents it from maintaining its bid, as long as the offeror was not involved in the adoption of this measure and the CNMV authorises the withdrawal.

26.11.4   Ineffectiveness of the offer

A voluntary bid ceases to have effect when, at the expiration of the acceptance period, the conditions to which the bid has been subject have not been fulfilled, unless the offeror waives such conditions and, in particular, when the bid has not been accepted by the minimum number of securities upon which the bid had been made conditional.

26.12   Competing offers

26.12.1   Conditions for competing offers

A takeover bid is defined as a "competing offer" when it affects securities for all or a part of which another takeover bid, the acceptance period of which has not yet expired, has previously been submitted to the CNMV.

Article 42 of the Royal Decree establishes a number of conditions for competing offers. A competing offer:

(a)   must be submitted at least five days before the acceptance period for the last preceding offer ends (whether that be the original offer or another competing offer). If a mandatory bid is triggered less than five days before the relevant period expires, the CNMV shall provide for an extension so that the mandatory offer will be subject to the rules for competing offers;

(b)   in the case of partial voluntary bids, must cover a number of securities that is not less than that of the immediately preceding offer; and

(c)   must outbid the last preceding offer, either by raising the value of the consideration or by extending the offer to a larger number of securities.

In addition, where the submission of a competing offer is mandatory, that mandatory offer must also comply with the requirements established in the Royal Decree in respect of mandatory bids.

26.12.2   Where there is more than one competing offer

Where more than one competing offer is submitted, Article 44 of the Royal Decree provides that the acceptance periods of all offers in existence will be consolidated into one single period, which will be the acceptance period for the last offer submitted, and will be published by the CNMV on its website.

26.12.3 Authorisation of competing offers

Under Article 41 of the Royal Decree, competing offers are processed in the order of their submission, such that a competing offer will not be processed until the preceding offer has been authorised, if applicable. As no specific period is provided for in the Royal Decree, the period for processing will be the period established for the processing of takeover bids in general (20 business days after receipt of the request for authorisation).

26.12.4 The effect of a competing offer on a takeover bid schedule

The primary effect of a competing offer on the schedule is the interruption of the acceptance period not only of the original bid but also of all competing offers previously submitted. As discussed above, the Royal Decree ensures that both the original bid and all competing offers subsequently submitted are processed together by consolidating the acceptance periods of all offers into a single period, which expires for all of them on the same day.

Under Article 44 of the Royal Decree, the acceptance period of competing offers is 30 calendar days from the day following the date of publication of the first announcement of the offer that has already been authorised.

26.12.5 The effect of competing offers on prior bids

26.12.5.1 Withdrawal
The authorisation of a competing offer may allow a bid to be withdrawn (*see* 26.11.3 above).

26.12.5.2 Improvements
The submission of a competing offer also enables prior offerors to modify (improve) the terms of their offers. The Royal Decree provides that improvements should take place once competing offers have been authorised, rather than merely announced. In this way the new regime allows for the terms of a bid to be improved in a continuous and unlimited fashion until the sealed envelopes must be sent, thus maximising shareholders' benefit. The new regime also allows the offeror to act in association or concert with third parties in order to improve the terms of the bid as long as certain requirements are satisfied (*see* 26.12.9 below).

26.12.6 The revocation of acceptances in the context of competing offers

The Royal Decree lays down no special rules as to the revocation of acceptance in the context of competing offers. Therefore, Article 34.3 allowing statements of acceptance to be revoked at any time before the last day of the acceptance period of the bid must be deemed applicable.

The new regime also allows multiple statements of acceptance. In this case, the order of preference must be indicated and the statements must be submitted to the various competing offerors.

26.12.7   The resolution of the competing offer process

The competing offers process ends when all of the offerors that have not previously withdrawn their offer send a sealed envelope to the CNMV within five business days following the end of the period established for submitting competing offers. In the sealed envelope the offerors will include a new improvement of their bid or their decision not to submit an improvement of the offer.

26.12.8   Advantages for the first offeror

The Royal Decree grants some advantages to the first offeror. This is justified by the fact that such first offeror has incurred search costs and greater risks than the other offerors. After the envelope submission stage has ended, the first offeror may make one last improvement, provided that:

(a)   the consideration offered by it in its sealed envelope was not more than 2 per cent lower than the highest consideration offered by competing offerors in their envelopes; and

(b)   the original offeror improves the price of the best offer made in an envelope by at least 1 per cent, or extends the original bid to a number of securities that is at least 5 per cent larger than that in the best competing offer submitted in an envelope.

26.12.9   Third party co-offerors

The Royal Decree prohibits those persons that act in concert with the offeror, those belonging to the offeror's group or those which act for the account of the offeror from submitting a competing offer. However, the new regime does allow association or concerted action between an offeror and a third party in order to improve a bid that has already been submitted as long as:

(a)   none of the entities participating in the bid has a direct or indirect interest in another offer regarding the same securities;

(b)   the offeror and the third parties acting in association or concert assume joint and several liability for the bid; and

(c)   the identity of the offeror group, including third parties acting in association or concert, is reflected in a supplement to the offer document.

26.13   Sell-out and squeeze-out

Articles 47 and 48 of the Royal Decree allow an offeror that holds at least 90 per cent of the voting capital of the offeree as a result of a takeover bid accepted by 90 per cent of the addressees thereof, the right to require the minority shareholders and the holders of the other securities to sell to the offeror all of their shares and other securities (squeeze-out). Minority shareholders have a corresponding right to force the offeror to purchase their securities (sell-out) under the same conditions, thus allowing shareholders that have been left in a truly minority position to opt out of the company.

The new regime grants squeeze-out and sell-out rights to the offeror and to the holders of the securities to which the original takeover bid was directed respectively. In the case of sell-out rights, such holders will be the shareholders that decided not to accept the bid and remain at the company as minorities, and any holders of convertible and exchangeable debentures, pre-emptive rights or any other instrument carrying an option to the acquisition or subscription of shares in the offeree.

26.13.1 Purpose of squeeze-out and sell-out rights

26.13.1.1 Squeeze-out

The squeeze-out rights contained in Articles 47 and 48 are designed to allow an offeror who has obtained a large majority of the offeree's share capital to more easily acquire the entire capital of that company. This will:

(a) allow the offeror to delist the offeree without having to follow the complex procedure applicable to delisting offers;

(b) facilitate the placing of the acquisition debt at the level of the acquired company ("debt push down") by means of a simplified merger, or the optimisation of the distribution of reserves of the offeree; and

(c) allow the majority shareholder to avoid exposure to abusive exercise by minority shareholders of their rights (e.g., the right to receive information, to challenge corporate resolutions or to hold the directors accountable). Such exercise of rights is not for the collective benefit of the shareholders, but rather in the individual interest of the minority as they seek to obtain an exorbitant price for their shares.

26.13.1.2 Sell-out

As stated above, the sell-out rights are designed to allow minority shareholders to opt out of the company. This serves as a fair counterbalance to the powers accorded to majority shareholders under the right of squeeze-out and mitigates the risk of abuse by the majority shareholder of the control obtained through the takeover bid, which may lead it to derive private benefits from the company to the detriment of minority shareholders or to modify the risk profile of the company by causing it to increase its indebtedness. Sell-out rights also:

(a) allow offeree shareholders a second chance to sell, thus freeing them from any pressure to accept the original bid; and

(b) allow minority shareholders to obtain adequate compensation for their shares once the market has lost liquidity as a result of the takeover bid.

26.13.2 Requirements for squeeze-out and sell-out

Squeeze-out and sell-out rights are conditional, in each case, on three requirements:

(a) the offeror must have made a takeover bid, whether mandatory or voluntary, for 100 per cent of the capital of the offeree;

(b) the offeror must hold, as a result of the takeover bid, securities representing at least 90 per cent of the capital carrying voting rights. Although the new regime does not clarify exactly how this percentage should be calculated, it will certainly include the shares already held by the offeror before submitting the bid in addition to the shares acquired under or during the takeover bid itself; and

(c)   the bid must have been accepted by holders of securities representing at least 90 per cent of the voting rights covered by the bid.

The right to squeeze-out and sell-out is therefore dependent not only on the possession of a large majority by the offeror, but also on the prior success of the bid in question. This measure effectively discourages the purchase of shares prior to the takeover bid, as any offeror holding a sizeable percentage of the offeree's share capital prior to a bid will have to acquire 90 per cent of the remaining shares at which the bid is aimed in order to acquire the right of squeeze-out.

26.13.3   *Offers conditional on the attaining of the squeeze-out percentage*

As discussed above, mandatory bids may not be subject to any condition. In contrast, voluntary bids are favoured by the new regime as they may be made conditional upon the acceptance of the bid by a certain number of offeree securities.

26.13.4   *The exercise of squeeze-out and sell-out rights*

The rights of squeeze-out and sell-out may be exercised by the offeror and by minority shareholders, respectively, within three months of the date of expiration of the acceptance period of the prior takeover bid. The offeror must exercise the right of squeeze-out in respect of all minority shareholders and must disclose the decision as soon as it is made. Such decision will be irrevocable. In contrast, minority shareholders may exercise their right individually and may also choose, acting individually, the consideration they wish to receive when an alternative is offered (cash consideration is assumed in the absence of such choice).

26.13.4.1   *Consideration*
Squeeze-outs and sell-outs must be carried out at an equitable price, such price being understood as being equal to the consideration paid in the prior takeover bid irrespective of whether the bid consideration was cash or securities. Therefore, the new regime avoids any speculation on the price for the squeeze-out or sell-out in order to discourage offeree shareholders from "holding out" on the original bid in the hope of obtaining a better price in a subsequent sell-out process.

26.13.4.2   *Settlement*
If the right is exercised by the offeror, squeeze-outs must be carried out simultaneously in respect of all minority shareholders on such date as the offeror elects within a period of 15 to 20 business days following notice to the CNMV, and the settlement takes place within the same period established in the offer document. In contrast, if the right of sell-out is exercised by minority shareholders (even after the exercise of the right of squeeze-out by the offeror), the sales must be carried out as the notices from the minority shareholders are received, and they

must be settled within the same periods as those established in the offer document, counted from receipt of each request.

26.13.4.3 Expenses

In the case of a squeeze-out (requested by the offeror), all expenses arising from the purchase and sale or exchange and the settlement of the securities are borne by the offeror, whilst in the case of sell-outs (requested by minority share-holders), all expenses are borne by the selling minority shareholders.

26.13.5 Squeeze-out/sell-out rights and delisting offers

Squeeze-outs or sell-outs whereby the offeror acquires 100 per cent of the voting rights in the offeree result in such company being delisted (unless the offeror has been forced to buy as a consequence of the exercise of the right of sell-out by the minority shareholders and the CNMV grants it a period within which to comply again with the requirements of dissemination and liquidity of the securities). Squeeze-out therefore constitutes a procedure for delisting the offeree that is clearly more advantageous than the procedure contemplated in Article 34.2 of the Securities Market Act and the regulations thereunder, to the extent that they spare the offeror the need to submit a new takeover bid at a price that is a product of the intervention of the CNMV. In this way, the offeror need not obtain the approval of the delisting offer by the shareholders at a general meeting of the offeree, nor does it need to prepare a fairness opinion, or to prepare and obtain approval for a new offer document or, in general, to go through the complexities of the delisting offer procedure.

26.14 Sanctions for failure to comply with the new regime

The sanctions for failure to comply with the rules applicable to takeover bids are set forth in the Securities Market Act.

26.14.1 Fines

26.14.1.1 Very serious violations

Article 99 of the Securities Market Act describes the following as very serious violations:

(a) Failure to comply with the obligations established in Article 60 (relating to mandatory bids when control of a listed company is reached) and Article 61 (relating to voluntary bids) of the Securities Market Act and in the set of provisions further developing thereof (i.e., the Royal Decree). The Act provides an illustrative list of potential instances of non-compliance which include, among others:
   (i) non-compliance with the obligation to submit a takeover bid;
   (ii) the submission thereof outside the maximum period or with material irregularities;
   (iii) submitting a takeover bid without the required authorisation;

    (iv)   failure to publish or send to the CNMV the information and documents to be published or sent to it; and

    (v)   publication or provision of information or documents on a takeover bid containing inaccurate, false or misleading information, when such information or documentation is relevant or the amount of the bid or the number of affected investors is significant.

(b)   Failure by the board of directors of the offeree to comply with its passivity duties established in the Securities Market Act and in the Royal Decree.

(c)   Failure to comply with duties relating to delisting and neutralisation (breakthrough) measures established in the Securities Market Act and in the Royal Decree.

Article 102 of the Securities Market Act sets forth a list of sanctions that may be imposed for committing very serious violations. Worthy of mention is the sanction consisting of a fine of not less than, or more than five times the amount of, the gross profit made as a result of the actions or omissions that constitute the violation; or, should such standard not apply, of up to the greatest of the following amounts:

(a)   5 per cent of the shareholders' equity of the violating entity;

(b)   5 per cent of the total funds of the entity or of third parties used in the violation; or

(c)   €300,506.

26.14.1.2 *Serious violations*

Article 100 of the Securities Market Act provides that the following shall be serious violations:

(a)   failure to publish or to submit to the CNMV the information and documentation that must be published or submitted as a consequence of actions requiring the submission of a takeover bid, within the course or after the completion thereof, when such failure does not constitute a very serious violation; and

(b)   the publication or provision of information or documentation relating to a takeover bid in which data has been omitted or which contains inaccurate, false or misleading information, when this does not constitute a very serious violation.

The Securities Market Act also establishes a list of sanctions that may be imposed by the CNMV for serious violations. Of note is the sanction consisting of a fine of up to the amount of the gross profit received as a result of the acts or omissions constituting the violation; or, in the event that such standard is not applicable, of up to the greatest of the following amounts:

(a)   2 per cent of the shareholders' equity of the violating entity;

(b)   2 per cent of its own or third-party funds used in the violation; or

(c)   €150,253.

26.14.2 Suspension of voting rights

In addition to any fines that may be imposed, Article 60.3 of the Securities Market Act provides that whoever fails to comply with the obligation to submit a takeover bid may not exercise the voting and related political rights attaching to any of the securities of the listed company, and presumes that such obligation has not been fulfilled by whoever fails to submit the bid, or submits it after the expiration of the applicable period or with material irregularities. It further provides that resolutions adopted by the decision-making bodies of a company shall be null and void if the securities whose voting and related political rights are suspended for such reason needed to be computed to convene the meeting or pass the resolution, and authorises the CNMV to take the necessary actions to challenge the resolutions.

Chapter 27

Sweden

Anders Lundin, Partner
Krister Skoog, Associate
Linnéa Ecorcheville, Associate
Gernandt & Danielsson Advokatbyrå KB

27.1   Introduction

A few examples of the recorded acquisitions during 2006 and 2007 are:

(a)   Cinven's acquisition of Ahlsell (2006);
(b)   EQT and Investor's acquisition of Gambro (2006);
(c)   MAN's aborted takeover offer for Scania (2006);
(d)   Investor and Morgan Stanley's acquisition of Mölnlycke Health Care Group AB (2007);
(e)   EQT's acquisition of Scandic Hotels AB (2007);
(f)   Milestone's acquisition of Invik (2007);
(g)   IBM's acquisition of Telelogic (2007); and
(h)   NASDAQ and Borse Dubai's joint offer for OMX (still pending at the time of writing).

Foreign takeovers are generally privately negotiated and made on an agreed basis, but they may also be effected by means of a public offer. Hostile takeovers occur.

The main securities market in Sweden is the OMX Nordic Exchange Stockholm. A number of additional marketplaces have been established, but the OMX Nordic Exchange Stockholm remains the most important securities market in Sweden.

27.2   Acquisition targets

Business in Sweden is generally conducted through limited liability companies (*aktiebolag* or AB) and, unless otherwise stated, this chapter deals exclusively with mergers and acquisitions of such companies. However, business may also be carried on through various forms of partnership.

In a general partnership (*handelsbolag*) the co-owners are jointly and severally liable for all obligations resulting from the operations of the partnership. The partners may be individuals or companies. A limited partnership (*kommanditbolag*) is a business consisting of one or more general partners (*komplementär*), and one or more limited partners (*kommanditdelägare*) who are liable only to the extent of the capital subscribed and/or invested by each of them. Business may also be carried on through incorporated associations (*ekonomisk förening*). This form of enterprise is used mainly for cooperative businesses.

A foreign limited liability company, lawfully registered in its home country, may operate through a Swedish branch office but the branch office must be registered in Sweden. Many foreign banks operate in Sweden through branch offices. It is also possible to conduct business in Sweden through a company set up within the territory of the European Economic Area ("EEA") in the form of a European public limited liability company (*Societas Europaea* or SE). Provisions in the Swedish European Companies Act 2004 supplement the European Council Regulation in respect of European companies which have their registered seat in Sweden.

It is also possible to set up European Economic Interest Groupings (EEIG) in Sweden.

27.2.1 ABs

Ownership of a limited liability company (an AB) is conferred by the holding of shares. All shares in an AB must carry voting rights, although different classes of shares with differing voting rights may be issued. However, no share may be issued with more than 10 times the voting rights of another. All shares in a company are recorded in a share register maintained by the company or, if the company is registered with a special authorised central securities administrator, by such central securities administrator.

Swedish law draws a distinction between public and private ABs. Only public ABs are allowed to turn to the public to procure new capital. The minimum share capital in public ABs is SEK500,000 whereas private ABs have a minimum share capital of SEK100,000. The share capital of an AB may also be expressed in euros.

27.2.1.1 Management

An AB is managed by a single board of directors. The board is normally elected by the shareholders, but it can be stipulated in the articles of association that one or more of the directors shall be appointed in another manner. As regards public ABs, more than half of the directors must be elected by the shareholders at a general meeting of shareholders. Control of more than 50 per cent of the voting rights in a company will confer control of the composition of the board of directors. As regards directors, the person (or persons) receiving the most votes (ordinary majority) at a shareholders meeting is elected director (or directors). The board may appoint a managing director and must do so where the company is a public AB. Unless the Swedish Companies Registration Office grants an exemption in a particular case, the managing director and at least half of the directors of a Swedish company must be resident within the EEA. In addition, where during the previous financial year the company has had at least 25 employees in Sweden and is bound by a collective agreement with a union, employees have the right to appoint two directors and two deputy directors. Employees are entitled to appoint three directors and three deputy directors if the company carries on more than one line of business and during the previous financial year has had at least 1,000 employees in Sweden. The employee directors may not outnumber the ordinary directors. The powers and duties of directors appointed by employees are essentially the same as those of the directors appointed by the shareholders.

27.2.1.2 *Powers of shareholders and voting*

Institutional investors and other companies often control the majority of the votes in Swedish publicly traded companies. As a rule, resolutions by the shareholders meeting require a majority of more than half of the votes cast to be adopted. A resolution to amend the articles of association will normally require approval by two-thirds of the votes cast and the shares represented at a shareholders meeting. Certain amendments to the articles of association require approval by higher majorities. For example, approval by all shareholders present at the shareholders meeting, representing at least nine-tenths of all issued shares in the company, will normally be necessary for an amendment which reduces current shareholders' rights to profits or other assets, restricts the transferability of already issued shares in the company, or alters the legal relationship between already issued shares. These majority requirements may be increased (but not reduced) by the provisions of a company's articles of association. As mentioned at 27.2.1.1 above, directors are normally elected by an ordinary majority. This majority requirement may be reduced (but not increased) by provisions in the articles of association.

Existing shareholders have pre-emption rights to subscribe for new shares in the case of new issues of shares. These rights can, as regards cash and set-off issues, be disapplied by a shareholders' resolution or by a provision in the articles of association in case the shares shall not have equal rights in the company's assets or profit or where the shares have different voting power. A resolution to issue new shares, or to authorise the board of directors to issue new shares, only requires approval by more than half of the votes cast, unless the resolution calls for a deviation from the shareholders' pre-emption rights or an alteration of the articles of association is necessary because the existing maximum share capital is insufficient to allow the proposed new issue. In the latter cases, approval by two-thirds of the votes cast and shares represented at the shareholders meeting is required. Any authorisation to the board of directors to issue shares or convertible securities must be for a specified period of time, expiring no later than at the next annual general meeting of shareholders. Authorisation for new issues is normally only given for specific purposes.

The Companies Act 2005 provides that all shareholders may exercise their voting rights in full, unless otherwise provided in the articles of association.

Minority shareholders have a number of rights for the protection of their interests. Holders of not less than one-tenth of all shares of a Swedish company may, among other things and subject to certain conditions:

(a)   have an extra auditor appointed by the County Administrative Board, who shall participate in the audit of the company together with the other auditors of the company;

(b)   have one or several special examiners appointed by the County Administrative Board;

(c)   institute an action for damages in favour of the company against a founder of the company, a member of the board of directors, the managing director, an auditor or another shareholder; and

(d)   request the payment of dividends computed by reference to the company's net profit for the year after certain deductions.

The Swedish code for corporate governance is based on the Companies Act 2005 and the tradition of self-regulation that prevails in Sweden. The code deals primarily with the organisation of corporate governance and management bodies and their work procedures and the interaction between these bodies, but not the division of power among the company's owners.

As most similar codes in other countries, the Swedish code is based on the principle "comply or explain". This means that a company can deviate from the code's provisions without this entailing a breach of the code. A company that intends to deviate from a regulation in the code must, however, explain why the deviation is occurring.

The code has been implemented in the rules of the OMX Nordic Exchange Stockholm and forms part of the requirements that a company must fulfil in order to be listed at the OMX Nordic Exchange Stockholm. The code applies to all Swedish companies that are registered on the OMX Nordic Exchange Stockholm and for other listed companies with a market capitalisation exceeding SEK3 billion

A revised Swedish Code of Corporate Governance has on 1 February 2008 been proposed by the Swedish Corporate Governance Board (a self-regulatory body supervising compliance with the Swedish code). One of the new features of the Swedish code will be that it will apply to all listed companies, regardless of market capitalisation, as from 1 July 2008.

27.2.2   Barriers to hostile acquisitions

There is no general prohibition on foreign persons or entities acquiring shares in Swedish companies. The shares of a Swedish company may be divided into different classes with different voting rights, and this may, in practice, impede the success of a hostile offer. It is not uncommon that shares are divided into two classes, with the shares of one class carrying 10 times as many voting rights as the shares of the other class. When a company goes public, shares conferring voting control are often retained by the initial shareholders. Furthermore, provisions granting rights of first refusal or post-sale purchase rights on transfers of shares to existing shareholders are commonly found in the articles of association of companies the shares of which are held by a small number of investors. Such transfer restrictions may also be found in the articles of association of companies with a large shareholder base. However, the class(es) of shares which are publicly traded on the OMX Nordic Exchange Stockholm may not be subject to such transfer restrictions.

27.2.3   Employment aspects

According to the Employment Protection Act 1982, an employee will, in the case of a sale of a business (in whole or in part), automatically be taken over by the purchaser of the business, provided the employee is not opposed to that arrangement. The employment agreements existing on the day of the transfer will be transferred to the purchaser. The purchaser of the business will be responsible (together with the seller) for monetary obligations which have arisen from the employment agreements prior to the transfer. These rules are based on EC law.

27.3 Exchange and investment control

27.3.1 Exchange control

Previously, Sweden had strict foreign exchange regulations, but exchange controls were abolished in the early 1990s and were replaced by a law on currency regulations. This law may be put into effect only under extreme circumstances, caused by, *inter alia*, war or extremely large short-term capital movements. Hence, there are at present no rules restricting fund transfers. However, provisions regulating the reporting of payments to and from Sweden exist and are used by the Central Bank (*Riksbanken*) to collect information in order to provide statistical information.

27.3.2 Foreign investment control

The acquisition of Swedish business enterprises by foreign entities is generally not subject to any restrictions. It is also possible to acquire real estate in the form of industrial property or commercial property without the need for a permit or licence.

However, companies involved in the defence industry may be subject to ownership restrictions. A government licence to manufacture and supply war materials may thus contain conditions limiting the total foreign ownership (whether direct or indirect) of shares in the manufacturer and breach of such conditions may result in the government revoking the licence.

Swedish limited liability companies licensed to conduct securities and clearing operations under the Securities Market Act 2007[1] are subject to certain provisions on ownership control. An acquisition of a securities or clearing company which results in the purchaser's total holdings constituting a so-called qualified holding may only take place pursuant to authorisation by the Swedish Financial Supervisory Authority ("FSA") (*Finansinspektionen*). Authorisation for an acquisition shall be granted where it can be assumed that the purchaser is suitable to exercise a significant influence over the management of the securities company. The Banking and Financial Business Act 2004 and the Insurance Business Act 1982 contain rules similar to those in the Securities Market Act 2007 for the acquisition or sale of banks, credit institutions and insurance companies, respectively. These rules mean that any purchase of shares constituting a qualified holding must be made conditional upon the FSA's approval and cannot be completed before such approval is obtained.

---

[1] This Act entered into force on 1 November 2007 as a result of the implementation of the EC MiFID Directive.

Acquisitions of farm property and apartment buildings also require (as a rule) permission. The acquisition of shares in a company whose main assets are apartment buildings can also (under certain circumstances) be subject to permission and a certain notification procedure must be adhered to as regards such acquisitions.

27.4   Merger control

The Competition Act 1993, which is based on EC law, requires that certain mergers and acquisitions be notified to the Swedish Competition Authority (*Konkurrensverket*). Notified transactions may, under certain circumstances, be prohibited by the Stockholm City Court (*Stockholms tingsrätt*).

27.4.1   Scope

The merger control rules of the Competition Act 1993 apply to concentrations, namely:

(a)   mergers where two or more previously independent undertakings merge; or

(b)   where control of an undertaking or a part thereof is acquired.

The Competition Act 1993 also applies to the establishment of fully functioning joint ventures.

The merger control rules apply in all cases provided the aggregate worldwide turnover of the undertakings concerned in the preceding financial year exceeded SEK4 billion and the turnover in Sweden of at least two of the undertakings concerned in the preceding financial year exceeded SEK100 million each. A negative prerequisite for the Swedish merger control rules is that the EC Merger Regulation does not apply.

If the purchasing party belongs to a group consisting of several companies under joint control or otherwise connected, the aggregate turnover of the group shall be deemed to be the purchasing party's annual turnover. If the purchaser is jointly controlled by two or more companies, the turnover of each of the groups to which the "parent" companies belong shall be included when calculating the turnover of the purchasing party. With regard to the target, only the turnover of the undertaking or business activities being transferred is relevant (and not the turnover of the seller).

With respect to partial acquisitions (e.g., the acquisition of some but not all of the shares in a company) the merger control rules apply only if the transaction enables the purchaser to exercise a decisive influence over the target. It follows that the merger control rules do not apply when somebody who already controls a company acquires additional shares in that company. However, the rules do apply to the transaction from joint to sole control since, in such a case, one form of decisive influence (joint control) is substituted for another form (sole control).

27.4.2 Notification

All transactions to which the merger control rules of the Competition Act 1993 apply must be notified to the Swedish Competition Authority. The Competition Act 1993 does not require that notification be made before consummation of the transaction; in fact no time limit whatsoever is stipulated.

When notification has been made, the parties may take no action to proceed with the acquisition for 25 working days (the standstill period), during which period the Competition Authority must decide whether to clear the acquisition or to carry out an in-depth investigation.

Since, as was noted above, the parties may complete the transaction before filing, the notification requirement is, in effect, of a post-merger nature, although the standstill period provided for is typical for pre-merger systems. Of course, the risk run by parties notifying after completion is that the Competition Authority eventually bans the deal and orders them to divest, something which normally would be both costly and impractical.

Failure to notify does not result in the imposition of fines. However, the Competition Authority may order the parties to a transaction of which it has become aware to notify and make compliance with such an order subject to a penalty.

27.4.3 Procedure

The Competition Authority has 25 working days from receipt of a complete notification to decide whether to clear the transaction or to carry out an in-depth investigation.

If an in-depth investigation is opened, the Competition Authority has another three months to decide whether to clear the transaction or to bring an action before the Stockholm City Court. This time limit may, under certain circumstances, be extended.

If proceedings are instituted, the Stockholm City Court may prohibit the transaction if:

(a) it creates or strengthens a dominant position which significantly impedes, or is likely to significantly impede, the existence or development of effective competition in the country as a whole or a substantial part thereof; and

(b) such prohibition can be issued without significant national security or supply interests being neglected.

By the reference to national security and supply interests, it is indicated that competition considerations may be overtaken by other considerations. Thus, the interest of maintaining competition must be balanced against other important interests.

If prohibited by the Stockholm City Court, the transaction shall be deemed to be null and void. Alternatively, if sufficient, the Stockholm City Court may require the purchaser to dispose of an undertaking or business activity, in whole or in part, or to take some other action having a favourable effect on competition.

Acquisitions that have been effected on a regulated marketplace, a corresponding marketplace outside the EEA, a multilateral trading facility as defined in the Securities Market Act 2007 or by a bid at a compulsory auction, shall not be prohibited. Instead, the purchasing party may be ordered to dispose of the assets acquired.

27.5   Regulation of the conduct of mergers and acquisitions

As a result of the implementation of the EC Takeover Directive, the Swedish takeover regime (earlier primarily set forth in the Rules Concerning Public Offers for the Acquisition of Shares, dated 1 September 2003 (as amended) issued by the Swedish Industry and Commerce Stock Exchange Committee (*Näringslivets Börskommitté*) ("NBK Rules") have been subject to major amendments (primarily as regards structure rather than content). As of 1 July 2006 Swedish takeover rules have been set forth in the Swedish Takeover Act 2006 and the Rules Concerning Public Offers for the Acquisition of Shares issued by the OMX Nordic Exchange Stockholm on 1 July 2006 ("Takeover Rules"). The Takeover Rules largely correspond to the NBK Rules. Furthermore, certain provisions as regards the offer document are set forth in the Financial Instruments Trading Act 1991, through which, *inter alia*, the EC Prospectus Directive has been implemented. It should be noted that the greater part of the takeover rules and regulations described herein also will be applicable to companies whose shares are listed on another regulated market in Sweden.

The Takeover Act 2006, the Takeover Rules and the Financial Instruments Trading Act 1991 generally apply to takeover offers (irrespective of whether such offers are made by a Swedish or foreign legal entity or physical person) to shareholders in companies listed on the OMX Nordic Exchange Stockholm to transfer their shares to the offeror on general terms. The rules cover public takeovers of shares listed on the OMX Nordic Exchange Stockholm, not only issued by Swedish companies but also, under certain circumstances, to foreign companies.

27.5.1   The Takeover Act 2006 and the Takeover Rules

Before a takeover offer is made, under the Takeover Act 2006 the offeror is obliged to enter into an agreement with the OMX Nordic Exchange Stockholm that includes an undertaking to comply with the Takeover Rules. As regards the target company, it is bound to comply with the Takeover Rules under the listing agreement with the OMX Nordic Exchange Stockholm. It this context, it shall also be noted that it is stipulated in the Takeover Rules that the press release announcing an offer shall include an undertaking to the shareholders of the target company to comply with the Takeover Rules and the sanctions that may be imposed by the OMX Nordic Exchange Stockholm in the event of non-compliance.

The primary aim of the Takeover Rules and the Takeover Act 2006 is to ensure that all shareholders of a target company receive sufficient information to enable them to make an informed decision on an offer. The Takeover Rules and the Takeover Act 2006 also seek to ensure that all holders of shares of the same class receive equal treatment, and that the board of the target company acts in good faith, directed only by the best interests of the shareholders.

The Takeover Act 2006 mainly includes provisions regarding mandatory bid requirement, frustrating measures by the target board, information to the employees and breakthrough clauses in a target company's articles of association and supervision, while other provisions regulating takeover offers are set forth in the Takeover Rules (other than those described at 27.5.2 below).

27.5.2 *The Financial Instruments Trading Act 1991*

The Financial Instruments Trading Act 1991 contains, *inter alia*, regulations on how trading in financial instruments shall be conducted, together with regulations regarding dispositions concerning financial instruments belonging to others and regulation on the disclosure of shareholdings (*see* 27.6.2.2 below). In particular, the Financial Instruments Trading Act 1991 provides a set of rules with respect to prospectuses and offer documents to be issued in connection with public offerings and takeover offers respectively.

The Financial Instruments Trading Act 1991 corresponds to the development on the international securities market and is based on EC law.

27.5.3 *Supervision*

The FSA supervises the adherence to both the Swedish Takeover Act 2006 and the Financial Instruments Trading Act 1991 and may in the event of non-compliance prohibit an offer and impose a "special fee" of up to SEK100 million. The OMX Nordic Exchange Stockholm supervises the adherence to the Takeover Rules and may also impose sanctions in the form of a special fee of up to SEK100 million (and in the case of companies whose shares are listed with the Exchange, delisting of the shares of the breaching party). Both the FSA and the OMX Nordic Exchange Stockholm have delegated some of their supervisory roles to the Swedish Securities Council (*Aktiemarknadsnämnden*), a private body with an established role on the Swedish stock market, including the right to grant exemptions from certain provisions of the Takeover Act 2006 and the Takeover Rules and to interpret the Takeover Rules. If rulings by the Swedish Securities Council are not complied with, the OMX Nordic Exchange Stockholm may issue sanctions. The Swedish Securities Council has been modelled on the Panel on Takeovers and Mergers in the UK. The Swedish Securities Council's opinions are made public on its website (with certain exceptions due to confidentiality considerations).

The influence of the Swedish Securities Council is not limited to the conduct of takeovers alone. The Swedish Securities Council also issues statements with respect to matters regarding what constitutes good stock market practice in Sweden in general. However, it has no legal authority to enforce compliance with its opinions, or to require that it be consulted in these matters.

27.6 Methods of acquisition and preparation for an offer

27.6.1 Structuring

In Sweden, acquisitions of shares are more frequent than acquisitions of business assets.

Generally, an acquisition by a foreign company will be made through a wholly-owned Swedish subsidiary. Foreign takeovers of Swedish companies are normally effected by means of private agreement, but may also be effected by means of a public offer. Legal mergers are not that common.

When structuring an offer, employee incentive schemes should be taken into consideration. Many listed companies have implemented incentive schemes (such as employee stock options, options with rights to subscribe for new shares, convertible debentures, etc.) for the employees and such schemes may sometimes result in a noteworthy dilution of the shareholdings in a company.

27.6.2 Stake building and disclosure

27.6.2.1 The mandatory bid rule

General

The Takeover Act 2006 includes a mandatory bid rule. According to the mandatory bid rule, an obligation to make a public offer to acquire the remaining shares in a stock market company will be imposed upon a shareholder who prior to the acquisition owns less than 30 per cent of the votes in the company and acquires shares to such extent that its shareholding thereafter equals or represents more than 30 per cent of the votes in the company. Also the shareholdings of certain persons related to the buyer and companies should be included when calculating the buyer's shareholding. If the buyer, within four weeks from the moment he became subject to the mandatory bid rule, sells shares in such number that his shareholding falls below the 30 per cent level, the mandatory bid rule no longer applies. The obligation to make a mandatory bid does not apply if the buyer obtains 30 per cent or more of the votes following completion of a voluntary public offer for all of the shares. A mandatory bid must always include an alternative with payment in all cash and may not be subject to conditions other than regulatory approval. Otherwise, mandatory bids are generally governed by the Takeover Rules.

Method of calculation

When a holding is calculated, according to the mandatory bid provisions, treasury shares held by the company itself shall be included. A buy-back of own shares may therefore not itself trigger an obligation for a shareholder to make a mandatory bid. The calculation is further made on an undiluted basis, that is, warrants or convertibles are not taken into account.

27.6.2.2 Disclosure

The Financial Instruments Trading Act 1991 requires disclosure of shareholdings in specified circumstances. The disclosure rules were amended on 1 July 2007 to comply with the EC Transparency Directive.

The Financial Instruments Trading Act 1991 requires that anyone who acquires or conveys shares in a Swedish company which has issued shares listed on a regulated market (and certain foreign companies which are not EEA resident), shall report the acquisition or conveyance, provided that the acquisition or conveyance leads to a total holding of shares or votes (including instruments that entitle or oblige the holder to acquire already issued shares) in the company reaching, exceeding or falling below 5, 10, 15, 20, 25, 30, 50, 66.66 or 90 per cent.

The acquisition or conveyance shall be reported to the company and the FSA in writing at the latest on the day after the triggering transaction. The FSA is under an obligation to make the information public before noon the day after the FSA has received the disclosure notice. The disclosure obligations remain applicable during a public offer. Furthermore, disclosure is also triggered when a threshold is reached, exceeded or fallen below as a result of a measure taken by the company itself (e.g., redemption of shares).

The Financial Instruments Trading Act 1991 requires various interests to be aggregated with those of a particular shareholder for the purpose of disclosure. These interests include, *inter alia*, the holdings of a shareholder's immediate family, of companies within the same group as the shareholders, and of third parties acting jointly with the shareholder. It is therefore not possible to avoid the disclosure requirement by making purchases through nominee companies. Certain exemptions from the disclosure obligations are available, for example for parent companies of investment funds.

27.6.3 Identity of shareholders

In preparing to make an offer, an offeror may wish to ascertain the identity of the shareholders in the target and, if possible, seek the agreement of substantial shareholders in the target to accept the offer once it has been made.

The share registers of Swedish companies are available for public inspection and all shares must be recorded in such a register. Publicly traded shares may be registered in the name of a nominee shareholder (*förvaltarregistrering*), in which event the name of the true owner will not be apparent from the register. A list of all true owners of more than 500 shares (registered in the name of a nominee) shall be available at the company and the central securities administrator and such list may not be more than three months old (however, it may be that true owners for practical purposes are not listed in such share register).

27.6.4 Other available information

In addition, a certain amount of information on Swedish companies is publicly available and can be obtained by a potential acquirer who is unable to (or does not want to) obtain details from the target company itself. The articles of association of all Swedish companies must be filed with the Companies Registration

Office where they are available to the public. Inspection of the articles of association is important in order to ascertain the voting and other rights attached to the issued shares of a proposed target company and any other available information of importance. Details of the issued share capital of all companies and of any increases in share capital must also be made available as well as the issuance of share-related instruments such as warrants or convertibles. It is also possible to obtain more-specific details regarding the company such as if there are any registered floating charges, historical changes in the share capital or the name of the company, etc. All Swedish companies must prepare accounts annually. These must be audited and filed with the Companies Registration Office. Furthermore, as described at 27.9 below, certain companies must publish interim reports.

In addition, all companies (the shares of which are listed on the OMX Nordic Stock Exchange Stockholm) must, according to the agreement with the OMX Nordic Stock Exchange Stockholm, publish details of decisions or events which are materially likely to affect the impression of the company (or, where the company has subsidiaries, of the group) created by the preceding annual report, interim report or other information in respect of the company or group, or otherwise affect the valuation of the company in the market.

In addition to the above, it is possible to obtain more extensive information from public registers such as, for example, a complete list of all Swedish real property owned by a company, including detailed information for these properties such as issued mortgages, etc. It is also possible to obtain a list of trade marks, designs and patents for which the company is a registered holder and to perform searches with courts to obtain information regarding cases where the company is a party. It is common for an offeror to conduct a preliminary review of publicly available information prior to making an offer.

27.6.5   Consultation

An offeror is not legally required to notify or consult with the board of the target company before making a public offer.

27.6.5.1   *Transfer of shares*
Where an intending purchaser is bound by a collective bargaining agreement, it will often need to consult the unions which are parties to the collective bargaining agreement before making a decision to acquire the shares. This can be carried out on a confidential basis, and the purchaser is not obliged to take into account the views of the unions in the event of a disagreement, that is, the unions do not have any right of veto. The same applies to the seller of the target company. Prior to making a decision to sell the shares in the target company, the seller may also be required to consult the unions which are parties to the applicable collective bargaining agreement.

27.6.5.2   *Transfer of business*
Where the transaction is structured as a transfer of business (e.g., an asset transfer or a merger), both the transferor and the transferee will need to consult relevant unions irrespective of whether the transferor and/or the transferee are bound by any collective bargaining agreement or not.

27.6.5.3 Damages

Notwithstanding that neither the purchaser nor the seller are obliged to take into account the views expressed by unions, failure to consult relevant unions can lead to legal action which may result in a Swedish court imposing damages.

27.6.5.4 Public offers

An offeror resident in Sweden must inform its employees as soon as a public offer for another company has been launched and as soon as the offer document has been made public. Furthermore, the board of directors of a target company must inform its employees of the offer, the offer document and the board's recommendation of the offer as soon as these have been made public. The information above shall be given to trade unions and directly to employees which are not represented by any union.

27.6.6 Shareholder approval

As regards Swedish companies, the acquisition or conveyance of another company, a business or other assets would require the approval of the shareholders only in exceptional cases.

27.6.7 Notification to the OMX Nordic Exchange Stockholm

Companies whose shares are listed with the OMX Nordic Exchange Stockholm are contractually required to inform the OMX Nordic Exchange Stockholm in advance of the announcement of a public offer. The OMX Nordic Exchange Stockholm must be notified immediately when the management of the offeror takes, or decides to take, certain preparatory actions (i.e., holding discussions on the possibility of an offer at board level, holding discussions with the management of the target company, beginning consultations with trade unions, or completing an investigation into the business conditions for a public offer). The OMX Nordic Exchange Stockholm will also be informed by the offeror as the offeror is under an obligation, before the launch of a public offer, to enter into an agreement with the OMX Nordic Exchange Stockholm that includes an undertaking to comply with the Takeover Rules and any sanctions in the event of non-compliance. The FSA must be informed of this undertaking before the launch of the offer.

27.7 Conduct of a public offer

27.7.1 Announcement

In Sweden, it is common for a foreign entity to set up a Swedish subsidiary that launches the public offer. The offer will be launched by means of a public announcement. According to the Takeover Rules the buyer shall, having decided to make a public offer, immediately issue a press release. The press release must, *inter alia*, include the following information:

(a) the identity of the offeror;
(b) the principal terms and conditions of the offer, including details of possible conditions of the offer;

(c)   how the offer is financed;

(d)   details of shares and voting rights in the target company which are held or controlled by the offeror;

(e)   the extent to which the offeror has obtained undertakings from shareholders of the target company to accept the offer;

(f)   the fact that the offeror has undertaken towards the OMX Nordic Exchange Stockholm, and undertakes towards the shareholders of the target company, to comply with the Takeover Rules (including the Swedish Securities Council's rulings in respect thereof) and be subject to the sanctions that may be imposed by the OMX Nordic Exchange Stockholm;

(g)   a summary of the reasons for the offer and the likely effect of the acquisition on the offeror's profits and financial position; and

(h)   the timetable for completion of the offer.

27.7.2   *Offer document*

The press release must be followed by an offer document. According to the Takeover Act 2006, an offer document must be prepared and filed for approval with the FSA by the offeror within four weeks of the announcement of the offer in the press release. As regards cross-border share exchange offers, it is common that the Swedish Securities Council grants exemption from the timing requirement. The offeror shall furthermore make public the offer document in accordance with what is set out in the Financial Instruments Trading Act 1991, for example by publishing the offer document on the offeror's website. The offer document shall be made public before the start of the acceptance period of the offer. Further, under the Takeover Rules, the offer document shall be sent to all shareholders of the target company.

The Takeover Rules and the Financial Instruments Trading Act 1991 contain detailed provisions as to the content of the offer document. The required content of the offer document is more extensive where the offer is a share exchange offer rather than a cash offer. Offer documents relating to share exchange offers shall include information equivalent to such information that is required in a prospectus under the Financial Instruments Trading Act 1991.

In recommended offers, it is common that the target company's board assists in preparing or verifies the information on the target company in the offer document. However, there is no obligation to provide such assistance. If the target company's board does not assist, the offer document must state this and contain information concerning the manner in which information about the target company has been obtained, for example from public documents.

27.7.3   *Offer period*

The Takeover Rules provide that an offer should be kept open for no less than three weeks and no more than 10 weeks. However, the offer period may be prolonged provided that the offeror has reserved the right to do so, or if an extension does not delay settlement with those who have already accepted the offer. Settlement may only be postponed if the offer document contains a provision to this effect. Extensions of the offer period are customary.

27.7.4 Funding of the offer

An offer may not be launched until the offeror has arranged for the financing of the offer. If the offeror is relying on external financing for the implementation of the offer and the lender stipulates conditions for payment of the loan, the offer may be made conditional on the provisions of such funds, and the conditions for payment shall be reproduced both in the press release and in the prospectus.

27.7.5 Full and partial offers

A public offer may be made for the entire issued share capital of the target company, but partial offers are also permitted. However, since the Takeover Act 2006 contains a mandatory bid rule (*see* 27.6.2.1 above) the possibilities for making partial offers are restricted. The Takeover Rules require that all holders of shares of the same class are treated equally.

The offeror is to a certain extent free to offer different terms to holders of shares of different classes and will normally be free to make an offer for one class of shares only. However, the offer must be extended to include other types of securities if the offer would result in the class of shares covered by the offer ceasing to be quoted, and this would have a substantial effect on the value of the other securities. An offeror may, therefore, be required to extend its offer to the holders of convertible securities or securities carrying subscription rights for new shares in the target company. Where the offer is a partial offer and acceptances in excess of the number of shares for which the offer is made are tendered, the offeror must scale down the acceptances of all shareholders on a pro rata basis unless he has reserved the right to acquire the additional shares.

27.7.6 Conditions

As a general rule, the offeror may not withdraw an offer after it has been announced. Only three exceptions to this rule are set forth in the Takeover Rules, all presuming that the offeror has made the offer subject to conditions in the press release launching the offer:

(a)   if the offer is conditional on the offeror acquiring a certain level of acceptance, for example acceptances from shareholders representing more than 90 per cent of the shares of the target company, or the general meeting of the offeror company or target company making a specific decision with regard to the offer, the offer can be withdrawn if it is clear that the condition has not or cannot be fulfilled;

(b)   the offeror may make the implementation of its offer conditional on the fact that no one else makes an offer to acquire shares in the target company on terms that are more beneficial for the shareholder than those offered by the offeror. If a competing offer is announced, the offeror is no longer obliged to implement its offer;

(c)   the offeror can withdraw the offer with reference to any other condition it has set if it is clear that the condition in question has not or cannot be fulfilled and that such non-fulfilment is of material significance to the offeror's acquisition of the target company.

It shall be noted that, typically, the conditions for the offer must be worded in such a manner that it is possible to determine whether or not the condition has been fulfilled. Further, the condition may not give the offeror a decisive influence over its fulfilment. This also applies to conditions related to the financing of the offer. However, one exemption from this principle is that the offeror may make the offer conditional upon receiving the necessary public permits, for example competition clearance, on terms that are acceptable to the offeror.

27.7.7   Result of the offer

After expiration of the acceptance period, the offeror shall issue a press announcement regarding the outcome of the takeover offer, including information on:

(a)   how many shares in the target company have been tendered in the offer and have been purchased by the offeror outside the offer (in proportion of the total share capital and total number of votes in the target company);

(b)   whether the conditions, if any, have been fulfilled and in the event of non-fulfilment of any condition whether the offeror has decided to complete the offer despite such non-fulfilment;

(c)   how many shares in the target company are controlled by the offeror (in proportion to the total share capital and total number of votes in the target company); and

(d)   when settlement is expected.

Where applicable, the press announcement must also include the further process of the offer (such as, *inter alia*, extension of the acceptance period and initiation of compulsory acquisition of the remaining shares).

27.7.8   No suspension of dealings

Dealings in the shares of the parties to a public offer are not suspended during the offer period. The offeror is free to purchase shares in the target company on the market during the course of a public offer. However, such acquisitions also need to be publicly disclosed under the Financial Instruments Trading Act 1991 while the offer remains open for acceptance (*see* 27.6.2.2 above) and may trigger the "cash trap" or the top-up requirement in the Takeover Rules (*see* 27.7.9 and 27.7.10 below).

27.7.9   Acquisitions in connection with a public offer

If the offeror (including certain persons acting in concert with the offeror) purchases shares in the target during the offer period, or (subject to certain exceptions) in connection with the offer, at a price which is higher than the offer price, the Takeover Rules require that the offer must be made at, or increased to, not less than the highest price paid (the top-up requirement). If less than six months have passed between an acquisition of shares and the announcement of the offer, it is presumed that the acquisition was made in connection with the offer. Furthermore, if the offeror, through transactions made within six months prior to an announcement of the public offer or in connection with the offer, acquires more than 10 per cent of the shares in the target company for cash consideration, the public offer must also give shareholders of the target company the opportunity to receive cash consideration for their shares (the "cash trap").

27.7.10 Increased and competing offers

There are no legal restrictions on the freedom of an offeror (including certain persons acting in concert with the offeror) to increase its offer once announced. An increase of the offer price will be required if the offeror purchases shares of the class for which the offer is made during the offer period, whether on the market or otherwise, at a price in excess of the offer price.

Competing offers are similarly free of restrictions. The making of a competing offer does not have any automatic effect on acceptances of the original offer which have already been tendered. Where the original offer is subject to any unfulfilled condition at the time a competing offer is made, target company shareholders who have accepted the original offer are permitted to withdraw their acceptances in favour of the competing offer.

There are no restrictions on the freedom of the offeror to make further bids for a target company following an unsuccessful public offer or partial offer. However, for a period of nine months from commencement of payment of compensation in accordance with an offer, the buyer may not acquire shares in the target company on terms which are more favourable to the transferor, either by means of a new public offer or otherwise, unless the offeror issues supplementary equivalent compensation to those who have accepted the previous offer.

27.8 Defences to a hostile offer

27.8.1 General principles

Defensive measures available to the board of directors of a target company, as well as other acts, measures and resolutions of it, are restricted by the general legal duty of the board of directors to act in the interests of the company and all shareholders. Furthermore, the Takeover Act 2006 provides that, once the board of directors or the managing director of a company has reasonable grounds to assume (based on information provided by the offeror) that a takeover offer will be made, or after an offer has been announced, the board of directors and the managing director of the target company may not take any steps which would typically be likely to have a negative impact on the prerequisites for making the offer or its implementation, unless it first obtains the approval of the shareholders at a shareholders meeting.

At least two weeks' notice is generally necessary to convene a meeting. As regards public ABs, the minimum notice period is four weeks if the shareholders meeting is the annual meeting or if the meeting shall consider an amendment of the articles of association of the company.

The restrictions on defensive measures above do not prevent a target board, acting in the best interests of the target shareholders, from seeking a competing offeror. Further, should an unsolicited competing offeror emerge, the target board is likely to have an obligation under its fiduciary duties to explore such a competing offer. However, there is no obligation to seek a competing offeror, even if the first offer is perceived as hostile, although this could be a feasible defensive measure.

27.8.2 Defensive measures

The restrictions and other provisions of the Takeover Act 2006 referred to at 27.8.1 above prevent the use of certain defensive tactics. Nevertheless, certain measures can be taken in advance of the announcement of an offer or the commencement of negotiations with an offeror.

Companies whose shares are listed on the OMX Nordic Exchange Stockholm sometimes hold mutually supportive cross-shareholdings in each other, thereby making it more difficult for a potential offeror to gain control and/or preventing a potential offeror from acquiring more than 90 per cent of the shares in these companies (*see* 27.11 below). Shareholders holding substantial percentages of the voting rights in such companies can enter into agreements giving the other parties to such agreements a right of first refusal with respect to sales of shares covered by the agreement. In addition, a company's articles of association, both public and private, may contain provisions conferring right of first refusal or post-sale purchase rights on transfers of shares in favour of existing shareholders. However, classes of shares that are publicly traded may not be subject to such restrictions. As a result of the implementation of the EC Takeover Directive in Swedish law, rules concerning provisions on breakthrough in the articles of association of a company entered into force on 1 July 2006. According to these, a company may include a provision in its articles of association to the effect that any restrictions on the transfer of securities provided for in the articles of association of the target company, or in contractual agreements, shall not apply vis-à-vis the offeror during the acceptance period of the offer. However, to the authors' knowledge, no such provision had been included in the articles of association of any Swedish listed company at the time of writing.

An example of a defensive provision is that only some members of the board of directors of a company may be replaced each year, combined with a provision that a member of the board of directors may be replaced during his term only if a qualified majority votes in favour of a resolution to that effect at a shareholders meeting. Such provisions prevent a purchaser of shares in the company from replacing the whole board of directors at once, unless the purchaser acquires shares representing more than two-thirds of the shares and votes in the target company and thereby is free to amend the articles of association of the company. Another example is a provision which requires that a measure, that would lead to the company's holding of shares in a subsidiary falling below a certain level, or assets of a certain value being sold, may be taken only if a qualified majority votes in favour of the resolution regarding such measure at a shareholders meeting.

27.9 Profit forecasts and asset valuations

The requirement to make public information which might be of importance for the valuation of the target company is contained in the Act on Annual Reports 1995 (which applies to the majority of ABs), in the Securities Market Act 2007 and in the agreement between the OMX Nordic Exchange Stockholm and each company listed on it.

27.9.1 The Act on Annual Reports 1995

The Act on Annual Reports 1995 applies to all ABs, except certain ABs in the financial and insurance sectors for which special acts apply (which, however, to a great extent refer to the Act on Annual Reports 1995). The Act on Annual Reports 1995 regulates the content of annual reports and interim reports.

27.9.1.1 Annual report – general

For each financial year an annual report shall, according to the Act on Annual Reports 1995, be published comprising a report on the administration of the company's affairs, a profit and loss account, a balance sheet and notes to the financial statements.

A parent company shall prepare consolidated accounts. A parent company need not prepare consolidated accounts if it has a parent enterprise which is subject to the laws of a nation within the EEA and the consolidated accounts of that parent enterprise have been prepared and audited according to the laws of that nation, provided that such laws are in accordance with the Seventh Council Directive 83/349/EEC on consolidated accounts. However, if shareholders representing at least 10 per cent of the share capital of the company request that the company prepares consolidated accounts or if the company's shares or other securities issued by the company are listed on a regulated marketplace, the company must prepare consolidated accounts.

Comparative figures for the preceding financial year shall always be presented.

Employee data shall be disclosed including remunerations to the managing director and the board of directors. Companies or groups operating in several countries shall disclose such data by country. The administration report shall include a proposal for the appropriation or the treatment of profits or losses.

Not later than one month after the adoption of the financial statements, and at the latest seven months after the end of the financial year, a certified copy of the annual report shall be filed with the Companies Registration Office, where it is available to the public.

27.9.1.2 Administration report

The administration report shall include a true and fair outline of the development of the company's operations, position and results of the operations. Furthermore, the administration report shall give information on matters that are not to be disclosed in the balance sheet, in the profit and loss account, or in the notes, but are of importance for the assessment of the company's assets and liabilities, its financial position and the results of the operations, and on events of material significance that have occurred during the financial year or after the end of the financial year. The administration report shall also give information about, *inter alia*, the company's activities as regards research and development and information about the company's future development and foreign branch offices. In addition, companies carrying on activities that require permission, or must be notified under the Environmental Code, shall always provide information about the effect of such activities on the environment.

27.9.1.3 Profit and loss account

According to the Act on Annual Reports 1995, Swedish companies may choose one of two layouts for their profit and loss account – one in the form of a report with type of cost division and one also in the form of a report but with function division. These layouts are based on Articles 23 and 25 of the Fourth Council Directive 78/660/EEC.

27.9.1.4 Balance sheet

The balance sheet must be in account form, corresponding to Article 9 of the Fourth Council Directive 78/660/EEC. Separate captions must show share capital which has been subscribed for but not paid, fixed assets and current assets, shareholders' equity, untaxed reserves, allocations and debts.

27.9.1.5 Cash flow analysis

According to the Act on Annual Reports 1995, the annual report of a larger company shall also include a cash flow analysis where the company's financing and capital investments during the financial year shall be presented.

27.9.1.6 Notes to the financial statements

In addition to the disclosure requirements mentioned above, additional information shall be disclosed in the notes. This additional information may instead be disclosed in the profit and loss account or balance sheet, provided that this is consistent with the general requirement that the annual report must be clearly arranged. This information includes *inter alia* valuation and translation methods, certain information about subsidiaries and other companies in which the company owns shares and over which the company has a considerable influence, details of changes in shareholders' equity and information about the average number of employees during the financial year.

27.9.2 The Securities Market Act 2007

A company listed on a regulated marketplace shall, according to the Securities Market Act 2007, make public such information regarding the business and securities as may be important when determining the market price of the securities.

Such company must also issue a semi-annual report and an interim statement (a less detailed interim report). If the company is under an obligation under a listing agreement to issue quarterly interim reports, no interim statement needs to be issued.

Semi-annual reports and interim reports shall be filed with the Swedish Registration Office as soon as possible but at the latest two months from the end of the period they cover. According to the Securities Market Act 2007, the Company must also provide the information to the relevant regulated marketplace on which the company is listed as well as to the FSA.

27.9.3 The listing agreement with the OMX Nordic Exchange Stockholm

The listing agreement between the OMX Nordic Exchange Stockholm and each company whose shares are listed on the Stock Exchange imposes certain duties to make public information about the company. Some of the information which might be important for an offeror is described below.

Immediately following the approval of the accounts for the year by the company's board of directors the company shall publish a press release containing the most important information from the forthcoming annual report.

Any forecasts in respect of profits and/or turnover prepared by the company for publication shall be made public immediately upon preparation of the forecast.

Each quarterly interim report shall, according to the agreement with the OMX Nordic Exchange Stockholm contain, *inter alia*:

(a) A summarised profit and loss account for the financial year and for the interim period and the last quarter with comparative figures for the corresponding periods from the previous financial year. The financial results shall include the estimated tax costs for the periods.

(b) The balance sheet in summary as of the close of the current reporting period including comparative figures from the expiry of the most recent financial year.

(c) A condensed cash flow statement for the financial year and interim period, including comparative figures for the same period during the previous year.

(d) A summary report showing changes in equity during the financial year and interim periods, including comparative figures for the same period during the previous financial year.

(e) Earnings per share for the financial year and the interim period for the previous quarter including comparative figures for corresponding periods during the preceding financial year. Information shall be provided both before and after dilution.

(f) Information regarding the number of outstanding shares at the close of the reporting period and both the average number of outstanding shares for the financial year and interim period and latest quarter including comparative figures for the corresponding period from the previous financial year. The information shall be provided both before and after dilution.

(g) Information regarding the company's own shares at the end of the reporting period as well as the average number of own shares during the interim period including comparative figures for the end of the immediately preceding financial year.

(h) Explanations of the earnings trend and financial position, including, *inter alia*, the effect of significant extraordinary events.

(i)   Where information relating to the future is provided, it shall also be evident what corresponding information was provided in the previous report as well as any changes published since the previous report.

(j)   Information regarding the time at which the next interim report or report of unaudited annual earnings figures will be published.

Where the company's board of directors or shareholders at a shareholders meeting have adopted a resolution in respect of the issuance of traded securities, or where the board of directors decides to propose such a resolution to the shareholders meeting, the company shall immediately disclose information about the issue publicly.

The company shall, in a press release from the general meeting of shareholders, immediately publish resolutions adopted in respect of dividends, changes in the board of directors and/or auditors and other information which is of material significance to the stock market.

The company shall also make immediate public disclosure of any decision or event which is likely to materially affect the appearance of the state of the company (or that of the group if the company is a parent company) as presented in the most recent annual report, six-month report, other interim report or in other information about the company (or the group), or otherwise affect the valuation of the company's securities which are listed on the Stock Exchange. Upon such disclosure, the company shall, where possible, set forth the expected effect of the decision or event on the company's earnings and position.

Should the activities of the company change in such material manner that the company, taken as a whole, may objectively be deemed to constitute a new undertaking, the company shall provide information within reasonable time to the stock market and to the Stock Exchange in accordance with the provisions governing prospectuses, or the company shall provide other information that describes the consequences of the changes.

27.10   Documents from the offeror and offeree board

An offer document shall be drawn up by the offeror in connection with a public offer for the acquisition of shares. The offer document shall contain all the information needed for a comprehensive assessment of the offer. These rules follow from the Financial Instruments Trading Act 1991, the Takeover Act 2006 and the Takeover Rules. These rules are described at 27.5 and 27.7.2 above.

27.11   Compulsory acquisition of minorities

The Companies Act 2005 permits the compulsory acquisition of minority shareholdings by a shareholder who owns shares representing more than 90 per cent of the capital of another Swedish company. The shareholder may be a natural person or a legal person of any nationality. Shares which are owned indirectly by the shareholder shall be included when calculating the threshold. However, any shares that the company holds in itself will not be taken into account when calculating the 90 per cent threshold. A majority shareholder who is entitled to require a compulsory acquisition of the shares in a company is also entitled to require compulsory acquisition of warrants and convertible shares in that company. In respect of convertibles, compulsory acquisition extends to both the value of the conversion right and the debt instrument as such. Similarly, in these circumstances, minority shareholders are entitled to require the majority share-holder to purchase their shares, warrants or convertibles.

The Companies Act 2005 provides that where the greater part of the majority holding has been acquired by means of a public offer, the consideration for the remaining shares must be the same as that provided under the offer unless there are special reasons for a different price, for example the length of time that has passed since the offer or a material change in circumstances affecting the value of the company. Otherwise, the price should be determined so as to correspond with the price for the share that can be expected at a sale during normal circumstances and the fact that such shares only represent a minority holding should be disregarded. With respect to shares quoted on the stock market, such price shall be the quoted price unless there are special reasons for a different price. With respect to shares not quoted on the stock market, etc. the basis for deciding the acquisition sum should be the same as with quoted shares, that is, on the basis of the real or calculated sales value of the shares. It should be noted that the minority shareholders shall always be paid in cash. Any dispute as to whether there is a right or obligation to purchase, or regarding the price to be paid, must be submitted to arbitration with three arbitrators. Where a majority shareholder wishes to acquire shares in a company through compulsory acquisition and no agreement is reached, the majority shareholder shall make a request in writing to the board of directors of the company that the dispute be referred to arbitration, and its arbitrator should be named. When the majority shareholder has initiated the compulsory acquisition procedure in respect of shares, convertibles and warrants may not be converted or exercised until the compulsory acquisition procedure is settled through a final award or decision. If the conversion or exercise period expires during the compulsory acquisition procedure, the holder of the security may however convert or exercise the security within three months from the arbitration award becoming final.

Unless all shareholders whose names are entered in the register and against whom the claim is directed have named a joint arbitrator within a prescribed time, which in practice never occurs, the board of directors of the company shall request the Stockholm City Court to appoint a legal representative to look after the rights of absent shareholders in the dispute.

If the right to compulsory acquisition is not questioned but the price for the shares is questioned, the shareholders are obliged to accept a full transfer of ownership of their shares to the majority shareholder provided the majority shareholder furnishes acceptable security for the purchase price including interest which has been approved by the arbitrators or the court. Such full transfer enables the offeror to disregard the interests of minority shareholders and will generally be obtained within six to eight months from the notice of the compulsory acquisition.

The costs for the arbitration proceedings will normally be borne by the majority shareholder. An appeal against an award of the arbitrators may be made to the Stockholm City Court within 60 days of the serving of the award.

27.12 Insider dealing and market manipulation

27.12.1 *Insider dealing*

27.12.1.1 *Selectively disclosed information*

In case of information which is likely to materially influence the valuation of the target company's listed securities, the principal rule under the listing agreement with the OMX Nordic Exchange Stockholm states that such information must not, except in special events, be disclosed other than by way of public announcements.

In its commentary to the listing agreement, the OMX Nordic Exchange Stockholm acknowledges that price-sensitive information may need to be disclosed on a selective basis in certain events which are important to the company. One example of this is preparations and negotiations of public offers. It is further mentioned that any price-sensitive information disclosed selectively should be eligible for subsequent public disclosure in order to neutralise the insider position of the recipient of the information. This obligation is further enhanced in relation to price-sensitive information to be provided on a selective basis in connection with public takeovers. The main rule is, pursuant to the Takeover Rules, that price-sensitive information disclosed to the offeror must be publicly disclosed in connection with the announcement (or during the acceptance period, e.g., in the offer documents) of the offer.

27.12.1.2 *The Market Abuse Act 2005*

Insider dealing is an offence in Sweden under the Market Abuse Act 2005 which is based on the EC Market Abuse Directive. The Market Abuse Act 2005 applies to dealings in financial instruments (i.e., stock market securities and other rights or obligations intended for dealings on the securities market). The Market Abuse Act 2005 prohibits certain dealings in financial instruments and also contains a prohibition regarding market manipulation. The Market Abuse Act 2005 is not limited to transactions on the securities market. It also applies to dealings in financial instruments admitted to trading on a regulated market in at least one EC Member State or for which a request for admission to trading on such a market has been made or a financial instrument not admitted to trading on a regulated market but whose value depends on such financial instrument, irrespective of whether or not the transaction itself actually takes place on that market.

The Market Abuse Act 2005 prohibits any person who has received information or knowledge about a circumstance which is likely to influence materially the price of financial instruments and which has not been made public, from buying or selling financial instruments before the circumstances have become generally known or has ceased to be significant for the price. In addition, such a person may not buy or sell financial instruments on behalf of another person or entity, nor may he cause any other person or entity to make such a purchase or sale by giving advice or by similar actions.

The prohibition on buying and selling financial instruments also applies to a person who has received information or knowledge about a circumstance which concerns a company in which he owns shares.

The FSA is the competent authority, holding both supervisory and investigatory powers, for ensuring that the Market Abuse Act 2005 is adhered to.

Further, the Act concerning Reporting Obligations for Certain Holdings of Financial Instruments 2000 imposes a duty upon persons with insider status in a Swedish stock market company (and certain foreign companies which are not EEA resident) to report holdings of and changes in holding of shares in the company in question to the FSA.

27.12.1.3 Public offers
A measure which is intended to, and is likely to lead to, a public offer consti- tutes a circumstance which is likely to materially influence the price of financial instruments and would therefore be regarded as inside information pursuant to the Market Abuse Act 2005.

In such cases, employees and advisers of the potential offeror, the target company and their respective parent enterprises, and others who are considered to belong to the categories of persons which are prohibited from buying financial instruments under certain circumstances, may not deal or procure others to deal in the shares of the target company (or, where the offeror is itself a stock market company, in the shares of the offeror) until the offer has either been announced or abandoned.

While the rules on insider dealing will prevent persons who have received inside information regarding a potential public offer from dealing in shares in the target company before the offer is made public, they will not prevent an offeror from buying shares in a proposed target company before the offer has been publicly announced.

27.12.1.4 Penalties
Insider dealing offences are punishable by a fine or up to four years' imprison- ment depending on the seriousness of the offence, and any gains made may be forfeited. In addition, in certain circumstances (e.g., fraud) insider dealing may constitute an offence under the Penal Code.

27.12.2 Market manipulation

The freedom of the board of the target company to take action to manipulate the market price of the offeror's or the target company's shares is limited by the provisions of the Takeover Act 2006, which prohibits the target company from seeking to hinder an offer unless their actions have been approved in advance by the target company's shareholders.

The Market Abuse Act 2005 contains a general prohibition with respect to persons engaging in "undue" market manipulation according to which it is a criminal offence for someone to act, on the securities market or otherwise, in a way which is likely to unduly affect the price of financial instruments or the conditions for transactions of financial instruments or otherwise mislead buyers or sellers of financial instruments.

The market manipulation crimes are punishable by a fine or up to four years' imprisonment depending on the seriousness of the offence.

In addition, an attempt to influence the market price of the shares in the offeror or the target company may constitute an offence under the Penal Code. It is a criminal offence to make public, or otherwise spread among the public, misleading information with the intention of influencing the price of securities.

27.13 Financial assistance

The financing of takeovers in Sweden can generally be characterised as rather conservative or conventional. If the financing is provided in Sweden, this is normally done by long- and short-term loans where the security provided is commonly mortgages on real property, chattel mortgages and guarantees.

According to the Companies Act 2005, a takeover may not be financed either in whole or part by the acquired company itself. Thus, the acquired company is not allowed to grant loans or security in connection with an acquisition of its shares. This prohibition is subject to criminal liability, that is, it is a criminal offence for the representatives of a target company to participate in such lending. In brief, a loan granted in violation of these rules is invalid and the loan amount shall be repaid.

These rules effectively preclude the possibility of acquiring the target company on the basis of a self-financing structure. However, it is possible for the acquisition finance loans that have been provided to an acquirer to be "pushed down" subsequent to the acquisition, provided that the acquisition financing was provided independently from the subsequent push down.

Also, where the acquisition is made through a Swedish company, the financing costs can in the future be partly covered by the target company making group contributions to its new parent company.

As regards refinancing of a target company's existing debts, there are generally no problems from a Swedish law perspective connected with the acquirer lending or procuring loans to the target company enabling the target company to repay its existing debts one for one, since the distribution of funds will be from a parent to a subsidiary.

Furthermore, there is a capital market in which trading in various long- and short-term financial instruments is carried out. Funds can be raised on the Swedish capital market by issuing bonds and commercial paper. Commercial paper is issued for short-term loans, normally with a duration of one to two years. The trading in the secondary market for commercial paper is usually very active.

The purchaser may also obtain funding through the OMX Nordic Exchange Stockholm or another marketplace or through a private placement. Only public ABs may use advertising to sell shares or other financial instruments issued by the company. Furthermore, only public ABs may offer more than 200 persons the right to subscribe to or acquire the shares.

In addition to these possibilities for raising capital, a company may also issue convertible debt instruments and warrants. Convertible debt instruments and warrants may be listed on a Stock Exchange or any other marketplace.

27.14   Some transaction costs

27.14.1   *Transfer tax and stamp duty*

Currently there is no stamp duty, transfer tax or similar tax on trading in shares and certain other equity-related securities in Sweden.

When a business combination is conducted as an asset transfer, a stamp duty is levied on the transfer of real property. The duty amounts to 3 per cent of the purchase price (or tax assessment value if higher) for a corporate buyer. The duty is generally paid by the buyer.

27.14.2   *VAT*

Value added tax at a rate of 25 per cent is generally payable on the sale of business assets (except the sale of a business as a whole or an entire branch).

Chapter 28

Turkey

Hergüner Bilgen Özeke
Istanbul

28.1 Introduction

28.1.1 General overview

In the past few years, Turkey has gone through a period of expansion and reform. Part of this reform is due to the efforts to harmonise Turkish legislation with that of the EU. Undoubtedly, the start of formal negotiations with the EU helped to create a more stable economy, resulting in a massive increase in the amount of direct foreign investment. Data released by the Central Bank of Turkey indicates that non-residents' net direct investment in Turkey recorded an inflow of $11,017 million USD in the January–May 2007 period compared to $8,521 million USD during the same timeframe in 2006. To put these in context, one should note that the total net direct investment for the period between 1984 and 2004 was $19.3 billion USD as opposed to $10 billion USD only in 2005 and $20 billion USD only in 2006.

Strict economic policies implemented by successive governments as a consequence of the 2001 financial crisis allowed the Turkish economy to achieve a sustained growth rate, not less than 5 per cent annually between 2002 and 2007. Meanwhile, inflation was also reduced to single digits for the first time in decades, followed by declining interest rates. Share prices at the Istanbul Stock Exchange and the foreign direct investment inflow both demonstrate an upward trend.

While the country is not insulated against possible changes in global trends, there is room for cautious optimism. Such optimism is reflected in the number of major privatisations and acquisitions that have occurred in Turkey since 2004. Together with the increasing number of privatisations and mergers and acquisitions in Turkey, the legal framework applicable to such transactions has also developed significantly.

28.1.2 Regulatory framework

Mergers and acquisitions ("M&As") in Turkey are mainly governed by the Turkish Commercial Code (the "TCC") and the Turkish Code of Obligations (the "TCO"). However, these codes, dating from 1957 and 1926 respectively (as amended from time to time), do not include specific provisions regulating M&A transactions. Therefore, as in most countries, an M&A transaction in Turkey requires the knowledge and evaluation of several legal disciplines, such as competition law, tax law and labour law. Furthermore, certain sectors are subject to special provisions with respect to mergers or acquisitions. For instance, the Banking Law sets forth certain limits with regard to the transfer of a bank's shares.

Historically, most M&A transactions in Turkey were structured as straightforward stock purchases between private parties. However, securities laws are becoming increasingly relevant as a greater number of listed companies are becoming involved in M&A transactions.

Acting as Turkey's capital markets regulator, and at the same time fulfilling the duties of a financial services authority, the Capital Markets Board of Turkey (the "CMB") supervises M&A transactions related to listed companies, and extends a great deal of effort to ensure a transparent environment that enables investors and publicly held companies to become part of a sound and prosperous market.

Publicly held companies are required to disclose all information that may impact investment decisions of investors and the prices of capital market instruments. The CMB legislation provides a non-exhaustive list of material information, developments and significant events that must be disclosed to the public. The type and scope of such information is considerably less detailed than the disclosure requirements in more-developed markets such as in the US or the UK.

Since 2003, the CMB has continued its efforts to enable publicly held companies to comply with the principles of the Corporate Governance Guide ("the Guide"). Subsequent to the Guide, the CMB took the matter one step further and issued a Board Decision ("the Decision") numbered 48/1588 and dated 10 December 2004 stating that all Istanbul Stock Exchange ("ISE") listed companies must report to the CMB as to whether or not they have applied the principles set forth in the Guide. This report is to be provided in a separate section of the companies' annual reports, setting out the relevant company's status by applying the principles and, if any, the reasons for failure to apply the principles. The CMB may also impose punitive and administrative sanctions upon companies that fail to comply with the Decision.

The ISE also plays a role in the implementation of Corporate Governance in Turkey, by having introduced the Turkish Corporate Governance Index ("the Index"). The purpose of the ISE Index is to encourage listed companies trading under the ISE to follow the Corporate Governance Guide published by the CMB, by rating the companies' compliance with the Corporate Governance Guidelines in relation to their price and return performances.

28.1.3   Recent legislative changes

There have been some serious legislative changes in recent years regarding the tax, banking and capital markets laws.

Turkey has recently experienced, arguably, the most rapid changes in its fundamental tax and fiscal laws. Highlights of some of the recent changes in the legislation that affect M&A transactions are in the Corporate Tax Law.

After protracted discussions, the long-awaited Corporate Tax Law was enacted on 23 June 2006. Some of the changes relate to the following matters:

(a)   transfer pricing;
(b)   thin capitalisation and equity to debt ratios;
(c)   tax havens;
(d)   controlled foreign entities;
(e)   liquidation;
(f)   spin-offs;
(g)   share swaps;
(h)   cost allocations;
(i)   withholding tax in dividend payments; and
(j)   sales of subsidiary shares and real estate.

Since June 2006, the Banking Regulatory and Supervision Agency (the "BRSA") has issued regulations dealing with various banking and financing-related matters. The new regulations mainly focus on issues such as the principles and procedures for applications to be filed with the BRSA, with the goal to strengthen the banking sector by improving supervision standards in line with international norms, through the enactment of several regulations.

Perhaps more importantly, a new Commercial Code and a new Code of Obligations are on the way, which were both in draft form at the time of writing. The new Commercial Code ("the Draft") is expected to be introduced early in 2008 if not sooner. According to the bill that was before the Turkish Parliament at the time of writing, the most salient novelties of the new Draft are as follows.

28.1.3.1   Single shareholder companies

Contrary to the current TCC requiring a minimum of five shareholders and a board of directors (a "BoD") to be formed with a minimum of three members for the establishment of a joint stock corporation (a "JSC"), the Draft provides that a JSC may be established by one shareholder and it may have a BoD consisting of only one member. Furthermore, non-shareholders and legal entities may be members of the BoD, which will enable professional directors to collaborate more efficiently. In adherence to corporate governance principles and guidelines, similar to the Banking Law and capital markets legislation, the Draft provides that at least half of the BoD members must hold a university degree in order to achieve more successful operations.

28.1.3.2   Online corporate information

The Draft intends to make use of today's technological developments by requiring JSCs to maintain a corporate website wherein they must publish official corporate announcements, important explanations for shareholders, audit reports and financial statements. Perhaps more importantly, the meetings of the BoD and the General Assembly may be audiovisual.

28.1.3.3   Minority rights

The Draft includes new minority rights for those owning 10 per cent of the shares in private companies and 5 per cent of the shares in publicly held companies.

According to the new rights contemplated by the Draft, minority shareholders may:

(a)   apply to a court for the appointment of a new company auditor;
(b)   require printed share certificates from the BoD;
(c)   demand the company's dissolution; and
(d)   nominate a candidate for the BoD.

28.1.3.4   Dividend distribution

The current TCC provides that BoD members may receive dividends on the net profit after the allocation of the statutory legal reserves, and distribution of dividends at the rate of 4 per cent to the shareholders. The Draft raises this rate to 5 per cent.

28.1.3.5   Mergers and demergers, spin-offs and transformations

The TCC is often criticised for inadequately covering mergers, divisions and transformations of JSCs. The new Draft intends to address this deficiency, and sets forth the legal provisions applicable to such transactions. According to the Draft, a "merger agreement" must clearly include corporate information regarding the merging companies and the new company, such as its head-quarters, company title and the exchange rate of the shares. Furthermore, a merger report determining the scope and results of the merger, approvals obtained from authorities, the exchange rate of the shares, and other relevant effects of the merger on employees and creditors of the companies must be prepared by the BoDs of the merging companies. Such report must be endorsed by an independent audit firm. The BoD must then present the merger agreement to the General Assembly (the "GA") for approval. The resolution regarding a proposed merger must be published in the Turkish Trade Registry Gazette. Similarly, these requirements are also applicable for demergers, spin-offs and transformations of companies.

28.1.3.6   Squeeze-outs

Squeeze-out mechanisms are currently not available under Turkish legislation. The Draft Commercial Code, on the other hand, introduces the "squeeze-out" mechanism to Turkish law. Article 208 of the Draft Commercial Code grants the squeeze-out right to shareholders representing 90 per cent of the share capital of a JSC if the minority shareholder acts in a manner that will block the company's operations, acts in bad faith or creates noticeable disturbance in the company. If this occurs, the majority shareholders may apply to the court to purchase the shares of the minority shareholder at the Stock Exchange price if the shares are publicly traded, or at the balance sheet value.

The other squeeze-out possibility available under the Draft Commercial Code may be exercised in the event of a merger. When an entity is merged into another, the shareholders of the merging entity are entitled to obtain shares in the surviving entity corresponding to the value of their shares in the merging entity. The Draft Commercial Code allows for the merger agreement to provide a squeeze-out mechanism. Accordingly, the minority shareholders of the merging entity will not be entitled to obtain shares in the surviving entity, but instead will be paid "squeeze-out compensation". If the merger agreement provides for such squeeze-out mechanism, the merger agreement must be approved by the shareholders with 90 per cent of the shares of the merging entity. Accordingly, shareholders with 90 per cent of the shares of the company may squeeze out the minority shareholders by paying squeeze-out compensation if there is a merger.

28.1.3.7   Risk analysis

The Draft requires that an "Early Determination of Risks Committee" (a "Committee") be established by the BoD in order to determine the causes jeopardising the existence, development and continuity of a listed company. Such Committee must be composed of members or non-members of the BoD, who will examine the said causes and take necessary precautions. In non-publicly held companies this Committee must be immediately formed if the auditor determines that its establishment is necessary and so informs the BoD in writing.

28.1.3.8   Company groups (holding companies)

The Draft includes provisions which relate to groups of companies. In this context, the Draft is also the first Turkish law to define the concept of "control". It addresses the direct or indirect control of a capital company by another capital company, leading to the establishment of "groups of companies" due to the means of control (such as having the majority of the voting rights; the right to elect the majority of the BoD; and using the majority of the voting rights, apart from individual voting rights, arising out of a separate control agreement). If the affiliated company acquires the shares of the controlling company, the affiliated company may not use rights related to more than a certain portion of the shares and votes of the controlling company. However, if a company directly or indirectly owns 100 per cent of the shares and voting rights of another company, the BoD of the controlling company may give instructions relating to the direction of the affiliated company, even to its detriment.

28.1.3.9   D&O insurance

The Draft introduces professional liability insurance for BoD members for damages they may cause during the performance of their duties. If a director is insured for an amount exceeding 25 per cent of the company's capital, then the Capital Markets Board should be notified of this in regard to publicly held companies and, if it is listed in the Stock Exchange, then the ISE must be notified.

28.2   Acquisition targets

28.2.1   Types of companies

There are a number of different business forms under Turkish law and these may be classified into two main groups, namely capital companies and personal companies.

The most common capital company forms are JSCs and limited liability partnerships ("LLPs"), both of which are limited liability business structures with the liability of shareholders limited to the share capital they subscribed to, as opposed to so-called personal companies, where the liability of the partners is unlimited. In both JSCs and LLPs, fields of activity, operations and other corporate matters of the company are governed by the company's articles of association within the mandatory framework set out in the TCC. The *ultra vires* principle is applicable under Turkish law.

From a practical point of view, JSCs are legal entities better suited for large operations; in particular corporate joint ventures, where the legal framework for the corporate governance of JSCs is more developed.

For US tax purposes, the preferred business form is the LLP, which allows substantial tax advantages for US-based investors due to its treatment under US tax laws. However, this business form has some of the characteristics of personal companies (such as no board of directors, special decision-making quorums higher thresholds for liability of shareholders, and the inability to issue and list share certificates). Therefore, JSCs are generally used for the purposes of larger operations and joint ventures allowing, among other things, more flexibility in corporate governance issues.

28.2.2 Publicly held companies

Publicly held companies are JSCs whose shares have been offered to the public, or shares that are deemed to have been offered to the public.

28.2.2.1 Companies that are deemed publicly held companies
JSCs having more than 250 shareholders are deemed to be publicly held companies and are subject to Turkish securities regulations applicable to publicly held companies.

As with all securities laws, Turkish capital markets regulations aim to protect investors investing in publicly held companies by ensuring proper disclosure and, therefore, they regulate the markets and participants extensively in their operations and activities. The acquisition of the shares of a publicly held company or a company that is deemed to be a public company is heavily regulated.

28.2.3 Closely held companies

Acquisition of a company's shares, other than a publicly held company, would be subject to:

(a) the articles of association of the company to be acquired or merged with;
(b) the relevant legislation, in particular, the provisions of the TCC; and
(c) the agreement of the parties involved in an acquisition or merger transaction.

If not provided for under its articles of association, matters that are not statutorily regulated under the TCC may be freely resolved through agreement of the parties in a transaction.

28.3 Methods of acquisition

28.3.1 *Private agreements*

A merger or an acquisition transaction most often involves the purchase of the current shares of the merging or acquired company, or through acquiring the company's participation in the acquired company's capital increase process by subscription to the newly issued shares.

The concept of "freedom of contract" is one of the main principles laid down in the TCO. Accordingly, the parties to a private contract are free to determine the content and the form of the contract as long as its provisions do not conflict with the mandatory provisions of the TCC or other laws. In this respect, under Turkish law, all warranties of the parties may be, with a few exceptions, excluded or extended through contractual provisions.

The parties to a merger or an acquisition are free to regulate agreements in accordance with the legal foundation and framework laid down by the respective articles of association of the two companies. Nonetheless, the TCO sets forth some implied warranties, and these warranties must be in harmony with the representations and warranties made in an agreement by their provisions.

Due to the increase in the number of foreign investors and capital in Turkey, foreign legal forms, especially US and English forms, have influenced acquisition agreements entered into between Turkish and foreign companies. Most often, the parties have no problem implementing these forms and associating them with Turkish laws.

For JSCs, there are no specific provisions requiring merger or acquisition agreements to be notarised in order for them to be effective. Nonetheless, depending on the nature of the acquired assets, notarisation of certain documents or the execution of certain documents before official authorities may be mandatory (e.g., real property transactions). For LLPs, the relevant legislation requires notarisation of certain documents.

Moreover, voting agreements, usufruct agreements and share pledge agreements are often used during the course of acquisition transactions.

As a main principle of law, and in light of the freedom of contracts principles, parties to an acquisition-related agreement are free to choose the applicable law and jurisdiction, taking into consideration the principle of reciprocity between the countries of the two parties.

28.3.2 *Mandatory public offers*

Some mergers or acquisitions may trigger mandatory tender offers in Turkey. The provisions regarding this requirement are explained at 28.8 below.

28.3.3 *Mergers and spin-offs*

28.3.3.1 *Under corporate laws*
Mergers and acquisitions in Turkey are mainly governed by the TCC and the TCO.

However, these Codes do not provide detailed regulations. Under the TCC, either:

(a)   an acquiring company must take over a target company, including its assets and debts in their entirety; or

(b)   two or more companies must be transferred into a new corporation along with all of their assets and debts.

The shareholders of the merged companies must obtain the shares of the acquiring company or the new company. A merger under Turkish law can only be effected between the same types of companies; that is, a JSC may only merge with another JSC, and an LLP may only merge with another LLP.

The acquiring company will be the successor of the target company, and as the surviving entity it will own all of the assets including contracts, permits, licences, incentives, etc., and will be liable for all of the obligations of the target company after registration of the merger with the relevant trade registry and upon the shareholders' approval of the target company. Upon the merger, the assets will be transferred to the acquiring company automatically by operation of law. In most instances, this will assist the acquiring or new company in the elimination of special procedures for the transfer of legal title to real property or in the application for new licences or permits. Consequently, an application to the relevant registries with notification letters and other requested documents should suffice in most cases.

Merger agreements may only become effective after the general assembly of shareholders of both parties approve the transaction.

Although spin-offs are not clearly regulated under the TCC, the CMB has issued communiqués covering particular aspects of spin-offs relating to the Turkish Capital Market legislation. In addition, the Ministry of Finance has issued a communiqué regulating partial division of JSCs and LLPs.

Under the CMB legislation, a spin-off of listed companies may only be realised by way of partial division. Partial division or contribution of a part of the target company's assets to a new company may be possible, subject to the rules set forth by the CMB, if the new company is incorporated via the transfer of more than 15 per cent of the listed company's assets as stated in its latest balance sheet.

28.3.3.2   Tax laws

Corporate tax is regulated under Corporate Tax Law No. 552. The Corporate Tax Law applies to profits earned by corporations, cooperatives, state-owned companies, economic enterprises owned by associations and foundations, and mutual funds and investment trusts governed by the CMB legislation.

There are two types of corporate tax liabilities under the Corporate Tax Law; namely "full" and "limited" liabilities. Full corporate tax liability applies to corporations with legal or business headquarters in Turkey (also known as "Resident Entities"), and corporations subject to full tax liability are responsible for the declaration and the payment of taxes on their worldwide corporate income. Limited tax liability applies when the corporation has no legal or business headquarters in Turkey (also known as "Non-Resident Entities").

Under limited tax liability, the corporation is only liable for taxes on corporate income earned in Turkey. Further, under the Income Tax Law, dividends, interest, dividends paid against profit/loss sharing certificates and similar income are defined as dividends, and interest income, income from the sale of the securities are deemed capital gains.

When a company enters into a sales agreement for goods/services (including payment of bonuses and wages) with "related parties" (the company's own shareholders, companies and/or individuals that are directly or indirectly related to the company) and does not apply the arm's-length principle, then the profits obtained from such a transaction may be deemed to constitute "disguised profits" and constitute transfer pricing. The consequences of transfer pricing are as follows: for resident entities the disguised profit will be taxed as dividend distribution under the corporate and income tax laws, whereas in the case of non-resident entities, such disguised profit will be taxed as profits transferred to the headquarters. Further, the amounts transferred via transfer pricing abuse may not be deductible for tax purposes.

In terms of share and asset transfers, in principle there is no separate capital gains taxation for legal entities. As a result, capital gains arising from such transfers are subject to the flat rate corporate tax. However, the Turkish tax system also provides certain tax exemptions or deferrals if such transfer is carried out in mergers, acquisitions or spin-offs that comply with Corporate Tax Law requirements. These requirements include the transfer to be carried of the book value on the balance sheet, and the transferee's assumption of the tax liabilities of the transferring entity. The losses are to be carried forward up to five years provided that they do not exceed the equity of the dissolving entity.

The tax free mergers, acquisitions or spin-offs are, in principle, exempted from VAT, stamp tax, real property transfer charges and any other fees, except for a 0.04 per cent fiscal liability of the increased capital paid as Competition Authority Contribution.

28.3.4 Joint ventures

Foreign investors who are unfamiliar with the dynamics of the Turkish market often prefer to enter into a joint venture relationship with a local company first. For this purpose, the partners normally establish either a JSC or an LLP in accordance with the provisions of the TCC. However, in certain business sectors, such as banking and insurance, the form of the joint venture must be a JSC.

28.3.5 Asset transactions

Investors also carry out asset purchase transactions, particularly if the seller company is not in good standing or is faced with organisational problems. Asset transactions assist the seller in eliminating unwanted liabilities, but at the same time reap the benefits from the assets of the seller. However, in asset transfers, the particular legal requirements for the transfer of ownership of relevant categories of assets must be observed for certain assets, such as real property. Generally, licences, permits and incentives related to the assets will not be transferred automatically to the seller, and the seller will be required to make re-applications. However, with respect to assignment and transfer of receivables, the debtor's consent is not required.

Depending on the nature and size of the asset deal, the issue of a transfer of an existing business (i.e., the transfer of a business enterprise with all of its assets and liabilities) may arise. The transfer of an existing business is specifically regulated under the TCO. Under Turkish law, if an existing business is transferred, the seller and the buyer continue to be jointly liable to the creditors for the debts of the transferred business for two years from the date of the transfer. Therefore, neither the transferor nor the transferee are free from exposure during this two-year period.

28.4   Investment and exchange controls

28.4.1   Foreign investment permission

The Foreign Capital General Directorate (the "FCGD") must be notified of the foreign investment transaction within one month following the completion of the relevant transaction for statistical purposes.

Foreign investors are free to repatriate their profits to countries outside of Turkey, subject to certain limited restrictions. They may also elect alternative dispute resolution for any commercial disputes arising from their transactions in Turkey. No FCGD notice or approval is required to make changes to the articles of association.

The Direct Foreign Investment Law ("Law No. 4875") allows foreigners to form any type of company permitted under the TCC rather than limiting them to JSCs and LLPs. While this is the case, incorporation of certain companies, such as banks, private financial institutions, insurance companies, factoring companies, holdings, publicly held companies, free-zone incorporators and operators, and companies engaged in the general retailing business are subject to permission from certain governmental authorities.

Foreign investors may freely invest in virtually all sectors open to Turkish investors. However, there are certain legislative restrictions relating to the rights and obligations of foreign investors. These legislative arrangements regulate specific sectors, most notably broadcasting, aviation and maritime transportation, and intend to protect and ensure national security, public order, and health and professional standards.

Accordingly, foreign investors are restricted to a maximum equity participation in the broadcasting sector of 25 per cent, and in aviation, maritime transportation and port services they are restricted to a maximum equity of 49 per cent.

28.4.2   Exchange controls

Foreign exchange regulations were substantially liberalised as early as the beginning of the 1980s through measures taken such as allowing for the exchange of proceeds from transactions in Turkish securities by foreign investors, permitting non-residents to buy foreign exchange without limitation, transferring such foreign exchange abroad, and permitting Turkish companies to invest abroad without any ministerial approval. There are no restrictions on the convertibility of the Turkish lira for current account transactions and foreign capital trans-actions. Only a certain percentage of the proceeds of export transactions must be repatriated to Turkey within a prescribed period, with a number of exceptions.

Foreign investors may transfer their benefits, dividends, sale and liquidation costs arising from the transactions and activities conducted in Turkey, values arising from licensing, management and similar agreements, and refund of the payments of interest on foreign credit to a designated country.

28.5   Merger control

28.5.1   Thresholds for mandatory notification

Turkish Competition Law is very closely modelled on EU competition law. However, some limited diversification exists in its interpretation by the Competition Board. The law restricts certain types of mergers or acquisitions. A merger or acquisition will be subject to permission from the Competition Board if:

(a)   the total market shares of the undertakings that are party to the merger exceed 25 per cent of the relevant product market within the whole, or in a part, of Turkey; or (even though their market share does not exceed this threshold)

(b)   their total turnover exceeds TRL25 million in the relevant product market within the whole, or a part, of Turkey.

Under the Competition Law, a merger or acquisition is comprised of:

(a)   the merger of two or more previously independent undertakings; or

(b)   the control or acquisition by any undertaking or person of the assets of another undertaking, or the whole or a part of its securities, or the means granting it the power to have a right in the management; or

(c)   joint ventures which emerge as independent economic entities possessing assets and labour to achieve their objectives, and which do not have any intent or effects in restricting the competition among the parties, or between the parties and the joint venture.

28.5.2   Procedure

An application to the Competition Board for permission must be made prior to completion of the transaction. In practice, considering the Competition Board's statutory 30-day review period, it is advisable that the notification be submitted at least 30 days before the closing date.[1] Generally, the Competition Board

---

[1] However, the clock stops if the Competition Board deems the application incomplete and thus sends out a formal request for additional information. The review period starts anew upon submission of the requested information.

notifies the parties of its decision to grant permission or to conduct further investigations at the end of the statutory review period. If the Competition Board conducts further investigations, its notice will also state that the merger is suspended until a decision is made and due to any other precautionary measures that the Competition Board deems necessary. A merger or acquisition agreement within the scope of the Competition Law will not become effective until it obtains the approval of the Competition Board.

If there is no reply within 30 days of the date of the application for permission, the transaction executed for the merger or acquisition will become effective and thus may be implemented.

In some cases, even if a notice of merger or acquisition is not required, for instance if the threshold criterion is not met, the merger or acquisition may still fall within the scope of the Competition Law if the agreement dealing with such merger or acquisition restricts competition (i.e., if it contains non-compete restrictions that may not qualify as ancillary restraints). In this case, the undertakings concerned may apply for individual exemption or negative clearance.

28.6 Regulation of the conduct of mergers and acquisitions

28.6.1 Preliminary steps and conduct of negotiations

According to the TCO, an agreement between the target company's shareholder and the acquirer is established when and if the shareholder of the target company accepts the sale and purchase offer. If the offer is subject to a condition, the agreement between the parties will be established upon fulfilment of the condition.

The parties may agree on the terms of their agreement in detail and thereby avoid the application of the general provisions of the TCO, other than the limited mandatory provisions.

The TCO sets out rules applicable to the pre-contractual phase of an agreement. The TCO regulates the offer procedure, the proper behaviour of the parties during the offer period, and the effect of an offer on the target company and its shareholders. However, it does not provide for any specific provision for the phase prior to an offer. Therefore, such phase would be subject to the general provisions of the TCO. As in other civil law countries, under the Turkish legal system, the *culpa in contrahendo* principle applies during the phase before the offer. During this phase, the parties must negotiate in good faith. If the offering party terminates the negotiations after giving the impression that an offer would be made, then such party may be liable for this wilful act or negligence, depending on the particular circumstances and damages inflicted.

28.6.2 Pre-contractual liability

It is common practice in Turkey for the parties to a merger or acquisition transaction to enter into letters of intent, memoranda of understanding and principle agreements. Such pre-contractual arrangements do not need to be in written form, but the parties must agree on material issues to be covered in the main agreement. As in other cases, freedom of contract reigns. Most importantly, it is advisable to clearly state in such an agreement which provisions are intended to be binding on the parties, and which provisions are merely intended to set out a framework for further good-faith negotiations or other procedures (such as due diligence) without creating binding obligations.

28.6.3 Disclosure obligations

CMB regulations adopt a disclosure-based approach with respect to changes in the capital structure and management control of a public company. According to the CMB's Communiqué on the Public Disclosure of Material Events ("the Disclosure Communiqué"), changes in the capital structure and management control of publicly held companies must be disclosed within the time periods set out in the Disclosure Communiqué.

Events that are deemed as "material", triggering the disclosure obligation, are listed in Article 5 of the Disclosure Communiqué, which provides that in addition to the material events requiring public disclosure that are listed in a non-exhaustive manner, any and all events that may have an effect on investment decisions and value of the securities shall also be disclosed to the public.

Material events that should be disclosed to the public are generally categorised under the Disclosure Communiqué as follows:

(a) events relating to share capital structure and management control (e.g., share transfers, voting agreements, etc.);

(b) events relating to asset sale, purchase, lease (e.g., sale, purchase, lease of assets exceeding 25 per cent of the total net value of assets provided in the recent balance sheet, asset purchases or leases that may affect service procurement, etc.);

(c) events relating to activities (e.g., change of scope of activity, discontinuance of manufacturing, starting of a new business line, etc.);

(d) events relating to investments (e.g., investment decisions exceeding 10 per cent of the total assets in the recent balance sheet or postponement or abandonment of the same, etc.);

(e) events relating to financial structure (e.g., initiation of a lawsuit against the company with a value exceeding 10 per cent of the total assets in the recent balance sheet, liquidation, providing collaterals, etc.);

(f) events relating to long-term financial assets (e.g., decisions regarding the acquisition or disposal of the long-term financial assets cumulatively amounting to 5 per cent of the total assets on the recent balance sheet, etc.);

(g) events relating to administrative/governance issues (e.g., management appointments, resignations, etc.);

(h) other events categorised as general terms (e.g., acquisitions of management, change of independent auditor, general assembly meeting-related issues, tender offer, issuance of capital market instruments, etc.).

Particularly in connection with changes in shareholding structure and control of management, the following should be disclosed to the public:

(a) changes in shareholding structure, voting rights or other rights granted by the articles of association or direct or indirect change of control of management;

(b) any acquisition of shares or voting rights, by an individual or a legal entity or by any other person(s) acting together with such individual or legal entity, as a result of which shares or voting rights directly or indirectly held by such person(s) exceed or fall below 5, 10, 15, 20, 25, 33.3, 50, 66.6 or 75 per cent of the total share capital of the public company; and

(c) information regarding voting agreements.

Naturally, there is a long list of matters and events that require disclosure, and specific care should be given in each individual case. In principle, any information that impacts the investment decisions of investors and the price of capital market instruments and changes in the business, control or management of the company, must be disclosed to the public in good time.

28.6.4   Due diligence

It is common practice in Turkey for an offeror to conduct a financial and legal due diligence review to have a full picture of the target company. Depending on the agreement of the parties and subject to confidentiality agreements, the scope of the due diligence may be either extensive or limited. The conduct of the parties during the due diligence may be important in the context of pre-contractual liability should a final agreement not be reached.

28.7   Corporate law considerations

28.7.1   Articles of association

The articles of association make up the primary document that gives a corporation its legal existence. The articles of association embody such information as the scope and purpose, management principles, shares, rights of shareholders, and all of the other regulatory matters of a company.

Companies may engage in any type of commercial activity, and shareholders may exercise their rights attached to their shares in any manner, provided that such activities and rights are exercised in accordance with the articles of association and the TCC. Therefore, the acquisition of the shares of a company is subject to the provisions set out in the articles of association of a company.

28.7.2   Authorised capital

Under Turkish law, a JSC that has not adopted the authorised capital system may only increase its share capital through a general assembly resolution of the shareholders up to an amount to be determined by its shareholders. JSCs established for the purpose of offering their shares to the public, or previously established JSCs intending to offer their shares to the public by increasing their capital, may adopt the authorised capital system provided that they obtain permission from the CMB. Rather than a general assembly resolution, which requires the approval of the shareholders, a board of directors' resolution on capital increase and the principles of sale of the newly issued shares would be adequate to increase the capital to the authorised capital ceiling previously determined by the general assembly resolution of shareholders. In the authorised capital system, new shares cannot be issued unless the shares already issued are completely sold and their value is paid.

28.7.3 Shares and privileged shares

In an LLP, a shareholder has a partnership share calculated in accordance with the nominal value of capital subscribed. The acquisition of shares is subject to major restrictions in LLPs and may be altogether restricted.

The capital of a JSC is divided into shares, each being separate and, unless privileged, conferring equal rights in proportion to their nominal value. Shares may be grouped in different classes and may enjoy certain privileges. Through its articles of association, a JSC may issue privileged shares that grant superior rights on certain matters (e.g., voting, dividends, board nominations, etc.) when compared to ordinary shares.

On the other hand, the CMB has adopted the principle of allowing no amendments to the articles of association of listed companies in relation to the creation of privileged share classes. While existing privileged share classes are unaffected, the CMB consistently rejects the creation of new privileges.

28.7.4 Board of directors and corporate governance

The board of directors of a JSC is authorised to resolve any matters with respect to the management of the company unless such affairs are specifically allocated to the authority and responsibility of the general assembly of shareholders. The board of directors is the body entitled to represent the JSC before third parties and to carry out the day-to-day management and operations of the corporation. Powers of the board of directors may be expanded or limited under the articles of association of the company to the extent permitted under the TCC. As a general rule, board members should also be shareholders. However, this rule does not apply to board members representing legal entity shareholders.

Members of the board of directors are required to participate in all activities relating to management of the company. In particular, they are required to attend board meetings, to raise questions and to give suggestions at such meetings, and to assert dissenting opinions in circumstances where they believe the resolutions being adopted are not in the best interests of the company.

Members of the board of directors must ensure that the business is operating in accordance with the legislation, the articles of association and in the interests of the company. A board member finding any sign of corruption must immediately warn the company's auditors.

LLPs do not have a board of directors. Instead, the TCC grants the right and establishes duties for each partner in an LLP to manage the company in the capacity of manager, and to represent it vis-à-vis third parties, unless otherwise provided for in the articles of association.

An LLP may be managed and represented by persons who are also partners of the company, or managers from outside of the company may be appointed. There is no difference in terms of authority and liability of a partner manager or a non-partner manager. The same duty of care imposed on JSC directors also applies to managers of an LLP, and they are required to act as prudent partnership executives in the performance of their duties.

28.7.5   General assembly of shareholders

The general assembly of shareholders is the body authorised to resolve substantial matters regarding the organisation, operation and management of a JSC, such as:

(a)   appointment of the members of the board of directors;
(b)   approval of balance sheets and profit and loss accounts;
(c)   distribution of dividends;
(d)   amendment of articles of association; and
(e)   release of members of the board of directors and statutory auditors from responsibility.

According to the TCC, a merger decision must be approved by the general assembly of shareholders of the merging entities. The articles of association of companies may also provide for the fulfilment of further requirements.

28.7.6   Minority rights

Under the relevant provisions of the TCC, minority shareholders' rights are defined as the rights of a shareholder or a group of shareholders owning shares representing at least one-tenth of the share capital of a joint stock corporation. The Capital Market Law has reduced the threshold to one-twentieth of the share capital for publicly held companies. The number of shareholders does not have any impact for the purposes of minority shareholders' rights. Even if only one shareholder owns shares representing one-tenth of the share capital of a company, such shareholder will still be able to enjoy the minority shareholders' rights.

The following is a list of rights granted to minority shareholders within the framework of the TCC:

(a)   to request the company to file a lawsuit against the board members and auditors;
(b)   to request the delay of balance sheet discussions;
(c)   in certain cases, to request the appointment of an independent auditor to conduct an investigation in relation to actions at the time of the incorporation, or acts of the board of directors, or infringement of the TCC rules and violation of the articles of association;

(d)   to file complaints before the statutory auditors of the company; and
(e)   to request the board of directors to call the shareholders for a general assembly meeting and to ask for the inclusion of additional agenda items.

28.7.7   *Trade registry*

A legal entity acquires its legal personality through the registration of its articles of association with the trade registry. Corporate records of companies are kept, registered, announced and made publicly available in trade registries. Any amendment to the articles of association of companies, general assembly resolutions and shareholders meetings, and certain major management decisions must be registered in the trade registry and announced in the *Trade Registry Gazette*.

In general, information announced in the *Trade Registry Gazette* becomes effective on the announcement date. Subject to the applicable provisions of the TCC, merger decisions become effective three months after the announcement of the merger decision in the *Trade Registry Gazette*. This time period may be reduced if the consents of merging companies' debtors are obtained.

28.7.8   *Taxation*

JSCs and LLPs are subject to the same taxation rules and ratios. Since introduction of the new Corporate Tax Law, the main change has been in the reduction of the corporate tax rate from 30 per cent to 20 per cent. This is the most significant decrease that has occurred throughout the world in 2006. Further, in line with the fiscal policy of establishing Turkey as a centre for the headquarters of multinationals, Controlled Foreign Company ("CFC") exemptions are available in addition to incentives in certain fields or activities (such as Real Estate Investment Trusts and Venture Capital Funds).

A withholding tax is applied to dividend distributions at 15 per cent to non-resident shareholders or Turkish real person shareholders. Yet, Turkey's extensive double-tax treaty network may provide more preferential rates as low as 5 per cent. For shareholder entities established in Turkey, a participation exemption is also available, making all dividend income exempt from the resident entity shareholder's corporate tax.

28.8   Capital market law considerations and tender offers

28.8.1   *Tender offer basics*

The principles regulating tender offers are set forth in the Capital Market Law and in the CMB's Communiqué Serial IV, No. 8. The third Chapter of Communiqué Serial IV, No. 8 states that the requirements must be fulfilled by either a voluntary or a mandatory offeror.

28.8.2   *Common requirements to be accomplished by the offeror*

In order to initiate a tender offer, the offeror must file the "information form" attached to Communiqué Serial IV, No. 8 with the CMB, together with a brokerage agreement.

28.8.2.1   *Content of the information form*
The information form must contain fair, sufficient and conscientious information and must include the following:

(a)   details of the target company;
(b)   information on the relationship between the offeror and the target company;
(c)   information relating to the features and types of shares to be collected;
(d)   tender offer price per share;
(e)   amount and nominal value of the shares owned by the offeror, if any;
(f)   business plan of the offeror if control over the target company is taken;
(g)   information relating to the broker; and
(h)   time schedule of the offer.

The CMB is entitled to request further information if it deems it appropriate. The approval of the CMB must be obtained prior to publication of any advertisement relating to the tender offer.

28.8.2.2   *Brokerage agreement*
The offeror must enter into a brokerage agreement with a bank or an intermediary institution which is organising the tender. The brokerage agreement must contain the following information, specifically:

(a)   amount and nominal value of shares subject to the tender offer;
(b)   start and finish dates of the tender offer;
(c)   tender offer price per share;
(d)   brokerage fee, commission, or any other benefits to be provided to the broker;
(e)   amount of money to be used during the tender offer and any fall-back plans if the money to be used during the tender offer appears to be insufficient;
(f)   responsibility sharing between the parties of the brokerage agreement relating to the publication of advertisements; and
(g)   information relating to the parties of the brokerage agreement, together with the date of the agreement.

28.8.2.3   *Timing issues*
The information form and the brokerage agreement must be submitted to the CMB 30 days prior to the initiation of the planned tender offer. Upon receipt of the CMB's approval, the information form must be published in at least two nationally distributed newspapers. The tender offer may remain open for a maximum of 30 days and a minimum of 15 days. Acceptance by the offeree shareholders must be made within the determined period to the bank or to the intermediary institution organising the tender offer.

28.8.3 Mandatory tender offer

If any party or parties acting together, directly or indirectly, through a block sale or series of sales or by any other means, acquire 25 per cent or more of the share capital and voting rights or control of the management of a publicly owned company, regardless of the specific amount of share capital, then the acquiring party is obliged to make a tender offer to the remaining shareholders to purchase their shares.

Furthermore, if any party or parties acting together own between 25 per cent and 50 per cent of the capital, and the voting rights of the company increase this percentage by 10 per cent or more in any given 12-month period, such party or parties are required to make a tender offer to the other shareholders to purchase their shares.

Upon reaching or exceeding the limits stated above, the documents required to make the tender offer must be submitted to the CMB within 15 days. If the limits stated above are reached as a result of a block sale (i.e., through a share purchase agreement), the tender offer application must be submitted to the CMB by the purchaser within 15 days of the closing/completion of that share purchase agreement.

28.8.3.1 Exemptions to mandatory tender offer requirement

The relevant CMB Communiqué provides that the CMB may grant an exemption from the obligation to make a tender offer under the following circumstances:

(a) if the acquisition of the shares and voting rights is necessary in order to strengthen the financial structure of the company. It is at the CMB's discretion to evaluate whether such action is necessary;
(b) the approval of the acquisition of the shares and voting rights by a general assembly of shareholders meeting to be held where the presence of shareholders or their representatives holding at least two-thirds of the share capital of the company is required. If the required ratio of shareholders is not made then the board of directors may convene a second session with a quorum of shareholders or their representatives holding at least one-half of the share capital. The decision quorum is a simple majority;
(c) if the acquisition of the shares and voting rights has no effect on the management and board structure of the company;
(d) if the acquisition of the shares and voting rights has been made due to a legal requirement or the thresholds have been exceeded unwillingly, the CMB may grant an exemption provided that the purchaser undertakes to sell the portion of shares necessitating the tender offer.

Exemption application may be filed upon signing, if obtaining an exemption is a condition precedent to Closing, but in any event no later than five calendar days following Closing. If the exemption request is refused, no appeal mechanism exists within the CMB. However, the relevant party may file a lawsuit before the administrative courts for judicial review against the CMB's decision.

Chapter 29

United Kingdom

Karen Davies
Clifford Chance LLP

29.1 Introduction

The UK continues to be one of the busiest public mergers and acquisitions markets in Europe. Whilst this is due in part to the proliferation of private equity driven activity, it is also due to the legal and regulatory regime which governs takeover offers in the UK.

The combined effect of provisions of statutory and common law, in particular the rules set out in the Takeover Code ("the Code") and the way in which the Code is flexibly applied by the Panel on Takeovers and Mergers ("the Panel"), is that it is the shareholders of the target company who ultimately decide whether the bid is successful. It is of paramount importance under the Code that bona fide offers are not frustrated and that shareholders are not denied an opportunity to decide an offer on its merits, that there is equivalent treatment of target company shareholders and that shareholders are kept properly informed.

In 2006, new UK companies legislation, the Companies Act 2006 ("CA 2006"), was given Royal Assent. The CA 2006 supersedes the Companies Act 1985 ("CA 1985") and is being brought into force in a number of stages between January 2007 and October 2009. Throughout this Chapter it is indicated, where appropriate, whether the CA 1985 or the CA 2006 is the governing legislation and, in the case of matters still governed by the CA 1985, it is indicated when it is anticipated that the CA 2006 will be bought into force.

29.2 Acquisition targets

29.2.1 Public and private companies

Companies that are the subject of takeover offers in the UK are usually public companies limited by shares. However, where the company being acquired is a private company limited by shares with a large number of shareholders, the logistical difficulty of getting all shareholders to sign a share sale agreement and the consequent need to make an offer, if 100 per cent ownership is to be obtained, by utilising the compulsory acquisition procedures referred to at 29.12 below, often lead to such an acquisition being effected by way of offer. In certain circumstances, offers for private companies are governed by the provisions of the Code (*see* 29.5.1 below).

29.2.2 Constitution of limited companies

It is usual for English companies to be managed by a board of directors whose members are appointed, and can be dismissed, by the company's shareholders in general meeting. English companies, whether public or private, do not have a dual board structure.

Assuming that there are no particular rights attaching to any separate class of shares in the capital of a company, some matters require a simple majority vote of shareholders to be implemented ("ordinary resolutions") and others require a 75 per cent majority vote ("special resolutions"). Voting is usually initially by a show of hands, which results in each shareholder having one vote, but there are usually provisions in the company's articles of association whereby a poll can be demanded which results in each share giving rise to an equal voting right. Matters which require an ordinary resolution include the appointment and removal of directors, an increase in authorised share capital and authorising the directors to allot share capital. Those requiring a special resolution include amending the articles of association or the memorandum of association of the company and authorising the directors to allot shares for cash other than pro rata to existing shareholdings.

Whilst companies which are not listed on the London Stock Exchange (the "LSE") may have in their articles of association provisions restricting the free transferability of shares, such provisions are not generally permitted in the articles of association of companies which are listed by way of primary listing on the LSE.

29.3   Exchange and investment control

There are no exchange controls currently in force in the UK. However, there are various statutory provisions regulating the acquisition of shareholdings in companies operating in certain sectors. For example, there are specific statutory clearances or consents which need to be obtained in respect of companies whose business relates to banking, broadcasting, insurance, newspapers or a water enterprise. Where the target company has assets or subsidiaries overseas, it may be necessary to seek governmental consents from the relevant overseas authorities. In addition, the UK Government has an unused power to prohibit non-UK persons from gaining control of certain manufacturing businesses.

29.4   Merger control

29.4.1 Enterprise Act 2002 ("EA 2002")

The EA 2002 is the main piece of UK legislation dealing with the competition law aspects of mergers. The provisions of the EA 2002 replace the merger control rules formerly contained in the Fair Trading Act 1973, and became fully operative on 20 June 2003. The EA 2002 establishes a scheme in which two separate institutions operate: the Office of Fair Trading ("OFT") and the Competition Commission ("CC"). In certain limited circumstances (namely where the merger raises a defined "public interest consideration") the UK system allows the Secretary of State for Trade and Industry to intervene in relation to mergers.

Transactions that qualify for review may be investigated initially by the OFT. The OFT has a general duty to refer mergers to the CC for detailed investigation if it believes there is a realistic prospect it will lead, or has led, to a substantial lessening of competition ("SLC"). Mergers qualify for review under the EA 2002 rules if:

(a) the merger produces the situation where any person (companies from the same group are treated as a single person) supplies or receives at least one-quarter of all goods or services of a particular description in the UK, or a substantial part of the UK; or

(b) the UK turnover of the business to be acquired exceeds £70 million.

A merger situation for the purposes of the EA 2002 can arise where one company acquires sufficient shares in another to be able "materially to influence" the conduct of its business. Depending upon the circumstances, a shareholding of 15 per cent or more may give the required degree of influence. The OFT might exceptionally consider that a lesser shareholding gave material influence, or that a shareholding which carried no voting rights did so.

29.4.2 Procedure

Whilst there is no obligation to notify the UK authorities of a merger which qualifies for review, in practice the parties to a qualifying merger often seek clearance prior to completing the transaction. Clearance may be sought either by a prescribed form of fixed notice which engages a timetable of up to 30 working days or by a submission which sets no formal timetable running. In practice, there may be little difference in how much time the procedure will take. Both procedures involve making submissions to the OFT as to the parties' businesses, the markets in which they operate and their views about the benefits or disadvantages of the merger.

Where a merger proposal has not been made public, in certain limited circumstances it is possible to obtain preliminary advice on a "confidential guidance" basis within about 25 working days. This is rarely done in the case of a public takeover and any guidance is non-binding.

29.4.3 Competition Commission

Merger references may be made either after or in anticipation of a merger. If a merger is referred to it, the CC must consider whether an SLC may be expected to result from the merger. Where the CC concludes that an SLC may be expected to arise from a merger, subject to rare exceptions, it must recommend remedies, which may be either structural or behavioural. The CC has wide-ranging and flexible powers in relation to remedies and, if an SLC has been identified, the CC can issue an order prohibiting the merger. At this stage also, the CC can require divestment by the parties. The CC's enquiry normally takes about six months: the first four months to reach provisional conclusions and, if these are unfavourable, up to two additional months to consider remedies.

29.4.4   The Code

The Code (Rule 12(a)) requires that a takeover offer subject to the Code must lapse if a CC reference is made. The Panel is generally prepared to exercise its discretion under the Code to stop the offer timetable running for a period if there is a significant delay in a decision as to whether or not the offer should be referred to the CC.

29.4.5   Powers of the OFT to seek undertakings in lieu

The OFT is able to seek and enforce undertakings from the parties to a merger in lieu of a reference to the CC. The OFT can, for example, consider requiring undertakings to divest which may take the form of a share sale, a sale of business or an asset disposal. Once undertakings in lieu have been accepted, no reference may be made of that merger unless any undisclosed material fact subsequently emerges.

29.4.6   EC merger control

Where a merger meets the criteria of the Council Regulation (EEC) No. 139/2004 on merger control ("the EC Merger Regulation"), exclusive jurisdiction over that merger will be with the EC Commission and UK domestic merger law will not apply.

29.5   Regulation of the conduct of mergers and acquisitions

29.5.1   The Code

The European Directive on Takeover Bids (2004/25/EC) ("the Takeover Directive") was implemented in the UK in April 2007 through the introduction of Part 28 CA 2006. Whilst this new legislation resulted in numerous changes to the wording of the Code, it did not have a significant impact on the content of the Code or the conduct of takeovers in the UK.

The Code remains the principal source of regulation of takeover transactions in the UK. The Code applies to takeovers of companies that have their registered office in the UK, the Channel Islands or the Isle of Man, and have their securities listed on the Official List or a Stock Exchange of the Channel Islands or the Isle of Man. It also applies to takeovers of public unlisted companies (including those whose securities are traded on AIM or PLUS (formerly Ofex)) which are resident in the UK, the Channel Islands and the Isle of Man and takeovers of private companies having certain public company characteristics.

Certain provisions of the Code may also apply to other companies in limited circumstances. Where a company is incorporated in another EEA Member State and its securities are traded in the UK (or vice versa) the Panel may, in certain circumstances, share jurisdiction over takeovers for such companies with the regulator in the other Member State. The shared jurisdiction requirements, which were introduced by the Takeovers Directive, are complex and early consultation with both sets of regulators on relevant transactions is essential.

The Code does not apply to offers for non-voting, non-equity share capital unless so required by Rule 15 of the Code which deals with securities convertible into equity share capital.

The Code applies to takeover and merger transactions, however they are effected, including by way of a takeover bid, statutory merger or court-approved scheme of arrangement ("a Scheme") (*see* 29.6.2 below), as well as other transactions which may effect a change or consolidation of control of the relevant company.

The Code comprises six general principles and 38 rules which amplify the general principles and govern specific aspects of takeover procedure. The Code's underlying objective can be summed up in three underlying principles. The first is that all shareholders of the same class in a target company must be treated equally and must have equal and adequate information so that they can reach a properly informed decision. The second is to ensure that a false market is not created in the securities of either the offeror or the target company and the third is to ensure that the management of the target company does not take any action which would frustrate an offer without first obtaining the consent of its shareholders.

Since the implementation of the Takeover Directive in the UK, the Code has been statutory in nature. It is acknowledged that it is impracticable to devise rules in sufficient detail to cover all circumstances which may arise in an offer. Accordingly, the general principles and rules are interpreted in accordance with their spirit as well as their precise wording to achieve their underlying purpose. Such flexibility means that the Code can be extended to apply in areas or circumstances which are not expressly covered by any rule, or can be relaxed as appropriate.

The Code is issued and administered by the Panel which is an independent body established in 1968. The Panel comprises up to 34 members drawn from major financial and business institutions.

The Panel's primary function is to ensure that shareholders are treated fairly and are not denied an opportunity to decide on the merits of a takeover and that shareholders of the same class are afforded equivalent treatment by an offeror. The Code is not concerned with the financial or commercial advantages of a takeover as these are matters for the company and its shareholders alone. Wider questions of public interest are dealt with by the Competition Commission, the Office of Fair Trading, the Department of Trade and Industry or the European Commission.

The day-to-day functions of the Panel are carried out by the Panel Executive which comprises both permanent and seconded staff. This arrangement ensures both continuity of approach and up-to-date experience of current takeover practices.

The Panel includes a Hearings Committee whose principal function is to review rulings of the Panel Executive. If a party is dissatisfied with a ruling of the Panel

Executive, it can appeal to the Hearings Committee. The appeal is usually heard in the presence of all parties. The Hearings Committee also hears disciplinary proceedings instigated by the Panel Executive when there has been a breach of the Code.

Any appeals against rulings of the Hearings Committee are heard by the Takeover Appeal Board which is an independent body. Any party to a hearing before the Hearings Committee may appeal to the Takeover Appeal Board against a ruling of the Hearings Committee or the chairman of the hearing.

The Panel has a range of statutory enforcement powers and sanctions, including the power to require disclosure to it of documents and information, the ability to require compensation to be paid to offeree shareholders, and the power to seek enforcement orders from the courts. These statutory enforcement powers and sanctions are relatively new, having been introduced as a result of implementation of the Takeovers Directive. At the time of writing, the Panel had indicated that it did not expect to exercise these powers, preferring to rely on the sanctions employed since its inception in 1968, including public or private criticism and public censure.

The Financial Services Authority ("FSA") supports the functions of the Panel by providing in its Handbook that an authorised firm must not act, or continue to act, for any person in connection with a transaction to which the Code applies if the firm has reasonable grounds for believing that the person in question is not complying or is not likely to comply with the Code (known as the "cold shoulder" principle). This principle reinforces the powers and sanctions of the Panel, and accordingly, anyone seeking to take advantage of the facilities of the securities markets in the UK should comply with the Code and the rulings of the Panel. Responsibility for compliance with the Code lies with the directors of both the offeror and the target company, as well as their professional advisers.

29.5.2 *Certain common concepts in the Code*

29.5.2.1 *"Persons acting in concert"*

For most purposes of the Code, holdings or acquisitions of shares in a target company by "persons acting in concert" are aggregated to those of the offeror. For the purposes of the Code, "persons acting in concert" comprise persons who, pursuant to a formal or informal agreement or understanding, cooperate to obtain or consolidate "control" of a company or to frustrate the successful outcome of an offer for a company. "Control" is defined in the Code as meaning an interest, or interests, in shares carrying in aggregate 30 per cent or more of the voting rights (*see* 29.5.2.3 below) of a company, irrespective of whether that interest gives de facto control. The Code provides that certain persons, including parent companies, subsidiaries, fellow subsidiaries, 20 per cent-owned associated companies, directors and pension funds are presumed to act in concert unless the contrary is established.

29.5.2.2 *"Offer period"*

For the purposes of the Code, the "offer period" is the period from the time when an announcement is made of a proposed or possible offer (with or without terms) until the first closing date or, if later, the date on which the offer becomes or is declared unconditional as to acceptances (*see* 29.7.3 below) or lapses.

29.5.2.3 *"Voting rights"*
"Voting rights" means all of the voting rights attributable to the capital of the company which are currently exercisable at a general meeting.

29.5.3 *The Listing Rules and the Disclosure and Transparency Rules*

The FSA acting in its capacity as the UK Listing Authority ("UKLA") is the UK's "competent authority" for listing securities. Its powers are conferred by the Financial Services and Markets Act 2000 (as amended) ("FSMA 2000") and it regulates, *inter alia*, admission to listing on the FSA's Official List and the continuing obligation of issuers through the "Listing Rules". Failure to comply with the Listing Rules may lead to private or public censure by the UKLA or suspension or cancellation of a company's listing.

A prospectus or an "equivalent document" is required to be produced where a takeover involves an offer of transferable securities to the public or an admission of such securities to trading on a regulated market.

If the offeror is a listed company and the takeover transaction constitutes a certain class of transaction pursuant to the Listing Rules, prior to the transaction being implemented the company may have to make an announcement or publish an appropriate circular to shareholders or obtain their approval. The Listing Rules classify transactions by assessing the size of the target company relative to that of the offeror on the basis of a number of different tests, and impose more onerous obligations the bigger the size of the transaction. For example, where a test shows that the size of the target company is 25 per cent or more of the offeror, the prior approval of the offeror's shareholders will be required.

The Listing Rules also require a listed offeror to obtain its shareholders' prior approval to any exceptional agreement or arrangement under which it agrees to discharge any liabilities for costs, expenses, commissions or losses incurred by another party, unless the maximum liability under such agreement or arrangement is within a specified limit. This would cover arrangements whereby the offeror's financial advisers purchase shares in the target company and the offeror agrees to indemnify the financial advisers against any loss they may suffer in acquiring the target shares.

The Disclosure and Transparency Rules ("DTRs") came into force in the UK in January 2007 and implement the European Transparency Directive (2004/105/EC). The regime for disclosure of major shareholdings is now found in Rule 5 of the DTRs which replaces Sections 198 to 220 of the Companies Act 1985. A shareholder must initially notify the company if it holds 3 per cent or more of voting rights in the company and of any subsequent increases or decreases of 1 per cent or more in its holding. The notification must be made as soon as possible and by no later than two trading days for UK companies and four trading days for non-UK companies. The notification must also be subsequently filed with the FSA. The notification only applies to shareholders of public companies admitted to trading on the main market of the LSE or the AIM or PLUS markets and is only triggered by the acquisition or disposal of voting rights, rather than the acquisition or disposal of interests in shares.

29.6   Methods of acquisition

29.6.1   Takeover offer

There are, in practice, two methods by which an offeror may acquire the entire issued share capital of a public company whose shares are widely held, namely a takeover offer and a Scheme. A takeover offer is the conventional method of acquisition and may be used whether the bid is hostile or recommended. Subject to the rules of the Code, the terms of the offer may be altered. If a 90 per cent level of acceptances is achieved within three months, an offeror may rely on the statutory procedure for compulsory acquisition of dissenting minority shareholdings (*see* 29.12 below). In addition, if this level is not met due to the existence of untraceable shareholders, the offeror may apply to the court for authorisation that this procedure may nevertheless be relied upon.

29.6.2   Schemes

As an alternative to the traditional takeover offer, it is becoming increasingly popular to use a Scheme structure to obtain control of a target company. A Scheme is a statutory procedure which is currently governed by Sections 425 and 426 CA 1985 and, from April 2008, will be governed by Sections 895 to 901 CA 2006. In the context of an acquisition, a Scheme is a proposal put forward by the target company to its shareholders which, if approved by a statutory majority, becomes binding on all shareholders once the High Court sanctions it and it is registered at Companies House. Until recently, the Code did not apply to the same extent to a Scheme as it does to a takeover offer and reliance was placed on unwritten practice in determining which elements of the Code were applicable when a Scheme was used. In response to the significant increase in the number of takeover offers being implemented by a Scheme, and to improve transparency and certainty in relation to the Code's applicability, a new appendix on Schemes was inserted into the Code as Appendix 7. The appendix came into effect on 14 January 2008 and largely codifies the Panel's existing practice as to when and how the Code applies to Schemes. At the time of writing, it is not envisaged that the introduction of Appendix 7 will result in a significant change to previous practice.

There are two different types of Scheme in this context:

(a)   a Scheme whereby the shares in the target not already owned by the offeror are transferred to the bidder. Stamp duty is payable on such a Scheme as consideration is paid by the offeror to the target shareholders in return for the transfer of target shares; and

(b)   a Scheme whereby the shares in the target not already owned by the offeror are cancelled by a reduction of capital of the target company. The offeror pays consideration to the target shareholders in return for the cancellation of their shares. The reserve created by the cancellation is capitalised and applied in paying up new shares which are issued by the target direct to the offeror. This is the more common Scheme due to the stamp duty saving of 0.5 per cent of the total consideration for the target shares as no transfer of shares takes place.

The two basic features of a Scheme are that it should be approved by both the shareholders (or the class of shareholders whose shares are involved in the Scheme) and by the court. A Scheme must be approved by a majority in number of each class of shareholders whose shares are the subject of the Scheme and who are voting at the meetings. This majority must represent at least 75 per cent in number of those shares. Once approved the arrangement is binding on the company and on all the shareholders involved.

The meetings of the shareholders are convened by the court and the documents sent to them must be approved by court officials. These documents include the formal Scheme, a letter from the chairman of the target company giving details of the terms of the acquisition and an explanatory statement to shareholders giving them all the material information needed to enable them to make an informed decision. Although a Scheme cannot itself be conditional, an offeror may require that the court order will not be filed until certain conditions, for example approval of its own shareholders, are satisfied.

29.6.3   Advantages and disadvantages of a Scheme

The fact that a Scheme is binding on all relevant shareholders provides certainty and makes it attractive to an offeror who is confident of gaining the support of target company shareholders holding 75 per cent of the shares but believes that the 90 per cent level needed for the compulsory acquisition procedures of Sections 979 to 982 CA 2006 to apply may be difficult to attain. Certainty also offers an advantage in respect of the offeror's ability to secure acquisition financing, as banks do not have the risk of providing finance without the security of knowing that control will be achieved. In certain circumstances, a Scheme can be structured to incorporate provisions which would otherwise be prohibited under the financial assistance rules. This is because anything done in pursuance of an order of the court under Section 425 CA 1985 is a permitted exception to Section 151 CA 1985. Furthermore, as mentioned at 29.6.2 above, stamp duty is not payable on a cancellation Scheme and, at present, Schemes are not subject to the restrictions of the Code to the same extent as takeover offers.

In general, however, a Scheme is a less flexible procedure, particularly because of the High Court constraints on the timetable. Also, it requires the cooperation of the target company and so cannot be used where the offer is hostile. In addition, there is no scope for altering the terms of a particular Scheme once it has been sanctioned by the Court. This is a distinct disadvantage if there is a likelihood of a competing offer from a third party.

In an extreme case, the court procedure may also deter an offeror from effecting a takeover by this method. The Court must determine whether "an intelligent and honest man, voting in his own interest" would approve the Scheme. Control of the target company will not pass to the offeror until the Court is satisfied and the order is filed. In contrast, there will be no judicial review of a takeover offer under the compulsory acquisition procedure unless a dissenting shareholder applies to the Court.

29.7 Preparation of an offer

29.7.1 *Announcement of an offer*

It is the announcement of a formal intention to make an offer that signals the commencement of the offer process, the offeror having to post its offer document within 28 days of the announcement. Both to protect target companies from having to defend themselves against offers which cannot be implemented and to avoid the creation of a false market in the shares of the target company and, where relevant, the offeror, Rule 2.5(a) of the Code provides that:

> "The announcement of a firm offer should be made only when the offeror has every reason to believe that it can and will continue to be able to implement the offer: responsibility in this connection also rests on the financial adviser to the offeror."

Rule 1(a) of the Code provides that the offer must be put forward in the first instance to the board of the target company or to its advisers before a public announcement of the offer is made. In the case of a hostile offer, the relevant communication may take place only a few minutes before public announcement, whereas in a recommended offer the period would clearly be significantly longer.

It is sometimes the case that the Code requires the making of an announcement before the parties would otherwise wish. An announcement is required by Rule 2.2 when, *inter alia*:

(a) following an approach to the target company, the target company is the subject of rumour or speculation or there is an untoward movement in its share price. This will be considered in the light of all relevant facts. One fact to consider would be the percentage movements of the target company's share price (a movement of approximately 10 per cent or a rise of 5 per cent in the course of a single day would be regarded as untoward for the purposes of Rule 2.2);

(b) before an approach has been made, the target company is the subject of rumour and speculation or there is an untoward movement in its share price and there are reasonable grounds for concluding that it is the potential offeror's actions (whether through inadequate security, purchasing of target company shares or otherwise) which have led to the situation; or

(c) negotiations or discussions are about to be extended to include more than a very restricted number of people (outside those who need to know in the companies concerned and their immediate advisers). An offeror wishing to approach a wider group, for example in order to arrange financing for the offer (whether equity or debt), where a consortium to make an offer is being organized or where irrevocable commitments are being sought, should consult the Panel.

Before the board of the target company is approached, the responsibility for making an announcement can lie only with the offeror. The offeror should, therefore, keep a close watch on the target company's share price for any sign of untoward movement. Following an approach to the board of the target company, the primary responsibility for making an announcement would normally rest with the board of the target company who, in turn, must therefore keep a close watch on its share price.

Except in the case of a mandatory offer under Rule 9 (29.8.3 below), until a firm intention to make an offer has been notified, it suffices to make a brief announcement that talks are taking place, without naming the potential offeror, or that a potential offeror is considering making an offer.

Where there has been an announcement of a firm intention to make an offer, the offeror must, except with the consent of the Panel, proceed with the offer unless the posting of the offer is subject to the prior fulfilment of a specific condition and that condition has not been met. A change in general economic, industrial or political circumstances will not justify failure to proceed with an announced offer.

On the other hand, an announced offeror need not proceed with its offer if a competitor has already posted a higher offer or, if the Panel consents, where the target company shareholders pass a resolution to approve frustrating action as envisaged by Rule 21 or the target company announces a transaction which would require such a resolution but for the fact that the transaction is pursuant to a contract entered into earlier or the Panel has ruled that an obligation or other special circumstance exists (*see* 29.9.2 below).

Further, a potential offeror should take care in making any statement as to its future intention or otherwise to make an offer. A person making a statement that he does not intend to make an offer for a company will normally be bound by the terms of that statement for a period of six months, unless there is a material change of circumstances or an event has occurred which the person specified in his statement as an event which would enable it to be set aside. The Panel should be consulted in advance about any such statement (Rule 2.8 of the Code).

Under Rule 2.4 of the Code the boards of the offeror and the target must inform their respective employee representative bodies or, if there are no such bodies, the employees themselves about the bid as soon as it has been made public. Once the offer document is made public, this too must be communicated to the employees by the offeror and the target (Rule 30.1). The requirements of the Information and Consultation Directive (2002/14/EC), the European Works Council Directive (94/45/EC) and the Collective Redundancies Directive (98/59/EC) are expressly referred to by the Takeover Directive (*see* 29.5.1).

29.7.2 *Secrecy*

It follows from Rule 20.1 of the Code, which provides that information about companies involved in an offer must be made equally available to all shareholders as nearly as possible at the same time and in the same manner, that it is vitally important before an announcement of an offer that absolute secrecy be maintained. The Code requires that all persons privy to confidential information, particularly price-sensitive information, concerning an offer or contemplated offer must treat that information as secret and may only pass it to another person if it is necessary to do so and if that person is made aware of the need for secrecy (Rule 2.1 of the Code).

29.7.3 Contents of an announcement

The announcement of the offer is required by Rule 2.5 of the Code to contain a number of matters, including the terms of the offer, the identity of the offeror and details of any existing holding of shares or outstanding derivatives, or options over shares, in the target company owned or controlled by the offeror or persons acting in concert with it. The announcement must also set out all the conditions to which the offer or the posting of it is subject. The offeror must ensure that all conditions of the offer are correct in the announcement as there will be no opportunity to change such conditions at a later date.

The offer will typically be subject to a number of conditions. It must normally be a condition of any offer that it will not be declared unconditional unless the offeror has acquired or agreed to acquire shares carrying over 50 per cent of the voting rights attributable to each of the equity share capital in the target company alone and the equity share capital and the non-equity share capital combined (Rule 10 of the Code). In addition to this condition ("the acceptance condition") which, except in the case of a mandatory offer under Rule 9 (*see* 29.8.3 below), is usually drafted so as to be conditional on 90 per cent acceptances but with the offeror having power to reduce this to shares carrying over 50 per cent of the voting rights, there will be many other conditions. Some of these will be in relation to formal matters, such as consents of regulatory bodies, the offeror's shareholders in general meeting, the UKLA and the LSE. Others will relate to the continuing nature and condition of the target company and its business. In any event, the conditions of an offer must not depend solely on subjective judgements by the directors of the offeror or on conditions the fulfilment of which are in the hands of the offeror (Note 3 on Rule 2.5 and Rule 13 of the Code).

The press announcement would also invariably set out the offeror's rationale for the making of the offer. It is standard practice to include detailed conditions in the press announcement, but the value of these may be limited. The Panel will not allow an offeror to invoke a condition to allow an offer to lapse unless the breach of condition is of material significance in the context of the offer.

29.7.4 Offers for other classes of shares and rights in respect of shares

Where a company has more than one class of equity share capital, a "comparable" offer must be made for each class of share (Rule 14.1 of the Code), whether such capital carries voting rights or not. A comparable offer does not have to be identical, but differences must be capable of being justified to the Panel; the Panel must be consulted in advance. No acceptance condition may be attached to a bid for non-voting equity share capital unless the bid for the voting equity share capital is itself conditional on the success of the offer for the non-voting equity share capital.

Where more than one class of shares is bid for, a separate offer must be made for each class (Rule 14.2 of the Code).

Any convertible securities, outstanding share options or other subscription rights must be the subject of an appropriate offer (Rule 15 of the Code). The offer must be enough to safeguard the stockholders' interests and secure equality of treatment, and it should be posted at the same time as the main offer (the Panel must be consulted if this is not practicable).

29.7.5   *Financing arrangements*

Although the entire offer consideration sometimes takes the form of securities in the offeror, it is common for some or all of the consideration to be in the form of cash. This cash could derive from the company's own resources or it could be raised, in whole or in part, by means of an underwriting of shares in the offeror. One method of underwriting in such circumstances is a so-called "cash under-pinning" where the offeror effectively arranges for its financial adviser to make a separate offer to the shareholders in the target company to acquire the shares in the offeror to which they are entitled as consideration under the offer, such offer being at a fixed price. Target company shareholders who wish to receive cash would accept such an offer. It would also be possible, although it is less common, for the underwriting to take the form of a rights issue.

Where the offeror funds some or all of the consideration from new bank facilities, it is necessary, in light of the requirement of the Code that the offeror be able to implement the offer, that the offeror should have available to it an unconditional loan agreement at the time of announcement of the offer, at least where a significant amount of the consideration is to be provided under that facility. The financial adviser of the offeror will also be concerned, in the light of its obligations in relation to the cash confirmation (*see* 29.11.3 below), that the cash under the facility be available for the purposes of the implementation of the offer. Accordingly, the financial adviser has an interest in ensuring that the facility be provided on terms that it will continue to be available until the entire cash consideration under the offer has been paid, notwithstanding that an event of default may have occurred or some other right to withdraw the funding may have arisen.

It is common for at least part of the consideration being provided to take the form of securities, even if only as a debt instrument, so as to give UK shareholders who are UK tax-resident and liable to taxation on capital gains the opportunity in appropriate circumstances of "rolling over" their gain into the consideration securities, thus deferring a charge to taxation.

29.7.6   *Due diligence*

The Code permits a target company to provide information in confidence to a bona fide potential offeror, and in recommended bids a broad range of non-public information is commonly requested by the offeror prior to announcing an offer so that the offeror can make a proper assessment of the target company. However, target companies are sometimes reluctant to comply fully with such requests due to Rule 20.2 which provides that any information which has been supplied to a potential offeror must on request be provided to any other potential competing offeror, even if that offeror is less welcome. Rule 20.2 extends to site visits and meetings with the target company's management in addition to information disclosed by other means. The target company and its financial adviser are responsible for ensuring, as far as practicable, that on request less welcome offerors are afforded access to management and site visits equivalent to that which any other offeror has been given.

If it is proposed to supply information to a potential offeror, the target company usually obtains a suitable confidentiality undertaking first. The agreement entered into with the original potential offeror may contain an undertaking not to buy shares or launch a hostile offer, but the target company is not permitted to make the provision of information to other less welcome offerors under Rule 20.2 conditional upon such a standstill undertaking.

To ensure that its intentions remain confidential, an offeror who does not anticipate a recommendation from the target company board usually has to rely only on publicly available information on the company. If the target company is a listed company, it will have published information about itself, principally in the form of its annual accounts and interim statements. In accordance with the Listing Rules, it should also have made announcements of any major new developments in its sphere of activity which may lead to substantial movement in the price of its listed shares. A significant amount of information on a listed offeree should therefore be publicly available, although this should not be relied upon as being comprehensive.

29.7.7 Stakebuilding

An offeror will often seek to acquire a stake in the target company before announcing the offer. This increases the chances of securing ultimate control of the offeree and may deter rivals by adding credibility and momentum to an offer and may lower the overall cost of the bid as it may be possible to buy shares in the market at a price below the eventual bid price.

Although there are tactical advantages in acquiring a strategic stake, it is worth noting that stakebuilding activities which come to the attention of the market are likely to force the offeree share price up and may establish a minimum offer price as under Rule 6.1 an offer must be made on no less favourable terms than any acquisitions of shares made in the preceding three months. There is also a risk that a loss will result if the bid is unsuccessful and no competing offeror emerges. Offerors should be aware of Rule 9 which requires that, when a person acquires 30 per cent or more of the voting rights of a company, that person must make a general cash offer to the remaining shareholders (*see* 29.8.3 below).

Stakebuilding is closely regulated by company law and the Code. The main restrictions to be aware of are set out in the paragraphs which follow.

29.7.7.1 Criminal Justice Act 1993 – insider dealing
It is a criminal offence for an individual who has inside information as an insider to deal in securities that are price-affected securities in relation to that infor-

mation, to encourage another to deal, or to pass on the information (*see* 29.13.1 below). Knowledge of an impending but unannounced offer will be inside information for the purposes of the legislation. However, it should not prevent stakebuilding by the offeror or its agents as there is a defence available to persons acting with a view to facilitating an offer if the only inside information they have is information about the offer, the offer price or the parties involved arising directly out of their involvement in the transaction. This defence would not, however, cover any confidential non-public price-sensitive information given to the offeror by the target company during the course of negotiations, the receipt of which will prevent an offeror dealing in the target company's shares until that information becomes public or a recommended offer is announced.

29.7.7.2 *Financial Services and Markets Act 2000 – market abuse*
An offeror must not engage in behaviour which amounts to "market abuse" (*see* 29.13.2 below). Broadly, market abuse is behaviour amounting to insider dealing (including dealing with inside information and improper disclosure) and market manipulation (including conduct likely to create a false market). In the context of a takeover, an example of market abuse is where, on the basis of inside information concerning a proposed bid, an offeror enters into a transaction in the target company's securities that provides merely an economic exposure to movements in the price of the target company's shares. Another example is where a person (other than the offeror, for example a director of the offeror) is aware that an offer is being contemplated and deals in shares or other securities in the target company for his own benefit. Knowledge of an impending but unannounced bid by a potential offeror is likely to constitute inside information for the purposes of the market abuse regime. Penalties for committing market abuse are either the imposition of unlimited fines or public censure.

Certain behaviour based on inside information relating to another company in the context of a takeover bid for the purpose of gaining control of that company does not of itself amount to market abuse, for example seeking irrevocable undertakings or letters of intent and making arrangements in connection with the underwriting of a securities exchange offer. This "safe harbour" covers inside information obtained by an offeror during the due diligence exercise and could be interpreted to permit pre-bid stakebuilding, but in practice the lack of an equivalent provision under the criminal insider dealing provisions generally prevents this.

29.7.7.3 *Rule 5 of the Code*
Rule 5 restricts a person (including his concert parties) who is interested in shares carrying less than 30 per cent of the voting rights of a company, from acquiring an interest in any other shares which would result in an interest in shares carrying 30 per cent or more of the voting rights in the company. In addition, a person interested in shares carrying between 30 per cent and 50 per cent (inclusive) of the voting rights may not acquire an interest in any other shares carrying voting rights in that company. There are various exceptions to the rule, such as where the acquisition is from a single shareholder and it is the only acquisition in a seven-day period. Rule 5 of the Code does not apply where the person has more than 50 per cent of the voting rights.

29.7.7.4 Listing Rules

Under the Listing Rules, a listed company cannot, without prior shareholder approval, acquire shares for a consideration equivalent to 25 per cent or more of its gross assets, profits, gross capital or its market capitalisation (*see* 29.5.3 above).

29.7.8 Irrevocable undertakings

An offeror will, particularly in the case of a recommended offer but more rarely in the case of a hostile offer, seek to obtain irrevocable undertakings from the directors of the target company or others, that is to say, undertakings that the relevant persons will accept the offer when made. As a result of negotiation by the persons giving the undertakings, such undertakings are sometimes expressed to be revocable in the event of a higher offer from an alternative offeror. Undertakings are also sometimes sought from, but very rarely given by, institutional shareholders. Unlike market purchases made before the posting of an offer document (*see* 29.7.7 above), shares acquired pursuant to the undertakings should, for the purposes of Sections 974 to 991 CA 2006, be treated in the same way as acceptances of the offer and so do not make it more difficult to apply the compulsory acquisition procedures. The provisions of Rule 2.1 of the Code should be borne in mind as these emphasise the vital importance of absolute secrecy before an announcement of an offer.

29.8 Conduct of a public offer

29.8.1 Timing

The Code contains detailed rules relating to the timing of offers. Amongst these are that:

(a) an offer must normally be posted within 28 days of the announcement of a firm intention to make it (Rule 30.1 of the Code);

(b) an offer must normally be open for acceptance for at least 21 days after it is posted (Rule 31.1 of the Code);

(c) the target company's directors must normally advise shareholders of their views within 14 days of the offer document having been posted (Rule 30.2 of the Code);

(d) any new information to be published by the target company must be published not later than 39 days after the offer is posted (Rule 31.9 of the Code);

(e) accepting shareholders have the right, if the offer has not become unconditional as to acceptances, to withdraw their acceptance from the day falling 21 days after the first closing date; this is therefore usually from 42 days after the posting of the offer document (Rule 34 of the Code);

(f) an offer may not normally be increased later than 46 days after it is posted (the combined effect of Rules 32.1 and 31.6 of the Code);

(g) an offer must normally remain open for acceptance for a further 14 days after it has become unconditional as to acceptances (Rule 31.4 of the Code), as must offers of alternative forms of consideration (Rule 33 of the Code), although, if certain conditions are satisfied, this does not apply to "mix and match" offers nor to cash alternatives by way of cash underpinnings (*see* 29.7.5 above) where the value of the cash underwritten alternative is at the time of announcement more than half the maximum value of the offer;

(h) an offer may not be extended beyond the sixtieth day after it was posted unless it has by then become or been declared unconditional as to acceptances (Rule 31.6 of the Code); and

(i) all conditions of an offer must be fulfilled within 21 days of the first closing date for acceptances or, if later, the date on which it becomes or is declared unconditional as to acceptances, failing which the offer must lapse (Rule 31.7 of the Code). Thus, if the offer is declared unconditional as to acceptances 60 days after it was posted, any remaining conditions must be satisfied or waived no later than 81 days after it was posted.

Note 3 to Rule 31.6 of the Code gives the Panel the discretion to stop the offer timetable running for a period if there is a significant delay in a decision as to whether or not the offer should be referred to the CC or as to initiation of proceedings by the European Commission.

Where a competing offer has been announced, the Panel will normally consent to the first offeror extending its offer beyond the sixtieth day even where the offer has not become unconditional, provided that such consent is sought before the forty-sixth day following posting of the competing offer document. Both the offerors will normally be bound by the timetable established by the posting of the second competing offer document (Rule 31.6 of the Code).

Except with the consent of the Panel, where an offer has been announced and has been withdrawn or lapsed, neither the offeror nor any person who is or was acting in concert with the offeror may, within 12 months from the date on which such offer is withdrawn or lapses, announce an offer or possible offer for the target company or put himself in a position whereby he would be obliged under Rule 9 of the Code to make an offer (Rule 35.1 of the Code). This is to prevent an offeror from putting a target company under continual siege. The notes to Rule 35.1 specify circumstances in which the Panel will normally grant consent for a further offer to be made notwithstanding that the 12-month period has not elapsed. These include where:

(a) the previous offer lapsed in accordance with Rule 12 (*see* 29.4.4 above) and the new offer follows a clearance of the CC or issuing of a decision by the EC (in such circumstances any offer must normally be announced within 21 days after the announcement of such clearance); or

(b) the new offer follows the announcement of an offer by a third party for the target company; or

(c) the new offer is recommended by the board of the target company, although in this case consent will not normally be granted within three months of the lapsing of an earlier offer in circumstances where the offeror was prevented from revising or extending its previous offer as a result of a no-increase statement or a no-extension statement or was one of two or more competing offerors whose offers lapsed with combined acceptances of less than 50 per cent of the voting rights of the offeree company (*see* 29.8.2 below).

29.8.2   *Revision of the offer*

Apart from where the offeror wishes to revise his offer, which can be done any time up to the forty-sixth day after the posting of the offer document, the offeror will be obliged to revise its offer in certain circumstances, for example where a cash offer is required under Rule 11 of the Code or where it purchases shares above the offer price (*see* Rule 6.2 of the Code mentioned at 29.8.4.3 below). However, offerors cannot use Rule 6.2 or Rule 11 of the Code as a device to permit revision after day 46.

If an offeror has made a statement to the effect that the offer will not be further increased, the offeror will be prohibited, save in wholly exceptional circumstances, from amending the terms of an offer unless it has specifically reserved its right to do so in circumstances specified at the time the statement was made and the circumstances which it so specified arise. If the offeror has made a no-increase statement and has expressly reserved its right to set the statement aside in the event of a competing bid and a competing offer subsequently arises, the offeror may choose to disregard the no-increase statement provided that notice to this effect is given as soon as possible within four business days after the announcement of the competing offer and any shareholders who accepted the offer after the date of the no-increase statement are given a right of withdrawal for a period of eight days following the date on which the notice is posted (Rule 32.2 of the Code). Rule 32.3 of the Code provides that if an offer is revised, all shareholders who accepted the original offer must be entitled to the revised consideration.

29.8.3   *Acquisitions over 30 per cent both before and during an offer period and mandatory offers*

The Code contains detailed provisions concerning acquisitions of shares giving rise to holdings to which are attached 30 per cent or more of voting rights, on the basis that such a holding gives rights of de facto control.

As mentioned below, if an offeror (including for this purpose any persons acting in concert with it) holds less than 30 per cent of the voting rights in a target company, it may not acquire any further shares carrying voting rights in that company which results in it holding, in aggregate, 30 per cent or more of the voting rights of that company (Rule 5.1(a) of the Code).

If an offeror (including for this purpose any persons acting in concert with it) holds 30 per cent or more of the voting rights in a target company, but less than 50 per cent, it is not permitted to acquire any shares carrying voting rights in that company (Rule 5.1(b) of the Code).

However, acquisitions are not restricted by the above if:

(a)   The purchase is from a single holder and it is the only acquisition within a seven-day period (Rule 5.2(a) of the Code). This exception will not apply where the purchaser has announced a firm intention to make an offer and the posting of the offer is not subject to a precondition.

(b) The purchase immediately precedes, and is conditional upon, the announcement of an offer which is publicly recommended by the board of the target company (Rule 5.2(b) of the Code).

(c) The offeror has announced a firm intention to make an offer (the posting of which is not subject to the fulfilment of any condition) and:

 (i) the purchase is made with the agreement of the target company's board;

 (ii) the offer (or any competing offer) has been publicly recommended by the target company's board;

 (iii) either:

 • the first closing date of the offer has passed and the Secretary of State has announced that the offer is not to be referred to the CC (or the offer does not come within the statutory provisions for possible reference) and it has been established that no action by the EC Commission will be taken in respect of such offer pursuant to the EC Merger Regulation (or such offer does not come within the scope of the EC Merger Regulation), or

 • the first closing date of any competing offer has passed and the Secretary of State has announced that such competing offer is not to be referred to the CC (or such competing offer does not come within the statutory provisions for possible references) and it has been established that no action by the EC Commission will be taken in respect of such offer pursuant to the EC Merger Regulation or such offer does not come within the scope of such EC Merger Regulation; or

 (iv) the offer has become unconditional in all respects (Rule 5.2(c) of the Code).

(d) The purchase is by way of acceptance of the offer (Rule 5.2(d) of the Code).

(e) Subject to the Panel's consent, the purchase is only part of a shareholding, such as where a purchaser acquires just under 30 per cent to fall outside the rule to make a general offer (*see* Note 6 to Rule 9 of the Code).

In certain circumstances, where the purchaser has a holding of more than 30 per cent but had previously sold shares, the purchaser may acquire shares provided that the level of shareholding does not exceed the highest percentage of such purchaser in the last 12 months, or the number of shares acquired under this exception does not exceed 1 per cent of the voting share capital for the time being, whichever is the lower (*see* Note 11 to Rule 9.1).

Notwithstanding that purchases may be permitted as referred to in this part, if:

(a) any person acquires (whether or not pursuant to a series of transactions or over a period of time) an interest in shares which (taken together with shares held or acquired by persons acting in concert with it) carry 30 per cent or more of the voting rights of a target company; or

(b) any person who, together with persons acting in concert with it, is interested in shares which, in the aggregate, carry not less than 30 per cent but not more than 50 per cent of the voting rights of a target company and such person, or any person acting in concert with it, acquires an interest in any other shares in that company which increase the percentage of its voting rights in which it is interested,

then such person will, except with the consent of the Panel, be required to make a mandatory offer to acquire all other equity shares in the company whether voting or non-voting and also to acquire any other class of transferable securities carrying voting rights (Rule 9.1 of the Code).

An offer will not be required under Rule 9.1 of the Code where control of the target company is acquired as a result of a voluntary offer made in accordance with the Code to all of the holders of voting equity share capital and other transferable securities carrying voting rights.

The following must be noted in relation to a mandatory offer:

(a)   the offer is permitted to be conditional only upon the offeror receiving acceptances which, together with shares acquired or agreed to be acquired before or during the offer, will result in the offeror or any person acting in concert holding shares carrying more than 50 per cent of the voting rights. The customary conditions referred to at 29.7.3 above will not therefore be permitted;

(b)   a mandatory offer must, where the offer comes within the statutory provisions for possible reference to the CC (*see* 29.4 above) contain a provision that the offer will lapse if there is a reference before the first closing date or the date when the offer becomes or is declared unconditional as to acceptances, whichever is the later. Where an offer would give rise to concentration with a Community dimension within the scope of the EC Merger Regulation, the mandatory offer must contain a term that the offer will lapse if, before the first closing date or the date when the offer becomes or is declared unconditional as to acceptances, whichever is the later, the EC Commission either initiates proceedings under Article 6(1)(c) of the EC Merger Regulation (also known as "Phase 2 proceedings") or, following a referral by the European Commission to a competent authority of the UK under Article 9(1) of the EC Merger Regulation, there is a subsequent reference to the CC;

(c)   the offer must be for cash or accompanied by a full cash alternative at not less than the highest price paid by the offeror or any person acting in concert with it for target shares from the period starting 12 months before the commencement of the "offer period" (Rule 9.5 of the Code); and

(d)   any purchase resulting in a mandatory offer becoming required must be immediately followed by an announcement that such an offer is to be made (Rule 7.1 of the Code).

Further in relation to Rule 9 of the Code, when the issue of new securities would otherwise result in an obligation to make a general offer under Rule 9, the Panel will normally waive the obligation if there is a vote to that effect at a shareholders meeting, known as a "whitewash". The person or group of persons seeking the waiver and any other non-independent party would not be entitled to vote at that meeting. The Panel will not normally give a waiver if the person to whom the new securities are to be issued, or any person acting in concert with him, has purchased shares in the company in the 12 months prior to the posting to shareholders of the circular relating to the proposals but subsequent to negotiations, discussions or the reaching of understandings or agreements with the directors of the company in relation to the proposed issue of new securities. Also, a waiver will be invalidated if any purchases are made in the period between the posting of the circular to shareholders and the shareholders meeting (Section 3 of Appendix I to the Code).

The Code (Rule 37) also contains provisions dealing with the impact of redemptions or purchases by a company of its own shares on the triggering of obligations under Rule 9.

29.8.4 Further rules relating to share purchases

The Code contains a number of further rules relating to purchases of target company shares, which are designed to ensure equality of treatment of target company shareholders.

29.8.4.1 Required cash offer
If:

(a) an offeror (together with any persons acting in concert) purchases for cash, during an offer period and within the 12 months prior to its commencement, 10 per cent or more of the voting rights of a class of shares in a target company; or

(b) the offeror acquires offeree company shares for cash during the offer period; or

(c) in the view of the Panel it is necessary to ensure that all target company shareholders are treated similarly,

then, except with the consent of the Panel in relation to (a) or (b) above, any offer for that class of shares in the target company must be made in cash or with a full cash alternative at not less than the highest price paid during the offer period (and in the case of (a) above, the preceding 12 months) (Rule 11.1 of the Code). Any such purchase must, if appropriate, be immediately followed by an announcement that an appropriately revised offer is to be made (Rule 7.1 of the Code).

29.8.4.2 Purchases made before an offer period
If an offeror or any person acting in concert with it has purchased shares in a target company:

(a) within a three-month period prior to the commencement of the offer period; or

(b) between any announcement of a possible offer and the announcement of a firm intention to make an offer; or

(c) prior to that period, if the Panel is of the view that there are circumstances which render it necessary to ensure that all shareholders in the target company are treated similarly,

then, except with the consent of the Panel in relation to (a) or (b) above, any subsequent offer by such offeror for that target company must be on no less favourable terms (Rule 6.1 of the Code).

29.8.4.3   *Purchases at above the offer price*

If, after the commencement of the offer period but before the offer closes for acceptance, an offeror or any person acting in concert with it purchases shares at above the offer price, such offeror must increase its offer to not less than the highest price paid on any such purchase (Rule 6.2(a) of the Code).

29.8.5   Sale of shares during the offer period

An offeror and persons acting in concert with it must not during the offer period sell any securities in a target company without having obtained the prior consent of the Panel. Panel consent will not be given where the offer is a mandatory offer as referred to at 29.8.3 above. Where consent is obtained, the sales will not be permitted to be made at a price below the value of the offer itself (Rule 4.2 of the Code). In addition, 24 hours' public notice must be given of any such proposed sale. Once an announcement has been made, an offeror or persons acting in concert with it may not make any further purchases and only in exceptional circumstances will the Panel permit the offer to be raised.

29.8.6   Special deals with favourable conditions

Rule 16 of the Code provides that, except with the consent of the Panel, an offeror or persons acting in concert with it may not make any arrangements with share-holders and may not deal or enter into arrangements to deal in shares of the target company, or enter into arrangements which involve acceptance of an offer, either during an offer or when one is reasonably in contemplation, if there are favourable conditions attached which are not being extended to all shareholders.

An arrangement made with a person who, while not a shareholder, is interested in shares carrying voting rights in the target company will also be prohibited by Rule 16 if favourable conditions are attached which are not being extended to the shareholders. For the avoidance of doubt, there is no requirement to extend an offer or any arrangement which would otherwise be prohibited by Rule 16 to any person who is interested in shares, but is not a shareholder.

29.8.7   Disclosure of dealings

As well as the provisions set out in Rule 5 of the DTRs (*see* 29.5.3 above), the Code contains provisions relating to disclosure of relevant share dealings with the aim of ensuring a fair market and transparency. Rule 8 of the Code imposes accelerated disclosure requirements in relation to dealings in:

(a)   target company securities (which include those for which an offer is being made or which carry voting rights), equity share capital and all securities carrying conversion or subscription rights into any of such securities; and

(b)   on a securities exchange offer only, the equivalent securities and securities which carry substantially the same rights as the consideration securities.

Dealings include entry into or closing out of options in respect of, or derivatives referenced to, securities and any action resulting, or which may result, in an increase or decrease in the number of securities in which a person is interested or in respect of which a short position is held.

During the offer period (which starts with the announcement of a proposed or possible offer), dealings by the offeror, the target company or any associates for their own account or for discretionary fund management clients have to be disclosed to a Regulatory Information Service by noon the next business day (Rule 8.1) and dealings by any person who has a 1 per cent or more long position in the securities of the offeror or offeree must be so disclosed by 3.30 p.m. on the next business day (Rule 8.3). Dealings by the offeror, the target company or any associate for non-discretionary fund management clients must be privately disclosed to the Panel (Rule 8.2).

"Associate" is defined very widely and includes any person who owns or deals in the shares of the offeror or target company and who has an additional interest, whether commercial, financial or personal, in the outcome of the offer. It encompasses, amongst others, members of the same group of companies as the offeror or target company (including 20 per cent associates), advisers to both sides (and persons in common control with such advisers), the directors of any members of the offeror's or target company's group, their pension funds and employee benefit trusts (*see* the Definitions section of the Code and Note 6 on Rule 8).

The financial adviser and broker to a target company are prohibited from acquiring interests in target company shares during the offer period (Rule 4.4). This is to address the concern that, particularly in hostile offers, such dealings might alter the final outcome of the bid and thereby frustrate the wishes of shareholders generally.

29.8.8 Restrictions on payments to directors

Sections 215 to 222 CA 2006 contain provisions relating to payments to directors for loss of office. Broadly speaking, for any compensation payment to be made by the offeror, the target company or any other persons, the payment must first be approved by the shareholders of the target company. A written memorandum setting out particulars of the payment must be made available to the shareholders before the resolution is passed. The duty to circulate this written memorandum rests on the target company. At the shareholders' meeting to approve the payment the person making the offer and any associate of his cannot vote at the meeting but they may attend and speak, be given notice of the meeting and, if present (in person or by proxy), count towards the quorum. Under the takeover provisions of the CA 2006, "associate" is widely defined and includes, in relation to an offeror, a nominee of the offeror, a holding company or subsidiary of the offeror and a person who is (or is a nominee of) a party to a share acquisition agreement with the offeror. Full particulars of any such payment or arrangement to which the offeror, or any persons acting in concert with it, is party must be disclosed in the offer document (Rule 24.5 of the Code).

29.8.9 Other provisions

The Code contains detailed provisions relating to the publication of advertisements in connection with an offer or potential offer, telephone campaigns, interviews and debates and having specified documents available for public inspection (Rules 19.4, 19.5, 19.6 and 26). Rule 36 sets out rules in relation to partial offers which are offers designed to result in the offeror owning less than 100 per cent of the target company.

29.9 Defences to a hostile offer

29.9.1 Restraints on action at law

Directors of a company are under an obligation at law to promote the success of the company for the benefit of its members as a whole. The statutory duty to promote the success of the company was introduced by CA 2006 in October 2007 and provides that directors must have regard to, among other matters, factors including the likely consequences of the decision in the long term, the interests of the company's employees and the need to act fairly as between members of the company. It seems that, in considering an offer, directors will now have to think about more than just maximising the offer consideration but, at the time of writing, the exact extent to which directors must have regard to these factors, and what this will mean in the context of an offer, remained unclear.

Directors are also under an obligation to exercise their powers for the purposes for which they are conferred. For example, it has been held that the issue of new shares by directors into friendly hands for the purpose of decreasing the possibility of an offeror gaining control of the company, rather than for the purpose of raising capital, constituted an improper use of the directors' powers.

29.9.2 Restraints on action under the Code

Rule 21.1 of the Code provides that, once the target board believes a bona fide offer to be imminent, or after such an offer has been communicated to it, it must not, without shareholder approval, act to frustrate the offer or to deny shareholders the chance to decide on its merits. Rule 21 of the Code particularises this prohibition by providing that the board should not, without the approval of shareholders in general meeting, during the course of an offer, or earlier if it believes a bona fide offer might be imminent, unless already contractually committed or otherwise bound to do so, act as follows:

(a) issue any authorised but unissued shares or transfer or sell, or agree to transfer or sell, any shares out of treasury or issue or grant options in respect of unissued shares;

(b) create or issue, or permit the creation or issue of, any securities carrying rights of conversion into or subscription for shares;

(c) sell, dispose of or acquire, or agree to sell, dispose of or acquire, assets of a material amount (10 per cent of assets is suggested by the Code as a guideline of what would be material); or

(d) enter into contracts other than in the ordinary course of business, for example for the significant enhancement of a director's terms of service.

It should be noted that, by means of aggregation, transactions of minor significance individually may be deemed frustrating action when considered together.

The law on directors' fiduciary duties provides that directors of the offeror and of the target company must always, in advising their shareholders, act only in their capacity as directors, exercise independent judgment and not have regard to their personal or family shareholdings or to their personal relationships with the companies. It is the shareholders' interests taken as a whole, together with those of employees and creditors, which should be considered when the directors are giving advice to shareholders. It is, on the other hand, interesting to note that circumstances could arise where there is a conflict between directors' fiduciary duties, which might compel them to act in a certain way, and the prohibitions set out in Rule 21 of the Code. Rule 3.1 of the Code obliges the board of the target company to obtain competent independent advice on any offer; this will ordinarily be from a merchant bank. An adviser to the target company who is rewarded on failure of a hostile offer or failure of an offer below an unrealistically high price will normally be disqualified from acting as an independent adviser due to a conflict of interest (Note 3 on Rule 3.3).

Other provisions of the Code are also relevant to the conduct of a bid defence. For example, if the target company has previously provided information to one offeror or potential offeror then, by reason of Rule 20.2, the same information must be given to another offeror or bona fide potential offeror, if it requests such information, even where that other offeror is less welcome or has not been named and/or no formal announcement has been made (*see* 29.7.6 above).

Also, during the offer period, financial advisers and stockbrokers (and persons under common control with them) to the target company are prohibited from purchasing target company shares and entering into other specified arrangements relating to the purchase of such shares.

29.9.3 *Other relevant legal provisions*

There are other provisions of law which might be relevant to proposed defensive action by a target board. Whilst market purchases of target shares by friendly parties may be an effective defence to an imminent or actual takeover offer, the target company cannot itself give an indemnity in respect of any losses that such a party might suffer, as this would constitute financial assistance (*see* 29.14 below).

Purchases intended to give the target's share price an artificial boost, for example by the false suggestion of a rival bidder, would amount to market manipulation (*see* 29.13.2 below). The same could apply to attempts to undermine a paper offer by selling the offeror's shares short. Finally, those with inside information must consider prohibitions relating to insider dealing (*see* 29.13.1 below) before dealing in the relevant shares.

Section 994 CA 2006 permits a shareholder to apply to court for an order under Part 30 of the CA 2006 on the grounds that the company's affairs are being or have been conducted in a manner which is unfairly prejudicial to the interests of its members generally or of some part of its members (including at least the shareholder) or that any actual or proposed act or omission of the company (including an act or omission on its behalf) is or would be so prejudicial. On a Section 994 application the court has wide discretionary powers to make such order as it thinks fit, for example to regulate the future conduct of the company's affairs, require the company to refrain from doing a particular act or provide for the purchase of the shares of any shareholder by any other shareholder or by the company itself.

29.9.4 Further practical implications

The combined effect of statute, common law and the Code is that a number of defensive tactics which might be available in some jurisdictions are not permitted in the UK. For example, so-called "poison pills", whereby it is ensured that a target company cannot be bid for or can only be bid for on unattractive terms, could not be adopted by the board of directors of a target company – firstly because, in all but the most extreme case, to do so would be a breach of fiduciary duty, and secondly because of Rule 21 of the Code (*see* 29.9.2 above). Also, where the poison pill would involve amending the capital structure of the target company or the rights attaching to its share capital, then the consent of the company's shareholders at a general meeting would be required prior to implementation.

However, that does not mean that there is no action that can be undertaken by the board of a target company. The board can, for example, take steps to ensure that, to the extent possible, it has the support of its major shareholders and financial institutions generally. Also, prior to any offer, the target company can, if it is a public company, monitor its share register by utilising its powers under Section 793 CA 2006 pursuant to which it may give a notice to any person (whether or not a registered holder of its shares) whom it knows, or has reason-able cause to believe, is or has in the last three years been interested in its shares to give details of his interests, and those of other persons, in the shares concerned. A response to the company's request must be given in writing within such "reasonable" period as may be specified in the notice which, towards the end of a hostile bid, could be 24 hours or less. Failure to reply to the notice is a criminal offence and may result in a reduction of the rights attaching to the shares in question.

Once an offer has been made, the extent to which action by the offeree board is permitted depends upon the view which it has properly formed of the offer. If, for example, the board has properly formed the view that the offer, if success-ful, would be damaging to the target company, then it might be possible (within the constraints of Rule 19.1 of the Code (*see* 29.11.1 below)) to take steps to reduce the prospects of success of an offer, for example by seeking to persuade a relevant regulatory authority that a consent required in order for the offer to proceed should not be given (e.g., the 1989 offer by Hoylake for BAT). On the other hand, the Panel has taken the view that the bringing of litigation to frustrate an offer would breach Rule 21 of the Code (e.g., the 1989 offer by Minorco for Consoli-dated Goldfields).

A further possibility is that the board of the target company may form the view that the offer does not value the target company sufficiently highly. In such circumstances, the target company will seek to persuade its shareholders as to the value of the target company. This may involve the preparation of a profit forecast or an asset valuation (*see* 29.10 below). Other legitimate means of persuading the shareholders of the target company of the company's value would be, for example, promising to pay to shareholders a special dividend in the target company should the offer fail or, alternatively, to effect a return of capital should the offer fail. Such proposals do not contravene Rule 21 of the Code. Where part of the consideration being offered by the offeror is shares in the offeror, it would be common for a target company to argue that such shares are less valuable than they might appear at first.

Where the directors of the target company are of the view that an offer does sufficiently value the target company, then they will commonly seek an alternative higher offer from a third party. Here, interesting legal questions arise where the directors are of the view that the party offering the higher price would, if the offer succeeded, take action detrimental to the business of the target company.

29.10   Profit forecasts and asset valuations

29.10.1   *Profit forecasts*

The target company or the offeror will often choose to make a profit forecast during the course of a takeover. This is a tactical decision which may be made by the target company to demonstrate that the value attributed to its shares should be higher, or by the offeror to support its own share price and its assessment of the value to be placed on any shares offered in consideration for the offer. Any profit forecast given therefore has the potential to greatly affect the outcome of the takeover. In deciding whether a profit forecast will be made, Rule 23 of the Code, which states that shareholders should be given sufficient information and advice to enable them to reach a properly informed decision, should be borne in mind.

Rule 28 of the Code contains provisions relating to profit forecasts and sets out the need for the highest standards of accuracy and fairness in any profit forecast made. It requires that a profit forecast is compiled with due care and consideration by the directors, whose sole responsibility it is. The following requirements are set out in Rule 28:

(a)   the assumptions upon which the directors have based their profit forecast must be stated. This provides shareholders with information to help them in determining the reasonableness and reliability of the forecast;

(b)   a profit forecast must include a report by the relevant financial adviser on the accounting policies and calculations for the forecast. If the profit forecast is contained in a press announcement the report should be sent separately to shareholders as soon as the press announcement is published. If a profit forecast is made before the start of the offer period it must be repeated in full together with the report in the document sent to shareholders.

Advisers should treat an estimate of profit for a period which has already expired as a profit forecast. A dividend forecast is not normally considered to be a profit forecast unless, for example, it is accompanied by an estimate as to dividend cover.

Any public statement which is viewed as putting a floor or ceiling on anticipated results will be regarded as a profit forecast, even if it is just a statement that the current year results will be an improvement on the previous year's. This was the case when Guinness plc made a statement in the press in connection with its offer for the Distillers Company. This statement predicted that the earnings per share of the enlarged group would be at least as great as the earnings per share of Guinness, whilst maintaining that this did not constitute a profit forecast. The Panel considered that this was a profit forecast for the purposes of the Code and Guinness then undertook to have the forecast reported on. Directors should therefore ensure that they do not inadvertently commit themselves to having a report prepared by making a statement which may be viewed as a forecast.

It may, however, be possible for a company to publish financial information which reflects the strength of its business whilst not actually committing itself to making a forecast. For example, in the Glaxo Holdings bid for Wellcome, Wellcome decided to publish its internal sales projections in its defence document to illustrate Glaxo's alleged undervaluation of the company.

Although directors may qualify a forecast by the statement that the forecast is made "in the absence of unforeseen circumstances", any shortfall may be subject to investigation by the Panel. The directors are potentially liable for negligent misstatement and may also be the subject of a contractual claim from the offeror in respect of a target company forecast, or from the target company shareholders in respect of an offeror forecast, if the takeover is successful. Auditors and financial advisers may now also owe a duty of care.

If earning enhancement statements are made that are not intended to be profit forecasts, an explicit disclaimer must be made that such statements should not be interpreted to mean that earnings per share will necessarily be greater than those for the relevant preceding financial period. The Panel should be consulted when including earning enhancement and merger statements with other financial information as these may be construed as profit forecasts.

29.10.2　*Asset valuations*

Asset valuations are primarily used when the directors of a target company desire a more accurate valuation of its assets in order to defend an offer or to argue for a higher price, although they could also be used by an offeror where there are consideration securities. During the Granada bid for Forte in 1995, Forte used various defences, including an asset valuation, which resulted in an increase in the price per share offered by Granada.

Rule 29 of the Code requires that when a valuation of assets is given it is supported by the opinion of a named, independent and appropriately qualified valuer. In contrast to the provisions relating to profit forecasts, such an opinion is only needed where a valuation is given in connection with the offer itself. Directors should be aware that this may not always achieve the intended effect as the valuation must be as objective as possible. Although the Code covers valuations of any type of asset, valuations would typically be used by property or oil companies or other companies where the share price is heavily dependent on the asset value.

The Code requires the basis of the valuation to be clearly stated in any document in which the valuation is made. In contrast to profit forecasts, the assumptions on which the valuation was based should not normally be included. However, if assumptions are permitted by the Panel, they should be fully explained. The Code sets out detailed provisions relating to the contents of, and procedures relating to, asset valuations.

29.11 Documents from the offeror and offeree board

29.11.1 Standards of care and directors' responsibility for documents

Rule 19.1 of the Code requires documents, advertisements or statements issued during the course of an offer to be prepared with the highest standards of care and accuracy. The directors of the parties to the takeover must take responsibility for documents issued by their respective companies and the documents must contain a responsibility statement to that effect as required by Rule 19.2 of the Code. The inclusion of such a statement may expose directors to liability for negligent misstatement to shareholders to whom the takeover documents are addressed.

29.11.2 General obligation as to information

Rule 23 of the Code provides that shareholders must be given sufficient information and advice to enable them to reach a properly informed decision as to the merits or demerits of an offer and the information must be available early enough to enable shareholders to make a decision in good time. The obligation of an offeror in these respects towards the target company's shareholders is no less than its obligation towards its own shareholders. Rule 27.1 of the Code provides for the updating of certain information where there has been a material change in information previously published during an offer period.

29.11.3 Offer document

The offer document contains the formal offer to the shareholders of the target company. It must usually be posted within 28 days of the announcement of a firm intention to make an offer and will normally contain a letter from the offeror, a formal letter from the offeror's merchant bank making the offer itself on behalf of the offeror and setting out its commercial terms and, where the offer is recommended, a letter from the chairman of the target company. The Code provides specified contents requirements for the offer document, some of which are discussed below. The offer document is accompanied by a form of acceptance to be used by shareholders of the target company to accept the offer.

The offer document must contain details of the offeror's intentions regarding the continuation of the target company's business and any major changes to be introduced. It must also state the offeror's long-term commercial justification for the offer as well as its intentions regarding the continued employment of the employees of the target company and its subsidiaries (Rule 24.1 of the Code).

Rule 24.1 requires that the offer document contains a statement of the offeror's intentions with regard to the future business and safeguarding the jobs of employees and management of both the offeree and offeror companies. This includes details of any material change in the conditions of employment, the offeror's strategic plans and the likely repercussions on employment and the locations of the offeror and offeree companies' places of business.

Rule 24.2(a) of the Code sets out the financial and other information regarding the offeror which must be contained in the offer document where the offeror is a UK listed company and the consideration includes securities while less detailed information is required if the consideration is solely cash (Rule 24.2(b)). Rule 24.2(e) requires that the same information must also be given in respect of the target company, whether or not it is listed. Where the offeror is not a listed company, it should disclose the information required of a listed offeror as far as is appropriate and any further information that the Panel may require (Rule 24.2(c)).

Rule 24.3 of the Code requires certain shareholdings and dealings to be disclosed, including the shareholdings of the offeror, and any directors of the offeror, in the target company and, in the case of a securities exchange offer only, the shareholdings in the offeror in which directors of the offeror are interested.

The offeror must have sufficient funds to be able to implement the offer in full. Rule 31.8 of the Code requires settlement of the consideration (in respect of acceptances which are complete in all respects) within 21 days of the first closing date or, if later, the date upon which the offer becomes or is declared wholly unconditional. Where the offer is for cash or includes an element of cash, Rule 24.7 of the Code provides that the offer document must contain a confirmation by an appropriate third party (e.g., the offeror's bank or financial adviser) that the offeror has sufficient resources available to satisfy full acceptance of the offer. The party confirming that resources are available will not be expected to produce the cash itself if, in giving the confirmation, it acted responsibly and took all reasonable steps to assure itself that the cash was available.

29.11.4   *Defence document*

Pursuant to Rule 30.2, the target board must, usually within 14 days of the publication of the offer document, publish a circular containing its opinion of the offer, making known the substance of the advice given to it by its independent advisers (Rule 25.1 of the Code). If the board is split in its views on the offer, the directors who are in a minority should also publish their views and the Panel will normally require that the minority views be circulated by the target company.

The target board must provide its opinion to its shareholders in good time with all the facts necessary to enable them, taking into account the recommendation of the target board and the target company's financial advisers, to make an informed decision whether to accept the offer. Rule 25 of the Code sets out the requirements for the content for the first major circular from the target board. These include requirements as to disclosure of certain shareholdings and dealings and directors' service contracts. Rule 25.2 of the Code provides that the target board should, insofar as relevant, comment upon the statements in the offer document regarding the offeror's intentions in respect of the target company and its employees.

In addition, the circular must set out the target board's views on the effects of implementation of the offer and of the offeror's strategic plans on all the company's interests and specifically employment and the locations of the company's places of business. The target company is also required to offer the representatives of its employees or, where there are no such representatives, to the employees themselves an opportunity to respond and to attach their opinion to the document. The document must be put on display in accordance with Rule 26 and its posting must be announced in accordance with Rule 2.9.

29.11.5   *Criminal sanctions*

Section 953 CA 2006 provides that it is a criminal offence if the offer document does not comply with the offer document rules. Liability arises for persons who either knew that the offer document did not comply or were reckless as to whether it complied and failed to take all reasonable steps to secure that it did comply with the rules.

Sections 21 and 397 FSMA 2000 re-enforce, with criminal penalties, the requirement for documents not to be false or misleading. Section 397(2) FSMA 2000 provides that it is a criminal offence where a person who either makes a statement, promise or forecast which he knows to be misleading, false or deceptive or dishonestly conceals any material facts or recklessly makes (dishonestly or otherwise) a statement, promise or forecast which is misleading, false or deceptive if, in any such case, he makes the statement, promise or forecast or conceals the facts for the purpose of inducing or is reckless as to whether it may induce, another person (whether or not the person to whom the statement, promise or forecast is made or from whom the facts are concealed) to enter or offer to enter into, or to refrain from entering or offering to enter into, an agreement, *inter alia*, to acquire shares or to exercise, or refrain from exercising, any rights conferred by an investment.

Section 397(3) FSMA 2000 provides that any person who creates a false or misleading impression as to the market in or the price of any investments, with a view to influencing dealings in those investments, is guilty of an offence. Rule 19.3 of the Code supplements the statutory provision by providing that all parties to an offer must endeavour to prevent the creation of a false market in offeror or target securities.

Section 21 FSMA 2000 provides that, as a general rule, an unauthorised person must not, in the course of business, communicate an invitation or inducement to engage in investment activity and imposes criminal sanctions in the case of breach of this rule. The prohibition will not apply if the content of the communication is approved for the purposes of Section 21 FSMA 2000 by an authorised person in accordance with FSMA 2000 rules. This means that communications in the course of a takeover must generally be made by, or with the approval of, an appropriately authorised financial adviser.

29.12 Compulsory acquisition of minorities

Section 979 CA 2006 provides that, once the offeror has acquired 90 per cent of the target shares, it can force an outstanding minority shareholder to accept its offer. This procedure is called the "squeeze-out" procedure.

Section 980 prescribes that the offeror must squeeze out the minority shareholders by the end of the three-month period following the period allowed for acceptance of the bid. The 90 per cent threshold relates to the value of, and voting rights attached to, the shares to which the offer relates. "Shares to which the offer relates" does not include shares held by, or contracted to be acquired by, the offeror at the date of the offer. Shares purchased before the offer document is posted cannot therefore be counted, but any bought during the course of the offer can be included.

Assuming that the 90 per cent threshold is met during the prescribed time, the offeror will then issue a notice to non-accepting shareholders enabling the compulsory acquisition of their shares – the compulsory acquisition notice. The shares must be acquired on the same terms and conditions as the final offer, with all alternatives offered initially being available to the non-accepting shareholders.

Similarly, Section 983 CA 2006 provides that the dissenting minority shareholders can force the offeror to buy their shares if the offeror does not seek to do so of its own volition pursuant to Section 979. The offeror must serve a notice on the dissenting shareholders within one month of acquiring nine-tenths in nominal value of the shares in the target company, unless a compulsory acquisition notice is served as set out above. The notice served on dissenting shareholders must give them the right, for a minimum period of three months from the end of the acceptance period, to require the offeror to purchase their shares on the terms of the final offer or on such terms as may be agreed.

If the offeror does not achieve 90 per cent acceptances it will not be able to use the compulsory acquisition provisions. In these circumstances the offeror may not mind being left with an outstanding minority or it may refuse to declare the offer unconditional as to acceptances and let it lapse. Alternatively, an offeror will often waive down the required acceptance level to below 90 per cent on the basis that declaring the offer unconditional as to acceptances will generally trigger further acceptances, which may result in the required 90 per cent threshold for compulsory acquisition being reached. The offeror cannot offer enhanced terms to the remaining shareholders for at least six months after the offer has closed as the Code requires equal treatment for all shareholders.

29.13 Insider dealing and market abuse

29.13.1 *Insider dealing*

29.13.1.1 *The offence*
The offences relating to insider dealing are contained in Part V of the Criminal Justice Act 1993 ("CJA 1993"). The CJA 1993 is supplemented by the Insider

Dealing (Securities and Regulated Markets) Order 1994, which defines the conditions that securities must fulfil to fall within the CJA 1993 and the regulated markets on any one or more of which the securities must be listed or traded. The legislation applies to all securities traded on a "regulated market" (which includes all EC Stock Exchanges and the SWX Swiss Exchange) and to depositary receipts, contracts for differences and warrants and derivatives (including index options and futures) relating to these securities, even if the warrants and derivatives are only "over the counter" or otherwise not themselves traded on a regulated market.

Section 52 CJA 1993 provides that, subject to exemptions, it is an offence for an individual who has non-public price-sensitive information to deal on a regulated market in securities whose price would be likely to be significantly affected by that information if made public. It is also an offence for such an individual to deal off market with or through a professional intermediary (a securities dealer or broker) or if the individual is himself a professional intermediary or an employee of one. Also prohibited are encouraging another to deal and disclosing price-sensitive information. Dealings include the procurement of dealings by others so that executives who authorised illegal dealings by their companies are caught.

Inside information must relate to an issuer or issuers of securities, or to securities, and be specific or precise. However, it is not necessary that the securities dealt in are the same as those to which the inside information relates or that they are issued by the issuer to whom the information relates. For example, if information relates to one company in a sector, it may be an offence to deal in the securities of other companies in that sector if the price of those other securities would be affected by the publication of the information.

Anyone is a potential insider if they have access to information by virtue of being, or their source being, a director, employee or shareholder of an issuer or someone who has access to the information by virtue of their employment, office or profession. However, it is not necessary for the individual's or the source's position to be one which is likely to give access to price-sensitive information.

If convicted, individuals may face up to seven years' imprisonment and/or an unlimited fine, although the dealing itself will remain valid.

29.13.1.2 Defences
There are three general defences and two defences based on the concept of "market information". It should, however, be noted that the burden of proof in respect of all defences is on the accused and one should be certain that a defence will apply before planning to rely on it.

The general defences are:

(a) the dealer has no expectation that the dealing would result in a profit (or avoidance of a loss) attributable to the fact that the information was inside information. This is an objective test and the motive of the dealer (whether or not he wishes to make a profit) is irrelevant;

(b) the dealer would have done what he did even if he had not had the information. This covers those dealing under some sort of compulsion;

(c)   the dealer deals after making limited disclosure to others involved in the transaction, such that no one participating is prejudiced. However, those to whom disclosure is made thereby become insiders and would be prevented from dealing further.

"Market information" is, broadly, knowledge about the details of impending or proposed transactions in securities. If an individual's information is market information, it is a defence to deal whilst in possession of it if it was "reasonable" for him to have acted as he did. Reasonableness is a difficult concept to apply in securities markets. However, if the individual is actually concerned in the transaction to which the market information relates, then there is no need to show reasonableness for any dealing which is entered into to facilitate the completion or carrying out of the transaction. This defence may be relied on by an offeror building a stake in a target company (*see* 29.13.1.3 below and 29.7.7 above).

Market-makers have a special defence for continuing to trade when they have price-sensitive information provided that they act in good faith in the course of their market-making business.

The Code also imposes restrictions on insider dealing. Other than the offeror, no one who has confidential price-sensitive information concerning a proposed offer may deal in target securities of any kind, or recommend another to deal in them, until the offer has been announced. Nor can there be such dealings in the offeror if the proposed offer is likely to have a material effect on the price of its securities. In general, the provisions of the Code in this area have been overtaken by statute which is invariably equally or more stringent.

29.13.1.3   Some practical implications
Although the offer and the gathering of irrevocable undertakings (*see* 29.7.8 above) take place off market, such dealings are within the CJA 1993 if they involve a "professional intermediary". The definition includes those carrying on the business of acquiring or disposing of securities (as principal or agent) or acting as an intermediary between parties to dealings in securities. There must also be a "holding out" of the person's willingness to engage in such activities. Unfortunately, this definition could include a merchant bank engaging in traditional activities on behalf of an offeror. If the merchant bank continues to act as agent of the offeror (e.g., by making the offer on behalf of the offeror) at a time when offeror and/or merchant bank have inside information in relation to the target's securities, it may be necessary to rely on either or both of two statutory defences:

(a)   that there is no expectation of any profit attributable to the inside information (because the information will be reflected in the offer price) (Section 53(1)(a) CJA 1993); or

(b)   that the offer would have proceeded anyway, at the same price, in the absence of the inside information (Section 53(1)(c) CJA 1993).

In both cases, the burden of proving the defence is, of course, on the person accused of insider dealing. An alternative may be for the offeror to make the bid in its own name, and not through the agency of the merchant bank, and to solicit irrevocable undertakings directly.

Stake building necessarily involves dealing on a regulated market, so that the insider dealing provisions cannot be avoided by ensuring that the merchant bank is not involved. In principle, therefore, both offeror and merchant bank would be prevented from making market purchases if they have inside information relating to the target's shares other than the fact that the offer is to be made. Thus, where, for example, the offeror has secured inside information about the target in negotiations with the target, or where an informal clearance has been secured from the relevant regulator of a utilities sector, market purchases would not be permissible until the particular item of information is made public. The "market information" defence is available to an offeror for straightforward stake building in the target where the only price-sensitive information is the information that the bid is under consideration or will be made (*see* 29.7.7 above).

29.13.2 Market abuse

Offences relating to market manipulation are set out in Sections 21 and 397 FSMA 2000 (*see* 29.11.5 above).

The criminal offence of insider dealing is also supplemented and extended by the statutory regime of market abuse set out in Part VIII FSMA 2000. The FSA has powers to impose unlimited civil fines on individuals and firms which commit market abuse. The lower standard of proof required in civil cases makes proceedings under the market abuse regime an attractive option to the FSA and aims to encourage higher standards of behaviour.

The FSMA 2000 identifies three types of behaviour as market abuse:

(a)   misuse of information;
(b)   conduct which may mislead market participants as to the supply, price or demand for investments; and
(c)   conduct likely to distort the market.

Guidance on the provisions of Part VIII FSMA 2000 is provided by the FSA in the Code of Market Conduct, which specifies behaviour which amounts to market abuse, safe harbours, and relevant factors in determining whether or not behaviour amounts to market abuse.

The FSA has endorsed the Code, and the FSA has agreed that it will not, except in exceptional circumstances, intervene during the course of a takeover bid (for market abuse in relation to stakebuilding *see* 29.7.7 above).

29.14   Financial assistance

29.14.1   Prohibition of financial assistance given both before and after an acquisition under the CA 1985

From October 2008 the financial assistance regime will change considerably as the provisions of the CA 2006 are bought into force (*see* 29.14.4 below). Until this date the financial assistance regime is set out in the CA 1985.

Section 151(1) CA 1985 provides that, where a person is acquiring or is proposing to acquire shares in a company, it is not lawful for the company or any of its subsidiaries to give financial assistance directly or indirectly for the purpose of that acquisition before or at the same time as the acquisition takes place. Section 151(2) CA 1985 provides that where a person has acquired shares in a company and any liability has been incurred (by that or any other person) for the purpose of that acquisition, it is not lawful for the company or any of its subsidiaries to give financial assistance directly or indirectly for the purpose of reducing or discharging the liability so incurred. There is no time limit within which the assistance has to be given and therefore the assistance could be given years after the acquisition.

Section 151 CA 1985 applies to an "acquisition" of shares and therefore covers not only a purchase or a subscription of shares in a company but also a share-for-share exchange. The prohibition not only applies where the assistance is given by the company whose shares have been acquired but also where the assistance is given by any subsidiary of such a company (other than any overseas subsidiary).

Section 152(1) CA 1985 partially, but not exhaustively, defines "financial assistance", namely financial assistance by way of gift, financial assistance by way of guarantee, security or indemnity, financial assistance by way of loan and any other financial assistance given by a company the net assets of which are thereby reduced to a material extent or which has no net assets.

If Section 151 CA 1985 is breached, the company giving the financial assistance will be liable to a fine and the officers in default will be liable to up to two years' imprisonment and/or a fine. A transaction in breach of Section 151 CA 1985 will be void and unenforceable and any money or asset transferred in the transaction will be irrecoverable unless the party to whom such property is transferred has knowledge of the facts and can be construed as a constructive trustee.

29.14.2 Exemptions from the prohibition against financial assistance

Section 153 CA 1985 provides a number of exemptions from the prohibition of Section 151 CA 1985. Many of these relate to procedures contemplated by the Companies Act 1985, such as the payment of dividends, the reduction of share capital, and the redemptions and purchases by a company of its own shares. In addition, Section 153(1) CA 1985 provides an exemption where the principal purpose of the company in giving the assistance is not to give it for the purpose of an acquisition of shares in it or its holding company, or the giving of the assistance for that purpose is but an incidental part of some larger purpose of the company and in either case the assistance is given in good faith in the interests of the company. (There is a similar exemption applicable to Section 152(2) CA 1985.) There are considerable doubts as to the precise scope of Section 153(1) and (2) CA 1985, largely in relation to the meaning of "principal purpose" and "incidental part of some larger purpose", and so it is often difficult for Section 153(1) and (2) CA 1985 to be relied upon in practice.

Sections 155–158 CA 1985 permit a private company to give financial assistance to acquire its own shares or the shares of any holding company (unless it is a subsidiary of a public company which is itself a subsidiary of that holding company). The company giving the assistance must be solvent and if the assistance reduces the net assets of the company, the assistance must be provided out of distributable profits. In order to fall within this exemption, a particular procedure must be followed (the so-called "whitewash procedure") which, as a minimum, involves each of the directors of the company giving the financial assistance swearing a statutory declaration of solvency (to which an auditor's report has to be attached) and the shareholders of the company giving the financial assistance, except where the company is a wholly-owned subsidiary, approving the financial assistance by means of a special resolution or a written resolution. If such a resolution is passed unanimously or no resolution is required, the assistance may be given immediately. If the resolution is not passed unanimously, the assistance may not be given for four weeks after the resolution is passed. During such a period, dissenting shareholders holding at least 10 per cent of the nominal value of any class of the company's issued shares may apply to the court for the cancellation of the resolution. There are also provisions as to the latest time for the giving of the assistance.

As this exemption is only available to private companies, any public company wishing to utilise it will need to re-register itself as a private company by passing a special resolution.

29.14.3   Practical implications

Section 151 CA 1985 prohibits, for example, the making of a loan by a target public company to a potential offeror to enable the offeror to buy target company shares. However, if properly structured, it may be lawful for the target public company to induce a potential offeror to make an offer by agreeing to meet a payment if the offer fails for certain specified reasons.

Section 151 CA 1985 will also apply to indemnities given by an offeror in connection with the purchase of its shares as well as to certain indemnities given by an offeror in respect of a share-for-share offer.

The exemption referred to at 29.14.2 above, permitting private companies to give financial assistance otherwise prohibited by Section 151 CA 1985, is often used in practice following a successful offer where the public company target (having been delisted, where appropriate) will be re-registered as a private limited company and then give security over its assets to banks who provided the offeror with funds with which to make the acquisition.

29.14.4   Prohibition of financial assistance under the CA 2006

From October 2008, Part 18 CA 2006 abolishes the prohibition on the giving of financial assistance by a private company for the purchase of shares in itself and the private company whitewash procedure. Therefore, private companies will be able to give such assistance without the need to go through the whitewash procedure. The provisions of Sections 155 to 158 CA 1985 will be repealed, but the prohibition on the giving of financial assistance is retained for public companies under Section 678 CA 2006, meaning that, following the implementation of the CA 2006 provisions, a public company will still need to be re-registered as a private limited company if it wishes to provide financial assistance.